Baker's

DICTIONARY
OF
CHRISTIAN ETHICS

Baker's

DICTIONARY

OF

CHRISTIAN ETHICS

CARL F. H. HENRY

Editor

BAKER BOOK HOUSE

Grand Rapids, Michigan

First printing, November 1978
Second printing, May 1981

PRINTED IN THE UNITED STATES OF AMERICA

PREFACE

The contemporary moral vagabond may be prone to regard ethics as an arena of private preferences; for such a one a dictionary of Christian ethics may seem much like an orderly introduction to an obsolescent past. Yet the flexious modern outlook offers no solid basis whatever for ethical norms; moreover, it inevitably leads to nihilism, to the loss of the worth and meaning of human existence.

As never before, the Biblical call to hear the Word and Command of the Lord remains man's one promising way into a hopeful future. Indeed, the philosophical exhaustion of our age and the constant technocratic encroachment on distinctively human values, are driving many persons to probing once again the heritage of revealed ethics and to asking what "creation" and "sin" and "grace" imply for man's present predicament.

This handbook on ethics provides more than illumination on the Christian life-style. It lays bare the very foundations of the Biblical ethic, expresses its content, indicates its impact upon man and society in the past, expounds its relevance to the problems besetting our own age, and wrestles some of the frontier moral dilemmas of the emerging future.

To be sure, a dictionary is not an encyclopedia; its purpose, rather, is to provide a succinct statement of essentials. The reader will often be referred to related articles, and the bibliographies suggest additional helps.

While this dictionary aims to be authentically evangelical, it does not impose upon readers a partisan view that obscures all differences between, for example, Calvinist and Arminian or pacifist and non-pacifist traditions. In some instances, such as Armament and Disarmament, contributors were deliberately chosen for their differing perspectives. Nor is the volume parochially evangelical; many contributions come from devout Christian scholars active not on evangelical but rather on secular campuses, including large universities, where the battle rages fiercely between the new morality and any commitment to fixed ethical values, and particularly to a revealed morality. Moreover, world-renowned scholars who have contended boldly for Christian positions on many frontiers of life have written crucial essays, such as Civilization, Social Change, United Nations.

Social critics almost everywhere acknowledge the rootlessness of contemporary man; intellectually and morally he is tossed about by winds of change. Purporting to offer escape from the emptiness and meaninglessness of modern life the drug culture searches for other selfhoods and a different world with more satisfying values. Marijuana is an accepted indulgence for millions of Americans and, worse yet, many of our big cities are deathly sick with the heroin plague. Moral shabbiness characterizes much of the social scene. Alcoholism plagues some nine million souls in the United States; drunken driving snuffs out twenty-five thousand lives annually, about twice the number as die by criminal murder. Overall crime is escalating by 11 percent a year.

In the past decade the United States spent some $20 billion getting men to the moon. Was this, as Senator William Fulbright has contended, "a distortion of priorities"? And if so, was Russia fully as eager to get there? Yet two-thirds of the world population goes to bed hungry each night, and someone on our planet starves to death every 2.6 seconds. World population increases by 120 every minute; at this rate the human race will have doubled to 7 billion persons by the year 2000. The U.S.A. comprises only 5.7 percent of the global population, although it consumes 40 percent of the earth's natural resources. The U.S.A. produces enough food to meet the daily caloric needs of all Americans as well as all Australians, Brazilians, Cambodians, Danes, Ethiopians, French, Greeks, Hungarians, Irish, Japanese, Koreans, Mexicans and many more, yet 10 million inhabitants in American go hungry each day. At the same time no nation in history has been so benevolent with foreign aid as has the U.S.A., and its reward seems to be a diminishing good will. The U.S.A. produces also half the world's pollution; vast factories annually pour 170 million tons of fumes and smoke and 165 million tons of solid wastes into the environment; Americans junk 7 million wrecked or obsolete cars each year, and discard enough bottles, cans, and rubbish to build an elevated expressway half way across the country. Some observers think that the problem of pollution has already passed a point of no return; the human species, they feel, can now only delay but not reverse a painful end to existence on the only planet known to be capable of sustaining human life. Others consider this reading too pessimistic, whether in view of technological possibilities, human reformability, or divine providence.

Disillusionment engulfs not only much of the scientific enterprise but of the political arena as well. Someone has said that frontier scientists cried when they had created in the atomic bomb a monster they could no longer control, and that they have been crying for help ever since; soon they may also be creating what additionally they cannot understand. In the U.S.A. the Watergate scandal, worst since Teapot Dome, brought the world's most powerful nation to a political watershed. The disappointing performance of many modern democracies, the frustrated hopes of those who relied on revolution and growing disenchantment with world political organizations—first the League of Nations and now the United Nations—has wrapped the whole cultural enterprise in a mood of gray doom. A number of responsible scholars consider the U.N. already senile and no longer a viable force; its philosophical even more than its fiscal deterioration has eroded the confidence of those who have witnessed its inability to resolve one crisis after another. Is the suppression of a clearly-defined national interest a reasonable expectation when the alternative is a murky global communality? Are nations facing extinction by totalitarian superpowers likely to agree that a global police force must replace any and every recourse to military response, if such agreements may portend their own eclipse? On the other hand, if national self-interest is to reign unchecked, in what dread calamity will modern history inevitably explode? It is no secret that the present course, if unaltered, could eventuate in full-scale nuclear warfare before the end of this century.

The connection between recent disenchantment with politics, science and even marriage, and modern man's naively excessive expectations from government, technocracy, and sex, should be clear. Our generation's theological dullness is apparent from its desire for instant millennium, from its disregard of and for the reality of original sin and the perversity of ongoing human transgression. This extravagant anticipation has come from adults who have effectively severed themselves from a rewarding spiritual life and from godly concerns, and whose balooning expectations are often projected to compensate for this loss; ensuing disappointment has often led them to infatuation with revolutionary novelty or to resignation with despair.

The Christian recognizes these particular temptations and fortunately may avoid them. His problem, however, may be lack of compassion or lovelessness for those immersed in other life-styles. Just because the believer, having brushed the very terrors of hell and glimpsed the demonic at its very worst through redemptive union with the substitutionary Saviour, now knows the incomparable splendor of God, he may underestimate the agonies and sufferings of unregenerate mankind, the personal aspirations of his fellow humans, and devalue the noblest achievements of civilization and culture. It becomes all too easy for the Christian, knowing the blessings of personal redemption, to concentrate on evangelistic and eternal matters, and to neglect other concerns that bind him to all mankind on the basis of a common humanity. Reinhold Niebuhr rightly complained that evangelists tend to overvalue conversion as having a millennium-producing potential. Despite his evangelistic mandate, the evangelical has no calling to ignore God's purposes through government as an instrumentality of justice and order in a fallen society; it is precisely in the world at large that he is to be salt and light. Yet Niebuhr's one-sided expectation of social justice mainly from public structures was no less a serious miscalculation. Hell is the only society now possible where all structures are sound but all citizens are uncoverted; requisite to an ideal society on earth are both personal religion and social justice.

Not since the fall of the Roman empire have social decay and political unrest been as widespread as today. When that classic empire collapsed, the Christians who were scattered abroad carried with them into the future the moral fortunes of the Western world. This dictionary of Christian ethics, a corporate effort by evangelicals of many traditions and callings, purposed to delineate once again the morally creative word of the Lord of the universe and of the nations. Just as in the creation narratives it is through the Word of the Lord that the primal desolation and waste becomes an orderly cosmos, just as the enslaved Hebrews in Egypt were lifted from bondage and became the most powerful moral force in ancient history through obedience to that Divine Word, so today the alternative to the Spiritual suicide of mankind and to ethical stagnation of our nations and cities lies in a renewed hearing of the Command and Will of God.

CARL F. H. HENRY

Arlington, Virginia
September, 1973

LIST OF CONTRIBUTORS

Alexander, John W., B.A., M.A., Ph.D.
President, Inter-Varsity Christian Fellowship, U.S.A., Madison, Wisconsin
  Cohabitation; Understanding; Youth

Alexander, Ralph H., A.B., Th.M., Th.D.
Assistant Professor of Bible, Wheaton (Illinois) College
  Abstinence; Desire; Impulse; Lying; Pity

Anderson, J. N. D., O.B.E., LL.D., F.B.A.
Professor of Oriental Laws, and Director, Institute of Advanced Legal Studies, University of London, England
  Islamic Law

Anderson, John B., A.B., J.D., LL.M.
House of Representatives, Congress of the United States of America
  Civil Disobedience; Civil Rights; Demonstration; Minority Rights; Protest; Rebellion; Resistance

Anderson, V. Elving, A.B., Ph.D.
Professor of Genetics and Cell Biology, and Assistant Director, Dight Institute for Human Genetics, University of Minnesota
  Environmental Pollution; Environment and Heredity; Genetics

Archer, Gleason L., B.A., LL.B., B.D., A.M., Ph.D.
Chairman, Division of Old Testament, Trinity Evangelical Divinity School
  Blasphemy; False Witness; Gods, False; Hosea; Isaiah; Jerusalem

Athyal, Saphir Philip, B.A., B.D., M.A., M.Th., Th.D.
Principal and Professor of Old Testament, Union Biblical Seminary, Yeotmal, Maharashtra, India
  Buddhist Ethics; Holiness

Augsburger, Myron S., B.A., Th.B. B.D., Th.M., Th.D.
President and Professor of Theology, Eastern Mennonite College
  Conscientious Objection; Disarmament

Aulie, Richard P., B.S., M.S., Ph.D.
History of Science Editor, Encyclopedia Britannica, Inc., Chicago
  Darwin and Darwinian Ethics

Babbage, Stuart B., A.B., M.A., Ph.D., Th.D.
Master of New College, University of New South Wales, Australia, and former Vice-President and Dean, Gordon-Conwell Theological Seminary
  Adoption; Bigamy; Desertion; Empathy; Gratitude; Philanthropy; Remorse; Sovereignty, Divine; Vows

Baird, Robert D., B.A., B.D., S.T.M., Ph.D.
Associate Professor of History of Religions, University of Iowa
  Hindu Ethics

Banks, Robert, B.A., B.D., M.Th., Ph.D.
History of Ideas Unit, Research School of Social Sciences, Australian National University
  Enemy; Neighbor; Peace

Barnette, Henlee H., B.A., Th.M., Th.D.
Professor of Christian Ethics, Southern Baptist Theological Seminary
  Alcoholism; Gambling; Highway Safety

Benjamin, Paul, A.B., B.D., Th.M., Th.D.
Department of Church Growth, Lincoln (Illinois) Christian Seminary
  Envy; Jealousy; Temptation

ix

Benjamin, Robert P., B.S.B.A., M.B.A., C.P.A.
Assistant Professor of Commerce, Catawba College
   Employment; Trusts; Unemployment

Beyerhaus, Peter, B.D., M.Th., D.Th.
Ordinary Professor of Theology, Tübingen University, and Director of Missiology and Ecumenical Theology
   Holy Spirit; Joy

Bird, Lewis P., B.A., B.S., B.D., S.T.M., Ph.D. (Cand.)
Eastern Regional Director, Christian Medical Society
   Medical Ethics; Sick, Care of the; Sterilization; Taoism and Ethics

Borchert, Gerald L., B.A., LL.B., B.D., Th.M., Th.D.
Dean and Professor of New Testament, North American Baptist Seminary
   Amusements; Athletics; Corporal Punishment; Enjoyment

Brobeck, John R., B.S., M.S., Ph.D., M.D.
Herbert C. Rorer Professor in the Medical Sciences and former Chairman, Department of Physiology, School of Medicine, University of Pennsylvania
   Drugs

Broger, John C., LL.D.
Director of Information for the Armed Forces, United States Department of Defense
   Armament; Conscientious Objection

Bromiley, Geoffrey W., M.A., Ph.D., D.Litt.
Professor of Church History and Historical Theology, Fuller Theological Seminary
   Barth, Karl; Canon Law; Casuistry; Celibacy; Censure; Compromise; Confession; Continence; Discipline; Dispensation; Virginity; Virtue, Virtues

Brown, Colin, B.A., B.D., M.A., Ph.D.
Dean of Studies, Tyndale Hall, Bristol, England
   Buber, Martin; Bultmann, Rudolph

Brown, Harold O. J., A.B., S.T.B., Th.M., Ph.D.
Associate Editor, *Christianity Today*
   Corporate Responsibility; Welfare State

Brubaker, Kenton K., B.S., M.Sc., Ph.D.
Professor of Biology, Eastern Mennonite College
   Defoliation; Famine

Bruce, Frederick F., M.A., D.D.
Rylands Professor of Biblical Criticism and Exegesis, University of Manchester, England
   Jesus, Ethical Teachings

Buehler, William W., B.S., B.D., D.Theol.
Associate Professor of Biblical Studies, Barrington College
   Peace and War

Burtness, James H., B.A., B.Th., Th.D.
Department of Systematic Theology, Luther Theological Seminary
   Bonhoeffer, Dietrich; Pride

Butler, Roy W., A.B., M.A., M.Ed., Ph.D.
Professor of Philosophy, Western Kentucky University
   Act, Action, Actor; Carnell, Edward John; Clark, Gordon Haddon; Henry, Carl F. H.; Intrinsinc, Instrumental Good; Ramsey, Paul

Chang, Lit-Sen, B.S., M.A., B.D., Lett.D.
Founder-President of Kiang-Nan University (China), and Special Lecturer in World Religions and Missions, Gordon-Conwell Theological Seminary
   Zen

Claghorn, George S., B.A., B.D., Ph.D.
Chairman, Department of Philosophy, West Chester (Pennsylvania) State College
   Liberalism, Ethical; Marx and Marxist Ethics; Phenomenology; Progress

Clark, Gordon H., A.B., Ph.D.
Chairman, Department of Philosophy, Butler University
Activism; Altruism; Anarchism; Antithesis; Aquinas; Atheism; Augustine; Behaviorism; Calvinistic Ethics; Capital Punishment; Cynicism; Determinism; Dewey, John; Egoism; Ethics, History of; Faith; Fate; Greek Ethics; Happiness; Hedonism; Humanism; Idealistic Ethics; Image of God; Intuition; Irrationalism; James, William; Kant; Legalism; Oaths; Pragmatism; Responsibility; Situation Ethics; Skepticism; Utilitarianism; Values

Cleath, Robert L., B.A., M.A., M.Div., Ph.D.
Associate Professor of Speech, California Polytechnic State University
Brainwashing; Prisoners of War; Propaganda; Public Opinion

Clouse, Robert G., B.A., B.D., M.A., Ph.D.
Associate Professor of History, Indiana State University
Free Will; Will

Daane, James B.A., Th.B., Th.D.
Professor of Practical Theology and Director of Pastoral Doctorate Program, Fuller Theological Seminary
Brotherhood; Intermarriage, Racial; Racism

Darling, Harold W., A.B., M.S., Ph.D.
Chairman, Social Science Division, and Professor of Psychology, Spring Arbor (Michigan) College
Defense Mechanisms; Oedipus Complex; Psychology

Davis, Richard, B.A., B.D., M.A., Ph.D.
Assistant Professor of Religion, Earlham College
Sermon on the Mount; Truthfulness

Dayton, Donald, W., B.A., B.D., M.S.
Assistant Professor in Bibliography and Research, Asbury Theological Seminary
Ebionites; Greed; Promise

De Koster, Lester R., A.M., A.M.L.S., Ph.D.
Editor, *The Banner*
Communism

Denlinger, Paul B., B.D., Ph.D.
Special Assistant to the Dean for Curricular Development, Asbury College, and former Professor of English, Tunghai University (Taiwan)
Confucian Ethics

DeVos, Peter A., A.B., A.M.
Associate Professor of Philosophy, Calvin College
Justice

Douglas, James D., B.A., M.A., S.T.M., Ph.D.
General Editor, *An Encyclopedic Dictionary of the Christian Church*
Chartism; Chivalry; Divine Right of Kings; Hoax; Honor; Neo-nephalitism; Nonconformity; Pacifism

Doll, Ronald C., B.A., M.A., Ed.D.
Professor of Education, Richmond College, City University of New York
Development; Motives and Motivation

Dully, A. J. Franklyn, M.A.
St. John's College, Bramcote, England
Guilt

Dunn, James D. G., M.A., B.D., Ph.D.
Lecturer in New Testament, University of Nottingham, England
Cullman, Oscar; Lord's Prayer; Repentance

Dymale, Herbert R., B.D., Th.M., Ph.D.
Associate Professor of Religion, Malone College
Hope; Totalitarianism

Eenigenburg, Elton M., A.B., B.D., Th.M., Ph.D.
Academic Dean and Professor of Christian Ethics and Philosophy of Religion, Western Theological Seminary
Aquinas and Roman Catholic Ethics; Roman Catholic Ethics

Ellis, E. Earle, B.S., B.D., M.A., Ph.D.
Professor of Biblical Studies, New Brunswick Theological Seminary
Adultery; Childlikeness

Ellul, Jacques, B.A., M.Lit., M.Droit, D.Droit, LL.D.
Professor of Law and Government, University of Bordeaux, France
Social Change

Erickson, Millard J., B.A., B.D., M.A., Ph.D.
Professor of Theology, Bethel Theological Seminary
Absolutes, Moral; Act Ethics; Fletcher, Joseph; Norms; Principles; Rule Ethics

Everett, Glenn D., B.A., M.A.
Washington newspaper correspondent and author, and Research Chairman for former Churchmen's Commission on Decent Publications, 1957-1965
Obscenity; Pornography; Smut

Farnell, Robert E. III, B.A., J.D.
Former Associate Judge, People's Court, Dorchester County (Maryland)
Accident; Homicide; Insurrection

Feinberg, Charles L., A.B., Th.B., Th.M., Th.D., M.A., Ph.D.
Dean and Professor of Semitics and Old Testament, Talbot Theological Seminary
Jewish Ethics

Feinberg, Paul D., B.A., M.A., B.D., Th.M., Th.D.
Assistant Professor of Philosophy, Trinity College, Deerfield, Illinois
Harnack, Adolph; Ritschl and Protestant Ethics; Troeltsch, Ernst; Tyrannicide, Tyrrany

Fitch, William, B.D., M.A., Ph.D.
Minister, Knox Presbyterian Church, Toronto, Canada
Affluence; Wealth; Widows

Forrester, James, B.A., M.A., Ph.D., D.D., LL.D.
Adjunct Professor of Psychology, Christopher Newport College of the College of William and Mary, and Director, Contact Peninsula, Inc., Newport News, Virginia
Clergy, Ethical Problems; Counseling, Ethical Problems; Draft; Guidance

Foulkes, Richard T., B.S., B.D., Th.M., D.Rel.Sc.
Professor of New Testament, Seminario Biblico Latinoamericano, San José, Costa Rica
Duty; Malice

Frame, John M., A.B., B.D., A.M., M.Phil.
Assistant Professor of Systematic Theology, Westminster Theological Seminiary
Reformed Ethics; Schleiermacher and Protestant Ethics

Fromer, Paul, B.A., B.D.
Formerly Editor, *His* Magazine
Leisure; Movies; Theater

Gaebelein, Frank E., A.B., A.M., Litt.D., D.D., LL.D.
Headmaster Emeritus, Stony Brook School
Bible; Dispensational Ethics; Passion

Garnet, Paul, B.A., M.A., Ph.D.
Assistant Professor, Loyola College, Montreal, Canada
Essene Community

Gasque, W. Ward, B.A., B.D., M.Th., Ph.D.
Assistant Professor, New Testament Studies, Regent College, Vancouver, Canada
Almsgiving; Fasting; Gluttony; Practice

Geisler, Norman L., B.A., M.A., Th.B., Ph.D.
Chairman, Philosophy of Religion Department, Trinity Evangelical Divinity School
Pessimism; Romanticism and Ethics; Superman; Utopianism

Genco, Peter, B.A., M.A., Ph.D.
Associate Professor of Philosophy, Eastern Baptist College
 Deontological Ethics; Emotivism; Naturalistic Fallacy; Objectivism; Positivism

Gerstner, John F., B.A., B.D., B.Th., Ph.D.
Professor of Church History, Pittsburgh Theological Seminary
 Apostasy; Doubt; Edwards, Johathan; Fundamentalism

Gish, Delbert R., A.B., M.A., Ph.D.
Professor of Philosophy of Religion and Christian Ethics, Nazarene Theological Seminary
 Descriptivism; General Rules Concept; Meliorism; Prescriptivism; Probabiliorism; Rigorism; Scrupulosity

Goppelt, Leonhard, B.A., D. Theol.
Professor of New Testament, Protestant Faculty of Theology, University of Munich (Germany)
 Grace

Gorman, Walter P. III, B.A., Ph.D.
Associate Professor of Marketing and Economics, School of Business Administration, University of Tennessee
 Credit; Debt; Money; Wages

Govig, Stewart D., B.A., B.Th., M.Th., Ph.D.
Associate Professor and Chairman of the Department of Religion, Pacific Lutheran University
 Self-denial; Self-examination; Selfishness

Groseclose, Elgin, A.B., M.A., Ph.D.
Financial Consultant and Writer, Washington, D.C.
 Inflation; Underdeveloped Nations

Grounds, Vernon C., B.A., B.D., Ph.D.
President, Conservative Baptist Theological Seminary
 Genocide; Murder; Naturalistic Ethics; Probabilism; Satan; Suicide

Guelich, Robert A., B.A., M.A., S.T.B., D.Theol.
Associate Professor of New Testament, Bethel Theological Seminary
 Jesus and the Law; Pharisaism

Guthrie, Donald, B.D., Th.M., Ph.D.
Professor of New Testament, London (England) Bible College
 Salvation; Schweitzer, Albert

Hall, Bert H., M.D., Th.D.
Professor of Philosophy, Azusa-Pacific College
 Arminius and Arminian Ethics; Children; Perfectionism

Hamilton, Kenneth M., B.A., M.A., Th.M., Th.D.
Professor, Department of Religious Studies, University of Winnipeg, Canada
 Niebuhr, Reinhold; Secularism and Secularization; Worldliness

Harris, Murray J., M.A., Ph.D.
Assistant Professor of New Testament, Trinity Evangelical Divinity School
 Habit; Mixed Motives; Unbelief

Harris, R. Laird, B.S., Th.B., Th.M., M.A., Ph.D.
Professor of Old Testament, Covenant Theological Seminary
 Asylum; Conviction (of Sin); Forgiveness; Omission, Sins of

Harrison, Everett F., B.A., M.A., Th.B., Th.D., Ph.D.
Senior Professor of New Testament, Fuller Theological Seminary
 Antinomianism; Chastening; Contentment; Forbearance; Gentleness; God; Humility; Kindness; Longsuffering; Patience; Self-control; Temperance; Tranquility

Harrison, R. K., B.A., B.D., M.Th., Ph.D., D.D.
Professor of Old Testament, Wycliffe College, University of Toronto, Canada
  Acquiescence; Aggression; Flagellation; Poor; Theocracy

Harrison, William K. Jr., LL.D., Lit.D.
Lieutenant General (Retired), United States Army
  Colonialism, Colonization; Diplomacy; Isolationism; Planetization

Hatfield, Charles, A.B., A.M., Ph.D.
Professor, Department of Mathematics, University of Missouri—Rolla
  Technocracy and Technology

Henry, Carl F. H., B.A., M.A., M.A. in Th., B.D., Th.D., Ph.D.
President of the Directors, Institute for Advanced Christian Studies, and Professor at Large, Eastern Baptist Theological Seminary
  American Council of Christian Churches; Christian Education; Ecumenism and Ethics; Metaphysics and Ethics; Moral Rearmament; New Testament Ethics; Political Theology; Prejudice; Prison Reform; Rape; Revenge; Slander; Terrorism; Watergate; World Council of Churches

Henry, Paul B., B.A., M.A., Ph.D.
Visiting Assistant Professor of Political Science, Calvin College
  Conservatism, Political; Liberalism, Political; Natural Law

Herrmann, Robert L., B.S., Ph.D.
Associate Professor of Biochemistry, School of Medicine, Boston University
  Old Age

Hesselgrave, David J., B.A., M.A., Ph.D.
Director and Professor, School of World Missions, Trinity Evangelical Divinity School
  Polygamy; Universalism

Hoffmann, Oswald C. J., M.A., B.D., D.D., LL.D.
Speaker, The Lutheran Hour
  Laity; Preaching

Holmer, Paul L., B.A., M.A., Ph.D.
Professor of Theology, Divinity School, Yale University
  Blessedness; Kierkegaard and Ethics; Pleasure

Holmes, Arthur F., A.B., M.A., Ph.D.
Chairman, Department of Philosophy, Wheaton (Illinois) College
  Just War Criteria; Marcuse, Herbert

Hook, H. Phillip, A.B., Th.D.
Assistant Professor of Systematic Theology, Dallas Theological Seminary
  Punishment

Houston, James M., B.Sc., M.A., D.Phil.
Principal, Regent College, Vancouver, Canada
  Environmental Perception; Sovereignty, National; Treaties

Hoy, W. Ivan, B.A., B.D., S.T.M., Ph.D.
Chairman, Department of Religion, and Professor of Religion, University of Miami
  Chance; Education and Morality; Sensuality

Hunnex, Milton D., A.A., A.B., M.A., Ph.D.
Chairman, Department of Philosophy, Williamette University
  Knowledge and Ethics

Hunt, Leslie, B.A., B.D., M.Th., D.D.
Principal and Professor of New Testament and Liturgics, Wycliffe College, University of Toronto, Canada
  Good Neighbor; Good Works; Hospitality; Indifference

Inch, Morris A., A.B., B.D., Ph.D.
Professor of Bible and Apologetics, Wheaton (Illinois) College
  Affinity; Benefience; Benevolence; Common Law Marriage; Concubinage; Dreams; Endogamy; Nullity

Jacobsen, Herbert K., B.A., M.A., Ph.D.
Professor of Religion, Wheaton (Illinois)
College
  Aspiration; Niebuhr, H. Richard; Scandal;
  Seduction; Sodomy

James, Gilbert M., A.B., M.A., Ph.D.
Professor of The Church in Society, Asbury
Theological Seminary
  Race Relations

Jeeves, Malcolm A., M.A., Ph.D., F.B.Ps.S.,
F.A.P.S.
Professor and Head of Department of
Psychology, University of St. Andrews
(Scotland)
  Emotion; Inhibition; Juvenile Delin-
  quency

Jekel, James F., A.B., M.D., M.P.H.
Associate Professor of Public Health, School
of Medicine, Yale University
  Health Laws

Jellema, Dirk W., A.B., M.A., Ph.D.
Professor of History, Calvin College
  Conformity; Custom; Ethos; Formalism;
  Negligence

Jewett, Paul K., B.A., Th.B., Th.M., Ph.D.
Professor of Systematic Theology, Fuller
Theological Seminary
  Brunner, Emil; Fall of Man; Neo-
  Orthodoxy and Ethics

Jocz, Jakob, A.B., Ph.D., D.Litt.
Professor of Systematic Theology, Wycliffe
College, University of Toronto, Canada
  Covenant; Talmud; Torah

Johnson, Alan F., B.S., Th.M., Th.D.
Assistant Professor of Bible and Religion,
Wheaton (Illinois) College
  Commandments; Conventional Morality;
  Disinterestedness

Johnson, John F., B.A., B.D., M.Th., M.Ed.,
S.T.M., M.A., Th.D.
Associate Academic Dean and Professor of
Systematic and Philosophical Theology,
Concordia Theological Seminary, Spring-
field, Illinois
  Mammon; Quietism; Saintliness

Johnson, Walter H., B.A., B.D., Th.D.
Chairman, Department of Philosophy, Seattle Pacific College
  Ambition; Character; Credulity; Excellence

Johnson, William C., B.A., M.A., Ph.D.
Associate Professor of Political Science
Bethel College
  Government

Kaiser, Walter C., Jr., A.B., B.D., M.A.,
Ph.D. (Cand.)
Associate Professor of Old Testament, Trin-
ity Evangelical Divinity School
  Decalogue

Kalland, Lloyd A., A.B., B.D., M.A., Th.M.,
Th.D.
Professor of Christian Ethics, Gordon-
Conwell Theological Seminary
  Population Control; Procreation; Re-
  marriage

Kamm, Samuel R., A.B., A.M., Ph.D.,
LL.D., D.H.L.
Professor of History and Social Science,
Wheaton (Illinois) College
  Bills of Rights; Constitutionalism; Free
  Enterprise; Independence; Laissez-faire;
  Social Darwinism

Kantzer, Kenneth S., A.B., A.M., B.D.,
S.T.M., Ph.D.
Vice President for Graduate Studies and
Dean of Trinity Evangelical Divinity School
  Man, Doctrine of

Kerr, William N., B.A., B.D., Th.D., Ph.D.
Professor of Church History, Gordon-
Conwell Theological Seminary
  Enlightenment

Kinlaw, Dennis F., A.B., B.D., Ph.D.
President of Asbury College
  Old Testament Ethics

Kitchen, Kenneth A., B.A.
Lecturer in Egyptian and Coptic, School of
Archaeology and Oriental Studies, Univer-
sity of Liverpool, England
  Egyptian Ethics

Klann, Richard, B.D., M.A., Th.D.
Associate Professor of Systematic Theology,
Concordia Theological Seminary, St. Louis
  Lutheran Ethics

Kline, Frank J., B.A., S.T.B., M.Th., Ed.D.
Dean, School of Religion, Seattle Pacific
College
  Family, Quarreling

Klooster, Fred H., A.B., B.D., Th.M., Th.D.
Professor of Systematic Theology, Calvin
Theological Seminary
  I-Thou Relationship; Merit; Super-
  erogation, Works of

Klug, Eugene F., B.D., M.A., Th.D.
Associate Professor, Concordia Theological
Seminary, Springfield, Ill.
  Household Codes; Military Chaplaincy;
  Parenthood

**Knudsen, Robert D., A.B., Th.M., S.T.M.,
Ph.D.**
Assistant Professor of Apologetics, West-
minster Theological Seminary
  Moral Theology

Koch, Kurt E., B.A., Th.D.
Author and Lecturer, Waibstadt, West Ger-
many
  Demonology; Witchcraft

Koop, C. Everett, A.B., M.D., Sc.D.
Professor of Pediatric Surgery, School of
Medicine, University of Pennsylvania, and
Surgeon-in-Chief, Children's Hospital of
Philadelphia
  Birth Control; Contraception

**Krishna, Purushotman Muthu, B.A., LL.B.,
M.Litt., Ph.D.**
Professor of Oriental Philosophy and Relig-
ion, Trinity Evangelical Divinity School
  Zoroastrian Ethics

Kromminga, John H., B.A., B.D., Th.D.
President of Calvin Theological Seminary
  Mysticism; Renaissance

Kucharsky, David E., B.A., M.A.
Managing Editor, *Christianity Today*
  Church Lobbies; Councils of Churches;
  Counsels; Food; National Council of
  Churches

**Kuhn, Harold B., A.B., S.T.B., S.T.M.,
Ph.D.**
Professor of Philosophy of Religion, Asbury
Theological Seminary
  Authenticity; Golden Rule; Humanitar-
  ianism; Relativism; Theism

Kusche, Roger W., A.B., B.D., Ph.D.
Chairman, Division of Language, Asbury
College
  Anger; Deliberation; Hate

Ladd, George E., Th.B., B.D., Ph.D., D.D.
Professor of New Testament Exegesis and
Theology, Fuller Theological Seminary
  Eschatology and Ethics; Interim Ethics;
  Kingdom of God, Kingdom of Heaven

Lake, Donald M., A.B., M.A., Ph.D.
Assistant Professor of Theology, Wheaton
(Illinois) College
  Berdaev, Nicholai; Bradley, F. H.; Mari-
  tain, Jacques

Larson, Reed, B.S.
Executive Vice President, National Right to
Work Committee
  Right to Work

Lazareth, William H., B.A., B.D., Ph.D.
Dean and Professor of Systematic Theology, The Lutheran Theological Seminary, Philadelphia
   Order of Creation and Preservation; Twofold Reign of God

Leitch, Addison H., A.B., B.D., Th.M., Ph.D., D.D., Litt.D.
Professor of Theology, Gordon-Conwell Theological Seminary
   Abandonment; Suffering

Leonard, Paul E., B.S., M.Th., Ph.D. (Cand.)
Associate Professor of New Testament, Trinity Evangelical Divinity School
   Freedom; Patriotism

Lewis, Jack P., B.A., M.A., S.T.B., Ph.D., Ph.D.
Professor of Bible, Harding Graduate School of Religion
   Courage; Despair

Linder, Robert D., B.S., B.D., M.R.E., M.A., Ph.D.
Associate Professor of History, Kansas State University
   Nationalism; Oppression; Protestant Ethic

Linton, Calvin D., A.B., A.M., Ph.D.
Dean, Columbian College of Arts and Sciences, and Professor of English Literature, George Washington University
   Abduction; Dante; Equality; Literature; Sin

Longenecker, Richard N., A.B., A.M., Ph.D.
Professor of New Testament, Wycliffe College, University of Toronto, Canada
   Pauline Ethics

MacKay, Donald M., B.Sc., Ph.D., F.Inst.P.
Professor of Communication, University of Keele, England
   Cybernetics

Maertin, Harvey A. II, B.S.M.E., M.B.A.
Associate Professor of Marketing Administration, College of Business Administration, University of Toledo
   Black Market; Cartels; Competition; Econometrics; Monopoly

Maier, Walter A., B.A., M.A., M.S.T., Th.D.
Professor of New Testament, Concordia Theological Seminary, Springfield, Ill.
   Dynamic; Enthusiasm; Generation Gap

Malik, Charles Habib, B.A., M.A., Ph.D., Litt.D., LL.D.
Distinguished Professor of Philosophy, American University of Beirut, Lebanon
   International Order; United Nations; World Government

Marshall, I. Howard, B.A., M.A., B.D., Ph.D.
Senior Lecturer in New Testament Exegesis, King's College, University of Aberdeen, Scotland
   Personal Ethics

Martin, Ralph P., B.A., M.A., Ph.D.
Professor of New Testament, Fuller Theological Seminary
   Cremation; Exogamy; Foolishness; Koinonia; Purity

Martin, William J., M.A., Th.B., Ph.D.
Vice-Principal, Regent College, Vancouver, Canada
   Immortality

McCallum, Floyd F., A.B., Th.B., M.A., Ed.D.
Head of Department of Psychology and Professor of Psychology, Houghton College
   Charismatic Movement; Church Covenants; Optimism

McCown, Wayne G., B.A., B.D., M.A., Th.M., Th.D.
Assistant Professor of Religion, Seattle Pacific College
   Compassion; Friendship

McCurtain, Edmund G., A.B., M.A., Ph.D.
Professor of Sociology and Anthropology, Drury College
Sociology and Ethics

McDonald, H. Dermot, B.A., B.D., Ph.D., D.D.
Vice-Principal, London Bible College (England)
Exception; New Morality; Robinson, John A. T.

McGee, Daniel B., B.A., B.D., Th.M., Ph.D.
Associate Professor of Religion, Baylor University
Aged, Care of; Human Experimentation; Senility; Vivisection

McIntire, C. T., B.A., M.A., M.Div., Ph.D.
Assistant Professor of History, Institute for Christian Studies, Toronto, Canada
Aristocracy; Natural Rights

McIntyre, John A., B.S., M.A., Ph.D.
Professor of Physics, Texas A & M University
Atomic Energy

McKenna, David L., B.A., B.D., M.A., Ph.D.
President, Seattle Pacific College
Capitalism

Menkus, Belden
Author and Lecturer, Bergenfield, New Jersey
Anti-Semitism; Consumer Fraud; Contracts; Industrial Espionage

Meye, Robert P., B.A., B.D., Th.M., D. Theol.
Dean of the Seminary, Northern Baptist Theological Seminary
Beautitudes; Chastity; Life, Sacredness of; Lynching

Mickelsen, A. Berkeley, B.A., M.A., B.D., Ph.D.
Professor of New Testament Interpretation, Bethel Theological Seminary
Interpersonal Relations; State

Mikolaski, Samuel J., B.A., M.A., B.D., D.Phil.
Principal, Baptist Leadership Training School, Calgary, Canada
Evil; Right and Wrong

Millard, Alan R., M.A., M.Ph., F.S.A.
Rankin Lecturer in Hebrew and Ancient Semitic Languages, School of Archaeology and Oriental Studies, University of Liverpool, England
Moses

Miller, Douglas J., A.B., B.D., Ph.D.
Associate Professor of Christian Social Ethics, Eastern Baptist Theological Seminary
Contextual Ethics; Revolution; Violence

Mills, Watson E., B.A., B.D., Th.M., M.A., Th.D.
Associate Professor of Philosophy and Religion, Averett College
Coercion; Extortion; Fornication; Lust; Provocation; Promiscuity; Theft

Minnema, Theodore, B.A., B.D., Th.D.
Professor, Department of Religion and Theology, Calvin College
Anxiety; Original Sin

Monsma, Stephen V., A.B., M.A., Ph.D.
Associate Professor of Political Science, Calvin College
Apartheid; Behavioralism and the Social Sciences

Mooneyham, W. Stanley, B.A., B.D., D.D.
President, World Vision
National Association of Evangelicals; Orphans

Moore, Merrill D., A.B., Th.M., D.D.
Executive Director (Retired), The Stewardship Commission, Southern Baptist Convention
Stewardship

Morris, Leon, B.Sc., M.Sc., M.Th., Ph.D.
Principal, Ridley College, Melbourne, Australia
Atonement; Expiation; Reconciliation

Mosteller, James D., A.M., B.D., Th.D.
Professor of Church History, New Orleans
Baptist Theological Seminary
   Anabaptists; Fanaticism; Pietism

Mouw, Richard J., B.A., M.A., Ph.D.
Assistant Professor of Philosophy, Calvin
College
   Language, Ethical

Mueller, William A., M.A., S.T.M., Ph.D.
Professor Emeritus, New Orleans Baptist
Theological Seminary and Visiting Lecturer,
PanAmerican University, Edinburgh, Texas
   Rauschenbusch, Walter; Religious Free-
   dom

Nash, Ronald H., A.B., M.A., Ph.D.
Head, Department of Philosophy and Relig-
ion, and Professor of Philosophy, Western
Kentucky University
   Force; Power; Rights

**Neill, Stephen C., F.B.A., D.D., Th.D.,
D.Litt.**
Anglican Bishop of Tinnevelly (Retired) and
Head of Department of Philosophy and
Religious Studies, University of Nairobi,
Kenya
   Human Nature

Nicholi, Armand M. II, B.A., M.D.
Faculty, Harvard Medical School, Harvard
University, and Private Practice of
Psychiatry
   Compulsion; Homosexualism and Homo-
   sexuality; Hypnotism; Masturbation; Sug-
   gestion

Nicholls, Bruce J. M.A., B.D., Th.M.
Theological Coordinator, World Evangelical
Fellowship, and Professor of Theology,
Union Biblical Seminary, Yeotmal, India
   Syncretism

Nicole, Roger R., Lic.Lett., Th.D., Ph.D.
Professor of Theology and Curator of the
Library, Gordon-Conwell Theological
Seminary
   Authority; Divorce; Pelagian Ethics

Oates, Wayne E., B.A., Th.M., Th.D.
Professor of Psychology of Religion and
Pastoral Care, Southern Baptist Theological
Seminary
   Sex; Social Class

**Olbricht, Thomas H., B.S., S.T.B., M.A.,
Ph.D.**
Professor of Biblical Theology, Abilene
Christian College
   Incarnation

Olthuis, James H., A.B., B.D., Ph.D.
Assistant Professor of Ethics, Institute for
Christian Studies, Toronto, Canada
   Marriage; Separation, Marital

Opitz, Edmund A., B.A., Th.B.
Senior Staff, The Foundation for Economic
Education, Inc.
   Socialism

Orr, J. Edwin, D.Phil., Ed.D.
Visiting Professor, School of World Mission,
Fuller Theological Seminary
   Christian Social Movements

Osterhaven, M. Eugene, A.B., B.D., Th.D.
Albert C. Van Raalte Professor of System-
atic Theology, Western Theological
Seminary
   Absolution; Dogma; Papal Encyclicals;
   Penance

Ostling, Richard N., A.B., M.S.J., M.A.
Religion Correspondent, *Time* Magazine,
New York
   Advertising; Mass Media; Plagiarism; Se-
   crecy; Television

Packer, James I., B.A., M.A., D.Phil.
Associate Principal, Trinity College, Bristol,
England
   Myth; Puritan Ethics; Revelation

Pattison, E. Mansell, B.A., M.D.
Associate Professor, Department of Psychiatry and Human Behavior, University of California-Irvine, and Deputy Director, Training, Orange County (California) Department of Mental Health
  Person and Personality

Paul, William W., A.B., A.M., B.D., Ph.D.
Head, Humanities Division, and Professor of Philosophy, Central College
  Decision; Dialectical Ethics; Existential Ethics; Infanticide; Melancholy

Payne, J. Barton, B.A., B.D., M.A., Th.M., Th.D.
Professor of Old Testament, Wheaton (Illinois) College
  Profit; Property; Usury

Pfeiffer, Charles F. B.A., B.D., S.T.M., Ph.D.
Chairman, Department of Religion, Central Michigan University
  Amos; Prophets

Pierard, Richard V., B.A., M.A., Ph.D.
Professor of History, Indiana State University
  Fascism; Weber, Max

Pinnock, Clark H., B.A., Ph.D.
Professor of Systematic Theology, Trinity Evangelical Divinity School
  Autonomy; Conscience; Heteronomy; Hypocrisy; Truth

Pippert, Wesley G., B.A., M.A.
Sunday Editor, Washington (D.C.) Bureau, United Press International
  Censorship

Powell, Ralph E., Ph.B., B.D., M.A., Th.D.
Professor of Theology, North American Baptist Seminary
  Consent; Deception; Destiny; Heroism; Meekness

Preus, Robert D., B.A., B.D., Ph.D., D.Theol.
Professor of Systematic Theology, Concordia Seminary, St. Louis
  Adiaphora; Law and Gospel; Propitiation

Redekop, John H., B.A., B.Ed., M.A., Ph.D.
Professor of Political Science, Waterloo Lutheran University, Canada
  Arbitration; Boycott; Guaranteed Income; Labor Relations; Strikes

Reid, W. Stanford, B.A., M.A., Th.B., Th.M., Ph.D.
Professor of History, University of Guelph, Canada
  Collectivism; Individualism; Industrial Revolution; Militarism; Military Service

Reilly, Christopher T., M.D., F.A.C.S., F.A.C.O.G., F.I.C.S.
Clinical Assistant Professor of Gynecology and Obstetrics, New Jersey College of Medicine and Dentistry
  Smoking; Sports

Reynolds, Stephen M., A.B., B.D., B.S., M.A., Ph.D.
Associate Professor of Old Testament, Gordon-Conwell Theological Seminary
  Euthanasia; Prudence

Rhee, Jong Sung, B.D., Th.M., Th.D.
President, Presbyterian Theological Seminary of Korea, Seoul
  Indigenization

Richardson, Peter, B.Arch., B.D., Ph.D.
Assistant to the Dean of Arts, and Assistant Professor, Department of Theological Studies, Loyola College, Montreal, Canada
  Justification

Robertson, Donald S., A.B., Ph.D.
Professor of Genetics, Iowa State University of Science and Technology
  Eugenics

Rodgers, John H., Jr., B.S., B.D., Th.D.
Professor of Systematic Theology, Protestant Episcopal Seminary of Virginia
　Monogamy

Rookmaaker, H. R., B.A., Dr.
Professor of the History of Art, Free University of Amsterdam
　Aesthetics; Art; Beauty

Rose, Delbert R., A.B., M.A., Ph.D., D.D.
Professor of Biblical Theology, Asbury Theological Seminary
　License; Liturgy; Vice

Roth, Robert P., B.D., M.A., Ph.D.
Professor of Systematic Theology, Northwestern Lutheran Theological Seminary
　Redemption; Tillich, Paul

Runia, Klaas, B.A., B.D., M.Th., Th.D.
Professor of Systematic Theology, Kampen Theological Seminary, Netherlands
　Law in New and Old Testaments; Separation, Ecclesiastical; Vocation

Rupprecht, Arthur A., A.B., B.D., M.A., Ph.D.
Professor of Classical Studies, Wheaton (Illinois) College
　Slavery

Rust, Eric C., M.A., B.D., M.Sc., Litt.D.
Professor of Christian Philosophy, Southern Baptist Theological Seminary
　Science and Ethics

Rutenber, Culbert G., Ph.B., B.D., M.A., Ph.D., D.D.
Professor of Philosophy of Religion, American Baptist Seminary of the West
　Magnanimity; Pantheism and Ethics

Ryrie, Charles C., A.B., Th.M., Th.D., Ph.D.
Dean of Doctoral Studies and Professor of Systematic Theology, Dallas Theological Seminary
　Women, Status of

Samudre, Vasant B., B.D., Th.M., M.A.
Professor of Religions, Union Biblical Seminary, Yeotmal, India
　Islamic Ethics

Saucy, Robert L., A.B., Th.M., Th.D.
Professor of Systematic Theology, Talbot Theological Seminary
　Mortification; Renunciation

Scaer, David P., B.A., B.D., Th.D.
Associate Professor for Systematic Theology, Concordia Theological Seminary, Springfield, Illinois
　Providence; Righteousness

Scanzoni, John H., B.A., Ph.D.
Professor, Department of Sociology, Indiana University
　Kinsey Report; Poverty; Prostitution

Scharlemann, Martin H., M.A., M.Div., Ph.D., Th.D.
Graduate Professor of Exegetical Theology, Concordia Seminary, St. Louis
　Abortion; Acts of God

Scholer, David M., A.B., M.A., B.D., Th.D. (Cand.)
Assistant Professor of New Testament, Gordon-Conwell Theological Seminary
　Gnosticism; Resurrection

Schultz, Arnold C., Ph.B., M.A., B.D., Th.D.
Professor of Near Eastern Studies, Roosevelt University
　Idolatry; Ignorance; Retribution

Seerveld, Calvin G., B.A., M.A., Ph.D.
Professor of Aesthetics, Institute of Christian Studies, Toronto, Canada
　Courtesy; Innocence; Kiss, Kissing; Modesty; Nudism

Shepherd, Norman, B.A., B.D., Th.M.
Associate Professor of Systematic Theology and Dean of the Faculty Westminster Theological Seminary
　Judgment

Shultz, Joseph R., A.B., M.R.E., D.R.E.
Dean, Ashland Theological Seminary
  Sanctification; Uncleanness

Sider, Ronald J., B.A., M.A., B.D., Ph.D.
Acting Director and Assistant Professor of
History, Messiah College Campus at Temple
University
  Allegiance; Communal Life; Conflict of
  Duties, Interest; Zeal, Zealot

Simmons, Paul D., A.A., B.A., B.D., Th.M., Th.D.
Assistant Professor Christian Ethics, Southern Baptist Theological Seminary
  Bestiality; Contraband; Hijacking; Open
  Housing; Piracy; Smog; Vote

Singer, C. Gregg, B.A., Ph.D.
Professor of Church History, Catawba
College
  Church and State

Singewald, Martin L., B.E., M.D., F.A.C.P.
Associate Professor of Medicine, School of
Medicine, Johns Hopkins University
  Artificial Insemination; Hippocratic Oath

Smalley, Stephen S., M.A., B.D.
Lecturer in New Testament Studies, Faculty
of Theology, Manchester University,
England
  Good, Goodness; Otherworldliness;
  Singlemindedness

Smick, Elmer B., A.B., B.D., S.T.M., Ph.D.
Professor of Old Testament, Gordon-Conwell Theological Seminary
  Animals; Cruelty; Hunting

Smith, Morton H., B.A., B.D., Th.M., Th.D.
Professor of Systematic Theology, Reformed Theological Seminary
  Contemplation; Prayer; Worship

Smith, Wilbur M., D.D.
Professor Emeritus of English Bible, Trinity
Evangelical Divinity School
  Antichrist

Snyder, John W., B.A., Ph.D.
Executive Vice-Chancellor, University of
California—Santa Barbara
  Democracy

Stahlke, Otto F., M.A., S.T.M.
Professor of Old Testament and World
Religions, Concordia Theological Seminary,
Springfield, Illinois
  Orthodox (Eastern) Ethics

Stanger, Frank B., A.B., Th.B., S.T.M., S.T.D., D.D., LL.D., L.H.D.
President, Asbury Theological Seminary
  Methodism; Prohibition; Prohibitions;
  Restitution; Secret Societies; Temper;
  Tradition

Stevens, Morris L., A.B., LL.B., M.A., Ph.D., J.D.
Chairman, Department of Social Science,
Kansas State College of Pittsburg
  Social Service

Stob, Henry, Th.M., Ph.D.
Professor of Christian Ethics, Calvin Theological Seminary
  Social Ethics

Story, Cullen I. K., M.A., Th.D.
Assistant Professor of Biblical Studies,
Princeton Theological Seminary
  Imitation of Christ; Johannine Ethics

Strauss, James D., B.A., M.A., Th.M.
Associate Professor of Philosophy and Christian Doctrine, Linclon Christian Seminary
  Ethical Relativism; Honesty; Maturity;
  Nihilism

Taylor, Willard H., M.A., B.D., Th.D.
Dean, Nazarene Theological Seminary
  Illegitimacy; Immorality; Incest; Licentiousness

Tenney, Merrill C., Th.B., A.M., Ph.D.
Professor of New Testament .and Former
Dean, Wheaton (Illinois) College Graduate
School
  Burial; Concupiscence; Conversion;
  Death; Depravity

Tepker, Howard W., M.S.T., Th.D.
Chairman, Systematics Department, and Professor of Theology, Concordia Theological Seminary, Springfield, Illinois
  Asceticism; Body

Thielicke, Helmut, Th.D., Ph.D., D.D.
Ordinary Professor of Systematic Theology, Hamburg (Germany) University
  Civilization

Thompson, Frank H., A.B., B.D., Th.M.
Associate Professor of Philosophy and Theology, Greenville College
  Obedience; Resignation; Rewards; Wisdom

Tinder, Donald, B.A., B.D., M.A., M.Phil., Ph.D.
Book Editor, *Christianity Today*
  Conservatism, Ethical; Cooperation, Ecclesiastical; Evangelism, Ethical Aspects

Tippett, Alan R., L.Th., M.A., Ph.D.
Professor of Missionary Anthropology, School of World Mission, Fuller Theological Seminary
  Animism; Cannibalism; Missions; Patricide; Suttee; Widow-Strangling

Traina, Robert A., A.A., A.B., S.T.B., S.T.M., Ph.D.
Vice President, Academic Administration, and Professor of English Bible, Asbury Theological Seminary
  Love; Temptations of Jesus

Travis, Stephen, M.A., Ph.D.
Lecturer in New Testament Studies, St. John's College, Bramcote, England
  Gospel; Wrath

Trueblood, D. Elton, A.B., S.T.B., Ph.D.
Professor at Large, Earlham College
  Quakers; Work

Tuel, John K., B.A., M.A., Ph.D.
Professor of Psychology, Oral Roberts University
  Persecution

Vanderlip, D. George, B.A., B.D., Th.M., Ph.D.
Professor of English Bible, Eastern Baptist Theological Seminary
  Heaven; Hell

Vandezande, Gerald
Executive Secretary, Christian Labour Association of Canada, Rexdale, Canada
  Collective Bargaining

Van Elderen, Bastiaan, B.A., B.D., M.A., Th.D.
Professor of New Testament Studies, Calvin Theological Seminary
  Petrine Ethics

Vincent, Merville O., B.A., M.D., C.M., F.R.C.P.(C)
Medical Superintendent, Homewood Sanitarium, Guelph, Canada
  Professional Ethics; Venereal Disease

Walters, Orville S., B.A., Ph.D., M.D., F.A.C.P.
Clinical Professor of Psychiatry, School of Medicine, University of Illinois-Peoria, and Assistant Medical Director for Psychiatry, Methodist Hospital, Peoria, Illinois
  Freud; Id; Instincts; Mental Health; Neurosis; Psychiatry; Psychoanalysis; Repression; Superego; Transference; Unconscious

Walters, Stanley D., A.B., B.D., Th.M., Ph.D.
Professor of Religion, Central Michigan University
  Mercy; Sacrifice

Wells, David F., B.D., Th.M., Ph.D.
Associate Professor of Church History and the History of Christian Theology, Trinity Evangelical Divinity School
  Reformation

Wenger, J. C., B.A., M.A., Th.D.
Professor of Historical Theology, Associated Mennonite Biblical Seminaries
  Evangelical Social Concern

Westphal, Merold, B.A., M.A., Ph.D.
Associate Professor of Philosophy, Yale University
  Alienation; Bergson, Henri; Nietzsche, Friedrich

Williams, Sidney A., A.B., Ph.D.
Professor of Economics, Hankamer School of Business, Baylor University
  Business Ethics, Industrial Relations

Willoughby, William F., B.S.
Religion Editor, *The Evening Star-The Sunday Star,* Washington, D.C.
  Crime

Wilson, Charles R., A.B., B.D., M.A., Ph.D.
Head, Department of Religion, Taylor University
  Self-love; Self-realization; Temperance Movements

Wilson, Donald R., A.B., M.Div., M.A., Ph.D.
Professor of Anthropology, Calvin College
  Anthropology; Cultural Relativism; Evolutionary Ethics; Primitive Ethics

Wirt, Sherwood E., B.A., B.D., Ph.D.
Editor, *Decision* Magazine
  Bennett, John C.; Sloth; Social Gospel

Wiseman, Donald J., B.A., M.A., D.Lit., F.B.A., F.S.A.
Professor of Assyriology, University of London, England
  Astrology; Babylonian Ethics

Wood, A. Skevington, B.A., Ph.D.
Senior Lecturer in Theology, Cliff College, England
  Cultural Mandate; Neutrality; Self-defense; Sunday; Temple, William

Woods, John E., B.A., M.D.
Organ and Tissue Transplantation, Mayo Clinic
  Heart Transplantation, Hospitals; Organ Transplantation

Woolley, Paul, A.B., Th.B., Th.M., D.D.
Professor of Church History, Westminster Theological Seminary
  Patristic Ethics

Wright, David F., M.A.
Lecturer in Ecclesiastical History, New College, University of Edinburgh, Scotland
  Monasticism

Yamauchi, Edwin M., B.A., M.A., Ph.D.
Associate Professor of History, Miami (Ohio) University
  Culture

Yorkston, Neil, M.B., M.R.A.C.P., M.R.C. Psych.
Associate Professor of Psychiatry and Medicine, School of Medicine, University of Minnesota
  Ego; Fear; Jung, Carl Gustave; Lesbianism; Paederasty

Young, Warren C., B.A., B.D., M.A., Ph.D.
Professor of Theology and Christian Philosophy, Northern Baptist Theological Seminary
  Faithfulness; Golden Mean; Royce, Josiah; Sanction; Subjectivism, Ethical; Voluntarism

Young, William, B.A., Th.B., B.Litt., Th.D.
Associate Professor of Philosophy, University of Rhode Island
  Moral Philosophy

TRANSLATORS

Ahlers, Rolf, Th.D.
Illinois (Jacksonville) College
 "Civilization" by Helmut Thielicke

Alsup, John, B.A., M.Div.
University of Munich, Germany
 "Grace" by Leonhard Goppelt

Borger, Ellen, M.A.
Calvin College
 "Social Change" by Jacques Ellul

Hunt, Paul A., B.Sc.
Egham, Surrey, England
 "Demonology" and "Witchcraft" by
 Kurt E. Koch

ABBREVIATIONS

HERE — *Hasting's Encyclopedia of Religion and Ethics*
IB — *Interpreter's Bible*
ICC — *International Critical Commentary*
JBL — *Journal of Biblical Literature*
TDNT — *Theological Dictionary of the New Testament*
TWNT — *Theologisches Woerterbuch zum Neuen Testament*
RGG — *Die Religion in Geschichte und Gegenwart,* 3rd ed.
ACCC — American Council of Christian Churches
NAE — National Association of Evangelicals
NCC — National Council of Churches
SCA — Student Christian Association
SCM — Student Christian Movement
SPCK — Society for Promoting Christian Knowledge
USA — United States of America
USSR — Russia
UN — United Nations
OT — Old Testament
NT — New Testament
WWC — World Council of Churches
Union SQR — *Union Seminary Quarterly Review*
CBQ — *Catholic Bible Quarterly*
FAO — Food and Agriculture Organization of the United Nations
JPSA — Jewish Publication Society of America

Baker's
DICTIONARY OF CHRISTIAN ETHICS

A

ABANDONMENT. See also *Existential Ethics; Infanticide.* The practice of abandonment has its sad history in the exposure of infants, the neglect of defectives, and the expulsion of the aged and infirm. In a godless society there is a sense of the self being abandoned in the existential combination of inborn moral demands, the dread of death and a universe of no moral resources. Positively, however, and traditionally, there has been the powerful ethical thrust of self-abandonment for the sake of others or for God. Christ's total subjection to his Father's will, made vivid in the Cry of Dereliction, is the supreme example.

ADDISON H. LEITCH

ABDUCTION. The act of leading or carrying away another person illegally, often by force or fraud. In law, abduction may be said to occur even if the abducted person goes willingly, if (as in the case of a child or wife) the person is thereby removed from the jurisdiction of those responsible for him. Ethically, abduction is the violation of another person's God-given right of self-determination and personal freedom, most obvious in abduction for the purpose of enslaving. A Biblical instance is the abduction of Joseph by his brethren and his consequent enslavement in Egypt (Gen. 37:12-36). CALVIN D. LINTON

ABJURATION. See *Oaths.*

ABORTION. See also *Birth Control; Infanticide.* Of all ethical decisions individuals confront in a culture growing continuously more secular few involve greater complexity in the application of basic principles than the matter of abortion. Any choice in this area of life embraces much more than definable human calculations, such as possible over-population and impending food shortages, since at best, such predictions suffer from the same fallibility which adheres to every human enterprise.

This does not imply that in offering ethical guidance from Scripture the church ignores or denigrates competent judgments made by professional persons. But it does indicate that God is still the Lord of history, and that he can and often does upset human calculations. More weight, therefore, must be put on a respect for basic theological principles set forth in the Biblical revelation.

Life is a gift from God. Men were created to live in response, chiefly to God's prior actions. As being created for life, men are endowed with that mysterious gift which they call life. Such life comes into being by an act which shares in the creative powers of God himself (Ps. 139:13). While there is considerable discussion as to the precise moment at which incipient life becomes human, in terms of potentialities, it is generally agreed that life starts when fertilization has taken place. The first origins of *individual* human life are thought to be established at the time of the blastocyst, which occurs about a week after such fertilization.

Such passages as Exod. 21:22-24 indicate that life in the womb must be thought of in terms of personal being. There the law of retaliation is made to apply in cases of injury to a mother or even a child in her womb, or to both. Jeremiah 1:5 speaks of the consecration of the prophet before he was born. The evangelist Luke, moreover, describes how the unborn baby in Elizabeth's womb leaped for joy at Mary's greeting (Luke 1:41).

Human beings are created for eternal life. Nascent life is of special value before God. Like every other human being he designed it to inherit eternal life (Ps. 139:16; I Tim. 2:4). This second consideration is of special import at a time when a concerted effort is being made, even within church circles, to remove from consideration everything which in some way relates to what is transcendental. In a formal sense, life stands in an enduring relationship to the Creator, whose will it is that his creatures live in his presence both now and forevermore. The beginning of human life may not, therefore, be cut short at will without risking the danger of disobedience and distorting God's intent.

At the same time, nascent life enjoys no independent existence. It is fully dependent on the maternal life that surrounds and sustains it. Accordingly, a conflict may develop between two destinies, so intimately linked as they are during the time of gestation. Incipient life may become a threat to the life of the mother. In that case, a choice needs to be made between two beings; and its primary thrust must be to save that life which is already functioning as a developed person. The latter takes precedence over the former because maternal life has come into being for fulfillment

and not for a death which can be prevented —in this case, by emergency action. Moreover, in most instances the mother is already involved in many other responsibilities of life, where her presence and assistance are needed. Under such circumstances, abortion is the indirect and unfortunate consequence of an action undertaken to preserve life. The ethical principle which has been applied in this instance is that of choosing the lesser of two evils.

Human life is created for fulfillment. The matter of fulfillment is the third factor to weigh in reaching a proper decision in the matter of abortion. The attainment of a fuller life, however, is not derived from a concern for convenience or a desire for comfort or self-centered pleasure. Not wanting to be a mother does not provide a proper justification for deciding to have an abortion. Fulfillment is often found in sacrifice for another human being and in trusting that God for whom no price came too high when it came to the task of redeeming mankind through his Son. The possibility or even the likelihood that a child-to-be-born will be a financial burden is not of itself sufficient reason for choosing to abort incipient life. Even very grave psychiatric considerations do not of themselves offer a justifiable ground for deciding on an abortion.

Instances of rape and incest create very special problems, requiring pastoral counseling of the most sensitive kind. Individuals trapped in such situations, with their attendant tragedy and heartache, deserve the best in guidance within the context and on the basis of major considerations set forth in Scripture.

Life and death belong to the province of God. The fourth guiding principle is that life and death belong to the province of God (Phil. 1:21-24). Therefore, no person has a right to extinguish human life by a decision of his own, made apart from general precepts that express God's will.

The commandment, "Thou shalt not kill," was given specifically to forbid murder; that is, killing with hatred and malice aforethought (cf. Matt. 5:21-23). It is hardly proper, therefore, to make a direct application of this commandment to every act of abortion, since no hatred or malice may be involved in a given case. Nevertheless, it must be kept in mind that life comes into being as a special creative act of God, and no gift of his can be either rejected or destroyed with impunity. Any decision on abortion must take this seriously.

Where a mistake in judgment has been made, Christians continue to live and serve in full assurance of forgiveness where there is repentance. However, the abiding availability of divine pardon suffers flagrant abuse whenever it is taken for granted and used as a basis for violating the cardinal principles relating to the creation and preservation of incipient life. Yet even flaunting God's will and abusing his grace are forgiven those who repent and accept the pardon offered in Christ.

Decisions in the matter of abortion are complicated by the fact that such choices normally involve not only medical but also legal aspects. States have laws on the issue of abortion. Furthermore, physicians work under the terms of the Hippocratic Oath (q.v.) which they take on entering their profession. The second section of that oath says in so many words, "I will not aid a woman to procure abortion." To be sure, some physicians elect to say the Prayer of Maimonides instead of the Hippocratic Oath; yet, even so, doctors are expected to understand the gravity of matters pertaining to a choice involving life and death.

MARTIN H. SCHARLEMANN

ABSOLUTES, MORAL. See also *Norms; Principles.* A distinction must be drawn in ethics between absolute judgments, which are always binding, irrespective of situation, and relative judgments, which apply only in certain situations.

God is the Christian's ultimate authority. His will therefore is absolute. God has spoken, and the Bible as the written Word of God carries this categorical authority. Within his Word, certain actions seem to be prescribed as always good, while some are unequivocally proscribed. Among the latter are such factors as murder and adultery, which are condemned in definite fashion. On the other hand, love and justice are among the qualities which seem to be depicted as always good and right. Yet, what love or justice require specifically will vary somewhat with the situation. Thus, there is a need for middle axioms, or defining rules, to lead to a definite action. In some cases, the absolute will be so specific as to be identifiable with a definite-action rule, while in others it will be a principle, from which the definite-action rule is derived. Even where ethical commands in the Bible are definitely culture-bound (cf. I Cor. 11:6, for example), certain absolute principles underlie them.

A number of criticisms have been raised against absolutes in ethics. One is the anthropological argument known as cultural relativism. Commands and taboos vary from culture to culture (q.v.). Thus it is concluded that absolutes are simply established by cultural agreement, and vary from society to society. This, however, seems to miss the point. Absolutes may not be identified correctly by all men. Indeed, apart from special revelation from God, man may make rather gross mistakes in attempting to isolate absolutes. The point, however, is that all cultures do seem to have the concept of absolutes and do invest certain practices with this quality. Furthermore, there is a small but growing list of "cultural constants" or values which are accepted by all cultures.

An epistemological problem is also sometimes raised. Being finite in intelligence and geographically limited as well, man cannot possibly know all the data and contingent variables, and thus formulate any absolute statements or standards. This, however, seems to exclude the Christian belief in an omniscient God, who has revealed his will to man. It also confuses knowing and being. There is a difference between saying that there are absolutes, and claiming that we know them absolutely.

Finally, Joseph Fletcher (q.v.) argues against absolutism on the basis of what might be termed "conflict of absolutes." He suggests that at most there can be only one absolute, because whenever there is a conflict between two absolutes, one has to be surrendered in favor of the other, and thus it is not absolute. In the use of his hypothetical cases, however, he overlooks or ignores the possibility that an omnipotent God providentially guides the events of life so that two absolutes do not occur in tension with one another. The evangelical Christian also believes that we do not now live in a perfect world, as it was when it came from the hand of God. In this sinful and distorted world, it is not always possible to realize the perfect good. It is sometimes necessary to choose the lesser of two evils, or the greater of two goods. This, however, does not mean that the values are not absolute, just as the mathematician does not abandon belief in straight lines, simply because he can only approximate such.

Without absolutes, any ethic ultimately slips into some form of subjectivism. Fletcher, who has been one of the most outspoken critics of absolutes, argues that the only absolute is love. Yet his own situations tend to slide in one of two opposite directions. In some cases, good becomes a quality of the *way* an action is done, rather than *what* is done. On the other hand, he sometimes makes very absolutistic statements, such as "no unwanted or unintended baby should have to be born." Some professed relativists become quite absolutistic in their condemnation of war, racial injustice, and other social ills. The issue then is not whether there shall be absolutes, but their nature, number and basis.

Charles Curran, "Absolute Norms in Moral Theology," in *Norm and Context in Christian Ethics*, Gene Outka and Paul Ramsey, eds., New York, Scribner, 1968; William Lillie, *Introduction to Ethics*, London, Methuen, 1961.   MILLARD J. ERICKSON

ABSOLUTION. From the Latin *absolvo* (set free), absolution is a theological term denoting the remission of sins through the redemptive work of Jesus Christ. In Roman Catholic theology it is the teaching that authority was given the Apostles and their successors to forgive sins in the sacrament of penance. Considered passively, it means the actual forgiveness of sins effected by the sacrament. Appealing to John 20:23, "If you forgive the sins of any, they are forgiven; if you retain the sins of any, they are retained," this interpretation holds that the priest, exercising the power of the keys (Matt. 16:19; 18:18), passes a judicial sentence in which sin is remitted and the sinner is immediately reconciled to the church, the body of Christ, and its divine head. It presupposes the sinner's repentance evidenced by his contrition, confession, and work of satisfaction. Historically, the rite of absolution has undergone extensive development, its present integration into the sacramental system having occurred during the age of Scholasticism. As practiced in some Protestant churches absolution is the declaration that God forgives repented sin freely through Christ.   M. EUGENE OSTERHAVEN

ABSTINENCE. See also *Prohibition; Temperance.* Abstinence is a voluntary self-denial and renunciation, usually of certain foods, alcoholic beverages, or fleshly enjoyments. Refraining from such items and from worldly contacts has been considered a way of perfection by those who regard the desires of the body as evil and as foes of the spirit. Jesus, in fulfilling his redemptive mission, did not flee the world or social life, but accepted hospitality from sinners, turned water into wine (John 2), and was called by his enemies a drunkard and glutton (Matt. 11:19).

Fasting is associated in Scripture with repentance and seeking God in times of difficulty or tragedy (II Sam. 1:12; Zech. 7—8). Its focus was Godward, not manward (Matt. 6:16-18), and it was merely ritually observed (Isa. 58:3; Zech. 7—8).

Israel was commanded to refrain from certain foods and acts for health reasons (Lev. 11—15). The Christian is exhorted to abstain from fleshly lusts (I Peter 2:11), impurity, immorality (Col. 3:5), coveteousness (Col. 3:5), fornication (I Thess. 4:3), strangled food, blood, pollution to idols (Acts 15:2, 29), drunkenness (Gal. 5:21; Eph. 5:18; I Tim. 3:8; Prov. 23:29-35), and from every kind of evil (Ps. 119:101; I Thess. 5:22). Out of love Christian liberty is not to be exercised when it becomes a stumblingblock to another Christian or non-Christian (I Cor. 8; 10:23-33). Temporary abstinence from sexual relations is permitted for married couples (I Cor. 7:5) if for positive reasons.

Scripture warns against false prohibitions such as forbidding to marry, eating meats approved by God, not handling, tasting, or touching specific things (Col. 2:20-23; I Tim. 4:1-3). These renunciations are encouraged by those who follow seducing spirits and the teachings of demons.

RALPH H. ALEXANDER

ACCIDENT. See also *Chance; Highway Safety.* An accident is an event having causes unknown to the persons involved or beyond their immediate ability to control. Even in accidents, those who follow Christ find solace in the words, "God works for good with those who love him, who are called according to his purpose," an assurance that nurtures confidence and reduces

fear. Christians have been found in the forefront of those working for legislation to reduce accidents and to minimize their harm.   ROBERT E. FARNELL III

ACCOMPLICE. See *Crime.*

ACCOUNTABILITY. See *Responsibility.*

ACQUIESCENCE. A passive condition indicating a state of satisfaction or compliance, characterized as much by an apparent lack of opposition as by an absence of avowed consent. As with waiver, acquiescence involves knowledge of fact, and therefore one cannot acquiesce in a misdemeanor while unaware that it has been committed.

R. K. HARRISON

ACT, ACTION, ACTOR. The term "act" may mean either the consequent (deed) of the execution (action) of an intention to act, or, as it is sometimes used by contemporary philosophical psychologists, a non-human physiological happening (e.g., raising one's arm). In both uses happenings have no moral meaning unless they are associated with human intention (raising one's arm to signal a turn). An action is intentionally performed by an actor—one who does an action. The ethical problem of action is, What constitutes the moral value of an action?

In teleological ethical theories, the moral value of an action depends on its effect (acts). A major weakness of this conception is the lack of knowledge of an intrinsic relation between a good act (e.g., economic security of the poor) and the action which attains it (e.g., "stealing from the rich"). For aetiologists, the value of an action depends on the intention of an action rather than any good attained. A major weakness of this assumption is that the intention to act bears no reliable evidence of its worth in any particular situation. Evangelical ethicists consider both good intention and valuable effects essential aspects of the rightness of an action. An action is right only if its intention conforms to God's purpose in creation, and its consequences are valuable only if they establish God's ends. Human intentions, actions, and goals attained in history are subject to the judgment of the Creator. But Christian ethics is characteristically an ethics of being (actor) not of doing or of consequences. What ought I to be? is logically prior to What ought I to do? or What ought I to achieve by my action? Actors or agents are active causes created by God in his intellectual and moral image. Man's superiority over other creatures is by virtue of his ability to know (mind) and love (will) his Creator. Without knowledge of norms prescribed by God there can be no responsible moral action or righteousness. Conscience is a universal, fallible source of the knowledge of God's law and therefore of man's responsibility to obey it. Specific, infallible, Biblical content of duty (especially the rules of the Decalogue and Sermon on the Mount), together with Biblically revealed goals of human action, are essential sources of knowledge for moral guidance not available to conscience alone.

Without will or causal response to God's purpose in creation, moral action is impossible. However, free will, the capacity to choose equally between two incompatible courses of action, is no more essential to finite moral agency than it is to the moral agency of God, who is necessitated by his nature to choose only the good. Human actors are responsible for their actions. "God . . . did . . . freely and unchangeably ordain whatsoever comes to pass; yet so, as thereby neither is God the author of sin, nor is violence offered to the will of the creatures, nor is the liberty or contingency of second causes taken away, but rather established " (*Westminster Confession of Faith*, Ch. III, 1).

Evangelicals acknowledge that the entire human race is involved in the fall of Adam. For Calvinists this means the entire loss of power to perform acts which fulfill the requirements of God's moral law, prior to supernatural regeneration. Other evangelicals consider human nature partially tainted with hereditary sin and hold non-Christians retain some ability to perform good actions. All evangelicals assume that supernatural regeneration is essential for righteousness. Morally good actions subsequent to regeneration are performed by strength which God the Holy Spirit imparts day by day and they are never perfect in this life.

In personal ethics, the emphasis is on the effects of action on the agent himself; while in social ethics, emphasis is on the effects of action on others. Evangelical social action is based on the assumption that redemption precedes social reorganization in the attainment of justice in society.

📖 Carl F. H. Henry, *Aspects of Christian Social Ethics*, Grand Rapids, Eerdmans, 1946; A. J. Melden and Paul Kegan, *Free Action*, London, Routledge, 1961; Paul Ramsey, *Deeds and Rules in Christian Ethics*, New York, Scribner, 1967.
ROY W. BUTLER

ACT ETHICS. See also *Rule Ethics*. An act ethic locates moral quality in particular acts, rather than in general moral rules. Its purest form gives no place to rules whatsoever. A moral judgment is not to be made on the basis of whether certain rules are fulfilled or violated; rather, a given act is simply compared to the principle or value espoused by the ethic, to see whether it fulfills that value. Thus a utilitarian ethic seeks not a fulfilling of rules, but rather whatever act will presumably accomplish the maximum good for the largest number of persons.

Implicit in this type of ethic is the assumption of the uniqueness of each act and situation. Facts about other situations and ethical conclusions arrived at in other situations are irrelevant and may even be misleading. Consequently no universally binding rules can be laid down. This assumption may be correlated with a view of the radical disconnection among various situations, so that reality itself is unsystematic; or it may derive from the belief that meaning and value are created by the decision and action of the individual himself. In this latter form, morality may not be a matter of what act is done. It may even derive the rightness of the act from the virtue of the person, such as "love, and do as you please."

A common form of Christian act ethic is act-agapism. The basic principle here is to act in such a way as to maximize love. The course of action, however, would not be decided upon by consulting any set of rules which somehow embody love, but simply by confronting one's loving will with the facts of the situation, and determining what is most loving (i.e., right). This could not be predetermined, but could only be arrived at within the actual situation of decision.

Less extreme is modified act-agapism, or summary-rule agapism. This does see a place for rules, but not really as guides to action. Rather, they are simply generalizations or summary statements of what kind of act has most frequently proven to be loving in past experience. In the situation of decision, one must choose the most loving course of action. He does this by measuring the act against love, not by recourse to any preformed code. Thus the summary rules are only acts of agape taken together. They are of informational interest only, although some summary-rule ethicists would say that the maxims are to be followed unless there is good reason not to do so (e.g., if keeping the rule is less loving than abandoning it). Since, however, one must decide in each situation whether the action dictated by the summary-rule is indeed the most loving,

some critics have argued that summary-rule agapism or modified act-agapism inevitably slips into pure act-agapism.

Pure act ethics is represented by existentialist ethicists. Most situationists would consider their view modified act ethics. Thus Joseph Fletcher (q.v.), and to even a greater degree, John A. T. Robinson (q.v.), would utilize rules based upon past observation. Both would, however, be prepared to abandon the rule if doing so were more loving.

A fault of act ethics is its seeming instability. The tendency is for acts to become so particularized that a virtual subjectivism arises. On the other hand, every attempt to make genuine moral judgments seems to lead one back to more general principles or rules. For the evangelical Christian, who believes that the Bible is a special revelation of God's will, acts are important, but they are always governed by the rules and principles of God's Word.

📖 Joseph Fletcher, *Situation Ethics*, Philadelphia, Westminster, 1966; William Frankena, "Love and Principle in Christian Ethics," *Faith and Philosophy*, Alvin Plantinga, ed., Grand Rapids, Eerdmans, 1965.   MILLARD J. ERICKSON

ACTIVISM. See also *Quietism.* Activism like its opposite, Quietism, comes in degrees. In its extreme form Quietism advocates the cessation of all volition and desire. "Absorption by God" is virtually Buddhist Nirvana in Christian dress. The extreme form of Activism would be a life all of action and volition minus any knowledge of what one is doing or should do. Obviously Christianity is neither the one nor the other. Disagreement concerning proportions oscillates between ivory-tower intellectuals and non-intellectual activists. In general European evangelicals are more intellectual while American evangelicals, even though they do not engage in the liberal's noisy demonstrations, are strongly activist.   GORDON H. CLARK

ACTS OF GOD. An expression used to refer to occurrences or experiences which seem to defy the ordinary principles of cause and effect (e.g., tornado; flood). In that sense the phrase offers at least indirect testimony to God's providential concern, even in a secular culture determined to remove from life and thought every vestige of belief in the Creator. In their usual setting these words echo an awareness of the dimension of some kind of general revelation (Rom. 1:20). In the sphere of special revelation the expression is at times modified by the adjective "mighty." In these instances, the words comprise an English translation of several Biblical terms which are used by the sacred authors to refer to those deeds of God which he performed for man's redemption (e.g., the Exodus, the Return, the Incarnation, etc.; cf. I Peter 2:9.)   MARTIN H. SCHARLEMANN

ADDICTION. See *Alcoholism; Drugs.*

ADIAPHORA. The term *adiaphora* (pl. of *adiaphoron,* meaning indifferent, neither good nor bad) denotes acts or church rites which in themselves are neither morally right nor wrong, but matters of Christian liberty. The notion of *adiaphora* assumes that there are ethical activities and goals that are not matters of indifference, and thus precludes antinomianism and ethical relativism. To discern what are truly *adiaphora* also protects one from the error of legalism.

The term is not found in the NT, but the underlying issue is clearly stressed by Christ and the apostles. Jesus and Paul, while denouncing drunkenness (Luke 21:23; I Cor. 5:11) leave the moderate drinking of wine an *adiaphoron* (John 2:1-12; Matt. 11:19; I Tim. 5:23). To Paul circumcision and eating certain meats were matters of Christian liberty *(adiaphora)* (e.g., I Tim. 4:3-5; Gal. 2:3; 5:6), although in certain circumstances, when the weak might be offended, Paul allowed circumcision and refrained from eating meat (Acts 16:3; Rom. 14:15 *passim).* The Church Fathers were the first to apply the term *adiaphora* to actions which in themselves were neither right nor wrong, e.g., eating meat, celibacy (cf. Chrysostom, *hom. 15.2 in Heb; comm. in Gal. 2:11ff.)*

During the Reformation the term *adiaphora* was applied primarily to church rites which were neutral, neither prescribed nor forbidden in Scripture, and could therefore be followed with a good conscience. Luther, for instance, in opposition to Carlstadt, maintained that forms of worship, practiced under the papacy but nor forbidden in the NT and not subverting the gospel, might be continued in a Reformed church.

After Luther's death a controversy concerning *adiaphora* ensued. The Melanchthonian party affirmed that certain rites imposed by Romish rulers could be followed in good conscience by Protestants (e.g., extreme unction, confession to the priest, abstaining from meat, Corpus Christi celebration, canonical hours, the Mass, etc.). The Lutheran majority, led by Matthias Falcius, denied this as syncretistic compromise. They also insisted that even acts in themselves indifferent *(res mediae),* if imposed upon the Christian community, should be rejected and disobeyed. Even certain vestments (e.g., the cope) should not be worn because they were associated with the adoration of the host in the Mass. The principle was: "Nothing is an *adiaphoron* when confession and offense are involved" (Flacius).

In the seventeenth century another adiaphoristic controversy broke out between Lutherans and Calvinists and also Lutheran pietists over the question whether amusements were *adiaphora.* Lutherans taught that amusements in themselves were neither good nor bad, but the person and circumstances made them right or wrong. Calvinists held that the Genevan code of discipline was a matter of conscience and not an *adiaphoron*. Certain pietists denied that any act in itself was an *adiaphoron*.

ROBERT D. PREUS

ADOPTION. See also *Orphans*. Adoption is the legal procedure whereby a child (usually either illegitimate or destitute of one or both parents) becomes the member of another family.

According to the Bible, God is the father of the fatherless and he sets the solitary in families (Ps. 68:5-6). Thus, one of the tests of true religion is a man's concern for orphans (James 1:27).

What is important in adopting parents is their ability to undertake this privilege and responsibility, their age, and the stability of their own relationship. Normally, it is undesirable that a single person should adopt a child: for satisfactory moral and psychological development, a child needs to relate to both a father and a mother. It would, of course, be improper for a couple to seek to adopt a child for the purpose of solving their own marital problems.

The Bible speaks of the way in which God "predestinated us unto the adoption of children by Jesus Christ to himself, according to the good pleasure of his will" (Eph. 1:5 KJV). The seal and confirmation of our adoption is that "God has sent the Spirit of his Son into our ears, crying, 'Abba! Father!'" By grace, we are no longer slaves, but sons, and, if sons, also heirs (Gal. 4:4-7 RSV; cf. Rom. 8:14-27).

STUART B. BABBAGE

ADULTERY. See also *Artificial Insemination; Marriage; Monogomy*. In the OT adultery involved the sexual intercourse of a married or engaged woman with someone other than her husband or fiancé. This violation of the Seventh Commandment was punished by the execution of both parties (Exod. 20:14; Lev. 20:10ff.; Deut. 22:22 ff.). Similar injunctions and penalties were contained in the Babylonian Code of Hammurabi (129) and (optionally) in early Roman law (Dion. Hal. *Roman Antiquities,* 2, 25, 6). The severity of the punishment suggests that ancient societies viewed adultery not just (privately) as a violation of the spouse's right to exclusive sexual enjoyment of the partner but also (socially) as a serious threat to the familial fabric of society. In the Biblical context this understanding of the offense was deepened by a prophetic word from God: in marriage the two "become one flesh" (Gen. 2:24). That is, a new "corporate" reality comes into being, a reality that both includes and transcends their individual persons. As a sin against marriage, adultery apparently has the character of murder either in robbing the husband of his selfhood (O. Piper, *The Biblical View of Sex and Marriage,* New York, Scribner, 1960, p. 150) or in destroying the corporeity that is created by the sexual union. In any case it is from the standpoint of Gen. 1-2 that Jesus speaks of the indissolubility of marriage and of its lifelong permanence (Matt. 19:4ff.; Mark 10:6-8; I Cor. 7:10f.).

In the NT the scope of adultery is broadened in several respects. First, Jesus gives a radical and inward interpretation of the commandment: "Everyone who looks at a woman lustfully has already committed adultery with her in his heart" (Matt. 5:28). With God, he implies, it is not only one's acts that are significant but also one's thoughts and intentions. By this word Jesus places all men under judgment, for who can say that he is not included in its scope? Indeed, Jesus regards as adultery "all thinking and speaking, action and conduct, which is inconsistent with and destructive of marriage and beyond this all perversion . . . in the life and relation of the sexes generally" (Barth, "Man and Woman," *Church Dogmatics,* Edinburgh, Clark, 1961, III, 4, p. 233).

"Whoever divorces his wife and marries another, commits adultery against her; if she divorces her husband and marries another, she commits adultery" (Mark 10:11f.). Unlike OT practice, and like the Qumran community of his own time (CD 4:20f.), Jesus equates divorce and remarriage with adultery and, by applying the teaching to both husband and wife, also excludes polygamy. That is, he calls his followers to exemplify God's original order in creation (Matt. 19:4ff.; Gen. 1:27; 2:24), an order destined now to be restored (Matt. 19:28).

Second, the OT depiction of idolatry as adultery against God. (Jer. 3) is given a different focus in the NT. Paul writes that an immoral sexual union and the union "with Christ" are mutually exclusive relationships. Therefore, fornicators will not inherit the kingdom of God (I Cor. 6:9-20). His rationale appears to be two-fold. First, because redemption is physical, the individual Christian's body belongs to Christ in a special way. Also, since Christians are members of Christ's corporate body, he and they are implicated when one of the members is involved in this sin (I Cor. 5:6; cf. 12:27; Eph. 5:28-31). Second, sexual immorality "implies not the mere possibility but the necessity of my being enslaved by an alien power. It occupies this relatively unique position because it can never take place 'outside' me and 'I' consequently cannot isolate myself from it" (H. Thielicke, *Theological Ethics: Foundations,* Philadelphia, Fortress, 1966, p. 91, cf. pp. 631-47). For both Jesus and Paul the sexual union is not merely what one *does;* it effects a qualitative change in who one *is* (I Cor. 6:16).

In this context it is impossible to justify adultery in terms of situational ethics (q.v.). Some violations of God's law may occur within the framework of God's love: for example, stealing to feed a starving person or lying to save an innocent person from a

murderer. But "there are certain conditions and attitudes with which the Holy Spirit cannot in any [situation] co-exist under the same roof in the same ego. . . . The first is fornication *(porneia)*" (Thielicke, p. 87). If adultery is not tolerable to God, neither is it the unpardonable sin. The word to the woman taken in adultery expresses the Lord's attitude toward the penitent: "Neither do I condemn you. Go and do not sin again" (John 8:11).   E. EARLE ELLIS

ADVERTISING. See also *Business Ethics; Consumer Fraud; Credit; Truth.* Advertising is information, particularly paid announcements, the purpose of which is to gain public attention for a product or idea. Advertising is thus closely akin to propaganda (q.v.), the usefulness of which was shown dramatically in the swift spread of early Christianity. Although forms of advertising exist in noncapitalist economies, it is most closely identified with capitalism, and is permissible insofar as capitalism is an ethically justifiable economic system for Christians. It should be noted that in capitalism, advertising income often serves to provide income for the mass media, which in turn distribute other kinds of necessary news and information, as well as entertainment.

Despite the widespread moral criticism of advertising and the similar field of "public relations," these practices are inherently good, not evil, because they are forms of public communication of information, a socially beneficial process. Commercial data is useful and helpful, and it would be difficult to find a job or purchase a house in a strange city, for example, without newspaper classified advertisements.

The controversy comes, first, over whether advertising fulfills the ethical demands of truth-telling. It is often not a simple task to define what the truth is. In advertising, the issue is usually not so much outright falsehood (though that is not unknown) as it is the use of hyperbole, or of half-truth. The intelligent consumer, at least, does not expect the advertiser to parade the drawbacks of his product along with its benefits, yet this admittedly falls far short of the example of candor in the Bible, with its reports on the faults of kings and apostles. The sinful nature of man leads naturally to self-interest in advertising. Consumer protection through "truth in lending" or "truth in packaging" laws is an example of government effort to counteract this human tendency.

A second ethical problem concerns advertising which promotes ethically neutral products, or promotes ethically neutral products for unethical reasons. Few doubt that advertising played a major role in the widespread use of cigarettes, a proven health hazard. As for motives, the seller can act out of greed, or play upon the basest yearnings for sexual glamor, possessions, or social status, because of a totally materialistic view of what is of value in human existence. Some appeals to social acceptability amount to psychological intimidation.

More broadly, advertising involves the complex question of the stewardship of both personal and social resources, and is thus intertwined with basic moral issues in economics. Much modern advertising has moved beyond transmission of basic data about available goods to a highly expensive craft dealing with motivational analysis and creation of needs or desires. Often consumers are encouraged to go into debt to purchase unneeded commodities. Such use of advertising demeans the concept of vocation, by making work important for the income it brings in, rather than as something with intrinsic value of its own. In his essay "Good Work and Good Works," C. S. Lewis argued that rather than creating *things* because they are wanted, our twisted society creates *wants,* so that people can earn money by producing goods—desirable or not—for which advertising has already engineered a demand. RICHARD N. OSTLING

AESTHETICS. See also *Art; Beauty.* Aesthetics is the philosophical theory of beauty. Since the eighteenth century it was pursued in an almost rigid intellectual way aside from the realities of art, though today it often comes much closer to the practical issues of art theory. Both are thus considered to be very close to art criticism. Of course, the development of these theoretical activities has always been related to the arts as such.

In ancient times two philosophers stand conspicuously at the beginning of aesthetics, defining its problems and offering two different ways of approach to the arts that have had a long and deep influence. Plato defined the artist (speaking of the poet, and not at this stage the artist working in the visual arts) as a seer, someone who through inspiration could see the Ideas and express them. Aristotle, however, defined art as mimesis, in a direct relation to experienced reality; for him the artist must concern himself with matters of probability, necessity, coherence, and completeness. Xenocrates followed Aristotle's art criticism, while the Romans took the main ideas over in a classicistic art theory. The Neoplatonism of Plotinus, in which "beauty" (and not in the first place "art") was a key word, defined the basic ideas for aesthetics and art theory that have been decisive up to the present century, often in the Christianized form of the work of psuedo-Dionysius the Areopagite.

In the middle ages, particularly through the work of Thomas Aquinas, Aristotelianism again became influential. The arts as we conceive them today, however, were considered under the heading of *artes technicae* (technology). The function of the work of art was the first consideration, in which the following notions were considered: the narrative or literal, the moral, the allegorical and the anagogical. By the latter was meant the influence of the work on the beholder, its total impact, its motivation and direction, and it is the highest and deepest effect a work of art can accomplish. The universal was experienced in the perception of the work of art, and it was the universal which imparted beauty to it.

At the time of the Renaissance, art theory again reverted to Platonic or Plotinian concepts, in the work of Ficino, Pico della Mirandola, Bembo, Michelangelo and many others. The sixteenth century is rich in art theoretical treatises, either in the Platonic or, particularly in Venice, a more Aristotelian vein. The latter type became once again the leading factor in the art theories of the seventeenth century, when Agucchi and Bellori influenced very strongly the ideas of Poussin and the French academy. The main trend of these theories, stressing the imitative and the ideal combined with a high regard for the arts of Graeco-Roman antiquity, exerted a deep influence on the following centuries: on Winckelmann, neo-classicism and on nineteenth century academicism.

Meanwhile, a more subjectivistic stream had gained priority. Its roots lie in the beginnings of the Renaissance, with its stress on *disegno* or conceptual form, the creative act of the artist. This changed the emphasis from the work of art to the artist. With Leonardo, the scientific, the intellectual and experimental were introduced. But with the Cartesian influence the aesthetic experience was more and more internalized, and made resident in the subject. Taste and rationality, and now also feeling, were determining thought on art. In this time too, the first philosophical aesthetics in the modern sense was written by Baumgarten, leading up to Kant, who determined later aesthetics through his *Critique of Judgment,* surpassed in influence only by Hegel's aesthetics.

The romantic movement reacted against the rationalistic ideas, often reverting to Platonic or Plotinian ideas, with great stress however on the idea of the artist as a genius, as e.g., with Schlegel, Schopenhauer, and Baudelaire, for whom the main motives were immediacy, intuition, idealization, inspiration and genius, while the symbolic replaced the older concept of allegory. Another line of thought in the nineteenth century is that of positivistic naturalism, particularly in Taine.

In the twentieth century, with Croce, Cassirer, Wittgenstein, and Susanne Langer, the stress is on language and symbolic expression. In addition much aesthetics is influenced by new psychological trends, or by phenomenology.

Encyclopedia of World Art, New York, McGraw-Hill 1961, IV, cf. "Criticism"; and V, cf. "Esthetics", with extensive bibliographies; H. R. Rookmaaker, *Synthetist Art Theories,* Amsterdam, 1959; H. Osborne, *Aesthetics and Art Theory,* an historical introduction, New York, E. P. Dutton 1970.   H. R. ROOKMAAKER

AFFECTIONS. See *Emotion.*

AFFINITY. Affinity is the relationship of one marriage partner to the kin of the other, and may provide a basis for restricting further union. The law prohibited marrying one's step-mother, step-sister, or daughter-in-law (Lev. 18:8, 11, 14). Two violations of the code are singled out in the NT, Herod Antipas' marriage of his brother's wife (Matt. 14:3-4), and a Corinthian's affair with his step-mother (I Cor. 5:1).   MORRIS A. INCH

AFFIRMATION. See *Oaths.*

AFFLUENCE. See also *Underdeveloped Nations; Wealth.* Affluence may be defined as an abundance of money, an expansive possesion of property, a wealthy holding of material goods. The affluent man is generally regarded as rich, prosperous, wealthy, well-off, and well-to-do. The affluent society is synonymous with prosperity, wealth, and success; and not infrequently rightly or wrongly carries a connotation of inconsiderateness towards others less gainfully placed.

There are degrees of affluence. There are the rich and super-rich. The United States of America is undoubtedly the richest, most powerful and affluent nation in the world. Yet most Americans own little more than their household goods, some few chromium-plated gadgets, and the clothes on their backs; while a great number of Americans live in shacks, tenements, ghettoes, and decaying apartment buildings. At the same time, a relatively small handful of Americans are extravagantly endowed almost like princes from some Arabian Nights tale. Similar conditions apply elsewhere—in India, England, Latin America, and Canada.

It was once believed (or at least said) that great wealth was either the reward for social service, or else represented the inevitable survival of the fittest with the unfit landing in the gutter. This was widely preached from many pulpits and editorialized in many a newspaper. It has also been broadly averred that if today all the world's money were equally divided among all people, within a generation it would be back in the same hands. No such division has ever been attempted—or is likely to be.

Affluence is not unknown in Biblical records. "Abraham was very rich in cattle, in silver, and in gold." The Bible does not regard this as wrong. The right of private possession is freely recognized and accepted by the Biblical writers. But the corruption that accompanies affluence is frequently exposed. Amos sternly rebukes the wealthy for their avarice and cruelty. "Your great houses shall be smitten to fragments and the little houses to bits" (Amos 6:11); "Woe to you who turn justice to wormwood, and cast down righteousness to the earth" (Amos 5:7). The oppression of the poor by the rich is an abomination in the sight of God. And Micah echoes the same cry: "What does the Lord require of thee but to do justice, to love mercy, and to walk humbly with thy God? (Micah 6:8).

It is the same message we meet in the words of Christ. He speaks of the "deceitfulness of riches" (Mark 4:19) and warns that "the cares of this world and the deceitfulness of riches can choke the Word and make it unfruitful" (Luke 8:14). Affluence, in his teaching, is always to be regarded as a sacred trust, to be used to glory of God and the amelioration of the help of the poor. "Sell your possessions and give alms. Provide yourselves with purses that grow not old, with a treasure in the heavens that does not fail" (Luke 12:33). The rich young ruler was told to "sell all you have and give to the poor and come, Follow me" (Matt. 19:21).

Christian discipleship obviously involves true stewardship of money. We own nothing by right. We are stewards and trustees. God means us to use his gifts for the sake of others. This obviously implies that rich men must give to the poor. Rich nations must give to poor nations. Developed, technologically efficient, national powers must support and not exploit the weak. There will be a judgment of the nations where even a cup of cold water "given in the Name of the Lord" will be recognized as of infinite merit. The Parable of the Good Samaritan has haunted the conscience of humanity ever since it was first told. Our Lord meant it should. To possess things that others do not, lays a moral obligation upon us to share what we have with them. Affluence thereby becomes a blessing—a veritable sharing of the life of God himself "who giveth liberally to all men and upbraideth not" (James 1:5).   WILLIAM FITCH

AGAPE. See *Love*.

AGED, CARE OF. See also *Family; Senility*. The moral and social problems associated with care of the aged arise from the paradox of an increasing number of elderly in our society and a corresponding decrease in their role and status. In the USA the average age at death lengthened from 45 in 1900 to 71 in 1960 and life expectancy has not changed significantly in subsequent years. This has resulted in an increase in the total population over age 65 from 3.1 million in 1900 to 16.6 million in 1960 and 20 million in 1970. This is an increase from 4.1 to 9.9 percent of the total population from 1900 to 1970.

The OT adduced a spiritual basis for the authority of the father as head of the household (cf. also Eph. 6:2). But the traditional veneration of the elderly as a source of wisdom and stability has declined with the development of a youth-valuing culture. This has created a crisis in care of the elderly in our society.

Among the most evident needs of the elderly are: (1) economic, (2) health care, and (3) housing. Other pressing emotional and social needs include (1) the need for a sense of worth, (2) emotional trauma caused by radical changes in their lives, (3) loneliness, and (4) adequate confrontation of the approaching reality of death. Without spiritual and moral anchorage, old age is an increasing battle against emptiness and hopelessness.

Traditionally three social institutions (the family, church, and government) have accepted responsibility for care of the elderly in our society. The role of families has declined because of the separation of family members by our mobile life style while the reduced size of families has weakened their potential to perform this service.

The church has for centuries supported programs of caring for the aged. Recently established social service agencies have reflected an increase in these services. There also is a renewal of interest in serving the needs of the elderly through local churches.

There has been a dramatic increase in the role of government in this area. As the size and complexity of the problem increases, this trend will doubtless continue.

DANIEL B. McGEE

AGGRESSION. Aggression is the initial act of hostility in a sequence of such events, or an unprovoked attack or injury leading to other reciprocal or contingent acts. In its most commonly-understood contemporary form, aggression normally leads to war between nations. In a non-political or non-military context it could comprise the beginnings of an acrimonious exchange such as a controversy or feud. Unprovoked hostility is one concomitant of fallen human nature, being particularly characteristic of an egocentric personality-orientation which seeks unrestricted accumulation of property or aggrandizement of status. Unless checked by restraints of a physical or moral order, aggression can seriously disrupt the fabric of personal and social life. In its most developed form it can enslave entire peoples to the designs of the aggressor. While it may represent an individualized expression of personality, the fact that aggression seeks to impose control over the freedom of others imparts to it a decidedly negative character, especially among those who cherish liberty and freedom of expression as rights to which mankind can lay claim.

As with other facets of human nature, aggression is amply characterized in Scripture, the capture of Laish by the tribe of Dan (Judg. 18:7ff.) being an outstanding example militarily. This was necessitated through failure to conquer Philistia (Josh. 13:3), and though the exploit was unopposed by God, who had given all of Canaan to Israel, it may account for the omission of Dan in Rev. 7:5ff.

The right of men to live at peace is a comparatively modern concept, although the New Testament commends this as part of normative Christian behavior (Rom. 12:18) while still recognizing it as an ideal.

In the ancient Near East it was generally only a pious expectation (cf. Ps. 122:6) apart from certain periods of political stability, since the inhabitants of cities usually lived in continual fear of invasion and enslavement, making for insidious feelings of insecurity.

Quite aside from the violence and the unwarranted destruction of persons and property resulting from military aggression, one important ethical objection is to the abrogation of individual freedom which aggression involves. This is particularly abhorrent to the Christian, who has been afforded liberty from bondage to various temporal elements by the atoning death of Christ (cf. Rom. 6:18; 8:2; Gal. 5:1; I Peter 2:16). Because aggression denies, ignores or represses the liberties of others, generally with a view to significant gain, it seems legitimate to resist it wherever practicable. Although often a calculated act, it is morally reprehensible because it views human rights in a cynical, irresponsible and culpable manner. It further encourages the domination of the weak by the strong, which frequently results in their exploitation or even extermination. Intellectual aggression, though more subtle in nature, is equally significant in its ability to bind and control.   R. K. HARRISON

ALCOHOLISM. See also *Prohibition; Smoking; Temperance; Temperance Movement.* Alcoholism is a chronic pathological condition caused by ingesting too much alcohol in the human body. An alcoholic is an excessive drinker who has become so physically and psychologically dependent on alcohol that he manifests mental disturbance, physical deterioration, and the inability to function adequately in society.

Alcoholism has become the fourth major health problem in the United States, exceeded only by mental illness, heart disease, and cancer. Approximately eighty million Americans drink alcoholic beverages and six million of these are excessive drinkers and classified as alcoholics.

There is a current debate as to whether alcoholism is a sin or a sickness. Some regard it as a sign of moral weakness and therefore sin. Specialists generally agree that alcoholism is a disease or at least a symptom of underlying personality disorders. A moral element is involved for God has created man as a responsible being. Therefore the alcoholic is responsible for his excessive drinking, for his actions, and for seeking to do something about the problem. It is therefore understandable that almost all alcoholics possess a sense of guilt and wrongdoing. Perhaps alcoholism can be viewed as stemming from a cluster of factors involving both sin and sickness.

Any attempt to deal with the problem of alcoholism must be based upon some understanding of the causative factors. Theories concerning the causes of alcoholism come under the general rubrics of physical, psychological, and socio-cultural. The physical theory holds that there is an inherited tendency, some unknown factor in the biologic make-up of a person, which makes it impossible for him to be merely a social drinker. Numerous psychological causes have been cited: intense anxiety, emotional immaturity, low self-esteem, a feeling of isolation, a sense of guilt, a low frustration-tolerance, compulsiveness, and social inadequacy. The socio-cultural factors include an inadequate family background, peer influences, social pressures, and an inability to adjust to environmental stresses.

Among the therapeutic resources for rehabilitation of the alcoholic are: hospitalization, psychiatric treatment, and counseling. Alcoholics Anonymous (AA) is considered to be the most effective organization in rehabilitating the alcoholic. Some of AA's Twelve Steps have religious overtones: "conversion," "commitment to a higher power," "confession," "prayer," "forgiveness," "restitution," "converting others."

Churches have a vital role in the redemption of the alcoholic through witnessing to man's individual responsibility to God, to the liberating gospel, counseling, radical sharing groups where he can find strength, and cooperation with community forces seeking to restore wholeness to him.

Howard Clinebell, *Understanding and Counseling the Alcoholic*, Nashville, Abingdon, 1968; David Pittman, ed., *Alcoholism*, New York, Harper and Row, 1967.　　　HENLEE H. BARNETTE

ALIENATION. The precise philosophical usage of this concept derives from Hegel and Marx. Hegel spoke of the alienation of Spirit from itself in nature and history and of the gradual overcoming of this estrangement in the historical process. Under the influence of Feuerbach, Marx understood this to mean that the overcoming of alienation was an abstract, intellectual, and otherworldly process entirely compatible with the deepest human degradation and oppression. The *Economic-Philosophical Manuscripts* of 1844 are his attempt to develop the concept of alienation in the concrete context of human labor.

For Marx alienated labor has four dimensions. In the system of wage labor and capitalism the worker is estranged from both the product of his labor, since the wealth he produces is not his own, and from the process of labor, since he does not participate in the decisions affecting his work. These two aspects of alienation express a structure which is often identified with alienation as such, namely that the products of man's own activity become his master. In this case it is the economic process, a product of human creativity, which gains independent status as The Market or The Economy, to which man becomes enslaved.

The third dimension of alienated labor involves the estrangement of man from his fellow man, since the system defined by alienated labor is a competitive war of all against all. Finally, this in turn involves man's estrangement from his "species being," his nature as a social and cooperative being. Concrete alienation for Marx, then, means not only that man is dominated by the products of his own creative activity, but also that he is fundamentally estranged from himself and from his neighbor.

Since there are many possible analyses of man's self-enslavement and of the estrangement of his existence from his essence, it is not surprising that the concept of alienation has come to stand for almost every variety of social and spiritual malaise.

MEROLD WESTPHAL

Revealed theology assures man's place in created reality by the fact the the Logos is the source of all the substance and the structures of life (John 1:3f.); the Logos of God is the divine agent in creation, redemption, and judgment. Biblical theology roots man's alienation not in his finiteness or creatureliness, contrary to many modern theories (cf. e.g., *Anxiety*), but in his moral revolt, and finds in redemptive revelation—in the sinner's knowledge of God in his judgment and grace—the only prospect of overcoming that alienation. Modernism, which forsook the supernatural, nonetheless affirmed man's assured place in a natural and social order which, although shaped by evolutionary causes, was declared to be benevolent. As that comfortable myth of progress collapsed, neo-orthodoxy postulated a haven from alienation in man's internal existential response to transcendent reality, but its lack of a reasoned validation opened the sluice gates to atheistic existentialism. In contemporary existentialism the secular man's sense of alienation from the cosmos and history reaches its peak, for man cannot be at home in a cosmos that originated in an explosive accident and whose activity consists at best of mathematical probabilities. On this view, man can overcome alienation, if at all, only by creatively forcing his own preferred values on an amoral environment. Human history thus returns to the alternatives of the Garden of Eden: the ultimacy either of the word of God or of man who would make himself god over all.—Ed.

ALLEGIANCE. See also *Faithfulness.* Allegiance is a citizen's fidelity to his sovereign and country. Without acceptance of this obligation, government would be impossible.

The Biblical doctrine is that governmental authority is ordained of God (Rom. 13:1ff.). Christianity, however, limits the individual's allegiance to government and country. Unlike Graeco-Roman and modern nationalistic thought wherein duty to the state is the highest virtue, Christianity affirms that Jesus, not caesar, king, or president is the Christian's ultimate Lord (Acts 4:19, 29; 5:29; Matt. 10:17-25; Dan. 3). The Christian cannot accept the slogan, "My country, right or wrong," or pledge unconditional allegiance to the flag. For the prophet who urged people to desert during wartime, allegiance to God relativized allegiance to the state (Jer. 21:8-9; 38:1-6).

RONALD J. SIDER

ALMSGIVING. The English word "alms" comes from the Greek *eleēmosunē,* meaning "kind deed," through the Anglo-Saxon *aelmaesse.* Originally it signified all works of mercy and material aid to the poor.

Although God's concern for the needs of the poor and needy is a regular OT theme (Exod. 23:10-11; Lev. 19:9-10; 23:22; Deut. 15:7-11; 24:19-22; 26:12-13; Ps. 17:12-14; 82:2-4; 140:12; Prov. 19:17; 22:22-23), the practice of almsgiving is rarely mentioned. The prophets condemn the rich for lack of compassion for the poor (Amos 4:1; 8:4-7; Isa. 3:14-15; 10:1-2; cf.

James 5:1-6), but their stress is more on justice than charity. In the NT our Lord included almsgiving among the religious practices of his disciples (Matt. 6:1-4), but he warned against self-righteousness and religious ostentation.

Fundamental to a Christian understanding of almsgiving is the concept of *stewardship:* God is owner of all things and alone has the right to distribute wealth; man is therefore responsible to use all his possessions for the glory of God. Sharing from God's bounty with those who are less fortunate becomes a privilege for the Christian, a token of thanksgiving to God for his loving care and an illustration of his grace.

Until modern times the practice of almsgiving has been essential for the survival of the poor, since there was little official provision for giving regular help to the underprivileged. However, the custom has its weaknesses. (1) There is the tendency to regard almsgiving as a means of earning God's favor (as in Inter-Testamental Judaism, Islam, and medieval Christianity), (2) It easily leads to paternalistic feelings of the wealthy toward the poor (quite contrary to the Biblical perspective), (3) It may lead to professional begging and passive dependence.   W. WARD GASQUE

ALTRUISM. See also *Egoism.* Altruism as an ethical theory arose in late seventeenth century England. In reaction to Thomas Hobbes' psychological hedonism, altruism tried to prove the existence of natural impulses to do good to other people. Hobbes had held that all natural impulses and motives are self-seeking. He had expressed himself, as one critic put it, in "delightfully repulsive" terms. For example, Pity is "the imagination of future calamity to ourselves proceeding from the sense of another man's calamity." Again he asserted that "the passion of laughter proceedeth from the sudden imagination of our own odds and eminency."

Francis Hutcheson (1694-1747) argued: "Had we no sense of good distinct from the advantage or interest arising from the external senses ... our admiration and love toward a fruitful field or commodious habitation, would be much the same with what we have toward a generous friend or any noble character. . . .we should have the same sentiments and affections toward inanimate things which we have toward rational agents; which everyone knows to be false."

Hutcheson's argument is obviously unsatisfactory, and Bishop Butler (1692-1752) removed the problem by identifying the effects of self-love and conscience. "Self-love then, though confined to the interest of the present world, does in general perfectly coincide with virtue. . . . Whatever exceptions there are to this, which are much fewer than they are commonly thought, all shall be set right at the final distribution of things. . . .Conscience and self-love, if we understand our true happiness, always lead us the same way."

In the nineteenth century, Utilitarianism, without the benefit of a final judgment, tried to harmonize the pleasures of all individuals, so that one's own pleasure and the pleasures of others were always consistent. They were not so successful as the good Bishop.   GORDON H. CLARK

AMBITION. See also *Pride.* The desire for fulfillment or achievement of the good for God is significant for the Christian. Paul expresses this in such colorful expressions as "press forward," "forgetting the past," "goal," "the race." Reinhold Niebuhr incisively analyzed the distortion of this good by pride and self-interest. The most idealistic dreams like the Babel tower and modern space ventures can end in tragic debasement of the human spirit if attempted without devotion to the moral and spiritual purposes of God.

WALTER H. JOHNSON

AMERICAN COUNCIL OF CHRISTIAN CHURCHES. See also *Ecumenism and Ethics.* This coalition of small denominations independent of the Federal Council (later National Council) of Christian Churches arose in protest against the ecumenical movement's monopolizing of Protestant chaplaincy appointments, growing control of foreign mission fields, and liberal orientation in theology and socio-political matters. Its moving spirit was the Rev. Carl McIntire of Collingswood, N. J. Hastily organized in 1941 in advance of the formation of the National Association of Evangelicals (q.v.), it demands, in distinction from NAE projections, an immediate and complete separation from "apostate" denominations and corporations, that is, from NCC-related movements, and institution of a rival council of churches. The *Christian Beacon* was its journalistic voice. Its denominational constituency assertedly totaled just under one million persons; claims to a much larger constituency of individual members from other churches were never supported by a published list. The international movement was known as the International Council of Christian Churches.

McIntire's emphasis was mainly polemical and negative. He assailed as compromisers evangelicals inside and outside the NCC (q.v.) who were not affiliated with ACCC. He captured extensive mass media coverage by publicly organizing counter-demonstrations against NCC political pressures. While eumenical churchmen pressed for USA withdrawal from Vietnam, McIntire vigorously urged bombing Hanoi for military victory.

The ACCC itself fell victim to internal strife, finally splintering over the issue of "McIntire-ism," or concentration of ACCC institutions and agencies (including Shelton College and Faith Theological Seminary, now disbanded) under his personal control. When ACCC leaders elected a rival leadership, McIntire in 1970 installed himself as president during a recess, purged the rolls of its incumbent leaders, propagandized through his radio "Reformation Hour" and the *Beacon,* and froze its bank accounts. ACCC leaders, entrenched in the movement's Valley Forge headquarters, and claiming to speak for most of the constituency, brought charges that McIntire had turned organizational solicitation to private purposes and had misappropriated funds. An out-of-court settlement ensued, in which McIntire agreed to relinquish all claims upon ACCC in return for transfer to his control of the International Christian Relief fund.   CARL F. H. HENRY

AMOS. Amos, from Tekoa in Judah, prophesied in the North during the prosperous days of Jeroboam II of Israel (786-746 B.C.). He was concerned that religious formalism had replaced true godliness. The ethical implications of the Law were largely neglected, and Amos foresaw judgment in the form of an Assyrian victory as a consequence.

Not only Israel, but her neighbors as well, would be punished for cruelty. The Syrians had "threshed Gilead" (1:3) as farmers using threshing sledges. Whole populations were enslaved (1:9) and the rights of the poor were violated (2:6-7). The women demanded that their husbands indulge their every whim, even if they had to oppress the poor to do so (4:1).

Luxury-loving inhabitants of Samaria reclined on fancy couches or beds of ivory. They sang the popular songs of the day, and enjoyed their pleasures unmindful of the misery around them, and unaware of the judgment soon to fall upon them (6:4-7). People brought sacrifices to the shrine at Bethel (Amos 4), but they ignored the ethical demands of the Law, and learned nothing from punishments which had al-

ready come on the land.
CHARLES F. PFEIFFER

AMUSEMENTS. See also *Leisure.* Refreshment in life is provided not simply through rest and spiritual renewal, but is also available during periods of relaxation and disengagement from the routine pursuits of life. In contrast to recreation, which usually involves physical and mental activity, amusements are generally understood to be lighter diversionary experiences of play, such as games, carnivals, and spectator activities involving sports and entertainment productions. Hobbies are sometimes included in this category.

When evaluating the legitimacy of various amusements the Christian must consider matters of finance and the use of time as well as whether or not the activities are depersonalizing, dangerous, or corrupting to the sensitive spirit. Contexts are often extremely important in decisions concerning amusements, as can be exemplified in the use of motion pictures, pool tables and cards, whether or not the spots and numbers are changed. While the Puritan aversion to enjoyment (q.v.) and amusements is a perversion of Christian discipleship, the growing overindulgence in amusements and pleasure-seeking escape activities within the contemporary Western world seems to be a clear sign of an increasing superficiality in interpersonal relationships.

In general, however, the need for a balance between duty and relaxation is vital to a zestful life. Though legitimate amusements may add little to man's understanding *per se,* they may as a by-product, nevertheless, add dimensions to life in terms of pleasant social relationships, and refreshment to either the busy and often tension-filled or the uneventful assembly-line type of existence.   GERALD L. BORCHERT

ANABAPTISTS. The term was (as early

as the fourth century) applied by opponents to groups who denied the validity of infant baptism and who "rebaptized" converts upon confession of faith; it is also used indiscriminately of the large "left wing" Reformation of the sixteenth century. The name was rejected as invalid by the latter, who preferred "Brethren," but it was nonetheless used frequently of the Baptists until the end of the eighteenth century (as in the German *Wiedertäufer* and *Täufer*). Misunderstood for four centuries after their appearance, both as to origin and character, these "radical" reformers are now receiving more objective evaluation by historians.

The movement began in Zurich in 1523, when several associates of Ulrich Zwingli, the Swiss reformer (cf. *Reformed Ethics*), separated on the issue that the church must be separate from the state to be free under Christ and maintain the local church as a fellowship of believers. In 1525 a small group, including Conrad Grebel, Felix Manz, and Georg Blaurock, reinstituted believers' baptism. Church discipline was administered internally by use of the ban, or exclusion from fellowship. Thus they emphasized a converted membership, separation of church and state, and religious liberty. Rapid expansion throughout Western Europe was met by severe persecution and, as had Theodosius in the fourth century, the Diet of Spires in 1529 decreed the death penalty throughout the Holy Roman Empire for adult Anabaptists, resulting in the death of tens of thousands.

There was wide diversity within the movement, but the majority were committed to the "restitution" or "restoration" of apostolic Christianity on the basis of the New Testament, rather than "reformation" of an apostate or "fallen" church. Concerned by the low moral level of medieval life, the Anabaptists concentrated on obedience to Jesus, centered in his ethical teachings in the Sermon on the Mount (Matt. 5-7) and the obligation of every Christian to witness (Matt. 28:19-20), thus demonstrating their love, patience, and suffering.

Baptists, Mennonites, Friends, Brethren, and Hutterites are modern denominations continuing various Anabaptist emphases: the believers, church principle, separation of church and state and religious liberty, peace, world relief, and social legislation.

JAMES D. MOSTELLER

ANARCHISM. Anarchism is a theory that rejects government and desires society to be regulated only by voluntary agreements. Not all anarchists propose to destroy government by violence. Others do.

Some proponents of secular anarchism are Proudhon, Bakunin, Kropotkin, Max Stirner, and the American, Benjamin Tucker (1854-1939). The theory assumes that human nature is good and needs no coercive laws.

Christian anarchists claimed freedom from law on the basis of liberation by Christ. They are represented by the Levelers and Diggers of the seventeenth century, the Anabaptists and Doukhobors, and William Godwin, who published an *Enquiry Concerning Political Justice* in 1793.

Augustine argued that sin necessitates civil government. Luther and Calvin continued this Biblical position.

GORDON H. CLARK

ANGER. Anger is attributed to deity as well as to men. Natural calamities in ancient religions elicited ambiguous interpretations of divine wrath, resulting in diverse expiatory rites (TWNT V, 385).

Divine anger is inseparable from the Covenant. As those chosen by God, Israel found that undeserved blessings (Ezek. 16:1-14) produced responsibility for obedience (Deut. 10:12-13) and certain wrath for violation (I Kings 14:15). Anger thus becomes God's response to Israel's violations of the Covenant. Wicked nations which are used as instruments of wrath themselves become objects of wrath (Isa. 10:12).

The severity of God's wrath is counteracted by his delay in executing anger, which is not partiality or weakness (II Chron. 19:7), but compassion, which gives opportunity for repentance (II Chron. 36:15-16; Rom. 2:4).

Greek philosophy viewed anger in men as predominantly an irrational passion, the source of many evils (*kaka,* TDNT V, 384).

Proverbs 14:29 extols the man "who is slow to anger," while in the NT man's anger does not work God's righteousness (James 1:20) but is an evil to be put away (Col. 3:8) or restricted (Eph. 4:26).

The anger of Jesus is aroused when men seek to bar others from the Kingdom (Matt. 23:13) or from his presence (Mark 10:14), over lack of faith (Matt. 17:17; John 11:33, 38), over opposition to God and perversions of his ordinances (Mark 3:5; Matt. 23:1-38; John 2:16). His ministry was in obvious contrast to the wretchedness of the leper (Mark 1:41; cf. Lev. 13:45, 46) and anger as well as compassion might be expected (cf. textual problem in TWNT, V, 427).

To the end of the age, neither wrath nor compassion excludes the other. The Lamb unleashes the Great Day of Wrath and overcomes God's enemies (Rev. 6:16) but even as he does, in love he redeems by his blood (Rev. 1:5) all who keep his testimonies (Rev. 20:4).

Walter Eichrodt, tr. J. A. Baker, *Theology of the Old Testament*, Philadelphia, Westnimister, 1967; R. V. S. Tasker, *The Biblical Doctrine of the Wrath of God*, London, Tyndale, 1951; A. T. Hanson, *The Wrath of God in the Former Prophets*, London, SPCK, 1957; H. M. Haney, *The Wrath of God in the Former Prophets*, New York, Vantage, 1960; Grether, Kleinknecht, Sjöberg Fichtner, Stählin Procksch, *TWNT* V, 382-447.   ROGER W. KUSCHE

ANIMALS. See also *Hunting; Vivisection.* Those who appeal to no authority beyond the human mind argue that maltreatment of animals encourages cruelty in general, which will eventually affect man. Others contend that we have duties to animals because they are in some elemental sense persons—that is, they have interests and therefore rights. Leonard Nelson in his *System of Ethics* (Yale University, 1956, pp. 137-144) questions whether we ourselves would consent to be used as mere means by another being far superior to us. He claims it is purely fortuitous that man has other beings in his power and is in a position to use them for his own ends. Were it only man's fully developed rationality gives him the right to prefer his own life over an animal's, then we could similarly disadvantage the feeble minded. No, says Nelson, it is an animal's "interest in life" that makes it mandatory that we treat it humanely. Since man is a rational being, he is invested not only with rights but duties. This is pure Kantian thought.

Christianity starts with God's creation of animals and man. God subordinated the animals to man and gave man a responsibility toward them which was similar to God's relationship to us. That responsibility was to care for them, as God cared. But as God may use all his creation to his own glory in the context of his good and holy nature, so may man use the animals, but with responsibility.

If one takes the teaching of the Bible as authoritative, he must work with certain basic premises. Isaiah 11:6-8 and 65:25 picture a time of Edenic renewal when predator and prey will lie down together and be at peace. Whether one spiritualizes this or takes it literally, it seems to say that violence in nature is not God's highest purpose. Genesis 1 discloses that God's purpose was that nature in its Edenic form be at peace with itself.

Tied to this is the premise that God made man as his representative to the animal kingdom and all nature (Gen 1:26). This dominion did not include the right to be a despot but as God's image bearer man was to treat nature with God-like kindness and goodness. Genesis 1:29f. implies that in the garden neither man nor the animals ate flesh. Only after the Flood were animals used for food (Gen. 9:1-3) and it is then that animals began to fear man (9:2).

A second premise is that animals were not made for eternal life. Without the fall of man and the subsequent curse on nature, animals would have died as did plants, without the violent and painful aspects of death in the natural world that result from the curse.

God approved animal sacrifice not because he approved of suffering and death, but because he disapproved of sin, and determined that blood, as the sign of life, should be the symbol of man's atonement. In the Bible God is merciful to animals as he is to man, but they do share God's wrath on man's sin, as in the case of the destruction of the world by flood. After the Flood the Noahic covenant included the animals also; they would never again be destroyed by water (Gen. 9:10, 11).

There are humanitarian aspects in the Biblical teaching on animals. Exodus 20:10 informs us they are included in the Sabbath rest. In Jonah God's mercy and goodness extends to the cattle of Nineveh. Nathan tells David the story of a man who raised a little ewe lamb as if it were his own daughter, and David is outraged by its senseless slaughter. Matthew 10:29 shows God cares for the sparrows although man is much more valuable in his eyes.

While animals and all life are to be respected, it is never at the expense of man. If rats need to be destroyed for human good, so be it. The extreme reverence for all forms of life in the Oriental religions is out of balance. A distinction must be made between killing and cruelty. This so-called "reverence for life" results in cruelty that allows diseased cows to live and vermin to spread filth. Christianity stresses the quality of life more than the duration of life. While no one would wish to denigrate pets, modern affluent society frequently puts more value on dogs than on people.

The Bible occasionally attributes to animals conduct for which the animal is held responsible and punished. In Exod. 21:28, if an ox that was not taught to gore, gored a man or woman, it was stoned. Biblical theology considers animals capable of being possessed of an evil spirit. Jesus allowed a demon to enter a herd of swine (Matt. 8:30-32). Do animals have moral conduct apart from these rare instances of demon possession? We would have to answer in the negative because morality centers around purposeful conduct, not just activity. And more than that, this must be purposeful activity that is directed by an idea, not merely instincts or outside stimuli.

The Christian is responsible toward the animal world not because animals are rational beings or that they possess special interests, or that they have inherent rights, but because God made them and us and put us together on this earth in a unique relationship by which we and they are obligated to honor the same Creator. He made us with many similarities, a certain kinship in that we are made by the same Creator, of the same stuff, in the same biological pattern. By God's decree animals have a right to exist and enjoy continued existence. When man, the rebel, is reconciled to God through Jesus Christ he begins to understand his proper relationship to other created beings. Then he seeks to restore the felicity of all creatures and all nature. Some who have not known this reconciliation come to understand their obligation to the created world by common grace. Others, sadly, who have known it fail to understand its fullest implications. No Christian dare wantonly outrage any part of God's creation. Not all forms of life, however, are equally sacred; there are levels of creation with man at the top. There should be no question of man's right to life above the animal world because he bears the Creator's image and has a spiritual nature.

ELMER B. SMICK

ANIMISM. The term "animism" *(anima, breath, soul)* was first used by Stahl (1720) as a philosophical "word-soul" concept, but introduced into anthropology and comparative religion by Taylor *(Primitive Culture,* 1871). A simple definition is "the doctrine of souls and spirits." Popular interest was then in origins. Religious belief supposedly evolved from the idea of souls, to spirits, to gods, as man became more civilized. Living "primitive" communities were considered survivals of earlier stages of human development. This unilinear evolutionary theory did not stand critical evaluation; yet much current comparative religion stands on this unstable base. Despite the commonality of religion itself, and the universal belief in spiritual phenomena, the regional diversity of historic religious patterns does not indicate unilinear evolution. The quest is futile and speculative. Much of the earliest evidence of man in social groups has accompanying evidence open for religious interpretation, and some of it quite complex, and quite varied.

Animism as the belief in spirits or spiritual powers impinging on the life of man can be classified for study. Some scholars prefer the term "tribal religions" but this permits an unreal exclusion of the great religions, and consequently avoidance of missionary responsibility. Hinduism, Buddhism, and frequently Islam and Christopaganism, are thoroughly animistic. Older evolutionists classified religions by complexity. The "primitive" conceptualized spirits in trees, rivers, animals and storms, and saw the activity of disgruntled ghosts in misfortune. His rudimentary religion supposedly had not evolved into organized cults, priesthoods and a hierarchy of gods. However, anthropology shows that complex organization can be quite animistic with identical philosophical undergirding and magical patterns.

The philosophy of animism recognizes an encounter of powers, called *dynamism.* Victims of evil spirit venom seek the *mana* of some stronger spirit to save them. People so orientated towards dynamism can understand a gospel message of one who can claim "all power is given unto me."

Christianity is competent for dialog with animism because they both (1) differentiate the material from the spiritual, (2) recognize the physical and mental limitations of man, and the operation of supernatural forces outside him, (3) reach out to draw on those supernatural forces, (4) differentiate between using one's own skill and knowledge (science) and appealing to the supernatural through prayer, sacrifice and worship (religion), and (5) accept the principle of dynamism, or spiritual encounter, with hope in the victory of the beneficent one. In this philosophical frame of reference, the idea of Jesus overcoming the powers is meaningful, and a gospel of salvation may be presented.

On the other hand Christianity and animism clash at two basic points. First, the animist serves a multiplicity of gods and spirits, differentiating their functional roles. The Christian is bound by Biblical law: "Thou shalt have no other gods before me." Second, the animist experiments with ways of manipulating the supernatural by magic and sorcery, practices forbidden to the Christian (Gal. 6:19-21) (cf. *Witchcraft*). As the converted animist will rely on religion to meet needs previously met by magic, careful nurture is essential. Failure here leads to *syncretism* (q.v.).

Converted animists normally demonstrate their response to Christ collectively by some ocular demonstration of their change of religious allegiance—fetish-burning, burial of skulls, destruction of groves or temples—a public, symbolic confession and validation of their change of faith.

Animist ethics stand on the concepts of communal cohesion and perpetuity. This has affinities with Christianity, which also demands responsibility to one's neighbor and social justice. However, when animist values are based on pagan eschatology, they lead to many forms of ceremonial *inhumanity* (cf. *Widow Strangling, Patricide, Infanticide, Suttee, Cannibalism*). The major difference between animist and Christian ethics is: first, "loving one's brother" is not enough, one should "love one's enemy"; and second, the ethics of any religious system stand on the character of its God. The Bible stresses the idea of "holiness unto the Lord." Animism has nothing like this; therefore again, conversion must be followed by careful nurture at this point.

Currently, under the pressures of acculturation and "world shrinkage" animism is breaking up in many lands. People are seeking new religions and ideologies; but Christianity cannot be one of the options unless the existing believers of Christian lands are obedient to the Great Commission (Matt. 28:18-20). Christian mission to animist lands is thus an ethical issue—a matter of Christian responsibility (Rom. 10:13-15).

A. R. Tippett, *Bibliography for Cross-Cultural Workers*, South Pasadena, William Carey Library, pp. 171-232.   ALAN R. TIPPETT

ANTHROPOLOGY. See also *Cultural Relativism; Culture.* Anthropology is the study of man—the whole man, both through time and in space, both as a biological organism and as a cultural being. Thus anthropology is divided into two main areas—physical anthropology and cultural (or social) anthropology. The central focus of anthropology is on those dynamic adaptive processes which enable man to make the necessary adjustments to living with respect to both the environment and to the group. The basic biological adaptive process is human evolution; the basic behavioral process is culture. These two processes are not independent and unrelated but rather are in a state of constant interrelationship and feedback.

One of the distinguishing characteristics of anthropology is its interdisciplinary nature. Anthropology is a natural science because it studies man as a biological organism, a social science because it studies man in terms of his social behavior, and a humanity because it studies the products of man's cultural activity—art, music, literature, and religion. Also, anthropology is both descriptive, in that it is concerned with recording the numerous variations that exist in man and his culture, and nomothetic, in that it constructs broad integrating and synthesizing generalizations which function as explanatory models.

Traditionally, anthropology has been primarily concerned with the study of primitive (or preindustrialized) peoples. The present trend, however, is to give greater emphasis to the peoples and cultures of complex societies.

Anthropology, particularly cultural anthropology, shares a common interest with sociology and psychology in its focus upon human behavior. The distinguishing characteristic of anthropology is its emphasis on culture, defined variously as the learned patterns of group behavior or as the value orientation of the group.

The basic analytical and methodological emphases and assumptions of anthropology are as follows.

1. Holism. This view of man insists on examining man as a total functional entity—biological, social, and cultural—and the interrelationships and mutual interdependence of these different aspects of his existence. It also implies a reluctance to accept the study of any part of man or culture in isolation from other parts.

2. Functionalism. This analytical ap-

proach to understanding culture determines the various contributions that different aspects of culture make to culture as a whole. These various aspects include art, social structure, political organization, religion, values, and ceremonies.

3. Field work. Anthropology emphasizes the direct observation of behavior in its natural setting. Participant-observation gives not only an intellectual acquaintance with the customs of the group but a sympathetic appreciation of the culture as an on-going adaptive system of behavior.

4. Comparative method. This analytical methodology constructs comparisons both within and between groups, and between the same features at different points in time. This method is used to highlight salient features, point up distinctive characteristics, and identify common processes when they are present in different groups.

5. Cultural relativism. This view holds that the behavior of the members of a group must be understood in relation to the values of that group. This view avoids making judgments on one culture from the value orientation of another culture.

The emphasis of early studies was on the wide variability that exists in all various cultural institutions. This variability was demonstrated by numerous descriptive and comparative studies concerning various aspects of culture, particularly linguistics, kinship, art, and religions. The emphasis of more recent studies has been on the uniformities between cultures and has concerned itself with the similarity of functions and the functional interrelationships in culture. In short, the shift in anthropological studies has been from an emphasis on differences to an emphasis on similarities, from an emphasis on form to an emphasis on function, and from description to comparison.

The goal of cultural anthropological studies is the understanding of behavior in terms of the values of the group. These values are in turn related to historical and ecological factors and are dependent upon the nature of man and the nature of social organizations. Anthropologists do not attempt to judge cultures by comparing them to a system of idea, transcultural standards, but they attempt to understand the culture in terms of its own dynamic system of values. However, at times the anthropologist, in applying anthropological principles to particular situations, must of necessity make judgments such as is often done by missionaries, diplomats, Peace Corps workers, etc.

Although the assumptions and methodologies of anthropology are essentially in agreement with traditional Biblical conceptions, two major areas of conflict have arisen. The first area relates to the problem of the origin and nature of human nature and its derived ethical systems (cf. *Evolutionary Ethics*). The second concerns the validity and applicability of the concept of cultural relativism. Cultural relativism as originally defined by M. J. Herskovits implies not only the recognition of cultural variability or the use of cultural relativity as a methodological technique, but also the acceptance of cultural relativity as a philosophical ideology. Such an acceptance requires the denial of transcultural values or behavioral absolutes. Herskovits' view was criticized by various individuals who have suggested different means for determining transcultural values—by David Bidney who suggested deriving transcultural values by rational analysis; by Robert Redfield who used the method of historical comparison of precivilized and civilized peoples; by Clyde Kluckhohn who used the empirical method; and by William Smalley and David Moberg who derived transcultural values from Biblical revelation. Although these men differed widely on the source of transcultural values, they agreed on rejecting cultural relativism as a philosophical ideology. Consequently, current texts (such as *Anthropology Today*) reject cultural relativism as a philosophy and define it as a methodology. Such texts today admit the possibility and value of using a non-relative perspective in understanding culture.

◁ Classic texts include A. L. Kroeber, *Anthropology;* M. J. Herskovits, *Man and His Works,* New York, Knopf. Among better contemporary texts are *An Introduction to Anthropology* by R. L. Beals and H. Hoijer, New York, Macmillan; *Anthropology Today,* C. Starr, ed. Applied anthropology to missions is present in E. Nida, *Customs and Cultures,* New York, Harper & Row; L. J. Luzbetak, *The Church and Cultures.* A comprehensive discussion of cultural relativity from a Biblical perspective is the article "Cultural Relativity and Christian Faith" by D. Moberg in *Journal of the American Scientific Affiliation,* 14:34-48 (June, 1962).   DONALD R. WILSON

ANTICHRIST. The name Antichrist is derived directly from the word *antichristos* occurring exclusively in the Epistles of John (I John 2:18, 22; 4:3; II John 7). The word implies a direct opposition to Christ, his claims, his redemptive work, and to the virtues which he practiced and taught: such as truth, peace, holiness and grace. A false Christ deceptively emulates the character and work of Christ, but Antichrist implies antagonism.

Since the entrance of sin into the cosmos there has been antagonism between God and Satan's revelation of his malignant self in antichrist. At the Fall of man (q.v.) the Lord said to the serpent, "I will put enmity between thee and the woman and between thy seed and her seed" (Gen. 3:15). This satanic program is often led by individuals dedicated to activities against the people of God and his Word, as in Antiochus Epiphanes, Judas Iscariot, Julian Apostate, and Adolf Hitler. Daniel predicts one to come who will make war with the saints and speak great words against the Most High (7:18-26; 8:23-27; 11:36-45).

Paul depicts the Antichrist (II Thess. 2:3-10) as the Man of Sin who showeth himself that he is God, who will be generized by Satan. He is significantly referred to as the Lawless One, whose appearance will be accompanied by a spirit of delusion, which Eadie rightly calls "an unparalleled hallucination indicating a mysterious state of mind and of society." In the Antichrist All law is discarded. All moral order is dethroned. Upon the ruins of shattered states and kingdoms the vast empire of Antichrist is built. The revolutionary conditions of society out of which the Antichrist and his dominion arise is clearly indicated by Daniel 7:2. Out of the same unstable and agitated element the beast of the Apocalypse issues forth. The sea, torn by the winds, is the graphic image of nations and peoples in Commotion and Revolution.

—William G. Moorehead

John speaks of the Antichrist as a liar who denies that Jesus is the Christ. Westcott says this denial "when grasped in its full significance—intellectual, moral, spiritual—includes all falsehood. . . . it takes away the highest ideal of sacrifice: it destroys the connection between God and man."

While the Apocalypse mentions many antagonists of truth, and the people of God, Chapter 13 represents Antichrist as the beast out of the sea (cf. 15:2; 16:10; 17:17; 19:19). It is almost unbelievable that *the whole earth* will worship both *the dragon* and *the beast* (vv. 3, 4). There will be much religion on earth, but it will be godless and blasphemous. This first beast is against God (vv. 5, 6); is satanically energized (v. 2); is militarily supreme (v. 4); possesses worldwide power (v. 7); and persecutes the saints of God (v. 7).

More than a century ago, a famous Swiss theologian, Karl A. Auberlen, made a statement concerning Antichrist and signs of his coming that describe conditions more world-wide today than when he wrote:

The apostasy will commence in a way which will be imperceptible to most people; it will have an appearance of Christianity and its outward form, as there were weeds which look like wheat;

yea, in some cases, the apostasy will pretend to be pure, and the only genuine Christianity. . . .

The false prophet asserts that the forms and doctrines of Christianity are of no importance; that everything depends on the fundamental ideas. Under which specious protest, however, he gets rid of everything in Christianity which is from above and against this world, the supernatural facts of redemption, the divine radical beginnings of life, and heavenly aims of life, in short, Christ the divine essence of Christianity. . . . This is the new heathenism sunk back into deification of nature and humanity, and of which it cannot be predicted what forms of folly and beast-nature it shall yet assume. . . . What is bringing thousands from Christianity, and preventing others from coming to a belief in a full and true Christianity, is nothing else but respect for these intellectual powers which rule in these days, for modern science and culture. But the worst thing is, that scarcely any one sees the depth of the evil.

The NT makes two references to the destruction of Antichrist. Revelation 19:21 asserts that immediately after the Battle of Armageddon the beast and the false prophet were both "cast alive into a lake of fire burning with brimstone." II Thessalonians 2:8 states that the Lord, returning in glory, "shall consume [him] with the spirit of his mouth, and shall destroy with the brightness of his coming." The verb here translated *destroy* occurs with great frequency in the NT (e.g., Rom 6:6; I Cor. 6:13; 15:24; II Cor. 3:7).

From the earliest post-apostolic writers down to this generation, Antichrist has been variously and erroneously identified with different individuals. Barnabas said that Antichrist was the Roman Empire; others that he would be Judas Iscariot raised from the dead, or Nero. The Reformers, including Luther and Calvin, named the papacy. Many designated Napoleon Bonaparte, or Napoleon III. In this century both Mussolini and Hitler have been so identified. Such inaccurate identifications of Antichrist should warn us against attempting to look upon any single individual of our own generation as the pre-eminent agent of Satan, and insisting that this one or that among contemporary world-leaders is Antichrist.

The subject was of interest to early Church Fathers. Hippolytus (170-236) wrote an entire treatise, *Christ and Antichrist*, clearly stating that the last of the seventy weeks of Daniel 9:24-27 is the period of Antichrist's reign and of the great tribulation. See also W. Bousset, *The Antichrist Legend*, Eng. tr. 1896; Arthur W. Pink, *The Antichrist*, 1923; G. Vos, *Pauline Eschatology*, Grand Rapids, Eerdmans, pp. 96-107; Wilbur M. Smith, *World Crises and the Prophetic Scriptures*, pp. 294-317; p. 294-317;_____,*This Atomic Age and the Word of God*, pp. 193-221; H. A. Hoyt, *The End Times*, Chicago, Moody, 1969, pp. 115-132. An article of great learning on Antichrist in McClintock and Strong, *Cyclopedia of Biblical, Theological, and Ecclesiastical Literature*, Vol. I, Grand Rapids, Baker, reprinted 1968, pp. 254-261; and an important article on the "Man of Sin" in John Eadie, *Commentary on Thessalonians*.

WILBUR M. SMITH

ANTINOMIANISM. See also *Justification; Law.* The word denotes that theological position which so radically opposes law and gospel as to maintain that the Christian, justified by faith, has no obligation toward the moral law. Paul contended against this view in dealing with the Corinthian church, where some believers seemed to think they were free to continue the practice of pagan license, especially in the area of immorality (I Cor. 5-6). It was a wrong conclusion from the apostle's teaching on grace (Rom. 3:8; 6:1ff.). Some Gnostic sects were antinomian, grounding their opinion on two basic tenets. One was the claim that the Mosaic law was given by Jehovah, identified as the demiurge who made the world, rather than by the true and living God who remains aloof from matter.

The other was the assertion that the spirit in man, in distinction from his soul and body, partakes of the divine nature, and this is all that counts. What happens to his physical and psychological constitution can not affect the life of the spirit. This doctrine opened the door for fleshly indulgence. In Reformation times antinomian views were maintained here and there as the outgrowth of Luther's teaching on justification by faith apart from works of the law (cf. A. H. Newman's article in the *New Schaff-Herzog Encyclopedia of Religious Knowledge*, Grand Rapids, Baker).

Antinomianism has been rejected by the church at large during its history, and with good reason. The view is damaging to the unity of Scripture which demands that one part of the divine revelation must not be opposed to another. It also contains a misunderstanding of the nature of justification, which is indeed granted apart from works of the law, but which retains the moral principles of the law, not as the objective of human striving but as inwrought by the Holy Spirit in the believer (Rom. 8:4; Gal. 5:22-23). This disposes of the objection that since the law is so demanding that it cannot be kept, therefore it is to be thrust aside completely as irrelevant to one who lives under grace. It should be recalled that in the very portion where Paul agonizes most over inability to meet the law's demands, he exalts it as holy, spiritual, and good (Rom. 7).

EVERETT F. HARRISON

ANTI-SEMITISM. Anti-Semitism embraces every aspect of hatred for—or hostility towards—Jews, both individually and collectively. (Some define it broadly to include active opposition to the State of Israel.)

"Jews generally are acutely aware of the history of Anti-Semitism, simply because it comprises so large a portion of Jewish history. . . . The pages Jews have memorized have been torn from our histories of the Christian era" (Edward Flannery, *The Anguish of the Jews,* New York, Macmillan, 1965).

Anti-Semitism has three facets (a) historical-political, (b) pseudo-scientific, and (c) religious.

Anti-Semitism is older than Christianity. It first appeared about 220 B.C. in the Greek colony at Alexandria. By 75 B.C. it had been refined as a philosophic principle by Cicero and other Roman leaders. A long succession of political opportunists have opposed Jews. Haman's complaint (Est. 3:8) epitomizes their charges of cultural-political separation.

About one hundred years ago, from the same German academic circles that spawned critical attacks on the integrity of Scripture, a pseudo-scientific rationalization for Anti-Semitism emerged. Attempting to counter the effect of the emergence fifty years earlier of Jews from ghettos into the social-cultural mainstream, these people attempted to demonstrate the purported social inferiority of Jews. Eventually, this theory was used by Hitler to justify the murder of over five million Jews.

Anti-Semitism gained acceptance in the church about the time of the Edict of Constantine (A.D. 323). Initially a reaction to rabbinic opposition to Christianity, it was an attempt also to protect the religious-political ascendancy of the church. Unfortunately, as the church came to dominate the affairs of the state, anti-Semitism continued. While anti-Semitism is clearly a denial of Jesus' command to be motivated by love (Matt. 5:43-45; 22:37-40; John 14:20; 15:12) many Christian leaders rationalized it as hatred of evil (Ps. 45:7; Heb 1:9). This ethical compromise has stained much of subsequent church history and permeates much classical Scriptural interpretation, sermonic material and educational literature (Bernhard Olson, *Faith and Prejudice,* New Haven, Yale, 1963).

Among other things, continued condoning of anti-Semitism has blurred the understanding by many Christians of the Judaic character of Scripture. The NT is not anti-Semitic; too many understand it in an anti-Semitic way.

While social and legal pressures restrain physical assault and most other overt acts, many covert vestiges of anti-Semitism still are present. On the part of churches there is too often an indifference to the presence of Jews in the community.

Anti-Semitism in all its manifestations is anti-Christian. Its proponents—both secular and pseudo-Christian—have sought to attack Christ through the Jews as a means of furthering particular ideology or institution. Too many Christians have ignored the theological, personal, and ethical implications of anti-Semitism. This is totally foreign to genuine Christian experience.

📖 Malcolm Hay, *Europe and the Jews,* Boston, Beacon, 1960; Raul Hilberg, *The Destruction of the European Jews,* Chicago, Quadrangle, 1961; Jules Isaac, *Jesus and Israel,* New York, Holt-Reinhart, 1971; Arthur Morse, *While Six Million Died,* New York, Random, 1968; Hans Schoeps, *The Jewish-Christian Argument,* New York, Holt-Reinhart, 1963.   BELDEN MENKUS

ANTITHESIS. See also *Irrationalism.* Antithesis as a term in modern discussions almost always has an Hegelian background. For Hegel truth resided in concepts rather than in propositions. Therefore his philosophy is a system of concepts.

The first concept, because it is the most universal, is Being. Plants and stones are qualified beings; pure, universal Being has no qualities. It is neither living nor inanimate, red nor blue, heavy or any other predicate. Therefore it is Nothing.

Being was the *thesis;* Nothing is the *antithesis,* obtained by the *dialectic* process of analyzing the thesis. By Aristotelian logic the process should end here in the mutual exclusiveness of contradictories. But Hegel adds a *synthesis* in which the contradictor-ies are reconciled, elevated, or preserved *(aufgehoben).* In this case, since Being became Nothing, the synthesis is Becoming. There are some two hundred such triads in Hegel's system.

Søren Kierkegaard reacted violently against the seeming omniscience and existential emptiness of "The System," and operated with a two-term dialectic of thesis and antithesis, without any synthesis. "Misled by the constant reference to a continued process in which opposites are combined into a higher unity . . . the System lacks an Ethic" *(Concluding Unscientific Postscript,* p. 272).

Kierkegaard also rejected Aristotle's position that one of two contradictories must be false. The principle of *Paradox* requires them both to be "true." Christian faith therefore consists in believing what is demonstrably *absurd.*

But if Hegel's System allows no Ethic, is Kierkegaard's repudiation of System better? One would then have to praise both theft and honesty, both adultery and fidelity.

This irrationalism characterizes atheistic existentialism and the dialectical theology of Karl Barth and his followers.

📖 S. Kierkegaard, *Concluding Unscientific Postscript,* tr by D. F. Swenson and Walter Lowrie, Princeton, Princeton University, 1941; W. T. Stace, *The Philosophy of Hegel,* London, 1923.

GORDON H. CLARK

ANXIETY. The term anxiety has been used of a wide range of human experiences in English translations of Scripture. From these translations no fixed ethical meaning of anxiety can be deduced. The term is probably most commonly associated with the Sermon on the Mount (q.v.) (Matt. 6:25-34). In this context Jesus brands anxiety as something inimical to Christian living. To be anxious is a denial of God's providence. It is the opposite of faith and trust in God.

In the nineteenth and twentieth centuries the term anxiety has accrued a more definite and specific meaning. It now has in certain contexts a theoretical status. In psychiatry anxiety has a highly refined and scientific meaning. In general it refers to a painful mental and emotional disorder accompanied by certain physical symptoms such as excessive nervous tension, insomnia, and loss of appetite. Through existentialism the term has been theoretically integrated into philosophy. Martin Heidegger, Karl Jaspers, and others employ the term anxiety in reference to extreme and threatening factors in the human situation such as death and mortality. Theologians and ethicists by means of certain existential motifs have made a specific kind of anxiety integral to their systems of thought. Among these Kierkegaard is a seminal thinker. In America Kierkegaard's conception of anxiety is reflected in the theology of Paul Tillich and the ethical thought of Reinhold Niebuhr. The current meaning of anxiety has gained special ethical implications through their pervasive influence.

Consistent with the modern ethical meaning of anxiety is an existential method which subjects human *consciousness* to radical analysis. This analysis proceeds on the assumption that the *self* has the capacity to transcend human consciousness. Through transcendence the self discerns the content and structure of consciousness. It ultimately confronts through transcendence the fundamental dimensions of reality (which Tillich describes as ontological reality). This reality upon analysis proves to be double dimensional. These dimensions are variously described as freedom and finiteness, spirit and nature, being and non-being.

Confrontation with the double dimensions of reality at the same time means participation. Participation means that the self is never a simple spectator to reality. It must inescapably identify with reality which in ethical terms means that the self must *choose*. But the double dimensional character of reality creates a moment of tension before the self chooses. On the one hand the self realizes that its identity is rooted in the dimension of freedom, an indefinite transcendence over all the concretions of human consciousness. On the other hand the self realizes its identity is involved in finiteness, nature and temporality. This moment preceeding choice is the context out of which anxiety arises. "Anxiety is the inevitable concomitant of the paradox of freedom and finiteness in which man is involved" (Niebuhr). This internal response of the self to its ambiguous position in freedom and finiteness Kierkegaard refers to as "dread" as well as anxiety.

The meaning of anxiety when arrived at through an existential methodology raises the question of its relation to Biblical revelation. Certainly in this approach the meaning of anxiety carries certain emotional overtones that have affinity with the subjective struggles a Christian experiences as he makes ethical choices. But an existential methodology gives an ethical normativity to human consciousness that tends to displace the normativity of Scripture. In Christ man and God (ultimate reality) are reconciled. Such reconciliation overcomes all ethical ambiguities. Consequently, for the Christian the moment in consciousness that should preceed ethical choice is more appropriately described as gratitude rather than anxiety.

Seward Hiltner, and Karl Menninger, *The Constructive Aspects of Anxiety*, Nashville, Abingdon, 1963. Søren Kierkegaard, *The Concept of Dread*, Princeton, Princeton University, 1946; Carl Michalson, *Christianity and the Existentialists*, New York, Scribner, 1956; Reinhold Niebuhr, *The Nature and Destiny of Man*, New York, Scribner, 1946; Paul Tillich, *Systematic Theology* Vol. I, Chicago, University of Chicago, 1950.

THEODORE MINNEMA

APARTHEID. Literally translated, apartheid means "separateness." It refers to the policy of strict racial separation pursued by the government of South Africa. Basically, apartheid is the forced separate development of white and non-white peoples. Native Reserves have been set aside for black Africans, where it is claimed the blacks are free to develop in their own way and at their own pace, without restriction on black land ownership, movement, or occupation. The rest of South Africa is reserved for the whites (plus those of Asian and mixed ancestry, who live under numerous special restrictions). When blacks venture off the Reserves they are subjected to restrictive regulations. The stated goal of the government is to help in the social, economic, and political development of the Reserves, with the ultimate goal of granting political independence.

The most serious moral problems raised by apartheid relate to the actual nature of the Reserves. In theory the Reserves are an answer to many of the possible objections to apartheid. In practice, however, they do not offer the black African the opportunity for separate development claimed for them. They are too small to support the black population: the Reserves constitute only 13 percent of the land area; the blacks constitute 68 percent of the population. Nowhere near the amount of money needed to make the Reserves viable economic units has in fact been spent on them. Thus less than half the blacks live on the Reserves, many being forced to seek employment off the Reserves in white owned industries, mines, and farms—where they are paid much lower wages than whites. Often 50 to 60 percent of the adult males are absent from their families in the Reserves for months at a time.

Thus the Reserves, instead of offering the opportunities for separate development, in practice run sharply counter to the Christian concept of social justice and to the Christian emphasis on the importance of family unity. In the process apartheid operates as an unchristian, discriminatory policy.

J. C. G. Kotze, *Principle and Practice in Race Relations according to Scripture*, Stellenbosch, S. C. A., 1962; Leo Marguard, *The Peoples and Policies of South Africa*, 4th ed., London, Oxford University, 1969.   STEPHEN V. MONSMA

APOSTASY. A Christian is one who continues in Christ's word (John 8:31). Already in NT times some professed faith without possessing it (John 2:23-25). Some "went out from us, because they were not of us" (I John 1:19). They had appeared to belong to Christ's disciples but their leaving revealed that they never really did. Thus Biblical apostasy seems to signify a process whereby a merely nominal believer is revealed by his separation to be actually an unbeliever. Apostasy is not from the church or body of Christ, but rather from an external association with the church. Branches which appeared to belong to the true vine but not in vital union were dead and therefore cut off (John 15:6).

In the postapostolic church there were three ways of wrongly leaving the church or apostasizing: by apostasy itself (renouncing the faith either directly or implicitly, as in the *lapsi*); by committing fornication; and by committing murder. For these there was no possibility of return. In the Middle Ages apostasy applied only to those who had renounced Christianity entirely (cf. Aquinas *ST.*, IIa-IIae, qq.11,12). The NT viewed as irreparably apostate the man who had committed the unpardonable sin (Matt. 12:31, 32). The church generally and historically has come to regard all other sins, however great, as forgivable.

There is general agreement that a denomination may become apostate by denying what is deemed essential to Christianity, but vast disagreement on what is essential to Christianity, and how defection from such is to be determined. Many today are wrestling with this problem, as Calvin did in the sixteenth century (cf. *The Necessity of Reforming the Church*). JOHN H. GERSTNER

AQUINAS. See also *Aquinas and Roman Catholic Ethics.* Thomas Aquinas (1225-74) as a dutiful disciple of Aristotle introduces his ethics by an empirical distinction between animals and men. Unlike inanimate objects that cannot determine their actions, animals have inclinations determined interiorly. The inclinations, however, are completely natural, and the animal cannot avoid desiring what he desires. But as one ascends the scale from inanimate, to animate, to men and angels, the nearer to God a being is, the more freedom it has—the more it is determined by itself.

Of course, man shares sensitivity with the animals, but in addition man has intellect and will. Sensitivity apprehends what is pleasant and what is useful to self-preservation, but only reason grasps the universal good. By reason man can know the end and the means to it, and so can determine his own inclination.

The main object of the will according to Aquinas, is the good as such: to desire it is a natural necessity for the will. But not all the acts of will are necessitated. Just as the intellect necessarily accepts the first principles of knowledge and cannot deny what follows from them, but does not necessarily accept contingent truths whose denial does not contradict first principles, so too the will necessarily wills the universal good but may or may not will certain particular goods. But goods that are necessarily connected with beatitude, the will wills necessarily, provided the intellect knows the connection. Clearly, an object must be known, before it can be willed. This explains why the fool does not even will God, since he does not know the necessary connection between God and beatitude.

The intellect is superior to the will in the sense that it apprehends universal truth. The object of the will, the general good, and the objects of the will, the particular goods, are included among the objects of the intellect, truth and being, and so the intellect is superior. However, if we consider the good as universal and the intellect as a special power of the soul, the will is superior, both because every item of knowledge is good and because the will sets the intellect in motion.

This defense of free will makes morality possible, for we could not deserve blame or earn merits if our actions were all unavoidable.

The will and the intellect develop habits. Man is not a pure substance, not a theoretical construction of intellect and will, but is affected by his own actions. Habit is a quality that modifies man's substance and is therefore either good or bad. (God, of course, has no habits because he is in no way potential.) The habit of grasping first principles is virtually innate (though habituation and innateness are mutually exclusive). Virtues are not innate but are developed by repeated actions.

Virtues are good habits, in that they conform to man's nature. Vice is a habit that leads in the opposite direction. To distinguish between them we must bear in mind man's natural end—beatitude or God. Some acts are in accord with reason and lead to God. Others are the reverse and are irrational. Some, like picking up a wisp of straw, lead nowhere and are morally indifferent. Thomas then continues by describing moral virtues and intellectual virtues, much as Aristotle had done.

Ethics must consider law as well as good. Law is an obligation founded on reason. Different types of law should be distinguished. The eternal law of God rules the whole universe; but as it is inscribed on human nature, it becomes the legitimate tendencies of our nature or natural law. The first law of all nature is self-preservation. The second law of sensitive beings is reproduction. The third law of rational beings is to live rationally. This includes living in communities (the family and the state) in order to achieve the good more effectively by cooperation.

There is also human law. A gap opens between the universal principles of natural law and the infinite complexity of particular actions. On these matters peoples and states disagree. Kings should deduce civil law from natural law; and if they do, a just man will conform to it with perfect spontaneity, as if the civil law did not exist. But unjust decrees are not law and need not be obeyed. It may be prudent to obey some unjust laws in order to modify them. But if a decree infringes on the rights of God, it should never be obeyed. GORDON H. CLARK

AQUINAS AND ROMAN CATHOLIC ETHICS. Thomas Aquinas (q.v.) gave Roman Catholicism its basic ethical theory. The massive structure, range of ideas, thoroughness of analysis, and interpretation of many moral matters is the heritage bequeathed to the future. Catholic ethicists today have to deal with Thomas' ideas at every significant point. His central moral theory is here summarized.

I. *Man a Created Moral Being*

A. A Rational Creature. Thomas gives man a significant moral quality in the framework of divine providence by describing him as a rational creature. As such, men are superior to other earthly creatures "in the perfection of their nature, and in the excellence of their end" *(Summa Contra Gentiles,* III, 91). Thomas places man midway between angels and animals in the created order. Like the former he has a rational soul and like the latter a physical body. The body is of lesser value. Ideally, the soul or spiritual element rules the body, having as its goal perfection in God in the heavenly state. A man's ordinary drives and impulses are his "appetitive faculties." As reason organizes them into acceptable patterns of behavior, he develops the desired virtues. His will seeks the good as reason determines what it is.

In Thomas' view man is not an autonomous thinker. His rational powers are divinely given and directed, and supplied with an intellectual or spiritual energy. Whatever a being is created for is that toward which he determinedly moves. Even the right goals are selected by God. Thomas does not share Augustine's dark view of the destructive impact of original sin upon man's whole nature, particularly upon his mental powers. He holds that man is left virtually intact after the Fall, though he suffers a certain blindness of reason and stubbornness of will. Weakened morally by the loss of the superadded gift of righteousness, man seeks sensuous gratification. Yet he retains a trustworthy thinking ability whose judgments, at their best, complement the truths given through revelation. Aristotle does supremely well in these matters, in Thomas' opinion, and the latter utilizes the "Philosopher's" schematic structures wherever possible. He adopts from Aristotle such important conceptions as the nature of causation, the play of the teleological factor in nature and man, the nature of virtue and the virtues, and the accent upon the "golden mean." Yet Thomas' ethics is not simply a synthesis of Aristotle's thought with his own. Numerous thinkers from the past, classical and Christian, have their part in his thought. His teacher, Albertus Magnus, contributes his bit. Thomas' understanding of the Bible is important in the finished product. His own creative genius figures in, too. He is no mere collector and arranger of other men's ideas.

B. Possessor of a Free Will. Man possesses a rational free will so that he is able to make choices. While Thomas' powerful emphasis upon the divine causation and control of everything might seem to exclude the will's freedom, he insists that divine providence is concerned to preserve that freedom, since it belongs to the will's perfection, yet not in such a way that the will is predetermined in a particular instance to produce a certain result. "God moves man's will . . . to the universal object of the will, which is the good. And without this universal motion man cannot will anything. But man determines himself by his reason to will this or that, which is a true or apparent good" (*Summa Theologica*, I-II, Q. 9, Art. v).

II. *Man Equipped for Moral Activity*

A. Man's Moral Goals Attainable. The four cardinal virtues of prudence, justice, temperance, and fortitude are possessed by all men as rational beings. They are "intellectual and moral" virtues. Thomas gives the highest marks to prudence, the intellectual virtue by which wise moral choices can be made. Reason is employed in determining correct general principles and in making specific decisions in relation to them. In this twofold activity the power by which general principles of morality are held and understood is called *synderesis*. When these principles are applied to specific actions in judging of their rightness or wrongness, *conscientia*, the exercise of the practical intellect, is called into play. Right action accords with right reason; evil action is contrary to it. Good moral habits or virtues result from doing good repeatedly, moving man ever closer to the goal of happiness.

Thomas agrees with Aristotle that man's ethical goal is *eudaimonia* or happiness, defined as a sense of well-being and well-doing, not as pleasure. But Aristotle's non-Christian concept is too limited. At this point Thomas presses his "moral theology" into service. To the four cardinal virtues he adds the three theological virtues of faith, hope, and charity. Their source is divine revelation. Supernatural grace is needed to sustain them in man. They direct him to his supernatural happiness, the intellectual vision of God. Faith functions in association with the intellect, laying hold upon the supernatural principles which are to be believed. Hope is created by the will, which marks the goal as attainable. Charity speaks of the spiritual union by which the will is transformed into the supernatural end. Charity is the most excellent of the virtues. It is basically one's love for God and his neighbor. The theological virtues supplement the natural, extending into areas of experience beyond the reach or capacity of reason. The natural lead man to the attainment of his "connatural end," the other to his supernatural end. Those outside the grace mediated through the church and her sacraments might satisfy the divine demand at the natural level, but come short with respect to the supernatural end. For them there is no vision of God in prospect.

B. Additional Divine Assistance. God assists man toward moral achievement by providing a structure of laws: (1) eternal law in the mind of God, furnishing the ultimate source of the distinction between moral good and evil; (2) natural law, the counterpart of the eternal law in the created world; (3) human or statute law enacted by governments; and (4) divine law, the revealed law found in the Bible. It agrees in part with natural law, but goes beyond it. Some of Thomas' finest accents appear in his discussions of the "new law," the New Testament part of the divine law (*ST*, I-II, Qs. 106-108). The Holy Spirit inscribes it upon the Christian's heart, creating an inner disposition of love of God. It is a written law secondarily. The right inner disposition provides the motivation which gives acts their proper virtue. Without it the act is without moral quality. While Protestant Reformers would later approve this emphasis, they would look critically upon his toning down of the gospel's radical demand in the ideal of the "golden mean," and upon his distinction between the standards of "evangelical counsels" for better Christians, and commandments in the divine law for others. The "reward for virtue" aspect of Thomas' ethics would also invite criticism, as would his optimism concerning the ability of unregenerate reason to function acceptably in this, as in other, areas.

Summa Theologica, I-II, II-II, and *Summa Contra Gentiles*, Book III, conveniently presented in *Basic Writings of Saint Thomas Aquinas*, Vol. II, edited by Anton C. Pegis, New York, Random, 1945; *Commentary on the Nicomachean Ethics*, translated by C. I. Litzinger, 2 vols., Chicago, Regnery, 1964.   ELTON M. EENIGENBURG

ARBITRATION. See also *Business Ethics; Industrial Relations; Labor Relations.* The term "arbitration" is usually associated with the settlement of labor disputes and is seen by many as a desirable alternative to the strike. In a voluntary arbitration situation both parties to the dispute agree to let a third party designated by them spell out the details of a settlement to be accepted by both sides. Compulsory arbitration normally involves government interference against the wishes of the employees, the employer, or both. In general governments are reluctant to intervene, and do so only when safety, public health, or national security are at stake or when the economic impact of a strike would be, or has already become, intolerable.

But governmental reluctance may be unwarranted when a strike by relatively few people can cause widespread havoc in our complex and interdependent society.

Arbitration appears to be a more satisfactory way to settle labor disputes than does a strike. It is preferable to arrive at a decision by rational assessment of the merits of conflicting views rather than to rely on the notion that might is right—that the side that can hold out longest economically has the best case and deserves to win.

It is important that arbitration arrangements be fair, that arbitration be employed only after negotiation and conciliation efforts have failed, and that a decision arrived at by arbitration be accepted in good faith and implemented fully by both sides.

Many Christian employers and employees have given whole-hearted support to the adoption of arbitration arrangements because these procedures virtually eliminate economic disruption, greatly diminish harsh feelings between employer and employee, and prevent the trampling of public interest or the infliction of harm on innocent bystanders.   JOHN H. REDEKOP

ARISTOCRACY. Aristocracy is a category of social class which in an earlier hierarchical society was an elite commonly based on birth into an ennobled family possessing a hereditary title (e.g., Duke, Baron, Earl), privileges, and usually landed estate. Members of the aristocracy obeyed unique social mores governing a grand style of life in their social manners, dress, language, worship. When functioning most smoothly, their social position required a relation of condescension toward, and deference from—not equality with—the non-aristocratic classes. Prior to the nineteenth century, at a lesser stage of differentiation, the aristocracy occupied the leading positions in the church and state, especially royal administration and the army, while their standards prevailed in art, architecture and education. Since the emergence of the democratic ideal, traditional aristocracy has been relegated to a more peripheral position, replaced by new elites, figuratively called aristocracy, based on wealth (the Rockefellers or Latin American oligarchs), education (scientists), good looks (entertainment personalities), or other criteria.
         C. T. McINTIRE

ARMAMENT. See also *Disarmament; Peace and War.* Scripture declares that government is divinely ordained and authorized to protect the general welfare of the citizenry and to provide protection and security against the predator. As "the minister of God" government is established to defend good works and to bear the sword in executing judgment on "him that doeth evil." Scripture ordains only that form of government which supports good and resists evil (Rom. 13:1-7).

Nations resist the ordinance of God to the extent that they seek by conquest to dominate others. To defend that which is good and to provide protection and security against the predator, every nation must be prepared to "bear the sword." This is armament, the means by which government is alert to the need to protect the general welfare of its citizens from external threat. Armament is also necessary to resist subversive threats to the internal well-being and security of a nation.

Bearing arms in the legitimate service of government either as a soldier or law enforcement officer does not conflict with the personal requirements of Christian faith and virtue. Jesus found the bearing of arms by the Roman centurion no spiritual barrier but commented on his great faith (Matt. 8:10).

The development of nuclear weapons, however, has created a dilemma for Christians. While nations should be able to protect themselves against their use and such an ability might actually prevent a nuclear war, the proliferation of nuclear weapons has posed the threat of destruction without any moral limits. Moreover, the soaring cost of armament absorbs funds needed for other purposes (cf. *Atomic Energy*).

Outlay for arms has doubled in the past fifteen years. The USA and the USSR are now spending close to one-tenth of their gross national product on national security. In 1969 this amounted to $80 billion for the USA and $60 billion for USSR.

Since 1969 the USA and the USSR have been holding Strategic Arms Limitation Talks (SALT) designed to control nuclear weapons. The USA is seeking a verifiable arms limitation agreement covering all offensive and defensive weapons. On May 26, 1972, the USA and the USSR agreed to limit antiballistic missile systems and approved an interim freeze on nuclear offensive systems for five years while seeking a more comprehensive agreement.

In the final analysis, it is not armament which is the cause of evil but the heart of man that must be changed. So long as greed and lust for power dominate some individuals and some nations, men and women of good will must be willing to support their government's use of defensive armament for a just cause and "that which is good."

JOHN C. BROGER

ARMINIUS AND ARMINIAN ETHICS. Jacobus Arminius (1560-1609) was ordained by the Reformed church of Holland in 1588 after studying at the University of Leyden and under Theodore Beza in Geneva. In Amsterdam he distinguished himself as an able preacher and expositor rising to the position of Professor of Theology at Leyden in 1603. His public lectures were opposed by Francis Gomar, a senior colleague, who held extreme Calvinistic views. Gradually Arminius came to express doubts regarding some features of Calvinism. Gomar persisted in accusations of heterodoxy and the sharp conflict between the two continued until Arminius' death in 1609.

After Arminius' death his followers crystalized his ideas in the *Remonstrance,* a five-point tract: (1) God's decrees are based upon his foreknowledge of man's faith, (2) Christ's atonement was for all men but is enjoyed only by the believer, (3) Man is depraved and needs the grace of God for salvation and goodness, (4) God's grace is the source of redemption but can be resisted by man, (5) Believers will experience final victory if they commit themselves to God and to the end.

Calvinists responded with the *Counter-Remonstrance,* setting forth the five points of Calvinism. The controversy continued until the authorities of Holland called the Synod of Dort in 1618 to unify the country. This synod disapproved the five articles of the Remonstrants and confirmed the Belgic Confession and the Heidelberg Catechism as the standard of orthodoxy. Remonstrant ministers were condemned and expelled from their pulpits. Many fled to England and France.

The salient principle of Arminian ethics is the idea of free will. If man is truly free, he alone is responsible for his choices. God's election and predestination are based on foreknowledge. The divine decrees are not compulsive either to sin or to grace. If man is free, he can resist the grace of God either when or after it is offered. Arminians thus reject the Calvinistic doctrines of irresistible grace and perseverance of the saints. The believer is one who has freely chosen the work and way of God. By faith he is justified and through the new birth enabled to live a good life.

Arminian ethics emphasizes human duties. Good works come out of the new life. Nevertheless, the new man in Christ must obey the commands of God as a condition of divine fellowship. The basic virtues of love, fear, trust, and honor give evidence to the world of Christ's presence in the Christian. The process of sanctification confirms man in holiness, enabling him to obey God. The Christian life is conditioned upon faith which expresses itself in obedience to God.

Arminius greatly influenced the Remonstrants and later the free will theology of John Wesley. Some of his theological and ethical ideas continue in the Wesleyan-Arminianism of the National Holiness Association and the Wesleyan Theological Society.   BERT H. HALL

ART. The modern schematization of the arts found its form in the eighteenth century. It distinguishes the fine arts from the applied arts or crafts, which without any well-defined boundaries are further differentiated from utensils, artifacts, etc., some of which in our days have once again gained some aesthetic significance under the heading of industrial design. Within the fine arts are distinguished the literary arts (prose and poetry), music, drama, dance, and the visual arts—architecture (which can be called "fine building," since building as such is often not considered architecture), sculpture, and painting, together with the minor arts, graphics (woodcuts, engravings), and drawing. Under the applied arts are considered (fine) ceramics, tapestry, textiles, gold-and silverware, etc. These distinctions have been created mainly by the collector of artistic objects, or with him in view, and by the art lover in general. The great tradition in European art, beginning with the Renaissance, looks to the work of art as the individual creation of an artist considered to be in line with poets, philosophers, and in general with men of letters. In other cultures and in the middle ages this system was unknown. The arts were considered under the *artes technicae,* distinguished from the seven *artes liberales;* in this system music was placed under mathematics, as a science of tones, and not as the actual music which was played or sung.

What is art? Is it to be defined by quality, or by structure? In the first sense a bad sculpture and a qualitatively poor novel are not art, while in the second they are, even if bad, art. This last offers advantages, as the normative approach is clearer, and an analysis of the structure of art can be accomplished; so e.g., we treat a painting simply as a painting and not either a work of "fine art" or a nonentity, which would conflict with experienced reality.

Art can be defined as man-made beauty, and as such has much in common with natural beauty (cf. *Beauty*). The beauty of a man-made thing is directly related to its meaningfulness, which as such includes its function, but is never identical with it. An ornament is beautiful if it is meaningful, just giving the accent needed at that spot, making the structure and use of the thing it adorns clearer, and adding to life and beauty in the human environment. An abstract (non-figurative) play with forms and colors can be beautiful and as such fascinating if it is meaningfully making the surroundings more agreeable, more humanely liveable, and at the same time serves the purpose of the place.

But human art can also express something, often by depicting human or natural forms, telling a story, singing about a situation, etc. This can be very meaningful: in this way we can honor the government in its head or hint at a great tradition, as on coins or stamps, or focus attention on that which gives meaning to a certain building, as a picture of the judgment of Solomon in a courtroom (not uncommon in previous centuries). Good quality in the work chosen for such use is a prerequisite; a bad and cheap painting is detrimental to the function just described, and impairs its meaning.

Before our own times works were never made just for the sake of art; art for art's sake is a very recent invention. A work of art was always given a meaningful place in a larger context. Think of the fountains by Bernini on the Piazza Navona in Rome, or the obelisk in the center of Washington, D.C. Altarpieces, frescoes with Biblical stories, capitals on the column in a building, mosaics on the floor, garden sculpture, all were chosen to play a meaningful part in a total man-made structure, in which they fulfill a function—although, the fact that they can be taken out of context and still remain beautiful shows that one cannot equate beauty and function. On the other hand, one can only understand the full beauty, e.g., of a Roman Catholic devotional image if one understands its intended use and considers the way it answers a specific religious need. The function the work of art has to fulfill specifies its form and therefore its beauty. Even cabinet paintings and the little decorative sculptures one has in one's room, which simply add to the humanity and life-quality of our surroundings, have a function that as such can never be equated with utility. In this we see a norm for art: it has to be in place. Marching music and chamber music can both be beautiful, but must be used according to their intended function.

The history of art shows that man has a need for depicting things dear or important to him—the human image itself, the portrait of the beloved, the animals around us, the scenery that is important to us. Man depicts the things directly around him, sings about things he knows, tells tales of the social world in which he lives. Or must we rather say, that these things to some extent become dear to us through depiction? The picture of the window view, the tale about the garden well, along with the objects with which we surround ourselves, such as old cartwheels and old weapons, help build emotional contact with, as well as an intellectual understanding of, those people or natural things around us, our environment. In this way art is related to life. It "works" in conquering realities for us, opening up their meaning, deepening our love for it, focusing our attention, in discovering hitherto unknown aspects. A humanity with little or no (figurative) art is poor in its relation to reality (therefore one finds clean and empty unadorned spaces where mystical people meditate, just because they want to break their contact with reality).

Art in this sense is constituted by reality as such, and, on the other hand, by our vision and understanding of that reality. In the tension between these two lies our appraisal and appreciation of the work of art: we like to see our vision affirmed, but we look for the true, the natural and real. Contrary to most critics today, we do not believe that quality is the last and maybe even only criterion for art. Quality is a prerequisite. When this fails, we never really come to assess the really important questions. The *what*, not the how, is the final test; quality is the first norm for art, but its final norm is love and truth, the enrichening of human life, the deepening of our vision.

Of course, this content can only become true, real, and expressive in the technical and artistic achievement. One can never sever content from form. The content can only be experienced through the form and, the form is created in order to express the content. In a good work of art one can almost say that form and content are an inseparable unity. Content here is more than only subject-matter. Subject-matter concerns that which the work of art talks about, while content means *what* it says about it. So a work of art—a song, a poem, a play, a picture—is not Christian by having a Biblical theme, but only if the understanding of that theme shows a Christian mentality and inspiration. Many Biblical stories are depicted in a humanistic or unbliblical sense, while a landscape or daily occurrence may be depicted in a Christian way with Biblical insight. Only on this level can any discussion of Christian art be fruitful.

🕮 E. Gilson, *Painting and Reality*, London, 1957; R. Berger, *Decouverte de la peinture*, Lausanne, 1958; R. Huyghe, *Dialogue avec le visible*, Paris 1955; F. Würtemberger, *Weltbild und Bilderwelt*, Vienna, 1958; H. Sedlmayr, *Kunst und Wahrheit*, Hamburg, 1958; E. Panofsky, *Meaning in the Visual Arts*, Garden City, N. Y., Anchor-Doubleday, 1955; J. Hospers, *Meaning and Truth in the Arts*, Chapel Hill, University of North Carolina, 1946; H. Read, *The Meaning of Art*, Baltimore, Penguin, 1949; H. Read, *Icon and Idea*, London, 1955; E. H. Gombrich, *Art and Illusion*, Princeton, Princeton University, 1960; R. Arnheim, *Art and Visual Perception*, London, 1956; K. Boulding, *The Image*, Ann Arbor, University of Michigan, 1956; W. Schöne, *Über das Licht in der Malerei*, Berlin, 1954; H. R. Rookmaaker, *Kunst en Amusement*, Kampen, 1962; H. R. Rookmaaker, *Modern Art and the Death of a Culture*, Inter-Varsity Press, 1970; Lawrence Lipking, *The Ordering of the Arts in Eighteenth-century England*, Princeton, Princeton University, 1970.

H. R. ROOKMAAKER

ARTIFICIAL INSEMINATION. The technique of artifical insemination is an ancient one, and goes back to at least the fourteenth century. Yet, this procedure has not been accepted by local governments, or by many churches. It is estimated that between ten and twenty thousand women in the United States annually become pregnant by this method (know as A.I.H. for artificial insemination, husband). By far, the largest number of such women are inseminated with their husband's sperm. The husband is known to be fertile, but for various reasons, is unable to fertilize the wife's ovum in usual coitus. Other women, whose husbands are not fertile, become pregnant by the artifically placed sperm of a carefully selected donor, whose genetic features match those of the husband. (This is known as A.I.D. or artificial insemination, donor.) Donor sperm may be fresh or the sperm may be frozen and stored in a "sperm bank."

Artificial insemination is medically sound, but A.I.D. has not been fully accepted legally. Some states have laws pertaining to this technique, but often they cloud rather than clear the legal air. Various courts have rendered contradictory opinions about cases that have come before them. Some lawyers and physicians hold that a formal agreement should be drawn up between the physician and the patient, but even this does not give complete protection. The law may consider the procedure as adultery (q.v.) and the physician may be considered a party to this. He may also be held liable for any inherited disease in the offspring.

In addition to legal pitfalls, the husband's delayed emotional reaction is extremely important. If he should undergo a psychological break, because of the feeling of inadequacy, then this might lead to a whole series of confusing problems. Evidently this tragedy does not occur often; parents of babies conceived by these techniques are often said to be among the happiest of parents.

Another important consideration is satisfying of the mother's desire to bear a child and to prove that she is really female. Many women prefer artificial insemination to adoption. Psychological disturbances in the mother have been reported, but are said to be rare. The divorce rate among such parents is considerably less than the usual rate in our society.

Religious bodies vary in their reactions. Most Protestant churches have not taken a firm stand. Orthodox Jewish groups, Lutherans, and Catholics have opposed it in the past, but Lutherans have recently relaxed their opposition, leaving the people involved to make a decision. V. Elving Anderson, Director of the Dight Institute for Human Genetics, University of Minnesota, writes:

> Artificial insemination using donor sperm is now used in families where the husband is infertile or carries harmful genes that would affect children. It is sometimes objected that this constitutes adultery, but this argument cannot be defended from the Bible. In the Sermon on the Mount, Jesus stressed the idea that lustful desire is the essential point of adultery. Furthermore, the Levirate law of marriage (in which a near kinsman of a deceased man is obligated to father an heir for the widow) is in essence a provision for donor insemination.— *Journal of the American Scientific Affiliation,* Dec. 1966

It would seem prudent for any couple considering this method of conception to consult their lawyer and their religious advisor, as well as their physician, before venturing into this controversial area.

↪S. J. Behrman and Robert W. Kistner, eds., *Progress in Infertility,* Boston, Little, Brown, 1968; C. H. Pommerenke, "Artificial Insemination, Genetic and Legal Implications," *Obstetrics and Gynecology* 9:189, 1957; James C. and Martin Hefley,

"Babies in Question," *Today's Health,* Aug. 1970, p. 17.   MARTIN L. SINGEWALD

ASCETICISM. See also *Abstinence, Self-denial.* Asceticism (from the Greek *askeesis*) originally meant "exercise," "practice," or "training" performed by an athlete or soldier in the attainment of a goal. Greek philosophers applied the term to moral discipline, virtuous conduct, and the practice of justice. According to modern usage it commonly denotes religious exercise involving self-denial and abstinence from certain comforts and pleasures.

In the history of religion, asceticism has played a most important role, being found especially in those religions which stress a dualistic view of the world and of man. Among the ancient Hebrews asceticism played a minor part. There is in the OT an elaborate system of dietary laws, but fasting usually occurred on a voluntary basis, especially as a sign of repentance in periods of national crisis (I Sam. 7:6; I Kings 21:9f.). Priests were required to abstain from wine before offering sacrifice (Lev. 10:9; Ezek. 44:21), and Nazirites were controlled by even more restrictive regulations (Num. 6:3-8). But asceticism never became an essential part of the religion of the ancient Hebrews.

In later Judaism asceticism became more common, especially in the form of fasting and tithing by such sects as the Pharisees (Matt. 9:14; Luke 18:12) and the Essenes.

The NT encourages Christian discipline and self-denial but opposes all forms of asceticism that are practiced to merit salvation. It retains the OT custom of fasting at the time of prayer (Matt. 4:2; Luke 2:37; Acts 13:2) and encourages an evangelical asceticism which exhorts the Christian to bear afflictions willingly (Matt. 10:38) and to exercise watchfulness, patience, self-control and love while awaiting the return of the Lord (Matt. 24:42; 25:13), but the mere performance of outward acts is without value (Matt. 6:2, 6, 16-18). Paul describes the Christian under the figure of an athlete who constantly trains and practices self-control to win the race of life (I Cor. 9:24-27; I Tim. 4:7f.), struggling to control his sinful nature (Gal. 5:17) and seeking to walk in the Spirit (Gal. 5:25).

Passages such as Matt. 5:29f. and Luke 14:26 do not establish ascetic regulations for entering Christ's kingdom, but are intended to emphasize that the Lord must come first in the life of the believer (Mark 10:29f.).

In post-apostolic times a more legalistic and outward type of asceticism entered the Christian church because of Hellenistic influences. Gnosticism, together with Montanism and Manichaeism, tended to distort the Christian concept of self-denial, teaching contempt for the material world, abstinence from marriage, and a severe moralism which denied all forgiveness for certain sins.

In the Middle ages asceticism assumed yet other forms. Christianity was thought of as consisting chiefly in the observance of certain holy days, rites, fasts, pilgrimages, etc. while the conscientious performance of one's tasks in the home and at work was regarded as worldy, imperfect, and without honor. The Protestant Reformers rejected medieval asceticism, considering it to be a perversion of the gospel. Luther in his *Freedom of the Christian Man* attacks medieval asceticism at a most vulnerable point, asserting that the Christian is free to enjoy all of God's gifts and blessings, and that depriving oneself of their use does not merit salvation.

The Reformers, however, did not eliminate true and God-pleasing forms of asceticism, performed in the freedom of the gospel. They too urged obedience to the moral law of God, love for one's fellowmen, sobriety, self-control, bearing affliction, and mortification of the flesh. Luther expressed the Protestant view regarding asceticism thus:

> Everyone can use his own discretion as to fasting and watching, for everyone knows how much he must do to master his body. Those, however, who think they become pious through works have no regard for fasting but only for the works and, imagining that they are pious when they do much in that direction, sometimes break their heads over it and ruin their bodies.—Luther, *Werke,* Erlangen Edition, xxvii, 27, 190

📖 Werner Elert, *The Christian Ethos,* Philadelphia, Fortress, 1957; *HERE,* ii, 63-111 (1910); "Treatise on Good Works," *Luther's Works,* American Edition, vol. 44, Philadelphia, Fortress.

HOWARD W. TEPKER

ASPIRATION. Aspiration is an act of intense desiring, generally a longing for position or possessions considered superior to one's present lot. It is used as a synonym for ambition, craving, or wish, and may involve covetousness (q.v.).

HERBERT K. JACOBSEN

ASTROLOGY. This method of divination from observations of the planets, stars or related phenomena to ascertain the future was practiced throughout the ancient Near East in antiquity. Lists of stars and omens are found from c. 2370 B.C. (Sargon of Agade) and in the following Old Babylonian period alongside elementary astronomical texts. References to stars in prayers and diverse omens (Venus observations) attest an earlier origin.

By the mid-second millennium B.C. at the latest a "canonical series" of c. 60 tablets (*Enuma Anu Ellil*- "when the gods Anu and Enlil") recorded omens based on the moon, sun, planets, fixed stars and meteorological data (thunder, hail, lightning, rain, earthquakes) with concomitant predictions for the whole country. These foresaw famines, epidemics, floods, war or inversely prosperity and peace; and, for the royal family, universal dominion, victory, revolution or death. Signs were drawn from the disappearance or reappearance of the moon, its relation to the sun, eclipses or, less extensively, from cloud formations, lunar halos, or planetary movement. It is noteworthy that these observations were never applied to individuals.

By the fourteenth century B.C. these texts were known to the Hittites, Elamites, and the west (Mari, Qatna). At Ugarit there were those who "knew the course of the stars" (I Aqht 50, 194. 201). That "the stars in their courses fought against Sisera" (Judg. 5:20) may, if not a poetic figure, reflect Hebrew knowledge of these practices. Strong Hebrew aversion to astrology was based on a Mosaic prohibition of its use with other forms of divination and augury (Lev. 19:26; Deut. 18:10-14). This rested on their exclusive monotheism, avoidance of the polytheistic practices of their neighbors who worshipped planets and stars, and belief in direct Divine revelation which rendered divinatory techniques unnecessary.

Astrology surpassed even extispicy in Assyria by the eighth century B.C. Isaiah warned against "astrologers, star gazers who foretell your future month by month" (47:13) as did Jeremiah (10:12) who told the Judeans not to be alarmed at "the heavenly portents" as were other nations.

Individual horoscopes are first attested in Babylonia (410 B.C., cf. Greece 4 B.C.) and may be connected with the introduction of the zodiac in the fifth century (others seventh century or earlier). These give the date of birth (or conception) with astronomical observations and a prediction of the child's future. Such genethlialogy passed to Egypt, Greece, and the west and made "Chaldean (Neo-Babylonian)" astrology widely known (Dan. 2:27; 4:7).

In the NT predictive astronomy was used by eastern savants (Magi) to foresee the birth of "the King of the Jews" (Matt. 2:1 ff.), as it will foreshadow his return and the final redemption and judgment (Isa. 13:10; Ezek. 32:7; Dan. 7:10; Joel 2:10; 3:15; Matt. 24:29; Mark 13:5; Luke 21:23; Rev. 6:13; 8:10-12; 9:1). The Biblical view is that the stars are always a reminder of God's prodigality (Exod. 32:13; Deut. 1:10; I Chron. 27:23; Neh. 11:12) and Divine control (Job 9:7). Beside God the stars are insignificant (Deut. 4:19; Acts 7:42f.).

DONALD J. WISEMAN

ASYLUM. The arrangement of asylum was a practical and reasonably effective way to punish the murderer and protect the innocent. OT law considers a person guilty until proved innocent. Murder was to be avenged immediately by the victim's next of kin. Therefore asylum was provided to protect both those falsely accused of murder and those who had committed manslaughter. Six cities of refuge were specified. If an accuser persisted in his case, the elders of the congregation tried the suspected murderer (Deut. 20:4-6) and delivered him up if found guilty. If found innocent he was detained in the city of refuge until a general amnesty was given when the high priest died.

The system of asylum is mentioned in Exod. 21:12-14; Num. 35:6-28; Deut. 4:41-43; 19:2-10; and Josh. 20:1-9. The early references outline the system in general terms. The three cities of Transjordan are first named in Deut. 4:41-43. Only after the conquest were the three cities in Canaan designated by name (Josh. 20:7).

R. LAIRD HARRIS

ATHEISM. See also *Skepticism; Theism.* Atheism, etymologically, names a philosophic view that denies the existence of God. In the nineteenth century the term Agnosticism was invented to designate a view that neither affirms nor denies the existence of God. Deism affirms a God who acts on the world only through the regularities of natural law. Theism (q.v.) allows for miracles and revelation. But the whole matter is not quite so simple.

In the first place, since there is no middle possibility between the existence and non-existence of God, agnosticism escapes atheism only in name.

Democritus, La Place, and Nietzsche were, no doubt, atheists; but Spinoza constantly talks about God, *Deus sive Natura,* God, i.e., Nature. But if God and Nature are identical, is not this atheism?

Kant postulated God, Freedom, and Immortality as the necessary bases of morality. But he also insisted that God is not a constitutive concept (a concept of an existing being) but a regulative concept (a rule for the direction of our conduct). Is this not atheism?

In our century, Paul Tillich and Bishop Robinson have denounced an anthropomorphic deity who is "out there," a cosmic policeman, and a theology of monarchic monotheism. For these authors God is not an entity besides the ordinary things of experience. He is being-as-such; which presumably means the common quality of existence in all that exists. But is this not as atheistic as Spinoza?

The trouble is that the word "God" is given no one definite meaning. Not only is Spinoza's God utterly unlike Pascal's, but on the level of positive religions Islam's Allah, Hinduism's Shiva, and the fetishes of animist have nothing in common. To say that "God" is the name of what one worships or serves does not give the term any concrete content. Nor does the definition of God as the "satisfier" (or alleged satisfier) of man's needs do any better, for men do not agree on what they need.

It is, then, relatively unimportant whether or not a man believes in the existence of God. Existence is a pseudo-concept. The important question is, What is God? To this Christianity gives a Trinitarian answer. And obviously the Trinity and Shiva have nothing in common.

For this reason one cannot discuss the ethical theory of atheism: there are too many varieties. Epicureanism, though it strangely asserted the existence of gods, was virtually atheistic; but no two ethical theories could be much more opposed than those of Epicurus and Kant. Similarly Spinoza and Nietzsche agree on nothing.

Twentieth century Humanism (q.v.) is a more unified movement and a measure of agreement in Ethics can be found among its exponents.   GORDON H. CLARK

ATHLETICS. See also *Body; Sports.* The primitive urge to play is basic to the development of athletics, whether related to man's challenge of natural forces like gravity in jumping or running, or of other men in contact sports such as football or wrestling. Objects like a ball or puck are employed to determine skills, and instruments like bat and pole or transportation means like roller skates and snowmobile are used to extend man's capacities.

Most athletics are justified in terms of promoting health and developing character, but the possibilities of sustaining injury and encouraging poor personality traits through intense competition are ever present and must be considered. Indeed, where money has become a significant factor—as in football, roller derbies, or boxing—the animal characteristics of man are encouraged for monetary purposes. Moreover, national interest in sports spectaculars has encouraged gambling. The Christian can ill afford to be insensitive to ethical implications in these amusements (q.v.).   GERALD L. BORCHERT

ATOMIC ENERGY. See also *Science and Ethics; Technocracy and Technology.* Atomic energy, extracted from atomic nuclei, has been made available through two processes: (1) the fission of a large nucleus such as in uranium into two smaller nuclei, or (2) the fusion of two hydrogen nuclei to form a larger nucleus.

Industrial application of the fission process is well underway. While different safety problems are associated with the industrial use of this new form of energy, no new ethical factors are introduced by generating power using nuclear fuel rather than the usual fossil fuels.

Such is not the case when nuclear energy is used for military purposes. Both fission (atomic) and fusion (H) bombs have been built and tested. The first fission bomb dropped on Hiroshima killed approximately 80,000 people. This bomb was equivalent in size to 20,000 tons of TNT. Since then H—bombs have been tested in the 50,000,000-ton range.

These facts cast doubt on the ethical propriety of ever employing such weapons. The Christian justification for using armed forces is the same as the justification for a police force: to protect the weak and to provide a stable social system. The police force must restrict its activities so that it will not damage the society it has been instituted to defend. It is this constraining feature that is missing when using nuclear weapons. Their destructive potential is so large that they cannot be used with discrimination except on isolated targets. Thus, the present strategic stalemate between the USA and the USSR is dependent upon the opposing powers holding hostage the civilians of the two nations. The inherent instability of such a "balance of terror" should be evident. Christians must deplore the announced threat to destroy millions of innocent people for national purposes.

Unfortunately Christian principles have not been applied to this problem in any significant way. J. Robert Oppenheimer, the first Director of the Los Alamos Laboratory, has eloquently expressed his disappointment over this state of affairs:

I find myself profoundly in anguish over the fact that no ethical discussion of any weight or nobility has been addressed to the problem of atomic weapons. . . . What

are we to make of a civilization which has always regarded ethics an essential part of human life . . . which has not been able to talk about the prospect of killing almost everybody, except in prudential and game-theoretic terms? Nuel Pharr Davis, *Lawrence and Oppenheimer,* Greenwich, Conn, Fawcett, 1968, p. 330

JOHN A. McINTYRE

ATONEMENT. See also *Reconciliation; Redemption; Salvation.* The Bible regards all men as sinful (I Kings 8:46; Ps. 14:3; Mark 10:18; Rom. 3:23). Not only so, but their sin is serious, for sinners are alienated from God and are his enemies (Rom. 5:10; Col. 1:21). Sin separates from God (Isa. 59:2), who is too pure to look on iniquity (Heb. 1:13). Awaiting sinful man is a fearful judgment (Heb. 10:27). And man cannot cope with the situation. He can neither keep his sin hidden (Num. 32:23) nor cleanse himself (Prov. 20:9). He can produce no deeds that will enable him to stand before God justified (Rom. 3:20; Gal. 2:16).

It is in this context that the atonement must be studied. It is not a casual gesture made to men who are in no trouble. It is the divine answer to a problem incapable of solution on the merely human level. The word atonement means "a making at one" and it signifies the process whereby those who were estranged are brought into unity. In the OT the divine forgiveness is mediated through the sacrifices in accordance with the words, "the life of the flesh is in the blood; and I have given it for you upon the altar to make atonement for your souls" (Lev. 17:11). There is nothing about the offering of an animal which in itself avails to put away the sins of a man. But God in his mercy had provided this way whereby the penitent sinner might approach him.

In the NT it is accepted that the cross of Christ is the one way whereby sins may be dealt with. Men were redeemed even from the transgressions committed under the old covenant only by the death of Christ (Heb. 9:15). He is that Lamb of God who takes away the sins of the world (John 1:29). There is no other than he by whom men can come to God (John 14:6), none other by whom they can be saved (Acts 4:12). The NT writers repeat in a variety of ways their basic conviction that Christ's death on the cross is the one means whereby God saves men.

Sometimes this is viewed as redemption. This way of looking at it is derived from practices of warfare whereby captives might be bought back out of their captivity by the payment of a price. Among the Hebrews the purchase might also be from a sentence of death (Exod. 21:30). Or God may be said to have justified believers (Rom. 3:26). This is most important for justification is a legal word pointing to a verdict of acquittal. It shows that God saves men justly as well as powerfully. The penalty has been paid. Sometimes atonement is seen as a process of reconciliation (Col. 1:21f.), or propitiation (I John 4:10). A new covenant has been established in Christ's blood (I Cor. 11:25). All that is involved in the rite of sacrifice is fulfilled in him (Eph. 5:2). Sometimes a particular sacrifice is singled out, such as the Passover (I Cor. 5:7). Christ bore our sins (I Peter 2:24) or our curse (Gal. 3:13). And there are other ways of viewing it.

No theory of the way the atonement works has ever been accepted by the church as the standard or orthodox doctrine. Three theories, in one guise or another, have won many supporters. One says that Christ won a victory over death and every evil; another that he paid the penalty for our sins; the third that he showed us how greatly he loves us and thus set us an example to follow. This last, taken by itself, is clearly inadequate. But all three are needed and even then we have not said enough. The atonement is too great and too comprehensive to be contained within any formula.

Men receive God's good gift by faith. But this is not to be understood as a simple credulity. In the NT sense faith brings a man into vital and living union with Christ. He is in Christ and Christ is in him. It is as he is in Christ that he receives the blessing of God.

📖 Anselm, *Cur Deus Homo;* G. Aulen, *Christus Victor,* London, S.P.C.K., 1931; K. Barth, *Church Dogmatics* IV, *The Doctrine of Reconciliation;* J. Denney, *The Death of Christ,* New York, Doran, n.d.; V. Taylor, *The Atonement in New Testament Teaching,* London, Epworth, 1945 (2nd ed.); L. Morris, *The Apostolic Preaching of the Cross,* Grand Rapids, Eerdmans, 1955; _____, *The Cross in the New Testament,* Grand Rapids, Eerdmans, 1965.   LEON MORRIS

AUGUSTINE. Unlike most philosophers, Augustine (354-430) lays great stress on ethics. In this, though in nothing else, he is similar to John Dewey, Friedrich Nietzsche, and the ancient Epicureans, and in this he differs from Aristotle, Descartes, the British Empiricists, and Bertrand Russell.

Strictly, ethical principles are not the logical basis of Augustine's philosophy. Truth is. But Augustine refutes skepticism (q.v.) and emphasizes the possibility of truth on the moral ground that truth and knowledge are necessary to our happiness. Skeptics try to act on probabilities; but the calculation of probabilities presupposes knowledge of various factors. This makes skepticism self-contradictory.

Everyone desires happiness, and Augustine simply could not credit a view of the universe that made happiness (q.v.) unattainable. Not only does skepticism conflict with ethics; the physical theories of the ancient Stoics and of the modern Nietszche also make happiness impossible. Their theory of eternal recurrence asserts that world-history, in every detail, must forever repeat itself. Such a view prevents anyone from being happy. If one is ignorant of the fact that he must repeat his life, without change, forever, he cannot be happy because he is deluded, and no deluded or ignorant person is happy. On the other hand, if he knows this, he knows that no state is permanent: whatever apparent good fortune he now enjoys was preceded by various youthful inconveniences and will be lost at death. But an essential characteristic of happiness is its permanence.

Since happiness must be permanent, it requires knowledge. One must know what to desire. Happiness is not the satisfaction of any random desire. The satisfaction of some desires brings tragedy. Therefore knowledge is essential. One must come to know what is permanent. To love what can be lost is to live in fear. Happiness is the immutable possession of an unchanging object. Now, the only unchanging object is Truth or God. Happiness therefore consists in having God.

Augustine does not crudely assume that knowledge is possible. He does not even restrict himself to proving that skepticism is self-contradictory. He positively defends knowledge on the ground that the laws of logic are indubitable. Mathematics also: we judge not merely that three times three is nine, but rather that it must be nine. It is a necessary truth.

Skepticism is usually based on an empirical or sensory theory of knowledge; and it is indeed a question whether sensation can furnish any knowledge at all. In his *Contra Academicos* Augustine agrees that sensation fails to prove the existence of any object similar to the sensation. But logic and mathematics do not depend on sensation. Further, even if I make innumerable mistakes, these are instances of thinking; therefore I know, without mistake, that I think and that I exist.

Intellectual intuitions, such as these logical and mathematical principles, make physical science unimportant for epistemology as it is also insufficient to guarantee happiness.

Every theory of ethics presupposes some view of human nature. For Augustine man is his will. Not only does morality require volition; intellectual learning and even sensation depends on voluntary attention. Memory requires an act of will.

Now, the innate tendency of the will is to seek happiness. Aristotle had said, "Every man by nature desires to know." Augustine insists everyone naturally desires happiness. This is called love. In Christian theology, contrary to some superficial contemporary opinions, love is a volition, not an emotion. It is a natural tendency that no one can destroy. The moral problem therefore is not whether one should love or not, but what one should love. Virtue is to love what one ought to love.

This returns the discussion to its starting point. One should love truth because it is immutable, but not all truth. The knowledge of physical nature, i.e., science, is unimportant. "O Lord, God of truth, does it suffice to know those things to please Thee? Unhappy is the man who, though he knew them all, does not know Thee; and happy is he who knows Thee, even if ignorant of them. As to him who knows them also, it is not those things which make him happy; he owes all his happiness to Thee" (*Confessions* V. iv. 7).

Augustine, *Writings of St. Augustine*, 15 Vols, C.I.M.A., 1948; V. J. Bourke, *Augustine's Quest of Wisdom*, Milwaukee, Bruce, 1944; Charles Boyer, *L'Idée de Vérité dans la philosophie de St. Augustin*, Paris, 1920; Etienne Gilson, *Introduction a l'etude de St. A.*, Vrin, Paris, 1929; B. B. Warfield, *Studies in Tertullian and Augustine*, New York, Oxford University, 1930.   GORDON H. CLARK

AUTHENTICITY. Basically the term means the possession of authority which is not open to challenge, or having inherent authority and consequently being entitled to respect. In recent thought, the word has acquired meaning which goes beyond the lexical, and in this usage is intimately related to existential modes of thought. Søren Kierkegaard, while not utilizing the term, anticipated the modern use of the motif in his definition of true individuality.

In his *Purity of Heart* (New York, Harper & Row, Sec. 13), he stresses the importance of individual willingness to act responsibly, apart from the support of the crowd, and praises the mode of life in which one is conscious of himself as an individual hearing the eternal voice of conscience.

In this century Martin Heidegger has emphasized the quest for authenticity in one's person. He has used the terms *eigentlich* and *Eigentlichkeit* with special emphasis upon the element of *eigen* — ("one's own"). Authenticity is defined by Heidegger in terms of the individual's assuming responsibility for the direction of his own life, rather than permitting himself to be determined by external factors. Man's ontological constitution is expressed by the term *Dasein* (roughly translated into English as "Being-there") which implies his "thereness," his finitude, and especially his vulnerability to death. The individual's *Dasein* is threatened by his "thrownness," responds in terms of anxiety, and finds a relatively stable form of existence as it becomes "free *for* one's own death" (*Sein und Zeit*, Sec. 264; see also Sec. 129, 184, 263, 268, 298).

John Macquarrie interprets Heidegger's view of authenticity in terms of the achievement of a unitary and stable character-form in which the antinomies of existence are held in balance, so that there may be an orderly actualization of individual potentialities (*Principles of Christian Theology*, New York, Scribner, pp. 64, 67). Authenticity seems within this context to connote individual integrity and self-reliance.

HAROLD B. KUHN

AUTHORITY. In ethics, as in everything else, supreme authority is vested in God, the creator and the ruler of heaven and earth, who has established the universe to conform to his will and to function in accordance with his law. Every constituted authority is subordinate to this primary rule, and possesses its warrant by a delegation of power from God (John 19:11; Rom. 13:1).

A rational agent's obedience to God is not to be viewed as renouncing free agency. True liberty and conformity to law, far from being mutually exclusive, are in fact complementary: it is only when man walks along the path delineated by God's commandments that he can realize true fulfilment of his personality. The law is not a tyrannical imposition, confining man and cramping his opportunity to enjoy life: on the contrary, it is God's gracious revelation of the structure of the spiritual universe, which teaches man to move along the cosmos' lines of force rather than at cross-purpose with his true destiny (cf. Ps. 119:1, 99, 130, 165; John 10:31, 36; James 1:25; etc.).

Man has an innate sense of the majesty of law (Rom. 2:14, 15), but because of the corruption of sin he suffers from a double disability.

1. Man does not discern adequately what God's law is and is subject to serious aberrations in this realm, although there is a wholesome general consent of mankind to condemn such misdeeds as murder, adultery, theft, lying, cowardice, etc. Sinful man has an imperative need to receive from God an authoritative revelation which will serve as a permanent norm.

2. Fallen man is incapable not only of rendering perfect obedience to the law of God, but even of living up to the light that he has. There is no one who does as well as he knows and God's redemptive grace is needed to deliver man from his plight (cf. Rom. 7:7-25, which probably describes this plight in terms of the Christian, and *a fortiori* of one not renewed by grace.)

Every theist, recognizing the authority of divine revelation, will naturally seek to safeguard its rights in his world-and-life view. But theists differ among themselves as to the scope of this revelation and as to the way in which it is communicated. The evangelical Christian confesses that the

Bible is "the only infallible rule of faith and practice." In this way he seeks to avoid the pitfalls on one hand of the views which pay homage to ecclesiastical tradition as coordinate with Scripture, and on the other hand of the views which locate God's voice supremely in some element of human nature, whether conscience (moralism), emotions (romanticism), or mind (rationalism). The common error of all these positions, the evangelical avers, is that they elevate some human word to a parity with God's Word, which should retain at all times its ultimate primacy. Whether the Word of God be diluted by accretions (traditionalism), or demoted by being subjected to screening in terms of some other norm (liberalism), the result is the same: man's voice assumes equality with, or even precedence over God's voice. Only when the unique Lordship of God (Christ) is acknowledged can man find the proper authority for life and death.

P.T. Forsyth, *The Principle of Authority*, London, 1913, reprint Naperville, Ill., Allenson, 1952, Norval Geldenhuys, *Supreme Authority*, London, 1953; Bernard Ramm, *The Pattern of Religious Authority*, Grand Rapids, Eerdmans, 1957.

ROGER R. NICOLE

AUTONOMY. See also *Heteronomy.* Autonomy is generally used in a political sense, meaning the right of self-government and self-determination. In ethics autonomy means adherence only to self-regulated morality, and complete freedom from external compulsion or restraint. It makes the individual morally sovereign, free to pursue whatever he reasons or intuits to be the right, and to reject any and all authority outside the self.

Kant (q.v.) introduced the idea into modern ethical discussion. By autonomy he meant the faculty of the will to be its own lawgiver. Universalizability was the main criterion of Kant's ethics. For him the only test for a moral maxim was to pose the question, Can I consistently will that this action be performed by all rational beings? Precepts which can be consistently universalized, Kant calls categorical imperatives.

Thus ethics is autonomous. It is rooted entirely in the good will of man doing its duty for its own sake, and refraining from acting on any premise which cannot be consistently universalized. The rational being utters the commands of morality to himself, and obeys no one but himself. The moral agent himself is autonomous, and accepts no moral criteria from any divine or other external authority. Man is a law unto himself, and has the power to bind himself by those rules which the self as such promulgates.

From one angle Kant's construction can be seen as a rational statement of his Golden Rule (q.v.). But stated as it is, the theory has serious difficulties. Kant completely overlooks the fact that with sufficient ingenuity practically any precept can be universalized, and, given a fallen world which Kant tried to ignore, can and will be. In addition, the Kantian principle is vacuous and empty. It gives no positive direction to the moral life. It cannot inform the self which moral ends it ought to pursue. For this reason it is parasitic on existing ethical systems. It tends to sanction the duties approved by the moral tradition of the day.

Autonomy in ethics reaches complete expression in existential (cf. *Existentialist Ethics*) thinking. authentic existence according to Sartre is to be found only in absolute freedom of choice. He absolutizes the individualist morality. The result is that we are tragically bound to the finite human situation. Each of us is compelled to choose the ends, rules, and virtues to which we wish to be bound. The person authenticates himself by a bare act of the will. Autonomy in ethics leads directly to arbitrariness in ethics.   CLARK H. PINNOCK

AVARICE. See *Greed.*

AXIOLOGY. See *Values.*

B

BABYLONIAN ETHICS. In ethics, as in religion, the Babylonians maintained a long tradition of mixed origins from the early third millennium B.C. until absorbed in the succeeding Persian and Hellenistic cultures. It is now usually impossible to distinguish between the philosophies and ideas of non-Semites (Sumerians) and Semites (mainly Amorites), many aspects of which scribes, traders, and armies carried to the rest of the ancient Near East by the thirteenth century B.C.

Philosophy. Sumerian epics describe their gods in anthropomorphic terms as largely amoral, reflecting both the prevailing philosophy of a moderate hedonism and the practical requirements of rival city-states dependent on a hard-won agricultural economy. The ideal was the past "golden age" when men lived in harmony without want, sickness, or old age and in unity of religious worship. The land, the city, and the individual was blessed or cursed (rewarded or punished) in relation to his standing with his god(s). An increasing tendency to henotheism (never actually attained) resulted throughout the first millennium B.C. from an ill-defined concept of some necessary moral purpose in the universe. Like the people themselves, moral standards were of mixed origins, a few were the result of cosmological thought, most were due to complex customs expressed as rites and taboos, while a few resulted from humanitarianism (or conscience, q.v.).

The universe was thought to be controlled by rules (*me*) which included truth, peace, goodness, and justice as well as governed by falsehood, fear, strife and other qualities within god, man and institutions (e.g., kingship). Evil was part of the inscrutable divine plan and as such was the subject of much theological speculation. Yet good was clearly preferable to evil. The god who supervised the moral order (Sumerian $^{d}u.tu;$ Akkadian $^{d}Shamash$) was omniscient and looked after all in special need. He punished the evil doer, the strong oppressing the weak, the unscrupulous judge, the one accepting a bribe or using false weights, the tyrant, the thief or the liar, and commended the just as well as the one who invested or traded well. He assumed the characteristics of earlier deities such as the goddess Nanshe lauded as the one who "knows the orphans and widow, knows the oppression of man over man. She is the mother of the orphan and cares for the widow. She administers justice for the poor, brings the refugee under her protection and provides shelter for the weary" (S. N. Kramer, *The Sumerians,* Chicago, University of Chicago, 1954, pp. 124f.)

Ethics and Law. The primary Babylonian concern was always social justice. The law was devised and administered to control abuse (so the collections of legal decisions by Urukagina, Lipit-Ishtar and Hammurabi). The king acted as servent of the god and was divinely called to act as a "just king" and to establish, and eventually report to his deity his effectiveness in maintaining, law and order. His conduct was thought to affect the future of the state through the reaction it would elicit from the gods. Thus the king bore an additional moral responsibility to record the events of his reign so that his successors might learn from it (*Cuthean Legend of Naram-Sin* l. 25). This element of "moral prophecy" integrated with the Babylonian view of history in that the significance of past events, which might recur, lies in their exemplicative value. Its weakness lay in their dependence on divination to ascertain the divine way of life to be followed on earth as compared with the clear and authoritative stipulations of the divine requirements in the Decalogue which controlled the O.T. tradition.

Ethics and Wisdom. Babylonian ethics was practical advice on living. Thus the ruler was the object of an extensive "wisdom" literature to aid him in office. In addition to essays, there are fables (cf. Judg. 9:8-15; II Kings 14:9), parables, riddles, folk tales, disputations, and dialogues to convey moral lessons. The primary mode of such teaching was through collections of proverbs and instructions (so also Prov. 30:1—31:9). All these provide almost the only extant evidence for the moral tone of Babylonian society. Thus a governor should never abuse a position of trust (*Counsels of Wisdom*), he must rule justly (*Advice to a Prince*). One of the oldest pieces of Sumerian literature, *The Instructions of Shuruppak* (before 2500 B.C.), is a corpus of moral teaching to be handed on after the Flood much as had Noah (Gen. 9:1-17). The tradition continued in Syria (Ugarit, 13th century B.C.) where, as *Advice to Shube' awēlum,* he was told of the proper behavior towards women, parents, in quarrels, or when choosing a wife or buying an ox.

Personal Ethics. Personal religion and practice followed the role set by the king. Individual responsibility in religion was clearly demanded: "Worship your god every day with sacrifice and prayer.... you will get your reward.... Reverence begets favor, sacrifice prolongs life, and prayer atones for guilt" (*Counsels of Wisdom,* 135-145). Personal action causing divine displeasure is equally listed: "One who walks in transgression and with a high hand, who transgresses established norms, violates contracts, looks with favor on evil ..." (cf. E. Reiner, *Surpu,* Archiv für Orientforschung, Beiheft 11, Graz, 1958).

Sexual Ethics. Unlike the OT these had no religious basis but followed customary law enforced by the state where abuse affected the community. Extant legal cases show grave concern with extramarital sexual behavior, adultery, rape, and seduction (*Journal of the American Oriental Society* 86, 1966, 356.). Thus betrothal was as sacrosanct as a marriage already consumated and violation of a betrothed girl was a

capital offense (Eshnunna Law 26); violation of a slave girl was no less a concern to Babylonian jurists than the rape of a free woman (Eshnunna 31), while that of an unmarried and unbetrothed virgin, normally considered as an economic injury to her father, or to her master if a slave, was condemned if she was not a willing consenting party (Middle Assyrian Laws, 55).

There was social concern for the moral conduct of respectable women. Married women and concubines had to be veiled in public, a right denied a prostitute (M.A.L., 40). Homosexuality was treated as a breach of general social decency, not as a crime or matrimonial offense (M.A.L., 19-20).

📖 W. G. Lambert, "Morals in Ancient Mesopotamia," *Ex Oriente Lux Jaarbericht* 15 (1957-8), pp. 184-196; *Babylonian Wisdom Literature,* Oxford, Clarendon, 1960; F. R. Kraus, "altmesopotamisches Lebensgefühl," *Journal of Near Eastern Studies* 19 (1960), pp. 117-132; S. N. Kramer, "Sumerian Theology and Ethics," *Harvard Theological Review* 49 (1956), pp. 45-62.

DONALD J. WISEMAN

BARTH, KARL. See also *Dialectical Ethics.* The name of Barth (1886-1968) is so integrally connected with theological issues that his important ethical contribution may easily be overlooked. In a real sense, however, Barth was driven to theological rethinking by the ethical breakdown of Liberal Protestantism. Nurtured in an optimistic social gospel with early socialist associations, Barth was severely jolted by the First World War and the feebleness of his German teachers demonstrated in their backing the war policies of the Kaiser. Acutely aware also of kerygmatic inadequacy, Barth concluded that the ethical failure was due to an underlying failure in theology. To find out what to do he had first to ask what to believe. Yet if the theological question now became the first and most urgent, the ethical question would still be re-set and re-answered in and with it.

Once this is understood the basic principle of Barth's ethics is immediately apparent. Ethics is theological ethics. A Liberal theology will produce a corresponding ethics, whether consciously or not. Similarly a theology which operates with two criteria, natural and supernatural or philosophical and theological, will produce an ethics of the same type. The task of the evangelical ethicist, then, is to derive his ethics from a Biblical and evangelical theology. To do this he does not necessarily have to be a dogmatician, nor to incorporate his ethics in dogmatics; he may build on the work of others. Barth himself, however, took the course of a combined dogmatics and ethics in which the latter would grow naturally out of the former.

This explains the structure of the *Church Dogmatics* and the place of ethics within it. After the manner of the New Testament epistles each volume contains an ethical section or chapter. The Prolegomena (I, 1 and 2) includes a chapter on the divine command alongside the divine election. The volume on creation (III, 1-4) has a concluding chapter (III, 4) on the ethics of creation. If completed, the volumes on reconciliation (IV) and redemption (V) would have concluded with similar chapters on the ethics of reconciliation and redemption. Barth did not live to complete the project, so that a full survey of his ethics is not possible. There is enough, however, to give us a general picture of his principles and conclusions.

In the ethical prolegomena (§18: "The Life of the Children of God") Barth makes several preliminary points. He shows that the question of conduct (i.e., obedience) is raised by the fact of revelation. The essence of the Christian life is love. Authentic love, however, is an answer to God's love. Love is commanded, yet Barth stresses that the command ("thou shalt") is also a future, a promise. Love of God is primary, but love of neighbor is also to be construed christologically in the light of the very humanity

of Christ. Works done in love are done in Christ represented by fellow man.

When Barth tackles more rigorously the foundation of ethics in the doctrine of God (II,2) his primary theme is that of the covenant whose essence is Jesus Christ. The covenant is two-sided. It consists of the promise: "I will be your God," and then of the corresponding command: "Ye shall be my people." The command is the theme of Chapter VIII and Barth develops it in four sections: first in relation to the problem of ethics, and then as the claim, the decision, and the judgment of God.

In the first section Barth explains and establishes more fully the interrelation of theology and ethics, i.e., promise and command, or law and gospel. What God wants from man can be known only as God is known. Knowledge of God carries with it knowledge of God's purpose and destiny for man. But the grace which grants this destiny (gospel) is also the grace which commands it (law). Man has to fulfill it both in the sense that he will and also in the sense that he ought. Grace itself puts man under the command. Law is thus implied in the gospel and established by it. The link between promise and command is ultimately christological, for Jesus Christ, electing God and elect man, is also the holy God and sanctified man. Hence Jesus Christ is the final ground and norm of ethics. The claim of God rests on the gift of grace in Jesus Christ, just as its content is conformity to him, and its fulfillment is made possible by him. Similarly, the sovereignty, definiteness, and goodness of God's command as decision concerning what we must do, are rooted in Jesus Christ. Finally, the command as judgment which condemns and justifies, thus excluding all legalistic ethics of self-righteousness and orienting ethics to eschatological fulfillment rests on the judgment which Jesus Christ has suffered vicariously for us.

Once this foundation is laid Barth can

take up specific aspects and issues under the three heads of the command of God as Creator, as Reconciler, and as Redeemer. Thus in III, 4 he handles the matters that arise out of creation. Two additional motifs are now interwoven. The first is a correlating of the ethics of creation with the Ten Commandments. The second is a grouping of issues according to the structure of fourfold relationship that Barth has discerned in human life, namely, relationship to God, to other men, to self, and to the natural boundaries of life. These relationships involve such matters as obligations to God, marriage, problems of force (war, capital punishment, abortion, suicide), the use of time and talents, and calling.

The treatment varies but we find many common features. Barth avoids casuistry and pleads for particularity. Yet this does not mean situation ethics, for right acts have a lasting theological foundation; the Biblical norm must be consulted, and criteria of right action may be discerned and stated. In most cases Barth, the former radical, tends to reach surprisingly conservative conclusions, although not by mere repetition of the familiar arguments.

In the development of his methodology Barth is not uniformly successful. Perhaps his greatest success is in the area of sex and marriage. Here the Bible itself presents a clear theological foundation and the Biblical material can be set out with corresponding force. In other areas the ethico-theological relationship is still strong and cogent, but occasionally a certain artificiality seems to threaten as though an individual theological source had to be found at all costs. The argument (in another essay) that the open publication of the gospel demands open diplomacy is perhaps the worst instance of this.

In one sense Barth's ethics stands or falls with his theology. Hence questions may be raised at the most radical level: the covenantal basis in God; the exclusive christo-

logical reference; the interrelating of law and gospel; the problem of pagan ethics; the application of theological insights or principles. Then the detailed judgments on specific issues will naturally give rise to questions and criticisms of their own, although here one may obviously expect an individual mixture of agreement and disagreement irrespective of premises.

Perhaps the main service of Barth is to confront Christian ethics with the final reality that beyond agreements and disagreements in specific issues certain fundamental ethical cleavages must be grasped and understood if a pure ethic and a powerful Christian life and witness are to be achieved. Barth also gives a convincing demonstration of the way in which a specific theological understanding can and will have important ethical implications and can and will provide ethics with an authentic imperative. Criticism of the way Barth himself works this out should not be an excuse for evading the task of tackling practical problems by first establishing the theological premises of action.

GEOFFREY W. BROMILEY

BEATITUDES. See also *Blessedness; Happiness; Sermon on the Mount.* The word "beatitude," derived from the Latin *beatitudo,* has a long history in Christian thought. Its primary meaning is "blessedness." From this derives its use to designate a literary form of Scripture commencing generally with the word "blessed," and declaring the well being before God of a devout man embodying the stipulated qualities.

Although "the Beatitudes" is generally used to refer to Matthew 5:3-12 — an initial section of the so-called Sermon on the Mount — the form is well represented in the OT (e.g., Ps.1:1; 2:12; 32:1; Prov. 8:32, 34; Isa. 30:18; Dan. 12:12). Here, the righteous man who keeps all the law of God is viewed as one who will receive such temporal blessings as length of days, abundance of heirs, peace and prosperity in the land, abundant life, and the blessing of worshipping God in the holy place. It is important to note that man in the OT is conceived as a totality, and the beatitudes affirm the presence of God in the totality of the righteous man's existence.

Although the beatitudes as a form are less frequent in the NT, their presence within the Sermon on the Mount has perhaps given them an even greater prominence here. They also appear in Rom. 4:7-8; 14:22, the Gospel of John (20:29), and seven times in the book of Revelation (1:3; 14:13; 16:15; 19:9; 20:6; 22:7, 14). Although they formally resemble the OT beatitudes, they differ materially in their stress upon the joys of the eschatological kingdom of God beyond the visible and tangible blessings of life.

Two types of questions or problems typically burden the interpretation of the Beatitudes. The first is more formal: How many beatitudes are there? How did they acquire their present form? Comparison of Matt. 5:3-12 with Luke 6:20-23 raises these questions, and is necessary to their resolution. However, they are not decisive for Christian ethics, and may be waived here.

More crucial is the question of the relevance, indeed, applicability, of the Beatitudes. A variety of perceptions have been brought to their interpretation. In *Understanding the Sermon on the Mount* (New York, Harper & Row, 1960), H. K. MacArthur documents no less than twelve primary and secondary approaches. The blessing (to cite only a few possibilities here) has been variously seen as a reward of perfect obedience *(perfectionist view),* an *impossible ideal* calculated to drive a man to repentance, or belonging to a brief interim period *(interim ethic)* preceding the final coming of the kingdom of God. These views, and other interpretations which essentially neutralize the relevance of the Beatitudes for Christian conduct today, are basically deficient when applied as a sole criterion of interpretation.

Above all else, the Beatitudes view the blessings of the kingdom as a gracious gift encompassing both this age and the future eschatological age. Thus, the blessing belongs today to those who in no wise seem blessed. The Beatitudes, in the same paradoxical way, confront man as promise and summons (Bornkamm). Only as the man of faith submits to the reign of God in the obedience of faith, does the gift of life become his; it is, nonetheless, totally a gift of God. And that is beatitude in the full Biblical meaning.

Günther Bornkamm, *Jesus of Nazareth,* tr. Irene and Fraser McLuskey, New York, Harper, 1960, pp. 75-81; George Ladd, *Jesus and the Kingdom,* New York, Harper, 1964; Joachim Jeremias, *The Sermon on the Mount,* tr. Norman Perrim, Philadelphia, Fortress, 1970 (4th ed.).

ROBERT P. MEYE

BEAUTY. See also *Aesthetics; Art.* As a concept, beauty stands in a line with truth, love, reality, life, righteousness. Like them it has a wide and all-pervading scope and importance and a tight definition is difficult. These universals however always manifest themselves in the particular, the individual, and the personal.

These concepts, moreover, are closely tied together, so that one cannot speak about one without also touching the other. Beauty will always be there where there is truth, love, life, and reality; while sin, lies, hatred, and death (in its deep sense), being negative reality, are ugly, and also lead to ugliness. In this sense a marriage, a group of people in their relationship, an action, a mentality, can be called beautiful, as they show love, unity, freedom, etc. In a certain respect one can call this inner beauty (cf. I Peter 3:3), but it will express itself in "outward beauty," visible, perceivable beauty. At this point one can also begin to speak about man-made beauty and art.

Beauty is always related to meaning and sense. In this it shows similarity to the beauty of nature, the distinctives of which also apply to beauty in human artifacts and in humanity itself.

Beauty in nature is related to meanings; e.g., the tree is beautiful as a tree. Trees are meaningful as such, being created by God. They have a meaningful place in the total structure of nature, together with mountains, rivers, sun and moon and their light, weather conditions, other plants and animals, the total ecological structure — man not excluded. They have a definite function in this whole, yet we should not define their meaning in a functional way, as their meaning is more than the sum of their functions. The concrete meaningful reality of the tree in itself, not referring to anything outside the tree — except God — even if always open to all kinds of relationship with other creatures, constitutes its beauty.

The beauty in nature as God's creation shows God's "style": endless variety and great unity. The unity is the result of the inherent simplicity of nature; e.g., all animals have a few peculiar qualities in common, as movement, perception (with a limited number of senses), feeding, breeding, some of them even in common with plants. Yet, within these basic simple structural patterns an almost endless variety of species, each having a specific place in the total ecological structure, is realized in creation. But the variety does not end here: even within one species each specific individual example is different from the others, not in a random way, but in relation to its place and environment, to its own history, its relation to other representatives of the same or other species.

In this way the beauty of nature becomes manifest in its meaningful totality, in which nothing is autonomous or stands by itself, yet everything has its own peculiarity and a meaning transcending the functional aspect.

It is a superabundant beauty, and as such is also open to man; in this God's creative love is discernable (cf. Rom. 1:20), for man has been placed in this abundance to use it and to guard it (cf. Gen. 2:15). Man discovers its possibilities, giving it names and putting it to use. He has to do so in love and with reverence to God's purposes and the meaning of things. Man's creativity (as he is in the image of God) lies in the opening up of the natural possibilities by adding to life, and in love, creating new beauties — whereas sin is always detrimental to life, "wounds" nature, brings death, and results in ugliness. Here we can point to the ecological problems of our time. In the same sense man, in his relation to other men and to God, can be creative in realizing harmony, mutual love, care, adding to life and enlarging its freedom, while sin leads to confusion, hatred, takes away freedom, leads to death and ends in ugliness. To do the truth (John 3:20f.) fulfills both life and freedom and inevitably also beauty.

H. R. ROOKMAAKER

BEHAVIORISM. See also *Determinism.* Behaviorism is an implication from materialism and as such is implicit in ancient Democritus and explicit in Thomas Hobbes. Contemporary behaviorism can be seen in William James (*Essays in Radical Empiricism,* Magnolia, Mass., Peter Smith, Chap. 1, "Does Consciousness Exist?"), but is more popularly known as originating in the works of John B. Watson. Watson was a psychologist; philosophical behaviorism is expounded by Gilbert Ryle (*The Concept of Mind,* New York, Barnes and Noble).

Both Watson and Ryle repudiate a soul, and Watson in particular deprecates introspection. The theory equates thought with bodily motions, at first motions in the larynx; thinking is called sub-vocal speech.

The motivation is to make psychology scientific and restrict it to what is observable, as mind is not. But if thought is laryngeal motion, then Watson's "observation" of my behavior is simply the motions of his larynx.

An objection specifically directed against laryngeal motion is that the removal of the larynx by a surgeon does not prevent the patient from thinking.

To get around this, John Dewey gave thought a wider base. "Habits formed in the process of exercising biological aptitudes are the sole agents of observation, recollection, foresight and judgment: a mind or consciousness or soul in general which performs these operations is a myth. . . . Knowledge which is not projected against the black unknown lives in the muscles, not in consciousness" (*Human Nature and Conduct*, New York, Modern Library, III i; cf. ibid. I vi, and *The Quest for Certainty*, New York, Putnam, pp. 86, 166).

If thinking is a motion of the muscles or, as Dewey adds, interaction between muscle tissue and motions of things outside one's skin, it would follow that two persons could not think the same thought and therefore could not communicate. The reason is that one set of motions is not another set of motions. The wiggles of my muscles are not the wiggles of your muscles, and if a thought is a wiggle we cannot have the same thought.

For the same reason it is impossible for one person to have the same thought twice. Since my wiggle today is *ipso facto* not my wiggle yesterday, I can never recover yesterday's thought. This makes memory impossible, prevents comparisons among disparate sensations, and destroys the foundation of knowledge.   GORDON H. CLARK

BEHAVIORALISM AND THE SOCIAL SCIENCES. Behavioralism is the study of human behavior by empirical means, in the hope of developing theories with explanatory and predictive qualities. Human behavior is defined broadly to include attitudes and opinions as well as overt acts. The empirical approach to the study of human behavior is used to develop precise, verifiable facts and generalizations. All values and facts which are not empirically verifiable (such as claims based on revelational authority) are excluded. Empirically based facts and generalizations are then used in an attempt to develop theories with explanatory and predictive qualities. The goal of behavioral science is to develop theories which explain why observed patterns of human behavior are true. Once these are established, it then also becomes possible to predict patterns of human behavior. For once one knows that a particular pattern of human behavior is caused by a certain factor, he knows that when this factor is present the particular pattern of human behavior and other logically deductible patterns will result.

Behavioralism in the social sciences poses two potential ethical problems for the Christian. The first revolves around the implicit if not explicit claim by most behaviorally oriented social scientists that empirical facts are the only trustworthy facts, values and facts based on revelation being regarded as untrustworthy. The Christian — with his acceptance of the authority and trustworthiness of God's Word — has a firm basis for the acceptance of certain values and facts apart from empirical means. The innate existence of life after death is, for example, a fact Christians accept on the basis of God's revelation, but one which most behavioralists would refuse to accept because it cannot be empirically demonstrated. The Christian must thus reject the claim of empiricism to the exclusive possession of truth and accuracy.

But this does not mean that the Christian cannot accept the accuracy of empirical facts. The Christian should, of all men, be concerned with accuracy and truth, and to the extent that empirical facts can advance our knowledge of the social world they are to be accepted and used. The Christian does not object to empirical facts, but only to reliance on them to the exclusion of all other facts and forms of truth. Thus the Christian can accept behavioralism as a way to fuller knowledge of the social world, but he also insists upon his right to move beyond pure behavioralism, integrating revelational facts and values with behaviorally obtained facts.

A second potential problem posed by behavioralism in the social sciences is its deterministic view of man and human behavior. Human behavior is seen as the consequence of the sum total of influencing factors acting upon man. If one can sort out those influencing factors, human behavior presumably becomes fully explainable and predictable. This view of man, however, leaves no room for man's will and for individual moral responsibility. Since man's behavior is regarded simply as the result of the sum total of influences acting upon the individual, his individual free will—and thus his individual moral responsibility—is ignored.

But it is not necessary for the Christian to accept a deterministic view of man in order to acknowledge the strong, pervasive impact that environmental influences have upon human attitudes and behavior patterns. One can in fact come to a better—even if not a complete—understanding of human behavior by the study of environmental influences. The Christian will only insist that man has the capacity to—and sometimes will—rise above or sink below his environmental influences and confound the predictions of the behavioral scientists.

📖 Bernard Berelson, *The Behavioral Sciences Today*, New York, Basic Books, 1963; Heinz Eulau, ed., *Behavioralism in Political Science*, New York, Atherton, 1969.   STEVEN V. MONSMA

BENEFICENCE. See also *Altruism.* Beneficence is well doing. "Let your light so shine before men," Jesus encouraged his disciples, "that they may see your good works and give glory to your Father who is in heaven" (Matt. 5:16). Aristides elaborated on second century obedience to Jesus' injunction: "Wherefore they do not commit adultery or fornication, nor bear false witness, nor covet what is held in pledge, nor covet what is not theirs. They honor father and mother and show kindness to their neighbors. If they are judges, they judge uprightly" (Aristides *Apology* 15). The Christian demonstrates by well doing God's universal concern, and the constructive life style commended to all men in general and those who believe in particular.

MORRIS A. INCH

BENEVOLENCE. See also *Beneficence; Philanthrophy.* Benevolence is well willing. It is the subjective disposition corresponding to good objective deportment (beneficence). The Psalmist appropriately distinguishes the concern: "For thou hast no delight in sacrifice; were I to give a burnt offering, thou wouldst not be pleased. The sacrifice to God is a broken spirit; a broken and contrite heart. O God, thou wilt not despise" (Ps. 51:16-17). The Biblical stress is not upon attitude to the exclusion of act or *vice versa,* but the concord of goodness.

MORRIS A. INCH

JOHN C. BENNETT. Since he wrote his first book (*Social Salvation,* Scribner, 1935) as a young assistant professor of theology at Auburn Theological Seminary, John Coleman Bennett (1902-   ) has been perhaps the most influential, and certainly the most normative, figure in the American social gospel movement (q.v.). At times his shifting views have followed the thinking of the liberal clergy; at times his views have shaped that thinking. Usually the two have closely coincided.

After being reared in the Presbyterian Church, U.S.A., and graduating Phi Beta Kappa from Williams College, Bennett won a Rhodes scholarship at Oxford's Mansfield

College. In 1930 he joined the faculty of Union Theological Seminary in New York City (which later united with Auburn) and there he was to remain throughout his teaching career except for a five-year stint (1938-43) at Pacific School of Religion. In 1939 he transferred his ordination to the more congenial fellowship of the Congregationalists (now United Church of Christ).

The forces that helped to determine Bennett's theological views, according to his statement, are many and varied. They included Baron von Hugel, F. R. Tennant, Nicolas Berdyaev, John Oman, William Temple, and more particularly Reinhold Niebuhr, his faculty colleague at Union with whom he founded and edited for many years the bi-weekly *Christianity and Crisis*. Bennett was influenced briefly by Frank Buchman and Moral Rearmament (q.v.). His third book, *Christian Realism* (1940), shows evidence of Barthian neo-orthodoxy as mediated by Niebuhr. He dealt with the depth and pervasiveness of human sin, an element that liberalism had tended to misjudge or overlook in history. For the next several years Bennett advocated a "chastened liberalism" which acknowledged the insights of the Barthians but rejected their concessions to traditional Christianity. Bennett views the Bible as the record of God's redemptive activity in history, but hardly as inspired written revelation.

As a teacher Bennett was stimulating, irenic, and brilliant. His seminars covered the gamut of theology from Origen to Augustine to Aquinas to Luther to Ritschl to Brunner. He displayed early a remarkable gift for reducing a consensus to writing. An active leader in the National Council of Churches, he drafted many of its major resolutions on social and political issues. An outstanding instance was the Cleveland document of 1953 which advocated USA recognition of Communist China. Bennett composed large sections of World Council of Churches reports at Amsterdam, Evans-

ton and New Delhi, dealing always with questions of social order. In his *Christianity and Communism* (New York, Association Press, 1962), he described Marxism, as had Temple, as a Christian heresy.

In later years Bennett took an increasingly active part in liberal social and political movements. He served as vice chairman of New York's Liberal Party from 1955 to 1965. His public espousal of the candidacy of Senator John F. Kennedy aroused national interest and helped to solidify eastern liberal support. Bennett early opposed involvement in the Vietnam war; his wife visited Hanoi as a member of an anti-war group. During the years 1964-1971 he served as president of Union Seminary and on occasion was challenged by theologs whom he urged to become political activists. At one time they seized his office and locked him out for several days. He now teaches in California.

While known to his students as a devout and catholic spirit, "the metaphysics of individualistic personalism" has never interested him much. Throughout his career he showed an apparent laissez-faire attitude toward the evangelical wing of the church. His contacts with evangelical leaders were few since the days when he traveled as a Student Christian Movement speaker in Britain.   SHERWOOD E. WIRT

BENTHAM, JEREMY. See *Hedonism; Utilitarianism.*

BERDYAEV, NIKOLAI. Berdyaev (1874-1948) was a Russian theologian who identified himself with Marxism in 1894, but later (1907) turned to Christianity. His vocal opposition to Marxism between 1917 and 1920 led to his imprisonment and a period of forced labor. He was eventually released and in 1920 was elected to the University of Kiev faculty. Further conflict, however, led to his imprisonment again and ultimately to his deportation from the

Soviet Union in 1922. After a brief stay in Berlin, he took up residence in Paris where he carried on an extensive literary career.

His theological orthodoxy is questionable, and his participation in the Orthodox Church was limited. His system of thought is basically ethical and is built upon four key principles. First, theology provides the fundamental norm for man's description and discovery of the good life. He lays heavy stress upon the divine image and the divine Spirit. This theological norm or foundation stands in bold contrast to the contemporary materialistic philosophies of the early twentieth century: naturalism, Marxism and bourgeois capitalism. Although Berdyaev regarded the Incarnate Christ as the supreme revelation of God, he argued that man comes to know God primarily in a mystical and intuitive way. Materialistic and naturalistic philosophies attempt to objectify man and nature with the result that both man and nature become objects, and consequently are placed within the framework of space, time, causality and rationalization. The end result of this distortion is the loss of meaning. Berdyaev's correction derives from a second element in his ethics: existential freedom. In one place, he states, "I have placed as the basis of my philosophy not being, but freedom." In *Spirit and Reality* (p. 115), he says: "Evil and suffering exist because freedom exists." A third principle, his concern for the human personality, reflects a general feature of Eastern Orthodoxy. Personality is a sort of synthesis of the human and the divine (Incarnational Christology). Consequently, evil and the Fall are associated with all depersonalizing attempts to make man a mere object rather than the *imago Dei*. Man can occupy center stage in man's ethical concerns because as God is *person,* so man derives his own *personhood* from God. Finally, the concept of *sobornost,* fellowship or community, connects his ethics with both ecclesiology—the world as a trans-

formed community—and eschatology—the Kingdom of God as the goal of history and lies beyond history.

Nicolas Berdyaev, *The Destiny of Man*, New York, Harper, 1931; Nicholas, *Meaning of History*, Meridian, 1921; Nikolai, *Slavery and Freedom*, New York, Scribner, 1944; Matthew Spinka, *Nicolas Berdyaev: Captive of Freedom* Philadelphia, Westminster, 1950.   DONALD M. LAKE

BERGSON, HENRI. Henri Bergson (1895-1941) made two important contributions to ethical theory. The first was his argument against determinism in *Time and Free Will* (1889, Eng. tr. by Pogson, New York, Macmillan, 1910). He argued there that the coherence of the determinist hypothesis is entirely dependent on a spatialization of time in the imagination. Whatever the scientific usefulness of this conception of time, it reveals itself to be merely a construct when compared with the immediate data of temporal consciousness. Thus determinism itself is found to be but a construct without support in experience.

In *The Two Sources of Morality and Religion* (1932, Eng. tr. by Audra and Brereton, New York, Holt, 1935), Bergson developed a phenomenological typology of morality and religion based on the categories "closed" and "open." That dimension of moral obligation which is derived from social instinct is called closed morality. Though it restricts individual egoism, it is not genuinely altruistic. It is rather a form of group selfishness, since it is the mechanism by which the self-interest of the social whole is made obligatory for the individual.

Open morality differs in both scope and source. It is radically universal, without any social distinctions between insider and outsider. Here a genuine altruism is possible. Further, this is a morality of aspiration. It derives, not from the compulsion of social pressure, but from the attraction which is mediated through charismatic individuals. For Bergson the Gospels are a paradigm of open morality, and he finds Christianity, against its background of the Hebrew prophets, to be the prime historical example of this type of morality. It is not clear that the concepts of aspiration and charismatic individuality can do justice to the importance for Jesus and the prophets of the unconditional nature of the divine imperative.

Bergson notes that open morality was not brought into the world by philosophers, and he argues that philosophy could never have done so. This is because morality, though always capable of rationalization, does not stem from reason but from the affective dimensions of the self. Closed morality springs from the sub-rational self, while open morality is rooted in the supra-rational self.

Although probably best known for his *Creative Evolution* (1907, Eng. tr. by Mitchell, New York, Holt, 1911), neither of Bergson's contributions to ethics is very closely related to his theory of evolution.

MEROLD WESTPHAL

BESTIALITY. See also *Kinsey Report; Sex.* Bestiality, or zoophilia, is the practice of sexual intercourse between humans and other forms of animal life. The term may also be applied to any sexual contact between humans and animals, such as oral stimulation or masturbation.

The Kinsey studies indicated that between 40 and 50 percent of the American rural male population had had some contact with farm animals. This is in contrast to a 4 percent contact among urban men, 1.5 percent of girls in pre-adolescence, and 3.6 percent of adult females. Most such contacts were occasional and did not represent pathological or long-standing attachment.

Human intercourse with animals is referred to in many ancient codes and laws. The Epic of Gilgamesh portrays Enkidu, the hunter, as having had intercourse with wild beasts (cf. J. B. Pritchard, ed., *Ancient Near Eastern Texts,* Princeton, Princeton University, 1955, p. 75). The OT is especially strong in its prohibition of such acts. They are condemned as "perversion" (Lev. 18:23 RSV); a curse is upon such persons (Deut. 27:21) and the death penalty is required (Lev. 20:15-16; Exod. 22:19). In the NT bestiality as well as homosexuality may have been included in the proscriptions against "dishonorable passions" which Paul relates to the sin of man and the wrath of God (Rom. 1:18-27).

Christian moral thought has almost universally condemned bestiality on several counts: (1) as a perversion, since human coital acts should be limited to male and female within the human race; (2) as violation of Biblical prohibitions, and (3) psychical and personal damage as guilt or sexual maladjustment.

Bestiality is considered a crime of sodomy (q.v.) in forty-nine of the fifty states. The Rhode Island statue describes it as "abominable and detestable crime against nature" and provides for a penalty of imprisonment for not more than twenty years and not less than seven years. Such laws reflect the long-standing social condemnation of bestiality throughout the history of Western civilization.

PAUL D. SIMMONS

BETTING. See *Gambling.*

BIBLE. See also *Authority; Revelation.* Although the Bible is the chief source of Judeo-Christian morality and ethics, some have challenged its authority on ethical grounds. They point to alleged moral discrepancies in the OT and also stress a contrast between the OT view of God and that presented in the NT. Others, in their advocacy of complete liberty of expression without any restraint upon obscenity, have charged certain Scripture passages as being "obscene."

The moral discrepancies most commonly cited relate to the conquest of the Promised

Land, during which many Canaanites perished at the hands of the Israelites (e.g., Josh. 8, 10, 11). The objection is made that for God to have commanded, as the OT states, the destruction of the inhabitants of Canaan was incompatible with a high view of deity. Several considerations shed light upon this problem. "Ugaritic cult worship revealed by cuneiform texts" shows the debased nature of Caanite religion with its ceremonial prostitution, homosexual as well as hetero-sexual (R. K. Harrison, *Introduction to the Old Testament,* Grand Rapids, Eerdmans, 1969, pp. 119f.), and its cruelty and bestiality (K. A. Kitchen in *The New Bible Dictionary,* J. D. Douglas, ed., Grand Rapids, Eerdmans, 1965, article, "Canaan, Canaanites," p. 186). Since the Israelites were the divinely appointed recipients and bearers of the revelation of monotheism, it was crucially important for them to avoid the moral and spiritual contamination of the cultic worship indigenous to Canaan. Thus God ordered the removal of these people as a surgeon excises a cancer. That the command was not completely obeyed led, as subsequent history showed, to the adulteration of Israel's religious and social life with the idolatrous practices that plagued them for centuries and ultimately brought the judgment of the captivities upon them.

Related to this objection about the moral inconsistency of the Israelites' appointment to destroy the Canaanites is the dichotomy some see between the God of the OT and the God of the NT. So there are those who speak of Yahweh as a vengeful deity in contrast with the loving heavenly Father of whom Jesus taught. But many passages in the OT speak of God's love for his people, and his mercy ("steadfast love," RSV) is one of the great concepts of Hebrew religion. To be sure, the OT places great emphasis on God's justice and the judgment aspect of his dealings with men. And it was Jesus who revealed most fully the Father-

hood of God and who made known in his teachings and, supremely, in his redemptive work the Father's love for humanity. Yet no OT leader or prophet spoke stronger words of judgment than Jesus in his excoriation of the scribes and Pharisees (cf. Matt. 23) or taught more specifically about the drastic nature of eternal punishment than he did (e.g., "the unquenchable fire ... where their worm does not die, and the fire is not quenched," Mark 9:43-48), and also the solemn close of the parable of the rich man and Lazarus, in which "a great chasm has been fixed" between those in paradise and the lost (Luke 16:19-31).

The doctrine of God is progressively revealed in Scripture. But progressive revelation must never be confused with discrepant views of God.

The charge of obscenity in the Bible stems from the tendency of some advocates of complete laissez-faire in literary expression to justify their position by alleging Scripture itself to be immoral. Such incidents as David's adultery with Bathsheba (II Sam. 11, 12), the rape of Tamar (II Sam. 13, occasional crudities of expression (e.g., II Kings 18:27), and the celebration of connubial love in the Song of Solomon are offered as evidence. One has only, however to read these passages in order to see how far removed they are from obscenity (q.v.) or pornography (q.v.). In keeping with its ancient oriental background, the Bible speaks plainly about the bodily functions but never in a scatological way. Its references to various acts of sexual immorality do not go beyond terse, unadorned statement of what happened. Never does the Bible portray sexual sin in the lascivious detail characteristic of pornography. Rather than lingering over the sinful acts, it portrays the consequences of these acts and, as in the story of David's great sin, relates the transgression to its judgment.

The Song of Solomon is a frank celebration of marital love. It is a poem replete with images taken from nature and from the environs of Jerusalem. The bride's charms are compared to doves, a flock of goats, a pomegranate, twin gazelles, a heap of wheat, pools in Heshbon, a tower of Lebanon, etc. One has only to read its most intimate passages such as 4:1-15 or 6:4—7:13 to understand how far removed from obscenity this superb poem is.

FRANK E. GAEBELEIN

BIGAMY. See also *Monogamy; Polygamy.* The Bible does not explicitly enjoin monogamy as the ideal marriage relationship (except in the case of "bishops" who must be the husband of one wife!) but monogamy alone does justice to the teaching of the Bible on the reciprocal nature of the marriage relationship and the equality of the sexes. Polygamy is marriage involving a plurality of spouses. In Western society the practice of polygamy is forbidden. The one who practices polygamy is guilty of the crime of bigamy, and no Christian can, with a good conscience, condone this. Bigamy is generally associated with deceit. Christians, Paul insists, are to do that which is honest in the sight of all men (Rom. 12:17).

STUART B. BABBAGE

BILLS OF RIGHTS. See also *Civil Rights; Natural Rights; Rights.* Bills of Rights are a series of constitutional documents enumerating the fundamental liberties of the people. They specify privileges of personal expression, such as freedom of religion, speech, press and assembly; privileges of political participation, such as the right to vote and to choose representatives to a legislative body; privileges of economic participation, such as the right to own property, and to have a voice in determining its use for public taxation; and the privilege of equality before the law, including the writ of habeus corpus and the right of trial by jury. Personal rights are attributed to God and to Nature. Rights of participation

and protection are considered essential to personal and community development.

Magna Charta (1215) is the first of the so-called bills of rights. It lists the traditional liberties of Englishmen under feudal custom and the "laws of the realm." Prominent among these were: government by "the law of the land," government by "due process of law," the right to trial by jury, and the principle of "no taxation without representation."

The Bill of Rights (1689) redefined and reconfirmed many of the privileges guaranteed by the Great Charter. By requiring the new English monarchs, William and Mary, to subscribe their support to these provisions, the Bill of Rights became the basic document in English constitutionalism (q.v.). Many of its provisions were copied later by constitution drafters in America and throughout the world.

Bills of Rights drafted by English colonists in the seventeeth and eighteenth centuries inaugurated the conception of rights as values to be achieved in a new society as well as privileges to be protected. Their sanction was found, not alone in the English common law, but in more general and subjective value systems such as Christian and humanitarian ethics. The first constitutions drawn by American states began with a declaration of rights based upon their experience under the English common law and assumed to be natural. The framers of the Declaration of Independence (1776), seeking a more universal sanction for a justification of their grievances, laid their claim for separation from British rule on the basis of alleged violation of rights affirmed by "the Laws of Nature and Nature's God." Those who drafted the American Bill of Rights, the first ten amendments to the Constitution of 1787, returned to the traditional English rights as a statement of limitations on the powers of the new government.

"The Declaration of the Rights of Man

and Citizen" (1789), drafted by the French National Assembly, identified rights as "natural and imprescriptible." Men were declared to be born and to remain "free and equal in rights." The nation, speaking through the general will, was named the guarantor and the determinant of rights. These were said to include the liberties of freedom from arbitrary arrest and excessive punishment as well as freedom of communication and the right of private property. By making the nation the sole determinant of human freedoms, natural rights gradually became civil liberties, i.e., those freedoms necessary to maintain republican institutions. Bills of rights included in the constitutions of the totalitarian democracies such as the Soviet Union (1936) and the People's Republic of China (1954) are neither natural or civil. They imply no limits on political power, but a sanction for state action in defense of their respective revolutions.

The International Declaration of Rights (1948), drafted by the General Assembly of the United Nations, seeks to make universal those human rights set forth in the constitutions of modern states. By the terms of the Declaration, and the opinions of jurists, human rights are attributed to man because of personhood. Such rights are conceived as safeguards to the dignity of the individual as over against the power of the state and the forces of the society in which he lives. One finds in the Declaration and in many new constitutions guarantees of such privileges as employment, education, health, social security, rest, leisure, and the enjoyment of the cultural benefits of modern technological society as rights for all men to enjoy.

SAMUEL R. KAMM

BIRTH CONTROL. See also *Abortion; Contraception; Sterilization.* In its broadest sense, birth control by inference includes any act or device which keeps apart two persons of opposite sex who have the potential for procreation, any act or device which renders male or female incapable of the performance of the totality of sexual function, any act or device which keeps apart sperm and ovum during or after sexual intercourse, and any act or device which destroys the product of conception (the zygote formed from male and female gametes) regardless of the age of the product of conception.

Birth control is to be distinguished from population control (q.v.) in that the latter by inference could concern itself with the destruction of selected individuals after birth and before natural death.

The Christian must be aware that the control of human reproduction is necessary in individual families as well as in geographical areas or in nations or in ethnic groups in the light of economics, the prevention of suffering, and the long term view of adequate food supply.

Isolated pregnancies may also be unwanted by individuals, families, peoples, or society in general, for a variety of reasons including desire, economics, convenience; pregnancy as the result of rape or incest; a known or presumed genetic defect in the fetus; or real or imagined medical risk to the pregnant mother.

Basic to this discussion is the conviction that sexual intercourse is permissible only in marriage. The Christian ethics of birth control are based upon the Biblical view of the sanctity of marriage and its resultant family life, on the sanctity of human life and our obligation to preserve it, and to some extent on our understanding of the sovereignty of God. As men we are bound by God's moral law, but we must acknowledge that we see moral law through the eyes of sinful men and are constantly in need of the Spirit's guidance as we attempt to understand God's Word in Scripture when no explicit commandment is given.

For the Christian, a dilemma is posed whenever ethical decision is attempted on the basis of the situation alone, when relationships in marriage are in jeopardy, when a pregnant woman's wellbeing is at stake, when the product of conception is unwanted for reasons of rape or incest, or for presumed congenital physical or mental defect. For the non-Christian, the dilemma may not be pressing, depending upon sensitivity of conscience. If the motivation for contraception is proper (i.e., in view of man's accountability to God) the technique is also proper.

The same cannot be said, however, for birth control, since one must take into account—at least theoretically—the life of the product of conception. Sperm and egg cannot reproduce themselves; they each have one-half the total number of chromosomes of the cells of the body that produce them. Once these two gametes, sperm and egg, have united, they form a zygote with the full complement of chromosomes. Unless something destroys that zygote it will develop into a human being; it has the potential for God-consciousness and for reproduction, and deserves to be treated in accordance with the Christian regard for the sanctity of life.

The size and weight of the fetus that will survive is provable. The time at which the product of conception becomes a soul is open to philosophical conjecture but not subject to empirical proof.

Abstinence from sexual intercourse, the practice of rhythm (i.e., intercourse only on those days when there is no probability of an ovum for fertilization) and coitus interruptus (withdrawal before ejaculation) are means of birth control with varying risks of failure that have the potential to produce marital discord, and expose one or both partners to the temptations out of marriage for what cannot be found within marriage.

Sterilization as a method of birth control is subject to the same moral principles as any other form of contraception. Vasectomy for the male is almost without risk while tubal ligation for the female is a procedure subject to greater risk and complication. All sterilization must be assumed to be irrevocable.

Of the various so-called contraceptive devices and techniques, whether mechanical barriers, washing, chemical or hormonal, all but the intrauterine contraceptive device prevent the ovum and the sperm from uniting. The IUCD on the other hand usually prevents implantation of the already fertilized egg on the uterine wall and is therefore an attack on the product of conception rather than a barrier placed against fertilization.

In light of the thesis already developed, abortion is the destruction of (potential) human life. To perform an abortion to preserve the life (not a spurious psychiatric indication) of the mother does not contravene. On other occasions, Christian compassion in a given situation may dictate abortion in the minds of some, but it contravenes the sanctity of human life.

If we all know how to love as Jesus Christ meant us to love, the laws we strive to erect as guidelines would be unnecessary. The Christian knows God's law, and he attempts to love with the love of Christ.

In an age where liberty becomes license the Christian must be on guard in all decisions, particularly in respect to intent and a good conscience.

📖 Walter O. Spitzer and Carlyle L. Saylor, eds., *Birth Control and the Christian: A Protestant Symposium on the Control of Human Reproduction*, Wheaton, Tyndale, 1916.

C. EVERETT KOOP

BLACK MARKET. Black market, or illegal market, tends to exist whenever excess profits can be made on scarce goods. It is through the price system that a free society puts into effect its decisions on how it will allocate its resources (inputs), distribute the output and then carry out and implement these decisions. When scarcities and gluts occur, price is not effective, the system breaks down, and a system of allocation or rationing arises. Rationed articles then become available illegally in the black market at inflated prices.

Missionaries usually confront black market conditions when the official exchange rate between the American dollar and local money varies considerably from the open market or free exchange rate. The inflated market price for goods places a missionary at a serious disadvantage when purchasing with official exchange rate money. Most missionary societies make all the exchanges in currency for the missionary so that he is not tempted to engage in unethical financial practices which would reflect on his Christian witness and the gospel message. Under inflationary conditions, money is of little value, so the sale of an article may be tied to the delivery of another usable article. King Solomon bartered for the needs of the Lord's house (I Kings 5:10). Missionaries can ethically trade for needs.

In Vietnam the variation between the official rate of exchange and that in the black market varied during the war from 50 to 200 percent, with illicit dealings amounting to ten million dollars a year. During 1935-1944, when price controls or rationing were in effect in America, 779 of the 980 decisions for black market operation violations were rendered against seventy large non-financial corporations as criminal offenses. Some 200,000 firms were punished as violators (*International Encyclopedia of Social Sciences,* Vol. 2, New York, Macmillan, 1968).   HARVEY A. MAERTIN

BLASPHEMY. As used in Scripture, blasphemy is a sin consisting of a verbal utterance or action grossly disrespectful of God, expressing an arrogant rejection of his majesty or authority, or casting contempt upon his providence, words or works. The basic sanction against blasphemy is found in the Second Commandment: "Thou shalt not take the name of Yahweh thy God in vain (or falsely, to no good purpose)." Blasphemy may be considered as the opposite to "blessing" the name of God; occasionally the Hebrew "bless" (berak) is even used euphemistically for a specific word for "curse" or "blaspheme" (e.g., in Job 1:5; I Kings 21:10, 13). The precedent-making case of blasphemy and its punishment occurred in Lev. 24:10-13, where an Egyptian-Israelite half-breed was stoned to death for his offense. It was on a trumped-up charge of the same nature that Naboth was executed at the instigation of Jezebel (I Kings 21:13-14), who induced false witnesses to affirm that he cursed both God and the king (Ahab).

The specific terms for "blaspheme" in the OT were: *giddēp, hārap* and *qabab.* (a) *Giddēp,* the commonest of these, originally meant "cut" "wound," hence "revile" or "blaspheme." This is illustrated in the servants of Sennacherib, whose doom was pronounced by Isaiah (Isa. 37:6, 23, and the parallels in II Kings 19:6, 22). The Psalmist (44:16) complains of the ungodly who "reproach" *(hārēp)* and "blaspheme *(giddēp)*"—the same combination of verbs as in Isa. 37:23. To Ezekiel God pronounces judgment on the Jewish forefathers who have blasphemed him by resorting to idolatry and its abominable practices (20:27-28).

(b) *Hārap,* "speak sharply against; reproach," is translated "blaspheme" just once in KJV: Isa. 65:7. (c) *Qābab,* "utter a curse against," occurs twice in Lev. 24:11 and 16. Besides these, *na'as* "contemn, spurn" (in the *piel*) is rendered "give occasion to blaspheme" in II Sam. 12:14; Ps. 74:10 and Isa. 52:5.

In the NT the term is *blasphēmeō* ("speak harmfully of")—used with God as its object (Rom. 2:24; I Thess. 1:20; 6:1; James 2:7; Rev. 13:6; 16:9, 11, 21), or Christ as God (Mark 3:28; John 10:36) or as usurping God's prerogative of forgiving sin (Matt. 3:29; Luke 12:10), or the word of God (Titus 2:5). This same verb is also used of "reviling" other men (Titus 3:2; Rom. 3:8; I Cor. 10:30; etc.), without connotations of sacrilege, unless those reviled are regarded as representatives of God, created in His image (James 3:9).

GLEASON L. ARCHER

BLESSEDNESS. See also *Beatitudes; Happiness; Pleasure.* The word "happiness" indicates a concept used widely in all cultures and societies, as a kind of "umpire" concept by which men evaluate and criticize their own lives and those of others too. There are a variety of words, even in English and other European languages, that have the same authority and power as does "happiness"; and, therefore, we can say that "happiness" is a concept, not always requiring the same verbal expression. It is quite clear that a life is not held to be meaningful if it is neither happy nor open to the possibility thereof. It is not unusual to warn someone, for example, not to marry that man, "for, he will make you unhappy." This is a token of how closely the issues of a meaningful life and a good act are tied up with happiness—and this not for the few but for the many.

The first lengthy philosophical reflections on happiness are found in Aristotle's *Nichomachean Ethics* and his *Rhetoric.* In the latter book, he says that public speakers must acknowledge that all men want and seek happiness, otherwise they will misaddress the populace no matter what cause they represent. But happiness has conditions, he says, and thus wealth, intelligence, health, and friends are among those necessary prerequisites; and only the fortunately placed will ever find happiness. Aristotle seems to think that being happy is a very general characteristic of the differentially endowed person. The happiness of the man is like health of the body. One is not

simply happy about this or that, any more than one is healthy in respect to this and that. Emotions require targets, so one is angry over this or that; but happiness has life in general as its context. Still one is made for it and tactics and strategies of life are only worthwhile within those conditions.

But Aristotle is wrong on this, for men have learned also how to become happy, despite those conditions or the lack of them. He is also wrong in thinking that one is, if well-placed, simply happy. For he leaves no room for that fact that in order to be happy one must also feel happy. The ancient Epicureans, as well as John Stuart Mill in the nineteenth century, discerned that happiness was something to be felt, but decided largely that happiness was a surplus of felt pleasures as over against felt pains. So, Mill also linked the seeking of pleasures with the fate of a liberal government, arguing that happiness, pleasure and the good life could be achieved if guided by the maxim, "The greatest good for the greatest number." Surely he was right in seeing that happiness had to have a psychological component; but he was wrong in thinking that it had to be made up of pleasure-states.

The psychological component of happiness is not a felt pleasure as much as it is an attitude. And one takes up and achieves an attitude. The particular attitude necessary for happiness is a very general acquiescence to the course of human life. But more, it is not simply passive, but active and therefore has a welcoming function. Here is where both the OT and NT also address a fundamental human condition, namely, the unrequited need for a deep and invulnerable happiness. The Bible, however, clearly shows us that God with all his power and love cannot make a man happy as long as he is envious, hateful, vengeful, self-centered and jealous. Despite the glories of God's grace and salvation, there is something in a man that prevents happiness on earth as well as his entrance to heaven. The question seems to be how and to what extent we will place ourselves in God's hand. And this means placing ourselves under the tactics and strategies of the Bible itself.

The Biblical promise is decidedly on the side of "blessedness." But this blessedness is neither an accident nor a simple achievement nor a wish. However, believing in God and obeying his commandments surely mean a radical and uncompromising view of the world and oneself in which blessedness and happiness thrive. Christian beliefs are like the river-bed for one's thoughts and emotions, within which contentment, peace, and joy can truly flourish. So much is this the case that the Apostle Paul can simply say, "Rejoice, again I say, rejoice," which command would ordinarily be impertinent without that river-bed within which human life can happily flow.

PAUL L. HOLMER

BODY. See also *Asceticism; Bestiality; Fasting; Gluttony; Resurrection.* The body of man is a marvelous creation of God, endowed by its maker with innumerable gifts, and elevated by him above all other earthly creatures. In its original state it was "very good," free from sin and its consequences, capable of living in the presence of the holy God, and possessing immortality. As a consequence of the Fall, however, sin has permeated and corrupted the whole nature of man. His body has become subject to suffering, weaknesses of many kinds, and finally death. Man's physical being, however, is neither intrinsically evil nor inseparably connected with sin. While the term "flesh" *(basar, sarx)* in both testaments may denote man in his frailty as distinguished from the divine essence, nowhere does Scripture suggest that the body of man in itself is evil, imprisoning the soul, and dragging it down into sin. When Paul describes the flesh as totally corrupt and continuously warring against the spirit (Gal

5:17 f.), he is not referring to man's physical being but to his fallen human nature.

The Bible speaks of man both as a unit and as dichotomous in nature, a being consisting of body and soul which operate in such close harmony that they are conceived of as one. John Gerhard states:

In life they (body and soul) are connected to each other by the closest bond, whence the affections and sufferings of the body flow over into the soul, and in turn the affections and sufferings of the soul flow over into the body; the soul does nothing whatever outside of the body, nor does the body do anything independently of the soul — *Loci Theologici* xvii, 149.

However, in describing death and the resurrection, the Bible suggests the dichotomy of man. It calls death a departure of the soul (Gen. 35:18), a putting off of the body (II Peter 1:14), a perishing of the body but not of the soul (Matt. 10:28), a return of the spirit to God (Eccles. 12:7; Luke 23:46), a condition in which the body is apart from the spirit (James 2:26; II Cor. 5:8). Scripture usually describes the resurrection as a rising of the body or corpse (Isa. 26:19; Phil. 3:21; I Cor. 15:44).

Though the resurrection body will be spiritual in nature (I Cor. 15:44), this does not necessarily imply an existence which is not material and physical. The body of Christ after his resurrection was one of flesh and bones which could be recognized and touched (Luke 24:39); and at his second coming Christ will change our lowly bodies so they will be like his glorious body (Phil. 3:21). The dead will be restored to life, but with new attributes: immortality, glory, freedom from physical weaknesses, from sorrow, and earthly limitations (Luke 20:36; Dan. 12:3; I Cor. 15:41ff.).

Alexander Heidel, *The Gilgamesh Epic and the Old Testament Parallels*, Chicago, University of Chicago, 1946; J. A. Schep, *The Nature of the*

Resurrection Body, Grand Rapids, Eerdmans, 1964.   HOWARD W. TEPKER

BONHOEFFER, DIETRICH. Relatively unknown during his lifetime, Bonhoeffer (1906-1945) has become a central figure in the church's contemporary struggle to clarify its message and to exercise its discipleship. His appeal is to a wide variety of people, partially due to the obvious attraction of his participation in the German resistance to the Nazi tyranny, for which he was eventually executed—but also to the fragmentary character of his most provocative theological explorations. Although Bonhoeffer's interpreters disagree on virtually every substantive issue, the main line is drawn between those who see in him the growth of an essentially stable point of view and those who see major shifts and radically new directions in his development. The latter see his outlook moving *"from* the church *to* the world" (the title of a book by East Berlin theologian Hanfried Müller), abandoning specific Christian claims for the sake of involvement in worldly concerns. The former see his development in terms of a gradually deepening commitment to Jesus Christ, in whom God and world come together. How one chooses to understand Bonhoeffer's development will have a great deal to do with one's judgment as to the helpfulness of his contribution.

In this writer's opinion, the continuities in Bonhoeffer's life and thought are far more impressive than are the changes. These continuities center in his persistent refusal to carve up reality. From the beginning of his study of theology to the time of his death he abhorred every notion of Christianity as separating a man from involvement in the pains and promises of God's world. When he spoke about the earth, he frequently added the words "in which the cross of Jesus Christ is planted." Perhaps the passage in which this rejection of dualism is most clearly stated is that en-

titled "Thinking in Terms of Two Spheres" in the *Ethics.* Bonhoeffer says that "since the beginnings of Christian ethics after the times of the New Testament the main underlying conception in ethical thought, and the one which consciously or unconsciously has determined its whole course, has been the conception of a juxtaposition and conflict of two spheres, the one divine, holy, supernatural, and Christian, and the other worldly, profane, natural, and un-Christian. . . . It may be difficult to break the spell of this thinking in terms of two spheres, but it is nevertheless quite certain that it is in profound contradiction to the thought of the Bible and to the thought of the Reformation, and that consequently it aims wide of reality. There are not two realities, but only one reality, and that is the reality of God, which has become manifest in Christ in the reality of the world. . . . There are not two spheres but only the one sphere of the realization of Christ, in which the reality of God and the reality of the world are united."

When one has grasped this central theme, all of the pieces of the Bonhoeffer phenomenon fall into place. It was *because of* his commitment to Christ, expressed so clearly in the books *(The Cost of Discipleship* New York, Macmillan, and *Life Together* New York, Harper & Row), that he wrote while training men for ministry in the "Confessing Church," and that he found himself involved in active resistance to Hitler, whom he considered to be Anti-Christ (q.v.). His famous formulations from *Letters and Papers from Prison* (rev. ed., New York, Macmillan, 1967) ("non-religious interpretation of Biblical concepts," "this-worldly transcendence," "holy worldliness," "world coming of age,") were all designed to center Christianity specifically in Jesus Christ rather than in general religiosity.

This found expression ethically, then, in Bonhoeffer's refusal to focus Christian decision-making on moral or religious abstractions (principles, ideals, values, ideas) and his insistence on following Christ concretely. He was a "situationist," or "contextualist," in that he saw the command of God as being always concrete. He differed from many contemporary situationists in that he grounded every facet of his position specifically in Christ and that he worked very hard at building structures which, though not "absolute," would provide corporate and historical dimensions to personal decision-making. His final significance will not lie in what he had to say on specific ethical issues (abortion, etc.) or even in his total "system," which he never completed, but rather in the very provocative suggestions which came from his brilliant mind and committed life.

📖 Eberhard Bethge, *Dietrich Bonhoeffer: Man of Vision-Man of Courage*, tr., Eric Mosbacker and others, Edwin Robertson, ed., New York, Harper & Row, 1970; Dietrich Bonhoeffer, *Ethics*, tr., Neville Horton Smith, New York, Macmillan, 1963; *The Cost of Discipleship*, tr., Reginald H. Fuller, New York, Macmillan, 1963.

JAMES H. BURTNESS

BOYCOTT. The term normally refers to a collective refusal to have dealings with an individual, a commercial concern, or a government in the hope that such action will produce a change in policy. Apparently the name derived from a certain Captain Boycott (1832-1897), the target of such collective action by irate Irish tenants seeking an end to their landlord's exploitative policies.

In modern times the boycott has been widely used to exert moral pressure on individuals and corporate groups of various kinds who continue their "evil" practices despite persistent requests for change. In most instances boycott action involves only peaceful activity such as refusing to buy goods, refusing to utilize services, and trying to convince others to follow suit.

Several major boycott actions of recent years have been supported or even championed by Christians. A widespread campaign against buying goods from South Africa was conducted for several years in an attempt to force the South African government to alter its apartheid racial policies. The late Martin Luther King organized major boycotts including a successful one against segregation on public buses in several USA cities. In some parts of the non-communist world there is a continuing boycott of goods produced in communist countries.

A major problem associated with boycott is that it is often very difficult to determine rightness and wrongness in a dispute. Often the moral issue is not as clear cut as boycott organizers would have us believe. Therefore this weapon should not be used without careful consideration.

A second problem is that the boycott is basically an indiscriminate weapon. The innocent may be hurt more than those presumably guilty.

Christians who quite rightly seek to promote justice and human dignity must thoroughly evaluate any potential or actual boycott situation in which they might participate. There is not much point in conducting a boycott against one party in a dispute if both are guilty, nor will there be any net benefit if the brunt of the boycott falls on innocent people.

In many situations a token boycott can be just as effective as general action. Limited activity which serves to bring the case at issue to the attention of lawmakers, the media, and the general public may be sufficient to produce the desired policy change.   JOHN H. REDEKOP

BRADLEY, F. H. (1846-1924), was the leading British idealist. Although Bradley never lectured at Oxford, where he was a fellow of Merton College, he exercised a wide influence through five major works written between 1874 and 1914. He drew upon Hegel and contemporary German philosophy in an attempt to counteract the British empiricism of J. S. Mill as well as the views of Immanuel Kant. In his *Ethical Studies* of 1876, he identified "Self-realization as the Ethical End." Bradley did not mean this in a strictly individualistic sense since, he argued, "self-realization" always implies a larger whole. This "larger whole" was social as well as metaphysical (and religious), i.e., the Absolute. "The object, which by faith the self appropriates," he says, "is in Christianity nothing alien from and outside the world, not an abstract divine which excludes the human; but it is the inseparable unity of human and divine. . . . It is known, in its truth, not until it is apprehended as an organic human-divine totality; as one body with diverse members, as one self which, in many selves, realizes, wills, and loves itself, as they do themselves in it."

Although the Absolute is the ideal toward which the self presses, Bradley stressed that there are intermediate stages in the ethical development of the self. Immediately each individual needs to recognize the communities and groups with which he is involved. These proximate ends in ethics are determined by the convergence of private or personal interests and the welfare of the communal group. The family, society and the state form the basic communal units of any society.

One of the major essays in *Ethical Studies* is "My Station and Its Duties" in which Bradley defends an aristocratic view of the state and society. Each individual is born into a particular family and nation, and the cultured classes have a higher ethical responsibility to lower classes. Bradley saw the English nation as playing a decisive role in shaping world history and the ethical ideals of man.

☞F. H. Bradley, *The Presuppositions of Critical History*, 1874; *Ethical Studies*, 1876; *The Principles of Logic*, 2 vols., 1883; *Appearance and Reality*, 1893; *Essays on Truth and Reality*, 1914.

R. W. Church, *Bradley's Dialectic*, 1942; H. Rashdall, *The Metaphysics of Bradley*, 1912.

DONALD M. LAKE

BRAINWASHING. See also *Propaganda.* Physical and mental torture have long been practiced but no assault upon the individual so insidiously exemplifies man's inhumanity to man as brainwashing. New knowledge in psychology has enabled barbarous men to rape the minds of men through systematic procedures of indoctrination, self-accusation, and conversion. Brainwashing violates the status of man as a free moral agent, by inhumanely reducing him to the level of an object in order to use him for political purposes.

Brainwashing first gained worldwide exposure in the Soviet Communist "purge trials" of 1936 when "Old Bolsheviks" confessed they were traitors to the Bolshevism to which they had dedicated their entire lives. Brainwashing also was employed by Nazis during World War II to induce betrayals of loyalties and by postwar communist satellite regimes to exact false confessions (e.g., Hungary's Cardinal Mindszenty).

To the Free World, however, brainwashing became most shocking through its use by Chinese Communists during the Korean War. At that time pro-communist publications published purported confessions by USA, British, and UN servicemen. North Korean propaganda broadcasts carried the voices of USA military men but the language was not their own. Peking announced that a group of USA servicemen had elected to remain with the enemy rather than return home. It became apparent that these prisoners of war had undergone brainwashing by the Communists.

Chinese Communists were able through normal interrogation to screen out from thousands of prisoners of war those susceptible to brainwashing. (Generally one person in five is highly susceptible to suggestion.) The men selected were then subjected to physical stresses and mental assaults that became an agonizing drama of mental death and rebirth. These men at first resisted. But forces upon and around them were so great that they found themselves finally drawn to confess and reform. Psychiatrist Robert Jay Lifton says, "This penetration by the psychological forces of the environment into the inner emotions of the individual person is perhaps the outstanding psychiatric fact of thought reform" (*Thought Reform and the Psychology of Totalism,* New York, Norton, 1961, p. 66).

Lifton sets forth twelve essential steps in the brainwashing process.

(1) *Assault upon Identity.* Along with relentless, incriminating interrogations, physical brutality, and painful and constricting chaining, the prisoner of war is constantly told that he is not really who he claims to be. This eventually leads to a hypnogogic state in which destructive impulses arising from within result in a renunciation of personal autonomy. This undermining of identity—a "dying to the world"—is the prerequisite for succeeding steps.

(2) *Establishment of Guilt.* Repeated accusations of existential criminal guilt and the need to *feel* guilty bring the prisoner to a sense of wrongdoing for which punishment is deserved and expected.

(3) *Self-betrayal.* Continuing accusations intensify shame and lead the prisoner to renounce the matrix of his previous existence: his people, organizations, nation, and behaviorial standards. Such betrayals bind him even stronger to his captors.

(4) *The Breaking Point: Total Conflict and Basic Fear.* Cut off from his former environment through loss of identity, sense of guilt and increasing self-betrayal, the prisoner experiences fear of total annihilation. Physical and mental integration break down and anxiety then may trigger suicidal thoughts, delusions, and hallucinations.

(5) *Leniency and Opportunity.* Relief comes through lessening pressure, friendliness, and guidance from his captors. He is offered "rest, kindness, and a glimpse of the Promised Land of renewed identity and acceptance—even freedom." He is now motivated to cooperate with officials as "a grateful partner in his own reform."

(6) *Compulsion to Confess.* Leniency has reinforced the need to confess in order to survive. He now assumes the identity of a repentant sinner seeking to excise the evil within him. Concurring in his captor's moral judgment, he begins to commit himself to the beliefs and values officially considered desirable in his present environment.

(7) *Channeling of Guilt.* Non-specific feelings of guilt are channeled into a paranoid, psuedo-logical system so that he now condemns himself less for what has been *done* than for what he has *been*—a guilty imperialist.

(8) *Re-education: Logical Dishonoring.* Group study leads him to recognize that his prior imperialist "evil acts" are related to historical forces, political happenings, and economic trends. His "evil acts" are seen to be the opposite of his cherished ideals. Following a dialectical thought pattern, he sees that his old life—his thesis—must be replaced by a commitment to his newly acquired outlook—his antithesis—which is rooted in Communist doctrine.

(9) *Progress and Harmony.* As the prisoner adapts and surrenders himself to the group, participates in the catharsis of confession, and enlists in the communist crusade of mass redemption, his living conditions are made more comfortable and he experiences the exhilaration of harmony with his milieu. He now achieves more intimate communication with his captors and feels they have accepted him.

(10) *Final Confession: Summing Up.* The prisoner's final all encompassing con-

fession in an atmosphere of harmony arises from self-accusations grounded in deep conviction. Complete acceptance of his criminality is a vital part of the re-education process.

(11) *Rebirth.* He now is urged to combine the special abilities of his old life (e.g., a physician, teacher, etc.) with his new role as a Communist reformer. The confluence of his identities—evil criminal, repentant sinner, student of communist doctrine, and the man originally imprisoned—constitute the new birth. Identified with his captors, he now sees the Communist world as peace-loving and is happy in his new faith.

(12) *Release: Transition and Limbo.* After a public trial formalizing his guilt and rebirth, the prisoner is finally released (sometimes following a period of "reform by labor") at a politically opportune time to go forth as a dedicated communist. His subsequent return to the Free World, of course, leads to a profound new crisis of identity. No longer shored up by the Communist environment, faced with the facts of life in the Free World, he must now decide what world—physically and mentally—he will live in.

Post-Korean war studies showed that men who successfully resisted Chinese Communist brainwashing were those firmly committed to faith in a particular way of life. In interviews with successful resisters Edward Hunter found "These three words—prayer, faith, and conviction—were closely linked in most minds. . . . At least one of these was mentioned in every case when a man thought back over what had given him his main support" (*Brainwashing from Pavlov to Powers,* Linden, N.J., Bookmailer, 1960, p. 272). For many prisoners, personal faith in Jesus Christ and the repeating of Biblical passages were bulwarks against the dehumanizing procedures of brainwashing.

The brutal, manipulative, false, and destructive practices of brainwashing are demonic as they seek to change free men into robots. All men of good will must totally condemn and seek to prevent their further practice.   ROBERT L. CLEATH

BROTHERHOOD. See also *Intermarriage, Racial; Koinonia; Racism.* The term brotherhood designates the bond of unity that exists between brothers. In its most elemental form this bond is not a voluntarily achieved association as in Rousseau's social contract or the local Lodge, but is a state and quality of human life that resides in the nature of man. In this brotherhood, inherent in the nature of man, lies the possibility of every voluntaristic form of human association: of city, state, teamsters, and manufacturers.

The Bible teaches two forms of brotherhood. The first the universal brotherhood of man which derives from the universal Fatherhood of God. All men are brothers because all men have one Father; because God created all men in the divine image, all are bound together in the unity that stems from a common origin. That all men are brothers, whether white, black, brown, or yellow, whether rich or poor, of whatever nationality, tribe, or culture, has wide and deep ethical implications for all forms of human relationships.

The second form of brotherhood taught by the Bible designates that bond of unity reconstituted by Christ and his Spirit that characterizes the people of God. Here the term brotherhood, as in Peter's exhortation, "Love the brotherhood" (I Peter 2:17), is another designation for the church. Between the creational brotherhood of man grounded in the universal Fatherhood of God and the reconstituted brotherhood grounded in Christ's recreation of man, lies the Fall. The Fall broke the relationship between God the Creator and man the creature, and that between men and man. As in the case of Cain and Abel, brother rises against brother in a self-assertion that destroys the brother. The brotherhood established by creation, broken by the Fall, is reconstituted by Christ in that new form of brotherhood—the new humanity, which the New Testament designates as the church. In this new community, men accept and call each other "brother," enjoy the communion of the saints because they have one Lord, one faith, one baptism, one spirit, and one God and Father who is over all and in all. As such the church is the concrete sign in history of the power and purpose of God one day to reconcile and unify in Christ all things in heaven and on earth, visible and invisible.

Until that day the relationship between the sin-broken creational brotherhood of all men and the Christ reconstituted brotherhood of the church, must be ethically assessed. Liberal theology stressed the Biblical truth of the universal brotherhood of man and its concomitant, the universal fatherhood of God, yet optimistically assumed that the brother relationship between men was, for all its brokeness, sufficiently intact for moral men of good will to reconstitute the brotherly relationship without the help of divine grace. Evangelicals reacted to this onesided distortion and the very language of universal Fatherhood and universal brotherhood became regarded as heresy. This exclusive recognition of a spiritual brotherhood only, for a long time foreclosed the possibility of a development of an authentically social ethic.

What must be recaptured is the Biblical teaching that the brotherhood constituted by Christ is a reconstitution of that brotherhood created by God and broken by the Fall. He who is the Elder Brother of those in the new Brotherhood of God, became what he is by means both of his Cross and his incarnational assumption of our divinely created and fallen human brotherhood. A truly social Christian ethic must take its stance and discover its imperatives neither from a created brotherhood, a fallen brotherhood, nor from that new brotherhood the

church, but from the Christ who stands between a created and fallen brotherhood and that brotherhood which he reconstituted into the form called the church. Any other understanding of brotherhood will foster an ethic that does less than justice to all the Biblical teachings about the creation, loss, and restoration of brotherhood.

JAMES DAANE

BRUNNER, EMIL. Emil Brunner (1889-1966) was born in Zürich, cradle of the Swiss reformation. After Gymnasium training he studied theology in Zürich and Berlin. He then came to Union Theological Seminary, New York, when religious liberalism was at the meridian of influence in America.

In 1912 Brunner was ordained a minister in the Swiss Reformed Church. He married Margrit Lautenburg, who bore him four sons, two of whom are deceased. When his second son died in a railway accident in the summer of 1952, Brunner wrote out of personal sorrow his *Eternal Hope* (Philadelphia, Westminster) a study of the Christian view of last things.

Brunner had been trained in his theological studies as a liberal. His first published book was a study of symbolism in religious knowledge in which he made an attempt, to use his own words, "to get beyond Schleiermacher"; but a profound change in his theological point of view began to take place as he pastored his first church at Glarus. No sooner did Barth (q.v.) publish his *Commentary on Romans* (1919)—which fell "like a bombshell on the playground of the theologians"—than Brunner openly avowed himself to be of this new theological persuasion in an enthusiastic review of Barth's book. He soon emerged as a leading exponent of Barth's theology and was appointed a *Privat-dozent* (an unsalaried lecturer) on the theological faculty of the University of Zürich. Here he established himself as a scholar in his own right with the publication of *Die Mystik und das Wort* ("Mysticism and the Word," Tubingen, Mohr, 1924, not translated), one of the most searching critiques of Schleiermacher's theology ever written. Soon after its publication, he was appointed professor of theology at Zürich, a post which he held (with some interruptions) until retirement in 1955.

In the early thirties Brunner became embroiled in a controversy with Barth over the question of natural theology. Brunner held that there is a "broken natural revelation" of God in the hearts of all men. That is to say, even though men are sinners, they retain some knowledge of the true God and some ability to hear and understand the gospel. Were it not for this point of contact, preaching would be useless. Barth replied with his *Nein!* ("No!"), subtitled, "An Angry Answer to Emil Brunner." Barth was terrified by the specter of religious liberalism with its doctrine of the divine spark in man that needs only to be fanned by environment and education into a flame of essential goodness. The Holy Spirit, he affirmed, does not need any "point of contact."

Meanwhile Brunner became interested in the Oxford Group Movement (cf. *Moral Rearmament*) and took part in the house meetings and Bible study groups, as meeting a need in the lives of lay Christians not being satisfied in the established churches.

As the controversy over natural theology raged between Brunner's disciples and Barth's, Brunner accepted an invitation to become a visiting lecturer at Princeton Seminary in New Jersey and at Union Seminary in New York. The theological right joined the theological left to challenge his position. From the side of conservative evangelicals, this challenge was provoked by his refusal to identify the Word of God with the words of Scripture and the sometimes cavalier manner in which he departed from the received doctrine of the church, notably

in his rejection of the virgin birth. Returning to his native Zurich from America, Brunner continued to lecture to large classes of cosmopolitan character. In 1947 he delivered the Gifford Lectures on *Christianity and Civilization* and the following year, 1948, was a delegate to the founding assembly of the World Council of Churches in Amsterdam.

In 1949 Brunner made a trip to Asia and the Far East, leaving, as he said, a part of his heart in Japan. Much to the surprise of the scholarly world, he returned to that land in 1953, at the age of sixty-three, to accept the chair of Christian philosophy at the International Christian University. He went, he said, that he might have a little part in making Japan a Christian country and use the last few years God had given him on the missionary battle front. Because of his wife's failing health he was forced to cut short his stay, however, and returned to his native Switzerland in July, 1955. The gruelling exertion of lecturing in English long hours in unheated classrooms took its inevitable toll. On the voyage home, he suffered a stroke which ended his teaching career and greatly curtailed his literary efforts. The third volume of his *Dogmatics,* composed largely by dictation, appeared in 1960. He died April 6, 1966, at home in Zürich.

Brunner's contribution to theology is appropriately noted in a dictionary of Christian ethics inasmuch as he was vitally interested in the practical implications of dogmatics and some of his most significant works were devoted to theological ethics. Basic to this interest was his anthropology, expounded in *Man in Revolt* (1937) in which, understanding man as a uniquely personal being, he uses categories and insights drawn from Kierkegaard and the Personalism of Ebner and Buber, philosophers who emphasized the relationship of the "I" to the "Thou." Man, as person, is responsible before God; but as sinner, is in revolt against him. The power to do the right comes from the indwelling Spirit of Christ, who makes a man a new creature by faith. The right act, according to Brunner, is one which is motivated by love and it is the Spirit who illumines the moment of decision so that one knows what love requires in that moment. This is God's command *(das Gebot)*.

The divine command, however, cannot be understood apart from the "ordinances of Creation" *(die Ordnungen)*, the divinely given structures of life (family, work, church, state, culture) through which God always makes known his will. This theory of ethics is principally set forth in Brunner's *The Divine Imperative* (1932). The social, political and cultural implications of this approach are set forth in his *Justice and the Social Order* (1945) and his *Christianity and Civilization* (1948-49). This approach, in certain respects, anticipated the current emphasis on "situational ehthics" (q.v.). How to mediate the absolute claims of love in the ever changing situation of the moment, so as to avoid legalism on the one hand and relativism on the other, is perhaps the most critical problem in Brunner's ethical theory. In his effort to illumine this matter, his contribution has been widely acclaimed. It is doubtful, however, that he would appreciate the conclusions of those who have seen in this effort the harbinger of the "new morality."   PAUL K. JEWETT

BUBER, MARTIN. Martin Buber (1878-1965) was one of the outstanding Jewish thinkers of our time. He was born in Vienna where he took his doctorate. In his earlier years he edited Zionist journals in Vienna and Berlin, and studied Hasidism (the spiritual and ethical movement which began in the eighteenth century). Buber was inspired by the ideal of the complete man, and dedicated himself to the proclamation of a humanism based on Jewish tradition.

In 1923 Buber moved to Frankfurt where he taught in the Free Jewish Academy founded by Franz Rosenzweig, with whom he began to translate the Jewish Bible into German. The same year he became Professor for Jewish History of Religion and Ethics at Frankfurt University, where he also taught the history of religions. Deprived of his post by the Nazis, he went to Palestine in 1938 and served as Professor of Sociology at the Hebrew University of Jerusalem until retirement in 1951. Here he sought by his teaching to win the state of Israel to a Hebrew humanism, based upon the Bible and Jewish tradition, which joined Jews and Arabs and which rejected narrow nationalism.

Buber's *I and Thou* (1923; Eng. tr. 1937) has exerted wide influence. Some Protestant theologians have adapted its ideas in stating their view of God and revelation. Buber contrasts the realms of the personal (I-Thou, q.v.) and the impersonal (I-It). He warns that even in the sphere of the personal the "Thou" tends to become an "It." But through our relationship with things, as well as with other people, we may discover the eternal "Thou."

Elsewhere Buber summed up the teaching of Hasidism in words which might well be taken as an expression of his own ideal: "God is to be seen in everything, and reached by every pure deed."

📖 Martin Buber, *I and Thou*, Edinburgh, Clark, and New York, Scribner (1937) 1960; *Between Man and Man*, Boston, Beacon (1948) 1955; *The Eclipse of God*, New York, Harper (1952) 1957; *The Kingship of God*, London, Allen & Unwin, 1967; *Tales of the Hasidim*, 2 vols., New York, Schocken, 1947-48, London, Thames & Hudson, 1955; *Hasidism*, New York, Philosophical Library, 1948; H. U. von Balthasar, *Martin Buber and Christianity*, London, Harvill, 1961; M. L. Diamond, *Martin Buber: Jewish Existentialist*, New York, Oxford, 1960; M. S. Friedman, *Martin Buber: The Life of Dialogue*, New York, Harper (1955) 1960; W. Herberg, ed., *The Writings of Martin Buber*, New York, Meridian, 1956; P. Schilpp and M. S. Friedman, eds., *Martin Buber*, La Salle, Open Court, 1967; R. G. Smith, *Martin Buber*, London, Lutterworth, 1966.

COLIN BROWN

BUDDHIST ETHICS. See also *Zen*. Buddhism is not a religion in the usual sense of the word. It is primarily an ethical theory addressed to the problem of suffering rather than moral evil, a philosophy of life which considers morality and intellectual enlightment as inherently interrelated, and a way *(dharma)* in which each one is his own saviour. Man's will is free, he is the sole guide of his destiny, and he has unlimited number of lives for his self development.

The beginnings of this faith are found in Gautama, an Indian prince of the sixth century B.C., who renounced his royal luxuries and privileges to set out as an ascetic seeking a way of deliverance for all men from suffering. After years of search he finally found answers to all his questions when he became the Buddha, the All-Enlightened One. Of the two main segments of Buddhism, Theravada or Hinayana (the Little Vehicle) in general follows the original teachings of Gautama while the other, Mahayana (the Great Vehicle), is more liberal and syncretic.

Buddhist philosophy of ethics may be summarized as follows:

1. *The Foundations of Ethical Theory: The Four Noble Truths (ARYA SATTYA).* First, there is suffering *(dukkha)*: all forms of existence everywhere at all times are subject to misery and pain both mental and physical. Second, there is a cause of suffering: every experience must have a cause and the cause of suffering is essentially the desire for individual existence. Third, there is a cessation of suffering: when the cause of suffering is removed suffering ceases to exist. Fourth, there is a way leading to the cessation of suffering; this is the Eight-fold Path which a person may follow to be completely detached from the wheel of birth, growth, decay and death.

2. *The Middle Way.* The term (cf. Aristotle's "golden mean") is applied to the Eight-fold Path because the two extreme ways, self-indulgence and self-mortification,

are futile. The eight steps that are taken in one's evolutionary development are: right views, that is faith in the four-fold truth; right resolve, to have wholesome and unselfish motives; right speech, using only words that are worthy and useful; right conduct, abstaining from killing any living being, stealing, hatred, sensuality and intoxication; right living, rejection of luxury and using one's life for the good of others; right effort, to avoid evil in a person by detachment from worldly desires and thinking on positive values; right thought, contemplation on the transitoriness of life and right concentration, meditation upon only one thing which leads one into a trance state of rapture and happiness. By the daily practice of these steps one ultimately attains full Enlightenment or Buddhahood.

The "fetters" which entangle a man hindering his journey through the Path are: the delusion of self that it is real, doubts which create mental idleness, false belief that rites and ceremonies can bring salvation, sensual desires, unkindness, desire for reward in the future world, spiritual pride, self-righteousness, and finally various types of ignorance. Mental exercises for the removal of these "fetters" comprise four "Meditations" of love, compassion, joy and peace.

3. *Self, Karma, and Rebirth.* Man is complete in himself needing no god or saviour, yet man is only a part of the constantly changing process. Each act of man is caused by a similar act and will be followed by a similar one. None can stop the consequence of a deed already done. The theory of Karma which the Buddha learned from the Hinduism, describes this universal law of cause and effect in the realm of man's actions. By mental effort man can control his present thoughts and actions, gradually bringing him closer to his goal. Man cannot learn all that he must and free himself during a single life; and he lives through many lives. Inequality among men

is explained in terms of rebirths. Each person is a product or fruit of his previous life. It pays one to be good for the consequence of good is good and of evil, evil.

4. *Attaining Nirvana*. The Eight-fold Path leads to the state of nirvana which is the final goal of all moral actions and intellectual developments. It is the "annihilation" of personal identity or separate individual life and one's immersion into the Universal Self, like a drop of water falling into an ocean. It is a state in which forces of Karma and limitations of selfhood come to an end.

> "Nirvana is, but not the man who seeks it
> The Path exists, but not the traveller on it."   (Visuddhimagga, 14)

The Zen or Meditation Sect holds that by contemplation rather than by knowledge one may receive a comprehension of one's true nature and be enlightened. The Pure Land Sect teaches that Amita Buddha has created a Pure Land where man has more favorable conditons under which he may receive nirvana rather than in this world. In Lamaism, the Esoteric Sect, man may receive help from Bodhisattvas, the spiritual giants, in his struggle to receive Englightenment, by the use of appropriate rituals, ceremonies and mechanical prayers.

Buddhist ethics contrasts sharply with Christian ethics in that it knows neither a personal God nor divine revelation and denies individual selfhood and the possibility of salvation through faith rather than through rigorous ethical and mental discipline practicable only to a few.

"Ethics and Morality (Buddhism)," *HERE*, New York, Scribner, Vol. V; Christmas Humphreys, *Buddhism*, Baltimore, Penguin, 1962; G. C. Pande, et al., *Buddhism*, Punjab University, 1969; Henry C. Warren, *Buddhism in Translations*, Cambridge, Harvard University, 1922.

SAPHIR P. ATHYAL

BULTMANN. RUDOLF. Bultmann (1884-   ), Professor of NT and Early Christian History at Marburg (1921-51), has been one of the most radical and influential contemporary theologians.

His *History of the Synoptic Tradition* (1921) pioneered form criticism, and his study of *Jesus* (1926) interpreted the gospel in existential terms. His famous essay on "New Testament and Mythology" (1941) outlined the program for demythologizing the gospel which he elaborated in later works.

Earlier liberals had claimed the presence of mythical elements (e.g., the virgin birth and the empty tomb) in the NT. Bultmann claimed that the whole ethos, thought forms and language of the NT is mythological, including the pre-scientific, three-decker view of the universe (heaven, earth, and hell). Angels and demons, sacramental grace, atonement by sacrifice, divine interventions, the coming of the heavenly redeemer, and eschatology derive from the mythical worlds of Jewish apocalyptic and Gnosticism. Taken literally and historically, they are obsolete and unacceptable to modern man. But the intention of myth is not to present an objective view of the world, but to express man's understanding of himself in his environment. The NT must, therefore, be demythologized and re-interpreted.

When Bultmann does this, the result has marked resemblances with the existentialism of Martin Heidegger, a point which Bultmann himself admits. The gospel presents man with the possibility of realizing his authentic existence by challenging him to choose between "human existence apart from faith" and "the life of faith." In the former, man is dominated by the "flesh," the sphere of visible, concrete, tangible reality (whether it be gross, sensual pleasure or pride of achievement). When man does so, he becomes weighed down with care. He loses his true life and becomes the slave of that which he desired to master. The authentic life of faith is based upon unseen, intangible realities. It means the abandonment of all self-contrived security. It is characterized in the NT as "life in faith" and "life after the Spirit" (Rom. 8:13ff.; Gal. 2:20ff.; 6:8; Phil 4:6). It is not an ascetic repudiation of the world, but keeping it at a distance in a spirit of "as if not" (I Cor. 7:29ff.; cf. Phil. 4:12).

The ground of the Christian life, is the gospel of the cross and resurrection of Jesus Christ. But in saying this Bultmann maintains a profound historical skepticism, which does not permit him to say what Jesus was like, but only that he lived and died. For we cannot penetrate beyond the Easter faith of the early church. It is in such faith that the believer today is said to understand himself and realize the "authentic life" or "self-commitment."

Through the gospel man is liberated from the flesh, the law and his own past. He is also liberated to love, which is man's "eschatological existence." "Love, as sheer existence for one's neighbor, is possible only to him who is free from himself" (Theology of the New Testament, I, p. 344). Faith is a renunciation of works and an act of decision in which man surrenders to grace. "Christ is the end of the law in that he gives man the freedom to live on a future basis and to live for the future, released from his past and himself" (Essays, p. 64).

Bultmann's rejection of an articulated ethical system follows from his view of the gospel, human existence and Scripture. The fundamental imperative is to love. This bids me love in such a way as to understand the claims of others who encounter me, and in discovering them I discover what to do.

Bultmann's radicalism goes beyond the older liberalism which stemmed from the Englightenment, and which presented Christianity as a form of altruistic morality. In many respects it is more Biblically orienta-

ted. At the same time it is more skeptical. Bultmann's understanding of myth, his principles of interpretation and his historical judgment have been challenged in many quarters. Bultmann's skepticism is unwarranted, his own teaching appears to be a sophisticated form of fideism which invites man to place blind trust in a message which Bultmann has been at pains to show to be in many ways untrustworthy. But if it is not, the relationship of faith and ethics to historical revelation requires a different approach.

📖 R. Bultmann, Theology of the New Testament, New York, Scribner, and London, S.C.M., I, 1953, II, 1955; Essays, London, S.C.M., 1955; Existence and Faith, London, Hodder, 1961; The Presence of Eternity: History and Eschatology, New York, Harper, 1958; Faith and Understanding, London, S.C.M., 1969; Jesus Christ and Mythology, London, S.C.M., 1958; Primitive Christianity, London, Thames and Hudson, 1956; The History of the Synoptic Tradition, Oxford, Blackwell, 1963; The Gospel of St. John, Oxford, Blackwell, 1971; H. W. Bartsch, ed., Kerygma and Myth, London, S.P.C.K., I, 1953; II, 1962; Carl E. Braaten and Roy A. Harrisville, Kerygma and History, Nashville, Abingdon, 1962; Ian Henderson, Rudolf Bultmann, London, Carey Kingsgate, 1965; C. W. Kegley, ed., The Theology of Rudolf Bultmann, New York, Harper, and London, S.C.M., 1966; J. Macquarrie, An Existentialist Theology, London, S.C.M., 1955; The Scope of Demythologizing, London, S.C.M., 1960; A. Malet, The Thought of Rudolf Bultmann, Shannon, Irish University, 1969; L. Malevez, The Christian Message and Myth, London, S.C.M., 1958; T. F. O'Meara and D. M. Weisser, eds., Rudolf Bultmann in Catholic Thought, New York, Herder, 1968; H. P. Owen, Revelation and Existence, Cardiff, University of Wales, 1967; W. Schmithals, An Introduction to the Theology of Rudolf Bultmann, London, S.C.M., 1968.

COLIN BROWN

BURIAL. See also *Cremation*. Burial is the interment of a corpse, including the accompanying ceremonies. Burial of the dead has been practiced longer than history has been recorded. The oldest memorials of human ·culture, some dating back to prehistory, are graves. With few exceptions, evidence points to a degree of ceremony attending the burial, for frequently tools, kitchen utensils, ornaments, and even horses, chariots, slaves, and wives were buried with the dead to insure proper comfort in the next life. Among the Hebrew people the highest respect shown to the dead was to be buried with his ancestors (I Kings 14:31). The greatest disgrace was to be crudely buried (Jer. 22:19), or left unburied for the dogs and birds to eat (I Sam. 17:46; II Kings 9:33-37). There is, however, no indication that Jews considered burial a necessary prerequisite to bliss in the afterlife.

Places of burial were caves (Gen. 23:1-9), within the environs of a city or fortress (I Kings 2:10; 11:43; 14:31), or in a private garden (John 19:41). Cremation was not generally practiced by the Hebrews; in fact, the idea was abhorrent to them as a violation of decency (Amos 2:1). The bodies of the honored dead were washed (Acts 9:37), and swathed in bandage-like wrappings in which spices were folded, and/or covered with a shroud (Matt. 27:59). A coffin was not generally used; ordinary burials simply interred the corpse with only a cloth wrapping. Formal mourning was customary (II Sam. 1:11, 12; Matt. 9:23).

The Christian church has generally preferred burial to cremation since the concept of the resurrection has deterred many from the voluntary destruction of the corpse. Elaborate funerary rites and burial were relatively unknown in Christian practice prior to the beginning of the twentieth century. MERRILL C. TENNEY

BUSINESS ETHICS. See also *Advertising; Capitalism; Credit; Industrial Espionage; Industrial Relations; Protestant Ethics; Work.* Business ethics is concerned with the moral implications of economic behavior.

"Business" is a generic term assigned to the array of socially-accepted customs and usages which allocate scarce resources and determine levels of output, income, and human welfare. Ostensibly, business activity—producing, exchanging, distributing and consuming—is undertaken to achieve the greatest good for the greatest number of people.

The moral principles which undergird business activity develop slowly over time. They proceed—just as business practices do—from the simple to the complex. They evolve through four stages. First, they emerge. Second, they become generally accepted and legally codified. Third, they are assaulted by forces which demand social change and which no longer accept the legally codified moral principles. And, finally, when they can no longer adjust to changing realities, the once-generally-accepted moral principles give way to new principles embodied in new institutions.

The American business ethic, which today is in the process of change, emerged from four ideological sources: namely, (1) the Protestant ethic, (2) classical economic theory, (3) social Darwinism, and (4) the social gospel.

The Protestant ethic, which served this nation from colonial times until just recently, emerged from the moralistic outlook of John Calvin's *Institutes of the Christian Religion.* But it did not stop there. As a work ethic, it took on peculiarly American connotations, rooted in the frontier spirit of individualism seasoned with large doses of pragmatism.

Basically, the American work ethic included the following principles: (1) God considers sloth, laziness, and idleness consummately evil, since "an idle mind is the devil's workshop." (2) Work is good because it is creative and because it is an act of Christian charity when the surplus from work supports others. (3) However, accumulation of wealth, as a concomitant of work, should not result in riotous or lavish living. It is good to produce, but it is evil to consume conspicuously. (4) Finally, it is not sinful to become rich, when men as stewards of God's bounty are frugal, save and invest. Capital expands, and the nation as a whole benefits.

Classical economic theory, based on the work of Adam Smith, supported a system of laissez-faire (q.v.), in which each man was responsible for his own welfare. In *The Theory of Moral Sentiments* (New York, Arlington), Smith asserted that man is motivated by greed and avarice. In *The Wealth of Nations* (New York, Modern Library), he turned man's selfishness to social advantage by explaining that free, competitive markets lead men, "as by an unseen hand," to socially desirable ends, since competition automatically regulates and harmonizes the selfish activities of men in the market place. Avaricious men, by competing with each other, benefit all by producing more goods at the lowest possible prices.

Social Darwinism (q.v.), made popular by William Graham Sumner's *Folkways* (New York, Dover), and Andrew Carnegie's *Gospel of Wealth* (Cambridge, Harvard University, 1962), stressed "survival of the fittest." Following the Civil War, there were many cases in which tough, avaricious men seized the nation's natural resources and instruments of production, all in the name of nature and "nature's God." Social Darwinists stood the Protestant Ethic on its head, by living ostentatiously and by disregarding the needs and rights of others, and they perverted Smith's competitive balance by erecting monopolies and quasi-monopolies, where prices were set by producers and not by markets.

The social gospel (q.v.) movement—coming at the turn of the century—was a reaction to the excesses of monopolistic, laissez-faire capitalism. Theologians such as Walter Rauschenbusch (q.v.) questioned the inevitability of poverty, subsistence wages, and excessive profits, and sought to substitute good works for the unseen hand of the unregulated market place. Social gospel theorists, however, did not believe that good works depend on the beneficence or charity of great capital accumulators. Instead, good works depend on the power of the state to put things right (cf. *Socialism*). Social gospel advocates, therefore, supported national socio-economic programs such as welfare, social security, minimum wages, guaranteed family incomes, child-labor laws and excess profits taxes.

In the 1960s and 70s, the tug of war between the competitive, individualistic ethic and the gospel of social amelioration became especially pronounced. Revolutionary communism, in the guise of the New Left, sought to exploit this situation, but made little headway. The social gospel, on the other hand, gained increasing approval from business leaders, legislators, jurists, and labor leaders. The American liberal establishment, compounded of all these elements, is rooted in Fabian socialism, but the old Puritan ethic comes through in the form of the gospel of good works, as liberalism seeks to save the nation through centralized monetary, fiscal, and social policies designed to expand human welfare.

In summary, the American business ethic emerged from the Protestant ethic. It became codified in a body of customs and laws, centered on Adam Smith's free, competitive market. It was turned upside down by monopolists in the 1880s and 90s, practitioners of *The Gospel of Wealth*. This business synthesis was assaulted by the social gospel theorists, who no longer recognized the legal and moral principles of laissez-faire.

Today, in consequence of this dialectical process, business morality is undergoing monumental change destined to usher in a new business ethic. The key to a generally-agreed-upon and accepted new business ethic is the balanced synthesis of individual freedom and social cooperation.

SIDNEY A. WILLIAMS

CALLING. See *Vocation.*

CALVINISTIC ETHICS. Calvinistic Ethics depends on revelation. The distinction between right and wrong is not identified by an empirical discovery of natural law, as with Aristotle and Thomas Aquinas, nor by the logical formalism of Kant, and certainly not by Utilitarianism's impossible calculation of the greatest good for the greatest number, but by God's revelation of the Ten Commandments. This revelation came: first in God's act of creating man in his own image so that certain basic moral principles were implanted in his heart, later to be vitiated by sin; second there were some special instructions given to Adam and Noah, which no doubt overlapped and expanded the innate endowment; third, the more comprehensive revelation to Moses; plus, fourth, the various subsidiary precepts in the remainder of the Bible.

Although the medieval church knew the Ten Commandments—in his defense of free will Pelagius even taught that it was possible to obey them perfectly, and the main body of the church came to hold that their observance earned merit toward salvation—Calvin initiated an almost completely new development in systematically using the Ten Commandments as the basis for ethics. In his *Institutes* II 8, he gives an Exposition of the Moral Law, approximately fifty pages.

His defense of such a long exposition is that "the commands and prohibitions always imply more than the words express . . . In all the commandments . . . a part is expressed instead of the whole . . . The best rule, then, I conceive will be that the exposition be directed to the design of the precept . . . as the end of the fifth commandment is, that honor may be given to them to whom God assigns it . . . " (II.viii.8).

In the main body of the exposition Calvin writes as follows on the sixth commandment.

"The end of this precept is, that since God has connected mankind together in a kind of unity, every man ought to consider himself as charged with the safety of all. In short, then, all violence and injustice, and every kind of mischief, which may injure the body of our neighbor, are forbidden to us. . . . The Divine Legislator. . . . intends this rule to govern the soul. . . . Mental homicide therefore is likewise prohibited. . . . 'Whosoever hateth his brother is a murderer' " (II. viii.39).

Following this lead of Calvin the Westminster divines devoted questions 91-151 of the Larger Catechism to the moral law. Take question 139 as an example:

Q. 139. What are the sins forbidden in the seventh commandment?

A. The sins forbidden in the seventh commandment, besides the neglect of the duties required, are: adultery, fornication, rape, incest, sodomy, and all unnatural lusts; all unclean imaginations, thoughts, purposes, and affections; all corrupt or filthy communications, or listening thereunto; wanton looks, impudent or light behavior, immodest apparel, prohibiting of lawful, and dispensing with unlawful marriages; allowing, tolerating, keeping of stews, and resorting to them; entangling vows of single life, undue delay of marriage; having more wives or husbands than one at the same time; unjust divorce or desertion; idleness, gluttony, drunkenness, unchaste company; lascivious songs, books, pictures, dancings, stage-plays, and all other provocations to, or acts of, uncleanness either in ourselves or others.

This highlights the difference in moral standards between Calvinism and Fundamentalism. In the USA Arminian churches have often required their members to avoid the movies on the ground that Hollywood was lascivious. At present (1973) the movies are sometimes worse than that: outright pornographic. But then, some books and magazines are pornographic. Should a church then forbid all books and magazines? Calvinism stays with the Bible and outlaws neither the movies nor books in general; but prohibits "lascivious songs, books, pictures, dancings, and stage-plays."

Further reading of the Larger Confession will show, to the surprise of some, how very ample and detailed the law of God actually is. Therefore Calvinistic ministers and writers have with some regularity expounded the Ten Commandments. An Anglican Example is Ezekiel Hopkins, Bishop of Derry, (1633-1689), whose exposition occupies 300 pages.

These expositions of the detailed application of the moral law are uniformly prefaced by some remarks on sin, grace, and legalism. The Romish merit system made this necessary. Today two other views necessitate the same theological background. First there is a pietistic view that depends for guidance on the direct instructions of the Spirit. The Scriptural directives are regarded as insufficient, or even as inapplicable in the age of grace. Therefore a person must receive an answer to prayer in order to know whether a particular action is right or wrong. Calvinism stays with the Bible and disallows later claims to special revelation.

The second factor that necessitates the theological background is liberalism's novel definition of legalism (q.v.). Legalism used to be the theory that man could completely or partially merit salvation by obeying the law; faith was then not the sole means of justification. But contemporary liberalism defines legalism as any attempt to distinguish right from wrong by rules, precepts, or commandments. The argument is that no rule fits every case—there are exceptions; or even that every situation is utterly unique so that rules are always impossible. Therefore each situation must be uniquely (not judged, but) perceived, and (usually) love decides what to do. Love then, of course, sanctions abortion, homosexuality, and anything one does lovingly. The Apostle Paul wrote to the Corinthians about this sort of thing.

Calvinism defines sin as any want of conformity to or transgression of the law of God. Saved by grace, that is, saved from sin and its effects, the Christian is sanctified by an ever more complete obedience to the Ten Commandments.

Gordon H. Clark, *A Christian View of Men and Things*, Grand Rapids, Eerdmans, 1952; _____, *Religion, Reason, and Revelation*, Nutley, New Jersey, Presbyterian and Reformed, 1961.

GORDON H. CLARK

CANNIBALISM. Cannibalism was worldwide when the modern missionary expansion began. Claims that it sprang from food shortage are not proved. Related to social organization, occupational rituals, war ceremonials and sacrificial systems, cannibalism institutionalized revenge in war and sorcery, humiliating an enemy, communal justice against manslayers and the acquistion of *mana*. (*Mana* is an impersonal supernatural force to which certain primitive people attribute good fortune, magical powers, etc.) Parts of dismembered bodies were given to persons in specific tribal roles to transmit the enemy's natural capacities— physical, intellectual, and procreational. Bodies offered for human sacrifice in temple-building, canoe-launching, war, and headhunting expeditions were shared by the group. Headhunting provided skulls with *soulforce* to strengthen the tribe and assure perpetuity. Outgroup cannibalism was vicious. Less common ingroup cannibalism was restrained, honorific and *mana*-transmitting. Missionaries encountered cannibalism as a basic pagan, demonic value system and attitude. Missions and governments have now virtually terminated cannibalism; nevertheless it sometimes re-emerges in antiwestern nativistic cults.

ALAN R. TIPPETT

CANON LAW. Canon Law is a codification of the rules of Christian life which are the basis of church discipline. The word "canon" reflects Gal. 6:15f., but in this context probably denotes the sum of canons. The "law" is basically the divine law revealed in Scripture; but then the human law developed in its application. The original rulings were made by early synods and councils in response to specific issues. Collections were already being made as early as the fifth century and a code of canons was recognized in France by the time of Charlemagne.

The final codification in the West came with papal centralization in the eleventh century and was primarily the work of Gratian, whose Decretum underlies the present *corpus iuris canonici*. With this codification the whole system of ecclesiastical discipline underwent astonishing expansion. Ecclesiastical courts flourished, with Rome as the court of final appeal. Ecclesiastical cases, which would cover all offenses by the clergy, were carefully distinguished from civil cases—the exemption of clergy from criminal law being the central issue between Henry II of England and Becket. Faculties of canon law, required to train personnel, rivaled those of civil law in the medieval universities.

Canon law covers four main areas: (1) personal, dealing with clergy and monks; (2) material, dealing with sacraments, liturgy, etc.; (3) judicial, dealing with marriages, etc.; and (4) penal.

Although it embodies divine law, canon law is primarily ecclesiastical, so that the church may change or amend it or dispense from it. Although some of its forms are obviously open to criticism, it is in itself unavoidable. Any church which orders its affairs is bound to have canon law, however simple.   GEOFFREY W. BROMILEY

CAPITALISM. See also *Communism; Competition; Corporate Responsibility; Socialism.* Capitalism is an economic system based upon private property, private profit and private initiative in business. Socialism as a counter-system substitutes the state for the individual in economic enterprise.

I. *History.* Capitalism developed in Medieval times when Europe moved toward a commercial economy. Distant markets for textiles required capital to fund increased production and shipping. By the seventeenth century, capitalism had replaced feudalism as the economic system of Europe.

The nineteenth century was the era of classical capitalism. Adam Smith argued for laissez-faire capitalism—self-regulation in a free market. His theory was the success formula for the Industrial Revolution (q.v.) in Europe and the USA. Individual initiative was stimulated, productivity increased, and the standard of living climbed upward. It was also the era when multimillionaires and giant corporations were made with the aid of government policies that favored domestic protection and international expansion of industry.

Capitalism was challenged by the Russian Revolution in 1914. Marx had foreseen the potential inequalities of free enterprise. In reaction, he said that the state must protect the worker and control the use of capital for the public good. Lenin, seeing that economic power was tied to the government, the church and class structure, called for a social revolution as the only alternative for changing the economic system.

Classical capitalism was also tested by the post-World War I economy in the USA. During the 1920s, international markets declined and production excesses grew. Consequently, unemployment and reduced consumer demands became key factors in The Great Depression. The public response came in Roosevelt's New Deal with the introduction of new controls on private trusts, individual wealth and individual initiative.

Since that time, the USA and other Western nations have become "mixed economies." Capitalism in the post-industrial society is a mixture of public and private control of the means of production. Examples of classical capitalism are still cited in West Germany and Japan. But every nation is under pressure to invest a greater share of its capital in human resources; e.g., education, health and safety. The hope is that this investment will give capitalism the new knowledge and the expanding market that it needs for the future.

II. *Ethical Issues.* Capitalism has been generally supportive of Christianity. The concept of private property has been a buffer against the establishment of a religious state. Private profit has been an incentive for economic growth that has raised the standard of living for all people. The freedom for individual initiative in business has helped maintain the margin of freedom for religious choice. But the compatibility of capitalism and Christianity has also produced problems that are looming large in the contemporary scene; produced problems that are looming large in the contemporary scene.

A. *The Nature of Wealth.* The early church opposed capitalistic trends because the sin of avarice was related to the accumulation of wealth and the sin of usury was said to be committed in money-lending. Jesus did not speak directly against wealth and money-lending, but he did emphasize the danger of riches and the rich man's responsibility for the poor. Evidently, the continuing test of the capitalist is the priority of his love and the purpose of his riches.

B. *The Doctrine of Man.* Classical capitalism was defined by Adam Smith with an optimistic view of man. He assumed "automatic harmony" in a free market because the goodness of man would ultimately check his competitive self-interest. Time and the success of capitalism have blurred this theological concept. As the roots of capitalism have come under attack, however, the doctrine of man is again a part of the debate.

C. *Culture and Christianity.* The Protestant Reformation was a reaction against the institutional domination of individuals. As every man was declared a priest and every occupation a divine office, the discipline of labor and frugal living became an ethic of work. In a rising capitalism system, it could also be expected that wealth might be a reward of that discipline. Therefore, capitalism, Protestantism and Western culture grew hand in hand. Radicals have singled out these same institutions for revolutionary change. The church is attacked, not only for the values that it holds, but also because it is part of the system. Capitalism may be compatible with Christianity, but if the two are inseparable, it could be fatal for both.

D. *Materialism.* Capitalism cannot stand still. It depends upon expanding markets for its existence. The inherent danger of that dependence is materialism. Products take on distorted values and wealth is measured by material goods. Then, as natural markets shrink, new consumer demands must be created by planned obsolescence. The result is a direct violation of Jesus' warning against the love of riches.

E. *Inequality.* Ideally, capitalism in a "pure market" would eliminate poverty because of full employment. In practice, however, capitalism produced greater relative inequality as new expectations divided the rich and the poor. Labor negotiations, anti-trust acts, income taxes, and governmental controls have been used to counteract this trend. Still, the revolution for economic equality continues. The question for the future is whether or not a "mixed economy" can retain the value of individual freedom while recapturing the sense of social responsibility. Evangelical Christianity has a stake in that question because it is a moral issue with implications for the future of the church.   DAVID L. McKENNA

CAPITAL PUNISHMENT. See also *Punishment; Retribution.* Capital punishment is specified both in the OT (Gen. 9:6) and in the NT (Rom. 13:4). It is implied in Gen. 4:14 and approved in Acts 25:11. Capital punishment is therefore an integral part of Christian ethics.

Contemporary efforts to abolish capital punishment proceed on a non-Christian view of man, a secular theory of criminal law, and a low estimate of the value of life.

The low evaluation of human life occurs in the liberal penology that holds criminal law to be solely for the purpose of rehabilitation. Not only does liberalism think that the murder of a human being is too minor a crime to justify execution; the theory consistently implies that no crime should ever be punished. Justice and punishment are deprecated as "irrational vengeance." This is a basic difference between Christian and liberal ethics. As such it can be resolved only by a decision on ultimate principles, to wit, whether ethical norms are established by divine decree, and secondarily what obligations God confers on civil government.

The liberal arguments are superficial. One is that capital punishment does not deter. Obviously it deters the executed criminal. If it does not deter others, the reply is that the law may not deter, but its enforcement will. In 1968 there were 7,000 murders and no executions, in 1969 there were about 8,500 and no executions, and in 1970 some 10,000 and no executions. But if the law had been enforced, and 5,000 murders had been executed in 1968, and 7,000 in 1969, could anyone doubt that there would have been fewer than 10,000 murders in 1970?

A worse argument is that only the poor are convicted and the wealthy escape. Actually the courts are so lenient and the public so permissive that nearly everybody escapes. If the objection were true, however, the answer would not be to abolish capital punishment and let the number of murders keep on soaring, but it would be to put honest judges on the bench and in the box jurors who are more compassionate toward the victim than toward the criminal.

The most impressive argument is that sometimes an innocent man might be executed. Once again, with our present courts, this never or almost never happens. Even murderers like Sirhan Sirhan, whose act was seen by a dozen witnesses, are not executed. Yet if just one innocent man is executed ...? Then consider: Do you prefer 10,000 murders to save one innocent man rather than one tragedy to save 5000 lives? But of course this type of argument is superficial and irrelevant. God gave the right of capital punishment to human governments. He intended it to be used wisely and justly, but he intended it to be used. Abolition of the death penalty presupposes the falsity of Christian principles.   GORDON H. CLARK

CARDINAL VIRTUES. See *Virtue, Virtues.*

CARNELL, EDWARD JOHN. Carnell (1919-1967) was primarily a Christian apologist. *Christian Commitment,* his major work in ethics, constitutes a moral argument for the Christian world view. Common moral judgments, the basis of human fellowship, evidence an "intuitive participation in the moral and spiritual environments" which are grounded in the nature of God. Carnell argued that moral right is what God wills, but that his will must be anticipated in human experience if its truth is to be recognized in the propositions of Scripture.
◻ E. J. Carnell, *Christian Commitment,* New York, Macmillan, 1957; _____, *Kingdom of Love and Pride of Life,* Grand Rapids, Eerdmans, 1960.   ROY W. BUTLER

CARTELS. See also *Monopoly.* Cartels are voluntary combination of independent private enterprises supplying like services or products to limit competition and control price. Each participant is given an exclusive geographic area, or a quota. The monopoly created is subject to invasion by non-member firms if profits are excessive and suppressing them may be impossible. Members may surreptitiously sell outside the syndicate or sell above quota or below price. Although illegal in America, cartels (called pools) are supported by some countries with government representatives on the board and special courts to enforce and to settle disputes. Through guarantees not to invade the realm of a monopolist, international cartels strengthen monopoly.

HARVEY A. MAERTIN

CASUISTRY. See also *Canon Law.* Although the word "casuistry" (from Latin *casus*) is usually associated with the Middle Ages and Roman Catholicism, one finds earlier examples in Stoicism and Judaism. In essence casuistry is simply the application of law or laws to the shifting circumstances of daily life. All conceivable contingencies are taken into account and a detailed list of rules is provided so that the permissibility or culpability of an act may be determined. The matter is complicated, of course, when motives and ends are also considered.

In its first proclamation Christianity was strongly opposed to legalistic casuistry, which, as Jesus saw, could easily corrupt or erode the divine commandments by human traditions. Nevertheless, the problem which casuistry was trying to solve, namely, how circumstances may alter cases, remained a genuine one; and it might be argued that our Lord himself practiced legitimate casuistry when, e.g., he showed that the claim of compassion takes precedence of the sabbath. In this case the point is, of course, that detailed rulings, even though right in themselves, may be overruled by the divine commandments.

Christian casuistry underwent its first main development, however, in connection with penitential discipline. As penitents confessed various offenses, it was quickly seen that even the same sins are not equally culpable because of the many variable factors (cf. the degrees of homicide in secular law). Penitentials were thus composed to try to assess precisely the degrees of culpability and the appropriate spiritual discipline. But penitentials also served a positive purpose in this regard, for they formed the basis of counsel as to the permissibility of certain lines of action. They could show how, given specific circumstances, an action is perhaps justifiable even though it would normally be wrong because (a) it is more right than the opposite, or (b) it is an exception to the command, or (c) it falls within a qualification of the command, or (d) a lofty inner motive transcends the external violation.

The growth of canon law obviously speeded the development of casuistry, since canon law provided a codification of rulings which called for detailed application and reciprocal counter-balancing. We thus find in the medieval period a new set of penitential *summae* in which the church's canons are applied in detail both to penitential systems and also to spiritual direction. After the Council of Trent a comprehensive system was worked out and training in casuistry was recognized to be an important part of preparation for the priesthood.

Inevitably differences of opinion arose in casuistical theory. Some groups took a more rigorous view of what is permissible, others took a moderate course, while others again, after the manner of attorneys seeking loopholes in tax laws, stretched the laws to the limit of credibility. The battle between the severe Jansenists and the elastic Jesuits in seventeenth century France is instructive here. The Jansenists were tutiorists, allowing an action only when there was overwhelming authority in its favor. The Jesuits, on the other hand, were probabilists (cf. *Probabilism*) allowing an action if some support could be found for it. The moral acrobatics which resulted from the Jesuit practice are devastatingly analysed in Pascal's *Provincial Letters*.

Casuistry bears a certain resemblance to situational ethics (q.v.), for both deal with action in the complicated circumstances of actual life. Situation ethics might ultimately build up a set of precedents (as in common law), which would fulfill much the same purpose as casuistry. Similarly, situation ethics can lead to some judgments in which wrong and right seem to switch places no less oddly than in casuistry. Nevertheless, situation ethics is not essentially legal as casuistry is. It operates with a much simplified master-criterion rather than a body of detailed rulings. It does not try to work out a schedule of culpability nor to offer a set of judgments in advance to cover possible contingencies. It sees only particularity in situations and therefore in moral acts.

In contrast casuistry presupposes codified law. It is the application of rules, many of them absolute, to practical situations. It does not operate with a master-criterion, although some rules obviously take precedence over others. It tries to cover every possible situation so that an authoritative judgment may be given on what should or should not be done. It allows little place for individual responsibility. It also tries to be comprehensive, so that not much room is left for the category of indifferent things in which contrary courses may equally well be adopted according to other factors. If situation ethics opens the door too broadly to individualistic standards, casuistry clamps it too tightly shut against ethical freedom.

The ethical weaknesses of casuistry are evident. It can be niggling in codification to the point of absurdity. It almost invites the reasoning which can make a thing legally right even when it is patently wrong from an ethical standpoint. It substitutes an externally legislated ethics for an inner ethics of responsibility. It represents a surrender of the individual to the skilled expert who can interpret and even manipulate the law. It threatens true morality at the root by attempting to impose a human scale of ethical value or guilt. Even when practiced with the greatest caution it can hardly avoid being legalistic in the bad sense. Even if self-justification is not expected from keeping the law, as may well be the case, life is still regulated by an intricate code which impedes moral growth on the one side and obscures the weightier matters of the law on the other.

Nevertheless, the principle of casuistry should not be thrown out with the abuse. If hard cases make bad law, life consists of cases, some of which are hard. The commands of God have to be worked out in the stuff of daily life, and, while right conduct is not so consistently obscure as some modern systems make out, many ethical choices are difficult. Casuistry recognizes that the commands of God are the criteria and not just a generalized concept. In ethics, therefore, some consideration must be given to the way in which these criteria apply in specific circumstances, and some guidance must be offered even if in the last resort the Christian must form his own judgment and bear responsibility for his own act. The point is, however, that the commands must not be endlessly multiplied. The ethical advice must not itself become a cramping law. Nor must the application be made in such a way that the ethically right can be evaded in favor of the legally possible. The aim of a true casuistry should be to help Christians develop a mature and responsible moral judgment as they tackle the business of being Christians, subject to God's commands, in a fallen world. But this after all is not just casuistry; it is Christian ethics as such.

GEOFFREY W. BROMILEY

CATEGORICAL IMPERATIVE. See *Duty; Kant.*

CATHOLIC ETHICS. See *Aquinas and Roman Catholic Ethics; Roman Catholic Ethics.*

CELEBRATION. See *Joy.*

CELIBACY. See also *Virginity.* Celibacy (from Latin *caelebs*) is the unmarried state. For no groups is this commanded in Scripture. Some disciples (e.g., Peter) were married and the bishop or deacon should be the husband of one wife. There might be voluntary celibacy, as for specific service. Jesus was not married. He speaks of those who become eunuchs for the kingdom's sake. Paul in I Cor. 7 shows why the widower or widow might better serve the Lord by not remarrying.

Emphasis on celibacy seems to have been promoted first by heretical dualism. Rejection of the physical as evil led to suspicion of marriage. Monasticism made celibacy an ideal and introduced the idea of permanent commitment. While dualism had some influence here, so too did the ideas of total consecration and following the evangelical counsels or counsels of perfection, i.e., things recommended but not commanded. By the third and fourth centuries many Fathers were extolling the superior merits of celibacy.

A movement was also developing to impose it on the clergy. Already it was preferred at Ancyra (314), and Nicea (325) moved toward a prohibition of marriage after ordination. This position of ordination of the married but not marriage of the ordained became the rule in the Eastern church. The West, however, pressed for complete celibacy. This was adopted at Carthage (390) and backed by civil enactment. It met strong resistance, however, and only after Gregory VII (1074) and Urban II (1089) threatened deposition for marriage

did it become established. Even then exceptions were made in the Uniate churches and unofficial unions replaced legitimate ones in many circles.

The Reformation effected a sweeping change in this area. Zwingli married in Zürich, Luther in Wittenberg, and Cranmer in England. Finding a wife for Calvin was an amusing interlude in Strassburg. As Erasmus wryly observed, what many called the Lutheran "tragedy" had really turned out to be a comedy, since it always ended in a wedding. Fortunately there were ex-nuns and widows to match with the new noncelibates.

In spite of pressure, Trent voted to retain celibacy, nullifying all acts performed by a priest after marriage. But the issue was not closed. Old Catholics have accepted marriage, modern states recognize the marriage of clergy, and in recent years there has been agitation thoughout the Roman Catholic world, resisted thus far, for the repeal of the celibacy rule.

The main arguments for celibacy are (1) the danger of hereditary priesthood, (2) the incongruity of marriage and ministry, and (3) the need for full consecration and hence for detachment from family cares. The third argument is strong and Biblical but it is hardly a basis for compulsory and permanent celibacy.

In contrast it may be said that (1) marriage is from God, (2) married clergy may often be better equipped to deal with personal problems, and (3) celibacy, while a calling and blessing for some, may be a burden if imposed on others. Above all, Scripture has no binding rule of celibacy for any Christians. Legislation to the contrary is thus invalidated from the very outset.

GEOFFREY W. BROMILEY

CENSORSHIP. Censorship comes from the Latin word meaning to value or tax. It refers to aggressive restriction or suppression of statements, opinions, or ideas, generally written, of such value, negative or positive, that the authority seeks to prevent their publication or dissemination.

Generally censorship is applied in two kinds of cases: (1) national security, and (2) religious doctrine and morals. It is usually carried out in two ways: (1) post facto, or suppression after publication, and (2) prior restraint, for instance, a court order prohibiting a periodical from publishing an article. Post facto censorship allows for publication subject to libel and civil suits for damages; prior restraint, which is particularly distasteful to civil libertarians, completely negates freedom of speech and the press.

Censorship poses the fundamental question of whether an authority, government, or church, should decide or whether men are competent to decide what should be published or read.

Scriptural Basis. It is difficult to find justification in Scripture for censorship involving national security or personal behavior. Jesus Christ is the source of truth (John 1:17), and indeed, is truth itself (John 1:14). The Lord's truth will endure forever (Ps. 117:2; Matt. 24:35), and therefore, believers ultimately need not fear falsehood, distortion, or dissemination of human information.

In the OT theocracy, those who preached idolatry, even a spouse or a friend, were to be put to death (Deut. 13:18). But this extreme censorship applied only to statements about "false gods," that is, idolatry. When Patricia Buckley Bozell, managing editor of the conservative Catholic magazine *Triumph,* rushed to the podium at Catholic University and struck a militant women's liberation advocate for remarks about the virgin Mary, Mrs. Bozell defended her action by saying that her first loyalty was to God and her responsibility against blasphemy was greater than her responsibility to act as a neutral journalist.

The Bible relates incidents of censorship, but generally these were ungodly acts. King Jehoiakim of Judah censored Jeremiah's scroll of prophecy from the Lord much as a World War II military censor snipped a GI's letter about combat maneuvers (Jer. 36). When King Ahab of Israel spurned the prophet Micaiah because his prophecies about Ahab were always bad, King Jehoshaphat admonished him, "Let not the king say so" (I Kings 22:8); this seems to say, "The king shouldn't censor the prophet." Christians burned their books about magic in Ephesus but this was not "book-burning" because these Christians acted voluntarily.

Historical Background. Plato, Augustine, and Machiavelli argued that those qualified to identify evil should be empowered to prevent its dissemination. Aquinas stated: "Human laws do not forbid all vices . . . but only the more grievous vices . . . and chiefly those that are injurious to others, without the prohibition of which human society could not be maintained." Aristotle, Justice Oliver Wendell Holmes, Jr., and John Dewey, contended that a man is free only so long as he can make his own choices.

During the days of the early church and the Middle Ages there was extreme censorship. The common law of seditious libel provided that persons could be prosecuted for "any comment about the government which could be construed to have the bad tendency of lowering it in the public's esteem or of disturbing the peace. . . ." But in the last half of this milennium, concomitant with the spread of Protestantism, government and church have both withdrawn many of their restraints.

In *Areopagitica,* a plea for unlicensed printing in England in 1644, John Milton argued that restraints are "an undervaluing and villifying of the whole nation." Licensing "hinders and retards the importation of our richest merchandise, truth," Milton said, adding that "a state governed by the rules of justice and fortitude, or a church built and founded upon the rock of faith and true knowledge, cannot be so pusillanimous." John Stuart Mill said in his essay *On Liberty* in 1859 that the sole reason for interfering with the liberty or action of another person is self-protection. "However positive anyone's persuasion may be, not only of the falsity but of the pernicious consequence—not only of the pernicious consequence but the immorality and impiety of an opinion," Mill said, "yet if, in pursuance of that private judgment, though backed by the public judgment of his country or his contemporaries, he prevents the opinion from being heard in its defense, he assumes infallibility. And so far from the assumption being less objectionable or less dangerous because the opinion is called immoral or impious, this is the case of all others in which it is most fatal." Said Meiklejohn: "When men govern themselves, it is they—and no one else—who must pass judgment upon unwisdom and unfairness and danger. And that means that unwise ideas must have a hearing as well as wise ones, unfair as well as fair, dangerous as well as safe, un-American as well as American."

Contemporary Situation. The First Amendment to the Bill of Rights interpreted literally, in the view of a minority including Justice Hugo L. Black, imperatively commands that no statement, even a libelous one, may be repressed.

Recognizing the problem of Mark Antony's funeral oration, which skillfully incited mob violence, and heeding Justice Holmes' aphorism that free speech does not apply to a man who yells "fire" in a crowded theater, the Supreme Court has adopted several· tests to balance authority and freedom, weighing legitimate government interest in the preserving of order against individual freedom of expression. Following the philosophy expressed by Justice Holmes in Abrams vs. U.S., 1919, "the best test of truth is the power of the thought to get itself accepted in the competition of the market," the court recog-

nized, in the words of Justice Louis D. Brandeis, in Whitney vs. California, 1927, "no damage flowing from speech can be deemed clear and present, where the incidence of the evil apprehended is so imminent that it may befall before there is opportunity for full discussion . . . only an emergency can justify repression."

Chief Justice Charles Evans Hughes wrote the Supreme Court opinion in Near vs. Minnesota, 1931, which struck down as unconstitutional a state law that allowed state officials to enjoin the publication of "a malicious, scandalous, and defamatory newspaper, magazine, or other periodical." Justice Hughes said the statute was of "the essence of censorship" because it "does not deal with punishments; it provides for no punishment, except in case of contempt for violation of the court's order, but for suppression and injunction—that is, for restraint upon publication."

National Security. While debating the Espionage Act of 1917, Congress deleted a provision that would have given the President broad powers in war time to prohibit the publication "of any information relating to the national defense, which, in his judgment, is of such a character that it is or might be useful to the enemy." In 1957 Congress rejected a recommendation by the U.S. Commission on Government Security making it a crime to disclose "information classified 'secret' or 'top secret.'"

In *The New York Times* vs. U.S. and U.S. vs. *The Washington Post,* the Supreme Court ruled that the newspapers could publish the so-called "Pentagon Papers" about the Defense Department's secret study of the Vietnam war. Justice Black stated: "Both the history and language of the First Amendment support the view that the press must be left free to publish news, whatever the source, without censorship, injunction, or prior restraints."

Obscenity (q.v.). The philosophic justification that allows even limited censorship for pornography (q.v.) becomes clear by applying the balancing test: the truly obscene is said to be totally worthless, and, therefore, cannot be balanced.

As of 1970 five federal laws prohibited distribution of obscene materials—dealing with mails, imports, broadcasts, and interstate transporation.

The U.S. Commission on Obscenity and Pornography in 1970 recommended repeal of all laws prohibiting the distribution of explicit sexual materials to consenting adults. The commission majority said it found no evidence that explicit sexual materials play a significant role in causing crime, deviancy, or severe emotional disturbance. Three commissioners, dissenting, called the recommendations "a magna carta for the pornographer." President Nixon, rejecting the recommendations, said "The warped and brutal portrayal of sex in books, plays, magazines, and movies, if not halted and reversed, could poison the wellspring of American and Western culture and civilization."   WESLEY G. PIPPERT

CENSURE. See also *Discipline.* This term, which comes from the Latin *censor*, has the general sense of blame, or correction. It corresponds to the Biblical admonition to be given to erring brethren. Its first use in the church is thus doctrinal, as in the censuring of heresies. Then the ecclesiastical censure is a specific penalty for grave faults. The censure is given by the church and may therefore be withdrawn by it.
                    GEOFFREY W. BROMILEY

CHANCE. See also *Accident; Choice; Free Will; Gambling.* Uncertainty concerning causes of events is designated as chance. Views of chance range from the seldom held belief that incidents occur without any preconditioning (Tychism), to the belief that everything happens as a result of foreordination.

"Probabilities" or "accidents" are terms used when the catalytic forces producing the happening are unknown. William James asserted that chance is the negation of necessity. Wagering is largely based upon this uncertainty.

Natural scientists in repeating their experiments exercise faith in a causality that inevitably produces identical results each time the experiment is performed. Natural law is generally accepted as unalterable and its reliability is seldom questioned. Man has no choice in many obvious aspects of life, such as the place, time, and nature of his birth.

Theists (cf. *Theism*) face the dilemma of desiring freedom granted by a God who requires accountability from man, or of wanting the comforting assurance that God has made all things and is intimately concerned with and has a plan for everyone. The first position can lead to belief in a transcendent God approaching Deism. The latter may result in a belief in a solely immanent Deity. The NT reconciles both emphases.   W. IVAN HOY

CHARACTER. See also *Development; Christian Education; Sanctification.* Character grows out of basic assumptions. This relation of being to ideas is often denigrated. But it was no accident that early Christians were first "believers" then the people of "the Way." We never advance behavior by depreciating belief or ethics.

A basic tenent of present academic "orthodoxy" is the repudiation of "Puritanism." Hugh Hefner and others have become very wealthy preaching this doctrine. The difficulty really is to find the dragon of Puritanism against whom the huge sword of *Playboy* is wielded. If we could find the enemy we would be assaulted by guilt-producing promoters of character, it is said. Although not radical Puritans, early American leaders were very concerned about morals and religion. Norman Cousins refers to extensive letters between Adams and

Jefferson in which they even had time to discuss the question of "interpolations" in the Bible and the relation of Scripture to morals and politics (*In God We Trust*, New York, Harper, 1958, p. 261). Early American character was guided by men of character and concern about Biblical truth and relevance.

The psychological approach to character contains many provocative suggestions. Personality is part of the person, and behavioral patterns can be classified and studied. Freud, as is well known, related behavior to childhood urges, particularly sex. Psychology has been interested in the adjustment and accommodation problems of what are sometimes called "strong characters." The common conclusions suggest that "strong characters" have major difficulties because they live in "a world of change." Socrates was faced with this dilemma having just read Heraclitus whose emphasis on change is hard to upstage. What is often forgotten in this context is that "strong characters" do not weep for themselves but for "adjustment people" who eventually must change because of "strong characters" such as Einstein, Socrates, and Jesus.

Adjustment in human relations is a continuing necessity; however, a climate of thought and ethics which eliminates all operational absolutes may be fast moving merchandise in academic circles but very unrealistic in business, society, or even communes.

Character as illustrated in a lonely stand by Luther may get few votes. Has anyone made a study of the limited number of major leaders in human history who were elected? Many such leaders were charismatic, dedicated people of basic belief and simple faithfulness. Some feel Luther was a foolish, impractical dogmatist. James Atkinson summarizes this view: "For Luther to take a lone stand against the church was to declare himself in the wrong and to forfeit his life and salvation" (*The Trial of Luther*, New York, Stein and Day, 1971, p. 65).

Others feel Luther was the relevant mind. When the crowd rushes to one side of the boat the relevant thing to do may be to lean as far the other way as possible. This demands character above limited humanism based on understanding valid relevance in the age. These may be found in both the Bible and the newspaper. As Karl Barth observed, "Both the language of the Bible and the language of the papers pointed to the same fact: history is not the bearer of humanization" (Ruben A. Alves, *A Theology of Human Hope*, Washington, D.C., Corpus, 1969, p. 44).

Only a new nature indwelt by the Holy Spirit has the character staying power needed in stress conditions. Many well-meaning humanists have become bitter under the continued discovery of human frailty, graft, cruelty and inhumanity to man in such occupations. Christian missionaries with the new nature of Christ have character which not only endures but transforms. Russia and China know they are vulnerable to this kind of character dedication, and they keep the various "curtains" pulled to such God-propelled persons.

Any man in any period of history with this kind of basic integrity will live in tension, not human relaxation. It is hard for vote-oriented minds to comprehend the strong dialog of Calvin, Luther, Zwingli, or Arminius. The fact which reveals character is that men stand and fight in the area of their greatest values. Calvin, Luther, Zwingli, and Arminius honestly felt the most significant values were in religion and faith and were willing to debate at that point. The world is richer because of them. We reveal our values and basic character when the only issue we debate with emotion is a change in pay scale.

WALTER H. JOHNSON

CHARISMATIC MOVEMENT. See also *Holy Spirit*. The term mainly designates those who stress the baptism of the Holy Spirit, subsequent to conversion, accompanied by speaking in a language unknown to the recipient. Glossolalia (speaking with tongues) is considered the initial evidence of having received the Holy Spirit in his fullness and is held to reproduce what occurred on the Day of Pentecost. The language received is thought to be not mere ecstatic utterance without meaning but a definite non-human tongue (rarely human). Although glossolalia is given primacy, divine healing with amazing results is a second charismatic emphasis along with interpretation of tongues. Pentecostalists affirm nine gifts: wisdom, knowledge, faith, healing, miracles, discernment of spirits, tongues, interpretation and prophecy. Though they trace their position through an intermittent history to the Early Church, Pentecostals are regarded as American in origin. Their immediate predecessors borrowed from the Holiness movement an emphasis on a "second blessing" subsequent to conversion. Through this the believer assertedly receives the Holy Spirit, the Spirit-led life, devotion to foreign missions wherein Pentecostals have had phenomenal success, and shuns "wordliness" as manifested in amusements, jewelry, use of cosmetics and luxury. Searching the Scriptures led some Holiness believers to expect and seek for gifts of the Holy Spirit along with his incoming.

The beginning of the charismatic movement usually is credited to Charles Fox Parham, director of Bethel Bible College in Topeka, Kansas, where tongues were reported January 1, 1901, although anticipated in North Carolina in 1896 under William F. Bryant. Of major influence was the renowned Azusa Street Revival of 1906 in Los Angeles, under the leadership of William J. Seymour (student of Parham). Throughout the 1960's glossolalia spread into various denominations, including some Roman Catholics.

Critics hold that the tongues given at Pentecost were actually human languages, not ecstatic utterances. They point to the difficulties Paul had with the Corinthian Church which emphasized tongues. Paul stressed the priority of faith, hope and agape over spiritual gifts. He preferred speaking in a language understood by his hearers. He urged all believers to be filled with the Spirit, but did not exhort or hold that all were to experience tongues. Opponents hold that Christ and many Christians have been Spirit-filled without them. They assert the Biblical test of being filled is the fruit of the Spirit of which love is the greatest. They doubt a position largely supported by experience, rather than grounded on the full teaching of Scripture. They look askance at urging seekers to turn their tongues over to God and to begin uttering words which supposedly assist in receiving tongues. Meantime, the movement's supporters believe their position represents the "full gospel" and point to their success as the fastest growing segment of Christianity.   FLOYD F. McCALLUM

CHARTISM. Chartism was a British political reform movement during a period of economic depression, and centered on the People's Charter of 1838. This document, the work of William Lovett and Francis Place, demanded annual parliaments, adult (male) suffrage, vote by ballot, abolition of the property qualification for members of the House of Commons, payment of members, and equal electoral districts. A direct result of working class disappointment with the 1832 Reform Bill, Chartism was marked by monster meetings, grandiose schemes, and bitter leadership differences about aims and methods. Newspapers were begun and charter unions were formed throughout the country (with a membership claimed to be about 40,000). The solidarity thus achieved was greatly to benefit trade unions and the cooperative movement. The cause faltered from 1842 when economic conditions improved, but briefly revived in 1848 when a petition reportedly signed by nearly six million people was presented to parliament. Chartism was finally discredited when the total proved to be as false as some of the signatures. Subsequent legislation has implemented all of the Chartist program except for annual parliaments.   JAMES D. DOUGLAS

CHASTENING. See also *Suffering.* In its Biblical usage the term "chastening" *(paideia)* has reference to God's dealings which are designed to instruct, correct, and improve his people. Instruction would suffice to accomplish the divine end if there were complete obedience, but since this is not so corrective measures are necessary. These may even bring pain and suffering, sometimes touching the body and most certainly affecting the human spirit (Ps. 32:3-4). The profit received is manifold, whether manifested in repentance or submission to the will of God or gratitude for things formerly accepted as a matter of course. Pride is rebuked. The relation of the human to the divine is brought into better perspective.

Throughout the experience of chastening God is to be perceived as fulfilling the role of Father. Therefore, it should be understood that the affliction involved is administered in love. The suffering is not to be viewed as punishment in a legal sense, but as part of a maturing process wisely administered by one who knows what is for our good. Chastening actually performs the function of providing assurance that we are true children of the heavenly Father (Heb. 12:7-8). God's righteousness is involved also, since failure to chasten his errant children would reflect on his character. Chastening demonstrates that election is not a species of favoritism. For example, it may be so severe as to bring death (I Cor. 11:30). When this happens, all the saints

learn afresh the necessity of walking in the fear of God (Acts 5:11). Through its functions of instruction and correction, the word of God is intended to render unnecessary the application of unusual chastening by the Father (II Tim. 3:16-17).
EVERETT F. HARRISON

CHASTITY. See also *Adultery; Asceticism; Body; Celibacy; Fornication; Marriage; Sanctification; Virginity.* Chastity is typically understood as abstention from any form of sexual relationship expressly forbidden by Scripture, as well as abstention from willful thoughts or actions conducive to unchastity. However, chastity must also be understood positively, as affirming and embodying that pattern of sexual relationships and attitudes ordained and blessed by God (Otto Piper, *The Christian View of Sex and Marriage,* New York, Scribner, 1960, p. 166). Thus, both virginity (II Cor. 11:2), and fidelity in marriage (Titus 2:5; II Peter 3:2), are described as chaste (Greek *hagnos*) conduct in the NT.

Neither the OT nor the NT (see Paul's teaching in I Cor. 7) provide a detailed description of the form of Christian chastity, within and without marriage. Nevertheless, recognition of the God-given unitive power—both to bless and to curse—of the ultimate sexual relationship (Mark 10:6ff; I Cor. 6:16) forms the foundation for the strongest possible language in the Bible regarding chastity and unchastity. Adultery and fornication are consistently condemned in the Bible as examples of gross sin (Jer. 3:8; Ezek. 16; Hos. 4:13; Mark 7:21; Rom. 1:29; I Cor. 6:9ff.). Jesus condemned unchaste attitudes with the harsh words that "everyone who looks at a woman lustfully has already committed adultery with her in his heart" (Matt. 5:28). The Apostle Paul warned that unchaste sexual relationship severs the Christian's union with Jesus Christ (I Cor. 6:15).

Although Paul understood that sexual

desire could become an instrument of sin (Rom. 1:24ff.; I Cor. 7:2), he also affirmed the honorable and holy, and therefore chaste, expression of sexual desire within the bond of marriage (I Cor. 7:1ff.; I Thess. 4:1ff.)—a fact only begrudgingly recognized by many critics of Paul's teaching.

There have been many deviations toward either sexual asceticism or sexual license in the history of the church. Unbiblical attitudes toward the material and bodily world soon led to a false stress upon sexual asceticism, virginity and celibacy (cf. *HERE*). Some Christians failed to see that although the urgency of the kingdom of God allowed, and even merited such practices, neither it nor the meaning of sex required them. In more modern times, veneration of the "human" sciences (anthropology, sociology, psychology), as well as inadequate views of the authority and meaning of Scripture, have frequently led to an abandonment of the Biblical teaching. Such modifications do not cope with real problems of modern man relative to sexual relationship because they do not match the depth in which the Scripture perceives the meaning of both sex and sin.

Peter Bertocci, *Sex, Love and the Person,* New York, Sheed and Ward, 1967; *HERE;* Otto Piper, *The Biblical View of Sex and Marriage,* New York, Scribner, 1960; Evelyn M. Duvall, *Why Wait Till Marriage?,* New York, Association, 1965.

ROBERT P. MEYE

CHILDLIKENESS. Many characteristics appropriate to children ordinarily are thought to be inappropriate in adults. As Paul expresses it, "When I became a man, I gave up childish ways" (I Cor. 13:11). However, the Scriptures commend certain childlike attitudes or attributes to all men. For example, "In malice be as children, but in thinking be mature" (I Cor. 14:20). Solomon pleases God when he confesses, "I am but a little child. . . . Give your servant, therefore, an understanding mind . . ." (I Kings 3:7, 9). So does Jeremiah (1:6) when

he responds to God's call: "I do not know how to speak, for I am only a child." Jesus thanks God for hiding his message from the wise of the world and revealing it to "babes" (Luke 10:21), and elsewhere his followers are addressed as "little children" (John 13:33; Gal. 4:19; I John 2:1, 12f.).

Between this age and the age to come, i.e., the kingdom of God, the NT sees a *principle of reversal* at work. Those now exalted will be abased, and the lowly will be exalted (Luke 1:52; 6:20-26; 14:11; Phil. 2:5-11; James 4:10; I Peter 5:5f.), the last will be first and the first last (Matt. 20:16; cf. E. E. Ellis, *The Gospel of Luke,* London, Nelson, 1966, pp. 187, 202). Childlikeness as a Christian virtue receives its most specific definition in this frame of reference. In the teaching of Jesus, "Whoever humbles himself like this child, he is the greatest in the kingdom of heaven" (Matt. 18:4). When the disciples keep children away from Jesus, he rebukes them. They have not perceived the meaning of his mission, i.e., that to such insignificant ones "belongs the kingdom of heaven" (Matt. 19:3). It belongs to children, not because of any subjective qualities in them—their innocence, humility, simplicity, etc.—but because of their dependent, helpless, and unimportant character and because God has chosen the weak things of the world (I Cor. 1:26-29; C. E. B. Cranfield, *The Gospel According to Saint Mark,* New York, Cambridge University, 1959, pp. 323f.). Therefore, Jesus says, "unless you turn and become like children you will never enter the kingdom of heaven" (Matt. 18:3).

The teaching that one must be "reborn" to see the kingdom of God (John 3:3, 5) rests on a somewhat different rationale: it expresses a *principle of discontinuity* between the life of this age and that of the age to come.   E. EARLE ELLIS

CHILDREN. See also *Adoption; Family; Marriage; Orphans; Procreation.* Christian ethics continues the high regard for children exhibited in the OT where, from Gen. 4 throughout Hebrew history, the family with children was the key unit of society. "Children are a heritage of the Lord . . .happy is the man that has his quiver full of them," says the Psalmist (127:3, 5). The author of Proverbs comments on childrearing, "Train up a child in the way he is to go, and when he is old he will not depart from it" (22:6). The OT placed high priority on the welfare and the education of the child. Parents are urged to teach the commandments "diligently unto thy children" (Deut. 6:7). Children are exhorted in the commandment, "Honor thy father and thy mother" (Exod. 20:12).

The NT, too, esteems children as a gift from God. Jesus reinforced the OT attitudes when he invited children to him, "Suffer the little children to come unto me and forbid them not, for to such belongeth the kingdom of God" (Luke 18:16). The apostle urged children to obey parents as long as their commands do not violate divine directives (Eph. 6:1-4; Titus 1:6). Childhood virtues such as innocence, faith, and love are transferred by analogy to Christians in their designation as "children of God."

Buttressed by the doctrines of divine creation and the dignity of human life, early Christians challenged the practices of infanticide (q.v.) and abortion (q.v.) in the pagan Mediterranean world. Christian orphanages began as early as the reign of Julian (361-363). Baptism of children, practiced from the second century, indicate their close relationship to the church.

The Medieval period witnessed the growth of a Christian theology of children. The "age of accountability" was fixed near twelve. Infant baptism, then almost universally practiced, brought children immediately into the family of the church. Education was encouraged by the church and the court school systems. The rising impor-

tance of children is seen in their inclusion in art forms and also in the famous Childrens' Crusades to the Holy Land in 1212, two attempts in which 50,000 German and French youths marched to free the Holy Land from the Turks.

The Protestant Reformation continued to minister to children and youth. Luther wrote children's hymns. Calvin was called to Geneva to set up an educational system and catechism. Reformed churches brought children into membership under the terms of covenant theology, while later Methodism considered them inheritors of the unconditional benefits of the atonement until they were able to exercise faith.

When the Industrial Revolution brought on an increase in child labor, Robert Raikes began the Sunday School Movement and F. D. Maurice promoted child labor legislation as the Christian ethic asserted itself against this evil.

The twentieth century has enlarged the Christian concept that children are worthwhile as individuals and their education and welfare must be the concern of society. Public and private schools offer compulsory education that reaches most children (59.2 million in USA) in the industrial countries. Church school enrollment in the USA has reached 47 million with a specialized literature of graded lessons for all ages (L. B. Whitman, editor, *Yearbook of American Churches,* New York, Council, 1969, p. 175). A. W. Cheek points out that "of more than 650 voluntary associations in our country, more than half of them are devoted in whole or in part to the welfare of children and youth" (M. J. Taylor, editor, *Religious Education,* Nashville, Abingdon, 1960, p. 371).

Despite the new attitude several ethical problems exist.

Christian ethics has not settled the problem of abortion (q.v.). Most Christians oppose "abortion on demand" arguing that the sixth commandment prohibits the taking of life, even of the unborn fetus.

Many children in countries of the undeveloped world are physically and educationally deprived. W. S. Grey reported to UNESCO that he estimated on the basis of the limited evidence available that 65-70 percent of the world's population falls below the level of functional literacy (J. S. Bruner, *Education and Training in the Developed Countries,* New York, Praeger, 1966, p. 66). While Christian missions have sought to alleviate this problem, the task is too great for the small missionary force. The Christian conscience is somewhat represented by national and international organizations like UNESCO and UNICEF.

The place of children in the family in a mobile, technological society does not seem as secure as in the earlier agrarian economy. This has led to juvenile delinquency and numerous problems of religious, psychological and educational retardation of children. It is estimated that one boy in every five will appear in court at least once between the ages of ten and seventeen (J. W. Kessler, *Psychopathology of Childhood,* Englewood Cliffs, Prentice-Hall, 1966, p. 298). In our large cities one out of every two children is culturally deprived. Evangelicals have sponsored such programs as Child Evangelism Fellowship and the Bible Club Movement.

Christian parents are often faced with the problem of whether to send their children to secular public schools or Christian private schools. The growing problems of violence and drugs among the young have given impetus to the Christian Day School Movement. The U.S. Office of Education reports that in 1968 there were approximately six million pupils in church related elementary and secondary schools. M. Fakkema reports a steady increase in evangelical day schools and the phenomenal growth of individual schools (J. E. Hakes, *An Introduction to Evangelical Christian Education,* Chicago, Moody, 1964, p. 376).   BERT H. HALL

CHIVALRY. See also *Courtesy.* Originating in the feudal system, chivalry (Fr. *chevalier,* "horseman," and thus "knight"), came to describe the ideal knight: gallant, honorable, protector of the weak, generous to foes. A rallying point and integrating factor came with the Crusades, during which the great religious and military orders came into being. A new dimension came when, for example, the Templars (1119) vowed to reject worldly chivalry that sought human favor and to "fight for the supreme and true King." Such soldier monks policed the road to the Holy Land, and in what was the golden age of chivalry championed the cause of pilgrims, widows, and orphans against the cruelty of pagans, marauders, and opportunists. In some cases the world won, and many guardians returned not a little corrupted by the East. Yet chivalry as a whole greatly benefited the Middle Ages, maintaining moral standards, bringing humane principles to the practice of war, and (to an extent on which historians disagree) raising the status of women. Even after the passing of the horse (symbol of superiority over the foot soldier) the concept of chivalry survived. Although it is now associated chiefly with the considerable romantic literature that sprang up about it, chivalry's lasting impact has been in the fostering of a tradition of personal ethics not limited, as was the early code of honor, to the upper classes.   JAMES D. DOUGLAS

CHOICE. See *Decision; Free Will.*

CHRISTIAN   EDUCATION. See also *Education and Morality.* Liberal learning is conceded almost everywhere today to be in trouble. The products of public education, steeped in a crisis of truth and morals, increasingly discredit the notion that ample budgets and facilities guarantee good schools and good students. By exalting tolerance as a supreme virtue modern learning has nurtured a loss of fixed truth and values, a collapse of respect for authority, and the forfeiture of a spiritual vision of life. The result has been a generation of youth unsure of who they are, what they ought to be and ought to believe.

The Western ideal of popular education stemmed from the Christian conviction that the inspired Scriptures encompass revealed information that must be shared with every man, woman, and child. To provide training for the clergy was the motivation for the founding of America's earliest prestigious colleges.

While the crisis of modern liberal education centers in the loss of objective truth and moral norms, Christian education in this century cannot be said to have communicated the truth of revelation with spectacular success. The reasons are numerous. For one thing, the USA policy of separation of church and state has prompted many elementary and secondary public schools to minimize religious instruction and involvement, thereby nourishing a younger generation of spiritual illiterates. Colleges and universities, which now show an expansive interest in religious studies, mirror a post-Christian bias in the conspicuous absence of evangelical scholars from many religion and philosophy faculties. In many strictly evangelical colleges an unfortunate isolation from the general academic milieu results in a paucity of literature that could effectively confront the secular mind. While non-denominational campuses frequently lack intellectual earnestness, many denominational colleges have lost evangelical authenticity.

The NT does not in principle require Christian schools alongside Christian churches, although their existence becomes a strategic necessity if and when the general educational process—as is often the case today—is highly erosive of evangelical beliefs and values. Although Roman Catholic parochial schools face mounting stresses, the Christian school movement has gained considerable evangelical support both from interdenominational and some denominational (e.g., Missouri Synod Lutherans, Christian Reformed) groups; in isolated cases the motivation has been racial as much as educational. Evangelical schools can effectively fulfill their mission only if Christian world-life perspectives serve to integrate human learning and behavior in contrast to the nihilistic tendency of nontheistic alternatives. The prime justification for evangelical education must be a concern for the victory of truth and justice and godliness; its purpose is not simply to compensate for the neglect of the Christian home or the failures of the local church, nor to provide personal shelter from the prevailing cultural milieu. Christian education is vital only when it raises up a nucleus of committed evangelical intellectuals who stand in the public arena unequivocally devoted to the truth and right of God.

The academic scene currently shows widespread indications of ideological exhaustion and intellectual fatigue, a development directly related to its evolutionary and relativistic outlook on reality and life. Modern education has no fixed center or cohesive content; it lacks rational unity. A pervasive naturalism obscures spiritual realities and moral absolutes, and refers the cosmos and man to evolutionary emergence alone, history to contingency, conscience to societal prejudice, and religion to personal preference. Revelational theism, on which virile Christian education rests, insists that nature is a commentary on the Logos of God (John 1:3) and that man, uniquely lighted by the Divine Logos (John 1:4, 9a), has a destiny in eternity; that history has its immovable center in the life and work of Jesus of Nazareth; that conscience hails man as sinner anticipatively before the judgment throne of the Creator; and that pure religion recognizes Jesus Christ as the incarnate Logos whose image is crucial for human life and destiny.

In the churches themselves the understanding of Christian education (sometimes called religious education) has too often been equated simply with organization and methodology, rather than with an intellectual and spiritual integration of the total ministry of the church. This faulty view has frequently been nourished by seminaries whose Christian education departments have neglected the priority and integrative role of revealed truth. The recent emergence of the Jesus-movement, with its discontents over the established churches, and such cultural changes as the four-day week, may bring pressures upon the traditional Sunday school for alternatives that realistically correlate Christian learning, vocational interests, and leisure.

📖 *Christian Liberal Arts Education:* Report of the Calvin College Curriculum Study Committee, Grand Rapids, Eerdmans, 1970; Gordon H. Clark, *A Christian Philosophy of Education,* Grand Rapids, Eerdmans, 1946; Frank E. Gaebelein, *Christian Education in a Democracy,* New York, Oxford, 1951; *The Pattern of God's Truth,* New York, Oxford, 1954, Moody paperback, 1968.

CARL F. H. HENRY

CHRISTIAN PERSONAL ETHICS. See *Interpersonal Relations; Orders of Creation and Preservation; Personal Ethics.*

CHRISTIAN SOCIAL ETHICS. See *Social Ethics.*

CHRISTIAN SOCIAL MOVEMENTS. See also *Evangelical Social Concern; Humanitarianism; Social Gospel.* The Great Commission of the church is to preach the Good News of Jesus Christ and to teach its disciples the truths declared by him. The concurrent ministry of the church, commended but not commanded, is to follow the Divine example of service and promote the welfare of mankind in meeting their temporal needs. No non-Christian is able to fulfill the Great Commission, which pertains to those regenerated by the Holy Spirit. Anyone of goodwill may join in ministering

to the temporal needs of humanity, and when society accepts its obligations, the will of God is advanced.

The sowing of the seed of social reform was aided by the eighteenth century Evangelical Awakenings. John Wesley denounced the greatest social evil of his days, slavery, and urged the reform of prisons, the education of the masses, and the like, as did other revivalists. It was in the extended nineteenth century—1776 to 1914—that a harvest of social reform was reaped in many a field of human concern.

The First Great Awakening (1725-1775) had raised up a number of American universities. A Second Great Awakening led to the founding of a monitorial school system for the masses of Britain and the founding of hundreds of colleges in the westering United States. The same revival of Napoleon's day raised up Wilberforce and other engineers of the abolition of the slave trade, followed by emancipation of the slaves in the British Empire (1834), in United States as a war measure (1863). At the same time, Evangelicals such as Elizabeth Fry promoted successful prison reform, while Fliedner in Germany followed suit in building homes for ex-prisoners, hospitals for the sick, asylums for the insane, orphanages for children, founding the order of deaconesses to staff them, all on evangelical impulse. Florence Nightingale, trained at his school, became the mother of modern nursing.

The decades following 1830 in American life have been called "the Sentimental Years," in which good works flourished as never before, the Revival producing societies to promote education, reform prisons, stop prostitution, recolonize Africa with freed slaves, advance the cause of peace, provide for sailors in port, promote temperance, and the like. The Awakening discouraged cruel sports, and produced societies everywhere for the prevention of cruelty to animals.

Great Britain was the first of the countries of the world to become industrialized, and its Industrial Revolution brought about a sorry exploitation of the toiling masses, caught in a treadmill of competitive labor which kept them straining for sixteen hours a day in appalling conditions.

Anthony Ashley Cooper, Seventh Earl of Shaftesbury, described himself as "an Evangelical of the Evangelicals," and harnessed the thrust of the Revival into a crusade for human betterment. He and his friends promoted legislation to cut the hours of labor in factories by half, to prohibit the use of women working in coal mines, of children in factories and farm gangs, to transform the lot of insane folk from abused prisoners to protected patients. He also promoted public parks, playing fields, gymnasia, garden allotments, working men's institutes, public libraries, night schools, debating and choral societies and other self-help.

The "Tolpuddle Martyrs," transported to the Australian penal colonies for refusing to work for less than a shilling a day, were evangelical lay preachers, except one who was later converted through their Christian behavior in convict camp. They gave a great impetus to the trade union movement in Britain. In later years, Keir Hardie, a convert of D. L. Moody, took up the cause of the working man, founded the Labor Party, and maintained until death an evangelical Christian testimony shared with various other leaders of the Labor movement, which (quoting Lloyd George) found many of its officers among converts of the Evangelical Revivals.

The Third Great Awakening (1858-59) in the United States and Great Britain and around the world, raised up a corps of Christian philanthropists who went straight to the slums with a practical Samaritanism, yet cooperated in wise legislative improvement. Numberless asylums, homes, refuges, homes, and schools were founded in Britain. Barnardo's Homes, founded by a convert of the Revival in Dublin, became the world's largest private orphanage system. Out of the same Revival grew the Salvation Army, an extension in evangelism and social action of the Awakening in which William Booth was an ardent evangelist. The impact of the Revival was felt in the immediate reform of thousands of prostitutes, and it was carried on by Josephine Butler in a campaign against the state patronage of vice, as was Bramwell Booth and W. T. Stead's crusade against the white slave traffic. Henri Dunant, a student evangelist in Geneva, founded the Red Cross in 1865. The Y.M.C.A., founded in 1844 in London, was vastly expanded by the 1858-59 Revival, becoming a social fraternity.

Some have said that the 1858 American Awakening lacked social benefits. Within three years, the nation was involved in the bloodiest war of the century, its energies otherwise absorbed. When peace came, new enterprises were transferred from Britain. Timothy L. Smith writes, "the rapid growth of concern with purely social issues such as poverty, working men's rights, the liquor traffic, slum housing, and racial bitterness is the chief feature distinguishing American religion after 1865...."

Another worldwide Awakening about 1905 was not only extraordinary in reviving the churches and evangelizing the masses of the United States and elsewhere, but infused social concern. Washington Gladden, "father of the social gospel," commended the movement for "creating a moral revolution in the life of the people."

Early advocates of "the social gospel" were often the warmest supporters of historic evangelism, winning individuals to Jesus Christ. Some of their followers, still sincerely motivated, diverged into the heresy of substituting social action for evangelism or identifying one as the other, generally to the detriment of evangelism. Unfortunately, a minority of Evangelicals reacted by denying the social obligation of the church, stirring Carl Henry's "uneasy conscience" over fundamentalism.

Wilberforce did not wait for the support of the Convocations of Canterbury and York, nor did Shaftesbury seek the approval of the Methodist Conference. They went straight to the seat of power with the heart of the matter, and spoke as enlightened churchmen possessing the privilege and responsibility of citizens. The forum of the church is not the fulcrum of reform; in parliament or palace, great decisions are made.

The missionaries—from William Carey on—secured the abolition of widow-burning and of child-sacrifices; they took the lead in the education of the people of India; they helped found the vernacular press; they introduced Western medical practice. In Africa, they discouraged polygamy, opposed trial by ordeal, fought the slave trade, challenged exploitation by unscrupulous traders, built schools and hospitals, and helped prepare the Africans for self-government—while sharing with rulers and traders the responsibility for cultural havoc. In 1875, there were in Malawi "no schools, no teachers, no pupils, nobody who could read." Within thirty years, Scottish missionaries operated more than 200 schools with 20,000 pupils. In a single generation, the Christian Missionary Society taught 200,000 to read in East Africa.

Following the 1858-59 Revival, medical missions spread in India, medical missionaries multiplying twentyfold in less than forty years. A survey in World War II showed that 90 percent of all nurses in India were Christians, four-fifths of them trained at mission hospitals. Missionaries have built Asia's biggest hospitals for leprosy, tuberculosis and the like; and Christian medical colleges pioneered in many countries.

A convert of the 1859 Revival, Timothy Richard, may be regarded as the founder of China's great universities. The educational system of Korea owed its beginnings to pioneer missionaries. A mission school became Japan's Imperial University, while a convert founded Doshisha University as an all-Japanese institution. Mission schools profoundly influenced the development of Brazilian education, and a team of teachers, largely impressed by the 1858 Revival, gave a teacher training system to Sarmiento's Argentine. And 70 percent of African students in American colleges are mission lads.

The years following World War II saw an extraordinary expansion of the evangelical missionary forces throughout the world, due in part to the reviving of the work of God at the mid-century. Their evangelism was matched by a social concern, as seen in the worldwide ministry of World Vision (begun in the 1950s) which promoted pastors' conferences on evangelism and revival overseas as well as maintaining a many-sided service of help in situations of the greatest emergency. Converts of the first Billy Graham Crusade of national importance, Los Angeles 1949, engaged in worthwhile social ministry—Jim Vaus in the gangland of New York and Louis Zamperini in the correctional farms of California, for example. While the significant civil rights campaign began without clearly Evangelical initiative, it could be said that the mid-century awakening had conditioned Evangelicals to accept a nobler standard of social injustice, and all but the obscurantists supported the drive for rights, though not some extreme methods employed by the few to obtain them. It seemed that American Evangelicals were reasserting the social conscience of the nineteenth century and of British Evangelicalism.

At the same time, Evangelicals protested the attempts of theological radicals to identify legitimate social action with evangelism, a classification resulting in abandonment of personal, group and mass evangelism entirely. Social action, however desirable, is no substitute for proclamation of the Good News of Jesus Christ. The solution of the race problem, the question of social and economic justice, and the problem of war, would place the American community in the same position as contemporary Scandinavia, with its equally great need of the gospel. The secular state—by revolution in the Soviet Union—has preempted all social service and prohibited Christians from engaging in such as Christians. The secular state—by evolution in the democracies—has taken over, more and more, the social work of the churches and voluntary societies. Christians, though not prohibited, are being displaced as Christians from such service. The time may come when only the preaching of the Good News will be left to them.

James Shepard Dennis, *Christian Missions and Social Progress*, New York, 1897-1906, 3 volumes; Timothy Lawrence Smith, *Revivalism and Social Reform*, Nashville, Abingdon, 1957; James Edwin Orr, *The Light of the Nations*, Grand Rapids, Eerdmans, 1965.   J. EDWIN ORR

CHURCH AND ETHICS. See *Ecumenism and Ethics.*

CHURCH AND STATE. See also *Persecution; Religious Freedom.* The problem of the relationship between church and state, between Christianity and its pagan environment, was inherent in the very nature of the Christian gospel and the church to which it gave birth. The fall of Jerusalem in A.D. 70 brought to the Roman government the realization that Christianity was not merely a sect within Judaism, but a new movement not entitled to that peculiar protection which the Roman Empire had accorded to the Jewish religion. This subjected the church in the Roman Empire to a series of persecutions during the first three centuries. The first dramatic change in the situation came when Constantine issued the Edict of Milan in 313 making Christianity a legal religion. The purpose of this edict was utilitarian and in essence made the church subject to the Roman state. For this new legal status of toleration the church paid a heavy price and the Eastern Orthodox Church has never been able to free itself from its secular shackles.

The pattern of church and state relationships developed quite differently in the West, although not without a severe struggle lasting for centuries. The basis for the pattern of development in the Western church was laid by Augustine's *De Civitate Dei*, with its division of humanity into two groups, the city of God on earth and the city of man. Holding that both church and state were ordained by God he taught that the state is concerned with civil affairs and that the church is responsible for man's spiritual life. Although Augustine laid the foundation for the Western view of proper relationship between the two institutions, the position he set forth soon received further clarification in a letter written by Pope Gelasius I to the Byzantine Emperor Anastasius I in 494. In this famous document Gelasius reasserted the position of the role of the two powers in his concept of the two swords, the spiritual and the temporal. But he also insisted that the priestly power is the much more important "because it has to render account for the kings of men themselves at the divine tribunal." Here the germ of the future claim of papal supremacy is quite visible, but the crowning of Charlemagne as Emperor of the Franks in 800 raised the question in a new way and this act was interpreted as one which clearly indicated papal supremacy over the civil ruler. However it is most unlikely that either Charlemagne or his immediate Carolingian successors regarded the crowning either as a precedent requiring papal confirmation of future emperors or an affirmation of the superiority of the spiritual sword. The appearance of the forged *Donations of Constantine,* emanating from the papal chancery somewhere between 750 and 800, gave added strength to the papal claims of supremacy over kings and emperors.

The question of the relationship between the church and state became very serious after 1050 with the emergence of the investiture controversy between the Holy Roman Emperor Henry IV and Pope Gregory VII. In his efforts to free the church from German control Gregory asserted in the most vigorous terminology yet formulated the doctrine of papal supremacy in the *Dictatus Papae*. Although this document may not have been his own work, it undoubtedly represented his position and it marked the beginning of a new era in the history of church and state relations and it served as the basis for the later claims of Innocent III and Boniface VIII, both of whom tried to extend the secular power of the Papacy. The failure of Boniface VIII in his conflict with Philip IV of France brought an end to the extreme claims on the part of the popes, but the controversy did not subside and able writers like Marsigilio of Padua vigorously contested the papal position.

With the coming of the Reformation the problem of the relationship between the state and church entered a new phase. Although Luther failed to enunciate a clearly defined Biblical doctrine on this issue and the Church of England fell into an Erastian position, Calvin at Geneva not only set forth in his *Institutes* the Biblical view, but also put it into practice in Geneva. For Calvin both the church and the state are ordained of God for the good of mankind and the proper order of human society. The church is responsible for the preaching of the gospel and the spiritual life of men while the state is responsible for civil affairs and the observance of the law of God as it is revealed in the Ten Commandments. Each institution is to operate in its divinely appointed sphere, the church as the instrument of special grace and the state the agent under common grace. This Calvinistic goal has always been difficult to achieve, even in a society committed to the Reformed theology. The rise of secularism and the emergence of pluralistic societies in Europe

placed the model at Geneva in a very difficult position, not only in Switzerland, but in the rest of Europe as well. In France the Roman Church by the Concordat of 1516 fell under the power of the French monarchy to such an extent that it became politically captive to the Bourbon monarchy and earned the scorn of the French people and became an object of attack during the French Revolution. This same development was repeated in Russia under the Romanov dynasty, so that the Russian Church became the popular object of attack during the communist revolution of 1917-1918.

In England Calvin inspired the Puritans to demand the separation of church and state both under Elizabeth and the Stuarts, but the English Revolution under Cromwell failed to bring a permanent separation of the two institutions. As a result, many Puritans left England for America where they revived the Geneva Model in New England. The result has often been called a theocracy, by which their critics mean a union of church and state in which the Puritan Church was predominant. This was not the case, however, for the Puritan leaders very clearly taught and practiced the concept of the two spheres, the spiritual and the civil.

By the time of the American Revolution the beginnings of a pluralistic society and the rise of the democratic philosophy brought about the demand for a new kind of religious liberty in those colonies which had established churches. The result was the disestablishment of the Church of England in Virginia under the leadership of Jefferson and Madison and elsewhere in the South. However, the Congregational Church was not disestablished in Massachusetts and Connecticut until the early decades of the nineteenth century. During the nineteenth century the Protestant ethic was widely accepted as normative for the conduct of American society and there were relatively few protests against a kind of ethical union between church and state. With the coming of the twentieth century and the rise of a secularized democratic outlook, this nineteenth century relationship began to be widely questioned, and after 1945, dissent against many previously commonly accepted practices became more widespread. Beginning with the McCollum Case in 1948 the Supreme Court began to rule against such practices as released time for religious education and the reading of the Bible and the use of prayers in the public schools of the nation.

The emergence of neo-orthodoxy with its various derivatives has also led to a reappraisal of the historic view of the relationship of church and state. Some, like Oscar Cullman, have even gone so far as to hold that the state is secretly God's kingdom, while Emil Brunner insists that there is a very clear distinction and that they operate in different realms with very little connection between them. Although the state was originally ordained by God it moves in a secular order, but both the church and the state are intended to serve the Kingdom of God.

Geoffry Barraclough, *The Medieval Papacy*, New York, Harcourt-Brace, 1968; John C. Bennett, *Christians and the State*, New York, Scribner, 1958; S. Z. Ehler, and John Morrall, *Church and State through the Ages*, Westminster, Md., Newman, 1951; Jacob Hoogstra, ed., *John Calvin, Contemporary Prophet*, Grand Rapids, Baker, 1959; F. Kempf, *Papsttum und Kaeserlum bei Innocenz III*, Rome, 1954; N. Q. King, *The Emperor Theodosus and the Establishment of Christianity*; Karl F. Morrison, *The Two Kingdoms*, Princeton, Princeton University, 1964; A. L. Smith, *Church and State in the Middle Ages*, reprinted, New York, Barnes & Noble, 1964; Ansom P. Stokes, and Leo Pfeffer, *Church and State in the United States*, Rev. ed., New York, Harper & Row, 1964; G. Tellenbach, *Church, State and Society at the Time of the Investiture Contest*, Oxford, 1940.

C. GREGG SINGER

CHURCH COVENANTS. See also *Covenant; Vows.* Church covenants are solemn agreements binding participants before God and man to certain obligations such as those concerning church membership and ministerial ordination. These compacts involve adherence to selected beliefs and practices while avoiding others. Historically, those subsequently changing their affirmations were expected to resign or face expulsion. Increasingly covenants are requiring less as conduct and doctrinal commitments are being restated in broader terms. Today they are often regarded as statements of ideals rather than binding agreements, yielding priority to individual conscience in interpretation. Conservative evangelicals require conscientious adherence to all vows.

FLOYD F. McCALLUM

CHURCH LOBBIES. See also *Counsels; Councils of Churches.* The USA requires all lobbyists to register with the federal government. But staff members of only one religious organization, the Friends Committee on National Legislation, have registered as lobbyists. A number of religious groups have special offices in Washington and in state capitals, but they are unwilling to state publicly that they exist primarily to influence legislation. Their "out" is that their lobbying role is only a minor aspect of their organization's goals. This subsidiary role enables them to retain a tax-exempt status.

As a result, church lobbies in Washington and Ottawa are not nearly as sophisticated as their secular counterparts. For clout they rely mainly on the vast number of citizens they purport to "represent." If, for example, the Roman Catholic Church and the National Council of Churches present a united front—as they have done with growing regularity—they can claim to represent nearly one-half the American population.

Church lobbies have assumed increasing importance in recent years as liberal clergy have become more infatuated with the notion that the way to change individuals is to change society. On social questions, generally speaking, these lobbies have been on the side of bigger government, and they have often been criticized for not authentically reflecting the views of their constituents, as well as for promoting legislative specifics that are not clearly identifiable with the New Covenant. The National Association of Evangelicals seldom offers testimony, but when it does it usually finds itself resisting the trend. The NAE normally advocates strict separation of church and state. It parted company with many church leaders when it argued for a constitutional amendment to authorize prayer in public schools.

Greater funding for public education has been a continuing cry of most church lobbies, this being a carryover from the old liberal reliance upon education as paving the way to utopia. The Amish Supreme Court case may have signalled an impending turnabout based on growing disillusionment with public education.

📖 The only substantial work on the subject in recent years is *The Growing Church Lobby in Washington* by James L. Adams. Although more descriptive than analytical, it is thorough.

DAVID KUCHARSKY

CIRCUMSTANCES. See *Interim Ethics; Situational Ethics.*

CIVIL DISOBEDIENCE. See also *Demonstration; Protest; Rebellion; Resistance.* Civil disobedience invariably has as its consequence the violation of a legal ordinance or statute. Hence it constitutes a challenge to the state or established authority. It can involve the act or acts of a single individual or the collective actions of a group. Although the laws thus violated are frequently penal in nature and often designed for the protection of property rights, those who engage in acts of civil disobedience are often stimulated not by a desire for personal aggrandizement, but by a desire to change some facet of the existing social, economic, or political order. They frequently justify acts of civil disobedience on the

basis of some higher law which in their view supersedes state authority and to which they feel answerable.

The gravamen of their complaint is that an injustice is being committed under the aegis of the state. It may be an allegedly unjust war, or discriminatory practices which deny equal protection of law to those of a particular race, or cartelized economic power in the hands of a few, or even a more general assault on the legitimacy of those wielding the power of the State. In this latter case civil disobedience can serve as a prelude to revolution, as in the case of the refusal of American Colonists to pay a stamp tax to the British Crown, which culminated in the American War of Independence. However, in its inception civil disobedience is essentially non-violent and sometimes even covert; e.g., the "underground railway" in pre-Civil War times challenged the existing legal concept of slaves as chattel property, but did so on a covert basis.

The twentieth century has seen the emergence of some truly historic figures who employed the tactic of civil disobedience. Mahatma Gandhi motivated the Indian masses to a desire for independence from British rule by conducting campaigns which involved passive resistance to the recognition of British sovereignty. In the USA, Martin Luther King, Jr., became an exponent of civil disobedience as a means to strike off the shackles which held millions of black Americans in legal bondage as second-class citizens. Southern legislatures, as well as some in the North, had legislated dual school systems, and "Jim Crow" laws ordained that the races were to be kept separate on railroad cars and in buses, in lunch counters, parks and swimming pools. Today, although the battle for equality under the law is not over, great gains resulted because Martin Luther King led marches and conducted protests in places where they were clearly illegal.

In the latter half of the decade of the 1960s, the Vietnam War became bitterly controversial. The refusal to step forward to take the oath to serve in the armed forces, or simply refusal even to register for the draft and the wholesale flight of possibly as many as 100,000 young Americans of draft age became a new symbol of civil disobedience.

The attitude and beliefs of the evangelical Christian regarding civil disobedience should be based on what the Scriptures teach. Romans 13:1-12, broadly implies that the ordinances of the State should be obeyed because the powers that be are ordained of God. Paul is speaking here of legitimate governments and just laws. There are clearly unjust and corrupt governments which promulgate laws that lack legitimacy. And a single act of civil disobedience, rather than mobilized contempt for law, will often serve to set in motion a higher juridicial test of discriminatory local statutes. Absolute obeisance to immoral or currupt practices by the state, whether codified by statute or carried out as policy, is not a price the Christian must pay to discharge his duty to recognize that governments are ordained of God. Even in a representative democracy like the USA, laws may be passed which conflict with conscience. Here the basic authority of the government is not to be challenged but a particular law or policy which seems to individual conscience to conflict with the higher law.

The Christian must be prepared in some instances to answer the call of that higher law, but be prepared also to accept the penalty of non-compliance with the authority of the state. His acts of civil disobedience must be non-violent in character and prayerfully inspired by the ethic of Christian love for his neighbor rather than by love of self. He must also be convinced that all other channels of effecting change are so obstructed that an act of civil disobedience is the only reasonable alternative.

JOHN B. ANDERSON

CIVIL RIGHTS. Civil rights are privileges and freedoms extended by law to the citizens of a particular society. Associated with the privilege of citizenship, they theoretically apply equally to all citizens, thus affording a rough measure of the freedoms valued by the society and what it means in human terms to be a member of it. However, in some purportedly egalitarian societies, including the USA, some civil rights have in practice been denied to certain groups of citizens even after the abolition of legal discrimination. And in other societies distinctions between different classes of citizens have been established by law, based on racial, religious, sexual, or other group characteristics; in these societies some groups are denied by law the civil rights that apply to others.

Some civil rights are traditionally considered inalienable; e.g., Thomas Jefferson noted man's inalienable rights to "life, liberty, and the pursuit of happiness" in the American Declaration of Independence. Most people, no matter what their nationality, take for granted the right to marry and raise a family, the right to own personal property, the right to move about freely within certain political jurisdictions, the right to try to find work of their own choosing, the right to water and air, and access to public property.

Other civil rights—the right to vote, the right to freedom of speech and thought, the right to redress of grievances—have not been so self-evident, and have been won in most democracies only through an historical process of struggle against the arbitrary power of kings. The Anglo-American tradition is a classic example. Though the Magna Carta of 1215 was a written document specifying the feudal rights and obligations of the English barons and their subjects, the English tradition was primarily an oral one, and the "rights of Englishmen" which formed the basis of the American Revolution—though clear enough to those who felt they had been denied—were nowhere written down. It was largely out of concern to avoid the possibility of such arbitrary tyranny in the new USA that many of these rights were spelled out in the Constitution and particularly in the Bill of Rights, the first ten amendments. As a result, to be an American citizen has traditionally meant that one has enjoyed the freedom to criticize one's government, to assemble and petition for redress of grievances, to bear arms, to worship in whatever manner one chooses, and to exercise the right to vote.

The denial of basic civil rights to millions of Americans who had been sold into slavery posed one of the great crises in the nation's history, and precipitated the Civil War. The Emancipation Proclamation and the thirteenth, fourteenth and fifteenth Amendments to the Constitution, adopted after the Civil War, were designed to guarantee these civil rights to black Americans. The equal protection clause of the fourteenth Amendment has proved to be one of the strongest weapons to achieve greater equality of treatment of minority groups by state and local governments.

Following World War II, the civil rights movement in the USA again flamed into action after more than three quarters of a century of relative quiescence. Unquestionably the 1954 decision of the U.S. Supreme Court in *Brown vs. Board of Education* specifying that separate but equal educational facilities represented an unconsitutional denial of equal protection of the laws, provided great impetus to a renaissance of the civil rights movement. The first important post-war civil rights enactment by the Congress was in 1957, and it dealt with voting rights. In 1960, 1964, 1965, and 1968 other important civil rights laws were passed but only after strenuous opposition and prolonged filibusters which often resulted in the passage of far weaker legislation than originally proposed. Gradually, however, the scope and application of civil rights laws have been expanded so that they go far beyond the guarantee of the franchise to vote. Equal accomodations, fair housing and equal employment opportunity have become the subjects of legislative enactment, and the courts and administrative tribunals and agencies have been given enforcement power in these areas.

Significant progress has been achieved in desegregating dual school systems in Southern States. Between 1968 and 1971 the percentage of black school children in majority-white schools increased from 18.4 percent to 43.9 percent, indicating substantial integration in areas where dual school systems still prevailed as late as 1968. Great controversy still remains, however, as to the extent to which federal, state and local authority should go in obtaining a racial balance in the classroom in those areas where children attend segregated schools because of residential patterns based on socio-economic factors; i.e., *de facto* as opposed to *de jure* segregation.

Christians have a clear duty to support efforts toward racial integration and full implementation of a broad scale of civil rights in the areas of education, employment, and participation in the political process. There is no Scriptural warrant or basis for believing that segregation based on some notion of racial superiority is pleasing in God's sight. The Scriptures enjoin us to believe that all men are of one blood (Acts 17-26), and clearly all are equal in God's sight in eligibility for his grace offered us through his Son, Jesus Christ. The moral strength of the nation will be dependent in a large sense upon the citizenry's willingness to lay aside prejudice and take up the challenge of building one society rather than two societies—one black and one white—which are separate and unequal.

JOHN B. ANDERSON

CIVILIZATION. See also *Culture; Decalogue*. The word "civilization" (from the Latin *civis*, "citizen") which originated in the eighteenth century in France, where it was used for the first time by Mirabeau in 1756. At that time the concept connoted generally man's rise above his primitive and original state—in other words, the humanization of nature. At this stage of development the concept "civilization" still unites inseparably subjective morality and objective condition of morals, that is, the realm of ethical motivation and the higher organization of society (laws, etiquette, urbanity, cultural forms of life). In this way it became inevitable—at least in France and England—that also in the nineteenth century amid the rapid development of natural science and technology the concept of civilization likewise implied the encompassing complex of humanization.

If on the other hand in Germany the decisive distinction was made quite early—since the Enlightenment—between culture and civilization, it is inappropriate to observe that this differentiation is merely an extravagant and spurious development. Rather, the thesis that civilization and culture are heterogeneous contains an important material problem.

Already in Kant the first indications of this differentiation are observable. Initially, of course, civilization is understood also here as the signature of the "finer man." With this phrase Kant understands that man who is not complacent in the state of nature, but who rather unites with others in a community "on the basis of an original contract which is dictated by man himself" (*Critique of Aesthetical Judgment*, § 41). In his *Idea of a General History of World-Citizenship* (7th paragraph) on the other hand that difference becomes already quite noticeable. Part of culture are morality and ethics, while civilization is understood as a pseudomoral organization of "external politeness"—in other words, as a socially

functioning mechanism: "By art and science we become highly *cultivated*. We become *civilized* to the point of the unbearable in all kinds of socially decent behavior. But it does not suffice at all to understand ourselves by these developments already *moralized*. For the idea of morality still belongs to culture; however, the use of this idea applied only to that which is similar (!) to morality in the love of honor and the external decency should be called merely civilization." Here we have a clear revaluation of culture as an *ens humanissimum* over against the merely external civilization. Pestalozzi mentioned in 1797 altogether in this sense that the mere external "observance of civilization" leads to moral decay, while alone "human love," in other words, a *moral* motive, creates culture (H. P. Dreitzel, in *Die Religion in Geschichte und Gegenwart*, 3rd ed., vol. VI, 1920).

Also Karl Marx assumes a critical position over against civilization: "Modern times, civilization . . . separates the *objective* nature of man as a merely external and material nature from him. It does not understand the content of man as his true reality" (*Kritik der Hegelschen Staatsphilosophie*, in K. Marx, *Die Früschriften*, ed. by S. Landshut, 1955, p. 99). Here that again and again varied basic thought of Marx confronts us, that the "external" products of man emancipate themselves from him and stand over against him as something strange which can therefore "estrange" him and insofar act in a dehumanizing manner on him. In this sense the external civilization can become as a material product an estranging power. Also here, therefore, civilization is separated as a phenomenon of material externality from culture, even if this juxtaposition is not explicitly made.

In Nietzsche we find a critique of civilization with slightly different emphases, but in no way less emphatic. The "first principle of civilization: Any custom is better than no custom" (*Morgenröte*, vol. 73, 21), to be sure also elevates civilization as the successor of the state of nature and makes it the representative of morality. But this civilized overcoming of nature is in no way to be interpreted unambiguously positively. He speaks of a "basic antagonism between culture and civilization" (*Der Wille zur Macht*, vol. 78, 88) which comes about, among other things, because the comfort of civilization "makes all good things accessible also to the coward" (73, 137) because civilization creates, while it grows, simultaneously an "increase of the morbid elements" (78, 585), and because it "results in the physiological decline of a race" (83, 397).

In Marx as well as in Nietzsche the antagonism between culture and civilization becomes more pronounced because both are witnesses to a world-changing development of the natural sciences and technology in the nineteenth century. Because of this problematic the descrepancy grows between the external technological-civilizatory progress and the inner retarded situation of man. In anticipation of this discrepancy Goethe has occasionally mentioned that mankind will certainly progress more and more, but that man *himself* will always remain the same. The mentioned witnesses of that stormy development of technological civilization would say in addition that technology would indeed mean regress for mankind and that technology estranges man from his real identity. It envelops him with an artificial world, with "secondary systems" (Freyer) and causes him to live a second-hand life. It also threatens to destroy the immediate relation between men and, therefore, personal communication, because the abstract and impersonal welfare-mechanisms, guided by computers, inject themselves *between* men, preventing the direct contact between them so as to create the "lonely crowd" (Vance Packard). Even so-called human relations become im-

personal rationalizations of love of neighbor, for they do not have in mind the personal center of man, but rather only the economic effectiveness of his working-capacity within the productive process. Also they would therefore belong to the technological civilization, and not to culture in the narrower sense of the word.

It is understandable that technological progress, which is determining civilization, is often seen critically in this way. The time of enthusiasm, which was triggered by the first epochs of civil, that is, scientific and technological progress, seems to approach its end and to make way for a certain "fatigue of civilization," of which already Nietzsche spoke (*Nachlasz* II, 83, 393). The modern radical and revolutionary movements of youth symbolize by means of their style of life and behavior the protest against an emptied civilization which appears to frustrate the freedom and the self-determination of man. Even the flight into the imaginary anti-world of drugs (q.v.) is to be understood as part of this protest. It is almost as if the perfection of the civilized world of comfort confronts man only so much more forcibly with its own imperfection, his helpless stagnation and his inability to change himself (instead of merely his world). Albert Einstein indicates this with his famous word that we live "in a time of perfect means but of confused ends." Civilization belongs to the realm of those "means" of conquering life, making it easier. It presents us with ever more smooth and trouble-free superhighways, but it does not show us where they lead us. It does not give us an answer to the question for the basis, goal, and meaning of our life. But the simplification of life causes the question for the purpose of this simplified life to be raised only so much more intensely.

It would be unchristian cantankerousness and would lead only to sterile criticism if one would make room for a general critique of civilization on the basis of the mentioned reasons. For civilization originates from the God-given gifts of creation; indeed, it is protected by the command, given at creation, to "subdue the world" (cf. *Cultural Mandate*). For that reason we are not asked, whether or not we are still permitted to *want* civilization and its progress. Of course, we must want it, the most obvious reason being that it is part of man's nature created by God. It is possible to provide also quite "worldly" reasons to make clear why man cannot withdraw himself from the law of the progress of civilization. The only question which is raised by the mentioned ambivalence is rather, in whose *name* do we further the perfection of civilization: whether we desire it for *its own* sake or whether we hope with its help to serve *man* who is created, called by name, painfully redeemed and sought out by God. If we further the progress of civilization only for its own sake, we do in blind naiveté—which, however, can be coupled with ingeneous intuition and high intelligence—everything in our power: we build means of mass-destruction, we destroy our environment by means of poisons, as biologists we tamper with the genes and we seek to manipulate man as a technical means. Should that happen, our civilization becomes in the end destructive and will provocate the self-destruction of man. It is probably the anticipation of this tragic development which is at the root of the disquietude of youth. Only if we retain in mind, that man was not created for civilization, but rather civilization for man, so that man is the "end," and the various aspects of civilization only the "means," only then are we on the right path. But in order to protect this monopoly of the *humanum*, we must have knowledge of the unconditionality of man and of his untouchable dignity. If we do not, he becomes without noticing in spite of all humanitarian slogans a mere function of the world of things. But how can we respect the tabu of human dignity other than in the knowledge that man stands in relation to God and that he for that reason is under a patronage which is removed from all pragmatic tampering?

That which we have said can be illustrated by a Chassidic tale: An old rabbi, who was famous for his wisdom, was visited by a man who was bitterly complaining about the damage done according to this opinion by the technological progress of civilization. He said: "Is not all of this technological rubbish completely worthless, if one considers the real values of life?" But the rabbi answered: "It is possible to learn from all things: Not only that which God has created, but also those things made by man can teach us."— "What can we," asked the man thereupon doubtingly, "learn from the railroad?"— "That one can lose everything because of one brief moment."— "And from the telegraph?"— "That every word must be counted and accounted for."— "And from the telephone?"— "That one hears hence and then that which we speak here and now." The visitor understood what the rabbi meant and went his way.— Buber, *The Tales of Chassidim*, 1949.

HELMUT THIELICKE

CLARK, GORDON HADDON. Only one of Gordon H. Clark's (1902-   ) books, *Readings in Ethics* (New York, Appleton, Century, Crofts), coedited with T. V. Smith, is wholly devoted to ethics. But ethics holds a prominent place in his *A Christian View of Men and Things* (Grand Rapids, Eerdmans), and *Religion, Reason, and Revelation* (Nutley, N. J., Presbyterian and Reformed, 1961) and bulks large in *The Philosophy of Gordon H. Clark* (Ronald Nash, ed., Nutley, N. J. Presbyterian and Reformed, 1968).

The task of ethics is moral guidance, which demands universal moral rules (alternative to moral skepticism), which in turn requires a theory of moral justification. Clark's revelational ethics is a theory of moral guidance based on what he conceives to be a rationally justifiable theory of moral rules. The source of moral guidance is propositional divine revelation (the Bible) in which are given definite universal laws governing such matters as capital punishment, war, and sex. He does not deny the difficulty of application or rules to some particular problems, but argues that competing systems can give no guidance at all.

Empirical ethical theories are logically unjustifiable, since they lack any valid inductive argument able to derive moral obligation from observable phenomena. The primary failure of deductive theories, on the other hand, is the lack of valid argument from abstract principles to specific situations. To avoid the failure of these theories, Clark proposes that moral reasoning start with the axiom of revelation, "The Bible is the Word of God." Biblical revelation is both absolutely true and factual, and in it is found the justifiable moral postulate, "The right is what God legislates." God is the sovereign creator of all things, including the moral law. Conceivably he could have created the world with a different physical order, and there is no a priori reason why this should not apply to the moral order also. On a theistic interpretation, "honesty is the best policy precisely because God has made the world that way. Anything God does is right because he does it" (*Religion, Reason, and Revelation*, p. 188). Apart from God's sovereign legislation, custom or habit is the only source of the expectation that honesty is the best policy.

Gordon H. Clark and T. V. Smith, eds., *Readings in Ethics*, New York, Appleton-Century-Crofts, 1931; _____, *A Christian View of Men and Things*, Grand Rapids, Eerdmans, 1952; _____, *Religion, Reason, and Revelation*, Philadelphia, Presbyterian and Reformed, 1961; *The Philosophy of Gordon H. Clark*, Ronald Nash, ed., Philadelphia, Presbyterian and Reformed, 1968.   ROY W. BUTLER

CLASSES, SOCIAL. See *Social Classes*.

CLERGY, ETHICAL PROBLEMS. See also *Preaching*. Most ministers in the Reformed tradition have interiorized Biblical codes of behavior which guide them in the many interpersonal relationships to which their profession commits them. A faithful devotional life will nourish spiritual sensitivity and ethical integrity. The ultimate criteria of their ethical judgments will be the glory of God. They can rely on the enabling presence of his Spirit who said "Lo, I am with you to the close of the ages" (Matt. 28:20).

Western culture is success oriented. Ministers of urban churches are often pressured by lay professional men and business executives who constitute their boards to develop programs which will result in quantitative expansion of members and finances. An imperceptible shift from the true ministry of the church will accompany a ministerial obsession to touch the human dilemma with the proclaimed Word in order to enhance the visible institution for its own sake. Concession to an ethic of expediency is an ever present temptation for the minister; any immediate "good" goal can be rationalized and may color his preaching. Sound Biblical criteria will dictate integrity in both mission and method.

Ethical relations between ministers are not regulated in most denominations by objective reference to codified standards. The American Medical Association articulates the principles of ethics for the practicing physician. The American Bar Association provides for a standing "grievance committee" which adjudicates ethical violations. In recent ecclesiastical history some denominations have modified the historic books of church discipline and order with some attention to ministerial behavior.

The minister's relation to his fellow ministers, involving also his predecessor and successor, is a sensitive area. When multiple staff association is involved, as well as in denominational political interchange, there is the inevitable hazard of ego conflict which may begin with lower than conscious level motivations and proceed to harmful division.

The history of congregational and denominational polarization suggests that, apart from fundamental matters of conscience, the ostensible and public reasons not infrequently disguise the unadmitted ego conflicts of clergy. Paul's exhoration "in honor prefer one another" (Rom. 12:10) concerns the interpersonal ethic applicable between the servants of Christ.   JAMES FORRESTER

CLONING. See *Genetics*.

COERCION. See also *Compulsion; Nonresistance*. Coercion is pressure exerted upon a voluntary agent to compel him to act or refrain from acting in a certain way. The pressure may come from another individual or from a social group or institution. The moral value of coercion depends upon the motivation of the agent applying the pressure and the results of the forced action (Matt. 27:17-18). At times there is but a thin line between legitimate and illegitimate coercive action. Criminal violence (Ps. 140:11; Luke 3:4), blackmail, and political tyranny are instances of illegitimate coercive action while the power or authority of state might exemplify the legitimate use of coercive force. When the individual being coerced is a member of the group doing the coercing, then this one may not feel that his moral freedom has been entirely sacrificed since he himself is a party to the coercion. This is precisely the case with representative governments which in regard to coercion occupy a very different moral stance than does the tyranny of mere force.

No authority can ultimately rest merely upon physical coercion for any sustained period (Ezek. 7:23). There are psychological dimensions in cases of enduring coercion where one being coerced places his entire personality at the disposal of those in authority (Matt. 10:28; Luke 12:4). He may do this either consciously or unconsciously. Historically, every case of submission to unfeeling coercion has proved to be both socially and personally demoralizing as in the case of slavery.

                                                        WATSON E. MILLS

COHABITATION. Cohabitation is living together as man and wife without a legal marriage. A narrower definition, sometimes employed, is coitus. Evidence indicates that cohabitation is increasing in the USA particularly at secular colleges and universities. The term "arrangement" frequently is used for a situation in which the pair cohabits. The abrupt drop in occupancy of college dormitories and the sharp rise in student occupancy of apartments in recent years correlates with this change in attitude and with a corresponding relaxation of college controls over student housing.

Is cohabitation wrong? If one's moral basis is relativistic, the answer may be either yes or no, depending on the person pronouncing judgment and his values. The pronounced swing toward relativism in the USA has spawned a sharp increase in the notion that there is nothing wrong with cohabitation for any pair who think they love each other and treat each other considerately.

But if one believes in moral absolutes, especially the absolutes which God presents in the Bible, cohabitation is wrong in a culture which recognizes legal marriage as the public testimony of a man and woman that they are committing themselves to one another, and thereby assume all the duties as well as privileges of marriage.

Most cohabitation appears to be temporary and suggests that the partners are interested in certain privileges of marriage without all the responsibilities.

God's Word clearly contains commandments forbidding adultery (Exod. 20:14) and fornication (I Cor. 6:18). Furthermore, God states that his commandments are given for our own good (Deut. 10:13). Hence, any person committed to loving and obeying the Lord of the Bible must conclude that cohabitation in our culture is morally wrong.   JOHN W. ALEXANDER

COLLECTIVE BARGAINING. See also *Industrial Relations.* Collective bargaining is considered the government-sanctioned, inviolable ritual by which management and organized labor privately settle economic self-interest disputes through reason or threat of or actual economic conflict. For balanced results, the adversaries must have equal bargaining power. Both sides are usually free to resort to coercive methods, such as layoffs, dismissals, lockouts, work-to-rule campaigns, slow-downs, boycotts and strikes, to reach a collective agreement—a short-term, cease-fire contract during which the warring parties must abide by hard-won terms of settlement.

Most corporations and unions alike thrive on this twofisted, competitive approach. Management considers collective bargaining the most efficient way of handling employee problems, while unions propagate it as the best vehicle for their members' economic advancement within a free enterprise system.

The antagonists are really bedfellows, idolizing power, cash, and economic security. This economistic collective bargaining ideology violates Christ's Word that man and creation serve him and mankind, not self. Life is not a struggle against flesh and blood or between classes. Its purpose is to gain hearts for the Lord's Kingdom, and to develop harmonious living in the redemption and spirit of the Liberator. The Father's workers, both employer and employee, are Creator-dependent-imagers called in Christ to seek each other's and the world's well-being. They are co-responsible for the creation, including the work-community, business enterprise, and nation, in which all have their respective co-authoritative place and task. Greedy collective bargaining sessions should give way to genuine service enterprises, meaningful work, on-going consultation, co-decision, and co-operation by work-communities responsive to justice, authority and joy in Christ and to the Father's good creation, and sensitive to the diverse needs and duties of fellow-creatures.   GERALD VANDEZANDE

COLLECTIVISM. See also *Communism; Individualism.* The fundamental idea underlying collectivism is that the whole social organism is more than the sum of its parts. The individual, therefore, must subsume his interest under those of "the general will," or at least the will of the majority. Usually this concept involves the absolute authority of the controlling element in society, which in many cases means a dictatorship, whether of a group or of an individual. Such a control claims to embody the will of the whole body in which all are equally under the ultimate authority.

Collectivism has always existed in history alongside "individualism." Frequently they appear as opposite sides of the same coin. It has been strongest at times of a threat to the established order—when those opposed to the collective ideal have been endeavoring to bring about a more individualistic type of social organization: political, ecclesiastical, or economic, or when a society has been threatened by external foes. It usually has been supported by a philosophy which holds that only collective action can give man the good life, by overcoming the "ultimate enemy," the atomism of the universe.

One of the earliest philosophic expressions of collectivism is found in Plato's *Republic.* Somewhat later the establishment of the Roman Empire took place to a large extent in the name of collective security as a result of the disintegration of the old republic. Some maintain that the most perfect example of collectivism in history was the medieval feudal society developed under the aegis of the Roman Catholic Church, which sought to set up the Kingdom of God on earth. With its ideal of an hierarchical society under the guidance of the church it endeavored, albeit unsuccessfully, to establish a completely collectivist civilization.

The sixteenth century saw a different approach to collectivism. Protestant Reformers such as Calvin and his followers and the Anabaptists thought in terms of a collectivism that would be more egalitarian than that of the Middle Ages and which would be directly under the Lordship of Christ, who speaks through his people as a whole. Meanwhile a secularist type of collectivism developed with the rise of absolute monarchs who sought to achieve economic and political self-sufficiency for their new national states. At the same time such works as Sir Thomas More's (1478-1535) *Utopia,* Jean Jacques Rousseau's (1712-78) *Le Contrat Social* and Claude Henri, Comte de St. Simon's (1760-1825) *Du System Industrial* advocated a type of collectivism often called "utopian." This Karl Marx (1818-83) took over, seeking to give to it a scientific basis in materialism and insisting that only "the dictatorship of the proletariat" would bring about a true collectivism.

More recent collectivist theories have been developed by writers such as C. Virgil Georghiu, Aldous Huxley, George Orwell and Herbert Marcuse who think of a collectivism imposed on a society by a minority from within or an invading force from without. In their projections they foresee not only a political and economic collectivism but even a uniformity of thought that will be determined by the governing power directed by a dictatorial system and operated by a bureaucratic elite using modern technology.

Largely under the influence of Marx, a number of attempts have been made in this century to establish a collective state. Communist Russia and its satellite nations with their public ownership of the means of production, their bureaucratic planning, their monetary controls, and their secret police have sought to put collectivist ideas into effect, but without entire success. National Socialism (Nazism) in Germany and Facism in Italy, both influenced strongly by Marxism, likewise sought to establish a national racial collectivism. The most recent example of such an endeavor has appeared in Communist China. Many so-called democratic nations also have been moving steadily in this direction with the development of the "welfare state" and what is called "participatory democracy." Yet history shows that collectivism is never complete or total. Something in man's makeup resists such totalitarian control.

Outside the political sphere also, we find collectivist thinking and action in the "free" nations. The joint-stock company, the trade-union and even the various churches, both Roman Catholic and Protestant, with their centralized managerial bureaucracies, have moved increasingly in this direction. The recent development of "communes" among the disaffected in Western society because of its conformism and uniformity, has likewise resulted in a collectivist counter-culture.

From the Christian point of view a true collectivism does exist, manifesting itself in the Christian community as "the body of Christ" and in the command to love one's neighbor as oneself. This is fundamentally a spiritual collectivism, not one that conforms to the humanist ideal. Both OT and NT emphasize that all men and all human organizations are under the sovereign rule of God in Jesus Christ, who is Lord of All.

The Christian, therefore, has always

stood in opposition to the usual "worldly" collectivism, since his ultimate responsibility is not to the humanly-devised "collective," but to the sovereign God. This is true in business, labor union, church, political government and all other spheres of human activity. Furthermore, since all collectives in this world are made up of sinners, none is ever perfect. Consequently no humanly devised collectivism can ever claim the Christian's total allegiance. Only when Christ's kingdom is visibly revealed will the true collective, to which he can adhere completely, be established.

📖 *Encyclopedia of Social Sciences*, New York, Macmillan, 1963, "Collectivism," "Individualism"; *International Encyclopedia of Social Sciences*, New York, Macmillan, 1968, "Communism"; *Christelijke Encyclopedia*, Kampen, Kok, 1958, "Collectivisme," "Individualisme"; B. Zylstra, *From Pluralism to Collectivism*, Assen, van Gorcum, 1969; H. van Riessen, *The Society of the Future*, Philadelphia, Presbyterian & Reformed, n.d.; J. Ellul, *The Technological Society*, New York, Knopf, 1965; H. Marcuse, *One Dimensional Man*, Boston, Beacon, 1966.   W. STANFORD REID

COLLISION OF MORAL CLAIMS. See *Conflict of Duties; Interest.*

COLONIALISM, COLONIZATION. See also *Isolationism.* Colonialism is "the policy of a nation seeking to acquire, extend or retain overseas dependencies." The government of the colonial power rules the population and territory involved.

Colonies have had different sources. Emigrants seek new homes overseas (e.g., the American colonies). Military conquest may support trade (e.g., British conquest of India). Treaties transfer colonies from one country to another (e.g., Puerto Rico to USA from Spain). A colony as a military outpost may protect the national interest (e.g., Guam for the USA). A people may ask for colonial status (e.g., Hawaii of the USA). Relatively defenseless peoples in strategic areas may become colonies or trusteeships in the interest of peace and stability in the general area (e.g., American trusteeship of Mariana Islands).

The motives and practices of all the peoples concerned determines the ethics of colonialism. Emigrants adopt a new homeland to which their lives and futures are bound. Interests of fatherland and colony diverge and sentimental ties decrease with new generations. Finally, the two populations are in fact separate nations, independence is demanded and granted or fought for (e.g., American Revolution).

Rule over people of different race and culture causes antagonisms. Generally the subjects are treated as second class citizens in their own country. They resent this and covet the status and material advantages of their overlords. To be ruled badly by their own kind seems preferable to good rule by aliens. Freedom is sought unless they have their own reasons for remaining a dependency (e.g., Puerto Rico).

If independence is right in principle for one man it is right for all. Similarly if a strong power has its right to freedom so does the small one. Might does not make right. Acquisition and exploitation of a colony for gain is without justification.

National self-determination is right in principle, but for the welfare of the many necessarily qualified in practice.

As freedom of the individual is not an absolute right if it harms the community, so likewise the welfare of the community of peoples may overrule the right of one people to political independence. In such cases the colonial power should allow the colony the maximum degree of home rule, develop its economy and prepare it for eventual freedom.

WILLIAM K. HARRISON, JR.

COLOR BAR. See *Apartheid; Race Relations; Segregation.*

COMMANDMENTS. See also *Decalogue.* In Biblical usage commandments may refer to orders by men with no valid reference to any binding divine obligation (Mark 7:7), or to specific divine commands issued through his servants (Lev. 27:34; I Cor. 14:37), or to the divinely obligating commands of Jesus (Matt. 28:20; John 14:15, 21; 15:10). Jewish teaching recognizes a minimum of 613 specific commands in the OT consisting of 248 positive injunctions and 365 negative prohibitions. Popular association connects the identification of the commandments especially to the Decalogue. Recent theological trends under the influence of certain existentialist philosophical theories and relativistic trends growing out of sociological studies have tended to abandon the idea of cognitive divine revelation in written form. Such emphasis away from the more objective character of divine revelation to the inward has resulted in a shift of focus from obedience to God's commands, which are now viewed as secondary human constructions and quickly set aside, to obedience only to God's command or non-cognitive Word in each individual situation (Karl Barth, *Church Dogmatics,* Vol II, part 2, Edinburgh, T & T Clark, 1957, p. 509). Others consider only the principle of love as binding and God's commands are reduced to illuminators and legal husks (Joseph Fletcher, *Situation Ethics,* Philadelphia, Westminster, 1966, p. 71). Paul, however, following Jesus (cf. Matt. 5:17), sees no antipathy between the commands of God and love. He indicates rather that the purpose of the law was to point toward loving action to the other person (Rom. 13:8-10) and that the Christian life involves the "keeping of the commandments of God" (I Cor. 7:19). When not limited by an inadequate view of divine revelation, the Christian perceives in the Biblical commands a disclosure from God which helps him more specifically to see what actually constitutes love for God and love for the neighbor in several of the crucial areas of life. When correctly interpreted and related

to the contemporary world these commandments constitute one of the concrete tests of our obedient love to God (I John 5:2, 3; II John 6). While the Christian is no longer under obligation to the Mosaic form and codification of the will of God (Rom. 6:14; Gal. 5:18), he is still under the rule of God as expressed throughout Scripture in the eternal moral commands of God. It is likewise clear that the purpose of God's commands are to awaken within us a consciousness of sin (Rom. 7:7), and lead us to repentance and faith in Christ (Gal. 3:24). God's commands were never intended as a means of justification before God for the sinner (Rom. 3:20, 28) though they no doubt serve in the human community at large as deterrents to sin and as the preserving and integrating core for more stable societies wherever they find expression in their laws.

📖 J. J. Stamm, *The Ten Commandments in Recent Research,* Naperville, Ill.: Allenson, 1967.

ALAN F. JOHNSON

COMMON GOOD. See *Utilitarianism.*

COMMON LAW MARRIAGE. See also *Cohabitation; Marriage; Nullity.* Common law marriage is a marriage based upon the mutual consent of the parties involved, but excluding either civil or religious ceremony. It would not be considered promiscuous, as implied by Jesus' rebuke of the Samaritan woman: "You are right in saying, 'I have no husband'; for you have had five husbands, and he whom you now have is not your husband; this you said truly" (John 4:18). Instead, common law marriage intends to legalize the union, legitimize children born of it, and protect the rights of the woman involved. The capacity of the couple to contract marriage and their mutual intent are assumed, as in a ceremonially recognized alternative. While the statutory law and court decisions covering common law marriage are exceedingly diverse, they contain references to such matters as cohabitation and reputation as that of husband and wife.

MORRIS A. INCH

COMMUNAL LIFE. See also *Cohabitation; Koinonia.* Common ownership of property and equality of consumption constitute the essence of communal life. Communes (sometimes called intentional communities) attempt to overcome the individualistic competitiveness of societies based on private property (q.v.).

Millions of people live in communes today. The vast majority however, reside in government controlled communes in the USSR and China. At least 125,000 persons have voluntarily chosen communal life. Approximately 80,000 persons live in kibbutzim in Israel. Some 20,000 Doukhobors and 15,000 Hutterites live communally. In the last few years hundreds of new communes with perhaps 10,000 to 20,000 members have sprung up in the USA.

The semi-communal character of the first century Jerusalem church has exercised a profound influence on all later communal experiments. "All who believed were together and had things in common" (Acts 2:44). Although they practiced equality of consumption, they apparently did not completely abolish private property (4:32).

Prompted both by the dire necessities of persecution and exile and also a zeal to restore the practice of the primitive church, the Hutterites, one important branch of sixteenth century Anabaptism, chose communal life. Their religious motivation and commitment to Biblical faith have enabled the Hutterites to survive four centuries of vigorous hostility. In their *Brüderhofe* in Canada and the USA, everything is owned by the community. Families have separate apartments, but all meals are taken together. All important decisions are made democratically by the male members.

In the centuries since the Reformation, hundreds of religious and secular communal experiments have emerged. Two important twentieth century communal groups deserve mention: the Israeli kibbutzim and the Society of Brothers. With no private property and absolute equality of income distribution, the kibbutzim have flourished since their beginnings in Palestine in 1909. Democratically elected managers receive no extra income for their additional responsibilities. Almost all aspects of life including care of children are handled communally.

The Society of Brothers is a highly successful Christian communal group with some seven hundred members in three *Brüderhofe* in the USA. Beginning in 1920 with Eberhard Arnold's belief that private property is the basic source of war and injustice, the Society attempts to establish a new society without any private ownership, interpersonal competition, class distinction based on sex or prestige, war or injustice. The Society manufactures Creative Playthings. The Society of Brothers believes that its most effective missionary strategy is to offer an attractive alternative to the decadence of American society.

A veritable torrent of new communal experiments gushed forth from the disintegrating "hippie" culture at the end of the sixties. Believing that if one wants to end the competitiveness embedded in American social structures, one must start with the individual person, thousands of young people established hundreds of communes all over the country in a desperate search for community. Some of these new communes are part of the Jesus movement. Dozens of new evangelical communes exist. By pooling economic resources, and by depending upon sympathetic financial supporters, these "Jesus People" are more free to carry on their evangelistic activities on the streets.

Communal life is an important contemporary phenomenon. The first University Center for the Study of Communal Societies was established at Temple University in 1972. By questioning basic assumptions of the dominant society and by keeping alternative models before us communes do play a constructive role.

📖 Donald G. Bloesch, "Koinonia Farm," *Centers of Christian Renewal*, Philadelphia, United Church Press, 1964, pp. 38-51; Harim Darin-Drabkin, *The Other Society*, New York, Harcourt, 1963 (on the Israeli kibbutzim); William Hedgepeth and Dennis Stock, *The Alternative: Communal Life in New America*, New York, Macmillan, 1970; Victor Peters, *All Things Common: The Hutterian Way of Life*, Minneapolis, University of Minnesota, 1965; Edward E. Plowman, *The Jesus Movement in America*, Elgin, Illinois, Cook, 1971; Calvin Rede-kop, "Church History and the Contrasystem: A Case Study," *Church History*, 40 (1971), 62-65 (on the Society of Brothers); Extensive current bibliography now available, mimeographed, from Calvin Redekop, Goshen College, Indiana, will be incorporated into *Contemporary Communal Societies*, soon to be published by Calvin Redekop and John A. Hostetler.   RONALD J. SIDER

COMMUNAL MARRIAGE. See *Marriage; Polygamy; Sex.*

COMMUNISM. See also *Marx and Marxist Ethics.* The Marxist reckons that Christian morality is deliberately designed by the dominant, exploiting class to justify suppression of the exploited classes. He rationalizes his conclusion as follows.

Historical. Ethical systems, according to Marxist theory, reflect (as does every form of human consciousness) the prevailing relations of production which underlie and characterize any historical epoch. This is the Marxist doctrine of historical materialism.

Relations of production are those sustained between the few who own and the many who operate productive enterprise. These relations always fall, consciously or unconsciously, into a pattern of class struggle—the inherent clash of interest between exploiters (those who own) and exploited (those who must sell, or give, their labor power in exchange for subsistence).

Class struggle is ethically significant because human consciousness and all its cultural and institutional forms take their character from conflict. All ethical systems reflect class interests, and change as the class structure itself changes in response to shifts in the mode and relations of production. The dominant ethical standards of any given epoch reflect the interests of the dominant (owning) class. Ethical dispute and casuistry, while presumably carried on at high theoretical level, in fact mirror tensions and changes in productive relations and class antagonism.

Marx distinguished a prehistoric and four historical epochs in human history. Prehistoric, primitive society emerges into history with the classical civilizations—based on slave labor and producing ethical systems reflecting the dominance of master over slave. Classical society gave way to feudalism—based on lord-serf productive relations and creating morality embodying the values of the princeling. Feudalism was overcome by capitalist production, in which the struggle between owner (bourgeoisie) and worker (proletariat) defines morals and all other forms of consciousness.

Historical change occurs because changes in the mode of production release dynamic in the form of class struggle. The historical process proceeds dialectically, in Hegelian terminology, each epoch generating the next as it antithesis, to merge together as synthesis—and new thesis. This is Marxist dialectical materialism (cf. *Dialectical Ethics*). Ethical systems tend, therefore, flatly to contradict each other, only to emerge at higher levels of synthesis.

In every era, the dominant class imposes upon society the means which will best serve its ends. Ethical theory comes to bless these means as "good," and all opposition as "evil," and religion serves to endow the prevailing morality with divine sanction. "The ruling class," writes Leon Trotsky in his pamphlet, *Their Morals and Ours* (Mexico, Pioneer, 1939, p. 15) "forces *its* ends upon society and habituates it into considering all those means which contradict its ends as immoral." (Remember that Aristotle thought of morality as habit-uation.)

Revolutionary. When, as in certain capitalist societies, the exploited classes (proletariat) achieve sufficient self-consciousness and awareness of the nature of class struggle, they achieve a new morality: that is "good" which forwards revolution against the oppressors, and that is "evil" which hinders it. Because only the vanguard of the proletariat, the Party or leadership, clearly discerns the nature, strategy, and tactics of the revolutionary struggle, in practice this leadership defines the right and the wrong. Tactics may require that today's right may be tomorrow's wrong, and *vice versa.* This "dialectic" is carefully expounded by Engels in *Anti-Dühring* (Moscow, Foreign Languages Publishing House, 1959).

Transitional. Should the revolution succeed, as in Russia, Cuba, China and elsewhere, morality takes a slightly different form. Now the victorious proletariat deliberately commits all power to its leadership—the dictatorship of the proletariat—to secure transition into the classless society, the final stage of history (cf. V. I. Lenin, *The State and Revolution,* Moscow, F.L.P.H., n.d.) and relevant parts in Anne Freemantle, ed., *Mao Tse-tung: An Anthology . . .,* New York, Mentor, 1962). Morality is now defined by fiat of the dictatorship on the principle: the "good" forwards progress toward the classless society (or defends the Party against its enemies) and "evil" hampers this progress (or endangers the Party). Again, the "line" may and does change, sometimes radically. Trotsky wrote, in the same pamphlet, "All is permissable which *really* leads to the liberation of mankind" (p. 45), and such "liberation" means "increasing the power of man over nature and the abolition of the power of man over man" (p. 45).

Personal. Personal morality has no Marxist status. The individual's interests and values are completely absorbed and defined by the Party. Personal decision consists only in absolute obedience—"To the Bolshevik," said Trotsky, "the party is everything" (ibid., p. 40).

Just as, in Marxism, "freedom" is defined as the discovery of historical and dialectical necessity, so Marxist virtue is found in complete submission to the dictates of the Party, even abject confession of error and acceptance of execution. Independence is rebellion; rebellion is political treason and ethical immorality, and is punished accordingly.

Final. The only absolute in Marxist ethics is materialism, which exerts its influence over history through economic relations which fuse the class struggle. The ethical systems which dominate historical epochs are transitory and time-bound. All morality, in the traditional sense, will disappear when the classless society is attained around the world, and the state withers away. Human relations will for the first time be truly human, as summed up in Marx's famous dictum: from each according to his ability and to each according to his need.

Summary. Engels writes,

We maintain that all moral theories have been hitherto the product, in the last analysis, of the economic conditions of society obtaining at the time. And as society has hitherto moved in class antagonisms, morality has always been class morality; it has either justified the domination and the interests of the ruling class, or, ever since the oppressed class became powerful enough, it has represented its indignation against this domination and the future interests of the oppressed. . . . A really human morality which stands above class antagonisms and above any recollection of them becomes possible at a state of society which has not only overcome class antagonisms but has even forgotten them in practical life —*Anti-Dühring*, pp. 131-32.

Evaluation. Marxism is man's most sophisticated effort to save himself in and through history. Ironically, Communist states so far demonstrate most succinctly the imposition of ethical norms by ruling power; class struggle has become Party tyranny, deadly and murderous. The classless society recedes more and more into visions of unattainable utopia.

Marxist ethical theory is essentially descriptive and hypothetical. Human relationships wholly determined by inexorable dialectical forces over which the participants have, in the last analysis, no decisive control, cannot be or become truly ethical relationships. The ocean waves can be described, but cannot be held accountable for their behavior—which is the key to ethics. Likewise, on Marxist materialist grounds, human behavior can be described— though the *choice* to do this already breaks the chain of necessity—but it cannot be defined, or judged, as ethical. Oppressor and oppressed are but figures in a mosaic, victims of history; morality has no place here.

Nor can absolute obedience to Party or dictator partake of morality, except perhaps in the initial and sustained choice of such self-negation. On Marxist grounds, rebellion against the system displays ethical consciousness.

The problem of "freedom" and consequent ethical decision has long been debated in Marxism, and in critiques of it. Hegel and Kant struggle with it, also. Marx denied absolute necessity in history—"we are not robots"—but his dialectical theory depends upon it. Until this paradox is resolved, Marxist morality can at best be descriptive of how human beings have behaved, and Marxist ethics remains rationalization for using any means to attain any desired end. It suffers thus from the severest indictment which Marxism mounts against class—and Christian—morality.

John Lewis, "Marxism and Ethics," in *Marxism and the Open Mind*, London, Routledge & Kegan Paul, 1957, pp. 94-131; "Ethik," in Georg Klaus und Manfred Buhr, *Philosophisches Wöorterbuch*, Leipzig, VEB Verlag, n.d., pp. 164-181 (first Marxist lexikon).   LESTER R. DE KOSTER

COMMUNITY. See *Civilization; Culture*.

COMPASSION. Compassion is love (q.v.) in action. It is applying Christian faith to human hurts. It is helping our fellow man. Compassion is burden-bearing.

Our Lord Jesus in his ministry seems to have acted precisely from this motive. "When he saw the crowds, he had compassion for them because they were harassed and helpless . . . " (Matt. 9:36). Compassion is following Jesus' example, that a man give his life for others.

Christianity regards compassion as an essential characteristic of the moral life. It is fulfilling Jesus' demand, that we love one another (cf. I John 3:11-18). "Brethen . . . bear one anothers burdens, and so fulfill the law of Christ" (Gal. 6:2; cf. 5:14).

Such loving sympathy is guided by an awareness of God's grace. ". . . Once you had not received mercy but now you have received mercy" (I Peter 2:10). "The pity of God becomes our own. By his forgiveness we are given a compassion of the same pattern as His" (R. Newton Flew, *Jesus and His Way*, London, Epworth, 1963, p. 147).

In Luke 10:29-37, Jesus depicts this Godlike compassion as a Good Samaritan. It is the active thoughtfulness of love which soothes the wounds with wine and oil, conveys the patient to an inn, and bears the cost of all charges.

The law of love Jesus here has translated into the business of life: (1) the Samaritan's focus was on the need of the other, not himself; (2) he directed his attention to the point of greatest suffering; (3) Jesus gives command, "Go, and do likewise"; (4) our obligation extends to every neighbor (q.v.) in need.

The lawyer's description of the Samaritan, too, is noteworthy: "The one who *acted mercifully with* the [wounded] man." The Samaritan not merely felt sympathetic, he did an act of kindness—not "upon" the suffering man, but "alongside" him (Greek: *met' autou*).

Pity or feelings of concern often elicit sympathy. But real compassion is not simply an emotional and passive thing; it is also a very powerful stimulus to action. "This emotion emerges into volition. . . . Genuine sympathy issues in active helpfulness" (Emil Brunner, *The Divine Imperative,* Philadelphia, Westminster, 1947, p. 323).

"Let us not love [merely] in word or speech, but in deed and in truth" (I John 3:18). WAYNE G. McCOWN

COMPETITION. See also *Capitalism.* Economic competition is seeking to gain some economic end which someone else is also seeking at the same time. It may be considered on the analytical-theoretical level, as by economic theorists, or in terms of the working or real world of business men and governing bodies.

Theoretically, pure or perfect competition exists when there are a large number of small independent buyers and sellers, each being perfectly informed with freedom of entry into the market, movement within the market, and exit from it, all products being homogenous and relatively unlimited and resources equally available to all. In a business sense a market is pure if no individual or group is large enough or has sufficient control to affect the market.

Imperfect competition results from the absence of one of these requirements for a pure market, usually a monopolistic factor involving control over prices. Common law defines unfair competition as misrepresentation, whereas the Federal Trade Commission Act defines it as monopoly-producing activity.

Workable competition is a concept that recognizes that pure competition does not exist in the real world and is practically impossible to obtain and maintain. Workable competition will exist when the buyer is protected from exploitation by the sellers through the existence of sufficient free choice among rival sellers. Scripture requires business men to be just and fair in their dealings: "But thou shalt have a perfect and just weight, a perfect and just measure shalt thou have: that thy days may be lengthened in the land which the Lord thy God giveth thee" (Deut. 25:15). "A false balance is abomination to the Lord: but a just weight is his delight" (Prov. 11:1).

Edward H. Chamberlain, *Theory of Monopolistic Competition,* Cambridge, Harvard University, 1962; Paul A. Samuelson, *Economics,* 8th Edition, New York, McGraw Hill, 1970.

HARVEY A. MAERTIN

COMPROMISE. See also *Casuistry; Situation Ethics.* In its technical use in ethics compromise is a comparatively late term. It achieved popular use only in the nineteenth century. Materially, however, the problem it denotes is an ancient one which occurs already in pagan ethics. In many situations a tension arises between conflicting duties, claims, or criteria. Thus natural law might be at odds with human law, convention, or tradition. Again, one command, although clear-cut in itself, might be in conflict with another command, or a command might be in tension with circumstances at a given point. In these instances there will have to be an element of violation no matter which way the decision goes. An ethical compromise is not, then, the compromising of a principle for the sake of advantage, gain, or expediency, as in common usage. It is the adjusting of various elements in circumstances where one principle or norm can be retained only at the expense of another. It is a balancing of criteria in which decision may favor one or the other, or an attempt may be made to do some justice to the conflicting criteria in some measure. Whatever the decision, there will be violation to the degree that absolute observance of the criteria is impossible, although in the event the decision may well be the right one and the act is, therefore, ethically good.

In Biblical ethics tension arises between command and command, as attempts are made to carry out the commands of God in daily life. Since a command of God is absolute, absolute obedience is demanded, but in the fallen world conflict arises. Sometimes the difficulty may be due to a specific command such as that which God gave Abraham to offer up Isaac in spite of the Biblical opposition to human sacrifice. In other instances general commands come into conflict, e.g., following Jesus and fulfilling the duty to parents, or preaching the gospel and obeying civil rulers who forbid further preaching. In many of these instances no great element of compromise is involved, since the Bible makes it clear that there is a precedence in commands. Worshiping the one God takes precedence over honoring parents, and obeying God, as Peter nobly states, must rank above obedience to civil authority even though this too is ordained by God. On the other hand the Mosaic law of divorce is a good example of a divinely permitted compromising of the original law of indissoluble marriage due to the hardness of the people's hearts. It is the hardness of the heart, the sin of man, that creates the situation in which compromise arises, whether it has immediate divine sanction, or whether it be man's own attempt to do the right in circumstances in which absolute observance of two or more divine commands is impossible.

The real tension, then, is not between one command of God and another, for in themselves the commands of God are fully compatible, and some specific commands would not have been given if God had not been legislating for fallen men. The tension is between the commands of God and the circumstances of the fallen world in which their pure fulfillment is impossible. Nowhere is this better illustrated than in the Sermon on the Mount. The Sermon on the Mount presents the divine commands in their most searching form, but for this very reason it has always been seen to have a certain impracticability in daily life, whether individual or more especially social. Some groups, it is true, have tried to live literally according to the injunctions of Jesus, but to do so they usually have had to evade other obligations. In the main, then, Christians have expounded the Sermon on the Mount in such a way as to produce compromise in actual fulfillment here and now. Thus the ethical teaching of Jesus is variously understood as an ideal, as an interim or pre-eschatological ethic, as an eschatological ethic, or as a dispensational ethic. Absoluteness is thus preserved for the teaching as such, but not for its observance in life today. At this level there is compromise. Oaths may be legitimately sworn, and friends entertained, and evil resisted according to other Biblical criteria.

It will be evident that compromise here is close to both casuistry on the one hand and situation ethics on the other. Casuistry is an attempt to work out compromises in advance so that a clear line of action may be followed even in detailed cases. Situation ethics stresses the uniqueness of each problem and tries to find a general command or criterion, e.g., love, which must never be compromised. Casuistry has to work with criteria while situation ethics proposes a distinction between relative criteria (which are negotiable) and the absolute (which is non-negotiable). Situation ethics presupposes that the act covered by the absolute criterion will be right even though it flout other laws, while casuistry more soberly allows that it may be a debatable act.

One has to realize, of course, that compromise may easily become a mere evasion of the right on the specious plea of conflicting standards or impossible circumstances. Along these lines, since many people might be hurt through obeying God rather than man, love could be invoked to justify obeying man. Compromise of this type is obviously indefensible. The real problem is when the issue is not so clear-cut, e.g., when in the case of commands of equal stature the first has to be compromised to fulfil the second, and the fulfillment of the second is to some degree compromised by the first. This situation arises easily and often in the observing of God's commands in the sinful here and now, and compromise is thus unavoidable. The important thing is (a) to see to it that only the right compromise is made, and (b) to remember that even though the resultant act may be right there is an element of wrongdoing in the violation incurred. Justification of a wrong act on the plea of valid compromise is a dangerous self-deception. But so, too, is the belief that a right compromise is really no compromise at all but an absolute fulfillment of God's absolute command.

GEOFFREY W. BROMILEY

COMPULSION. Compulsion refers generally to a state of being compelled. Psychiatrically, compulsion refers to a morbid, undesirable, and uncontrollable urge or impulse to action which, when expressed, leads to a compulsive act. These impulses often accompany obsession—ideas or thoughts—which also are persistent and unacceptable. Compulsions and obsession when occurring together comprise the obsessive-compulsive syndrome.

Compulsive acts do not usually express the impulse directly but are attempts to modify or ward off the anxiety caused by the impulse. A form of compulsion commonly observed clinically is repetitive handwashing. Compulsive handwashing accompanies the obsession that any dirt on one's hands will contaminate people one touches.

Compulsive acts may also express themselves in complex highly elaborate, rituals which when deviated from produce great anxiety in the individual.

ARMAND M. NICHOLI II

CONCUBINAGE. See also *Common Law Marriage.* Concubinage is the habitual practice of intercourse between a man and a woman without the sanctions or status of marriage. Instances of concubinage are frequent in OT Scriptures. While the issue of the union might share in the inheritance (Gen. 21:10), there was no guarantee, and both he and his mother could be readily disowned, as with Hagar and the child she bore to Abraham (Gen 21:14). The concubine hoped to enjoy the affection of her partner (Judg. 19:1-3), and generally had the house privileges of a wife. The practice of concubinage among the Hebrews is best appreciated in the light of their desire for offspring consecrated as a religious hope: "Lo, sons are a heritage from the Lord, the fruit of the womb a reward" (Ps. 127:3). The practice, so consistent with the portrayal of patriarchal times, became increasingly the privilege of the royal rich, and disappeared as implications of the monogamous ideal became more evident (cf. Matt. 19:8).   MORRIS A. INCH

CONCUPISCENCE. Concupiscence is an archaic word used by the KJV to translate the Greek *epithumia* (see Rom. 7:7, 8; Col. 3:5; I Thess. 4:5). The Greek word may refer to the legitimate desire or appetite, as in Jesus' expression of longing to eat his last passover with the disciples (Luke 22:15). Its more common reference is to evil lust (II Peter 2:11), especially sexual passion (Rom. 1:24; I Thess. 4:5). The most definitive occurrence of this word is Rom. 7:7, 8, translated *covetousness* by the ASV and the RSV. The connotation may vary with the context, but the term usually means an overpowering selfish desire to obtain and possess that which is not legitimately one's own. Concupiscence describes appetites which are the perversion of natural desires or drives, and which thus become the cause of foul or malicious behavior.

MERRILL C. TENNEY

CONFESSION. See also *Repentance.* Confession of sin has played an important ethical role. Confession to God is obviously an integral part of genuine repentance. In a general sense, then, the renunciation of sin expressed in early baptisms is also a form of confession. In the early church penitential readmission after discipline for open faults included confession; this was public confession to the whole congregation. Gradually, however, private confession began to oust the original public confession. It seems to have begun in monasticism with the confession of inner faults (e.g., of thought) to the abbott. In spite of opposition it was extended to the clergy and finally made obligatory for the laity. Thus the Fourth Lateran Council in 1215 enjoined auricular confession, although not with any frequency. Only in the sixteenth century were attempts made to enforce regular confession, e.g., weekly in the case of priests. With confession a form of absolution came into use. This was originally a prayer ("May the Lord absolve thee"), but later it became a priestly declaration ("I absolve thee"). At the Reformation some churches retained forms of private confession. Thus the Church of England recommends that anyone burdened in conscience should come to some "discreet and learned Minister of God's Word, and open his grief." Most of the Reformation churches, including the Anglican, introduced into public worship an opportunity of general confession with the declaration of the divine promise of forgiveness to those who repent and believe. It has also been customary to recommend that offenders confess their faults, with restitu-

tion where possible, to those against whom they have offended. The practice of shared confession has not found general support as a correct interpretation or fulfillment of the injunction in James 5:16, but it occurs in some groups. One may conclude that, in addition to confession to God, there ought to be an opportunity of confession in the church too, not necessarily in a single form. The criteria of true confession are (1) that it should not become a mere form or duty, (2) that it should not suggest that men have actual power to remit sin, (3) that it should serve to maintain right relationships, and (4) that it should be a means of assurance.

GEOFFREY W. BROMILEY

CONFLICT OF DUTIES, INTEREST. A conflict of duties exists when one seems to have an ethical obligation to do two or more mutually exclusive things. If an act is truly one's duty, however, a contradictory act cannot also be one's duty. In practice, however, situations arise where moral reasons seem to support the performance of incompatible acts. For instance, one might seem to have an obligation both not to lie (cf. *Lying*) to the policeman of a totalitarian state and also to save the life of an innocent person for whom he is searching (cf. Gen. 22; Judg. 11:34-40; Matt. 8:21-22). The person who recognizes conflicts of duties does not thereby become an ethical relativist; the latter denies objective ethical standards, whereas the former merely acknowledges that the Christian must sometimes decide which of two or more revealed ethical principles has priority.

There is no easy ethical calculus to solve such conflicts. The Bible does teach that some duties (to show love, justice and mercy) outrank others (Matt. 23:23; I Cor. 13; Luke 14:5). The Christian must rely on the Holy Spirit, not as an anti-intellectual rejection of painstaking analysis, but in a joyful confidence that the Spirit will guide his careful deliberation (John 14:16, 26;

16:13; Acts 13:1-2; 20:22-23; Rom. 7:6).

Conflict of interest of a government official or a professional person arises when his private advantage clashes with the rightful public interests or those of a client. Two general rules are helpful for public officials: they should not participate in governmental action which would directly affect their private interest nor accept private gifts.

📖 W. D. Ross, *Foundations of Ethics*, Oxford, Clarendon, 1939; Helmut Thielicke, *Theological Ethics, Volume 2: Politics*, Philadelphia, Fortress, 1969; Vernard Eller, *Promise: Ethics in the Kingdom of God*, Garden City, Doubleday, 1970; *Conflict of Interest and Federal Service*, Cambridge, Harvard University, 1960.

RONALD J. SIDER

CONFORMITY. See also *Custom; Tradition.* In general, conformity refers to a voluntary act of an individual by which he makes either his patterns of action or his beliefs or both to coincide with a given set of values, ideals, practices, usages, or the like. Outward conformity (involving outward actions only) should be distinguished from inward conformity (involving beliefs). The term can also be used for similar action on the part of a social group. It most frequently refers to an individual following a given pattern of usages or beliefs affirmed by a social group. In the most profound sense, however, it has in view forming one's actions and indeed one's self after the model of an archetype. Thus a Platonist would seek to conform to the divine Ideas or Patterns of which Plato spoke. The Christian's task is to conform himself and his actions to the image of God in Christ (Rom. 8:20), an emphasis which is one of the major motifs of the New Testament. The theme of Christ as archetypal model, or the theme of holy conformity, is thus an important and recurring theme in devotional literature (cf. such disparate works as Thomas á Kempis, *The Imitation of Christ,* and Charles Sheldon, *In His Steps*). Ultimately, we choose to conform to one of two: Christ or Antichrist. Conforming to

Christ obviously implies not conforming to the sinful world (Rom. 2:23). The danger of worldliness is a constant one. Expediency usually dictates compromise (q.v.) with the world. A church, like an individual, can go through periods when there is compromising of the demands of holy conformity, and a turning towards conforming to the codes of whatever establishment holds secular power.

Two special usages of the term should be noted. In church history, it appears in connection with the ritual of the Anglican Church (the established Protestant church in England): in the sixteenth century, and thereafter, those who refused to conform to the ritual were known as Non-Conformists (cf. *Nonconformity; Puritan Ethics*). In current parlance, the term is often used in a pejorative sense: to conform is to blindly follow group customs. In this context, recent sociological research has shown the powerful influence of peer-group pressure: individuals will often adopt plainly erroneous evaluations of physical facts provided a peer-group holds (or claims to hold) such errors.

📖 "Conformity," *Encyclopedia of the Social Sciences,* ed., E. R. Seligman, New York, Macmillan; David Riesman, *The Lonely Crowd*, New Haven, Yale University Press, 1950. DIRK W. JELLEMA

CONFUCIAN ETHICS. In Western culture, ethics is a sub-system of religion; religion provides the context of ultimate meaning of which ethical actions form a part. Religion, generally organized into a tight social organization, gives the individual a context within which he finds his destiny and provides society with the ethical reinforcement necessary to check anarchy and tyranny. Religion without ethics is as inconceivable as ethics without religion.

Chinese culture knows no such fusion. Religion generally operates in the individual sphere. The ethical system with its own context of ultimate meanings provides the social norms which undergird society. This philosophical-ethical system is Confucianism, for two thousand years the most determinative element in Chinese culture. Confucianism has been for China what Christianity has been for the West.

In the twentieth century there was much discussion as to whether Confucianism is a religion. The early Chinese missionaries considered it such and stoutly opposed it. Modern Chinese scholars, many with Western secular training, praised Confucianism for its rationalistic rejection of religious beliefs. This argument hinges on the definition of religion. If, by religion, we mean a theistic system of ultimate meanings, Confucianism is not a religion. But if by religion we mean a system of ultimate meanings that can be agnostic or even atheistic, then Confucianism is a religion. In this article, we will consider religion to be a theistic system; Confucianism is thus a philosophical system of ultimate meanings subsuming an important and powerful system of ethics.

Confucius lived (550?-478 B.C.) in a critical period of Chinese history; the land was divided into an unstable number of constantly warring states. Rulers were corrupt and ruthless and the people in despair. Confucius taught an alternative; but his plans were not adopted until two-and-a-half centuries after his death.

Confucius taught there is a moral law written into the nature of the universe; an impersonal arbiter of justice called "Heaven." Because it is just, Heaven rewards good and punishes evil. One studies history for illustrations of this moral law. Confucius collected and taught as "The Classics" dynastic annals, a divination manual, and a collection of poetry, all carefully annotated from a moralistic point of view. This heterogeneous collection drawn from the divided and warring states became the classic foundation of a unified Chinese culture.

Confucian ethics deal with the individual, the family, and the state. Individual virtue (jen[2]) is the basis on which a person becomes human (tso[4] jen[2]); the human ideal is a scholarly gentleman (chün[1] tzu). By nature's design, man finds fulfillment in the family. Confucian support of the Chinese family, sometimes even at the expense of the state, gave China a social stability through political upheavals that few nations have equalled. "Filial piety" means respect to elders, including elder siblings. The superior respect given parents gives them added responsibility in the practice of virtue.

Politically, the Confucian ideal is a paternalistic state in which the Emperor is a father to all, in deed as well as in name. He is the "Son of Heaven"; the superior respect he enjoys gives him special ethical responsibilities toward Heaven. If he is a despot, he rules in name but not in deed; he has lost "the mandate of Heaven"; his subjects have the right to rebel. Social and political ranks and virtues are thus arranged in parallel hierarchies. When society is corrupt, the rank and virtue are not equivalent and a "rectification of names" (cheng[4] ming[2]) is required to make fathers real fathers and emperors really virtuous.

Confucianism perpetuated its teaching and prepared people for social and political roles by the establishment of private schools, usually with some charitable provision for the talented poor. Confucius is revered as the great teacher. Confucianists educated China in the same way that the Christian church educated the West. An Imperial Civil Service Examination System which survived 1600 years, completed the educational process and provided entrance into government service. In theory and often in practice, the system ensured that those with the highest appointments were best qualified in terms of education and virtue.

The end of the empire in 1911 began an eclipse of Confucian philosophy and Confucian ethics. Republican, Democratic, Socialist and Communist ideologies from the

West fascinated modern Chinese. But both Republican and Communist China, increasingly disappointed with their Western infatuations, are turning back to traditional indigenous forms in which Confucianism is as important as ever.

📖 Fung Yu-lan, *History of Chinese Philosophy*, Derk Bodde, tr., Princeton, Princeton University, 1952; J. K. Shryock, *The Origin and Development of the State Cult of Confucius*, New York, Century, 1932; C. K. Yan, *Religion in Chinese Society*, Berkeley, University of California, 1961.

PAUL B. DENLINGER

CONSCIENCE. The word "conscience" (the "inwit" of Chaucer and Joyce), is derived from the Latin *conscientia* which, like the Greek root *suneidesis,* means co-knowledge. It denotes an inner witness to moral responsibility, the inherent human capacity to distinguish between good and evil. It is the guide to decision-making, and points to its moral dimension.

Conscience is not an OT term. The emphasis there is upon God's transcendent law which is given to man to obey. Conscience is an idea in the realm of introspection. Without using the word as such, however, the OT describes experiences of conscience. "David's heart smote him " (I Sam. 24:5; II Sam. 24:10). The idea of conscience is implicitly present wherever man's responsibility is presented. The OT teaches man's responsibility to God, to hear his word and to accept his will. Jeremiah deals with the idea of conscience when giving the oracle: "I will put my law within them, and I will write it upon their hearts" (31:33).

New Testament scholars often connect conscience with the ideas of Stoicism. But this derivation is dubious. The term is very rare in the Greek inscriptions and papyri. The word does not appear in Epictetus, Plutarch, or Marcus Aurelius. There is no literary source from which Paul can be fairly said to have borrowed the idea. More likely, the NT writers (it occurs chiefly in Paul, Hebrews, Peter) came across the word in everyday speech, took it over, and developed it in the light of the Christian revelation. The term is absent from the Gospels (John 8:9 is inauthentic), though the idea appears in Matt. 6:22-23, "the light that is in thee."

In the NT conscience has central significance. By his conscience man knows himself to be confronted with the demands and judgments of God. His conscience is open towards God (Acts 24:16; II Cor. 1:12). Depending on the life he has lived his may be a "good" conscience (I Tim. 1:5; II Tim. 1:3; Heb. 13:18) or a "bad" conscience (I Tim. 4:2; Titus 1:15; Heb. 10:2, 22). According to Paul, all men are a "law unto themselves" because God's demands are "written on their hearts" while their conscience also "bears witness" (Rom. 2:14-15). Evidently the conscience is a natural property of all men, the inner counterpart to the process of "wrath" Paul sees working in the natural order and society (1:18). Paul elaborates the idea of the imperative conscience which precedes the act and speaks with the authority of God, obliging man to act in a certain way. It is the capacity in man which enables him to take stock of his life and which passes favorable or unfavorable judgments upon it. In the redeemed man, the conscience can with the Holy Spirit bear witness to the truth (Rom. 9:1).

Paul's generous use of the term in I Cor. suggests it may have been in use in that city. Elsewhere Paul employs precisely the same idea without using the term at all (e.g., Rom. 14:5, 15). In I Cor. 8 and 10 Paul makes several points. We are to avoid injuring the conscience of weaker brethren (8:10). At the same time the freedom of the strong conscience is not to be fettered by the scruples of the weak (10:29). The weak conscience may be due to a lack of knowledge, force of habit, or inability to comprehend the actions of others (I Cor. 8:7, 10). Conscience must not be ignored in our dealings with men. Though prone to error and often mistaken, conscience should be heeded and respected. A person ought to act in faith on the basis of his convictions (Rom. 14:1-23).

According to the NT man has in the depths of his personality a moral monitor which sin has affected but not destroyed, placing him in touch with the objective moral order of the universe. That order is translated into human awareness by means of the conscience. That it does not arise from the cultural mores can be seen when men press for moral reforms that directly challenge the existing social patterns. The relation of God's objective norms given in special revelation should not be thought to compete with conscience as an alien authority. The law revealed in covenant disclosure is intimately related to the moral reality given in conscience. A good conscience is the basis for accepting transcendent law, and a bad conscience the self-judgment which God will complement in the future in his own judgment (Rom. 2:16). God's word here finds inner endorsement in the heart of man.

At the same time Christianity does not idealize the conscience. It cannot be revered as the veritable voice of God. It can through sin and faulty training be weakened to the point of being practically ineffective. Conscience can be mistaken, and even "seared" (I Tim. 4:2). Man's interior moral sense is not sufficient for the complete moral life. The light that is in us can become darkness (Luke 11:35). Man in revolt is often able to silence and suppress its demands. The varying demands of conscience in different cultures in part reflect the effect of sin in human life.

Although the act according to conscience is not always good, the act against it is necessarily bad. We are called to obey the voice of conscience and never to resist it.

CLARK H. PINNOCK

CONSCIENTIOUS OBJECTION I. See also *Military Service; Pacifism; Peace and War.* While many men object to participation in war for humanistic reasons others conscientiously oppose war on purely religious or Christian grounds. These are of various types, but the clearest expressions of Christian pacifism have come from the Mennonite, Brethren, and Quaker churches. Even among these, however, some expressions of pacifism are determined more by humanistic considerations—such as the sanctity of human life and the concern for brotherhood among men—than by considerations of Christian discipleship.

The more consistent position of Christian discipleship in conscientious objection to war has often been distinguished from pacifism by the designation of "New Testament non-resistance." This is not simple pacifism, but an active kind of missionary non-resistance. "Turning the other cheek" is the strategy of love. Rather than a simple pacifism, this seeks to register an influence of redemptive love in society. In this perspective alone can we understand an evangelical conscientious objection to war.

The evangelical Christian is committed to Christ as Lord and, as a consequence, lives as a member of the Kingdom of heaven here and now (John 18:36). Thus committed, such a Christian cannot take the life of a person for whom Christ died, but seeks to win his enemy to become his brother in Christ. Such an approach may be made at the expense of his own life, as has been the lot of missionaries in other circumstances.

As a member of society, the conscientious objector to war gives his total life in sacrificial living and does not take this position simply in relation to the draft. While others in society live at another level of action, the conscientious objector lives by love and self-sacrifice, finding it quite often necessary to declare, "We ought to obey God rather than men." (Acts 5:29). Further, those holding this position see the

Kingdom of Christ as global; in the event of war, they ask, "How can a Christian of one nation take the life of a Christian of another nation when both live for the same Lord?" This allegiance to Christ as Lord means that the line of separation between Church and State is drawn horizontally, rather than vertically, and the State as a part of God's order is on a lower level. The disciple of Christ serves the will of God while the non-disciple serves the State as the highest level of commitment. In Rom. 13, Paul makes clear that the powers are ordained of God, and as a consequence, God is continually above the powers of State. He alone deserves our ultimate allegiance. The C.O. stands in society as a witness to the will of God for human behavior.

The C.O. faces the charge that he is a parasite in society. There is a twofold answer: first he serves society in many other ways than those measured by the criterion of carrying a gun; and second, the true C.O. is willing to face his enemy on the basis of his stance in love and is not asking to be protected by others. In a society of order he respects the State and its right to punish the evil and protect the good, accepting that protection. But in the event of revolution or war he stands alone by his integrity and love. Such a position is best held as the strategy of a believing minority.

There are C.O.'s who do not accept the NT biblicism of the preceding interpretation. Their position is more humanistic or "religious," resting on premises related more directly to the supreme value of human life or on the will of God to create a covenant people on a global basis.

It is a tribute to the quality of the USA Government that there is legal provision for the C.O. position and for alternate service as a demonstration of the C.O.'s integrity. While a voluntary army may wholly replace the recent draft (q.v.) system, something would nonetheless be lost were the C.O.

position not held and promoted by Christians for peace.   MYRON S. AUGSBURGER

CONSCIENTIOUS OBJECTION II. Since the first century Christians have sought to reconcile duty to country with the dictates of conscience, and they have wrestled with the issues of opposition to arms-bearing and any type of military training and service. Scripture teaches that when the demands of civil law militate against the supreme law of God, men ought to obey God rather than man. But scripture, and Christian teaching over the centuries in view of this, has also sanctioned governmental force to restrain evil (cf. *Armament; Government*).

Some Christians conclude that the waging of war by a nation and participation in war by an individual are wrong under any circumstances. They point out that Christ refected war as a means of spreading his teachings and advocated only forbearance and nonviolence.

Equally sincere Christians believe that armed resistance with all of its consequences may in some cases be preferable to acquiescing to evil. Reinhold Neibuhr, a pacifist at the time of the First World War, came to accept this view. During World War II he argued that it was impossible to avoid sin by simply refusing to engage in violence and that by failing to act to preserve decency and justice against tyranny and injustice the Christian himself becomes involved in sin (cf. Charles W. Kegley and Robert W. Bretall, *Reinhold Niebuhr, His Religious, Social, and Political Thought*, New York, Macmillan, 1956, pp. 69-70).

In recognition of the right of the individual to follow the dictates of his conscience in the matter of arms bearing and participation in war, some Western nations (e.g., the USA, Great Britain, the Commonwealth countries that have conscription, and Scandinavian countries to some extent) permit alternate service to those whose moral outlook will not allow them to engage in physical conflict. The USA has endeavored to frame and administer its draft laws in keeping with the principle that respect for a man's religious beliefs is more essential than to force him to serve in the Armed Forces. Coercion of conscience can recruit only an unwilling body, while mind, spirit, and a willing body are likely to serve society more fully in alternate tasks not repugnant to individual conscience.

During World War I several thousand Americans refused to perform military service. World War II produced an estimated 25,000 conscientious objectors, most of them reassigned to some form of noncombatant duty. A small number of young men were granted conscientious objector status during the Vietnam conflict although exact figures are not available.

"The number of young Americans who opposed the Vietnam War philosophically to the extent of applying for non-military alternative service was relatively low, even in peak war years. Selective Service granted permission to a low of slightly more than one-half of one per cent of the applicants in 1965 to a high of slightly more than one percent in 1970 " (Selective Service System, December 15, 1971).

Statistical Year	1-O Category (those who applied and were granted alternative service)
1965	.58
1966	.88
1967	.81
1968	.98
1969	1.07
1970	1.18

In 1971, of a total registration of 17,400,278 young men, 36,713 sought and secured alternative service.

What would happen if 50 percent of the manpower refuses to bear arms? A modern nation that will not defend itself is inviting suicide. Are the objectors entitled to the fruits of military protection if they renounce arms-bearing as evil? Many believe that a Christian should willingly assume all duties of citizenship including the bearing of arms in a war that is just and defensive in nature. Force must sometimes also be employed to establish the preconditions for justice, public order and freedom.

Each Christian must satisfy his own conscience under God and should with his fellow men have the right to choose his role as combatant, non-combatant or conscientious objector. But the question remains, Is there a spiritual basis for defending the society or the nation from predatory power? Since God intends that all creation exist in an orderly manner, he ordained civil government as the process by which good is protected and evil punished (Rom. 13:2; I Peter 2:13-16). Even though the Christian must above all else follow the dictates of his conscience (Acts 4:19; 5:29) there must be a recognition that liberty paid for in time past exacts its price in responsible citizenship today. Otherwise society would be chaotic and liberty would soon disappear. In order to reap the benefits of a free society enough individuals must be willing to perform the obligations of citizenship in bearing arms to insure that good is defended and evil suppressed (Rom. 13:1-7; I Peter 2:13-16).   JOHN C. BROGER

CONSENT. Consent is voluntary agreement, assent, or acquiescence to that which is proposed or desired, or compliance with a course of action. Since consent may not necessarily imply complete agreement, it may involve a hesitation or reluctance to agree with or yield to the thought or action proposed. Appearances as well as overt actions may be involved.

Responsibility varies with the nature and degree of consent. Mere permission is undeniably a type of volition but usually bears a different responsibility from that which involves active participation or full cooperation. It may often be difficult to determine the degree of responsibility involved.

Living in social relations with individuals and groups inevitably involves making decisions on what others propose, including the requirements of various authorities and co-operation with activites with which we may be unfamiliar or toward which we may not be altogether favorably disposed. We may be asked to give consent without being able to pass judgment upon the merits or faults, the right or wrong of the entire situation. The most one can do is to search the Scriptures, seek the will of God, commit one's way to the Lord, and then consent or dissent in good conscience. Often this involves dependence on the insights of others, particularly mature and wise Christians.

Since consent involves voluntary agreement, a person cannot be said to have given his consent if he has been forced to make a certain decision or yield to a course of action. Such an act does not constitute consent since the person has not given his free acquiescence (q.v.).

The matter of consent is important in several areas of ethics, such as marriage, divorce, military involvements, and civil government. A pertinent consideration is that of the dilemma of many clergymen who disagree with denominational pronouncements affecting theological issues or particular social action programs, when these are made in the name of the entire constituency. Failure to protest such situations where there are important and basic disagreements may appear to constitute consent.

In law, actual or implied consent is a necessary element in every contract or agreement. Different ages are determined by law (the age of consent) to establish particular periods of life when persons are bound by their words and acts for certain categories of human activity, such as consent in marriage, choice of a guardian, making contracts, and so on. The age of consent is sometimes higher for 'males than for females.   RALPH E. POWELL

CONSERVATISM, ETHICAL. See also *Conformity; Conventional Morality; Revolution; Social Change.* Understood as the view that behavioral standards should change slowly if at all, ethcal conservatism has never been compatible with Christianity. The primitive church forthrightly denounced the views of the Roman world regarding such matters as sexual relations, non-recognition of the personhood of slaves and of women, and drunkenness. A radically distinctive ethic, based on both the OT and the teachings of Jesus was proclaimed by the apostles and a sincere attempt made to practice it.

Almost everywhere the wide gap between Biblical and conventional standards has persisted. In some places many Christian standards—though not necessarily the performance of them—have been incorporated into civil law and social convention. When others seek to change these standards, Christians superficially appear to be cast in the role of ethical conservatives. However, their true commitment is to their understanding of Biblical ethics—to be achieved where not present, to be conserved where achieved. Christianity has nothing in common with traditional thinkers and societies that argue for conservatism because change is upsetting. Viewed historically and globally Christianity is notable not for conservatism, but for its drastic ethical innovations. Indeed, sometimes, to be sure, religious innovation (e.g., abstinence from marriage) goes beyond explicit Biblical guidelines.

DONALD TINDER

CONSERVATISM, POLITICAL. See also *Liberalism, Political.* Political conservatism is a tradition of political thought having its origins in reactions against the libertarianism and individualism of the French Revolution of 1789. Its earliest spokesman was Edmund Burke (1729-1797) who in his *Reflections on the Revolution in France* (1790) attacked the theoretical and abstract notions of liberty being voiced by the French revolutionaries. Burke maintained that a priori declarations regarding the rights of man were meaningless until given substantive applications within the historical context of a given society. Governing a society, argued Burke, was a matter of practical wisdom stemming from the historical experiences of a given people. Hence, the reform of political life could not be achieved simply by abstract declarations based on a priori argumentation. Accordingly, Burke stressed the importance of history and tradition as a basis for social and political change, and he argued that a society is a partnership not only of the living, but of the dead and those yet to be born. Burke's conservatism was not based simply on opposition to all change, but rather on the belief that change must always be incremental and evolutionary and generated from the self-consciousness and historical traditions of a given society.

Twentieth century political conservatism has been characterized by several recurring themes. First, political conservatives have generally acknowledged some sort of universal moral order. Thus, when they speak of such political matters as liberty, power, and law, they are equally concerned with the moral circumscriptions pertaining thereto. Second, political conservatives concede the inconsistencies and imperfections of human nature. Hence, they are cautious in their attempts at social reform, recognizing that progress in human affairs can never be regarded as certain or automatic. Third, political conservatives are generally agreed that some inequalities within society are both natural and beneficial. While there is disagreement as to what the bases for social differentiation should be (e.g., property, blood, education), there is agreement that social orders and classes provide valuable

safeguards against majoritarian impulses within societies. Each station in society carries its own particular moral responsibility of service to society at large. Fourth, political conservatives stress that man must be regarded as more than simply a purely rational being; symbols, traditions, and feelings are important to men, and hence to the governing of society. Political knowledge must therefore transcend theoretical knowledge about society and be informed by practical knowledge gained from experience in human affairs.

The principles of political conservatism suggest a critical attitude toward attempts at socio-political change and innovation. Thus those benefiting most from the prevailing socio-political arrangements within a given society often utilize conservative principles to facilitate their defense of the *status quo*. In Europe—where a strong and viable tradition of political conservatism may be said to exist—political conservatism is often associated with support for established national churches, the rights of property and aristocracy, and general support for imperial interests. In its more extreme embodiments, it has sometimes been associated with nationalism, monarchism, and imperialism. Many European political conservatives found themselves in sympathy with fascistic critiques of the moral vacuity of Western civilization in the 1920s and 1930s, but very few gave open support to the totalitarian practices of the fascistic regimes.

There is some debate as to whether a genuine tradition of political conservatism exists in the USA. American political conservatism has been strongly influenced by the *laissez-faire* capitalism of the Manchester economists and the social philosophy of the Social Darwinists (cf. *Social Darwinism*), and thus bears striking similarities to the classical political liberalism to which Burke himself was opposed.

From the perspective of Christian theology, there are certain obvious points of affinity between political conservatism and Christianity. The Christian concept of sin corresponds to the conservative's view of man's fallibility and consequently with the conservative's reluctance to engage in efforts directed toward utopian reform of the social order. The Christian concept of the state as having been ordained by God corresponds to the conservative's insistence that the state is a moral order and thus cannot be viewed simply as the product of a social contract. The Christian rejection of a purely rationalistic concept of human nature relates to the conservative's reaction against the rationalism of much modern philosophy. On the other hand, the conservative's concern for order and authority within society often blunts his sensitivity to the need for social change or to the rights of individuals as unique objects of God's creation. The Christian concepts of eschatology and the radical implications of Christ's teachings as in the Sermon on the Mount are likewise difficult to reconcile with the somewhat historicist temper of political conservatism.

📖 F. J. C. Hearnshaw, *Conservatism in England,* London, Macmillan, 1933; Russell Kirk, *The Conservative Mind,* 2nd. ed., Chicago, Regnery, 1954; Clinton Rossiter, *Conservatism in America,* 2nd. ed., New York, Knopf, 1962; Peter Viereck, *Conservatism from John Adams to Churchill,* Princeton, N. J., VanNostrand, 1956; Reginald J. White, ed., *The Conservative Tradition,* London, N. Kaye, 1950.   PAUL B. HENRY

CONSTITUTIONALISM. Constitutionalism is the doctrine that order and justice can be maintained in the political community only through the rule of law. It is grounded in the observation that human governments tend to be both despotic and demonic in their use of power. Moral principle, couched in a popularly approved body of governing rules, is invoked to offset this amoral tendency. Some believe this law to be divinely revealed in the Bible. Others hold that it is rationally discernible to all men through reason. Others contend that it is readily discernible through the light of human experience. In each instance both ruler and ruled are expected to live in accordance with the law.

Advocates of constitutionalism have employed the Platonic model of the just man, the Aristotelian model of the temperate man, the Ciceronic model of the rational man and the Biblical model of the covenantal man as a basis for theoretical analysis. Institutional models have been drawn from the Greek polis, the Hebrew commonwealth and the Roman corporation. Speculative philosophers and Christian theologians developed concepts of natural law, natural rights, limited sovereignty and human equality to implement their theories of constitutionalism.

They were first applied by sixteenth century European states where religious minorities were granted rights of toleration and cities or trading companies were authorized to govern themselves under the terms of charters. In each instance the charter defined the rights and privileges of the group and placed limits upon the powers of the national sovereign. The Puritan Revolution in seventeenth century England enlarged the demand to include certain rights for all the people. This movement, culminating in the Revolution of 1688 and the Bill of Rights (1689), laid the foundations of constitutionalism in both England and America (cf. *Bills of Rights*).

Constitutionalism is closely associated with the demand for written constitutions as a limitation upon governmental power. Certain features appear in most of these instruments: a bill of rights, a description of the chief institutions of government with a listing of their respective areas of jurisdiction; general qualifications required for participation in government; and provisions for alteration of the original document.

Recent judicial opinions indicate that constitutionalism is conceived positively as a doctrine to be invoked in the extension of equal social and economic rights to all as well as a restraint upon the arbitrary acts of government in violation of civil and political rights already established.

SAMUEL R. KAMM

CONSUMER FRAUD. Continued mutual trust between buyer and seller is essential for the operation of a healthy economy. Consumer fraud is any omission or misrepresentation that tends to subvert that trust. On the part of the seller, this can include such things as distortion of reports of product performance and cost, misrepresentation of sales performance and equipment maintenance capabilities, as well as design and production of products known to be less than reasonably safe and reliable. On the part of the buyer, this can include such things as theft of goods (shoplifting) or services, as well as misrepresentation of goods presented for exchange or repair.

Both types of consumer fraud appear to be as old as human history. The deceitful merchant is condemned repeatedly in the OT (Lev. 19:36; Deut. 25:13-16; Prov. 11:1; 16:11; 20:10; Amos 8:5 Micah 6:11). Legislatures and government agencies have attempted with varying success to curb seller frauds. Yet, buyer frauds seem to have become an accepted part of the economic system.

The basic Christian ethical quandry is obvious: Why not cheat or defraud if everyone else is doing it? The Christian employee of a seller involved in fraud has a secondary problem: Should I condone my employer's deceit or risk losing my job? However, the buyer faces a more complex problem: How can I be sensibly honest when deceit and fraud are basic business policy assumptions, as when an insurance company routinely substantially reduces all claims payments—even legitimate ones—to discount claimant fraud possibilities? Collectively the local church congregation faces two other problems: Are we obligated to help individual members face and resolve these problems? And, does our toleration of members who commit these frauds cause us to share their guilt and weaken our testimony in the community? It is insufficient merely to invoke pious aphorisms. The needed solutions can be found in a new understanding of Micah 6:8.

BELDEN MENKUS

CONTEMPLATION. See also *Mysticism; Worship*. Contemplation is a type of experimental knowledge, intuitive and not discursive, involving admiration of its object. Aristotle considered contemplation the highest form of human activity, since this is the sole activity of God (*Nicomachean Ethics*). Plato sees philosophic contemplation as a recollection of true beauty from man's pre-natal existence (*Phaedrus*). Neoplatonic thought influenced patristic Christianity with a contemplative mysticism, involving world-renunciation in quest of ecstatic union with the One.

The contemplative life, characterized by solitude and prayer, has been practiced since the early Christian period and is important in Roman Catholic monasticism. Catholic theologians espouse three levels of theological contemplation: first, natural theological contemplation based on the knowledge of God acquired by reason (modern Roman Catholic scholars, e.g., Karl Rahner, question the validity of such knowledge of God); second, acquired supernatural contemplation based on knowledge of God through faith and love; third, mystically infused contemplation involving an intuitive experience of union with God. This is assertedly experienced in degrees of contemplative prayer, from prayers of simple union, and finally transforming union, or total surrender to God and transformation in God.

The Protestant emphasis on justification by faith is principally opposed to the ideal of man's ascent to God by the mystical ladder of contemplative process. Nygren in *Agape and Eros* considers this sort of mysticism and intrusion of the egocentric eros-principle as opposed to the descending agape-love of God bestowed freely on the sinner. Some Protestants, however, stress the Spirit's indwelling, and elaborate this into an "inner light" principle, as do German pietists and the English Quakers.

MORTON H. SMITH

CONTEMPORARY SOCIETY. See *Social Change*.

CONTENTMENT. See also *Tranquility*. Contentment is a rare word in Scripture, but the idea is common to both Testaments. Said David, "The Lord is my shepherd; I shall not want." Contentment is based on confidence in God, and that in two respects: the assurance that he does all things well and the realization that personal knowledge of him and fellowship with him constitutes the supreme good, exceeding by far all creaturely blessings. Jesus' teaching is germane, especially his reminders of the Father's loving care of his own, which renders anxiety both unnecessary and sinful (Matt. 6:25-34). The conception is further illuminated by the Apostle Paul, who asserts that he has learned to be content in the midst of any earthly condition, whether it be need or abundance (Phil. 4:11-12). The word he uses for "content" means self-sufficient, but in a sense which distinguishes it from the Stoic ideal of independence of outward circumstances because of an indomitable spirit. Rather, Paul is self-sufficient because the redeemed self includes the strength-imparting Christ who dwells within him (Phil. 4:13). The same apostle, after denouncing those who try to make financial gain out of religion, goes on to say that godliness, when accompanied by contentment, is great gain (I Tim. 6:6). In other words, godliness thrives in an atmosphere

unsullied by a craving for self-enrichment. The remainder of the chapter conveys the truth that contentment is stimulated by hope as well as faith, for God has provided not only for this life but for the life to come.

EVERETT F. HARRISON

CONTEXTUAL ETHICS. See also *Situational Ethics*. In the discipline of Christian ethics, contextualism is, broadly speaking, a method by which moral evaluations of persons, acts, courses of action, or policies are made on the basis of psychological considerations, socio-political relations and structures, philosophical insights, and Biblio-theological perspectives. In this approach, the substantive consideration of Christian ethical decision-making varies, but has most characteristically found expression in the attempt to make ethical evaluations in light of the emerging historical possibilities of a more mature manhood (human wholeness or interrelatedness) and a more human world (social inclusiveness). Some of the more important Christian ethicists who have adopted this methodology are Paul Lehmann, Gibson Winter, Gordon Kaufman and Joseph Sittler.

Contextualism as a method in ethics arose in response to legalistic ethics or ethical absolutism. According to the contextualist, the absolutist affirms that conduct is to be designated as ethically good when it conforms in some degree to a standard which is to be applied "to all people in all situations in exactly the same way" (Paul Lehmann, *Ethics in a Christian Context*, New York, Harper, 1963, p. 125). The contextualist believes that this approach invariably yields an unbridgeable gap between absolute standards and the particular case. Taking this gap seriously the contextualist asserts that the primary ethical reality ought not to be formulated in terms of principles, maxims, or precepts, but rather in terms of functions and relations.

This could be misinterpreted in at least one of three different ways. First it ought not to be inferred that directional factors are never important to the ethical situation. Rather the point is that directional factors are not the most prominent consideration in ethical decision making. Secondly, it should not be thought that contextualism and situationism are to be equated. The contextualist would deny that all ethical factors are specified simply *by* the situation itself. Rather, the contextualist would claim that the situation itself must be illuminated by empirical or theological factors which the situation may delineate, but may not provide sufficient understanding. Thirdly, contextualism ought not to be interpreted as either an ethic of self-interest or as a strictly relativistic ethic. While self-fulfillment may be considered, ethical decision making is to be located in the context of the fulfillment of the total historical community. Also, while granting that ethical reality is dynamic and changing, contextualism moves beyond relativism by claiming that there is always a matrix of meanings and values which are emerging from human action or from the conditionings of the past and the pre-given structures of society.

The contextualist claims that moral decisions can be made as one begins to understand the context of particular behavior or the content of socio-political structures and policies. This entails perceiving the human significance of human action, structures, or policies in light of the values which might possibly be emerging. From a Christian perspective this would include sensitivity to and re-enactment of what God himself is doing in the world to effect harmony and wholeness. This had led some contextualists to claim that the primary ethical reality does not lie in the divine imperative, "What does God command?" but rather in the divine indicative "What does God do?" (Lehmann).

Certainly contextualist writers have brought important insights to bear upon Christian ethical decision making. For instance Lehmann's suggestion that God's self-disclosure in Jesus Christ ought to have formative power in the Christian's life, is, for sure, a necessary condition for making moral decisions. Furthermore the contextualist has pointed out the necessity of gaining perspective and understanding before making important decisions on issues as well as on strategies for action.

Yet contextualism as a methodology is replete with difficulties. While scientific and Christological factors are necessary considerations of decision making, they are not sufficient conditions. Rational and revelational principles are also necessary features. One of the issues at stake here is the place of "ought" in Christian ethical reflection. While not denying the imperative mood which the term "ought" suggests, the contextualist claims that priority must be given to the indicative mood. Two points need to be noted. First, in rejecting a contractual view of the concept of "ought" the contextualist feels he must reject any meaningful use of the concept altogether. However, to scrap one use of the term does not necessarily entail a rejection of all uses. Secondly, suppose that in a particular situation, after all contextual considerations have been taken into account, we could act in either one of two ways to bring about the same amount and kind of humanization. One way the end might be realized would be to engage in forceful but speedy activity, whereas the other way would entail slower rational persuasion. In such cases the contextualist could not make any *prima facie* case for the moral preferability of one course of action as opposed to the other. Yet most morally sensitive people would likely make *prima facie* moral claims about the moral priority of one means (persuasion) over the other (force). In fact many Christian moralists would argue that love is in-principled in a variety of revelatory and reasonable precepts.

Lastly, contextualists are correct in claiming certain formal rules of reason are not sufficient when making moral decisions. However, the contextualist has not shown that certain "material rules of reason," such as maturity and wholeness, are sufficient for making these decisions. It would be possible to create more wholeness in the world at the expense of some minority group. Formulating morality in such a way that material rules of reason take precedent over formal rules of reason is to misconstrue the dialectic of moral decision making. Rather, action or policy must be submitted to the tests of both kinds of reason before a sufficient moral account can be given. So also God's self-authenticating activity in the area of moral decision making ought to be compatible with both the material and formal principles of reason. The principles of universalizability, reciprocity, and constancy are just as important in determining what God is doing in the world as one's sensitivity to God's action which one gains by participating in that community in which the human meaning of behavior is being unveiled.

📖 James M. Gustafson, "Context Versus Principles: A Misplaced Debate in Christian Ethics," *New Theology No. 3*, Martin E. Marty and Dean G. Peerman, eds., New York, Macmillan, 1966; Gordon Kaufman, *The Context of Decision*, New York, Abingdon, 1961; Paul Lehmann, *Ethics in a Christian Context*, New York, Harper & Row, 1963; Paul Ramsey, *Deeds and Rules in Christian Ethics*, New York, Scribner, 1967; Gibson Winter, *Elements for a Social Ethic*, New York, Macmillan, 1966.   DOUGLAS J. MILLER

CONTINENCE. See also *Abstinence; Temperance.* Basically continence means restraint or temperance in relation to the appetites. But then a twofold restriction modifies the original sense. Continence takes on the nuance of abstinence and comes to be applied specifically to sex relations. Hence the customary use is for sexual restraint or for the practice of abstinence.

This is taught by Scripture, although not in the form of a binding law that might be imposed on certain groups. Fornication is a sin, and extra-marital continence is thus commanded. Temporary continence is also enjoined on married Israelites at Sinai. Jesus can speak of those who are eunuchs for the Kingdom's sake; this would seem to suggest voluntary continence either for a period or for the whole of life. Paul teaches similarly. While marriage is good, there may be periods of agreed continence within it and some Christians may accept celibacy rather than marriage (or remarriage) for the specific purpose of service.

It is to be noted in this connection (1) that continence is not commended as the one right way, the sex relation being wrong, (2) that continence is not necessarily a higher virtue, since every man has his own gift from God in this field, and (3) that there is no question of an external obligation, only an inner commitment.

In Christian history, however, continence very quickly came to rank higher than a proper use of sex in marriage and it also came under legislative control. In the monastic movement continence was an integral element from the very first and with institutionalization a lifelong vow of continence was imposed, and it became a sin no less heinous than adultery to break this vow. Soon attempts were made to impose a similar obligation on the clergy. This might be done in different ways, e.g., by ruling that no clergy should marry after ordination, by commanding that married clergy should either separate from their wives or live with them only as brother and sister, or by having none but unmarried clergy.

The results of this legislated continence provide a sorry chapter in Christian history. Perhaps not the least unfortunate consequence has been the loss of a true understanding of continence and its value. Continence has indeed a place. It is commanded absolutely outside marriage. Within marriage it is a useful discipline which may be voluntarily practiced for agreed periods, and sexual incontinence is certainly to be avoided. Beyond that some may have, either temporarily or permanently, the divine gift and calling of celibacy, which they are to exercise humbly in God's service and to God's glory. For the imposition of continence by ecclesiastical rule, however, there is no Biblical or ethical basis apart from the banning of fornication.

GEOFFREY W. BROMILEY

CONTRABAND. Contraband is any item prohibited by law from being smuggled into or out of a country. An obsolete usage refers to goods a nation may seize to cut off an enemy's overseas commerce. Contraband may include people, such as political prisoners or criminals. Items concealed to avoid USA customs charges are contraband and are subject to seizure and the levy of penalties three times their worth, in addition to imprisonment and up to $5,000 fine for the tourist. Military arms are frequently smuggled to guerrilla forces or belligerent nations. Illegal drugs, especially heroin, have recently been the most common and profitable items of contraband. Such traffic, although an international menace, has involved diplomats as well as underworld figures.   PAUL D. SIMMONS

CONTRACEPTION. See also *Abortion; Birth Control.* Contraception may be defined as the prevention of conception or impregnation by any of various artificial techniques or devices. In common parlance, this definition would cover all such devices usually called contraceptive devices except the intrauterine contraceptive device which does not prevent fertilization but rather prevents implantation of the already ferti-

lized ovum. There is not complete consensus on the modus operandi of the IUCD. It is known to increase tubal peristalsis and pass the ovum quickly out of the tube into the uterus. The IUCD keeps the walls of the uterus apart and could interfere with normal implantation. It has not been demonstrated that fertilized ova are aborted from the uterus; nevertheless, ovulation takes place, sperm are not blocked from entering the fallopian tube, the tubes are not blocked to ova, and implantation does not occur.

It is assumed that contraception discussed here is contraception within marriage. Scripture provides no proof text on the subject of contraception. But the Biblical view of God, of man, of marriage, and of the family can lead one to a Scriptural premise. God created male and female and each with sexual desire and the ability for a sexual relationship both physically and emotionally. Men and women in exercising the right to the sexual union do so within the moral law established by God and in the free will, reason, and decision which is part of God's creation in man. Marriage was ordained by God and it is clear in the Genesis account that woman was not created solely for the purpose of propagation of the race but for the outworking of man's social relationship in companionship and love. The NT explains the love of marriage and likens it to the relationship of Christ and his church. It also makes clear that the sexual function of marriage is ordained of God.

The Bible clearly teaches that sexual union has purposes other than procreation. Indeed, Paul implies that frequent sexual intercourse in marriage is natural and indeed, advisable. Certainly there is no implication in the Bible that union for the fulfillment of the sexual drive in man is wrong. There is no Biblical justification for the view, sometimes expressed, that sexual intercourse is not an independent good unrelated to the procreation and rearing of offspring.

If then, sexual intercourse has non-procreative ends, marital partners have the right to control conception. This is true for the individual family for a variety of reasons, and true also for all of society in view of the evidence that without population control we would before long populate this planet in excess of its ability to sustain us with food.

The various devices worn by male and female to prevent fertilization and the various medicaments, foams, and douches used by females as spermatocidal agents are liable to the risk of failure in varying degrees. In the USA "the pill" is the most widely discussed form of contraception and probably has altered moral patterns more than any other scientific advance in this field. Whether the hormone in question is estrogen or progesterone or a combination thereof, the action is to prevent ovulation— the extrusion of the egg from the ovary— and hence keeps egg from sperm for possible fertilization. The high degree of success of this method coupled with the ease of procurement as well as administration has made it consumer-acceptable in spite of a few specific medical contraindications to its use.

The "morning-after pill" (post-coital birth control with diethylstilbestrol), like the IUCD, does not aim at isolation of sperm from egg but seeks hormonally so to alter the lining of the uterus that implantation of the fertilized egg is impossible. The same ethical considerations, therefore, apply as were mentioned for the IUCD.

The contraceptive pill, although quite acceptable in an affluent, educated society, is less so in an underprivileged, uneducated setting because of its cost and the need for precise timing of administration for twenty-eight consecutive days before a few days rest. The IUCD, on the other hand, is cheap, usually needs only one fitting, and is adaptable to large masses of uneducated females. This advantage alone of the IUCD presents a Christian dilemma to those who see its advantages as a mass "contraceptive" device, yet believe it destroys the product of conception with all of its potential for the formation of a human being oriented toward God.

📖 Walter O. Spitzer and Carlyle L. Saylor, eds., *Birth Control and the Christian:* A Protestant Symposium on the Control of Human Reproduction, Wheaton, Tyndale, 1969.

C. EVERETT KOOP

CONTRACTS. See also *Business Ethics.* The contractual relationship is as old as human history. Contracts (together with what might be called treaties, pacts, covenants, and mortgages) are mentioned in many places in Scripture (Gen. 21:27, 30, 31; 26:28, 29; 31:50; I Sam. 11:1, 2; Neh. 9:38; 10:1; Ezek. 17:12-20; Luke 6:34; and elsewhere). Breaking of contractual agreements is one of the specifically named sins of the Mosaic Law (Num. 30:2, 4, 12). The supreme examples of the contractual relation are the agreements between the parties to a human marriage (whose details are written by Orthodox Jews in the *ketubah,* a formal document), and God's covenants with Israel and with the redeemed in Christ.

Legally a contract is an agreement, given sufficient valuable consideration, between two or more parties, to perform, or to refrain from performing an act. Contract provisions may be specified in writing or may derive, without a written document, from some already existing relation. The ideal contract is a face-to-face agreement between principals to a transaction. Basically, it broadly obligates each party to do whatever is necessary and right in the transaction. However, the more realistic contract is one that leaves nothing to chance or the essential good faith of the parties involved. It carefully details every possible obligation of each party to the transaction. The Christian concept of the contractual relation, following the Scriptural mode, moves a step beyond detailed transactual commitments to an implicit pledge of personal loyalty to the other contracting party, even when that person is not a Christian.

Two deceptions subvert the desired trust between contracting parties: misrepresentation of contract terms and willful evasion of contractual responsibilities. A continuing rise in these deceptions has clogged the courts causing a serious deterioration in the quality of civil justice and a growing general suspicion of the motives of individuals and business organizations (cf. *Consumer Fraud*).

Obviously the Christian is obligated to discharge fully all contractual commitments (I Thess. 4:12). However, a dilemma arises when the other contracting party refuses to meet contractual obligations. At first glance, the answer seems to lie in the forebearance envisioned in Matt. 5:39, 40, but this is difficult to maintain when loss of income or prestige may result from the default.   BELDEN MENKUS

CONTRITION. See *Repentance*.

CONVENTIONAL MORALITY. See also *Custom; Tradition*. Conventional morality refers to a set of norms, behavior patterns, and ethical values which are generally accepted by a more or less stable society. A conventional view of morals arises when the speakers within the society agree upon the descriptive meaning of the chief moral terms. One obvious result of the convention can be seen in the society's ability to distinguish a good man from an evil man and to formulate laws which promote the former and limit or eliminate the latter from the community. The sociological relativist argues that all customary morality is completely dependent upon the diverse cultural environments, so that right and wrong are merely matters of local convention with no universal agreement between cultures. In opposition to this view it has been pointed out that underlying the differences in cultural expression is found a common goal that suggests a basic moral conviction which varies in its expression due to differences in current opinion on matters of fact or inaccurate perception of the true moral values. From a Biblical standpoint there appears to be evidence from Paul's writings that he taught that God's will was in some manner revealed to all men (Rom. 1:19) and that at least to some degree all societies embodied in their moral codes a witness to this higher will which would be the basis of God's final judgment (Rom. 2:14, 15). Thus conventional morality may be seen as a mixture of both the divine will and human values requiring the Christian's selective affirmation of certain norms and the constant transformation and modification of others in the light of the revealed will of God in Scripture.

Philip Wheelwright, *A Critical Introduction to Ethics*, 3rd ed., New York, Odyssey, 1959, pp. 30-40.   ALAN F. JOHNSON

CONVERSION. In its most general sense conversion means to turn from one use to another, or from one faith to another form of religious belief. In the Biblical sense it is derived from the concept of *turning* (Heb. *shub*, Gr. v. *anastrepho*, n., *anastrophe*), generally used in relation to spiritual and moral status. The noun appears only once in the NT with reference to the conversion of the Gentiles (Acts 15:3), but the verb on several occasions is used to describe the initial change of attitude and will that brings men into relation with God. The fullest description occurs in the words spoken to Saul of Tarsus at his own conversion: "to open their eyes, that they may turn from darkness to light and from the power of Satan unto God, that they may receive remission of sins and an inheritance among them that are sanctified by faith in me" (Acts 26:18 ASV). A similar statement appears in the Pauline Epistles: "ye turned to God from idols, to serve a living and true God, and to wait for his Son from heaven" (I Thess. 1:9, 10). Conversion involves a renunciation of evil deeds and false worship, an entrance into a new relationship with God, forgiveness of sins, and the prospect of a place among the people of God.

Closely allied to the concept of conversion are repentance (q.v.) and faith (q.v.), the negative and the positive attitudes implied in the change of relationship. Conversion involves a profound moral dissatisfaction with one's existing status and beliefs which motivates a turning to a different position, and also a confidence that the position to which one turns will be both more rational and more satisfactory. Conversion is not merely a superficial exchange of one set of beliefs or of one pattern of behavior for another, but in the fullest Christian sense means a whole-hearted turning to God.

The inward aspect of conversion is defined by the new birth (John 3:3-8), a transformation of the mind, emotions, and will so radical that it can be described only by the figure of birth into a new life. As an infant enters the physical world with a totally new existence, and grows in a new experience, so conversion, in this sense, is a new beginning in relation to God. Regeneration is the divine act which prompts and is concomitant with conversion.

The event of conversion may differ with the individual. That of Saul of Tarsus was sudden and radical; the conversion of Lydia (Acts 16:14, 15) seems to have been easy and voluntary. In all Biblical instances, however, conversion was marked by a definite committal to the commandments and program of God, and by a clear change of attitude and direction of life.

MERRILL C. TENNEY

CONVICTION (of Sin). The Westminster Shorter Catechism affirms conviction to be the work of the Holy Spirit and a first step toward salvation (Q. 30). Quickened in conscience, Christians repeatedly experience conviction for sins committed after conversion.

The OT provides many examples of conviction of sin. The best known is David's repentance (q.v.) under the accusing finger of Nathan. David's penitential psalms, especially 32 and 51, attest the depth of his conviction.

In the OT ritual the sin offerings and trespass offerings were ordained particularly to express a person's confession (q.v.) of sin. On the annual day of atonement the high priest, representing all Israel, was to make a general confession of the sins of the nation over the head of the escape goat which would then symbolically carry them away (Lev. 16:21-22). Hebrews clearly points to Christ as the anti-type of the goats of the sin offering (Heb. 13:11-13).

Christ brought the Samaritan woman to conviction of sin and through this to himself (John 4:17, 29). His teaching regularly included the rebuke of sin which was intended to produce conviction in his hearers (John 8:24, 44; Matt. 21:33-45). At Pentecost the assembled crowd was "pricked in their heart for their sin against Christ and many repented to salvation (Acts 2:37).

There is a remorse (q.v.) for sin which, while akin to conviction, does not lead to repentance and faith. Cain and Judas were sorry for what they had done. Felix trembled at Paul's preaching (Acts 24:25) but his conviction was not deep enough to bring him to seek Paul's Christ.

Many efforts have been made to explain away conviction of sin. Bushnell's idea of

Christian nurture minimized its necessity; a child properly nurtured, he held, would routinely grow into Christian experience. Edward S. Ames in his *Psychology of Religious Experience* (Boston, Houghton Mifflin, 1910, pp. 258ff.) likened conviction of sin to psychological experiences of subjective perplexity and tension. Conviction is thought by such writers to be a product of internal factors and neither caused by the Holy Spirit nor necessary to a healthy emotional life. Some consider the sense of sin harmful.

It is, of course, true that conviction is a psychological state just as is earnest faith. But the Bible grounds the conviction of sin in a basic experience in which a sinner is keenly aware that he has transgressed God's law and is therefore guilty. The attitude of conviction, confession, and trust continues throughout the Christian life after one experiences God's forgiveness in Christ.

R. LAIRD HARRIS

COOPERATION, ECCLESIASTICAL. See also *Separation, Ecclesiastical.* Cooperation among individual Christians within congregations and specialized agencies and fellowships, and cooperation among such groups, is widely indorsed in principle, but in practice disagreement abounds over forms, limits, and methods. Where there is agreement, implementation is incomplete.

The Bible teaches there is unalterably only one church, the body of Christ, into which all Christians are placed by God (Eph. 1:22, 23; 2:15, 16; 4:4-6). The Bible envisages all true Christians in each place and globally cooperating as the various parts of one body, with their distinctive functions and styles (I Cor. 12:12-26). When one's bodily members functions uncooperatively he is sick, handicapped, or dead. A major ethical failure of Christians is their inadequate demonstration of body-like cooperation for which Jesus prayed, so that "the

world may believe" he was sent by the Father (John 17:21).

Realizing its importance, most subapostolic Christians sought cooperation through the leadership of bishops, one for each place. Resolutions of episcopal disputes were attempted by councils or the pope. Instead rival bishops and popes resulted. Episcopacy has never achieved genuine cooperation and through political associations has impeded it. (Moreover, evangelicals think many bishops claiming apostolic succession, as well as many leaders in the "ecumenical movement," have not conformed to apostolic doctrine, hence have not genuinely been church leaders.) At least episcopacy attempted to exhibit a cooperation which non-Christians could see. With the development of Protestantism even this attempt was abandoned.

For sixteen centuries all .Christians believed there could be only one organized expression of the church in each place. The concept of denominationalism arose when several groups, though independently organized throughout England, recognized each other as brethren.

Each denomination traditionally claimed to be the most Biblical, but never the only (as do sects), expression of the church. As conditions for membership denominations set doctrinal and ethical standards which were narrower than their definitions of the church. This was an impediment to all Christians in each place cooperating as do the parts of one's body.

Denominations have facilitated cooperation among distant congregations, but they have hindered full cooperation among adjoining congregations. The inevitability of denominations can be explained historically, sociologically, and psychologically, but denominations cannot be justified Biblically. Strife within the church at Corinth was severely censured (I Cor. 1:10-13). Paul strongly stressed that all races and classes are spiritually one in Christ (Col. 3:11). The argument that denominations are like army divisions would only apply if platoons fought interspersed while answering to uncoordinated commanders.

As much as possible Christian individuals and groups should embrace in thought, word, and deed all fellow residents whom they deem brethren, not just those sharing their specific views, even on cooperation. (The proper Corinthian response to "Paul's" and "Apollo's" factions was not "Christ's" faction, but a "we are all Christ's" attitude.) Fundamental doctrines and practices which one thinks separate Christians from non-Christians must be clearly distinguished from secondary doctrines on which true Christians disagree. Cooperation should begin where any agreement is found, not waiting for full concord. Especially in times of revival and persecution and in "interdenominational" specialized ministries such attitudes prevail. Cooperation could be more permanent and generalized if Christians were truly "eager to maintain unity ...forbearing one another in love" (Eph. 4:3, 2). Meanwhile, God patiently works through inadequate expressions of cooperation while calling us through his Word to fuller obedience. DONALD TINDER

CORPORAL PUNISHMENT. See also *Prison Reform; Punishment.* The courts have defined corporal punishment as involving action on the body in contrast with pecuniary punishment or fine and execution (cf. *Capital Punishment*). Usually it involves whipping or the pillary, though some jurists include imprisonment. In many countries criminal codes specifically provide whipping as a punishment for armed burglary, choking, drugging and various sex crimes. Placing a prisoner in irons, even at common law, was considered unlawful except to prevent escape. Where corporal punishment is not prohibited in the USA confinement to a dungeon in irons and limiting food to bread and water has been held valid (cf.

Howard v. State, 28 Ariz. 433). Where prohibited by state codes, three slaps across the face of a disobedient prisoner is a violation.

To the ancients, underworld torture offered the pattern for punishment. By illustrations like vultures picking the liver of Tityus and the inability of Sisyphus to complete his stone rolling sentence, Homer represents punishment in the hereafter as vindictive retaliation (*Odyssey* xi). Some scholars view future punishments in the Bible similarly (cf. Luke 16:23).

While shedding of blood in the OT requires life to cleanse the land, Hebrew law seems primarily directed to recompensing the person who suffered loss (cf. Exod. 22:1ff.). Corporal punishment such as flogging was employed to correct deviant behavior (Deut. 21:18; 22:18), but a limit was prescribed to prevent degrading the brother (25:1-3).

Most parents recognize some connection between a type of corporal punishment and reformation (cf. Prov. 13:24). But the Christian considers that such punishment, without support and concern for the individual, may lead to brutalization and rebellion. Wholesome concern for prisoners should not, however, be confused with permissiveness within contemporary society. Failure to recognize instability patterns in criminals has often led to recommendations for treatment appropriate to stable persons. To achieve reinstatement in society the unstable deviant will probably be stabilized more by positive reinforcing factors in reconditioning than by negative means such as flogging. But experience with the hardened criminal does not offer much optimism for reform. GERALD L. BORCHERT

CORPORATE RESPONSIBILITY. See also *Business Ethics; Industrial Relations.* Responsibility in theology is typically seen as an attribute of the individual: God speaks to men, and they are individually responsible (answerable) to him. The vis-a-vis of the individual and God appears as the ultimate source of human personhood, particularly in recent religious existentialist thought.

Although God assuredly speaks to individuals, we also find in the Bible, the concept of the solidarity and accountability (a) of mankind as a whole, (b) of Israel, (c) of other individual nations, and (d) of the church. However, this general or corporate accountability never relieves the individual of personal responsibility to God, nor does it bind the obedient man over to condemnation because he is part of a disobedient community. In fact, the concept of corporate accountability offers an important counterpoise to the modern atomistic individualism (q.v.) for which evangelical religion is often blamed, but which owes more to eighteenth-century Rationalism and modern Existentialism.

In both ancient and medieval times and in many non-Western societies even today, the life of the individual was dominated by his membership in a body or bodies of various kinds: nations, tribes, churches, castes, guilds, clans, and so on. The individual craftsman, for example, was responsible to his guild, which in turn answered to the town authorities for his conduct and the quality of his work. The Moslem conquerors of the Near East made the bishops responsible for the behavior of their Christian subjects. In the Latin West, the confessional was the church's means, not always effective, of exercising responsibility for its members. The Reformation broke up this penitential discipline, and the French Revolution accelerated the disappearance of responsible intermediate bodies from Western society.

The extreme individualism of bourgeois democracy and laissez-faire (q.v.) capitalism goes beyond any Biblical warrant, for the Scripture does hold nations as well as individuals accountable. A good, moral man who is loyal to an evil state may be responsible for its misdeeds. After World War II, the War Crimes Trials refused to accept the idea that the perpetrator of an evil deed is innocent if he was following the orders of his lawful government, and sought instead to hold individuals responsible for government actions, at least to the extent that they did not oppose them. The ambiguous situation of the morally good individual who is integrated into an unjust corporate or national system has been examined at length by Reinhold Niebuhr (q.v.) in *Moral Man and Immoral Society*.

As moralists from the Allied countries argued that German and Japanese soldiers should have refused to obey immoral orders during World War II, a growing number of citizens, supported by clergy, now claim the right and the duty to decide whether they will cooperate with government decisions, such as recent USA involvement in Viet Nam.

Corporations are legal persons and have certain legal responsibilities which resemble those of natural persons. While the law usually defines such responsibilities only in the financial sphere, recent thought has begun to hold corporations responsible for all the implications of their actions. Thus, e.g., the Dow Chemical Company is widely condemned on moral grounds for the manufacture of napalm, and Harvard University is criticized for expanding its campus at the expense of existing low-income housing. The profit-making motive which dominates industry and advertising, calling for increasing production and consumption of unnecessary or even undesirable products, has been excoriated at various levels and for different reasons by people as diverse as Herbert Marcuse and Ralph Nader.

If theologians of the past have tended to view their own governments and important corporate bodies such as industries and labor unions as immune from moral accountability, there is now a contrary tendency to see only corporate and social problems as moral questions and to over-look individual moral responsibility. The religious individualism which ignores the question of the morality of national or corporate actions has given way to a religious collectivism which preaches to the nations about war or to corporations about pollution but which says very little to individuals about personal moral issues such as divorce, self-indulgence, or dishonesty. Certain subcultural groups seem to think of themselves as a chosen band who can do no wrong as individuals because their stand on great issues is more righteous than that of other elements of society. For Christians, a concern for collective responsibility should be developed as a corrective to individualistic indifference, but collective responsibility must not be allowed to obscure the fact that in the last analysis it is individual human persons, not nations or corporations, which must stand before the judgment seat of Christ.

📖 Jacques Ellul, *The Political Illusion*, New York, Knopf, 1967; Norman L. Geisler, *Ethics: Alternatives and Issues*, Grand Rapids, Zondervan, 1971; James M. Gustafson, *Christian Ethics and the Community*, Philadelphia, Pilgrim, 1971; Reinhold Niebuhr, *Moral Man and Immoral Society*, New York, Scribner, 1932; _____, *The Children of Light and the Children of Darkness*, New York, Scribner, 1944.   HAROLD O. J. BROWN

COUNCILS OF CHURCHES. See also *American Council of Christian Churches; National Association of Evangelicals; National Council of Churches; World Council of Churches.* Basically, councils of churches can be described simply as being the ecclesiastical counterparts of trade associations. At the local and state-province level, individual congregations and intermediate denominational judicatories make up the membership of councils of churches. At the national and international level, whole communions and denominations are the main (and in the case of the National and World Councils of Churches, the exclusive) constituents.

There are no formal organizational ties between any of the councils, but most consider themselves manifestations of the ecumenical movement. There have been widespread fears that conciliar ecumenism was the prelude to creation of a super-church, but that possibility seems to be growing more remote. When the ecumenical euphoria of Vatican II subsided, many councils began diminishing in importance. The most obvious common bond currently is not the desire for unity per se but the campaigning for alleviating social problems through government intervention.

Evangelical "councils" ordinarily prefer to go by some other name such as "fellowships." They are not nearly so numerous, active, or conspicuous as those composed of churches with theologically liberal leadership.

Theologically liberal councils pride themselves for having advocated positions which at first were unpopular but which eventually became public policy. They are eager to outrun their constituencies with "prophetic" stances, always arguing that grass roots dissent must not be regarded as an ethical criterion. Yet when the positions do become public policy they regard it as ethical vindication. They seem to consider that the public can be wrong before the fact, but not after.

The theologically liberal councils also tend to be highly selective in the issues they confront. In its first twenty years, the National Council of Churches tackled a number of political questions, but devoted little or no study to such pressing concerns as pollution, traffic safety, pornography, medical ethics, and crime. It campaigned against capital punishment but had nothing to say about reducing the suicide rate. It called for measures to be taken against South Africa for its oppression of non-whites, but was virtually silent on the suppression of religious liberty in Communist countries. It remained neutral on the Israeli-Arab conflict.

In the late sixties and early seventies the theologically liberal councils apparently began to feel some frustration with the political process. Economic clout was being explored increasingly as a means of social change.   DAVID KUCHARSKY

COUNSELING, ETHICAL PROBLEMS. Parish ministers are called upon to counsel individuals either as part of their shepherding mandate or in other situations involving human crisis. In urban areas counseling relates largely to pre-marital and marital concerns, youth needs, depressions, anxieties of middle-age persons and of the lonely aged. The minister is one of the most available resources in family crises involving such experiences as an accident, combat casualty, emotional breakdown, or threatened or attempted suicide.

A prime ethical requirement at such critical junctures in another human life is that the minister have no doubt about his role. This implies realistic assessment both of his competence and limitations with respect to the particular need. The minister, as God's man in every relationship, should not abdicate this role to become a legal, financial, medical, or psychiatric specialist. He should make referrals in a professional manner to a specialist where this is indicated. Referral carries an ethical obligation to remain in a supportive roll.

All counseling involves an obligation to accept the counselee as a person—and just as he comes. This implies a posture which is non-judgmental and empathetic. It means also listening to all that is being communicated by verbal propositions, but also in the non-verbal language of emotion. It is an ethical violation for the minister to use another's distress to pre-empt the time with his own concerns or with psychological theories. The minister should be aware of the dynamics of "transference" and "counter transference" inherent in every interpersonal encounter. Even without psychological sophistication in his training, ethical considerations should keep him from returning hostility for hostility, either verbal or physical, and from reciprocating in kind affectional advances with sexual overtones. The latter is too frequently a swift path to moral scandal. The minister must reckon with his own elemental drives.

It is unethical for a minister to betray the confidences reposed with him by a counselee. The distresses of parishioners should not become illustrative material for sermons. Nor is advice-giving ethical when it erodes the individual's responsibility for making a necessary and important personal decision.

Ethical considerations call for restraint in exploiting the counseling situation for theological indoctrination. Yet a minister sensitive to intimations of God's Spirit and aware of the psycho-dynamics involved may find opportune the judicious use of Scripture and of prayer.   JAMES FORRESTER

COUNSELS. See also *Church Lobbies.* By this term some Christian ethicists denote special advice on behavior, not intended to be binding on all. Counsels are thus distinguished from precepts, which are universally binding. The so-called "counsels of perfection" or "evangelical counsels" are those associated historically with monastic life: poverty, chastity, and obedience. The Biblical rationale most often cited for counsels is Jesus' advice to the rich young ruler to sell his possessions and give to the poor (Matt. 19:21), which is generally recognized as not being incumbent on every believer.

Contemporary relevance for the term lies particularly in social ethics where means and ends are often hard to distinguish. Many Christians today feel impelled to take some constructive position with respect to major public issues but (1) are unable to find appropriate Biblical warrant for specific courses of action, and (2) realize the great difficulty of determining which courses will give the desired results in an unregenerate society. Given this ambiguity the Christian seems obliged to rely on his own conscience while respecting the consciences of others. A serious consequence of this view is that it seems to undercut the possibility of absolutes in social ethics. By contrast, church lobbies today, which are generally allied with the ecumenical movement, convey the impression that they are promoting precepts rather than counsels. There is some irony in this, because many religious lobbyists tend to be ethical situationists (cf. *Situational Ethics*), and situationism makes little or no room for precepts. DAVID KUCHARSKY

COURAGE. Courage *(andreia)* along with wisdom, justice, and temperance, made up the four cardinal virtues of the Greeks (Wisdom 8:7). Defining courage as the ability to act rationally in the face of fear, the Greek philosophers attempted to indicate those things worthy to be feared. While the soldier's courage was the outstanding example of courage, to have ethical value courage must arise from the choice for that which is noble rather than from mere physical strength or from ignorance that danger is real. The example set by Socrates in choosing death challenged the Greek world to accept also the concept of the courage of wisdom.

While valuing and praising the warrior, the Hebrews valued the moral courage fostered by confidence in God: "Hope in the Lord and be strong" (Ps. 27:14). The martyr chose death rather than be faithless to his religion (I Macc. 2:21, 22).

While *andreia* (courage) does not occur in the New Testament and while the corresponding verb *andrizomai* is used only once (I Cor. 16:13), *tharsos* is rendered courage (Acts 28:15), and the Christian is called upon to be steadfast. Cowardice ranks among the mortal sins (Rev. 21:8). The Christian can be of good courage out of faith in the God who rules the world and in Jesus who in overcoming death overcame the greatest of men's fears. Not only is the courage of the martyr who endures to death (Rev. 7:14) idealized, but there is also the moral courage of him who following his Lord (Heb. 12:2) is undaunted by tribulation and willingly endures pain and temptation. JACK P. LEWIS

COURTESY. Courtesy gets at the pleasantries and deferential decorum that go with manners in a polite society. Courtesy, as we have known it in Western civilization, stems from the patterns of gentility initiated at the Provencal court of the eleventh century by the few womenfolk there, who set the tone of propriety and a habit of decent companionship for the throng of men round about them. An early pagan tradition had held sacred a roughhewn hospitality and respect for the stranger guest. Non-Christian, oriental custom kept social courtesies highly ritualized (e.g., tea service, niceties of conversation). But only in this feudal, miniature court society where a Christian germ of man-to-woman protective chivalry (q.v.) was at work did etiquette differentiate itself, for the first time, as a specific code or norm for social intercourse. Courtesy is first of all a matter of social mores—that unformulated, diffuse, integrating, normal usage a given community assumes for personal interaction—rather than an item with peculiarly ethical dimensions. (Morals—ethical decisions—however, will not long be considered norms where mores—social practices—are thought to be arbitrary conventions rather than also *norms* posited by men for a different but complementing sort of human activity.) Courtesy and the Christianized Western fabric of civility is breaking down today because it has become largely a fake routine trying to substitute for ethical bonds, void of an original Christian animus. If our present-day courtesies are not shored up by a widespread renewal of Biblically insightful manners, the liberating practice of genuine compliments and social neighbor love we have witnessed in history will degenerate into something close to the habits of clan life or a social pressuring protocol determined by a tyrannical will of the majority.

CALVIN G. SEERVELD

COVENANT. Our approach to the meaning of covenant as we meet it in the Bible may be governed by purely historical presuppositions. In that case we would adduce archeological data to illustrate and explain the idea of covenant between God and Israel (cf. Delbert R. Hillers, *Covenant— The History of a Biblical Idea,* Baltimore, Johns Hopkins, 1969). But it is questionable whether such an approach allows sufficient weight for the theological aspect of covenant so prominent in the Bible.

On Biblical evidence there appears to be two aspects of covenant—one on the level of human relationships, and the other in relation to God.

As a sociological phenomenon, covenant has a long and primitive tradition. Anthropologists have shown the importance of contractual pacts in primitive society (cf. Sir James George Frazer, *Folk-Lore in the Old Testament, I,* New York, St. Martins, 1919, 391ff.). From archeological data we know that the same applies to the ancient East. The Hebrew expression "to cut a covenant" *(kharat berit)* already points to primitive practice which involves sacrificial rites (cf. Gen. 15:9-21). The ancient Greeks used a similar phrase. An additional feature of such contractual agreements was the solemn oath before witnesses (cf. Gen. 21:28-31). A treaty, for example, could be concluded between individuals (I Sam. 18:3), between king and nation (I Chron. 11:3), between king and guards (II Kings 11:4ff.), and between chieftains (Gen.

21:32; 26:28). The validity of the contract depended upon the loyal adherence of both parties.

Scholars have seen a parallel in the treaty between a great king and his vassals and YHVH and Israel (cf. G. E. Mendenhall, *Law and Covenant in Israel and the Ancient Near East,* 1955, p. 26). Such a treaty would be based upon clearly defined terms by the suzerain to which the vassal submits. But this does not appear to fit the relationship between Israel and his God. Even Exod. 19:5 contradicts the idea of imposition: "If you will obey my will and keep my covenant, you shall be my special people among all nations." What happens if Israel breaks faith and refuses to obey?

This was the very problem confronting the prophets. The question was raised early in Israel's history.

After the idolatrous worship of the golden calf Moses is confronted with the problem. He refuses to accept the annulment of the covenant: "If thy presence will not go with me, do not carry us hence" (Exod. 33:15). In the end YHVH reveals himself as "a God gracious and merciful, slow to anger and abounding in steadfast love and faithfulness" (Exod. 34:6).

These two nouns: *ḥesed ve-'emet* go to show that it is impossible to treat covenant in the Bible in purely sociological terms. There is no way of avoiding the theological implications: *ḥesed*—for which there is no English equivalent—the RSV translates "steadfast love," i.e., a love which goes beyond contractual arrangements. YHVH remains faithful to his promise: "How shall I give you up, O Ephraim! How can I hand you over, O Israel!" (Hos. 11:8). God is himself *ḥesed* and he desires *ḥesed* rather than sacrifice (Hos. 6:6; cf. Matt. 9:13; 12:7). *'Emet* ("truth") in the covenantal context enforces the meaning of *ḥesed.* Here "truth" means: faithfulness; "steadfast love" means faithful love. *'Amen* derives from the same root as *'emet*: God is *'Elohe*

'Amen: the faithful, or faith-keeping God (Isa. 65:16 as against RSV). Rev. 3:14 provides us with the meaning of 'amen: "faithful and true" (cf. Ps. 100:5 RSV).

There would be no explanation for the conditionless covenant with Noah (Gen 9:9) and Abraham (Gen. 15:18) except for the fact that the God of Israel is a God of ḥesed.

The NT has taken over the LXX rendering of covenant as diathēkē ("last will" or testament); this does not strictly correspond to the Heb. berit (cf. Gal. 3:15). It is only when diathēkē is related to God's promises (Gal. 3:16) that it acquires the meaning of berit as the prophets understood it. In the case of the Last Supper some important aspects of the OT berit come into play, chiefly the sacrificial aspect, whereby the Messiah as the victim vouches for God's faithfulness to his promise. This is beautifully expressed in Zechariah's song: "The God of Israel visited and redeemed his people. . .to perform the mercy promised to our forefathers and to remember his holy covenant" (Luke 1:68 ff.).

This raises the question regarding the connection between the Old and the New Covenant. Some scholars have argued for a new beginning, pointing to Heb. 9:11ff. and II Cor. 3:7ff. (cf. Hillers, op. cit., pp. 178ff.); others hold that the Old is only preparation for the New (cf. E. Przywara, Alter u. Neuer Bund, 1955, p. 115). In theological perspective Calvin's view appears more accurate—the New Covenant is a renewal of the Old, for the promises of God are inviolable (cf. Jocz, The Covenant, Grand Rapids, Eerdmans, 1968, pp. 163ff., 296). Covenantal (or federal) theology subsequently played an important part in Protestant thinking and was recently revived by Karl Barth in his Church Dogmatics (New York, Harper & Row).   JAKOB JOCZ

COVETOUSNESS. See Greed.

CREDIT. See also Debt; Usury. In the credit relationship, the creditor gains some control over the debtor. The misuse of power over another is always a serious moral error. Loans in OT times were not of a commercial sort, but were intended to relieve poverty. The creditor was to suspend the demand for payment every sabbatical year (Deut. 15:2). Under no circumstance was he to exact usury from the poor (Exod. 22:25). Moreover, the creditor may be morally obligated to lend in circumstances of need. The preferred Christian position is, of course, giving to those in financial distress.

Personal attitudes toward debt have been liberalized by the concept that promoting high levels of demand through expanding credit contributes to economic prosperity, the invention of new credit instruments, and the governmental example of deficit spending. Many consumers now finance foreign travel and other non-essentials under debt arrangements with little moral reservation. Non-payment lawsuits have flooded the courts. Universal credit cards, a convenience to many, have been instrumental in numerous bankruptcies. (A national credit card could be used in lieu of money by a totalitarian government to control its subjects.) Consumer credit has lowered the price of some goods by allowing mass-production economies, has permitted earlier enjoyment of durable goods by young families, and has redirected family income in some cases from undesirable goods through the forced savings of installment payments. Many families, schools, and churches, however, have over-mortgaged future incomes and reduced present purchasing power through high interest payments.

Credit becomes the basis of a capitalistic economy by permitting production and distribution before ultimate buyers pay for goods. Credit capital permits economic growth and innovation. It allows governments to exert limited control over unemployment and inflation by controlling the supply of money. By furnishing capital injections advanced economies can create multiple expansion effects in underprivileged nations where little surplus above subsistence exists. Whenever a favorable position is enjoyed and the needs of the less fortunate are evident, assisting is a Christian opportunity.   WALTER P. GORMAN III

CREDULITY. Credulity or "easy belief" is commonly attributed to the hill country of Appalachia. Those who have spent time in Appalachia and modern universities are quite aware that geography is not the determining factor. Somewhere in every sizable gathering of humans the pride of doubt or skepticism is found. In fact, contemporary academia in certain of its "now" word-games merely revives a skepticism (q.v.) prevalent in 4-5 B.C. Some current metaphysics, epistemology, ethics and linguistics recall the non-cognitivism and relativism of Gorgias: "Nothing exists; if it did we could not know it; if we could know it we could not communicate it."

Eric Hoffer observes that the common man discerns with remarkable perception overstatements and fallacies of the credulous academic world. The average man may not accept the old time religion but does believe that "some kind of religious theology is humanly more satisfactory than the theology of the naturalist" (Gustav Weigel, *The Modern God,* New York, Macmillan, 1959, p. 34). Sophisticate (derived from Pre-Socratic Sophists) parents influenced by modernist unbelief in the supernatural sometimes find the Biblical beliefs of their children credulous, whereas many children find the easy skepticism worn as a badge of maturity by such parents exceedingly naive.

Many credulous moderns simply accept the notion that there can be a society without norms. This apparently innocuous view is at the root of most ethical tensions at all levels of present thought. It is appealing because it is the Hugh Hefner philosophy verbalized in varied contexts. While not new (cf. Gen. 3:6; Prov. 14:15), it is a current expression of man's amazing credulity.   WALTER H. JOHNSON

CREMATION. See also *Burial.* This is one of three ways in which man has disposed of his dead, the other being burial and exposure to birds of prey. Within the Biblical tradition cremation is known only as an exceptional method, occasioned by unusual circumstances (e.g., I Sam. 31:12, where the men of Jabesh-Gilead burned the corpses of Saul and his sons to prevent desecration at the hands of the Philistines) or severe conditions, such as criminal execution (Gen. 38:24; Lev. 20:14; 21:9; Josh. 7:15, 25). The horror with which cremation was normally regarded is seen in Amos 2:1 where the burning of the bones of the King of Edom is treated as an outrage because his Moabite enemies were thought to be pursuing their vengeance to the underworld.

Cremation as a method of disposal of the dead is not attested in the NT, the only possible exception being in a variant textual reading (I Cor. 13:3 RSV). But even this is death by martyrdom rather than cremation after death. The Christian fathers preferred "the ancient and better custom of burying in the earth" (Minucius Felix, *Octavius,* 34, written in early third century) to cremation which was practiced in the Roman world. Christian belief in the resurrection of the body was a powerful deterrent to the adoption of this method. Also association with fire for burning was too closely reminiscent of the belief that the wicked are punished in hell-fire. Dislike of cremation prevailed in Europe through the Middle Ages and up till the nineteenth century.

In 1874 a congress at Milan, Italy, was called to discuss the legal, hygienic and religious implications of cremation. In England in the same year a society to advocate this mode of funerary disposal was formed, but it met opposition. In USA the first crematory was built in 1876. In the twentieth century the practice has gained in popular acceptance, due mainly to improved disposal methods (use of gas and electricity), a more dignified setting in crematoria and the economic factor of shortage of ground for burial-plots in crowded European countries. From a Christian standpoint resurrection hope does not require a literal identity between the deceased corpse and his "spiritual body" (I Cor. 15:42-44). This has made cremation more acceptable to Christians.

In Buddhism as in Hinduism cremation is a normal way of disposing of the dead, and in predominantly Buddhist lands (in S.E. Asia, for example) this method is more usual. Climatic condition and religious beliefs contribute to its acceptance.

📖 *A Dictionary of Comparative Religion,* S. G. F. Brandon, ed., New York, Scribner, 1970.

RALPH P. MARTIN

CRIME. Crime occurs when an act is committed or omitted in violation of public law deemed necessary for the protection and general welfare of persons governed by such law. The laws and the punishments vary in each political entity, depending much on a combination of cultural, religious, social, economic and legal interlacing over the year. Generally, however, such anti-social actions as rape, treason, murder and burglary are punishable in all societies, while adultery, homosexuality, or drunkenness may, in some jurisdictions, be considered not crimes but sicknesses.

At best, any legal system by which crime is determined is an attempt to get justice (q.v.) for as many people as possible. Laws change to meet the demands of justice, there being inherent injustices in any set of laws. Legislative bodies are the authors of laws; the courts the arbiters and refiners of them.

On any given day in the USA there are 1.2 million persons in jails and prisons, about 210,000 of them serving long terms for serious crimes, known as felonies. Although there is a growing incidence of crime, paralleling urbanization of the USA, the total detained in prisons has declined from almost 10 per 100,000 population in the first part of the twentieth century to slightly under 5 in 1970.

But while the prison population is declining, prisoner problems are increasing. Some states are adopting a "local parole" system whereby the state pays counties and cities to supervise locally the reform of those convicted of lesser crimes, instead of tempting them to aggravated stages of crime by contact with more hardened criminals. This segregation, however, leaves the prisons with only the more difficult prisoners, resulting in an increasing number of in-prison atrocities and revolts.

A rash of revolts such as at the Attica, N. Y., prison in the early 1970s incensed the nation to take a more serious look at conditions existing in the penal system and to review what largely has been only a theoretical objective of the system— rehabilitation. Church spokesmen, who had been silent on prison reform (q.v.), suddenly became the most ardent champions of reform. The silence dated almost as far back as William Penn and the Quakers who established in 1682 in Pennsylvania a penal code of exceptional mildness. A hallmark of that reform was establishment of houses of correction, with the emphasis on humanitarian reform the theoretical basis of the modern system.

Prison systems have never really coped with the reform problem as a practical matter. Instead, they have been functioning more as detainment centers, deterrents to crime and protection to citizens. FBI statistics since the middle of the twentieth century, point up the rehabilitation failure;

the range of those returning to prison is 40 to 60 percent.

There is Biblical precedence for penology that both demands justice and yet acts compassionately toward the offender. Before there were governments to act as intervenors, God established that Cain should be punished, but within well-defined bounds (Gen. 4:11-16). Societies disregarded these principles until the vengence tendencies of anarchy forced them into legal codes for their own protection. The Biblical "an eye for an eye, a tooth for a tooth," for all its austerity, nonetheless was humane compared to the law of vengeance which set no limitations.

Jesus placed a particular significance on compassion toward the prisoner (Matt. 25:36). Notwithstanding, the history of Catholic and Protestant theologians in Europe and America has left them largely silent on reform, lending, at the least, tacit religious sanction to the existing penal systems.

The biggest crime problem, however, is not reform and rehabilitation, but prevention. Thus, it also becomes foremost a youth problem. Testifying before a congressional committee in 1967, U.S. Attorney General Ramsey Clark said,

> Of all the statistics in the crime picture, the one that is the most incredible is that. . .four out of five, 80 percent, of the people convicted of felonies were at an earlier time convicted of another crime, nearly always a misdemeanor and nearly always while they were kids.

> Here you are talking about a predictability of 80 percent of your serious crimes. If we address ourselves early enough to these people to prevent them from committing the first misdemeanor, or if we miss that opportunity, we at least make every effort on a tailormade basis to give that violator an opportunity for a lawful existence, we can reduce a major part. . .of serious crime.

If the church believes that crime is not merely against society as such, but against God who created man in his image, then the mandate—and even the program—for action becomes apparent from Clark's words. So far the vocations of the church have been inordinantly light in this area.

📖 C. Beccaria, *Crime and Punishment*, 1764; Daniel Glaser, *The Effectiveness of a Prison and Parole System*, Indianapolis, Liberal Art Press—Bobbs Merrill, 1964; Robert M. MacIver, *The Prevention and Control of Delinquency*, New York, Atherton, 1966; *Editorial Research Report*, Vol I, 1970.   WILLIAM F. WILLOUGHBY

CRUELTY. See also *Animals; Hunting; Sports; Suffering; Vivisection.* Some think the Bible, especially the OT, is a primitive document sanctioning, even authorizing, gross cruelty—for example, the sacrifice of Isaac, the exterminating of the Canaanites, eye for an eye retaliation, and extreme utterances of the imprecatory Psalms (137:8, 9; 139:21ff.). The Bible, however, is not a book which sanctions pointless suffering.

Cruelty cannot be defined solely in terms of physical suffering, nor is a definition adequate that fails to reckon with man as he is, a sinner. The sacrifice of Isaac was not fulfilled and ultimately taught just the opposite of human sacrifice which was practiced in the ancient world. The extermination of the Canaanites was a command of God based on the principle of the choice of lesser over greater evil; had they lived, more suffering would have resulted than in their extermination. The eye for an eye principle was not meant as retaliation at all, but was the lifting up of the principle of equal justice for all in courts of law. The imprecatory Psalms are variously interpreted, but perhaps most wisely as the extreme expression of men who were capable of hating what opposed God and his kingdom. God must hate evil, not because he is cruel but because he is just.

Job thought God was cruel until he came to realize that the Creator has the right to use even Satan's cruel ministrations to bring about his higher purposes for the creatures on whom he has placed his love. The prophets teach of God's plan to bring an end to war, man's greatest instrument of cruelty and horror. The Biblical law of love, of compassion, of bearing one another's burdens, of healing the sick and caring for the widow and orphan is theologically based on that appallingly cruel human act, the crucifixion of Christ in which God paid the ultimate price designed to bring an end to the multiplication of cruelty in the world.

ELMER B. SMICK

CULLMANN, OSCAR. Oscar Cullmann was born in Strasbourg in 1902. From 1938 he was Professor of New Testament and Early Church History at Basel, and from 1949 also Professor of Early Christianity at the Sorbonne, Paris.

The most notable modern exponent of the *Heilsgeschichte* (Salvation history) school, his major theological contributions are *Christ and Time* (London, SCM, revised 1962) and *Salvation in History* (London, SCM, 1967). Fundamental is his theme of the "Already and the Not Yet"—the "already" being Christ's first coming and Resurrection, the "not yet" his second coming (Parousia). "We stand in a section of time in which we are already redeemed through Christ. . .but in which also the sin characteristic of the entire period before the Parousia is not done away" (*Christ and Time*, p. 92). "It is characteristic of all NT salvation history that between Christ's resurrection and his return there is an interval the essence of which is determined by this tension" (*Salvation in History*, p. 202), i.e., between the "Already" and the "Not Yet."

The present therefore has to be conceived of essentially as an interval—an interval between the decisive events of the past and the completion yet to be, between D-Day and V-Day. This temporariness of the present is normative for ethics. The possibility of Christian ethics derives wholly from the decisive victory of the past. The urgency of Christian ethics derives from the nearness of the End—the interval is also the End time.

Ethical conduct therefore involves both an indicative and an imperative. "In Primitive Christianity ethics without theology is absolutely inconceivable. All 'Ought' rests here upon an 'Is.' . . .We have received the Spirit; this means that we should 'walk in the Spirit.' In Christ we already have redemption from the power of sin" (*Christ and Time,* p. 224). This tension between the Already of the indicative and the Not Yet of the imperative is most clearly expressed in Rom. 6:1-11 (indicative), 12-19 (imperative). See also *Baptism in the New Testament* (London, SCM, 1950), where Cullmann understands faith as (ethical) *response* to the grace of baptism.

The Holy Spirit typifies the present—being both the decisive "first installment" of salvation, the "Is," and the power who enables the "Ought." His working shows itself chiefly in *dokimazein* (testing), i.e., "the capacity of forming the correct Christian ethical judgment at each given moment" (*Christ and Time,* p. 228), and in *agape* (love), the new principle of application characteristic of the Christian ethic.

The nature of the present also means that Christian ethics are not characterized by a negative renunciation of the world. The Christian recognizes that the structures of the world share in the impermanence of the present; but he also recognizes that they have a positive God-given role to play in the present. And so long as they fulfil that role and content themselves with that which is Caesar's the Christian is bound to respect them (Rom. 13:1ff.). (Cf. *Church and State;* Cullmann, *The State in the New Testament,* New York, Scribner, 1956.)

JAMES D. G. DUNN

CULTURAL MANDATE. See also *Civilization; Culture.* The recognition of certain divine mandates, contained in Scripture and reflecting the design of creation as it affects human society, is a feature of neo-Protestant ethics. Brunner sometimes followed Luther in speaking of orders, but also referred to mandates, as did Bonhoeffer. Both included culture in this category.

Brunner's definition of culture was restricted to "that activity in which the intellectual element is not a mere means to an end, as in civilization, but is a relative end in itself, that is, in the main, science, art, and education" (Emil Brunner, *The Divine Imperative,* London, Lutterworth, 1947, p. 483). He regarded it as a relatively autonomous sphere to be entered by Christians with a view to impregnating it with the distinctive ethos of obedience and faith.

Man's innate impulse towards cultural development is not to be explained in purely naturalistic terms. It arises from the urge of his spirit and is one of the marks of his divine creation which is not wholly impaired by the fall. The Biblical basis for the cultural mandate is found in Gen. 1:26-29. As Sauer points out, this passage not only declares man's vocation to rule but calls him to progressive growth in culture (Erich Sauer, *The King of the Earth,* London, Paternoster, 1962, pp. 80, 81). So far from being in conflict with God's will, these advances in science and the arts are expressions of it. In Gen. 4:21, 22 we trace the birth of both music and technology. "Only complete misconception of the simplest laws of revelation could charge Holy Scripture with obscurantism and hostility to culture" (*op. cit.,* p. 81). Hence culture is at once God's gift and man's duty.

On the other hand, culture has clearly been affected by the incidence of sin. It is incapable in itself of achieving what it might have done had not man been driven from paradise by disobedience. It aspires to an absolute autonomy which would usurp the divine perogative. It also inclines towards a certain abstraction and impersonality of which men are more than ever aware of in Western technocratic society. Culture always aspires to erect another and more successful Babel, and in so doing tends to lose touch with man as well as to ignore God. Hence the continuing need for culture to be reminded of its provenance in the divine plan and its need of redemption by Christ.

Reinhold Niebuhr claimed that the issue between essential Christianity and modern culture lies in the question of confidence; is it to be placed in man or in God (*An Interpretation of Christian Ethics,* London, SCM, 1936, pp. 131, 132)? The fact that man still clings to the illusion that through the refinement of culture he can regain his lost paradise provides current evidence of his fallen condition. But the fact that his culture is allowed to remain and expand is due to God's gracious mandate.

Emil Brunner, *The Divine Imperative; A Study in Christian Ethics,* London, Lutterworth, 1947; Dietrich Bonhoeffer, *Ethics,* London, SCM, 1955.

A. SKEVINGTON WOOD

CULTURAL RELATIVISM.

I. *Definitions and History*

Cultural relativism has three separable meanings in contemporary social science. Confusion of these meanings has resulted in considerable misunderstanding and, at times, a blanket rejection. The misunderstanding is unfortunate and the blanket rejection unnecessary.

The first use of this concept implies merely the existence of wide cultural variation (subsequently be referred to as CR-1.) This use makes no value judgment concerning these variations; rather, it merely recognizes their existence. The second use refers to the analytical or methodological technique which attempts to understand the customs and culture of a group in terms of its own value system (referred to subsequently as CR-2). This use implies neither the agreement or disagreement of the analyst with the value system of the group being studied. It is not a position of ethical indifference, but rather a position of cultural neutralism maintained in order to gain a better understanding of the functioning of a particular group. The third use refers to a philosophical position which accepts all value systems and all systems of behavioral norms as having equal dignity and validity (referred to subsequently as CR-3). Consequently, valid judgments can never be made across cultural lines. Put another way, this philosophy denies the existence of any type of transcultural values, regardless of their origination or determination.

This third use (or the concept CR-3), which has a long history, has been a basic assumption of many social or behavioral scientists during the twentieth century. It has been articulated primarily by two social scientists, William Graham Sumner of Yale University early in the century, and Melville J. Herskovits of Northwestern University in the 1940s. Sumner, a sociologist, after noting the great variability of group customs in his classical work, *Folkways* (1906), concluded that "mores can make anything right." Thus he argued that principles of rightness and morality are entirely cultural; culture itself becomes the final authority of rightness and morality.

Herskovits, in *Man and His Works* (New York, Knopf, 1948), based his development of this concept on the principle that "judgments are based on experience, and experience is interpreted by each individual in terms of his own acculturation" (pp. 61-79). One's cultural experience then became the ultimate judge of all customs, behavioral principles, and morals. He emphasized that CR-3 refers not only to perception and cognition, but to moral structures as well. While not denying the existence or the necessity of moral codes, he did deny the existence of transcultural

moral principles. To him, the existence of cultural variability (CR-1) necessitated the relativistic methodology (CR-2) which, in turn, logically necessitated the acceptance of relativism as a basic philosophical principle (CR-3). To him, CR-1 and CR-2 inevitably required the acceptance of cultural relativism as "a philosophy which, in recognizing the values set up by every society to guide its own life, lays stress on the dignity inherent in every body of custom" (i.e., CR-3). CR-3 in this view was merely the inevitable and logical extension of CR-1 and CR-2.

II. *Criticisms of CR-3 by Other Non-Christian Anthropologists*

Although Herskovits' position became for many the accepted position of anthropology, it was not in any sense universally accepted. In fact, many voiced considerable criticism of it. Although some of the criticisms unfortunately were based on a misunderstanding of Herskovits' position, many were valid. These are:

1. That cultural relativism as a philosophy is logically self-contradictory in that, by denying the existence of absolutes, it is in reality stating an absolute; or that by denying the existence of transcultural values, it is actually subscribing to one such value.

2. That the derivation of cultural relativism as a philosophy (CR-3) from CR-1 and CR-2 is a fallacious deduction. In the words of David Bidney this commits the "positivistic fallacy" (i.e., deriving the "ought" from the "is"), a logically unacceptable procedure (*Theoretical Anthropology*, New York, Schocken, 1953, pp. 428-429).

3. That if no cultural position is absolute because each is the product of an enculturative experience, cultural relativism, having been similarly enculturated, consequently cannot hold an absolute position.

4. That CR-3 logically and inevitably leads to the position of individual relativism, an initial step toward social anarchy.

If no transcultural absolutes are admitted, the unanswered questions facing cultural relativism are: Where does the group derive the authority to become the source of values? and, Why does not this authority ultimately rest in the individual? Such individualization of values would render social existence impossible.

5. That CR-3 is useless as a basis of cross-cultural interaction and understanding. As a practical policy it is applicable only in situations of total cultural isolation, which situations rarely, if ever, exist. Consequently, it has no practical or useful application in the world today.

6. That CR-3 goes contrary to man's basic moral nature and conscience, which affirm the existence of moral norms.

Admittedly, not all of these criticisms are equally valid, nor does any one of them singularly disprove CR-3. However, taken as a group, the criticisms are relevant and point up many of its logical inconsistencies and difficulties.

III. *Proposed Methods of Determining Transcultural Values*

Although many non-Christian anthropologists agreed in rejecting the type of total cultural relativism proposed by Herskovits, they did not agree on the method by which transcultural values should be determined. Three methods were suggested:

1. Rational analysis. This position, advocated by David Bidney, a philosopher/anthropologist from the University of Indiana, assumes that transcultural values can be established by the disciplined exercise of man's rationality. Bidney believes that the real problem relates not to accepting or rejecting the existence of transcultural values, but rather to the source of nature of those values. To him the real choice lies between accepting rationally derived norms or accepting irrational supernatural or mythological absolutes. He obviously opts for the former.

2. Historical analysis. The second method, proposed by Robert Redfield of University of Chicago, is that transcultural values can be established by the comparative historical analysis of civilized or precivilized societies (*The Primitive World and Its Transformations,* Ithaca, N.Y., Cornell University, 1953, pp. 139-165). This method is based on the premise that man's moral consciousness matured into a form with greater moral sensitivity and that this maturation is associated with the development of civilization. Thus, Redfield believes that judgments of the true and the good are objectively attainable by comparison of the moral systems of precivilized and civilized peoples, and that the analysis of the total trend of history is an instrument of establishing truth which is inherently better, not just relatively better to the judgment impressed on man by his culture.

3. Scientific investigation. A third method was proposed by Clyde Kluckhohn of Harvard University, "Value and Value Orientations in the Theory of Action," in *Toward a General Theory of Action* (eds., Talcott Parsons and Edward A. Shils, New York, Harper & Row, 1959, pp. 417-421). Accepting the idea that anthropology does not as a matter of theory deny the existence of moral absolutes and that values are not completely relative to the cultures from which they derive, he argues that these values are in fact the givens of human existence. They are founded, first, on the fundamental biological similarities of all human beings, and secondly, on the necessary circumstances of human social existence. Kluckhohn holds that these values can be determined by the rigorous application of the scientific method to the study of the nature of man and the nature of the group. He is quick to point out, however, that it would be difficult to apply the descriptive "absolute" to these values, because like all scientific judgments scientific propositions about values are subject to revision, and because new knowledge or

radically changed circumstances of man's existence may also alter such universal values. Consequently, he favors speaking of "conditional absolutes" or "moving absolutes" (in time).

IV. Current Status of the View

Because of the above criticisms and because these various methodologies have been proposed for establishing non-relative values, the type of cultural relativism proposed by Herskovits has become less popular with anthropologists during the decade of the 1960s. While acceptance of CR-1 (fact of cultural variability) and CR-2 (methodological relativism) remained equally strong, the commitment to CR-3 (philosophical cultural relativism) gradually waned. The presentation today, as in a typical text such as *Anthropology Today* (1971), distinguishes between understanding, an intellectual exercise (CR-2), and judging, a moral exercise (CR-3). In this text CR-2 does not imply an approving judgment of the group values being studied, and furthermore, an anthropologist reserves the right to assert universal moral standards if he so desires. As described by this text, "This anthropologist can practice cultural relativism without excluding other perspectives, especially because the nonrelative perspectives give him understandings that relativism cannot" (pp. 326-327). It further notes that CR-2 does not preclude taking a nonrelative perspective.

V. Christian Reactions to Cultural Relativism

Christians have rejected both the cultural relativism of Herskovits (CR-3) and the methodologies for establishing transcultural values proposed by non-Christian anthropologists. They almost universally accept divine revelation as the only source of transcultural values. Although agreeing on this point, their reaction to cultural relativism has ranged from vehement renunciation and rejection to sympathetic hearing. Eugene Nida, in his *Customs and Cultures*

(New York, Harper & Row, 1954), rejects the relativism of Herskovits because it is derived from a view of a total relativism which he finds unacceptable. On the other hand, he emphasizes that the Bible supports a type of relativism. "The relativism of the Bible is relative to three principle factors: (1) the endowment and opportunities of people, (2) the extent of revelation, and (3) the cultural patterns of the society in question." He states that the Christian position is not one of static conformance to dead rules, but of dynamic obedience to a living God, and that only such a relativism permits growth, adaptation, and freedom, under the Lordship of Jesus Christ. As for what is absolute, his answer is, "The only absolute in Christianity is the triune God. Anything which involves man, who is finite and limited, must of necessity be limited, and hence relative. Biblical cultural relativism is an obligatory feature of our incarnational religion, for without it we would either absolutize human institutions or relativize God." So Nida recognizes no absolutes with reference to norms of human behavior. And although he does not claim to be a total relativist, practically or functionally speaking, he appears to be a total "cultural" relativist.

In contrast to Nida, William A. Smalley believes that certain norms of behavior are divinely revealed and ordained. These he calls the "Superculture," which term "should be reserved for that which is truly beyond culture—for God himself, His nature, attributes and character, for the moral principles which stem from what He is" ("Culture and Superculture," in *Practical Anthropology*, 2:3, 1955). He considers the Ten Commandments as close to superculture as any statements in Scripture, although he finds touches of the cultural in them.

The single most extensive study of cultural relativism by a Christian social scientist is by David Moberg entitled "Cultural

Relativity and Christian Truth" (*Journal of the American Scientific Affiliation* 14:2, 1962, pp. 34-48). He points out that the following two contradicting ethical perspectives may be observed among Christians: (1) that perspective which specifies rules which are absolute and authoritarian, and (2) that which emphasizes principles of conduct as being guiding models, broad rules, or generalized patterns. The former perspective, Moberg believes, reduces Christian morality to the legalistic obedience to the rule; consequently he prefers the latter. He finds these absolute norms in the Commandments, in Christ's two-fold principle of loving God and of loving one's neighbor and numerous New Testament exhortations. But, since man does not behave in a non-cultural vacuum, the social situation will decree how these absolutes should be interpreted and applied in any given group as well as in any particular person's life. He says "God's Word provides the Christian with principles for living, not absolute standards. It allows for a type of cultural relativity within this framework."

Many have recognized that at times situations arise in which Biblical emphases, if literally followed, would not constitute the most appropriate behavior. Such an example, admittedly extreme, would concern answering the German Gestapo about the location of Jews in hiding. Consequently, they argue that even these principles are not totally absolute in nature. They have variously called them "relative absolutes," "situational absolutes," or "conditional absolutes." Such terms unnecessarily weaken their intended force. The connotation that all Biblical norms must be judged by the situation is unfortunate. A necessary and helpful distinction is between the supercultural imperative (those divinely revealed principles that must always be obeyed) and supercultural ideas (those principles that should be obeyed in all normal or ordinary situations). In the first category would be

God's twofold command to love, and in the second, such principles as the Ten Commandments and exhortations about the structure of the family (monogamy). The imperatives are attitudinal in nature; the ideals may be attitudinal (as in fruits of the Spirit), or may refer to more specific behavioral patterns of the group or to social structures.

VI. *Values of the Concept*

The concept of cultural relativism is a valid and valuable concept if properly used. It helps us to distinguish the surface structure of the cultural expressions of behavior and the deep structures of behavioral attitudes and meanings which must be rooted in basic Biblical principles. Only when one becomes fully aware of both the cultural and supercultural aspects of our behavior will he avoid the unfortunate error of absolutizing purely cultural phenomena or relativizing Biblical absolutes. Only when such distinctions are clearly in mind, one can become all things to all men (I Cor. 9:19-23), without violating Biblical imperatives. Jesus did not automatically obey all the cultural practices of his day; in fact, his violation of them often appalled the legalistically-minded Pharisees.

VII. *Conclusion*

Improperly understood and misused, the concept can be destructive. Misapplied, the concept can undercut the idea of any type of a transcultural ethical system which in turn undercuts the validity and authority of Scripture. Furthermore, if behavioral norms are made totally relative, cultural relativism would almost inevitably result in individual relativism, making the existence of a structured society impossible and producing anarchy. Moreover, as a substitute for traditional religious views, it assumes the character of a new and competitive religion.

In short, cultural relativism, as recognition of cultural differences (CR-1), and as a methodological technique (CR-2), does not conflict with Christianity and can, in fact, be an extremely valuable and helpful analytical tool in understanding culture. But as a philosophy (CR-3), it stands in direct contradiction to divine revelation and its derived system of ethics, and hence must be rejected.   DONALD R. WILSON

CULTURE. See also *Civilization; Cultural Mandate.* The word "culture" is ultimately derived from the Latin root *colere,* "to till or to cultivate." In current usage the term has both a humanistic and an anthropological sense. Matthew Arnold in his *Culture and Anarchy* (New York, Cambridge University, 1869) popularized the humanistic concept of culture as "a pursuit of total perfection by means of getting to know . . . the best which has been thought and said in the world." T. S. Eliot has spoken of culture as "that which makes life worth living" (*Notes toward the Definition of Culture,* New York, Harcourt, Brace, 1949, p. 26).

More prevalent today than the idealistic sense of culture is the descriptive use of the term. This latter usage was first articulated by E. B. Tylor in 1871 as "that complex whole which includes knowledge, belief, art, morals, law, custom, and any other capabilities and habits acquired by man as a member of society." Modern anthropologists use the term to designate the distinctive way of life of a given society, including values, manners, morals, habits, and artifacts.

That which above all distinguishes man from even the most advanced animals is the possesion and transmission of culture, including language.

Anthropologists note the great variability of cultures. It is true that certain basic needs are common to all human societies. Within the community murder, incest, lying, and stealing are universally condemned. But how people regard such matters as property, family relations, time, and work, how they eat, drink, clothe themselves, are attitudes and activities which vary from society to society. Because of such variations anthropologists caution us that each society's actions and mores must be judged in the light of their total cultural complex.

This does not mean, however, that moral standards are dispensable. According to M. J. Herskovits:

Cultural relativism must be sharply distinguished from concepts of the relativity of individual behavior, which would negate all social controls over conduct. The existence of integrative moral forces has been remarked in every human society. Conformity to the code of the group is a requirement for any regularity in life.—*Man and His Works,* New York, Knopf, 1949, p. 63

In view of the complex inter-relatedness of the various features of a culture, anthropologists such as Bronislaw Malinowski have argued against missionary efforts, which they regard as an interference which threatens to upset primitive cultures. In reply, W. F. Albright notes that, "The history of Christian missions since the first century A.D. is the most conclusive demonstration of the fact that cultures can change their religions without national suicide" (*History, Archaeology, and Christian Humanism,* New York, McGraw-Hill, 1964, p. 49).

We are faced with the fact that God's revelation in history was originally mediated through the Jews of Old and New Testament times who represent a variety of cultures quite different from our own.

Even within the confines of the New Testament one can detect cultural differences. Jesus makes no reference to the Greek athletic games which provided the Apostle Paul with many sermon illustrations. Pentecost did not obliterate the cultural differences between the Hebraist and Hellenist Christians (Acts 6). Paul was able to perceive the difference between the supracultural message of the gospel and its flexible adaptability to various cultures. In his desire to reach all groups with the gospel, he declared that he was ready to be "made all things to all" (I Cor. 9:22), without, however, compromising the gospel.

The relationship of Christians to their culture is a problem which has elicited various responses. In a perceptive study (Christ and Culture, New York, Harper, 1951), H. Richard Niebuhr has classified the reactions to culture as follows: I. Christ against Culture; II. The Christ of Culture; III. Christ above Culture. A. Synthesists, who view Christianity as the fulfillment and restorer of human values. B. Dualists, who view man as subject to two moralities, the Christian and the cultural. C. Conversionists, who believe that God comes to man within his culture in order to transform man and his culture.

The outstanding exponent of Christ against Culture was Tertullian. Trained in Roman law, Tertullian rejected participation in political life. Most vehemently he rejected the use of Greek philosophy to expound Christianity, exclaiming, "What indeed has Athens to do with Jerusalem?" Yet Tertullian was indebted to certain classical concepts and to Roman rhetoric even in expressing his rejection of pagan culture.

At the other extreme, The Christ of Culture, Origen and Clement of Alexandria so extensively used Neo-Platonic philosophical concepts that it is difficult to decide whether they were Platonic Christians or Christian Platonists. A more recent example of the Christ of culture may be seen in the quest of liberal scholars who sought to uncover their ideal of an ethical teacher in the so-called "historical" Jesus of the Gospels.

Thomas Aquinas is a representative of the synthesist, who views the church as the fosterer of true culture. The difficulty here is that a particular type of culture tends to be absolutized. Luther and Roger Williams are representatives of the dualists, who view man somewhat as an amphibian—in Niebuhr's words—living in two realms. The conversionist position which looks to the transformation of culture and society by Christ is represented by Calvin and Wesley.

Our modern culture is so different from that of Biblical times that critics such as Bultmann have dismissed the Bible as cast in the form of myth. On the other hand, some extreme conservative Christians like Carl McIntire have sought to find Biblical justification for the American way of life. The missionary statesman, Hendrik Kraemer, deplored the unconscious identification of Christianity with Western culture by missionaries.

Just as missionaries have translated the gospel into a multitude of languages, so too the Holy Spirit can work in a variety of cultures (Col. 1:27-28; 3:11; Rev. 5:9). For the Bible to be meaningful today, we must: (1) understand the cultural settings of the original Biblical passages; (2) understand the receptor culture, whether our own or that of others; (3) apply the supra-cultural Biblical principles in a culturally relevant way.

Kaj. Birket-Smith, The Paths of Culture, Madison, University of Wisconsin, 1965; Émile Cailliet, The Christian Approach to Culture, Nashville, Abingdon, 1953; Charles N. Cochrane, Christianity and Classical Culture, New York, Oxford University, 1957; C. Dawson, Religion and the Rise of Western Culture, New York, Sheed and Ward, 1950; W. Jaeger, Early Christianity and Greek Paideia, London, Oxford University, 1961; Hendrik Kraemer, The Christian Message in a Non-Christian World, New York, Harper and Brothers, 1938; Eugene Nida, Customs and Cultures, New York, Harper and Brothers, 1954; Richard H. Niebuhr, Christ and Culture, New York, Harper and Brothers, 1951.   EDWIN M. YAMAUCHI

CUSTOM. See also Conformity; Conventional Morality; Tradition. In general, the term refers to the habit patterns or habitual usages of an individual or social group. The customs of an individual or social group reflect in a general way the values held, and are a powerful means of inculcating at least outward respect for these values. So the young Jesus, "as his custom was, went into the synagogue on the sabbath day" (Luke 4:16). The custom of regular religious observance tends to strengthen values. Deviation from the customs of a social group can result in social pressures and, in extreme cases, social ostracism. Churches, being social institutions, generate customs of varying kinds, e.g., the custom of having two services on Sunday, of having the preacher wear a robe (or not wear a robe), of men wearing ties to church services, and the like. Customs can be morally good, morally neutral, or morally bad. The NT recognizes this in dealing with custom (cf. Luke 1:9, John 18:39; Acts 16:21; I Cor. 11:16). The Christian standard for evaluation of custom is God's revelation. Recognition of this ultimate standard, however, does not necessarily produce agreement among Christians. Is the custom of foot-washing one to be followed today? Is the custom of having only male preachers valid?

In pre-modern societies, the custom of the group was often regarded as having divine sanction: thus, to violate the tribal custom was considered to incur divine wrath. Custom likewise was widely regarded, in pre-modern Christian societies also, as "unwritten law." The legal codes of the Germanic tribes were basically codified custom. In Medieval times, feudal customary law was highly respected. English law (and thus American law) is based essentially on "common law" which was customary law, for a long time unwritten. There is an important tradition, in short, of law as based essentially on custom rather than on legislative enactment (cf. the late-medieval and early-modern conflicts between Germanic customary law and Roman prescriptive law).

Custom can be viewed as the best source of law, since it represents the desired action patterns of the community. Such an attitude has parallels in religious history: thus, for example, the Jewish rabbinical stress on religious custom as unwritten law; the Russian schismatic Old Believers and their insistence on God's sanction for traditional religious custom rather than church-imposed reforms: medieval Roman Catholicism's respect for religious custom as in some sense God-given. Catholic canon law still regards local religious custom as binding under certain conditions (basically, the custom must be compatible with canon law, and followed by the community for a long time), and sees the Holy Spirit at work in forming the customs, traditions and usages of the Roman Church. The Reformation objected to medieval Catholicism's stress on the validity of religious custom, and insisted that all religious custom and tradition be tested by the Word of God (which left some questions unresolved, e.g., Should a religious custom not specifically mentioned in the Bible be followed or not?) (cf. *Adiaphora*).

DIRK W. JELLEMA

CYBERNETICS. Derived from the Greek *kybernetes,* "a steersman," the term denotes the science of control and communication, whether in human societies, individual organisms, or artificial automata. This embraces all types of process that depend on the flow and exchange of *information,* rather than simply of *energy.* Self-regulating mechanisms, signalling systems and computers are typical examples of "cybernetic" devices.

Cybernetics raises ethical questions at three different levels.

1. Increased understanding of the mechanisms of self-regulation in society e.g., in economics or politics—both enhances the responsibilities of government and at the same time gives increased scope for the manipulation of society by "social engineering." There are however no grounds for expecting computerized decision-making to solve all problems of social stability, as long

as human value-systems themselves are unstable (cf. Vickers, *Value Systems and Social Process,* London, Tavistock, 1968).

2. The study of the human brain as a cybernetic mechanism throws fresh light on the nature of man as a scientific phenomenon. It has become clear that some of the most characteristic features of human behavior may be explicable in cybernetic terms as dependent on the peculiar *organization* of our brains rather than on any exemption they might enjoy from the laws of physics. The suggestion is inevitable (though far beyond present knowledge) that perhaps all human behavior, even in moral choices or religious devotions, may be similarly explicable.

Here it is vital not to confuse *explanation* with *debunking.* A warning signal in Morse code might be completely explained in terms of the physics of the transmitter; but this would be no reason for ignoring what it says. Similarly, even a complete cybernetic explanation of human behavior would offer no reason for devaluing its personal significance. Mechanistic and personal or spiritual accounts of human actions are logically not rivals, but complementary.

3. The rapid development of "artificial intelligence" over recent decades is sometimes imagined to hold a threat to the Christian doctrine of man. A digital computer is essentially a device for manipulating symbols according to set logical rules. It can do so at rates above 100 million operations per second, and can perform logical as well as numerical calculations. It can also change its own rules, within limits, as calculation proceeds. To claim that such machines "think," however, would be a solecism, just as it would be to claim that a man's brain, rather than the man himself, thinks.

It has been proved ("Turing's Theorem") that any precisely specifiable logical task in principle can be performed by a general-purpose computer. Note however that this does *not* mean that "computers can do whatever a man can do." They are limited in principle by our inability to understand, let alone specify fully, all that a man can do.

The "brain like" powers of computer systems are nevertheless remarkable. Fair comparison requires the computer to be augmented by artificial sense organs and means of action and locomotion. "Conversational modes" of interaction with human beings, including synthetic speech, can already provide convincing imitations of dialog with a purposive and intelligent agent. Although "computers do only what they are programed to do," the sensitivity of such systems to signals from their environment and their power to modify their own programs can rapidly make their behavior as unpredictable as that of a human being.

It is sometimes argued that the artificial production of a conscious intelligence would "usurp the prerogative of the Creator"; but this is to confuse *creation* with *reproduction.* There seems to be no Biblical issue at stake here, however implausible the notion may be for technical reasons.

An important distinction in computer technology is that between "hardware" (the physical equipment) and "software" (the logical program governing its behavior). The complementary relation between the two has been likened to that between physical and mental aspects of human nature, and the parallel may prove instructive in relation to the "mind-body problem."

Are brains themselves computers? Opinion is unanimous that parts of the brain, such as the cerebellum, compute—though on different principles from digital machines. Other brain functions, however, are less well understood, such as the setting of priorities, the initiation of spontaneous action, and the mediation of our conscious experience. These may involve processes quite other than computation, though not necessarily any less mechanical.

G. Guilbaud, *What is Cybernetics?* London, Heinemann, 1959; D. M. MacKay, *Information, Mechanism and Meaning,* Cambridge, Massachusetts Institute of Technology, 1969; G. Vickers, *Value Systems and Social Process,* London, Tavistock, 1968; N. Wiener, *The Human Use of Human Beings: Cybernetics and Society,* Garden City, N.Y., Doubleday Anchor, 1954.

DONALD M. MACKAY

CYNICISM. See also *Despair; Nihilism; Pessimism.* Cynicism, whose founder would rather go insane than feel pleasure, was a school of Socratic inspiration. Virtue can be taught, thundered Antisthenes, although he and his disciples had little epistemology and sometimes employed the tawdry fallacies of the Sophists. This seeming inconsistency disappears when one realizes that the teaching was not dialectic disputation, but practical exercise in action. Hercules was their hero, and they assumed the role of hero or at least of example to other men.

Therefore they practiced asceticism (q.v.), braved the rigors of the weather, despised riches, begged bread from those whom they despised, and in rebellion against effete society, lived like dogs. Diogenes threw away his tin cup to be consistent and ordered Alexander the Great to get out of his sunlight.

As time went on the movement, because of its mendicancy and animalism, developed hedonistic tendencies. Its good points were absorbed in Stoicism and were furnished with an epistemological foundation.

The modern meaning of the term cynicism is an inaccurate but natural development from the Greek background. With their ascetic virtue the early cynics despised society. Thus today a cynic is one who entertains a contemptuous disbelief in men's sincerity. The factor of moral athleticism is gone.

GORDON H. CLARK

D

DANTE. Dante Alighieri (1265-1321), probably (with Shakespeare) one of the two greatest writers of the Western World, sums up with vast learning and massive comprehensiveness the religious beliefs of Medieval Christendom. A mystic (that is, he believed that the soul can, through a long process of purification, blend, in ecstasy, with God) and an allegorist (that is, he believed that objects, persons, and events "stand for" things other than themselves, and have multiple significance), he tried to encompass the whole history of man, past, present, and future, in *The Divine Comedy.* (In Medieval usage, "comedy" is a story that begins tragically—the Fall—and ends happily—Redemption; "Divine" because his story is of sacred things.) From Augustine he derived his emphasis on love as the central flame of man's life, and the central reality of the universe in the Empyrean (heavenly) fire of God's love; from St. Bernard he derived mystical vision; from Thomas Aquinas (who codified and interpreted Aristotle for Christian purpose) he derived the complex view of the hierarchy of all life (that is, the belief that all things exist in an inter-related pattern of higher and lower); and from Virgil he derived his structure, the journey or pilgrimage which Dante takes through Hell, Purgatory, and Paradise. His ethical system is built upon the concept of the "ladder of love" *(scala d'amore),* by which man can rise step by step to Heaven (ecstatic union with God) by a process of purging one's sensual desires and expanding one's spiritual consciousness of God. The complexity of his ethical system is matched by that of his allegory and symbolism. Central to his symbolism is

Beatrice, upon whom he concentrated his love when he was nine, she eight, and who comes to stand (with a mingling of identification with the Virgin Mary) for divine beauty and love. By rising step by step from devotion to the earthly personage (he barely knew Beatrice—whom scholars have not certainly identified) to the spiritual virtues she embodied, Dante in his journey, like the journey of the soul of all men in this life, reached the Beatific Vision. En route through *The Divine Comedy* sins and virtues are categorized and placed in a hierarchy of great complexity (cf. "seven deadly sins" under *Sin*), reflecting the Medieval ethical system, which was essentially a system of "works."   CALVIN D. LINTON

DARWIN AND DARWINIAN ETHICS.

See also *Evolutionary Ethics; Social Darwinism*. Although naturalistic explanations of ethics were advanced long before Darwin, his work raised anew the question of man's moral nature. In his books, *The Origin of Species* (New York, Dutton) and *The Descent of Man* (New York, Modern Library), he argued that all living things, including man, are the result of progressive change in time. Students of evolution have since attempted to show that man's ability to make moral judgments is also a product of the same process of hereditary divergence that Darwin used to explain anatomical similarity and variability. These naturalistic attempts underscore the pitfalls involved in deriving ethics from evolution.

Attempts in Darwin's time emphasized only the struggle for existence to form the old tooth and claw ethic while discounting other aspects of evolution. However, Herbert Spencer tried to soften this harsh view by insisting that individual survival was the greatest good. Though in his *Descent* Darwin agreed that natural selection would be socially beneficial, yet his *Origin* was strongly empirical; he observed that eliminating the weak would betray "the noblest part of our nature." Thomas Huxley, arguing that goodness opposed the struggle for existence, discredited this "gladiatorial theory" because it denied sound ethical principles—but he did not know from where they came.

More recent attempts stress the findings of science, notably genetics and anthropology, as clues to man's unique characteristics—and continuing use of non-biological language in ethical formulations. Julian Huxley, while denying his grandfather's view that social progress must defy the cosmic process, finds inspiration in the flowering of human individuality if man would but guide his own evolution. New evolutionary possibilities must therefore be valued for their own sake. George Gaylord Simpson seeks ethical standards in the promotion of knowledge, as essentially good, and the application of human responsibility, which is "rooted in the true nature of man."

Critically evaluating these views, Theodosius Dobzhansky wonders what criteria might measure Huxley's evolutionary possibilities, and notes that the "highest wisdom" was once given to Galilean fishermen. Allowing that "ethics are the products of evolution," he holds that modern science tells us *how* we obtain our standards of right and wrong, but not why we *ought* to view them as such. By contrast, C. H. Waddington suggests that evolution may have provided man, not with ethics, but with the ability to acquire them. Wise ethical behavior means promoting human evolution—but he cannot say how we learn what behavior is in tune with evolution.

Laudable among naturalistic moralists are their emphases on individuality, human responsibility, and wise ethical choices. But the proponents of such ethics, though ingenious and diverse their attempts, are limited by their monistic assumption that nature alone is real. Eschewing ultimates, they extrapolate ethics from essentially biological descriptions of events in nature, thus departing from the accepted use of the scientific method. Holding that ethics are derived from the cosmic process, they cannot agree on how man should act, nor resolve the dilemma of why man does not act as he ought. And none is free from the Spencerian misrepresentation of Darwin.

↪ Th. Dobzhansky, *Mankind Evolving*, New Haven, Yale University, 1964; J. Huxley, *Knowledge , Morality, and Destiny*, New York, 1957; T. H. Huxley, and J. Huxley, *Touchstone For Ethics*, New York, 1947; G. G. Simpson, *The Meaning Of Evolution*, New Haven, Yale University, 1967; C. H. Waddington, *The Ethical Animal*, New York, Athenium, 1961.   RICHARD P. AULIE

DEAD SEA SCROLLS. See *Essene Community*.

DEATH. See also *Organ Transplantation*. Death can be defined as the termination of the biological processes on which the activities of life depend and the consequent beginning of decay. The exact point of death is sometimes difficult to determine. Modern medical science tends to fix it at the point where the brain ceases to function, even though the use of artificial means may keep many of the bodily functions alive for some time afterwards. Such artificial means, however, really prolong activity but not life, for the person concerned has ceased to act independently.

Death is not merely a sudden accident, though it may so occur, but more generally is the end of a process of decline that begins in middle life. After childhood, there is a brief plateau of existence in which the forces of vitality and decay seem evenly balanced, after which the powers of the body decrease slowly until resistance is so weakened that the strain of life takes its final toll.

Because life is regarded with reverence, the normal ethic directs that it shall be preserved as long as possible. Death, therefore, poses certain difficult ethical questions: (1) Should life be preserved when it will mean only pain and uselessness for the person concerned? (cf. *Life, Sacredness of; Senility*). (2) When death or a "vegetable existence" seems inevitable, is euthanasia (q.v.) permissible? (3) Does the modern technology of organ transplants to preserve the life of an otherwise doomed person warrant allowing another to die in order to provide the organ? (4) At what point or for what causes should abortion (q.v.) be legalized? (5) Who should make the decision in cases such as these? (cf. *Medical Ethics*).

A scientific age tends to regard death simply as a material event with no emotional or spiritual significance. Since it is the common lot of all men, its universality promotes the attitude that it is the inevitable outcome of life, and therefore to be accepted simply as one accepts all facts.

While the scientific definition of death may change from time to time, the theological definition of death remains. For man it is the ultimate penalty of alienation from God, of which physical death is only a part: "The wages of sin is death" (Rom. 6:23). Jung has suggested that "Life is an energy process . . . in principle irreversible, and is therefore unequivocally directed toward a goal. That goal is a state of rest. . . . The curve of life is like the parabola of a projectile which . . . rises and then returns to a state of repose." So far this implies a normal and universally observable phenomenon, but then he adds: "The psychological curve of life . . . refuses to conform to this law of nature" (Carl A. Jung, "The Soul and Death," in *The Meaning of Death*, Herman Feifel ed., New York, McGraw Hill, 1959, pp. 4, 5). Consciousness does not diminish as bodily powers decrease. Though Jung does not argue for immortality, he admits that there is a lack of parallelism between the psyche and the body. This indicates that death is not merely a physical process, but that spiritual factors are also involved.

The Biblical doctrine of death holds that death is an abnormality for man, since he was created for life. Though it is universal, it can be reversed by the intervention of the power of God.

The promise of new life gives a different perspective on the current phenomenon of death by making it a crisis to be passed rather than a final denial of all meaningful existence. This hope helps to remove the fear of death that plagues both the young and the old, for it means not only the transcendence of death but the continuation of purposeful life to further undisclosed goals.

The Christian perspective aids in formulating answers to ethical questions attending death. The value and potential of any life should be carefully guarded, though in hopeless cases the artificial prolongation of physical life might be withheld. Transplants of organs may be legitimate if they can be effected without shortening the life of the donor. Most cases of heart transplants have proved ultimately futile, since the recipients did not long survive the operation. Abortion may erase a life of promise and usefulness, and should be confined to those cases where physical danger to the mother demands the choice of one life or the other. If life is God's designed destiny for man, it must not be treated lightly; and if death is "the last enemy" (I Cor. 15:26), its ravages should be withstood as long as possible.

☙ For modern views on death, see Herman Feifel, ed., *The Meaning of Death*, New York, McGraw Hill, 1959; Liston O. Mills, ed., *Perspectives on Death*, Nashville, Abingdon, 1969; Christopher T. Reilly, "The Diagnosis of Life and Death," in *The Journal* of the Medical Society of New Jersey, 66 (Nov. 1969, No. 11) pp. 601-604. The first of these deals with physical and psychological research; the second with a religious and ethical viewpoint; the third chiefly with the definition of death.

MERRILL C. TENNEY

DEBT. See also *Credit.* The staggering escalation of public and private debt is one of the features of our day. Money from governmental debt when repaid, unlike private debt, usually flows back into the economic unit. The doubling of private debt in the last decade (*Statistical Abstract of the United States,* 1970, p. 394), the debt financing of leisure activities, and even the practices of churches and seminaries of financing luxurious buildings at the expense of future generations may be less defensible. Debt is used in Matt. 6:12 as a synonym for sin. Jesus' payment of man's sin debt on the cross frees believers under grace and permits Christian service without the guilt burden (Rom. 4; 6:23).   WALTER P. GORMAN III

DECALOGUE. The Ten Commandments (or the "ten words" as they are designated in Exod. 34:28; Deut. 4:13; 10:4) are recorded in Exod. 20:1-17 and Deut. 5:6-21. Some minor differences occur between the accounts in Exodus and Deuteronomy but a harmonization is now possible from the Nash Papyrus of the second century B.C. found in the Fayyum area of Egypt in 1902 (cf. bibliography on the Nash Papyrus in H. H. Rowley, *Men of God,* London, T. Nelson, 1963, p. 3, n. 1).

Many deny a Mosaic origin for the Decalogue and ascribe it rather to the period of the prophets (Rowley, *ibid.,* p. 1, n. 2) or even to the time of the exile (*ibid.,* p. 1, n. 3) rather than to a 1440 B.C. date. Recently, however, that tide has begun to turn and many have returned to a Mosaic origin and a Sinaitic setting (*ibid.,* p. 2, n. 1 and 2; also J. J. Stamm and M. E. Andrew, *The Ten Commandments in Recent Research,* Naperville, Ill., Allenson, 1967, pp. 22ff.). The principle evidence has been the favorable comparisons of the literary form of the Decalogue and the whole book of Deuteronomy with the second millennium Hittite Treaties *vis a vis* the literary form of the first millennium treaties (M. G. Kline, *The Treaty of the Great King,* Grand Rapids, Eerdmans, 1963).

It would appear that there are three positive expressions of God's will in the Decalogue to which the negative statements are subordinate, *viz.,* "I am the Lord your God" (20:2a), "Remember the Sabbath day" (20:8a), and "Honor your father and your mother" (20:12) (J. J. Owens, "Law and Love in Deuteronomy," *Review and Exposition*, 61, 1964, pp. 274-83). These three non-finite verbal forms introduce the three spheres of man's morality.

1. *Man's Relationship to God* (20:2-7). Like Ps. 50:7, the opening affirmation is to be translated with the Greek and Latin versions, "I am Yahweh, your God." It is a revelation and a basis for faith more than just a command. Moreover, the context for everyone of the ten commands is God's grace and redemption, for the Covenant had already been initiated by the divinely engineered exodus from Egypt (20:2b).

Immediately there follow the three negative commands which implement a right relation to God internally, externally and authentically. There are no other gods even to turn to when one leaves Yahweh. (On the phrase "beside me" see W. F. Albright, *From Stone Age to Christianity*, New York, Doubleday Anchor, 1957, p. 297, n. 29). Further, no idols were to be made of these non-gods for external and material worship. Finally God's name, i.e., his person (Ps. 20:1), attributes, authority and doctrine (Micah 4:5; Ps. 22:22; John 17:6, 26) is not to be abused or misused for empty and unlawful purposes. If one borrows the name of God, he must adopt the person, and the purpose of this God in that usage.

2. *Man's Relationship to Worship* (20:8-11). The second positive statement is moral in that it declares that this sovereign God has a right to man's time. Therefore he set aside the Sabbath for rest and service to God. It is partly ceremonial, when it specifies the seventh day, but moral and eternal when it points to a stewardship of our time. The motivation for this function of rest and service is given in the double explanation of God's example in creation (Exod.) and redemption from Egypt (Deut.).

3. *Man's Relationship to Society* (20:12-17). The third positive injunction starts with the basic unit of the family and subjoins to it the sanctity of life, marriage, property, truth and internal desires.

The sixth commandment uses the word *rasah* which means any illegal killing, hence our "murder." In all of its forty-six occurrences, it is never used like *harag* (165 times) or *hemit* (201) for killing someone in battle or the destruction of someone who has fallen under divine judgment (J. J. Stamm, Sprachliche Erwagungen zum Gebot, "Du sollst nicht toten," *Theologische Zeitschrift I* 1945, pp. 81-90; also John Murray, *Principles of Conduct*, Grand Rapids, Eerdmans, 1957, pp. 107-122). This word upholds the integrity of a man's life.

Adultery is a violation of the oneness established by God for marriage in Gen. 1:27; 2:18, 21-24. Joseph saw sexual sins already in pre-Mosaic times as an offense against God as well as against society (Gen. 39:9) (cf. Murray, ibid., pp. 45-81).

Stealing and lying are prohibited by the God who owns everything and is the truth himself. While the ninth commandment points primarily to the courtroom situations, texts like Exod. 23:1-3 and Lev. 19:16 show how the informal situation is also part of this word. The preceding nine commandments are all to be judged not from an external point of view only, but also from the aspect of a man's heart desire. Covetousness is one of Baal's characteristics, but not one for God or his creatures (C. H. Gordon, "A Note on the Tenth Commandment," *JBL*, 31, 1963, pp. 108-09; and "The Ten Commandments," *Christianity Today*, 8, 1964, pp. 625-28).

The Decalogue may be summarized by the one word "love." This was Moses' inspired teaching in Deuteronomy (e.g., 4:6) and Paul's in Rom. 13:10 and I Tim. 1:5. Hence both testaments stress the priority of an internal response. Likewise the prophets never stopped expostulating the people for their externalized religiosity without any internalized bases.

Jesus also stressed this same point in the Sermon on the Mount. The Ten Words were put in the form of synecdoche, for when it forbade any particular sin, it also encouraged every opposite precept. For example, "Thou shalt not murder" means that I should seek to aid and help the life of all men. Thereby these words became all encompassing, reaching even to the occasions, and inducements leading to these sins as well. Finally, the form of the law makes no difference, for every moral act is double sided; it commands and prohibits. Therefore all moral acts are a choosing of one way and a refusing of another. Moral commands are not fulfilled merely by inactivity (which equals death in the moral sphere) but by choosing one action or another.

The Decalogue is part of the moral law of God. Since it is based on his nature and being, it remains permanently valid for Christians as long as God is God (the so-called third use of the law). While many deny that the civil and ceremonial aspects of the law can be isolated from the moral law, their Lord commands them to do just what they think is impossible (Matt. 23:23; 9:13; 12:7).

📖 Thomas Watson, *The Ten Commandments*, London, Banner of Truth, 1965 (r.p. 1692); Ezekiel Hopkins, *A Practical Exposition upon the Ten Commandments*, Edinburg, A. C. Black, 1841 (r.p. 1701); John Calvin, *Institutes*, II, vii, viii; Ernest F. Kevan, *The Moral Law*, Marshallton, Del., Sovereign Grace, 1963; Robert C. McQuilkin, *God's Law and God's Grace*, Grand Rapids, Eerdmans, 1958.   WALTER C. KAISER, JR.

DECEPTION. See also *Advertising; Consumer Fraud.* Deception is an intentional misleading of another person with the aim of getting him to accept falsehood as the truth. It involves more than a lie. It deliberately seeks to confuse through a false idea or device, or by deceptive appearances or pretensions, in order to further one's own purpose.

Deception may be achieved by suppression of truth, misrepresentation, or fraudulent practices. Cleverly-worded statements are used, and something is skilfully or craftily implied but not actually stated in order to sound or look like what it is not. Hence the truth may be perverted to induce another to part with something of value or to surrender a legal right.

Contemporary life must contend against such deceptions in family relations, business practices, mass media, local and national politics, and international affairs. The well-known credibility gap (q.v.) in all these areas has led to the demand for truth-in-advertising, truth-in-lending, truth-in-testimony laws.   RALPH E. POWELL

DECISION. A decision is an act of choosing which can be thought of as issuing from and involving the total being of a man. This includes man's past and future as well as what he is in the present.

Existentialists have called attention to the interrelation in experience of passion, thought, decision, and action. This is obviously true in the choice of the overriding moral values and broad goals which an individual takes as indispensable to his vision of life. So for Sartre to decide to be a Marxian or for Paul to determine to commit his life to Christ is to be an active partisan, vitally and persuasively engaged.

One of the functions of Christian ethics is to clarify how such life-commitments influence both general and particular judgments of moral obligation and value. By virtue of their centrality these commitments have a bearing on the kinds of programs one actively favors, on the means one is willing to employ to attain goals, and on the way one treats persons and responds to principles. They may, as well, influence certain prudential, conditional, and technical decisions of significance for moral life in the contemporary world.

The above account points to the depth and complexity of the problem of choice.

Existential voluntarism (q.v.) is, perhaps, an over-reaction against the traditional Western understanding of ethics as an intellectualistic discipline. There moral decision is seen as coming at the climax of a deliberative process in which an individual has considered reasons for and against alternative courses of action and has made a selection expressable in the form of an intention to do x rather than y. On this view explanations of actions thought to result from deliberation are made in terms of giving reasons for the action of the chooser. It may be supposed that he was following some moral rule such as promise-keeping. Or, if we know the individual well, we may say that he actually decided on utilitarian grounds, or that he took into account the persons and circumstances making up the situation.

There is little doubt that an ethical theory adequate to the *total* phenomenological complexities of moral experience must be prepared to incorporate both perspectives. Men do have to "make up their minds" when moral principles conflict. There are times when the desirability of certain ends and the suitability of certain means have to be thoughtfully weighed. Christians who seek moral direction from Scripture are not relieved of the cognitive responsibility for discovering precisely what principles of moral action are taught there, for looking into their import in their original historical-cultural context, and then determining how the divine command relates to specific contemporary situations.

It is well to remember that ethics belongs to the realm of practical decision where perplexity and anxiety are often present, and where choices may be influenced by feelings of love and hate, by desires and wishes, by our intentions exercised in good or bad faith, by our proneness to self-deception and rationalization, and by our sense of duty in terms of the scruples and sanctions of society. A Christian ethic grounded in the redemptive revelational perspective can provide a practical and theological basis for the response of the total man, including the need for careful reflection leading to responsible, concerned conduct.

Certainly the Bible itself exemplifies a variety of approaches. The OT contains, for example, a record of centuries of the practice of casuistic (If . . . then . . .) law which parallels much of the Near Eastern case law as it was brought over and set within the covenantal relationship of God's redemptive love. There is the apodictic law (Thou shalt . . .) with its Ten Commandments and the supreme command to love God and neighbor. Beyond this are the Biblical teachings which take the forms of proverbs, parables, prophetic warnings, and narratives. One reads of the intense struggles of Job and Abraham, of moments of moral weakness and also of injunctions like the "golden rule." The Apostle Paul speaks of the law as a schoolmaster to lead us to Christ who is the paradigm of the Christian's moral life. All this and much more points to the richness of factors which may influence the formation of Christian character and which, under the guidance of the Spirit as well as sound reasoning, can issue in Christ-honoring decision in daily life.

Traditional speculative ethics centers the decision problem in a contest of duty, natural law, an ideal good, happiness, or utility. In religious ethics the current trend is to appeal to "love" (cf. *Situational Ethics*).

While it is too much to expect that the study of Christian ethics will resolve all moral problems, it should have a clear framework of understanding. On specific issues it may help the Christian establish sound moral reasoning, perceptive contextual analyses, and an ability to appropriate guiding principles of Christian conduct. Nothing, however, can replace a sensitivity to the counsel of God (Ps. 1) and a sense of radical obedience—to "do justice, love mercy, and walk humbly with thy God" (Mic. 6:8).

📖 Dietrich Bonhoeffer, *Ethics*, New York, Macmillan, 1955; William F. Frankena, *Ethics*, Englewood Cliffs, Prentice-Hall, 1963; Arthur F. Holmes, *Faith Seeks Understanding*, Grand Rapids, Eerdmans, 1971; Gene Outka and Paul Ramsey, eds., *Norm and Context in Christian Ethics*, New York, Scribner, 1968; Alvin Plantinga, ed., *Faith and Philosophy*, Grand Rapids, Eerdmans, 1964, essay by William Frankena; Paul Ramsey, *Deeds and Rules in Christian Ethics*, New York, Scribner, 1967; Mary Warnock, *Ethics Since 1900*, New York, Oxford, 1966.   WILLIAM W. PAUL

DEFENSE MECHANISMS. Defense mechanisms are techniques used as means of coping with impulses, feelings and thoughts which are not acceptable at the conscious level. They are employed to minimize and/or avoid anxiety. Used moderately, many of these may be adjudged normal and helpful in reducing anxiety, and not socially unacceptable. Others, however, overly depended upon, result in bizarre behavior. These are obviously ineffective in reducing frustration, and may be judged as abnormal. Freud, in 1894, defined defense as a psychic mechanism set up by situations in which the ego is confronted by experiences, ideas or feelings producing such pain that the individual resolves not to think of them or push or suppress them from consciousness.

More recently the term has been used to cover only the *unconscious* techniques used to cope with unwelcome, undesirable, and instinctual tendencies that are anxiety-producing. These tendencies threaten the integrity of the personality and as such must be defended against as one would defend against physical blows, only unconsciously.

A dozen of the more common and best understood defense mechanisms are presented alphabetically, with brief descriptions.

Compensation: responding to failure in one area by entering into another realm of activity where one can and does succeed, thereby minimizing his inferiority in the first area.

Displacement: redirecting an aggressive impulse toward a substitute person or object rather than toward the one originally responsible for the frustration.

Fantasy (daydreaming): retreating into a world of make-believe where one's wishes, thwarted in the world of reality, can be satisfied.

Nomadism: a physical withdrawal, involving wandering continually from place to place, job to job, etc., in an attempt to escape frustration.

Overcompensation: similar to compensation, except that because of his exaggerated attempts to succeed in the seond realm, he only alienates himself further from his fellow man.

Projection: attempting to rid oneself of an obnoxious tendency, which cannot be consciously faced, by assigning it to another.

Rationalization: attempting to give a rational justification for one's own behavior which if not explained would most likely hurt his self-esteem or social approval.

Reaction formation: repressing socially unacceptable desires by taking on conscious attitudes and behavior that contradict one's true, but unconscious, wishes.

Regression: reverting to earlier modes of behavior characteristic of a previous developmental stage in which one felt more secure and adequate.

Repression: excluding from consciousness that which will cause pain, shame, or guilt.

Sublimation: choosing an alternate, substitutionary manner of satisfying sexual impulses, which meets social standards.

Substitution: similar to sublimation, but the choice of activity is socially unacceptable, thus producing guilt or loss of self-esteem.

While it may be useful to know about the various defense mechanisms we employ, such knowledge has two inherent dangers. First, the labels applied to us either may be objectionable or may encourage us to take on behavior to correspond with the label. The other danger is that, by being given labels, we may feel justified in our clearly irresponsible behavior. (Although not all defense mechanisms are irresponsible, many are.) Paul described men thus: "Their own conscience accuses them or sometimes excuses them" (Rom. 2:15 *Living Bible*). The Christian worker's task is to help us discard our defensive, excusive behavior and thus facilitate our moving toward "actually becoming all that God has had in mind for us to be" (Rom. 5:2 *Living Bible*).

HAROLD W. DARLING

DEFOLIATION. See also *Environmental Pollution*. Defoliation or the removal of leaves from trees through the use of herbicides has recently been extensively employed for military purposes in Vietnam. Weed killers applied to forests and cropland from low-flying airplanes are estimated to have killed almost one-half of South Vietnam's mangrove forest, millions of board feet of good timber, and enough crops to feed one-half million people for one year. The object was to prevent ambush, to assist in detection of enemy movement, and to deny local food supplies to Viet Cong. But destruction of created reality in view of man's responsibility "to dress and to keep" the garden (Gen. 2:15 has stimulated ecological concern over massive destruction of natural life and resources (cf. Deut. 20:19-20).

Mounting criticism from scientific organizations and others, especially during 1970, as well as apparent failure of some aspects of the defoliation program, probably were responsible for the scheduled phase-out of spraying in 1971. Major issues were the increasingly apparent ecological and psychological devastation.

Philip M. Boffey, "Herbicides in Vietnam: AAAS study finds widespread devastation," *Science* 171:43-47, Jan. 8, 1971.

KENTON K. BRUBAKER

DELIBERATION. Deliberation designates in moral philosophy the process by which men make moral choices.

Since moral choice is made with reference to some standard which is regarded as normative, it must proceed from a consideration of the values expressed in the various alternatives. Objects or qualities which for the chooser have value in themselves are of intrinsic value and receive prior consideration over those things whose value is instrumental, i.e., their value is only a means to the fulfillment of a need (cf. *Intrinsic, Instrumental Good*). Similarly, when the choice is between two or more objects or issues of intrinsic value, the moral choice will rest upon the one with the greater value to the chooser.

Inevitably in such discrimination of values, two questions arise: What is right? and What is good? If the decision concerning value is based upon the former, i.e., some articulated form or standard of right, the ethical approach is designated as formal; if the decision is based upon the latter, in which the consequences of the choice are the basic consideration, the ethical approach is teleological.

The relationship between the question of the right (q.v.) and the good (q.v.) raises a further dilemma. Judgments based solely on the right are conditioned by psychological and sociological factors which often blur the meaning of right as it is applied to diverse situations; consequently, without some reference to what is good, judgments may become arbitrary. On the other hand, strictly teleological judgments are subject to the futility which man experiences when he acts without reference to the creative process of the universe (Harold H. Titus and Morris Keeton, *Ethics for Today*.).

For the Christian, Dietrich Bonhoeffer attempts to resolve the tension between right and good in asserting that the call to be good and to make the world good through action is fulfilled only as the realities of self and the world are embedded in the ultimate reality of God in Christ (*Ethics*, edited by Eberhard Bethge, New York, Macmillan, 1965, pp. 188-89). The conception of God as the Ultimate Reality and Sovereign Ruler left no room for disobedience in Biblical history (Josh. 24:24), but the God who is to be obeyed is also the God who shows himself concerned for the quality of the life of the world and its inhabitants (Mic. 5:8; Isa. 5:7). If the first command to God's. people was "Love the Lord your God . . . " (Deut. 6:5), the dialectical relationship between God and Israel yielded the further responsibility, "Love your neighbor as yourself . . . " (Lev. 19:18).

The NT continues Judaism's recognition of the relationship between the commands to love God and to love one's neighbor (Matt. 12:30-31, etc.) but the ultimate ground for the ethical responsibility of the Christian is not in the formal demand of God but in the nature of his being: "We love because He first loved us" (I John 4:19 RSV; John 3:16; cf. similar expressions in Deut. 4:37; Hos. 11:1). Thus the right and the good are inseparably joined in the NT as the highest ethical conduct of man is a direct expression of the being of the One who gave the command.

Dietrich Bonhoeffer, *Ethics*, Eberhard Bethge, New York, Macmillan, 1965; Jacques Ellul, *To Will and To Do: An Ethical Research for Christians*, Tr., C. Edward Hopkin, Philadelphia, Pilgrim, 1969; Harold Titus and Morris Keeton, *Ethics for Today*, 4th ed., New York, American, 1966.

ROGER W. KUSCHE

DEMOCRACY. Democracy refers to rule by the people *(demos)* ancient Greek, used to distinguish rule by common citizens from rule by the aristocracy. The Bible has much to say about government (q.v.), but little if anything explicitly about democracy.

Through much of history, governments called "democracies" granted very little political power to the lowest levels of their societies. Athenian democracy offered no votes to the resident aliens who may have outnumbered citizens. After Magna Carta (A.D. 1215), seven hundred years and the passage of the Corn Laws were required before its ideals settled upon common Englishmen.

Whatever the official designation of the government, actual rule always requires communication and the distribution of risk and power. So democracies have their cabinets, and limited monarchies their ministries; even the Peoples' Republics have their Comintern or Party Presidium. Failure to follow this realistic limitation of power has usually produced demagoguery where great masses of people follow a single, charismatic leader for the short period of time his promises can hold their attention.

Democracy may have begun with Sumerian city-states in the third millennium B.C., but its earliest documented development is with Greek governments in the sixth and fifth centuries B.C. There it forestalled anarchy as oligarchies were forced to surrender control to the people. It began with small and tight aristocratic government living off the labor of workers who gradually were being deprived of their own lands by an unfair system of land distribution and court justice. However, changes in warfare on land and sea during the sixth century greatly increased the effectiveness of the nearly landless peasants. Now needed for army and navy and in alliance with middle-class merchants interested in trade and political stability, they were able to overthrow the aristocracy. Usually, after a period of one-man tyranny, revolution in these Greek cities ended with the establishment of democracy.

The best-known of these, Athenian democracy, was very carefully balanced by the annual election of a chief magistrate, the *archon,* who presided over the assembly of all the citizens, the *ecclesia*. Various other devices, such as the control of the military and the special competence of a council of elders, the *gerousia*, also helped to block the return of tyranny through the oratorical success of a would-be demagogue. When these systems broke down in the course of the Peloponesian War between Athens and Sparta, Athenian democracy blundered from one bad decision to the next. It included the execution of Athens' greatest philosopher, Socrates, after his lifetime of corrective service and occasionally irritating debate. Thereafter, *democracy* had an odious reputation in the ancient world.

Roman experience, prior to the rise of Julius Caesar a half-century before Christ, improved upon the Athenian formula for democracy, profiting from the political insights of Aristotle and Roman frontier pragmatism. This brought into being the system of checks and balances lauded by Polybius to the Greeks and to the rest of the literate world by Cicero. This system balanced political power between the people, meeting in popular assembly, the wealthy and elderly senate, and the chief civil and military leaders, the consuls. In general, the people either acquiesced or denied requests for going to war, levying taxes and the holding of office by individuals. The popular assembly was usually led in these actions by middle-class merchants acting as supporters of the consuls. The Senate was the deliberative assembly of the state. Its members could pose actions for the Senate itself or for the popular assembly. The consuls had important rights of veto over each other (always there were two) and over any specific public action.

This system of checks and balances proved irresistible to the founding fathers of the USA, and exists to the present in the form of the Congress, the Presidency, and the Supreme Court. Constitutionally-prescribed competence for each limits legislation and advice and consent for presidential action to the Congress, judicial decisions to the Court, administration and command of the armed forces to the President. It is generally recognized, however, that the American Presidency has developed far more power than initially accorded it and at times is now able to counterbalance the weight of Congress.

In England the limited monarchy has taken the form of parliamentary democracy, ruling without a constitution and with a strong presumption of party domination both of cabinet appointments and total policy of the prime minister. Essentially a two-party system, England has avoided the complexities of most European democracies which must form coalitions among the many parties to achieve sufficient majority in parliamentary votes to form a government. Such majorities often prove unstable in times of stress. Even in periods of stability, factions within the coalition are sometimes unable to provide the clear policy directives of an ideological majority.

In Communist countries, the votes for single-party candidates are massive; the issues few. Yet even in the USSR clear signs are appearing of the necessity for allying government with the middle-class.

People's Democracy, checks and balances, and demagoguery attest that democracy's record in history is one of constant need for effective and statesmanlike control from its leaders.   JOHN W. SNYDER

DEMONOLOGY. See also *Witchcraft*. In pre-Christian animism, nature religion, demons were believed to be ethereal or intermediary beings who had the power to influence men's good, but especially evil, fortune.

This primitive concept spilled over into Greek philosophy, and, during the age of Empedocles, Plato, and Plutarch, the idea of a hierarchy of demons evolved. The demons themselves were thought of as spirits of the dead. They were considered to be partners to magic and mantic, and the cause of disease, catastrophes, and possession.

The OT differentiates between the angels of God (Ps. 91:11; Dan. 9:21) and the fallen angels (Gen. 6). The idea of spirits of the dead is barely touched upon (I Sam. 28:13; Isa. 8:19). Intercourse with departed spirits is forbidden and classed with sorcery (Deut. 18:10-12). In contrast with animistic and Hellenistic beliefs, the OT describes the unbridgeable gulf which exists between good and evil spirits.

In the NT the word "demon" is mentioned only once. On the other hand the adjective "demonic" occurs fifty-five times in the Gospels, and "unclean" or "evil" spirits twenty-eight times. There is no mention of the spirits of the dead. The angels of God (Matt. 22:30; Luke 12:8; 15:10; John 1:51) and the angels of Satan (Matt. 25:41; II Cor. 12:7; Rev. 12:7) again stand in sharp contrast to one another. Contact with demonic powers can result from participation in heathen rites (I Cor. 10:20) and through sorcery, and there are strong warnings against such practices (Gal. 5:20; Rev. 9:21; 18:20; 21:8; 22:15). The NT describes the battle between the *civitas dei* and the *civitas diaboli*—the kingdoms of God and Satan—a war in which mankind is also involved (Eph. 6:12; I Peter 5:8). Illustrations of this conflict are not only to be found in the life of Jesus, but also in the several reports of exorcism of evil spirits (Mark 5; Luke 8: Acts 16). At the name of Jesus Satan has to flee.

Liberal and modern theologians not only deny the existence of the devil and his demons, but also that of the angels, and more recently, even God himself. In their eyes Jesus was a child of his times caught up in the mythological outlook of the ancient world. For them the demonic is merely the sub- or super-human within man, and possession only a form of mental or psychical illness. But this does justice neither to the Bible nor to the experience of Christians today.

The NT differentiates clearly between mental illness and possession (Matt. 4:24; 8:16). In fact these two phenomena are characterized by a completely different set of symptoms. If one prays authoritatively for a mentally-ill person, he or she will remain calm throughout. A possessed person on the other hand would begin to storm and to rage. Likewise the possessed can quickly fall into a state of trance during times of spiritual counsel, or become clairvoyant, or begin to speak in a language or languages they have never previously learned—symptoms which are never present in cases of mere psychological disturbance.

Kurt E. Koch, *Occult Bondage and Deliverance*, Grand Rapids, Kregel; _____, *Christian Counselling and Occultism*, Grand Rapids, Kregel; _____, *Demonology, Past and Present*, Grand Rapids, Kregel; Merrill F. Unger, Biblical Demonology, Winona Lake, Scripture Press.

KURT E. KOCH

DEMONSTRATION. See also *Protest.* Demonstration is physical action, as contrasted with mere verbal expression, designed to protest an act or policy of a governing authority. It is usually a collective action and is designed to bring about a change in the action or policy being protested. Common forms include marches, mass meetings, boycotts, sit-ins, picket lines, and individual or group fasts; less common forms range from pray-ins to self-immolation.

Demonstrations have been a form of protest throughout modern history. In America in the early 1960s they became associated with the civil rights movement and particularly with the theory of nonviolence preached by Martin Luther King, Jr., who combined Gandhi's concepts of peaceful resistance with appeals for social justice. King led the 1956 bus boycott in Montgomery, Alabama, which as much as any one event opened the "black revolution," and also led the March on Washington in the summer of 1963—one of the biggest demonstrations in modern America and certainly one of the most successful because of its impact on passage of the 1964 Civil Rights Act.

Characteristic civil rights demonstrations included student sit-ins at public lunch counters, "freedom rides" on integrated buses, prison fasts, and mock election campaigns to dramatize votelessness. The white counter-revolution was characterized by demonstrations against school integration, open housing, and busing of students. In the late 1960s opponents of the Vietnam War took over demonstration techniques from black civil rights leaders; this movement reached its zenith with the March on the Pentagon in 1968 and the November Mobilization of 1969.

Many activist clergy have been prominent in the leadership of civil rights and anti-war demonstrations. Essentially this form of protest is an act of conscience, reflecting personal moral concern or outrage against what is perceived as blatant injustice or evil. Usually it is directed against an objectionable government policy or law, but it may also be aimed against a private institution or individual. Disadvantaged or minority groups have found that the combination of an appeal to conscience and a dramatic format is an effective way of getting their message across in a democratic society where politicians tend to speak for the advantaged or the majority, since the mass media will give a major demonstration the same treatment as a major speech.

JOHN B. ANDERSON

DEMYTHOLOGY. See *Bultmann; Existentialist Ethics; Myth.*

DEONTOLOGICAL ETHICS. In Opposition to teleological theories, deontological theories set forth the view that the rightness or wrongness of an action or rule is not contingent (at least not in toto) upon its results. That is, one's moral obligations do not depend entirely upon the intrinsic value of the actual or anticipated consequences that a particular act or rule brings or may bring into existence. Instead, a deontologist holds that morally right actions or correct moral rules are determinable either solely by a consideration of the *nature* of an act or rule, or by a consideration of several factors—some of which are or may be the results of that action or rule. Immanuel Kant, for instance, contended that the *nature* of a moral rule should be such that it can be consistently universalizable. Hence all maxims, or particular rules of conduct, can be judged morally right or wrong according to this general criterion of universalizability. William D. Ross, on the other hand, lists six characteristics of acts, each of which counts either as a positive or negative factor in determining the rightness or wrongness of an act, *one* right-making characteristic being the promotion of the maximum possible intrinsic good.

Joining hands with Kant, Ross, and several other deontologists, are those theologians who, like them, give credence to the deontological thesis. They adhere to the position that right actions or correct moral rules either are, or are directly related to, specific commands that have issued from God. The guarantee for the moral acceptability of the commands he prescribes is thereby rooted in God's infinite goodness, for he commands only those things that he knows to be good. Subsequently, as a deontologist, the believer is obliged to act in accordance with his commands, and not on the basis of calculated consequences alone.

K. E. M. Baier, *The Moral Point of View*, Ithaca, Cornell University, 1958; Immanuel Kant, *Critique of Practical Reason and Other Writings in Moral Philosophy*, tr. Lewis W. Beck, Chicago, Liberal Arts Press—Bobbs Merrill, 1949; W. D. Ross, *The Right and the Good*, Oxford, Clarendon, 1930; Stephen Toulmin, *An Examination of the Place of Reason in Ethics,* Cambridge, Cambridge University, 1951.   PETER GENCO

DEPRAVITY. "Depravity" is a technical theological term relating to the state of man after the Fall and his consequent alienation from God. It describes the inherent flaw in his nature which renders him incapable of complete obedience to the law of God or of attaining holiness by his own effort. "Total depravity" does not mean that every man is utterly debased or that he necessarily possesses criminal inclinations. It does mean that he is totally a sinner because he disobeys God, and because even in a struggle for virtue he may be prompted by pride and self-interest. The "image of God" in man is not wholly obliterated, for he still retains high potentialities and may be motivated by good impulses. He is, however, constantly subject to selfish and impure motives which vitiate the good deeds that he may perform.

The evidence of this depravity is manifested in the moral history of the human race. The initial formation of any ethnic group may begin with high motives and a code of just laws, but ultimately declension begins which inevitably ends in moral decay. Man has sometimes succeeded in improving his knowledge and his culture, but he has not permanently elevated his nature. No civilization has yet existed which has eliminated completely political corruption, the degradation of some of its constituents, or an indifference to moral and spiritual values.

To the extent that human nature is permeated by depravity, the will (q.v.) is affected so that its choices are distorted by selfishness. The choices may or may not involve malicious acts, but they are formed without regard or little regard to the declared will and purpose of God. The Biblical statements, "All we like sheep have gone astray; we have turned every one to his own way" (Isa. 53:6), and "All have sinned and come short of the glory of God" (Rom. 3:23) bear witness to this fact.

In theological terms, total depravity is related to original sin (q.v.), which does not refer to sinful acts but to a condition or nature inherited from Adam, whose sin alienated him and his descendants from God. This has been the view of the Augustinian theology, perpetuated by the Reformers. Pelagianism, originated by a British monk, Pelagius (A.D. 401-409), contended that man is unconditioned by environment or by heredity, but is always capable of choosing freely good or evil. Pelagius denied the existence of inherited evil in human nature, and affirmed that man could live a perfect life if he chose to do so. The doctrine of total depravity is realistic, neither overlooking the better side of human nature nor disregarding its fatal flaws.

          MERRILL C. TENNEY

DESCRIPTIVISM. See also *Prescriptivism.* In ethical discourse descriptivism refers to methods attending primarily to factual data as the basis for deciding moral issues. Sociology and kindred sciences may supply the facts, or these may be obtained from the immediate situation or context in which the decision-maker acts. Christian descriptivists will be guided by the way God works with man in the world. Because the method calls for decisions to be based upon what *is* (the indicative mood) rather than upon what law, tradition or duty may *prescribe* (the imperative), it contrasts radically with the authoritative character of the inherited morality.   DELBERT R. GISH

DESERTION. See also *Abandonment; Divorce; Separation, Marital.* Desertion poignantly illustrates the pain and tragedy of our human situation, whether we think of the desertion of one spouse by the other, or whether we think of the desertion of a child by its parents. In either case there is suffering and there is always sin.

The Bible draws a sharp contrast between man's unfaithfulness and God's steadfast love, between man's hardness of heart and God's compassion.

Hosea was deserted by his wife Gomer, and from this bitter, hurtful experience Hosea learned to understand something of God's anguish and heartbreak in Israel's chronic apostasy. In spite of Israel's deep ingratitude and infidelity God sought to allure Israel from her idols and spoke tenderly to her (Hos. 2:14). Such is his magnanimity; such is his grace.

The Bible uses not only the marriage relationship to illustrate the nature of God's unchanging, unfailing love, but also the parent-child relationship. In answer to the question: "Can a woman forget her sucking child, that she should have no compassion on the son of her womb?" God says: "Even these may forget, yet I will not forget you" (Isa. 49:15).

If desertion always involves sin, are there circumstances which would justify a Christian deserting his spouse? The answer is no. Nevertheless, if an unbelieving partner departs, the other partner is free (I Cor. 7:15).

STUART B. BABBAGE

DESIRE. Desire is a longing for, a craving, or a wish. Moral connotations are not inherent in the term. The virtue of desire depends on its usage and attitude. Sexual desire is correct in marriage (I Cor. 7:2-6) but wrong outside of marriage (Matt. 5:28).

Scriptural criteria for the morality of desire are twofold. (1) Biblical commandments declare what one should or should not desire. Desire to serve Christ or help the poor is good (Isa. 26:8-9; Matt. 19:21); desire to kill or covet is wrong (Exod. 20:13; Deut. 5:21). (2) A non-Christian cannot fulfill the Spirit's desires because the Spirit does not indwell him (I Cor. 2:9-14). He follows his sinful nature's desires which

are evil (Prov. 21:10), impure (Rom. 1:24), Satanic (John 8:44), enslaving (Titus 3:3), enticing (James 1:14-15), and fruitless (Ps. 112:10). The Christian is indwelled by the Spirit (Rom. 8:9), whose desires war against those of the sinful nature (Gal. 5:17). The Christian refrains from the sinful nature's desires (Rom. 13:14; I Peter 4:2-3) by walking in the Spirit (Gal. 5:17). The Christian refrains from the sinful nature's desires (Rom. 13:14; I Peter 4:2-3) by walking in the Spirit (Gal. 5:16), realizing his sinful nature and its desires have been crucified with Christ (Gal. 5:24).

God desires steadfast love, the knowledge of God, truth among men, and also that none perish (Ps. 40:6; 51:6; Hos. 6:6; II Peter 3:9). He grants the desires of the righteous and meek (Prov. 10:24; Ps. 10:17) who delight in him (Ps. 37:4) and fear him (Ps. 145:19).

RALPH H. ALEXANDER

DESPAIR. See also *Cynicism; Melancholy; Nihilism; Pessimism.* Despair, the opposite of hope, is that state in which one abandons all expectation of salvation. A positive act of the will, the state may arise from a lack of recognition of one's dependence upon his fellow men, from a conviction of the excessive magnitude of one's sins, from a conviction that the demands made are too great for his capabilities, from a lack of trust in the grace of God, or from a combination of these. Incompatible with a life of faith (II Cor. 4:18) and at the opposite extreme from presumption, despair moves into the area of sin by questioning the goodness, mercy, and faithfulness of God who in all things works for good to those who love him (Rom. 8:28) and by rejecting the duty to seek perfection and salvation.

Though occurring infrequently in the Bible, "despair" *(exaporeein)* is used once in the NT for despairing of life when in great danger (II Cor. 1:8). Paul described the plight of the Gentiles as "without hope and without God in the world" (Eph. 2:12).

A distinction is to be made between discouragement, anxiety (q.v.), and despair. Discouragement is encountered by all men who meet with great difficulties; anxiety is due to excessive fear; but neither need entail abandonment of hope. The NT contrasts it with perplexity (II Cor. 4:8). Despair is the abandonment of the pursuit of the final goal. Sloth, immersion in pleasure, and lack of gratitude for God's blessings may predispose a man to despair.

📖 S. Kierkegaard, *Sick unto Death*, tr. Walter Lowrie, Princeton, Princeton University, 1941, 231 pp.; W. Molinski, "Despair," *Sacramentum Mundi*, II, 69-70.   JACK P. LEWIS

DESTINY.   See also *Astrology; Eschatology and Ethics; Fate; Providence.* Scripture attests the reality of a final goal or end which God has established for his creation in general and for mankind in particular. In revelational perspective, God's providential guidance and sovereign rule in history and for his people is undeniable. This does not reduce man to a puppet of unalterable fate; no deterministic force sets aside man's free and responsible being. The idea of an indifferent, inscrutable necessity to which everything is subject is a non-Christian concept and is foreign to the Bible. The common dictionary definition of destiny as a predetermined course of events invincibly decreed by a resistless power or agency is inappropriate to Biblical realities.

Non-Christian thinking incorporates a wide range of ideas regarding destiny, including views that are clearly deterministic and those which provide for free decision on the ground that man is destined to be free. The former posit some inscrutable, objective power to which everything is finally subject, though a distinction is sometimes made between the manner in which the resulting inevitability affects personal and impersonal agents. The latter insist that one's destiny is the basis of one's freedom,

and yet that freedom participates in shaping destiny: only he who has freedom has a meaningful destiny.

The Greeks often conceived destiny as a curse hanging over a noble house (a backdrop for the Greek tragic spirit); and at times as a weakness or defect of individual character. Freudian thought attempts to combine these two motifs in the tragedy of destiny concept, Freud's Oedipus complex.

In Spengler's elusive development, destiny is mystical and vague in nature and attempts to draw together a futureless Greek theory of natural cycles with Christian eschatology.

In much contemporary thinking destiny stands in polarity with freedom, each limiting the other (whereas fate is the simple contradiction to freedom). Destiny is not the contradictory of freedom, but points to its conditions and boundaries. It is not meaningless fate, but necessity united with meaning.

Dominating vast areas of modern thought is a deterministic notion of destiny as that posited in dialectical materialism, which leaves no place for freedom or divine providence. In Marxism man's destiny is the total State with the nationalization of the whole of life in an ideal classless society. Notable in Communist-dominated nations today, however, are the motifs of liberty and individual responsibility that appear in the writings of influential intellectuals who are dissenting from official Soviet doctrine.

For various reasons many modern nations assert that a special destiny is assigned them or their people, as evidenced by the term "the Third World."   RALPH E. POWELL

DETERMINISM. See also *Free Will.* Determinism has many forms. The three most important are physical, logical, and theological.

Physical determinism or mechanism is most popularly associated with the term.

Democritus in antiquity, Spinoza, Kant, La Place, and generally nineteenth century science, followed by behaviorism in the twentieth, hold that all motions, including the motions of human bodies, can be described by differential equations. Kant, who permitted freedom in the noumenal world, asserted clearly that men in the visible world, following their inclinations, are in no way free. Since the determinism is strictly mathematical, no statement of purpose is possible. Spinoza added, though this is not generally true of mechanists, that what does not happen is logically impossible.

The second form is logical determinism, of which the ancient Stoics and the nineteenth century Hegelians were separate examples. They were not mechanists; they allowed for purpose; and therefore they might be called rational or teleological determinists. The universal Logos controls all that happens, or Absolute Reason unfolds itself in history. Whatever happens, must happen; and, more consistently than in Spinoza, what does not happen is logically impossible. The Stoics added their theory of eternal recurrence (cf. *Stoicism*).

The Stoics also stressed ethics and held that the good life is a life of virtue. Mechanistic determinism may make morality meaningless (though Spinoza's great work bears the title of *Ethics*), but teleological determinism can be strongly ethical. Since too the Stoic Logos is God, this provides a transition to the third form of determinism, theological determinism; i.e., God foreordains whatsoever comes to pass. Note here that Josephus (*Antiquities of the Jews*, XVIII. i. 3.) reports that while the loose-living Sadducees believed in free will, the meticulous Pharisees and the strict Essenes were determinists: "The Pharisees . . . live meanly and despise delicacies in diet, and they follow the conduct of reason . . . and when they determine that all things are done by fate, they do not take away the freedom from men of acting as they think fit; since their notion is that it has pleased God to make a temperament whereby what he wills is done, but so that the will of man can act virtuously or viciously."

Romanism holds to free will, and Erasmus made this his main point against Luther, who replied in his masterpiece *The Bondage of the Will*. Melanchthon in this as in many other points repudiated Luther. Calvin, Knox, the Irish Articles of Religion, the Westminster Confession, and the Reformed position as a whole was thoroughly deterministic. Arminius in the early seventeenth century repudiated the Reformed faith and took a step backward toward Romanism.

📖 William Cunningham, "Calvinism and the Doctrine of Philosophical Necessity" (pp. 471-524), *The Reformers and the Theology of the Reformation*, London, Banner of Truth, 1967; John Gill, *The Cause of God and Truth*, Marshallton, Del., Sovereign Grace Book Club, 1957 (?); Jacques Loeb, *The Mechanistic Conception of Life*, Chicago, 1912; Augustus Toplady, *Philosophical Necessity Asserted*, pp. 784-819, in *Complete Works of*, London 1869.   GORDON H. CLARK

DEVELOPMENT. See also *Character; Christian Education; Evolutionary Ethics.* Development is the process of the human organism "unfolding" as it interacts with its environment. The terms "growth" and "development" are often used interchangeably, but growth is only a part of the total developmental process.

Traditionally, biology has contributed much to the study of human development. Since the 1930s, however, psychoanalytic viewpoints and logitudinal investigations by social scientists and educators have added new dimensions. Both heredity and environment play important roles in the development of man. A person's sense organs, his endocrine system, and his mind receive stimuli from his environment, and respond by differentiating and integrating the intake to form patterns of behavior. While general behavior patterns usually remain stable and consistent throughout his lifetime, a person's specific, variable behaviors are believed to result from immediate requirements exacted by both heredity and environment. The interactive relationship between hereditary factors environmental influences seems to be universal, but the culture in which a person is reared seriously affects the particular ways in which he develops. For instance, the ideas which the culture sanctions and the methods by which the culture permits the individual to express his emotions help to pattern his behavior. Despite the strictures imposed by the culture, however, the individual creates, to some extent, a pattern of behavior that is uniquely his own. Recent theory, with evident implications for Christian education, states that experience gained early in life contributes much both to the quantity and the quality of human development.

The area of human development in which moral and ethical character has been studied intensively is the social-emotional domain. Specialists in Christian education have perhaps too often relied on the resultant psychological and sociological data for understanding how Christian ethical character develops. The Character Education Inquiry which Hartshorne and May reported in three volumes seemed to reveal that conscience is not a "unitary trait" because many children show little consistency in moral and ethical behavior from one situation to another (Hugh Hartshorne and Mark A. May, *Studies in the Nature of Character*, New York, Macmillan, 1930). These authors and Berkowitz have reinforced the findings of many practitioners in education that merely possessing moral and ethical knowledge does not cause a person to behave morally and ethically (Leonard Berkowitz, *The Development of Motives and Values in the Child*, New York, Basic Books, 1964). Psychologists have tended to explain the

ability of an individual to resist temptation by saying, for instance, that the individual has a "strong sense of self."

The theorist and researcher who has probably had greatest impact on character education is Piaget, who postulated a developmental sequence in moral and ethical judgment which he attributed to combined maturational and environmental influences. Piaget's three stages of character development are: (1) the stage of constraint, at which parent or teacher actually determines the child's morality and ethics for him; (2) the stage of cooperation, at which the child agrees with peers and adults concerning acceptable standards; and (3) the stage of comprehension, at which the child can understand the implications of ideals which he himself has formulated (Jean Piaget, *Moral Judgment of the Child*, New York, Harcourt, Brace, 1932). Piaget's followers have shown that religion, social class, occupations of parents, and nationality help to determine the ages at which children move through the stages. Still other investigators have turned their attention from Piaget's concern for the intellectual components of character development to selected emotional components. They have emphasized the importance of familial love, children's internalizing of family value systems, and consistency in adult behavior (A. William Kay, *Moral Development*, New York, Schocken, 1969).

Though some of the ideas stated above accord in a general way with New Testament teachings, the Christian finds in none of them the irreplaceable significance of faith in patterning human development.

RONALD C. DOLL

DEWEY, JOHN (1859-1952). Dewey's philosophy, unlike that of Aristotle and Augustine, is basically ethical because all research, logical as well as physical, has for him the purpose of solving life's problems.

Knowledge for knowledge's sake is anathema to him.

Since there are both efficient and awkward ways of solving life's problems, and since problems change from time to time and place to place, he concludes that there are no fixed norms for human action. "We institute standards of justice, truth, esthetic quality, etc. . . . exactly as we set up a platinum bar as a standard measurer of lengths. . . . The superiority of one conception of justice to another is of the same order as the superiority of the metric system . . ." (*Logic, The Theory of Inquiry,* New York, Holt, Rinehart, & Winston, p. 216). Another and better illustration is that the rules of morality, like the rules of grammar, are the unforeseen and unintended results of custom. There are no antecedent ideal standards. (See *Human Nature and Conduct,* New York, Modern Library, I, Section 5.)

Scientific method can determine what customs at a given time and place are best. We should neither distrust the capacity of experience to develop ideals and norms, as Christians do in their belief in divine law; nor unthinkingly enjoy pleasures irrespective of the method used to produce them, though this is a better attitude than theism. Values are fugitive. A method is needed to discriminate among them on the basis of their conditions and consequences. The reason for enjoying a value is often (to have a conclusive argument Dewey should have said *always*) that the object is a means to or a result of something else.

Nothing is valuable in itself. A genuine good differs from a spurious good because of its consequences. Nor are the consequences good in themselves. They too are good only as a means to something further. Nothing carries its own credentials; everything is instrumental; there is no final, intrinsic value on which the value of other things depend.

Science can establish norms, or at least

show which customs are best, because the problem is not one of intellectual certainty as rationalists and Christians think, but of security. Chemistry improves the food supply; and so science, by studying the conditions by which values are made more secure, solves the problems of ethics.

Again, science is the solution because not all enjoyments are *de jure,* rather than *de facto,* values. "Enjoyments that issue from conduct directed by insight into relations have a meaning and a validity due to the way in which they are experienced. Such enjoyments are not to be repented of; they generate no aftertaste of bitterness" (*Quest for Certainty,* Minton, Balch, 1929, p. 267). For example, heating and lighting, speed of transportation and communication, have been achieved, not by lauding their desirability, but by studying their conditions: "Knowledge of relations having been obtained, ability to produce followed, and enjoyment ensued as a matter of course" (*Quest for Certainty,* New York, Putnam, p. 269).

The examples of heating, lighting, and communication concretize Dewey's view that there are no intrinsic values. But if there are no intrinsic values, why should one engage in arduous scientific investigations to make heating and lighting more secure? If Dewey answers, "to obtain something further," the question repeats itself: Why should one arduously develop them as means to something further, which itself has no intrinsic value? The moral question is not, as Dewey says, how to make values more secure, but, rather, how to select which values to secure.

Dewey admits that there are wrong ideals. Without aesthetic enjoyment mankind might become a race of economic monsters (*Reconstruction in Philosophy,* New York, Holt, 1920 p. 127). But why not choose economic monstrosity? If *de jure* value is conferred by a scientific study of complicated means, not only economic monstrosity but nearly any other imaginable purpose is justified.

Dewey also gives the examples of murder and wanton cruelty (*Ethics,* with Tufts, pp. 251, 265, 292). But it is significant that Dewey with communistic massacres and Spanish bullfights before him nowhere gives a scientific proof that these are evil.

There is a reason why Dewey dare not try to prove that murder is bad. To do so would result in a fixed rule, a hierarchy of values, and intrinsic qualities. Therefore Dewey makes all moral judgments aesthetic determinations in single cases. Each contemplated case of murder must be decided singly and individually. Hence in some cases murder may have beneficial results.

The final criticism is then that scientific technique cannot select any goal. It can be used for opposite purposes. Scientific methods of communication are efficient for preaching the gospel and equally efficient for totalitarian subjugation of the Hungarians, Czechs, and Vietnamese. And this means that Dewey has not solved the problem of morality.

   Gordon H. Clark, *Dewey,* Nutley, N.J., Presbyterian and Reformed, 1960; P. A. Schilpp, *The Philosophy of John Dewey,* New York, 1951.

GORDON H. CLARK

DIALECTICAL ETHICS. See also *Barth; Brunner; Buber; I—Thou Relationship; Kierkegaard.* An ethical philosophy is dialectical whenever the interpretive principles it requires for giving meaning to the moral life are viewed as pointing to conflicting (contrary) elements held in tension in the moral life itself.

Initially, as in Plato, dialectic was a critical form of dialog used to discover ethical truth by considering conflicting opinions about the virtues that go into a life of excellence. A modern religious version of ethics as dialogical can be seen in Buber's influential *I and Thou.* For the Stoics and medieval theologians the term became a synonym for logical reasoning in which propositions and counter-propositions were debated. Modern usage begins with Kant's "Transcendental Dialectic" which asserts that theoretical reason employed apart from an understanding of empirical phenomena runs into contradictions or "antinomies" expressable as theses and antitheses. So, in the freedom vs. determinism controversy, this reasoning defines freedom as "lawlessness" while the practical reason decisive for ethics properly understands freedom as an independence from coercion. Thus for Kant, dialectics is useful in warning theoretical reasoning of its limitations and in pointing to the possibility of practical moral truth.

Although it is commonly supposed that Hegel completed the dialectical triad by adding the idea of "synthesis," this development was worked out by his predecessors Fichte and Schelling. It is also thought that he viewed theses and antitheses as logical contradictories, whereas careful study shows that most of his examples stress antithetical *tendencies* manifested in natural and historical processes and in much of human thinking. Hegel is most significant in his discussion of dialectic as a *cultural-historical* process which involves a continual interplay of opposites as rational freedom is realized in the history of nations. Hegel also believed that all of these natural, cultural, and individual developments are part of the self-conscious manifestation of the Universal Spirit. As is well known, Marx rejected Hegel's religious and ethical idealism and interpreted history in terms of a dialectical necessity—the movement of economic classes through struggle and revolution. Both men contributed to the understanding of cultural dynamics although with clearly different emphasis.

For Christian ethics no single recent line of development has been more important than that which comes through Kierkegaard. He rejects the possibility of syntheses as overcoming all antitheses. What remains are the two terms of the *paradox*. Jesus Christ as the God-man is *the* Paradox by which the intellect of man is completely stunned and man is driven by passionate faith to respond "inwardly" and existentially to the Incarnation.

The early writings of neo-orthodox theologians like Karl Barth and Emil Brunner became known as dialectical theology because of their reaction against both orthodox and liberal thinkers who made unqualified assertions about God. Like Kierkegaard, Barth, and Brunner affirm a paradoxical relationship between the Creator and the creature. For Barth divine revelation is paradoxical; it comes in human language and truth and must therefore be participated in existentially. For Brunner the object of faith is always absurd in the sense of being paradoxical. As he applied this in Christian ethics he makes his appeal not directly to the commands of God in Scripture but to imperatives received from God "afresh each time through the voice of the Spirit. . . . God's command does not vary in *intention*, but it varies in *content*, according to the conditions with which it deals." The supreme principle of love is not predefined "for it means being free for God. . . . Love is 'occasionistic.' She does not know the Good beforehand" (*The Divine Imperative*, Philadelphia; Westminster, 1947, pp. 111, 134).

Barth's later thinking illustrates his willingness to use dialectical thinking to get at existential truth about abortion. The divine "No" comes from the sixth commandment and from recognizing that the fetus is a relatively independent human being, endowed with life from God and therefore belonging to Him. On the other hand, if a particular act of abortion is a case of murder, it is also a sin which can come under divine forgiveness. So, in the case where the life of the mother is at stake, for example, there may come the divine "Yes." On the basis of the same sixth commandment, but with an exceptional situation, he says, "we can learn that when a choice has to be made between the life or health of the mother and that of the child the destruction of the child in the mother's womb might be permitted and commended" (*Church Dogmatics*, Edinburgh, Clark, 1961, III, Part IV, p. 421). Barth here moves beyond a mere statement of paradox to the development of a reasoned decision-making process which aims to take seriously the written command of God.

This dialectical and situational approach leaves unsatisfied those who feel that ethics should be built on the revealed truths of the Word as such. Carl Henry, for example, has reasoned that while Brunner's emphasis on the love of Christ has the *form* of Christian ethics it forfeits much of the cognitive *content* that is available to guide man in his choices. The fountainhead of Christian ethics, he says, is the will of God "received in the Divine confrontation of man by commandments, statutes, and laws, and face-to-face in the incarnation" (*Christian Personal Ethics*, Grand Rapids, Eerdmans, 1957, p. 193). This emphasis on the Bible as ethically normative is hardly intended to deny that the Scriptures must be interpreted and applied with great care and Christian concern to specific situations. But, as Henry sees it, the successors of Kierkegaard, for all of their re-emphasis on sin and the cross, may leave men adrift amid existential ambiguity and the tensions of the dialectic (p. 371).

The dialectic of assertion and counter-assertion in ethics and the paradoxical character of revelational truth continues in various forms through the writings of Reinhold Niebuhr, Rudolf Bultmann, and Paul Tillich. For the latter, Christian ethics—by virtue of being theological—is at the same time reflective, dialectical, and paradoxical. It is dialectical because the moral life itself is always full of tension and struggle; it is paradoxical because it seeks to go beyond rational, philosophical ethics and against man's limited self-understanding and expectations to a "new reality" in Christ.

By and large dialectical talk seems to have been replaced in the "new morality" by a pluralism—by discussions in terms of situations, persons, and contexts. The central issue is the understanding of love, the *agape-principle*, in Christian ethics. The situational ethics (q.v.) approach of Joseph Fletcher (q.v.) claims to be dialectically located between legalism and antinomianism, but it clearly flirts with the latter since its sole guide is to "do the most loving thing." Critics have pointed out that Fletcher uses "love" in a variety of senses, that he assumes a maturity of moral experience, and that his person-centered ethics of response is actually a form of act-utilitarianism. His anti-absolutism prevents him from saying, for example, that racism is always wrong, yet when he is opposing the Catholic view on abortion he easily slips into a statement like *"No unwanted and unintended* baby should ever be born" (*Situation Ethics: The New Morality*, Philadelphia, Westminster, 1966, p. 39). The failure to get a Biblical perspective on "law"—to see it in the convenantal context of God's redemptive love—is perhaps situationalism's most serious mistake.

Dietrich Bonhoeffer, *Ethics*, New York, Macmillan, 1955; Martin Buber, *I and Thou*, New York, Scribner, 1958; Rudolf Bultmann, *Theology of the New Testament*, New York, Scribner, V.I, 1951; Soren Kierkegaard, *Concluding Unscientific Postscript*, 1941, *The Concept of Dread*, 1957, *Philosophical Fragments*, Princeton, N. J., 1936, 1962; Edward Long, *A Survey of Christian Ethics*, New York, Oxford, 1967; John Macquarrie, *3 Issues in Ethics*, New York, Harper & Row, 1970; Thomas Oden, *Radical Obedience, The Ethics of Rudolf Bultmann*, Philadelphia, Westminster, 1964; G. H. Outka and P. Ramsey, eds., *Norm and Context in Christian Ethics*, New York, Scribner, 1968, essays by J. Fletcher, Basil Mitchell, and Donald Evans; H. L. Smith and L. W. Hodges, *The Christian and His Decisions*, Nashville, Abingdon, 1969; Warren E. Steinkraus, ed., *New Studies in Hegel's Philosophy*, New York, Holt, Rinehard & Winston, 1971; Paul Tillich, *Systematic Theology*, Chicago, University of Chicago, 1957, v. II; Sidney Hook, *From Hegel to Marx*, Ann Arbor, University of Michigan, 1962.   WILLIAM W. PAUL

DIPLOMACY. Diplomacy is the art, science or practice of conducting international negotiations. Contacts between nations are unavoidable. Some relate to a common objective, others to conflicts of interest. In theory, negotiations are conducted in order to reach a mutually acceptable agreement even though neither side secures all or most of its objectives. In practice, negotiations may be simply a tactical maneuver to gain an advantage.

When one contemplates the terrible costs of war and corruption in society it becomes evident that peace, equity and progress would best be served were government to heed the Biblical emphasis that they serve as ministers of justice.

History shows that Biblical principles are more "honored in the breach than in the observance." To give the appearance of integrity and good will may be intended only to deceive and thereby gain an unfair advantage.

Reputation is built more on what one does than what he professes. A government which consistently demonstrates its probity is the more likely to negotiate just settlements, and this should be its aim. Every government is charged with the protection of the persons, rights, and property of its citizens. It should therefore always be on guard against efforts by the other side to deceive it by fair words and promises. If the other government is honorable and capable of carrying out its agreement, guarantees may be minimized or neglected. If experience shows that the other party often uses diplomatic negotiations as a means of deception to gain advantage which it subsequently exploits, then the government must have guarantees that it can itself supervise. This guard by a government against deception and treachery in no way implies that it should adopt similar dishonest tactics.

Some Christians serve their country in positions where they may influence the national foreign policy or serve as negotiators. Their primary purpose should be that they seek to glorify God (I Cor. 10:31) rather than men (Col. 3:22, 23). They should apply the Golden Rule in relations with their official superiors and with their associates. Biblical ethics should not be abandoned in the interests of expediency. They may have to choose between obeying God or man, in which case the faithful Christian should not hesitate to pay whatever his obedience to God might cost (Acts 5:29). In his decision however he should make sure that what he is asked to do is actually contrary to the will of God as expressed in the Bible. Too often men do what they want to do and try to justify the action by claiming that they are doing God's will. It is not difficult to misuse the Bible if one chooses.

In negotiations with the other side the Christian diplomat should be courteous but firm, adhering faithfully to his government's policy. Here, too, accuracy of statement is essential. Since the world so often practices and expects deception he must try to establish his own credibility. He can do this only by being consistently truthful. Efforts of the other side to attack him and his country by lies and insults of various kinds should not disturb him, for, if God be for him who can be against him? (Rom. 8:31). Allowing oneself to become emotionally embroiled with the other side cannot help but may actually do real harm to the success of the negotiations. Because of their good will toward others, Christians may often be naive. This is not a demonstration of Christian virtue but a failure to be realistic as to the hearts of men. By being wise as serpents and harmless as doves (Matt. 10:16), the Christian may by God's

help be able to achieve respect and confidence that would bring success to an otherwise hopeless negotiation.

WILLIAM K. HARRISON, JR.

DIRECTION, SPIRITUAL. See *Guidance.*

DISARMAMENT. See also *Armament; Peace and War.* A most serious problem for future existence is the threat of an all-out nuclear war. For nations to continue to arm themselves with the ultimate weapons is to increase the probability of such a holocaust. It is highly probable that the development of nuclear armaments to maintain a balance of power will ultimately lead to someone's using that power.

The exponents of disarmament recognize that "power corrupts, and absolute power corrupts absolutely." They recognize that violence begets violence, and advocate finding ways to establish "good neighbor" policies with all. They advocate a national attempt at being good neighbors to opposing nations, and to achieve mutual well being. They contend that war is basically a concomitant of economic problems and advocate the establishment of an economy built on helping peoples. War has never been a long-range cure for man's problems.

The fact that disarmament must begin where we are, with major powers already armed with nuclear power, does not require that one power should suddenly and totally disarm and be completely vulnerable. But a program of mutual reduction in arms ought to replace the arms race. One nation will need to run the risk of moving first in good faith. If this is not done, the future can only offer the risk of nuclear destruction of the world.

Man was created in and for community. All that lends itself to man's destruction is a violation of that community, of human life, and consequently of the will of God for man.   MYRON S. AUGSBURGER

DISCIPLINE. The Biblical basis of church discipline is Matt. 18:15-18 along with the application in I Cor. 5 (incest), I Thess. 3:6 (idleness), and II Tim. 2:17 (error). Discipline was taken seriously in the early church, especially where there was relapse into paganism. In the second century permanent excommunication could be imposed, but official opinion, backed by *The Shepherd of Hermas* and formulated by Calixtus of Rome and Cyprian of Carthage, permitted readmission after protracted probation culminating in public confession.

New and mostly unhealthy developments occurred from Gregory I to the Council of Trent. Penances were imposed for less offenses with possible financial commutation. Private confession to the priest established itself. Purgatory became a supposed extension of temporal discipline, and to avert this many of the worst medieval abuses arose, e.g., indulgences and private masses. The elaborate system of church courts formalized discipline but to no great spiritual profit. Serious offenders could also be handed over to the civil power for punishments the church was not allowed to impose.

The Reformation ended the medieval system but found the disciplinary problem a hard one. Sometimes the state exercised it as the supposed representative of the laity. Calvin put it in the hands of the consistory or ruling elders. The Anabaptists exercised it through the ban, though unfortunately this caused a good deal of inner disruption.

The modern church is in the main distinguished by an erosion of discipline. The state system has mostly broken down, while pluralism makes inner enforcement difficult. There is even the risk of civil actions for slander where the church's moral standards differ from those of the state.

Discipline is Biblical, but it has seldom if ever been applied successfully. If lack of discipline weakens the inner life and outer mission of the church, perversion of discipline carries serious dangers of legalism, disruption, and even hypocrisy. The achievement of a true Biblical and evangelical discipline which will serve both doctrinal and ethical edification is perhaps one of the most urgent tasks on the church's agenda.

GEOFFREY W. BROMILEY

DISCRIMINATION. See *Prejudice; Race Relations; Segregation.*

DISINTERESTEDNESS. See also *Good Neighbor.* To describe the peculiar character of love for neighbor enjoined upon Christians in the NT, some use the term disinterested love. To love the neighbor "as oneself" means to love the other person *for his own sake* without ulterior motive or self interest—thus to love disinterestedly. Thornton Wilder's Julius Caesar illustrates well the idea:

Would it not be a wonderful discovery to find that I am hated to the death by a man whose hatred is disinterested? It is rare enough to find a disinterested love; so far among those that hate me I have uncovered nothing beyond the prompting of envy, of self-advancing ambition, or of self-consoling destructiveness. It is many years since I have felt directed toward me a disinterested hatred. Day by day I scan my enemies looking with eager hope for the man who hates me "for myself" or even "for Rome."—*The Ides of March*, Harpers, 1948, pp. 218, 113

If one asks how this disinterested love can be separated from interested love, perhaps Jesus' words help: "But I say to you, Love your enemies . . ." (Matt. 5:43f.). If love persists despite continued hostility, then the love is truly disinterested. Jesus' parable of the Good Samaritan also teaches this same quality of neighbor-love (Luke 10:25f.). The Samaritan with no apparent thought of recompense or self-interest showed mercy to the helpless man. Again, the expression to love the neighbor "as thyself" carries with it the same type of idea. You love yourself for your own sake. Christian love is this type of disinterested self-love inverted.

In contrast to this genuine disinterested Christian love for the neighbor, one might recall the numerous recent and glaring incidents of muggings, rapes, and even murders, such as the famous New York City incident, where the cries for help of the victims were ignored by nearby people who, by refusing to come to their aid, were displaying a basic self-interested view of neighbor love.

◯ Paul Ramsey, *Basic Christian Ethics,* New York, Scribner, 1950, pp. 92ff.

ALAN F. JOHNSON

DISPENSATION. A dispensation is a suspension of canon law or of ecclesiastical rules in certain cases and for special reasons. Thus if the church has a rule that no one should be ordained to the ministry under the age of twenty-one, any exception to this will be by dispensation. As early as the fifth century, when the rulings of synods came to be collected into canon law, the power of dispensation was recognized. With the increasing codification of canon law, and especially the centralization of the western church in Rome, a detailed system of dispensation was worked out. Some power was granted to bishops in local matters, in emergencies, or as papal legates. In the main, however, the power to grant dispensations was vested in the papacy on the principle that the church's rules came from the pope and could not be changed or waived except with his sanction.

Strictly, dispensing belongs to the pastoral office of the church and this means that it ought to be without charge. The establishment of a complicated legal machinery, however, entailed considerable expense and it was customary, therefore, to charge fees for the costs incurred. Since canon law covered so many things in the lives of church members, great numbers of dispensations were needed, and dispensations became a lucrative source of revenue for the Roman church.

Some dispensations might be granted very beneficially. Thus when celibacy was finally imposed on the clergy by Gregory VII, dispensations could still be granted, as in the so-called Uniate churches. Similarly, rules of fasting might be relaxed in the case of the sick and elderly. In some instances, of course, the rules contained built-in exceptions, as the Benedictine Rule does in relation to sick monks. In other instances dispensations for various causes might become established procedure.

Yet the system of dispensations also opened the door to grave abuses which impaired the spiritual and moral health of the church. Two examples may be taken from the Reformation period. The indulgence scandal, which led to Luther's epoch-making protest in 1514, was itself occasioned by an expensive dispensation allowing Albert of Mainz to be a pluralist in spite of the clear rules against this and the financial evils and pastoral neglect involved. Then the marriage of Henry VIII of England to Katherine of Aragon had originally taken place by dispensation, since she had already been (technically at least) married to his deceased elder brother and thus came within the prohibited degrees. Incidentally, dispensations were more or less essential for all marriages once the fantastic system of spiritual relationship increased the risks of marrying even unknowingly within the prohibited degrees. All this was grist for the papal mill, and its moral value is not too apparent, especially when one remembers that at a pinch dispensations could even be given for bigamous unions.

Another dubious element in the whole system of dispensations is the claim of the papacy that it can dispense Christians from oaths of loyalty to civil rulers. This was an important matter in the violent conflicts between popes and secular powers in medieval Europe. Thus Gregory VII wrote concerning Emperor Henry IV: "I absolve all Christians from the bond of the oath which they have made to him or shall make" (Feb. 1076). Similarly English Roman Catholics were encouraged to revolt against Elizabeth I, to try to assassinate her, and finally to make common cause with the Spanish Armada (1588) in an attempt to depose her. Although claiming the power to dispense from oaths as a right, the papacy also tried to substantiate it by claiming an ultimate civil overlordship as well.

In principle, the power of dispensation applied only to ecclesiastical law and not to divine or Scriptural law. This could be an important distinction, for the marriage suit of Henry VIII rested on the argument that dispensation from the prohibited degrees of Leviticus is unlawful. Yet observing the distinction in practice was often very difficult. Levirate marriage, for example, is another Biblical rule which led the Lutherans to oppose Henry's suit. Dispensations for bigamy might also be defended on grounds of patriarchal precedent. Similarly, if Paul seems to demand absolute loyalty to civil rulers in Rom. 13, the Old Testament can record a *coup d'état* (e.g., that of Jehu) commissioned by God himself, and Peter and the apostles could also practice civil disobedience.

Nevertheless, the principle is a sound and important one in ethics. No law of man, however sound in itself, can claim the same absolute authority as divine and Scriptural law. From Scriptural law there is no dispensation by any other court. Even when circumstances in this fallen world make its pure observance impossible, there can be no infringement of this law without sin. Ecclesiastical rules may be relativized by historical, geographical, or cultural factors, but care must be taken that this not become a deliberate or automatic dispensing from Biblical law as well by simple relativization.

GEOFFREY W. BROMILEY

DISPENSATIONAL ETHICS. Dispensationalism as commonly held by a considerable number of evangelicals today not only sees progressive revelation in the Bible as carried forward under seven different dispensations or economies through which God governs the affairs of the world; it also makes a basic hermeneutical distinction between passages relating to Israel and those relating to the church (cf. *Dispensationalism Today*, C. C. Ryrie, Chicago, Moody, 1965, pp. 43-46). This distinction, coupled with the radical differentiation between the dispensation of law and that of grace, has led to a view of the Sermon on the Mount (q.v.) that, stressing the Jewish and Messianic aspect of Matthew's Gospel, emphasizes the application of Matt. 5–7 to the eschatological Messianic kingdom. Thus critics of dispensationalism have charged it with ruling out any present application of Christ's moral teaching in the Sermon and so evading personal responsibility for obedience to this part of his ethic.

While the teaching of some dispensationalists, particularly those holding an ultradispensationalism, have lent credence to the charge, a fair contextual reading of the mainstream of dispensationalism fails to substantiate it. Nor is the term "dispensational ethics" used generally, if at all, by theologians or expositors of dispensational persuasion. Such writers, though indeed holding the central and ultimate relation of the Sermon on the Mount to be eschatological, also teach that it has a proximate ethical application to readers today. As the *Scofield Reference Bible* (New York, Oxford University Press, 1909, 1917) says after identifying the Sermon as containing the principles of the future Messianic kingdom, "But there is a beautiful moral application to the Christian . . ." (note on Matt. 5:2); and the New Scofield Reference Bible

(New York, 1967), following a discussion of how Matt. 5–7 shows Christ's use of and relation to the Mosaic law, declares that "both the Mosaic law and the Sermon on the Mount are a part of Holy Scripture which is inspired by God and therefore 'profitable for doctrine, for reproof, for correction, for instruction in righteousness' (II Tim. 3:16) for the redeemed of all ages" (note on Matt. 5:3). Moreover, M. F. Unger, a leading dispensationalist, writes of the Sermon: "This remarkable discourse has first of all an omnitemporal moral application, and hence its principles are applicable to the Christian. . . . However, in the Jewish slant of Matthew, presenting Christ as king, premillennialists frequently hold the application is literally to the establishment of the future Davidic kingdom" (*Unger's Bible Dictionary*, Chicago, Moody, 1957, p. 997).

Rather than holding a special kind of "dispensational ethics," dispensationalist exegetes and theologians, while facing the same problems of literal application of every statement in the Sermon on the Mount that non-dispensationalists face, find likewise in it principles determinative for Christian ethics. Indeed, the attitudes of dispensationalists toward such things as divorce, lust, anger, and hypocrisy reflect this discourse. They recognize, moreover, the relation of the great ethical passages in the epistles to the Sermon on the Mount and see in them an extension of Christ's teaching in the Sermon and elsewhere in the Gospels. In short, they base their ethics on Christ's law of love and on the whole body of relevant NT teaching. And if they do not find the way of salvation explicitly set forth in the Sermon on the Mount, in this they agree with nost non-dispensationalists. (Cf. this statement by R. H. Mounce in the *New Bible Dictionary*, Grand Rapids, Eerdmans, 1965, "The Sermon on the Mount," pp. 1161f.: "By no stretch of the imagination can it be considered 'good news' to one depending upon fulfilment of its demands for entrance into the kingdom.")

FRANK E. GAEBELEIN

DIVINE RIGHT OF KINGS. See also *Prophets.* In its extreme form the theory affirmed that monarchs derive their authority from God, are responsible to him only, and can demand unlimited and unquestioned obedience from their subjects on pain of divine as well as kingly displeasure. Some scholars trace its origins to the new line of "God's anointed" initiated when the OT Jews substituted monarchy for theocracy; others identify the theory with the later practice of "sacring" Eastern and Western emperors at their coronation, by which process they were thought to have acquired some special divine attribute. Nevertheless in medieval times the concept seems to have been restricted to the belief that rulers had divine (but not unlimited) authority.

With the growth of nationalism kings were not slow to realize the possibilities of Divine Right as a counter-balance to papal claims; thus was fathered the notorious principle *cujus regio ejus religio* that made the religion of the subject dependent on the will of the monarch. Neither Luther nor Calvin seems in practice to have had a strong and consistent attitude toward Divine Right, but in England the theory entered a new phase when Henry VIII broke with Rome. The Church of England came to identify itself with a somewhat modified doctrine of Divine Right, perhaps because it served equally well against Rome on one hand, Puritanism on the other—and at the same time ensured the English Church's position in the state. Wrote Bishop John Jewel in words acceptable to Elizabeth I: "We publicly teach, that princes are to be obeyed as men sent by God; and that whosoever resists them resists the ordinance of God," a declaration echoed in 1626 by William Laud, later Archbishop of Canterbury.

But it was in Scotland, paradoxically, a land with a record of conspicuous disrespect for its kings, that Divine Right was more authoritatively enunciated. Despite George Buchanan's warning to his pupil in *De Jure Regni apud Scotos* (1579), James VI was later to assure his son that "as to dispute what God may do is blasphemy, so is it to dispute what a King may do in the height of his power." While admitting that parliaments were expedient, the Stuart kings steadfastly maintained that members sat there only through a special privilege accorded by the ruler. When Charles I, king of the by then united kingdom of Scotland and England, deprived them of that privilege, it led to civil war, a period of military dictatorship under Cromwell, and (after a further period of Stuart supremacy) the toppling of a dynasty, and the discrediting of what had always been an indefensible theory. It lingered on in varying forms on the mainland of Europe, but did not survive the close of the eighteenth century.

J. N. Figgis, *The Divine Right of Kings*, 2nd ed., 1914.   JAMES D. DOUGLAS

DIVORCE. See also *Marriage; Remarriage.* Divorce is legal dissolution of the bond of marriage, involving permanent separation of the spouses, and the right in law to contract another marriage.

In the OT, divorce, while never mandatory, was tolerated in certain cases whose precise nature has long been and is still a matter of controversy (Deut. 24:1-4). The Mosaic legislation prescribed that a written bill of divorcement be given to the repudiated wife, thus safeguarding the woman's rights more than was the case in surrounding cultures.

The Lord Jesus condemned divorce (Matt. 5:31, 32; 19:3-12; Mark 10:2-12; Luke 16:18), stigmatizing as adultery the marriage of a divorced person. The statement appears without qualification in Mark and Luke, but Matthew preserves an exception-clause "unless it be for sexual impurity." Considerable debate has centered on the meaning of this expression. Three major views may be indicated:

1. The "sexual impurity" in view is unchastity before the marriage. This view is open to the objection that the Mosaic law provided a specific way of dealing with this problem (Deut. 22:13-21). Furthermore, it might undermine the stability of all marriages in which one of the spouses was not a virgin at the time of union.

2. The "sexual impurity" in view is due to a degree of consanguinity which would make the marriage incestuous according to the Mosaic law (Lev. 18:6-18). It is noteworthy that in the law this type of relation is mentioned in the same context (Lev. 20:10-21) with some of the gravest sexual disorders (homosexuality, bestiality, etc.). This view also might account for the presence of the exception clause in the Gospel of Matthew, written for people of Jewish culture, and for its absence in Mark and Luke, for whose audience this consideration would have less relevance. One difficulty with this view might lie in the unusual sense of the word for "sexual impurity" (although Acts 15:29 and I Cor. 5:1 might be parallel cases). One would think that the solution of a situation like this would be annulment not divorce, since the marriage should never have taken place.

3. The "sexual impurity" in view is an act of adultery. Since sexual congress, even of a casual kind, does bring about that the two partners become one flesh (I Cor. 6:15, 16), it would seem to follow that adultery actually dissolves the marital bond. The spouse who has remained faithful, upon discovering what has taken place, may seek to legalize the break of the marriage and may, without adultery on his (or her) part, contract another union. Naturally, he (or she) may also choose to forgive and to reinvigorate the union with his (or her)

spouse. This appears to be the most natural interpretation of Jesus' statements in Matthew. The term "sexual impurity" rather than "adultery" might have been used for variety of style, or in order to indicate that some other forms of grievous sexual immorality (such as homosexuality, bestiality, etc.), beside adultery strictly speaking, might provide ground for the dissolution of the marriage. Mark and Luke may have refrained from recording the exception-clause, because in this way Christ's intention to discourage divorce, which is the main point of this saying, would be more forcefully presented. This silence could hardly be used to disallow the exception expressly contained in Matthew.

Paul's teaching is in keeping with the above (I Cor. 7:10-15; Rom. 7:1-3). Some have interpreted I Cor. 7:15 to mean that desertion by an unbelieving spouse, as well as adultery, can be a ground for divorce. This has sometimes been called the "Pauline privilege," and is a possible interpretation, but it is not completely clear that the statement "the brother or sister is not under bondage in such cases" implies that the deserted believer may contract another marriage. In Rom. 7, Paul uses wedlock as an illustration of man's relation to the law, and is obviously not intending to set up a complete code for marriage and divorce. The fact that he does not include Christ's exception-clause is, therefore, no indication that he meant to disallow adultery as a legitimate ground for divorce.

In view of the general laxity that prevails in the twentieth century respecting marriage and sex, some may wonder whether the strict view of the NT on this subject is still enforceable. It is obvious that the lives of many people have become ensnarled in grievous complications because of a general disregard of the divine law: these must be dealt with in compassion and understanding. Yet to those who would plead for a relaxation of NT principles in order to provide accommodation to the times, we would propose the following questions.

Can we assume that God's laws must be adapted to shifting human opinions and sinful practices, rather than to stand in the midst of human relativity as the permanent standard?

Did not Christ, the Apostles and the early Christian church face a world with a laxity equal to, or even worse than that of our times, and yet proceed on the strict basis established in the NT?

Who knows better what is good for man than God who created man "male and female" and established marriage in the first place?

James M. Boice, "The Biblical View of Divorce," *Eternity* XXI, 12 (December, 1970), 19-21; Oral Collins, "Divorce in the New Testament," *The Gordon Review* VII, 4 (Summer, 1964), 158-169; Kenneth E. Kirk, *Marriage and Divorce*, 2d ed., London, 1948; John Murray, *Divorce*, Nutley, N.J. Presbyterian and Reformed, 1953; J. Ridderbos, *Gereformeerd Theologisch Tijdschrift* xxii, 1-4 (May-July, 1921), 1-17, 49-67, 103-116.　　　　　　　ROGER R. NICOLE

DOGMA. See also *Aquinas and Roman Catholic Ethics; Papal Encyclicals.* From the Greek *dokein,* "to think," or "to seem," dogma originally referred to distinctive teachings of various schools of philosophy or to public decrees. This second sense occurs in the LXX in Esther 3:9; Dan. 2:13; 6:8. In Luke 2:1 dogma is the decree of Augustus; in Acts 16:4, the decrees of the apostles; and in Eph. 2:15 and Col. 2:14, the judgments of the law against sinners.

In the church of the first centuries the word was used loosely to refer to any Christian teaching. In the late fourth century, however, it came to mean the truths of revelation which the Holy Spirit has given the church. Today dogma signifies established Christian teaching derived from revelation and officially defined by the church.

Inasmuch as dogma is necessarily expressed in the language of the day in which it is written and is subject to the limitations of language, it does not, according to Protestant belief, bear the absolute character of revelation but must ever be examined in the latter's light. There is then always the possibility of the church having erred in its formulation of dogma. With Luther, Protestantism regretfully but firmly acknowledges that church councils have erred and do err, and it denies the teaching of the infallibility of the church and its dogmatic pronouncements.

In its teaching of the development of dogma the Roman Catholic Church holds that the Holy Spirit keeps the church free from error in dogmatic pronouncements. This "infallibility" does not imply the perfection of church formulation of its official teaching but it does imply irreversibility. Currently, Roman Catholic theology emphasizes the historical conditioning and incompleteness of all dogmatic statements, the negative aspects of the teaching on infallibility, i.e., that the Holy Spirit is said to have kept the church only free from error, and the impossibility of recovering the exact setting in which a specific dogmatic utterance was promulgated in history.

M. EUGENE OSTERHAVEN

DOUBLEMINDEDNESS. See *Mixed Motive; Singlemindedness.*

DOUBT. See also *Unbelief.* Paul Tillich has written: "If faith is understood as a thinking that something is true, doubt is incompatible with the act of faith. If faith is understood as being ultimately concerned, doubt is a necessary element in it" (*Dynamics of Faith,* New York, Harper & Row, p. 137). Tillich relates truth only to the finite and concern to the infinite. But Scripture relates both to the infinite God. The real difference, therefore, between faith and doubt does not concern their object but the subject. Logically one either believes or

disbelieves (doubts). Psychologically one can both believe and disbelieve (doubt), though not at the same time and with the same referent. Such fluctuation happens not because the evidence for truth changes, but because the believer changes in his evaluation or feeling about the evidence. If Christians always saw clearly and rightly, doubt could not occur; since they do not always see clearly and rightly, evaluation fluctuates and doubt occurs. As the Psalmist says: "these doubts are my infirmity" (Ps. 77:10).

Must we then fall into the neo-orthodox pit of thinking all men are both believers and unbelievers—thus obliterating the distinction between believers and unbelievers? Not according to the Bible. Unconverted men, though presented with the evidence, do not savingly believe it. Christians are those who continually (though not continuously) believe (John 8:31). Under their infirmity, they may occasionally doubt. But non-Christians are never true believers, though they may seem to be (John 2:23-25; cf. *Apostasy*); Christians are never true unbelievers, though they may seem to be (John 8:31).   JOHN H. GERSTNER

DRAFT. See also *Conscientious Objection; Pacifism; Peace and War.* Most free societies have modified the mandatory requirements for military service to accommodate the "conscientious objector." His obligation may be discharged in forms of service not involving the personal use of lethal weapons. In most instances men identified as bona fide ministers of religion or seminarians have been exempt from draft in the USA.

Christians react to compulsory military service in varied ways. Although the Quakers have been traditionally pacifist, and other denominations have made formal pronouncements about military resistance, all ministers are ethically involved in terms of personal religious stance, draft-eligible counselees and response to the law of the land. In good conscience the minister must maintain a position consistent with his inner convictions in respect to the will of God. He cannot ethically persuade counselees to evade the law. Although he may try to change the law by constitutional means, he cannot ethically and consistently endorse illegal acts as means of bringing this about.

The Vietnam war and wide possibilities of nuclear war produced a new form of ministerial activity in the form of church centers to counsel and even house and arrange transportation to Canada for those seeking to avoid military service. Often young lawyers were used as legal consultants in collaboration with the minister. There is serious doubt about the morality of the clergy when they participate in subversive activities incident to such centers; certain of these "ministries" seem in fact to be illegal.   JAMES FORRESTER

DREAMS. A dream is a seeming reality experienced during sleep. It appears to be related to physical conditions—such as water flicked into the face giving rise to the imagery of standing at the bow of a boat—or to a psychological state. As an illustration of the latter, Paul Tournier confidently observes: "During the night I had had a dream which was clearly the manifestation of my unconscious reactions to our discussions on the previous day" (*The Meaning of Persons,* New York, Harper, 1957, p. 56).

The Bible, contrary to a commonly held viewpoint, gives relatively little consideration or significance to dreams. While occasionally dreams are mentioned as a medium for divine communication (Gen. 20:6; I Kings 3:5; Dan. 7-8), they are not the usual means and certainly not the only manner in which God reveals his will. The New Testament gives even less place to dreams than the Old Testament, with only seven references to dreams or dreamers and all but a

citation of Joel's prophecy (Acts 2:17) are bunched in Matthew's gospel.

Since Sigmund Freud (q.v.), and eminently through the work of Carl Jung (q.v.), dreams have been considered an important avenue to the subconscious. It is also generally believed that they provide a means for working out certain frustrations and discharging hostilities. In considerably less cases, dreams have been means of significantly altering the course of men's lives, as with Adoniram Judson Gordon's vivid recollection of how Christ came to church.

Dreams, then, are human phenomena, sometimes valuable incentive, more often a means of release and potential insight when professionally interpreted, and, in the sovereignty of God, a possible channel for God's communication.   MORRIS A. INCH

DRINKING. See *Alcoholism; Temperance.*

DRIVES. See *Instincts.*

DRUGS. See also *Suggestion.* A drug is a chemical that is taken or administered because it has a desired effect upon some biological system, except that those carbohydrates, lipids and proteins that serve as foodstuffs are not considered to be drugs. There is no sharp distinction between the valid use, the misuse or the abuse of a drug.

This brief review is limited to only a few drugs, those that have a rather prompt action upon the central nervous system leading to changes in mood, emotion, perception, or behavior. Some of these drugs are used very widely, indeed, and are not usually regarded as hazardous (see classification, Category A). Others (Category C) are subject to misuse that is known as "abuse." In the USA and other countries with similar customs and laws drug abuse is almost always a consequence of self-administration by the user.

CLASSIFICATION OF DRUGS
ACCORDING TO USE AND POTENTIAL FOR ABUSE

Category	A	B	C
Typical drugs	Aspirin Caffeine (coffee) Theophylline (tea) Theobromine (chocolate) ———— Nicotine	Amphetamines Tranquillizers Barbiturates Alcohol Marijuana	Cocaine Opium Morphine Heroin LSD, other hallucinogens
Potency as used	Low	Intermediate	Generally high
Tolerance	Yes, except for aspirin	Definite	Obvious
Hazards	Insignificant, except for cigarette smoking	Personal hazards from any if misused Societal hazards from amphetamines and alcohol	Personal and societal hazards from each one
Risks of addiction	Negligible, except for tobacco	For alcohol and marijuana, said to be 1 in 10 for users	Almost universal among users (but uncertain for LSD)
Control of use	Not controlled; sometimes taxed	Controlled (alcohol, amphetamines, barbiturates Taxed (alcohol) Prohibited in U.S. (marijuana)	Controlled, prohibited or restricted to prescription by physicians
Public acceptance of self administration	Almost generally accepted	Accepted, with strong protest from some individuals and groups	Not accepted; approved only by small number of users

Some critics have supposed that certain of the personal and societal hazards of drugs of Category **C** stem from attempts to control their distribution and use. It is true that such control leads to definite problems; it does not follow, however, that legal prohibition is therefore unwise. The number of users and therefore of potential addicts varies with the availability of any drug. In countries, cities, or cultures where opium has been freely available the user population has been characterized by indifference to social, economic and even personal well being. This indicates that making opium available is morally not much different from deciding to tranquilize a population by adding some chemical to a city's water supply.

The repeated and regular use of most of the drugs in this table is accompanied by two phenomena that are of considerable scientific as well as practical interest. The first is *tolerance,* in which a given dose of the drug has a smaller effect upon a regular user than upon a nonuser. When the drug is usually present in the body, nerve cells seem to acquire the ability of resisting its action. The second phenomenon is *dependence;* once the neurons are capable of resisting the action of the drug, they may become unable to function normally if it is taken away.

Habituation and *addiction* are psychological phenomena that arise from tolerance and dependence. Habituation involves subtle neural changes related to learning, experience and memory, whereas addiction is a result of more definitely physicochemical changes in the nervous system. In habituation the withdrawal of the drug leads only to changes in mood, emotion or behavior; addiction, by contrast, is signified by all of these plus physiological changes such as salivation, sweating, vasomotor responses, nausea, and other symptoms when the drug is withdrawn.

Drugs in Category B are the subject of most of the current dispute over drug abuse. Availability of alcohol in the USA since the end of prohibition has led to addiction of perhaps 9 million persons; yet a return to prohibition is scarcely considered by the public. Marijuana is likewise easy to obtain although illegal. Yet there is little evidence that addiction to this substance is about to become a problem of any consequence. It is interesting that students in contact with the "drug culture" rank drugs in order of risk in almost exactly the same order as do pharmacologists—with the exception that students being less familiar with schizophrenia are less apprehensive than physicians are about the use of drugs such as LSD that produce at least temporarily a state similar to schizophrenia.

A Christian view as to self-administration of drugs of Category B might include the following points: (1) They are used solely for the purpose of altering central nervous function in a direction that sooner or later impairs that function. (2) They induce tolerance, dependence, and perhaps outright addiction such as alcoholism. (3) Their use may be illegal (marijuana). (4) The effects their use is intended to evoke are said in the NT to be the work rather of the Holy Spirit in the personality of each Christian believer.

L. S. Goodman, and A. Gilman, *The Pharmacological Basis of Therapeutics*, New York, MacMillan, 4th ed., 1970; L. Lasagna, *Life, Death and the Doctor*, New York, Knopf, 1968.

JOHN R. BROBECK

DUTY. Duty is action required by moral or legal obligation, or the force of such obligation. Duty has an imperative character stemming from some kind of mandate. There is general recognition of the fundamental difference between duty as that-which-ought-to-be, and things-as-they-are; the former is considered to have a normative existence quite apart from whether or not it is put into practice. The nature and source of this mandate give exact meaning to duty in general, as well as to specific duties, whether the source be nature, reason, the deity, the human race, or a system of values.

In antiquity, and even through the Middle Ages, reflection on this subject has almost always been reflection on particular duties, since, previous to Kant, almost all moral systems were concrete ones in which the content itself of the laws and commandments mattered more than their form (on the exceptional nature of the Biblical revelation cf. *Law*).

For moral systems of a naturalistic bent, duty is deduced from nature (cf. *Natural Law*). Thus for the Stoics duty implies primarily living according to universal reason. For the moral system of an idealistic type, on the other hand, duty is deduced rather from a supreme categorical imperative. Kant (q.v.) tolerated no external authority such as divine commandments. But his insistence that duty be self-legislated rests on the enormous assumption of man's direct moral continuity with the divine. Furthermore, his definition of duty, whatever its clear implications for the form of ethics, leaves its content wholly in doubt, an omission which can only be considered serious.

In an anti-rational reaction to this idealistic deification of the moral life, existential ethics (q.v.) has taken two forms: the atheistic and the theistic. For the former, duty is not an imperative which confronts man in advance; rather, the valuable becomes valuable in the choosing. For the latter, duty has roots in passionate inwardness and loses its universally valid character even when appeal is made to the Biblical revelation.

Often in the course of discharging one duty, the ethicist runs into another which seems to conflict with it. One of the principle tasks of ethics is to establish priorities in these conflicts, as the Lord Jesus did in the parable of the Good Samaritan (the positive principle of doing good, even to an enemy, takes precedence over the negative one, of avoiding contamination through contact with a "corpse," Luke 10:25-37) and in the teaching about leaving one's gift at the altar (reconciliation with an offended brother, who is bound to me in covenant love, takes precedence over my ritual expression of love to God, Matt. 5:23). Taken together, the Scriptural injunctions follow the order of duties: to God, to others, to self; but as the foregoing illustrations prove, all reality is so interrelated that every case must take into consideration the whole moral context.

The commandments of God release the believer from bondage to casuistry without denying his freedom as a moral agent. Thus he can overcome the tension introduced into the ethical life when pleasure and duty are set in opposition. A duty such as prayer, for example, is a delight as well, because the person in whom God is at work "inspiring both the will and the deed" (Phil. 2:13) desires to keep the commandments as the very means of expressing his love for God. It is often forgotten by those who criticize the ethic of obedience that the sense of obligation need not spring only from a bad conscience; according to Gen. 1-3 even unfallen man was under divine command. Judging from the fact that in the apostolic age newly-saved Gentiles were expected to become familiar with the Mosaic legislation, and from the ethical admonitions of the Gospels and Epistles, hearing the commandment is requisite to the understanding of duty. But just as the Decalogue is prefaced with a reminder of God's saving action, so the NT commands are heard "in Christ," where redemption is at work from within. Since the Redeemer is also the Creator who put his image in man, his expressed will

accords perfectly without needs for fulfillment and humanization. So in the case of the obedient Christian the tension between heteronomy and autonomy is superseded by a fruitful theonomy in which man can be free.

Of the two commands with which Jesus summarized the Law (love to God and neighbor love), the latter implies a proper self love, and enlightened unselfishness which depends on the first command and works itself out toward the neighbor (q.v.). This implies the duty of developing and using all of one's natural capabilities, as part of his vocational service grounded in Christian love for others. Then he can move beyond rights and claims and see his duty to his neighbor as one to whom he learns to attribute worth without necessarily first finding it (cf. again the parable of the Good Samaritan). But as Jesus implies in the parable, the Christian cannot take refuge from full maturity by merely fulfilling what is commanded; there must come the bold stroke of the deed done with holy joy. Such a creative view of individual or collective duty is possible only to those who exist in grateful obedience before God and for the neighbor.   RICHARD T. FOULKES

DYNAMIC. See also *Holy Spirit*. The word "dynamic" may be used as an adjective or a noun. The adjective means either "characterized by energy and forcefulness" (as in "a dynamic personality") or "producing the effect of energetic movement, action, change" (e.g., "the dynamic gospel"). The noun signifies a particular energizing force, producing action (e.g., "a Christian's ethical dynamic").

"Dynamic" is related to the Greek word *dunamis,* power. In the NT *dunamis* is said to be the possession of, and to be exerted by, each of the persons of the Holy Trinity (Eph. 1:19; II Peter 1:3; Rom. 15:13). Thus it may refer to divine omnipotent might. A *dunamis* is also the possession of the Lord's people, a power which they have received from God (II Cor. 4:7; Eph. 3:20); from the Holy Spirit (Acts 1:8; Eph. 3:16). As the Almighty exercises his *dunamis* through his Word (Heb. 1:3; Rom. 1:16, the gospel; I Cor. 2:4-5), so the believers' possession of *dunamis* is associated with the divine Word, with their knowledge of it (Col. 1:9-11; Eph. 6:10-17; Rom. 14:1–15:7; cf. Acts 1:8 with John 14:26).

According to the Scriptures, the Holy Spirit uses the gospel and the sacrament of baptism to work faith in Jesus as Savior from sin in the hearts of those whom he saves. Through faith a man is united spiritually to Christ and experiences the regeneration of his inner being; the Christian becomes a new creature within, endowed with the basic power to conquer sin and live to God's glory (I Cor. 12:3; James 1:18; II Cor. 5:17; Rom. 6:1-14). The believer is subject to the Spirit's further strengthening, when he obtains additional knowledge of the divine will and Word. He is moved increasingly to make strides in holy living. He is impelled, in particular, to cultivate love, trust, joy, and hope in the Lord; to bear bold witness of him and his gospel; to exhibit steadfastness in Kingdom work and loving service of fellow men; to glory in sufferings for Christ's sake; to do all things the Lord requires through Christ who strengthens him (Phil. 4:13; see above passages, and others). Faith in the fact that in Christ and through the Spirit he has sin-destroying might enables the believer to make use of that power and progress in the obedience to God's will. It may, then, be stated that the Holy Spirit, Christ, the Word of God, faith, or the power he has received from God, or the combination of these factors of influence, is the Christian's ethical dynamic, prompting his godly living.

WALTER A. MAIER

E

EBIONITES. The term refers to a sect of Jewish-Christians who in the first few centuries of the Christian era attempted to accept Christianity while maintaining the practice of Judaism. Reconstruction of their history, belief, and practice is difficult because it must be based primarily on fragmentary and polemical reports by the Church Fathers. The name first appears in Iraenaeus (*Adv. Haer.* 1.26.2). The Church Fathers traced their origin to a man named Ebion, but it is now generally agreed that the source of the name is the Hebrew word for the "poor," either as an epithet revealing their economic status or conveying the more spiritual connotations of the word in the Psalms or the Beatitudes of Jesus. Some scholars note similarities to the Essenes or the Qumran community of the Dead Sea Scrolls. Variations existed within Ebionism.

Some scholars discern three groups: (1) the Nazarenes who held a more orthodox Christology and associated with Gentile Christians, (2) the dominant group that refused to associate with Gentiles, and (3) a syncretistic form revealing affinities with Gnosticism (Justin Martyr *Dialogue* xlvii and Epiphanius *Haer.* xxix). All appear to have died out by the fifth century.

In general, the Ebionites viewed Jesus as a man, "the true prophet" promised by Moses (Deut. 18:15). Jesus became the Christ by virtue of his perfect obedience to the law (Eusebius HE iii.27 and vi.17). The Ebionites therefore opposed the teachings of Paul and advocated a strictly legalistic ethic, insisting on circumcision, Sabbath observance, and other features of Judaism. There is also some evidence of asceticism, especially among the more syncretistic groups who ate no flesh, drank no wine and despised marriage. Somewhat inconsistently such practices led them to the rejection of the OT sacrificial system (Epiphanius *Panarion* xxx.16).

> Jean Danielou, *The Theology of Jewish Christianity*, Chicago, Regnery, 1964, pp. 55-67; H. J. Schoeps, *Theologie und Geschicte des Judenchristentums*, Tübingen, Mohr, 1949.
>
> DONALD W. DAYTON

ECCLESIASTICAL INFLUENCE. See *Councils of Churches; Ecumenism and Ethics; Papal Encyclicals; Roman Catholic Ethics.*

ECOLOGY. See *Beauty; Environmental Pollution.*

ECONOMETRICS. The application of mathematics or quantification techniques to economic data either to develop or to test theory may be called econometrics. Usually a mathematical model consisting of an equation or equations expressing quantative relationships is developed. The model is then applied to data or is tested. The cycle is repeated while the relationships and the data are refined possibly through additional experiments. Although Augustin Cournot used mathematics as an analytical tool in 1838, only in the last two decades have significant efforts been made to develop the types of data necessary. Science has recently provided more powerful analytical methods and computers capable of working large problems.

The Keynesian theories gave great impetus to the econometric study of national economics as well as a basis for the study of its components. The input-output technique analyzes the distribution of the resources supplied and of the end products obtained. Certain input-output ratios must be kept constant in most studies. Time series studies indicate the values and relationships of economic variables over successive time intervals. Most time series data are affected by consumer activity. Cross section analysis deals with a survey of data classified by geographic area or some other dimension at a given time or within a short time period. It is sometimes difficult to isolate temporary and permanent elements. Regression analysis establishes average relationships between variables as a causitive (independent) variable changes. Variations can be discussed in statistical terms of amount and probability. Economic studies are complicated by the tendency for relationships or parameters taken as fixed to vary over time. Since all possible variables or data cannot be taken into account, results may have a built-in error or bias, particularly when used for forecasting.

> Robert Dorfman, Paul A. Samuelson, and Robert M. Solow, *Linear Programming and Economic Analysis*, New York, McGraw Hill, 1964; Paul A. Samuelson, *Foundations of Economic Analysis*, New York, McGraw Hill, 1965.
>
> HARVEY A. MAERTIN

ECONOMIC AID. See *Underdeveloped Nations.*

ECONOMICS. See *Capitalism; Communism; Socialism.*

ECUMENISM AND ETHICS. The term "ecumenism" designates a complex transdenominational phenomenon whose character has undergone considerable change. As a movement, the transcendence of post-Reformation denominational barriers is rooted in evangelical cooperation for evangelistic and missionary purposes which, as early as 1819, enlisted Baptists, Anglicans and Methodists in London for mutual ends. This same concern to fulfill the Church's evangelistic mandate was reflected on a global scale at the World Congress on Evangelism (Berlin, 1966); its participants included representatives of churches both outside and inside the World Council of Churches, none of whose numerous world conferences had been devoted to evangelism.

Conciliar ecumenism (e.g., the Federal Council of Churches and its more recent successor, the National Council of Churches) devoted itself more largely to concerns of social ethics than to those of theology or evangelism. This was due primarily to a modernistic leadership that tended to be metaphysically agnostic in its religious outlook, was experience-centered and devoted to the social gospel (q.v.). In the absence of historic Christian belief in transcendent divine revelation, Modernism allowed a wide span of metaphysical notions, and opposed any credal test of Christian authenticity; it proposed, rather, to promote church unity through cooperative devotion to social ends and the structural merger of existing denominations. Its proponents insisted, as Edwin A. Burtt puts it, that "a far more effective church . . . can be formed out of people who agree . . . on socialism and pacifism, while differing in their cosmology, than out of persons who hold the same metaphysical creed but strongly diverge on . . . pressing social issues" (*Types of Religious Philosophy*, New York, Harper & Row, 1939, p. 434).

Ecumenical espousal of specific positions in debatable areas, often in the absence of any persuasive derivation from governing Biblical principles, precipitated extensive ecclesiastical controversy (cf. *National Council of Churches; World Council of Churches*). Critics contended that politically-minded churchmen had no divine mandate, authority or wisdom to speak in Christ's name in the area of legislative particulars and military tactics. The weaknesses of such neo-Protestant involvement in social ethics are reflected in a recent reference work, *Dictionary of Christian Ethics* (1967) edited by John Macquarrie, which faces moral concerns largely in the context of modernist presuppositions. In its shift from historic Christian theology it not only omits any essay on "Sacrifice," but in line with the *ad hoc* nature of liberal social concern also lacks any treatment of "Ecology" or environmental pollution.

The first reaction of evangelical churches to ecumenical enthusiasm for socialism and pacificism and optimistic notions that history is secretly divine and man essentially good, was to withdraw from social and cultural concerns and to concentrate instead on redemptive evangelism and missions. These vitalities, while they continue to be notably dwarfed in conciliar circles, remain a hallmark of evangelical Christianity. But during the past generation evangelical Christians have sensed afresh the need for a distinctive socio-cultural involvement on Biblical premises. Their earlier tendency to champion capitalism as if it could do no wrong, against an uncritical modernist devotion to socialism, and in some instances to communism, has yielded to an awareness that all cultural expressions are subject to searching divine scrutiny and judgment.

Ecumenical provocation arose not merely from controversial political pronouncements; it derived also from neglecting evangelism and replacing the evangelization of the individual with the changing of social structures as the essential task of the church. In order to redress this trend, Key '73 emerged in the USA as an effort by some 140 denominational and church agencies to evangelize cooperatively at the community level. It is noteworthy, however, that in recent years major evangelical gatherings have not viewed evangelism and social concern as alternatives; they have insisted, rather, on the Biblically-oriented basis and necessity of both. The opening address of the World Congress on Evangelism (1966) expounded the evangelical task in fidelity to "the God of justice and of justification" and the Jerusalem Conference on Biblical Prophecy (1971) viewed the impending Lord's return as a stimulus not only to world evangelization, but also to summon men and nations to recover the personal and public righteousness intended by the Divine Creator and to be reenforced by the Coming King.

Carl F. H. Henry, *The Uneasy Conscience of Modern Fundamentalism*, Grand Rapids, Eerdmans, 1947; *Aspects of Christian Social Ethics,* Grand Rapids, Eerdmans, 1964; *Evangelicals at the Brink of Crisis,* Waco, Word Books, 1967; *A Plea for Evangelical Demonstration,* Grand Rapids, Baker, 1971; Paul Ramsey, *Who Speaks for the Church?,* Nashville, Abingdon, 1967; C. C. West, "Ecumenical Movement, Ethics in," in John Macquarrie, ed., *Dictionary of Christian Ethics,* Philadelphia, Westminster, 1967.   CARL F. H. HENRY

EDUCATION AND MORALITY. See also *Christian Education.* The term "education" comes from a root meaning "to rear" or "to nourish." "Morality" is derived from the root denoting "custom" or "measure." As "custom" it is the type of conduct expected by society and as "measure" it relates to a standard or guiding rule of life. The Hebrew-Christian tradition strongly emphasizes both.

From earliest times Judaism commanded parents to teach their children diligently by precept and example to love God and to serve him. These Biblical admonitions (Deut. 6:4-9; 11:13-21; cf. 4:9) were taken so seriously that they were encased and affixed to the doorposts of the homes. As further reminder the same passages, together with Exod. 13:1-16, were enclosed in leather boxes (phylacteries) which were bound daily on the arm and head. "Keeping the covenant" came to mean "strict adherence to the Mosaic Law." When Jews were scattered abroad the synagogue developed and provided adult male education. It claims the distinction of originating public schools. Judaism has continually stressed the importance of education and morality.

Early Christianity perpetuated home training and added catechetical instruction to preserve, protect and propagate the faith. The teachings of Jesus were stressed. Centuries later, cathedral schools were designed to produce leaders. Gradually the European university emerged, staffed by churchmen, with theology as the "queen of the sciences." Even after religion was banned religious morality continued to permeate the educational process.

This religious heritage reinforced by spiritual influences like Log College and the Great Awakenings led to the establishment of numerous Christian educational institutions in the USA.

State institutions of higher learning became competitive only after the Civil War. The clergyman surrendered his avocation as teacher of community youth to the public school. As a supplement, but not as a substitute, the Sunday School was imported. Due to many factors, including religious rivalry, religion began to play a diminishing role in public education. McGuffey Readers with their Biblical selections and stories with morals gave way to plastic juvenile actors who never need moral solutions to problems.

Legal issues concerning religion in the schools, starting with the McCollum case, produced Supreme Court rulings interpreting the phrase in the First Amendment ("Congress shall make no law respecting the establishment of religion") as an erection of a wall of separation between church and state or religion and education. Suprisingly the court suggested the study of religion in the public schools.

It might well be said that one's education is not complete without a study of comparative religion or the history of religion and its advancement of civilization. The Bible is worthy of study for its literary and historic qualities. Nothing . . . indicates that such study, when presented as a part of a secular program of education, may not be effected consistent with the First Amendment." (374, U.S. 203, p. 225).

Until recent years the perpetuation of the Judeo-Christian ethics has been uppermost among the goals of education in Western civilization. There are irrefutable evidences that science, not theology, is now on the educational throne. Strong emphasis upon the acquisition of knowledge and skills without a conscientious consideration of their proper use has already produced an educated populace that squanders resources and surpluses, and pollutes water, air, and food in a world that is filled with hunger, nakedness, disease, and warfare. Situational ethics (q.v.) has been converted by some receptive minds to no personal ethics at all.

Modern education has concentrated upon theoretical techniques, electronic gadgetry, and proper racial balance but seldom addresses itself to factors of moral development.

Institutions of higher education too frequently are transformed into thought factories contracting with government and industry for studies, tests, and surveys resulting in masses of data pouring from computers. Meanwhile students, for which the institutions were established, receive their stamp of approval after having gone through a curriculum assembly line, which largely ignores ingredients of moral commitment and service.

William Temple characterized this as a "cut flower civilization." It appears beautiful, but is cut off from its roots, the value system, which nourished it. Signs of withering may be detected in increased criminality, salaciousness, profanity, vulgarity, and an uncontrollable drug culture. Instead of emphasizing values proven by years of societal experience, liberal education has frequently capitulated to the demands of pressure groups that have never been exposed to, or have never gained an appreciation of, these values. Legitimate criticism has asserted that often in the past morality has been taught but not practiced. But it is infinitely more difficult to practice if it is not taught. Freedom of inquiry need not be accompanied by freedom from morality. It should demand the opposite.   W. IVAN HOY

EDWARDS, JONATHAN. In an unpublished sermon on Rom. 3:11 entitled "All That Natural Men Do Is Wrong," the New England Puritan divine, Jonathan Edwards

(1703-1758) defines the good as: first a right heart, spirit, or attitude; second, a spiritual service; and third, an aiming at the glory of God in all actions. Although everything that fallen man now does is evil from all three aspects, he was originally created upright by God. But he "sought out many devices" (Eccles. 7:29; *Original Sin, passim*). Evildoing came about by man's refusing to submit his own self-interest to the control of the divine Spirit.

Though man is now fallen and totally depraved so that he is far more vicious than the fiercest animals and, if able, would kill God (Rom. 4:10 sermon), he is required to repent. Unable to do so because of his depraved disposition he is not thereby excused. Spiritually unable to deliver himself he is still responsible. The fact that only God can now overcome his evil, does not make God the responsible author of man's sins, any more than darkness prevails (*Original Sin* and in numerous sermons). Though depraved, man may and often does deeds of external morality that are, formally speaking, good, though not materially so. These bad good works do not meet the ethical demands of God—in fact, they too are materially evil, and require repentance no less than bad works.

God commands moral perfection of all men but he gives the grace to achieve it only to the elect. Thus they are regenerated, a new ruling disposition prevails in their hearts, and good (not perfect) good works certainly follow. Sanctification was probably Edward's principal homiletic concern. His key concept is "universal obedience" to the will of God. A new man in Christ strives to follow Christ in all he commands while determinedly resisting all Christ forbids. Though the regenerated elect never cease their endeavor after holiness—most convincingly shown in their doing of good works (*The Religious Affections*)—they never perfectly achieve it. The nature of true virtue is a God-given disinterestedness or a disinterested love to being in general *(Nature of True Virtue)*. Although some of Edwards' followers extended this concept to the point of desiring to be damned, if necessary, for the glory of God, Edwards himself denied that a true Christian can ever will to be damned, because that would involve separation from the God whom he unalterably loves *(Miscellanies,* 530).   JOHN H. GERSTNER

EGO. See also *Person and Personality; Psychology.* "Ego" is the Greek and the Latin word for "I." The word has been given many special definitions in both philosophy and psychology, but it usually conveys the idea of "I myself." Ego is the I whom I know. In contrast, after an unexpected outburst of anger or tears, I might apologise saying, "I was not myself then."

Psychoanalytic theorists postulate three divisions of personality which form different power groupings, almost different personalities within the person, each with its own function and name. The *id* (q.v.) (L., "it") is responsible for basic biological behavior. The *ego* (L., "I") which learns from practical experience, controls the id and conducts the business of waking life: it feels, remembers, flees, adapts, and takes action. The *super-ego* (q.v.) (L., "above me"), which derives from the expectancies of society, either curbs the ego or spurs it on to action.

Different psychoanalytical schools vary in their precise use of these terms. Furthermore, these conceptual divisions do not correspond (as has been suggested) with Biblical terms such as "the old man," "the new man," and "conscience." The terminology of psychoanalytical theory, which at best is obsolescent, is therefore better kept distinct from the terms used in the word of the Lord which endures for ever (I Peter 1:25).   NEIL YORKSTON

EGALITARIANISM. See *Equality.*

EGOISM. See also *Altruism.* Egoism is the theory that one's own good either is or ought to be the sole motive operative in human choice. The term has attracted to itself some disagreeable connotations. For example, Thrasymachus argued that the tyrant who could get away with brutality and murder is the happiest man. Plato repudiated this view and enjoined justice; but Plato was equally an egoist. He asked everyone, Do you want what is really good for you or do you want what really harms you? He expected everyone to answer in the affirmative to the first option.

Plato of course did not identify the good with pleasure. In his middle period he taught that pleasure was actually evil. Justice, wisdom, temperance, and courage are good. If therefore a man chooses injustice or intemperance, it is because he does not know what is good for him.

In the Middle Ages the problem was not acute because Christians agreed that God adjusted the interests of all men.

Thomas Hobbes sharpened the matter by insisting that by an inviolable scientific law the sole motive of choice is one's personal pleasure (q.v.). To this egoistic psychological hedonism (q.v.), Jeremy Bentham (q.v.) tried, inconsistently, to add a universalism (q.v.): each man ought to promote the pleasure of all. As with Plato, failure is due to lack of knowledge.

Henry Sidgwick also tried to unite egoism and universalism; but he saw that this was impossible, unless, with Bishop Butler, we assume that God eventually redresses present injustices. Sidgwick hesitates before a theistic assumption; the other utilitarians are more outspokenly anti-theistic.

Since the time of Freud (q.v.) the discussion has not been carried on in precisely the same terms.   GORDON H. CLARK

EGYPTIAN ETHICS.
I. Scope of Sources
Almost the whole span of pharaonic

history (c. 3100-330 B.C.) yields relevant data in regard to Egyptian ethics. From the Pyramid Age (c. 2700-2200) come "wisdom-books" (Kagemni, Hardjedef, and especially Ptahhotep) in later Mss, and contemporary "autobiographical" texts from tombs of notables. The First Intermediate Period (of weakness) and renewed power of the Middle Kingdom (together, c. 2200-1780) offer further wisdom and social tracts (e.g., Merikare, Man Tired of Life, Eloquent Peasant), more autobiographical texts from tombs and stelae, and the Coffin Texts (funerary spells). The Second Intermediate Period has left little. But the New Kingdom or Empire Period (c. 1550-1085) yields a varied wealth of data: more "wisdom" (Aniy, Amenemope), further autobiographical texts including of the "humble poor," and the Book of the Dead (funerary spells), among others. The Late Period of declension is likewise characterized by wisdom and autobiographies (Onkh-sheshonqy, Petosiris). While variations of emphasis occur, these 3000 years of cultural history show remarkable continuity.

II. Scope of Subjects

A. *Key Concepts.* For the Egyptian, the basic concept governing all of life—gods, king, people alike—was *maat*. This omnibus concept included truth as opposed to falsehood; justice as against injustice; righteousness as against evildoing; and a right world order as against chaos and disorder. *Maat* and its opposites thus cover the overall field of right and wrong; but also include ritual matters that modern moralists exclude from ethics.

B. *Specific Spheres and Values*

1. *Personal and Family Relationships.* Marriage was man's customary state, with offspring in mind (Hardjedef, Ptahhotep, Aniy). But he was to care for his wife and all her needs, leaving household matters to her (*ibidem*). Children should honor their mother (Aniy), and obey their parents if they would have parental favor (Ptahhotep).

Monogamy was perhaps common but polygamy accepted. Wisdom-writers and teachers warned against amorous adventures; adultery could bring the death penalty on both parties (Papyri Westcar, D'Orbiney). There was much familial affection, a quality frequently reflected in tomb-inscriptions and stelae.

2. *Social Values and Relationships.* Negatively, theft and fraud (e.g., falsifying documents [re] moving landmarks). lies, especially against a third party, and murder and violence all stood condemned (Book of the Dead, ch. 125; wisdom-books, passim; autobiographies). Positively, values esteemed included reliability in service, compassion on the needy (as for the hungry, thirsty, and naked in tomb-inscriptions), deference to the great but impartiality in judgment. Discretion and skill in speech were both valued in their respective spheres. A favorite contrast made by the "wisdom-writers" is one between the "heated man" (cf. our "hothead") and the self-controlled, "silent man" (e.g., Amenemope).

3. *The State.* Pharaoh was the keystone of society, intermediary by virtue of his office between gods and men. He especially was charged publicly to uphold *maat* in all its aspects—in serving the gods, in defense of the realm, and as fountainhead of legal and social justice. In turn, loyalty to the throne was considered a prime duty of Pharaoh's subjects and also their best hope of advancement. This double aspect of loyalty to the crown was incorporated in politically motivated "wisdom-books" (Sehetepibre, Man to his Son) produced under the auspices of the Twelfth Dynasty (c. 1900 B. C.) (cf. Kitchen, *Oriens Antiquus* 8, 1969, pp. 189-208).

4. *Ethics and Religion.* Proper reverence was to be shown the gods, their offerings and festivals (Merikare, Aniy). Specifically, the gods were invoked as ultimate sanction—executors of blessing or curse—for respect or transgression of contracts, bound-

aries, etc. Of particular interest is a series of inscriptions of "the humble," by the royal workmen who cut royal tombs in the Valley of Kings (thirteenth-twelfth centuries B.C.). They confess their transgressions, accepting subsequent sickness or trouble as punishment from the gods, seeking restoration, and giving thanks for deliverance. The outward Egyptian attitude to sin was ritually to deny having committed any; but behind this facade, its reality was acknowledged as on these stelae and occasionally elsewhere (e.g., Merikare).

5. *Role of Magic.* Positively, magic was "a weapon to ward off what might befall (one)" (Merikare), used for protection or healing alongside other means. However, magic had less happy applications. It could be used in order to harm others, a legally-punishable crime. Or, more subtly corrupting, it could be used to circumvent ethical and moral requirements and penalties; for example, the spell on the heart—scarab amulet and chapter 125 of the Book of the Dead (both declaring one's innocency) when simply included in a burial could be taken to ensure a blessed hereafter regardless of one's earthly conduct, and circumventing magically judgment after death.

6. *Conclusion.* In many basic things, the ancient Egyptians shared various ethical norms and attitudes with other cultures into modern times. Overall, as Gardiner pointed out, they were a practical rather than a speculative people; no wonder, then, that prominent sources for Egyptian ethics are works dealing with everyday life and concrete issues, wisdom and "autobiography," not philosophical treatises. And in common with all mankind, of course, their practice did not always match their explicit ideals.

Texts in: J. B. Pritchard, ed., *Ancient Near Eastern Texts,* 3rd. ed., Princeton, Princeton University, 1969; T. G. Allen, *The Egyptian Book of the Dead,* Chicago, Chicago University, 1960; General: A. H. Gardiner, *HERE* 5, Edinburgh, Clark, 1912, pp. 475-485. KENNETH A. KITCHEN

EMANCIPATION OF WOMEN. See *Women, Status of.*

EMOTION. To experience emotion is to become aware of larger than usual differences in the continuous changes in feeling which are experienced by all normal healthy people in the waking state. Such changes in feeling are normally accompanied by bodily changes—such as, in circulation, breathing and sweating—and when very strong may also be accompanied by intense and impulsive actions. The experience of emotion is the opposite of calm relaxation. At times the experience of emotion may be the goal towards which behavior is directed; at times it may simply accompany ongoing behavior; and at yet other times it can be the motivating force causing the behavior.

Theories of emotion proposed by psychologists and physiologists over the past one hundred years may be roughly categorized into those where physiological changes are believed to precede the conscious awareness of emotion and those where such changes are concurrent with or follow conscious awareness. Theories currently most widely held and best supported by available evidence, while paying due regard to cortical influences, also lay great importance on the role of sub-cortical brain mechanisms in the control of emotion. According to such theories, emotion and the general arousal level of an organism are closely linked. Such theories in their psychological aspects point out that moderate arousal levels result in better performance on a variety of tasks and that too much arousal leads to a loss of control and consequently less efficient performance. The specific form which an emotional response takes will depend, among other things, upon the thoughts of the individual relevant to the particular emotion provoking situation; the specific features of the situation; upon a process of learning resulting from imitation of others in similar situations; and upon the way such situations were reacted to in the past. Maturation is fundamental to this process; in many instances, however, emotional reaction depends upon prior experience and learning.

Many writers on the psychology of religion note that one factor leading to religious belief is affective or emotional. This is often expressed as a sense of an intimate pervading presence, of a deeper significance in everyday things and the events of one's life. More recently it has been pointed out that similar experiences can be brought about by the action of certain drugs. Apart from drugs it is held that the principal agents commonly used for inducing emotional experiences during religious services are the use of ceremonial—including ritual, music, and emotional oratory. The derogatory label of emotionalism has in recent years become a predictable response from some vocal critics of mass evangelism. While the combined effect of a large crowd, massed choirs, bright lights and somewhat emotional hymns, heightens emotions in many people, the lasting effects in the changed lives of many converted at such crusades cannot be adequately accounted for solely by such factors, but must properly be attributed to the work of the Holy Spirit.   MALCOLM A. JEEVES

EMOTIVISM. According to the ethical emotivist, traditional ethical theorists became embroiled in knotty moral issues because of a failure to comprehend that there are no concepts in normative ethics, but only factually meaningless ejaculations used to express or arouse emotions. The utterance "Stealing is wrong" functions primarily not as a statement-making sentence but rather as a vehicle for expressing one's attitude or feeling about stealing (A. J. Ayer) and also as an evocative expression intended to generate a similar attitude in the hearer (C. L. Stevenson). In any case, the question of truth or falsity does not

arise because ethical utterances, being composed of terms such as "boring," "right," or "good"—which have no factual import—express feelings without *stating* anything at all.

📖 Alfred Jules Ayer, *Language, Truth and Logic,* New York, Dover, 1946; C. L. Stevenson, *Ethics and Language,* New Haven, Yale University, 1944.
                 PETER GENCO

EMPATHY. See also *Compassion.* This term, "empathy," as first used in the beginning of this century in connection with art, denotes the capacity to enter into and lose one's identity in the feelings and works of others. In psychoanalysis it means the capacity to adopt, in relation to someone else, an attitude which is nonjudgmental and accepting.

Christians are obligated, by their faith, to speak the truth in love (Eph. 4:15). Both emphases are important: the Christian man is required to be both honest and compassionate. Christians are to enter into the experiences of others, imaginatively and sympathetically; they are also enjoined to speak the truth to each other (Eph. 4:25).

The polarities are truth and discernment on the one hand and love and compassion on the other. We ought to abstain from making judgments which are hasty and ill informed; the danger is that, in our desire to avoid this error, we will abstain from making any judgments at all. Jesus indicates the nature of the distinction: "Do not judge by appearances, but judge with right judgment" (John 7:24 RSV). As Jesus talked to the woman by the well of Sychar, so we need to learn how to empathize if we are to minister, faithfully and tenderly, to those in need.   STUART B. BABBAGE

EMPLOYMENT. See also *Unemployment; Work.* Employment is the relationship existing between an employer (master) and employee (servant) for a voluntary service by the employee for the mutual benefit of both parties.

In this relationship, the employer, unless restricted by law or contract, has the right to determine exactly how the service is to be performed.

The difference between master-servant and master-slave lies in the involuntary service of the slave versus the voluntary service of the servant (employee).

An employment relationship does not exist where the person performing the service has the inherent right to determine how the service is to be performed: this is a client-independent contractor relationship (e.g., building contractor, lawyer, television repairman).

The employer has certain obligations to his employees. The employer should provide a safe and healthy place of work for the employees. The employer must also pay the employees the compensation voluntarily agreed to by both parties at the beginning or during the employment period; such an agreement may be on an individual basis, collective through a union contract, or set by law. Unless prohibited by law or agreement, the employer may vary the compensation to his employees performing the same work (Matt. 20:1-15). The employer must fulfill his part of the employment contract. The employer also has the implied obligation to treat his employees in a dignified and respectful manner (Eph. 6:8-9), and to encourage the employees to have pride in their work.

The employee has expressed and implied duties to his employer. The employee must fulfill the expressed terms of employment. Implied obligations include being obedient (Eph. 6:5-8), performing the best possible work, avoiding stealing the employer's time through idleness, slowness, or lack of punctuality, and, finally, being loyal to his employer (Titus 2:9-10).

ROBERT P. BENJAMIN

ENCYCLICALS. See *Papal Encyclicals.*

ENDOGAMY. See also *Exogamy.* Endogamy, opposite of exogamy, is marriage within the tribe. Probably the prime example of endogamy is the caste system of India, where marriage is carefully regulated, a violation of which loses one his social standing. Priesthood and royalty are also often cases in point. A Biblical illustration was Abraham's charge that his servant secure a wife for Isaac, not from "the daughters of the Canaanites, among whom I dwell," but from "my kindred" (Gen. 24:3-4). The endogamous ideal was recognized, and Rebekah responded to Abraham's bidding as the will of God.

MORRIS A. INCH

ENEMY. See also *Interpersonal Relations.* In the OT the word is quite wide-ranging and may refer to opponents in war, the Gentile nations, personal enemies, the unrighteous, and to those rebellious against God. Personal, political, and religious factors are generally intertwined thoughout these writings since God's covenant with Israel and the demands associated with it contain more than purely religious instruction. However, a transition to a more exclusively religious enmity occurs in such passages as Isa. 1:24ff. where the reference is to God's enemies within Israel. This is developed further in Ps. 6:10; 54:3 ff., and elsewhere.

A similar usage is to be found in the NT and not only in passages quoting from the OT (Rom. 12:20; cf. Prov. 25:21-22 and Mark 12:36 par; Acts 2:34 ff.; I Cor. 15:25; Heb. 1:13; 10:13 citing Ps. 110:1). *Echthros* refers to military foes (Luke 19:43), other nations (Luke 1:71, 74), personal opponents (Rom. 12:19-21; Gal. 4:16), enemies of Christians (Matt. 10:36; Rom. 11:28; Rev. 11:5, 12) and to those antagonistic towards God (Luke 19:27; Acts 13:10; Rom. 5:10; Phil. 3:18). An extension of OT views is present when the enemies of God also include death and supernatural powers (I Cor. 15:25 ff.; cf. Col. 2:15) and ultimately Satan (Matt. 13:39; Luke 10:19).

Most striking in this connection is the apparent reversal of OT attitudes in Jesus' injunction to "love your enemy" (Matt. 5:43ff.). While it is true that no direct parallel to "hate your enemy" occurs in the OT, there are passages which approach it in spirit (e.g., Deut. 20:16-18) and instances in which individuals express such an attitude (Ps. 26:5; 31:6; 139:21-22). The problem is solved if the word "hate," as elsewhere in the gospels, is related in a comparative rather than antithetical manner to "love" (cf. Luke 14:26), and not pressed too literally. Jesus' reply in Matt. 5:44 is to be viewed as a response to the whole of v. 43 and not merely to the clause concerning love of one's enemy. Its sense, then, is not "love your neighbor and love your enemy also," for with the command to love the enemy the distinction between neighbor and enemy is annulled.

While a general background to this teaching is provided in those places in the OT where some form of kindness to the enemy (or stranger) is enjoined (Exod. 23:4,5; Lev. 19:34; Job 31:29; Prov. 24:17; 25:21) and by similar sayings in the rabbinic writings (Gen. R. 38:3; Midr. Ps. 41:8; b. Ber. 10a; Tos. Bab. Kamm. 9:29) all such passages fall short of this comprehensive principle uttered by Jesus (Matt. 5:44) which is elsewhere exhibited by him in practice (Luke 23:34) and insisted upon by Paul (Rom. 12:19-21). ROBERT BANKS

ENJOYMENT. Enjoyment is frequently linked with the sense of satisfaction and well-being attained when the physical organism adapts to pleasant elements of the environment such as odors, foods, and sights. The concept of enjoyment, however, is much broader. Indeed, enjoyment of life is a basic mark of an integrated personality. because man is often unable to relate appropriately to society or the environment, his spontaneous experience of joy or well-being is significantly dwarfed. Moreover, when, as one catechism reminds us, enjoyment of God is part of man's chief end, the relationship of enjoyment to personality integration becomes more definite.

The sense of enjoyment flows from creativity and discovery, from refreshment and recovery, from meaning and purpose, and from reconciliation and community. Accordingly, the decisions and actions of the individual and society have important ethical implications for the enjoyment potential of the self and of others.

To the Christian whose life touches reality in two worlds and whose sense of confidence flows from Christ's victory over death, the participation in suffering does not necessarily imply non-satisfaction of life, since it can be matched with the hope of glory presently guaranteed through the Holy Spirit. Thus, though it may mean affliction to choose the difficult way of righteousness, love and equity in a world of dishonesty, hate and evil does not *per se* vitiate the sense of enjoyment in life (cf. James 1:2-3; I Peter 1:6-9; Phil. 2:17; Matt. 5:12). GERALD L. BORCHERT

ENLIGHTENMENT. The Enlightenment was an eighteenth century movement which began with publication of Isaac Newton's *Principia* (1687) and ended with the French Revolution, though its lineage precedes Newton and its influence was felt long after 1800. Principally it emphasized man's ability by reason to discover truth imbedded by a divine architect in nature and man's consciousness. It was believed that the right use of truth would promote a harmony by which man could perfect himself and society to the ultimate end of securing happiness for the largest number. In erecting its humanistic structure the Englightenment established a base for human conduct resting on the imperfect conscience of natural man rather than on a Christian social and personal ethic.

The Enlightenment was highly confident of progress. This optimism derives in part from the Renaissance (q.v.) and the concept of hope imbedded in the Puritan application of Reformed theology to history. The new science and its philosophical thinking on man and his world was directly the source of this faith in the triumph of good in the world now as a result of the effort of enlightened man.

A new cosmology emerged as Aristotle and Aquinas were set aside. Truth in nature was sought, not deductively from a theological precept or theme as in scholasticism, but by observation. Copernicus, Kepler and Galileo viewed the world through scientific eyes. Descartes followed with his *Discourse on Method* (1637) in which he gave a philosophical garb to scientific methodology (Cartesian doubt). Bacon in *Atlantis* presented a visionary glimpse into a world transformed by science. It was, however, left to Newton to provide the canon of scientific methodology in which these pioneer works were synthesized. *Principia* became the handbook for the enlightened seeker after knowledge.

Newton was a traditional Christian but his Enlightenment followers viewed the universe mechanistically with unvarying laws and man as a thinking machine. The role of God was drastically diminished, revelation eliminated and the importance of man immensely inflated. Man was of value for his own sake as a self-conscious being. As Pope in his *Essay on Man* has it,

Know then thyself, presume not God
  to scan;
The proper study of mankind
  is man.

The beginnings of the examination, of how man was to function in this new world are found in John Locke's *Essay Concerning Human Understanding* (1690). Man is shaped by those stimuli which he encounters, and his mind as a *tabula rasa* records these. He is molded by his environment but is able through educational reform to improve his society and thus change the character of men. Locke brought the significant questions about man and society under the scrutiny of this type of reason.

The deeply penetrating impact of the Enlightenment can only be explained by the presence of a large number of remarkably able men contemporary with each other who were committed to the application of the scientific method to all disciplines of life. These men had a freedom unknown in the medieval age and found ready support from the new wealth. The common endeavor found stimulation in the exchange of books, monographs, and journals possible because of the printing press. The universities largely rejected new ideas but this was offset by the founding of scientific societies such as the Royal Society of London (1662). Here the scientific observer and mathematician met and instructed the merchant, politician, and often cleric. The philosophy of the Enlightenment comes into its own, however, in the salons of Europe where dilettantes discussed the significance of the new learning and planned practical applications of its principles to government and society. These non-professional philosophers are the "philosophes."

Though British in origin, the Enlightenment influenced Western culture most in its French dress. Voltaire learned much during his three year exile in England and, with his remarkable ability to communicate made this knowledge popular. He scorned the traditional, lauded natural science, acclaimed the natural rights of man and expressed confidence in man's perfectibility. Above all he saw reason as the answer to all as it used natural laws (q.v.). Voltaire was opposed to violence—and especially to war, injustice, superstition and reasonless authority. He denied the romantic tenet that "this is the best of all possible worlds" but felt man's duty was to strive, since improvement was possible. Rousseau also developed these principles especially in his *Social Contract*. He accepts man as a creature of reason, but not primarily, for feeling must be given place.

We should remember here that Enlightenment leaders were limited in their plans to apply the fruits of their movement to all men. The benefits of freedom were for the elite intellectual coterie of which they were a part.

The Enlightenment while rejecting traditional religion, and often attacking it, had religious overtones. These are expressed in English deism, French naturalism, and German rationalism. Deism as a religion failed since its principles were so obvious and it lacked all those elements which satisfy the human heart. Generally God was considered an absentee landlord who had created and withdrawn, so that only nature remained. Men could know the moral law inherent in nature and no special revelation is needed. All true religions are basically the same and what they foundationally hold in common is truth.

How did the church respond? Certain elements became more rigid and merely turned back to the traditional. Others adopted a latitudinarian stance and compromised by absorbing the new ideas while changing to ritual. Many continued in the strong strain of evangelicalism and participated in the Evangelical Revival. Law, Berkeley and Butler gave strong answers to Enlightenment advocates and provided an intellectual base to accompany the religious experience of advocates of Biblical faith.

WILLIAM N. KERR

ENTERTAINMENT. See *Amusements; Leisure.*

ENTHUSIASM. The term "enthusiasm" is derived from the Greek noun *enthusiasmos,* which means the state of having a god

in oneself, of being inspired by an indwelling deity. The English word is commonly employed to designate the conviction held by various individuals and groups in the course of Christian church history that they happened to be under the unique influence of the Holy Spirit; that they enjoyed his special enlightenment and inspiration, and (frequently) other extraordinary charismatic gifts. The designation is also applied to the behavior or activity of such persons.

Though enthusiasm has appeared in many forms, certain additional characteristics, discernible in numerous variations, are noteworthy. Enthusiasts, seeking a return to the type of living which they presumed characterized the members of the early church, have rigorously stressed holiness of behavior for the members of their society. They have frequently supposed that, through the powers of the new life given them in regeneration, they can and do achieve sinlessness.

Enthusiasts have chafed under the restraints which traditional church bodies have imposed upon their teaching and practice, and have regularly banded together as independent groups to conduct their spiritual affairs in the freedom of charismatic (as opposed to institutional) Christianity. An enthusiastic ideal is the restoration of theocratic government on earth. Many of the enthusiastic sects have espoused a millennialism of some type. Enthusiasts have tended to minimize the importance of the sacraments. Glossolalia, violent emotional experiences, convulsive bodily movements, and other ecstatic phenomena have not uncommonly been a characteristic.

Evidences of enthusiasm have appeared in Christendom in every period of church history from apostolic days until the present time. At the time of the Reformation the term was applied to the various sects claiming divine inspiration, such as the Anabaptists and Schwenkfeldians. Lutherans have regarded as enthusiastic all groups who believed that the Holy Spirit works immediately, that is, apart from the Scriptures and the sacraments. In USA religious bodies traits of enthusiasm are discernible in the Swedenborgians, and some Quakers and Pentecostals, and in some aspects of the charismatic renewal which began in the mid-1950s.   WALTER A. MAIER

ENVIRONMENTAL PERCEPTION. The appraisal of environmental quality in ecological alarms over such issues as pollution have brought to public attention the relevance of environmental perception. No real body of theory has yet developed, although geographers have begun to take it seriously in the last ten years as a significant new field of research. The whole environment external to man is the objective geographical environment. Within this largest sphere is the operational environment, or the sphere within which man operates. Man is aware of only a portion of this, and this is the extent of his perceptual environment. The awareness may be derived from physical sensitivity to it or from learning experience. At this level, a portion of the environment is symbolic: the behavioral environment is that portion which elicits a behavioral response.

Most geographical research has been devoted to the perception of natural hazards such as frequency of floods in river valleys, or drought. The perception of risk has been shown to have correlation with the decision-making process of innovation of new techniques. The perception of architectural space, and neighborhood units, the visual quality of cities, the formation of map images, the evaluation of wilderness, and national outlooks on landscape values, are new fields of investigation that did not exist ten years ago. Other studies are historical, viewing landscapes and other geographical concepts through the minds and eyes of previous observers. Perception of environment at the broadest level involves national stereotypes, ethnocentrism, xenophobia, national attitudes, and national character. The importance of mental images such as racism, the mirror image of national judgment upon other states, and other forms of ethnocentric perception is a vast subject. This inter-disciplinary field within the social sciences will provide richer insights, and modify an extroverted view of the world.

D. Appleyard, et. al, *The View from the Road*, Boston, Massachusetts Institute of Technology, 1964; Commission on College Geography, Association of American Geographers, *Perception of Environment*, No. 5, 1969; Edward T. Hall, *The Hidden Dimension*, New York, Doubleday, 1966; Davie Lowenthal, ed., *Environmental Perception and Behavior*, Chicago, University of Chicago, Dept. of Geography Research Paper no. 109, 1969.
                              JAMES M. HOUSTON

ENVIRONMENTAL POLLUTION. See also *Atomic Energy; Defoliation*. Among the causes of environmental pollution are population growth, affluence, and the misuse of technology. All three have important moral and ethical implications. Technological solutions will not be sufficient, however, since changes in attitudes and values are required. From a theological point of view, we need a new understanding of God as Creator and of man as steward.

1. Causes of Pollution

Population. Highly industrialized societies tend to assume that population problems are serious only in less developed nations. But the highly visible evidence of pollution has demonstrated the consequences of growth in the size and density of populations. Furthermore, it has cast serious doubt upon "growth" as a self-sufficient measure of the health of a city or of the economy in general.

Affluence. Higher "standards of living" involve greater per capita drain upon natural resources and more pollution of the environment. Perhaps the most serious aspect is energy demand. In the USA the annual rate of population growth is somewhat over

1 percent, while the production of electrical energy increases 6 to 8 percent per year.

Misuse of Technology. Barry Commoner (*The Closing Circle,* New York, Knopf, 1972, pp. 140ff.) thinks that the main issue is not the amount of goods used, but their nature. Pollution has risen about ten times faster than the gross national product. He traces the onset of severe pollution to about World War II when new products that cannot be recycled by nature were developed as short-cut solutions to specific narrow problems. Convenience is almost always bought at the cost of a debt to nature.

An adequate solution requires attention to all three factors, but there is the additional claim that the present state is a moral, not merely a scientific, crisis. Engel (*Zygon,* 1970, 5:227) feels that man's violence toward his surroundings is just as sinful as his violence toward his fellows. Sittler (*Zygon,* 1970, 5:179) holds that pollution is "Christianly blasphemous."

2. Evidence from Ecology

Ecology is the study of the interrelationships of organisms and their environments. Commoner (*op. cit.,* pp. 33ff.) has summarized the basic principles in four "laws." (1) "Everything is connected to everything else." In the ecosphere every effect is also a cause. (2) "Everything must go somewhere." In nature there is no "waste." It is impossible to throw anything "away." (3) "Nature knows best.... The artificial introduction of an organic compound that does not occur in nature, but is man-made and is nevertheless active in a living system, is very likely to be harmful." (4) "There is no such things as a free lunch.... Because the global ecosystem is a connected whole ... anything extracted from it by human effort must be replaced. Payment of this price cannot be avoided; it can only be delayed."

Commoner (*op. cit.,* pp. 15, 295) claims that the present situation has arisen in large

part from the illusion that through our ingenuity we have escaped from our dependence upon the natural environment. The real fact is that the "vaunted productivity and wealth of modern, technology-based society" have been gained by "rapid short-term exploitation of the environmental system." Pollard (*Man on a Spaceship,* 1967, Claremont, Calif., Claremont Men's College) has insisted that we must replace a "frontier" view of inexhaustible resources with a "spaceship earth" concept that recognizes the need to care for life-support systems.

3. Individual and Society

Hardin (*Science,* 1968, 162:1243) used the "tragedy of the commons" to illustrate the tension between individual and public morality. Imagine a pasture open to all. Each herdsman considers it to his advantage to add one more animal to his herd, since all the others will share the harmful effects of overgrazing. "Each man is locked into a system that compels him to increase his herd without limit — in a world that is limited.... Freedom in a commons brings ruin to all."

This parable can apply to overpopulation, to depletion of natural resources, or to environmental pollution. A large portion of the true costs of productivity are hidden, and hidden costs usually are social costs. The world-wide distribution and the long persistence of DDT, for example, have extended the meaning of "neighbor" to include the entire world community as well as the next generation. Furthermore, ecological and economic issues overlap, and we must weigh choices between pollution and employment.

4. View of Nature

White (*Science,* 1967, 155:1203) insisted that what we do about the environment depends upon our beliefs about human nature and destiny. Specifically, he claimed that "we shall continue to have a worsening ecologic crisis until we reject the Christian axiom that nature has no reason for existence save to serve man."

The problem indeed has an important religious component, but it is seriously misleading to place the entire blame on a Christian view of nature. The squandering of natural resources is not a recent development. Environmental crises have arisen in all highly technological societies, regardless of the dominant religion. Furthermore, the Biblical view is not fairly described as "arrogance toward nature."

White proposed that St. Francis be considered the "patron saint for ecologists" and that the Franciscan view of the "spiritual autonomy of all parts of nature" be substituted for the idea of man's limitless rule. Francis Schaeffer (*Pollution and the Death of Man*, Wheaton, Ill., Tyndale, 1970, p. 30) cautioned that this is a pantheistic answer which is inadequate both theoretically and practically. René Dubos (*A Theology of the Earth*, p. 5) suggested that St. Benedict would be a truer symbol because of his insistence that monks should learn to manage the land.

5. God as Creator

It is apparent that theology has focused on human nature and has generally disregarded the world of nature. Yet God's provision for all forms of life is clear in Ps. 104. The sabbatical year (Exod. 23:10) was intended to provide food for the poor, but a concern for the fertility of the land may be involved as well. God's covenant with Noah (Gen. 9) included every living creature. Schaefer (*op cit.*, p. 47) claims that nature has value in itself because God made it.

The view of God as Creator will prevent the nature worship that could otherwise characterize the environmental movement. The understanding that the earth is the Lord's (Ps. 24:1) encourages respect for nature without the temptation to worship it.

It is unfortunate that interest in the doctrine of creation too often has been limited to the problem of origins, thus obscuring the view of God as both Creator and Sustainer.

6. Man as Steward

Some have asked whether man is to be viewed as *in* nature or *over* nature, but a reasonable answer is *both*. Man is a part of God's creative work, but God has given him a unique role toward the rest of nature. It is important to realize, however, that dominion does not mean exploitation. The command to subdue and have dominion (Gen. 1) is balanced by the instruction to dress and keep the land (Gen. 2).

C. F. D. Moule (*Man and Nature in the New Testament*, Philadelphia, Fortress, 1967, p. 3) holds that responsible authority is God-like. God "is not responsible to another; but he cares for his creation in the sense that he makes it his concern and responsibility." Man is responsible in the sense that he must render an account before God.

The terms "steward" and "stewardship" are not common in the Bible, but the concepts are. Stewardship has been stressed for many years in forestry and conservation, but in Christian circles generally often has been limited to money and abilities. Environmental concerns should be made an important part of stewardship programs in churches.

7. Hope for the Future

Acute awareness of environmental problems has given a new meaning to exhortations to "repent or perish." The difficulties are real and serious, and will not respond to weak efforts. Nevertheless, a sense of hope is needed to avoid the fatalism that can paralyze effective action.

The environmental action movements have shown that energies can be enlisted and that attitudes can be changed. Nature has recuperative powers that we should seek to understand. Sittler (*op. cit.*, p. 180) believes that ecology " is the only theater vast enough for a modern playing out of the doctrine of grace." Schaeffer (*op. cit.*, p. 82) calls for Christians to demonstrate that man can exercise dominion without being destructive.

Perhaps we can find new meaning in God's promise (II Chron. 7:14 RSV) that "if my people who are called by my name humble themselves, and pray and seek my face, and turn from their wicked ways, then I will hear from heaven, and will forgive their sin and heal their land."

V. ELVING ANDERSON

ENVIRONMENT AND HEREDITY. Environment and heredity usually are viewed as two opposing forces. Heredity is assumed to be fixed, while environment is highly modifiable. Therefore, environmentalist views have been favored as being more optimistic.

This approach is now known to be incorrect. Both heredity and environment are involved in all human traits. The relative contribution of these two factors can be estimated for a specific situation, but no general answer will fit all circumstances. If the environment were made more uniform, then more of the observed variation would arise from genetic differences. If heredity were made constant (as in identical twins), then environmental factors would account for the variation.

A significant part of the variation in body height results from genetic differences. Yet, over the past few centuries the average height has increased by several inches, mainly as a result of improved nutrition. Thus a trait may be under fairly strong genetic control, but the whole distribution can be shifted if the environment is changed.

It has sometimes proved difficult in practice to modify environments, however, partly as a result of social inertia. Furthermore, the importance of early environment may be underestimated. Fetal development can be modified by drugs taken by the mother or inadequate nutrition. Severe malnutrition in the first months of life can irreversibly limit the number of small interconnecting neurons in the brain. Early experiences can modify aspects of behavior that might not be noticed until months or years later.

There are at least three gene-environment pathways, each with interesting ethical implications.

1. *Environment may influence the genes.* Radiation or certain chemicals can alter the genetic material, producing mutations. There is a strong ethical obligation to identify causes of added mutations and try to keep them to a minimum. Harmful mutations were weeded out by natural selection, but medical advances (a change in environment) extend the lives of carriers and increase the chances of passing the genes on. This newly won right to reproduce must not be used arrogantly without regard to the welfare of future generations.

2. *Genes can influence the environment* by affecting the ways in which individuals select environmental niches in which to live, or actually modify the environment. Identical twins reared apart from early age often are found to be living in similar circumstances. We are not merely creatures of our environment, but participate in selecting it. Furthermore, different species have characteristic ways of altering their environment, an obvious reflection of their own genetic constitution. Man is genetically able to alter his surroundings more drastically than any other organism, but this capacity has led to the "environmental crisis."

3. *Genetic and environmental factors can interact* and thus jointly influence the development of a trait. A few people have a genetic defect of an enzyme needed to repair ultra-violet damage to chromosomes. They develop pigmented spots on the skin which can change into tumors, but the problem is greatly reduced by staying out of direct sunlight (a precaution not needed by

most people). Individuals differ genetically in their patterns of response to many other aspects of environment. Parents and teachers realize that children react quite differently to the same circumstances. Children start life with different genetic repertoires. Life experiences develop part of each person's genetic potential, while much remains untapped. The combined effect of differences in genetics and experience leads to rather marked variation in behavioral patterns.

The psychotic disorders represent this type of interaction. In the case of schizophrenia the risk to identical co-twins is about 50 percent, while the risk to other siblings is about 10 to 15 percent. Children of schizophrenic mothers, when reared by adoptive parents, have about the same risk as such children reared by their own affected mothers. The most reasonable interpretation is that people differ genetically in their tendency to become psychotic, but that the actual illness may be precipitated by specific aspects of the environment.

In many populations somewhat over half of the variation in measured IQ can be traced to genetic differences. It is also reported that the average IQ for blacks is generally lower than for whites. We cannot conclude, however, that the IQ discrepancy results from racial differences in genetic potential, since the environments are not equivalent. Thus both the requirements for fair evaluation and a humane concern for the welfare of ethnic minorities argue for providing adequate environment and education.

What, then, is an appropriate ethical response as we consider the welfare of others? Some genes are deleterious in any environment. We should seek ways to prevent or reduce their effect. Some environments are disastrous for any genetic combination. These too should be eliminated. Beyond these extreme cases we should recognize the genetic uniqueness of individuals and seek to make possible the differing environments needed for expression of their potential.   V. ELVING ANDERSON

ENVY. Envy is the resentful and even hateful dislike of the good fortune or blessing of another.

It is a sin covered by the Tenth Commandment, and also expressly forbidden in the NT. Paul lists this sin as a cognate with murder and with hating God (Rom. 1:29), and declares it a work of the flesh which can debar a person from the Kingdom of heaven (Gal. 5:19). In the Pastorals, Timothy is warned against becoming the kind of unsound teacher whose "morbid craving for controversy and for disputes about words" leads to envy (I Tim. 6:4). Titus is reminded of the worldling's addiction to envy which is done away through Christ (Titus 3:3). Its heinousness may be seen full force in Jewish leaders who delivered up Jesus Christ to be crucified because of envy (Matt. 27:18). Even Pilate recognized their motivation (Mark 15:10).

Envy appears in a positive light only once in the NT. God's intense love for man causes him to be "envious" for man's friendship (James 4:5). It is also possible for envy to result in good to others. Paul can rejoice that the gospel is being preached in Rome even though the proclaimers are motivated by envy (Phil. 1:15).

                                                    PAUL BENJAMIN

EPICUREANISM. See *Greek Ethics; Hedonism.*

EQUALITY. Equality is a relationship of identical worth or quantity between two or more entities, concrete or abstract. This writing is concerned only with the latter: abstract or qualitative equality as among human beings.

Human beings are obviously unequal in numberless ways, including: health, opportunities, abilities, energy, moral character, and contribution to society. It is essential, therefore, in asserting the equality of all men to delineate the nature and the source of that equality.

In Christian ethics the nature of the equality is that all men are equally to be loved — not equally admired, or emulated, or praised; but equally loved. The source of equality, and the basis of the Christian's love of his fellow man, is God's love for all men. It is the relationship of the first and second of the two great commandments which establishes the "right" of all men to be called equal. At its highest, the love that is equally extended to all men is *agape*, self-generating, selfless love, of which God alone is perfectly capable; at a lower (non-Christian) level it is philanthropy.

The practical political consequence of equal love for all men is the declaration (as in the Constitution of the United States) of their equal worth under the law, and of the equality of their rights and duties as citizens. The social consequence is the extension of equal respect to all men, as creatures of God.

Such equality and such ideals are a rare, not a normal, characteristic of human society in history. At the height of ancient Athenian democracy, for example, the great majority of the population were slaves, with no civil rights whatever. Throughout the history of Europe down to the seventeenth century few questioned a natural inequality of status and rights, based largely on the class into which one was born. Many voices cried in the wilderness, and many knew the medieval egalitarian query: "When Adam delved and Eva span, who then was the gentleman?"; but most people would have agreed that to assert the legal, civil, and social equality of all men would be to fly in the face of "natural law." Indeed, the terms "state" and "citizen," which our generation uses in any discussion of equality of rights, were unknown until the late Renaissance

(q.v.). At the simplest, a three-fold distinction separated all males into the classes of clergy, nobility, and worker (agricultural, of course). Women had practically no rights, as a class, at all.

The modern concept of equality in Europe and America in the seventeenth/eighteenth centuries is founded on religious and philosophical, not political, principles. In very significant ways, the movement toward equality grew out of the Reformation insistence on the equality of all men before God. If equality is to be conceived of as a permanent right, it must derive from something higher than the whim of kings, governments, or society, for what these powers give they can also take away.

Widely divergent religious and philosophical views were held by such advocates of equality as Milton, Burke, Rousseau, Shelley, and Jefferson, but all agreed that the right of equality is inalienable. The Founding Fathers of this nation, too, held different religious beliefs, but they found a broad theistic, not humanistic, foundation for their declaration of the rights and equality of all men. They conceived themselves to be acting, and the nation to be established, "under God."   CALVIN D. LINTON

ERASTIANISM. See *Church and State.*

EROS. See *Love.*

ESCHATOLOGY AND ETHICS.
I. Jesus
A. The Problem. The interpretation of Jesus' ethical teaching, particularly the Sermon on the Mount (q.v.), will be largely conditioned by one's understanding of the Kingdom of God. "Old liberalism" discarded the apocalyptic element in Jesus' teaching as a time-conditioned form which contained the kernel of his pure ethical teaching: the Fatherhood of God, the brotherhood of man, the infinite value of the

individual soul, and the ethic of love. The "consistent eschatology" of A. Schweitzer radically changed the situation by the insistence that Jesus' view of the Kingdom was thoroughly and exclusively eschatological. This ethic was an interim ethic (q.v.) designed only for the short interval before the apocalyptic Kingdom would break in. It was an ethic of repentance designed to enable men to enter the approaching Kingdom. C. H. Dodd's "realized eschatology" understands the Kingdom as the inbreaking of the eternal order into the temporal, and Jesus' ethic therefore is not conditioned by futuristic eschatology but is a moral ideal given in absolute terms and grounded in timeless religious principles. Dispensationalism insists that Jesus' message about the Kingdom of God involved an offer to Israel of the promised earthly Davidic Kingdom. The Sermon on the Mount, like the Mosaic law, is legislation for the Jews in the coming Kingdom. It is not an ethic for Jesus' disciples living in the world; it is a legalistic ethic which is designed for the (Jewish) millennial kingdom.

The view taken in this article is that the Kingdom of God (q.v.) is first of all the rule of God which has come to man in history, which will be manifested at the end of the age to establish the glorious eternal order. Thus the primary sanction of the ethics is the will of God manifested now and in the future.

B. Ethics of the Reign of God. Jesus' brought the reign of God to men in history. His disciples are those who have received the reign of God (Mark 10:15), who receive the word of the Kingdom (Mark 4:20). It is an ethic designed to be lived out in this world in history; otherwise the word about salt and light is meaningless (Matt. 5:13-16). However, this ethic has an eschatological perspective in two ways. Jesus introduces a new righteousness which stands in contrast to the righteousness of the preceding age (Matt. 5:20). This is why Jesus reinterpreted the Old Testament law, annulling its ceremonial requirements (Mark 7:19). Furthermore, possession of this new righteousness is the condition for entering the eschatological Kingdom of heaven (Matt. 5:20).

C. An Absolute Ethic. Because it expresses the will of God, Jesus' ethic is absolute. The Sermon on the Mount is in a sense an ideal; it is a picture of the man in whom God perfectly rules. This means absolute kindness, absolute purity of heart, absolute honesty, perfect love (Matt. 5:21-48). This is why many scholars have felt that Jesus' ethic is impractical and unattainable. In fact, it is both attainable and unattainable. It can be attained, but not in its full measure. "In so far as the Christian is part of the church . . . the ethics of Jesus is a practical ethic. In so far as he is part of the world, it is relevant but impractical" (S. M. Gilmour in *Journal of Religion* XXI [1941], p. 263).

D. Ethics of the Inner Life. The context of the Sermon on the Mount is the OT law as interpreted by the scribes and Pharisees (Matt. 5:20). The illustrations of this principle contrast with current rabbinic teaching. The scribes emphasized outward conformity to the law as they interpreted it, as a casual reading of the Mishnah shows (see Matt. 23:23). Jesus emphasizes the inner character which underlies outward conduct: malicious anger is sin as well as murder, a lustful heart is sin as well as adultery, a broken word is sin as well as a broken oath. A spirit of revenge is sin; God's rule demands love.

E. The Attainment of Righteousness. The most basic demand which Jesus laid upon men was for a radical unqualified decision to follow him. Following Jesus is equivalent to receiving the Kingdom of God. "He who receives me receives him who sent me" (Matt. 10:40). A man must make a decision so radical that he must be willing, if need be, to turn his back on all other relationships. It may involve forsaking one's home (Luke 9:58), but Jesus did not lay this demand upon all his disciples. The demand of the Kingdom must take precedence over normal human relationships (Luke 9:60); it may also involve the rupture of the closest family relationships (Luke 9:61). A man must be willing to renounce every other affection when he renders a decision for the Kingdom (Luke 14:33). In fact, he must be willing to renounce his very life (Luke 14:26). He must deny himself and take up his cross (Matt. 16:24). This is not self-denial; it is renunciation of one's own will that the Kingdom of God may become the all important concern in life.

F. An Ethic of Grace. Jesus often speaks of rewards in the Kingdom (Matt. 5:12, 46; 6:4, 18), but never of merit. In fact, the very reward is a matter of grace. When a man has exercised the largest measure of faithfulness, he still deserves nothing, for he has done no more than his duty (Luke 17:7-10). The reward is the Kingdom of heaven itself (Matt. 5:3, 10) which is given to those for whom it has been prepared (Matt. 20:33; 25:34). Reward therefore becomes free unmerited grace and is pictured as all out of proportion to the service rendered (Matt. 19:29; 24:47; 25:21, 23; Luke 7:48: 12:37). While men are to seek the Kingdom, it is nevertheless God's gift (Luke 12:31, 32). It is God's free act of vindication which acquits a man, not the faithfulness of his religious conduct (Luke 18:9-14). The parable of the laborers in the vineyard is designed to show that the divine standard of reward is utterly different from human standards of payment; it is a matter of sheer grace (Matt. 20:1-16). The gift of the Kingdom includes both a blessedness while men are still in this life (Matt. 5:3-10), and the eschatological Kingdom in the age to come (Luke 12:32).

In summary, ethics of the Kingdom of God as present in Jesus and the eschatological Kingdom are inseparably related as two phases of the single reality: the reign of God and its blessings.

II. Paul

Eschatology plays an important role in Paul's thinking about Christian conduct. Christians as well as the world must stand before the judgment seat of God (Rom. 14:10) and of Christ (II Cor. 5:10), "so that each one may receive good or evil, according to what he has done." While believers have not received the spirit of bondage to fear (Rom. 8:15), they are nevertheless exhorted to "make holiness perfect in the fear of God" (II Cor. 7:1). Slaves are exhorted to exercise obedience in fear and trembling (Phil. 2:12); wrong-doers will be paid back for the wrong they have done (Col. 3:25). He who "sows to his own flesh will from the flesh reap corruption" (Gal. 6:8). Paul exercises severe self-discipline because he is engaged in a race to win an imperishable prize which is the goal of all Christians — eternal life (I Cor. 9:24).

The place where eschatology influences Pauline ethics more than anywhere else is in his attitude toward the social structures of his day. The basic structure of Paul's theological thought is the apocalyptic dualism of this age and the age to come. He sees the present age to be in the grip of evil powers, so that Satan is called the god of this age (II Cor. 4:4). This is, however, different from Jewish apocalyptic, for Christ has given himself to deliver us from this present evil age (Gal. 1:4), so that we need no longer be conformed to this age (Rom. 12:2) but may be renewed by the indwelling power of God.

While the Christian is individually renewed by the indwelling of Christ in the Spirit, Paul does not view this as a world-changing power. While he sometimes has a historical perspective which sees the salvation of Israel at some indefinite future time (Rom. 11), at other times his view of the future is foreshortened and he seems to reckon with such an imminent end of the world that one's situation in the social order is of little importance. In fact, he expressly says, "In view of the impending distress, it is well for a person to remain as he is" (I Cor. 7:26). Married people should not seek to break the marriage bond, Jews should not try to appear like Gentiles and vice versa, slaves should not seek to be free even if the opportunity presents itself. The context of the passage is one of indifference to one's situation in the social structures of the age. "Everyone should remain in the state in which he was called" (I Cor. 7:31).

The "impending distress" (I Cor. 7:26) and the shortness of the time (I Cor. 7:29) have been differently interpreted. The present distress may refer to the inevitable tension which arises between the new creation in Christ and the old age, or to the idea that the eschatological woes (the great tribulation) are immediately impending and are already anticipated in the sufferings of Christians. In any case, Paul clearly is dominated by a sense of the imminence of the Parousia and the end of the world which rendered questions of social ethics comparatively irrelevant. "In the New Testament perspective, the interadventual period is short, however long it may be from our historically oriented viewpoint" (John Murray, *Principles of Conduct*, p. 72). From this Murray draws the conclusion, "The eschatological perspective should always characterize our attitude to things temporal and temporary" (*loc. cit.*). This is difficult in our modern world if it means indifference to the impact of the gospel upon social structures. The cultural situation and the structure of the church is very different from that of first century Christianity, and the modern Christian cannot apply the teachings of Scripture in a one-to-one relationship but must seek the basic truth underlying the particular formulations in the New Testament.

📖 *Gospels:* C. H. Dodd, "Ethical Teaching of Jesus," in *A Companion to the Bible*, ed. by T. W. Manson, Edinburgh, Clark, 1939, pp. 378-381; C. F. H. Henry, *Personal Christian Ethics*, Grand Rapids, Eerdmans, 1957, pp. 278-326; Hans Windisch, *The Meaning of the Sermon on the Mount*, Philadelphia, Westminster, 1951; A. N. Wilder, *Eschatology and Ethics in the Teaching of Jesus*, New York, Harper and Row, 1950; G. E. Ladd, *Jesus and the Kingdom*, Waco, Word, 1964, Chap. 12; W. Schweitzer, *Eschatology and Ethics*, Geneva, World Council of Churches, 1951; J. Jeremias, *The Sermon on the Mount*, Philadelphia, Fortress, 1963.

Paul: John Murray, *Principles of Conduct*, London, Tyndale, 1957; M. S. Enslin, *The Ethics of Paul*, New York, Abingdon, 1975; R. Schnackenburg, *The Moral Teaching of the New Testament*, New York, Herder, 1965; V. P. Furnish, *Theology and Ethics in Paul*, Nashville, Abingdon, 1968.

GEORGE E. LADD

ESSENE COMMUNITY. The group of Essenes which lived by the Northwest shore of the Dead Sea (modern Qumran) for most of the period 150 B.C.-A.D. 68 produced the Dead Sea Scrolls. On the question of the Essene identity of the Qumran Community see M. Mansoor, *The Dead Sea Scrolls* (Grand Rapids, Eerdmans, 1964, pp. 143-152).

Sections I-III below summarize the Community's main ethical tenets; the final section compares these with the NT.

I. *Raison d'être.* This semi-monastic community believed that Israel had become ritually and morally unclean under her existing leaders. They separated themselves, therefore, from the rest, to constitute a faithful remnant as a starting-point for the Messianic age, which was soon expected to be ushered in with the repentance of the masses of Israel (1QSa 1.1-5).

II. Principles. Qumran's highest ethical ideal was the righteousness of God. The link between this *summum bonum* and concrete ethical precepts was the revealed will of God. They believed that God had not ceased to reveal his will. Out of his faithfulness to his covenant with the Fathers he had raised up the Community to be a remnant and showed it what he was doing with Israel, what he was about to do and what its duties were under these circumstances (CD 1.3-12). All this was set out in the Community's *Damascus Document*.

The Members' acceptance of God's righteous will as their highest good was not so much conditioned by the hope of reward as a loving response to God's faithfulness and wonderful electing grace to them in spite of their unworthiness. Fear of punishment was certainly present as a motive, but it was coupled with acceptance of punishment along with all God's righteous judgments (1QS 10.11-13).

This ethic involved a demand for perfection, both outwardly and inwardly. It was supported by strong sanctions. Members were disciplined through fines, expulsions, and even death (1QS 6.24-7.25, CD 9.1). They were also admonished through solemn curses and blessings, indicating sanctions to be imposed by God himself. The emphasis here was on man's relationship with God in this life and eternal bliss or punishment hereafter.

All this implies moral responsibility, but the Community believed in predestination too, without any feeling of incompatability. They held to double predestination (1QH 15.13-22), ethical dualism (1QS 3.15-4.26), total depravity and universal human sinfulness. There was a cosmic dimension to their ethic: man has an obligation to praise God in time with the movements of the heavenly bodies which obey him perfectly.

III. Precepts. The obligation to love extended only to those whom God loved. There was a parallel obligation to hate those whom he hated, but this was not to be translated into general action until the Day of Vengeance, in the final holy war against all the forces of evil in which the Members would participate (1QS 10.17-21, 1QM 1.1-14). Their pacifism was not absolute. Akin to the patience of God, it awaited the last day (cf. Philo *Quod omnis probus* 78). Similarly, their abstinence from Temple sacrifices was only temporary. In the last days their priests expected to lead the worship in a purified Temple (1QM 2.1-7; cf. Josephus *Ant.* xviii.1.19 and Philo *Quod omnis probus* 75).

Celibacy and the practice of the community of goods were the two most striking features of their *mores* to outside observers (e.g. Philo *Apol. pro Judaeis* 4-17, Pliny the Elder *Hist. Nat.*, v.17.4), but to the members themselves neither was very fundamental. Not all Essenes were celibate (Josephus *De bell. Jud.* 11.8.160f., CD 7.6-9). The practice probably originated from the desire for strict ceremonial purity and the consciousness of living in a conflict situation similar to a holy war (A. Marx, "Les racines du célibat essénien," *Rev. Qum.*, VII, pp. 323-342).

Many of their precepts can be paralleled with those of Christ. They were opposed to swearing, foolish speaking, abuse of vows, anger, revenge and covetousness. The Essenes' teaching on the Sabbath was the furthest removed from Christ's and even more extreme than that of the Pharisees.

IV. Relationship with early Christianity. There are some striking differences between the NT ethic and Qumran. Besides those already mentioned (law of love, Sabbath observance), the NT demand for perfection was qualitative rather than quantitive (W. D. Davis, *The Setting of the Sermon on the Mount*, New York, Cambridge University Press, 1964, pp. 209-219), its community sactions far more flexible and its tone more apodictic. Instead of curses it has woes, expressing pity for the erring, not hatred.

The resemblances remain important, but are best explained in terms of a common background in "sectarian" (i.e., non-Pharisaic) Judaism. There are no verbal parallels or signs of direct borrowing.

📖 H. Ringgren, *The Faith of Qumran*, Philadelphia, Fortress, 1963; G. Vermes, *The Dead Sea Scrolls in English*, Baltimore, Penguin, 1968.

PAUL GARNET

ETHICAL LANGUAGE. See *Language, Ethical.*

ETHICAL RELATIVISM. See also *Contextual Ethics; Interim Ethics; Situational Ethics.* Ethical Relativism is ultimately contingent on epistemological-cultural relativism. The fact of cultural variation has been acknowledged at least since Herodotus wrote his *History* in the fifth century B.C. Plato's *Protagoras* contains a myth concerning the relativity of moral standards. In Plato's *Republic,* a Sophist character named Thrasymachus maintains that right is determined by the laws and conventions of each society. But the fact of cultural variations does not logically imply any particular theory of truth and ethics. Plato, Aristotle, and other moral philosophers are as fully aware as the Sophists that standards of morality and truth vary. But they insist that truth and the good are objective and absolute, and that society fragments and human life loses worth when relativism is championed and practiced.

The contemporary theological ethicist, like his philosophical counterpart, maintains that all ethical ideas are either culture-bound or impractical. *Vox populi* replaces *vox Dei.*

Interim Ethic. The first quest for the "historical Jesus" maintained that Jesus' austere ethical demands (Matt. 5–7) are impractical for daily life. Wrede and Schweitzer (q.v.) presented an eschatological interpretation of Jesus' ethical teaching. Jesus' demands were valid only in view of the imminent end of the world; such "interim ethics" loses power and validity with the delay of *parousia.* But the early church neither abandoned its "perpetual expectation" nor reduced the vigorous moral demands of Kingdom-participation.

Contextual Ethics. Paul Lehmann says that "It is not the situation which makes the context ethical; but the context which makes the situation ethical." This position entails at least two serious problems: (1) Since there are many contradictory contexts, how is one to discern whether he is operating in a Christian context? Are we to assume that Lehmann's position necessitates commitment to a proper religion in order to attain a proper ethic? Why not a Zen or Hindu ethic? (2) If context provides the dynamic origin for all ethical decision, how then resolve the contradiction presented, for example, by the Paris peace talks. Position A is contextually moral; position B is contextually moral, but they are contradictory and thus cannot resolve the moral dilemma. Contextualism produces a pluralism, but cannot resolve the conflicts between mutually exclusive contexts. Pluralism is only theoretically viable: in the existential situation the elite decision-maker will make the concrete decision. Consistent contextualism would produce chaos.

Situational Ethics. The "new morality" maintains that love is the only norm for the moral. If one reads all of Joseph Fletcher's (q.v.) examples, two things become apparent: (1) All examples are extreme situations; (2) There is always something "valued" which is not derived from a given context. In each case, someone is transformed into a thing to be used; this violates the indicated love-criterion and principle (what is its transcendent source?): love people, use things. In a fallen world many situations do not present a simple choice between the moral or immoral, but God's forgiving grace is available to those who ask; and the Christian is to act conscientiously in view of the Biblical standard.

Nineteenth Century "Cultural Copernican Revolution." The classical statement of the cultural relativity thesis is found in Mannheim's *Ideology and Utopia* (Trans. L. Wirth, E. Shils, New York, Harcourt, Brace & World). "The historical and social genesis of an idea would only be irrelevant to its ultimate validity if the temporal and social conditions of its emergence had no effect on its content and form. .... The very principles ... (by) which knowledge is to be criticized, are themselves found to be socially and historically conditioned." The historical relativity thesis establishes at best only a contingent causal relation between a man's social commitments and his canons of cognitive validity. What is the cognitive status of the thesis that a social perspective enters essentially into the content as well as the validation of every assertion about human affairs? Is this thesis meaningful and valid only for those who maintain it and who thus subscribe to certain values because of their distinctive social commitment? or is the thesis singularly exempt from the class of assertions to which it applies, so that its meaning and truth are not inherently related to the social perspective of those who assert it? If so, it is not evident why the thesis is so exempt. The thesis is then a conclusion of inquiry into human affairs that is presumably "objectively valid" in the usual sense of this phrase—and, if there is one such conclusion, it is not clear why there cannot be others as well. It is therefore not self-evident that a broader epistemological-cultural relativism supports ethical relativism.

Mere description of behavior cannot sustain the objective values of truth, a person, love, and justice. Only the God of revelation can support their normative character against their socially and personally lethal contradictories. JAMES D. STRAUSS

ETHICS, HISTORY OF. See also *Evolutionary Ethics; Greek Ethics; Kant.* Ethics, in its history from Plato to Jeremy Bentham, has been closely conjoined with politics. Political decisions require ethical judgments; an individual man cannot be separated from society; therefore there is no clear-cut distinction between ethics and politics, or between so-called personal ethics and social ethics.

To maintain some distinction, a degree of difference is inserted in the definition, making ethics a little more individual and politics a little more social.

Henry Sidgwick, the great ethical scholar of the nineteenth century, acknowledging the vagueness of ethics' boundaries, defined the subject as a rational procedure for determining what individual human beings "ought" to seek to realize by voluntary action. Ethics could also be defined as the study and eventually the justification of criteria by which one human life can be identified as better or worse than another.

Although some of the main views can be described by a title (e.g., Hedonism, the theory that pleasure is the supreme good; Altruism, the theory that not every natural impulse is selfish; Instrumentalism and Situationism, the theory that there are neither final ends nor fixed rules, and that each decision must be an individual aesthetic intuition), it is almost impossible to classify the historical views with exactitude, for there is too much room for cross classification.

If one should divide theories of ethics into teleological (those in which the value of an act is determined by some purpose) and ateleological, the only representative of the latter would be Kant; and this makes an unbalanced classification. Then too, teleological systems are so various that their similarity (of being based on purpose) seems superficial.

For the Epicureans the purpose of a good act is the sense pleasure of the individual. For the Utilitarians it is the pleasure (maybe sense pleasure, maybe not) of the whole human race. For Aristotle the purpose of man, by nature, is happiness, and this is a combination of intellectual and moral activity in which pleasure plays but a small role. For contemporary existentialism the good life is anything one chooses, provided he does not choose to conform to his society.

Christianity, in detail, is not teleological. One does not determine a right from a wrong choice by calculating the probability of its achieving a purpose. Neither are its rules determined by formal logic alone, as Kant's categorical imperative is. The particular rules of morality are the commands of God. Yet these have a purpose in glorifying God and advancing man's blessedness. But no man has any knowledge of just how this is accomplished.

Since, too, philosophers frequently agree on ethics while disagreeing on metaphysics and epistemology, and vice versa, the best procedure is to study each view in its historical matrix.   GORDON H. CLARK

ETHOS. The term generally refers to the operative values in a given society or social group. Thus one might, e.g., speak of the Puritan ethos as stressing hard work as a virtue (as Max Weber does in his well-known *The Protestant Ethics and the Spirit of Capitalism* New York, Scribner); or, describe the American ethos as one which admires technological advances; or, discuss the post-Renaissance Western ethos as one emphasizing the value of individualism. The Christian ethos would thus be a network of operative values, centering around the concept of love as defined in Scripture. In practice, however, the ethos of any Christian church or group has been and is an uneasy combination of the Christian ethos and the ethos prevailing in the culture and society in which the church finds itself. The operative values of the Russian Orthodox Church were heavily influenced by the ideas of Holy Russia and the historical mission of the Tsar which were prevalent in ecclesiastical circles; the Byzantine Church similarly found it difficult to disentangle its supposed Christian ethos from the imperial ambitions of Constantinople; the medieval Roman Catholic Church had operative values heavily infiltrated by feudal ideals; and the modern Protestant churches have often taken the ethos of capitalism and nationalism as the only God-given systems. It is understandable that the visible churches in the present state of imperfection can never attain a purely Christian ethos, though the attempt must always be made. Any given church, in its particular time and place, can perhaps, however, hope in practice to stress one or even several aspects of the Christian ethos which have not been sufficiently stressed by churches in other times and places. And, indeed, they should always strive to avoid giving allegiance to any ethos besides the Christian ethos.

DIRK W. JELLEMA

EUGENICS. See also *Genetics*. Eugenics is a movement that began the latter part of the last century and has as its goal the improvement of the hereditary endowment of the human race. Positive eugenic programs are designed to encourage hereditarily "superior" individuals to marry early and produce an above average number of children and negative programs are designed to discourage or prevent the marriage and propagation of hereditarily "inferior" persons.

In the first quarter of this century, eugenists actively lobbied for laws that would provide for the institutionalization of the less desirable elements of the population (e.g., the feeble minded and insane); for the sterilization of these groups as well as criminals; and for outlawing the marriage of the mentally deficient. Their efforts met with considerable success and most of the laws passed by the states in these areas were the direct result of the eugenics movement.

Many eugenists were convinced of the superiority of the Anglo-Saxon race and were alarmed at the influx into this country of what they considered to be inferior races. This racist bent along with uncritical genetics that characterized the early eugenic research lead ultimately to its almost complete demise by the 1930s. The coup de grace of the movement as originally conceived was the demonstration by Nazis Germany of what could be accomplished if a state took seriously the programs expounded by the eugenists. The institution in Germany of human breeding, mass sterilization (q.v.), euthanasia (q.v.) for the unfit, and genocide (q.v.), were all logical extensions of many an eugenic program.

Even if these programs are not carried to the extreme of Nazi Germany they are still open to question. On purely genetic grounds, there is nothing that insures that couples with outstanding abilities will necessarily have "superior" children. The shuffling of genes during sexual reproduction permits the production of offspring that can vary considerably from the norm of the parents. While many of a person's characteristics and abilities are genetically controlled, a very large environmental factor enters into their determination. Since there is still much to be learned on the relative importance of nature and nurture in the development of the total individual, is it morally acceptable to restrict the reproduction of what today appear to be inferior types before more is known about what made them "inferior"? How can the laws necessary to make an eugenic program succeed be applied in a democracy without abridging basic human freedoms? Superior physique, intellect or ability does not necessarily mean that a person will have superior moral character. An unusually gifted person can use his talents for altogether unworthy ends and in the end be a greater burden on society than one less gifted but with higher moral principles.

Today, while few people call themselves eugenists, there is still considerable interest in conserving and improving the hereditary endowment of mankind, primarily by geneticists. For example, the Nobel Prize winner, the late H. J. Muller, and others have suggested that this could be accomplished through artificial insemination (q.v.) by a donor (AID). Semen of outstanding men would be stored in sperm banks from which couples who wanted one or more children derived, at least on one side, from germinal material of an outstanding person, could make a selection. For the Christian, however, the use of artifical insemination raises some moral questions with respect to the Biblical view of sex and marriage which are not easily answered.

Another geneticist and Nobel Prize winner, Joshua Lederberg, has suggested that in the future it may be possible to make many copies of a given individual. This has been done with frogs and it may just be a matter of making use of some of the techniques already developed in man and perfecting a few new ones before this becomes a reality. If it ever is possible, should it be attempted? There are some real psychological and moral questions that need considering before such a program is undertaken.

Information on the inheritance of many human disorders now is made available through hereditary clinics, where couples who have reason to suspect they might pass on a heredity disorder can get genetic counseling. The parents, once informed, reach their own decision concerning having children. Should this be the case? Do parents that know they have a high risk of having a defective child have a right to have children? Certainly there are moral implications here, not only from the eugenic point of view of improving the race but also with respect to alleviating human suffering.

These eugenic programs deal solely with the physical betterment of man, with little or no thought about spiritual or moral implications.   DONALD S. ROBERTSON

EUTHANASIA. Euthanasia is the act of putting to death a person suffering from incurable, distressing disease. It is a violation of the Sixth Commandment: "Thou shalt not kill [murder]." If the sufferer consents to his own destruction, he becomes guilty of suicide (q.v.). Such consent does not relieve the killer of guilt for the sin of murder.

Giving drugs to relieve pain, however, is permitted. Proverbs 31:6, for instance, recommends the use of alcoholic drinks to relieve the suffering of the dying. Because alcohol is a narcotic drug, we may by analogy assume that other such drugs may be given for constructive purposes. Yet, the use of any drug with the intent to kill or to hasten death has no support, explicit or implicit, in the Bible.

The law in most jurisdictions where Christianity has prevailed is uncompromisingly against euthanasia. Bishop F. R. Barry of the Church of England would "with some misgiving" agree to a change in the law which would "provide that it is not an offence for a qualified medical practitioner to accelerate the death of a patient who is suffering from severe pain in an incurable and fatal illness, unless it is proved that the act was not done in good faith and with the patient's consent" (*Christian Ethics and Secular Society,* London, Hodder and Stoughton, 1966, p. 256). It is entirely possible, however, that if the laws were changed to legalize euthanasia, persons with ulterior motives might be more inclined to put pressures, subtle or otherwise, on patients and medical practitioners to bring about "mercy killings." Bishop Barry, incidently, does not support his reserved approval of euthanasia with arguments from the Bible.

On the other hand, that classical representative of Protestant interpretation of the Bible, *The Westminster Larger Catechism,* does not include mercy killing as a permissible reason for taking human life. In 1950, the General Assembly of the Presbyterian Church in the United States of America approved an overture pointing out that legislation which permits euthanasia is in direct conflict with the interpretation of the Sixth Commandment as given in the Constitution of the church. This interpretation is in harmony with Scripture. Job, for example, although he suffered excruciatingly and knew no reason for his sufferings, refused to "curse God and die." Now it is known that his suffering had meaning in God's plan, and we can infer from this that other sufferings may not be without purpose. Moreover, the possibility always remains that a cure will be discovered for a supposedly incurable disease.

📖 Glanville Llewelyn Williams, *The Sanctity of Life and the Criminal Law,* New York, Knopf, 1957.   STEPHEN M. REYNOLDS

EVANGELICAL SOCIAL CONCERN. See also *Humanitarianism; Socialism; Social Service.* Christianity burst into a corrupt world with a brilliantly new moral radiance. The New Testament represents Christ as coming in the fulness of time (Gal. 4:4). The old pagan faiths were disintegrating, the prevailing cyclical view of history offered no real hope to mankind, and even Israel's holy cultus was losing its appeal. The moral level of society was dismal, and sin prevailed in many forms. Life without God did not fill men with holy joy and with a purpose for life. Into this discouraged world came Christ and his Spirit-transformed disciples, filled with holy joy, motivated by a love which the pagans could not grasp, and proclaiming Good News—the message that God has provided a Saviour for individual sinners and for the race. These Christians lived in tiny communities knit together in the power of the Holy Spirit, little colonies of heaven. They thought of themselves as pilgrims on their way to the celestial city, but they were very much concerned to manifest the love of Christ in all human relationships. Their *Kyrios* (Lord, emperor) was the resurrected Christ, enthroned at the right hand of God and destined to come in the glory of the Father with all his holy angels.

These early Christians insisted on bringing all of life under the lordship of Jesus Christ. Not only had Christ by his atoning death reconciled men to God (II Cor. 5:19); he had also taken away both the guilt and bondage of sin, and had vanquished the devil as well (Rom. 3:21—8:39; Heb. 2:14, 15). Such sins as moral inpurity were not even to be mentioned in the new holy community (Eph. 5:3). This was the answer of the early disciples to all forms of prostitution, including liaisons with *heterae.* Marriage was to be only in the Lord in the new Kingdom of God (I Cor. 7:39), and believers were to be strictly faithful to their spouses in a lifelong union of love (Matt. 5:32). This was the answer of the early church to the divorce evil of the Roman Empire. It is men and women of this kind of moral purity who build into society a strong fabric of integrity and strength. Such people are the salt of the earth and the light of the world (Matt. 5:13, 14).

Life was cheap in the pre-Christian world: murder, abortions, infant exposure, war: people died in great numbers without anyone being troubled in conscience. The early Christians brought a new concern into society on these points. Murder was regarded as a serious violation of God's majestic moral law. Abortions and the exposure of infants were vigorously condemned also. And for a variety of reasons (the sacredness of life, the military oath of allegiance to the earthly emperor, the Roman *Kyrios,* the required offering of incense to the emperor) the early Christians for the first century and a half rejected even the profession of being a soldier. In the 170s Celsus chided them for their disloyalty to the Empire, a charge which Origen vigorously rejected seventy years later. Origen insisted that by their prayers for peace, and by their inculcation of piety in the youth, Christians were making a greater contribution than those who went onto the field of battle for the emperor.

The pagans simply could not grasp how it was that the early believers so deeply loved one another. Did their terms, brother/sister for fellow-believers, perhaps imply incestuous relationships? The second-century apologists had stoutly to defend the moral integrity of the Christian community, while the Christians went right on living by love. "We always keep together," declared Justin at the middle of the second century in his first *Apology.* That is, they lived in close Christian fellowship—not in a new type of economic system, but in *agapē* love that so modified economics that they shared richly with those in need (cf. Acts 4:34, 35:)

The New Testament reminds us that our *politeuma* (citizenship, commonwealth) is in heaven (Phil. 3:20). Christians therefore live in this life with a somewhat loose attachment to the concerns of this world: wealth and other earthly matters (cf. I Cor. 7:29-31). Christians are deeply concerned for the welfare not only of their own fellow citizens in their homeland, but for all men around the globe.

In summary Christians relate to all men in *agapē* love. It is the love of Christ which constrains Christians. The intent of Christ's death was that his disciples should henceforth not live unto themselves but unto Christ. And the Christ who reconciled us to God has committed to us to the ministry of reconciliation (II Cor. 5:14-21).

Evangelism is the greatest commission Christians can undertake in the area of social concern. But Christian love is not confined to "souls," but extends necessarily to the needs of total persons: spiritual, physical, social. Pious remarks are no substitute for social action, in feeding and clothing the poor, for example (James 2:14-26). But neither is social action an adequate expression of evangelical concern. All eleemosynary work is to be undertaken "in the Name of Christ." It is in his name that the sick shall be visited, the poor fed, those in prison assisted (Matt. 25:31-46; cf. also Heb. 13:3). Evangelical scholars and leaders such as John Wesley were concerned for the reform of prisons. And the Colonial John Woolman was burdened for the voluntary manumission of slaves. Christian concerns of this type expressed in Christ's name should lead ultimately to an aroused national conscience and to the prevention of social evils by federal law.

⇀ Ray C. Petry, *A History of Christianity, Readings,* New York, Prentice-Hall, 1962; Karl Heussi, *Kopendium der Kirchengeschicte,* J. C. B. Mohr, Zwoelfte Auflage, 1960; C. J. Cadoux, *The Early Church and the World,* New York, Scribner, 1925.   J. C. WENGER

EVANGELISM, ETHICAL ASPECTS. Those who deny the propriety of any evangelism (which they often label "proselytism") should, but rarely do, oppose efforts to persuade others to change their minds on any subject. To argue that people should be left to their original religions reveals both disbelief in the historic Christian claim to be the only true religion and a fundamental misunderstanding of evangelism. With few exceptions, Christians in recent centuries have opposed forcing "conversion," recognizing that only voluntary belief of the gospel is valid. Today the ethical problem is the use of force by many governments to hinder voluntary conversion.

Those who approve evangelism in principle also use the term "proselytism" more narrowly to mean evangelistic methods deemed unethical. The term is further applied to efforts to persuade recognized Christians to change their allegiance from one group to another. It is understandable that leaders have difficulty believing their followers would depart unless unethically enticed. In principle, however, the same motivations for evangelism also produce efforts by some to convince their fellow Christians to change their understanding of Biblical teaching.

Proselytism and other evangelistic abuses do occur, but no one seems to admit to them. Christians should therefore seek to formulate clearly in advance their own ethical guidelines and procedures. Many abuses are related to the presumed need to report large numbers of converts. (The only converts numbered in the NT were Jewish.) What the evangelist sees as voluntary response, the detached observer might sense as psychological manipulation or materialistic inducement. Evangelistic work among youth requires special sensitivity to the unethical coercion which elicits emotional decision without genuine persuasion. Evangelistic appeals must be based on adequate communication of the facts of the gospel. When persons are urged to believe without telling them what, it should not be surprising to find numerous relapses.

Evangelistic work, well supported among unresponsive populations, may continue at the expense of intensifying outreach and follow-up where people are believing in large numbers. The "church growth" approach to evangelism focuses attention on this common problem. One can be out-of-step with the Holy Spirit either by moving ahead or lagging behind.

Some dishonest persons have practiced itinerant evangelism. This has long beclouded the profession of evangelism as a whole, especially among those who know little of the far more numerous sincere evangelists.

⇀ *Church Growth Bulletin, Evangelical Missions Quarterly* and *International Review of Mission,* regularly discuss ethical questions related to cross-cultural evangelism. Unfortunately nothing comparable deals with intra-cultural and youth evangelism.   DONALD TINDER

EVIL. See also *Sin.* Evil is among the most intractable of human problems, touching as it does the natural as well as the moral order. The distinction between surd evils and moral evil further raises the issue of their relationship. In the history of man we observe at least four forms of evil: ignorance (evil often results from even well-intentioned acts), ugliness (distortion of life and environment), suffering (due to disease, catastrophe and evil intent), and sin. Of these, Christians identify sin as the worst form of evil because it is the corruption of man's inner being. It is not curable by human progress, is an obstacle to man's dealing with other evils, and hinders faith in God the Creator.

As to the co-existence of good and evil in the world, five possibilities present themselves. (1) Only good is real and evil is illusory, as in certain types of Idealism (Christian Science is a modern religious form). Such idealism attempts to cure evil simply by thinking it away. (2) Only evil is real and good is illusory. Some contemporary forms of pessimism over life and the world order reflect this tendency to deify evil and satanic powers. (3) The very distinction between good and evil is illusory, as held by some monistic mystical systems. (4) Good and evil co-exist as eternal competing principles, as for example, in Manicheanism. (5) Only good is eternally and ultimately real, but evil is a present reality within the created universe. This last possibility expresses Christian belief as based upon the Biblical revelation. Evil for the Christian, like contingency and freedom, must be accepted as realities within the created order which cannot be explained away or dissolved into some more ultimate reality.

Reference to the created order points to the prior and crucial significance of cosmic models in one's thinking about the problems of evil. Systems of Idealism since Plato and Oriental religions such as Hinduism see God as the Absolute and evil as nonbeing or illusion from which philosophy offers escape. Modern process philosophers like E. S. Brightman and A. N. Whitehead see evil as a built-in element of the natural order against which God as finite must struggle in quest of his own ultimate perfection.

Ancient forms of Materialism and modern naturalistic variants are also reductionist in expounding evil. If the world is a unilinear one-level process then no criterion exists by which to judge the better or worse. Reality is then ultimately a blind and meaningless surge of energy.

The problems of evil appears at its sharpest in Biblical teaching because Christians believe in the goodness, omniscience and omnipotence of God. Central to Christian understanding is the doctrine of creation *ex nihilo*. Genesis 1-3 are not accidental first chapters of the Bible; rather, creation of the world by God is the key to all further understanding. In contrast to Idealism and Materialism, the Biblical creationist view in relation to evil is neither escapist nor reductionist.

The doctrine of creation implies that ultimate reality is of the nature of personal life, mechanism is not the mode of the relation between God and the world, contingency and freedom are real, and grace is not illusion. The full implications of the doctrine of creation relieve Christians of any need to resort to notions that evil is non-being, privation of goodness, or illusion. Christians reject merely verbal solutions to the real problem.

If God is good, whence is evil? Christians rest their view ultimately upon the Biblical revelation of God's purpose. Of the various forms of evil, sin seems to be the primeval one. The doctrine of the Fall expresses the truth that evil has originated within creation through creaturely rebellion. While some (like N. P. Williams) have postulated the fall of a world-soul, the traditional doctrine of the pre-mundane angelic Fall coheres with the doctrine of creation because it makes of persons and personal relations the ultimate nature of reality (Matt. 25:41; John 8:44; II Peter 2:4; I John 3:8; Jude 6). Thus while evil has forms other than sin, the moral model of the universe which Christians hold in contrast to the illusionist and determinist models places the origin of evil in sin.

For Christians evil is cured by God's action alone, involving no solution short of the redemptive death of the Son of God. By the doctrine of creation Christians assign to God responsibility for creating the conditions in which evil and sin could arise. Yet our person responsibility and guilt for evil choices, correlated with the fall of Adam (cf. *Fall of Man*) though they be, is vast and terrible. By the doctrine of the Atonement (q.v.) Christians acknowledge that God is dealing with evil and sin by himself bearing them in the incarnate Lord's perfect sacrifice. The moral relations between God and the world have been transformed by the triumph of Christ over sin and death (Col. 2:13-15; Heb. 2:14). This triumph constitutes the moral basis of the Christian life in its relations to evil in this world (Rom. 12:17; II Cor. 4:10; I Peter 4:12-13). The Christian's response to evil is taken up into Christ's own victory (Rom. 8:17). Through the Cross and Resurrection of Christ there is anticipated God's final triumph when the natural order and redeemed men together will be delivered from the bane of evil (Rom. 8:19-25; Rev. 21:1-8).

📖 P. T. Forsyth, *The Justification of God*, Naperville, Ill., Allenson, 1957; John Hick, *Evil and the Love of God*, Brooklyn, Fontana, 1968; Leonard Hodgson, *For Faith and Freedom*, I, Oxford, Blackwell, 1956; H. E. Hopkins, *The Mystery of Suffering*, Inter Varsity Press, 1959; C. E. M. Joad, *God and Evil*, London, Faber, 1943; C. S. Lewis, *The Problem of Pain*, London, Macmillan, 1940; F. Petit, *The Problems of Evil*, 1959; Nelson Pike, ed., *God and Evil*, New York, Prentice-Hall, 1964; James Orr, *The Christian View of God and the World*, 1897; J. S. Whale, *The Christian Answer to the Problem of Evil*, SCM, 1957.

SAMUEL J. MIKOLASKI

EVOLUTIONARY ETHICS. See also *Cultural Relativism; Darwin and Darwinian Ethics; Social Darwinism*. The concept of evolutionary ethics as used by various authors refers to four separable ideas. Consequently, each of these ideas must be considered individually.

1. The first use of the concept of evolutionary ethics is for the ethical system which results from the logical extrapolation of the principles of bilogical evolution into the field of ethics. Darwinian evolution made popular the concepts of struggle, competition, selection, survival, and extinction. Evolutionary success is survival of the most fit at the expense of the least fit. Therefore, some evolutionists constructed an ethic derived from those concepts which accepted the functional necessity of hate, war, famine, and interpersonal hostility because only through the exercise of these attitudes and actions can the survival of the fittest be assured. Such an ethic is obviously opposed to Biblical ethics. Thus, Sir Arthur Keith rejected Christian ethics because " . . . the ethic of Christianity is in fierce opposition to that sponsored by human nature—the human nature which has been fashioned in the course of evolution for evolutionary purposes" (as P. Kropotkin, *Evolution and Ethics*).

Other individuals equally committed to biological evolution, have denounced the overemphasis on conflict and hostility and have emphasized that evolution does not refer to a process of the individual but of the group, and that success is to be measured in terms of group survival. Group survival is dependent on the altruistic behavior of individual members who put group interest above individual interest. Therefore, group concern or altruistic behavior becomes a virtue. In this way an attempt is made to derive an ethic which is more consistent with traditional Judeo-Christian ethics. This attempt, however, is unsuccessful.

2. The second use of the concept refers to an ethic which has resulted from an assumed evolution of man's moral nature. Here ethics are viewed as arising as a direct result of the appearance of self-awareness in the growing human consciousness. Socially-oriented, learned behavior, that is, social consciousness, is viewed as evolving first, as

is demonstrated in the social carnivores such as dogs and wolves. But the development of a human ethic necessitates more than this, for it is the result of social consciousness and self-awareness. Ethics arise when man finds that he has to make conscious choices in a social context. Man's activity was no longer directed by the straightforward actions of an unthinking brain but by the conscious functioning of the human mind which can foresee the altruistic and anti-social, the good and the evil results of its actions.

3. The third use of the concept refers to the development of human ethical systems through the history of man. The emphasis of this aspect is one of development, not of origin. Implicit in this idea of development is the concept of progressiveness. So it implies not only change through time but also a direction—a direction from simpler to more complex, from naiveté to sophistication, from lower to higher. Such emphasis is found in the nineteenth century social evolutionism of Lewis Henry Morgan who postulated the division of human history into three basic stages—savagery, barbarism, and civilization. With each level in his unilinear sequence of cultural levels he postulated an accompanying social ethic.

4. The fourth use of the concept of evolutionary ethics emphasizes the adaptive nature of ethical systems. In fact this is not evolution in the generally understood sense of the word. Rather, ethical systems are not viewed as static sets of rules but as dynamic and adaptive systems of values. They are adaptive first to varying social conditions, such as the size and composition of the group. Consequently, as group size changes, so do the social norms defining appropriate social relations. These changes are not considered to be universal, inevitable changes which would imply ethical progression or advancement. This concept is consistent with the concept as proposed by Julian Steward. Here no evaluative transcultural

judgments could be made on the different ethical systems that result in various situations. A basic emphasis of Julian Steward is that basic value systems are largely the result of exploitative techniques utilized in a particular environment (cf. *Primitive Ethics*).

Because of these various usages, it is difficult to make a judgment concerning evolutionary ethics that is equally valid or applicable to these different usages. With respect to use number 1: it must be objected that it is not methodologically valid to extrapolate a principle derived from the study of one type of phenomenon to another type of phenomenon—i.e., the application of a biological principle to an ethical system. This is true whether one is using this methodology either to deny or to support Christian ethics. Rejection of this methodology of extrapolation is entirely independent of the acceptance or rejection of biological evolution as a valid biological principle.

With respect to use number 2: the evolutionary development of man's moral nature —the Biblical perspective attributes man's moral nature, defined as the image of God, to a specific creative act of God and indicates that man's moral nature was not the product of an evolutionary development.

The Biblical concept of the fall and the resulting alienation from God makes the view of evolutionary ethics, as expressed in use number 3: unacceptable, because a progressive development of ethics from lower to higher is not evidenced in man as a counterpart of the development of civilization. It appears that man's moral nature has not experienced such a development throughout human history.

Thus view number 4, which is quite independent of the evolutionary concept as generally understood, would be the only acceptable and valid use of the concept of evolutionary ethics. For here the emphasis is on the dynamic and adaptive nature of human ethical systems rather than on unilinear, progressive development.

An early comprehensive survey is *Evolutionary Ethics: A Review of the Systems of Ethics Founded on the Theory of Evolution* by C. M. Williams. Other noted books are *Morals in Evolution* (2 vols.) by L. T. Hobhouse, 1906; *Evolution and Ethics* by T. Huxley, 1893; *Ethics, Origin and Developments* by P. A. Kropotkin, 1936; *Evolution and Ethics* by Sir A. Keith, 1946; and *The Ethical Animal* by C. H. Waddington, New York, Athenium, 1960. A recent brief work is *Evolutionary Ethics* by A. G. M. Flew, New York, St. Martin, 1967.   DONALD R. WILSON

EXAMPLE OF JESUS. See *Imitation of Christ.*

EXCELLENCE. See also *Perfectionism; Virtues.* To excel is to go beyond the average and at times to achieve the best. The history of philosophy and ethics has made "perfection" and self-realization important themes that have challenged man to stretch toward moral and spiritual excellence. Jesus commands our aspiration to perfection: "Be ye perfect."

When the theme of excellence has been inordinate it has resulted in destructive guilt feelings. Fromm feels Protestant Christianity has created unhealthy ethical and psychological results. Fromm considers Protestantism as guilt-producing religion. "It creates the problem which its message of salvation is intended to answer" (J. Stanley Glen, *Eric Fromm: A Protestant Critique,* Philadelphia, Westminster, 1966, p. 197).

Concern about excellence is often denigrated as "Puritanism" or "Victorianism." However, if relevance means active involvement with current ethical norms it is difficult to find much "Puritanism" over which to be concerned. A more appropriate concern may be "Neo-Puritanism" which gives many people guilt feelings for their inability to enjoy and practice present norms of sensate orgy ethics touted by fiction and theater.

The positive values gained from stress on excellence include awareness of the inescapable factors of human limitations. We are at best "earthen vessels." However, it is better to aim at stars and live in tree tops than aim at snails and be certain of an abode in muck.

Post-Sputnik education spurred stress on excellence in American schools. But present hyper-permissive trends have affected both the educational and ethical climate. The "do your own thing" creed unites a growing army of mediocrity. "Your own thing" has become the opposite of freedom and individualism—a contemporary dogmaticism.

The Christian is not to be an isolated monk either at a monastery or Walden Pond, but is to be a tough-minded realist who must with God's help do the best he can with his gifts great or small.

Dedicated Marxists and other non-Christians continue to challenge world purpose and will with Sputniks and ideas. If non-Christians enlist so much energy and excellence, can Christians afford the luxury of less than their best?   WALTER H. JOHNSON

EXCEPTION. The English word "exception" (deriving from the Latin *capio* "take," and *ex* "out," through the French *excepter*) relates to the act of excluding a particular issue or item from a general description or to the state of being so excluded.

Some to spring from thee, who never
  touch'd
Th' *excepted* tree. . . .
        (Milton, *Paradise Lost,* xi. 426)
In ethics *exceptionism* has become a vogue word. The question it poses is, If moral principles are absolute, how can there be any justifiable exceptions? The problem arises whether the ethical norm is conceived of as love, utility, self-realization, the general good, or whatever.

1. *The exception becomes the rule.* Contemporary situational ethics (q.v.) and the

new morality (q.v.) give credence to this judgment by the contention either that exceptions arise out of particular situations which determine their ethical significance or that they are the result of intuitive responses to unique occasions. In the first case the tendency is towards moral anarchy in that contrary acts can be equally justified. For if an *agapaic* qualification be held to give a beneficial quality to an act in one situation and another quality to a similar act in another situation then each situation becomes itself an exception. Thus love could in one instance require chastity while in another it would justify fornication. On the other hand, where the exception is regarded as an intuitive response to a unique occasion it presents itself as a featureless act exhibiting no characteristics for moral appraisal. Here the tendency is towards naturalism in that the moral act is read as a natural response to a given stimulus; and this in its turn leads on to subjectivism (q.v.) by making the acting individual himself the creator and judge of what is ethically justifiable.

2. *The exception proves the rule.* Here it is argued that if exceptions are allowed only as exceptional then the rule is the more firmly established. Justifiable exceptions far from breeching the dike serve rather to strengthen the ethical rule or principle in those realms where the excepted case has not its home. The problem here is to make clear why the moral rule or principle does not hold in a particular case. The tendency in this context is towards sophistry and rationalization.

3. *The exception negates the rule.* The Christian who regards the Bible as providing the divinely appointed ethical norm and demand, particularized in Jesus Christ and elaborated in the New Testament record, will hesitate to admit exceptions. For him the New Testament sets forth an absolute ethic grounded in the character of God which allows of no escape-clauses.

David Holdcroft, "A Plea for Excuses?", *Philosophy*, vol. XLIV, No. 70, Oct., 1969; Leonard G. Miller, "Rules and Exceptions," in *Ethics*, vol. lxvi, July, 1956, pp. 262-270; I. T. Ramsey, *Christian Ethics and Contemporary Philosophy*, London, SCM, 1966; Paul Ramsey, "The Case of the Curious Exception," in *Norm and Context in Christian Ethics*, Gene H. Outka and Paul Ramsey, eds., New York, Scribner, 1969, ch. 4.

H. DERMOT McDONALD

EXISTENTIALIST ETHICS. See also *Bultmann; I-Thou Relationship; Knowledge and Ethics.* Existential moralists seek to gain ethical perspective through describing and evaluating "the human condition." The fundamental moral claim is that man is truly human to the extent that he discovers his own value-nature (essence) through decisive action (his "existence") as opposed to starting with some received moral system.

Actually the label since 1940 has become a broad umbrella. It would be misleading to suppose that writers as diverse as Kierkegaard (q.v.) and Nietzsche (q.v.) in the nineteenth century and such successors as Heidegger, Sartre, Marcel, and Bultmann share one ethical philosophy. Some existentialists are atheistic, others religious. Yet all are committed to a philosophy of personal involvement and to a revolt against "systems" which—pushed to an extreme—requires a subjectively relativistic ethical stance. In practice, however, most escape that extreme by appealing to the humanistic, Marxian materialist (Sartre since 1960), or to theological perspectives to bridge the gap between the subjective and the objective, and to move from an individualistic approach to the makings of a social ethic.

Despite the diversity, certain basic characteristics bearing on ethics are noteworthy. Existentialist literature offers valuable phenomenological insight into man's moral life. At the same time it evidences striking philosophical and theological weaknesses.

Beginning with Kierkegaard stress has been placed on (1) *subjective individuality,* or personal involvement, as distinguished from being merely theoretical and detached, in making moral choices. Sartre says, "existence precedes essence," subjectivity must be the starting point for genuine understanding. This characteristic is therefore set alongside another: (2) a strong *opposition to "systems"* which, like Hegel's, tend to fit human existence into abstract or pre-conceived molds. At its best existentialism urges each individual to discover for himself what his own "authenticity" as a person requires in a given ethical situation. It calls for setting aside the rationalization of behavior and mere conformity to the "crowd."

Taken as a pair these two themes, subjective individuality and opposition to "systems," have considerable justification. Certainly the stress upon the individual can be viewed as a corrective revolt against an abstract anthropology. Kierkegaard uses the terms "subjectivity," "inwardness," and "passion," to lay stress on the interpenetration in experience of thought, action, and decision. So it is also with Heidegger, Sartre, and Jaspers. Due in part to the ambiguities present in existentialist writings, interpreters disagree as to how close the position comes to irrationalism. A careful reading shows that existentialists wish to avoid that extreme as well as that of rationalism. Kierkegaard allows that the methods of science may have their proper place, but understanding is not an objective and detached apprehension nor is thinking reducible to a purely theoretical activity. Existentialists agree that knowledge of one's self arises only in situations where one is already involved in decision and action. The high point of "subjectivity" for the religious existentialists comes with "revelation," the interaction between God as Subject and man as subject. All existentialists are concerned with a phenomenological study of man's existential subjectivity: starting with the immediate content (phenomena) of

lived experience and proceeding to analyze and describe that content. Out of this has come a new "system" created by Heidegger, using such existential categories as anxiety, ambiguity, estrangement, self-deception, and authenticity.

A third claim, made in its most dramatic form by the atheistic existentialists is that (3) *human existence is basically absurd* (Sartre, Camus), that man has been thrown into a world that lacks cosmic meaning (Heidegger). Nietzsche's proclamation through Zarathustra of the death of God helped to mold this perspective. Life is not simply paradoxical, as in Kierkegaard's view; life is absurd in the fundamental sense that there are no rational theological or philosophical categories for explaining it. Man must accept the reality of his "being towards death" (Heidegger) without Kierkegaard's hope in God who meets the man who reaches out in faith from his "sickness unto death." For Nietzsche no appeal can be made, for example, to the Christian spirit of self-sacrifice; this runs counter to man's natural desire for survival, and is also being used by the church to create men of weakness and hypocrisy. In contrast, he offers the self-sufficient superman who finds his values in himself through creative self-assertion. He breaks with all prevailing systems of morality, and transvalues all existing ideas of the good to create his own positive values.

These existentialists are perhaps most persuasive at that point at which they agree with the Christian perspective in planting absurdity firmly in man's own moral folly. This is expressed graphically by Camus through the character of Meursault in *The Stranger* (New York, Knopf, 1942) who is depicted as drifting along and turning his life into a meaningless pursuit of momentary pleasure. He becomes a total stranger to his own past and refuses to accept responsibility for it. But Camus, too, fails to distinguish between man's moral absurdity and the supposition that life must be lived within a classical, cosmic fatalism. In *The Myth of Sisyphus* (New York, Knopf) where man is pictured as doomed to roll the stone up the hill only to have it roll down again, man's dignity as a conscious being lies in his adoption of projects in spite of the basic futility of life.

Why not settle then for nausea and despair? Perhaps there is a partial answer in existentialism's basic contention: (4) *the inescapable freedom to choose,* which is the fundamental fact of being human and the *sin qua non* for a qualitative existence. All existentialists agree that the quality of life is up to the individual to determine. Whether he moves in a religious or in an atheistic-humanistic direction must be determined by the individual's own radically free decision in concrete situations. So Kierkegaard in *Either-Or* and in *Stages on Life's Way* points to alternative ethical life-styles from among which all men, even if by default, choose. He contrasts three ways of life: aesthetic, ethical, and religious. The first centers in the pleasures of self-interest, the pursuit of happiness and security either by following the crowd or by loosing oneself in rational speculation. Drifting is a fundamental sign of inauthenticity. By contrast the ethical man is one who makes decisions and seeks with passion and concern to follow them through. The ethical way is not simply a rational morality of rule keeping (Kant) or of supposing that the problems of ethics can be solved by cognitive means. It does take into account one's duties to others but it sees these as arising in the accepting of one's self as involved with others, as a historical being with a past and a future, a being conscious of freedom. So viewed, the ethical way merges easily with the religious. Here, however, consciousness of sin and of estrangement from God enter in along with the existential significance of suffering, forgiveness, and faith. At its best the religious way includes the aesthetic and the ethical

dimensions of life and puts them into a new perspective.

Sartre leaves us with a more radical and puzzling conception of freedom. It is also incomplete in that he has never fulfilled the promise of *Being and Nothingness* to develop his existentialist ethics and has since forsaken the project in favor of promoting his own version of Marxism. As an existentialist Sartre offers an analysis of man who is what he is due to pure contingency, with all the feeling of futility, disposability, and sense of absurdness that this may bring. But this same man can apparently achieve authenticity as he becomes conscious of his freedom and accepts the anguish that comes with realizing that there is nothing which commits him to choosing in any particular way. With the death of God all things are possible, even the project of trying to make himself God. There are no rules save the ones he sets for himself as he defines himself and his values. Unlike most humanists, Sartre appeals to no rational directives for conduct, and in that sense he has no ethics at all (cf. *Decision*). But that he was a humanist as well as existentialist is reflected in his claim that the authentic man is one who accepts responsibility and treats his choices as ones which are made for all mankind. The "norm" of *Existentialism Is Humanism* (New York, French and European Publications, 1945) is "so act as to let others be free while oneself remaining free." Beyond that he has been largely negative—giving us some vivid phenomenological descriptions of life as ordinarily lived in "self-deception."

Sartre has left it to others, like Hazel Barnes, to suggest how ethics may be grounded in radical freedom without God. Clearly, to justify and apply to social ethics one's private choice of values requires appealing to a larger philosophy and theology. Heidegger, while trying to remain neutral religiously, sought to show that the decision which one makes authentically in solitude must include being-with-others. Still others like Jaspers, Marcel, Barth, Brunner, Bonhoeffer, Bultmann, and Tillich have in various ways made central for the ethical outlook Kierkegaard's Christ who becomes contemporary in man's act of existential faith (cf. *Dialectical Ethics*).

📖 Hazel E. Barnes, *An Existentialist Ethics*, New York, Knopf, 1967; James Collins, *The Existentialists*, Chicago, Regnery, 1952; Paul Edwards, ed., *Encyclopedia of Philosophy*, New York, Macmillan, 1967, V. 3, Kai Nielson, "Problems of Ethics," & Alasdair MacIntyre, "Existentialism"; Jerry Gill, ed., *Philosophy Today No. 1*, New York, Macmillan, 1968, Arthur Lessing, "Marxian Existentialism"; Martin Heidegger, *Being and Time*, New York, Harper, 1962; Walter Kaufmann, *Existentialism from Dostoevsky to Sartre*, New York, Meridian, 1956; Søren Kierkegaard, *Stages on Life's Way*, 1940, *Concluding Unscientific Postscript*, 1941, and *Either/Or*, 1949, Princeton, Princeton University; Jean-Paul Sartre, *Existentialism*, 1947, and *Being and Nothingness*, 1956, New York, Philosophical Library; Calvin O. Schrag, *Existence and Freedom*, Evanston, Ill., Northwestern University, 1961; Mary Warnock, *The Philosophy of Sartre*, London, Hutchinson, 1965; Julius Weinberg & Keith Yandell, eds., *Ethics*, New York, Holt Rinehart & Winston, 1971, essays by Jean-Paul Sartre, and Alvin Plantinga.   WILLIAM W. PAUL

EXOGAMY. See also *Endogamy*. This term as used in social anthropology implies the restriction of marriage to those partners who are outside (Greek, *ex-*) one's own tribal or clan group. The terms of membership within the group are variously reckoned, sometimes being understood territorially but more often in regard to consanquinity, i.e., blood-relationship. Thus marriage is universally prohibited between parent and child, brother and sister.

Marriage ethics in the Biblical tradition take cognizance of this factor in the Levitical law (Lev. 18:6-16; cf. Deut. 27:23). Incestuous relationships are abhorrent to God (Lev. 20:23; cf. I Cor. 5:2, 5).   RALPH P. MARTIN

EXPEDIENCE. See *License*.

EXPIATION. This term signifies the removal of a sin or a crime. It is an impersonal term, which may be the reason it is used in RSV and other recent translations in passages where AV reads "propitiation." This latter term means the taking away of wrath and it applies to persons. It can scarcely be doubted that the modern preference for "expiation" is due to a dislike for the concept of the wrath of God. If God is not really hostile to men on account of their sin there is no need for propitiation and no place for it. Then expiation may be held to sum up all that Christ did in his atoning work.

We need not doubt that expiation may fitly be applied to what Christ did for men. He really did take away our sin. But the term is an inadequate one. It overlooks far too much. In the first place, it is not a good translation of *hilaskesthai* and its cognates (see evidence in my *The Apostolic Preaching of the Cross*, London, Tyndale, 3rd ed., 1965, chaps. V-VI). These words mean that wrath is put away by an offering, not simply that sin is dealt with. They apply to relationships between persons. They show that in part man's forgiveness must be understood as the putting away of the wrath of God by the offering of Jesus Christ on the cross.

In the second place, not only is expiation a bad translation, it is also an inadequate concept. Those who favor it but reject the idea of the wrath of God never seem to face questions like, "Why should sin be expiated?" If there is no such thing as the wrath of God there seems no reason for expiation. But if there is such a thing we need something more. And if personal relationships are involved we need a more personal term.   LEON MORRIS

EXPOSURE. See *Abandonment; Infanticide; Nudism*.

EXTORTION. Reliance upon methods of extortion is regarded by the Biblical writers as the antithesis of trust in God (Ps. 62:1). The Psalmist warns against trust in extortion and robbery (Ps. 109:11; cf. Isa. 16:4) because any benefit derived thereby will end in delusive hopes (Ps. 62:10). Surely extortion cannot be depended upon for salvation (Ps. 49:5 ff.). Ezekiel mentions extortion as a crime when expounding the truth that God deals justly and retributively with everyone (Ezek. 18:18).

Jesus accused some Pharisees of extortion and rapacity (Matt. 23:25). Paul reminds Corinthian Christians that extortioners shall not inherit the Kingdom of God.

WATSON E. MILLS

F

FAITH. Faith is a concept that raises two main problems: (1) its definition or psychological analysis and (2) its function. The second of these, concerned chiefly with the doctrine of justification by faith alone, will be treated only briefly.

Augustine was probably the first to define faith. In his treatise *Concerning the Predestination of the Saints* he said, "Thinking is prior to believing. . . . To believe is nothing other than to think with assent. For not all who think believe . . . but all who believe think; and they think believing and believe thinking." To the present day the Roman church defines faith as assent, "fiducial assent" (cf. *The New Catholic Encyclopedia,* New York, McGraw-Hill, 1967).

The Reformers, though more concerned with justification, of necessity considered faith. That faith or belief had an intellectual content was universally accepted. Aside from the mystics, Kant was the first to speak of a faith without knowledge. Jacobi, Schleiermacher, some Modernists, and more particularly the contemporary dialectical theologians follow this line. Brunner (q.v.) states, "God and the medium of conceptuality are mutually exclusive." But the Reformers unanimously agreed that belief requires a known object.

The second element in belief is assent. A person may know or understand a proposition and yet not believe it. To believe is to think with assent. Assent is an act of will: it is the voluntary acceptance of the proposition as true.

By combining knowledge and assent Calvin was able to oppose the Romish idea of implicit faith. The *Institutes* (III.2) complain that the schoolmen "have fabricated the notion of implicit faith, a term with which they have honored the grossest ignorance. . . . Is this faith—to understand nothing? Faith consists not in ignorance, but in knowledge."

The early Reformers were inclined to include assurance of salvation in their definition of faith. But there were many variations. Cunningham (cf. bibliography) reports seven different views. Later Reformed theologians definitely excluded assurance (cf. the Westminster Confession), but came to add *fiducia* as a third element in addition to knowledge and assent. They failed, however, to give an intelligible account of *fiducia,* restricting themselves to synonyms or illustrations (cf. Thomas Manton, *Exposition of the Epistle of James,* pp. 216ff., Marshallton, Del., Sovereign Grace Book Club, 196-). This defective view is so common today that many ministers have never heard of the earlier Reformed views.

The doctrine of faith, like all doctrines, must be deduced from Scripture. One cannot make an empirical analysis of experience and hope to arrive at the Christian position on faith, regeneration, or anything. Because the Scriptural material is so copious, all that can be offered here is a sample study restricted to John. John speaks of faith about one hundred times; more accurately it should be said that John uses the term *faith* only once, while the other ninety-nine times he uses the verb *believe*. Consonant with this, John puts great emphasis on the intellectual content of faith and supports his emphasis by asserting that Christ is the Logos or Reason of God, who himself is truth.

Sometimes the object of the verb believe is a noun or pronoun: name, doctrine, Son, Moses, me, him. No one should conclude from this that belief in a person is any different from belief in a truth, for in most cases it is easy to see the doctrine or proposition in the context even when the word-object is a pronoun (John 4:21; 5:38; 8:31, 45, 46; 10:37).

Twenty-five percent of instances of the verb *believe* have the propositional object written out in full, if not in the verse itself, at least in the context (2:22; 3:12; 4:21, 41, 50; 5:47; 6:69; etc.). These two sets of references show that the immediate and proper object of faith or belief is a proposition. To believe the Son, or me, or Moses, is to believe what the person said.

In contrast, the Liberals of the twentieth century want a "faith" in a god who is unknowable and silent because he is impotent to give us any information to believe. This anti-intellectualism undermines all good news and makes gospel information useless.

But according to John, and Paul as well, assent to doctrine or information is not useless. "If thou shalt confess with thy mouth that Jesus is Lord and believe in thy heart that God has raised him from the dead, thou shalt be saved." Likewise John tells us that those who believe in his name, i.e., believe he is the Messiah, have the right to be children of God (1:12; 3:15, 36); and those who don't, don't (3:18). Those who believe have already crossed over from death to life (5:24). Faith or assent is not the cause of life: it is the evidence of life. Similar ideas are found in 6:40, 47; 7:38; 8:31; 11:25; and particularly 8:51, 52, "If

any one keeps my doctrine, he shall not see death ever." Obviously this is consistent with the doctrine of justification (q.v.) by faith.

  Gordon H. Clark, *The Johannine Logos*, Nutley, N.J., Presbyterian and Reformed Publishing Co., 1972; William Cunningham, "The Reformers and the Doctrine of Assurance" in his *The Reformers and the Theology of the Reformation*, London, Banner of Truth Trust, 1967; I. A. Dorner (Lutheran), *A System of Christian Doctrine*, Vol. IV, pp. 192-238, London, T & T Clark, 1882.   GORDON H. CLARK

FAITHFULNESS. Faithfulness is that quality which characterizes one who abides in the attitude of obedience and faith. The faithful person is marked by fidelity, allegiance and devotion to a person or cause. In the OT two passages illumine its essential attitude. God is said to hide his face from his children who lack faithfulness (Deut. 32:20). But the truly righteous one is he who lives by his faithfulness (Hab. 2:4). Faithfulness is not just an act, but that which characterizes the one who walks by faith. Abraham is commended for his unwavering loyalty to God's promise; hence, he is called an ideal example for emulation by the Christian believer (Gal. 3:6-9; Heb. 11:8-10). Paul includes faithfulness as one of the fruits of new life in Christ (Gal. 5:22). The believer in life is to be characterized by complete commitment and loyalty to Jesus Christ. That is, he is to live a life of faithfulness. The opposite is faithlessness, an attitude of unbelief referred to as sin. Paul contrasts faithlessness of God's people with the faithfulness of God to them (Rom. 3:3).   WARREN C. YOUNG

FALL OF MAN. See also *Image of God; Man, Doctrine of; Sin.* The Christian doctrine of man affirms his unique relationship to God as created in the divine image. Whatever differences of opinion there may be as to the exact meaning of the term "image," there is a general consensus that it implies a moral likeness to God. Man, as originally endowed by the Creator, was one who loved God and submitted to his will in all things. However, by sinning against God, man lost his original integrity and thus, while still uniquely related to God, he is now in revolt against him and at enmity with his neighbor. This first sin is called *the fall*, in contrast to the many subsequent lapses (falls) which characterize human experience because it marks the beginning of human folly and is a defection for which there is no remedy apart from divine grace. It is called the *fall* because it is an event in which man's original righteousness is lost; he now comes short of the glory of God (Rom. 3:23). The word "fall," though an ancient figure of speech, is most apt, in our day, to describe man's moral ruin because of the contemporary effort to construe man's past history in terms of evolutionary progress. The notion of human progress has disposed many a thinker to express an unfounded optimism about man's moral ability which can lead only to disillusionment.

The story of the fall in Gen. 3 evidences amazing simplicity and inescapable insight in its account of the origin of man's sin and misery. One should not overlook the historical form in which it is cast. The plain intent of the author, who is ultimately the Spirit of God, is to say that the fall is an historical event; man did not fall *into* history, as Plato supposed, but *in* history. It is not because of his creaturely finitude but because of his willful disobedience that man is a sinner.

Distilling the basic themes of the fall narrative, theologians and ethicists have emphasized the following points.

1. Man is so created that while his nature and destiny, like all the rest of creation, is given him by his Maker (Gen. 1:27; 2:7), yet in a sense he is free (cf. *Free Will*) to determine his own nature and destiny. He is created upright but mutable, and it is his to decide whether he will attain the highest good, eternal life (symbolized by the tree of life, Gen. 2:9), or lose all by choosing evil

through the wrong use of the tree of the knowledge of good and evil (Gen. 2:17). He is required to render obedience to God or suffer the consequence which is the curse of death (Gen. 2:17). Man makes the fatal choice and is confirmed in sin. This is his fall.

2. The fall takes place under the double circumstance of probation and temptation (q.v.). Probation is a testing with a view to confirming man in moral rectitude; temptation is a solicitation to evil with a view to destroying man. Probation is of God; temptation is of Satan (symbolized by the Serpent, Gen. 3:1f.).

3. Man's fall into sin is occasioned (not caused) by temptation, which teaches us that moral evil in the universe is prior to and greater than man's rebellion. Though man's first sin appears of little consequence (eating the forbidden fruit, Gen. 3:6) man is deceived if he supposes such to be the case. It is the art of a superior power to make the evil appear of little consequence, even as good, and so ensnare man in hell's larger revolt against heaven. Because of this demonic dimension of moral evil, man cannot simply undo what he has done; moral evil is beyond him. Neither reformation nor resolution, neither psychiatric adjustment nor social uplift, but only the sovereign promise of a Deliverer, the Seed of the woman who shall bruise the serpent's head (Gen. 3:15), can ever redeem man from his sinful alienation. It has been further suggested that while the role of the tempter hints at the larger canvas on which man's sin is drawn, at the same time, because man's sin is suggested to him, not self-originated, therefore man is redeemable. His sin is not Satanic sin; at least this side of hell he is not confirmed in sin beyond hope. (But cf. I John 5:16, with its reference to "the sin unto death.")

4. If man fell by a free act of disobedience, what caused him to yield to temptation? In probing the mysterious motives

that provoke a free and responsible agent to act in a given manner, theologians have differed. Some have suggested pride, others unbelief as the root of all sin. Actually these are but two sides of the same coin, for if man distrusts God (unbelief), he will be brought to an inordinate trust in himself (pride). Here the narrative in Genesis is most instructive. The temptation begins with a questioning of the divine veracity ("You shall not surely die," Gen. 3:4) and ends with a flattering appeal to the human ego ("you shall be as gods, knowing good and evil," Gen. 3:5).

5. The sin of the first man is not an isolated, private act. Adam's fall is every-man's fall, according to the Bible. In Adam all die (I Cor. 15:22). This principle of man's solidarity in sin, so graphically under-scored in the narratives which constitute the sequel of the fall (Cain's murder of Abel, Gen. 4:8; Lamech's song of the sword, Gen. 4:23-4; the deluge which destroys man, the thoughts of whose heart are only evil continually, Gen. 6-9; the confusion and alienation of Babel, Gen. 11), is the aspect of the Biblical doctrine of the fall most bitterly arraigned. From the standpoint of modern day individualism (q.v.), it has been declared impossible to accept the notion that the sin of one man should be imputed to all. Yet vicarious ethical action is no scandal for the writers of Scripture. In fact it is central to the NT interpretation of the death of Jesus. His death is an act of obedience on the part of one by which many are made righteous (Rom. 5:19). Hence the apostle's comparison of the work of the two Adams, so utterly different in nature (disobedience vs. obedience) and result (condemnation vs. justification), yet so fundamentally alike in that both acted in a public way as representative men on behalf of "the many" (Rom. 5:12-21).

📖 Charles Hodge, *Systematic Theology*, Vol. 2, Eerdmans, Grand Rapids, 1952; Reinhold Niebuhr, *The Nature and Destiny of Man*, Scribner, New York, 1953.   PAUL K. JEWETT

FALSE WITNESS. See also *Lying; Truth-fulness.* The Ninth Commandment fur-nishes the primary sanction against false witness: "Thou shalt not bear false witness [more literally: "answer as a false witness"] against thy neighbor." In Exod. 20:16 the phrase is *'ēd šeqer:* "a witness of deception, falsehood"; in the parallel Deut. 5:17, it is *'ēd šāw':* "a witness of emptiness, worthless-ness". The key passage dealing with the punishment to be meted out to false wit-nesses (Deut. 19:15-19), provides that any-one convicted of false witness shall be compelled to suffer the same penalty as the person he accused would have had to endure had he truly been guilty: "Then shall ye do to him as he thought to do to his brother; so shalt thou put away the evil from the midst of thee.... And thine eye shall not pity; life shall go for life, eye for eye, tooth for tooth, hand for hand, foot for foot." It is interesting to note in this connection that the very first law in the Code of Hammurabi back in the late eigh-teenth century B.C. contained this same measure in connection with a false charge of murder; in such a case the false witness himself should be put to death. *'ēd šeqer* also occurs in Deut. 19:16, 18; Ps. 27:12; Prov. 6:19; 14:5 (the plur. *šeqārīm* in Prov. 12:17; 19:5, 9). *'ēd šāw'* also appears in Prov. 25:18. The NT term is *pseudo-martyreō,* "give a false witness," and usually appears in references to or applications of the ninth Commandment (so Matt. 19:18; Mark 10:19; Luke 18:20; Rom. 13:9). But it also occurs in connection with the false testimony lodged against Jesus in his trial (Mark 14:56, 57).   GLEASON L. ARCHER

FAMILY. See also *Household Codes; Marriage; Procreation.* The word "family" is used to indicate not only a man with his wife and children, but also an aggregate of kinfolk, a community, a tribe, clan, nation, or even the human race. The family is affirmed in the Bible and recognized by social anthropology as well as the first institution in society. It is the oldest institution known, antedating both the state and the church. It is universal. We shall here use the term restrictedly of the universal relationship between a man and a woman in some recognized form of mutual responsibility.

The Bible unfolds a picture of society based on the family which became a tribe, then a nation, and then was scattered throughout the world. The family-tie from the first was made sacred by an act of God, when he gave man and woman to each other (Gen. 1–3).

The OT mirrors the impact of God the Father in family life. Matthew begins the NT account of the birth of Christ with a genealogy of families. In a sweeping statement on world families and Father-God, Paul in Eph. 3:14 affirms that "every family *(patria)* is so named after and by the Father (Pater)." God as Creator is the Father of all; he precedes all the families—clans, tribes, homes, and nations of earth. Without this understanding we cannot even speak of families on earth as related to the Father in heaven. As Gottlob Schrenk says;

> According to the total Hebrew understanding, the question of the nation is viewed from the standpoint of the family and of the father ... creation stands in the background ... and families are created ... by Him who is Father in Christ ... (Gerhard Kittel, *Theological Dictionary of the New Testament*, Grand Rapids, Eerdmans, 1967, Vol. V. pp. 1018f.).

According to the Hebraic understanding of mankind and his relation to God, each and every family on earth sustains an evident relation to every other family on earth. Inherent in these Creator-Father and human-family inter-relationships, then, are the bases of Christian society and social development. Indeed, the family is the very

cradle of much of the development of society itself as well as national selfhood.

From the psychological point of view, the human need of man and woman for each other is emphasized as the basis for the original relationship made possible by God's creative act (Gen. 2:18-20). Writing in *The Family in the Sexual Revolution* (E. Schur, ed., Bloomington, Indiana University, 1964, p. 157), Seward Hiltner says that sex (q.v.) is only one of the needs for which God has so richly provided the family. The need to belong, the desire and urge for companionship, individual and group security, socio-economic, cultural, religious and other avenues of personal development are initially faced and thoroughly provided for in the family.

Basic to the definition of family in Biblical literature, then, is the relationship of husband and wife; around this develops the full orbit of mutual responsibilities and activities of the family. Rose Laub Coser of Harvard holds that family activity in a given society is the basic force that creates social structures, *The Family,* New York, St. Martin's, 1964, p. xiv). This takes place as the family becomes the instrument that brings together individual and group attitudes. There is quite general agreement that these attitudes emerge in the form of organizational attributes of family existence. The family finds its origin in marriage; consists of husband, wife, and their children; is united by socio-economic, legal, moral, and religious factors and emerges in the society it helps to form. In this context the family universally serves as an agent determining status and function in society. Similarly, the family serves as an agent of all kinds of control and instruction. At the heart of these family responsibilities is the universal recognition of some ritual which formalizes the marriage act as basic to family functioning. Never, points out Dr. Coser (*op. cit.*, p. xv) has the promiscuity of random mating been a characteristic of human society—not in Occidental or in Oriental society, not even in the societies practicing either polygamy (q.v.) or polyandrism.

The infinite variety today in accepted family styles, however, and the current emphasis on the power of innovation and change, serve as a threat to the stability of the family in our land as elsewhere. Current articles, television, and recent books emphasize a change even in the role of motherhood. Some of these authors think that marriage will probably not continue to be as universal as it is now; that the drive for equality of sexes will increase unless there is a violent upheaval; and that women who do marry will tend to do so for what they call "more personally satisfying" reasons rather than merely wanting the "security of a family" or the "prestige of marriage."

Likewise, urbanization challenges the stability of the family. It tends to sever the threads of family patterns. The young family, for instance, no longer resides in the tribal abode or on the old family estate. In today's urban society children are no longer the economic asset they were to their rural forebears. Similarly, matters of health, education, protection, life-fulfillment in daily work and needed recreation all add up to a myriad number of changes that challenge the family. Yet, as noted in the *Encyclopedia Britannica* essay on "Family" (Vol. 9, p. 55), there remains a "modified form of extended family co-operation . . . in the form of parental subsidies and gifts to get started in marriage. . . ."

What, if anything, ties this family idea together in a vision of wholeness that would give purpose and meaning to life? Do human beings need the family for their own best development?

As far back as Plato it was proposed to take children from selected upperclass parents and commit them and their education to the state. Currently, some states are experimenting with this idea in a way that tends to reduce the role of family, and to increase state controls, even relative to procreation, education and other functions of the family. Similarly, some individuals are experimenting with varying degrees of control and seeming nonchalance in reference to the influence of the home on children.

In contrast, the Judeo-Christian society emphasized monogamous (cf. *Monogamy*) marriage with mutual responsibility shared by both parents and by the children as the norm expected of a family. The family is then responsible as an entity within the society in which it exists, for individual and group development to the fullest possibilities in man and to the glory of God. The first two chapters of Genesis present the divine norm of a man leaving his own parental family to "cleave unto his wife, and they shall be one flesh" (Gen. 1:27; 2:24; 5:21). In this family scene the husband is named the head (3:16), and children are urged to honor their parents (Exod. 20:12; Deut. 5:16). The same emphasis is reiterated and elaborated in the NT (Col. 3:30, 31; Eph. 6:11-14). The sacredness of the family is highlighted in the Biblical position on marriage-faithfulness. Jesus' comment on divorce (q.v.) (Mark 10:2-12) as it was allowed in the OT Scripture (Deut. 24:1-3), points out that even when allowed it was an accommodation to man's weakness. Jesus in his Sermon on the Mount is less permissive, and gives his strong opposition to divorce (Matt. 19:1-12; 5:27-32). Three-way mutual responsibility—father, mother, and children—is the keynote in Biblical literature for a successful family. Mutual responsibility is the correct translation of the picture of family partnership at its best as given in Eph. 5:21-25 and Col. 3:18-19. The strength in this Biblical family is closely related to the foundation laid in family life in the OT. The foundation is thoroughly placed in the monogamous family. God had to tell Abram six times (Gen. 12-18) "Thy wife . . . shall bear thee a son."

The repetition of these two words "thy wife" and the events they heralded, left no doubt but that God expected Abram to have a son by his real wife and that God would bless that son as Abram's heir. Abram and Sarai had not prayed when they decided that Abram should take Sarai's handmaid to wife. They shared a need. They wanted an heir. They bypassed God as a possible factor in meeting that need. It took years for them to understand God, but Abram finally learned his lesson. God is the god of the impossible, and God has his pattern for marriage and for the family. Man is to have one wife. The children of such a union are the blessed heritage of such a family.

Christian society is based on the monogamous family. In evaluating this Christian concept in modern society, it is instructive to keep in mind its relation to the basic human needs of man. The list below can be enlarged by observations of many socio-anthropologists. It is evident that the family fulfills the need of man and woman for each other and provides the initial life-needs of children. No wonder Dr. Hiltner (*op. cit.*, p. 167) remarks, "Some unbiblical moderns will marvel at the modernity of the Bible. Biblically-minded readers may well be surprised at how Biblical some of the modern findings sound." We continue paraphrasing him, and Coser, in summaries of man's human needs as they are met in an astoundingly wonderful way in the family.

Man is a whole or total being. The family may be adjudged good to the extent that it serves the fulfillment of man as a total being.

Man's total self finds its very existence and fulfillment to the highest degree in the community of others.

Sex in human life is aimed toward the development of the progressive personality-integration of a man with a woman. Together, they grow "more like each other" through several levels of life-style, both as individuals and as a couple, within the limits of the human family. They gladly accept the mutual responsibilities of an organized society which they help form.

Human sex requires both intensity and steadfastness. Together, these merge in a relationship which depends on security and trust for its highest fulfillment but in which trust sex is never an end in itself.

The ultimate standard for good is the righteousness and love of God, of which the Christian community may at times be the representative.

All of these points may be repeatedly related to the pattern of the Judeo-Christian family life. The Bible (notably Eph. 4-6 and Col. 3-4, and negatively Rom. 1:18-32) builds on these same human factors and motivates man to his fulfillment in the context of both religious and human sanctions.

Family life is under greater strain today than it possibly has ever faced. This does not mean that the objection of youth to parental patterns is new. To obey or not to obey was man's first challenge to authority. The challenge is age-long.

The fact remains, however, that the forces of change are more widespread, better communicated, and more drastically addressed to the foundations of social order and Judeo-Christian "decency" than ever before. Trends are evident that indicate an erosion of the foundations of the family and society. It is much more than the trend from the large, "patriarchal, consanguineous type" of family to the small, "equalitarian conjugal type." Part of this a-morality is the new so-called "morality" which is so widespread that it threatens to wipe out the very basis of moral judgment developed throughout history. The basic challenge, however, seems to be against Biblical revelation and the idea of a God-given standard. This humanistically and relativistically defined "morality" supplants revelation with individual or collective caprice; it is already part of a modern way of life that by-passes family responsibilities and concepts that have been developed by societies all over the world. It by-passes history, refuses to accept tradition and does not consider revelation as having any validity or authority in today's world.

We are faced, so report the medical-social pundits of Haight-Ashbury, California, with "the crumbling structure of the American family" (David Smith and John Luce, *Love Needs Care*, Boston, Little, Brown & Company, p. 96). Society, then depends on our decision. Over two million young people, these authors tell us, have passed through this hippie center in San Francisco. Their free medical clinic has probably as direct an insight into the problems of the American "family" as any. While maintaining that some 2 percent are sincere, they officially believe that very few of these millions of our youth would have been there at all if they had "had sufficient reason to stay home"!

It remains to be seen whether we will maintain our commitment to the value of some kind of family institution, or whether we will cop-out for a relativistic definition of "individual freedom." This freedom calls for the one-person-centered development of personality with a demand for sex-centered equality and equal participation in decision making. There is good here. But such freedom does not nor should it demand the exclusion of family, group, synagogue, or church norms. Freedom may never be ego-centered as opposed to the God-ordained and God-revealed value system based on mutual responsibility of human beings.

This value system is in no way a demand for large families; the true value and equal importance of women has long been a Judeo-Christian theme; no one needs to demand thorough and loving respect for elders if and when it is not earned; nor should one insist on an obedience to authority that is capriciously wielded and never applied equally to the one wielding it.

Balanced authority and a family acceptance of agreed norms do not, however, depend on paternalism or legalistic authoritarianism. There is that which is integral to the well-being of human-kind which develops best within a family and society based on mutual responsibility. Mutuality of responsibility is a natural accompaniment of the successful implementation of the fact that "all men are created equal" It works best when it thankfully recognizes and is blessed by Eternal God. These are the factors which make for a healthy and balanced unit in society. Family life, based on these principles, demonstrates an actualized vision of wholeness that generates orderly unity and love in human living patterns. This reflects modern realization of the truth of Aristotle's statement that "Friendship is among equals." It also demands obedience to Christ's exhortation "Thou shalt love thy neighbor as thyself." Such relations are a must for the future of mankind.

The basic human factor underlying this is the Biblically proclaimed principle of an acceptance of mutuality of responsibility as necessary to family and social continuity (Col. 3-4; Eph. 4-6). Some such agreed commitment to a basic norm and the value of family life as part of personal and group continuity is definitely needed. Human beings need some way of banding together for mutual good; some way to strengthen each other, the weak and the strong; some planned pattern to insure time for life together in dialogue, play, work, culturally pleasing exchanges, worship, and sharing in each other's sorrow and hurts as well as joys. These are a must for the fullest life of which man is capable.

These are needs we all share: to love and to be loved; to work and to be helped to work; to play and to be taught to play; to serve and mutually to serve together in the needs of one's own group and of others as well. This is human. It is also divine. It is the fulfillment of that best which is commonly present in all men, for these basic needs and urges are the product of a divine creative act wrought by God into the being of all mankind.

The family that develops some such a life together; that has some values they mutually accept and respect together; that even develops what may seem to be somewhat ritualistic forms and functions of the family life they cherish—this family builds a strong society and nation in which an increasing number of others find security and satisfaction. In *Ritual in Family Living* (Philadelphia, University of Pennsylvania, 1950, p. i) J. H. S. Bossard emphasizes that "those religions with the most elaborate and pervasive rituals best retain the allegiance of their members," and those "families that do things together prove to be the most stable ones."

The close relation of family-togetherness in Biblical literature on one hand, and the close relation of family to the historical development of tribe and nation on the other hand, demonstrate again the close relation between revealed Biblical data and a true grasp of the best that is in man and family. If one believes in God as Creator as well as Heavenly Father of us all, this is to be expected. As such, God is involved in naming all families of the earth as his, for they were created by Him. So, obviously, he is working through history so that all men of all families on all the earth may have an opportunity to know and to worship him in the name of his self-revelation in Jesus Christ our Lord. The divine goal, then, is the families of earth gathered into the household of God—forever! FRANK J. KLINE

FAMILY PLANNING. See *Birth Control; Contraception; Procreation.*

FAMINE. The most devastating famines have been recorded in India and China where, until fairly recent times, their occurrence has been tragically frequent. In India three million people died in the famine of 1769-1770, 800,000 in 1837, one million in 1863 and again in 1900. Two to four million died in West Bengal in the famine of 1943. Several million Chinese are also thought to have perished in periodic famines, the worst being in 1877-1879 and 1920-1921. Widespread starvation has occurred in many other countries, including Egypt, Russia, France, and Ireland.

Famines are caused by natural disasters such as floods, crop failures, and war. Obviously countries with dense populations, non-diversified agriculture, and poor food distribution facilities are most severely affected. In many poor countries "pre-harvest hunger" is an almost annual occurrence due to food shortages when harvests are delayed.

Massive shipments of food from wealthy, grain-rich countries have helped avert widescale famine in recent times. However, the FAO of the United Nations still estimates that 20 percent live on diets inadequately nutritious. *Starvation* generally results from inadequate food and produces the typical famine disease, *marasmus,* characterized by extreme emaciation. *Malnutrition* due to improper balance of food, especially lack of protein, produces the disease called *kwashiokor.* Generally seen in children, especially infants recently weaned, kwashiokor is characterized by apathy, hair pigment changes, growth failure, liver enlargement, drop in blood serum proteins and edema (swelling).

Children suffering from starvation are usually more susceptible to infectious diseases and parasites, and death may result more directly from infection than lack of food. One tragic consequence of sustained hunger in infants is irreversible brain damage.

Paddock and Paddock estimate that 12,000 persons die daily of starvation and associated complications. Over half the people in the world exist on less than the minimum calorie recommendation. The most famine-vulnerable countries include India, Pakistan, China, Indonesia, Iran, Turkey, Egypt, Colombia, Peru and Haiti.

India recently startled the world with an announcement that it was canceling an order of 400,000 tons of USA wheat because of record wheat and rice crops. They attributed this to an agricultural by-product of new "miracle" rice, new wheat and corn varieties, as well as to increased use of fertilizer and irrigation. Only four years earlier experts had doubted that all the grain in the world could save India when the great famines of 1975-1980 would arrive. India shares with China, Japan, Egypt, and several other countries in southeast Asia and western Europe the dilemma of having less than one acre of productive land per person. Diets in such countries must of necessity be mainly vegetarian unless exports generate enough cash to import high protein foods.

The long-term solution to world hunger requires improved local productivity, population control, public health, and economic growth. Meanwhile, Paul Simon considers massive government aid essential. This involves reduction of trade barriers, expansion of food and technical aid, and maximum food production for export.

The Christian church alone does not have resources to meet the challenge of world famine. Simon's plea of church-state cooperation is one alternative. Another involves more personal involvement in small pilot programs as part of the church's work of compassion around the world. In either approach, decisions will need to be made as to who is helped and who left to starve.

William and Paul Paddock, *Famine—1975! America's Decision: Who Will Survive?*, Boston, Little, Brown, 1967; Paul Simon, *The Christian Encounters a Hungry World*, St. Louis, Concordia, 1966.   KENTON K. BRUBAKER

FANATICISM. Fanaticism is an attitude of extremism or irrational enthusiasm, es-pecially in religious matters. The term is generally used of individuals or groups in a disparaging sense. The OT depicts the prophets of Baal in this light (I Kings 18:28) while the NT implies this of the Jewish hostility to Christ (John 19:15), their stoning of Stephen (Acts 7:57ff.) and Saul's persecution of the church (Acts 9:1).

Basically, the word relates to the area of psychology. Psychologists usually detect psychopathic, schizoid, or paranoid tendencies in such cases. At best this is judgmental, demanding responsible evaluation. If fanaticism is measured by degree of intensity, energy or enthusiasm, it is relative. The person described as a fanatic generally reveals certain personality traits which doubtless aggravate or accelerate the drive for expression, whether verbal or physical. These include: prejudice, narrow-mindedness, hatred, extreme credulity, or extreme skepticism, highly subjective values and intense individualism. But external pressures may contribute to individual or mass hysteria and retaliation—hunger and famine, plague and war, or a restrictive, totalitarian regime. Asceticism, either Christian or non-Christian, also has a tendency to carry persons to the extremes of fanaticism. In the drive to conquer or subjugate the body, self-mutilation, flagellation and harmful fasting commonly occur.

Fanaticism is most dangerous when it spreads from the individual by contagion to mob hysteria and action, whether it be in the form of a posse, street rioters, or an efficient army driven to a frenzy by hate or fear. Politics also has its diary of fanaticism, but religion consistently has been the foremost arena. The annuls of history are filled with records of persecution in the cause of religion, from the burning of witches to the Crusades. The Inquisition used scourging, branding, the rack, fire, and imprisonment for its methodical extirpation of heresy. The Wars of Religion in Europe (1618-1648) have been matched by the fanatical zeal displayed in Ireland today, in which religion, economics, and politics are inextricably woven together.

JAMES D. MOSTELLER

FANTASY. See *Joy.*

FASCISM. Polemical and inexact usage of the term renders fascism difficult to define. The official spokesmen of some regimes (Italy and Spain) proudly identified themselves as fascist, while communists freely use it to smear and discredit those who for any reason seem to hinder communist objectives. Adherents of "left-wing" positions often indiscriminately label more conservative individuals as fascists. Fascist movements arose in most European lands in the 1920s and 1930s—Italy, Germany, Spain, France, Belgium, Great Britain, Norway, Finland, Poland, Hungary, Rumania, Austria, Croatia, and Slovakia—and outside Europe as well—in Japan, the United States, Argentina, and among widely scattered groups of anti-Soviet Russian emigrés. Since World War II it has not been a significant political force in Europe.

Fascism is a blending of three philosophical traditions: absolutism—governmental power in the hands of one man whose duty is to maintain and expand the state; organicism—the nation-state an organic unity like a human being and thus a superperson whose will is that of its members but superior to the interests of any individual person; and irrationalism—the deliberate repudiation of reason in favor of sentiment, passion, intuition, will, and violence which in turn reveals itself in such powerful modern myths as nationalism and racial superiority.

A fascist movement is characterized by a reactionary ideology based upon a mythical vision of the nation's glorious past that is intended to inspire political action, and by an effective mass organization to carry out fascism's basic objective of effecting a na-

tional regeneration. The "leader," possessing personal dynamism and magnetism that can arouse crowds to frenzy, is venerated like a saint and is exempt from criticism. Fascism draws supporters from almost all classes and groups, but those who are uprooted and threatened by social and economic change are especially responsive.

Although fascism is attractive to many Christians because of its emphasis upon discipline, authority, selfless devotion, and patriotism, its characteristic violence, scapegoating, militarism, and deification of the nation, race, and *Volk* clearly make it an unacceptable option for them. The inclination of theologically conservative churchmen, both Protestant and Catholic, to take reactionary stances toward modern ideas and institutions partially accounts for fascism's pre-war strength in Europe and the more recent appearance of fascist tendencies in South Africa and the USA.

Hannah Arendt, *The Origins of Totalitarianism,* Cleveland, Meridian, 1958; Ernst Nolte, *Three Faces of Fascism,* New York, Holt, Rinehart & Winston, 1965; Hans Rogger and Eugen Weber, *The European Right: A Historical Profile,* Berkeley, University of California, 1965; "International Fascism, 1920-1945" *Journal of Contemporary History,* No. 1, January 1966; F. L. Carsten, *The Rise of Fascism,* Berkeley, University of California, 1967; John Weiss, *The Fascist Tradition,* New York, Harper & Row, 1967.

RICHARD V. PIERARD

FASTING. See also *Famine; Gluttony.* Fasting is the act of voluntarily abstaining from (all) food (and drink) for a limited period of time for moral or religious reasons.

In the OT fasting is a sign of mourning (I Sam. 31:13; II Sam. 1:12; etc.), or of repentance (Joel 2:12-13; Neh. 9:1-2), or of serious concern before God (Ps. 35:13; 69:10; 109:24; Dan. 9:3). It is often coupled with prayer. Though there were many occasions of national fasting, only one fast-day is prescribed by the Law, namely the Day of Atonement (Lev. 16:23;

Num. 29:7). There was always the danger of fasting degenerating into legal observance—thus the prophets' protestations (Isa. 58; Jer. 14:12).

The NT says very little on the subject. Jesus probably occasionally fasted (Matt. 4:1-2; Luke 4:1-2), but he lays no stress on the custom. Only two dominical sayings refer to the practice: Matt. 6:16-18; 9:14-15 // Mark 2:18-20 // Luke 5:33-35. (The AV contains additional references, but these are not in the best manuscripts; cf. RSV and NEB.) The former recognizes the value of the custom but contrasts the simple and sincere devotion to God and his glory which is expected of the disciples of Jesus with the ostentation and desire for human praise among religious "show-off"; the latter indicates that Jesus did not lay down any definitive rules for his disciples concerning fasting as John the Baptist and the Pharisees for their disciples. In Acts the Christian community is pictured as fasting and praying (13:2-3; 14:23) on solemn occasions, but it does not appear to have been a prominent feature of its existence.

Fasting became a more regulated custom in the church toward the end of the second century, and especially from the fourth century onward. Although in the early church fasting was simply a sign or symbol of an inner attitude, it became more and more linked with an ascetic or legalistic theology and the concept of meritorious works. For this reason the traditional fasts were rejected by the Reformers, though the custom itself was not disapproved.

A modern approach has been to link fasting with the call to love one's neighbor and to see it as a symbol of the Christian's identification with the poor and hungry of the world. Thus Pope Paul VI in his Apostolic Constitution *Paenitemini* of February 17, 1966: "Nations who enjoy economic plenty have a duty of self-denial, combined with an active proof of love towards our brothers who are tormented by poverty and hunger." In some Christian circles there is the custom of meeting to partake of a very simple meal and giving the cost of a normal meal to relieve the world's hunger. There has also been the revival of the custom of fasting in Pentecostal and charismatically oriented fellowships, and here it is generally regarded as a spiritual exercise.

↪ *HERE* 5 (1912), 759-71; *RGG* 2 (1958), 881-85; *TDNT* 4 (E.T. 1967), 924-38.

W. WARD GASQUE

FATE. See also *Astrology; Destiny; Eschatology and Ethics; Providence.* Fate and fatalism, so far as written records go, seem to begin with the Greek myth that Clotho spins the thread of life, Lachesis measures its length, and Atropos cuts it off. Apparently only the date of one's death is fated. Moslems today sometimes hold such a view, as did a number of soldiers in the World Wars, who talked about one's number being on the fatal shell, while no other shell could hurt them.

Stoicism held the more consistent view that all events are determined by the divine providence that permeates all nature. The Stoics defended this view, first, by an appeal to the law of natural causation. No motion can occur without a cause. An event is always explained *because;* the cause produces or necessitates its effect. In the second place the Stoics defended fatalism by an appeal to logic. Every proposition must be either true or false. Events described by true propositions in the past tense cannot be altered. All people admit that some statements in the future tense describe the inevitable; e.g., Caesar will die. But consistency requires one to say that the statement, "Caesar will die by the hand of a friend," if true, is also inevitable. A false proposition in the future tense states an impossibility. Therefore the future is as unchangeable as the past.

The objection was raised, and still is popularly raised today, that if every event is inevitable, there is no need to do anything. If a general is fated to win a battle or a student is fated to flunk, neither need exert himself, for the one will win anyway and the other will fail anyway. No, not any way, replied the Stoics. The general is fated to win by exerting himself. He wins only in this way; and the exertion is as much fated as the victory.

So too Christ was foreordained to die, but not just any way; for Pontius Pilate, the Jews, and Judas were gathered together to do what God had predetermined to be done (Acts 4:28).

Augustine, as he grew older, paid more and more attention to predestination; but earlier he replied to the popular, astrological fatalism that says the stars determine our careers. This is false because two men, even twins, born under the same astrological signs, often have extremely different careers. Conversely men born under different stars sometimes live very similar lives.

Augustine also notices those who reserve the name of fate for natural causation and the will of God. Cicero objected to this Stoicism and denied divine foreknowledge. But, says Augustine,

> their opinion is more tolerable, that ascribe fate to the stars, than his that rejects all foreknowledge.... Nor let us fear that we do not perform all our actions by our own will, because He, whose foreknowledge cannot err, knew before that we should do thus or thus .... Our very wills are in that order of causes, which God knows so surely ... so that He that keeps a knowledge of the causes of all things, cannot leave men's wills out of that knowledge.

Since the Reformation the term *"fatalism"* has been relegated to popular superficialities, and the important problems are discussed under the secular rubrics of Scientific Law and Mechanism, or the Scriptural doctrines of Foreknowledge, Predestination, and Providence. Augustus Toplady insisted on philosophical necessity; William Cunningham, less successfully, argued that the Scripture neither requires nor forbids this view. The Arminians, abandoning the Reformed faith in 1620, deny that God foreordains whatsoever comes to pass.

Augustine, *The City of God* (V, viii, ix). John Calvin *The Institutes of the Christian Religion*, III iii; Gordon H. Clark, *Biblical Predestination*, Nutley, N. J., Presbyterian and Reformed, 1969; John L. Girardeau, *The Will in Its Theological Relations*, New York, 1891; D. D. Whedon, *The Freedom of the Will*, Philadelphia, 1864. GORDON H. CLARK

FEAR. Christians are often encouraged by the Scriptures not to fear. Conversely, they are also warned to fear. The difference lies in the cause of the fear (a principle useful in examining any emotional state).

Christians learn to overcome some causes of fear. In the light of Biblical teaching they can learn to view a situation differently. For example, Christians can be delivered from the fear of death (Heb. 2:15) or of man (Heb. 13:6).

But there are some causes of fear to which Christians should not let themselves grow accustomed. For instance, they are to work out their salvation with fear and trembling (Phil. 2:12). They are to learn to submit to each other in the fear of God—or of Christ (Eph. 5:21). Living in the fear of Christ is not craven fear or forced submission. It is a sensitive fear, an awareness of the first sign of grieving Him. "The fear of the Lord is the beginning of wisdom" (Ps. 111:1; Prov. 9:10). NEIL YORKSTON

FEMINISM. See *Women, Status of.*

FETICIDE. See *Abortion; Infanticide.*

FIDELITY. See *Faithfulness.*

FLAGELLATION. The act of beating, whipping, or scourging, usually by a rod or lash, was frequently employed in the ancient Near Eastern cultures, being particularly prominent in Egypt. Spartan youths submitted to the lash to inculcate indifference to hardships, but among the Hebrews, who found corporal punishment distasteful (cf. Exod. 5:14ff.), the rod was used only for crimes of considerable severity. In such cases the offender was beaten in the presence of his judges (Deut. 25:2f.), and was never permitted to receive more than forty stripes. Slaves could be beaten with rods, but never to the point of death (Exod. 21:20). The "scorpions" (II Kings 12:11f.) mentioned by Rehoboam were probably scourges with knots tied in one end. In NT times Christ used a scourge

In NT times Christ used a scourge on the money-changers (John 2:15), and predicted that he and his disciples would also be accorded such treatment (Matt. 10:17; 20:19). Christ's crucifixion flagellation was, however, a Roman rather than a Jewish punishment.

Paul received the traditional Mosaic sentence (Acts 16:22; II Cor. 11:24f.) which had long been reduced by one stroke to keep within legal limits. The beating occurred before the authorities realized that he was a Roman citizen (Acts 16:37), who as a class were exempt from such indignities. In the cult of Cybele the priests scourged themselves and the worshippers alike, holding this to be a sacred act. Paul's words in I Cor. 9:27 have been interpreted to mean self-inflicted chastisement, but since the Greek verb means metaphorically "to mortify," the sense of scourging seems precluded (cf. Luke 18:5) in favor of the general indication of mortification. In the seventh century flagellation was used as a popular form of punishment, but was also becoming common as a private means of doing penance or chastening the flesh. From the tenth century the scourge was used widely in self-flagellation, coming to a climax in the thirteenth century fanatical sect of the "Flagellants." Sentences involving whipping have become unpopular in contemporary Western society.

R. K. HARRISON

FLESH. See *Asceticism; Body.*

FLETCHER, JOSEPH. See also *Absolutes, Moral; Dialectical Ethics; Situational Ethics.* Joseph Fletcher was born in Newark, New Jersey, April 10, 1905. He received his B.A. from the University of West Virginia and B.D. from Berkeley Divinity School and also studied at Yale and London. Following pastoral ministry, he served as Paine Professor of Social Ethics, Episcopal Theological School, Cambridge, Massachusetts, 1944-70. He became one of the most influential spokesmen for "situation ethics." He has authored several books, notably *Morals and Medicine* (Boston, Beacon, 1954); *Situation Ethics: the New Morality* (Philadelphia, Westminster, 1966); *Moral Responsibility* (Philadelphia, Westminster, 1967); as well as contributions to *The Situation Ethics Debate and Norm and Context in Christian Ethics* (H. Cox, ed., Philidelphia, Westminster, 1968). He teaches Medical Ethics at the University of Virginia Medical School.

MILLARD J. ERICKSON

FOOD. See also *Health Laws.* Most Christians recognize the immorality of gluttony (q.v.) and of letting others go hungry. Many also consider the use and/or abuse of alcohol, tobacco, and other drugs as sinful. But some are beginning to see an even greater ethical dimension in diet, especially as the public becomes more aware of the chemical composition of the foods we consume and of food additives and their effects upon our bodies. One need not resurrect the OT ceremonial law (cf. Acts 10:15) to justify a careful selection of food for physical as well as spiritual well-being. The popular distinction between so-called natural and synthetic foods, however, is not very helpful, for either can be harmful.

DAVID KUCHARSKY

FOOLISHNESS. In OT perspective background the word "foolishness" can best be defined by its opposite. Wisdom is expressed most clearly by a fear of the Lord and a turning away from all that is evil (Job 28:28; cf. 1:8). Foolishness characterizes a man who denies God's reality and lives in practical ignorance of him (Isa. 32:6; Ps. 14:1; cf. 10:4). The obvious example of such a man is Nabal (I Sam. 25:25) whose insensitivity to human need and spiritual blindness meant that he lived up to his name (nābāl is Hebrew for "fool"). Other Hebrew words in the same family indicate that the "foolish man" is not primarily an illiterate ignoramus or uneducated misfit in society; he is the man who forsakes the source of wisdom in God and relies upon his own native strength and intellectual prowess. He lacks perception of spiritual issues (Prov. 1:7; 10:14; 12:15; 15:5) and is guilty of obstinate stubbornness (Jer. 4:22; 5:21).

In the NT foolishness is a term of abuse (Matt. 5:22). But its deep significance is reserved for a spiritual blindness and obstinacy which refuses to see God's wisdom in Christ's cross and turns away from his saving act by treating it with contempt and derision (I Cor. 1:18-30). The reasons for this sad rejection of the cross are given in the context. Top of the list is fallen man's unbridled confidence in his own ability to save himself and his reluctance to admit his need of God. This is "boasting," which effectively excludes a man from God's presence (v. 29). Only a humble trust in God's mercy and grace revealed in the cross of Jesus can meet and overcome man's pride and folly (v. 21).

Christians are counseled not to remain in a state of foolishness by disbelief (I Cor. 15:36) or wilful ignorance of God's ways (Eph. 5:15-17).   RALPH P. MARTIN

FORBEARANCE. As with so many other ethical terms, forbearance is used both of God and of man. The divine forbearance (anochē) is celebrated in connection with God's kindness and patience (Rom. 2:4), which provide the motivation for his stay of judgment to permit man the opportunity to repent of sin. The Greek word denotes a truce in its classical usage, which is somewhat relevant to the meaning in this passage, since the refusal to act in judgment is a temporary measure. The word has similar force in Rom. 3:26, where the forbearance of God is linked to his parēsis or temporary suspension of judgment during the pre-cross period, since he had in view a future basis of decisive dealing with sin, namely, in the death of his Son, through which full forgiveness is made possible for all who will believe (cf. Acts 17:30-31).

The self-restraint demanded in exercising forbearance is not easy. Even the Son of man confessed to difficulty in putting up with a faithless generation (Mark 9:19). Within the body of Christ offenses take place, and these are a threat to unity. But love is equal to the situation (Eph. 4:2-3), and this manifests itself in a readiness to forgive the offender, as the offended party recalls that God's forgiveness is the basis of his own position in grace (Col. 3:13).

EVERETT F. HARRISON

FORCE. See also Coercion; Pacifism; Power; Violence. Force is the strength or power to control, constrain or compel another by physical coercion or persuasion. Force is used against a man whenever something is done which he does not want done but which he is powerless to prevent or when a man is prevented from doing something he wishes to do.

Force and violence are not the same. Violence is the use of force in an illegal or immoral way. But it must be recognized that one man's force is often another man's violence, i.e., an act may be considered force by those who view it as immoral.

There are several reasons why the Christian cannot disavow the use of force *per se*. (1) the Biblical teaching regarding human sinfulness entails the need for restraints and checks on human actions. Man has an inherent tendency to take what liberties he has and turn them into a license for evil. As Alexander Hamilton wrote, "Why has government been instituted at all? Because the passions of men will not conform to the dictates of reason and justice, without constraint" (Federalist XV). (2) Paul's words in Rom. 13:1-6 constitute an endorsement of the apparatus of civil government. Consistent opposition to both the state and the use of force would require the Christian to decline the protection of the military and police. One cannot consistently abhor all use of force and then avail himself of the benefits derived from the fact that his nation offers him military and police protection. (3) Scripture recognizes that force is legitimate in child-training. (4) Scripture permits the use of force to resist evil, to punish evildoers, and to enhance conditions for good. As Augustine wrote, "It is the duty of a blameless person not just to do no wrong, but to keep others from wrongdoing and to punish it when done, so that the one punished may be improved by the experience and others be warned by the example" (*City of God* XIX, 16). Civil authorities are divinely given both the right and the duty to use force under law to discourage disorder within the state and aggression from without. Matthew 26:52 should not be taken as an indictment of the legitimate use of force in civil society, for in context, Jesus asserts that he himself could use force to resist his capture. Jesus did not indict those who were professional soldiers. Jesus himself used force when driving money changers from the temple (John 2). Nor does Matt. 5:39 forbid a proper use of force; The Sermon on the Mount simply warns against vengeance or hatred when one resists or punishes evil.

According to Augustine, the purpose of the state is the maintenance of a peace on earth that will permit men to live in harmony and attain their rightful goals. This purpose is realized through two primary means: the use of force and the fear of punishment (q.v.). Augustine taught that a province "must be governed by instilling fear" (*Epist.* 134, 3). The society that would not need the apparatus of force (law, courts, police, prisons) would not be a state but the city of God brought down to earth. The force used by earthly states is a necessary means in the restraint of evil men. Only as wicked men fear punishment will peace and security be possible. The state differs from other human organizations in its need for and ability to use force. Politically, the use of force is a necessary condition for the existence of any civil order. Force is needed to forstall violence, discourage criminals and aggressors, encourage obedience to law, and attain social co-operation. The elimination of force would in effect destroy the state with whatever potential it has for good.

Of course, the state also has potential for evil. This evil is realized most frequently in either of two circumstances: (1) when the state fails to exercise the proper amount and kind of force required to prevent other evils such as crime, or (2) when the state exercises too much force or the wrong kind of force. The use of force by the state must be limited to duly authorized institutions, e.g., the police, the courts. The state cannot preserve its unity by force alone. But it cannot hope to survive without some means of insuring that its laws will be obeyed and its institutions respected.

There must be checks on the use of force. Force must be applied lawfully and without caprice or discrimination. Law is needed to prevent the indiscriminate use of force (against people for no lawful reason) or discrimination (selective use of force against a few for no lawful reason). Law without force is impotent; but force without law is blind. Force is, in a sense, the other side of the coin we call law. It is implicit in all law, a latent sanction. But when resistance to law arises, force must be used.

The Christian must reject the view that force is the ultimate ground of the state's authority. The "might is right" doctrine that has served as the basis of many modern tyrannies is unchristian at its core and incapable of sound philosophic justification.

The use of sheer physical force should always be a last resort. Civilized human relations no doubt require the use of force, but whenever possible that force should be moral and rational rather than physical.

📖 Will Herbert, "Christian Faith and Totalitarian Rule," *Modern Age,* 1966, pp. 63-71; H. R. Davis and R. C. Good, eds., *Reinhold Niebuhr on Politics,* New York, Scribner, 1960; Helmut Thielicke, *Theological Ethics,* Philadelphia, Fortress, 1966.   RONALD H. NASH

FORGIVENESS. In general "to forgive" involves releasing a person from the consequences of some wrong action and restoring a breached relationship. Thus one person may forgive another for some slight or a damaging action. More specifically, forgiveness of sin is the releasing of a person from God's judgment and from the penalty which is the sinner's due. In this sense forgiveness is a divine act whereby God for his own special reasons pardons sin and releases the sinner from punishment in hell. This is the major use of the word *forgiveness* in the Bible. Similar expressions are *to pardon* and *to cleanse.*

I. *Biblical Analysis.* The important Hebrew words signifying *forgiveness* are first, *nāsa'* which has the idea of lifting up and removing sin, and second, *sālah* which means to pardon the sin with its consequences. The NT uses the word *amphiēmi* to suggest that the sin is put away from the person and the word *charidzō* which emphasizes that God becomes gracious to the forgiven sinner.

In his climactic self-revelation to Moses on Mount Sinai God proclaimed himself a God who forgives iniquity, transgression and sin (Exod. 34:7). This is his character as a merciful God. The word *forgive* here used means that the sin is lifted off and taken away. David in Ps. 32 calls the man blessed whose iniquity is forgiven (taken way) and his sin covered.

Since sin is a breaking of God's law, none can forgive sins but God only, as the Pharisees knew (Mark 2:7). Jesus accepted this challenge and proved his right to forgive sins by showing his divine power to heal (Mark 2:10-11). On the Cross Christ prayed the Father to forgive those who crucified him for they acted in ignorance (Luke 23:34). I John 1:9 assures us that if we confess our sins, God will forgive our sins and cleanse us from all unrighteousness. Here, forgiveness refers to the removal of the penalty of sin; cleansing refers to removal of its stain. Forgiveness is a judicial act; cleansing is a spiritual operation of God's Spirit on the human soul. The judicial aspect of forgiveness is never to be separated from the spiritual work of conversion, conviction and the exercise of faith. Faith, regeneration, justification and the beginnings of sanctification are all interrelated.

In the secondary sense, Christians are enjoined to forgive those who injure them. Hebrew and Greek language employs the same words for human forgiveness as for divine. Indeed the parallel is drawn explicitly in Eph. 4:32. Christians are to forgive because God for Christ's sake has forgiven them.

II. *The Basis of Forgiveness.* The verse just referred to raises an important point, the basis of God's forgiveness. God is a forgiving God, but he is also just and punishes sin (Exod. 34:7). How can God at the same time be just and yet justify the ungodly? The Biblical answer, both in the OT and the NT, is that this problem is resolved through the atonement. The word meaning *atone* in the OT is best taken as a verb derived from the noun for *ransom*. The many OT sacrifices providing atonement for sin involved the substitution of life for life (Lev. 17:11). Forgiveness consisted not merely in ceremonial cleansing but also in divine action, and it required an adequate basis. It included a radical blotting out of iniquity. The broken spirit and contrite heart referred to by David were not cited in place of atoning sacrifices, but as the evidence of sincerity on the part of the one who would offer true and proper sacrifices (Ps. 51).

The NT makes abundantly plain that the adequate basis for God's forgiveness is nothing less than Christ, the atoning Lamb of God (John 1:29). Because Christ paid the awful price, God can be "just and the justifier of him who believeth in Jesus" (Rom. 3:26). But Christ is not a third party to whom God in capricious fashion could transfer man's guilt. Rather, Christ is God incarnate and therefore could himself assume and bear our sins in his own body on the tree (I Peter 2:24). The love of God underlies his forgiveness, but the basis of forgiveness is God's own Son (John 3:16), and the means of our securing that forgiveness is belief and trust in Christ the divine Saviour.

📖 John Owen, *The Forgiveness of Sin,* New York, American Tract reprint 1845; Hugh R. Mackintosh, *The Christian Experience of Forgiveness,* London, Nisbet, 1927; James Denney, *The Christian Doctrine of Reconciliation,* London, Hodder & Stoughton, 1917; Leon Morris, *The Cross in the New Testament,* Grand Rapids, Eerdmans, 1965.

R. LAIRD HARRIS

FORMALISM. See also *Legalism; Pharisaism.* Formalism is excessive devotion to form rather than substance, especially, reliance on the forms, rituals, and ceremonies in use in a given social institution, with little or no thought or regard for the values which originally gave rise to the forms. Some random examples are: undue emphasis on the rituals and ceremonies involved with royalty, at the expense of allegiance to the values which kingship represents; elaborate attention to the details of the ritual of saluting the flag, at the expense of acting on the values which the flag represents. In connection with religion, formalism is "having the form of godliness, but denying the power thereof (II Tim. 3:5), and is closely related to legalism. Formalism can be seen in such things as concern for liturgical details while forgetting the real meaning of the liturgy; debate as to details of the formal aspects of church regulation, while ignoring the purpose such regulation is to serve; a desire to produce formal codes of minutely prescribed behavior, while disregarding the law of love which should underline them.

In church history formalism usually occurs as part of a period of decay and loss of vitality, following a period of maturity and establishment, which itself follows an era of innovation and vitality. This pattern recurs frequently, and produces anit-formalistic movements in reaction. Thus the late-medieval Roman Catholic Church, in a decadent period, seemed to many to be formalistic; the Reformation rebelled against this formalism. The Pietists and Methodists rebelled against the formalism of the decadent Reformation churches. The Jesus movement of the 1970s may someday be seen as a reaction against formalism. Such reactions, in turn, face the danger of the other extreme, replacing formalism with a lack of good order, a drift to sectarian enthusiasm, and excessive reliance on emotion. Historically, the church's problem has been to avoid both rigid formalism and chaotic irrationalism. For NT comment on various aspects of formalism, cf. II Tim. 1:3; Matt. 7:18ff., Rom. 2:20.

DERK W. JELLEMA

FORNICATION. See also *Sex.* The term *porneia* may denote voluntary sexual intercourse between unmarried persons (as distinct from adultery) or may express sensuality in general as well as every kind of sexual transgression. In a broader sense it may mean "adultery" (Matt. 5:22; 19:9), "sodomy" (Jude 7), or "incest" (I Cor. 5:1). The Christian must avoid fornication for the sake of purity (I Cor. 6:18).

WATSON E. MILLS

FORTITUDE. See *Courage.*

FRATERNITY. See *Brotherhood.*

FREEDOM. In a universe wherein natural order prevails, the subjects of that universe are free to function only within limits of their particular order. Given a theistic pre-supposition, there is a divinely established order, in the physical, social and spiritual worlds. Violation of the order in any sphere leads to a corresponding loss of freedom. Cooperation with the order results in the greatest possible degree of freedom.

Two factors complicate the question where man is the subject. In the first place, the details of God's order are not always comprehended by the unaided rational intellect. The use of revelation as a medium of communication involves man's spiritual sense as a necessary tool in understanding his spiritual environment. If the spiritual sense is itself askew, then man finds himself at odds with his environment. Secondly, man has a certain responsibility not only to interpret the divinely established order, but also to maintain it, thus frequently finding himself confronted with questions of an ethical kind.

In the world of physical natural law, there can be no argument that submission to law is a necessary prerequisite to freedom. This is true, whether in the development and use of machines (i.e., spacecraft, designed and operated according to certain well-known laws of flight and thus freeing man from earth, at least temporarily) or the use of man's body itself, with the necessary prerequisite in observing the lawful demands of nutrition, rest and learning.

It is in the spiritual sphere that argument may be raised, due to the interpretive responsibilities of the subject himself. However, given the theistic presupposition and given that we are intellectually engaged at the moment with the specifically Christian concept of freedom, we are limited in this discussion to a consideration of the Biblical teaching on the subject and the ethical implications of our conclusions.

The tension between freedom and bondage is one of the crucial dual themes of Scripture. Beginning with the Genesis account of the Fall, humanity lost a freedom it possessed in primeval innocence. It lost the freedom to converse with God and to live in Paradise; man lost the freedom to eat without toilsome endeavor, and the freedom to live without dying; woman lost a certain freedom in coming into a new relationship to man; the serpent lost its freedom of mobility and as a representation of Satan had the earnest of extinction stamped upon it by the promise and curse. From that moment of traumatic loss, the history of God's involvement in the affairs of men has been one of active intervention so as ultimately to secure once again man's freedom. Whether it be physical freedom from Egypt or Assyria, or spiritual freedom from Satan or self, God's hand is always the sovereign instrument of deliverance.

In the NT the Apostle Paul is clearly the chief expositor of this Christian concept of freedom (Gal. 5:1). He emphasizes the nature of true freedom as intrinsically associated with the new relationship of believers with Christ. Furthermore, true freedom in this life is not necessarily related to social freedom, though in practice the application of the principles should lead to freedom in this sphere (i.e., Philemon). However, the teaching of

Paul has its roots in the teaching of Jesus.

In Jesus' teaching one passage is crucial. In a confrontation with a group of Jewish believers he said, "If you abide in my word, then are you truly my disciples; and you shall know the truth, and the truth shall make you free" (John 8:31). In reply the Jews refer to their Abrahamic descent, concluding they have always been free men, as their forefather was. Jesus however makes it clear that freedom is not a matter of ancestry. It is one of individual responsibility, obtainable only to those who become Jesus' disciples and through him come to know truth. "If therefore the Son shall make you free, you shall be free indeed" (John 8:36). The Jews were slaves to sin and therefore not free at all. But how could they be free? The answer lies in Jesus' own summation of the nature of the Christian life and its relationship to his redemptive act. "For verily the Son of Man came not to be ministered to, but to minister, and to give his life a ransom for many" (Mark 10:45). He had also said to his disciples that ". . . whosoever would become great among you, shall be your minister; and whosoever would be first among you, shall be servant of all (Mark 10:43b-44). This "truth" is discovered to be the central paradox of the gospel. To be mastered by Christ who was the pre-eminent servant, is to partake of the benefits of his redemptive death. To base one's behavior on the principle that the Christian leads his fellows by serving, is to be a truly free man. This is the Christian perspective from which all truly ethical questions must be viewed.

Carl F. H. Henry, *Christian Personal Ethics*, Grand Rapids, Eerdmans, 1957; John MacQuarrie, *A Dictionary of Christian Ethics*, Philadelphia, Westminster, 1967; Herbert J. Muller, *Freedom in the Ancient World*, New York, Harper & Row, 1961; Otto A. Piper, *Christian Ethics*, 1970; Heinrich Schlier, *TDNT (eleutheros)*, G. Friedrich, ed., Vol. II, 1964.   PAUL E. LEONARD

FREEDOM OF INFORMATION. See *Secrecy.*

FREE ENTERPRISE. See also *Capitalism; Laissez-Faire; Socialism.* Free enterprise denotes an economic system in which free choice prevails for enterprisers, consumers, and workers. It is based upon the assumption that freedom of decision will provide both individual incentive and socially desirable rewards in the production and distribution of goods and services. This is in direct contrast to any system which advocates centralized decision making through either a business or government elite.

The free enterprise system is generally associated with laissez-faire capitalism where private ownership and control of capital and property, the means of production, prevails; where each individual enjoys freedom of decision in matters relating to the economy; and where income is distributed roughly in proportion to an individual's input of labor, skill, or resources. Profits and losses determine the firms that will continue to operate in the economy.

Additional features characterize the free enterprise system: (1) freedom of competition among producers and workers; (2) freedom of investment for private capital in any productive enterprise enjoying legal status; (3) freedom of choice in profession, vocation or job; (4) freedom of contractual relations in all transactions; (5) freedom to determine the kinds, quantity, quality, and price of goods and services in compliance with consumer demand; (6) freedom to save a portion of current income for future use; and, (7) freedom to organize among producers, workers or consumers for mutual advantage. Government is held responsible for the enactment of legislation guaranteeing these freedoms to all competitors.

Philosophic underpinnings for free enterprise may be traced to the economic liberalism of Adam Smith. His stress upon the constructive role of individual desire in a world of natural harmony governed by the "invisible hand" of Providence gave utilitarian assurance to the development of an economy free of public monopolistic controls. "Every individual," wrote Adam Smith in *The Wealth of Nations* (1776), "is continually exerting himself to find out the most advantageous employment for whatever capital he can command. It is his own advantage, indeed, and not that of the society, which he has in view. But the study of his own advantage naturally, or rather necessarily, leads him to prefer that employment which is most advantageous to the society." This utopian dream has been most effective where governments have regulated ensuing competition by statute.

The popularity of free enterprise is due largely to its efficiency in stimulating economic growth and the magnitude of the gross national product. Asiatic countries, such as Japan, have experienced beneficial results when the principles of free enterprise have been applied. Yet it must be said that negative factors continually embarrass its defenders. Growing poverty, the alienation of minority groups from employment opportunities, the destruction of natural resources, the pollution of air and water, not to speak of the rapid increase of entrepreneurial monopolies, retard the successful operation of free enterprise systems. It can be maintained only where personal integrity of laborer, producer and consumer are united in support of the rules of law designed to keep the facilities of free enterprise open to all who would participate in the system.   SAMUEL R. KAMM

FREE WILL. See also *Decision; Determinism; Fall of Man; Will.* The truly free will exists only on the level of *voluntas.* On the level of *liberum arbitrium* I am free completely in the sense that I can direct my consciousness to any object whatsoever. I am free spontaneously to will to walk up a wall but, on the level of *voluntas,* reflection and deliberation takes place, and I must consider the universal law that all bodies gravitate. What appeared to me to be the most free alternative was not truly free because it did not consider the law of gravity. In the same way, I have a duty to will good action, not just any action. Evil actions arise when I do not consider my duty, and fall into self-will. An evil act absolutizes itself as my duty or the good when in fact it is not.

In any given situation only one course of action is good or right. There cannot be any conflict of duties in a situation since there is only one good. Willing to do the good is willing the universal which is in accord with God's will. In a sense, discussions about determinism and the possibility of the individual free will can only take place on, or refer to, the level of *voluntas.* No one would deny that my spontaneous will of *liberum arbitrium* cannot take anything whatsoever as its object. Determinism is not really a problem until consciousness reaches the level of *voluntas* and on this level one would have to concede that the range of possibilities for action is limited. Only in this sense in respect to the level of possible courses of action has determinism any validity. Many Christians believe that sin has twisted man's will so as to make only evil or self-will choices. Others try to refute this by appealing to the fact that not all people act in their own self-willing interest. An example of this would be a person who disregards his own safety and saves a small child from an oncoming car. However, such selfless acts can be accounted for by the fact that even fallen man has something of the image of God remaining in him.

For the believer in Christ, the will is modified by the spiritual union between his soul and the Saviour. As the apostle Paul stated: "I am crucified with Christ: nevertheless I live, yet not I, but Christ liveth in me: and the life which I now live in the flesh I live by the faith of the Son of God, who loved me, and gave himself for me" (Gal. 2:20). One of the results of this union is to cause the believer to increasingly do the will of his Heavenly Father. Still, even in the light of this spiritual dynamic men can never completely escape the bondage of the will due to sin.   ROBERT G. CLOUSE

FREUD, SIGMUND. See also *Psychoanalysis.* A devout Jewish father and a Roman Catholic nursemaid provided some of Sigmund Freud's (1856-1939) early religious nurture, but the Comtean positivism that captivated European thought in the last half of the nineteenth century soon took precedence in the young scientist's thinking. So complete was young Freud's break with Judeo-Christian faith that he opened his office for the practice of psychiatry in Roman Catholic Vienna on Easter Sunday. Even his reverent biographer, Ernest Jones, conceded that this seemed like "an act of defiance."

After several years spent in scientific research at the University of Vienna, Freud tried to establish a scientifically sound link between his psychoanalytic theory and neurophysiology. He was justifiably dissatisfied with the result and at length released *The Interpretation of Dreams,* even though he realized that the publication of this book would cut his ties with the scientific community. The verdict of his university colleagues, that psychoanalysis is philosophy rather than science, has never been conclusively refuted, even though Freud continued to claim scientific standing for his method and the observations growing out of it. He disclaimed any concern for philosophy or ethics, but espoused "an erroneous metaphysics that is unaware of itself" (Maritain).

Freud early attracted a circle of disciples who were eager to become associated with psychoanalysis. However, he was intolerant of any digression from his own theories, and several of the deviants—Jung, Adler, Rank and others—separated to establish their own variant systems of psychoanalysis.

To his life's end, Freud continued to struggle with unsolved problems of personality. He produced a great volume of psychoanalytic literature, most of it highly theoretical and multistoried, with each layer of theory assuming the truth of preceding theory. Freud's empirical observations were underlain by assumptions concerning the place of the unconscious in personality, as were his explanatory hypotheses.

Freud was fifty-three before he turned his talent for theory to an examination of religion. In an essay written at that time, he ventured the suggestion that religion is a universal obsessional neurosis. Twenty years later, in *The Future of an Illusion,* the suggestion became an assertion. Freud paid little attention to criticism, although he conceded that his antagonism toward religion was a personal philosophy and not a necessary part of psychoanalysis.

His prediction that psychoanalysis would bring the third great revolution in human thought after Copernicus and Darwin remains unrealized, although Freudian theory has indeed permeated psychology, psychiatry and many other disciplines. Freud's emphasis upon the primacy of the unconscious is declining rather than spreading, but his originality, industry and creativity have been generally appreciated. His courage and continuing productivity in the closing years of life as he fought a losing battle against cancer have been universally acclaimed.

📖 Ernest Jones, *Sigmund Freud, Life and Work,* London; Hogarth, 1956; Benjamin Nelson, *Freud and the 20th Century,* New York, Meridian, 1957.
                                ORVILLE S. WALTERS

FRIENDSHIP. Friendship is really a love (q.v.). And this love is of an eminently spiritual kind. It is a relation between men at their highest level of authentic personhood.

Of late, *philia* has lost favor because of

infatuation with *agape*. Few moderns think friendship a love of comparable value or even a love at all (cf. C. S. Lewis, *The Four Loves*, New York; Harcourt-Brace, 1960, p. 87). Perhaps few value it because few experience it.

The basis of friendship is delight in another, as a *person*—and mutual attraction. Through this intimate relation between persons enters the ethical demand, love of neighbor. As Emil Brunner says, "The more that friendship is concerned with the whole personality, the more it becomes a bridge leading to the ethical realm" (*The Divine Imperative*, Philadelphia, Westminster, 1947, p. 517).

In friendship love matures into a singularly robust and well-informed kind. We can know and love nobody so well as our "fellow." Every step of the common journey tests his metal, and we empathize. "You will not find the warrior, the poet, the philosopher or the Christian by staring in his eyes as if he were your mistress: better fight beside him, read with him, argue with him, pray with him" (Lewis, ibid., p. 104).

Christians learn from Jesus the profound meaning of true friendship. "Love one another as I have loved you. Greater love has no man than this, that a man lay down his life for his friends. You are my friends if you do what I command you" (John 15:12-14). WAYNE G. McCOWN

FUNDAMENTALISM. Although the term "fundamental" or "essential" of the Christian faith had long been used in classical theology, the movement called Fundamentalism is American and modern. Europeans today speak of *amerikanische Fundamentalismus* because around the turn of this century many concerned American conservatives believed that even the irreducible minimum of a supernatural Christianity was being abandoned or questioned by the liberal movement. To resist this trend Bible conferences and schools came into existence. The "five fundamentals" seem first to have been defined at the Presbyterian General Assembly in 1910. The 1910-1915 *The Fundamentals* were published through the generosity of the Stewart brothers of California. The early phase united traditional Reformed and Arminian theologians of the major Protestant denominations, and dispensational conservatives usually found in the smaller, independent groups, in defending the fundamentals of the faith which all shared, despite many important differences over non-fundamentals.

During the last half century there has been a slight shift in the use of the term Fundamentalism. Conservatives in the major denominations are not so often called Fundamentalists (partly because their denominations are not identified with such bodies as the "National Association of Evangelicals," "American Council" and the like); the term Fundamentalism has come to be associated more exclusively with the smaller, independent groups. J. Gresham Machen is possibly the last famous scholar in a major denomination commonly to be so designated, though his position is still shared by many in his own and other major denominations. Because of the growing association of the term with separated bodies having lesser educational systems and constantly involved in polemics, the term has come in general parlance to represent not only the advocates of the traditional fundamentals of the Bible but also a militant ("fighting fundamentalists"), schismatic, anti-scholarly mood, and is also widely associated with dispensational, premillennarianism. (According to Sandeen, premillennarianism was the background movement that came into expression as twentieth century Fundamentalism; but this seems to make the tail wag the dog.) This characterization is not accurate because, for one thing, many who are not militant, schismatic, anti-scholarly, or even dispensational or premillennarian are, nonetheless, proponents of the fundamentals. But these pejorative adjectives are so generally associated (fairly or unfairly) with the movement, that many staunch defenders of the fundamentals hesitate to accept the designation lest it convey an image they do not embody.

The late Edward John Carnell (q.v.) was a case in point. His extremely able defense of fundamental Christianity was beyond dispute. Yet he became increasingly uneasy about the term and preferred to distinguish between "classic" and "cultic" fundamentalism. In fact, the term "neo-evanglical" or "neo-fundamentalist" has now come into wide use by men to the right of conservative center (e.g., Robert Lightner) and to the left of it (e.g., William Hordern) to locate the difference between classic and cultic and even to suggest that the difference is substantially greater than supposed. Yet within the fundamentalist movement a group is emerging which seems to question even some of the fundamentals (particularly inspiration) while still regarding themselves and being regarded by some others as fundamental (e.g., Dewey Beegle). All the while, the generality of nonfundamental ministers suppose that the movement is passé and that fundamentalists do not exist anymore. An instant cure for such wishful thinking on their part would be to consult the bibliography in Sandeen's *Roots of Fundamentalism* (1970) or read one of

Christianity Today's polls or Kersten's study of the situation in the Lutheran churches in this country (*The Lutheran Ethic*, not listed 1971). In addition to the older works of Furniss and Cole, a rash of major writings on our subject have appeared within the last decade by Hebert, Packer, Ryrie, Krauth, Sandeen, Gasparri, and others. Without distinguishing between cultic and classical we will mention a few more prominent living fundamentalists: Carl Henry, Bernard Ramm, Billy Graham, John Walvoord, Francis Schaeffer, Cornelius Van Til, Gordon Clark, Kenneth Kantzer, Addison Leitch, John Montgomery, John Murray, Clark Pinnock, Carl McIntyre, Oral Roberts, Rex Humbard, H. J. Ockenga, Robert Lamont, Cary Weisiger, Bob Jones, Leighton Ford.

With reference to ethics, significant differences appear among fundamentalists. Something very close to antinomianism is stressed by some, in the presumed interest of grace ("easy believism"). On the other hand, most are vigorous in their emphasis on Christian duty and the absolute necessity of good works as a corollary of true faith. The Fundamentalist reaction against social involvement (cf. Henry, *The Uneasy Conscience of Modern Fundamentalism*) has largely been reversed. Fundamentalism of all shades has become more socially expressive, as can be seen by the wide reception given Robert L. Ferm (ed.), *Issues in American Protestantism* (Magnolia, Mass., Peter Smith, 1969).   JOHN H. GERSTNER

G

GAMBLING. See also *Chance*. Gambling involves the transfer of something of value from one person to another on the basis of mere chance. Three basic factors appear in the process of gambling: the payoff, the

element of pure chance, and the agreement to pay by the bettors. While there are some risks in buying stocks on the stock market, it is not considered pure chance because the money is risked to provide for the development of industry. Purchasing insurance involves some risks, but these are greatly reduced. Chance is not a predominant and controlling factor in either case.

Gambling dates far back in human history and has been an almost universal practice among nations. Dice with numbers on four sides have been found in Egypt dating thousands of years before Christ. In the ruins of Pompeii, gaming tables have been discovered. Tacitus, the Roman historian who lived about A.D. 100, noted that gambling was very common among the tribes of Germany.

In the Bible, particularly in the OT, the casting of lots was common (Num. 26:52-56; I Sam. 10:20-21; I Chron. 24:5). Judas' successor was chosen by lot (Acts 1:26). The casting of lots was a means of ascertaining the will of God. It should be noted that after Judas' successor was chosen by lot, this method was not employed again by the church. Decisions thereafter were made in relation to the guidance of the Holy Spirit.

Gambling in the sense of transferring something of value from one person to another on the basis of chance is not sanctioned by the Scriptures. The NT view of work, stewardship, love of neighbor, and the proper use of influence rule out the practice of gambling (II Thess. 3:10-12; Eph. 4:28; I Cor. 10:23; Gal. 5:13-14; Matt. 22:37; I Thess. 5:22; Rom. 12:9).

There are many forms of gambling. The lottery is used for raising money. A promoter sells numbered tickets, duplicates of which are placed in a container, later drawn out, and the persons holding the tickets bearing the numbers drawn win the prize offered. In 1612, an English lottery supported the settlement in Jamestown. Lotteries have since been used in America to support state and local governments, schools, and even churches.

Other forms of gambling are racetrack betting, the numbers game, slot machines,

dice and card games, rouletee, chuck-a-luck, punch boards, pinball machines, raffles, and bingo. Bookmakers take illegal bets on horse races, prize fights, elections, and athletic contests. In some states betting is legal at the race track where a part of the money goes into the public treasury.

More than fifty million Americans engage in some form of legal or illegal gambling. Some six million of these are compulsive gamblers. Hence, about as many people are addicted to gambling as to alcohol.

Studies show that the compulsive gambler has certain characteristics. He habitually takes chances; gambling absorbs all of his interests; he is optimistic and never learns from losing; he never stops while winning; he risks too much; and he enjoys a strange tension between pleasure and pain (Edmund Bergler, "The Psychology of Gambling," in Robert Herman, ed., Gambling, New York, Harper and Row, 1967, pp. 114-117).

People gamble for numerous reasons: to win money; for thrills and excitement; belief in luck; and the compulsion to see defeat, humiliation, and pain.

The consequences of gambling can be devastating. The gambler may suffer loss of income, job, get deeply in debt, resort to stealing in order to get betting money, strained family relations, and divorce.

Resources for rehabilitating the gambler are psychiatric aid, counseling centers, and Gamblers Anonymous (GA). Patterned after Alcoholics Anonymous, this organization is a fellowship of men and women who share their experience, strength, and hope with one another in order to solve their common problem and to help others in the same condition. Requirement for membership is the desire to stop gambling. GA has established Gam-Anon for wives of gamblers to help them to understand their husbands' problem and how to help them.

Unfortunately some churches promote gambling by the use of games of chance such as bingo for charitable purposes. It is held that the end justifies the means. Gamblers can rationalize their own practice of gambling by noting that churches approve of gambling.

Churches, instead of promoting gambling, should aid the gambler through pastoral counseling and referral. By providing literature and seminars on the nature and results of gambling, members can better understand the problem. Above all, Christians can set the right example by not participating in games of chance.

HENLEE H. BARNETTE

GENERAL RULES CONCEPT. Some moral philosophers believe that there are rationally- and experientially-validated principles of right and obligation which demand universal acceptance. The formulation of such principles is one kind of philosophical contribution toward simplifying the making of moral decisions. A general rule or principle does not specify concrete acts to be performed, but indicates a more or less broad basis for determining right actions. General rules exhibit varying degrees of generality. Some, like Kant's categorical imperative, require much interpretation in order to provide direction to particular cases of decision-making. Others, like the so-called "middle axioms," need less explanation to make clear what acts of conduct they require.

The question arises whether general rules are simple prudential guidelines for conduct, or whether they must be accepted as prescriptive. They belong to the province of meta-ethics. Many ethical theorists would agree that although they are valid and meaningful statements, they offer little help to practical morality. Christian moralists, insisting that "love is the fulfilling of the law," must consider whether love is to be understood as displacing all other rules and making them superfluous; or whether it is simply the power in the lives of Christians which enables them to meet the requirements of all rules. DELBERT R. GISH

GENERATION GAP. The expression "generation gap" in current usage refers to the present-day alienation of many young people in our country from their parents and from elders in society generally. In this day of rapid technological, social, and ideological change, these youth have become disenchanted with and opposed to the traditionally accepted viewpoints, values, manners, and morals that have long constituted the American cultural consensus. Many older members of the community have reacted antagonistically to the youthful protesters and rejected young people's differing ideas concerning politics, education, war, racial and urban problems, dress, sex and morality, the new theology, and other issues.

The welfare of our society requires that the generation gap be narrowed. This can be accomplished, if both groups will make the serious endeavor to communicate with and understand one another, and together work for the solution of the problems facing our nation and world.

In Christian circles generational antagonism can be dispelled when genuine love for God and for fellow believers, born of common faith in Christ, will lead young and old to a sincere concern for one another and a readiness to let the Word of God chart the basic course of behavior each group should follow for the glorification of God.

WALTER A. MAIER

GENETICS. The public understanding of genetics has changed from a sense of fatalism (as though nothing could be done) to one of apprehension (as though too much might be done). This transition has resulted from recent discoveries about genes, chromosomes, and genetic variation.

Genes guide the development of an organism by determining how amino acids are put together to form proteins. Some proteins are enzymes which regulate chemical reactions, but mutations may cause defective enzymes. On the average each person carries about five harmful genes which could be expressed in a child if the other parent carries the same gene. Over 1800 different genetic traits can be recognized at present. About 150 of these cause severe mental retardation, and there is growing evidence that other aspects of human behavior are genetically conditioned.

The discovery of a serious genetic defect in a child draws heavily upon the inner resources of parents. They may need help to cope with their own distress, to avoid blaming themselves or others, and to be ready to accept help.

Fortunately, some of the effects can be alleviated by medical intervention. Special diets limit the intake of those foods the body cannot handle. Hormones and other missing gene products can be administered. In a few conditions an enzyme can be supplied by injections or organ transplant. In the future it may become possible to add new genetic material, perhaps by using a carrier virus. These procedures seldom involve ethical problems, since they are intended to repair a specific defect.

When parents know that there is a sizable risk of producing another child with a serious defect, the responsible approach is to consider setting aside the privilege of further reproduction (cf. *Birth Control*) in order to protect the "rights" of children to be born with reasonably good health. Paul Ramsey stressed the need for an "ethics of genetic duty," adding that taking chances with another pregnancy is genetic imprudence and gravely immoral (*Fabricated Man,* New Haven, Yale University, 1970, p. 57).

The new option of prenatal diagnosis and selective abortion (q.v.) is more controversial. Some parents face a 25 per cent chance that their next child will die by two years or require continuing institutionalization. If pregnancy occurs in spite of efforts at contraception, there is a difficult choice. Terminating the life of a fetus is never desirable in itself, but continuing the pregnancy under these circumstances also has serious ethical implications. In certain genetic conditions the analysis of fetal cells from the amniotic fluid will change the risk to zero or to 100 per cent. Termination need not be considered if the fetus is shown to be normal.

Much more disturbing are speculations about "cloning," a term which includes nuclear transplantation and multiple embryos (so that a number of genetically identical children could be produced). It may be years before this or similar types of "genetic engineering" become technically feasible, but more fundamental objections can be raised. (1) Essential decisions about reproduction would be moved from the family to the laboratory. Some argue that technological advances have doomed the biological family, but Kass (*Science,* 1971, 174:784) has insisted that "the elimination of the family would weaken ties to past and future, and would throw us, even more than we are now, to the mercy of an impersonal, lonely present." (2) Restrictive choices would be made on behalf of the next generation. The resulting children may have different values. (3) Genetic control of this type infers agreement about ideals for positive selection. Kass (*op. cit.,* p. 786) commented on "the folly of arrogance, of the presumption that we are wise enough to remake ourselves."

A consideration of genetics thus forces us to examine our view of human nature. (1) *Wholeness.* We should view man as both biological organism and responsible self, as Ian Barbour has insisted (*Science and Secularity,* New York, Harper & Row, 1970, p. 83). Means to alleviate genetic defects are welcome indeed. Yet a Biblical view of man does not stress human frailty so much as distorted personal relationships and responses toward God. (2) *Responsibility* (q.v.). Just as we are stewards of God's other good gifts, we are also stewards of the human gene pool. (3) *Freedom* (q.v.). Not all parents will choose alike, but decisions based on a prayerful search for guidance should be respected by pastors, physicians, and friends. Authoritarian uses of genetic control should be discouraged if they seriously limit personal freedoms. (4) *Family* (q.v.). Although the Bible says little about genetics, it does say much about the family. Reproductive problems should be handled so as to strengthen its role.

V. ELVING ANDERSON

GENOCIDE. See also *Euthansia; Suicide.* The willful policy of seeking to exterminate a particular group of people seems to be the most extreme violation of the Sixth Commandment conceivable, that Commandment which teaches that human life as God-derived possesses an inviolable sacredness. Yet in the first half of the twentieth century that policy became a cornerstone of the Nazi regime. As Eberhard Jäckel has irrefutably demonstrated, Adolf Hitler as early as 1919 was advocating a "rational anti-Semitism" the "ultimate goal" of which "must be unalterably the elimination of the Jews altogether" (*Hitler's Weltanschauung: A Blueprint for Power,* Middletown, Connecticut, Wesley University, 1972, p. 48). Years later, in 1945, he said, "I have fought the Jews with an open visor. I gave them a final warning when war broke out. I left them in no doubt that they would not be spared this time should they once more thrust the world into the war—that the varmin in Europe would be exterminated once for all" (ibid., p. 165). Hitler's diabolical veracity in carrying out this policy is written indelibly into the pages of history with the blood of—more or less!—six million human beings. Age and sex made

no difference: the crime of belonging genetically to a certain group served as an individual's death warrant (cf. the ghastly details given by Erich Kahler in *The Tower and the Abyss,* New York, George Brazeller, Inc., 1957, pp. 72ff.; also Robert Cecil, *The Myth of the Master Race: Alfred Rosenberg and Nazi Ideology,* New York, Dodd Mead, 1972). It is doubtfull whether the deportation or decimation of any conquered people in the past offers a parallel to so evil and efficient an exercise in sadistic cruelty. If any proof of man's depravity is required, the Nazi concentration camps and gas chambers supply it overwhelmingly.

Does the immorality of genocide need to be laboriously argued? Everything that can be said against murder can likewise be said against this national policy of wholesale murder. Underlings in a governmental structure cannot exonerate themselves from guilt by pleading obedience to superiors. As the Nuremberg Tribunal contended, there are "international duties which transcend the national obligations of obedience imposed by the individual state" (quoted by Telford Taylor, *Nuremberg and Vietnam: An American Tragedy,* New York, Bantam Books, 1970, p. 84). Nor can a government act as a law unto itself in the policies it initiates and pursues. An unwritten Law transcends all the laws which the rulers of a *de facto* state may enact. And difficult as that Law may be to define and apply, it is humanity's bulwark against inhumane barbarism.

But troublesome questions therefore arise concerning the use of genocidal weapons as well as, say, the American intervention in Viet Nam (Jerome D. Frank, *Sanity and Survival,* New York, Random, 1967, pp. 14ff.). These questions are compelling a reassessment of long-standing concepts of just and aggressive wars, subjecting them to a sustained criticism in the light of both Biblical principles and existential realities.

VERNON C. GROUNDS

GENTLENESS. For the most part "gentleness" is the translation of the Greek *epieikeia,* although *ēpios* is properly rendered "gentle" in I Thess. 2:7 and II Tim. 2:24, and *praütēs,* ordinarily rendered "meekness," may occasionally have the flavor of gentleness. The concept has something in common with other terms such as kindness, patience, forbearance, and graciousness.

The original idea of *epieikeia* was bound up with what is reasonable and right. Then, on the ground that a man who is fair and equitable can afford to be concessive without loss of principle, the idea of moderation and yieldingness came into prominence. As Trench points out (*Synonyms of the New Testament*) the element of condescension plays an important role in the usage of the word. This is true in the Biblical as well as the classical context. It was God's willingness to humble himself to David's low estate which made this shepherd lad great (II Sam. 22:36). Paul utilizes the gentleness of Christ as the pattern of his own moderation in dealing with the unruly Cornthians (II Cor. 10:1). Here the background is the royal majesty of the Son of God which he was willing to forego as Mediator (Phil. 2:5ff.). The apostle has authority from him and is prepared to act with something of the same gentleness toward Christ's church. Similarly, the bishop, by the very fact that he is overseer of the flock, must be gentle toward those for whom he is responsible. The linkage grows longer when the relationship of the Christian community toward outsiders is included. "Let your gentleness be known to all men" (Phil. 4:5). As recipients of grace and candidates for glory, believers have a position of strength and blessing from which to deal with "sweet reasonableness" towards all men.   EVERETT F. HARRISON

GLUTTONY. See also *Fasting.* Gluttony is the vice of excessive eating and is termed as one of the "seven deadly sins." Surprisingly, gluttony does not have any great prominence among the sins of the flesh in the Bible. The term "glutton" appears six times in the RSV (Deut. 21:20; Prov. 23:21; 28:7; Matt. 11:19; Luke 7:34; Titus 1:12). The two Gospel references are epithets hurled at Jesus by the Pharisees because of his non-ascetic life-style and his association with "sinners"; the Titus passage is a quotation from the pagan writer, Epimenides.

One of the reasons gluttony is seldom mentioned is that it is specifically the rich man's sin and it is his *attitude* of scorn for the poor and needy which is generally singled out for condemnation rather than his personal self-indulgence. In addition, over-eating does not have the same social ramifications as other sins of the flesh such as drunkeness, immorality, theft, or murder. Nevertheless, the fathers who classified gluttony as one of the cardinal sins were certainly correct. The glutton is not only guilty of sinning against his own body, but he also is guilty of displaying a singular lack of concern for his fellow man, since most men are and have always been poor and without enough to eat. The story of the rich man (who is appropriately disignated "the rich glutton" by the Vulgate) and poor Lazarus of Luke 16:19-31 vividly illustrates the point.

W. WARD GASQUE

GNOSTICISM. Gnostic ethics are rooted in gnostic theology, cosmology, and anthropology. The absolute cosmic dualism in which the purportedly true God is totally separate from the universe, which he neither created nor governs, is reflected in the nature of man. The gnostic *pneumatic,* in whom the true divine spirit has been "awakened" with knowledge (*gnosis*), thus relates to the world as either an ascetic or libertine. The ascetic gnostic expresses his possession of the true *gnosis* and freedom from the evil cosmos by abstention from the world; the libertine gnostic by indiscriminate abandonment to the world and the body. Both ethical attitudes are, although opposite in practice, expressive of the same gnostic anti-cosmic pattern of thought.

Our knowledge of gnostic ethics, usually in the form of an exposé of the moral excess of libertine gnostics, is mediated primarily through the writings of the early Christian heresiologists such as Irenaeus *Adversus haereses* (e.g., i.6:2-3), Hippolytus *Refutatio omnium heresium* (e.g., vi. 14) and Epiphanius *Panarion* (e.g., xxvi. 4-5). Plotinus, the third century A.D. non-Christian Neo-Platonist, also describes the gnostic ethical stance in his work *Against the Gnostics* (*Enneads* ii. 9:15-18).

The most systematic and extended treatment of the full range of gnostic ethics is Clement of Alexandria's discussion of marriage and sexual gnostic groups (*Stromateis* iii; for comment and translation see John E. L. Oulton and Henry Chadwick, *Alexandrian Christianity* . . . , Philadelphia, Westminster, 1954, pp. 22-23; 40-92).

Since no primary gnostic ethical treatise is extant, the accuracy of the patristic data is debatable. Although Plotinus says (*Enneads* ii.9.15) that the gnostics had produced no treatise on virtue, Clement of Alexandria quotes from the sons of two prominent gnostic leaders: Isidore, son of Basilides, *Ethics* (*Stromateis* iii.2-3) and Epiphanes, son of Carpocrates, *Concerning Righteousness* (*Stromateis* iii.6-10). The Nag Hammadi Coptic gnostic texts discovered in 1945, although not completely published, presumably do not include any ethical treatises (see David M. Scholer, *Nag Hammadi Bibliography 1948-1969*, Leiden, Brill, 1971). These texts do use sexual imagery in describing the gnostic ideal as the elimination of sexual *differentia* (e.g., *Gospel of Thomas* 37; 114; *Gospel of Philip* 77-79).

Some scholars have interpreted certain NT letters as directed against gnostic ethical positions, such as Colossians against ascetic gnostics and Jude against libertine gnostics (e.g., F. F. Bruce, *The Defence of the Gospel in the New Testament*, Grand Rapids, Eerdmans, 1959, pp. 74-82).

Hans Jonas, *The Gnostic Religion*, 3d ed., Boston, Beacon, 1970, pp. 46-47, 270-77; Edwin M. Yamauchi, *Gnostic Ethics and Mandaean Origins*, Cambridge, Harvard University, 1970, pp. 24-34.   DAVID M. SCHOLER

GOD. See also *Atheism; Gods, False.* Here we are concerned not with the existence of God or his knowability, but only with his character. Since this is part of the data of special revelation, we need not resort to speculation. Nor are we shut up to analogy so as to make use of comparison between ourselves and God on the basis of man's creation in the divine image. The effects of sin on mankind have to be reckoned with, and even without this factor such comparison must be taken as suggestive rather than precisely determinative. God is pleased to adapt himself to our limitations for educative purposes, but he cannot be pressed into the human mold. The divine character can be known through the acts of God and through his words. Frequently the words help to interpret the acts. Statements about his character by writers of Scripture add to our store of knowledge. Above all, God is made manifest in his Son (John 1:18); to come to grips with the Son is to confront the Father (John 14:9). Being without sin, the Son is able faithfully to reveal God in his own person.

There is a certain peril in dwelling on individual attributes of God in detached fashion. The approach becomes impersonal and we lose the sense of totality and interrelation; God becomes a symbol bearing a variety of labels. All that God is, he is all the time. He does not cease to be righteous when he is gracious. As though to emphasize this, the Bible not infrequently joins together characteristics of the deity that we think of as antithetical, such as mercy and truth (Ps. 85:10), kindness and severity (Rom. 11:22 RSV).

In the OT God has revealed himself as the self-existent one (Exod. 3:14) who does not stand aloof from his people but is touched by their afflictions (Exod. 3:9) and willing to intervene on their behalf, exhibiting covenant faithfulness (Exod. 3:6, 17). Yet this God who draws near in deliverance and even in personal communion (Gen. 15:1) insists on making known his holiness, keeping his redeemed people at a distance when the law is given (Exod. 19), prescribing ceremonial cleanness for them in minute detail (Lev. 11-17), and communicating this central feature of his being through solemn angelic reiteration (Isa. 6:3).

Closely allied to holiness is righteousness, which might be called holiness in action. If holiness is what God is in himself, righteousness is what he is in his dealings with others. Along with the assertion of his goodness and graciousness to Israel is the declaration of his readiness to punish the sins of his people (Exod. 34:6-7). Seeing that this is the covenant nation, the obligation to reflect his righteousness in human relations is mandatory (Amos. 5:24).

By his own announcement the God of Israel is a jealous God (Exod. 20:5). He cannot tolerate recognition and worship for deities of human devising. He will not share his glory with another. This in itself demonstrates that Israel did not originate its own deity inspired by the desire to be like the nations. Her god was different from all others.

When the record of Israel's unfaithfulness to God her husband is unfolded in Hosea, what is emphasized is not divine jealousy but indestructible, patient love that seeks the unfaithful wife and takes her back. This is the zenith of the revelation of the character of God in the OT.

In the NT two features stand out. One is the immediacy of the disclosure of the divine character in the person of the Son of God. As Jesus of Nazareth rubs elbows with the children of men, he is revealing God on the human level amid all sorts of situations. Since few recognized him as God manifest in the flesh, his character had to win its way without the benefit of status. Obviously it had to disclose itself through a truly human medium.

What our Lord had to say about God is largely gathered up in his teaching concerning him as Father. He taught benevolence through the impartiality of God's provision on behalf of all the children of men (Matt. 5:45), his gracious and abundant care of his own, so that anxiety becomes a needless affront (Matt. 6:25-34), and the privilege of praying to him with confidence that he hears (Matt. 6:5-13; 7:7-11). His teaching on the perfection of the Father seems especially designed to underscore his love (Matt. 5:48; cf. I John 4:8). He does not fail to mention the readiness of the Father's response to all who love his Son (John 14:23; cf. Rom. 8:39). In the gospel message the truth is stressed that God did not hide his love, but commended it to us by the gift of his Son as the Redeemer to die in our place for our sins (Rom. 5:8).

The Bible is prone to set forth the perfection of God by the use of the term "glory." In the heavens we discern the glory of God in terms of wisdom and power, while in the fecundity and beauty of the earth the glory shines forth again. The glory is personally reflected in the Son (Heb. 1:3) for believing eyes to see (John 1:14). The glory of God is restored to men as they are renewed in Christ and refashioned in the divine image (II Cor. 3:18). Those who refuse the Son must taste the bitterness of judgment, which is the fruit of rejecting God's love and grace in Christ. This is the shadow of the divine glory. God is no less perfect here than elsewhere. "I am God, and there is no other; I am God, and there is none like me" (Isa. 46:9 RSV).

EVERETT F. HARRISON

GODS, FALSE. From the standpoint of Biblical revelation, all deities other than Yahweh Elohim are imaginative products of fallen man's mind, so corrupted by sin as to be unable to see that mere artifacts of metal, wood or stone are utterly devoid of life, reality, or power. They were to be despised as "the work of men's hands," unable to see or hear (Deut. 4:28), and utterly helpless to deliver those who called upon them, since they were devoid of real existence.

Sennacherib of Assyria failed to realize that his easy conquest over other nations and their impotent gods (whose images he cast into the fire) resulted from their non-existence: "For they were no gods, but the work of men's hands, wood and stone" (II Kings 19:18). But in his contemptuous defiance of Yahweh he would find that he had to do with the one living and true God. Hezekiah in his prayer affirmed: "Thou art the God, even Thou alone, of all the kingdoms of the earth; Thou hast made heaven and earth" (19:15).

Isaiah boldly affirms as Yahweh's spokesman: "I am he; before me there was no god formed, neither shall there be after me. I, even I am Yahweh, and besides me there is no Savior" (Isa. 43:10-11). To Israel he has proved this by his miraculous deliverances and his clear prediction of coming events, events related to his program of redemption and of judgment upon the ungodly: "I have declared and I have saved, and there was no strange god among you; therefore ye are my witnesses, says Yahweh, And I am God" (v. 12). The heathen who worship false gods fail to see that the deities who images they adore lack objective reality beyond the material which men contribute to the idols. It is to the residue of the wood chopped down for use in the fireplace or stove, shaped into anthropoid figures, that the heathen bow down and pray, saying, "Deliver me, for thou art my God!" (Isa. 44:13-17).

Among heretical or syncretistic Israelites this clear distinction between the one true God and the non-reality of all other "gods" was not found. Numerous references appear in the OT to the maintenance of idolatrous cults alongside the worship of Yahweh—a fact misinterpreted by some modern scholars to indicate that all Hebrews from Abraham until Amos or even the post-Exilic period were aware of the ontological existence of other gods, while bound to Yahweh by a tribal or national loyalty of some sort. But Hebrew Scripture consistently affirms that the knowledge of Yahweh as the only true and living God was cherished by the recipients of special revelation from Adam onward, and the leaders in the development of Israel as a covenant nation from the time of Moses onward clearly understood that no other deities, no matter how firmly believed in by pagan nations, have any genuine existence. "Their idols are silver and gold, the work of men's hands . . . .They have eyes but they see not . . . .They that make them shall be like unto them; yea, everyone that trusteth in them" (Ps. 115:4-8).

Yet as the Israelite nation came under the influence of the surrounding pagan culture, it was difficult for the people to believe that all the heathen were totally mistaken in their metaphysical world-view. From the very beginning there was a constant struggle to escape idolatry. Jacob had to command his household to discard their idols (Gen. 35:2-4); Moses had to suppress the worship of the golden calf by the destruction of 3000 of its devotees (Exod. 32:27-28), and likewise in connection with the worship of Baal-Peor (Num. 25:1-9). The cult of Baal, so widespread among the Canaanites and Phoenicians, continued to plague Israel after the Conquest. Baal-berith (thought by some to refer to Yahweh as "Lord of the covenant") was worshipped after the death of Gideon (Judg. 8:33). Ahab was induced by his Phoenician wife to build a temple to Baal and his consort, Asherah, in his capital city (I Kings 16:31-33). This temple was later (842 B.C.) destroyed by Jehu, after the massacre of all of the worshipers within it (II Kings 10); yet down to the very end of the Northern Kingdom Baalism continued to flourish (cf. Hos. 2). Other deities mentioned in the OT were: the Babylonian Bel (Jer. 50:2; 51:44-52) Merodach or Marduk (Jer. 50:2); the Mesopotamian astral deities, Sakkut and Chiun (Amos 5:26); the Philistine Dagon (I Sam. 5), Ashtoreth, the goddess of love and war (Judges 2:13; 10:6; I Sam 7:3; I Kings 11:33); Tammuz, the vegetation-god (Ezek. 8:14), and the goddess Asherah (frequently mentioned as Baal's consort, but especially worshipped by the queen-mother, Maacah—I Kings 15:13).

GLEASON L. ARCHER

GOLDEN MEAN. The doctrine of the Golden Mean lies at the heart of the ethical system of Aristotle (384-322 B.C.). It expresses the Greek concept of moderation in all things. The moral goal of the good life is the harmonious development of all moral aspects and functions, under the guidance of reason. In general it can be stated that the ideal lies between two extremes. Courage is the mean between rashness and cowardice; self-control between overindul-

gence and repression (*Nicomachean Ethics,* II). Yet Aristotle does not suggest by this that the ideal is always a mid-point between extremes, nor even that it is the same for all men. Indeed he points out that the soldier ought to have more courage than the artist or farmer. Furthermore, Aristotle never claims that the principle is universal in application. Some actions, such as adultery, theft, and murder are always wrong, not just in excess or deficiency. And in the case of such virtues as perfect self-mastery there is no excess or defect for the mean should be considered to be the highest possible state. The mean, then is to be understood as a general principle for moral guidance, not as an absolute rule that allows for no exceptions. It is not necessarily the same for all individuals nor under all circumstances, but is relative to ourselves and "determined by reason, or as a right-minded man would determine it" (*Nic. Ethics,* II).

WARREN C. YOUNG

GOLDEN RULE. This term has been given in modern times to the statement of our Lord in Matt. 7:12 and Luke 6:31. The usual form is Matthew's, "So whatever you wish that men would do to you, do so to them; for this is the law and the prophets" (RSV) The name Golden Rule appears first in English about the middle of the sixteenth century; it occurs in similar form in German, *goldene Regel,* and in Dutch, *de gulden regel* (cf. the Spanish *la regla aurea* and the French *la regle par excellence*).

The negative form appeared in the literatures of antiquity. Confucius is quoted as saying, "What you do not like if done to yourself, do not to others," and Isocrates said, "Do not do to others that at which you would be angry if you suffered it from others." Similar mandates are found in the Buddhist Dhammapada (10, 129f) and in the Mahābhārata (12, 924f, 5, 1517, and 13, 55711f.) where in the latter section it is called "the sum-total of *dharma.*"

When asked for a short summary of the Law, Rabbi Hillel, a contemporary of our Lord, is reported to have said, "Whatsoever you would that men should not do to you, do not that to them." A similar negative rendition is found in Tobit 4:15, while in the early post-Christian literature (the *Didaché* and *The Apology of Aristides*) it seems to have been a catechetical form. The nearest approach to an affirmative form for the Rule in antiquity is found in Confucius' principle of "reciprocity" although some modern Hindu and Buddhist thinkers believe it to be found with positive implications in the ancient Sanskrit and Pali literature.

Our Lord's enunciation of the Golden Rule is reminiscent of the command in Lev. 19:18, but in reality his words inaugurate a new era in person-to-person relationships. He went beyond the best of the formulations of the ancients, who saw this conduct-mode as a restraining or limiting principle, a guide for what ought not to be done. The Golden Rule as enunciated by Jesus becomes a rule of benevolence, of universal application, which goes beyond the merely prudential. It enjoins a role of detachment, shaped by a reflective benevolence in which one finds ethical guidance in the imaginative placing of oneself in the position of another. The guiding principle is, what one would wish done to himself if he were in another's total context. The Golden Rule implies a broad understanding of what is good, and enjoins an individual discerning of the highest good for the self and for others. It is less a scientific definition of Good than a moral precept, in which is implied the prior impartation of a benevolent spirit by which the individual participates sympathetically in the needs and moods of others. The positive thrust of the Golden Rule is in the direction of the extension of help and enhancement, upon the basis of an intelligent anticipation of the well-being of another. It is the duty of the Christian to initiate and sustain this quality of conduct.   HAROLD B. KUHN

GOOD, GOODNESS. See also *Kindness*. The Biblical terms for good and goodness possess a wide range of meaning. In the OT the Hebrew word *tob* ("agreeable," "joyful," "pleasant") is used for something or someone reaching the required practical or moral standard (Exod. 3:8; Gen. 24:16; Prov. 13:22). The LXX translates *tob* by the Greek *agathos* (the normal term for physical or moral goodness; Eccles. 9:2), or *kalos* ("beautiful," "noble"; Job 10:3). The two Greek words are used synonymously in the NT (Rom. 7:12, 16; both *agathos* and *kalos* there describe the law). Paul uses *agathoosune* for the goodness of the Christian (Gal. 5:22), and *chrēstotēs* of the goodness (kindness) of both the Christian and God (Gal. 5:22 and Rom. 11:22); the corresponding Hebrew term for God's goodness is RSV "steadfast love," as in Ps. 136:1ff.).

The distinctive contribution of the Biblical writers to the concept of good(ness) relates to their theocentric understanding of it, as opposed to the man-centered view typical of thinkers in the Greek tradition. Unlike the Greeks, they "define good in terms of God," and not the reverse (J. I. Packer, *NBD*, p. 482). The Bible thus teaches that the essential nature of God is good; He is holy and therefore perfect (Lev. 11:44f.; Ps. 100:5). This is no abstraction, since his works and gifts are themselves good, and reveal God's character of goodness (I Tim. 4:4; Acts 14:17). Within the covenant relationship between God and his people, God's spiritual good gifts are assured for the believer; and of these, material gifts (especially in the OT) are sometimes the mark (Rom. 8:28; cf. Job 42:10). The ultimate and active pledge of this beneficence is to be found in God's gift of his Son for man's salvation (Rom. 8:32). On the basis of the Scriptural doctrine of God in both creation and new creation, it is the clear and logical teaching of the Bible that the law of God itself is good (Ps. 119:39), and so is man's obedience to it (I Tim. 2:2f.).

The Christian view of good(ness) obviously impinges on the thought-world of secular philosophy and ethics. But it offers in addition a unique ethical understanding of the concept, proceeding from the Biblical teaching just surveyed. This is the proper starting-point for the evaluation of any Christian ethic. "Good" may be defined in ontological terms, as the actions man should perform (Plato), the goal at which all things aim (Aristotle), physical pleasure (Epicureanism), reason without passion (Stoicism), or the ultimate source of all things (Plotinus). But, as Augustine and Thomas Aquinas saw, ontological good (while desirable) is impermanent, and without reference to the final purpose for which man was created. On the Christian showing, good must also be defined in these (moral) terms. The Augustinian and Thomist meaning of the good thus builds on the Platonic and Aristotelian, but goes beyond it. Augustine regarded the good as "being," and as a degree of perfection given to man by divine grace. Moreover, since goodness is ultimately to be identified with God, the transcendent and sovereign Creator, man's own goodness must be related to his end, which is to grow in goodness and finally enjoy God forever. Aquinas similarly argued for God's existence as "first cause" and "necessary being," to provide a basis for the change and multiplicity in creation; he then insisted that this "highest being" is synonymous with the good. Man himself must not only exist (and "being" is good), but also develop morally by a creative act of choice, for moral and ontological goodness in the thought of Thomas, following Augustine, are not necessarily identical.

The concept of the "supreme good" debated by the rationalist philosophers tends to be subjective (existential) in character, and relative in content (cf. the work of Spinoza, Kant, Hegel and Sartre). On the other hand, the Christian conception is objective and unique. It does not deal in propositional intellectualizing, but claims that the ground of the good is in a personal, living God who has revealed himself as love and goodness in Jesus Christ. Good(ness) is an absolute quality, which can be seen perfectly in Christ; and its total content and meaning cannot thus be defined pragmatically. Moreover, good is partly to be defined in terms of its opposites, evil and sin. The Biblical doctrine of man makes clear that evil is not only the absence of perfection (as the scholastics held), but also the temptation to choose wrong rather than right, man rather than God (cf. Rom. 1:25); and this, when yielded to, is sin.

There are three further characteristic features in the Christian view of the good. First, man being what he is can only become good through Christ. Goodness, like salvation, is an undeserved gift of God's Spirit (Gal. 5:22). Secondly, man's good works similarly follow from his trust in Christ and obedience to God's commands. They do not lead to salvation, but they should be the mark of it (James 2:18). Finally, man's goodness is related to his final end, and to the purpose of God for his church and for all creation (Rom. 8:19-23). Meanwhile the Christian is called to grow in grace (II Peter 3:18), and to be changed into the likeness of the Lord by the Spirit (II Cor. 3:18).   STEPHEN S. SMALLEY

GOOD NEIGHBOR. In the original meaning of the word "neighbor" there was a geographical implication, for it meant one who lived nearby, a fellow countryman. Neighborliness held an important place in the social ethics of Judaism where there were strict obligations required (Exod. 20:16-17) and strong exhortations to fulfil them (Lev. 19:18).

In the NT the relationship to one's neighbor takes on a new dimension. Jesus teaches that love toward God is the great fundamental demand made upon those who would enter the Kingdom. He goes beyond his nation's ethical tradition and lifts love to new levels so that all other commandments are included in it. Jesus points out (Matt. 22:37-40) that all the law and prophets are summed up in this basic concept of love to God and to one's neighbor. Love to God is not just an exalted religious feeling. It is a relationship with God which by its very nature expresses love to man. This becomes the fundamental motive of Christian action. This places an inseparable connection between the love of God and the love of a neighbor. A member of Christ's Kingdom is confronted with the fact that he cannot truly love God and not be a good neighbor. The Synoptic writers all give it a place of importance (Mark 12:30-31; Matt. 22:39; Luke 10:27).

In this parable of the Good Samaritan (Luke 10:25-32) Jesus moves beyond the more exclusive concept of Judaism in regard to the definition of neighbor and fills it with new meaning. The Good Neighbor of the Kingdom is not bound by local, racial or geographical implications, but rather is motivated by love and compassion wherever he meets need. The Samaritan in the parable had no problem recognizing a neighbor in the man who fell among thieves, and acted generously (Luke 10:35) because it was neighbor love which motivated him. The NT epistles commend this time and again (Rom. 13:9; Gal. 5:14; James 2:8). The living faith of the Christian believer grounded in love calls for action to be the good neighbor to all men.

Carl F. H. Henry, *Christian Personal Ethics*, Grand Rapids, Eerdmans, 1957; A. B. Bruce, *The Parabolic Teaching of Christ*, Armstrong & Sons, 1908; B. H. Branscomb, *The Teachings of Jesus*, Nashville, Abingdon, 1931; E. Clinton Gardner, *Biblical Faith and Social Ethics*, New York, Harper and Brothers, 1960; G. Quell and E. Stauffer,

"Love," *Bible Key Words* from Kittel's *Theologisches Worterbuch*.   LESLIE HUNT

GOOD WORKS. See also *Justification; Merit*. At the center of the teaching of Jesus is love toward God. The basic requirement for members of the Kingdom is obedience to God's will (Matt. 7:21). In teaching about life in the Kingdom Jesus pointed to a greater righteousness than mere conformity to the Law. It meant living in a relationship as sons in imitation of the Father (Matt. 5:48). This involved complete devotion to God and loving service to one's fellow man (Luke 10:27). The NT teaches that good works must be the pattern of Christian living (Titus 2:7).

The principle of merit and rewards for good works had a prominent place in the ethical teaching of Judaism. Jesus, however, rejected the idea that God is under any obligation to reward the believer for good works (Matt. 20:8ff.). Good works are God's due and the Christian must be engaged in good works but not for the purpose of merit or reward. Indeed the man who does good deeds openly to be seen and to gain reward loses it (Matt. 6:1). The motive must be a believer's love toward God and towards his neighbor.

The Epistle of James lays great stress on the importance of good works in Christian living. Some have made considerable issue out of the seeming contradiction between Paul's frequently repeated saying "justified by faith" (Rom. 3:28; 5:1; Gal. 2:16) and that of James "by works a man is justified" (James 2:24). At first sight these two statements seem to be at variance, but upon closer examination we discover them to be supplementary and not contradictory. Paul taught that faith was the basis of justification before God. This faith is not a mere intellectual belief about God but a self-surrender of one's life to him. This is the initial act by which God accepts the believer and starts him on the Christian way. Faith then proves itself in good works. It is not real faith unless it does. The strong position of James is not directed against Pauline doctrine but rather a distortion of it. Some Christians laid hold of Paul's doctrine of justification by faith and ignored what was required of a believer in the matter of good works. This distortion Paul himself rejects vigorously (Rom. 3:8; 6:1-2). James seeks to correct the distortion by laying great emphasis on good works and sees justification as more than the initial act but part of the progress of the spiritual life.

📖 Lindsay Dewar, *An Outline of New Testament Ethics*, London, London University, 1948; Carl F. H. Henry, *Christian Personal Ethics*, Grand Rapids, Eerdmans, 1957; B. H. Branscomb, *The Teachings of Jesus*, Nashville, Abingdon, 1931; William Barclay, *Letters of James and Peter*, St. Andrews Press, 1958.   LESLIE HUNT

GOSPEL. See also *Grace*. This characteristic term for the Christian "good news" (Greek *euangelion* occurs seventy-five times in the NT) and the verb "preach good news" (*euangelizomai*, fifty-one times) are comparatively rare outside early Christian literature. The NT usage stems from passages in Isa. 40-66 which speak of a messenger announcing the return from exile, proclaiming the establishment of God's rule (Isa. 40:9; 41:27; 52:7). The key passage is Isa. 61:1-2: "The Spirit of the Lord God is upon me; because the Lord has anointed me to preach good news to the poor. . . . "

In his sermon at Nazareth Jesus referred Isa. 61:1-2 to himself (Luke 4:16ff.): He had come as bearer of the promised salvation. The content of his message was the Kingdom, or rule of God: "The time is fulfilled, and the Kingdom of God is at hand; repent, and believe in the gospel" (Mark 1:15). This means that the time of blessing to which the OT looked forward, when God's gracious authority would be asserted in a new way, has begun to be realized through the coming of Jesus.

Through his ministry (Matt. 12:28) and death (Mark 10:45) God is dealing with men's bondage to evil, offering them forgiveness (Mark 2:10), joy and peace (Luke 2:10, 14) and knowledge of God (Matt. 11:27). God's kingdom will not be finally established until the return of Christ (Mark 13:26-27); meanwhile men are challenged to enter the kingdom (Mark 10:15; Matt. 18:3), since their fate in that eschatological consummation will depend on their relationship to Jesus and his proclamation of the kingdom (Mark 8:38).

From speeches in Acts and pre-Pauline fragments in Paul's epistles (e.g., I Cor. 15:1ff.; Rom. 1:1-4), C. H. Dodd concluded that in the evangelistic preaching of the primitive church there was a fixed pattern consisting of the following points: (1) The age of fulfillment has dawned. (2) This has taken place through the ministry, death and resurrection of Jesus. (3) By virtue of the resurrection Jesus has been exalted to God's right hand as messianic head of the new Israel. (4) The Holy Spirit in the church is the sign of Christ's present power and glory. (5) The messianic age will shortly reach its consummation in the return of Christ. (6) This proclamation closes with an appeal for repentance, the offer of forgiveness and the Holy Spirit, and the promise of salvation (*The Apostolic Preaching and its Developments*, London, Hodder & Stoughton, 1936).

Critics of Dodd's thesis have rightly objected to the impression he gave that the apostolic gospel was rigid and invariable (cf. R. C. Worley, *Preaching and Teaching in the Earliest Church*, Philadelphia, Westminster, 1967). But Dodd clearly demonstrated that there was a central core of facts and convictions about Jesus—albeit expressed in many different ways—which regularly formed the basis of the early preaching.

We should note well the similarity between this outline of the apostolic message and Jesus' gospel of the Kingdom. But whereas Jesus' message was about the Kingdom of *God,* the church's message was about *Jesus* (Acts 5:42; 8:35; 11:20; 17:18). The one who came proclaiming the gospel has become the content of the gospel! This is striking evidence of the significance which the early Christians attached to the person of Jesus.

Although Paul sometimes speaks of "my gospel" (Rom. 2:16; 16:25) and urges that he "did not receive it from man" (Gal. 1:12)—i.e., his recognition of Jesus as messiah and his authority to preach the gospel derived from his personal encounter with Christ—he agreed with other Christians about its basic contents (I Cor. 15:11; Gal. 2:1-10). There can be only one gospel (Gal. 1:6-9).

Paul's characteristic terms for interpreting the death and resurrection of Christ—"justification" (q.v.), "reconciliation" (q.v.), "redemption" (q.v.)—may be found in Rom. 1-8, where he comes nearest to a systematic exposition of the gospel.

The source of the gospel is God (Rom. 1:1); its subject, Christ (Rom. 1:3-4); its purpose, the salvation of all who believe it (Rom. 1:16).

Although the NT writers oppose the notion that man can earn God's favor by his good works (Luke 18:9-14; Rom. 3:27-28), they insist that faith must prove its genuineness in a manner of life consistent with the nature of the gospel (Matt. 18:23-35; Phil. 1:27) (cf. *Good Works*).

In Jesus' preaching repentance is demanded of those who would enter the Kingdom (Mark 1:15), and his moral teaching (e.g., Matt. 5-7) is presented as a life-style for subjects of the Kingdom. To follow Jesus means to be different from other men (Mark 10:42-44); it demands discipline and costly obedience (Mark 8:34-38; 9:43-48; cf. Gal. 5:19-21).

Paul deals with ethical problems by appealing not to general principles but to the gospel. Thus in Rom. 6:1-11 he explains the relationship between baptism and Christ's death and resurrection, and in verses 12-23 shows how this should affect one's life (cf. Col. 3:1-4; Gal. 5:13-26). This combination of indicative ("God has done...") and imperative ("therefore do...") is characteristic of all Biblical ethics. God's grace and man's response are held in tension, and Biblical religion is thus preserved from antinomianism, which is a denial of the purpose of the gospel, and from legalism, which is a denial of its essential character.

📖 In addition to works already cited, see G. Friedrich in *TDNT,* Vol. II, pp. 707-737; M. Green, *Evangelism in the Early Church,* London, Hodder & Stoughton, 1970; R. H. Mounce, *The Essential Nature of New Testament Preaching,* Grand Rapids, Eerdmans, 1960; R. H. Strachan, "The Gospel in the New Testament," in *IB,* Vol. VII, pp. 3-31.
                                               STEPHEN TRAVIS

GOVERNMENT. See also *International Order; Sovereignty, National; State; World Government.* Government is most often defined as that institution established by law or custom to exercise control over the behavior of the members of a society. It consists of a series of offices whose holders have the authority to make and apply rules, and of the procedures and standards that apply to such action. More generally, government may also be seen as the social process whereby behavior is controlled; the Greek root of the word refers to the helmsman of a ship who directs its course. In either case, the central concern is with maintaining a sufficient level of justice (q.v.) and order so that desired social interaction can take place. Governments employ a variety of means to carry out this function, including moral persuasion, material incentives, and physical coercion.

A broader concept, *political system,* is increasingly used by social scientists to encompass such extralegal entities as political parties and interest groups, which exert great influence over the objectives and policies of their respective governments.

Many of the ethical considerations discussed here also apply to the behavior of these groups. The term *politics* is ordinarily defined as the process whereby persons are selected to hold governmental office and make decisions on the rules with which the society is governed.

Government is universal, found in the simplest primitive communities and in the most complex technological societies. Many theories exist as to the origins of government in human hiatory, but the basic source lies in the conflicts between individuals and groups that spring from the sinful nature of man. When these conflicts cannot be settled by those involved, the community must intervene, both to protect itself from the consequences of that conflict and to prevent or limit future conflicts. The experience of ancient Israel, in which Moses appointed a hierarchy of judges to settle disputes among the people, illustrates the primacy of this function (Exod. 18:13-26).

The institution of government is ordained by God as a means of checking the evil tendencies in the behavior of his creatures, and for channeling their actions for socially beneficial purposes. All political authority is ultimately rooted in God's will (Rom. 13:1-7), but this fact does not automatically bestow his approval on all actions of each individual ruler. Those who govern are held responsible to him for implementing the divine standards of justice to the extent possible by and among sinful men. The political system which consistently fails to maintain an adequate level of order and justice is subject to God's judgment, and he may remove its officials or overthrow the entire regime by means of his choosing (Amos 9:8-10).

The Biblical concept of justice embodies several applications, including impartiality and accuracy in legal judgments (Deut. 16:18-20), liberation and protection of the oppressed and helpless (Amos 2:6-7), supply of the physical needs of those who cannot care for themselves (Isa. 58:7), and the punishment and correction of law-breakers (Rom. 13:3-4). To these basic functions may be added such governmental activities as are necessary to uphold the spirit of these standards and guard the society's integrity. Among these are presumed the duty to go to war to defend one's rightful territory. The specific activities which governments may legitimately undertake will vary with their circumstances. Thus, a nation which lives at a high level of social and technological interdependence needs a much larger volume of regulations and services for its governance than does a relatively simple rural community. Similarly, no "ideal" form of government is to be found in Scripture. Systems ruled by one, the few, or the many are all capable of justice and injustice, depending on their ethical standards and political objectives. However, some measure of responsibility of rulers to the citizens as well as to God is prescribed in the OT (II Sam. 5:3).

Scripture also provides standards for the behavior of the individual citizen toward his government. In the NT he is seen exclusively as a subject; this was the status of Christians in the Roman Empire then. He is told to pay his taxes, and to honor and respect those in authority and pray for them, and obey the laws (Rom. 13:1-7; I Tim. 2:1-2; Mark 12:13-17). Rome did provide a considerable degree of justice and order for her subjects, from which Christians and nonchristians alike benefited, and obedience was commanded for pragmatic as well as ethical reasons. In general, modern governments should be respected and supported as well, even though they may follow principles that are far from Christian otherwise.

However, it is clear that the Christian's obligation to obey is not absolute or unqualified. He must not accede to a law or command which would compel him to violate a commandment of God (Acts 5:29), and should seek by peaceful means to have it changed. By implication, he may also seek, through legitimate procedures if possible, the replacement of those in authority and even of the very institutions of government, should they grossly and consistently violate the divine standards of justice. Indeed, in such cases, he may be called to serve as an instrument of God's judgment on unworthy governors, which may come through violence (q.v.). This course of action is not to be chosen casually, for the price of forced political change is high, and any action should be taken only with a clear understanding of both the moral and the practical realities.

The Christian who is a conscientious subject should also use such opportunities as he has to influence the goals and policies of his political system. In democratic nations he has many avenues for participation, and thus he bears a share of the responsibility (however small) for the behavior of his government. The commands and admonitions which God addressed to the leaders and kings of Israel are therefore relevant to him, in parts, as they express his universal standards for the performance of all human government. It is quite proper for him to seek and hold public office; indeed, it is an honorable calling if he discharges well his responsibilities to God and his fellow citizens (Ps. 72:1-7).   WILLIAM C. JOHNSON

GRACE. Whenever Christians speak about grace they have meant since apostolic times the grace of God. The word grace is a religious term. And our understanding of grace directly determines the matter of how we think about the relationship between God and man, in particular the possibility of man's living according to the will of God; in short, how we think about the meaning of a Christian ethic. The question of what the grace of God is and how it works has been for this reason throughout the cen-

turies the central theme of theology.

Today, far-reaching consensus can be found among Catholic and Protestant theologians on the basic premise: Grace alone can make a man whole! Grace, nevertheless, is understood among Catholic theologians more as a supernatural power which is passed on through the sacraments while in the Reformed tradition it is understood more as God's personal offering of himself through the preaching of the gospel and having fellowship as its goal. To be sure, not a few Protestant theologians are showing a tendency to volatilize the grace of God as simply a love-principle which is supposed to have the desired psychological effect of producing loving people.

In view of these varying perspectives it is imperative that we listen to the theologian who introduced the term into theology, namely the Apostle Paul. He used the Greek word *charis,* which had religious meaning neither in Hellenism nor in the LXX, in order to express in a pregnant way how he had come to a new human existence (I Cor. 15:10) and how the same is to be expected for others (Rom. 3:24; 5:15). The Greek word *charis* means basically "that which makes joyous" and in the Hellenistic world it had become a standing expression for a benevolent deed of a ruler. Along with this Greek word Paul combines the OT notion expressed in the Hebrew word *chesed.* Normally, the LXX translates the term by the Greek word *eleos,* kindness, which appears in the more recent English translations as "grace." According to the OT the "chesed of God" means: God addresses himself as a person to the person of man in order to help him in accord with his covenant. Paul says with the Greek word *charis* something similar and yet coins something new as well. The meaning of this term is to be taken above all from Romans. For Paul grace and love (q.v.) are coordinates (Rom. 5:2). Grace is the demonstration of God's love which overcomes the largely unconscious rejection of the Creator by his creation. In Rom. 9-11 the term used frequently for grace in connection with Israel is mercy (Rom. 11:5f. and 9:15f.; 18:23; 11:30f.). And yet, grace for Paul, while including forgiveness, mercy, and love, has the additional meaning: the final, ultimate, and abiding address of God to men, that to which a man may cling so that he "stands in grace" (Rom. 5:2; Gal. 5:4). It is an unearned bestowal (Rom. 5:15) contradicting a man's desire for autonomy and his achievement categories (Rom. 4:4; 11:6). He who would "help along" his salvation through his own efforts surrenders the grace which is the exclusive medium of salvation in Christ (Gal. 2:21).

Grace, however, is not merely the benevolent decree of a ruler. Rather God gives himself as the gift. Grace is not only something offered, but also a power as well which draws men into service and at the same time frees them from the power of evil (Rom. 5:20f.). So it is that the grace of God operates in the same way as his righteousness (Rom. 6:1f., 18f.) or his Spirit (II Cor. 13:13). For this reason the Spirit-given capabilities of man to act through the utilization of natural talents for God's work of salvation in the world are to be understood as the "gifts of grace" (charismata)—originating in the grace of God (Rom. 12:6; I Cor. 12:4-6). Those talents given the designation "gifts of grace" are only those specific acts of Christian service which directly serve to establish and strengthen faith (Rom. 12:6). Nevertheless, for Paul loving your neighbor (Rom. 12:9-21) and acting as a Christian in society (Rom. 13:1-7; cf. Col. 3:18—4:1) also rest upon grace. In Rom. 12:1 the entire Christian ethic, developed in exemplary fashion in Chapters 12f. takes its rationale from the phrase: "I implore you by the mercies of God. . . ."

Just how the "mercies" of God free men

for a new conduct is explained in Rom. 6-8. According to Rom. 12:2 a man's thinking is "transformed" through grace; he thinks now from the perspective of faith in God the Creator and Redeemer. For this reason he can "test what the will of God is"; he can discover and do that will. Because grace communicates everything that makes men whole, all Paul's letters begin and end with an expression of grace (e.g., Rom. 1:7; I Cor. 1:3; 16:23). Through Paul grace became one of Christian theology's basic terms; it is used by all of the post-Pauline authors of the NT.

Paul correctly interpreted with this term the basis for Jesus' ministry; Jesus did not speak about grace, but his ministry gave grace its definition. The meaning behind Jesus' every word and deed is that God through him addresses men in a new and final way to make them whole. This address is not motivated by the attitude of men nor by that of Israel as the chosen people. All saving transformation which Jesus brings about in men—being made whole, forgiven and brought into discipleship—is not the consequence of human goodness, but is exclusively the consequence of his love. The followers of the Rabbis, for example, selected their teachers; Jesus' disciples, however, were called by him. All positive behavior of men in relationship to Jesus is an answer. They incorporate that activity of Jesus encountered on a person to person basis into life through discipleship, i.e., faith. The fundamental realization of conversion to the Kingdom of God, a conversion demanded by the imperatives of the Sermon on the Mount, is constituted by discipleship and faith; in them the wellspring of a new conduct is to be found. Because God addressed himself through Jesus' words and actions and finally through his death and resurrection to men captive to themselves, a new man has come into existence. The unconditional address of God, i.e., grace, has become the principle of

Christian ethics (cf. John 1:14, 16f.).

LEONHARD GOPPELT

GRATITUDE. Gratitude is the response of the believing man to the goodness and grace of God in creation and redemption. It is the authentic hallmark of the Christian man. The Christian knows that there is nothing which he has not first received. The Christian is one who has a doxology on his lips.

God is the author and giver of every good and perfect gift (James 1:17). We are therefore debtors to God for all that we are and all that we have. "We love him," John testifies, "because he first loved us" (I John 4:19). Our love is always responsible: it is because he has taken the initiative on our behalf that we are enabled to love.

Gratitude is the characteristic attitude of the redeemed man. Kierkegaard gives memorable expression to this fact. "I am," he confesses, "a poor wretch whom God took charge of, and for whom he has done so indescribably much more than I ever expected ... that I only long for the peace of eternity in order to do nothing but thank him" *(The Journals)*.

Gratitude is what motivates the Christian man to service. Paul writes: "I beseech you therefore, brethren, that you present your bodies a living sacrifice, holy, acceptable unto God, which is your reasonable service" (Rom. 12:1). The ground of the apostle's appeal is "the mercies of God": it is the awareness of God's unmerited favor and goodness to us in Christ that should move us to present our bodies as a living "liturgy" to God.

The apostle Peter uses the same argument. Christians, he says, are to show forth the praises of him who has called us out of darkness into his marvellous light (I Peter 2:9). Gratitude expresses itself in thankfulness. The psalmist speaks of the glad joy of the returning exiles when God turned again the captivity of Zion. "Then was our mouth filled with laughter, and our tongue with singing: then said they among the heathen ... the Lord hath done great things for us, whereof we are glad" (Ps. 126:1-2).

The life of the Christian man, rightly understood, is not only a life of joyful thanksgiving, but also a life of service. The man of the world is a man of cold and selfish calculation; the life of the redeemed man is, by contrast, one of glad and generous self-giving. Christ admonished his disciples: "freely ye have received, freely give" (Matt. 10:8).

The expression of God's grace in forgiveness and acceptance causes a man to sing. Thus Paul bids the Ephesians to give thanks always for all things, and to do this in psalms and hymns and spiritual songs, making melody in their hearts to the Lord (Eph. 5:19-20).

Gratitude, expressed in praise and thanksgiving, is the atmosphere in which a Christian lives. "In everything give thanks," the apostle commands, "for this is the will of God in Christ Jesus concerning you" (I Thess. 5:18).

STUART B. BABBAGE

GREED. The word refers to an inordinate and absorbing desire for material possessions. Greed is closely related to avarice, excessive desire for money, and covetousness, the desire for another's possessions. The tenth commandment (Exod. 20:17 and Deut. 5:21) deals expressly with it, while others are concerned with related vices. Jesus warned of the power of possessions (Luke 12:15; Matt. 6:19-24; 19:16-22; etc.). In the Pauline lists of vices (Rom. 1:29ff.; I Cor. 5:11; 6:9; II Cor. 12:20; Gal. 5:19f.; Eph. 4:31; 5:3; Col. 3:5ff.), greed is second in prominence only to sexual sins. This is confirmed in later Christian teaching and experience. The list of the seven "deadly sins" formulated by Gregory the Great included avarice.

Greed is essentially idolatry (Col. 3:5).

The desire for possessions easily becomes all consuming, thus shaping human life in a way that only God should. Besides disrupting social life (Prov. 28:25) and leading to other sins, greed is wrong because it gives ultimate value to a temporal good and leads to apostasy (Ps. 10:3). One must finally choose between God and Mammon as Jesus taught (Matt. 6:24). In the middle ages men were taught to fight greed by cultivating the opposite virtue of generosity or liberality. While not without value, this solution tends to legalism and is less than Biblical and evangelical. Instead we are to will only God and let other values find their penultimate valuation in relationship to him. In the words of Augustine, "Let not these occupy my soul; let God rather occupy it" (*Confessions* x.51)   DONALD W. DAYTON

GREEK ETHICS. Greek ethics during the Pre-Socratic period did not exist in any systematic form. Heraclitus (c. 500 B.C.) condemned drunkenness on the ground that the cosmic principle is fire and therefore dry. Protagoras (c. 440 B.C.) and the other Sophists were relativists and concluded that whatever anyone thinks is just, is just for him. The mystery religions, over several centuries, imposed some irrational taboos (e.g., do not eat beans) and engaged either in ascetic or licentious practices.

Plato (427-347) not only pursued ethical studies systematically, but made them essential to his whole philosophy. His early Socratic dialogues seek to define the several virtues: piety, justice, courage, and so on. So doing he concludes that virtue is knowledge and that no one does wrong knowingly. The reason is that no man wants to harm himself, and if he knows, really knows, that injustice and cowardice will harm him, he will avoid them.

In the period of the *Gorgias,* the *Phaedo,* and the *Republic,* Plato, under Pythagorean and Orphic influence, not only attacks Hedonism (q.v.), the theory that pleasure is the greatest good, but even adopts an asceticism (q.v.) in which pleasure is actually evil. This is combined with arguments for the immortality of the soul and an epistemological theory of suprasensible Ideas, among which the Idea of Good is supreme and even superior to God. On this broad and profound philosophy, Plato advocates a civil government in which philosopher-kings enforce a totalitarian control of art, education, and business so as to promote temperance, courage, justice, and wisdom, along with promiscuity and the abolition of the family.

Aristotle (384-322) made an even more detailed study of ethics than Plato, but the subject is more detached from his main system and is of less importance than it was for his famous teacher. Aristotle was just as totalitarian: the state is the supreme community that includes all others, and since communities are always organized for some good, the all inclusive state aims at the all inclusive good. The family, however, and other lesser communities, are natural and should not be abolished, but merely regulated. The good for man (Aristotle drops Plato's suprasensible Idea Good) is determined by nature, human nature. Since "all men by nature desire to know," as the *Metaphysics* says in its opening line, the highest good is the practice and enjoyment of contemplation and philosophy.

The moral virtues, as distinguished from the higher intellectual virtues, are such things as courage, liberality, temperance and so on. He defines these as the right amount (not too much, not too little) of feelings and action. Too much fear is cowardice; too little is foolhardiness; the right amount is courage. So too with liberality; but Aristotle reflects Greek custom when, so far as his means permit, he will keep up with and outdo "the Joneses."

He also investigates distributive and corrective justice, weakness and badness of will, the criteria of responsibility, and adds a long chapter on friendship. The whole, quite secular, is devoid of Plato's religious enthusiasm.

During their life-time Plato and Aristotle overshadowed two very minor schools that had been stimulated by Socrates. The Cynics stressed virtue, and Diogenes with his lamp searched for an honest man (cf. *Cynicism*). The Cyrenaics on the contrary searched for the grossest pleasures of sense. Both schools refused to develop a full philosophy and were essentially anti-intellectual. They are mentioned only because they gave rise, respectively, to the Stoics and the Epicureans.

The Epicureans accepted Hedonism; but unlike the Cyrenaics they defended their theory with a little logic and an extensive system of physics. Since pain is evil, and since religion causes the greatest crimes and worst pains, especially the fear of divine punishment in a life after death, one's first principle must be that nothing ever comes from nothing by divine power. The universe is a collection of atoms and all phenomena are explained by their bumping each other.

Rejecting the complete mechanism of Democritus, the Epicureans asserted that atoms occasionally swerve for no reason or cause at all. Otherwise men, whose bodies are composed of atoms, could not have free will. Aside from this swerving, the Epicureans explained physical phenomena mechanically in order to show that the gods have nothing to do with the world.

Unlike the Cyrenaics the Epicureans did not recommend gross sensual pleasures. Though good in themselves, intense pleasures produce pains, and therefore the calmer pleasures should be sought. Epicurus even gave a semi-recommendation of celibacy. More to his taste were good meals, dozing in the sun, while avoiding politics and family life. Unjust actions must also be avoided because, even if one escapes civil punishment, one cannot escape the fear of detection, and this fear or pain overbalances the pleasures derived from injustice.

Finally, since the atoms of our body disperse at death, since therefore no pain will be possible, even from the gods, the life of pleasure is best.

Stoicism, in opposition to Hedonism, defined the rational life as a life of virtue. Besides ordinary personal virtues they insisted, against the Epicureans, on political and family responsibilities. It was necessary to insist that most men, maybe all men but Socrates, are totally evil. There are no degrees of evil: a man drowned in two feet of water is just as dead as if drowned in two hundred fathoms. One cannot grow from death to life or evil to wisdom. Moral regeneration must be complete and instantaneous.

A life of virtue and reason was defended on the ground that the substance of the universe itself is a rational fire or energy. Man is a spark of the divine fire and should therefore live according to reason. The Stoics were indeed materialists, or, better, like Heraclitus, hylozoists. They were not atomists. Nor did they allow irrational swerving or uncaused events in their universe. The divine Reason has intelligently planned all things with the result that there can be no free will. After the present cosmos finishes its history in a universal conflagration, things start over again on the exact same course.

Augustine, although he spoke kindly of the Stoic doctrines of fate, providence, and rational causation, deplored eternal recurrence as a pessimism without hope. Christians might also note that the Stoic emperor, Marcus Aurelius, was a cruel persecutor of the church. Then too Christianity sees a flaw in the virtue or wisdom that permits suicide when the going gets difficult.   GORDON H. CLARK

GUARANTEED INCOME. See also *Unemployment; Work.* One aspect of our society which disturbs many Christians is the fact that in the midst of plenty and at a time when per capita income is higher than ever before, millions of people are unemployed and many are destitute. The Christian ethic compels us to consider their need and to assist those who through no fault of their own have no income.

In earlier times the needy often received assistance from relatives, from their closely-knit community, or from voluntary organizations including the church. In our time, however, governments at various levels have assumed a general responsibility to provide the basic necessities of life. Many citizens, although they still donate to charities, feel that they have basically done their part when through taxation they pay for welfare and other assistance plans.

If we assume that it is appropriate that governments should carry a general responsibility for the unemployed, the question arises whether it is equitable that every person who normally would be part of the work force should be guaranteed at least a minimal annual income. What is society's responsibility towards those who because of automation, economic recession and similar reasons are unable to provide for themselves? Many Christians believe that traditional welfare programs are inadequate. It is argued that often the assistance is insufficient, that it undermines the incentive to work, that the system is demeaning and embarassing and that the screening and supervision of welfare recipients is inefficient and expensive.

Some observers suggest that the adoption of a general guaranteed income plan with a built-in work incentive scheme would overcome at least some of these problems. The size of the income in such a plan should be sufficient to permit family units and single people to maintain a pattern of living conducive to health and general well-being but not so large as to discourage a continuing attempt to gain regular employment.

We cannot assume that the problem will disappear with the passing of time; for years it was believed that unemployment would disappear at least during wartime but it is now clear that even during wartime the problem remains.

Those fortunate enough to have steady employment carry a continuing responsibility for less fortunate fellow countrymen. For Christians this responsibility has special significance, for the Biblical emphasis on loving one's neighbor in practical ways cannot be set aside.   JOHN H. REDEKOP

GUIDANCE. The Bible has given rise to an unbroken tradition of the "man of God" as guide. In the OT this is implicit in the shepherding concept of the pastoral ministry. It is explicit in the ministry of our Lord Jesus Christ. Guidance is a function of the Holy Spirit (John 16:13). It is also an aspect of contemporary Christian ministry.

The minister has an obligation to stand in such vital relationship to Christ that he can by creative and imaginative ways bring the light of God's Word to bear upon the pathway of the common life he shares with his parishioners. The minister as guide has an ethical obligation to keep the springs of his own life pure and vibrant. If he is to guide men to God by the living Christ he personally must know him who is the Way. A vital personal experience is the minimal condition for an ethical assumption of the responsibility of a spiritual guide. Likewise the man who knows the Way and fails consistently in pulpit or pastoral ministry to point to Christ, violates the ethic of his role as guide.

Guidance as a ministerial function is carried on by both direction and indirection. Paul and Silas influenced their fellow prisoners at midnight by indirection when they "prayed and sang praises" in the inner cell of the prison (Acts 16:28).

Guiding is characteristically also a one-to-one relationship. It involves a need on one hand and a competence on the other. The bridge of rapport will be an essential minimal condition of effective guidance. The counselor is ethically obliged to perceive the real problem of the counselee in terms of the counselee's frame of reference and then to introduce the relevant new data into the phenomenal field of the counselee in such a way as to assist him to his own insight.

Guiding must have as its goal the development of autonomous motivation on the part of the counselee. It is unethical to perpetuate dependence upon the guide, however flattering to him. The Christian minister will be effective only as his guidance brings his parishioner to full spiritual competence.

Christian direction may involve confession, guidance to Christ, guidance to mature spiritual living, guidance in a stress situation such as a terminal illness or bereavement. The minister in his ordination vows assumes the responsibility to give guidance at critical junctures of human confusion. He is ethically obligated to respond with his best competence, being himself guided by the dynamic Biblical principle that "whatever ye do, do all to the glory of God" (I Cor. 10:31).   JAMES FORRESTER

GUILT. Guilt is basically a legal concept. A court declares a man guilty, and therefore liable to censure or punishment, if convinced that he has broken a law to which he is subject. Guilt is thus not a quality of his act in itself but in relation to a legal system, the rules of which determine what acts incur guilt and how far, if at all, the agent's motives and knowledge of law or circumstance affect the verdict.

For those who see morality primarily as a matter of self-realization or the harmonization of individual goals, moral law and moral guilt are determined by convention—useful at best, but not an ultimate fact of our existence. If, on the other hand, morality is the recognition of an objective moral

law, there is a place for the notion of moral guilt: the conscience appears as prosecutor and judge, punishing the wrongdoer through a sense of lost integrity. For the theist, both the moral law and the verdict of conscience gain their authority from God, their Creator, and the penalty is not merely alienation from self but from him. The Christian doctrine of the Fall, however, involves the consequence that man's conscience and the guilt feelings that it generates no longer necessarily reflect the moral situation as God sees it.

Subjective feelings of guilt, therefore, must be distinguished from the objective reality. Psychologists generally agree that the former originate in the experience of pre-school years and that methods of upbringing affect their character and intensity, guilt feelings being strongest in those whose parents treated them with a combination of warm affection and firm discipline. To Freudians guilt is connected with the formation of the "super-ego" as an inner policeman controlling those basic drives which bring parental disapproval and hence loss of well-being. By identifying himself with the disapproving parent and hence turning back his angry frustration on himself, the child seeks to avoid an estrangement too painful to admit to consciousness. Thus as an adult he is prevented from recognizing guilt feelings for what they are, and, because they still speak with the parents' imperious voice, he invests them with an authority perhaps undeserved.

For the Christian, guilt is a fact of the human condition, even when man is loathe to acknowledge it (Rom. 3:19). The fact that guilt feelings are a product of upbringing does not contradict this, granted that the human family is not a biological accident but an institution ordained by God as a microcosm of his own relation to his creatures (Gen. 1:27-28; Eph. 2:14-15). However the strength of guilt feelings or their occasion may vary between individuals; no one can grow up to maturity without some measure of conditioning to the feelings of his fellow men and of identification with a parent-figure as the source of his well being, and therefore without some capacity to feel guilt. Sin, not least through spoiling the family relationship, has made it impossible for our guilt feelings accurately to reflect God's law. Nevertheless, their existence is a pointer to our fundamental estrangement from him. However, guilt, seen as a quasi-legal category, related to an impersonal moral law, is not the whole of that alienation.

Biblical usage reflects this. Hebrew *'asham* is not exactly equivalent to "guilt," covering both the condition of the offender and the offering by which he makes atonement. The circumstances under which this is offered suggest that sometimes ritual uncleanness rather than guilt is at stake (Lev. 5:1-6:7). Both moral offenses and ritual pollution barred fellowship with God, and therein lay their seriousness. Furthermore, though only the offender's punishment can atone for guilt before an impersonal law, fellowship can be restored, though only on the initiative of the guiltless party. The gospel is the proclamation of this initiative. The Christian no longer *is* guilty before God and needs no longer *feel* guilty, because in Christ God has borne the consequences of his sin and offers him reconciliation despite what he deserves (I Peter 3:18).

Persistent guilt feelings in the absence of an adequate occasion or after assurance of its forgiveness are a common spiritual problem, often associated with depressive neurosis and requiring sensitive counseling and sometimes psychiatric help. The same is true of the compulsive offender, who may feel intensely guilty for acts for which, if they are genuinely beyond his conscious control, he cannot be held responsible. In both cases the causes are often deeply buried in the unconscious and normal pastoral resources may bring no instant relief and even make the sufferer think that he has committed the "unforgiveable sin" (q.v.).

The cure lies in enabling him to face the repressed causes through faith in Christ and confidence in undemanding support from his counselors; but this is often a lengthy and demanding process.

📖 Paul Tournier, *Guilt and Grace*, London, Hodder & Stoughton, 1962 (from the standpoint of a Christian psychiatrist); John G. McKenzie, *Guilt, Its Meaning and Significance*, London: Allen and Unwin (relates the theology and psychology of guilt, from a not entirely conservative point of view); *Concilium*, Vol. 6, No. 6 (June 1970) (contains a stimulating Roman Catholic symposium).   A. J. FRANKLYN DULLEY

H

HABIT. See also *Conventional Morality; Custom; Instincts.* Man is commonly described as "a creature of habit" or as "a bundle of habits." In his *Human Nature and Conduct* (New York, Carlton, 1922), John Dewey (q.v.) sets forth "a belief that an understanding of habit and of different types of habit is the key to social psychology" (Preface).

In psychology, a habit is an automatic (or motor) response to certain situations, which is acquired by learning, reinforced by repetition and is relatively invariable and simple. As the product of learning, habit is clearly distinguishable from instinct; whereas instincts are inherited, habits are acquired. Yet some habits may arise from instincts. The instinct of self-preservation, for example, prompts the habit of complying with major traffic regulations.

More generally, a habit is a specific way of acting or thinking which characterizes a person in certain circumstances and has become almost automatic and sometimes compulsive.

Habits, says the Spanish proverb, are at first cobwebs, then cables. But in their effect habits may be beneficial. The power and influence of a good habit may be as great as the harmful result of a bad one. Since character is largely shaped by habits, to sow good habits (see e.g., Acts 17:11, study of the Scriptures; I Peter 4:9, hospitality) is to reap good character. The Christian is to strip off his old nature with its sinful habits and put on the new nature which is being habitually renewed in the image of Christ through the mighty inward strengthening of Christ's Spirit (Rom. 13:12-14; II Cor. 3:18; Eph. 3:16f.; Col. 3:9f.).

As acquired patterns of behavior and thought, habits may be gained by either unconscious or conscious imitation or emulation. Many lasting habits are formed early in life; the child naturally adopts his parents' habits of speech and conduct. The Christian's habits are to be patterned on those of Christ (John 13:15; II Cor. 8:9; 10:1; Phil. 2:5; Heb. 3:1; 12:1f.) and formed under the Spirit's directions; we are to walk in Christ's steps (I Peter 2:21) and according to the Spirit (Rom. 8:4, 12-14; Gal. 5:16-18, 22f.). There is, in Christian ethics, both an *imitation Christi* and a *repetitio Christi*.   MURRAY J. HARRIS

HALLUCINATORY DRUGS. See *Drugs*.

HAPPINESS. See also *Blessedness; Pleasure*. "Happiness" (*eudamonia*, from which we derive *eudaemonism*) is the term Aristotle used to designate the goal of life. It is an end in itself, never a means to anything else. "Honor, pleasure, intelligence, and all forms of virtue, we choose both for their own sakes, . . . and we also choose them for the sake of happiness. . . . But no one chooses happiness for the sake of honor or

pleasure, nor as a means to anything else at all" (*Nic. Ethics*, I, vii, 1097 b1-6).

Though the one term "happiness" seems to designate a single end, it actually consists of several parts, all necessary. Two factors to be chosen voluntarily are virtuous and rational activity. The virtues are courage, temperance, liberality, and so on. Rational activity is a matter of studying physics, metaphysics, etc. The reason is that these are the natural functions of man as man. The purpose of a flute is to produce music; the purpose of a fish is to produce fish; the purpose of a shoemaker is to produce shoes; but the purpose of man as man is to live virtuously and rationally.

There are also some involuntary factors in happiness. A life of tragedy or disgrace (even unmerited) is not a happy life. Nor can a man be called happy if his children suffer tragedy. Therefore it is impossible to know whether a man is happy until after he is dead.

Augustine's ethics was also eudaemonism. The good life is one of happiness (*beatitudo, beatitas;* both terms coined by Cicero). All men desire happiness (*De Trin.* X, v, 7). "No one lives as he wishes unless he is happy" (*De Civ. Dei,* XIV, 25). Now Augustine would not disparage virtues such as courage and temperance; nor would he belittle rational thought. In fact, no one can be happy without knowledge of the truth. In this there is similarity to Aristotle. But Augustine replaces Aristotle's secularism with Christian content. God is truth and to know God is wisdom. Therefore the happiness Augustine recommends becomes blessedness or beatitude.

More explicitly: wisdom (q.v.) is not the knowledge of some heathen god, nor even of, say, Spinoza's first principle. To have wisdom is to have Christ. Christ is the truth (q.v.); Christ is the wisdom of God.

One reason for making truth the aim of our endeavors is that if we love what can be lost, we cannot be happy. But God, Christ, and truth are immutable, and if we have this, our blessedness is permanent.

Eudaemonism therefore should not be confused with Hedonism (q.v.), as is sometimes ignorantly done; the two form a contrast.   GORDON H. CLARK

HARNACK, ADOLPH. Adolph von Harnack (1851-1930) was born at Dorpat, Estonia, where his father, Theodosius Harnack, was professor of practical theology. He was educated at Dorpat and at Leipzig, where he became *Privatdozent* in Church history (1874) and professor *extraordinarius* (1876). Subsequently, he served as full professor at Giessen (1876-86), Marburg (1886-89) and the University of Berlin (1889-1921). As a noted Church historian he was recognized in his time as the leading authority on the Ante-Nicene period.

Harnack's intellectual pilgrimage led him through the orthodoxy of Dorpat and the historical-critical approach of the Tübingen school to the liberalism of Ritschl, who was primarily concerned with the relation between Christianity and culture. For Harnack religion was essentially a practical affair, having as its goal the proper ordering of life. Such an ordering was possible through the power and revelation of God which Jesus Christ brought. Therefore, he taught that the dogmatic and theological elements should be reduced to a minimum.

He considered the development of dogma in the early church to be the natural outgrowth of a community seeking standards for membership. These standards, according to Harnack, tend to obscure that which is essential in Christianity. Thus, there is need to penetrate back to the practical teachings of Jesus, particularly those dealing with the Kingdom of God. A rediscovery of Jesus was imperative and a continuing reformation was essential.

The Kingdom of God (q.v.) concept was the embodiment of the ethical ideal. In it was found the teaching of the fatherhood of God and the infinite worth of a soul. Christ therefore becomes in his teachings and example, the hero of the human race. The Christian life then is achieved by following his teachings and example, and in realizing the Kingdom characterized by brotherhood and love, and ruled benignly by a somewhat obscure heavenly Father.

Harnack's views soon found a wide following. However, in more recent years support has sharply declined because of criticism by Alfred Loisy, Albrecht Schweitzer and Karl Barth.

PAUL D. FEINBERG

HATE. The Greek word *misein* (classics, LXX and NT) and the Hebrew *sânê'* (OT) express a variety of meanings besides the common understanding of hate as strong aversion or hostility.

1. *Instances in which hostility is absent or virtually absent.* Jacob "loved Rachel more than Leah . . . Leah was hated . . ." (Gen. 29:3-31 RSV) indicates preference for Rachel or distaste for Leah. One of the inscrutabilities of election is Esau's hatred by God (Mal. 1:3; Rom. 9:12-13). Renunciation (q.v.) (hatred) of family and even one's own life (Luke 14:26; cf. Matt. 10:37; John 12:25) is demanded by Jesus of his disciples (cf. A. Carr, "The Meaning of 'Hatred' in the NT," *Exp.* VI Ser., XII ('05), 153-60: Natural affection receives Jesus' highest sanction elsewhere in the NT).

2. *Instances in which hostility is present and endorsed but subordinate to the idea of strong rejection.* Hatred is commended where the integrity of God or a basic principle is at stake, e.g., idolatry (Deut. 12:31); insincere worship (Amos 5:21-23); evil as an expression of opposition to God (Zech. 8:16-17); or where the integrity of the community is threatened (Mal. 2:16). Evildoers themselves are hated (Ps. 5:5; cf. Jude 23 and Rev. 2:6 where there is strong rejection of association and deeds but not of the persons themselves).

3. Instances in which hostility is condemned. In the Greek world, as the evil consequences of hatred become apparent, mercy, love and goodwill are urged (TWNT, IV, 684-85). In the OT the prohibitions against hating one's neighbor (Lev. 19:17) did not originally apply to aliens or to the ungodly (cf. Isa. 56:3-7), but in judging the penalty for slaying another, the presence of hate was the basis for the death penalty (Deut. 19:6, 11). A similar relationship between anger, killing, and guilt is expressed by Jesus (Matt. 5:21-22). With the coming of Christ, hatred of one's brother is described as bondage to darkness (I John 2:9; cf. Titus 3:3) which nullifies one's love for God himself (I John 4:20). The issue of loving or hating is not national or religious but cosmic: God is love (I John 4:8); to love is to know him (I John 4:7) and those who belong to the world hate him (John 15:24) as well as their brother (I John 2:9). Hatred by the world is inevitable for the righteous (John 15:18-19) but even in rejecting evil they do not act under the power of hate (Jude 23) but of a love which overcomes natural and legal customs (Luke 6:27-30).   ROGER W. KUSCHE

HEALTH LAWS. See also *Uncleanness.* The many and varied health related laws found today are the result of the impact of modern medical science on the values of Western civilization as contained in its legal traditions, which have their roots in the Judeo-Christian faith, the law of Greece and Rome, and the English common law.

1. *Health Laws in the Bible.* The earliest known comprehensive set of health laws is found in the OT, although they are not specifically set apart as such. Rather the key concept is found in Lev. 19:2, "Ye shall be holy: for I the Lord your God am holy." Holiness (q.v.) is defined in Lev. 10:10, " . . . that ye may put difference between holy and unholy, and between unclean and clean." This is interpreted to include personal cleanliness (Lev. 11:28; 15:5, and Mark 7:1-3.); purity of the water supply (Lev. 11:32-36); proper disposal of body wastes (Deut. 23:12-14); quick burial of the dead (Deut. 21:23); use of clean foods (Lev. 11; 19:5-8; Deut. 14:21); and isolation of persons contaminated by the dead (Lev. 5:2), by unclean discharges (Lev. 5:3; 15:1-13), and by skin diseases (Lev. 13). Terminal disinfection has provided for both people and things that were contaminated (Lev. 14:34-48; 15:1-13). Isolation of women following childbirth (Lev. 12:1-8), although interpreted in a different way from today, was nevertheless an effective method of preventing childbed fever. Venereal diseases were effectively controlled by the promulgation of sexual morality (Exod. 20:14; Lev. 18:1-20). Provision was made for the enforcement of these laws by the provision of a kind of health officer, the priest (Lev. 13, 14). Health was seen, then, not to be found in nostrums but rather in a holy and clean way of life, and in the cleansing of body and spirit (Lev. 15:13-15). These laws were given to the Israelites at a time when their government was theocratic, and scientific knowledge as such was not great. Every aspect of their lives was to be lived in relationship to God.

2. *Nature of Health Laws.* In the now largely democratic countries of the West, health laws were developed by legislatures. The impact of the Bible was indirectly felt through its influence on the values and beliefs of those who made the laws. Man's obligation to God was seen increasingly in the context of individual freedom. In order to insure and maximize these freedoms, constitutional government was established. The constitutions were responsible for defining the nature and limits of police power, which has been defined as the power "to enact and enforce laws to protect and promote the health, safety, morals, order, peace, comfort, and general welfare of the

people" (Frank P. Grad, *Public Health Law Manual*, New York, A.P.H.A., 1965, p. 5). Although legislatures have the power to make health laws, within the limits of the constitution and the common law, they may, and frequently do, delegate their authority to administrative bodies with greater technical competence in the health field, such as boards of health. This is required by the great number and complexity of certain kinds of health regulations today, and by ongoing scientific and technological developments.

There is frequent tension between the goal of individual freedom and the goal of maximum protection of the health, safety, and welfare of the public. Some religious groups have questioned whether the state has the right to require vaccination of individuals against their wishes in order to protect the public's health; the courts have consistently upheld the right of the state to require immunizations which are known to protect the public's health (Jacobson v. Massachusetts, 197 U.S. 11, 1905). Other issues include requirements for individual disposal of sewage and refuse, searches and seizures, compulsory isolation or hospitalization, the condition and manner of operation of motor vehicles, control of individual incineration, and control of firearms.

3. *Control of Pollution and Consumer Protection.* Another and more complex area concerns the tension between the public's right to health, safety, and a pleasing environment, and the rights of individuals and corporations to do business for profit. Two large problems that develop from this tension are the questions of environmental pollution (q.v.) (to what extent may manufacturers pollute the environment?) and consumer protection (to what extent must the producer insure the safety and purity of his products?). Legislatures and governmental control agencies are struggling with the problem of how to reduce industrial pollution of air, water, and soil without unfairly penalizing one company, business, or an entire industry, and without increasing the cost of the product to such an extent that there is public outcry. The quality of life, and perhaps the survival of mankind, are at stake in this issue (Gen. 2:15).

In the area of consumer protection, originally the legal principle of "caveat emptor" (let the buyer beware) guided the courts regarding the safety of products for sale. However, first in the area of bacteriologic safety, and now in physical and chemical safety as well, courts and legislatures are insisting that the public deserves safe products. Thus, foods, whether packaged and sold at a market or served hot in a restaurant, have standards of bacteriologic and chemical purity. The requirements to kill tuberculous cattle and pasteurize milk were originally considered by the dairy industry to violate their freedoms, but were ultimately shown to be wise not only in the great advance in public health which resulted, but also in the increased profits the industry realized from having healthy herds. However, the standards required for public safety frequently increase costs and decrease profits. Therefore the electorate, through their representatives, ultimately must decide how much safety they will require from consumer products.

4. *Control of Medical Practice.* Another large area of problems for legal control concerns the practice of medical care (cf. *Medical Ethics*). All states use their police power to limit the practice of medicine, dentistry, nursing, and other specialty fields of practice to persons of demonstrated training and competence; this is done through licensure of individuals and institutions. The state also uses its police power to obtain certain kinds of information which is possessed only or largely by health practitioners. Thus states require physicians to report causes of death, to attest to the facts of birth and death, and to report any cases

seen of certain diseases considered dangerous to the health of the public, such as
many infectious diseases. The need for
surveillance and investigation of disease
raises the problems of confidentiality of
medical information.

The rapid advance of medical technology
has created over a relatively short space of
time a large number of issues for which
ethically satisfying answers are difficult to
find. Such capabilities as organ transplants
(q.v.), artificial organs, and maintenance of
life on artifical kidneys present serious
ethical problems. Who should receive the
benefits and at whose expense? Is ability to
pay or individual social usefulness really a
satisfactory criterion by Biblical standards?
Life can often be maintained for weeks or
months by modern technology, albeit often
at a terrible cost in money and suffering for
patient and his family. When have the
attending physicians done what is morally
necessary, so that withholding further
heroic methods (often at the request of
patient and family) does not constitute
euthanasia (q.v.)? The question of abortion
(q.v.) has two levels: under what circumstances, if any, can the Christian consider
abortion as morally acceptable for his
family (Walter O. Spitzer and Carlyle L.
Saylor, *Birth Control and the Christian,*
Wheaton, Tyndale, 1969)? Second, even if
the individual Christian responds negatively
to this question, should he attempt to
enforce his convictions in this controversial
area upon others through legislation?

5. *Health and the Welfare State* (q.v.).
Another category of health legislation directs the allocation of governmental resources to provide health care for individuals or to see that such is provided. The
basic ethical question is, Is health care a
right or a privilege? The answer is not
simple, because adequate health care by
modern standards requires a tremendous
amount of society's resources, and it must
compete with other values that may be

considered the "right" of each citizen in a
wealthy society: adequate housing, food,
and education. If the individuals and voluntary organizations in a society cannot or
will not meet these basic needs of the poor,
should not Christians then support governmental efforts to provide them?

In conclusion, Christians should be reminded that the Bible places greater emphasis upon man's obligations to God and to his
neighbor than upon personal "rights" and
freedoms. These latter values, particularly in
the health field, are dependent upon individuals and the society as a whole first
meeting their responsibilities and obligations to maintain a safe and clean environment, and to provide adequate health care
for all.   JAMES F. JEKEL

HEART TRANSPLANTATION. See also
Medical Ethics; Organ Transplantation.
Nothing particularly unique about cardiac
transplantation sets it apart from other
types of unpaired organ transplants. Because of its name association with the seat
of the emotions, its pulsatile property and
its equation with life itself, its transplantation in the earliest instances attracted a
great deal of dramatic press coverage. Although its cessation of function may end
life more abruptly, it is not more essential
to life than either the liver or the lungs,
both of which have been transplanted in
human beings. It is entirely possible that
because of its purely mechanical function,
as compared to other transplantable organs,
an artificial substitute will be successfully
developed within the next few years. Many
ethical problems will then no longer be
germane.   JOHN E. WOODS

HEAVEN. The word for heaven (Hebrew, *shamayim;* Greek, *ouranos,* pl.
ouranoi) has sometimes a strictly physical
meaning and on other occasions is used with
a distinctly religious significance. In the
former usage it refers to the sky and to

outer space. Here the birds fly (Gen. 1:20), the clouds are formed and from it the rain descends (I Kings 18:45; Matt. 16:2, 3). It is also the realm in which we see the sun, the moon, the stars and the planets (Gen. 15:5; Deut. 4:19; Heb. 11:12).

When used with a religious meaning it is the dwelling place of God (I Kings 8:30, 32; Ps. 2:4; Isa. 66:1; Matt. 5:16; 6:9). Matthew sometimes has "kingdom of heaven" where the other gospels read "kingdom of God." This substitution of "heaven" for "God" may stem from Jewish reticence to speak the divine name. In the OT heaven is not spoken of as the future inheritance of the believer in the way in which it enters into NT teaching (cf. *Immortality*).

The Son of God has come down from heaven (John 3:31) and at his ascension returned to heaven (Acts 1:11; I Peter 3:22). In heaven he is in the presence of God ministering on behalf of the saints (Heb. 9:24; Rom. 8:34; Col. 3:1). From heaven Christ will come in glory and in judgment, the saints to be gathered to himself, the disobedient to be punished (Acts 1:11; I Thess. 1:10; 4:16; II Thess. 1:7-9). Believers will be with God in heaven (Col. 1:5; I Peter 1:4). In the new Jerusalem which comes down from heaven God will dwell with men and "God shall wipe away all tears from their eyes; and there shall be no more death, neither sorrow, nor crying, neither shall there be any more pain; for the former things are passed away" (Rev. 21:3, 4).

In the first century world heaven was generally thought of as being "up" and in the realm of the stars. This is symbolic language and while we recognize its limitations we continue to speak in much the same manner because in areas which transcend human experience we can sometimes best proceed by means of analogy. What is important is not a spatial reference but the presence of God. The concepts of fellowship and of relationship are the central

ideas. God transcends limitations of space and time.

The NT leaves much unsaid about the future life and about the nature of heaven. "It does not yet appear what we shall be, but we know that when he appears we shall be like him, for we shall see him as he is" (I John 3:2). Enough has been given in Scripture to still our anxieties and to give us a firm and confident assurance about the future, even though many questions which pique our curiosity remain unanswered. Where human knowledge fails we can be confident that the power of God will not fail. We have seen the evidence of that power in the resurrection of Jesus Christ from the dead (Rom. 1:4).

Christians are sojourners in this world, i.e., their stay is transitory (I Peter 1:1) for their real citizenship is in heaven (Phil. 3:20). From it they await a Saviour, the Lord Jesus Christ.   D. GEORGE VANDERLIP

HEBREW ETHICS. See *Jewish Ethics; Old Testament Ethics.*

HEDONISM. See also *Greek Ethics; Happiness; Pleasure; Utilitarianism.* Hedonism is the theory that pleasure is the good. Egoistic hedonism plausibly restricts pleasure to the pleasure of the individual. Utilitarianism defines the good as the greatest possible amount of pleasure for all sentient beings. Psychological hedonism, which Jeremy Bentham (q.v.) inconsistently incorporated in his utilitarianism, holds that as a matter of scientific fact, pleasure is man's only motive.

Plato mentions some Sophists who were hedonists; but the first school of hedonism were the Cyrenaics. They restricted pleasure to sense pleasures and tended to stress the most licentious. This form of hedonism has the advantage of providing a clear cut definition of pleasure.

The Epicureans, while they enjoyed eating and acknowledged the pleasure of sex, put more emphasis on peace of mind. Thus they would refrain from injustice because, even if one were not arrested by the police, there would always be that disquieting possibility. As for sex, Epicurus actually recommends celibacy (q.v.). These moral advances over the Cyrenaics are purchased by the failure to given a clear cut definition of pleasure. True, the Epicureans defined pleasure negatively as the complete absence of pain. But as Plato had earlier noted, a broad definition of pleasure allows for such different types of life that, if one of them is good, another cannot be.

Bentham's Utilitarianism suffered implicitly from the same defect; and Mill's explicitly. He distinguished between the pleasures of a man and those of a pig. But this is equivalent to denying that pleasure as pleasure is the good.   GORDON H. CLARK

HELL. See also *Judgment.* Three words in the Scriptures are sometimes translated as "hell." These are *sheol* (in the OT) and *hades* and *gehenna* (in the NT). Another word, *tartarus,* appears in verbal form in II Peter 2:4. This last word was used among the Greeks to refer to a place of punishment located in or under *hades.*

Sheol was the realm of the dead, the underworld. The Hebrew view was that everyone went to *sheol* at death (Gen. 37:35; Isa. 14:11, 15; Ps. 88:3). It was described as dark and gloomy and as a place without return (Job 7:9; 17:13). Here was no work, knowledge or wisdom (Eccles. 9:5, 6, 10). Belief in a resurrection appears later. Some will be raised to everlasting life, some to everlasting contempt (Dan. 12:1, 2).

The Septuagint regularly used the word *hades* to translate the Hebrew word *sheol. Hades* originally referred to the god of the underworld in pagan mythology. As in the case of *sheol* in the OT, *hades* is spoken of in the NT as the place of the dead (Acts 2:27, 31). There is presented the further

thought, however, that death brings an immediate separation of the righteous from the wicked (Luke 16:19-31; Acts 7:59; Phil. 1:23). This distinction did not begin in NT times but had been expressed earlier in Jewish literature. Christ has the keys of death and of *hades* (Rev. 1:18).

Gehenna refers to the valley of the sons of Hinnom, a ravine south of Jerusalem. There, according to popular Jewish belief, the Last Judgment was to take place. In the Gospels it is the term used to speak of a place of punishment after death (Matt. 5:29, 30; 18:9; 23:33; Mark 9:43, 45, 47; Luke 12:5). In the NT *gehenna* is used eleven times in the Synoptic Gospels and once in James 3:6, and nowhere else. The valley of Hinnom was infamous because in Jewish history children had been offered there to the god Moloch (II Chron. 28:3). In later years it became a refuse heap for Jerusalem, and there the rubbish of the city was destroyed by burning. Hence it came to be used symbolically for divine punishment of sin. Whereas *sheol* and *hades* did not originally carry the concept of punishment, *gehenna* did. The opposite of *gehenna* was *paradise* (Luke 23:43). Here were the righteous dead.

The Scriptures focus on the love of God in the proclamation of the gospel more than they do on the terror of punishment if men do not turn to God. Many warnings are given, however, and we cannot escape the fact that not only the Scriptures but our own experiences in life remind us that present decisions and actions carry future consequences, and in the matter of salvation eternal ones.   D. GEORGE VANDERLIP

HENRY, CARL F. H. Carl F. H. Henry (1913-   ) has authored the most thorough study of evangelical ethics in the twentieth century. His writings cover both individual and social ethics.

In *Christian Personal Ethics,* an exposition of the system of Biblical ethics, Henry shows that non-Christian ethical systems lead to a content different from the system of Christian ethics since the controlling ethical assumptions of each differ. Evangelical assumptions—the good as identical with the will of God, man as a fallen bearer of the image of God, justification by faith and the birth of the spiritual man by regeneration—are derived exclusively from Scripture. Not even the *imago dei,* as a recognized point of contact between non-Christians and Christians, constitutes a sufficient moral guide; man in sin requires additional revelational instruction.

The Uneasy Conscience of Fundamentalism (1947) gave impetus in America to an evangelical turning from social withdrawal to social involvement. This was followed by *Aspects of Christian Social Ethics* (1964), supplying broad guidelines for an evangelical strategy of social action. Since God is governor of all things including civil government, regenerate persons are obligated to apply Christian moral principles to social as well as individual problems.

Henry argues in *A Plea for Evangelical Demonstration* that evangelical demonstration is imperative and must always be for the sake of God's larger spiritual and moral purpose for man. Yet social action must not be ventured merely as "an indirect evangelistic ploy" (p. 112). Christianity proclaims the God of justice and of justification. The "double basis of social action" is man's common humanity and "Christian concern and commitment." However, since Christian social action springs from Biblical principles, evangelicals engaging in general social action must either identify their position or, preferably, initiate social action on Christian principles.

C. F. H. Henry, *The Uneasy Conscience of Modern Fundamentalism,* Grand Rapids, Eerdmans, 1947; _____, *Christian Personal Ethics,* Grand Rapids, Eerdmans, 1957; _____, *Aspects of Christian Social Ethics,* Grand Rapids, Eerdmans, 1964; _____, *A Plea for Evangelical Demonstration,* Grand Rapids, Baker, 1971.

ROY W. BUTLER

HEREDITY. See *Environment and Heredity, Genetics.*

HEROISM. Heroism consists of noble courage and extraordinary bravery which is willing, when necessary, to endure great suffering for the benefit of others. It involves intense love for one's neighbor without regard to cost to oneself. A hero risks or sacrifices his life for his fellow or for a stranger. Among the characteristics of heroism are virtue and purpose far above that of ordinary men, illustrious achievement, fortitude in the face of danger, resolute fearlessness and endurance. Often a hero allows or helps someone else to be a hero at his own expense.

RALPH E. POWELL

HETERONOMY. See also *Autonomy.* Heteronomy in ethics means the derivation of a person's moral principles from a source outside the self, such as divine revelation or the concept of universal happiness. Kant (q.v.) condemned it sharply in the belief that ethics is autonomous and that moral principles arise from the rational self. Scripture, with its emphasis on the law of God, contains a heteronomous ethic, though revealed morality need not be considered incompatible with an intrinsic morality mediated through general revelation.

CLARK H. PINNOCK

HIGHWAY SAFETY. Auto accidents on American highways have become a major problem due to carelessness, reckless driving and intoxication. The National Safety Council reports that one-half of the deaths in vehicle accidents are related to drinking drivers.

Positive steps toward greater highway safety are: higher standards for possessing a license to operate a car, periodic inspection of automobiles, uniform traffic laws, and stricter control of drunken driving.

Manufacturers continue to design cars that are dangerous and easily damaged in accidents. These damaged cars must be repaired by costly parts available only from the manufacturers. Producers of cars have demonstrated a reluctance to invest money in safety features. Thus laws and their effective enforcement are needed to force the manufacturers to produce safer cars.

Practical things that every driver can do to make for safer travel are: defensive driving (anticipating the wrong action of other drivers); maintenance of vehicles; refraining from driving when tired, sleepy, or intoxicated; obeying traffic laws; and practicing the Golden Rule: "Drive unto others as you would have them drive unto you."

HENLEE H. BARNETTE

HIJACKING. Hijacking involves stealing valuable items while they are intransit and/or the seizure of persons or items such as airplanes as hostage for ransom, or to gain political objectives. Modern criminals, who stand in the unenviable lineage of "inventors of evil" (Rom. 1:30) have merely updated ancient sins.

Skyjacking, the seizure of planes, if often a dramatic political maneuver as those led by Palestinian guerrillas. Airlines are also the special object of left-wing terrorists who threaten destruction of planes with or without passengers aboard, often seeking passage to another country or large ransoms to further revolutionary aims.

More serious economically is truck hijacking where losses run as high as a billion dollars annually. In 1970, 22,000 cases were reported involving such items as cigarettes, meats, clothing, furs, liquors, and home appliances. Often masterminded by organized crimes in collaboration with insiders, such efforts provide a cheap source of merchandise for legitimate businesses operated by the thieves (such as saloons, restaurants, grocery chains) or delivered to a "fence" who disposes of the items.

PAUL D. SIMMONS

HINDU ETHICS. The designation "Hindu" comes from the Sanskrit *sindhu* ("river") and was applied particularly to the Indus river. The Persian form was *hindu* and the Greeks omitted the *h* and came up with *India*. Hence the term "Hindu" refers to India and "Hinduism" to the religion(s) found there. "Hindu" was first used as a religious designation by Muslim invaders (c. 1000) to distinguish the native inhabitants from themselves. Even excluding the "Jains" and "Buddhists," "Hindu" has been applied to an amorphous body of divergent beliefs and practices.

As early as the *Upanishads* (500 B.C.), the concepts of karma and rebirth were part of Indian thought. Karma (from *kar*, "do") is the application of the law of cause and effect to the spiritual and moral realm. It means that every action (mental as well as physical) has inevitable effects upon the agent. Karma was linked with rebirth for some karma was seen to bear fruit in the same life while other karma reached fruition in subsequent lives. Karma was elaborated to account for various combinations of favorable and unfavorable aspects of the spiritual, mental or physical life. Injustice was thus impossible, and the future depended upon how one handled his present possibilities.

The valuation of life as suffering was joined to asceticism as a means to liberation. To reconcile the ascetic ideal of renunciation with social responsibility, Indians advanced the notion that there were four stages (*aśramas*) in life: student (*brahmacārin*), householder (*gṛhastha*), forest dweller (*vānaprasthya*), and homeless wanderer (*atyaśramin*, "one who is beyond the *aśramas*). While the ethical life had certain universal aspects, duties were significantly determined by one's stage in life.

In addition to the *aśramas*, there developed classes (*varṇas*), which were later determinative for ethics. *Brahmins* were thought to be men of learning, wisdom and spirituality, *Kṣatriyas* were princes or warriors, *Vaiśyas* engaged in commerce and trade, while *Śudras* contributed manual labor and service.

The *Bhagavad Gītā* brings these principles together. Arjuna, a *kṣatriya*, is unwilling to participate in battle. Krishna tells him that if he does not follow his class duty *(varṇadharma)*, he will reap the effects and the social order will be thrown into confusion. But to achieve liberation *(mokṣa)* he must remain unattached. The *Gītā* teaches a dualism between psycho-physical activity *(prakṛti)* and soul *(ātman)*. Renunciation as inactivity is impossible because of the eternal action of *prakṛti*. The perfect act is duty done without attachment.

Another way of organizing these principles is offered by Sankara (788-820). For Sankara, Reality is one. All multiplicity is ultimately illusory *(māyā)* and provisional. As a dream, multiplicity appears to be real as long as it lasts, but can be subrated by the realization of unity. Perfection arises when one experiences unity and realizes that there is no distinction between oneself and Ultimate Reality *(Brahman)*. The *jīvanmukti* (one who is liberated while living) realizes that the body is only appearance. When the karma which produced his body has exhausted itself, the body perishes and the disembodied non-dual state of *videhamukti* results.

If *Brahman* is beyond all distinctions, there are ultimately no ethical distinctions. The *jīvanmukti* transcends all distinctions of good and evil. While he would probably not become involved in social action, neither would he commit acts which presuppose egoism or attachment. On the provisional level of multiplicity, ethical distinctions are necessary for ordering existence. Those actions which lead to liberation and tend to minimize ego-involvement are good, while actions leading to ego-involvement are bad. All acts of the unliberated are involved somewhat in selfish desire. This makes

ethical norms necessary on the provisional or phenomenal level where one would follow his duty as dictated by class and stage in life.

Ethics are a means to liberation. In the yoga system of Patānjali, there are eight steps toward liberation, the first two of which are ethical. The first includes five restraints: against injury to life, falsehoods, theft, unbridled passions, and accepting unnecessary gifts which might lead to greed. The second includes five observances: purifying the body through washings and eating food not likely to increase the passions, contentment with what one has, austerities, study of religious texts, and devotion to god. Without a prior moral life, meditation was considered pointless.

Not all Indian thinkers saw Ultimate Reality as one. Ramānuja (1017-1137) saw liberation not as the realization of nonduality, but as the intuition on the part of the soul that it is a mode of god. Modern thinkers emphasize the reality of the world and place a correspondingly greater emphasis on social concern. Radhakrishnan and Vivekananda both admit that the world of distinctions is provisional, but are emphatic that while distinctions remain ethical concern is imperative. Aurobindo Ghose and Rabindranath Tagore both held to the ultimate reality of the world. Aurobindo appropriated the notion of an evolutionary ascent of the soul from matter through animal to human consciousness. From the human, the soul is ready to advance to the stage of "Supermind." This is a higher level of humanity where a newly constituted gnostic being is brought into existence who will be involved in action while indifferent to its fruits. The life of such a one is not governed by external laws but by the Divine Life within. It was Aurobindo's hope that groups of gnostic beings would form communities in different parts of the world and that their number would grow until hu-

manity itself reached a new level of human existence.   ROBERT D. BAIRD

HIPPOCRATIC OATH. See also *Medical Ethics.* The Oath of Hippocrates reads (translated from the Greek by W. H. S. Jones, *Hippocrates,* Cambridge, Harvard University Press, 1952-58, the Loeb Classical Library, Vol. I, pp. 298-301):

"I swear by Apollo Physician, by Asklepius, by Health, by Heal-all, and by all the gods and goddesses, making them witnesses, that I will carry out, according to my ability and judgment, this oath and this indenture:

"To regard my teacher in this art as equal to my parents; to make him partner in my livelihood, and when he is in need of money to share mine with him; to consider his offspring equal to my brothers; to teach them this art, if they require to learn it, without fee or indenture; and to impart precept, oral instruction, and all the other learning, to my sons, to the sons of my teacher, and to pupils who have signed the indenture and sworn obedience to the physicians' Law, but to none other.

"I will use treatment to help the sick according to my ability and judgment, but I will never use it to injure or wrong them.

"I will not give poison to anyone though asked to do so, nor will I suggest such a plan. Similarly I will not give a pessary to a woman to cause abortion. But in purity and in holiness I will guard my life and my art.

"I will not use the knife either on sufferers from stone, but I will give place to such as are craftsmen therein.

"Into whatsoever house I enter, I will do so to help the sick, keeping myself free from all intentional wrong-doing and harm, especially from fornication with woman or man, bond or free.

"Whatsoever in the course of practice I see or hear (or even outside my practice in social intercourse) that ought never to be published abroad, I will not divulge, but consider such things to be holy secrets.

"Now if I keep this oath and break it not, may I enjoy honour, in my life and art, among all men for all time; but if I transgress and forswear myself, may the opposite befall me."

This oath is generally attributed to the writings of the celebrated Greek physician Hippocrates, a native of the Island of Cos (c. 460—c. 357 B.C.).

It is thought by Edelstein and some others to be derived from the rites of the Pythagoreans.

This oath became the basis of medical ethics in the West. It was translated many times and was sworn to by graduating students of some medical schools until present times. It shows the ethical heights reached by medical practice even in the early medical schools of Greece.

The Hippocratic Oath continues today to be an excellent code for professional conduct. The present generation of medical students and of younger physicians, not unlike their elders, have serious concern for the problems of the real world. They want to help cure the socio-economic ills that exert great influence on the impact of the practice of medicine. The Hippocratic Oath still speaks to them and to all physicians in our permissive society.

L. Edelstein, *The Hippocratic Oath*, Bull. Hist. Med. Supp. #1, 1943, Baltimore, Johns Hopkins; W. Penfield, *The Torch*, Boston, Little, Brown, 1960.   MARTIN L. SINGEWALD

HOAX. A hoax is a deceptive trick or story, usually propounded for mischief or sport. Sometimes a hoax is journalistically "planted" (cf. *Neo-Nephalitism*) in order to expose plagiarism (q.v.). JAMES D. DOUGLAS

HOLINESS. See also *Perfectionism;* "Holiness" more than any other term describes the essential nature of God as infinitely great and unapproachable. It belongs to a complex of terms that describe God's awesomeness, greatness, and power. To regard God as Holy is to regard him with fear and dread (Isa. 8:13); Ps. 96:9). Holiness is closely related to the idea of God's terribleness, judgment, and wrath (Ps. 111:9; Lev. 10:1-3; Ezek. 36:21-24; cf. Heb. 10:31; 12:26-29). It is also associated with fire representing judgment, and theophanies symbolizing God's cleansing and grace (Exod. 3:2-5; Lev. 2:3; Isa. 6:6-7).

The term is applied to men, things, places, and times as related to God, and bears on man's conduct, worship, history and destiny. The Biblical prophets relate holiness to the covenant relationship of God and Israel (e.g., Hosea's "Holy One in your midst" and Isaiah's repeated epithet for God, "Holy One of Israel"; cf. Christ's use of "Holy Father", John 17:11.) The distance and nearness of God are brought together as one reality (Isa. 57:15; 41:14). In the NT the prayer, "Hallowed be thy name" (Matt. 6:9; Luke 11:2) expresses the hope of the coming of God's Kingdom in power and glory. The Book of Revelation often associates holiness with power and greatness of God (4:2-11; 16:4-7).

Holiness is specially affirmed of Jesus Christ. Of his birth Gabriel announces, "therefore the child to be born will be called holy" (Luke 1:35). The demons recognizing him as their destroyer call him, "The Holy One of God" (Mark 1:24; Luke 4:34). Peter uses the same title (John 6:69). Signs and wonders are performed in the name of "the holy servant Jesus" (Acts 4:30). Holiness is specially associated with the Spirit. Christ's baptism is with "the Holy Spirit and with fire" (Luke 3:16). To receive the Holy Spirit is to receive power (Acts 1:8; 2:1-4).

While the word "holy" cannot be equated with moral perfection or righteousness, the term carries clear ethical significance throughout the Biblical writings. "The Holy One" is "of purer eyes than to behold evil and canst not look on wrong" (Hab. 1:12-13; Isa. 1:2-15; Exek. 28:18; II Chron. 30:17-20).

God's people are called to be "partakers of his holiness" (Heb. 12:10). God's holiness is not a static "otherness." He imparts his holiness to his people and particularly to their leaders. The central precept to Israel, "You shall be holy for I the Lord your God am holy" is explained in terms of a righteous and moral life rather than cultic purity (Lev. 19). Uprightness of heart and blameless life are the qualifications for approach to and worship God (Ps. 15:1-5; 24:3-6). The NT Church understood itself as "the holy people" standing in the tradition of Israel (I Peter 2:9-10; Heb. 12:18-24; Rom. 11:13-16). The whole church is built together as a "holy temple in the Lord" (Eph. 2:21). The calling to belong to Christ is the calling to be "saints (Rom. 1:7; Eph. 2:19; I Cor. 1:2). This calling is inseparable from purity of life and moral conduct (Eph. 5:3; Col. 3:5-17; Titus 1:8; I Peter 1:15).

Throughout the Bible holiness in the highest sense is applied to God expressing his awe-inspiring character. To those who stand in right relationship to him, his holiness becomes the controlling source of their total life, conduct and witness.

SAPHIR P. ATHYAL

HOLY SPIRIT. The word "spirit" and its original Biblical equivalents (Heb., *ruach;* in Gk., *pneuma*) contain a wide variety of concepts like wind, breath, life, consciousness, personality, intellect, mental power, ghost. The gradual Biblical revelation of the Holy Spirit both used and purified such previous connotations. In the OT and parts of the NT the Holy Spirit appears more as emanation of God's creative life force and holy nature than as a person. The personal identity breaks through in the writings of Paul and John: the Holy Spirit as intercessor and paraclete. Apostolic Christianity had an experimental knowledge of the Holy Spirit. The Council of Constantinople expressed the doctrine with conceptual clarity when in A.D. 381 it defined him as third person of the Trinity, equal to God — Father and Son.

The dispensation of the Holy Spirit is unfolded in the history of salvation. In the OT the term "Spirit of the Lord" refers to God's life giving and restoring activity in creation and the leading of Israel. He is given to charismatic leaders like judges, kings, and prophets to enable them for their redemptive and mediating tasks. The Holy Spirit as connecting link between God and men and principle of moral regeneration clearly appears in Ps. 51:12-13. The prophets announce the coming of an eschatological Messiah endowed with the fulness of spiritual gifts (Isa. 11:2) and a general outpouring of the Holy Spirit at the end of times in connection with Israel's renewal and the coming Kingdom (Joel 2:28ff.).

In the NT the life and work of Jesus Christ stand in closest relation to the Holy Spirit. In his farewell speeches (John 14-16) Jesus promises to send his disciples the Holy Spirit as paraclete, i.e., counsellor, comforter, and advocate, who will through them continue his redemptive work in the world. This promise is fulfilled at Pentecost, which is also interpreted as a coming true of the OT prophecies of eschatological outpouring of the Holy Spirit (Acts 2:1-21). The reign and presence of Christ between Pentecost and his second coming is enacted by the Holy Spirit. He prepares the consummation of history and will be the regenerating force in the new creation.

The work of the Holy Spirit is both corporate and individual. He builds up the life of the church by establishing the mystical bond between Christ the head and the church his body. Through this work the real presence of the Lord is sensed in the worship of the congregation. He equips her for her mission through vocational ministries and services. As convicting advocate he paves the way into the unbelieving world. The complementary *charismata,* i.e., spiritual gifts, unite all Christians as members into one body for mutual service (I Cor. 12).

By means of inspiration the Holy Spirit is the agent of God's revelation and as such both the living force and the guarantee of reliability and unity of the Biblical Word. While through the OT prophets the Holy Spirit pointed forward to the coming Messiah, in the NT dispensation the Holy Spirit unfolds the truth and relevance of Christ's words as well as the significance of his completed and forthcoming work. As such he is the guide of God's people during the temptations and afflictions of its eschatological pilgrimage.

To the individual believer the work of the Holy Spirit means the application of the redemptive work of Christ and personal connection with him through regeneration and sanctification. Because of his sinful deprivation fallen man is unable both to believe in God and to obey his commandments (Rom. 7). The Holy Spirit is the source of divine life given to the believing and repentant sinner and dwelling in him. He counteracts the sinful inclination of the flesh, i.e., natural man. In Rom. 8 Paul describes Christian life as a constant but hopeful warfare between Spirit and flesh. The Holy Spirit assures us of our divine adoption and mediates our prayer life. In the present tension between the old and the coming new eon our affliction is alleviated by the gift of the Holy Spirit who is the initial experience of the full eschatological life. His sanctifying work is to transform us gradually into the image of Christ (II Cor. 3:18). The evidence is the fruit of the Spirit (Gal. 5:22).

Thus Christian ethics is an unfolding of the life in the Holy Spirit. Since He always takes the initiating and enabling part, the believer's responsibility consists in abiding within the realm of the Holy Spirit, which is identical with fellowship with Christ, and in remaining sensitive and obedient to his promoting of conscience through the Word. Negatively it means not to quench, i.e., willfully to disregard the Holy Spirit which can lead to the unforgivable sin of consciously rejecting him (Matt. 12:32).

Christian responsibility consists also in discerning the Holy Spirit from the camouflages of demonic spirits who through human mediums intrude the church with an usurped prophetic authority or a pretended mediation of charismatic power. I John 2:18-19 identifies such spirits as foreshadowing the Antichrist. The danger of false spiritualism is its disregard of the intimate relationship between Christ and Spirit as well as Spirit and Word. Since the Holy Spirit speaks nothing of his own (John 16:13) but comes to glorify Christ, the decisive test is the truthfulness of the inspired document of revelation, faithfulness to Jesus Christ in his genuine Biblical features, and emphasis on belief in his atoning sacrifice as sole foundation of salvation.

H. Berkhof, *The Doctrine of the Holy Spirit*, Richmond, John Knox; René Pache, *La personne et l'oeuvre du Saint-Esprit*, Editions Emmaus, Switzerland, Saint Legier sur Vevey.

PETER BEYERHAUS

HOMICIDE. See also *Murder.* Homicide is the taking of a human life by a human. Some authorities exclude suicide from the definition.

Homicide may be divided into the categories of lawful (generally termed "justifiable") and unlawful. This recognizes the fact that the taking of life by another human is regrettable even if permitted by law. In the Bible the most obvious examples of justifiable homicide are executions of condemned criminals (Gen. 9:6 and Num. 31:7, 8). The Bible enumerates other examples of justifiable homicide which form a part of almost all modern legal codes; for example, killing an assailant who breaks into one's house at night (Exod. 22:2).

Excusable homicide is a killing that is actually unlawful but is excused for some compelling moral reason. An obvious example is killing by a person who is insane. This is based on the ethical concept that society would be wrong to punish as legally capable those who are mentally deranged. Here is one of the clearest illustrations of the influence of Christian ethics.

Modern law recognizes a distinction between unlawful homicide which is intentional and that which is accidental. The Bible makes this exact distinction in Num. 35:27. The first unlawful homicide in history is Cain's slaying of his brother Abel (Gen. 4:8). God knew of the crime (as he always does) and punished it on the spot. The punishment, banishment, was so severe that Cain wailed that he could not bear it (Gen. 4:12).

The Sixth Commandment clearly condemns unlawful homicide. The Second Commandment given by Christ, love for neighbor as yourself, also embodies it (Matt. 22:29).

The OT regards murder as one of the most terrible crimes, an offense for which no bail bond can be posted, and carrying the punishment of death (Num. 35:31).

The growing modern practice of not always executing murderers depending on the circumstances is clearly consistent with the examples given of justifiable homicide in the OT (cf. *Capital Punishment*). Christ extended the principle of sparing those guilty of a capital crime in the case of the woman caught in adultery (John 8:7). Yet the NT condemns unlawful homicide and sanctions the just punishment of criminals, including punishment for murder (I Peter 2:13, 14).   ROBERT E. FARNELL III

HOMOSEXUALISM AND HOMO-SEXUALITY.

See also *Lesbianism*. Homosexuality refers to sexual behavior between members of the same sex. Authorities agree on what constitutes homosexual behavior, but they have found it difficult to arrive at a clear definition of the homosexual. Some describe a homosexual in terms of overt activity, others in terms of desire, i.e., a preferential attraction to members of the same sex. One may have strong homosexual desires, however, without ever engaging in homosexual activity, or may engage in homosexual activity while having a strong preference for members of the opposite sex. In the latter case, circumstances such as alcoholic influence or prison confinement may help precipitate homosexual experience. The term "bisexual" refers to individuals who engage in both homosexual and heterosexual activity. These individuals may be predominantly homosexual or predominantly heterosexual.

Regardless of how one defines homosexuality, no precise means exist for determining its prevalence. A few studies have indicated that about 4-5 percent of the white male population remain exclusively homosexual after adolescence, and about 10-20 percent engage in sexual behavior with both sexes regularly. Studies carried out in the armed forces during World War II indicated that about 1 percent of the men in the services were homosexual. Researchers estimated that another 1 percent remained undetected, bringing the total to 2 percent. All in all, the statistical evidence now available indicates homosexuality is relatively uncommon.

History records homosexuality in many ancient civilizations. The OT and NT mention the practice and make explicit strong prohibitions against it. Some cultures, for example the ancient Greeks, apparently accepted the practice with little if any disapproval. Though most modern day cultures struggle with the problem, no trace of homosexuality has been found in a number of societies.

The cause of homosexuality has not been clearly established. Theories abound, and may be summarized under two categories. The first may be termed "genetic," and postulate that an individual inherits a predisposition for homosexuality. Such theories draw evidence from studies of twins revealing a much higher incidence of homosexuality among identical twins than among non-identical twins. This second group of theories might be classified as "psychogenic." These theories postulate that family constellation and other environmental factors determine a person's sexual identity. These theories point to the common denominators among the families of many homosexuals. Current research indicates that the family most likely to produce a homosexual boy comprises an overly intimate, possessive, and dominating mother and a detached, hostile father. Mothers tend to be puritanical, sexually frigid, and involved in forming an alliance with her son against the father, whom she demeans. The son becomes excessively submissive to his mother, turns to her for protection, and sides with her in arguments, especially against the father. Fathers of homosexuals often are detached, lacking warmth and affection, and critical of the son. They tend to minimize and humiliate the boy, spending little time with him. The attitude of the boy toward his father involves fear, hatred, and lack of respect. Some researchers feel the relationship of the boy to his father may be more influential in forming sexual identity than the relationship with his mother. These researchers feel strongly that no possibility exists of a child becoming homosexual if he has a warm loving father.

In some homosexuals, fear of the opposite sex appears to be more a dynamic factor than deeply rooted attraction to the same sex. Once these fears are resolved in therapy, heterosexuality prevails. Current research does not consider seduction by other homosexuals, particularly by other boys, a significant causal factor. Latent homosexuality refers to emotional conflicts similar to those of the overt homosexual but without awareness of or overt expression of these conflicts.

Lesbianism refers to female homosexuality. As with male homosexuality, prevalence is unknown. Here the family constellation also appears to play an important role. Recent research indicates that many mothers of Lesbians tend to be hostile and competitive with their daughters. They interfere with establishing a close relationship with the father as well as with boy friends. The fathers of female homosexuals seldom appear to play a dominant role in the family and have considerable difficulty being openly affectionate with their daughters.

Both male and female homosexuals tend to be lonely, isolated people and have difficulty forming satisfactory relationships with their peers even as children. In adolescence and young adulthood, they rarely date. Most homosexuals become aware of their homosexuality before the age of sixteen and many before the age of ten. They tend to gravitate toward large cities and form their own social system, with their own rules, dress, and language. Recently, national organizations have been formed to improve their image, and most of these organizations tend to deny that homosexuals are sick or abnormal.

The layman often asks whether homosexuality ought to be considered sickness or sin. One does not preclude the other. Those who base their faith on the OT and NT documents cannot doubt that their strong prohibitions of homosexual behavior make homosexual activity a direct transgression of God's law. On the other hand, the preponderance of current medical opinion views the homosexual condition as a form of psychopathology that warrants medical intervention.

Many in our society today deny the pathology of homosexuality, refuse to consider its moral implications, and tend to view it as a form of sexual expression that merely "differs" from the statistical norm. Such attitudes, though appearing humane and altruistic, act to destroy the well-being of the homosexual. They not only discourage his seeking available help, but also encourage him to resign himself to a life which clinical evidence reveals to be increasingly lonely and frustrating, regardless of how permissive and accepting our society becomes.

Another question frequently asked involves the attitude of the church toward homosexuals. The homosexual often encounters an insensitive ear and a closed door within the Christian community. Such a reaction intensifies the anguish, the pervasive loneliness, and utter despondency that haunt him and not infrequently leads to his suicide. Christ, while taking strong action against sickness and sin, reached out to both the sick and the sinner with understanding and compassion. The church can ill afford to do less.

The wide coverage afforded homosexuality in the news media, resulting from the recent activity of national homosexual organizations, has made homosexuality more acceptable as a topic of discussion. Thus, the church undoubtedly will become more aware of the problem among some of its members. This ought not to be surprising for at least two reasons. One is that loneliness, intense need for human contact, and the image of himself as a misfit, cause the homosexual to see the Christian community as a refuge and a possible source of comfort. Additionally the high incidence of cold, rejecting fathers within the family background of homosexuals produces within many a yearning for a warm, accepting, loving father. The appeal of Christianity in meeting this particular emotional need is obvious.

Various forms of psychotherapy have been used in treating the homosexual with varying degrees of success. As with all psychotherapy, success depends on multiple factors, the motivation of the patient being important. Homosexuals tend to lack motivation, thus posing one of the more difficult problems for psychiatrists to resolve. Clinical experience has demonstrated that motivation to change plus conscious feelings of guilt significantly increase the prospect of therapeutic success.

ARMAND M. NICHOLI II

HONESTY. Paradoxically our post-Christian civilization despite the death of its absolutes, is most vocal in its demand for honesty (private and public). The search for honesty is apparent in the revolt against doubtful values in architecture, cinema, and painting. But if there is no truth, there is no honesty; if no honesty, then no integrity or wholeness of personality.

Intellectual integrity. It is easy to lie in our technological age through manipulatory power of propaganda and controlled media, but even the manipulators are aware that something "real" is being manipulated.

Emotional health. Wholeness entails an "ethic of honesty." Freud, and others, demonstrate the need for honesty in their emphasis on the psychological well-being of the person. Honesty overcomes fragmentation in thought, word, and action.

Christ and honesty. All forms of hypocrisy (role playing, feigned holiness, spiritless literalism) are denounced by Jesus (Mark 6:14; 23:25-28; Mark 2:27). "We stand in need of folk who have determined to speak directly and unmistakably and come what may, to stand by what they have said" (Camus).

The unity of word and deed is expressed by *kalos* which means honest in the Latin sense of *honestus*, i.e., winsome, attractive behavior (Matt. 5:16; Rom. 7:16; II Cor. 13:7; Gal. 6:9; I Thess. 5:21). Honesty in the Christian sense is more than telling the truth; it is making the truth attractive.

The Christian and Yes or No. Against charges of equivocation and compromises we must always be able to say "in him it is always yes" (II Cor. 1:20). God's love entails his honesty; his honesty entails integrity and trustworthiness. "Let your yes be yes and your no, no." JAMES D. STRAUSS

HONOR. See also *Chivalry; Conscience; Virtue.* The esteem due or paid to worth (cf. Matt. 13:57). At its highest it denotes an excellence of character that preempts all lesser demands, expressed in Richard Lovelace's classic words, "I could not love thee, dear, so much, Loved I not honor more." As in the Biblical commandment to honor parents, honor can involve conformity to strict norms of conduct, expecially in obedience to the dictates of conscience. For those acknowledging such standards violation is a serious offense (Edmund Burke refers to "that chastity of honor which felt a stain like a wound"). The Bible indicates that all men are to be honored (I Peter 2:17), but cites particularly the holders of certain offices such as ruler, priest, and judge. Honor is distinct from, and may be achieved in spite of, the praise of men; the latter response might indeed be an enemy (John 5:44). Although honor is to be sought after, the quest must be carefully controlled lest baneful motives creep in and a clash is provoked with truth and righteousness. That honor (*doxa,* "glory") which comes from the Father is the perfect kind (John 8:54). Over the years numerous peripheral terms have sprung up to claim kin with honor, from the earnest assurance "word of honor," down through academic and funeral "honors," to the somewhat tarnished gambling allusion to "debts of honor."

JAMES D. DOUGLAS

HOPE. See also *Eschatology and Ethics.* The word "hope" has traditionally been understood as the conviction that God will judge the evil of the world and create a new heaven and a new earth with righteousness. The OT prophets tell us that the whole of history is divinely ordered, and interpreted even the most hopeless hours in the light of the coming victory of God. A new age will replace the present one and end all woe and sin.

The NT takes up the theme of the OT idea, but elucidates, sharpens, and specifies it at the same time. Jesus through his life, suffering, death, and resurrection laid the basis for that final intervention of God in history and human experience. Christian hope is concerned with the future of every human being, but it does not end there. The overarching concern encompasses the new humanity or Christ's church.

A controversy is raging today in regard to interpreting this hope in the Kingdom of God. Is this to be understood in apocalyptic terms, in existential terms, or in historical terms? Some, like Bultmann (q.v.), argue that the apocalyptic concept cannot be understood in the context of the world, history, or time, and must therefore be interpreted existentially. Cullmann holds the view that the new era will be the final stage of a continuous time process with the resurrection of Christ being the midpoint. Still others, the "theologians of hope" among them, want to rewrite theology in terms of categories of change, whereby the God-world polarities are reversed (Walter H. Capps, ed., *The Future of Hope,* Philadelphia, Fortress, 1970, p. 28). With change becoming the source or context of theological affirmations, a total restructuring takes place where God is seen as part of the changing process. The basic assumption is that the future is amenable to our plans and actions.

For evangelical Christians, hope will continue to denote the fulfillment and comple-

tion of history when we together with creation will be freed for a glorious new life. This hope is the secret of strength even under the most adverse conditions and is nurtured by God's steadfast love, as promised in the Scriptures, demonstrated in the resurrection of his Son, and experienced by Christians in the past and present.

📖 Jürgen Moltmann, *The Theology of Hope,* New York, Harper, 1967._____, *Religion, Revolution, and the Future,* New York, Harper, 1969; Oscar Cullmann, *Christ and Time,* Philadelphia, Westminster, 1950. HERBERT R. DYMALE

HOSEA. Hosea was a prophet to the Northern Kingdom of Israel (and evidently a citizen) from about 755 to 725 or a little later. This was an age of gross moral and theological decline beyond remedy or reform, and it was his melancholy task to explain to his countrymen why their land was doomed to extinction as a political entity. The distinctive feature of Hosea's ministry was his emphasis upon the heinousness of Israel's sin as a betrayal of God's love. Immoral and ruthlessly materialistic behavior resulted not simply in the violation of the rights of man, but involved trampling the holiness and honor of Yahweh, to whom their forefathers had bound themselves by solemn ties of covenant faithfulness and commitment. With flagrant ingratitude men gave their worship, allegiance and thanks to the degenerate nature-gods of their heathen neighbors, Baal and Ashtoreth and all the rest, rather than gratefully ascribing their fruitfulness and prosperity to the bounty of the one true God. As Hosea, anguished by the adultery and desertion of his unfaithful wife, Gomer, was nevertheless bidden to buy her back from slavery and shame, so it was Yahweh's purpose to redeem his apostate people, or at least that remnant of them who would eventually repent and turn back to him with full purpose to walk with him once more in covenant faithfulness. While there would never be a restored national Kingdom of the

Ten Tribes (Lo-ammi and Lo-ruhamah—chap. 1), yet this remnant (and possibly the Gentile believers who would fill in the gap left by their apostates) would yet experience his mercy and grace.

GLEASON L. ARCHER

HOSPITALITY. In the ancient world the entertainment of a stranger as a guest in one's home was widely recognized as a prime duty. The motive was not always one of generosity, but often the awareness that the giver might one day need hospitality himself. Through the centuries it came to be regarded as a virtue of great importance and the laws dealing with its observance were widespread.

In the OT there is ample evidence that hospitality was observed as a sacred duty (Gen. 18:1-8; 19:1-11), and to refuse to offer it was a serious offense.

In the NT hospitality has a place of prominence at the heart of the mission of Jesus. He came into the world to be received and he certainly counted on the hospitality of men (Luke 2:7; 9:58). During the days of his ministry we find Jesus depending on and accepting the hospitality of others (Matt. 8:20; 9:10; Luke 7:36). There seems to be no question in his mind that it would not be available as he sends out his disciples (Matt. 10:5-15; Mark 6:7-11). It was an accepted fact in the missionary journeys of the early church (Acts 16:15; 18:27).

The ethical basis is seen in the teachings of Jesus and especially in his parables (Luke 10:34ff.; 11:5; 14:12) where he presents a new dimension of hospitality. The motive should not be based on whether the recipient could ever repay or the possibility that the giver might have need himself (Luke 14:12). Membership in the Kingdom of God meant being like God and doing his will. The Christian is a steward of the things he possesses and should give evidence of this by sharing God's gifts with others. Hospi-tality becomes much more than a sacred duty to be observed or a law to be obeyed. It arises spontaneously from one's response to God who is the bounteous Giver.

E. Clinton Gardner, *Biblical Faith and Social Ethics*, New York, Harper and Brothers, 1960; B. H. Branscomb, *The Teachings of Jesus*, Nashville, Abingdon, 1931.   LESLIE HUNT

HOSPITALS. See also *Body; Sick, Care of the; Christian Social Movements; Medical Ethics*. Hospitals have existed in one form or another throughout recorded history, although references to them are fragmentary. Sumerians are believed to have had hospitals in 4000 B.C. According to Pliny there was a college of physicians in Egypt by the eleventh century B.C. and "there were official houses to which the poor went at certain times." In the third century B.C., an edict was published in India by Asoka commanding the establishment of hospitals throughout his dominions. These were still in existence six hundred years later as places where the poor, the destitute, the cripples and the diseased might repair for shelter and every kind of requisite help. The inspiration for these institutions was derived from the Buddhist belief that all life is sacred. Hospitals were established not only for people but for animals and insects. One such institution was still in existence in India in the early nineteenth century.

While hospitals and compassion for the sick did not have their origins in the Christian faith, there is no doubt that hospitals received their greatest impetus from the church in the centuries after Christ. The oldest Christian hospitals were not for sick travelers but rather for the healthy. Usually they provided shelter for pilgrims making journeys to holy places. They were managed by religious orders and brotherhoods, often supported by bequests from the well-to-do for services rendered, or as tangible thanks for supernatural benefits.

The earliest hospitals in the sense that we know them today appear to have been established by the Christian church as a means of propagating the faith. There were outstanding hospitals in Alexandria, Cappadocia, Caesarea and Constantinople, all of which were apparently founded on the basis of instructions to bishops by the Council of Nicaea in A.D. 325 to establish a hospital in every cathedral city.

With the Crusades, leprosy came to Europe in almost epidemic proportions. Hospitals were founded to care for these unfortunates. These institutions were known as lazar-houses. A lazar was any person having a loathsome form of skin eruption. The word referring to Lazarus, the beggar afflicted with sores who was later enfolded in the Father's bosom, as referred to by Jesus.

The oldest existing hospital is probably the Hotel Dieu at Lyons, dating possibly from A.D. 542.

The close alliance between modern missions and medicine is well known. As instruments of evangelization they have served with varying success. There are those who feel that the only justification for their existence is as a part of a missionary effort to spread the gospel. Careful examination of the ministry of Christ, however, reveals that his healing was not always directly related to a specific spiritual ministry, and that he healed because he was moved with compassion. The Christian ethic demands that its adherents minister to the needs of the whole man, both spiritual and physical. The hospital may thus be viewed simply as one of the many avenues through which members of the body of Christ express redemptive concern for their fellow men. That such expression is implemented during the particular stress of physical and often mental affliction, lends added impetus to this outreach of compassion. When the healing ministry offered by a hospital is devoid of compassion, it is often inferior. Secular and religious hospitals may offer equal care, but in numerous instances, patients of alien faith in developing countries afforded a choice between the two types of institutions have largely chosen the latter on the basis of Christian concern for the individual. Love, thus demonstrated in action, is one of the most effective means of Christian witness. This is not to imply that the Christian church should involve itself with the tremendous economic burden of financing hospital construction. Rather, with the urgent need for personnel to man existing secular and government hospitals, especially in developing countries, it would seem appropriate that Christian individuals, both lay and physician, meet the challenge.

JOHN E. WOODS

HOUSEHOLD CODES. The family (q.v.) belongs among the basic, natural orders of creation. Life within a family unit, in an ordered manner, is an inescapable, existential fact; no people, however primitive in culture, has ever existed without its benefit, and a household code. Rules of life have been strictest in the simplest, agrarian cultures; more permissive and more indifferent to moral codes in the sophisticated and more "advanced." By genealogical descent and familial connection each person (father, mother, son, daughter, etc.) has his "station" in the family; also in society, since the family is the microcosm for mankind as a whole. Certain basic rules or commandments are implicit with the "household"— narrowly or broadly conceived—under the sovereignty of God. Standards of morality, or notions thereof, do not differ widely even in pagan cultures from those in the Biblically-oriented world.

But Christian life begins with faith. Good works (q.v.) in Scripture's definition and in Christian theology, proceed out of faith, in accord with God's commandments. Faith has but one subject, Christ, and diligently delights in God's Holy Will. Luther added a "Table of Duties" (Haustafeln) to his Small Catechism, and reminded each Christian to consider "his station according to the Ten Commandments, whether you are a father, mother, son, daughter, etc. . . . " For the Christian, according to his "station," God's commandments become the glorious possibilities of life in his service, especially in terms of NT explication. Husbands and wives find new life for life together in the hortatory, or parenetic, passages in God's Word, sharing love, faithfulness, honor, and respect, and extending forgiveness for each other's failings (Eph. 5:21-33; Col. 3:18,19; I Tim. 2:8-15; Titus 2:4-6; I Peter 3:1-10; Matt. 19:6ff.); parents (cf. *Parenthood*) look upon their children as precious gifts, sacred trusts from God, to be brought up in his nurture (Ps. 127:3; I Tim. 5:8; Eph. 6:4; Col. 3:21; Prov. 22:15); and children, in turn, see that "God has assigned this estate (i.e., parents) the highest place, yea, in his own stead upon earth," as Luther puts it in his Large Catechism, thus drawing the Fourth Commandment into obvious close relationship with the First, for it is godlessness to show contempt, disregard, disobedience, and dishonor to parents (Rom. 1:30) and, moreover, "honor does not comprise love alone, but also deference, humility, and awe, as if we were in the presence of majesty there hidden" (Luther).

Respect for constituted authority has its beginning and end in the household, or familial, unit and rules of life, spreading its antenna horizontally into every aspect of life, social, economic, political, religious. Elert states: "For the center of life where the problem of authority arises, and the only place where it can be solved, is the family circle" (*The Christian Ethos*, 86). In faith and baptism the Christian finds new dynamic, as well as dimension, for triumphant and godly living. On this the apostolic exhortation is grounded (I Cor. 6:11; II Cor. 5:17; I Peter 1:23; 3:21; I John 4:10, 11; 5:4). No household code has ever transcended the "perfect love" of Christian faith acting thus, within the household of faith, in obedience to the Lord and his revealed will. EUGENE F. KLUG

HUMAN EXPERIMENTATION. See also *Human Rights*.

Human experimentation refers to the use of humans as subjects in medical, psychological, social or educational experiments. This practice has grown dramatically in the twentieth century for two reasons: first, the rapid development of those sciences which directly affect human life, and second, at some stage in their development, new techniques, procedures and medicines must be tested on human subjects. The moral issues relate to the rights of the individual and the good of the total community.

Issues related to human experimentation sprang to world attention with the discovery of the atrocities practiced in Nazi Germany in the name of experimental medicine.

The debates following World War II resulted in professional codes that prescribe behavior designed to protect both the rights of the individual and society. The best known codes are *The Declaration of Helsinki*, *The Declaration of Geneva* and *The Nuremburg Code*. In general these call for the following protections: (1) only qualified professionals shall perform such experiments; (2) human subjects are to be used only after extensive laboratory research and animal experimentation has been completed; (3) if possible, consent of the subject should be secured; (4) the research should be significant enough to warrant whatever risk may be involved for the subject.

As the debate continues, other questions have been raised. Should captive groups (prisoners, military personnel, etc.) be asked to serve as subjects? What is the status of those who cannot give informed consent (children, comatose patients, the mentally incompetent)? Should subjects be coerced with payments or rewards? How can social scrutiny by those outside of the profession of the researcher be effectively established?

The caution that is expressed in the area of human experimentation grows out of the Christian's high regard for human life, especially life that is weak or defenseless. (See Exod. 22:22; Deut. 24:17-18; Isa. 1:17; Matt. 25:37-40).

📖 Henry K. Beecher, *Research and the Individual*, New York, Little, Brown, 1970; *Daedalus*, Spring, 1969; World Council of Churches, *Experiments with Man*, New York, Friendship, 1971.

DANIEL B. McGEE

HUMANISM. Humanism in America is the result of two related factors, Unitarianism and Modernism. The latter was the more extensive in its influence and the more philosophical in its principles, though the less consistent in its earlier forms.

Schleiermacher initiated Modernism by replacing written revelation with religious experience, and thus replacing theology with psychology. Our knowledge of God is the result of analyzing experience, precisely the experience of the feeling of dependence. In this way, Schleiermacher believed, the essential doctrines and values of Christianity could be defended against secular scientism, and only the unessential husks of religion would be discarded.

Early Modernism was inconsistent because it retained too much Christian content that could not be obtained by psychological analysis. Humanism is the result of a consistent application of Schleiermacher's principles by which everything Christian is repudiated.

This is most fundamentally seen in the argument about God. The nineteenth century modernists almost without exception believed in God. In Hegelian fashion they may have doubted his personality, but they believed in God.

However, the logic of the matter soon showed that psychological analysis of feelings, in addition to losing the God of Abraham, Isaac, and Jacob, never arrived at anything that could clearly be called God. The more consistent thinkers then asked, Why should the term God be retained when none of its common historical meaning remains?

What can be retained is a set of values, of which the integration of personality is not only one, but, as many humanists say, the highest. They use this as an argument against Christianity. Christianity used to be successful in integrating personality, they contend, but recent experience has shown it less successful. Buddhism and secularism are equally successful. Therefore Christianity is not essential.

This argument, however, leaves Christianity unscathed because Christians do not admit that integration, in this life at least, is the highest good. Furthermore the argument injures Humanism because humanists admit that Christianity in some cases produces integration. Now, if integration is the highest good, Christianity in these cases is better than Humanism, and Humanism has no claim on these people for acceptance. But a philosophy that is "true" or useful only part time and has no logical claim on some people, is not true and cannot make a universal demand.

Other values that Humanism discovers in experience are truth, friendship, and beauty. On these Humanism bases its ethics, or religion if one wishes to retain the term.

This is also another point at which the Christianity of verbal revelation, and even secular philosophy, can easily attack the modernist-humanist line of thought. The reason is that experience can justify nothing. Nietzsche is more convincing than any humanist when he asserts that falsehood is usually a greater value than truth. It is even more difficult to justify beauty—if the word has any definite meaning at all. And friendship, developed into some socialistic or communistic political theory, has no empirical argument in its favor. The most that empiricism can say (and more skeptical considerations would dispute even this) is that such and such is the case: e.g., truth seemed useful to John Doe's purposes on a given date; or, Little Lord Fauntleroy thinks the Sistine Madonna is beautiful. But to say that Mr. X on one occasion thought that Y was a value, or that many X's so thought, is far from proving that Y is a value.

Ethics requires normative principles that never follow from descriptive premises. Therefore Humanism cannot prove that Humanism itself is of any value.

GORDON H. CLARK

HUMANITARIANISM. The term denotes an attitude which has given impetus to a variety of historical movements designed to improve the condition of mankind. The ideological roots of modern humanitarianism are found in ancient civilizations, and more especially in the literature and praxis of the ancient Hebrews.

The Hebrew ethical and social system was distinctive among the systems of antiquity for its concern for the defenseless in society. Particular provision was made for the widow, the orphan, and the "stranger," groups which were frequently the targets for discrimination and exploitation in the ancient world. The Cities of Refuge also provided protection to those involved in false or ambiguous charges of having taken life. Refugees were, under Hebrew law, to be given shelter and assistance in integrating into Hebrew society.

Indic thought, particularly under the influence of the system of the Buddha, contained humanitarian strains. These were derived chiefly from the insistence upon the unity and value of all life, including that of man. The Buddhist antagonism to the growing caste system of ancient India reflected a concern for human equality, and led to the exclusion of Buddhism from the accepted stream of Indian life from about the beginning of the Christian era.

In classical times, despite the aristocratic social models proposed by Plato and Aristotle, humanitarian ideals were expressed by the Pythagoreans especially in their Italian communities. Later the Stoics, probably as a result of their concept of universal Reason, inculcated sympathy with the needs and sufferings of fellow men.

The Christian message introduced new dimensions into classical humanitarianism, especially that of love for the neighbor. By precept and by example, Jesus Christ embodied neighbor-love as "the second and great commandment." The Sermon on the Mount, and especially the Beatitudes, commended mercy and opened the Kingdom to the humble, making the child the paradigm of the citizen of that Kingdom.

The mood and message of our Lord inspired, through his concern for human need and human suffering, the saints and orders of medieval life, especially of St. Francis of Assisi, whose example embodied Christ's dimension of concern for the welfare of all living creatures.

Humanitarian ideals permeated the Renaissance, part of whose thinkers severed humanitarianism from its other-worldly bearings, and restricted the thrust of Christian ideals to man's present predicament. This severance has continued to the present, so that alongside the specifically Christian expression of humanitarian concern there have existed many humanistic emphases and movements.

Immanuel Kant gave formal expression to the secular forms of humanitarianism in his ethical principles, centering in his formulation of the "categorical imperative." Here the emphasis was upon the pursuit of that pattern of behavior which was suitable for extension to the whole of mankind. His stated ethical criterion represents an unacknowledged debt to our Lord's formulation for conduct known as the Golden Rule (q.v.).

Strong humanitarian emphases emerged

within the Christian movement of the seventeenth and eighteenth centuries. German Pietism led to the founding of institutions for the care and nurture of orphans. In England the Quakers pioneered in prison reform and in the amelioration of conditions in the alms houses. Responding to the needs of those impoverished and displaced by the industrial revolution, the Methodist Societies in England, and later their churches in America, expanded their charitable services and sensitized the public conscience to the needs of the unfortunate.

The awakened social conscience led to the establishment of secular agencies, outstanding among which was the British Royal Humane Society which dates from 1744, and its counterpart established in Boston in 1786. Foundling hospitals and public dispensaries appeared in both England and Colonial America in the eighteenth century. Similar movements worked for more humane treatment of the mentally ill.

Christian and secular agencies shared in the development of humanitarian movements which proliferated in the nineteenth century. Clergy and secular reformists joined hands in agitation for the abolition of slavery, and in the combatting of drunkenness among the working classes whose lives were left empty by the spread of the industrial revolution.

Among those responsible for the development of the secular aspect of humanitarianism, Benjamin Franklin is regarded as something of an embodiment of its principles. In his writings, he combined folk-wisdom with a natural benevolence, and commanded wide respect as one deeply concerned for his fellow man. His principles were given a more philosophical and systematic treatment in the nineteenth century by Auguste Comte, who popularized the term *altruism* (q.v.) and who sought to found a Religion of Humanity in which each acted for the interest and welfare of others, rather than out of self-love.

Since 1850, societies for the protection of children and of animals have been established and enlarged. Settlement houses have been maintained in the immigrant sections of large cities. The impetus for these has come largely from Christian sources, whether at first- or second-hand. The Social Gospel (q.v.) movement has sought to find in humanitarianism the essential message of Christianity.   HAROLD B. KUHN

HUMAN NATURE. See also *Fall of Man; Image of God; Man, Doctrine of.* Human nature can best be studied in the one in whom it has been exemplified, the Man Christ Jesus. In him we see that a truly human existence involves total acceptance of the will of God, the sense of vocation to a great enterprise, total self-forgetfulness in the service of others, and faithfulness unto death. These together result in freedom, creativity, fellowship, and joy.

Man as He Is

The mystery, obscurely expressed by the term "Original Sin," is that, though all men have been created for this true humanity, none but the Son of man has ever realized it. Man's true nature is set out in Gen. 1:27 in the phrase that man is created in the image (q.v.) of God (q.v.). This is best understood as meaning that man is made with the capacity for fellowship with God, and also with the impulse "to feel after him and find him" (Acts 17:27). Man is distinguished from the animals in many ways—by the upright carriage, by the size of the brain, by the movable thumb, by the use of tools, by the use of fire. More important than any of these is the sense of the divine, the unseen. Ethnologists have sought in vain for a people without religion. It seems that awareness of the unseen, as menace, as command, or as fulfilment, is inborn in the race, and has existed since man as man first appeared on the earth.

Man can best be studied in terms of his relationships. Full and rounded human existence demands balanced and harmonious relationships in four directions—down, in, out, and up. Man is related to the whole physical universe; in the splendid picture of Genesis, he was put into the garden to dress it and to tend it. All too often man has become the wrecker and the pillager, instead of the priest of the world, creating deserts and dustbowls where God had created fertility and beauty. Man's many gifts should produce inner harmony; with the dislocation called sin, these gifts fall out of balance. For example, the beautiful and wonderful sexual apparatus, strong and creative as a servant, becomes a raging and destructive monster. Man can no longer live with himself. Since he cannot live with himself inwardly, he cannot live with others outwardly. The other, instead of being complement and fulfillment to man, becomes the threat, the aggressor, the enemy. Hence, strife within the family, contention in society, and on the international scale wars and rumors of wars. All this has come about because the basic relationship upwards to God has become disturbed; the place of the true God has all too often been taken by idols, cruel and capricious, of man's own devising.

The doctrine of total depravity was put forward to guard against the idea of the mystics that there is in the soul of man a divine spark, which has never been touched by sin. This is not so; no part of man's nature has been safeguarded against the ravages of sin. But this is not to say that man has totally yielded to sin; if he had done so, he would have ceased to be human. Even in his alienation, man is capable of great achievement. The modern world still has to turn to the Greeks for instruction in the art of thinking and the apprehension of beauty, to the Romans for instruction in the meaning of law and discipline. The thought of God has never been absent from the minds of men. But man's alienation cannot be healed by man; it can be healed only by act of the living God.

The New Man in Christ

We are saved by the death of Christ. It is often forgotten that we are saved by the death *of Christ*. The new thing was that one Man had lived for more than thirty years in perfect submission to the will of God and in unbroken fellowship with him. This was the consummation for which the universe had waited from the beginning. Because of this, in the death and resurrection of Jesus, the whole universe was born again and the new creation is already here (II Cor. 5:17). Faith in Christ, of which baptism is the outward sign and seal, means incorporation into the body of the risen Jesus. The God of love is restored to his rightful place as Lord and sovereign over human life; when this relationship is renewed, the relationships in the three other directions come also to be renewed; in the dignity of the last Adam, man can recover all that was lost in the failure of the first Adam (I Cor. 15:42-50). But this is not achieved in a moment. The old is subdued but it is not destroyed; hence the element of conflict in the life of the believer, and in the life of the church; two worlds co-exist, and the old is ever striving to reassert its lost sovereignty. This is the condition under which the church is called to serve until the final victory of Christ.

In the recovery of true manhood there is an element of changelessness and an element of change. The changeless is the perfected character and victory of Jesus Christ, the same yesterday today and forever (Heb. 13:8). The changing element is the work of the Spirit, through whom the transformation of human nature after the image of Christ (Col 3:5-11) is gradually worked out. The characteristic of this new life is freedom (II Cor. 4:17-18), the freedom of sons in their Father's house (Gal. 4:4-7).

The Destiny of Man

We are saved in hope (Rom. 8:18-25).

The perfect fulfillment of our hopes lies the other side of the final triumph of Christ. Of the nature of that triumph little has been revealed in Scripture; all that we can say with certainty is that for us it will mean "to be with Christ, for that is far better" (Phil. 1:23). We can be assured that, however splendid our imaginations of that world may be, what God has prepared for us will far surpass the highest flights of our imagination. We know that life will mean the fulness of fellowship with the Father and with all those who are in the body of Christ; the fulness of service, without the imperfections and frustrations of all our service here; and unimpeded progress in the knowledge and love of God, which will continue throughout eternity.

If little is revealed in detail of the destiny of those who are in Christ, still less are we told of those who have not known him or who have continued in rebellion. Universalism is one of the most popular of modern heresies, but it has no foundation in Scripture. Each one of us, in his own heart, knows all too well one man or one woman who could be lost eternally. But we know that the Father of all is far wiser and far more compassionate than we; he may have ways beyond our imagining of bringing the lost son home to himself. We have the absolute assurance that the Father of our spirits will bring each human spirit that he has created to its own place. And we are warned against idle speculation in one of the most alarming of the words of the Lord himself; when asked "Are there few that be saved?" (Luke 13:23), he replied sternly, "Strive to enter by the narrow door; for many, I tell you, will seek to enter and will not be able."   STEPHEN C. NEILL

HUMILITY. See also *Meekness*. If pride is the supreme sin, it follows that humility, its opposite, should be given a primary place among the virtues. Augustine (q.v.) was one who recognized that primacy. The OT gave it a central position in true piety (Micah 6:8) at a time when the pagan world, especially the Greeks, thought of it as weakness, the mark of a servile spirit. The truth that God shows favor to the humble (Prov. 3:34) received verification in the choice of Mary as the mother of the Saviour and was the burden of her song of exultation (Luke 1:46-55).

However, the great change in the estimation of the worth of humility came with the impact of Jesus Christ upon mankind. His incarnation was a breathtaking manifestation of it as the Son of God took his place among the sons of men, and not in regal majesty or power but in obscurity and poverty (II Cor. 8:9). His teaching magnified its necessity for conversion (Matt. 18:3-4) and for discipleship (Luke 14:11). By his own declaration, he was "lowly in heart" (Matt. 11:29). One can be lowly in his worldy status but unless one is lowly in heart he is not truly humble. In the case of Jesus, humility could co-exist with the most exalted claims for the reason that the claims contained no exaggeration nor were they the expression of an aspiring and ambitious spirit. This observation provides help for the Christian who seeks to avoid the pitfall of false humility. He is not expected to depreciate himself. In deed as well as in word our Lord was humble. The washing of the disciples' feet was not a spectacle for the world to see, but a lesson that his own must never forget (John 13:3-17). Shortly thereafter came the climactic event in which occurred the supreme self-humbling. As Paul reminds us, this act of humiliation at the cross was undertaken by one who had already assumed the likeness of man, and for this reason he can be our pattern in this crucial area of life. This same apostle, remembering that he was chief of sinners because of persecuting Christ through his church, was bound to make humility a fundamental element of his ministry (Acts 20:19). He recognized that it was essential for the peace and progress of the Christian community (Phil. 2:3ff.).

Humility may be promoted through the experience of suffering, through reflection on the truth that we have nothing that we have not received, and through reminding ourselves constantly that we are utterly dependent on the mercy and grace of God.

EVERETT F. HARRISON

HUNTING. See also *Animals; Cruelty.* The Bible does not teach that hunting pursued to meet the true needs of man is wrong. Hunting for sport or profit may be another question, but one that is not easy to answer. It is less cruel for the population of some animals to be kept under control by hunting than for excess animals to die of disease or starvation. But there would be no disease or starvation had there not been a curse on nature as a result of sin. The Christian must find an answer that centers around God's purpose in putting animals on the earth. God's command that Adam and Eve multiply and subdue the earth (Gen. 1:28) was not an invitation to destroy nature. God's image bearer should behave like God toward nature. Every beast of the field and fowl of the air was placed on the earth to honor God and for man's good.

ELMER B. SMICK

HUSBAND AND WIFE. See *Family; Household Codes; Marriage.*

HYPNOTISM. See also *Suggestion.* Hypnotism refers to the act of inducing hypnosis, a trancelike state of heightened concentration and increased suggestibility.

Hypnosis (from the Greek *hypnos,* meaning sleep) has been known in one form or another for centuries. Its first recorded therapeutic use occurred in the eighteenth century when Franz Mesmer, a European physician, described a treatment that became known as mesmerism. Physicians continued to experiment with this process and

in the middle of the nineteenth century, James Braid, an English doctor, coined the terms hypnosis and hypnotism. A resurgence of interest in the medical uses of hypnosis occurred during the 1950s when the British and American medical associations formally approved its use.

Though we have little understanding of what occurs during the hypnotic trance, many different theories have been proffered. The trance differs from sleep in that the subject is conscious, his awareness is limited and focused, he experiences progressive relaxation, becomes highly suggestible (but not to pronouncements against his will) and shifts his attention from the outside world to his inner self.

Hypnosis has been used in the treatment of many physical and emotional illnesses and as an anesthetic in surgery, obstetrics, and dentistry.

The danger of hypnosis lies in its abuse by unethical or untrained and uninformed persons. Although hypnosis can not be induced without the subject's willingness, an unskilled hypnotist may precipitate untoward reactions—e.g., criminal behavior in a person with latent criminal impulses or an intensification of psychiatric symptoms in a person not amenable to hypnosis.

ARMAND M. NICHOLI II

HYPOCRISY. Originally a technical term in Greek drama, designating the act of playing a part and the one who plays a part, hypocrisy came to mean feigning or pretending to be what one is not. The outward appearance bears no relation to the inward being. In English its dominant meaning is an insincere simulation of goodness or piety.

In the Bible hypocrisy goes deeper morally than simply the idea of pretense, though the latter nuance is not absent. The chief priests sent spies, "pretending to be sincere," that they might implicate Jesus in some crime (Luke 20:20). Jesus indicated the Pharisees for serious moral discrepancy in their lives: "So you also outwardly appear righteous to men, but within you are full of hypocrisy and iniquity" (Matt. 23:28). Jesus opposed outward religious ostentation which so often exists apart from genuine piety (Matt. 6:2, 5, 16). He criticized as hypocrites those who could clearly see the speck in a brother's eye, and fail to see the log in their own (Matt. 7:5). It is likely, however, that Jesus had more in mind than pretense when he condemned the Pharisees as hypocrites. Parallel to "hypocrisy" in Mark 12:15, we find "malice" in Matt. 22:18 and "craftiness" in Luke 20:23. In Luke 12:46 we find the reading "unfaithful" in place of "hypocrites" in Matt. 24:51. Hypocrisy includes radical opposition to God and wickedness. The Pharisees were not criticized just for pretending to be good and relgious; they were self-righteous and convinced of their own goodness, so much so that they set themselves against the gospel and stood in the way of others accepting it. "But woe to you, scribes and Pharisees, hypocrites be-cause you shut the kingdom of heaven against men; for you neither enter yourselves, nor allow those who would enter to go in" (Matt. 23:13).

In Antioch, when Peter withdrew from eating with Gentile Christians, Paul accused him and Barnabas of acting like hypocrites (Gal. 2:13). Their outward behavior did not line up with their inward convictions. More than that, it was a breach of faith against the gospel of grace. In his first letter, Peter couples hypocrisy with malice, guile, envy, and slander (I Peter 2:1). Paul reproaches false teachers for hypocrisy, meaning their falsification of the true faith (I Tim. 4:2). Hypocrisy may be conscious or unconscious. Because of social pressures, we adopt attitudes and actions acceptible to the group.

Conforming to public opinion instead of following the dictates of conscience is what existential philosophers generally mean by inauthentic existence. It also opposes the Biblical insistence on truthfulness in word and deed.   CLARK H. PINNOCK

I

ID. The id is one of the elements, along with ego and superego, that make up a tripartite model of personality in the structural theory devised by Sigmund Freud. This hypothetical system replaced Freud's earlier topographic theory, which divided personality into unconscious, preconscious and conscious. Freud regarded the id as the undifferentiated, primitive, unconscious portion of the psychic apparatus. According to his theory, as the organism encounters reality, driven by the instinctual urge for gratification, the ego develops as a kind of mediator, to bring the untamed urges of the id under control. Freud likened the id and ego to a horse and rider, the horse being the stronger, but usually controlled by the rider. The id does not relate itself directly to external reality, but seeks gratification by following the pleasure principle. The ego develops to bring the id into line with the reality principle.

By attributing all the driving power of personality, both functional and creative, to energy derived from the instincts of sex and aggression, Freud created an id-psychology based upon conflict—pleasure versus reality, the primitive irrational versus the rational. In recent decades, this id-psychology has largely been supplanted, even within psychoanalysis, by an ego-psychology in which autonomy of the person is acknowledged. Such recognition of purpose and decision in human destiny may easily be harmonized with Biblical teaching on the nature of man.

Sigmund Freud, *An Outline of Psychoanalysis*, New York, Norton, 1949; Robert W. White, *Ego and Reality in Psychoanalytic Theory*, New York, International Universities Press, 1963.

ORVILLE S. WALTERS

IDEALISTIC ETHICS. Idealistic ethics specifically designates the ethics of Hegel, his Kantian predecessors, and immediate disciples; the inclusion of Berkeley, Leibniz, and Plato (all idealists in virtue of the term's elasticity) would leave no common ethics to be discussed.

Hegelian ethics develops out of Kant's attempt to escape Spinozistic mechanism. Kant agreed that all bodily motions, including the motions of the human body, are mathematically determined by the inviolable laws of causation. But morality, to which Kant was fervently attached, presupposes God, freedom, and immortality. To harmonize these two themes Kant postulated two worlds: the sensory world of space, time, and causality, and the noumenal world of things in themselves, free transcendental egos, and God. This solution encounters both epistemological and ethical difficulties (cf. *Kant*).

Johann Gottlieb Fichte (1762-1814) admitted that there is no logical flaw in scientific mechanism. But though mechanism cannot be disproved, it is morally unacceptable. No philosophy can demonstrate its own principles, and in these matters one is faced with an ultimate choice. Whether a man chooses Spinozism or freedom depends on what kind of a man he is. Fichte chose morality and freedom.

The moral self, now accepted as the fundamental principle of philosophy, also removes the epistemological difficulties of an unknowable world. Kant had analyzed knowledge into two components; the *forms* of the mind, such as space, time, and causality, which it imposes on experience,

and the *contents* that are *given to* the mind by experience. *Das Gegebenes*, the data, required an unknowable source. If, however, we commence with the moral self, the objects of nature become constructions of my consciousness. I *give* them to myself, and no unknowable source is needed.

This idealism avoids the great absurdity of materialism. The latter denies fundamental reality to mind, as for example the twentieth century behaviorists deny even the existence of consciousness; but knowledge can begin only with some sort of *Cogito*. Philosophy and experience both start with the self. But if this is the starting point, the objects of nature are derivative. Having so deduced them, a philosopher cannot then reverse himself and profess to explain the self as a result of nature.

The moral self also solves the problem of solipsism. The moral self has obligations. But neither Humean images nor Kantian phenomena have. Therefore the self is not a phenomenon. Furthermore no obligations are due to images or phenomena. Obligations can exist only among persons. Therefore solipsism is impossible and I am a member of a world of free spirits.

If these free spirits were totally independent, the world would be a chaos. Beyond the plurality is a single, all inclusive Absolute Self.

Fichte's Absolute Self is by no means the personal God of Christianity. Fichte opposed Christianity: its people are hedonistic (since they desire heaven) and therefore immoral; and what is worse, its God is also hedonistic because he created the world for his own pleasure. Such a God is the devil.

Therefore Fichte concludes, "It is not doubtful . . . that there is a moral world order . . . that every good action succeeds and every evil fails, that for those who love only the good, all things must work for the best. . . . It can as little remain uncertain . . . that the concept of God as a particular substance is impossible and contradictory."

Hegel, in conformity with his triadic method, divides the general subject into Abstract Right, Morality, and Social Ethics. Although abstract right is supposed to concern externalities, like property, and morality concerns inner motivation, the former includes a theory of the person that lays the foundation for early twentieth century personalism.

A person is a consciousness that knows itself, as animals do not, and therefore has rights. Things have no rights. Therefore property is justified. The exercise of property rights may be possible only in a State, but the right itself is inherent in the individual. This means that not merely property is justified, but private property.

How far Hegel would have approved of latter developments may be hard to decide. Even communism can argue that the State does not abolish private property but merely distributes it—the food one actually eats must be private.

A consideration of crime and punishment brings morality into focus. Crime reveals an opposition between the will of one individual and the universal will. But since the latter is the essence of the former, a criminal will does not conform to what it ought to be. Thus it violates its own personality. It negates its own right. Punishment is the negation of the negation. Morality consists in the conformity of the individual will to the universal.

But morality is a one-sided abstraction that must be completed by social ethics. Freedom, the rational goal of man in history, is the individual's subjection to the State. The State is the individual's true self, and if, as is sometimes the case, an individual must be sacrificed to or for the State, it is a sacrifice of the individual to his own higher self.

Hegel went into many details about marriage and the family, agriculture and industry, the judicial system including the police, the forms of government, and world history—none of which can be included here.

Hegel's influence on Marx (q.v.) must also be omitted to allow space for a disciple who was more orthodox and more interested in Ethics. Thomas Hill Green (1836-1882), an English idealist, was very much interested in refuting utilitarianism. Empiricism had resulted in skepticism; evolution had reduced morality to a vestigial fear inherited from animal ancestors; and physics explained all phenomena mechanically. Green gave the idealist reply.

To begin with, knowledge cannot be explained empirically or mechanically. Natural change does not know itself. Knowledge of change is not a part of the changing process, for, if it were, it could not know any process as a whole but would be confined to the moment.

Since, therefore, man is free, rather than a natural product, morality is possible. Green is not concerned with an indeterminism that asserts unmotivated willing; he wishes to maintain the existence of moral motives that are not natural phenomena. This rules out animal wants. Such appetites do not lead to distinctively human action. Morality requires a self-conscious subject and the idea of self-satisfaction or self-realization.

Such a man and such a morality cannot exist in the world that materialistic science pictures. The universe must be conceived as personal. We can conceive of such a world, a world that is an object to a single mind, and a connected whole, only because we are conscious objects to ourselves. The irreducibility of this self-objectifying consciousness to mechanistic science compels us to regard this our consciousness as the presence in us of the mind for which the world exists.

This divine mind or God is not merely a Being who has made us; he is a Being in whom we live and have our being. We are one in principle with him. He is all that human spirit is capable of becoming.

Therefore morality consists in self-realization. It cannot consist in utilitarian pleasure. Our aim must be a state of self-conscious life that is intrinsically desirable, the full realization of our capabilities.

📖 A. C. Bradley, ed., *Prolegomena to Ethics*, Oxford, Oxford University, 1883; G. W. F. Hegel, *The Philosophy of Right*, tr., T. M. Knox, Oxford, 1942; Sidney Hook, *From Hegel to Marx*, New York, 1936; W. T. Stace, *The Philosophy of Hegel*, London, 1924; E. B. Talbot, *Fundamental Principle of Fichte's Philosophy*, New York, 1906.

GORDON H. CLARK

IDOLATRY. See also *Gods, False*. Idolatry is the worship, or rendering of divine honor, to a false god represented by some object or image in which he is thought to be present. The word is used generally to include dendrolatry, litholatry, necrolatry, pyrolatry, and zoolatry.

The Genesis narratives presuppose monotheism as the original religion. Archaeological evidence indicates that the earliest attempt to worship a man-made image was in the form of a mother goddess in the South Russia steppe from which point the worship of images spread to play a significant role in the fertility cult corruptions of ancient Near East religions and then around the world.

Hebrew idolatry included the worship of false gods by images or otherwise, and also the worship of Yahweh through visible symbols (Hos. 8:5, 6; 10:5). The first of the Ten Commandments prohibits idolatry: "You shall have no other gods before [or besides] me." In the New Testament there is added to this conception of idolatry a metaphorical form which ascribes an idolatrous attitude to human desires when such desires supplant the will of God (I Cor. 10:14; Gal. 5:20; Col. 3:5). In the last of these references the word *eidōlolatreía*, the usual word for idolatry is used, and it describes the sin of covetousness or "mammon worship." Christian moral theology insists that any inordinate desire which views the object of that desire to be the ultimate source of good and the ground of one's being is idolatry.

The state of the mind of the idolater is radically incompatible with the faith of monotheism. Idolatry is evil because the devotee instead of placing his trust in God puts his trust in an object from which the desired good cannot come and instead of submitting himself to God submits himself to some degree to the perversion of values that the image represents.

ARNOLD C. SCHULTZ

IGNORANCE. The law controlling English-speaking societies, as did Roman law, generally does not allow ignorance of the law to be grounds for escaping the consequences of an act. The OT contains many references to sins of ignorance (Gen. 20:9; Num. 22:44; Deut. 22:8). Among the Hebrews the fact that one was not aware of breaking the law did not excuse him (Lev. 4:13; 14, 22, 23, 27, 28; 5:2-4; 22:14; Num. 15:24). A penalty was required and specific sacrifices were made which provided grounds for forgiveness. But culpability and moral responsibility were somewhat modified in sins of ignorance by attaching to them a minor degree of guilt (Lev. 14; Num. 15:22-32). This principle is further illustrated specifically in the incident of inadvertant manslaughter or manslaughter without premeditation in which case cities of refuge were established to provide opportunity for the defendant to escape the more severe penalty (Deut. 19:4-10; Josh. 20:2-6, 9).

Paul indicates that the OT period of ignorance of God is due in part to the "ungodliness and wickedness of men who by their wickedness suppress the truth" (Rom. 1:18 RSV). The NT recognizes the difference in some respects between the pre-Christian "times of ignorance" (Acts 17:30), and the later knowledge that came with Christ (I Tim. 1:13; I Peter 1:14). But there are suggestions in the NT that sins of ignorance modify responsibility (Luke 23:34).   ARNOLD C. SCHULTZ

ILLEGITIMACY. Illegitimacy means birth outside of wedlock. The OT employs illegitimacy as a broad term denoting incestuous origin (Gen. 19:30-38), mongrel peoples (Zech. 9:6), and the child born to an unwed mother. The illegitimate child and his descendants to the tenth generation were excluded from the assembly of the Lord (Deut. 23:2). The one NT instance (Heb. 12:8) refers to Christians who refuse to be disciplined by God.

It is estimated that in the USA 400,000 babies may be born out of wedlock in 1980, should present trends continue.

Greater freedom in extra-marital relations, communal living, and abortion have eroded significantly the public stigma of illegitimacy. Long-standing laws have been erased so that an illegitimate child can recover damages for the wrongful death of a parent, and insurance companies must pay a deceased father's workman's compensation benefits to a child born out of wedlock. Social Security Act amendments in 1965 enable a child to collect federal benefits irrespective of legitimacy.

The Commission on Population Growth and America's Future stated: "The word 'illegitimate' and the stigma attached to it have no place in our Society." But the Biblical indictment of fornication remains as firm as ever.   WILLARD H. TAYLOR

IMAGE OF GOD. See also *Fall of Man; Imitation of Christ.* The image of God in man is asserted but not precisely explained in Gen. 1:26-27; 5:1; 9:6; I Cor. 11:7, and James 3:9. Something of an explanation comes in Col. 3:10 and Eph. 4:24, where one may infer that the image consists of knowledge or rationality and righteousness or holiness, from which proceeds dominion over the creatures. Romans 8:29 confirms this by describing salvation as a process of conforming the predestinated saint to the image of Christ.

Other passages also, such as Heb. 2:6-8 with its appeal to Ps. 8, and Acts 17:26-29, are examples and contribute at least implicitly to the doctrine. When, too, empirical philosophers deny innate ideas, inherited corruption, and a priori forms of the mind, Rom. 2:15 and Ps. 51:5 give the Biblical reply.

To avoid error, one must note that the image does not consist in man's body. First, animals have bodies but were not created in God's image. Second, God is spirit and has not body; for which reason idolatry is sin (Rom. 1:23).

Man is not two images, as a fanciful exegesis would interpret *image* and *likeness* in Gen. 1:26. Note that *likeness* is not repeated in Gen. 1:27. Nor can the single image be divided into parts. Dominion over the creatures is not an extra part, but one of the functions of unitary rationality. Not even morality is a second part, as if knowledge and righteousness are two components. Righteous action is a function of the unitary image. In fact, the unitary image is not something man has: the image *is* man. "Man is the image and glory of God" (I Cor. 11:7).

The reason some theologians have asserted a duality in the image, rather than the unity of the person and the plurality of his functions, is the occurrence of sin. Since Adam remained Adam after the fall, these theologians thought that some part of the image had been lost. Unfortunately this view allows the remaining part of man to be untouched by sin and so conflicts with the doctrine of total depravity.

Although sinful men, especially very sinful men, do not seem to be God's image, these men could not sin unless they were. Sin presupposes rationality and voluntary decision. Sinning always starts in thought. Adam thought, incorrectly, but nevertheless thought that it would be better to join Eve in disobedience than to obey God and be separated from her. Sin has interfered with but does not prevent thought. It does not eradicate the image but causes it to malfunction. Responsibility (q.v.) depends on knowledge. Animals cannot sin and are not morally responsible because they are not rational or intellectual creatures. Therefore man remains the image of God even after the fall.

The image must be reason or intellect. Christ is the image of God because he is God's Logos or Wisdom. This Logos enlightens every man that comes into the world. Man must be rational to have fellowship with God. II Peter 1:2-8; 2:20; 3:18 emphasize knowledge and state that the means through which God grants us all things that pertain to life and godliness is theology—our knowledge of him. This idea is important for the late twentieth century when the dialectical theologians deny the image of God in man, calling God *Totally Other,* or define image ridiculously as the sexual distinction between man and woman (Karl Barth), and insist that God cannot put his "truth" into language, thus denying that the Scriptures are revelation and even reducing them to false pointers to something unknowable.

Secular objections to the image of God in man can be based only on a general nontheistic philosophy. Evolution views man as a natural development from neutrons and protons, through plants and animals, until in Africa, Asia, and the East Indies human beings emerged. Therefore evolution cannot insist on the unity of the human race as Christianity does in Acts 17:26.

Evolution as an explanatory principle must apply to the mind as well as to the body. There can then be no divine image, no eternal principles, no fixed truth or logic. The mind operates only with the practical results of biological adaptation. Reason is simply a human method of handling things. Earlier man had and future man will have other forms of logic. The syllogism called Barbara is valid now but will become a fallacy after a while.

If this be so, that is, if evolutionists have used evolutionary logic in the nineteenth and twentieth centuries in order to sustain their theory, then their arguments will prove fallacious in the next evolutionary advance and evolution will then be a fallacy.

The Biblical doctrine alone makes eternal truth possible (and "truth" that is not eternal is not truth). Reason makes possible both sin and fellowship with God. Sin has caused a malfunctioning of man's mind, but redemption will renew men in knowledge, righteousness, and holiness, so that in heaven we shall no longer make mistakes even in arithmetic.

   📖 G. C. Berkouwer, *Man: The Image of God,* Grand Rapids, Eerdmans, 1962; John Laidlaw, *The Bible Doctrine of Man,* London, T. & T. Clark, 1895.   GORDON H. CLARK

IMITATION OF CHRIST. To understand imitation as the accomplishment of disciples (so Thomas à Kempis) who thereby obtain a life like Jesus, "exalts man and abases Christ" (H. Thielicke). *Imitatio Christi* is more accurately interpreted as the gospel promise to sinful men who find forgiveness and sonship through faith in Christ. "It is not the imitation that makes sons; it is sonship that makes imitators" (Luther). As sons, the forgiven are *already* conformed *(summorphoi)* to the image of God's Son (Rom. 8:29). Hence the promise is fulfilled, though the goal to be like him (I John 3:2) is *not yet* realized. Thus, for the present time, imitation means following Jesus in daily life. The verb *akoloutheisthai,* (to follow) always active in voice, pervades the four gospels. Periodically, capricious crowds follow Jesus (e.g., Matt. 12:15; 14:13; Mark 3:7-8; 5:24; Luke 7:9) until his words offend them (cf. John 6:60, 66). Disciples follow more seriously, sensing that they must abandon the familiar security of home and possessions to share in the itinerant and uncertain life of the Master (Luke 9:57-62; cf. Mark 10:21, 28). Care-free Corinthians learn that true freedom means to sacrifice for others as Jesus did (I Cor. 11:1, "Become imitators . . . of Christ; " cf. 8:1 – 11:1). Status conscious Philippians need to imitate the mind of Christ (Phil. 2:5-11). Discipleship, however, connotes no personal acquisition or merit of Christ-likeness. Contrariwise, a qualitative distance separating disciple from Master is suggested, e.g., by the centurion who recognizes in his military calling a faint imitation of the infinitely higher mission of Jesus. "If soldiers execute my orders, how much more will the authoritative word of Jesus heal my slave" (Luke 7:6-10). Like the triumphant saints (Rev. 14:3-4) who follow the Lamb because of his redeeming love, so disciples must learn to follow Jesus. By graphic example (John 13:15), Jesus urges them to imitate his love (John 13:1-11 and 34-35). Since, however, love is of God (I John 4:7), their imitation is only possible because love is *given* to them (John 13:34; cf. I John 4:19). And, love sacrifices for others (John 15:13).

Imitation means also fellowship with Jesus in suffering. The Synoptics basically agree that the disciple—like Jesus—must bear a cross (Matt. 16:21-24; Mark 8:31-34; Luke 9:21-23). Their agreement suggests that the "cross" of Matt. 10:38 is anachronistic. (Logically, Matt. 10:38 *is* in place as part of Jesus' instruction to the twelve, instructions from various periods condensed into a single discourse.) Since his disciples actually failed to comprehend Jesus' repeated saying about his death (Mark 9:9-10; cf. 9:31f.; Luke 18:34), his crisp words about their cross proved unintelligible also. They were well aware that each crucified Galilean Jew (cf. Josephus, *Antiquities* XVII. 10. 10) did not bear a cross; the cross bore him! Apparently, therefore, suffering like Jesus' remained a mystery while he was on earth;

later the meaning became clear. For some followers, imitation of Jesus meant violent death like his, e.g., Stephen (Acts 7:59-60) and James (Acts 12:2); his cup and baptism became theirs (Mark 10:39). For Peter, the imitation was more precise—crucifixion (John 21:18f.). For others, however, imitation implied self-sacrifice and suffering. Some were challenged to become "imitators of God" who freely forgives men in Christ (Eph. 5:1; 4:32). At Thessalonica, imitation of Christ implied that men believed the Word amid severe opposition like that which Christ and his apostles faced when they proclaimed the Word (I Thess. 1:6). Paul personally claimed to share in Christ's sufferings (II Cor. 1:5; 4:10; Phil. 3:10), even to fill up what is lacking of Christ's afflictions (Col. 1:24)! Is his meaning mystical, i.e., Christ suffers with his church (e.g., A. S. Peake, F. F. Bruce)? Is the sense eschatological, i.e., as Christ's sufferings inaugurated the end-time, Paul's afflictions consummate it (e.g., H. Schlier, Ch. Masson, O. Cullmann)? A practical sense seems preferable. Paul rejoices that the sinless Master bequeathed sufferings to his unworthy servant (J. B. Lightfoot). Certainly in Colossians as elsewhere, Paul proclaims that only the suffering of Christ redeems. Nevertheless, servants who carry the redeeming message also suffer (John 15:20). Imitation of Christ thus implies that Jesus suffered, leaving behind an example, so that in life and suffering, men can follow in his steps (I Peter 2:21). Peter's words once inspired Charles Sheldon to write the novel, *In His Steps,* but Sheldon's question, "What would Jesus do?" is—at best—secondary. The primary NT question is: "What has Jesus done and how may redeemed disciples follow him in daily life and suffering to show God's great redemption in him?"

CULLEN I. K. STORY

IMMODESTY. See *Modesty; Nudism; Obscenity.*

IMMORALITY. Immorality is conduct contrary to established principles of morality. More specifically it connotes sexual impurity or irregularities. Standards of sexual morality were clearly enunciated in the Decalogue and the Mosaic materials. All who failed to abide by the prescriptions were duly punished.

Jesus seldom dealt with the matter of immorality, principally because he preached in the Jewish context where personal purity was taken for granted. His central concern was to demonstrate that sins of the flesh cannot be cured by fierce denunciation of them apart from their inner motivation and that abstaining from the grosser sins of the flesh does not necessarily make a man acceptable before God. He focused on the inner disposition of man. Thus, he could say that anyone who "looks at a woman lustfully has already committed adultery with her in his heart" (Matt. 5:28 RSV). Lustful thinking is for Jesus just as serious as lustful acting. It is better to sever an offending member of the body than to allow it to become an occasion for immorality (Matt. 5:39, 30).

Adultery *(moicheia)* and fornication *(porneia)*, translated "immorality" and "unchastity" in the RSV, were singled out by Jesus for special condemnation. *Moicheia* is generally defined as sexual intercourse of a man with another man's wife. Jesus speaks of this sin in connection with divorce. A man who divorces his wife, except for fornication or unchastity, commits adultery if he cohabits with another. A man who marries a divorced woman commits adultery (cf. Matt. 5:32; 19:9; Mark 10:10-12; Luke 16:18). *Porneia* appears to be a wider term and incorporates all sexual perversities, including adultery, prostitution, sodomy, and the like. Prostitution was sufficiently common among Jesus' listeners to make his reference to it intelligible.

Working in the Gentile world, which was rampant with sexual corruptness, the Apostle Paul was compelled to say much about immorality. See his description in Rom. 1:18-32. His epistles contain several lists of vices (Rom. 1:29-31; I Cor. 5:11; 6:9, 10; II Cor. 12:20; Gal. 5:19-21; Eph. 4:31; 5:3; Col. 3:5-8; I Tim. 1:9, 10; II Tim. 3:2-4; Titus 3:2, 2), and with the exception of two, each list includes specific sexual sins, namely, fornication *(porneia)*; uncleanness, meaning sexual impurity *(akatharsia)*; licentiousness *(aselgeia)*; and passion *(pathos)*. He lists fornicators *(pornoi)*, adulterers *(moichoi)*, homosexuals *(malakoi arsenokoitai)* (cf. I Cor. 6:9; I Tim. 1:10, Sodomites; cf. Jude 7).

The prevalence of, and moral indifference to, sexual promiscuity, presented a serious challenge to the Christians as they labored among the pagans. Thus, Paul and others insisted on continence before marriage, fidelity in marriage, purity of body, and restraint of desires for all men. The body is meant to bring glory to God as a temple of the Holy Spirit (I Cor. 6:18, 19).

Christian condemnation of adultery (q.v.), prostitution (q.v.), sodomy (q.v.), and homosexuality (q.v.) roots in the teaching of Christ which is based upon the Hebrew tradition as a whole. These divisive evils testify to the depraved condition of the human heart (Rom. 1:18-32). The stability of the home, the family, and society in general depends on a divinely ordained propriety in matters of sex. Furthermore, early Christian teaching asserted that the judgment of God would fall upon the immoral and adulterious (Heb. 13:4).

WILLARD H. TAYLOR

IMMORTALITY. See also *Death; Eschatology and Ethics; Resurrection.* The belief that the spirit or soul of man was indissoluble was widespread in the ancient world. It was reflected in the burial customs of the ancient Egyptians, whose religion was in a sense a religion of the dead. The Pyramids stand as a visible monument to this belief. The frequent references to the abode of the dead in Akkadian literature, the royal tombs at Ur, the attainment of eternal life by Ut-naptishti, the Babylonian Noah, show how firmly established was this belief. The Greeks believed in a realm of the dead (Hades), and the Romans had more than one word for the spirits of the departed (*Manes, Lemures, Lares*).

In contrast with the prominence given to the cult of the dead in the ancient world (archaeology's debt to the contents of tombs is immense) explicit statements in the OT concerning immortality are relatively few. The question there is not about the possibility of existence after death, but about the nature of that existence. In the OT a "beyond" is clearly presupposed.

The OT presentation of God as a living and a life-giving God (Num. 14:21; Ps. 42:2; I Sam. 2:6) was doubtless the main ground for the belief in a life beyond death. Man at his creation acquired something of divine origin—"the breath of life" (Gen. 2:7; cf. Job 33:4). From Gen. 3:22 we may conclude that man, apart from sin, would not have been subject to the dislocation of death, but that he would have lived for ever.

The first clear reference to the transitional character of death is the account of the translation of Enoch (Gen. 5:24). That this was understood by later writers as an actual circumvention of death is seen from such passages as Ps. 49:16, and 73:24 where the context refers to survival after death and the verb of the Genesis passage is used: "He (God) took him." Elijah also was taken without having to experience death (II Kings 2:11).

The case of Saul's attempt to make contact with the deceased Samuel is surely incontrovertible proof of a common belief among the Israelites in survival after death. Saul evidently believed: (a) that Samuel although disembodied still existed, (b) that there was a continuity of his personality, (c) that he was in possession of his mental faculties, including memory. Hebrew possessed not only a well-known word for the abode of the dead (Sheol) but also a word for the spirit of a dead person (*ōb*) (cf. Lev. 19:31; Deut. 18:11, and Isa. 8:19).

A number of passages speak with unmistakable assurance of immortality. There is for instance, Isa. 26:19: "Thy dead will live, and thy corpses will arise. Awake and rejoice, O dwellers of the dust. For the dew of lights is thy dew, and thou (Judah) will overthrow the realm of shades." A similar passage is Hos. 13:14: "From the power of Sheol I will redeem them, and from death I will ransom them. Where are thy plagues of death, where is thy destruction, O Sheol?" It is to this passage that Paul alludes in I Cor. 15:55. Another passage is Isa. 25:8: "Death is swallowed up for evermore" (There is nothing to prevent one's taking the verb here as a passive form, as Paul has done).

Other passages that may well refer to survival beyond the grace are Gen. 37:35 and II Sam. 12:13. The various accounts of the raising of the dead show that God has power over death (cf. I Kings 17:17-22; II Kings 4:18-37). Ezekiel's vision of the miracle in the valley of dry bones typified the resurrection power of God (chap. 37).

The optimism present in so many of the Psalms speaks of something greater than earthly prosperity: Ps. 36:9, "For with thee is the source of life, in thy light we shall see light"; Ps. 41:13, "In my completeness thou hast laid hold of me, thou hast set me before thee for ever"; Ps. 23:6, "And my dwelling will be in the house of the Lord for length of days." The word "house" could also be translated "household," "family." It cannot here refer to the Temple, which was not yet built. The great passage in Job 19:25f., whose introductory asseveration couched in the most solemn terms has not prevented some translators from reducing its content to a mere triviality, can surely only be a statement concerning ultimate reality. The passage is admittedly difficult, but a possible translation would be: "I know that my kinsman-redeemer is alive, and that he will arise [or "prevail"] over death [lit. "dust"], for after men deprive me of my frame, then away from my flesh I will have a vision of God, whom I myself will behold and my eyes will see, for he is not a stranger."

Those passages in the OT that seem to speak of death as cessation, must be taken in the light of the entire context. In Ps. 49:12, "And man in honor will not stay, he is like cattle that are cut off," is not, however, the writer's final word on the subject, and the countercheck comes almost immediately: "Surely God will redeem my soul, from the power of Sheol he will take me" (v. 15). Ecclesiastes is commonly thought to express unqualified pessimism about man's future state in such passages as, "The destiny of men and the destiny of beasts is one; alike they die" (3:19), or "For the living know that they will die, but the dead know nothing at all" (9:5). Nevertheless, before the book ends, we find one of the strongest and plainest statements about man's ultimate destiny: "And the dust will return to the earth as it was, and the spirit will return unto God who gave it" (12:7). Incidentally, in the light of this and similar passages, there is little support from the Hebrew text rightly understood for the view that the OT is mainly concerned with the materialistic aspect of man's nature.

The imprecision of the OT is replaced by clarity in the NT where immortality is made to include the resurrection of the body. Our Lord's words to Martha (John 11:25) and to the dying thief (Luke 23:43) leave no room for doubt. Again his words of comfort to his disciples (John 14:3) convey the sense of absolute assurance. On the other hand he does not hesitate to paint in the darkest colors the fate of the wicked (Matt. 10:28; John 5:29). Among the apostles, Paul is the most eloquent on the theme of

immortality and resurrection (I Cor. 15; II Cor. 5; Phil. 1:23). The book of Revelation contains many descriptions, often with imagery borrowed from the OT, of the blessedness of the future state of the righteous (Rev. 7:9-17; and chaps. 21 and 22).

WILLIAM J. MARTIN

IMPERIALISM. See *Colonialism, Colonization.*

IMPULSE. Impulse is a motive or tendency which is not instinctive nor governed by reason and which leads to sudden incitement to action. Scripture declares people fools who lack self-control (Prov. 13:3), live impulsive lives, or are short-tempered and hasty (Prov. 14:16-17; 21:5). Man's sinful nature can suddenly lead him astray (Rom. 7:13-25) resulting in rash statements like Saul's (I Sam. 14) and impulsive action like Moses' (Num. 20). Men are warned not to be hot-headed and to act rashly (Prov. 25:8-10; Eccles. 5:2; Acts 19:36). In contrast, the Holy Spirit gives self-control (Gal. 5:22) and enables one to respond spontaneously to life from a divine perspective (II Cor. 10:5-6).   RALPH H. ALEXANDER

INCARNATION. The English word is derived from *incarnatio* (Latin) which means to be made flesh. The Word which is God (John 1:1) "became flesh" (1:14). Christ came in the flesh (*en sarki,* I John 4:2). For the Hindu the incarnation of the divine (Brahma) is all pervasive, so that no significance is attached to personality and individuality. The Christian incarnation is distinctive, because this apex of divine revelation is personal, in a particular life. The revelation in Jesus Christ takes the form of a man (Heb. 1:2), not a rule, a law, an idea, a theology, nor an all pervasive force or spirit. The manner in which the incarnation informs ethics is by outside motivation rather than from forces internal

Mainstream Biblical ethics are revelational rather than natural, so that the avenue of incarnational ethics is the revelation of God in Christ. Natural ethics are found in the Wisdom literature of the Old Testament in that the proper ethical course is built by God into the natural order (Prov. 8:22-36; Job 28) and is there discovered by the wise person. In the NT Paul distinguished between those under special revelation and those who are not. "God judges those outside" (I Cor. 5:13). Those under the law are judged by the law (Rom. 2:12), those in Jesus Christ are judged by his word and work (I Cor. 5:12), but those under neither are judged by "the law ... written on their hearts" (Rom. 2:15).

Because of the importance of John for incarnational ethics his writings are first discussed, then the synoptic Gospels, the Petrine letters, and Hebrews.

Incarnational ethics are found in John's Gospel in Jesus' washing of the disciples feet. The one undertaking this menial task "had come from God and was going to God" (John 13:3). He is addressed as Lord (*kurios* 13:6, 13, 14) by which the early church bestowed on him *Yahweh*, God's special name (Exod. 6:3). It is thus God incarnate who washes the disciples' feet. Through taking on human flesh and this service he commends to his disciples a life of service. Specific ethical acts are not itemized, but the basic Christian ethical life style is declared. Because Christ came as a servant *(incarnatio)* the Christian lives to serve.

I John is addressed to a church from which Christians who claim spiritual superiority have departed. They claim a similar superiority for Jesus by denying that he came in the flesh (I John 4:2). John charges that their heretical Christology leads them to imporoper ethical action in severing fellowship with those whom they consider their spiritual inferiors. Jesus Christ became flesh (I John 1:1) so as to share *(koinonia)* the life of God with man (1:3). Since Jesus

willingly shared his deity with man, spiritual men should in turn share their life with their inferiors (1:7). It is only by so doing that they emulate Christ and appropriate his death. Christ shows his love for man through his incarnation (4:9); therefore "Beloved, if God so loved us, we also ought to love one another" (4:11). This love takes the concrete form of assisting the brother in need (3:17) and being in fellowship with him (1:7).

Paul typically grounds ethics from other theological beginnings than the incarnation, for example, the crucifixion or the eschaton, but II Cor. 8:8ff., and Phil. 2:2-10 are exceptions. In II Cor. 8 Paul encourages the church to collect funds for the poor in Palestine. He refers to Jesus coming as a man as a theological reason why the rich should help the poor: "Though he was rich, yet for your sake he became poor, so that by his poverty you might become rich." Scholars argue that Phil. 2:2ff. is a hymn of the early church borrowed by Paul. Even if so, the theology is not foreign to Paul. Internal dissention disturbed the body of Christ at Philippi. Paul sought to diminish these rifts by declaring that the Christians should "in humility count others better than yourselves" (2:3). If they will do so they will take seriously the ethical implications of the incarnation, for Christ "emptied himself, taking the form of a servant, being born in the likeness of men" (2:7).

The ethical implications of the incarnation are missing in the synoptics unless found in Mark 10:45 (cf. Matt. 20:28). If the phrase "Son of Man" implies a divine figure (see Dan. 7:13) then the ethical life style of the incarnated Lord is commended, for the Son of man came "not to be served but to serve." Indirectly certain actions of Jesus might point to incarnational ethics, for example, the incarnated Lord eating with tax collectors and sinners (Matt. 9:10-13).

The doctrine of the incarnation is found in Petrine materials (I Peter 1:20; 5:4, II Peter 1:16) but no ethical implications are set out. The writer of Hebrews gives emphasis to the incarnation but only indirectly spells out ethical implications (Heb. 2:9-18). The Christians to whom this letter is addressed have become indifferent (12:12) and neglectful (10:25). Should they seriously consider what the incarnated Lord has done and is doing for them, however, they would take up the Christian race with new vigor. He was once man on earth but is now a heavenly man as high priest. Inasmuch as he became man, Christians should boldly request his assistance (Heb. 2:18; 4:14-16; 5:1-10). As the result of his help those who are his should "stir up one another to love and good works" (10:19-24) and "Strive for peace with all men, and for . . . holiness" (12:12-14).

The ethical implications of the incarnation are that the Christian is to live as a servant, in fellowship with his brother, in love, and in good works. Jesus himself created this ethical style by for a little while taking up humanity.

"Incarnation," *Interpreter's Dictionary of the Bible,* Nashville, Abingdon; D. M. Baillie, *God Was in Christ;* James Orr, *The Christian View of God and the World,* Grand Rapids, Eerdmans, 1947; Victor P. Furnish, *Theology and Ethics in Paul,* Nashville, Abingdon; T. F. Torrance, *Space, Time and Incarnation.*   THOMAS H. OLBRICHT

INCEST. Incest is sexual union between persons related within familial boundaries prohibited by law. The Bible adduces a number of examples of this crime (Gen. 19:30-35; 35:22; 49:4; II Sam. 13:7-14; Ezek. 22:10-11; I Cor. 5:1-5). Ancient society's concern to preserve the family through the birth of male offspring often precipitated incestuous involvements. Penalties ranged from death (Lev. 20:11-17) to excommunication (I Cor. 5:1-5). In this latter instance the man had married his "father's wife." Paul commands deliverance of the offender to the satanic order that bodily suffering might evoke repentance. The ethical issue in incest includes the moral as well as the physical degeneration of the family.   WILLARD H. TAYLOR

INDEPENDENCE. See also *Sovereignty, National; United Nations; World Government.* Independence is a political doctrine and movement of the modern age. It asserts that the right of national self-government is necessary to the political, economic, cultural and moral development of a people. Historically, it gained recognition because of its association with the anticolonial movement of the eighteenth century. The right of political revolution as a legitimate basis for the claim to national sovereignty acquired status in the American Declaration of Independence (1776). Simultaneously, Adam Smith's *Wealth of Nations* with its doctrines of laissez-faire (q.v.) and freedom of trade offered a utilitarian sanction for economic independence. These doctrines became a powerful force in support of the demands of colonial peoples for political and economic independence. Nineteenth century nationalism, with its plea for political sovereignty as a means to cultural freedom, provided an added dynamic. By the twentieth century independence had assumed the form of a utopian myth which offered the millennium of modern technological society to colonial peoples still living in underdeveloped areas of European overseas empires.

The American Revolution became a model for independence movements throughout the world. During the nineteenth century it motivated the claims of Central and South American provinces in Spanish and Portugese empires for political and economic freedom. Simultaneously, it set in motion a demand for greater liberties within the British Empire culminating in the Statute of Westminster (1931) which accorded independence to the major dominions and colonies within the Commonwealth of Nations.

Twentieth century independence movements were most prominent in Europe following World War I and in Asia and Africa during and after World War II. Central European members of the Austro-Hungarian and Russian Empires, and the various component elements of the Ottoman Empire in the Middle East and North Africa, all plead the Wilsonian doctrine of national or cultural self-determination as the basis of political independence. India laid claim to sovereignty during World War II and was granted such in 1950. Pakistan established its independence in 1956. Religious, cultural and political freedom were the justifications advanced by these states.

The Indonesian provinces of the Dutch Empire in Southeast Asia proclaimed their independence in 1945, a status given full recognition in 1949. Vietnam, Cambodia and Laos were awarded independent status by the French in 1954. The Vietnamese Declaration of Independence (1945) employed language from the American Declaration of Independence and the French Declaration of the Rights of Man in justification of their plea for national sovereignty.

Independence as a revolutionary and utopian myth has had its greatest influence in Africa. The North African states secured independence during the period 1947-1962. West, Central and East African states began with Ghana in 1957. By 1968 twenty-eight new states appeared, including three within South Africa.

The Declaration on Rights and Duties of States, authorized by the United Nations General Assembly (1947), declares that "every state has the right to independence." Historically, this has often been of little effect unless backed by the military power of neighboring states and the moral force of international political organizations. But that is not all. Although modern nations pursue their political concerns as if God were an irrelevance, the Apostle Paul reminded the Athenians whose nation had once been the ruling world power that God "hath determined the times . . . and the bounds" of man's habitation (Acts 17:26). The role of tiny Israel, long preserved while powerful surrounding nations lost their independence, attested God's truth: "Not by might or by power, but by my Spirit . . . " (Zech. 4:6).   SAMUEL R. KAMM

INDETERMINISM. See *Determinism; Free Will.*

INDIFFERENCE. Indifference may be defined as an absence of feeling for or against a matter, an unconcern or apathy. The word certainly conjures up a negative, do nothing concept.

In the teaching of Jesus we find him not only dealing with negativism, but attacking indifference as a serious sin. His whole approach to life was positive, creative and progressive, and so he took a serious view of indifference which so often meant just doing nothing. In the parable of the Good Samaritan (Luke 10:30) standing in sharp contrast to the man who was a good neighbor are the priest and the Levite. We would have expected them to have taken some action but they just passed by on the other side. It must be noted that they broke no moral law and in no way contributed to the plight of the victim of the thieves. Their sin was indifference. They just did nothing. The same fact is true in the parable of Dives and Lazarus (Luke 16:26). There is no reason to believe that Dives was a cruel man or that he did any harm to Lazarus who lay at his gate. Busy with his own affairs he was just indifferent to Lazarus' condition and did nothing.

In preaching the Kingdom of God, Jesus denounces indifference with grave severity. In the parable of the Great Judgment (Matt. 25:42f.) the condemnation is because "I was hungered and ye gave me no meat, I was thirsty and ye gave me no drink, naked and ye clothed me not, sick and in prison and ye did not visit me." They were indifferent and had done nothing, and Jesus condemned it. The seriousness of the offense may be measured by the drastic punishment meted out (Matt. 25:46).

To Jesus loving God was the first requirement. But no man can love God and not keep his commandments (John 14:15). Basic to God's command to obedience was his call to responsible action. Jesus was a person of action and from his youth he was concerned to be about his Father's business. He called for involvement in the Kingdom, the very opposite to indifference. In proclaiming the Kingdom he taught that there could be no neutral position for the believer (Matt. 12:30). With deep insight he saw the nature of the struggle against forces of evil. Consequently indifference was treated harshly and excuses for non-involvement were denounced (Luke 14:16-24).

LESLIE HUNT

INDIGENIZATION. The term "indigenization" is derived from the Latin word *indigenus*. It designates a conscious effort to root in the native soil in order to produce or share a cultural character peculiar to the land. This effort is found wherever racial, cultural, and religious intercourse occurs. When religions confront each other either they will repel each other or become syncretic. Though a noteworthy tendency toward indigenization is found in the past, it is more common in the modern period.

There seem to be two reasons for the emphasis on indigenization in modern times. First, it is a concern among the underdeveloped countries which fear cultural and religious invasion by the developed countries. Second, at the end of missionary enterprise initiated by the Western churches the question of the indigenization of the gospel is believed to be the most urgent problem for more effective expansion of the Christian message in non-Christian countries.

Christian evangelism from the beginning has been a movement of indigenization, even before the term acquired controversial overtones. Having been sown, the seed must take root in the new soil and necessarily become a neighborhood church. Christians were united and found themselves in the church of the province, state, or country.

However, advocates of indigenization in modern times tend to overlook a very important and serious fact: that the gospel has been in many ways indigenized wrongly. As we have already pointed out, the gospel belongs to a certain local church as soon as it is preached. The listeners hear what the preacher has to say and they absorb it as they understand it. If there are parts of the message and any words which they cannot understand, they accept only those words and meanings which they can understand while they leave aside what they do not understand. This is the inevitable process of communication in any intercourse of culture or religion. Consequently there is a twisted absorption of the content. This happened in the early churches, in the church of Corinth in particular. One of the main struggles of Paul was against "a different gospel" (II Cor. 11:4; Gal. 1:6, etc.), or even "another Jesus" (II Cor. 11:4).

The real question for indigenization, therefore, is how to make the gospel relevant to each circumstance while preserving its universal character. If relevance is emphasized at the cost of universal validity, the gospel becomes a partially true gospel, which is contrary to the one which Jesus himself preached. If the universal character ignores the cultural situation, its relevance will be jeopardized. Therefore, the history of Christian theology has been an attempt to avoid this dilemma. The attempt has been only partly successful, but for the Biblical and evangelical Christian this is not very satisfactory.

The presentation of the gospel has always been tainted with local color which in many cases is incompatible with the gospel. There are various degrees of this type of indigenization. In the theology of younger churches in particular the God of the Scriptures, Christ and the Holy Spirit, are identified with their own spiritual forerunners. A few references will be sufficient. Christ is identified in Korea by some believers with Lee-Doryung who was the deliverer of his mistress just before her execution, or with Moon-Sun-Myung, founder of the Unification Movement of the World Spirit and author of "The Divine Principles," who claims that he is the Second Coming of Christ to complete what Jesus failed to fulfill in his earthly life. But the Christ of authentic Christian faith cannot be identified with any particular national heroes or with some other living modern person.

For this reason, a theory of three-stage indigenization seems the best solution. According to this theory, when the gospel is preached to another nation it is naturally· interpreted and understood in their own particular terms (the first stage). When it is re-examined for its validity by the people it is usually found to be wrongly indigenized and understood. At this stage the gospel must be *de*-indigenized (the second stage). As soon as it is de-indigenized it must be *re*-indigenized in their own context to retain the fundamental content of the gospel, in order to become the real good news, for the gospel of Jesus Christ is not a vain teaching but the power of salvation.

JONG SUNG RHEE

INDIVIDUALISM. See also *Collectivism.* Individualism is the view or belief that the individual is completely autonomous and ultimate in his decision and actions. While the individualist may hold that the individual person may enter into voluntary association with others and may also become bound by a voluntarily accepted contract, no external force or authority is acknowledged to determine his actions within society unless he is contravening the freedom of others. In this the individualist apparently stands in direct opposition to collectivism (q.v.), although he frequently finds it necessary to accept a collective or dictatorial regime in order to curb the egoism (q.v.) manifest in what is threating to become a completely atomistic order of society.

Individualism has been current in human society since the days of Cain (Gen. 4:9). Usually it receives support when society is developing and prospering; or when individuals wish to free themselves from the controls, restrictions, and taboos of established society. They then rationalize their position by positing the natural ability, goodness, and freedom of man, although in actual fact they usually apply these attributes only to themselves and their social group. Thus, while individualism is not necessarily egoism, an egoist is always an individualist.

Although the term was not employed until the nineteenth century, first being used by Alexis de Tocqueville (1805-1859), the idea appears at the beginning of the OT in the expressions of Cain and Lamech's "Song of the Sword" (Gen. 4:9ff., 23ff.), and in Greek thought in the philosophies of Heraclitus and Epicurus. The philosophical atomist of the earlier Greeks carried over into the thinking of the Stoics who stressed the superiority of the individual to all circumstances. This outlook had much to do with the eventual collapse of the Roman Republic and its supplanting by the Empire. In the Middle Ages individualism was not popularly accepted, although with the growth of the merchant class, the rise of national monarchies and the adoption of classical ideas which led to what is known as the Renaissance (q.v.), it gradually became very influential.

Among Renaissance thinkers Pico della Mirandola (1463-94), Niccolo Machiavelli (1469-1527) and Baldissare Castiligne

(1478-1529) were typical exponents of this point of view. They believed that there was an élite class of men of *virtu* who could make of themselves whatever they wished by means of their will and reason, and that they could and should act as completely autonomous—which usually meant without much concern for others.

The Protestant Reformation of the sixteenth century, on the other hand, while emphasizing the importance of the individual, thought of him (or her) as God's creature who had fallen into sin, but who could find redemption through God's offer of grace and forgiveness in Jesus Christ. This was the basis of Luther's (1483-1546) doctrine of "justification by faith alone" and of Calvin's (1509-1564) doctrine of God's election of the individual to eternal life. At the same time both Reformers also stressed the Christian's position as a member of the church, "the body of Christ." Following the Reformation (q.v.), there grew up in some Christian circles a pietism and a quietism that adopted the view that the Christian should not take part in society and frequently not even in the church, but should simply concentrate on his own individual relationship with God. This has not been an uncommon attitude in some Protestant and Roman Catholic circles down to the present.

With the growth of trade and industry in the sixteenth and seventeenth centuries, which culminated in the Industrial Revolution (q.v.) of the eighteenth and nineteenth, individualism became a powerful element in western thought. Jeremy Bentham (1748-1832), Adam Smith (1723-90) and John Stuart Mill (1806-73), the last particularly in his early days, all stressed the importance of individual freedom in every aspect of life. The best government was that which governed least, a point of view that fitted in well with the views of the rising middle class and the pioneers on colonial frontiers in America and elsewhere. Often this philosophy came into direct conflict with the disadvantaged and those who sought to help the "underdog," as well as with bureaucratic governments. The result has been the ever growing interference of the state in economic and social affairs, in order to protect those who are unable to protect themselves.

Trade unions, cooperatives and similar movements have also been a collective answer to individualism. In the nineteenth century, facing an individualistic middle class who believed in "freedom of contract" and government abstention from economic regulation, the laboring classes found it necessary to combine in order to defend themselves against exploitation by their employers. Many of these organizations, however, have now become as anti-individualistic as any large capitalistic corporation.

From the Christian perspective as expressed in both the OT and NT, the individual is important as created in the image of God, and as having a direct relationship to God. Christianity also stresses the supreme requirement of man's faith in and obedience to God. Moreover, Christ and the apostles insisted that he had come to save his people whom God had given him before the foundation of the world John 6:37ff.; 17:9ff.; Eph. 1:4ff. These he calls by his Word and Spirit to be his people and the citizens of his kingdom. Therefore, their "individualism" is always under his Lordship and is involved in "his body," the church.

The Christian consequently finds himself opposed equally to a humanistic collectivism and a humanistic individualism. He rejects the idea of autonomous man. He also realizes that under God he is responsible for his brother's welfare both spiritual and material. This results in his recognizing both evangelism and social action as his responsibilities. Yet he fulfills these obligations not in any individualistic manner, but as a citizen of the Kingdom of Christ, seeking in all things to glorify him. W. STANFORD REID

INDUSTRIAL ESPIONAGE. Rapid growth in the sophisticated use of computers emphasizes the increased value of information to business management. In most instances, available information is the organizations' most valuable asset; its loss or compromise could seriously weaken or destroy the organization's effectiveness. Industrial espionage encompasses all conscious efforts to secure unauthorized access to proprietary or other privileged organizational information.

It exists in tension with the legitimate business intelligence function of management, i.e., to gather and systematically analyze all available information about the economic environment in which the organization must function. Some organizations integrate the two functions. For instance, management may employ computer programs used to analyze their company's planning data to perform identical analyses of comparable surreptitiously secured competitor data.

Efforts to protect valuable organization information against intrusion are complicated by its inherently intangible nature, general lack of employee awareness of the value of this information, and the ability to duplicate and remove this information from organizational custody without evidence of its compromise.

Apart from its inherent dishonesty, industrial espionage can subvert almost every aspect of business activities. As examples: pseudo merger negotiations may be initiated to gain access to the other organization's confidential information, or a key competitor employee may be hired only for the proprietary information to be extracted from him.

Industrial espionage is rationalized as a necessary means for assuring corporate survival or, at least, maintaining one's position in a highly competitive market. Yet it remains unvarnished theft (q.v.) of the assets of others. The Mosiac Law was very severe in the punishment stipulated for thieves (Exod. 22:1-4), and the NT views thievery no less severely (I Cor. 6:8, 10).

BELDEN MENKUS

INDUSTRIAL RELATIONS. See also *Business Ethics; Collective Bargaining; Contracts; Labor Relations.* " Industrial relations" is both a term and a method. It attempts to explain and to ameliorate conflicts of interest within the productive process.

Advanced, industrialized countries experience a constant three-way tug-of-war between firms, workers, and the public. The aims, aspirations, and needs of these groups —while overlapping—are often antithetical, and compromises must be negotiated, if complex societies are to survive.

It is the function of "business ethics" to provide a climate of reasonableness and goodwill in which conflicts of interest can be negotiated. And it is the function of industrial relations to bring conflicting groups together, so that socially-acceptable adjustments (procedures and institutional patterns) can be worked out.

Interests of firms were once centered almost solely on profit-making. This is no longer true, though—in an expanding economy, where investment in capital-deepening is vital—profits are of paramount importance.

Profits depend on the spread between prices at retail and the costs of production— the costs of property, resources, and labor, and the social costs of operating in an increasingly state-dominated system. Profits also depend on volume of sales. Low costs and high sales mean more profits.

Firms, therefore, strive to keep resource costs low, wages suppressed, and taxes minimal. They strive to expand output per man-hour, by using more machines and keeping the workday constant. They strive to expand sales by maintaining a "good public image" through public relations campaigns and institutional advertising. They struggle to expand sales by maintaining high quality-control standards and by extending the time and scope of warranties. More recently firms seek a good public image by making gestures in the direction of pollution control.

Security of the firm—its continuity and survival—involves strong, often very expensive, programs in "research and development." The firm must invent "new products" if it is to survive in a rapidly-changing and competitive world. And the firm must maintain good government relations, at local, state, national, and international levels. It must be conscious of a fantastic maze of overlapping jurisdictions, laws, codes, and customs, if it is to survive. All this adds to cost and little to service or profits.

While struggling to maintain reasonable labor costs and a balanced relationship with the public, it is inevitable that the firm will come into conflict with these groups. Rising costs based on labor inefficiency and increasing demands for pollution control are but two of many areas of conflict.

Interests of workers still center on AFL President Samuel Gompers' original nineteenth century demands of labor unions— higher wages, shorter hours, and better working conditions. With passage of the Anti-Injunction Act and the National Labor Relations Act during the 1930's, labor was able to realize Gompers' goals on a steadily expanding basis. Other goals were added. Once basic living needs have been met, wage increases, *per se,* are not so important. Workers desire more "fringe benefits." These include: health and accident insurance, improved safety standards, higher pensions and earlier retirement, longer vacations, job security, provisions for promotions and on-the-job training, protection

against the speed-up, and protection against autocratic or criminal union leaders.

Workers are also increasingly conscious of their relationship to the community, and a whole array of demands on government— involving expanding social costs—are being made. They include: fair employment practices, community services, neighborhood maintenance, support of education through the college level, expanding recreation facilities, police protection, proximity to shopping centers, and proximity to clinics and hospitals. These expanding "demands" of workers involve conflicts of interest with both business firms and the public. Sabotage, featherbedding, slowdowns, wages which increase more rapidly than productivity, sloppy work, etc., all add to the cost of production and deterioriation of quality. Both firms and the public feel the impact of these manifestations of labor power and are constrained to combat it.

The public interest is consumer-oriented. This means that the public wants reasonably (competitively) priced products which will hold up a reasonable length of time. The public expects warranties to be clearly stated and of sufficient duration and coverage. When products break down, the public wants reasonably priced, efficient, and fairly quick service. But the public has little power of its own and must depend on government to protect its interests as between giant firms and monopolistic labor unions.

The public wants labor-management peace. It is "sick and tired" of costly strikes that tie up whole regions of the country for months. It wants a pollution-free environment, and is anxious for government to pass and enforce pollution-control legislation. Finally, the public wants adequate social services for reasonable taxes, and it wants welfare rolls to be made-up exclusively of those unable to work.

The public is in conflict with labor unions and firms. Labor exhibits a self-centered attitude which ignores public interest, and firms, by and large, act as though the public is their own oyster to be exploited at will.

Ethical industrial relations, therefore, depend on men of goodwill bargaining in good faith—with all special-interest groups represented. Since the 1930s, collective bargaining (q.v.) has been viewed as a process for resolving conflicts of interest between labor and management only. This narrow concept of bargaining cannot continue. The time has come for all interests in collective bargaining to be represented—including the public.   SIDNEY A. WILLIAMS

INDUSTRIAL REVOLUTION. The Industrial Revolution began in the latter half of the eighteenth century in Great Britian. It introduced the idea of mass production, distribution, and communication of goods, services, and information, largely by means of power-driven machinery or new techniques related to its use. From Great Britain the revolution—so named by the social reformer and economist Arnold Toynbee (1842-1883)—spread first to Europe, then to America and in the twentieth century to the whole world. Many current technological, economic, and social developments are a continuation of the same movement.

Because of basic changes it has made in the production, distribution, and consumption of goods and services, the Industrial Revolution not only has had a radical influence on finance, communications, and other aspects of economic life, but has also faced twentieth century man with social and ethical problems unprecedented in human history.

The change in the whole pattern of production from the craft and domestic to the factory method, led to the uprooting of thousands of industrial workers who became mere "hands" employed for wages by the factory owner. The first result was frequently gross exploitation, since workers were usually very much underpaid. At first unorganized and unprotected by government, they had no means of defending themselves. This in turn led to widespread poverty, such as had been unknown in earlier days, since the poor no longer had any connection with the land but were concentrated in towns and cities without subsidiary means of support or even clean water or clean air.

While the laboring classes were suffering from the effects of the Industrial Revolution, the same developments brought about a radical change in the whole social structure. No longer in Great Britain, Europe, or America were the great landlords the dominant element. This position was taken by the industrialists, the merchants, and the financiers who were increasing rapidly in wealth. Usually, at least at first, they gained control of the economy by hard work, thrift and aggressive action. Men such as Josiah Wedgewood, Matthew Boulton, Alfred Krupp, Andrew Carnegie and Henry Ford were all of this type. The appearance of the joint stock company, the trust, the mutual fund has tended to spread the wealth more widely. At the same time, with the rise of large corporations, trade unions and socialist governments, the direction of economic affairs has tended to fall into the hands of a managerial or technocratic class.

In this development of the past two and a half centuries the Christian can see certain elements. On one hand, he recongizes that this is part of man's fulfillment of the cultural mandate to "subdue the world and replenish it." On the other hand, the exploitation of men and resources, the materialism, the waste and pollution which have resulted indicate clearly that man's sinfulness always perverts the good gifts of God. The Industrial Revolution has faced the individual Christian and the church with a mass of ethical questions that remain to be fully understood and answered. The need today is a massive Christian attack upon these pressing problems.

While the Industrial Revolution has undoubtedly brought many benefits to man, not only in providing him with more and cheaper goods, but also in advancing his knowledge and use of the physical environment, so enabling him to fulfil his cultural mandate "to subdue the world and rule over it" (Gen. 1:28; 9:1-7), it has also permitted him to misuse and misunderstand God's good gifts. (1) It has frequently led to the unprecedented exploitation of the worker and his economic and social degradation in direct contradiction of Biblical socio-economic principles (Lev. 19:13; Amos 8; Mal. 3:5; Luke 10:7; Eph. 6:9; Col. 4:1; I Tim. 5:18) (2) Through the industrial exploitation of the physical world it has stimulated the rape and pollution of the environment to a dangerous extent, thus denying the Christian teaching that man is the steward of creation for the glory of God and the benefit of his fellow man (Gen. 1:28; 9:1-7; Lev. 25:1-17) (3) Most important of all, however, it has fostered the belief that the material is ultimate, and consequently that the acquisition of material goods and wealth is man's principal means of attaining happiness. One result of this has been the widespread acceptance of materialistic philosophies, such as Marxism, which reject the Christian view that the love and glory of God is "man's chief end" (Deut. 8:3; Matt. 4:3); 16:26; Luke 12:13ff.; II Cor. 10:17, 31). In all of this the Industrial Revolution has shown how man sinfully perverts and misuses every good gift of God. While some Christians such as the seventh Earl of Shaftesbury in the early days of the economic changes sought to mitigate its worst effects, in more recent times many Christians have shown themselves generally indifferent to the problems raised by the Industrial Revolution.

📖 H. Hamilton, *The Industrial Revolution in Scotland*, London, Cass, 1966; L. C. A. Knowles, *The Industrial and Commercial Revolution in Great Britain in the 19th Century*, London, Routledge & Kegan Paul, 1933; P. Mantoux, *The Industrial Revolution in the 18th Century*, London, Cape, 1937; M. Beard, *A History of Business*, Ann Arbor, University of Michigan, 1938; J. H. Clapham, *Economic History of Modern Britain*, London, Cambridge, vols. 1 & 2, 1935; A. Toynbee, *Lectures on the Industrial Revolution of the 18th Century in England*, London, Longmans, 1927.

W. STANFORD REID

INEQUALITY. See *Equality*.

INFANTICIDE. See also *Abortion; Birth Control*. Sacrificing a child for religious reasons—offering one's most precious possession to the deities occurred in ancient Egypt, India, Greece and Rome. This practice comes under strong attack in the OT. The worship of the Ammorite god, which included the burning of offspring before Molech, was punishable with death by stoning (Lev. 18:21; 20:2-5; Deut. 12:31; 18:10). Its condemnation by Josiah and the prophets intimates that the pagan practice increased up to the Babylonian captivity and became associated with Baal worship (Jer. 32:35; Ezek. 16:20, 21). The completeness of Ahaz' apostasy is evidenced by his offering of his son as a sacrifice (II Kings 16:3; 21:6). It is thought that the Phoenicians helped spread the practice to Carthage and thus to the Roman world.

The account of Abraham and the offering of Isaac teaches that obedience is better than sacrifice. The God Abraham worshipped delighted not in destroying life, but rather in saving and sanctifying it. The contrast with pagan religion is clear in Exod. 13:15 where Jehovah says, "but all the first-born of my sons I redeem."

Christian faith arose in a world where killing of a new born child, directly or by abandonment, was widely practiced. By some it was viewed as a means of population control or of meeting economic pressures, or of disposing of weak or deformed infants. For whatever reasons infanticide was practiced, its inconsistency with Christian ethics is not hard to see. The concept of the Creator God implies that every life has its value from God and not solely by cultural standards. To take an innocent life is murder and to sacrifice a life to deity is in addition, demonic. Beyond this stands the high value established in the Bible for precreation and responsible family relationships, including loving concern for those who may be handicapped.

In our contemporary world the question has been raised as to whether abortion-on-demand is a matter of infanticide or, as Paul Ramsey has suggested, of "feticide." Induced abortion has been generally condemned by Christian theologians.

In the present state of discussion, including the definitional problem of the fetus as a person, the analogy between abortion and infanticide is not clear. The issues, both in their personal and demographic dimensions, provide an instructive instance of the impact of contemporary medical technology upon matters of Christian moral concern.

WILLIAM W. PAUL

INFLATION. In economics, inflation is commonly defined as a disproportionate and sudden increase in the quantity of money or credit, or both, relative to the amount of exchange business, with consequent higher prices. Historically, this has resulted at times from the discovery or capture of quantities of the precious metals, as following the Roman conquest of Spain, the Spanish conquest of Peru, and the nineteenth century and later developments of large gold deposits in California, the Klondike, Australia, and South Africa. Most commonly, however, it has come about from reducing the amount of metal represented by the unit of account, thereby giving an illusory increase in the amount of real money.

Mosaic law forbad tampering with the weights and measures ("just balances, just weights, a just *ephah* and a just *hin* shall ye have: I am the Lord your God," Lev. 19:36) but such prohibitions were not in the moral code of surrounding pagans. The process of inflating the currency by clipping, alloying, or otherwise reducing the precious metal content of the coinage became an accepted statecraft in the Western Roman Empire. The first recorded instance of deliberate debasement by the State was in connection with the Solonian reforms in Athens in 594 B.C. when the Lawgiver authorized debtors to discharge their debts in *drachmas* lightened by 27 percent. Thereafter, apparently sobered by this experience, the Greeks adopted a law forbidding tampering with the coinage, and the tradition of a pure coinage of fixed weight persisted in the Eastern Roman Empire throughout the period of Byzantine greatness, so that the *bezant* became during the Middle Ages a standard of account from the Baltic to Ceylon.

With the advent of paper making in Europe, in the thirteenth century, warehouse receipts for coin and metal left with the Italian bankers circulated as money, and among unscrupulous bankers the technique of inflation became that of issuing receipts for more money than was actually held.

With the establishment of the Bank of England in 1694, the practice received official sanction, and with the creation of the U.S. Federal Reserve System in 1913 obtained universal respect. In 1922, the Federal Reserve officially adopted—though somewhat fearfully—the policy of manipulating the quantity of paper currency and credit in the interest of a stable price level, which resulted unfortunately in a steady depreciation of the money measured by a price level that rose by nearly four times in the interval. Today, an annual increase in prices of around 3 percent is considered normal (but a rate of 6 percent reached in 1970, as inflation). As a consequence, the dollar defined by law and Presidential proclamation as the equivalent of 1/35 oz. fine gold actually has no relation to such standard: citizens can neither obtain gold for their currency nor hold monetary gold, and to all practical purposes the dollar is irredeemable abroad.

Elgin Groseclose, *Money and Man*, New York, Ungar, 1961.   ELGIN GROSECLOSE

INHIBITION. As a technical term in physiology and psychology, inhibition carries different operational definitions according to its theoretical context. Technically it is as ethically neutral as terms like force, friction, and energy in physics. Most of the various definitions agree that it usually denotes a suppressive action between two or more processes, whether in the physiological, behavioral, mental, or social realm. While Diamond and others have shown (S. Diamond, R. D. Balvin, F. R. Diamond, *Inhibition and Choice*, New York, Harper & Row, 1963) that in all higher organisms tonic inhibitions play an indispensable part in nervous control, it remains highly speculative whether writers such as W. Sargant (*Battle for the Mind*, New York, Heinemann, 1957) adequately portray the part played by such inhibition in the process of establishment of religious and political beliefs. In any case no ethical and moral stakes seem to be involved in deciding among competing scientific models, of which Sargant's is but one example, and which are presently proposed by brain scientists as explanatory mechanisms of the process of inhibition.

Among psychologists, as Diamond (ibid.) points out, the technical usage of the term often lacks precision; the reader is left with the impression that inhibition is merely a close synomyn for repression (q.v.) in the Freudian sense. Freud (q.v.) very early abandoned the attempt to establish a physiological foundation for his psychological theories and in his published works he does not discuss the problem of neurological inhibition. The fact remains, however, that Freud's fundamental propositions regarding inhibition were developed in the early period when he was still dealing with neurological problems. Recent years have witnessed a sustained critical reassessment of the Freudian view of inhibition (meaning repression); in the USA this has been led by O. H. Mowrer and in Britain by H. J. Eysenck. The debate will doubtless long continue in scientific circles. In the meantime it is disturbing to realize that psychoanalysis (q.v.), in which the Freudian concept of inhibition figures so large, has had its greatest impact, not as an individual therapy, but as a broad social ideology and personal philosophy. Equally disquieting, as O. H. Mowrer has pointed out (*The Crisis in Psychiatry and Religion*, New York, Van Nostrand, 1961), has been the tendency of some theologians, overzealous to be abreast of the scientific hounds, to incorporate the supposed latest scientific theory into their theology, when they lack the skills necessary critically to assess the evidence for and against the theory they so readily embrace.
                                                    MALCOLM A. JEEVES

INNOCENCE. Innocence designates a privative quality or condition of men. The innocent are *not* guilty, are *not* harmful, are *un*sullied by evil, *in*experienced, *without* guile. Therefore, to be innocent is to be pure, simple, utterly single and open to development, a naive, just person. Adam and Eve were innocent creatures before the devil tempted them in Paradise; they did not know evil until they sinned. After their childlike, obedient relationship with God was broken, their life got a crease in it, and they forfeited their innocence.

Most pagan cultures postulated an original Golden Age of Innocence from which our present world had fallen. Their mythological depictions of this blissful, pristine period are really bastard accounts of Eden, transmitted by word of mouth through generations of ethnic peoples and matter-of-factly lamented as gone. The

Greek ethic did not praise innocence. In fact, the Homeric hero, (never-at-a-loss) Odysseus, was the very apotheosis of experienced deceit and guile. Innocent, simple people came to be associated somewhat contemptuously in the Hellenic mind B.C. with harmless, simple-minded, easily duped youth or hoi polloi.

Patristic churchmen, however, synthecized, by and large, the comment of Christ about being childlike (Mark 10:13-16) with the ancient belief of Hellenistic cynic philosophy that the state of uncomplicated nature is ideal. Then *innocentia* or *simplicitas* became the ground-level, necessary state of sanctity one needed to be saved. Some believers felt compelled to exercise their holy innocence by a rigorous, ritualized life of prayer and abstinence so as to become more perfect (cf. *Monasticism*).

Secular modern man has taken two different tacks on innocence. (1) A "Romanticist" primitivism, stretching from the Enlightenment (Rousseau) through German Idealism (Schelling) to American transcendentalism (Walden, Brook Farm community), has been anti-historical enough to encourage mankind, complicated by culture, to recapture a condition of utterly sincere naiveté and uncorrupted innocence supposedly native to man. (2) A positivistic tradition, with leaders like Durkheim, Lévy-Bruhl and F. M. Cornford, have evolutionistically acclaimed the movement of humankind from a mythopoeic simplicity to our present logical level of societal consciousness that makes science possible—you can't go home again to innocence.

It is important not to confuse *religious* innocence before God, the forgiveness men can have as a gift of grace through faith in Jesus Christ, with an *ethical* mode of action men should practice in society. Religiously innocent men, those who are pure in their heart, are blessed because they shall be able to see God (Ps. 32:1-2; Matt. 5:7). Ethical innocence, however, if it is understood to

mean men should anticipate the attainment of a blank, clear conscience, is not a Christian calling but a frustrating fiction. Ethical "innocence" makes Christian sense only if it describes the unassuming, non-judgmental demeanor children of God show who live normed by the Biblical imperative to be prudent and unsophisticated (Matt. 10:16), and as such willing to trust all kinds of things believingly, with great expectations, taking setbacks without complaint, covering for others in everything possible (I Cor. 13:7).   CALVIN G. SEERVELD

INSTINCTS. Freud created a psychological system in which instinctual energy was considered the motive power of personality. He defined an instinct as a stimulus arising within the organism itself and exerting a continuous force. The instincts were regarded as a borderland concept between the mental and the physical, representing somatic demands upon the mental life. Instincts were conceived as needs residing in the id (q.v.), which was considered the most primitive element of personality and the bearer of everything that is inherited. The instincts are thus basically biological in nature. Instinctual energy is conceived as streaming into the ego from various parts of the body, the ego having no energy of its own.

In an effort to reduce the phenomena of personality to their most fundamental terms, Freud came at length to postulate two instincts, love and aggression. His elaboration of these two described Eros as the forward-driving life instinct, and the destructive tendency as a drive toward death and dissolution. "The goal of all life is death." The concept of a death instinct was rejected by many of Freud's followers, although it has also been defended by pointing to the varieties of self-destruction, both slow and rapid, that are practiced by mankind. Such unconscious compulsions are indeed found in neurotic persons, but evidence is lacking to make this component of psychopathology a universal characteristic of human personality.

Since instincts often cannot be expressed in raw form, Freud imagined their conversion into socially acceptable, or even highly artistic or altruistic forms, a process he called sublimation. According to this concept, the noblest of deeds are simply the transfigured end-product of biological instinct, arising from the unconscious id. The dual instinct theory and the concept of sublimation are Freudian constructs that have no empirical foundation. The individual that foregoes some specific gratification in favor of another type of activity is more likely to be exercising a choice than diverting instinctual energy.

Academic psychology, in its study of motivation, has largely passed over the term *instinct* in favor of the term *drive*. Indeed, the German word, *Trieb,* used by Freud, might better have been originally translated drive instead of instinct. Efforts to derive all adult motives and interests from primitive urges are inadequate, since adult drives are infinitely varied and contemporary. Even childhood activities are often unrelated to erotic or aggressive goals.

A movement known as ego psychology has arisen within psychoanalysis which denies that the instincts are the sole source of motive power for personality. Instead of calling upon deflected or transformed instinctual drives to account for human motivation, ego psychology recognizes autonomy within the ego or the self, and acknowledges the primacy of conscious, purposeful intentions and values. In this development, ego psychology has converged upon a number of other psychologies more compatible with Christian faith, which holds that human achievement is not limited by biological endowment in the form of instincts, but may change and grow in response to the dynamic forces of purposeful living and striving.

Franz Alexander, *Fundamentals of Psychoanalysis,* New York, Norton, 1963, Chapter IV; Gordon Allport, *Pattern and Growth in Personality,* New York, Holt Rinehart & Winston, 1961, p. 201ff.; Sigmund Freud, *Beyond the Pleasure Principle,* London, Hogarth, 1922, Ch. VI; ————, "Instincts and Their Vicissitudes," *Collected Papers,* London, Hogarth, 1957, Vol. IV, p. 60-83;————, *The Ego and the Id,* New York, Norton, 1962, Ch. IV.   ORVILLE S. WALTERS

INSTRUMENTAL GOOD. See *Intrinsic, Instrumental Good.*

INSURRECTION. Insurrection may be broadly defined as revolt against civil authority or established government. David gives a vivid description of it in Ps. 55.

One must carefully distinguish obedience to God's laws as supreme authority from revolt against civil authority. The Bible teaches the former and opposes the latter.

A classic illustration of the supremacy of the laws of God is found in Daniel. The king had prohibited prayers to anyone save himself. This law was clearly contrary to devotion to God, and Daniel openly refused to obey, esteeming devotion to God above obedience to the specific law. However, he made no effort to overthrow the Persian government. In the lion's den he was shown God's favor and protection. The result was the establishment of the worship of God as a national policy. It is doubtful that violence would have had such a result.

Few governments have been as cruel or corrupt as that of Rome. Insurrection was one crime that the Romans punished swiftly and severely. If Jesus could have been convicted of it, he surely would have been. He was not.   ROBERT E. FARNELL III

INTENTION. See *Motives and Motivism.*

INTERCOURSE. See *Marriage; Procreation.*

INTEREST. See *Credit; Usury.*

INTERIM ETHICS. Interim ethics is the term used by Albert Schweitzer (q.v.) to characterize his understanding of Jesus' ethical teaching. The prevailing interpretation of the Kingdom of God before Schweitzer was the "old liberal" view. The Kingdom of God consists of several universal spiritual values: the universal Fatherhood of God, the brotherhood of man, the ethic of love, the infinite value of the human soul. The eschatological-apocalyptic teachings of Jesus were only the time-conditioned husk which encased his pure spiritual teaching (A. Harnack, *What Is Christianity,* New York, Putnam, 1901).

Schweitzer rocked the world of contemporary German scholarship by insisting that in the teaching of the "historical Jesus," his preaching of the Kingdom was altogether eschatological and apocalyptic and in no sense a present spiritual reality. His books were published in Germany in 1901 and 1911. He believed that Jesus looked for an imminent supernatural inbreaking of God to end history and inaugurate his glorious Kingdom. In this, Jesus was one with contemporary Jewish apocalyptists. He was not a great ethical teacher of universal truths, but a first-century Jewish apocalyptist. When Jesus sent the disciples on a preaching tour, he expected the Kingdom to come before they returned (Matt. 10:23). When this did not happen, he changed his plans. The coming of the Kingdom must be preceded by the Messianic woes. Jesus decided to go to Jerusalem, to compel the Jewish leaders to bring about his death, and thus by suffering the Messianic woes in his own person to force the Kingdom to come. He expected to be exalted by God to be the heavenly Son of man in the apocalyptic Kingdom. When this did not happen, he died on the cross crying out to God for having forsaken him. In short, Jesus was a deluded first-century Jewish apocalyptist whose message has no relevance for succeeding centuries.

Thus, interim ethics contends that Jesus' ethical teaching must be interpreted in light of his eschatology. It is not an ethic of the coming Kingdom; when the Kingdom comes, all will be perfection. It is not an ethic for the future conduct of men in history, for Jesus' entire life and mission was conditioned by his expectation of the imminent end of the world and the inbreaking of the supernatural Kingdom of God. His demand was one primarily of repentance to prepare men for the coming of the Kingdom. Jesus' ethical teaching was designed only for the short interim which he believed would intervene before the Kingdom would come. It was an emergency ethic to tide over the brief interval before the imminent end. Only a few central ideas, such as the commandment of love, are valid for all time, even after Jesus' expectations have proved erroneous. Interim ethics is an essential element in Schweitzer's "consistent eschatology."

Albert Schweitzer, *The Mystery of the Kingdom of God,* London, Black, 1925; *The Quest of the Historical Jesus,* New York, Macmillan, 1969.

GEORGE E. LADD

INTERMARRIAGE, RACIAL. See also *Marriage; Race Relations.* Because the Scriptures nowhere explicitly speak about the permissability of a racially mixed marriage, the Christian must find his answer by way of his own ethical decision. He need not, however, decide on the principle that what the Scriptures do not prohibit they allow. The Scriptures provide positive teachings enabling the Christian to make moral decisions in confidence.

The Scriptures attach no significance to race or matters of race. The Scriptures teach that God is the creator of all men and that he created them in his own image. Since skin color is not a part of the image of God in man, it cannot take precedence over what constitutes the most distinctive feature of man. Nothing that is incidental to our humanity can override the Psalmist when he asks, "What is man?" and answers, "But thou has made him but a little lower than God, and crownest him with glory and honor" (Ps. 8:4, 5). In the light of this, the significance of skin-color fades and other racial differences dissolve into insignificance.

Christ died for men of every tribe, nation, and tongue, and the church is a house of prayer for all peoples. Biblical thought sees a definite distinction between Jew and Gentile, grounded in election, but Biblical theology does not consider man's color and never raises race into an ism (cf. *Racism*).

Scripture makes only one stipulation about any Christian's marriage. Man is required to marry "in the Lord." The Scriptures do not limit a Christian's right to marry a Christian of another race or color. Consequently, no State or human society, or church, has the Biblical right to forbid interracial marriages.

Interracial marriage in the USA rose from 0.44 percent in 1960 to 0.70 percent in 1970—in either case a tiny portion—of the census-recorded married couples (44.6 million in 1970). Most occur between black men, frequently with high education and earnings, and white women.

This freedom to enter a racial intermarriage, however, does not relieve the Christian contemplating such a marriage from ethical decision. Christians live in a society. Whoever contemplates a racially mixed marriage must solemnly and conscientiously decide whether to subject himself, his spouse, and his children to the heavy toll that racist societies and cultural considerations impose on mixed marriages and families. Not only do the Scriptures take a dim view of divorce, but marriages that issue in families are in fact indissoluble.

As regards marriage the Christian is free within the stipulation "in the Lord." What the Scriptures allow, none should disallow in self or another. But such freedom includes the freedom to decide, in the light of the concrete situation, not to do what one is before Scripture free to do.

JAMES DAANE

INTERNATIONALISM. See *Nationalism*.

INTERNATIONAL LAW. See *United Nations; World Government*.

INTERNATIONAL ORDER. A Christian believer holds that the international order is governed by a deeper invisible order. God holds the world in his hands including all political and social relations. Nothing escapes God's rule, and whatever is could not have been and cannot continue to be without his will and power. Even if we cannot "prove" this in every detail, it remains nevertheless a firm article of faith. The laws of nature, the laws of development, the moral law whereby nations rise, mature, decay, and disappear, are all created and allowed by God. Augustine in his *City of God* outlines the principles of a Christian interpretation of history and therefore of all international order. In this sense Christ, being Lord of lords and King of kings, is affirmed by faith as the Lord of history.

Keeping all this in mind, we wish nevertheless to concentrate on the visible international order. The nation, as the unit of this order, is a juridical international entity determined by a distinct territory, a distinct people with their special customs and relations, a distinct government, and distinct laws. What constitutes a nation formally is the unity which its government and laws impose upon its people and the recognition by other nations of its distinctness and independence. This recognition is expressed by respecting its territorial integrity and political independence, and by exchanging diplomatic representation with it. A nation may exist without every other nation recognizing it, but no nation can juridically exist if no nation recognizes it. Recognition is of the essence of a nation.

Just as the world of matter is made up of some 104 chemical elements (theoretically scientists speak of another 50 or so possible but highly unstable elements), so the world of men is made up of (strange coincidence!) some 150 nations, of which 132 constitute the United Nations. And just as in the world of matter there are highly stable and highly unstable elements, so in the world of men there are stable and unstable nations. The order that obtains between these juridical collective entities is governed by six sets of laws.

There is first the recognized laws of international intercourse which together form a corpus known as international law. Such laws always existed, at least in some incipient form, between international political communities. But it was Grotius (1583-1645) who, more than any other man in history, first identified them as constituting a distinct subject matter for rational inquiry and elaboration. International law covers all kinds of regulations and usages between the nations, both in time of war and in time of peace (diplomatic exchanges and usages, elementary courtesies and proprieties, reciprocal rights, the form and character of treaties, how sovereigns or heads of state or members of government are addressed or treated from one nation to another, the treatment of prisoners of wars, etc.). The nations in their dealings with one another submit in varying degrees to this immense body of international law.

There is second the law of the United Nations (q.v.)—its Charter as well as its cumulative jurisprudence—which applies, at least so far as matters relating to international peace and security are concerned, to all nations, whether or not members of the world organization. The nations keep this law in mind all the time, because, should they violate it, a complaint might be lodged against them in the appropriate organ of the United Nations, and a decision could be taken against them.

On top of these two elements of international order, nations regulate their dealings with one another by all sorts of special treaties or agreements or arrangements or instruments, covering military, defense, economic, commercial, legal, or cultural matters. When they conclude these treaties or arrangements they make sure that their terms do not conflict with international law or the law of the United Nations. Without mutual trust between the contracting parties, international treaties would be impossible. The proof of the sway (at least partially) of the moral order in international affairs is that no nation would want that it be said of it that it broke its plighted word.

There are further commercial or cultural dealings which are not covered by special treaties or general international law. When a commercial deal is concluded between, say, General Motors and a private company in France, or when an American university engages French professors or uses French books, or when these two nations listen to each other's radio broadcasts or see each other's works of art, these dealings need not come under any special agreement between France and America. But they help to govern and constitute the international order.

Then there are underlying cultural affinities between peoples and nations uncovered either by international law or by special treaties or by private transactions. Thus, for example, there are common unformalized customs and mentalities between the English-speaking peoples, or between the Slavic peoples, or between the nations of Europe, or between other groups of nations with common traditions. These communities of mind and mores help to determine and constitute the international order.

Finally, there are certain norms and standards which belong to human nature as such, and which need not be codified by international law or embodied in special agreements. That it is not in a nation's interests to insult or attack another, that the more a nation finds that its trust of another nation is well founded the more this trust is likely to continue, that the stronger a nation is, both materially and spiritually, the better for its security vis-a-vis other nations, that it is in a nation's interests to increase the circle of its friends, to promote mutually advantageous relations with other nations, and to have a favorable image of itself cast abroad, that self-defense is a sacred natural right, all these and a myriad other such norms are taken for granted in any international order, and no nation need that it be taught them or that it subscribe to them in any formal pact, because they all spring from the given nature of things. As such, they, too, enter into and constitute the international order.

When the international order breaks down on a large enough scale, we have war. But so long as it lasts, this order is determined and constituted, in varying degrees and modes, by the law of nations accumulated over the centuries, the special international organization of the moment, special treaties and agreements which have been concluded between the nations, unformalized private transactions between persons and cultures, such communities of mind as exist between certain groups of nations, and all that belongs to what might be termed the human law of nature.

World order is far more determined by the intercultural than by the international order. Nations come and go, and if there are 150 such units today, it is almost certain that the number will be different a hundred years from now—some breaking up, some merging together. Who can predict the exact political order, fifty or a hundred years from now, between the two Koreas, the two Viet Nams, the two Chinas, the two Germanys, the two Irelands; or within such large nations as Canada, India, the Peoples Republic of China, the Soviet Union, the United States; or among the twenty Latin American nations, or the fifteen or more Arab states, or the thirty African nations? What appear to be far more abiding in world history are a few fundamental world outlooks. There are six such outlooks, each capable of further refinement and discrimination: the Western European world, including the whole of the Western Hemisphere; the Eastern European world, including Russia; the Islamic world; the Chinese world; the Indian world; and the African world.

These worlds, each more or less coherent within itself, have different outlooks on matter, mind, law, man and his destiny, the nature of history, the nature of society, the nature of truth, the nature of morality, and the nature of the supreme being. A composite world outlook has been developing in recent years, but, in fundamental matters, it is still most precarious and unstable. In general, one can still speak—and doubtless one will continue for a long time to speak—of six distinct world cultures. Intercultural world order is the fundamental thing, and world history is not so much the history of the nations as the history of the development of these six cultural worlds, both internally and in their fateful interactions with one another.

The world has become, physically, more or less one; the same world, however, contains a multiplicity of apparently irreducible cultures with different and, in important respects, contradictory outlooks. It would appear that the only possible order in a world that has become physically one but continues to be spiritually many is an order of freedom and respect—freedom for each of the many in itself, respect when the many interact so as to produce a unitary effect.   CHARLES H. MALIK

INTERPERSONAL RELATIONS. See also *Ethics, History of; State.* Relations between or among persons focus on how an individual relates himself to another individual or to those within a group. This is in contrast to national or tribal groups where the group as a whole is friendly or hostile to another group as a whole.

Basic to all Christian interpersonal relations is loving God with the whole heart, soul, mind, and strength, and loving one's neighbor as one's self (Mark 12:30-31). Interpersonal relations of love are impossible for anyone who cares only for himself. If he tries to love his neighbor as himself but has no love for God and does not know God's love for himself, he will lack the motivation for loving all varieties of neighbors. When one loves his neighbor as himself, the neighbor can no longer be an object of observation or of malicious or negative criticism. A loving person is not blind to weaknesses, needs, and various kinds of sin, but he seeks to restore to wholeness the neighbor in need. The energy for such love comes from God.

When a person loves another, he does not think of giving back evil for evil; rather, he gives constant forethought and careful consideration for all that is noble in the presence of all men (Rom. 12:17).

Both the OT and NT tell in great detail what practices are detrimental or helpful in living with other people.

Friction. Throughout the NT there are comprehensive lists of vices and virtues that either destroy or establish a man. In the works of the flesh mentioned in Gal. 5:19-21, particular aspects of sexual immorality and drunkenness are mentioned. Yet equally destructive of interpersonal relations are idolatry, sorcery, enmity, strife, jealousy, outbursts of anger, outbursts of selfishness, dissensions, factions, and envies. Paul says that self-centered hostile living characterized men before God's kindness and love for mankind appeared (Titus 3:3-4). Paul describes conceited controversialists (I Tim. 6:4-5) as also being self-centered egotists (II Tim. 3:1-5). Their way of life is a way of pain.

Harmony. The qualities that bring harmony are not the self-generated products of human endeavor. The fruit of the Spirit (Gal. 5:22-23) refers to a harvest in the lives of Christians for which the Holy Spirit supplies the nurture: love, joy, peace, forbearance, kindness, goodness, faithfulness, consideration, and self-control. These qualities make interpersonal relations blossom. Living in harmony with others results from agreement on basic issues (Phil. 2:2; 3:15; 4:2; II Cor. 13:11; Rom. 15:5-6). Those who live in harmony maintain a positive spirit even in the face of petty strife (II Tim. 2:24-25). The servant of the Lord does not fight, but instead is gentle to all, skillful in teaching and bears evil without resentment (II Tim. 2:24). The man of God pursues uprightness, piety, faithfulness, love, endurance, and gentleness (I Tim. 6:11). These factors bring harmony and demand a delicate sensitivity to others. At the same time, the man of God is insensitive to personal abuse. This is an outstanding combination.

Basic Attitudes toward God, Self, and Others. We must seek first the Kingdom of God and his righteousness (Matt. 6:33). Christ must have first place in everything (Col. 1:18). Since we live by the Spirit, we are to follow the Spirit (Gal. 5:25). We are to make God the central focus of our lives.

When a man becomes a disciple of Jesus Christ, he denies his self-centeredness (Matt. 16:24-28; Mark 8:39—9:1; Luke 9:23-27) but never his self-hood. He gradually learns to make better self-appraisals (Rom. 12:3). He has a sense of being transformed (II Cor. 3:18). With God in right focus, he gets self in the right perspective.

The Christian is to work for the good of all, especially for those who belong to the household of faith (Gal. 6:10). He seeks to benefit all men, yet he has a particular loyalty to his fellow Christians.

A. BERKELEY MICKELSEN

INTERRACIAL RELATIONS. See *Intermarriage; Race Relations.*

INTRINSIC, INSTRUMENTAL GOOD. Intrinsic good is the property of being valuable as an end in itself or of having internal value. In classical philosophy it is the notion that virtue is its own reward and moral excellence is to be sought for its own sake. For Aristotle happiness is the intrinsic human good since it is "something final and self-sufficient, and the end of action" (*Nichomachian Ethics*, Book I, Ch. 7, 1097 b). Intellectual, moral, and aesthetic values have traditionally been considered intrinsic goods.

Instrumental goods are properties which are means only, or goods in the service of other ends, usually intrinsic goods. Health and wealth usually are considered means to religious or intellectual good.

There is some criticism of the category of means and ends as an accurate guide for identifying and discriminating values. "Means and ends shade into one another in experience," and no value at all may belong to one of them apart from the other (R. Sorley, *Moral Value and the Idea of God*, Cambridge University, 1918, p. 41), and values which are ends in themselves are to have less value than the value of the whole of experience of which they are parts. Dewey and H. R. Niebuhr deny the validity of any distinction between means and ends, and consider all goods as instrumental. X is a means to y, and y to z, *ad infinitum*. "But unless some things were good-in-themselves and not only as means, nothing would be of any use at all. To value everything only as a means would be to do everything for the sake of a future benefit which never came" (A. C. Ewing, *Ethics*, New York, Free Press, p. 13).

The Biblical concept of intrinsic good opposes all non-Biblical theories because of its emphasis on the transcendence of God and absolute creation Evangelicals, recognizing the validity of the distinction between instrumental and intrinsic values, believe that the argument for intrinsic values can be pushed back to God's relation to creation. All created goods are instrumental. The will of God then is the only intrinsic good.

God wills himself necessarily and human ends freely. His free will is not arbitrary but grounded in his attributes, yet his will is free with reference to creation. The significance of the concept that "intrinsic good is God's will" is that no simple deduction of specific human ends from the nature of God is possible. The non-Christian doctrine of continuity, the continuity of the being of God and the World, is denied, over against classical Greek philosophy, modern idealism and scholastic philosophy under the influence of Aristotle. Evangelical Christianity sharply opposes a doctrine of the continuity of being since it conflicts with the doctrine of creation *ex nihilo*. God is not merely first in the order of being and value, but sovereign creator of all being other than himself, and his will is recognized as the source of the order of their worth.

ROY W. BUTLER

INTUITION. Intuition, if there be such, is the grasping of an individual object without using inference or general rules. It is an *immediate* knowledge, knowledge without means.

The most frequent form of intuition is sensation. By the sense of sight, for example, one sees, grasps, or "knows" this chair, this desk, or this pen. John Locke, because of his empiricism, would deny that we intuit this chair. We intuit the color brown by sight, the quality hard by touch, and then we combine these sensations to produce a chair.

For Kant the only pure intuitions are

those of space and time. These two are strictly individual. There is only one space and one time, whereas there are many chairs and desks. Though we cannot see or touch space and time, they are intuitions of sense in that they are the forms of empirical intuitions. A single chair is seen in space somewhat as railroad tracks converge in perspective. This is how the mind works. Railroad tracks do not really converge; nor do chairs in themselves occupy space. Space is just our way of seeing them.

In opposition Hegel denies that there is any immediate knowledge. His argument includes the point that the individualizing "this" of space and time is the most universal and empty term of all; so that what empiricists take as the richest knowledge is the poorest, in fact no knowledge at all.

By an analogy between the physical seeing of a sensory individual and the figurative intellectual "seeing" of a truth, the term intuition has been stretched to include the grasp of ultimate or first principles. Since axioms cannot be inferred, they must be seen immediately in their intuitional self-evidence. There is no geometrical proof whatever that two sides of a triangle are longer than the third side. One must simply "see" that only one straight line can be drawn between two points.

In ethics, Ralph Cudworth (1617-1688) used the intuitionism of Platonism to establish morality. Henry More (1614-1687) was closer to the geometrical ideal. He posited moral axioms—two dozen of them. But if six Euclidean axioms can imply several books of geometrical theorems, it seems cumbersome to have twenty-four in Ethics. The more serious objection, however, is the difficulty of convincing an opponent that such and such a proposition is axiomatic and self-evident, when he does not "see" it.

In the present century behaviorism (q.v.) and linguistic analysis have tried to explain what actually lies behind the belief in intuitions. The purely linguistic theories are, in the writer's opinion, pedantic trivialities, and behaviorism faces other difficulties. In any case their discussions of intuition have nothing specifically to do with ethics.

Brand Blanshard, *Reason and Analysis*, La Salle, Ill., Open Court, 1962; Gilbert Ryle, *The Concept of Mind*, London, 1949; Henry Sidgwick, *Methods of Ethics*, London 7th ed., 1907.

GORDON H. CLARK

IRRATIONALISM. Irrationalism was a nineteenth century reaction against Hegel that has grown into the secular existentialism (q.v.) and religious dialectical (cf. *Dialectical Ethics*) theology of the present.

Hegel, by eliminating the impossibilities of Kant's unknowables, claimed, or seemed to claim, that he had produced the final, rational solution to all philosophic problems.

Kierkegaard (q.v.) insisted that Hegel had lost the existing individual—not merely the individual pen or desk, but much more seriously the living, suffering, dying, human individual. Man is basically emotional and irrational. His destiny requires Christian salvation, and this depends on a passionate and deliberate choice to believe absurdities, for there is no rational explanation of the Incarnation.

Nietzsche (q.v.) was a secular or atheistic irrationalist. There is no such thing as a mind. What Descartes mistook for an ego is a multiplicity of conflicting desires and urges—a theory Freud took over. The whole apparatus of knowing is a simplifying device, directed not at truth but at the utilization of the world for our purposes. Logic, whose basic principle is the law of contradiction, is an evolutionary product. At a prior date the law had not developed, and even yet frogs and fish do not think as we do. At the moment we cannot think otherwise, for evolution has imposed our logic on us. In the future we shall outgrow the law of contradiction, for evolution has not stopped. But neither ancient, modern, nor future logic can be considered true. No such law is a law of reality. Logic is simply our way of handling the universe.

This is essentially the view of William James (q.v.) and John Dewey (q.v.) also. French existentialism is equally illogical, but inherits from Kierkegaard a greater emphasis on irrational decision in moral affairs.

Among theologians Karl Barth (q.v.) accepted Kierkegaard's view of Paradox, and though in his later writings he restricted its extent, he never repudiated it. In the early pages of his *Church Dogmatics* he says that the law of contradiction is acceptable in theology only upon conditions that are scarcely tolerable to a scientific theologian. Emil Brunner (q.v.) more pointedly held that faith should curb logic: we must believe certain things and disbelieve what they necessarily imply.

Besides these recent developments, we always have with us the mystics and all those who think of religion as essentially emotional and non-doctrinal.

In conclusion, it should be made clear that if with Kierkegaard we must believe absurdities, we are at liberty to believe any absurdity we choose, for there is no *reason* for thinking that one is better than another.

Nietzsche should be warned that if logic distorts reality, the arguments by which he tried to establish his philosophy distort reality, and therefore his evolutionism cannot be true.

If faith curbs reason, no reasonable limit can be set for the curbing. We could have faith that Jesus is truly God, but refuse to draw the inference that he is eternal or omnipotent. In other words, faith justifies insanity.

Gordon H. Clark, *Karl Barth's Theological Method*, Nutley, N.J., Presbyterian and Reformed, 1963; ———, *Thales to Dewey* (chap. 11) Boston, Houghton Mifflin, 1957; Paul King Jewett, *Emil Brunner's Concept of Revelation*, London, 1954.   GORDON H. CLARK

ISAIAH. Isaiah was the most outstanding prophet of OT times. His ministry extended from 740 to about 680 B.C., while Judah was governed by godly kings like Uzziah, Jotham, and Hezekiah, and very wicked rulers like Ahaz and Manasseh. Isaiah 6 records his confrontation by God in his majesty and holiness during a vision the prophet saw in the Jerusalem temple. There he came to know Yahweh as the "Holy One of Israel," i.e., as the faithful Protector, Chastener and Redeemer of his covenant people (a concept which dominated his entire preaching ministry, for this distinctive title appears at least twenty-six times in his sixty-six chapters). Humbled and repentant for his own impurity in the presence of the holy seraphim, Isaiah was nevertheless forgiven and cleansed by the gracious atonement of God, and commissioned to preach his truth, even though it would be rejected by his gospel-hardened countrymen (6:9-10), and would eventuate in their ultimate devastation and exile. But he was also assured that after the Captivity there would be a restoration of a believing remnant ("a tenth") to Palestine, and the eventual appearance of "a holy Seed from their root-stump" (6:13)—a verse which clearly shows that the eighth century Isaiah foreknew the Babylonian Captivity and the Restoration under Cyrus.

There is in the book of Isaiah more prediction concerning Christ than in any other. He is to be born of a virgin (7:14) as the incarnate God (Immanuel means "God with us"), combining in himself divine attributes as well as human (9:6-7). His gospel, preached under the full enduement and anointing of the Holy Spirit, will bring liberation to the enslaved, sight to the blind, and restoration to those in captivity and exile (61:1-4). But he will accomplish redemption by personal suffering, rejection by his people, and by surrendering his life as a vicarious, substitutionary atonement (53:1-9)—emerging triumphant as One who lives on after death, and obtaining ultimate victory for God (53:10-12). Furthermore, he is to sit as final Judge of all mankind, and as Davidic king in authority over a warless earth (11:1-5; 32:1-3), having established peace and righteousness throughout the whole world (2:1-4; 11:5-10). Christ alone will be God's Mediator and Redeemer, gloriously succeeding where Israel has failed (59:16-20).

But despite his preoccupation with Christology and predictive prophecy, Isaiah has much to say about the great moral issues of his own generation and the Divine imperative for social justice. Not only do the heathen nations stand under the judgment of Yahweh, who will destroy their power and glory when their time is up (chaps. 13-23), but even the covenant nation of Israel is found inescusably guilty before him. It has trampled upon his fatherly love and thanklessly rebelled against his rule (1:2-4). It has disregarded his warning chastenments of military disaster and invasion (1:5-8), and insolently attempted to buy him off with blood-sacrifices, services of worship, and solemn public prayers which do not represent any sincere repentance for sin or purpose to lead a godly life (1:10-15). Only a complete about-face and a whole hearted contribution, claiming the undeserved grace of God for cleansing from sin, can avert disaster (1:16-20).

In the ringing indictment of Chapter 5 the prophet declares that God's moral law is not subject to any kind of modernization or amendment so as to conform to the emancipated views of modern, eighth century B.C. man. Nor will he adapt his standards to the level of morality attained by the majority; no referendums are possible for his holy laws. "Woe to those who call evil good and good evil, who put darkness for light and light for darkness.... Woe to those who are wise in their own eyes and prudent in their own sight! Woe to those who are mighty to drink wine . . . who justify the wicked for a reward and take away the righteousness of the righteous from him." Their asserted enlightenment and emancipation, their cynical materialism was powerless to annul one syllable of the moral decrees of God, and they were therefore doomed to defeat, invasion and ultimate doom (5:24-25).

It was to this stern warning that Isaiah's generation turned a deaf ear, scoffing at his old-fashioned, outmoded emphasis upon the conventional morality of the past (chap. 28). They preferred to fritter away their day of grace in alcoholic dissipation as they scoffed and derided Isaiah's Bible lessons as mere pablum for kindergartners (28:9-10). Only the sincere remnant would ever enjoy the safety of trusting in the foundation-stone of Christ (v. 16). Although King Hezekiah made earnest effort to bring his nation back to God, even he turned a deaf ear to God's warnings against turning to Egypt for deliverance from Assyrian might (30:1-5), and hence brought Judah to the brink of disaster in 701 B.C., the year of Sennacherib's invasion. By dint of an anguished appeal to the Lord, Hezekiah prevailed upon him to rescue his beleagered people. Yet the nation soon proved ungrateful and eagerly followed Hezekiah's son, Manasseh, down the pathway of apostasy and utter abandonment of the moral law (59:1-15).

Yet the scope of Isaiah's vision did not end with Judah's disaster. After the fall of Jerusalem and the exile of Babylonia would come the conquest of the conqueror at the hands of the Persian deliverer, Cyrus, whose name (to the scandal of all antisupernaturalists) is spelled out (44:28—45:4) as God's anointed agent to restore the Jewish captives to their homeland. Out of the chastenment of exile would emerge a remnant of sincere believers who would completely eschew idol-worship and serve the Lord as sincere witnesses to the one true Sovereign of the universe, who alone could foretell the future (44:1-23). Final and complete deliverance would come only through the Messianic Servant of the Lord, who would in his own person constitute true Israel, and offer his life as an atonement for their sins (chap. 53). But he would come not only to restore the dispersed of Israel (cf. 11:10) but also as a light of salvation to the Gentiles, even to the very ends of the earth (49:6), suggesting the world-wide expansion of the Christian faith. GLEASON L. ARCHER

ISLAMIC ETHICS. See also *Islamic Law.* Islamic ethics is based on two sources, the Quran (or Koran) and the Traditions (Sunna). The Quran contains specific commandments of God on the faith and manner of life for every believer, and according to which all men, Muslims and non-Muslims, will be judged and rewarded or punished. The Traditions (Sunna) supplement the Quran. Since the Quran did not give details of conduct for every circumstance of life, Muslims recalled the way of life of Mohammad, the founder of Islam, as the pattern of life to be followed.

Islam in its genesis and development was to some extent influenced by the moral ideas of the ancient Arab tribes; hence traces of tribal ethical customs are found in Islamic ethics. In the early stages of the development of Islam, Mohammed stood forth as a reformer, demanding personal belief and personal morality. Good intentions are commended, while unpremeditated lapses from virtue are leniently judged. Allah is forgiving and merciful towards the faithful.

The ethics of the Quran might be summed up in the trite formula: "Believe and do right" (*HERE* Vol. V, p. 501). Muslim ethical behavior is grounded in belief in: God (Allah) the Merciful, to whom absolute submission is essential; the angels who record the deeds of men; the Prophets, Mohammed being the last; the Resurrection and the Day of Judgment; the predestination of all actions, good and evil, from eternity; the Books, the Quran being God's final revelation.

In the light of these essential beliefs, a Muslim must shape his everyday conduct by "doing right." Of human virtues, the Quran gives primary inportance to beneficence—the bestowing of benefits, especially in the form of alms, upon the poor, the needy, the orphan, the stranger, the slave and the prisoner. The duty of voluntary almsgiving is frequently enjoined in the Quran (Sura 2:274, 275). According to one of the traditions, Mohammed says, "The best of alms are those given by a man of small means, who gives of that which he has earned by labor, and gives as much as he is able." Again, "God says, Be thou liberal, thou child of Adam, that I may be liberal to thee." Because of the Quran's emphasis on virtuous action, the practical ethics of Islam *(Fiqh)* is all-important and rigidly governs the religious and social actions of the Muslim. There are at least five types of ethical actions found in the Quran and in the Traditions, each with its corresponding rewards and punishments. They are as follows:

1. Obligatory *(Fard).* This is a required duty. You will be rewarded if you do it and punished if you don't.

2. Preferred *(Mustahabb).* You will be rewarded for doing it, but not punished if you don't.

3. Permissible or allowed *(Halal).* You may or may not do it. There is neither punishment nor reward for doing or not doing it.

4. Disliked *(Makruh).* Such actions are disliked, but not forbidden. If you do them, you will not be punished, but if you do not do them, you will be rewarded.

5. Forbidden *(Haram).* These must not be done under any circumstances, otherwise punishment ensues. Abstinence brings reward.

No Muslim is exempt from obligatory duties, except under special circumstances. The five obligatory "pillars of religion" are:

1. Reciting the Kalima, "There is no God but Allah and Mohammed is his prophet" *(Tashahhud)*.

2. Reciting the daily prayers generally five times a day *(Namaz)*.

3. Observing the Fast in the month of Ramzan *(Roza)*.

4. The giving of alms *(Zakat)*.

5. Undertaking the pilgrimage to Mecca in person or by proxy *(Hajj)*.

The moral actions of a Muslim are also governed by the Islamic idea of sin, i.e., "What Allah forbids is sin." The Quran repeatedly stresses that some things are "halal" (permitted) and others are "haram" (forbidden). Muslim theologians divide sin into the two categories of *Kabira* or "great sins" and *Saghira* or "little sins." *Kabira* includes murder, adultery, disobedience to God or parents, evading *Jehad* (holy war), drunkenness, usury, neglecting Friday prayers and the fast of Ramzan, forgetting the Quran after reading it, swearing falsely or by any other name "than that of God," indulging in magic, gambling, shaving the beard. Such sins can only be forgiven after repentance. The sin of sins is heresy *(Shirk)* i.e., the sin of associating a partner with God. This is the unpardonable offense. *Saghira* includes lying, deception, anger, lust. Sins of this class are easily forgiven if the greater sins are avoided and if some meritorious actions are performed. The Quran says, "Observe prayer at early morning, at the close of the day and at the approach of night, for the good deeds drive away the evil deeds" *(Sura 11:116)*.

Islamic ethics permits polygamy. A Muslim is allowed to have up to four wives but only if he treats them equally. Divorce in Islam is very easy. It is exclusively the prerogative of the husband. A Muslim can divorce his wife at any time and for any reason, by repeating thrice the formula, "I divorce thee." Traditionally, Islam has sanctioned slavery and the slave trade, though Muslims are enjoined to treat slaves mercifully. Islam prohibits the manufacture and use of intoxicating liquors. It also forbids music, dancing, gambling and the use of religious images and pictures, and of certain meats and foods. VASANT B. SAMUDRE

ISLAMIC LAW. See also *Islamic Ethics.* Traditionally, Islam has been dominated by two sciences: theology and the sacred law (the Shari'a, or path of God's commandments). If theology tells a Muslim what he should believe, the Shari'a teaches him what he should do or leave undone; and Islam is far more explicit about the conduct God requires of man than about the nature of God himself. The Shari'a, moreover, covers every aspect of life: not only law as understood in the West—national and international, public and private, criminal and civil, substantive and procedural—but also matters of morality, religious observance and social conduct.

The Shari'a, then, is regarded as a divine law, firmly based on revelation. In the classical doctrine its sources were the Koran (as the *ipsissima verba* of God, written from eternity in Arabic in heaven, and vouchsafed to the prophet Muhammad as occasion required); the *sunna,* practice or teaching of Muhammad himself (as equally inspired in content, if not in form); the *ijmā',* or consensus of Muslim jurists (as yet another sure indication of the divine will); and *qiyās,* or analogical deduction from these three primary sources. Modern scholarship indicates that this traditional view of both *sunna* and *ijmā'* were in fact later developments; and that the raw material of the Shari'a was customary law and the administrative practice of the Ummayyad period, systematised by scholar-jurists in the light of Islamic principles.

It is clear, therefore, that the Shari'a was not only a "divine" law but also a lawyers' law; for it was built up, directly or indirectly, on their deduction from the sacred texts. Eventually four Sunnī or "orthodox" schools of law established themselves, together with several "heterodox" systems; for the early jurists enjoyed a wide scope for independent deduction *(ijtihād)*, Soon, however, this faculty was regarded as having fallen into desuetude, and the law became progressively more moribund.

During the first century Islamic law was somewhat influenced by those general concepts of Roman law known to early converts; and the same is probably true of Rabbinical concepts. But these foreign elements were soon absorbed into a vast and highly sophisticated system which is distinctively Islamic, which has held Muslim peoples together through the ebb and flow of political fortune, and which still represents one of the great indigenous legal systems.

Until recently, moreover, the Sharī'a largely prevailed throughout the Muslim world. True, it was never the only law, for customary law and the will of the executive always vied with its requirements; and the courts of those judges devoted to its application, the *qādīs*, were paralleled by courts presided over by local governors, the police and even the Ruler or his deputy. But the Sharī'a was the law to which all paid homage; and the *qādīs'* courts were the courts of basic and residual jurisdiction.

About 1850, however, this began to change, initially in the spheres of commercial, criminal, and constitutional law, where the Sharī'a had never been fully applied. Now, however, it was progressively replaced, in most Muslim countries, by statute law based on Western models, and this legislation was commonly applied by a new system of "secular" courts. Thus judicial enforcement of the Sharī'a became restricted largely to family law, where it was still applied in the old way, uncodified and

unreformed, by personnel trained in the traditional fashion.

From about 1915, however, many Muslim governments began to find it necessary to introduce reforms even in family law, which had always been the core of the Sharī'a. But here all except the Turks felt they could not adopt an alien law, but that family law must remain distinctively Islamic. So the reformers were faced with the acute problem of how a law based on divine revelation could be reformed by men. In the event they resorted to four expedients: an eclectic choice between the wide variety of opinions attributed to jurists of the past; a procedural device which forbade the courts to enforce the law in specified circumstances; a resort to new interpretations of the sacred texts; and administrative regulations based on these principles or represented as "not contrary to the Sharī'a." By these means notable reforms have been introduced in most Muslim countries, and the legal position of women greatly improved.

Still more recently, Muslims have argued that the same principles should be applied to other parts of the Sharī'a, which could then replace legislation of alien inspiration. So the most recent Civil Codes represent an amalgam—in varying proportions—of sections based on European and others on Islamic sources. The fact that the family law is also being progressively codified has, moreover, enabled some Muslim countries to unify their courts. But it is noteworthy that, even where the Sharī'a still prevails, it is commonly applied today under the authority of legislative enactments—a principle which would have been utterly abhorrent throughout the classical period.

J. N. D. ANDERSON

ISOLATIONISM. See also *Colonialism, Colonization.* In hope of avoiding troubles and dangers inherent in associations with other countries, many propose isolationism as a national policy. This policy advocates national self-sufficiency and freedom from all foreign political and economic alliances.

All human government is accountable to God, the policies and actions should be judged by the ethical principles of Scripture. Modern nations no less than ancient Israel are to use righteously the material means and methods available to them.

Among Christians alliances of various kinds are necessary and moral (e.g., marriage, contracts, community organization including laws and police, etc.). If alliances are in principle ethical in Christian relationships, they must be so also for governments. The morality of a particular alliance depends on the purpose for which it is intended and on the purpose for which it is actually employed. A major difference between an alliance of Christians and one of governments is that the Christians are believers enjoined not to be "unequally yoked together with unbelievers" (II Cor. 6:14), whereas alliances of governments are not.

A government is directly responsible for the security, peace and welfare of its citizens. In this modern age of expanding populations, industry and technology, the interdependence of nations is increasingly apparent. Trouble anywhere may have serious repercussions in distant places. A government seeking the welfare of its own people can hardly avoid concern for that of other nations, especially those with which it has important relations. A rich and powerful country having much to lose and much with which to act inevitably bears some responsibilities for all.

It is doubtful that any country can be truly self-sufficient. Imports of products and raw materials are essential to maintain certain production. Exports are needed to pay for imports. A country which tries to be self-sufficient would forfeit manufactured products which require imports of materials. Loss of production would mean loss of jobs. Export income would decrease.

This adds up to serious social and economic loss and military weakness might expose a nation to blackmail or conquest by a powerful aggressor. The capability of helping to improve world conditions would be greatly reduced. Isolationism is not a viable solution to the national ills and dangers. A nation should fulfill its role as responsible member of the community of nations. Alliances are a valid and not unethical means of doing so. The fact that many alliances are unwise or intended for evil purposes does not invalidate the principle itself.

In the light of its responsibilities a government seeking to employ alliances in an ethical manner should possess a just intent. Its need should be clear. It should include provision for its disollution by either party under specified conditions. It should avoid commitments which might involve the nation in matters beyond the original intent of the agreement. It should not extend the national commitments beyond its capabilities.   WILLIAM K. HARRISON, JR.

I-THOU RELATIONSHIP. See also *Dialectical Ethics; Existential Ethics*. The terms "I-Thou" and "I-It" were coined by the Jewish philosopher-theologian, Martin Buber (q.v.) who published his famous book *Ich-Du* in 1923. It appeared in English in 1937 as *I and Thou* and was reissued in 1958 with an important postscript by the author. The I-Thou concept has deeply influenced contemporary Jewish, Roman Catholic, and especially Protestant thought. Its influence is evident in contemporary philosophy, theology, ethics, psychology, sociology, and education.

Although the Enlightenment (q.v.) emphasized the autonomy of man and liberal theology was "faith in man," the offspring of Enlightenment thought was a depersonalized world. Modern science with its aim of objective inquiry led to positivism and historicism. The effort to describe scientifically the world of nature and history led to the elimination of personal reality, decision, and purpose. Soren Kierkegaard and others paved the way for the reemphasis on the personal, but Buber gave the I-Thou relationship its classic form.

Buber's book, fragmentary and poetic in style, states that "to man the world is twofold, in accordance with his twofold attitude." Two sets of "primary words" express this dual attitude—"I-Thou" and "I-It (he, she)". The I-It relation is objective, detached, and disinterested. Here the I experiences and uses persons and things for observation, objectivication, and manipulation. On the other hand the I-Thou relation is one of mutuality, dialogue, openness, receptivity, and engagement. One's whole being is then involved in the sphere of mutuality and dialogue. Only the I-Thou relation enables man to achieve his authentic existence in loving encounter with God and his fellow man. Buber also conceives of an I-Thou relation with animals which has a "latent twofoldness" and stands on "the threshold of mutuality." Similarly in the sphere of nature things stretching from "stones to stars" can stand on "the pre-threshold or preliminal" stage of mutuality. And also in "the sphere of the spirit" an I-Thou relation is possible with authors and past characters of history in "the sphere above the threshold, the superliminal." The I in each of the two primary attitudes of I-Thou and I-It is a different I. How and what one's relation to others is determines who and what he really is.

The Protestant neo-orthodox theologians —Barth, Brunner, Friedrich Gogarten, Karl Heim, H. Richard Niebuhr, Reinhold Niebuhr, Tillich and others—have been deeply influenced by the personalistic philosophy of Buber. This has led to an emphasis upon the dynamic, actualistic categories in contemporary theology. Brunner's *Truth as Encounter* reflects the most direct influence of Ferdinand Ebner and Buber: "Here I saw the rationalistic thought-scheme of object and subject overcome by understanding the human person as basically related to the divine Thou and by the distinction between the I-Thou world and the I-it world. Through this I came to see what was the heart of the Biblical concept of man" (*The Theology of Emil Brunner*, ed. C. W. Kegley, Macmillan, 1962, p. 11). The price of this concept of revelation as encounter in an I-Thou relationship is the denial of Scripture as the Word of God written. It also involves an actualizing of the doctrines of God and man.

Whatever insights one may gain from Buber's penetrating psychological analysis of the I-Thou relationship, his total perspective remains Jewish. That means a unitarian view of God; for all his admiration of Jesus as engaged in Jewish renewal, he rejects him as divine Messiah.

For a more authentic Biblical context for the I-Thou relationship, one may profitably turn to the *Institutes* of Calvin. The opening words of that classic of the Reformation stress the intensely personal character of the knowledge of God: the mutual interrelations of the knowledge of God and of ourselves. We know ourselves only when we truly know God and vice versa. Yet Calvin's emphasis upon the personal never turns into personalism or subjectivism. The reality of God as creator and redeemer, the created character of man as image of God—these considerations are basic to the I-Thou relation. In and through the creation-revelation God continues to confront man as his creator. And Scripture as the Word of God written is the means God employs to bring about the encounter with man for the purpose of salvation through Jesus Christ in the fellowship of the Holy Spirit. Calvin thus holds together the objective and the personal whereas modern theology displays the disastrous consequences of an I-Thou relationship which sacrifices the former.

FRED H. KLOOSTER

J

JAMES, WILLIAM. See also *Pragmatism.* William James (1842-1910) popularized Pragmatism. Ideas are said to be plans for action; they become true insofar as the action is successful.

Huxley and Clifford insisted that believing anything without scientific evidence is the depth of immorality. James replied that in practical matters scientists violate this principle every day. The scientific viewpoint itself is accepted without conclusive evidence.

Furthermore, faith often makes fact. If I refuse to unbend until you have furnished me scientific evidence that you like me, you never will. But if I have faith that you like me, you will reciprocate.

Pragmatism is thus an ally of religion. Suppose God asked, Do you want to take part in a world capable of being saved only if every man does his level best, or do you prefer non-existence?

James is quick to answer: If you are healthy-minded, normally constituted, and not a coward or a morbid Buddhist, you will find such a universe exactly to your liking. Faith in a finite God and faith in your fellow man will greatly reduce the danger. And, says James, "this pluralistic and moralistic religion . . . is as good a religious synthesis as you are likely to find."

But, we ask, since some men have not done their level best, would it not be better to side with the forces of evil? They may seem to have a better chance of winning; and if they do, their view presumably will be the truth.

⌒ Gordon H. Clark, *William James*, Nutley, N.J., Presbyterian and Reformed, 1963.

GORDON H. CLARK

JEALOUSY. As a descriptive term for human behavior, "jealousy" usually is regarded negatively as an ethical minus.

The Hebraic etymology is somewhat uncertain, but the root perhaps means "to become red in the face." In NT Greek, the basic sense of jealousy is "to well up" or "to bubble," with "to boil" as a secondary designation. These ideas relate primarily to a passionate emotion regarding a person or cause.

Turned selfishly inward, jealousy can spawn a furious hatred. The OT abounds with examples. Jealousy caused Joseph's brothers to sentence him to slavery in Egypt (Gen. 37:11f.). A murderous Saul hunts David like an animal with the songs of the women of Israel stinging his ears: "Saul has slain his thousands, and David his ten thousands" (I Sam. 18:7).

In the NT, Jewish leaders in Antioch are filled with jealousy when they see the crowds gathered to hear Paul and Barnabas. Consequently, they stir up the leading citizens of the city against them (Acts 13:45, 50). Jealousy and its twin, "envy" (q.v.), are "works of the flesh" mentioned in the NT vice-lists along with immorality and drunkenness (Gal. 5:19-21).

Jealousy, however, also has a positive side. God is jealous for his people and wants to keep them from being contaminated by pagan idols (Exod. 20:4-5; cf. Deut. 4:24). In Nahum, God becomes the Avenger against pagan nations because of his single-minded devotion to Israel (1:2). Israel's apostasy causes God to be jealous for his holy name among the people he has chosen (Ezek. 39:25).

Jealousy for a cause can produce a zeal and devotion in human beings which is admirable. Paul, anxious for the spiritual welfare of the Corinthians, feels a "divine jealousy" for them (I Cor. 11:2).

Unlike envy which is used almost exclusively in a bad sense in the NT, jealousy which inspires concern for a righteous purpose can be ennobling. Thus, for example, parents jealous for the godly conduct of their children will themselves undoubtedly be enriched spiritually (Eph. 6:1-4).

PAUL BENJAMIN

JEREMIAH. Jeremiah was called by God to his prophetic ministry in the thirteenth year of Josiah's reign, about 626 B.C., when he was barely twenty years old. Although the spiritual climate was favorable to his message of repentance all during Josiah's reign, he faced constant opposition from those who succeeded Josiah, who died at the Battle of Megiddo in 609 B.C. King Jehoiakim went so far as to slice up and cast into the fire the earliest copy of his prophecies (Jer. 36:22-24); the predominating party of the nobles branded him a traitor (because of his urging to submit to Nebuchadrezzar), and even the priestly class fiercely opposed him, even though he was himself of a priestly family. His own relatives in his home town of Anathoth plotted his death.

He had to stand almost alone in his defense of God's truth, and often became discouraged enough to quit (20:14-18), despite his deep and abiding love for the word of God (15:16). Vilified as a tool of Chaldean imperialism, misunderstood and maligned by his compatriots, thwarted in all his efforts to make his apostate, self-willed nation believe the warnings he brought them for God, forbidden to live normally as a married man, Jeremiah was compelled to lead a life of unrelieved sorrow and frustration.

His only consolation was found in his close relationship with the Lord, and the assurance that he was speaking the truth, even though his people would not listen. There was the added satisfaction of knowing that after the fall of Jerusalem (in 587) a time of restoration from exile and bondage was in prospect, and some day a godly remnant of Judah would return to the Holy Land (31:23-26). Moreover the Lord would yet write his law upon men's hearts, inaugurating the New Covenant (31:31-34), and God's people would be governed and protected by the Messianic descendant of David, whose name would be called Yahweh our Righteousness (23:5-6; 33:14-27).

As for his own apostate generation, Jeremiah defined their basic sin as outrageous ingratitude towards God, whose covenant faithfulness they had abandoned for the false nature-gods of their heathen neighbors (2:4-13). Utterly groundless was their hope that Yahweh would feel compelled to deliver them, regardless of their wickedness, simply to protect his temple from destruction by their foes (7:4-11). Their abominations had already so defiled his temple that to save it was pointless. Their only hope lay in complete and thoroughgoing repentance, forsaking idolatry, murder, injustice and oppression of foreign residents, of widows and orphans (7:3-7), in order to renew themselves in loving submission to God and to keep his covenant. For before giving them the Ten Commandments in the days of Moses, Yahweh had bidden them first and foremost to obey his voice, even before anything was said about sacrifice and ritual (7:22-26; cf. Exod. 19:5-6). Sincere gratitude (q.v.) and honest obedience were indispensable conditions for the bestowal of all the glorious blessings promised to his covenant people, or for any people who would walk in fellowship with him (30:8-9).

GLEASON L. ARCHER

JESUS AND THE LAW. Apart from Jesus' clear rejection of scribal interpretation (Mark 7:8), his actions and teachings pertaining to the Mosaic Law constitute an apparent paradox. While stressing the Law's continuing validity (Matt. 5:18f.; Luke 16:17), he sets the Law's demands aside (Mark 7:18f.; 10:2-12; Matt. 5:38f.). While teaching the observance of the Law (Mark 1:44; Matt. 5:19; 23:2f.), both he and his disciples are accused of unlawful behavior (Mark 3:1-6; 2:23-28). This very anomaly appears clearest in Matt. 5:17-48, the classic passage on Jesus and the Law.

Of the sayings of Jesus Matt. 5:17-20 is the closest to a programmatic statement on the Law. At first glance Jesus appears to affirm the Law's enduring validity in each verse: he comes "not to annul but to fulfill the Law" (5:17), the Law remains intact "until heaven and earth pass away" (5:18),the doing and teaching of the "least of these commandments" is rewarded (5:19), and a righteoness exceeding that of the Scribes and Pharisees is necessary to enter the Kingdom (5:20). However, in the subsequent verses (5:21-18) Jesus places his "But I say to you" in antithesis to the Law.

If one takes seriously the antithetical format, Jesus actually countered the validity of the Law (cf. Matt. 5:38f.). Yet Jesus did not annul the Law with liberalizing statements, rather he radicalized and, at times, reversed the Law by his own demands. Whereas the Law condemned adultery, Jesus condemned lust; the Law condemned perjury, Jesus demanded total honesty; the Law provided restitution, Jesus demanded giving rather than taking; the Law taught discriminatory love, Jesus demanded love for all men. These demands presuppose a totally new situation. Essentially they demand a "wholeness" comparable to that of the Father (5:48). Such demands could not only come from an idealistic utopian or from one who brings a new situation for mankind, the age of salvation, when man's hard heart becomes a "new heart" (Ezek. 36:26) and God's Law is written in one's heart (Jer. 31:33). The Gospels bear witness to the latter.

This is precisely what Matt. 5:17-20 attests. Matthew 5:17 actually states that Jesus came "to fulfill the *Law and Prophets*," a phrase meaning the Scriptures. Jesus, in other words, came as the fulfillment of the OT promise, the bringer of the age of salvation. Matthew 5:18bc, implying that the Law is a part of this perishing age, states that it will remain intact "until heaven and earth pass away." Yet 5:18cd states that it remains "until all things come

to pass." In light of 5:17 and the primary emphasis of Matthew, "all things came to pass" in Jesus' coming. Therefore, the Law remains binding for those of this age (5:18bc), but it has no binding force for those of the new age of fulfillment (5:18cd; cf. Rom. 10:3) whose conduct stems from a new heart (cf. John 3:3) and a new relationship with God (Matt. 5:3-12). A product of this new relationship between God and man is God-pleasing conduct toward one's fellow man (5:21-48) which is the greater righteousness of Matt. 5:20. Since, however, this age and the age of salvation overlap for Jesus and his followers until the consummation, a tension remains. Although the Law had been superseded in Jesus it still remains God's ordering principle for this age. To the degree that it accomplished God's purpose in sinful society, one is free to keep and support it as commended in Matt. 5:19.

Such an understanding of Matt. 5:17-48 explains Jesus' anomalous relationship to the Law. Whenever the Law impeded the redemptive work of God (Mark 3:1-5) or shielded one from God's new and ultimate demand (Matt. 5:20; 19:20f; 23), Jesus set it aside without programmatically annulling it. Yet to the degree that the Law was a valid expression of God's will for this age, Jesus kept the Law (Mark 1:41) and taught others to do likewise (Matt. 5:19; 23:3f.). Jesus brought neither a better interpretation of the Law nor a new Law, which could lead to its own form of legalism. Rather he brought a radical demand presupposing a new relationship between God and man, a relationship which he himself was establishing as the fulfillment of God's promise (cf. Jer. 31:31ff.). Therefore, when asked about the greatest commandment, Jesus responded that the love-commandment was the pivotal point for the Law and Prophets (Matt. 22:40).   ROBERT A. GUELICH

JESUS, ETHICAL TEACHINGS. See also *Imitation of Christ.* The ethical teachings of Jesus were given as part of his proclamation of the Kingdom of God. Only by his death and vindication could the divine rule be effectively established on earth, but even while it was still in process of inauguration through his ministry its principles could be embraced and translated into action in the lives of those who accepted his message, thus becoming "sons of the Kingdom." The most familiar collection of these principles is that known as the Sermon on the Mount (q.v.) (Matt. 5–7), which was addressed to his disciples and aimed at showing not how men in general ought to live in order to bring in the Kingdom of God but how those who were already sons of the Kingdom ought to live.

While Jesus' ethical teachings are thus eschatologically (cf. *Eschatology and Ethics*) orientated, they have not a merely "interim" (cf. *Interim Ethics*) validity; if we understand them in relation to their primary context we shall be able to apply them to the most varied aspects of personal and community life. Their primary context includes the social, political and religious state of early first-century Palestine under the Roman occupation; there is much detail in the teaching which is intelligible only in this setting. For one thing, Jesus' teachings are concerned with the situation of subjects much more than with that of rulers, whom he rarely had the opportunity of addressing. 1. *Jesus and the Law of Moses.* Jesus emphasized the ethical quality of the Torah (q.v.) by summarizing it in terms of its two commandments enjoining love to God and man: "You shall love the Lord your God ..." (Deut. 6:5) and "You shall love your neighbor as yourself" (Lev. 19:18). The second of these was alternatively formulated in the words of the Golden Rule (q.v.) (Matt. 7:12). He did not claim uniqueness or originality for his ethical teaching: it was, he said, but the fulfillment of the law and the prophets. Yet there was a distinctiveness and freshness about his exposition of the

law and the prophets, as he made pronouncements on his personal authority— "You have heard that it was said ... but *I* say to you ... " (Matt. 5:21ff.)—and affirmed that only in listening to his words and doing them could men lay a secure foundation for life (Matt. 7:24-27; Luke 6:47-49).

As for the interpretation and application of specific commandments, he did not adopt the methods of the rabbinical schools of his day. Indeed, he dismissed their orally transmitted rulings, "the tradition of the elders," as too often prone to obscure or nullify the original purpose of the commandments. He appealed to that original purpose and held that a commandment was best observed when the purpose for which God gave it was fulfilled. Thus, since the sabbath was instituted for man's rest and relief, it was most worthily honored by acts of healing: instead of reluctantly conceding that such acts might be done on the sabbath in an emergency, he maintained that the sabbath was the most appropriate day for doing them, since they promoted the divine purpose in instituting that day.

Again, the question of divorce (q.v.) was settled by an appeal to the original marriage ordinance of Gen. 2:24f.; since husband and wife were made one by the Creator's decree, divorce was an attempt to undo the work of God. If, later, Moses (q.v.) contemplated divorce in certain situations (Deut. 24:1-4), that was a concession to men's hardness of heart, but it was not so in the beginning and it should not be so for citizens of the kingdom of God. It should not be overlooked that in contemporary Jewish society this ruling amounted to a redressing of the balance in favor of women, who were liable to be divorced without the right of appeal or of initiating any comparable action themselves.

2. *Inwardness and Higher Standard.* Jesus' radicalization of the ethical principles of the Torah is bound up with the fact that

he was not imposing a new set of statutes which could be enforced by material sanctions but prescribing a way of life for his followers. The act of murder (q.v.), forbidden in the Sixth Commandment, was punished with death (Exod. 21:12-14), and conduct or language likely to provoke a breach of the peace (like the insulting words quoted in Matt. 5:22b) could also incur legal penalties. But no human law can detect or punish the angry thought; yet it is here, according to Jesus, that the process begins which, if unchecked, leads to murder; therefore, "every one who is angry with his brother shall be liable to judgment" (Matt. 5:22a), but the judgment is God's, not man's. This saying was early felt to be such a hard one that an editor tried to render it more tolerable by adding the qualification "without a cause" (cf. KJV), a qualification which naturally won rapid and widespread acceptance.

Similarly the law could penalize a breach of the Seventh Commandment which prohibited adultery (q.v.), or similar actions of the same general character. But, as Jesus put it, the overt act was but the outcome of the illicit thought; hence "every one who looks at a woman lustfully has already committed adultery with her in his heart" (Matt. 5:28), but no earthly court can take cognizance of adultery in the heart.

With this inwardness in Jesus' ethical teaching goes the insistence that more is expected of his followers than the ordinary morality of decent people, more even than "the righteousness of the scribes and Pharisees" (Matt. 5:20). "If you love those who love you, what credit is that to you? For even sinners love those who love them" (Luke 6:32). The higher standard of the kingdom of God called for acts of love to enemies and words of blessing and goodwill to ill-wishers and persecutors. The children of that kingdom would not insist on their legal rights but cheerfully relinquish them in the interests of the paramount law of love.

3. *The Way of Non-Violence.* The inculcation of non-violence is too deeply embedded in Jesus' teaching at all levels of the gospel tradition for us to entertain seriously the suggestion that this pacific ethic has overlain an earlier phase marked by hostility to the Romans and their collaborators in the Jewish establishment and by active sympathy with those whose policy was to take up arms against both. In Jesus' references to the "men of violence" who tried to seize the kingdom of God and bring it about by force he gave no sign that he approved of their aims or methods. On the contrary, he advocated the way of peace and submission, and urged his hearers not to retaliate against injustice or oppression but to turn the other cheek, to go a second mile when their service was commandeered for one mile, to take the initiative in returning good for evil. If this way of peace was repudiated in favor of the way of resistance and rebellion, then disaster would overtake the nation as surely as it overtook the Galilaean pilgrims who on one occasion were massacred in the temple court by members of the Roman garrison in Jerusalem (Luke 13:1-3; cf. 19:41-44).

The division which Jesus foresaw in society and even within families when some members followed him and some did not (Matt. 10:34-36; Luke 12:51-53) inhered in the nature of the situation: it was not something desirable in itself. The coinage which bore Caesar's name and likeness should most appropriately be given back to Caesar. If, on Passover Eve, a dozen men of his company could muster only two swords between them, they were far from resembling a band of Zealots, and when one of these swords was used in his defense a few hours later, the action incurred his rebuke. The teaching of non-violence was unpopular; it is not really surprising that the activist Barabbas was preferred to Jesus when an opportunity arose to have the one or the other reprieved. But the spirit that called for the release of Barabbas was the spirit that would one day lay Jerusalem level with the ground. Despite his being sentenced on a charge of sedition against Rome, it is not as a heroic liberationist that Jesus has come down in Jewish communal memory, as he would have done had he really been a Zealot sympathizer.

4. *The Supreme Incentive.* Various incentives are held out in Jesus' ethical teaching, including the prospect of reward and punishment on the final day of judgment or in the more immediate course of history. Any courting of human applause is discouraged. But the highest of all incentives is the example of God himself. There was nothing new in this: one section of Leviticus is known as the "law of holiness" because of its insistence on the principle: "I am the Lord your God . . . ; be holy, for I am holy" (Lev. 11:44; etc.). In the same spirit one of the Targums on Lev. 22:28 (a passage enjoining humane treatment of animals) says: "As our Father is merciful in heaven, so you must be merciful on earth." This is a close parallel to Luke 6:36, "Be merciful, even as your Father is merciful," or Matt. 5:48, "You, therefore, must be perfect (i.e., all-embracing in your love), as your heavenly Father is perfect." God's children should reproduce their Father's character; if he does not discriminate between good and bad in bestowing sunshine and rain, they should not discriminate in showing kindness to all.

5. *The Example of Jesus.* That Jesus' own life was the practical manifestation of his ethical teaching is the unanimous testimony of the Gospels; this testimony is specially explicit in relation to service and sacrifice. It is to provide an example to his disciples that he declares that the Son of man "came not to be served but to serve and to give his life as a ransom for many" (Mark 10:45; cf. Luke 22:27; John 13:15).

This motif of the *imitatio Christi* (cf. *Imitation of Christ*) pervades the NT epistles, not least the writings of Paul, who was not personally acquainted with Jesus during his Palestinian ministry. He can beseech his converts "by the meekness and gentleness of Christ" (II Cor. 10:1), he can encourage them to imitate him as he himself imitates Christ (I Cor. 11:1), and when he wishes to recommend the practice of all those graces which are both inculcated and exemplified by Jesus in the Gospels, he says, "Put on the Lord Jesus Christ" (Rom. 13:14). So by various writers Jesus is presented to the readers of the NT documents, and of much subsequent Christian literature, as the one who left them an example that they should follow his steps (I Peter 2:21). In this ethical *imitatio Christi* the peculiar genius of true Christianity has been widely acknowledged. "The character of Jesus," wrote W. E. H. Lecky, "has not only been the highest pattern of virtue, but the strongest incentive to its practice, and has exerted so deep an influence, that it may be truly said, that the simple record of three short years of active life has done more to regenerate and to soften mankind, than all the disquisitions of philosophers and than all the exhortation of moralists" (*History of European Morals*, ii, London, Longmans, 1869, p. 88).

Joseph Arthur Baird, *The Justice of God in the Teaching of Jesus*, London, SCM, 1963; Bennett Harvie Branscomb, *Jesus and the Law of Moses*, New York, R. R. Smith, 1930; William David Davies, *The Setting of the Sermon on the Mount*, Cambridge, Cambridge University, 1964; Robert Newton Flew, *Jesus and His Way*, London, Epworth, 1963; Joachim Jeremias, *The Parables of Jesus*, London, SCM, [2]1963; John Knox, *The Ethic of Jesus in the Teaching of the Church*, Nashville, Abingdon, 1961; Thomas Walter Manson, *The Teaching of Jesus*, Cambridge, Cambridge University, [2]1935; *Ethics and the Gospel*, London, SCM, 1960; Amos Niven Wilder, *Eschatology and Ethics in the Teaching of Jesus*, New York, Harper, 1939; Hans Windisch, *The Meaning of the Sermon on the Mount*, Philadelphia, Westminster, 1951.

FREDERICK F. BRUCE

JEWISH ETHICS. See also *Essene Community; Old Testament Ethics; Talmud; Torah.* In Judaism ethics and religion are inseparably related. The survival of the Jews has been attributed as much to their peculiar morality as to their religion. The purity of traditional Jewish family life is due to their ethics. Jewish ethics has been divided into (1) Biblical, (2) Apocryphal, (3) Rabbinical, (4) Philosophical, and (5) Modern. This article deals with the first three, usually assigned to the classical periods.

Sources. The sources of Jewish ethics are the Bible (OT), the Talmud, Talmudic Midrashim, and religious works. But "beside and above all literary sources, the living, traditional, constantly growing spirit of the whole Jewish race may be and must be considered the front of instruction upon the ethics of Judaism" (M. Lazarus, *The Ethics of Judaism*, Part I, Philadelphia, *JPSA*, 1900, p. 105). Two main sources that have had a directive influence in Judaism are the maxims and aphorisms found throughout the entire literature, and the ethics implied and enunciated in the codes of law and ritual practice (Harold M. Schulweis, "Jewish Ethics and Its Civilization," in *Ethics of Morals*, by V. Ferm, ed., New York, Philosophical Library, 1956, p. 254). On the other hand, the source of Christian ethics is in the OT and NT, where character and action proceed from the new relationship to God (A. T. Mollegen, "Ethics of Protestantism," in *Patterns of Ethics in America Today*, by F. E. Johnson, ed., New York, Collier, 1962, p. 67).

Basis. Jewish ethics rests on the monotheism of the OT which originated in divine revelation. Ethical concepts derive from the unity and holiness of God. God has placed an ethical ideal before man because he is created in God's image (E. G. Hirsch, *et. al.*, "Ethics," in *The Jewish Encyclopedia*, Vol. V, pp. 245ff.; cf. also the Talmudic section "Ethics of the Fathers").

The basic principle of all rabbinical ethics is that God and his law require moral perfection (Lev. 19:2). Morality is the express will of God. Jewish ethics is based on the premise that the universe operates under purpose and law; that is, there is a moral order directed by a personal God whose nature excludes evil. In rabbinic literature the attempt to emulate God's moral attributes is the reason for morality. God is both the Source and Ideal of morality (K. Kohler, *Jewish Theology*, Cincinnati, Riverdale, 1943, p. 477.

In the pagan world man's desire for ethical perfection was fragmentized, because he thought of deity under the form of many and warring gods; in the Biblical world the unity of God was enunciated with transcendent implications for the integration of human nature. Furthermore, the concept of covenant between God and Israel demanded the existence and enjoyment of a basic mutuality (Jacob B. Agus, "Jewish Ethics," in John Macquarrie, ed., *Dictionary of Christian Ethics*" Philadelphia, Westminster, 1967, pp. 178, 179).

No writer on Jewish ethics will deny "an implicit theocentric source of Jewish ethics" (Schulweis, *op. cit.* p. 260). God is the only authority who can define the limits of right and wrong and good and evil. Thus the ultimate reason for an ethical system is the holiness of God; man formed in his image is meant to strive for the highest standard (M. Gaster, "Conscience (Jewish)" in *HERE*, IV, pp. 41, 42).

Scope. Most non-Jewish writers on Jewish ethics stress the position that Judaism saw only the personal and national in the realm of conduct. This is erroneous; Jewish ethics is personal, social, national, and international or universal. First, rabbinical ethics took into account the totality of human life. Man has obligations toward himself: the enjoyment of life, the preservation of his life and health, study of the Law, labor, marriage, and family. In his own life man must resolve the tensions of daily living psychologically, philosophically, and sociologically. In the first area he must allow the full function of the good desire *(yezer tov)*; he must sublimate the evil desire *(yezer hara)*. In the second sphere he must achieve an integrated design of life. In the third realm he must submit to law and order (Agus, *op.cit.*, p. 178). Second, Jewish ethics embraced more than the individual Jew; it took into account his neighbor. Social ethics demanded the avoidance of fraud of every kind, benevolence, truth, and peace. The rabbis held that all Isrealites are responsible for each other, hence all the confessions of the Day of Atonement are made in the first person plural. Without bypassing individual responsibility, the morality of the individual Jew was set against the background of his place in society. Third, ethics in Judaism had a universal thrust. As a corollary to the doctrine of ethical monotheism the rabbis of Mishna and Talmud broadened the sphere of personal and social ethics. Yet, despite the record, it is held that ethical obligations in Israel did not go beyond national bounds, so that universal or international ethics was no more prevalent in Israel than in any other nation of that time (C. H. Toy, *Judaism and Christianity,* Boston, Little, Brown, 1891, p. 48).

Character. Jewish ethics is generally recognized to be ethically grounded in personal monotheism. It is theistic ethics.

It has, moreover, been characterized as emphasizing not love, but justice. A religious nomianism, it is said to be optimistic. The claim is made that Jewish ethics instills faith in man and the future. It has been described as autonomous, because it sees the divine spirit in man. For this reason Jewish ethics makes much of the free will of man, whereby he is self-redemptive through prayer and repentance. Liberal Jewish authors habitually characterize Jewish ethics as idealistic, universal, optimistic, rational, anti-ascetic, and humanistic. Orthodox Jewish writers portray the matter as nomian, other-worldly, particularistic and ritualistic.

The differences can be laid to polemics and apologetics. Each group is able to adduce numerous citations from sources to fortify its position. The reason for the differences is threefold: (1) these elements are not systematized in the Scriptures or Talmud; (2) there is no single authority in rabbinic literature; and (3) ethical expressions in Judaism cover a long and diversified history, from OT times through the Talmudic period (c. sixth century, A.D.) to the medieval philosophers, the mystics, Hasidim, the age of enlightenment, the Reform movement, and contemporary religious and secular viewpoints (Schulweis, *op.cit.* p. 253).

Christian ethics, on the other hand, deals with man as a victim of the fall with no self-redemptive ability in an abnormalistic world, and standing in desperate need of divine interposition through regeneration.

Motivation. The motive for all moral action was to be genuine love and reverence for God. Motivation in conduct was not to be prosperity or fear of punishment. It was the urgency to be true to the nation's holy calling as a priestly nation.

Virtues. In the main the rabbis expanded on OT duties. As for family ethics the emphasis was on reverence for parents (Exod. 20:12). Monogamy is the norm (Gen. 2:24). Chastity is of greatest importance (Lev. 18:6ff.). Strangers, the poor, widows, and orphans were due special concern (Exod. 22:21; Lev. 19:18, 34). Honesty and truthfulness were absolutely required. Stealing and falsehood of any kind were forbidden. The reputation of others was sacred (Exod. 23:1). Reverence for old age was enjoined. Correct weights and measures in business dealings were indispensable (Exod. 23:3; Lev. 19:15, 18). Animals, let alone servants and culprits, are to be shown kindness (Exod. 23:4). Obscene speech was to be avoided. Stress is placed on blessing and wrath in kind *(lex talionis)* in the noncanonical Jewish writings (Enoch 50:5;

51:1; II Macc. 9:5, 6). Kindness and graciousness are extolled (Ecclus. 16:12; 35:20). Giving to the poor should be abundant; it should not be lacking even if one's means are limited (Tobit 4:8). Numerous rewards are cited for benevolence (Ecclus. 29:12, 13; Tobit 4:9; 12:9): freedom from trial, forgiveness of sin, and deliverance from death (Ecclus. 40:24; Tobit 4:10). Those to be granted benevolence are widows, orphans, strangers, homeless, aged, weak, and blind (Baruch 6:38; II Esdras 2:21). Wisdom is highly esteemed and advocated (Ecclus. 14:20-15:8). Thrift and industry are worthy traits to be inculcated and practiced (Tobit 2:11, 12). Traits of love to God, patience, and humility are recognized (Ecclus. 1:23; 3:17, 23). Justice (IV Esdras 5:114) and patriotism (Judith 12:8) are commended. Calumny, deceit, scolding, backbiting, slander, swearing, and perjury are decried (Test. Benj. 6:4-6). Hate is to be avoided (Test. Gad 4:5, 6). Violence and warfare are denounced (Wisd. Sol. 14:25). Various sexual sins are excoriated (Ecclus. 9:5; 26:6; Wisd. Sol. 14:26). The worst of sins is idolatry (I Macc. 1:47) (Abraham Cronbach, "Ethics in Noncanonical Jewish Writings," in *The Interpreter's Dictionary of the Bible*, Vol. II, Nashville, Abingdon, 1962, pp. 161-167). Rabbinic ethics stressed personal purity (*Yoma* 9b), care for the sick, the widow, and orphan (*Moed Katon* 6a), and prayer and study of the Law. The great Hillel was able to condense all Jewish ethics in his famous dictum: "Do not unto another that which is repugnant to you" (*Babylonian Talmud,* Sabbath 31a). Moses was taken as the ideal personality and revered for his modesty. "Modesty may be regarded as the key to all the virtues which were supposed to be engraved on the souls of the best among men" (A. Steinberg, "Jewish Morals," in *The Jewish People*, Vol. II, New York, Jewish Encyclopedic Handbooks, 1948, p. 251).

Goal. The goal of Jewish ethics is the hallowing of life; that is, what the rabbis termed "the sanctification of God's name." Israel was not only to sanctify the name of God, but to prevent that name from desecration among non-Israelites. Because of God's love for the patriarchs and his choice of them as his people Israel is expected, individually and socially, to maintain godlikeness—"to be holy" (Exod. 19:6; Lev. 19:2; Deut. 14:2). The clear obligation is to be like him.   CHARLES L. FEINBERG

JOHANNINE ETHICS. Johannine ethics are based on the incarnation of the Son of God (John 1:1-14). Jesus inaugurates a new existence and thus introduces a new ethic for the elite of society (John 3:1; 4:46ff.) as well as for the injured (John 5:1-9; 9:1-7) and insulted (John 7:53—8:11). To a Samaritan woman at the lower end of the social spectrum (John 4), Jesus reveals himself as fully incarnate ("Give me a drink"). Moreover, though quite aware of her dark past ("Go call your husband and come here"), he promises life to her (John 4:14). She, in fact, receives the promise and becomes Christ's witness to others (John 4:28-30). At the other end of the social spectrum Jesus encounters a highly-esteemed religious leader (John 3). Nicodemus exhibits the autonomy of the one who regulates life by himself and congratulates the other whose behavior shows a high religious ethic (3:1-2). Yet, without a new birth, Nicodemus reflects a basic uneasiness with mere obedience to the law. Though he may have changed later (John 7:50-52; 19:39), his repeated inquiry "How" (3:4, 9) reveals the uncomfortable truth that a great gulf separates his own life in Judaism from the new life in the Spirit.

Specifically, the new life means that Jesus effects a radical change in everyday existence. Disciples are called (1:39, 43), chosen (cf. *eklegesthai* in 6:70; 13:18; 15:16, 19), and given by the Father to the

Son (17:6). Divine choice could conceivably imply divine arbitrariness and/or human passivity. Nevertheless, a love that encompasses the world (3:16), which sends Jesus into conflict and danger (e.g., John 7-8) with a witness who invites a response from all, is a love that reveals an amazing depth of divine concern.

The Response of Faith. Amid a rich imagery of terms which depict the human response (e.g., come, eat, drink, receive, hear), the verb *pisteuein* possesses a unique importance. It suggests not mental assent or passive acquiescence but the commitment of oneself unreservedly to another (John 2:24), a decision to act upon his naked word (4:50; 5:9; 9:7; cf. 2:7-8) ("Jn achieves a unity of Proclaimer [the person] and Proclaimed [his word]," R. Bultmann, *TDNT* VI, 222, writing on *pisteuein*), and a readiness to follow him as sheep follow a shepherd (10:1-5). In John 1–12 the verb generally occurs in the aorist (c. 24 times) or the present (c. 37 times) tense. The aorist means definite decision, e.g., of the disciples (2:11) and the nobleman (4:50, 53) at Cana and of men in Samaria (4:39, 41) and Bethany (11:45). The present tense implies dogged reliance on Jesus (cf. John 6). Realistically, the miracle of the loaves relieved momentarily physical hunger but the sequel reveals Jesus' *continued* offer of himself to the spiritually hungry. The present tense of *pisteuein* (7 occurrences in John 6:29-64) issues the challenge to accept the offer.

The Fruition of Faith in Fellowship and Service. John's contemporary, Epictetus, based the good life upon the training and control of the will and upon self-esteem. John's ethic is neither self-contained nor primarily concerned with self-realization but leads believers into the fellowship and service of the incarnate Jesus. The vine-and-branches imagery declares that the fellowship is indispensable (John 15:5) but the imagery also demands fruit issuing from

service (15:4, 16). Here and elsewhere the *declaration* affirms a relationship—"we are children of God" (I John 3:1; John 1:12), "you are the branches" (John 15:5), "you are my friends" (John 15:14), "you are of God" (I John 4:4), "begotten of God" (I John 5:1), "beloved" (I John 2:7; 3:2, 21; 4:1, 7, 11), and "sanctified" (John 17:17, 19). The *demand* is ethical, appearing in numerous imperatives. Always it expresses an obligation or responsibility (cf. *opheilein* in John 13:14; I John 2:6; 3:16; 4:11; III John 8) which requires daily performance. (Nearly 65 percent of all verb forms in I-III John occur in the present tense.) What ultimately counts, however, is not man's work but the work wrought through man by God's Spirit (John 7:37-39), that "other" Counsellor like unto Jesus (John 14:16). Precisely in the unbelieving world, the Spirit creates the situation where faith can operate (John 16:7-11). At the same time he leads the listening disciple into a deeper understanding of Jesus (John 16:13-15; I John 2:20-27). Hence, the demand is to "receive" the Spirit (20:22), to "abide" in the vine (15:5), and thus to "bear" fruit—in the fellowship and in the world (13:33-35; 20:21; cf. I John 1:3-4). To bear fruit means to manifest love in action (I John 3:18). Indeed, love is the very essence of Jesus' life and of the new commandment given to his own (13:1, 34-35; cf. *hupodeigma* in 13:15). Love for God is an empty delusion unless it includes love for brothers (13:34-35; I John 3:11ff.; 4:20-21).

Viewed in the larger context of witness (15:16; 20:21), Christian love in John is not exclusive as A. Nygren contends (*Agape and Eros*, New York, Harper & Row) but comparable to Christ's love (15:12; 17:26). To bear fruit also means to manifest truth and righteousness. As the "righteous one," Jesus becomes the defense attorney for all who sin (I John 2:1-2) so that he who does righteousness bears the hallmark of him who is righteous (I John 2:29). Moreover, as "truth" incarnate (John 1:14; 14:6), Jesus liberates men (8:32). They discover that his flesh and blood are true sustenance (6:55), that they are *of* the truth (18:37; I John 2:21; 3:19; cf. 5:20), and hence, called to *speak* the truth (I John 1:6, 8) and *do* it (John 3:21; I John 3:17-18). And whatever be the outward expression, the scene of ethics is the world because Jesus came to where men live (John 16:28). And, while Jesus chooses disciples out of the world (John 14-17) to share in his kingdom (John 3:3, 5; 18:36), he also sends them into the world (20:21). Their mission is thus comparable to his (17:18; 20:21). To be sure, their service lies in enemy territory (14:30; I John 5:19) but they are confident that the enemy is defeated. Thus their victory is assured through faith in Jesus (I John 3:8; 5:4-5). For them, life offers not only relationships and meaning now but it holds out hope for the future, because the Incarnate one will surely return (I John 2:28-3:3). They anticipate his return and thereby purify their lives so that they become unashamed before God and unflagging in service (I John 3).

CULLEN I. K. STORY

JOY. Joy is the pleasant emotion resulting from a satisfaction of man's unquenchable thirst for a fuller life. Such participation in a greater portion or in higher values of life can take place on different levels: sensual, aesthetical, intellectual, moral or religious, and in various degrees. Joy can be individual or social in nature. Liberation, recovery and reconciliation mean joyful restoration of life lost; enrichment, advancement or discovery give access to larger realms of life not known before.

According to universal human experience any joy is transitory: our emotional capacity is limited, or the attained values prove to be passing or mistaken. Popular industries of amusement now try to pro-

duce ready available stimuli to our senses and instincts. Hedonistic philosophies seek by refinement and escapism to cultivate the art of enjoying. Contrary to this, original Buddhism declared human desires as such to be the cause of suffering, and commanded their mortification.

The Bible on the basis of its doctrine of creation fully recognizes man's privilege of enjoying nature, art (music), and community. The whole man in his spirit, heart, and body is the recipient of joy. Such joy in the creational sphere is purified and intensified by one's relation to God as the fountain of all life. The Bible clearly realizes the transitory character of earthly joy (Eccles. 2:1-12; I Cor. 7:30) and warns against sinful pleasures which harm our neighbor or lead to idolatry by substituting the created good for the creating God.

The gospel as such is a message centered on joy. It reveals everlasting communion with God himself as the ultimate fulfillment of man's thirst for joyful participation in life. The Psalms constantly exhort Israel, the nations, or creation to rejoice. The Christmas message announces great joy to all people (Luke 2:10). The normal mood in the early church is joy, which the apostles serve to increase (II Cor. 1:24). The content of Biblical joy is the redemptory and promotional self-disclosure of God to man in order to impart to him everlasting life. The realization of God's coming kingdom, which is centered in the two liberating comings of the Messiah, makes this joy also a societary experience. This joy is partly aroused by the witness of redemption already experienced in new communion with God and fellow man. Partly it is a joy in anticipation.

Christian joy is often overshadowed by temporal afflictions (John 16:20-22). But under the layer of pain and anxiety it is constantly kindled by the Holy Spirit as the pledge of the full life still to come (Rom. 8:22-30). The endurance of suffering for

Christ's sake is the precondition for sharing the bliss of his eternal glory.

PETER BEYERHAUS

JUDGMENT. See also *Eschatology and Ethics; Heaven; Hell.* God discriminates between right and wrong among men and angels according to the criterion of his own law, and pronounces a verdict issuing in eternal weal or woe.

The Judge and the Judged. In the ultimate sense God alone is lawgiver and judge (James 4:12; Ps. 50:6). God searches the heart (Jer. 17:10), weighs the actions of men (I Sam. 2:3), avenges wrong (Heb. 10:30), and rewards the righteous (Mark 10:30). The scope of judgment is such that only the omniscience of deity is adequate to it. God's love of righteousness guarantees that the judgment will be according to truth (Gen. 18:25; Ps. 96:13; Rom. 2:2).

Although God the Father is judge (I Peter 1:17), he exercises this judgment through the Son (Acts 17:31), not simply by virtue of the intertrinitarian union, but because he has given judgment to the Son as Mediator (John 5:22, 27). The final redemptive judgment of the Son is in continuity with the promises and threats which he made during his earthly ministry, and brings his mediatorial reign to successful completion. Jesus' advent was for salvation (John 3:17-19), but since redemption is inseparable from condemnation of the wicked, he is also said to have come for judgment (John 9:39). Angels and saints are associated with Christ in the final judgment (Matt. 25:31; I Cor. 6:2, 3).

All men without exception will be judged. When the Judge appears, every eye shall see him (Rev. 1:7) and all must appear before the judgment seat of Christ (II Cor. 5:10). For this purpose the earth and the sea will give up their dead (Rev. 20:13). Since God is no respecter of persons (I Peter 1:17), there will be no preferences based on social, economic, or ethnic considerations.

Distinction will be made only in view of works done in the body, whether good or bad (II Cor. 5:10). For this reason, the eternal destiny of the individual is fixed at death and does not change in the intermediate state before the final judgment. Not only men, but also preternatural beings are subject to this judgment (II Peter 2:4).

Certainty and Publicness of Judgment. There are in this present life anticipations of the judgment to come. The discipline of the Father has, as its purpose, escape from the final condemnation (I Cor. 11:32). The discipline of Christ administered through the officebearers of the church serves similar ends (I Cor. 5:3-5). Men receive rewards and punishments which are not be to construed simply as the natural consequences of good or evil behavior, although these divine providences serve the purposes of moral order. God gives the wicked up to a reprobate mind (Rom. 1:28) while granting prosperity with the promise of eternal life to Christ's disciples (Mark 10:30). The perplexing discrepancies observable in this life are removed in the final judgment. More profoundly, believers already enjoy eternal life together with peace of conscience while the wrath of God and hardening in sin rest upon the reprobate (John 3:36).

The time of the final judgment in absolute terms is unknown (Matt. 24:36). The final judgment is therefore not a present immanent process but takes place on a day appointed by God (Acts 17:31) at the end of calendar history. The simultaneous redemption of the covenant people of God and destruction of their enemies evident in the time of Noah, Moses, and the Restoration point to the simultaineity of the final judgment of the just and the unjust in the resurrection unto life, and unto condemnation (John 5:29). For believers, resurrection is public vindication of their justification secured in the resurrection of Christ (Rom.

4:25). The resurrection is coincident with the return of Jesus from heaven to visit destruction on the disobedient and to be glorified together with his saints (II Thess. 1:7-10). The appointed day of judgment (I John 4:17) is a day of wrath (Rom 2:5) and of redemption (Eph. 4:30). The certainty of the judgment to come (Heb. 9:27) gives rise to the urgency of the call to repentance.

The final judgment is not to be internalized but is public, corresponding to the publicness of the revelation of Christ, the resurrection, and cosmic cataclysm. Its purpose is not to ascertain the future state of man but to ratify the judgment determined at death and to display the glory of God in righteousness and holiness.

Criterion and Consequences of Judgment. The criterion of judgment is the revealed will of God. Those outside the pale of redemptive revelation show the work of the law written on the heart. They pervert and sin against the light which they enjoy and therefore perish. Those who have redemptive revelation (both Law and Gospel) are judged by it (Rom 2:12-14). None are without excuse (Rom 1:20), and since all have sinned, none can escape judgment unto condemnation apart from Jesus Christ. The Gospel demonstrates that the Law is the criterion of judgment because it is in terms of the penalty attached to the perpetually binding law of Scripture that Jesus died in the place of his people. Believers who are savingly joined to Christ are acquitted in the day of judgment because their sin is imputed to Christ and his righteousness according to the revealed will of God is imputed to them for justification (Rom. 5:19). Neither their faith nor their works contribute to their acceptability with God. Since good works (q.v.) are, however, intrinsically pleasing to God, they are rewarded as such (I Cor. 3:8); and the more intense the sin, the greater the condemnation (Luke 12:47, 48). The wicked are consigned to the punishment of hell as eternal as the blessed-ness which the redeemed enjoy (Matt. 25:46).

James P. Martin, *The Last Judgment*, Grand Rapids, Eerdmans, 1963; Leon Morris, *The Biblical Doctrine of Judgment*, Grand Rapids, Eerdmans, 1960.   NORMAN SHEPHERD

JUNG, CARL GUSTAV. C. G. Jung (1875-1961), a pastor's son, studied medicine, specialized in psychiatry, and developed a variation of psychoanalysis which the Jungians term analytical psychology. He founded the International Psychoanalytic Society, of which he was the first president, but within two years the differences between himself and Freud (q.v.) lead to a break.

His approach to a psychological problem was to keep working around it again and again. He began his approach to psychology with clinical practice in which he exhaustively analyzed the experiences of individual patients. He extended his studies by experimental methods, for example by observing the reaction time and the response to a given stimulus word. He read the classics, mythology, comparative religion, and Oriental literature, and enjoyed personal discussion with scholars of foreign cultures. He examined ancient tribal cultures by himself living with African and North American tribes. He was impressed by the similarities of the imagery or symbolism of the people from the most diverse cultures, and suggested that there are common ways in which mankind grasps experiences. He regarded these ancient or "archetypal" ways of perceiving as evidence of a "collective unconscious."

Jung was concerned to embrace and unify diverse and paradoxical positions, often finding a unity is symbolism. This interest is reflected in his descriptions of introverts and extraverts; the mask of performance (*persona*), and the underlying shadow; the female aspect of a man (*theanima*), and the male aspect of a woman (*theanimus*).

He thought that both mental health and the progress of civilization depended largely on a suitable religious expression. In his view Christian civilization had proved hollow, so he developed a process of "individuation" in which the patient becomes what he really is. The quest for wholeness was a process of suffering to find a god within. The problems of the second half of life (after 35) are, he thought, not so much those of sex or aggression, as stressed by Freud and Adler, but of finding the undeveloped side of the personality. The solution he regarded as religious. His "natural religious function," of course, is not Christianity.   NEIL YORKSTON

JURISPRUDENCE. See *Law.*

JUST WAR CRITERIA. See also *Pacifism; Peace and War; Revolution.* The "just war theory" in Christian ethics has taken shape slowly. The Church Fathers, like the Biblical writers, lamented the tragic consequences of war and urged believers to seek peace and to love their enemies. Some early Christians refused military service (q.v.), but the Church Fathers did not challenge the right of governments to wage war. Ambrose rebuked the Emperor Theodosius for atrocities committed at Thessalonica, but no organized proposals were offered for applying Christian principles to the practice of war (Tertullian *On the Military Crown* xi; Origen *Contra Celsus* viii. 73-75; Ambrose *Letter* li).

The pagan Cicero provides the first organized statement of a just war theory. In the ideal state where law is based on right reason rather than utility (1) the only just cause for war is the defense of national honor or safety, (2) war is a last resort when all negotiations fail, (3) it must be formally declared, in order to give due warning, (4) the purpose may not be conquest or power, but the securing of a just peace, (5) prisoners and all who surrender should be spared and (6) only those who are legally soldiers should be involved (*De Republica* iii. 22-29; *De Officiis* i. 11-12).

In Christian ethics, discussion has centered less on these criteria, which are largely accepted, than on their basis (moral and political philosophy) and application. Their purpose, moreover, is not so much to justify a war as to limit its evils and to bring justice and love into its conduct.

Augustine (q.v.) (*City of God* xix) criticizes Cicero's ideal state as unrealistic. Natural law (q.v.) and universal reason afford no basis for peace and justice because society is ridden with the desire for honor and power and wealth. Justice becomes the orderly pursuit of these common desires. But the Christian relates justice to man's highest end, which is love for God and so for fellow men. No war is ever fully just. A just peace is desirable, however, and war may be legitimate in order to secure peace and reduce injustice. But it may only be waged on the authority of the rulers, and then with mercy. The soldier should fight in repentance, lest in the heat of conflict love be turned into lust or hate.

Thomas Aquinas (*Summa Theologica* ii. 2. a. 40) also stresses the necessity of a just cause and rightful intention. The moral question focusses there rather than on the consequences of war. The intention must be to secure the peace, not to kill nor to conquer nor to gain honor. Justice is determined by law, and law is "an ordinance of reason for the common good" (*Summa Theologica* ii. 2. Q. 57-61). A just war, therefore, is one that is governed by laws which derive from natural law, and thence from the eternal law of God. Thomas' view of war laid the foundation for Roman Catholic ethics to the present day.

The Reformers renew Augustine's emphasis on the sinfulness of man and cite the Biblical teaching that the state is an agent of retributive justice, to support war in self-defense and for the righting of injustices (Rom. 13:1-5; I Peter 2:13-14. Calvin, *Institutes* iv. 20).

The just war theory is also evident in modern political thought. John Locke realizes that war is sometimes necessitated by the absence of any international authority to whom appeal might be made. Yet force may only be used against unjust and unlawful force; even the just side, if victorious, has no power over either non-combatants or their property and must allow a defeated people to form its own new government. Authority depends on popular consent (*Of Civil Government* ii. 3, 16-18).

Aquinas ties his just war theory to his view of civil law. The Dutch jurist Hugo Grotius develops the concept of international law from the Renaissance (q.v.) notion of natural rights, and formulates a detailed body of international laws to control both the causes and the conduct of war (*The Law of War and Peace*, Indianapolis, Bobbs-Merrill, 1962). His work lays foundations for the League of Nations, the Geneva conventions, and the United Nations (q.v.). International law and the growth of an international political body are commended by both Catholic and Protestant moralists today as a needed alternative to international conflict.

Meantime, Augustine's criticism of Cicero's unrealism must be kept in mind. The rule of law offers hope for the prevention of wars, but the mistaken judgments and sinful intentions of men and nations persist. Participation in war is only justifiable as the lesser evil in the hope of lessening its evils still more. The Christian must bring love and justice into existing conflicts.

The just war criteria accordingly receive continued discussion, and renewed attempts are made to apply them to the dilemmas posed today. War for ideological reasons is accordingly condemned. But are either retaliatory or preventive war ever justified?

How can the requirement of immunity for non-combatants be sustained in an industrial society, mobilized to produce and transport arms and munitions, or in guerrilla warfare in Southeast Asia? With a view to the immunity of non-combatants and the limited use of force, can the just war theory allow indiscriminate saturation bombing and the use of nuclear weapons? Is it justifiable to stockpile for deterrent purposes the weapons of total warfare, which must never be used if the human race is to survive? Since not every war is just and every conflict has its moral ambiguities, should the right to selective conscientious objection (q.v.) be guaranteed by law? These are typical questions currently discussed in application of the just war criteria.

📖 Paul Ramsey, *War and the Christian Conscience*, Durham, N. C., Duke University, 1961; *The Just War*, New York, Scribners, 1968; *Pacem in Terris*, Encyclical Letter of Pope John XXIII, National Catholic Welfare Conference, 1963; Roland Bainton, *Christian Attitudes Toward War and Peace*, Nashville, Abingdon, 1960; *The Evanston Report*, World Council of Churches, 1954, pp. 130-158; Ralph B. Potter, *War and Moral Discourse*, Richmond, Virginia, John Knox, 1969; Albert Marrin, ed., *War and the Christian Conscience*, Chicago, Gateway, 1971.

ARTHUR F. HOLMES

JUSTICE. See also *Rights; Responsibility.* Christian ethics, like the ethics of the ancients, views justice as a virtue, but, unlike the ancients, as flowing from and tempered by faith, hope, and love. But since "justice" has a variety of meanings, it is necessary to distinguish these in order to see in what senses justice is a virtue.

In its widest meaning, "justice" is very nearly synonymous with "righteousness" (q.v.). Among its more narrow senses are those of distributive justice, remedial justice, and retributive justice.

Distributive justice concerns both the *distribution* of goods or services by an agent to a group of recipients and the *expropriation* of such by an agent from a group of contributors. Since distributive justice concerns a wide variety of goods and services distributed (such as money, health care, honors, educational opportunities, and protection from threats to life and limb) by a wide variety of agents (such as fathers in a family, employers in a business, civil government, and even God, who distributes his favors to good and evil alike) to an equally wide variety of recipients (such as children in a family, employees, citizens and businesses), distributive justice is an important concept not only for ethics but also for theology and for political and social theory.

Many conditions must be satisfied in order for an act of distribution (or expropriation) to be a just one. The more important of these are discussed below.

1. The agent must be legitimately empowered to distribute (or expropriate) what in fact he does distribute. Although a father is legitimately empowered (as God-ordained head of the family) to require performances of household chores by his children, he is not so empowered to require the same of his neighbors' children. Civil government is legitimately empowered to distribute and expropriate some types of goods and services but not others: there are limits to its authority. Of course, the question of *who* is legitimately empowered to distribute (or expropriate) *what* is a difficult one to answer. The Christian sees the resolution of the problem as resting not in sheer convention and custom, but in a Biblically-oriented view of the nature and source of authority, and of the proper divisions and limits of authority.

2. Those to whom goods and services are distributed must be legitimately entitled to a share of the goods and services distributed; it must be theirs by *right*. (cf. *Rights*). Likewise, those from whom such is required must be legitimately required to contribute their goods or services; it must be their duty (q.v.) to give. Thus justice, right, and duty are correlative notions.

3. The distributing agent must also distribute (or expropriate) fairly and impartially; each individual must be treated equally. As Paul says, "Masters, give unto your servants that which is just and equal. . ." (Col. 4:1). This is the core of the meaning of distributive justice. But to treat each equally is not to treat each exactly alike. The government which requires of each of its citizens exactly the same amount in tax money has not thereby treated all equally and justly. Difference of income, in this case, is a relevant difference for determining each citizen's just and fair *share* of the burden; of course, difference in skin color is not. Thus, the distributing agent must determine each recipient's (or contributor's) share of the goods and services distributed (or expropriated) on the basis of *relevant* differences and only on the basis of relevant differences. But how are relevant differences to be determined? Although this matter is a difficult one, a direction towards a solution can be gained if we note that distributions and expropriations are done for a purpose. Assuming that the purpose is a legitimate one, to treat people equally is, in the case of distribution, to give to each recipient the same chance at realizing the purpose for which distribution is made; and, in the case of expropriation, to require of each contributor the same sacrifice towards realizing such a purpose. Some recipients need more than others to achieve the purpose of the distribution, and some contributors must give more in order to sacrifice equally. These differences which account for such variations in need and sacrifice are the relevant ones for determining just and fair shares in distribution and expropriation. What constitutes a relevant difference, then, depends upon the precise nature of the distribution and the purposes for which it is intended.

Remedial justice is the present correction of a past case of unjust distribution effected by giving to those unfairly treated that share of the distribution to which they were entitled by right but did not receive. Remedial justice is not simply the changing of an unjust mode of distribution so that *henceforth* the distribution will be more just; rather, it is correction of past injustice. The recent cry for social justice in the USA originally concentrated on changing unjust modes of distribution (of job opportunities, educational opportunities, voting privileges, and the like); more recently, that cry has become a cry for remedial justice. Unfortunately, no theorist has as yet sufficiently delineated the conditions which must be met in order for such remedial corrections to be just ones. This presents a challenge to the contemporary Christian theorist.

Retributive justice concerns the restoration of a right violated (or the giving of recompense for such violation). The state is one of the authorities empowered to mete out justice (Rom. 13). It arbitrates cases of alleged infringement, and requires those responsible for violation of right to restore the right or to render recompense. Fathers, teachers, and others also mete out retributive justice in their spheres. Most evangelical Christians, with an eye to the substitutionary atonement of our Lord, would include in the concept of retributive justice the right or duty to punish the transgressor, thus including a punitive, as well as compensatory, element in retributive justice.

There have been different views concerning the basis of justice, in whatever form. The Stoics viewed justice as rooted in the rational order of things; the Sophist Thrasymachus, in power and coercion; still others, such as Hume and the logical positivists, in convention and custom. The Christian, however, sees justice as rooted in the loving will of God, a will directed towards the good of the beings he created and exemplified in his dealings with men.   PETER A. DE VOS

JUSTIFICATION. Justification answers man's persistent question: How is God gracious and how can I have fellowship with him? Its meaning depends upon the legal background in both Hebrew *(tsadaq)* and Greek *(dikaioō)*—to declare righteous, to acquit, to treat as righteous (in both languages "righteousness" and "justification" have the same root). Presupposed by the word is man's guilt (q.v.) because of his sin (Ps. 143:2; Rom. 3:23) and its solution by a declaratory act of God (Isa. 64:5ff.; Rom. 3:26; 4:5; Heb. 10:1-10). God declares acquitted of guilt (but not innocent!) those who trust in Christ's atonement for sin.

The grounds for this declaration are: (a) the righteousness (q.v.) of God, viewed in terms of purity and also of his relationship with his creation (Isa. 42:5ff.); (b) this relationship from man's side issues in faith (trust) between man and God (Isa. 45:18ff.); (c) the NT affirms that faith is a new possibility with the life, death and resurrection of Jesus Christ and that man can be justified through faith alone (Gal. 2:15ff.); (d) Jesus Christ is the righteousness of God; he is wholly sinless and does fully the will of God (Heb. 9:11ff.; I Cor. 1:30).

Paul expresses most clearly this view of justification through faith, particularly in his polemically motivated passages in Rom. 1-6 and Gal. 2-4. (Paul uses the noun justification only twice in Rom. 4:25; 5:18; generally he uses the verb.)

His view is that no man can be justified by doing what the Law demands (Rom. 3:30; 4:13ff.; Gal. 2:21) because one must then keep the whole Law, which is impossible (Gal. 3:10ff.; 5:3). Faced with despair (Rom. 7) man prefers to think that good and bad deeds will be weighed at the last judgment (so Pharisaic Judaism). But God has provided man's escape from bondage to sin through his own righteousness, mediated to man in Jesus Christ's sacrifice for sin (Rom. 8:1; Eph. 1:7). He treats as righteous all men (Rom. 1-3) who are incorporated into Christ (Gal. 2:17ff.).

This view is found explicitly nowhere else; similar terminology is found elsewhere only in James 2:18ff. where James counters an incorrect deduction from Paul's view. But the same view of God's righteousness, graciousness and his ability to save apart from man's attempted meritorious works is found throughout Scripture. Paul extracts especially the implications of Jesus' teaching (e.g., Luke 18:14), his function of offering forgiveness freely (Mark 2:6ff.), and his role as a ransom on behalf of many (Mark 10:45). These he puts together with Hab. 2:4 in which "life" is understood to follow from justification through faith (Rom. 1:16f.).

The ethical issues arise from the fact that justification means to *declare* righteous and not to *make* righteous. What then is the relation between justification and sanctification (q.v.)? Between the objective act on the cross and the subjective appropriation of it? Justification means more than that a person is treated *as if* he were righteous (a legal fiction); it means less than that he has attained moral rectitude (perfection). Rather, judgment has been given now because his subsequent life will conform to the act on his behalf ("Christ justifies no one whom he does not at the same time sanctify" —Calvin, *Institutes*, iii.16.1).

Both OT and NT evidence the closest relationship between justification and the ethical life of the justified (Isa. 59; Rom. 5-6; I Peter 2:24). Forgiveness of sin leads not to antinomianism but to a radical No! to evil, based on the Spirit's activity (Rom. 8:9ff.). The justified man is to be a new creation (II Cor. 5:17), full of the fruit of the Spirit (Gal. 5:22), knowing victory over sin (I John 3:7ff.) conformed to the image of Christ (Phil. 3:8ff.). He is "in Christ," a part of the Body of Christ.

The justified man lives, then in a new corporate context where he wrestles afresh with the ethical issues posed by the demands of the sharing of new life among Christians, particularly matters like freedom, law, purity (I Cor. 6:12ff.; 8:9ff.; Rev. 2-3). But he lives not only in the corporate Christian context; he lives also in the world which provides another set of issues the justified cannot shirk (I Cor. 9:19ff.; John 17). Justification by faith provides the basis on which the Christian, knowing he is accepted by God, relates to others, whether Christian or not, openly and graciously.

📖 G. Quell and G. Schrenk, *dikē* in *TDNT* II, Grand Rapids, Eerdmans, 174-225; E. D. Burton, *Galatians*, *ICC*, London, T. & T. Clark, 460ff.; W. Sanday and A. C. Headlam, *Romans ICC*, London, T. & T. Clark, 24ff.; J. Calvin *Institutes*, iii, ch. 11-18; M. Luther, *Christian Freedom;* G. C. Berkouwer, *Faith and Justification*, Grand Rapids, Eerdmans, 1952; K. Barth, *Church Dogmatics* IV, 1, London, T. & T. Clark, 514-642; E. Brunner, *Dogmatics*, London, Lutterworth, III, ch. 14ff.

PETER RICHARDSON

JUVENILE DELINQUENCY. Behavior which is opposed to the tenets held by society and the law of a particular culture is defined by and within that culture as delinquent. Loosely speaking, the major offenses are stealing, truancy, vandalism, and all degrees of cruelty up to murder.

The study of delinquents does not fall neatly within the scope of any one scientific discipline. Lawyers, sociologists, psychologists, anthropologists, psychiatrists, geneticists, and others, with different aims in mind, have sought an understanding of delinquent behavior. Many different classifications of delinquents have been proposed. However, as P. D. Scott has pointed out ("Delinquency," chap. XVI, *Modern Perspectives in Psychiatry*, J. G. Howells, ed., Edinburgh, Oliver & Boyd, 1965, p. 375) in general, classifications are of three sorts: "those which are based upon an offender's specific behavior, those based on his personal qualities, including his motivation, and those based on his interaction with others." Yet as Adelaide M. Johnson reminds us ("Juvenile Delinquency," chapter 42, *American Handbook of Psychiatry*, S. Arieti, ed., New York, Basic, p. 841) only a few years ago "many investigators telescoped all delinquents into one category." Johnson believes that study of the causation of delinquency leads to the conclusion that broadly speaking there are two categories of anti-social behavior, "the unconsciously driven individual delinquent from the so-called 'good or normal' family, and the gang or sociologic group operating at an economic level." Scott (*op. cit.*, pp. 375-377) on the other hand, finds a fourfold classification more meaningful: (1) by parental attitude, referring to the quality of parental discipline and its importance in determining child behavior, (2) by first classifying the characteristics of the delinquent children and then noting the characteristics of their home background, (3) using a rating scale to classify delinquents into pro-social (those from stable home backgrounds), anti-social gang members, with lax parental discipline, and a-social, those who for a variety of reasons have experienced early and severe parental rejection, and (4) on the basis of a typology which looks at the course of normal psychological development and examines the stage at which a delinquent's development went wrong and the causes for the aberrations.

Whatever particular classification is chosen tends to reflect the emphasis given to intrinsic and extrinsic factors in the causation of delinquent behavior. The greater part of research into the causes of delinquency has in the past been concerned to study the extrinsic factors, that is, social and environmental factors. Yet, as Cowies, et al, observed in a recent research report (J. Cowie, V. Cowie, E. Slater, *Delinquency in Girls*, London, Heinemann, 1968, p. 174) "The relative contribution of hereditary and environmental factors to the causation of

adult criminality remains an open question. The preponderance of opinion favors the greater importance of social and environmental factors in determining whether an individual falls into criminality or he does not; but the type of crime into which he may drift, and the extent to which his life is governed by criminal tendencies, would seem to be largely a reflection of his personality, with genetical factors lending much that is most characteristic." Certainly early studies of delinquency laid great emphasis on poverty, overcrowding and the economic disadvantages of the homes from which delinquents came. Added to this were the effects of others in the home, of disturbed family life, of broken homes and of educational deprivation. However, as many workers have pointed out, correlates of delinquency are not necessarily causes. To take one recent example, W. R. Little and Ntsekhe (*British Journal of Delinquency, 10,* 130, 1959) quoted by Scott, using unusually representative and satisfactory sampling techniques, show that in London, the shift is now towards the middle social class of the Registrar General's classification. Cowie (*op. cit.*) also urges that while the effects of maternal separation and deprivation form part of several theories of delinquency, nonetheless an uncommitted assessor of the evidence must conclude that as yet this general impression is an unproven hypothesis.

More recently, along with rapidly increasing knowledge of genetics (q.v.), there has been a renewed interest in physiological causal factors. Here there are broadly two different kinds of theories: those that make physical factors directly causative of delinquency and those that consider the connection less straightforward. The latter argue for a predisposition to delinquent behavior which then develops under certain circumstances. The strongly and directively causative views of genetic factors is not consistently supported. What emerges is a view of physical factors as predisposing via temperamental traits to delinquent behavior, in association with other factors such as social ones. The effect of such theories is to focus attention upon the criminal rather than upon the legal system or upon social environmental factors.

Finally, it is significant that one of the most recent research reports, already referred to (Cowie *et al*) concludes that "The evidence seems quite overwhelming that disturbance of home life is one of the main causes, if not the main cause, of juvenile delinquency." In the face of the pressures of the permissive society, their further comment is significant, that "There is growing recognition that the child needs a system of rules which he can clearly understand, and that an unduly permissive upbringing does not lead to his health or happiness, or to his becoming a tolerable member of society." They add that the child "never faces a world without prohibitions, for when those of childhood are superseded, those of an adult society remain," and that, "Discipline in its proper sense in training in self discipline." Finally commenting on inconsistency in parental behavior they point out that "most unfavourable of all is haphazard variation between one extreme and the other, leaving the child after any and every act unable to know what he has to expect. These findings are just what might have been predicted from our present knowledge of conditioning theory."

In this regard the Christian response would surely be to advocate the clear, consistent, loving, and compassionate application of Christian moral and ethical standards. Since Abrahamic times a child has been considered a priceless home blessing (Gen. 15:2). Training a child in the way of duty to God and man is a parental responsibility (Prov. 22:6), and love, respect, and obedience for parents a duty of children (Eph. 6:2).

In short, then, the many complex problems which emerge when we attempt to understand juvenile delinquency, and which we have outlined above, cannot be completely isolated from considerations of the part played, in some instances, by parental delinquency.   MALCOLM A. JEEVES

K

KANT. Kant (1724-1804) stood in awe of the starry heavens above and the moral law within. But the mechanism of the one seems to conflict with the freedom of the other.

Since empiricism results in skepticism (q.v.), as Hume so clearly showed, knowledge is possible, Kant held, only because sensory content is molded or formed by a priori categories. One of these categories is causality. Therefore whatever we see, whatever occurs in time, must be causally determined. Scientific law is inviolable and human bodies are as mechanical as the starry heavens.

However, morality, obligation, or duty is as irrefragable a fact as any scientific law. Moral imperatives are also categorical. To explain:

Moral law is a priori and cannot be deduced from experience. An empirical morality would be hedonistic (cf. *Hedonism*). But if pleasure were the end of action, the end would justify any efficient means. Yet means as much as and even more than ends are subject to moral praise or blame.

Further, if doing right depends on calculating future consequences, only the most intelligent would have a chance of being moral. Even they would have little chance; and surely morality ought to be within the reach of all. Therefore moral laws must not be degraded into the hypothetical imperatives of prudence, calculation, or science, They cannot be empirical. Moral laws are categorical imperatives.

The test of a moral law is necessity and universality. Suppose someone, in order to avoid embarrassment, considers making a promise with the intention of breaking it. This is wrong because it involves a logical contradiction in our will. If all broke their promises, there could be no promises because promises depend on the universal principle that they are made to be kept. The contradiction is that this man recognizes the *universality* of the principle (since he makes a promise) and yet intends to make an *exception.* Moral law therefore is categorical, a priori, universal, and necessary.

The fundamental law of morality is, "Act in conformity with that maxim and that maxim only which you can at the same time will to be a universal law." Particular duties, like telling the truth, are special applications of this fundamental law.

The motive of a moral act must be reverence for law. The only thing that can be absolutely good is a good will. Other things, money and even health, may sometimes be bad. A will is good if it is motivated by reverence for law. A will motivated by pleasure, by a desire to produce some result, or by anything other than reverence for law is not a good will, even if the act is objectively moral.

This system of morality requires the transcendental presuppositions of God, immortality, and freedom. Though desire for happiness is immoral, a good world must find them combined; and only God can guarantee the coincidence of virtue and happiness. Next, moral progress to the goal of perfection is an infinite process; therefore man must be immortal. But the most serious problem for morality is freedom.

The category of causality, an a priori form of the mind, compels us to construct out of chaotic sensations a world in which every temporal event is the effect of a cause. Not only bodily motions but desires, inclinations, psychological events also are subject to mechanical law. In such a world freedom is impossible.

But the categorical imperative of morality is an undeniable, a priori fact. And from this fact freedom can be deduced. Here then is the problem: Are not mechanism and freedom contradictory? The very possibility of knowledge requires mechanism. The very possibility of morality requires freedom. Must not Kant discard one or the other?

Kant's solution lies in the existence of two worlds. The mechanical world is the world of phenomena, the world of space and time, the world we "see," or, rather, the world we construct by imposing our forms of perception on sensory stimuli. In this world there is no freedom.

However, there must be another world. Since what we perceive are phenomena or appearances, since the sensory stimuli must come from somewhere other than our minds—only the forms come from the mind —there must be a world of noumena, a world of things-in-themselves, of things as they do not appear. To these things the category of causality cannot apply, for the categories are imposed only on appearances. This implies, to be sure, that we cannot know things as they are in themselves, for knowledge is a composite of form and content. The things-in-themselves have no form.

God may also be a resident of the noumenal world; though there is some doubt here. Kant had said that God, or at least the idea of God, is necessary to morality. On the other hand, he also said that God is not a constitutive idea (an existent component of the universe), but a regulative idea. That is, God is a rule of conduct. At any rate, God cannot be known; and someone has quipped, We cannot know there is a God, but we must live as if there were one.

Another resident of the noumenal world is more closely connected with ethics, namely, ourselves. Hume had described the empirical self, not as a soul-entity, but as merely a collection of images. Kant insisted that a collection requires a collector. Therefore behind the empirical self stands a self-in-itself, a transcendental self, a noumenon. Unknowable, of course.

Now, if freedom and mechanism were both attributed to one world, we would be enmeshed in contradiction. But no contradiction arises if the empirical self in the world of space and time is mechanically determined, and the noumenal self is free.

But though this is not a formal contradiction, a difficulty in application arises. A particular act of theft, i.e., the visible, temporal motions of surreptitiously putting your friend's credit card in your pocket, is a mechanical necessity of the causal world. It is inevitable; it cannot be otherwise; it is devoid of freedom. This, however, is only the appearance or phenomenon of theft. The theft-in-itself, the noumenal theft, could occur only in the noumenal world where we are free. Hence the theft-in-itself could have been avoided, but the appearance of the theft could not have been avoided.

Kant sagely concludes: "While therefore it is true that we cannot comprehend the practical unconditioned necessity of the moral impulse, it is also true that we can comprehend its incomprehensibility; and this is all that can fairly be demanded of a philosophy that seeks to reach the principles which determine the limits of human reason" (*Fundamental Principles of the Metaphysic of Morality,* Chap. III, end).

GORDON H. CLARK

KIERKEGAARD AND ETHICS. See also *Dialectical Ethics; Existential Ethics.* Søren A. Kierkegaard (1813-1855) wrote about thirty-five books, most of them in a brief nine year period, from 1842 through 1850. Much was published under pseudonyms, not so much to disguise his authorship as to force the reader to come to grips with idealized authors, whose emotions, form of life, dispositions and thoughts were of a discernible quality. Therefore, Kierkegaard designed his literature to help his reader get a strong impression, first, of what the qualitatively distinct ways of living really were and, secondly, to enable that reader to understand himself with vividness and acute conceptual detail and, thirdly, to stimulate him to become a Christian. Thus the literature aims to tug the reader into self-consciousness but not to leave him there, but, rather, to motivate him to become a truly responsible man and even a Christian.

Thus, there are four distinct contexts in which Kierkegaard might be said to describe and to discern issues of ethics. First, Kierkegaard's entire authorship has a broadly moral aim and that very much like Socrates', as described in Plato's *Apology.* There Socrates castigates the Athenians for spending so much time earning money and reputations and neglecting what is most important—"the improvement of their souls." To this extent, at least, Kierkegaard is very much like Socrates, for his entire work has a moral and, in a deep sense, an upbuilding and edifying, aim. So, though the literature combines humor and style, a variety of essays and literary genres, it is also carefully calculated to cause the reader to remember what is required to exist as a spiritual man. But, secondly, the literature as a totality also contains a sub-literature, in fact, several pieces, *Fear and Trembling* (trans. Walter Lowrie, Princeton, Princeton University, 1941), *Either/Or* (Magnolia, Mass., Peter Smith, 1959), and the *Stages on Life's Way* (trans. Walter Lowrie, New

York, Schocken, 1967). in which an ethical way of life is sketched in great detail.

About this latter "stage" or qualitatively distinct way of living a human life, Kierkegaard is at great pains to be both discerning and solicitous. In *Fear and Trembling,* he shows how the faith of Abraham and also that of the NT cannot be only a moral life now decked out in religious terminology. Rather it is his thesis that neither OT nor NT can be adequately discerned as Kant had said, only moral laws conceived as the will of God. But in *Either/Or* and the *Stages,* he also clarifies an ethical way of like in contrast to an enjoyment and aesthetic way of life. He is very much like Aristotle in intellectual manner, trying to show the distinctive moral concepts and their relations to distinctive moral pathos and feelings. Above all, he is doing an analytic job of intellectual discrimination, separating moral categories and subjectivity, from the aesthetic varities on the one side, and from too easy an assimilation into a religious and Christian way of life on the other.

It is not a mistake to see Kierkegaard here as levelling an attack upon the theological and philosophical pedagogy of his century which followed Kant in assuming that ethical thought was formal and categorical and, in the manner of a liberal religiosity, that Christianity could be construed wholly in moral terms. Instead, he shows how impulse, feeling and other kinds of subjectivity, do in fact correct Kant's formalism and that once one gets moral concepts straight that Christianity is not simply a moral teaching which can do without distinctively Biblical concepts.

But this brings us to a third sense in which Kierkegaard is an ethicist. For he also saw that Christian orthodox theology, especially that of a Lutheran sort, had become a peculiar kind of Protestant indulgence. So, he begins to search out the morphology of a distinctively Christian consciousness, that of a man nurtured in the Bible, on Luther and

Calvin, and the liturgy of the historic churches. He does not correct that theological lore; but he does attack the way it has been taught and assimilated. So, he shows in the *Postscript, Works of Love* (New York, Harper & Row), and *Training in Christianity* (trans., Walter Lowrie, Princeton, Princeton University) that one cannot know the God of Old Testament and New without a radical difference obtaining in one's subject-life. Just as one cannot be truly said to know a great danger unless one feared it so we cannot know God without fearing him. Once Kierkegaard begins, there are no end of connections he finds between what he calls "dialectic" and "pathos," between discerning Christ's teaching and one's subjectivity. This, of course, is a new kind of ethics, yet it is also very much like the teaching of the NT and the early church fathers. It is even argued that Jesus Christ is everyman's truth, not only to be thought about, but also to be assimilated as a new life, new emotions and feelings, and a radically different kind of consciousness. Kierkegaard's charge is that Christian orthodoxy had made being a Christian too easy by insisting upon a cheap kind of belief. He chooses to make it harder, but not any harder than the NT.

This is, fourthly, to make a certain kind of thinking once more a pursuit of wisdom. Kierkegaard brings matchless gifts of satire, irony, and humor, as well as relentless logic and clarity, to the search for the truth by which men can live. This he does in order to show that even grace and thinking can intertwine to make thoughtful preoccupation with oneself—rather than thoughtlessness—a means of securing what is needful in order to live as a person. Here Kierkegaard is a model with those ancients who thought wisdom and philosophy were one. But he also sought to be a Christian who found that "logos" in Jesus Christ—but not by being thoughtless or careless. Rather it was by the study of himself in the light of the

Scripture that both God and man could be known and a worthy life could be forged.

PAUL L. HOLMER

KINDNESS. In the OT this term usually reflects the Hebrew word *hesedh,* for which the RSV supplies the felicitious rendering "steadfast love." This loving kindness can be either divine or human, and covers both attitude and action. In the NT the basic word is *chrēstotēs.* The most pressing problem is to distinguish kindness from goodness, which is necessary if for no other reason than that the two stand side by side in Gal. 5:22 and therefore cannot be treated as identical. Usage seems to bear out the judgment that kindness is the fitting term when benevolence is extended not simply to one in need but to one who is undeserving and possibly unreceptive. God is said to be kind toward the unthankful and the wicked (Luke 6:35). But the divine kindness is not soft indulgence, for it is coupled with the severity of God which must operate when his gifts, especially his saving mercies, are rejected (Rom. 11:22). The kindness of God has provided for mankind a Savior (Titus 3:4-5; Eph. 2:7; cf. I Peter 2:3) and it seeks to bring men to repentance (Rom. 2:4).

It is in imitation of this kindness that Christians are enjoined to be kind and forgiving toward one another (Eph. 4:32–5:1; cf. Col. 3:12-13). Paul is careful to advance the reminder that love is kind (I Cor. 13:4). The apostle is able to claim for himself a ministry marked by kindness (II Cor. 6:6) that commended the gospel to the unsaved and exemplified the spirit of Christ to the redeemed (cf. Matt. 11:30).

EVERETT F. HARRISON

KINGDOM OF GOD, KINGDOM OF HEAVEN. Jesus' central message was the coming of the Kingdom of God. Matthew alone uses the expression, the Kingdom of the heavens (34 times), but he also has the Kingdom of God (Matt. 12:28; 19:24 (?); 21:31, 43). Heaven was a common Jewish substitute for the divine name (cf. Luke 15:18); "The Kingdom of the heavens" occurs frequently in rabbinic literature (G. Dalman, *The Words of Jesus,* Edinburgh, Clark 1909, pp. 96ff.). The two phrases are identical in meaning.

The phrase "Kingdom of God" does not appear in the OT, but the idea permeates the prophets. God is regarded as the heavenly King whose right it is to rule over the earth. "Kingdom" derives its basic meaning from the OT *malkuth* which has a dynamic meaning: reign, rule, and not the realm over which a king rules. In this sense, God is viewed as the eternal King who is actively ruling over men. "Thy kingdom is an everlasting kingdom, and thy dominion endures throughout all generations" (Ps. 145:11, 13). "The Lord has established his throne in the heavens, and his kingdom rules over all" (Ps. 103:19).

However, it was obvious that something was wrong with the world—both nature and man. The earth yielded its fruit only after hard labor. A curse of evil rested upon the world. Men were full of sin and rebellion. Idolatries, hatreds, wars, and injustice marked human society. Men worshipped idols and false gods. Therefore it was necessary for God to act in his kingly power to establish effectively his reign in the world and among men.

The OT frequently pictures a coming of God to shake the old fallen order, to judge men, and establish his rule (Isa. 2:12-22; Mic. 1:3-4). This will mean both judgment and salvation; judgment on the physical world because of its evils and judgment on wicked men. But out of the ruins of judgment will emerge a new order on the earth where peace and righteousness will prevail and a redeemed people will gladly worship their King.

Frequently in the OT, the reign of God will be established by God himself; there is no messianic agent in Amos, Micah, Zephaniah, or Joel. Sometimes the Kingdom is established by a Davidic King who is supernaturally endowed to destroy the wicked and cause peace and prosperity to prevail throughout the earth (Isa. 9, 11). Once we meet a heavenly figure—one like a son of man, who represents the saints of God, who comes to God to receive the kingdom, and then establishes the divine reign forever on the earth (Dan. 7).

Jesus claimed that in his person and ministry, the Kingdom of God had come among men and the OT hope was being fulfilled (Luke 4:21). In answer to the question of John the Baptist as to whether he was the Messiah, Jesus pointed to the fulfillment of OT messianic prophecies (Matt. 11:5-6). His claim raised questions among both leaders and people, for Jesus acted neither like a victorious conquering king nor a heavenly superhuman sort of man. In fact, Jesus radically reinterpreted the OT hope. His victory was the conquest of satanic bondage to evil and bringing man into a new relationship with God, as children of God.

Herein lay "the mystery of the kingdom" (Mark 4:11). Contemporary Judaism looked for the fulfillment of the OT hope in the appearance of a Davidic king who would be supernaturally endowed of God to conquer the Roman legions and free Jerusalem and the Jews. from political bondage (see Pss. of Sol. 17). Others, meditating on Dan. 7, looked for the coming of a heavenly Son of Man who would raise the dead, judge the wicked, and gather God's people together in peace and righteousness.

Jesus, however, refused to be a conquering king (John 6:15); although he claimed to be the Son of Man, his present mission was to be one of suffering and death, like the suffering servant of Isaiah 53 (Mark 8:31). The presence of the Kingdom was to be experienced in the spiritual realm, not in the political or economic sphere. This was indeed a mystery—a new revelation of the divine purpose (Rom. 16:25-26). The Kingdom was present in the humble person and word of Jesus, but instead of destroying the wicked, it waited for a human response to be effective (the four soils). The rule of God in Jesus must be received by men as little children receive a gift (Mark 10:15). Jesus called those who received the Kingdom his *ekklesia*—the new people of God (Matt. 16:18). The Kingdom is never to be identified with the church. The Kingdom is the redemptive reign of God which has come to men in the person of Jesus and the realm of spiritual blessing into which they enter. The church is the people who receive God's rule and enter the spiritual blessings it provides.

However, the Kingdom is also an eschatological event. He who came as the meek and humble one to suffer and die will yet come in power and glory as the heavenly Son of Man to judge the wicked, destroy Satan, and gather God's people into an eternal realm of blessing. This apocalyptic event will include the resurrection of the dead (Luke 17:35). In brief, the NT sees the OT hope accomplished in two stages: a fulfillment in history when Jesus brings God's rule to men who will willingly receive it, and a consummation at the end of history to usher in the eternal state of the age to come.

📖 H. Ridderbos, *The Coming of the Kingdom*, Philadelphia, Presbyterian and Reformed, 1962; R. Schnackenburg, *God's Rule and Kingdom*, New York, Herder and Herder, 1963; G. E. Ladd, *Crucial Questions about the Kingdom of God*, Grand Rapids, Eerdmans, 1952;_____, *Jesus and the Kingdom*, Waco, Word Books, 1964.

GEORGE E. LADD

KINSEY REPORT. See also *Sex*. The first Kinsey volume on sexual behavior of the American male was published in 1948; the second, on the female, in 1953. In spite of technical problems, especially with sampling, Kinsey's studies represent a major landmark in efforts to apply the scientific method to the study of sexual attitudes and behavior. Great indignation and disbelief emerged among many Americans not only because of the findings themselves, but also because of the assumption on the public's part that the findings prescribe what should be. This assumption is unfounded—Kinsey's and later similar studies simply describe what *is*, never what should be. Some major findings include: 25 percent of the women born before 1900, and 50 percent born afterwards, reported premarital coitus; some 90 percent of the men reported premarital coitus; the less the education, the more likely it is that persons will have had premarital coitus; blacks are more likely than whites to have had premarital coitus, but this seems to reflect educational and economic deprivations.

Religion was found to be an extraordinarily important determinant of premarital sexual behavior patterns for women. For men, however, religion was of little significance. Twenty-one percent of "religiously active" and 56 percent of "inactive" Catholic women had premarital coitus; for Protestant women, comparable percentages are 22 and 48. The differences in sex behavior *between* denominations were never as great as differences between persons who were "religiously active" vs. those who were not, irrespective of religious group label. Catholic women who were the most "religiously active" were the least likely of all women to have been premaritally sexually active.

Regarding extra-marital sex, 26 percent of the wives and 50 percent of the husbands in Kinsey's sample reported coitus outside marriage. The less the education of the men, the more likely they were to report extra-marital coitus. For Protestants, Jews, and Catholics (men and women), the less religiously active they were, the more likely they were to have had extra-marital coitus. Persons who lose their spouse through

death, separation, or divorce tend to remain sexually active, though this is more true for men than for women.

The Christian needs accurate knowledge regarding all areas of human behavior, including the sexual. He neither opposes this kind of research nor is led by this knowledge self-righteously to condemn other people's behavior. In the past (and occasionally now) Christian identification with certain laws and pronouncements gave the impression that Christians were trying to *impose* a set of sex ethics on nonChristians.

Robert R. Bell, *Premarital Sex in a Changing Society,* Englewood Cliffs, Prentice-Hall, 1966; _____, *Social Deviance,* Homewood, Ill., Dorsey, 1971; A. C. Kinsey, et al., *Sexual Behavior in the Human Male,* Philadelphia, Saunders, 1948;_____, *Sexual Behavior in the Human Female.* Philadelphia, Saunders, 1953; Reiss, I. L., *Premarital Sexual Standards in America,* New York, Free Press, 1960; Letha Scanzoni, *Sex and the Single Eye,* Grand Rapids, Zondervan, 1968.

JOHN SCANZONI

KISS, KISSING. A kiss is a complex human touch which evidences or assumes intimacy. The pressure of one's lips upon another person's body has the special poignancy of sealing some kind of promise with one's total existence. In cultures less differentiated than our present Westernized world, kissing was often a ritual act of honoring authority and celebrating (political) peace. Pagan societies also, not uncommonly, naively turned the intimacy and existential completeness of kissing into matters of sacral veneration and tabu. The early Christian community used a "holy kiss" semi-liturgically as a pledge of friendly brotherhood. Within our modern, secularized society kissing is still frequently a proper social greeting or way to say farewell, like a handshake. The nuclear meaning of a kiss, however, lies in its promise character, its vowed sealing of affection, respect and loyalty. Therefore, kissing appears most normally and richly within the ethical bonds of family, friendship and marriage. Integral to the private love play between man and woman, kissing affords deep mutual pleasure within the joyful freedom of creationally normed relationship. Erogenous kissing void of promissory commitment and selective jealousy denatures the act—a happy gift of God to open up men to their sexual humanity—reduces kissing to a psycho-physical, sucking stimulus.   CALVIN G. SEERVELD

KNOWLEDGE AND ETHICS. See also *Conscience; Ignorance.* Human culpability is universal. "All have sinned and fall short of the glory of God" (Rom. 3:20). Those who "have sinned without law shall also perish without law: and as many as have sinned in the law shall be judged by the law" (Rom. 2:12). Those "having not the law are a law unto themselves" (Rom 2:14) because "the law (is) written in their hearts" (Rom. 2:15). The apostle makes it clear that the unrighteous are "without excuse" because "the invisible things of him . . . are clearly seen, being understood by the things that are made. . ." (Rom. 1:20). Thus together with the ubiquity of sin is the ubiquity of knowledge and responsibility.

Everyone has access to moral knowledge if only the requisite effort is made. One's sense of sin alone reminds one of failure. And although knowledge of sin does not of itself give moral knowledge, it does indicate that one's duty needs to be determined. And if again one fails to determine his duty, one is nonetheless responsible for failing to do it.

There are at least two sides to the question of moral knowledge: letting the indwelling Christ motivate the believer in whatever he thinks or does and taking care to justify decisions. But what of those for whom there is no indwelling Christ? They are the slaves of sin rather than of Christ. Even so they can justify their acts no less than can believers. They have a "law written in their hearts." They have a conscience (*syneidēsis*) which links them to the laws of all creation and to God himself. Conscience—as Paul understood it—approves as well as condemns and forbids (Rom. 9:1). The nonbeliever can estimate the consequences of his acts no less than can the believer. But sin may distort his thinking. Thus although no less guilty of wrong doing than the believer, the nonbeliever is seriously handicapped in his effort to know the right and to do it.

Moral knowledge consists of knowing the right things to do and reasoning rightly about them. One is not limited merely to knowledge that one ought to love God and neighbor as situationalists argue. One must know the Scriptural injunctions that ought to be followed. Jesus reminds us that if we love him we will obey his commandments.

To be sure there may be difficulty in determining what Scriptural injunctions entail or what would count as instances of obeying them. Yet it cannot be argued that these injunctions are not binding simply because some applications of them are unclear. There *are* clear cut examples of application, and although the nonbeliever is handicapped by sin he also knows clear cut examples of what he ought to do. This will be true whatever may be the problem of borderline cases.

It has been customary for philosophers since Hume to follow his claim that moral reasoning is spurious on the grounds that the only kind of reasoning that can produce rational conclusions is deductive or inductive reasoning. Thus since moral judgments cannot be proved in the "hard" sense of being deduced from factual premises or even shown to be probable by inductive reasoning, they must be subjective. All forms of ethics which concur with Hume hold that a moral judgment is binding not because of the reasons that are given in support of it but because of the way the agent feels about it or the moral principles that would entail it.

Reasoning, however, is not limited in such a way as to make it inapplicable to moral judgment. Reasons do logically justify the moral judgments they support even though they do not entail them in the deductive way that skeptics require. One can, for example, give all kinds of reasons—including Biblical injunctions—to justify a particular moral judgment. And one can take these reasons to be *rational* grounds for the particular judgment and not merely the psychological causes of it. Hence what we know Jesus specifically enjoins us to do may cause us to do it if we are his followers. But it may also provide logical grounds for our doing it.

Moral knowledge no less than any other knowledge rests on the reasons that justify it even if those reasons do not prove the knowledge claim in the "hard" deductive sense. Moral knowledge claims resemble other metaphysical claims in that they necessitate drawing conclusions of one kind —in this case moral—from non-moral premises, i.e., premises of a different logical kind. Hence moral knowledge is no less objective than knowledge of other minds, e.g., or objects independent of mind. The skeptic makes his case by restricting reasoning in such a way as to make moral knowledge impossible.

There are many clear-cut cases of right and wrong by comparison with which believer or unbeliever can know right from wrong. One cannot set aside the claims of these cases since it is by virtue of these very cases that moral language is learned in the way it is used. Hence moral language itself reflects the law "written in our hearts."

Moral knowledge is in principle real knowledge no less than any other kind of knowledge. The New Testament claims that all men know or could get to know what is right if only they would consider the evidence before them including the workings of their consciences. For the nonbeliever the problem of knowing and doing is particularly acute because of sin. Nonetheless he is responsible. MILTON D. HUNNEX

KOINONIA. This Greek word has a variety of NT meanings. The basic idea is that of sharing in something with someone. Hence the simplest translations are "communion," "fellowship," "partaking."

Recent studies of NT language usage have led to a firm conclusion, namely that the root idea of *koinonia* is participation in something rather than human association with others. This is an important conclusion for NT interpretation and Christian ethics. For it means that a common interest in and concern for the realities of the gospel are for the writers more vital issues than the popular modern idea of a personal association with fellow Christians (such as our use of the word "fellowship" of a friendly atmosphere in a public meeting or worship service). Among the "realities" in which Christians share are (a) their call to salvation by God (I Cor. 1:9), (b) a celebration of the gospel at the Lord's table (I Cor. 10:16), and (c) an experience of suffering as Christians in a hostile world (II Cor. 1:7; Heb. 10:33; Rev. 1:9).

Secondary meanings of the term are "generosity" as a Christian virtue (e.g., Rom 15:27; II Cor. 9:13) and a pooling of material resources for the good of the Christian brotherhood (Acts 2:42).

"Koinonia ethics" is a phrase used to emphasize the interdependence of believers within the body of Christ, the church (Eph. 4:25).

Ralph P. Martin, *Paul's Epistle to the Philippians*, Tyndale NT Commentaries, Grand Rapids, Eerdmans, 1959, p. 46.   RALPH P. MARTIN

L

LABOR RELATIONS. See also *Industrial Relations; Strikes.* A gospel of "costly grace" has widespread social consequences for all aspects of life including labor relations. It tells us not only that there is dignity in all honest work, that work (q.v.) is part of the order of creation, and that for Christians work ought to be particularly meaningful and creative, but also that a Christian workman is responsible first to God, then to his employer, and then perhaps to his union. "Whatever your task, work heartily, as serving the Lord and not men, knowing that from the Lord you will receive the inheritance as your reward; you are serving the Lord Christ" (Col. 3:23f. RSV).

In labor relations, as in all other endeavors, the notion of justice (q.v.) is an indispensable ingredient in a Christian code of ethics. Justice is part of God's nature and of his norm for us (Deut. 10:18; Ps. 33:5; Mic. 6:8). Even more to the point Jeremiah proclaims: "Woe to him who builds his house by unrighteousness, and his upper rooms by injustice; who makes his neighbor serve him for nothing, and does not give him his wages" (Jer. 22:13 RSV). "To do righteousness and justice," we read, "is more acceptable to the Lord than sacrifice" (Prov. 21:3 RSV). But the Christian concern for justice is a peculiar one: it is primarily a concern to do justice and only secondarily a concern to obtain justice. Clearly, this norm is equally applicable to employer and employee.

Obedience (q.v.) is a second ingredient of the Christian ethic. We identify with Peter and the other apostles when they answered the queries of the priestly council by saying: "We must obey God rather than men" (Acts 5:29 RSV). Such an orientation which permits no ethical compartmentalization may evoke hostility or even rejection by others but it is no less valid for that reason.

Genuine love (q.v.) constitutes a third and perhaps the most consequential component of a Bible-based ethical system; a love that is prepared to go beyond justice and a love exemplified by our Lord himself (I John 3:11; John 15:10; Gal. 5:6). Justice, obedience, and love as well as the other Christian virtues are not unrelated standards but form an integrated whole. They constitute a normal, as well as essential, ethical imperative for both the individual Christian and a Christian brotherhood. To ignore this imperative, in labor relations or elsewhere, is to deny the claims of Christ.

In keeping with the above, the Christian does not view management and labor as ultimately hostile opponents. He does not bring distrust and hostility with him either to his place of work or to either side of the negotiating table. His ethic has no place for exploitation, for using people as a means to a selfish end, or for seeing them primarily as economic units. Rejecting the adversary system of rigid confrontation he adopts and implements a problem-solving approach.

Although most employees in the USA, Canada, the United Kingdom, and other democratic countries are not unionized, the term "labor relations" connotes activity involving organized labor partly because union leaders are prominent in the labor scene and partly because many important ethical issues are associated with labor as a pressure group. Thus we must consider some problems usually associated with labor unions, all the while reminding ourselves of three crucial points: labor unions arose mainly as a reaction to abuse and injustice practiced by concentrations of managerial power often brutally exploitative; labor leaders are quite right when they argue that they got rid of 72-hour work weeks, child labor, starvation wages, and a callous indifference towards safety standards by long and bitter union struggles and that, by and large, they did this without the leadership or help of the church; and that most union pursuits in our own day are at least as legitimate and praiseworthy as the activities of management.

Yet the fact remains that many labor unions are plagued by problems and that some of these are particularly relevant for Christians. One of these categories of problems might be termed "inherent." Let us consider the problem of power. In itself social power, any concentration of power, is neither ethical or unethical. But where there is organized power there tend to be ethical problems because leaders, especially, are generally unable to resist the temptation to misuse their power. Associated with this power-drive, in labor, management, and elsewhere, is the common assumption, sometimes called secular or humanistic, of self-sufficiency. The custom is to act as if—or even assert that—there is no higher authority than man. Lacking long-term objectives, often only a short-term vague or stark materialism underlies policies. The result is that work is seen only as a means to a selfish, material end. One need not be a Christian to realize that the "good life" which both employee and employer seek to achieve cannot be found in this fashion since it necessarily consists of more than economic gain. Yet most major unions are still almost wholly interested solely in money. Who can deny that despite all its talk, organized labor, as well as its managerial counterpart, often lacks both an integrative or directional philosophy? Christians have an obligation to assert the importance of non-economic values as well as to proclaim and exemplify the nature of these values.

A second category might be termed "specific problems." These tend to be associated with unions although they cannot simply be assumed. A class-struggle orientation is a case in point. A union-shop situation which makes union membership a condition of continued employment is

another. Laws which permit only one union to represent all employees in an establishment might be cited as still another. Christians must be careful not to sell out their personal freedom or compromise their accountability to God. On the other hand, Christians should constantly be searching for positive alternatives. A carefully conceived profit-sharing plan, more employee involvement in decision-making, and improved grievance procedures may result in mutual benefit to all concerned.

A third category of problems could be called "circumstantial"; these are problems not necessarily associated with unions but which may occur more or less incidentally in the course of events. Failure to bargain in good faith, "feather-bedding," insistence on outrageous settlements, misuse of union funds, the insistence that all union-controlling legislation is "vicious," open defiance of the law, and gross corruption are some major examples. Obviously a Christian will have to make his views known on these matters and refuse to participate in what he knows to be evil. Fellow Christians have a major responsibility to assist someone who finds it necessary to give up his job in order to save his integrity.

One is tempted to spell out clear-cut directives concerning union membership generally, membership in unions whose leadership is unworthy, office-holding, participation in strikes, responsibility for the allocation of dues, and numerous other aspects, but one must be cautious. The Bible, despite clarity on guidelines, does not address itself to these specifics and, furthermore, discerning Christians often disagree on what constitutes proper conduct in a given situation. Some try to avoid problems in labor relations by hanging back, but these often seem to be frustrated. A few make specific efforts to make their commitment effective where they work; their lot is not easy but it is Biblical. Many, apparently, try to skirt the issue by leading double lives; at best their response is inconsistent. An increasing number, although still a minority, have opted for separate Christian-oriented unions such as the Christian Labor Association of Canada. The option which their outspoken and courageous leaders enunciate warrants careful consideration. Whatever our personal response to specific dilemmas might be, let us not forget to practice Christian tolerance and to remember that the actions of workmen and managers, of the A.F.L.-C.I.O. and the Manufacturers Association, as well as the countless unorganized individuals must all be measured by the same ethical yardstick.

Harry Antonides, *The Freedom to Work*, Rexdale, Christian Labor Association of Canada, 1968; E. A. Keller, *The Case for Right-to-Work Laws*, Chicago, Heritage, 1956; John H. Redekop, ed., *Labor Problems in Christian Perspective*, Grand Rapids, Eerdmans, 1971; H. E. Runner, *Can Canada Tolerate the CLAC?*, Rexdale, Christian Labor Association of Canada, 1968; E. L. H. Taylor, *Reformation or Revolution*, Nutley, N. J., Craig, 1970.   JOHN H. REDEKOP

LAISSEZ-FAIRE. Laissez-faire is the doctrine which holds that government must follow a policy of limited interference in the activities of individual enterprisers. The phrase, more popular than scientific in nature, originated with the physiocrats in France. It became associated with the campaign of Adam Smith and other individualists to secure a revision in British mercantilist policies. Smith and the physiocrats based their claims on a beneficent view of the world of nature as one of harmony and justice. Man, it was believed, would find similar laws at work in the national economy and would be guided by God or the "unseen hand" in following these universal principles.

Utilitarianism (q.v.) early provided an ethical basis for a claim to radical individualism in economic enterprise. Social Darwinism (q.v.) with its stress upon the natural law of competition in human life, came to dominate the interpretation of economic individualism (q.v.) under Herbert Spencer in England and his American disciple, William Graham Sumner. Both argued for freedom from government interference in business. Both contended that any regulatory legislation must be in accord with scientifically determined laws of economic competition. This is the laissez-faire doctrine which came to influence public policy in America during the decades after the Civil War.

Simultaneously in both England and America the new liberalism (q.v.) laid the basis for an expanding intervention of state power in promoting fair competition. Individual enterprise was regulated through antitrust legislation, minimum wage laws and social welfare legislation, thereby laying the foundation for the welfare state (q.v.).

SAMUEL R. KAMM

LAITY. The early church was one people of God in Christ, gathered about the ministry of the apostles, the direct emissaries of Christ. All together thought of themselves as a royal priesthood (I Peter 2:4-10). The *laos* or people of God through daily witness and contact with the world propelled the message which the apostles preached publicly (Acts 5:12-16), and the witness of the people became a cardinal facet in the spread of the gospel (I Peter 2:11—4:11), climaxing in the martyrdom of their *martyria*. The second generation of the church supplanted the leadership of the apostles with elders or bishops or pastors; as the church grew larger, special administrators were devised for greater responsibilities, and a distance set in between clergy and laity.

The danger in splitting clergy from laity. For the clergy, this distinction tempted to obscure the meaning of servanthood, which Jesus Christ himself had set up as the criterion of redemptive ministry (Matt. 20:28). The spin-off from this situation was authoritarianism, when ethical or doctrinal principles were enforced by prescription rather than by the power of the gospel; or status supported by outward signals, draining the resources of the church into the support of human prestige rather than the care for human need. At the same time the vocation of lay people was denigrated, and "secular" callings were viewed as essentially inferior to "clerical" or "spiritual" ones, whereas the gifts of the Spirit were intended to give the Spirit's power and purpose to all human callings by which other prople are helped, including the humblest (cf. I Cor. 12 or Rom. 12). In this procedure preaching became moralizing rather than evangelizing; the pastorate became group administration rather than the cure of souls; the church became a power complex rather than God's arm and Christ's body among men.

The danger in merging clergy and laity. Ever since the Christian era reaction against clericalism has thrust the Christian community into a one-class form; whether in the spiritual direction, as with the monastic bodies or the utopian and anti-clerical sects; or in the secular direction as contemporary declericalized lay vocations. Overlooked in this process is the Spirit's gift of the combination of word of wisdom, word of knowledge, utterance, direction, and service, which is the pastor. Therewith the special student and witness to the word of the Bible and the message of Christ, the starter of God's own chain reaction of the gospel, is apt to be silenced. The pastor can take the lead among his people to help all sanctify their callings, out in the world, and so make the gospel of Christ meaningful where they live (cf. Eph. 4:1-16; John 17).

📖 *Work and Vocation,* John Oliver Nelson, ed., New York, Harper, 1962; Georgia Harkness, *The Church and Its Laity,* Nashville, Abingdon, 1962; Hendrik W. Kraemer, *A Theology of the Laity,* Philadelphia, Westminster, 1958.

OSWALD C. J. HOFFMANN

LANGUAGE, ETHICAL. When we say that a person is morally good, or that an action is morally right, what, if anything, are we *asserting*? If we *are* asserting something when we employ terms such as "good" and "right," how might (and/or ought) we go about *justifying* what is asserted? The intense interest in these questions on the part of twentieth-century Anglo-American philosophers has resulted in the formulation of a variety of theories concerning the meaning and justification of moral judgments.

The contemporary discussion of these issues was initiated in the 1903 publication of G. E. Moore's *Principia Ethica* (New York, Cambridge University). Moore insisted that in saying that something is "good" one is asserting something, i.e., making a claim about a state of affairs. But one is not making a claim about an empirically observable or subjective-psychological state of affairs. For if the claim that something is good *means* that it is productive of pleasure, then the question whether the production of pleasure is itself good is not a significant question. But since the latter *is* a significant question, "good" must denote some distinct property. This Moore took to be a unique, indefinable, simple, "non-natural" property which is known by rational "inspection."

The non-cognitivist view of ethical language defended by the logical positivists (cf. *Positivism*) was based on a denial of the assumption shared by both Moore and his "naturalist" (or "definist") opponents—the assumption that ethical language is used to *assert*. According to A. J. Ayer, sentences employing ethical terms are vehicles for the *expression* of feelings of approval or disapproval. (This view must be distinguished from a cognitivist-subjectivism which would understand moral judgments as *descriptions* of feelings of approval or disapproval.) Thus on Ayer's view, to say "Stealing is wrong" is not to do anything more than what one would be doing if one said "Stealing!" with a tone of disgust. Other non-cognitivi•ts understood moral judgments to be prescriptions, commendations, or instruments of non-rational persuasion.

In recent decades there has been a general consensus that no one of these earlier views was, by itself, adequate. Non-cognitivism fails to account for the apparent significance of moral disagreement. The attempt to understand moral judgments as disguised assertions about empirical or subjective states of affairs also seems to fail to do justice to what *is* being said when moral terms are employed. On the other hand, Moore's non-naturalism carried with it both an ontology and an epistemology (with an intuitionist, "moral sense," flavor to it) which failed to gain currency. More recently, some writers have attempted to combine in various ways what they take to be the worthy *emphases* of these earlier positions. Thus, R. M. Hare has argued that moral judgments have both a descriptive and a prescriptive element; and J. O. Urmson has suggested that moral terms function in a way analogous to "grading" labels: e.g., to say that an apple is a "super" is to refer to the presence of certain objective characteristics (of size, shape, etc.) which it has, but it is also to *commend* these characteristics, which commendation is in turn related to subjective (or trans-subjective) tastes.

Two recent developments in the continuing discussion of these issues are of special interest from a Christian point of view. One is the insistence, by several recent writers, that in making a moral judgment one is implicitly appealing to certain criteria which one takes to be universally binding; or, as William Frankena has argued, one is implicitly claiming that all perfectly rational beings who assessed the situation in the light of all relevant facts and from the moral point of view would share one's position of approval (or disapproval). If it could be argued convincingly that the making of moral judgments involves an implicit appeal to the assessment which an "ideal observer"

might make, then an ethical system in which the revealed directives of an omniscient, omnibenevolent deity have a central, authoritative role might be seen as providing satisfactory (or at least *relevant*) answers to questions which arise out of the examination of the very "logic" of moral discourse.

The second development is a growing concern with the question of whether the "meta-ethical" investigation of normative ethical language can itself be carried on from a normatively "neutral" perspective. It must at least be granted that many of the accounts put forward have *not* been neutral with respect to normative ethical systems. Some theorists, e.g., fail to keep clearly in mind that "moral" can be used in contrast to both "non-moral" and "immoral." Consequently, their accounts of moral judgments often have the effect of relegating some apparently *im*moral judgments to the realm of the *non*-moral. (For example, the view that moral judgments implicitly appeal to criteria which have to do with the promotion of social harmony has the implication that an individual egoist, if consistent, does not make moral judgments. Or, a theory which requires that a moral judgment be characterized by "impartiality" would seem to rule out the possibility of a racist moral judgment.)

Whether normative biases are a *necessary* part of meta-ethical investigation is, of course, arguable; and it is a matter which ought to be explored further. Such exploration will be of importance to Christian thought, which has a special—if not vested—interest in the general question of "neutrality."

Even where the question of the *possibility* of neutrality has not been raised, there have been growing complaints that the neutral meta-ethical posture is one which *ought not* be adopted. Some have seen that posture as a subtle form of "conservatism" which explicates the morality of the *status quo,* without calling existing moral criteria into question. Others see the meta-ethical posture as just one more aspect of the abdication of social and moral responsibility, in the name of "value-free inquiry," on the part of the twentieth-century academic community.

Christians must be sensitive to these charges; but they must temper them by a recognition of the positive benefits which can be derived from the work of those who have analyzed ethical language. The examination of the way in which moral views are in fact proposed and defended can give us valuable insight into the interrelationships which exist between moral beliefs and other (e.g., religious, metaphysical, political, economic, etc.) beliefs; it can teach us something about the role which *reason* plays in our moral deliberation, and thereby provide us with an occasion for a better understanding of ourselves, our "rationalizing," our self-deception, and perhaps even our created nature as it reflects the *imago dei.* And not the least, it can equip those whose calling it is to articulate a Christian vision of our moral life with the tools of logical analysis and with a sensitivity to subtle distinctions.

A. J. Ayer, *Language, Truth and Logic,* London, Gollancz, 1936; William K. Frankena, "On Saying the Ethical Thing," *Philosophy Today,* No. 1, Jerry H. Gill, ed., New York, Macmillan, 1968; Alan Gewirth, "Metaethics and Moral Neutrality," *Ethics,* April, 1968; R. M. Hare, *The Language of Morals,* New York, Oxford University, 1952; G. E. Moore, *Principia Ethica,* New York, Cambridge University, 1903; J. O. Urmson, "On Grading," *Logic and Language* (Second Series), A. G. N. Flew, ed., Oxford, Blackwell, 1961.

RICHARD J. MOUW

LAW AND GOSPEL. The concepts behind the terms "Law" (God's demands upon man, God's immutable will) and "Gospel" (God's promise, good news of salvation through Christ) are found throughout Scripture.

The two concepts are most consciously and closely related to each other, however;

in Paul's writings, particularly as he deals with justification by faith and the function of the Law (Rom., Gal.). To Paul both Law and Gospel are revealed by God (Rom. 1:18-19; Gal. 1:12 *passim*) and both are concerned with man's justification before God and man's salvation. But no one can obey God's Law and thus achieve righteousness before God in that way. The Law serves therefore to condemn man and reveal his sin (Gal. 3:10; Rom. 3:20; 4:15). The Gospel is something quite different to Paul and its function is different. The Gospel is the good news of all that God has done in Christ for fallen and sinful man. It is the message concerning the work of God's Son, our Saviour incarnate, who has obeyed God's Law in our place, suffered God's wrath against sin, died and risen to save us forever. But it is more than a mere report, much less a transcendental dogmatic formulation. It is in itself a vehicle of God's power to save (Rom. 1:16; I Cor. 15:2). As Gerhard Friedrich says, "It takes hold of men in actual life, shapes them and creates of them a congregation. . . . Since the Gospel is God's speech to men (*euangelion theou,* I Thess. 2:2, 9), it challenges men to decision and works in them submission (Rom. 10:16; II Cor. 9:13). . . . The Gospel is not an empty word, but a creative word which brings about what it says because its author is God (Rom. 1:1; 15:16; II Cor. 11:7; I Thess. 2:2, 8, 9; I Peter 4:17; I Thess. 1:5)" (Gerhard Friedrich on *euangelion* in Gerhard Kittel, *TWNT*). Because the content and function of Law and Gospel are so radically different it is of great concern to Paul that the two teachings which must both be taught in the church be rightly distinguished (II Cor. 3:6 *passim*; Gal. 2:16-21; Rom. 3:20-31).

In the post-apostolic age Augustine (q.v.) did more than anyone else to retain the Pauline doctrine of Law and Gospel. This he did in his anti-Pelagian writings, especially his *De spiritu et littera* (412 A. D.) which seeks to interpret and apply II Cor. 3:6. Interpreting the passage in the light of Paul's Romans, Augustine takes "letter" to denote the Law in its full sense and "Spirit" to mean the work of the Holy Spirit. He denies justification by the works of the Law. The Spirit alone can give life, that is, save a lost sinner and work in him newness of life. But much of the Pauline doctrine is lost in Augustine with the latter's non-Pauline understanding of grace. And in the ensuing centuries the notion of Gospel came more and more to be understood in terms of Law.

A radical change took place in the Reformation (q.v.) when the Pauline doctrine was again emphasized. To the Reformers all Scripture could and should be divided into "two chief themes," Law and Gospel. "In some places it presents the law. In others it presents the promise of Christ; this it does either when it promises that the Messiah will come and promises forgiveness of sins, justification, and eternal life for his sake, or when, in the New Testament, the Christ who came promises forgiveness of sins, justification, and eternal life. By 'law' in this discussion we mean the commandments of the Decalogue, wherever they appear in the Scriptures" (*Apology of the Augsburg Confession*, IV, 5-6). The proper distinction between Law and Gospel therefore became a necessary hermeneutical tool and pre-understanding for the right understanding (acceptance) and application of Scripture. The great error of the Romanists was centered in their using Law passages of Scripture to mitigate against the Gospel into a new Law and undermining the all-sufficient and saving work of Christ.

To Luther (cf. *Lutheran Ethics*) everything depended in the theological enterprise upon making the proper distinction between Law and Gospel and not confusing the two. "This distinction between Law and Gospel is the highest art in Christendom which should be grasped and understood by all who call themselves Christians. Where this is not done, a Christian may not be distinguished from a heathen or a Jew. So much depends on this distinction." Again he said, "Therefore, whoever has mastered this ability to distinguish the Law from the Gospel place him at the head and call him a doctor of Holy Scripture. For without the Holy Spirit it is impossible to make this distinction" (W^2 9, 798ff.). Luther saw the proper distinction between Law and Gospel to be imperative not only for correct exegesis and polemics against false teachers, but also for effective pastoral work.

Luther's emphasis was shared by Melanchthon and other Lutherans of the sixteeth century. Reformed theologians, particularly those under the influence of Melanchthon (e.g. Zachariah Ursinus), also made much of the distinction between Law and Gospel, and in some cases structured their theological works according to these categories. But for the most part Calvinists constructed their theological systems according to other categories.

Calvin also recognized the importance of the distinction between Law and Gospel (*Institutes*, 3.17.T). But it was not central for him as for Luther (cf. *Calvinistic Ethics*). And he employs the terms more loosely than Luther. At times the terms denote the Old and New Testaments respectively; the Law the period of waiting, the Gospel the period of fulfillment (*Institutes*, 3.11.10). At other times Calvin uses the terms in a more "Lutheran" sense to denote "the merit of works" as contrasted to "the free imputation of righteousness" (*Institutes*, 3.9.4). But Law for Calvin also means the "rule for righteous living" which God requires of us. Here his emphasis differs from Luther's. Luther too understood the term "Law" to mean God's norm for human behavior (*Large Catechism*, I, 311 *passim*). But in his many discussions concerning Law in its relation to Gospel he understood "Law" metonymically for the work and function of the Law to bring man's sin to light, to condemn the sinner (*Smalcald Articles*, III, II, 4-5). To Luther *Lex semper accusat*, the Law always accuses a man, judges him to be a sinner before God—whatever other functions it may play upon society or the individual. It is never only a rule for human behavior, not even for the Christian.

The proper distinction between Law and Gospel functions to protect an evangelical theologian from legalism on the one side and antinomianism on the other. Antinomianism (q.v.), the view that the Law need and ought not be preached and applied to Christians, was ·introduced into the Lutheran Church in 1526/7 by John Agricola of Eisleben. Luther answered Agricola more than once, contending that both Law and Gospel must be preached to Christians, since daily contrition which is necessary for the Christian can only be wrought by the Law. Furthermore, the Gospel cannot be understood without the Law, for the Gospel is God's answer to the accusations of the Law and there are nomistic and forensic aspects in the proclamation of the Gospel. Later as the controversy persisted in Lutheran circles the *Formula of Concord* settled the matter in an article on the "Third Use of the Law." There it was stated that the Law does not produce faith or good works in a Christian, but it must nevertheless be preached because of every Christian's flesh and because it is "a certain rule and norm for achieving a godly life and behavior in accord with God's eternal immutable will" (*FC SD* IV, 3).

Since the sixteenth century Protestant theologians, primarily Lutherans, have continually occupied themselves with the problems of distinguishing Law and Gospel in the face of various forms of legalism, antinomianism and Classical Liberalism with its denial of the wrath of God and the need for a vicarious atonement.

📖 Werner Elert, *Zwischen Gnade und Ungnade*, Munich, Evangelischer Pressvergand für Bayern, 1948; Gerhard O. Forde, *The Law-Gospel Debate*, Minneapolis, Augsburg, 1969; C. F. W. Walther, *The Proper Distinction between Law and Gospel*, St. Louis, Concordia, 1929; Francois Wendel, *Calvin*, Tr. by Philip Mairet, London, Collins, 1965; Adopf Köberle, *The Quest for Holiness*, Minneapolis, Augsburg, 1938.   ROBERT D. PREUS

LAW IN NEW AND OLD TESTAMENTS. See also *Jewish Ethics; Law and Gospel*.

I. *Old Testament*. The concept of law plays a predominant role in the OT. The terminology used is rather varied (Ps. 119, which sings the praises of the law, uses such words as law, testimony, way, precept, stature, commandment, and ordinance). The main term, however, became the word *torah*, which occurs about 220 times. Its meaning is wider than that of "law" in the strict sense; it stands for divine instruction, and gradually became the name for the whole Pentateuch.

A. *The Mosaic Law*. The law in the OT is the law given by God through the intermediary of Moses. This law is both complex and comprehensive. It consists of many parts and covers almost the entire life of the individual and of the nation.

1. *Law and Covenant*. To understand the nature of the Mosaic law one must keep in mind that this law was given within the framework of the Sinaitic Covenant. This covenant, just as that with Abraham, was essentially a covenant of grace, originating in the electing love of God (cf. Exod. 19:4, 5). The law itself is a gift of grace. The actual promulgation of the Decalogue (Exod. 20, Deut. 5) is preceded by the announcement (Exod. 19:5, 6) or reminder (Deut. 4:37; 5:2) of the covenant (cf. also the introduction of the Decalogue itself, Exod. 20:21; Deut. 5:6). The Lord also commanded Moses to put the tables containing the Ten Words in the ark of the covenant (Deut. 10:2). All this means that the law is not the way to obtain grace, but issues from grace; its main function is to

show the way of love and gratitude in response to grace.

2. *Implications.* This place of the law within the framework of the covenant also explains many features of the Mosaic law. The following implications can be mentioned. (a) There is no place for the idea of a "contract." The keeping of the law is not Israel's achievement, offered to God as part of the "contract," but is a matter of simple obedience to him, to whom they belong on the basis of his gracious Lordship. (b) The law is absolute and unconditional. There is no place for "ifs", the people are called to unconditional obedience. (c) Many commandments (cf. *Decalogue*) are given in a negative form. God's people are simply forbidden to do anything which will break the existing covenant-relationship. (d) The law has a totalitarian character. "It is not only the cult of Yahweh, but the whole of life which stands under the law. The claim of this God to rule leaves no neutral zone" (Gutbrod).

3. *Three kinds of law?* It is quite common in both Protestant and Roman Catholic theologies to distinguish three kinds of laws within the Mosaic law, namely, moral, ceremonial, and civil. The usual line of argument is that the NT believers are bound only to keep the moral laws, while the other laws have been abrogated by Christ. Although this distinction is not without merit, it must be used with great caution and supplies no simple answer to the question to what extent the Christian is still bound by the law of Moses. (a) The OT itself never makes this distinction. The various aspects are usually intertwined, even in the Decalogue (cf. the fourth and fifth commandments). (b) The NT does not make this distinction either. The *whole* Mosaic law has been fulfilled by Christ: the moral aspects in the obedience which he learned by his suffering; the civil or legal aspects in his satisfaction to the justice of God; the ceremonial aspects in his sacrifice of Calvary

(A. A. Van Ruler, *De Vervulling der Wet,* 1947, pp. 359, 491). For this reason the *whole* Mosaic law, including the Decalogue, is no longer binding upon the Christian as a *legal code.* Only "Seventh-Day" bodies venture to keep the fourth commandment in its original, legal formulation.

B. *Law before Moses.* The law as given by Moses (q.v.) is a clearly dated revelation of God's will to his people. It included many legal aspects common to the Near Eastern world, as evidenced by several other ancient law codes discovered in the last hundred years (cf. A. van Selms, "Law," *New Bible Dictionary,* London, Inter-Varsity Fellowship, 1962, p. 720). The concept of law, also of divine law, is much older than the Mosaic law. God himself, e.g., commanded Abraham to walk before him and to "be blameless" (Gen. 17:1). The Covenant with Noah contained several explicit commandments (Gen. 9:1-7). In fact, the concept of divine law must be traced back to the creation. Admittedly, the creation story does not contain anything that resembles the Mosaic law or even the Decalogue, but the story does point out that from the very beginning man is a religious and moral being, called by God to serve and obey him as his child (cf. Gen. 1:26, 27). It also mentions a special prohibition (Gen. 2:16, 17). From these data has developed the doctrine of the Covenant of Works (cf. Westminster Confession VII, 2). Although the terminology may be debatable, the religious-moral-legal relationship between God and man is a fact firmly embedded in the whole of Scripture (cf. Lev. 18:5; Rom. 10:5; Gal. 3:12; cf. especially Rom. 2:14, 15, which speaks of the knowledge of the "works of the law" even with the Gentiles, due to God's general revelation; cf. also Rom. 1:18, 32; 2:12).

C. *Law after Moses.* The introduction of the kingship did not mean an essential change in the law. Although naturally the king became the supreme court in legal matters (cf. II Sam. 15:2-6), he himself was not outside the law but subject to it. At the same time the priests continued to play their important part as interpreters of the law (cf. Deut. 33:10; Hos. 4:6; Jer. 5:4f.). Later on the prophets also recognized the authority of the Torah (cf. Hos. 4:1f.; 9:12; Jer. 11:1ff.; Ezek. 22:1ff.). At times they were very critical of the ceremonial system (cf. Amos 5:21ff.; Hos. 6:6; Micah 6:6ff.; Isa. 1:11ff.; Jer. 7:21ff.), not in negation of the system, but in criticism of the wrong attitude of a people that lived in gross sins and yet continued to bring formal sacrifices. In general the prophetical books clearly represent a further stage in the history of salvation. On the one hand, they radicalize the law by emphasizing that God looks upon the heart (cf. Jer. 4:4). On the other hand, they show a new messianic-eschatological perspective by indicating that when the messianic era has come the whole Mosaic law in its form of legal code will be superseded (cf. Jer. 31:31ff.; also 3:16; Zech. 14:20, 21). In the meantime the exiles who returned to Palestine began to emphasise the observance of the law as the only escape from further judgments, an attitude that during the inter-testamental period led to such extreme positions as held by the Pharisees in NT days.

II. New Testament.

A. *Jesus and the Law* (q.v.). In Jesus' attitude towards the law as portrayed in the Synoptic Gospels there seem to be two contrasting lines. On the one hand, there is a clearly positive line. Jesus himself recognizes the validity of the Mosaic law (cf. Matt. 5:17ff.; 22:36ff.) and also keeps it (he goes to the synagogue on the sabbath; keeps the great festivals; pays temple tribute; wears garments prescribed by the law; etc.). He also commands others to keep it (cf. Matt. 7:12; 8:4; 11:15f.; 19:16f.; Luke 16:27ff.). On the other hand, there is also (at least seemingly) a critical line. In the Sermon of the Mount (q.v.) he sets his own

teaching over against that of tradition (Matt. 5:21ff.). He eats with publican and sinners (Matt. 9:9ff.). There is also his attitude toward the sabbath (cf. Matt. 12), things clean and unclean (cf. Matt. 15:1ff.; Mark 7:1ff.) and divorce (Matt. 19:3ff.). Quite often these two lines are regarded as contradictory, but a careful analysis shows that such a view is untenable. (1) Jesus never attacks the law itself, but only the interpretation given in the oral tradition. Over against the latter he upholds the law as the revelation of God's will for his people. (2) In fact, he radicalizes the law by putting it within the new context of the Kingdom of God. Not a formal but only a radical repentance and obedience will do for the Kingdom. (3) At the same time there are indications in his teaching (especially in Matt. 9:14-17, cf. also 5:18) that in the near future a shift will take place. In fact, the change is already taking place, for his own coming means that an entirely new situation is arising. The full change, however, awaits the completion of his work in death and resurrection and in the outpouring of the Spirit.

B. *The Primitive Church and the Law.* Fairly soon in the life of the young church the problem of the law came to the fore. No great problems arose as long as the church consisted mainly of converts from Judaism, but as soon as Gentile congregations were established the problem became pressing. Over against Judaizing tendencies the Conference of Jerusalem (Acts 15) decided that Gentile converts should not be burdened with keeping the whole Mosaic law, while at the same time it drew up certain practical rules which all parties concerned should keep.

C. *Paul and the Law.* Paul in particular has struggled with the problem of the law. His letters abound with references to the "law," a term he uses in several ways, but usually for the whole Mosaic law (cf., e.g., Rom 7:22, 25; 8:7; I Cor 9:9; Gal. 3:17).

His view can be summarized in the following points. (1) He utterly rejects every possibility of obtaining salvation by means of the law (cf. Rom. 3:20; 4:13; Gal. 3:11). (2) Yet he recognizes the goodness and holiness of the law itself (Rom. 7:12, 14). In itself it is the way of life for everyone who keeps it (Gal. 3:12). But due to sin no one can keep it any more. Even worse, the rebellious heart is incited by the law to indulge in sin (Rom. 7:7ff.) and thus the curse of the law (i.e., of God himself) rests heavily upon the sinner (Gal. 3:13; cf. Rom 4:15; 7:9, 10; I Cor. 15:56). (3) All this is true not only of the life of the individual, but Paul also sees the law in the wider context of the whole history of salvation. The law as given through Moses belonged to the interim period of the Sinaitic covenant. It came 430 years after the promise given to Abraham (Gal. 3:17) and had a dual function, namely, to make Israel aware of its sin (cf. Rom. 5:20) and to act as its custodian until Christ came (Gal. 3:24, 25). (4) When Christ came, he took the curse of the law upon himself (Gal. 3:13). He also abolished the law's function as a custodian. Believers are no longer little children under the custodianship of the Mosaic law (Gal. 3:25; cf. Rom. 10:4), but in Christ they are (adult) sons of God (Gal. 3:26). Time and again Paul emphasizes this new freedom of the believers (cf. Gal. 4:4f., 21f.; 5:1ff.). Those who are led by the Spirit are not "under the law" (Gal. 5:18). The Mosaic law as a legal code is no longer binding upon the believers. (5) Yet Paul does not simply reject the law as of no lasting value. Though rejecting the binding nature of the law as "pure" law, i.e., as code, he regards it still as the revelation of God's will. Again and again he refers to the OT law to describe the content of the new obedience (cf. Rom. 8:3, 4; 13:8-10; I Cor. 7:19; 9:21; Gal. 5:14; 6:2). But three emphases stand out: (a) He always holds the old law in the light of Christ; whatever has the function of a "shadow of what is to come" (Col. 2:17) is no longer binding. (b) He emphasizes that God's will as revealed in the law is directed at persons (cf. Gal. 5:14; Rom 13:10). (c) The new obedience is possible only when the Spirit dwells in a man (cf. Rom. 8:1ff.; Gal. 5:16ff.).

D. *The Rest of the New Testament.* In *Hebrews* we find a basically similar approach, although the emphasis is on the ceremonial aspects of the law. Now that Christ has come and has completed his priestly and sacrificial work, the ceremonial aspects of the law are no longer binding. *James,* like Paul, emphasizes the principle of freedom (cf. 1:25) but also urges his readers to be "doers of the word" and not only "hearers" (1:22f.; 2:14f.) The *Gospel of John* does not deal specifically with the problem of the law. Several times it stresses the superiority of the revelation in Christ over that given in the law (cf. 1:17; 6:32; 8:12, 16; 9:5; 15:1), but it also maintains that the OT (including the law) is God's revelation to his people (cf. 8:17; 10:34; 12:34; 15:25) and points to Christ (cf. 1:45). Very significant is Jesus' statement about the new commandment to love one another (13:34), which actually is the summary of the Mosaic law (cf. Matt. 22:34ff.; Rom. 13:8ff.). Yet it is "new," because it now functions within the context of the Kingdom of God that has appeared in Christ himself (cf. also I John 2:7-11).

A. Alt, *Die Urspruenge des isrealitischen Rechts,* 1945; B. H. Branscomb, *Jesus and the Law of Moses,* 1930; G. Brillenburg Wurth, *Het Christelijk Leven,* 1949; Alfred De Quervain, *Die Heiligung,* 1942; C. H. Dodd, *Gospel and Law,* Irvington-on-Hudson, Columbia University, 1953; P. Fairbairn, *The Revelation of Law in Scripture* (1869), 1957; Carl F. H. Henry, *Christian Personal Ethics,* Grand Rapids, Eerdmans, 1957; E. F. Kevin, *The Evangelical Doctrine of Law,* 1955; E. Kevan, *Keep His Commandments,* 1964; H. Kleinknecht and W. Gutbrot, *Law,* 1962 (Kittel, *TWNT,* Vol IV. 1016-1084); G. A. F. Knight, *Law and Grace,* Naperville, Allenson, 1962; T. W. Manson, *Ethics and the Gospel,* New York, Scribner, 1960; R. C. McQuilkin, *God's Law and God's*

Grace, 1958; G. Oestborn, *Tora in the Old Testament,* 1945; H. N. Ridderbos, *When the Time Had Fully Come,* 1957; H. N. Ridderbos, *The Coming of the Kingdom,* Nutley, N. J., Presbyterian and Reformed, 1962; H. N. Ridderbos, *Paulus, Ontwerp van zijn theologie,* 1966; J. M. P. Smith, *The Origin and History of Hebrew Law,* 1931; J. VanderPloeg, *Studies in Hebrew Law, CBQ* 12, 1950, 248-259, 416-427; 13, 1951, 28-43, 164-171, 296-307; A. A. VanRuler, *De Vervulling der Wet,* 1947.　　　　　KLAAS RUNIA

LAW AND JESUS. See *Jesus and Law.*

LEGALISM. See also *Fundamentalism; Phariseeism.* Legalism, in the history of theology, is the theory that a man by doing good works or obeying the law earns and merits his salvation. Pelagius argued that since man has free will, he is able to keep God's commandments perfectly. The Pharisees, who denied free will, gave greater scope to grace, in that if a man's sins and merits were in balance, God would graciously remove one's sin.

The evangelical doctrine is justification by faith alone, and that faith itself is a gift of God. The merits are all Christ's.

The Apostle Paul considers the objection that justification by faith alone removes all need for good works and allows the regenerate man to continue in sin. His reply is that redemption is salvation from sin and that justification irresistibly issues in sanctification.

In the present century the term legalism has been given a new meaning. Situation ethics (q.v.) despises rules and laws. Anyone who conscientiously obeys God's commandments is regarded as legalistic. Therefore Joseph Fletcher approves the breaking of every one of the Ten Commandments. He thus transfers the evil connotation of legalism to the historical morality of Protestantism.　　　　　　　GORDON H. CLARK

LEISURE. See also *Amusements; Pleasure.* The industrial revolution (q.v.) has given many people the forty-hour week and in some cases the four-day week. The result is an increase of leisure, i.e., off-work hours. The Office of Economic Development defines leisure as "(2) Opportunity offered by freedom from occupations. (3) The state of having time at one's disposal; time which one can spend as one pleases; free or unoccupied time." It quotes Samuel Johnson as distinguishing idleness from leisure. Johnson felt that he was so idle he was having to pay a "fine" by having no leisure. Ruskin says, "The first volume of *Modern Painters* took the best of the winter's leisure."

How do we handle our leisure time? "In whatever you do, in word or deed, do everything in the name of the Lord Jesus, giving thanks to God the Father through him" (Col. 3:17 RSV). The heart of the gospel is, "Jesus Christ is Lord" (cf. II Cor. 2:5). We are fortunate that Christ has not abandoned us here but willingly gives us direction. (See also I Peter 1:15.) This comes through Scripture (Ps. 119:105) which is a lamp to our feet, a light to our way. The Christ of Scripture is Lord of our leisure.

What does he want? He wants us "to glorify God and to enjoy him forever" (cf. Eph. 1, etc.).

At least nine prominent uses of leisure are found in Scripture. (1) *Worship* and (2) *Rest* are commanded (Exod. 20:8-11; 31:12-17; Heb. 10:25; etc.). If we lose worship, we also lose rest. Our culture, losing worship, is restless and up-tight. Mark 2:27 says the sabbath is for man; so loss of rest and worship hurt him. (3) *Service.* Deacons (Acts 6) and elders (I Tim. 2) use some non-work hours for service or ministry to the church. I Peter 4:9 calls for hospitality from all believers. Social service is a leisure activity too. (4) *Evangelism* is an off-hour pursuit of each believer (Matt. 28:18-20). (5) *Health.* Deliberate bodily exercise is necessary for survival (cf. I Tim. 4:7b-9). "For no man hates his own body but nourishes and cherishes it ... " (Eph. 5:29). (6) *Creative avocations.* For instance, regarding music, David invented musical instruments (Amos. 6:5), was the "sweet Psalmist of Israel" (II Sam 23:1), and played the lyre day by day (I Sam 18:10). (7) *Celebration.* The marriage feast of Matthew 25 and at Cana (John 2) show this use of leisure. (8) *Amusement* vs. asceticism (q.v.), Christ came "eating and drinking" (Matt. 11:16-19). He enjoyed himself. Some leisure should be spent in fun, not for a serious purpose. For example, sports fall here (but if done with more purposeful intent, under (5) above. (9) *Delight,* as with God's creation. Hiking need not be only for health or amusement, but for sheer delight in enjoying God's creative hand (cf. I Tim. 6:17; Ps. 8).

Misuse of leisure can represent self-indulgence and egoism. In Amos 6:4-7 this led to indifference, suffering and injustice as is widely true in the USA now. In Haggai 1 men lived in paneled houses but the temple was a wreck, so leisure led to indifference to God. Wisdom, pleasure, laughter and money—without God—led to emptiness as described in Ecclesiastes. Boredom, frustration and despair follow if leisure is not under Christ's lordship (cf. Eccles. 12:1).

PAUL FROMER

LESBIANISM. See also *Homosexualism and Homosexuality.* During the Golden Age of Greece, six hundred years before Christ, the poetess Sappho encouraged young women on the island of Lesbos to appreciate beauty and affection, and, in the worship of Aphrodite, to develop mutually erotic relationships. Erotic practices between women became known as sapphism or (more often) as lesbianism, and a woman taking part as a lesbian. Encouragement by another person, often combined with loneliness and with a fear of heterosexual relations, seem important factors in a woman becoming a lesbian.

The Biblical view of lesbianism contrasts sharply with that of the ancient Greeks, who extolled it as admirable. The Bible describes it as sinful in the sight of God. However, Scripture draws a second distinction—between God's approach to lesbianism and to a lesbian. It is the difference between his attitude to sin and to a sinner: he abominates sin, but he loves a sinner. Christians sometimes find it difficult to learn these distinctions. They may be misled by the increasing publicity ("education") that any sexual relationship between consenting adults is acceptable. Alternatively, they may allow loathing of the sin to extend into disdain for the sinner.

The Biblical approach to lesbianism exemplifies the complementary bad and good news of Christianity. The bad news is the "the wrath of God is revealed from heaven against all ungodliness and unrighteousness of men" (Rom. 1:18ff.) Male homosexuality and lesbianism are indicted; so also are the proud, boasters, unmerciful, and not only those who do these things, but those who take vicarious pleasure through them. The good news is the gospel of Christ, which is the power of God to save all who believe and turn from their wicked ways. This includes those who have relations with their own sex. "Such were some of you," wrote Paul to the Christians at Corinth, "but ye are washed, but ye are justified in the name of the Lord Jesus, and by the Spirit of our God" (I Cor. 6:9-11).

NEIL YORKSTON

LIBEL. See *Slander.*

LIBERALISM, ETHICAL. See also *Conservatism, Ethical.* Derived from the word "liberty," liberalism means to free or loosen from restraint. The term has been used in different ways at different times, however, to signify freedom from different things. In early modern history (1500-1789), for example, liberalism favored the individual against the system (church, state or feudalism). In the twentieth century, liberalism calls on the system (government, organized labor, social agencies) to free the individual. The earlier variety stressed laissez-faire (q.v.) and political egalitarianism, to promote the interests of the middle class. Contemporary American liberalism advocates social control and economic egalitarianism, to benefit especially the "disadvantaged" and certain minority groups (cf. *Liberalism, Political*).

Liberalism considers itself the champion of people, of freedom, relativism, tolerance, and openness to change. It stresses rights and self-expression. While liberalism does not condone violence, it "understands" violence as a "natural reaction" to unjust conditions. Liberals also tend to oppose war and to regard police activities skeptically.

On the personal level, liberals believe that ethical questions are to be decided by the individual alone, without reference to codes. This opens them to the charges of antinomianism (q.v.) and anarchism (q.v.).

On the social level, liberals are environmentalists. They rely on changing conditions to change men. They apply ethical terms such as "justice" and "injustice" to situations, although those terms are undefined. The ultimate goal may be unknown; the direction unsure; the measure of progress toward it, undetermined. Nevertheless, liberals believe that a given project is not a stop-gap, short-run expedient, but a concrete, positive benefit.

Liberals are found under diverse labels. They can be naturalists or supernaturalists, rationalists or irrationalists, emotionalists or not, and so on. Leading liberals have often criticized Communism (q.v.). In turn, Communists have lashed at liberalism for not being radical enough.

Liberalism views conservatism as being: rigid; dogmatic; legalistic; repressive; unwilling or unable to change; and more mindful of laws and vested interests than of human needs. Conservatism, on the other hand, regards liberalism as: ignoring principles and ideals, which are wise summaries of experience and valuable future guides; lacking an organic view of life; improvising overmuch; and disparaging of responsibility, self-discipline, law and order.

A number of factors currently encourage ethical liberalism. Ethical philosophers are increasingly disinterested in practical moral questions. They hold such discussions to be trivial, resembling "advice to the lovelorn." Hence, they concentrate on high-level meta-ethical questions. Further, some influential modern ethicists designate ethical judgments as purely emotive, subjective, or meaningless. The libertine's outlook is as good as the saint's. Another theme is that of rights, taken to extremes, to justify all sorts of promiscuity. Regardless of religous command or moral precept, any action is acceptable if "authentic," performed "in the right spirit." Again, a liberal, while seeking to establish social relationships, often tends to isolate personal ethical acts. He judges each by its immediate, discrete circumstances.

Representative recent ethical conservatives are Brand Blanshard, *Reason and Goodness*, New York, Humanities; Jacques Maritain, *Moral Philosophy*, New York, Scribner; and Eliseo Vivas, *The Moral Life and the Ethical Life*, Chicago, Regnery. Recent ethical liberals include Joseph Fletcher, *Situation Ethics*, Philadelphia, Westminster; Bertrand Russell, *Religion and Science*, New York, Oxford University; and Charles L. Stevenson, *Ethics and Language*, New Haven, Yale University.   GEORGE S. CLAGHORN

LIBERALISM, POLITICAL. See also *Conservatism, Political.* Political liberalism refers to that tradition of modern political thought seeking a society which will maximize the free self-expression and self-fulfillment of the individual. It is opposed to all laws, traditions, and beliefs which it believes to be restrictive of human freedom. It is associated with an attitude of mind which values liberty, is receptive to change, pragmatic in its methodology, and distrustful of tradition.

The origins of political liberalism reach back to the Renaissance transition from the medieval to the modern world. Challenging traditional concepts of authority and order, liberalism espoused a philosophy of individualism (q.v.) and libertarianism. In religion, liberals emphasized the priesthood of the believer as opposed to the authority of the church. In economics, liberals advocated the open-market system as opposed to mercantilist and protectionist trade policies. In philosophy, liberals tended toward empiricist epistemology and utilitarian ethics. In politics, liberals opposed absolutist regimes and argued for constitutional restraints on government and the protection of individual liberties.

The growth of political liberalism is associated with the industrial revolution and the political demands of the newly emergent bourgoisie which challenged the traditional privileges and authority of the landed aristocrats and remnant feudal interests of the seventeenth century. Thinkers such as John Locke (1632-1704) argued that government was the creation of a social contract designed to keep order which, in turn, would make more secure the innate rights of individuals to life, liberty, and the pursuit of property. Liberals argued for representative institutions in government to help insure that government would be responsible to those people who established it. Within the framework of representative government, toleration of differing political viewpoints and freedom of expression were to be allowed insofar as the chief test for truth was viewed as its ability to compete and survive in a free marketplace of ideas.

During the seventeenth century, a still commonly accepted Christian heritage placed limitations on the individualism and anti-authoritarianism implicit in political liberalism. Thus, while John Locke was an empiricist and spoke of the rights of the individual, he nonetheless justified his political philosophy on the grounds of a higher moral law and insisted that the rights of man are innate. By the eighteenth century, however, political liberalism had become explicitly rationalistic, anti-religious, and utilitarian. Jeremy Bentham (1748-1833) and the French encyclopedists are illustrative of this shift to a more radical liberalism. In the eighteenth century, such political liberals generally shared in the belief that man is essentially rational and good. Evils in society were ascribed to a lack of knowledge or to environmental conditions which thwarted mankind from realizing his true nature. Hence, the technical progress of the industrial revolution was equated with moral progress as it offered man the opportunity to remake and control his environment. Education, social reform, the spread of technology, and freedom against arbitrary government would bring about a new age qualitatively different from that of all past epochs in human history.

The nineteenth century saw several fundamental shifts in liberal thinking. John Stuart Mill (1806-1873) argued that happiness must be measured *qualitatively* as well as quantitatively when seeking to define the political good. Thus, while Mill considered himself a utilitarian in the Benthamite tradition, he sought to reintroduce moral measures which would suggest the uses to which human freedom should be put. Mill also advocated changed strategies in liberal tactics which he felt were necessary if the working classes were to achieve the same benefits of social emancipation as the middle-classes had already won against the old aristocratic and feudal classes. Mill believed that the particular plight of the working classes could be relieved by turning to the positive use of government power to combat social and economic threats to the freedoms of the working classes. This positive concept of the state is quite distinct from the very limited and negative role envisioned for the state by earlier liberal thinkers. Hence, the distinction is sometimes made between classical (or early) liberalism and the revisionist liberalism of Mill and those who follow him in advocating positive and interventionist uses of government power for social goals. (In the USA many individuals calling themselves political conservatives actually espouse the principles of classical liberalism.)

The basic philosophical assumptions of political liberalism have increasingly come under attack in the twentieth century. World wars, economic depressions, and racial strife have brought into question the optimism of the liberal's faith in the inevitability of progress. Freudian psychoanalytic theory and behavioral research have raised serious doubts that man's basic motivation is rational.

From the viewpoint of Christian theology, the political liberal's concern for human freedom may be said to correspond to the concept of the *imago dei* within each man, which suggests that each man's individuality possesses certain inviolable rights. The political liberal's concern for social and political reform may be matched to Christian insistence on the pervasiveness of sin, suggesting that no socio-political order has achieved perfection and that change is always necessary in the pursuit of justice. On the other hand, the political liberal's concern for freedom often implies a model of a purely atomistic society composed of autonomous individuals responsible to no authority other than their own self-interest. The political liberal's concern for social justice often neglects the reality that justice can never be achieved without order, nor order without authority.

John Dewey, *Liberalism and Social Action*, New York, Putnam, 1963; Leonard T. Hobhouse, *Liberalism*, New York, Oxford, 1964; Guido de Ruggiero, *The History of European Liberalism*, translated by R. G. Collingwood, Boston, Beacon, 1959; Harold J. Laski, *The Rise of European Liberalism*, London, Allen & Unwin, 1958; J. Salwyn Schapiro, *Liberalism: Its Meaning and History*, New York, Van Nostrand-Rheinhold, 1958.   PAUL B. HENRY

LIBERTY. See *Freedom.*

LICENSE. See also *Antinomianism; Situational Ethics.* License is here understood not as "formal permission from a constituted authority" to act by or to deviate from the rules and conventions of a particular society, but as willful departure from basic moral and Biblical precepts.

In the Greek NT the word *aselgeia* probably most closely designates what Christian ethics means by license. *Aselgeia* is nearly always translated "lasciviousness" in the Authorized Version and as "licentiousness" (q.v.) in the Revised Standard Version (Mark 7:22; Rom. 13:13; II Cor. 12:21; Gal. 5:19; Eph. 4:19; I Peter 4:3; II Peter 2:7, 18; Jude 4). In other versions, "indecency," "lewdness," "sensuality," or "lustfulness" characterize such behavior.

Jesus and Paul agree that the source of licentiousness is man's unregenerate nature (Mark 7:20-23; Gal. 5:19-21). According to William Barclay, license (*aselgeia*—licentiousness) is "the action of a man who is at the mercy of his passions and his impulses and his emotions, and in whom the voice of calm reason has been silenced by the storms of self-will." At worst, license "is violent, insolent, abusive, audacious ... completely indifferent to public opinion and to public decency" (*Flesh and Spirit*, Nashville, Abingdon, 1962, pp. 31-33).

Early Christians confronted a licentious and vice-ridden world in which sin was condoned "as natural and normal." Some misunderstood the nature of Christian liberty proclaimed by the Apostles and adopted antinomianism (Gal. 5:13; Eph. 5:3). But NT ethics (q.v.) rules out all "debauchery and licentiousness" (Rom. 13:13; II Cor. 12:21). To love the God of purity and morality is to keep his commandments (I John 1:5-7; 5:3).

From early Gnosticism (q.v.) (Jude 4,

RSV) to twentieth-century "situationists" various movements have arisen advocating a "spontaneous and unprincipled morality." Such license is a revolt against both legalism and the disciplined liberties of Biblical Christianity (I Cor. 6:18-20; 10:31-33).

DELBERT R. ROSE

LICENTIOUSNESS. Licentiousness, from the Latin *licentia* (freedom, license), means a state of unrestrained behavior, lawlessness, or immorality. More precisely, it connotes lewdness and unchaste behavior. Lasciviousness, lustfulness, and wantonness are proper synonyms. In the NT "licentiousness" translates *aselgeia* ("lasciviousness" in KJV), the exact derivation of which remains obscure. Apparently the distinctive element is the highly provocative and unabashed nature of the behavior. Lightfoot comments that "a man may be *akathartos* (unclean) and hide his sin; he does not become *aselgēs* (wanton) until he shocks public decency."

Jesus expressly mentioned licentiousness among the many evils generated in the heart of man (Mark 7:22, 23). Man apart from God approves and practices sexual license, illustrated graphically by Sodom and Gomorrah (II Peter 2:7). The whole pagan world in the first century was licentious, according to Paul (Eph. 4:19; II Cor. 12:21). In his list of the "works of the flesh" Paul includes this deplorable trait (Gal. 5:19). He exhorts the Romans to "wake from sleep" and to conduct themselves as men of light and not as men of darkness, who practice reveling, drunkenness, debauchery, and licentiousness (13:13). Christian teaching calls for personal purity, which in turn obligates the Christian to exercise discipline over his body, especially the sexual drive. The body is to be a servant of the mind and spirit under Christ (cf. I Cor. 9:24-27). One is called upon to offer his body a living sacrifice, holy and acceptable to God (Rom. 12:1). Furthermore, this purity demands

respect for the body and personal worth of every individual and for society as a whole.

WILLARD H. TAYLOR

LIFE, SACREDNESS OF. See also *Abortion; Feticide; Image of God; Infanticide; Lynching; Medical Ethics; Senility.* The Christian view of the sacredness of human life rests upon the vigorous affirmations of the whole of sacred Scripture. It is rooted in the revelation that man was uniquely created by God, a crowning part of the created order, and that God created man in his own image (cf. *Image of God*). It is also based on the Biblical account of God's redeeming work, which declares the care of the living God for man, and the reconciling, searching love which offers life to man, ultimately in Jesus Christ, in the place of death, the rightful judgment of God upon man the sinner.

The sacredness of life is affirmed from the very outset of Scripture. The sin of Cain, the first-born son of the first parents was murder (Gen. 4:1-16), and because of this God intensified the curse already laid upon man for his disobedience (Gen. 4:11). Despite the mark of God upon Cain, as a man bearing God's image and sign no man should slay him (Gen. 4:15). Because of violence which filled the earth, God destroyed the race (Gen. 5, 6), preserving but a small remnant with whom he made covenant to sustain and protect life in the future (Gen. 8:21-22; 9:1-17).

In the continuing self-disclosure of God to Israel, the dignity of man's life is affirmed both by negation and affirmation. The sixth commandment of the decalogue commands man not to kill (Exod. 20:13; Deut. 5:17). Beyond this, the law, in numerous commandments, makes positive provision for the life of man, even to the temporary protection of the manslayer in cities of refuge (Num. 35:9-34).

Jesus reaffirmed the injunction of the decalogue and the affirmations of the OT regarding life (Mark 12:28-33) extending the judgment of God even to the spirit of hate (Matt. 5:21-22, 43-47). Moreover, in fulfillment of his divine mission he everywhere affirms the life of man, whether in his teaching or in his healing ministry, Mark 3:1-5 providing a classic illustration of the union of the two in Jesus. Beyond all else that he did, Jesus affirmed that he came to give his own life for the life of man (Mark 10:45), that in himself, freely offered to all, was the very gift of life, a particularly strong witness of the Fourth Gospel (see John 5:26; 10:10; 11:25; 14:6; etc.).

This latter truth brings us to a recognition of the duality in the Biblical understanding of life. Man is a body-soul unity, and the Scriptures speak of life at both of these levels, not infrequently in the same context. Not only in his teaching regarding a spirit of hate, but in his call to discipleship as well, Jesus warned that a man could save his life, and yet lose it (Mark 8:35ff.). Thus, although discussion of the sacredness of life is concerned first of all with corporeal existence, the inner existence of man in his freedom and in his own relationship to God, is always in view. This fact is also underscored in such texts as Deut. 8:3 and 32:47, where life is defined in terms of obedience to the Word of God. Ultimately, life is seen in responsible relationship to God and to man; thus, the Christian view permits no willful severance of man from life lived in these free and responsible relationships.

Two persistent issues—capital punishment and the permissibility of Christian participation in war—have constantly troubled Christian conscience. Is it right to take the life of a man as recompense for his own willful act of murder (cf. *Capital Punishment*)? The Bible seemingly allows capital punishment when justly decreed by due process of law. Another question is that of Christian participation in national conflict (cf. *Peace and War; Pacifism*), traditionally justified through a just-war theory appealing es-

pecially to Rom. 13:1ff. and to I Peter 2:13ff. Apart from the demonstrable futility of war and the complexity and perennial unrighteousness of international politics, it seems doubtful that the depth and breadth of the Biblical teaching of the sacredness of human life can be fully perceived where it is flagrantly and violently taken by Christian people.

The medical profession has long since avowed the sacredness of life from conception to death in the form of compassionate and expanding medical care. Nevertheless, scientific advance and the world wide population explosion (itself due in large measure to progress in medical care) have sharpened a number of issues in medical practice. For example, at the same time that abortions have been readily available and relatively safe, and therefore one possible safeguard against threatening population explosion, science has perceived how far back into the fetal stage the fetus bears the main signs of "life" characteristic of man. The issue is sharpened as medical science is able to detect malformation or other defects in the fetal stage. If life is more than bodily existence, but consists also in relationship, the Christian must be at least reluctant to make judgments upon sheerly physical indications—significant as they are for fullness of life.

Both Christian conscience and the medical profession have persistently rejected mercy-killing or euthanasia (q.v.). This practice is deficient in that its basic appeal (to compassion) fails to cope with the fullness and sacredness of life in its relationships.

The fact that medical skill now enables the prolongation of life, sometimes in an unconscious state for long periods of time, raises still other issues. How much care is due an unconscious and dying patient? Is it wrong to deny (say) extraordinary medical care when that care can quite possibly extend life for longer periods of time? Although it is wrong willfully to hasten the death of another, death is not the supreme evil, and Christian conscience must give regard to all factors constituting the "life situation" of the patient. A wise procedural question here is: Does this procedure offer a *reasonable chance* of an *appreciable duration* of *desirable life* at an *acceptable cost* of suffering? (Douglas M. Jackson, *Human Life and Human Worth,* London, Christian Medical Fellowship, 1968, p. 10). Whatever answers Christians give to these questions, it is clear that Scripture calls Christian conscience to continual care for others as for persons created in God's image and sustained by the loving care of one who as Creator, Lord and Judge of all men, ultimately holds the gift of life.

📖 John Murray, *Principles of Conduct,* London, Tyndale, 1957, pp. 107-122; Vincent Edmunds and C. Gordon Scorer (eds.), *Ideals of Medicine,* London, Tyndale, 1958; D. M. McKinnon (ed.), *Making Moral Decisions,* London, SPCK, 1969; Thomas Wassimer, *Christian Ethics for Today,* Milwaukee, Bruce, 1969, pp. 193-227.   ROBERT P. MEYE

LIQUOR TRAFFIC. See *Alcoholism; Prohibition; Temperance; Temperance Movements.*

LITERATURE. Literature, as preserved either in oral tradition or in written form, is the use of words in such a way as to invest them with permanent aesthetic worth. Writing may serve many purposes, worthy or unworthy, practical or fanciful; but writing can claim to be literature only by reason of its power to gratify man's artistic sense, his innate response to order and to meaning, his capacity to recognize beauty, not by reason of its gratification of his need or desire for information.

Though the literary value of a piece of writing is not dependent upon, nor derived from, its subject matter or purpose, yet certain topics and purposes are more likely to generate literary qualities than others. For the greater part of human history, it has been believed that the highest and most appropriate purpose of literature, as of other art, is worship. Certainly in Western literature, from Plato to the early nineteenth century A.D., the idea that the divine (as God, the gods, the Muses, or other supernatural identities) breathes into (inspires) the writer, and chiefly the poet (for his work is more elaborately artistic than prose), has been a persistent and often dominating view of literary creation. Though this view is less prevalent today, so modern a writer as Robert Graves still insists that all literature, knowingly or unknowingly, is a form of worship of the ancient Mother Goddess (see his *The White Goddess,* New York, Farrar, Straus, & Giroux). And Dylan Thomas declared that he wrote for the love of man and the glory of God. A Christian view of divine inspiration is best seen in the words of John Milton, notably in the first twenty-six lines of Book I, the first fifty-five lines of Book III, and the first thirty-nine lines of Book VII of *Paradise Lost.*

Although both prose and poetry can exhibit three major devices for arousing emotion—rhythm, sound, and imagery—poetry, because it employs these devices more intensively, has always been considered the primary form of literature. In Greek and Roman theory (the basis for literary criticism in the Western World), prose was considered largely utilitarian, a means of communicating information and thought—histories, philosophies, scientific treatises, and the like. As Thomas De Quincey puts it in his *Letters to a Young Man,* "All that is literature seeks to communicate power; all that is not literature to communicate knowledge." The "power" he refers to is a power to *move* the reader—not merely to inform him, but to alter his outlook, his sensibility, and (in consequence) his conduct. Matthew Arnold declares that all art affects conduct, be it ever so slightly. If, therefore, conduct is susceptible of being described as being either good or bad, all art (and chiefly literary art) is morally and ethically influential. There is no such thing as ethically neutral literature, for one's conduct will inevitably be altered by it, for better or worse.

To probe this thought more deeply it is necessary to comment on two primary elements in literature—indeed, in all art: content and form.

Content is, so to speak, what literature *says*. It is the paraphrasable content of a piece of writing, the part that can be expressed in other words without factual loss. It is the plot of *Hamlet* without the poetry and its rhythm, music, and metaphor. (Analogously, it is the melodic theme of the Ninth Symphony; it is the identification of the person or event depicted in a piece of sculpture.) Music and the visual arts may exist without paraphrasable content (that is, as "pure form"). Literature, because it uses words, which are inextricably associated with meaning, must possess content. (Modern efforts, as in the late works of James Joyce, to eliminate paraphrasable content, and to duplicate the condition of music, are too complex to be treated here.)

Form is that which is lost from *Hamlet* when one merely tells its plot. Form is a much more complex, subtle, and profound concept than content. As a result, the temptation is to oversimplify it, and to conceive of it as relating only to such important but merely exterior matters as whether a piece of writing is in the "form" of a play, novel, sonnet, or similar mechanical pattern. The truth is far more vital and interesting. Form is that which gives aesthetic pleasure, which gratifies the artistic sense; in short, that which gives literature its power to *move* the reader, as distinct from merely *informing* him.

One of the most interesting, as well as mysterious, features of form is that it appears to solicit its response from something innate within the human spirit, as well as from what may be termed "educated anticipation." As to the latter, the truth is clear: until the reader becomes sufficiently familiar with literature, he does not know what to anticipate; hence his pleasure is, at first, slight. When he develops, through reading, familiarity with the way literature works, he develops an "educated anticipation" which is gratified when what he expects to happen actually does. The sophisticated reader has, for example, experienced the effect of many poems written in the sonnet form. He has come to anticipate (as the neophyte reader cannot) the aesthetic effect of that form, and to enjoy it when the expectation is gratified. Unlike the desire for information (the content of a piece of writing), the desire for form is not subject to satiety. The more one reads, the more numerous and comprehensive become his "educated anticipations," and the more pleasure he is capable of deriving. This is a hallmark of true literature: that it can be read and re-read with pleasure; for its power is not chiefly derived from its gratification, through content (mere information), of the satiable condition of ignorance, but from its appeal to the insatiable desire for form. This is why a person will return to see a favorite play over and over, hear a favorite musical composition many times, read and re-read a favorite poem—even though he already knows "how it comes out."

But a deeper question remains: What is there innate in the human spirit that anticipates, and is gratified by, that which true literature (and all true art) provides? Probably, a sense of order, of meaning, and of purpose, moral as well as intellectual. To the Christian, these characteristics are implanted in man, and compose part of man's similarity to the "image" of God imparted to Adam at his creation.

The ethical significance of literature, therefore, derives from both content and form. Through form, it reflects the orderliness, meaningfulness, and purposefulness of creation (nature). Aristotle, whose critical theories have probably had more effect on Western literature than those of any other writer, declares that true art reflects nature as in a mirror, and high literary art always has a moral purpose (see his *Nichomachean Ethics*). Like his contemporary, Plato, Aristotle taught that man possesses a dual nature: a material body and "form," the latter being (at least as corporate Man) immortal and characterized by "reason," which is the image of the divine, and to which the form of literature appeals.

Through content, literature teaches directly (is "didactic") through ideas, the elucidation of ethical principles, exhortations to good conduct, and so forth.

In general, modern literature exhibits not the classical belief in cosmic order and in art as that which reflects (or should reflect) nature, but rather the "romantic" emphasis on individualism and the unique personal vision, emphases which have been prominent since the revolution of sensibility that occurred in the late eighteenth and early nineteenth centuries. Hence the familiar themes of fragmentation, alienation, rebellion, and despair in such modern writers as Camus, Joyce, Lawrence, Beckett, Sartre, Hemingway, Greene, Updyke, and many others. In T. S. Eliot the fragments are brought together to create a new and blazing Christian mosaic, formed through stylistic devices that have had a profound influence on widely diverse writers.

Contemporary emphasis on the inner man, and on the individual vision, has often produced a clearer vision of the nature of good and evil, of the burden of sin, and of the need for personal redemption than is presented by many contemporary theologians. Thus, by its power to inform and to move, literature continues to confront man with his own nature in the midst of his physical, moral, aesthetic, and religious environment.   CALVIN D. LINTON

LITURGY. See also *Mysticism*. In ecclesiastical literature the word "liturgy" (from the Greek *leitourgia,* used in both LXX and NT) refers to officially authorized forms and rituals of corporate worship, particularly those followed in celebrating the church's sacraments. Christianity's basic patterns of liturgy include Psalms, prayers of confession, thanksgiving, adoration, dedication and intercession.

By the sixth century A.D. the classic liturgical rites of Eastern and Western Christendom were formulated. Drastic liturgical reforms, however, were initiated by Luther, Calvin, and Zwingli on the Continent and by Cranmer in England. These new movements, though differing in many respects from each other, unitedly insisted on two things: the vernacularization of the church's worship services, and the Bible's authority in determining what the church should believe and practice. More radical views were propagated by Anabaptists and some Puritans, who opposed all liturgical forms, insisting upon "the free inspiration of the Holy Spirit in Christian worship." Some evangelicals and charismatics presently champion this viewpoint.

For over a century a liturgical revival and reform has been spreading across Christendom. By vernacularizing her rituals, increasing lay-participation, recognizing charismatic manifestations and the need for proclamation, Roman Catholicism has moved closer to Protestantism. Much of Protestantism has moved closer to Roman Catholicism's stress upon altar-centered sanctuaries, vestments, processions, and litanies. This liturgical change has both stimulated and been promoted by the ecumenical movement. Currently, numerous liturgists are experimenting with innovative musical forms and litanies.

Donald G. Bloesch, *The Reform of the Church,* Grand Rapids, Eerdmans, 1970.

DELBERT R. ROSE

LONGSUFFERING. It is so difficult to distinguish this term from patience that the translators of the RSV showed wisdom in dropping it entirely. From its components, one would estimate its meaning as denoting a drawn-out condition of suffering, as from an incurable disease or a deep sorrow. But actually in its usage it indicates a readiness to bear injury or neglect without retaliation, with no great stress upon the time element. The Greek word *makrothumia* means long temperedness. God exhibited this trait repeatedly in his dealings with the disobedient nation Israel. He showed his longsuffering by refusing to destroy a people who had broken the covenant bond, even though in righteousness he could not refrain from chastening them. The Lord Jesus manifested this quality by refusing to punish the inhospitable Samaritans (Luke 9:51-56), by hearing accusations against himself in silence (Matt. 27:12) and by refusing to meet reviling with counter reviling (I Peter 2:23). In his risen state his bearing is the same, despite the possession of all authority and power, permitting Saul to ravage his church until the chosen moment for interposing his self-revelation and transforming the persecutor into a loyal and obedient servant (I Tim. 1:16). In putting on Christ (Rom. 13:14) the believer receives the ability to clothe himself with this element of his Master's character along with others (Col. 3:12).   EVERETT F. HARRISON

LORD'S PRAYER. The "Lord's Prayer" comes to us in two versions—Matt. 6:9-13, Luke 11:2-4. Luke is briefer, omitting "Our ... who art in heaven," "Thy will be done on earth as it is in heaven," and "But deliver us from evil" (RSV) or "the evil one" (NEB). Three other variations do not substantially affect the sense. The concluding doxology is not original to either version.

In the most recent scholarly study Jeremias concludes: (a) that the shorter text of Luke is to be regarded as original in *length*, but that the text of Matthew is to be preferred in general *wording;* (b) that it was intended by Jesus not only as a *model* for proper prayer, but also as a *formula of recognition*, a distinguishing badge of his disciples; (c) that it was first intended as an *eschatological* prayer—that is, it was for use by those who were conscious that they were living in the last days, the expression of their faith and hope in the light of the imminence of the end. Hence the petitions: "Let your kingdom come (speedily)"; "Give us today the bread of tomorrow" (literally) —that is, "let us even now begin to share in the bread of the end time, the time of salvation, viz., the bread of life"; "do not bring us to the test," i.e., the last great trial which the faithful will have to undergo prior to the end; "do not let us fail that final test, preserve us from apostasy."

Ethical Corollaries. (a) The attitude and life of discipleship expressed in this prayer springs from a relationship of childlike trust between the disciple and God. He addresses God with the intimate word *abba* (Father), and thereby acknowledges his dependence on God to direct and provide (cf. Matt. 6:25-34). (b) The disciple affirms that his first loyalty is to God: his primary concern is that God should be given his due honor, that *God's* rule should be accepted by men, and that *God's* will not his own should be done (cf. Mark 14:36). Likewise, the later doxology gladly confesses that the whole life of discipleship begins, continues, and ends with God. (c) The eschatological orientation of the original prayer indicates that the true ethical life is lived from the perspective of the future and draws its nourishment from God's future purpose. Note the variant for "Thy kingdom come" in Luke's version: "May your Holy Spirit come upon us and cleanse us"; the power of the new age is the necessary presupposition for discipleship in the present. (d) "The only prior condition for the disciples' prayer mentioned by Jesus is a *readiness to forgive*" (Jeremias). Discipleship involves acceptance of and openness to others. Without this two-sided forgiveness discipleship is impossible (cf. Matt. 5:23-24, 38-45; 6:14-15; 7:1). (e) The prayer closes with a confession of weakness: the disciple does not ask to be spared from suffering, but to be preserved through it, recognizing that such suffering is an inevitable corollary to discipleship (cf. Matt. 5:10-12; 16:24).

📖 J. Jeremias, *The Prayers of Jesus,* London, SCM, 1967.   JAMES D. G. DUNN

LOTTERY. See *Gambling.*

LOVE. Agape-love is rightly described as "the centre of Christianity, the Christian fundamental motif *par excellence*" (Anders Nygren, *Agape and Eros,* Philadelphia, Westminster, 1953, p. 48). This estimate is supported by the entire Scriptures, but especially by the teachings of Jesus, Paul, and John.

The key NT word for love is *agapao,* the OT counterpart of which is *ah-hav'.* These words are used for human love, such as the love of man for woman (Gen. 29:18; Eph. 5:25), of parents for children (Gen. 37:3), and of men for each other (Isa. 20:17; Matt. 22:39). They are also employed to describe God's love for man (II Sam. 12:24; John 3:16) and man's love for God (Deut. 6:5; Matt. 22:37). In addition the NT uses *agape* for the Father's love for his Son, Jesus Christ (John 15:9), the Son's love for the Father (John 14:31), and the Son's love for man (John 13:1).

In view of this rich usage, *agape-love,* when used of God, man, or the Son of God, may be defined as a warm, affectionate devotion to and desire for its object, issuing in a genuine concern for the interests and activities of the beloved. *Agape* shares with *eros* of pre-Biblical Greek, which is not found in the NT, and with *philos,* which is found in the NT, the element of deep feeling. However, whereas *eros* is self-acquisitive, even in its highest Platonic form, with the "I" at the center, *agape* is self-giving, with the "Thou" at the center (I Cor. 13:5). And whereas *philos* often expresses feeling without understanding and without decision, *agape* suggests a volitional act based on a genuine appreciation of its object (John 21:15-17).

In spite of the commonality in personal usage which makes possible a general definition, the specific meaning and expressions of love will vary, depending on the subject and object. God's love for man will differ in some respects from man's love for God, and man's love for God will differ from man's love for his fellow man. Consequently, though all interpersonal love has a common core, it is dangerous to absolutize the characteristics of love, as do some.

The point of departure for understanding the Judaeo-Christian view of love is God's love for man, which is the origin and norm of all genuine love. Thus the Biblical view of love is essentially theological. As Nygren notes, the Scriptures give the same answer to the religious question, "What is God?" and the ethical question, "What is Good?" namely, love. God is said to love the Israelites, not because of their superiority, but because he loves them (Deut. 7:7-8). The supreme expression of this love is seen in its continuation in spite of Israel's harlotry (Hos. 3:1). In such instances, God's love is graciously unrelated to the merit of its object. It does not follow that the object is worthless, but merely that whatever value he may have, he is not deserving of God's loving action. God loves because God is love, and because He chooses freely to act in accordance with his being (I John 4:8).

In the NT God's *agape* is Christo-centric: it is most fully revealed in the loving life and the cross of Christ (John 15:13; Rom. 5:8; I John 4:9-10). God's affectionate concern is supremely expressed in the sacrificial giving of his Son for the pardon of all mankind and for the fullest realization of man's possibilities, both here and hereafter.

Christ not only reveals God's love but also mediates it. He mediates both the forgiving love of God and the gift of love through the Holy Spirit (John 15:9; Gal. 5:22; II Cor. 5:14). It is only when the Spirit of God becomes the indwelling, motivating force in human existence that *agape* is realized. Thus the love ethic is freed from a humanistic interpretation as mere good will or philanthropy. To love, as Moffatt points out, is to seek God's ends for human personality. It is solely through communion with God in Christ that such love exists.

Since Christ is the Divine love incarnate and therefore its revealer and mediator, the Christian love ethic must be derived from him as its model. His teachings and deeds are the yardstick for measuring love.

Jesus Christ saw no conflict between a God who loves and a God who judges. He realized that in the last analysis love is interpersonal and bilateral, and that experiencing the benefits of God's love requires a loving response by man. Such a response must be voluntary, for interpersonal love exists only within the context of freedom. If man deliberately chooses not to reciprocate God's love, the result is self-imposed separation from God and from life (John 3:16-21).

Christ is the model not only for God's love for man, but also for man's love for God. When Jesus urged that man love God with all his heart, soul, strength, and mind, he was doing more than quoting an OT teaching; he was describing his own relation to the Father (Matt. 22:37). This relation involved affectionate, undivided devotion issuing in radical submission to the Father. The result was a spiritual, joyful obedience to the Father's will regardless of the sacrifice. Thus Jesus' love for the Father was both internal and external. It included his disposition and intention, because it sprang up from the very depths of his personality. But it necessarily resulted in overt conduct pleasing to the Father. Jesus practiced the principle that to love God is to love God's law and to submit his whole being to the control of his Father.

Because Jesus was divine, he demanded the same kind of loving devotion and obedience owed to God. Thus Jesus rightly insisted that there be no divorce between love and obedience with regard to him and his commandments (John 14:15). He recognized that a legalistic type of obedience is possible without love but that there is no genuine love without obedience.

As regards man's love for his fellow man, Jesus also becomes the model and inspiration. In requiring man to love his neighbor as himself, Jesus is essentially reflecting the teachings of the old covenant (Matt. 22:39; Lev. 19:18). The genuinely new dimension of the love ethic of the new covenant is Jesus himself. Whereas the *nomos*-piety of the old covenant considered self-love the norm for loving one's neighbor, Christ ultimately insisted that his disciples love as he loved (John 13:34). This encompasses but also transcends the old commandment. Though this new commandment relates specifically to brotherly love, by extension it may be applied to all men, since Christ's love is all-inclusive.

Accordingly, Jesus extended the concept of the neighbor beyond the concentric framework of the old covenant to include all men in need, even one's enemies and those of other races (Matt. 5:44; Luke 10:29-37). They are to be loved because Christ loves them and as he loves them. For to love God in Christ is to love those whom he loves, and to view all men as having great worth. Moreover, this love is to include the whole man, not merely his soul. For just as Christ expressed God's love by dealing with the physical, mental, emotional, as well as spiritual problems of men, so must those who follow him.

In its expression, Jesus' love is a relative absolute. He was not bound by a *nomos*-piety which restricted love to compliance with a codal system. His "new wine" required doing what was good for man (Mark 3:4) and the redemptive work of the Father (John 5:17).

Therefore, any effort to absolutize or to codify the love ethic is doomed to failure, because it runs contrary to the spirit and life of Christ. The command to love is always absolute, but its particular outworkings are related to concrete situations. Consequently, a Christlike love ethic requires the divine wisdom to analyze situations so as to determine how to express such love in varying circumstances.

Above all, the love ethic which uses God in Christ as its source will differ radically from *eros*-piety. It will not use God or men as means to the egocentric ends of success, health, and prestige in the present age, or even heavenly bliss in the age to come (I Cor. 13). Rather the love ethic will make God and men ends in themselves. It will express affectionate devotion to God for the sake of fellowship with God and to men for the sake of God and men. It is this love ethic which is indispensable and supreme, because it is the purpose of all else, including faith and hope (I Cor. 13:1-3, 8-13).

📖 E. Brunner, *The Divine Imperative,* Philadelphia, Westminster, 1937; J. Burnaby, *Amor Dei,* London, Hodder, 1938; M. J. D'Arcy, *The Mind and Heart of Love,* New York, World, 1945; C. F. H. Henry, *Christian Personal Ethics,* Grand Rapids, Eerdmans, 1957; T. Kagawa, *Love, The Law of Life,* Chicago, Winston, 1929; S. Kierkegaard, *Works of Love,* New York, Harper, 1962; C. S. Lewis, *The Four Loves,* New York, Harcourt, 1960; J. Moffatt, *Love in the New Testament,* London, Hodder, 1929; R. Niebuhr, *Love and Justice,* New York, World, 1957; G. Quell and E. Stauffer, "Love," *TWNT,* Vol. I, Grand Rapids, Eerdmans, 1963.   ROBERT A. TRAINA

LOYALTY. See *Faith, Royce, Josiah.*

LUST. The Biblical terms usually rendered by this word are generally used in a negative sense. The translations vary, but they carry the meaning of "passionate desire," especially "sexual desire," or sometimes, "desire for worldly pleasure." Greek ethicists treat the subject in some detail as a moral issue.

In the OT. "sensuous sexual love" may be imputed to all the Israelite's (Ezek. 33:32) or to foreign nations (Ezek. 23:5).

In the NT *epithumia* is used positively on occasion as in Luke 22:15 and II Thess. 2:17, but its negative connotation is more frequent. In such cases it may be rendered "desire." In Matt. 5:28 the term is used specifically of "sexual desire." Jesus forbids a man to look at a woman "in lust." In the NT epistles the meaning is more precisely fixed, e.g., as a description of sexual passion. Paul warns that God may give up the unrighteous "in the lusts of their hearts to impurity" (Rom. 1:24) and admonishes Timothy to "shun youthful passions" (II Tim. 2:22). "Passion and evil desire" should be put to death (Col. 3:5) and "fleshly lusts" avoided (I Peter 2:11) because such produce corruption and evil in the world (II Peter 1:4: 2:10).   WATSON E. MILLS

LUTHERAN ETHICS. Luther's rediscovery of the gospel on the basis of a fresh examination of the Scriptures, specifically the Epistles of Paul, led to a renovation of his ethical teachings. Major expositions are his *Large Catechism* (1529), his interpretation of Christ's *Sermon on the Mount* (1532), and his *Commentary on the Epistle to the Galatians* (1532). His lesser writings include *The Freedom of the Christian Man* (1520), *Treatise on Good Works* (1520), *On Usury* (1519 and 1524), *Obedience to Government* (1521 and 1523), *On Marriage* (1522 and 1530), *On Military Service* (1526), *On Ecclesiastical Vows* (1530). Luther's *Table of Duties,* consisting of selected quotations from Scripture, and appended to Luther's *Small Catechism,* was an important means of ethical instruction for the young in Lutheran congregations for four centuries.

1. Ethical Teachings of the Lutheran Confessions

Theological principles of Lutheran ethics were formulated, and sometimes given immediate applications, in the *Augsburg Confession* and its companion, the *Apology*, in such articles as "The New Obedience" (Art. VI), "Order in the Church" (Art. XIV), "Church Usages" (Art. XV), "Civil Affairs" (Art. XVI), "Faith and Good Works" (Art. XX). In addition to his catechisms, the Lutheran Confessions also include Luther's *Smalcald Articles* (1537), important for the understanding of Lutheran formulations of theological ethics. The articles of the *Formula of Concord* (1580) were adopted by the Lutheran Churches in response to their struggles to maintain the proper distinction of Law and Gospel for the sake of preserving the sum of the gospel, the doctrine of the justification of the sinner before God alone by grace, on account of the person and work of Jesus Christ, to be accepted in faith, and lived in santification. Articles IV ("Good Works"), V ("Law and Gospel"), and VI ("The Third Function of the Law"), are basic theological formulations on these topics. Article XII sets forth the churches' ethical judgments toward Rome as well as forward the Enthusiasts and Anabaptists.

2. Ethical Instruction Derived from the Lutheran Confessions

Lutheran ethical instruction centers upon the proper response of the new being in Christ living in his forgiveness. It is, therefore, a study of the Christian ethos (q.v.) in answer to the question: What sort of person ought a Christian to be? (II Peter 3:11). Lutheran ethical instruction must maintain simultaneously the context of "old aeon," of fall-redemption-fulfillment, for its theological perspective.

The Lutheran Confessions, specifically the Formula of Concord, Art. IV, V, VI, assert that the view of the Christian man as simultaneously sinner and saint, that is, as a forgiven sinner who continues as a sinner to live in the forgiveness of God, so that the whole life of the Christian on earth is a life of repentance, is properly understood and explicated by rightly dividing the Word of Truth according to its application as Law and Gospel. Christian ethics is thus seen as the effort to understand Christian living in terms of the fitting truths or dynamics of Law and Gospel. Other axial Biblical terms provide a parallel context: sin and grace, enslavement and liberation, fall and restoration, creation and fulfillment.

It is the Lutheran confessional understanding that "strictly speaking, the law is a divine doctrine which reveals the righteousness and immutable will of God, shows how man ought to be disposed in his nature, thoughts, words, and deeds in order to be pleasing and acceptable to God, and threatens the transgressors of the law with God's wrath and temporal and eternal punishment" (F. C., S. D., Art. V, 17). Since the entire will of God, encompassing all aspects of his creation, is thus seen as Law, it is also correct to say that all descriptions of the human condition or explanations of the relation between God and man under his judgment are expositions of the Law. The function of the law is never seen apart from the fallen condition of man, so that "everything that rebukes sin is and belongs to the law, the proper function of which is to condemn sin and to lead to a knowledge of sin" (Rom. 3:20; 7:7).

"The Gospel, however, is that doctrine which teaches what a man should believe in order to obtain the forgiveness of sins from God. . . . Everything which comforts and which offers the mercy and grace of God to transgressors of the law strictly speaking is, and is called, the Gospel, a good and joyous message that God wills not to punish sins but to forgive them for Christ's sake."

The Lutheran understanding of the Christian man as simultaneously sinner and righteous, or as forgiven sinner, so that the righteousness of the Christian is always a gift of God received in faith and bestowed in every moment on account of the merit and Person of the Mediator, rejects both sin and righteousness as ontic characteristics or substantive possessions of the nature of man. As sin is above all else rejection of God and rebellion against his sovereign majesty, so forgiveness and acceptance is a gracious gift of God.

Since the sanctification of the Christian is never an ontic quality of his nature, he needs the instruction of the Law in order to know which work or service is pleasing to God. In this respect, the Christian no longer lives *under* the Law (legalism), nor *above* the Law (antinomianism), but *in* the Law. That is the congruence of the will of the Christian with the will of God in sanctification. The Christian never asserts any kind of moral or ethical autonomy. Christian discipleship is obedience to God's will.

3. Social Implications of Lutheran Ethics

Since the Lutheran understanding of Christian ethics is governed by the promise and hope of the Christian faith according to the revealed will of God, and not by descriptive or prescriptive norms devised after philosophical reflection upon prudential considerations of human and historical realities, it would follow that there can be no specially Christian ethics of government, business, education, science, or ethics of a particular calling both uniquely valuable and distinct from another one. Luther's axiom, "the work is what the person is," denies the attribution of intrinsic values to particular callings. Whatever his calling or his competence, his fidelity to his Lord's will in his calling renders the Christian's calling as a service to the neighbor acceptable to God.

While such an understanding of Christian ethics rejects normative descriptions or prescription for a social order, the affirmation is retained that God wills social order and not chaos. Lutheran ethical teaching asserts the existence of "orders of creation," such as marriage, the family, or the community, and all that pertains to their maintenance. These orders of creation provide the historical context for the Christian's response in his sanctification to the gift of faith, so that the Christian understands himself as living between two aeons. He is both a pilgrim on earth and a citizen of the heavenly commonwealth.

Rejecting any political, economic, or sociological monism as uniquely appropriate for the Christian life in this aeon, Lutheran ethical teaching recommends maximal accommodation to uncongenial structures on the principle that it is better for the Christian life to endure a lesser evil than to strive for a worse remedy, but always under the principle that God is to be obeyed rather than men. This is a rejection of any form of tyranny on principle and is also expressive of the basic interest that an imperfect society is better than social chaos.

Werner Elert, *The Christian Ethos*, Carl J. Schindler, tr., Philadelphia, Muhlenberg, 1957; Donald R. Heiges, *The Christian's Calling*, Philadelphia, Board of Publication of the United Lutheran Church in America, 1958; Albert G. Huegli, ed., *Church and State Under God:* A Re-evaluation of Church-State Relations with Special Reference to Emerging Trends in Political and Social Life, St. Louis, Concordia, 1964; Harold J. Letts, ed., *Christian Social Responsibility.* Vol. I *Existence Today*, Vol. II *The Lutheran Heritage*, Vol. III *Life in Community*. Philadelphia, Muhlenberg, 1957; Paul E. Meehl, ed., *What, Then, Is Man.*, St. Louis, Concordia, 1958 and 1971; Helmut Thielicke, "Theological Ethics," Vol. I *Foundations*, Vol. II *Politics*, William H. Lazareth, ed., Philadelphia, Fortress, 1966 and 1969; Gustav Wingren, *Luther on Vocation*, Carl C. Rasmussen, tr., Philadelphia, Muhlenberg, 1957.   RICHARD KLANN

LYING. See also *Truth; Truthfulness.* Lying is the intention to deceive when we are bound to speak or do the truth. God's

Word is truth (Hos. 10:13; Amos 2:4; Rom. 3:4; I John 2:4, 22), whereas Satan is the author of lies (John 8:44), manifesting them through man's sinful nature (Col. 3:9-10) by filling man's heart to lie (Isa. 59:13; Acts 5:3). Men think lies are warranted when they are seeking security (Isa. 28:15-17), concealing hatred (Prov. 10:18), and fearing man (Isa. 57:11). Lying leads to discord (Prov. 6:19), betrayal (Prov. 14:25), mankind's ruin (Isa. 32:7), and worthlessness (Prov. 12:19).

Concealment of truth does not necessarily constitute lying. Man is not always obligated to reveal everything (cf. I Cor. 2:11). He can even refuse to answer. The Hebrew midwives (Exod. 1:19-20) and Samuel (I Sam. 6:1-2) did not lie; they were not obligated to disclose information to their questioner or observer. Intentionally leading an aggressor astray in battle or by censorship is not lying: one is not obligated to divulge military intentions (cf. II Kings 6:14-20). Neither is deception through ignorance or mistake a lie.

Scripture forbids lying (Exod. 20:16), calling it sin (Ps. 59:12) and an abomination to God (Prov. 12:22). God never lies (Num. 23:19) nor ever approves lying. Lying never brings about good (Rom. 3:5-8). Man should trust in a sovereign and almighty God rather than in lies. Lies and liars do not escape God and his punishment (Acts 5:4; Ps. 101:7; Prov. 19:5, 9; Rev. 21:8). Their salvation is in Christ alone.

Righteous men hate lying (Prov. 13:5), continually ask God to remove it from them (Ps. 119:29), and speak truth, for their old nature has been put off (Eph. 4:25; Col. 3:9-10).   RALPH H. ALEXANDER

LYNCHING. See also *Life, Sacredness*

of. Lynching is an act of mob violence, generally defined as the willful and summary execution by several or more persons of another for alleged offense against law or custom, without benefit of due process of law. Lynching is, from every perspective, inimical to Christian conscience. The wresting of justice from lawful authority, violation of man's personal rights and freedom, and above all, willful taking of the life of another are all condemned by Scripture.

Despite this, lynching has occurred within as well as without the boundaries of Christendom. Although widely practiced in frontier America, one of the most shameful chapters in the history of lynching is the white violence against Negroes before, and especially after, the Civil War. Such organizations as the Ku Klux Klan lawlessly intimidated Negroes throughout the South—and did so in the name of law and order based upon a doctrine of white supremacy which, despite frequent appeal to Scripture, has no basis in the Bible. Fairly reliable data record the lynching of between three and four thousand Negroes between 1882 and 1951.

Christian ethics is bound to draw a lesson from Scripture here, namely, the relationship of sowing and reaping, that violence begets violence (Gen. 9:6; Matt. 26:52; Rev. 13:10). Although black resistance to lynching was generally impossible in earlier times, the history of lynching has provided a fateful precedent and court of appeal for the descendants of former victims living in the ghettoes of urban America. Moreover, the fact of violence in national life on even broader scale in present time continues to be nurtured with images out of a violent past.   ROBERT P. MEYE

M

MAGNANIMITY. In a famous passage in the *Nicomachean Ethics* Aristotle describes the man who possesses great souledness or highmindedness (Lat. *magnanimitas*) as a man who has goodness in the highest degree, is well aware of that fact, and hence has justifiable self-esteem which expresses itself, in part, in a preference for giving benefits rather than receiving them.

Descartes *(The Passions of the Soul)* discusses *generositas* as the equivalent of the medieval *magnanimitas,* which he defines as meaning justifiable pride. *Generositas* he defines as that which causes us to esteem ourselves at a just value.

Spinoza, picking up Descartes and Aristotle, identifies *generositas* with goodness and defines it as "the desire by which, from the dictates of reason alone, each person endeavors to help other people and to join them to him in friendship" (*Ethics,* Bk. III).

Some Christian writers, dissatisfied with the Aristotelian concept of magnanimity for obvious reasons, have sought to relate magnanimity to the NT idea of longsuffering, that Christian grace by which we endure the wrongs and evil-doings of others without retaliation or anger. Thus "love suffers long" (I Cor. 13:4)—i.e., is magnanimous.

Magnanimity as a Christian virtue is that enlargement of self which sees events and actions in the perspective of God's eternal purposes. It includes longsuffering (q.v.) the acceptance of the insignificant as divinely significant, rejoicing in others' success, being generous in praise and attention and money, being large hearted towards God and man.   CULBERT G. RUTENBER

MALICE. Malice is the desire to inflict injury or suffering on someone else. The OT recognizes that such ill-will persists (Ps. 41:5; 73:8), sometimes taking the form of spiteful glee over someone's ill fortune (Ezek. 25:6) and sometimes of violent vengeance (Ezek. 25:6; as our legal term, "with malice aforethought"). Malicious defiance can be directed to God (Ps. 139:20), but is especially pernicious in the form of a lying witness against innocent men (Exod. 23:1; Deut. 19:16; Ps. 35:11; Dan. 3:8). In the NT too, the Lord Jesus is aware of the evil intent of his opponents (Matt. 22:18; here the word is *ponēría*), and the Apostle John recognizes the power of malevolent criticism (III John 10).

But the most common word in the NT for malice is *kakía*. Pagan Greek thought had invested it with negative connotations, as though it designated mere moral deficiency or lack of virtue. But in the light of the gospel, *kakía* came to mean positively "the evil which men do to each other," either generically (I Cor. 14:20; I Peter 2:16) or in single acts (Act 8:22). Since it came upon men as a punishment, the result of their breaking off fellowship with God (Rom. 1:28f.), it is among men, too, a force which destroys fellowship. Therefore *kakía* stands in several lists of vices intolerable in the Christian community, a permanent element in the oral catechism of the churches (Eph. 4:31; Col. 3:8; I Peter 2:1; James 1:21; cf. Titus 3:3; I Cor. 5:8), usually in connection with the command to "strip away, throw off." The positive command which follows is to put on kindness, compassion, forgiveness, or sincerity.

RICHARD T. FOULKES

MAMMON. "Mammon" (*mammōnas,* meaning wealth or property, and probably of Aramaic usage) is not the name of an idol but was often personified to refer to valued possessions. Comparative Semitic roots possibly provide evidence of Arabic and Syriac origin and have a meaning of gift or bounteous. The term apparently was current enough among Greek speaking Christians so as to require no translation (e.g.,

Luke 16:13; Matt. 6:24; cf. Luke 16:9, 11). Mammon is also personified by the author of II Clement (6:1). In what is generally recognized to be part of his Sermon on the Mount (q.v.), our Lord warns his followers against love of things, i.e., material possessions, over love of God. Jesus speaks in terms of the slave and his master. A slave was to be totally devoted to his master. It was therefore impossible for him to serve a second master while properly serving his first or rightful one. For the Christian, Jesus Christ is Lord, Saviour, and Master. The believer in Christ loves his Lord and Master because he puts his full trust in him for pardon, peace, and salvation. We love him because he first loved us! The Christian cannot, therefore, acknowledge the lordship of Christ in his life and then love and serve (slave for) a foreign lord, for example, things that one can possess, sell, manipulate, use, and hoard. One is to continue serving first the kingdom which consists in righteousness, joy, and the Holy Spirit. Things, i.e., material goods and necessities, will be provided as blessings of God to be enjoyed and used to the glory of God. Jesus' warning against Mammon reminds us to "fear, love, and trust in God above all things" (Luther).   JOHN F. JOHNSON

MANAGEMENT. See *Corporate Responsibility; Industrial Relations.*

MAN, DOCTRINE OF. See also *Fall of Man; Image of God; Sin.*

1. *Modern Optimistic Interpretations.* The dominant stream of modern Western thought, building on Greek Aristotelianism and medieval Thomism, revitalized by Renaissance humanism, culminated in the optimistic idealism of the nineteenth and early twentieth century. It viewed man as a "spark" of the Absolute Spirit, inherently immortal, ethically good or at least morally neutral, and destined by evolution to self-perfection and complete union with the divine.

2. *Contemporary Pessimism about Man.* Much contemporary thinking about men roots in pessimistic views (Feuerbach: *Der Mensch ist was er esst*—"Man is what he eats"), and receives characteristic expression in the despair of modern existentialism (Heidegger: man is "being unto death," or Sarte: "Man is a useless passion").

3. *Biblical Realism as the Basis for a Doctrine of Man.* Biblical man is neither a complicated machine or ephemeral value nor a divine being needing only time and opportunity to achieve perfection. Rather, he lives in daily tension between the tragic perversion of what might have been and the glorious foretaste of what may be and, indeed, what in God's good grace will be.

The Christian revelation at its center points to the doctrine of creation, according to which man was "made a little lower than God" (Heb. 8:5), crown of the entire creative process (Gen. 1:26; 2:3), declared "very good" by God himself, entrusted with possession of the earth (Gen. 1:31), instructed to rule over other earthly creatures (Gen. 1:26; Ps. 8), and commanded to subdue earth and its resources for human well being (cf. Gen. 1:28-30), the Biblical foundation for a Christian philosophy of science and modern ecology). In sum, by contrast with the rest of earth's creation, man was made to be godlike (Gen. 1:26, 27) for personal companionship with God (Gen. 3:8).

Just as the Christian doctrine of man as created is today frequently interpreted in terms of a naive, unrealistic optimism, so the Christian doctrine of man as fallen was in an earlier day often misunderstood in a radically pessimistic way. Biblical realism sees man as a finite creature who conquers nature only in a struggle that ultimately ends in death. Man is frail "flesh," weak in power over the elements (Isa. 51:12) and, especially as expressed in Pauline writings, morally weak (Col. 2:11). Man has become a rebellious sinner who defiles the image of God, is enslaved to moral turpitude, divinely condemned for his sin, alienated from God, from fellow men, and from himself, without power to reinstate himself into right relationships. Even so, fallen man retains signs of the divine image which distinguish him from the animal (Gen. 9:6; James 3:9), enable him to know right and wrong (Rom. 2:14, 15), mark his life as of infinite value, and enable him to receive grace and good from the hand of his heavenly Father.

4. *Biblical Man as Community.* By creation man is a social being. God made man for fellowship with himself, and woman to provide human fellowship for man (cf. Gen. 2:18-25). The intimate circle of family love afford a prototype for all humanity.

Only Biblical revelation adequately undergirds the equality of all races. All human beings are descended from one and are interrelated, thus sharing equally in the image of God and in benefits of his creation (Acts 17:26). Although man by the fall lost this perfect relationship and became Spiritually alien, humans remain one race of one blood (Rom. 5:12ff.).

While woman by creation shares equally with man the image of God, Biblical woman and man are not on that account identical. Each has a distinctive divine calling, a role mutually supplementary to the other and of equal honor. The curse upon women (Gen. 3:16) to serve and suffer must be understood as penal and descriptive, not definitive of essential womanhood (cf. *Women, Status of*). Biblical passages restrictive of women are in some instances directed to a particular historical situation (Cor. 7, and presumably I Cor. 14:34, 35), in other cases explicitly derived from the order of creation (II Tim. 4). The Biblical teaching supports a kind of "headship" for man; man is the head of the family in the sense that he is the presiding executive in an earthly miniature of the heavenly society of perfect love.

Sex in itself, as God's creation, is good; far from reckoning sexual intercourse as evil or a result of the fall, it is Biblically commanded of the believing partners in marriage (I Cor. 7:4, 5). Sex is a legitimate and even necessary right of husband and wife; to omit it or neglect it is to defraud the other of what is rightfully his (or hers) by creation. Scripture condemns only perversions of sex.

5. *Constituent Elements.* Biblical vocabulary does not yield a precise scientific psychology. The meaning of terms varies from context to context, and different terms are frequently employed as loose synonyms. The Scriptural emphasis, moreover, is relational, tending to describe the human psyche from a functional rather than from an ontological viewpoint.

Man is derived from the ground and shares with the beasts a physical body of flesh. Especially in the NT, the "flesh" and "body" depict the moral weakness of man and in Paul occasionally describe the sinful nature of man. Always, however, the context excludes any intent to consider the physical body of itself sinful. Man also is derived from above with soul or spirit infused at creation. Bultmann's claim that man does not *have* a body, but *is* a body, accords only with certain Scriptural emphases; man *is* also a soul and in some contexts can be described as *having* a body.

According to both OT and NT man is more than physical body (Eccles. 12:1; Ps. 16:4ff.; 17:15; 49:15; 73:30; Phil. 2:22-24; II Cor. 5:6-9). The soul is generally presented as the seat of life and consciousness, viewed in conjunction with the body. Man may thus be said either to have a soul or to be a soul. The spirit is the same seat of life and consciousness regarded distinct from the body. Ordinarily, the Scriptural formula is that man *is not* a spirit (unless disembodied); but he *has* a spirit (I Cor. 2:11). The body is not an inferior part of man eventually to be sloughed off so as to free the spirit, but integrally essential to man's being. Human existence as disembodied soul or spirit is incomplete and undesirable. Complete redemption means not disembodied spirit (II Cor. 5) but resurrected body. This wholeness of man, with stress upon the body, is distinctive in the Biblical doctrine of man's makeup. The center of this unity is the heart. Contrary to wide contemporary usage, the heart in both OT and NT is not merely the seat of emotions (more often referred to the liver—Prov. 7:23, the kidneys—Jer. 11:10, or the bowels —Isa. 16:17). By contrast, the heart is more frequently designated the seat of the intellect (Matt. 9:4). It is also the focal center of the will (cf. I Cor. 4:5). These aspects are viewed in Biblical psychology not as separate faculties but as functions of one integrating ego, the heart as the center of human personality.

6. *Origin of the Soul.* No clear statement of Scripture indicates the precise time and manner in which the unity of man's immaterial and material being is attained. The pre-existence view, according to which God created souls in a pre-incarnate state, later assigning one each to man's body (sometimes defended Biblically by reference I Sam. 2:6; Job 1:21; Ps. 139:15), was declared heretical and no major Christian group any longer holds it. Creationism, or that God creates each individual spirit as he joins it to its body, is held by the Roman Church and most traditional Reformed theologians. Lutherans and most contemporary evangelicals prefer the traducian view, which regards the immaterial aspect of men as inherited. Though not insisting that it is directly taught by Scripture, they maintain that it offers fewer difficulties and best accords with Biblical data. Additional arguments may be drawn from such passages as Heb. 7:9, 10, and the inheritance of sin and bodily and other characteristics of the whole man.

Still less clear than the derivation of the soul is the time at which the soul is united to body (creationist view) or the body soul becomes truly human (traducian view). Generally the assumption is made that the life of the spirit begins at conception with the beginning of the body.

7. *Man's Destiny.* Man's ultimate destiny is glorious beyond all human measure (Eph. 4:20-21). Created by God a little lower than himself, man fell to awesome depths of sin; but in God's grace, through Christ's ministration by the Holy Spirit man is transformed into the perfect (moral) likeness of God. Man's final end, therefore, is even better than his beginning.

Although death registers sin's final victory over man, even death's sting is withdrawn from the believer. Entrance into the very presence of Christ brings unalloyed joy and compensates for the terror of the dissolution of man's body (Phil. 1:24). Only a fearsome expectation of final judgment (Heb. 10:27, 31) awaits those who have rebelled against God and the good in unbelief.

Man's ethical destiny is complete conformity to Jesus Christ—the God-man. Man's goal, therefore, is not a selfish realization of his own potentiality or some abstract perfectionism; rather he achieves his ultimate good as his loving heavenly Father in infinite wisdom works out for and in him what is best for him as a unique individual (Rom. 8:28). Like Christ, man is to be motivated by an absorbing passionate love for God and for his fellow men as revealed in Scripture (Matt. 23:34, 35).

Man's social destiny is participation in a universal kingdom of love in which he will know God and enjoy his fellowship forever; and, in knowing and enjoying God, will also be freed to know and enjoy his fellow men.

Physical creation, now functioning in apparent disorder as a divine provision of the appropriate environment for fallen, sinful mankind, will be transformed into a perfect world—the proper habitation for redeemed men. In this way God will demonstrate a perfect "worldly" society and reveal that the evil on earth is not inherent in creation but arises out of the evil will of man and is necessarily judged by a holy God.

📖 Both general works in OT and NT Biblical theology and standing systems of theology are of primary importance. See among older monographs: James Laidlaw, *The Bible Doctrine of Man*, Edinburgh, T. and T. Clark, 1905; Franz Delitzsch, *A System of Biblical Psychology*, Grand Rapids, Baker, 1966; James Orr, *The Christian View of God and The World*, Grand Rapids, Eerdmans, 1947. especially chapters on "Sin and Disorder"; and more recent works such as G. C. Berkouwer, *Man: The Image of God*, Grand Rapids, Eerdmans, 1962; Karl Barth, *Christ and Adam: Man and Humanity in Romans 5*, T. A. Smail, tr., New York, Harper, 1957; *Church Dogmatics*, Vol. III, Part I: *The Doctrine of Creation*, G. W. Bromiley and T. F. Torrance, ed., Edinburgh, T. and T. Clark, 1958; Emil Brunner, *Man in Revolt*, New York, Scribner, 1939; E. DeWitt Burton, *Spirit, Soul and Flesh*, Chicago, University of Chicago, 1918; David Cairns, *The Image of God and Man*, New York, Philosophical Library, 1953; Walter Eichrodt, *Das Menschenverstandnis das Alten Testaments*, K. and R. Gregor Smith, trs., Chicago, Allenson, 1956; John Murray, *The Imputation of Adam's Sin*, Grand Rapids, Eerdmans, 1959; Reinhold Niebuhr, *The Nature and Destiny of Man: A Christian Interpretation*, New York, Scribner, 1949; Russell Philip Shedd, *Man in Community*, Grand Rapids, Eerdmans, 1964; C. R. Smith, *The Biblical Doctrine of Man*, London, Epworth, 1951; Thomas Torrance, *Calvin's Doctrine of Man*, Grand Rapids, Eerdmans, 1957; Walter Zimmerli, *Das Menschenbild im A.T.*, Munchen, Kaiser, 1949.

KENNETH S. KANTZER

MANICHAEISM. See *Gnosticism*.

MARCUSE, HERBERT.

As a neo-Marxist social philosopher Herbert Marcuse (1898-   ) has been influential in rise of the New Left. He was born in Berlin and emigrated to USA in 1934. A student of modern political thought and life, he criticizes advanced industrial society in both East and West for creating needs to which it enslaves men. Government, education, mass media (q.v.), industry, "law and order," all repress liberty by determining the forms of modern life. This "establishment" must be broken by revolution (q.v.) if a new society is to emerge without war, poverty, pollution and overproduction. Utopia is now technologically possible.

📖 H. Marcuse, *One-Dimensional Man*, Boston, Beacon, 1964; *Essay on Liberation*, Boston, Beacon, 1969.   ARTHUR F. HOLMES

MARITAIN, JACQUES.

Jacques Maritain (1882-1973) was an influential French, Roman Catholic, Neo-Thomist philosopher. He was baptized into the French Reformed Church. After his marriage to the Russian Jewess, Raissa Oumansoff, the Maritains were converted to Roman Catholicism in 1906. Maritain immediately began an intense study of Thomas Aquinas' *Summa Theologica* in which he found support both for his rejection of positivism and materialism as well as his affinity for philosophical realism. Maritain's academic career began in 1914 as professor of philosophy at the Institut Catholique in Paris. During the war years, he taught at Columbia and Princeton as well as the Pontifical Institute of Medieval Studies in Toronto. After 1945, de Gaulle appointed him to serve as French Ambassador to the Vatican, and from 1948 to his retirement in 1953, he taught again at Princeton. He was also active in the Second Vatican Council.

The foundations of Maritain's ethics lie in both his metaphysics and his epistemolgy. Metaphysically, following Thomas the *good* can only be properly defined in terms of God and his purpose for all created beings who share in the essence of being-itself. The lopsided emphasis of existential subjectivism as well as the nearsighted perspective of objective positivism can be overcome only when the subject-object dualism (Cartesianism) is approached from the vantage point of God who knows me as subject. Similarly, the knowledge of God (and consequently myself as well) involves intuition, reason and revelation. There is, therefore, a natural order of things each with its own gradation of being and purpose. There is an ascending scale to God. "The concept of existence," says Maritain, "cannot be detached from the concept of essence . . . at that instant the intellect says (in a judgment), *this being is* or *exists* and at the same time (in a concept), *being.* . . . To say *that which exists* is to join an intelligible to a super-intelligible; it is to have before our eyes an intelligible engaged in and perfected by a super-intelligibility" (*Existence and the Existent,* pp. 24-25, 34-35). Negatively, evil is defined as "neither an essence nor a nature nor a form nor an act of being—evil is an absence of being . . . the privation of the good that should be in a thing" (*Saint Thomas and the Problem of Evil,* p. 1).

Although Maritain is highly critical of modern anthropocentric humanism, and finds its sources in Luther, Descartes, Rousseau, and Kant, he would substitute an "integral humanism" which he describes as theocentric. "Such a humanism would recognize all that is irrational in man, in order to tame it to reason, and all that is supra-rational, in order to have reason vivified by it and to open man to the descent of the divine into him" (*The Range of Reason,* p. 194). He proposes no utopian scheme but does define the political structure of this "integral humanism" as "a genuine democracy" (ibid., p. 198). Maritain was not optimistic that Christian regeneration will be able to bring about the moral and spiritual transformation of the world. He has been highly critical of younger Roman Catholic theologians, i.e., Küng, Schillebeeckx, and Metz, for a compromising stance before secular anthropocentric humanism.

▭ Jacques Maritain, *Existence and the Existent,* New York, Pantheon, 1948; *Moral Philosophy,* New York, Scribners, 1964; *The Range of Reason,* New York, Scribners, 1952; *The Responsibility of the Artist,* New York, Scribners, 1960; *True Humanism,* Geoffrey Bles, 1946.

DONALD M. LAKE

MARRIAGE. See also *Common Law Marriage; Concubinage; Monogamy; Polygamy.* Marriage is an exclusive lifelong bi-unitary community of fidelity or troth between husband and wife sealed in physical intercourse. In marriage "a man leaves his father and mother and joins himself to his wife, and they become one body" (Gen. 2:24). And Christ added: "So then what God has united, man must not divide" (Matt. 19:6).

Although physical intercourse is important, troth is the key concept in marriage. Obedience in marriage to the central love-command means fidelity to one's partner. Troth involves loyalty, trust, devotion, reliability: a husband can count on his wife, and she on him. Without masks or pretenses, husband and wife grow together and strengthen the bond of love (troth) between them. "Wives, give way to your husbands, as you should in the Lord. Husbands, love your wives and treat them with gentleness" (Col. 3:18, 19; cf. Eph. 5:22-33; I Peter 3:1-7).

Marriage is between one wife and one husband. Polygamy does not refer strictly to a husband having many wives, but to a husband involved in many marriages. And that is impossible. One cannot be joined in the fellowship characteristic of marriage with more than one woman. The Biblical norm is monogamy.

In marriage the husband is the head of the wife (cf. Gen. 2:18; I Cor. 11:3, 7-9; I Tim. 2:13; Eph. 5:23). Headship does not mean that in every detail the husband leads or decides. The husband is to take the lead in setting the religious direction of the marriage, its meaning, goals and purposes. Once the basic question is settled as to which vision of life is going to norm activities, who decides and leads in the day-to-day affairs of the marriage depends on the persons and situations involved.

If marriage is not considered a permanent trust for life, it is in permanent crisis. If the "freedom" to leave is regarded as a real option, it becomes a specter which haunts the marriage. Consequently, there is not the requisite freedom to develop an authentic relationship. Only within the bonds of troth is a marriage truly free. Such a troth relationship is not an automatic gift but requires attention and devotion. And since marriage is not a human invention or convention, neither is marital troth subject to the arbitrary whims of the partners. Husband and wife live under God's word of troth for marriage and are duty-bound to live by this norm.

Troth in marriage involves the becoming of one body in many ways. Intercourse is required in many matters: economic, aesthetic, educational, social, confessional, political, etc. Physical intercourse is the sealing or consummating of this troth-intercourse. Reducing troth to physical sex is to reduce human sexual intercourse to animal copulation. Physical intercourse is a good gift of the Lord which ought to stay in the marriage-room of the creation. If sex in principle can be had with anyone—so-called free love—without exception elements of selfishness, exploitation and insecurity enter in. (This is not to claim that intercourse in marriage is always perfect, but rather that physical intercourse loses its created place when indulged in outside of marriage).

"You shall not commit adultery" is an OT way of republishing the word for marriage and not a prohibition aimed at holding down man's evil sexual lusts. It emphasizes that only in marriage can physical intercourse be the totally joyful culmination of daily life activities together. Adultery is warned against because it breaks God's word of troth, destroys mutual freedom and leads to unhappy people. The word is a cryptic warning protecting marriage.

Physical sexual intercourse is not the divine sweet mystery of life without which one cannot be happy. Nor is it the inevitable fate of man as if the physical sex drive is an evil tyrant which just has to have an outlet in animal-like fashion. Sex is not candy, just a consumption article in which one tries a man or woman as he tries a ball point pen.

Troth is not physical sex, nor is it romance or sentiment, e.g., the "free love" of the romantics à la Schlegel's *Lucinde*. Although couples are usually mutually attracted because of psychic congeniality (romance), the tension-relaxation pattern of human psychic life means that the romantic feelings involved are in themselves too capricious and uncertain to serve as the dominant factor in marriage. If marriage were dependent on psychic feeling it would be an uncertain business.

Since marriage is a bond of moral troth in which two people marry (betroth) each other before the Lord, it may not be considered either basically a legal (civil) or ecclesiastical institution. Even though in God's plan marriage is made serviceable for and enriched by beginning a family, a marriage is not a la traditional Thomist doctrine a legal institution whose "essence" is its natural purpose of procreation. It is not, whether conceived sacramentally or legally, a "remedy for sin." Further, even if sanctioned by civil or canon law, it is not a contractual agreement giving two persons the right to each other's body à la Immanuel Kant.

The roles of the state and church, although important, are external to the troth relationship itself. In more recent times by means of a marriage license (and bill of divorce) the state, concerned to safeguard marriage, simply acknowledges the life (or death) of a marriage. If the couple are in Christ, they seek the blessing and support of the cultic worship community. A minister does not marry a couple; he only acknowledges that in their vowed promise God marries them. A wedding ceremony is the rite by which a couple, seeking support and sharing joy, publicly pledge their troth in the presence of God, friends, family, church, state, and enter marriage.

Marriages can be broken in as many ways as they can be built. Adultery covers all the ways in which infidelity in marriage can take place. Due to the structure of marriage, infidelity of various kinds usually leads to infidelity on the physical level. Since adultery—the breaking of troth—is simply wrong, there are no grounds for marriage breakdown (cf. Matt. 5:32; 19:9; Mark 10:11-12; Luke 16:18; I Cor. 7:10,16).

Not every infidelity need foster and eventually lead to total marriage break-up. Every husband and wife has been unfaithful in diverse ways and in various degrees. He who looks lustfully at a woman, says Christ, has already committed adultery with her in his heart (Matt. 5:28). However, even in cases where infidelity leads to physical intercourse outside of marriage, divorce ought not to be automatic. A spirit of forgiveness should rule. There should—as in the case of any marital difficulty—be repeated, concentrated efforts by various outside parties to heal the marriage.

But sometimes the marriage continues to flounder and over a period of time it dies. There is prolonged total marriage breakdown. In such cases the state acknowledges the fact and grants a divorce (q.v.). Such a bill is simply the legal recognition that the bond of troth in marriage no longer exists.

In its subjective realization a marriage, affected by sin, can often be a caricature of what it ought to be. Then God's word for marriage becomes a judgment to man. Obedience to the norm of troth in contrast leads to blessing. In Christ a marriage can futher deepen in meaning, and take its place in the Kingdom of God. Then Paul sees in the intimacy, tenderness and troth of the husband-wife relationship a comparison to the relationship of Christ and the church (cf. Eph. 5:21-33).

Derrick S. Bailey, *Sexual Relations in Christian Thought*, 1959; Emil Brunner, *Divine Imperative*, Philadelphia, Westminster, 1947; Helmut Thielicke, *The Ethics of Sex*, 1964; Edward Westermarck, *A Short History of Marriage*, New York, Humanities, 1926.   JAMES H. OLTHUIS

MARX AND MARXIST ETHICS. See also *Communism; Capitalism.* Karl Heinrich Marx (1818-1883), revolutionist, prime leader of modern socialist and communist thought, was born in Trier, Germany. He studied at Bonn and Berlin, receiving his Ph.D. in philosophy from Jena University in 1841. His radicalism deepened during his student years. Economics and politics captured his attention. He determined to make them his lifelong study.

Marx began his writing career with a controversial newspaper at Cologne in 1842. The following year, he married and moved to Paris. There he met Friedrich Engels, a young German industrialist with background and outlook similar to his own. Engels became Marx's collaborator, patron, and closest friend.

In 1849 Marx settled in London, where he resided most of the rest of his life. Plagued by poverty, hunger, sickness, and bereavement, he was, nevertheless, a tireless researcher and prolific writer. He died in London.

All history, according to Marxism, is a struggle between two forces, the exploiters (bourgeoisie or capitalists) and the exploited (proletariat or workers). This will only cease with the destruction of capitalism (q.v.), elimination of capitalists, and the ushering in of the classless society. Prior to this, the poor will get poorer (law of increasing misery), the rich, richer (law of accumulation of capital), and the profit system will rob workers of just rewards (theory of surplus value). The golden age will come when private property (q.v.), bourgeois marriage, nationality, and religion are abolished. Marx thought the proletariat would accomplish this; Lenin counted on cadres of intellectuals. The state will control finances, education, production, and distribution. Peace and harmony will prevail.

Marxists consider ethics to be a reflection of class interest. If moral principles arise from the proletariat and promote communist goals, they are "good," otherwise, not. Marx held the class to be basic "substructure." Law, morality, and religion belong to the "superstructure." Every alteration in the substructure brings a corresponding change in the superstructure. Change conditions and you will change men.

Marx viewed religion as a tool of oppression, opium of the people. He repudiated conventional ethics and idealism for the same reasons. Marx said, the communists "preach no morality." Engels and Lenin continued the attack. In 1947, however, Zhdanov called for a philosophic reawakening. Stalin added impetus in 1950, contending the ethical superstructure could even modify the base, for the better. The outcome was a new moral code in 1961, which dominates contemporary Russian ethical thought.

"The moral code of the builder of communism" is a twelve-point platform. Included are devotion to the communist cause and the socialist motherland; conscientious labor; concern for public health; high sense of public duty; collectivism and comradely assistance; humane relations toward others, mutual respect; honesty, truthfulness, moral purity, modesty; family loyalty and concern; an uncompromising attitude toward injustice, dishonesty, and opportunism; friendship and brotherhood, intolerence of national and racial hatred; an uncompromising attitude to enemies of communism, peace, and freedom; fraternal solidarity with working people everywhere and with all peoples.

These norms are offered as the "golden foundation" of life. However, the necessary relationship between them and communism is not shown. In fact, they combine many noncommunist ideals with some patently Marxist doctrines. Class hatred is not forbidden. Fraternal solidarity presumably does not include capitalists, who are marked for extinction. "Peace" and "freedom" have communist definitions.

Marxist ethics has been criticized from a number of standpoints. For example, Marxists oppose practically all Western philosophies (except naturalistic materielism), but seldom from a philosophic standpoint. They refer to social structures and the Marxian theory as basic, and so are often said to have no real philosophy of their own. They appeal to "justice," yet do not regard it as a valid ideal. Traditional ethical concepts like punishment, responsibility, value theory, and love receive no extended treatment. Marxists spurn reform, thus opposing ethical meliorism (q.v.). Social rather than individual morality is discussed. The present is sacrificed to the future.

In China, Mao Tse-tung reigns as chief theoretician, Liu Shao-Ch'i having been purged. Major themes are contradiction (the unity of opposites); criticism, particularly self-criticism; the necessity of struggle; and the unity of theory and practice. Chinese philosophers grapple with the relation of Western thought, including Marxism, to their own rich heritage.

Marx saw man alienated from himself and his fellows by work, under capitalism. Although the task may be the same communism overcomes the alienation. Through submission to historical necessity (communism), the laborer finds fulfillment and freedom. Authority for the communist is expressed by Party pronouncements; they are "fact," "truth," and "science," not to be questioned. Despite these limitations, moral questions are being increasingly discussed in the Soviet Union. Several philosophic dictionaries published there recently may spur this activity.

↪ The works of Marx, Engels, Lenin, and Mao Tse-tung are available in many editions. Note especially the *Communist Manifesto* (Marx and Engels, 1848) and *Capital* (Marx, first vol. in German, 1867); John Lachs, *Marxist Philosophy: A Bibliographical Guide*, Chapel Hill, University of North Carolina, 1967); Isaiah Berlin, *Karl Marx*, New York, Oxford, 1963, ed. 3; Robert Payne, *Marx*, New York, Simon and Schuster, 1968; William deBary, ed., *Sources of Chinese Tradition*, New York, Columbia, Vol. 2, 1964; Richard T. DeGeorge, *Soviet Ethics and Morality*, Ann Arbor, University of Michigan, 1969; R. N. Carew Hunt, *The Theory and Practice of Communism*, New York, Macmillan, 1959, 5th ed. chap. VII; Eugene Kamenka, *The Ethical Foundations of Marxism*, New York, Frederick Praeger, 1962; *Studies in Soviet Thought* containes up-to-date reviews and articles on these topics. Note also works of Karl Kautsky, Ernst Bloch, and George Lukacs.

GEORGE S. CLAGHORN

MASS MEDIA. See also *Advertising; Censorship; Movies; Pornography; Propaganda; Secrecy; Television.* Mass media are the methods by which identical material can be communicated to people: notably the press and its modern extensions, motion pictures, radio, and television. The press, for centuries the only mass medium, played a key role in the development of Protestantism. The classic case for the freedom to publish was made not by a libertarian, but the great Puritan John Milton. Though he did not favor absolute freedom, he argued on theological and pragmatic grounds that truth is best served when publishing is controlled by neither church nor state.

Communications media are wholly consonant with belief in a God who is intelligent and self-revealing. Since God is Truth, truthfulness is the divine standard for all communication. Though ethically good in principle, the media in practice are finite and flawed by sin.

The media raise two basic moral problems: distortion of reality, and dehumanization of man. Distortion is most dangerous in news coverage (see below) but has important effects elsewhere. For example, television dramas constantly set in extravagant homes can lead to social disquiet by giving those with less material possessions a false image of how others live. On the other hand, a truthful representation can add to impetus for just social changes. As for dehumanization, blacks and other minorities once had little part in most media, except in specialized or caricatured roles. Moreover, the media, perhaps increasingly, glorify and trade upon violence and sex. Though experts differ on the influence of the media upon behavior and attitudes, even among children, there seems little doubt that these tendencies give direction to social behavior in the long run, and extend the range of what is considered acceptable. Social control of pornography is a long-standing press issue.

Politically, the media can be valuable in uplifting and unifying a people. But they can also add to totalitarian centralization of power. Even in free societies, concentration of media ownership in the hands of persons with a particular social status or ideology can similarly inhibit a free flow of ideas. The media also face potential influence from advertisers and pressure groups.

In the evolution of media from early printing to modern electronic systems, the apparent changes have been the growing size of audiences and the increasing speed of information flow. In the 1960s, communications theorist Marshall McLuhan cast new light on the special qualities of the electronic media, though his dictum that the medium itself is more influential than the content it conveys is far from proven. Related to McLuhan's theories on the electronic media is the growing impatience with or distrust of verbalization. For Evangelical Christianity, with its theology of the Word and its dependence on Bible-reading and preaching, this tendency could have an increasingly negative impact.

The importance of the media increases in modern culture, in part, because there no longer is a compact body of knowledge shared by all educated persons. Without a commonly understood tradition to explain man and society, and with increasing gaps among specialized fields of knowledge, journalism is necessary for social cohesion. Interpretative journalism and the spread of more objective information, or "news reporting," lie at the center of the media. For instance, libel law protects an individual's right to good reputation, while later development justifies printing of libelous material if it is truthful and devoid of malice. More recently, courts have stemmed pre-trial publicity about defendants to ensure an impartial jury.

Other issues are in the formative stages. One is the way in which the media themselves become news or influence what is news, rather than neutrally conveying it. Television's need for pictorial news has encouraged demonstrations to publicize grievances, and some argue that the presence of TV cameras influences events. Some suspect that suicides increase if news of previous suicides is reported prominently. Far worse, media have been accused of consciously staging or creating news events to be covered.

A final problem is the media's judgment on what constitutes news. One danger is that the public assumes that everything which is real or important is contained within the limited purview of the media. In a sense, if an event is not mentioned in important newspapers, it "never happened." The media tend to prefer the dramatic or amusing event, or the simplified two-sided conflict, to the subtle social trend. Official government acts, once the major source of change in largely stable societies, continue to receive inordinate coverage; such complex areas as religion were long neglected. Publicity-seekers learn the art of conforming to the unexamined assumptions of the media on what is worth reporting. The post-television generation has been exposed to news

through a medium of dramatic entertainment. Yet not all important developments are dramatic, or easily pictorialized.

📖 Bernard Häring, *The Law of Christ*, Vol. III, pp. 626-673, Westminster, Md, Newman, 1966; Kyle Haselden, *Morality and the Mass Media*, Nashville, Broadman, 1968; John Milton, "Areopagitica," 1644; Pontifical Commission for the Means of Social Communication, "Pastoral Instruction," Vatican City, May 23, 1971.

RICHARD N. OSTLING

MASTER AND SLAVE. See *Household Codes; Industrial Relations; Labor Relations; Slavery.*

MASTURBATION. Masturbation refers to sexual stimulation without a partner. The stimulation may or may not continue to orgasm.

Masturbatory activities occur early in life, often as early as the second year when the child discovers pleasurable sensations on touching parts of his body. Masturbation occurs frequently in adults, both male and female, especially when they have no regular sexual outlet.

During the middle ages, religious institutions condemned sexual activity other than intercourse between husband and wife with the express purpose of procreation, and regarded masturbation as sinful and perverse. Perhaps because compulsive masturbation often occurs in severe mental illness, physicians once considered masturbation the cause of the illness. The preponderance of current medical opinion, however, does not consider masturbation physically or emotionally harmful. Nor is it considered a symptom unless it becomes a compulsion beyond willful control. Medical authorities realize, however, that masturbation and the accompanying daydreams often result in conscious and unconscious guilt which may evoke anxiety or depression. Though most physicians do not in any way encourage parents to sanction masturbation, they also warn against an overreaction that condemns or threatens the child.

ARMAND M. NICHOLI II

MATURITY. Paradoxically, Bonhoeffer's *Mündigkeit* and Kafka's *Metamorphosis* come at a time that could signal the end of depersonalized man. But the Word of God alone brings the transforming power which can make men new and empower them for spiritual growth. Maturity (attainment of a goal) and transformation (source of attainment) are central themes of the gospel. James 1:14 exhorts "... let steadfastness have its full effect... be mature *(teleioi)* and complete. . . ." In Col. 1:28, Paul's concern is "... to present all men mature in Christ *(panta anthropon teleion en Christo)*." Paul affirms of Christians that "we all, with unveiled face, beholding in a mirror the glory of the Lord, are being changed *(metamorphoumetha)* into the same image from glory toward more glory; for this comes from the Lord who is the Spitit." A grammatical form of *metamorphoustai* appears three times in the NT (Matt. 17:2; Mark 9:2; Rom. 12:2; II Cor. 3:18). Paul continues, "Do not be comformed... but be transformed *(metamorphousthe)* by the renewal of your mind, so that you may prove. . . what is the good and well-pleasing and mature *(teleion)*." Christian maturity entails growth in both private and public arenas of faith.

JAMES D. STRAUSS

MEAN, DOCTRINE OF THE. See *Golden Mean.*

MEDIAEVAL ETHICS. See *Aquinas and Roman Ethics; Augustine; Ethics, History of.*

MEDICAL ETHICS. See also *Abortion; Heart Transplantation; Organ Transplantation.* As defined by *Dorland's Medical Dictionary,* "medical ethics are the rules or principles governing the professional conduct of medical practitioners." While historically the term ambiguously has included both medical etiquette and medical ethics, only the latter is in view here. By medical ethics the relationship of the physician to his peers, his patients, and the general public is intended, with stress given to the morality of medical relationships, procedures, techniques, therapies, and counsel.

Roman Catholic moral theologians and medical schools have devoted considerable casuistic argumentation to this subject. Catholic physicians have found a forum for discussion in both the National Federation of Catholic Physicians' Guilds (founded 1932) and the Guild of Catholic Psychiatry (founded 1948). Few Protestant theological scholars have written extensively here until the public debate of the past several years focused attention on the whole range of issues facing the medical profession. Evangelical physicians and dentists formed the Christian Medical Society (incorporated 1946) in large part to discuss problems of a medico-moral nature. Evangelical medical societies from most of the nations of western Europe and the Orient have met triennially since 1963 to present papers in conference fashion (Amsterdam, 1963; Oxford, 1966; Oslo, 1969; Toronto, 1972). In 1961 the American Medical Association established its Department of Medicine and Religion to foster discussion between doctors and clergymen on patient care.

Medical schools, particularly those with no religious affiliation, have been slow to sponsor formal courses in medical ethics. It is significant that Harvard Medical School founded the George Washington Gay Lectureship for this purpose in 1917; distinguished physicians, jurists, theologians and scientists have lectured annually. Only with the general public's ground swell of ethical concern during the past decade coupled with the various new and overwhelming medical procedures have medical schools inaugurated special courses or convened forums in order to focus the attention of the medical community upon them. One survey suggests that at least 40 percent of American medical schools now offer some form of formal discussion on medico-moral issues.

Codes of Medical Ethics. Concern for medical ethics is as old as recorded history. While not a formal code of ethics, the Mosaic hygienic laws evidence a revelatory concern for human health and welfare (cf. *Health Laws*). The Hellenic Asclepian cult joined mythology with medicine for moral prescription. Aristotle urged ethical inquiry: "the philosopher should end with medicine; the physician commence with philosophy."

With the Oath of Hippocrates (cf. *Hippocratic Oath*) (approx. 400 B.C.) medical ethics received its first important Western formulation. Eastern medicine can trace the Oath of the Hindu Physician back through the *Charaka Samhita* to a considerably earlier period (c. 1500 B.C.). Jewish medicine knew the Oath of Asaph by the sixth century A.D., while Maimonides added his extensive literature to Hebrew medical ethics during the twelfth century A.D.

Modern codes date from the ethical code for English physicians written by Sir Thomas Percival in 1803. From this stimulus the American Medical Association in 1846 first published its code of ethics. Recent codes of importance include the *Nuremberg Code* (1946-1949), the *Declaration of Geneva* (1948), the *International Code of Medical Ethics* (1949), the *Ethical and Religious Directives for Catholic Hospitals* (1955), and the *Declaration of Helsinki* (1962). These codes are by nature idealistic, giving the profession of medicine a moral frame of reference; their power is that of moral suasion, not legal enforcement.

Universal Principles of Medical Ethics. An analysis of these various codes reveals that at least seven distinct principles emerge which have universal appeal and form the basis for professional discussion: (1) *primum, non nocere* ("first of all, do no harm"); (2) the sanctity of human life; (3) the alleviation of suffering; (4) the sanctity of the physician-patient relationship; (5) the right to truth; (6) the right to informed consent; (7) the right to die with dignity. The first three principles largely apply to the physician; the last three essentially to the patient.

These principles can be found throughout the history of the various medical traditions. They are readily compatible with a thorough-going Christian ethic. Their application to particular cases may well be a cause for considerable debate and disagreement, both among medical professionals and Christian ethicists. To enumerate these principles is one thing; to provide the inner motivation which humanely and consistently translates these principles into daily practice is another. Unique to the Evangelical physician should be the compelling motivation which the Great Physician provides, both as ethical Model and abiding Presence.

The Church and Medical Science. Historically, the conflict between science and religious faith has had its counterpart confrontations within the healing profession. Christians in the early church continued Christ's healing mission toward bodily ailments (thus rebuking the Gnostic depreciation of the body). They established the first hospitals (q.v.) in the Western world which cared for the general populace. Clement of Alexandria, Theodore of Laodicea, and Eusebius, Bishop of Rome, combined theological reflection with medical practice.

Unfortunately, they also fostered significant controversies. Those Christian students who studied under Galen were excommunicated by church officials as followers of "pagan" medicine. Pope Innocent III forbade monks to practice medicine (A.D. 1212); the study of anatomy through human dissection was pronounced sacrilegious by Innocent IV (1248). Some Christians condemned the discovery and use of ether for surgical and obstetrical cases as being contrary to nature and maternal retribution (Gen. 3:16, "in pain you shall bring forth children"). But other Christians such as Sir James Simpson, familiar with theological casuistry, cited the account of Eve's creation ("and the Lord God caused a deep sleep to fall upon Adam," Gen. 2:21) as a merciful and pertinent precedent. In more recent times conflicts continue over faith healing, psychiatric illness and therapy, contraception, artificial insemination, sterilization, abortion reform, euthanasia, human experimentation and organ transplantation (cf. separate essays).

Indicative of the fresh approach religious bodies have taken more recently concerning the church's relationship to the healing sciences is the 1960 report of The United Presbyterian Church (USA), "The Relation of Christian Faith to Health." The Tübingen Consultation (1964), "The Healing Church," correctly acknowledges medical care to be within the mission of the church: "the specific character of the Christian understanding of health and of healing arises from its place in the whole Christian belief about God's plan of salvation for mankind." In addition, the treatment of the "whole man" has emerged as a needed emphasis, thus encouraging a larger concept of total patient care.

Medical Research and Future Ethics. Any review of current biomedical research is, of necessity, both awesome and overwhelming. Laboratory investigations and clinical experimentations combine to call in question many of the ethical conclusions of traditional medicine. Traditional principles, though useful in the past, appear to offer only fragmentary and tentative guidance before the onslaught of medical science's vast new cornucopia of discoveries. Experimentation with the aging process, organ regeneration, disembodied brains, animal-human chimeras, gender selection, etc., threatens Orwellian consequences. Modern man, having lost his innocence both in the Garden and at Hiroshima, is now confronted with questions which imperil his very birthright. Some areas of special concern:

a. *Cellular Experimentation.* One of the truly great discoveries of modern science was the uncovering in late 1953 of the double-helical shape of deoxyribonucleic acid (DNA)—the master molecule containing the blueprint of life. Finally biochemists could understand and explore at the most fundamental level of life the processes which govern genetic coding and cellular division. Further research has given man the potential means to control and to alter significantly our basic life processes. The possibility of "gene surgery" exists whereby DNA microsurgery (probably by radiation) might remove specific defects, or insert new coding. Consequently, the awesome prospect of biogenetic engineering would permit man to tamper with his own inheritance.

At this point more questions are raised than answered. Christians must ask whether or not this research constitutes a legitimate modern response to the Creation Mandate ("have dominion over... every living thing," Gen. 1:28; Ps. 8:6). Who will determine the ideal genetic profile of future man? Will future parents be denied their own natural fruits of conception if such offspring will not measure up to a predetermined prototype?

b. *Human Embryo Experimentation.* It is but a step from genetic inquiry and manipulation to embryo experimentation. Inovulation permits the surgical removal of unfertilized eggs from a woman's ovaries, their fertilization *in vitro* ("in glass"), and their reimplantation in the uterus. Artificial insemination (q.v.) (using either the husband's [AIH] or a donor's [AID] sperm) already permits egg fertilization. Efforts are being made to achieve fetal gestation outside the uterus—the creation of an "artificial womb." A sexual reproduction through genetic "xeroxing" might one day create innumerable, virtually identical, individuals (called "cloning" from the Greek word for throng). Already available for problem pregnancies is a technique for sampling the amniotic fluid (amniocentesis) in order to determine genetic disorders. Nearly seventy can be detected.

c. *Mind Manipulation.* Striking results for schizophrenia through drug therapy have already been achieved; as further research demonstrates the degree and interplay of electrical and chemical components in the brain, further behavior control will be possible. The electrical stimulation of brain sites can now trigger fantastic memory recall, pacify destructive aggression characteristics, and excite erotic "pleasure centers." Current research is focused on mood, memory, and intelligence quotients. Should future neurosurgeons or psychiatrists view the mind simply as matter to be manipulated, the political and military implications of such procedures will vastly exceed behavioral and sociological considerations. If thought control, mood control, and controlled amnesia or recall become possible, are they desirable? If human personality is to be preserved inviolate, what guidelines need to be established? Is it realistic to speak of "brain transplantation"? These questions, and many more, confront medical research and future man.

Obviously, many unnerving ethical problems face Christian thinkers. With modern medicine having already redefined death, Promethean man may have to redefine life. If evangelical biomedical scientists are to be a part of this new age, interdisciplinary teams of Christian scholars must provide a focus on a forum for any needed reinterpretation of traditional theology or reapplication of traditional ethics. The possible control of global man by unprincipled governments and military machines appears

to demand that international limits be placed on some of this research. The age-long paradox of the Parousia suggests that both a distant hope and present homework remain.

↪ Representative medical-ethical studies include: for Protestant studies, Vincent Edmunds and C. Gordon Scorer, eds., *Medical Ethics: A Christian View*, London, Tyndale, 1966 (Evangelical); Joseph Fletcher, *Morals and Medicine*, Boston, Beacon, 1954 (Situational); for Roman Catholic studies, Edwin F. Healy, *Medical Ethics*, Chicago, Loyola, 1956; Thomas J. O'Donnell, *Morals in Medicine*, Second Edition, Westminster, Md., Newman, 1960; for Jewish studies, Immanuel Jakobovits, *Jewish Medical Ethics*, New York, Bloch, 1959; for secular studies, Leroy Augenstein, *Come, Let Us Play God*, New York, World, 1968; for symposium results, Daniel H. Labby, ed., *Life or Death: Ethics and Options*, Seattle: University of Washington, 1968, Kenneth Vaux, ed., *Who Shall Live?*, Philadelphia, Fortress, 1970.

LEWIS P. BIRD

MEEKNESS. See also *Virtues.* The root idea of meekness is gentleness, humility and modesty. Meekness endures injury with patience and without resentment. Meekness does not indicate a deficiency in spirit or courage. The common idea that meekness implies such inadequacies as weakness, effeminateness or timidity is fallacious.

Aristotle regarded meekness as a mean between irascibility (hot temper) and sluggishness (apathy); hence, not a positive virtue but merely a balance between two opposite faults. In general, the quality of meekness is quite contrary to the spirit of Greek philosophy with its emphasis on self-confidence and self-assertion. Any approach to life that regards power as determining the course of reality ("might makes right"), as with followers of the ancient Thrasymachus or of moderns like Machiavelli, Hobbes, Nietzsche, or Marx, despises meekness as an evidence of weakness.

The example and teaching of Jesus Christ provide the true meaning of meekness (Matt. 11:29; II Cor. 10:1). The NT regards it not merely as a natural virtue, but as a Christian grace and one of the fruits of the

Spirit (Gal. 5:23). Like humility (q.v.) it described an inner attitude of complete dependence upon God and an ideal outer relationship toward one's fellows (Eph. 4:2; Col. 3:12; I Tim. 6:11; II Tim. 2:25; Titus 3:2; James 1:21; 3:13; I Peter 3:15).

Christians are exhorted to cherish meekness and to emulate Christ's example, especially in relation to one another. The meek man does not fight for his own rights or insist upon vindication of his personal honor. He does not repay in kind when injustices are done to him. His is not the spirit of retribution; instead, he commits himself and his cause to God and leaves vengeance with divine justice and mercy. Thus, meekness is not incompatible with legitimate self-regard, but it does not assert itself for its own sake. Meekness is the opposite of pride (q.v.), which is basically a reliance upon and assertion of one's self independent of God, and thus the root of sin.   RALPH E. POWELL

MELANCHOLY. See also *Meliorism; Pessimism.* Melancholy is a feeling of gloom or depression. It had settled over much of the ancient world into which Christianity came with "good news." Existentialist literature establishes a close alliance between melancholy and boredom. Both Kierkegaard and Heidegger make the point that one may be bored either with particular experiences or simply with one's self and one's being in the world. Paul Tillich said of Nietzsche, "In him the feeling of meaninglessness became despairing and self-destructive" (*The Courage to Be,* New Haven, Yale University, 1952, p. 143).

In the modern world many are "with it," or abreast of all the "in things," and yet they appear melancholy. Blaming "the system" is for some merely a means of escape—what Sartre would call an instance of "bad faith." Christian concern with contemporary morality cannot ignore either the socio-psychological or the existential and theological aspects of boredom. The whole gospel for the whole man within the totality of his cultural life must be addressed to those who suffer loneliness and anxiety. God in Christ comes to us with gifts of his Spirit which transcend our moods of disillusionment and apathy (Gal. 5:22; Rom. 14:17).   WILLIAM W. PAUL

MELIORISM. See also *Optimism; Pessimism.* Meliorism defines the moral condition of man to be neither as good nor as bad as possible. It tends to be an unstable position, for whoever advocates it finds himself driven by contrary evidence, now toward optimism, now toward pessimism. Ideas of progress and evolution brought optimism in their train, while twentieth-century breakdowns in morality have raised doubts about human perfectibility. Nevertheless meliorism appears attractive to realistic minds. Christian moralists have differed over the issues it raises, some contending that fallen man has wholly lost the image of God while others insist that remnants of the image remain.

DELBERT R. GISH

MENTAL HEALTH. See also *Psychology; Psychiatry.* The mental health movement began early in the present century largely through the efforts of Clifford Beers, a psychiatric patient who, after several hospitalizations, wrote a book exposing some of the objectionable practices in mental hospitals. Beers' book, titled *A Mind that Found Itself* (New York, Doubleday), became very influential in focusing attention on mental hospital reform. With a number of prominent physicians backing him, Beers established the National Committee for Mental Hygiene, the principal forerunner to today's movement. Contemporary efforts are aimed not only at improved patient care, but at greater understanding and sympathy for the mentally ill. A further objective of the movement is to discover ways of prevention and effective early intervention in mental illness at the level of family, school and community.

Recent emphasis upon mental health has evoked many efforts to define the concept. The term usually signifies the absence of disease, following the common medical model. Another concept using psychopathology as a reference point emphasizes maturity. By enumerating the objectionable characteristics of the immature person, a list of opposites may be compiled which describes a composite ideal of mental health. The resultant is likely to bear little resemblance to any real person.

Still another concept of mental health considers adjustment to environment. By this definition, conformity becomes the criterion. While such adjustment may reduce interpersonal friction and enhance an individual's acceptability to his fellows, it is likely to do so at the cost of creativity and to eventuate in mediocrity. Mental health is not synonymous with a statistical norm or mode.

Health is clearly more than adjustment to physical and social requirements. Apart from some perceived objective, human motivation never becomes activated, or else it undergoes atrophy. The ability to discern purpose in human life depends upon a satisfying interpretation of the universe and man's place in it. Such a construct must necessarily be philosophic, since a value-free science has neither the insight nor the means of achieving it to penetrate the meaning of existence.

An inward hunger for spiritual meaning has been a constant characteristic of human personality. Religion has tried in every century to satisfy this universal vacuum. Christian theism, by drawing upon historical and Biblical sources, has sought to mediate between seeking man and transcendental meaning. Most emotional disorders arise within the realm of values, from which a fact-gathering science is barred. Anxiety and guilt, indicators of maladjustment within personality, signify conflict and some threat to cherished values.

Any definition of mental health must take into account this need for intelligible meaning and a coherent world view, for without it, man lacks a basis for ethical conduct and inner poise. Freud acknowledged that religion possesses a philosophy of incomparable strength and consistency, one that exerts power over the strongest human emotions and that has successfully resisted severe criticism. This remarkable observation is not vitiated by Freud's reductionist depreciation of religion. The psychiatrist increasingly has come to recognize that his work lies in a dimension pervaded by religious values and that he must reckon with these values in directing his patients toward mental health.

📖 *Action for Mental Health*, New York, Basic, 1961, Ch. III; Orville S. Walters, "Have Psychiatry and Religion Reached a Truce?" *Christianity Today*, October 8, 1965.   ORVILLE S. WALTERS

MERCY. See also *Grace.* The Christian understanding of mercy grows out of Biblical usage, particularly the OT concept of *hesed*, "assisting faithfulness" (Bultmann). Thus mercy consists of acts done by God to man and by man to man, particularly within the circle of loyal commitment to God.

God's mercy is his faithful help to man in all his weakness and need. It is much broader than forbearance towards sin (cf. Ps. 6:4; 143:12; Isa. 63:7), although salvation is certainly an expression of it (Exod. 34:6; Luke 1:58; Eph. 2:4; I Peter 1:3; Titus 3:5). Forgiveness (q.v.) as such is usually expressed in the Bible with the vocabulary of sacrifice (q.v.) rather than of mercy.

The divine arbitrariness sometimes inferred from Rom. 9:15 is not present in the idiom of the original (Exod. 33:19) which implies God's absolute freedom to act mercifully, but not whim or disregard for man's moral intention (Paul Joüon, *Grammaire de l'Hébrew Biblique,* Rome, 1947, § 158 o). Since the covenant is defined partly by obligations which men are to meet (Exod. 20:6; I Kings 8:23; Ps. 103:11, 17; cf. Hos. 6:6 NEB, "loyalty is my desire, not sacrifice"), we may assume that God takes human actions seriously. By the same token, the divine openness does not mean that God regards sin lightly. Mercy and judgment are not in conflict, even as love and holiness together describe the essence of God's character.

In men, mercy denotes acts of compassionate kindness, such as that of the Good Samaritan (Luke 10:37) or the one who forgave a debt (Matt. 18:33). Such deeds are part of true Christian commitment, as Jesus stressed (Matt. 25:31-46; cf. James 1:27). They do not establish one's reconciliation with God, but flow from the personal renewal which such reconciliation effects. In spite of the covenant connections of mercy (OT *hesed*), the NT does not imply that man's mercy to man is to be limited to fellow-believers.

H. R. Mackintosh, *HERE 8,* pp. 455 f.; Rudolf Bultmann, *TDNT 2,* pp. 447-87.

STANLEY D. WALTERS

MERIT. See also *Good Works; Justification; Supererogation, Works of.* Merit concerns the worth or value of good works in earning a reward from God. Non-Christian religions generally stress the merit of man's actions, while Christianity emphasizes God's grace in Jesus Christ. Within Christianity, the concept of "merit" points to a fundamental difference between Roman Catholicism and Protestantism.

The merit of works was stressed by the Jewish legalists within Israel and by the Pharisees in Jesus' day. This emphasis reappears in differing ways in Pelagianism and Liberalism as well as in Semi-Pelagianism and Arminianism.

In connection with the medieval penitential system, the emphasis upon merit was developed by the Schoolmen who distinguished a merit of condignity (worthy of reward) and a merit of congruity (fit to be rewarded) and linked this to the church's "treasury of merit" and the sale of indulgences. The Council of Trent restated the Roman doctrine in the face of the Reformers' objections, though adding subtle distinctions. Rome acknowledges that grace is needed to enable one to perform good works, but these works are said to merit eternal life. Some saints are held to perform works of supererogation that the church can apply to others in need. The role of meritorious works stands out especially in connection with the sacrament of penance. One whose sin has led to the loss of the justifying grace received in baptism must regain this grace in the sacrament of penance through his own works of contrition and confession, and must perform works of satisfaction to cover the temporal punishments of his sin.

In repudiating this doctrine, Luther and Calvin emphasized that Jesus Christ, through his perfect life and sacrificial death, fully merited eternal life for believers. Merit was denied because of the Biblical doctrine of total depravity and fallen man's total inability to do any saving good. Even the believing sinner has no merit which contributes to his salvation or deserves God's reward. But good works are necessary as the fruit of salvation, as the evidence of true faith, and as the expression of gratitude for unmerited salvation.   FRED H. KLOOSTER

METAPHYSICS AND ETHICS. See also *Ecumenism and Ethics; God.* The basic structure of the ultimately real world is determinative of the nature of ethical decision and its consequences. Speculative or philosophical approaches deeply differ concerning the ultimate structure of reality; classic Graeco-Roman and modern idealist thinkers insist that it is teleological while others, including Spinoza as well as humanists or naturalists, view it as a realm of impersonal events ideally statable in mathematical formulas. This controversy is lifted to a revelational level by orthodox Judeo-Christian theologians, who insist that the ultimate nature of reality be defined in view of God's self-disclosure, and not simply on the basis of human intuition, experience, reflection, or desire. For historic Christianity, what is decisive for ethical concerns is the fact that the sovereign God is the self-revealed creator and judge of all, and the redeemer of the penitent.

Roman Catholic scholars, in agreement with Aquinas (q.v.) and Aristotle, hold that without any appeal to revelation, and solely on the basis of empirical considerations, the cosmos can be logically demonstrated to be tending towards good and away from evil, and that absolute good or God can be proved to be the ultimate cause of all events. In recent decades neo-supernaturalistic theologians have assailed this downgrading of revelational considerations in establishing a theistic ethic; neo-Protestant moralists, on the other hand, have at the same time, in contrast to evangelical Christianity, abandoned the logically consistent and intelligible nature of Divine disclosure (cf. *Dialectical Ethics; Existential Ethics*).

Apart from Divine revelation it is indeed difficult to resist reducing speculative arguments for teleology to simply a rationalization of subjective factors. The fact that man's desires are often disappointed, and that what seems at times to be good not infrequently turns out to be otherwise, undergirds the argument that exact knowledge of external reality must be stated in mathematical relationships. This line of argument has been nurtured by technocratic scientism (cf. *Technocracy and Technology*), in which the outer world is levelled to a realm of impersonal sequences expressible in mathematical equations. If this is the case, that external reality is a continuum of impersonal events, then—over and above internal or subjective desire and postulation—no possibility remains in the externally real world for personal reality, thought, agency, purpose or providence, whether Divine or human. This exclusion of human values from the externally significant world is one factor that provoked the revolt of counter-cultural youth in the mid-1960s and the search for a transcendent world which, unhappily, it probed in terms of mysticism and hallucinatory drugs.

While the effort of Kant (q.v.) to mediate between teleological and non-teleological theories of reality has lost its force, it became an influential option for a time. Before Kant, not only Judeo-Christian theology but philosophical idealism or rationalism as well insisted that one's world view *(Weltanschauung)* determines one's life view *(Lebensanschauung)*, that is, that the nature of the ultimately real world is fundamentally decisive for ethics. Kant assumed that, because of the postulated limits of reason, man cannot have cognitive knowledge, revelational or otherwise, of the noumenal world. Basing the case for theism on the moral nature of man, that is, on the sense of duty, he argued that God is to be postulated by faith as the "Thou shalt" demanded by the inner "I ought" of conscience. This view not only brushed aside the cognitive metaphysical significance of the Hebrew-Christian Scriptures, but also substituted a profoundly optimistic view of the moral nature of man; this moral nature was now viewed as so essentially continuous with the Divine that God could be projected in man's moral image. On Kant's view, ethics determines metaphysics, rather than vice versa. Kant assumed that the world of physical nature is entirely mechanical, yet that ultimate reality is to be viewed as a moral order. Later philosophers erased this mediation alternative, and insisted that reality must be interpreted consistently either in teleological or in impersonal categories.

Evangelical ethics emphasizes the importance of intelligible Divine revelation for a purposive grasp of the universe; in view of this fact, it stresses the complications posed by sin (q.v.) and evil (q.v.) in a fallen world. According to this view, evidences of dysteleology are not at all incompatible with the insistence on God as all-perfect source of the cosmos and of man. At the same time, evangelical ethics notes the inability of speculative views to vindicate any moral norms whatever. The ethical considerations on which nontheistic views insist are devoid of persuasive supports; if followed consistently, these views would subordinate both man and nature to impersonal fate or chance.

Non-revelatory views tend to regard sin and evil as illusion, or as due to the finite character of the world and man, and seek escape from the evils of life either through private union with a mystical divinity or rely chiefly on evolutionary optimism for significant personal and social amelioration. This has stirred insistent counterdemands for greater recognition of the seriousness of evil. Regrettably, these calls have led in recent decades not to a widespread recovery of Biblical perspectives so much as a resignation to naturalism. The result has been the steady erosion, through evolutionary theory, of the enduring significance of human reason and of moral ideals, as well as loss of belief in an afterlife; human history becomes but a transient episode in an unending drama of cosmic development.

Against nontheistic perspectives the Biblical revelation of creation, fall, and redemption offers a compelling alternative; claiming more than merely speculative sanction, it sets both goodness and sin in serious context, and through its offer of personal regeneration imparts to the penitent an incomparable dynamic for moral change. The history of ethics incorporates as one of its irreducible contrasts that between speculative moralists who seek perfection through the gradual reorganization of social structures and the refinement of unregenerate human nature, and Biblical scholars who insistently call for the crucifixion of the old self and the birth of a new self by the Spirit of God.

📖 Gordon H. Clark, *A Christian View of Men and Things*, Grand Rapids, Eerdmans, 1952; C. F. H. Henry, *Christian Personal Ethics*, Grand Rapids, Eerdmans, 1957.   CARL F. H. HENRY

METHODISM. See also *Arminius and Arminian Ethics; Holiness; Perfectionism.* Methodism is the religious movement which traces its origin to John Wesley (1703-1791) and his brother Charles (1707-1788) and in a lesser degree to George Whitefield (1714-1770). John Wesley was an evangelist, administrator, educator, philanthropist, social reformer, author; Charles, an evangelist and hymnist (author of more than 6000 hymns); George Whitefield an evangelist both in England and America.

The name "Methodist" was first given in derision to the members of the "Holy Club" at Oxford, which included the Wesley brothers, because of "the exact regularity of their lives as well as studies."

John Wesley's conversion at Aldersgate Street in London on May 24, 1738, marked the beginning of Methodism as a distinct and aggressive evangelistic movement. At the outset there was no thought of separation from the Established Church. But the course of events gradually made this inevitable, despite Wesley's long struggle against it. The official separation took place in America in 1784 with the organization of the Methodist Episcopal Church, and in England after Wesley's death.

Methodism during Wesley's life-time was dominated by his strong personality, organizing genius, extensive evangelistic activities, and intellectual leadership. Prominent features were field preaching, lay preaching, strict discipline, and militant religious zeal. Significant contributions were made to public life and morals. After Wesley's death a world-wide missionary activity was gradually inaugurated.

A number of schisms within Methodist ranks occurred during the nineteenth century. But in this century a marked tendency toward reunion has issued in many significant mergers (British Methodism in 1932; in the USA, The Methodist Church in 1939, and The United Methodist Church in 1968).

Methodist theology centers in the idea of human freedom, the freedom of contrary choice in relation to spiritual decisions. Methodist theology has always emphasized religious experience. According to Wesley the only genuine religion is experienced religion. Methodism has sought always to make dogma subservient to life. Methodist theology offers a universal salvation (procured for all and offered to all); a free salvation (sovereignty and dignity of man demands freedom of choice); a full salvation (Christian perfection is the heart and center of Methodism); a sure salvation (spiritual certitude based on the witness of the Spirit within a person).   FRANK B. STANGER

MILDNESS. See *Meekness.*

MILITARISM. See also *Nationalism; Pacifism; Peace and War.* "Militarism" is a term frequently employed to describe any government because of its readiness to use military force. The term is properly applied only when war is regarded by any group, society, or nation as of primary ethical or political value. Militarism, however, is by no means limited to the fighting forces since many civilians often have the same point of view.

The forces producing militarism are many and varied. External pressures on a nation resulting in fears of being conquered, or threats to internal security by anarchism and general disorder, may bring a nation to regard military force as the only hope of continuance and development. Coupled with these general causes, may go personal ambition on the part of politicians, of army officers, or of political parties, who seek to use the armed forces to gain control of a country for their own ends. An alliance between the military and the industrial-commercial complex may also result in a militaristic state. Frequently the presupposition of such thinking is the view that man is ultimately only a belligerent being. Therefore, the way to keep him happy is to give him the symbols of militarism and allow him periodically to indulge in the violence of war.

Militarism in one nation usually leads to war with others. With a large military establishment in existence, a militaristic nation usually feels that it should employ its war potential to bring others to submission or to prevent them from attacking it. Ambition on the part of military, political, or business leaders may also have a place in such ventures. Usually, however, the militaristic state ends by being defeated. One reason for this is that frequently the technical aspect of war is neglected because of the cost of change, or because the leaders are so confident of their strength that they ignore technical advances in warfare elsewhere. The other cause of defeat is the breakdown of morale in the face of the loss of man power, the suffering and the privation that continuing war entails.

As militarism has been a constantly recurring phenomenon of history, men have long sought for a means of obviating the rise of such thinking and action. The usual view has been that to achieve this the armed forces of a country must be subordinate to the civilian government. Furthermore, the freedom of such forces should be limited by law. The one problem has been, however, that society as a whole may become infected with a militaristic type of thinking, preliminary to the rise of a militaristic regime.

From the Christian point of view as

expressed in Rom. 13, civil government is a creation of God for the maintenance of justice and equity. To fulfill its responsibility a government may use the power of the sword both to preserve internal peace and to protect the citizens from external aggression. Yet the government may never make the so-called military virtues primary or ultimate. Armed force must always be employed subject to the responsibilities of the state of God. Only as this principle is observed does it seem possible to prevent the rise of militarism and all its disastrous consequences.

📖 "Militarism," *International Encyclopedia of Social Sciences,* New York, Macmillan, 1968; S. Andreski, *Military Organization and Society,* Berkeley, University of California, 1968; S. P. Huntington, ed., *Changing Patterns of Military Politics,* New York, Glencoe, Free Press, 1962. A. Vagts, *A History of Militarism,* New York, Free Press, 1967.   W. STANFORD REID

MILITARY CHAPLAINCY. The military (or institutional) chaplaincy in the USA takes its authorization under the great commission of Christ to carry the gospel to the world (Mark 16:15) and under the guarantees of the first amendment in the Bill of Rights, that "Congress shall make no law respecting an establishment of religion, or prohibiting the free exercise thereof...." Christ's mandate to his church is clear and simple; the meaning of our founding fathers also is not hard to determine: government shall not establish religion to the exclusion of or infringement upon the rights of others, nor shall religious liberty be denied to anyone in the free exercise of his faith, nor any hindrance be placed in his way. With the sorry history of Europe fresh in their minds, our forebears were convinced that religion, specifically Christianity, would flourish best and with greater purity *without* the aid of government, but government must also not interpose obstacles.

Military chaplaincies grew in this soil and have been notable exceptions in the process of keeping church and state separate. They existed already in the revolutionary army, prior to the Declaration of Independence, and they have had a continuing history ever since in all branches of the military. Longevity of existence by itself is no proof of rightness. But every test before the law, under the Constitution, chiefly Art. VI (concerning test of religion), and the Bill of Rights, first amendment (concerning freedom of religion) and fourteenth (concerning due process), has failed to prove unconstitutionality. In fact, the Supreme Court has repeatedly cited the military chaplaincy, to show that our forefathers never conceived of the separation principle in terms so severe as to preclude benign interaction between government and the churches at certain critical points. One of these was the right of the individual to freedom of religious exercise while in the military, a right which must not be impaired by the government's own machinery and demands upon its citizens. This has never implied abandonment of the separation principle, but accommodation. As a matter of fact, the Supreme Court has recently ruled strictly on other issues involving contact points between church and state, e.g., religion and prayer in the public schools, or support of parochial religion. Thus, provisions for religious services in the armed forces by permitting the churches to supply qualified clergymen in uniform for ships, stations, posts, and armies in the field, has never been judged to be in violation of the neutrality principle. The government has no design to promote religion but to protect the religious freedom of those whom it isolates for a time from civilian life. In the same line of reasoning, the high court has not seen fit to strip away other traditional usages that touch on common law and rights, such as religious phrases on our coins and insignia, oaths in court, reference to God in the pledge of allegiance, prayers in Congress, the reverent opening of the Supreme Court itself each day when in session, or the flying of the church flag over "Old Glory" when church call is sounded in the military. No breach of the "wall" has occurred in these instances, the Court has ruled.

Obviously certain dangers persist. Over-zealous officials from either side, government or the churches, could fashion the working arrangement of the military chaplaincy into an "establishment" of religion by and under the government, or the churches could conceivably become militaristic pawns in the hands of the government. To prevent this, vigilance is needed: government must be concerned to maintain the provisions and safeguards of the Constitution and the Bill of Rights; and churches, in turn, must refrain from pressing for favors from government beyond the ecclesiastical function of ministering spiritually to the needs of the military man.

➲ See the military manuals governing the chaplaincy, Army, Navy, Air Force, U. S. Government Printing Office; E. F. Klug, "The Chaplaincy in American Public Life." in *Church and State under God*, Concordia, 1964, pp. 365-393; Anson P. Stokes, *Church and State in the United States*, 3 vols. New York, Harper, 1950; C. M. Drury, *History of the Chaplain Corps, U. S. Navy*, Government Printing Office, 1949; R. J. Honeywell, *Chaplains of the United States Army*, Government Printing Office, 1958; Carl Zollmann, *American Church Law*, St. Paul, West Publishing, 1933; E. F. Klug, *The Military Chaplaincy under the First Amendment*, U. S. Army Chaplain Board, 1967; W. G. Katz, *Religion and American Constitutions*, Evanston, Northwestern University, 1964; P. B. Kurland, *Religion and the Law*, Chicago, Aldine, 1962; Leo Pfeffer, "The Case for Separation" in *Religion in America*, World Publishing, 1958.

EUGENE F. KLUG

MILITARY SERVICE. See also *Militarism*. Three types of military service have existed. First, in the voluntary-temporary type of service citizens of a country or members of a group assume the responsibility of military service to meet a specific crisis, i.e., a militia. Secondly, there is voluntary-professional service, in which in-

dividuals volunteer to serve for a period of years, thus becoming professional soldiers. Finally conscript service is that in which all males, and sometimes females, within certain age limits are required to enter the nation's armed forces, either in an emergency or as a regular practice in view of the possible need for trained personnel in case of war (cf. *Draft*).

In the ancient world some states such as Sparta had what might be called a conscript system, although this was not common. More frequently, as in the Roman Empire, the army was of the voluntary-professional type. During the Middle Ages feudalism was a system of both civil organization and military service by which each holder of a fief had to serve at his own expense in the national forces for forty days a year. In some countries such as England the *levée en masse*, or *ferd*, could be raised to meet special emergencies. From the fourteenth century on voluntary professional armies (whether the condottieri of Renaissance Italy or the mercenary troops of France and England in the Seven Years War became increasingly common. The French Revolution introduced once again the *levée en masse* and during the nineteenth century conscript armies became the rule in Europe. In the American Civil War a modified form of conscription was adopted. Since 1914, even though some countries do not have universal conscription in peacetime, practically all impose it in time of war.

In some Christian circles military service has always been held to be inconsistent with Christian ethical standards, not only because of oaths the soldiers may have to take, but also because they believe that Christians must never resort to violence. During the Reformation of the sixteenth century the Anabaptists strongly advocated such views, largely because they believed that all civil government was only for non-Christians; Christians, not needing such controls, should avoid such mundane matters. The problem, however, is whether Christians can accept the protection afforded by the state without offering anything in return.

A contrary Christian view has been that military service is justified on the basis of Rom. 13 and similar passages. Its proponents believe that at times the necessity of using force does arise, a position borne out by the OT history of Israel. Yet they also hold that the Christian can never accept uncritically a government's dictum as to the righteousness and necessity of any particular war. He must always place his responsibility to obey God above the demands of a civil government. If he feels that a war is unjust and immoral he must not only refuse to serve in the armed forces, but must also oppose the action taken by his government, even though this may lead, as it has in some cases, to imprisonment and even death.

W. STANFORD REID

MINORITY RIGHTS. See also *Civil Rights.* The post-war activism in the field of civil rights was concerned initially with the plight of the largest racial minority in the USA, Negro Americans. More recently Mexican and Spanish-speaking Americans (Chicanos), Indians and numerous other ethnic groups have challenged their underprivileged status in American society. The implementation of equal voting rights has been virtually guaranteed by passage of the Voting Rights Act of 1965 which was extended for five years in 1970. Hence, the emphasis on minority rights has shifted to such areas as employment and housing. Charismatic leaders like Caesar Chavez have attempted through the organization of agricultural workers into unions in states like California and Florida to use the economic weapon of the strike and boycott to improve the terms and conditions of employment of farm workers, largely Mexican and Spanish-speaking migrants.

However, as the cause of minority rights has expanded, it has gone far beyond the scope of racial and ethnic groups. Welfare mothers have united to seek more adequate benefits under the welfare laws of the federal government and the several states. Women, although not a numerical minority in the general population, have launched a Women's Liberation movement which is based on the premise that in many areas of American life they are not accorded the full economic and social rights to which they are entitled. At the outer penumbra of minority rights are the Gay Liberationists who seek to assert the minority rights of the homosexual community.

Some offer as an explanation for this explosion of interest in minority rights, with emergence of many different groups, each asserting the rights of a particular minority, the passing of the American dream. They reject the melting pot theory of the Americanization of successive waves of immigrants. This then becomes a rationalization for various groups to insist on maintaining their identity while they assert their right to full acceptance by the dominant power structure and majority culture.

Christ was deeply concerned during his earthly ministry with the underprivileged who are most often to be found in the various minority groups. He preached good news to the poor, the captives, the blind, and the oppressed (Luke 4:18-19). If we would see "judgment run down as waters, and righteousness as a mighty stream" (Amos 5:24) we cannot be indifferent to the wrongs that exist in society and which often find expression in mistreatment of minorities. Evangelical Christians have the foremost responsibility of communicating the good news of the gospel. But this priority must not imply indifference to constructive efforts to improve the lot of disadvantaged minority groups. Intelligent and dedicated Christian social action will defuse frustration and embitterment that has led some of these groups to resort to bizarre, if not violent, means of gaining public recognition.

There are heartening signs that the evangelical community does perceive its necessity of playing a role in advancing the cause of minority rights. It can thereby restore credibility to the promise of rest addressed to "all . . . that labor and are heavy laden."   JOHN B. ANDERSON

MISSION(S). See also *Humanitarianism; Universalism.* Missions, the human organizations, must be distinguished from *mission,* the assignment received as a mandate from our Lord. Discussion of one also involves the other. The validity of the church's institutionalized program depends on the validity of the *idea of mission,* namely, that Christ commanded his followers to bring the lost to him for salvation.

The ethical validity of this idea is under attack from inside and outside the church, and especially from universalists. Against evangelistic (converting) missions it is popularly reasoned that Christian exclusivism (Christ being claimed as the *only* way—John 14:6; Acts 4:12) (1) is an affront on rational human personality, (2) is monological proclamation in a day which demands dialogue, (3) fails to recognize the divine in non-Christian religions, (4) is divisive and hinders ecumenicity, and (5) savors of antequated revivalism and church extension when new forms are needed. These critics would redefine such terms as *evangelism* and *mission* to suit a day "when man has become of age." Service often substitutes for mission rather accompanies it. Much current missionary terminology—dialogue, Christian presence, development, humanization—is ambiguous, liberal, or conservative as the speaker desires.

The evangelical position, while granting the current need for new techniques and modes of communication to suit the day, nevertheless denies our right to change either the *motive* or *message* of our Lord's

mission. The rightness of the idea of mission, seeking the lost and bringing them in repentance to Christ, may be postulated by sociological, ethical, Biblical and theological arguments.

The sociological argument rests on the statistical fact that millions of non-Christians (especially animists) are currently in the process of changing their religion. Under the effects of acculturation and the "shrinking" of the globe, old gods and fetishes are being called on to perform functions beyong their capacity. Medicine men are less and less effective. Animists are questioning, testing, seeking, experimenting and making decisions as never before. Moslem, Buddhist, Bahai and Communist "missionaries" are operating in these dynamic situations. It seems just plain sociological common sense that decision for Christ should be at least one option put before them.

The ethical argument is that of Christian responsibility: the old issue of the "haves and the have-nots." Has not the Christian a duty to share both physical and spiritual blessings? This does not mean in paternalism, so often characteristic of the old type of missions; but rather fraternally and towards self-help. The former establishes a dependent, foreign, station church; the latter moves toward responsible indigeneity.

The Biblical or exegetical argument recognizes several themes running through Scripture: the idea of "the people of God" responsibile for bringing the nations to God; the idea of the diffusion of "the knowledge of the Lord"; the NT idea of the church itself, the growing fellowing or disciple group, persons "called out" and "not of the world," but doing the work of Christ "in the world." Although all Christians should witness, the mission is the task of a corporate body—the church "which is his Body," ministering the mind, love and message of Christ to the world. Then there is the direct commission of Christ to his followers, in space (to all nations) and time (by his promise to be with them to the end of the age).

The theological argument stands on the character, purpose, and revelation of God, who declared his intention to save man from sin. The *theological negative* is his pronouncement against idolatry, witchcraft, and phallic cults (e.g., Gal. 5:19-20), which deny man his inheritance of the Kingdom of God (v. 21). The *theological positive* is the evangelical Christian's commission to missionary activity, bringing men to commitment to Christ (e.g., Rom. 10:13-15). The word of reconciliation in Christ is committed to his followers (II Cor. 5:14-19). The *theological potential* of Christian mission is that "strangers and foreigners" may become "fellow-citizens" in the "household of God" (Eph. 2:11-22).

The clash between these opposing philosophies of mission is reflected in their respective operations. Those who "demythologize" Scripture must interpret the idea of mission to suit the projects they feel the world situation needs. Their theology and ethics are, therefore, situational, and often anthropocentric and universalist. Evangelicals, on the other hand, accept Scripture at its face value, and operate from the Biblical frame of reference in encountering their situations. The former appear to be surviving mainly on the strength of an evangelism of an earlier generation. Where statistics show great church growth the concept of mission invariably turns out to be evangelical. Each generation must hear the call of mission for itself. Each must see the opportunities of its own day—even unto the end of the age.

Stephen Neill, *Call to Mission*, Philadelphia, Fortress, 1970; G. F. Vicedom, *The Mission of God*, St. Louis, Concordia, 1965; *Church Growth Bulletin.*   ALAN R. TIPPETT

MIXED MOTIVES. See also *Motives and Motivation; Singlemindedness.* A motive is anything which, consciously or uncon-

sciously, moves a person to action, anything that impels or induces him to act in a certain way. Whenever a person performs an action from two or more motives, one of which predominates, his motives may be said to be mixed. For example, the scribes and Pharisees, in practicing their piety before men in order to be seen by them (Matt. 6:1; 23:5-7; Mark 12:40), were acting from mixed motives; their desire for men's praise, rather than simply their love for God, motivated much of their religious practice.

Most human action seems to be prompted by a variety of motives. There is Biblical justification for believing that although the overriding motive for all the Christian's thought and action should be to glorify God or Christ (Rom. 14:8; I Cor. 10:31; II Cor. 5:9), this need not exclude the simultaneous operation of subsidiary motives such as gratitude for forgiveness (Col. 3:13), filial reverence for a holy Father (I Peter 1:15-17), the hope of final perfection (I John 3:2f.), accountability to Christ (Col. 3:23f.), or the recognition of the brevity of life (James 4:13-15). Singleness of heart (I Chron. 29:17; Eph. 6:5) or singlemindedness should therefore not be equated with singleness of motive. Paul can appeal to the two motives of redemption and retribution in support of ethical injunction (see e.g., Rom 8:12f.; Gal 6:8). The variety and richness of Christian motivation find their unity in the person of Christ, who is at once the supreme motive, model and end of the Christian's new life.

The periodic examination of one's motives for and intention in acting in a particular way is both imperative and healthy (I Cor. 4:5; 11:27-29). Yet experience teaches that preoccupation with purity of motive tends to deaden motivation and can easily lead to unhealthy introspection.

Action performed, or known to be performed, from mixed motives (in the pejorative sense of "ulterior motives") is not necessarily morally worthless. An act of benevolence, such as the return of a lost article to its owner, remains a dutiful and commendable act although it is carried out in the hope of monetary gain as well as from a sense of duty. The impurity of motive, however, makes the action less praiseworthy and to some extent robs it of its basic "rightness."

📖 Jonathan Edwards, *Freedom of the Will*, Paul Ramsey, ed., New Haven, Yale University, 1957; Norman H. G. Robinson, *The Claim of Morality*, London, Gollancz, 1951, pp. 233-5, 261f., 319-21; Archibald B. D. Alexander, *The Ethics of St. Paul*, Glasgow, Maclehose, 1910, chap. 6.

MURRAY J. HARRIS

MODERATION. See *Golden Mean; Temperance; Virtues.*

MODERNISM, ETHICAL. See *Liberalism, Ethical.*

MODERNITY. See *Conformity; Culture; Social Change.*

MODESTY. Modesty is a habit of measured action which is normed by some sense of shame. A woman who dressed modestly shows a taste for clothes that honors the privacy of her body. A man who exercises authority is modest if he uses the power with restraint, based on sober judgment of the limits to his personal competence. People with means whose life style is thrifty and unassuming exemplify modesty. To be modest is to live without show, but with caution, tact, and reserve.

Conformity to the ancient, Eastern customs that prohibited openness (e.g., veiling of women) did not, properly speaking, promote modesty. It takes a developed consciousness of personhood and the mettle of voluntary discipline, rather than a reticence dictated by tabu to constitute modesty. Medieval Western culture largely mixed a realization of human sinfulness together with the ubiquitous Stoic virtue of *apatheia* (unfeelingness) to conceive and forge the quality of modesty with an ascetic cast. Saintly modesty meant unadorned simplicity, carefully suppressed passions, a prim demeanor. In more subjectivistic, modern times that characteristic developed into the practice of pseudo-modesty: affected self-depreciation. Mainstream secular thought has little use for modesty, not even as a strategy, for a humble estimate of one's gifts in today's world seems too much like timidity, a lack of self-reliance.

In Christian perspective, however, modesty gives one the strength of thrift. A modest man or woman's reliability is the more solid because modesty keeps it uncluttered by pretense, not potholed with conceits, just carefully and straightforwardly dependable. The healthy, self-*appreciative* awareness of one's blemishes and failings gives quiet grit to the person's whole character. The modest do not lord it over their neighbors either, and therefore may also claim the promise Christ makes to the meek (Matt. 5:5). CALVIN G. SEERVELD

MONASTICISM. See also *Asceticism; Continence; Virginity.* Monastic life down the ages has assumed diverse forms, ranging from solitary abandonment of civilization to a separated community's active involvement in the world, and embodying differing and even contradictory ideals, most of which are observable in the early and mediaeval centuries. The pioneer hermits (men of the "deserts" of the Levant) or anchorites (who "withdrew" from the world), like Antony of Egypt (d. 356), lived alone (Greek *monos*) or in loosely grouped colonies, at first eschewing even the church in pursuit of perfection (Matt. 19:21). This individualistic cultivation of discarnate existence on earth encouraged a competitive heroism, emulating the martyr's struggle with demonic powers by feats of endurance typified by the Syrian pillar-saints.

The hermit ideal, classically presented in Anthanasius' *Life of Antony* and never wholly absent from the monastic scene, has periodically experienced significant revivals, e.g., in eleventh century Italy and fourteenth century Russia, often in rejection of decadent institutional monasticism, and has frequently been combined with elements of a coenobitic ("common-life") regimen, especially for worship, as in the early Palestinian *lavra,* individual cells grouped under one "father" *(abba),* and the enclosure of cells round a cloister and oratory in the twelfth century Carthusian houses.

The coenobitic monasticism pioneered by Pachomius (d. 346) in Egypt introduced obedience to a superior within the discipline of a rudimentary "rule," but it remained for Basil the Great (d. 379), bishop of Caesarea in Cappadocia, not only to ecclesiasticize monasticism but also to abjure solitude and exalt life in community as alone expressive of brotherly care in the body of Christ. Though eastern monasteries, Byzantine and modern, have generally structured their regimens around Basil's informal *Rules,* especially as supplemented by Theodore of Studios (d. 826), they have rarely preserved the community service performed by Basil's orphanage and hostels. Eastern monasticism has been mostly coenobitic, with Byzantine foundations frequently sited near cities and their monks engaging in religious and political controversy. But the monastic colonizing of Mount Athos from the tenth century foreshadowed the remoteness of later Russian establishments. Orthodox monasteries have not been noted for outgoing enterprises but as centers of pilgrimage, religious art and timeless devotion, with "holy men" often eclipsing abbots. Hesychasm, a somewhat mechanical form of quietist contemplation ensuring the beatific vision, became prominent in the fourteenth century.

In the West monastic beginnings, though inspired by Oriental anchoritism, especially in Gaul (Martin of Tours and John Cassian), soon developed along more refined, churchly and even clerical lines under the lead of Ambrose, Jerome and Augustine. Celtic monasticism alone perpetuated hermitic rigors, but fused a penal discipline with a questing adventurousness which looked upon missionary monks like Columba and Columban as exiles in Christ's service. In the Celtic realms, where urban society was almost unknown, monasteries became centers of a vigorous Christianity and Latin culture.

Benedict's highly influential *Rule* (c. 540) rejected the harsh athleticism of the solitaries and married a moderated ascetic schooling to a flexible but well-ordered common life of prayer, work and devotional study, insulated from the outside world. Monasteries of this pattern, sometimes merging with more austere Celtic foundations, dominated subsequent centuries and gave birth to important reform movements such as the Cluniac in the tenth century and the Cistercian in the twelfth. Abandoning Benedict's isolation they developed a commitment to missionary extension (e.g., Boniface), charitable services, learning, art and education. Monasteries became increasingly the chief seats of civilized and cultural life. Manual labor disappeared and devotional exercises multiplied, encouraged by the notion of vicarious worship and intercession on behalf of the unfortunate world. Later mediaeval protests against the monasteries' increasing wealth, sophistication and secularism contributed to the emergence in the fourteenth century of the new active mendicant orders of Franciscan and Dominican friars, which coupled a recall to poverty and simplicity with works of mercy and teaching, especially in the universities.

The modern flowering of monasticism, in Protestant as well as traditional fields, displays continuing diversity. Attempts to integrate disciplined community life with active service in society are to the fore. Though a

Biblical perspective, following the Reformers, refuses any distinction between a "religious" life and normal Christian existence in the world, any élitist estimate of monastic vocation as the only perfect following of Christ, and any ascetic abnegation that denigrates God's good creation, it may freely appreciate the monastic witness to the priority of the claims of Christian allegiance over all earthly concerns, including marriage (Matt. 19:12). While the ideal of solitude and permanent withdrawal (which has sometimes been tantamount to escapism) is highly questionable, life in community under specific norms of discipline may have much to commend it in certain circumstances.

H. B. Workman, *The Evolution of the Monastic Ideal*, London, 1913; D. Knowles, *Christian Monasticism*, London, 1969; F. Biot, *The Rise of Protestant Monasticism*, New York, Helicon, 1963 (with chh. on Reformation attitudes); D. J. Chitty, *The Desert a City*, New York, Ferndale, Oxford, 1966; C. Butler, *Benedictine Monachism*, 2nd. ed., London, 1924.   DAVID F. WRIGHT

MONEY. See also *Economics; Inflation; Mammon; Wealth.* Money plays a legitimate role as a medium of exchange and a storehouse of value to facilitate economic transactions. But Christians are warned that love of money is the root of all evil, and coveting money causes erring from the faith, and sorrow (I Tim. 6:10). Jesus spoke of the highly corrupting role of money in his encounter with the rich young ruler (Luke 18:18-30). Money, may readily become a popular false god, like intellectual pride, self-image, and sex. Selfish use of money in the face of great need is a common sin. All things are gifts of God and should be used to his glory. This includes money.   WALTER P. GORMAN III

MONOGAMY. See also *Common Law Marriage; Concubinage; Marriage; Polygamy.* Marriage has been variously understood and organized in human society. In general marriage is one of the central social institutions by which a society orders the relations between the sexes and provides for the relation of children to that society. Monogamy in the widest sense of the term is that understanding and organization of marriage which defines the married state as consisting of one man and one woman at any given time. Christians and many other peoples add to this the understanding that the one man and one woman enter into the married state intending and promising a life-long union of mutual trust, service, and love. It is a Christian conviction that marriage so understood is the true understanding of marriage which corresponds to the intention of the Creator and which alone will meet the needs of human society.

The teaching of Christ concerning marriage makes it clear that God intended monogamous life-long union to be the proper form of marriage from the beginning. Only such a union will provide a setting in which the human needs of mutuality can be met by giving both the security of belonging and the exclusive intimacy which such a relationship needs to flourish and be itself. It is in this setting that sexual intimacy may rightly be exercised both to express mutual love as well as to conceive and rear children. The writers of the NT all place the same emphasis upon the inner content of marriage and presuppose its monogamous, life-long state (Matt. 19:3ff.; Eph. 5:21ff.; I Tim 3:2; 4:3; 5:14).

As a covenant of intimate love for the well being of man marriage can be likened to the covenant of redemption which God has effected with man by his choosing a people in Christ and indwelling this people intimately as the Holy Spirit. Thus marriage is dignified by its likeness to God's relation with his church. At the same time the likeness is not that of identity; this makes it clear that marriage like all the institutions of fallen man stands in the need of redemption. Marriage can find its true stability, service, and fulfillment only as Christ is the gracious Lord of the married couple. It is for this reason that Christians solemnize their marriages in prayer to God in Christ in the context of God's people, and beg God's blessing to enable them to keep the vows which the couple makes one to the other (Isa. 1:21; Jer. 3:1-20; Hos. 2; Matt. 9:15; II Cor. 11:2; Eph. 5:23-32; Rev. 19:7; 21:2, 9; 22:17).

It is true that polygamy is to be found in the OT, but the OT cannot be cited in favor of polygamy. In the covenant people polygamy is begun by Abraham's lack of trust in God's promise of an heir, continually gives rise to jealousy and second-class status for wives who are not most favored, and is the occasion for much disobedient and selfish behavior. Christ interprets God's allowance of polygamy in the covenant people through Moses as a concession to the hardness of Isreal's heart (Gen. 16:4, 6; I Sam 1:6; II Sam. 9, 13; I King 9:1-8).

JOHN H. RODGERS, JR.

MONOPOLY. Monopoly may be defined as control by individuals, business concerns, groups, or governments permitting them to fix prices or regulate output on one or more articles or services. This may be entirely ethical and commendatory when based upon necessity or practical exigency.

Monopoly privileges or grants were common in Europe and especially in England in the fifteenth and sixteenth centuries. Examples are: exclusive privileges to trade in certain countries such as India and parts of Canada, to import or export certain articles; or, to practice certain arts or trades.

Today, public monopolies exist in federal postal service, toll highways, municipal electric, water and sewage services, telephone service, and currently under consideration, a national railroad.

Private monopolies may originate from privileges granted by governments, through possessions of patents or copyrights, through possession of superior know-how, skill or talent or from ownership capital. Examples are superior musical or entertainment ability, franchises for products in exclusive areas, and the limitations on entry into high cost industries such as steel, automotive, petroleum products. Monopolists consider the differences between selling price and production costs at various levels of output with the objective of maximizing highest net revenue. However prices are subjected to public regulation if they are exhorbitant; so a lower price in the short run may mean a better profit in the long run. High prices mean high profits and this invites competition. Restricted output may mean the development of substitutes and the decline of the market. Several public laws have been enacted to eliminate abuses and exert control.

To increase profits, a monopolist may increase quality or increase promotion when these are more effective than price cuts. When there are close substitutes but differentiation created by advertising, branding, packaging, styling, etc. the term monopolistic-competition is used. Oligopoly refers to a few sellers with retaliation to price changes so that one becomes the price leader establishing prices above the competitive level. Monopsony refers to only one buyer. When a small market exists with tariff barriers or high transportation costs, cutthroat competition may occur until one firm remains and becomes the monopolist. When it reaches this level monopoly is clearly and evidently contrary to Christian ethics which is based upon the principle of loving God above all, and our neighbor as ourself.

John F. Due and Robert Clower, *Intermediate Economic Analysis,* 5th ed., Homewood, Ill., Richard D. Irwin, 1966, chap. 10.

HARVEY A. MAERTIN

MORALITY AND METAPHYSICS. See *Metaphysics and Ethics.*

MORAL PHILOSOPHY. See also *Metaphysics and Ethics*. An approach to moral philosophy in terms of Christian ethics must be grounded on Biblical revelation. A basic datum is the teaching of Rom. 2:14, 15, as to natural moral law. This law, obscured but not eradicated by sin, makes possible moral knowledge and responsibility and, on the theoretical level, moral philosophy and ethics as a special systematic discipline. Ethics in the special sense is theory dealing with the content of natural moral law. Moral philosophy is theory dealing with the foundations of ethics and interdisciplinary questions involving ethics. Moral philosophy in this sharply defined sense may be termed meta-ethics, as distinguished from ethics as moral science. Is it right to take human life and if so when? is a question of ethics. The meaning of "right" and the foundations of right are questions of meta-ethics.

Contemporary Anglo-American meta-ethics, under the influence of the thought of Ludwig Wittgenstein and J. L. Austin, tends to center moral philosophy in an account of the language of morals. Some very recent work of this type, however, exhibits a trend toward openness to broader philosophical questions. Distinct from the ordinary-language methodology is the promising investigation of the formal logic of obligation and related notions (deontic logic). Christian moral philosophy may not ignore ordinary language and, if it aims at rigor in argument, must express the highest competence in logic, so far as logic is related to ethics.

A Christian moral philosophy, while maintaining the highest standards of philosophical method, must be firmly grounded in the Word of Scripture. It is to the credit of Herman Dooyeweerd that he has insisted on this in opposition to an ethics based on a Pelagian or humanistic optimism as to the ability of man as he is, to know and to will the morally good. On the other hand, Dooyeweerd may unduly limit the scope of ethics as a special science to love in human relations. It appears arbitrary to deny that the two great commandments of the law are determinative of the scope of ethics. This consideration about ethics is a fundamental issue of moral philosophy.

Sketch of Christian Moral Philosophy.
The moral subject may be considered as conscience (q.v.) in relation to moral action. Conscience as a permanent disposition of the soul or synteresis is the repository of innate and acquired moral knowledge and belief. As an activity of the soul, conscience has the form of a practical syllogism. The major premise is universal, derived from natural or revealed moral law. The minor premise is factual, dependent on a typical or individual situation. The conclusion is the judgment of conscience as to the right behavior in the given situation. The will is the capacity of the soul for rational activity or the exercise of that activity. The will is not an isolated or independent faculty, but functions in accordance with judgments of the intellect as to what is or appears best. In no state of the soul, does the will enjoy a freedom of independence from predetermining divine Providence. In a fallen state it is in bondage to evil, and liberated only by the grace of Christ. Freedom is not indeterminacy, but rational spontaneity, fully realized in the deliverance from the possibility of sin.

The moral law was written on the human conscience by nature. This writing has been defaced, but not obliterated. A clear and correct knowledge of the moral law requires the republication of the commandments, summarized in the Decalogue as the permanent and unalterable rule of man's duty on earth. Virtue is conformity to this norm in heart as well as in practice. The so-called virtues of the heathen were correctly characterized by Augustine as "splendid vices."

The moral end, or highest good, is the glory of God. In declaring by word and deed the perfections, especially the moral perfections of the most High, man finds true happiness. The Kingdom of God is the partial and ultimately the complete realization of this goal both inwardly and outwardly, individually and corporately. The conflict of the two cities and the ultimate triumph of the heavenly city is the theme of a Christian understanding of history which may thus be regarded as a branch of Christian moral philosophy.

Archibald Alexander, *Moral Science*, New York, 1852; William Ames, *De Conscientia et eius iure, vel Casibus*, Amsterdam, 1630; John Calvin, *Institutes of the Christian Religion*, Bk. II, c.8; III6-10, 19; Herman Dooyeweerd, *A New Critique of Theoretical Thought*, Vol. II, 140-162, Nutley, N. J., Presbyterian and Reformed, 1969; Jonathan Edwards, *Freedom of the Will; True Virtue* in *Works*, Vol. I; Theophilus Gale, *The Court of the Gentiles*, Part IV: Of Reformed Philosophy, Bk. I, London, 1677; Thomas Aquinas, *Summa Contra Gentiles*, Bk. III; *Westminster Larger Catechism*, Questions 91-152.   WILLIAM YOUNG

MORAL REARMAMENT.

Earlier known as the Oxford Group (sometimes designated Buchmanism), Moral Rearmament became an energetic movement aimed at personal spiritual recruitment. Its founder, Frank N. D. Buchman (1878-1961) was a Lutheran minister who, after many differences with associates in successive posts, in 1922 launched a global evangelistic crusade based on personal divine guidance and individual life-changing. Its call for spiritual surrender in accord with the "four absolutes" (honesty, purity, love, unselfishness) enlisted thousands of persons through "house parties" in England, the Netherlands, America, and elsewhere. Many followers were conventional Protestants in formalistic churches that lacked an emphasis on vital personal experience.

The movement's stress on religious immediacy tended to obscure the mediatorial work of Christ, however, and the objective authority of Scripture. Many "key persons" including the wealthy—the "up and outers,"

as Buchman called them—were attracted. The theological outlook was simplistic and vulnerable, however, and the socio-political thrust highly individualistic. After World War II Buchman, who was criticized as being sympathetic to the Nazis, widened his appeal to followers of all faiths. These developments dissipated much former support. A large headquarters on Mackinac Island, Michigan, which together with a center in Caux, Switzerland, served as a training ground, was sold in 1971 because of financial pressures.

CARL F. H. HENRY

MORAL THEOLOGY.

See also *Casuistry; Moral Philosophy; Religion and Ethics; Roman Catholic Ethics*. The meaning of "moral theology" will vary depending on the meaning in combination of the terms "moral" and "theology." It is a term used to refer, however, most often in Roman Catholic thought, to the science of the principles of human action that derive from the supernatural revelation of God and that have as their end the saving union of the believer with God in Christ. As *moral* it differs from dogmatic theology, which deals cognitively with the revealed truths of the faith. On the contrary, moral theology deals with the revealed principles of action. As *theology* it differs from moral philosophy (ethics), which treats of the principles of action that pertain to man as man, that are known by the power of natural reason, and that provide guidance with respect to temporal life. Moral theology, on the contrary, is said to do with the revealed supernatural truths that pertain to the elevation of man to God and to eternal life.

Moral theology has often had a very intimate connection with casuistry, namely, with the science of stipulating rules of action, particularly as they relate to individual cases. At times the two terms have been virtually identified with each other. It has been stressed by Roman Catholic theologians, however, that the principles of moral theology should not be treated apart from the end they have in view, namely, the union of man with God in Christ. It has become customary, therefore, in Roman Catholic circles to give casuistry a subordinate place, making certain that rules of action and their application to specific cases do not become divorced from what is regarded to be the end of theology in its grand sweep, namely, the vision of God.

In the Roman Catholic church there has been continuous study of moral theology. Gabriël Vázquez (1549-1604) was the first to set forth the idea that moral theology was a distinct science. The most famous Roman Catholic moral theologian was Alphonsus Liguori (1696-1787). Other prominent ones were Lehmkuhl (1834-1918) and Prümmer (1866-1931). Prominent moral theologians of the Church of England in the seventeenth century were Jeremy Taylor, R. Sanderson, and J. Hall. A contemporary representative is Kenneth E. Kirk.

In the above sense, moral theology also appears in more distinctly Protestant thought, although not so extensively. A reason is often given that Protestant theologians have been disinclined to specify rules of action in such detail, preferring to restrict themselves to general principles. There is, however, a deeper explanation for the difficulty of rooting moral theology in Reformation soil.

In Reformation thought there is less room than in Rome for the term "moral theology." That is because there is less room, on the one hand, for the distinction between natural and supernatural theology, and, on the other hand, for the distinction between a science of action that relates to man as man, acting by the light of natural reason, and a science of action based on supernatural truths that relate to man's ascent to God. Put more strongly, it belongs to the genius of Reformation thinking to reject the idea of natural theology. Reformational thinking does not allow for a knowledge of God that man may attain as man by the light of reason, i.e., independent of divine revelation. Instead, it maintains that men are always confronted with the personal self-disclosure of God, to which they are always responding, either in an attempt to shut out this true knowledge (the attitude of the natural men) or in a joyful acceptance of it (the attitude of the spiritual man). The true knowledge of God and service of him with the whole heart should characterize human activity in its entirety. One should reject a conception of ethics, therefore, that refers it to what man can attain as man by the light of reason. Ethics should focus on man responding to God with all of his heart, as this estate has been restored in Christ. Having its root in Christ, the obedience expected of all men is an evangelical obedience.

Thus the distinction between ethics as moral philosophy (based on reason) and moral theology (based on supernatural divine revelation) falls away. In its place comes an ethics that is informed with the revelation of God, particularly as that revelation comes to its fulfillment in Jesus Christ. In agreement with these reformational principles, the Christian life is not regarded first of all as an ascent to blessedness by way of obedience to supernaturally revealed principles of action but as a life of gratitude to God for the salvation that has already been received in Christ.

📖 F. Bordeaux and A. Danet, *Introduction to the Law of Christ*, Staten Island, Alba, 1966; B. Häring, *The Law of Christ*, 3 vols., Westminster, Md., Newman, 1963; Kenneth Escott Kirk, *Some Principles of Moral Theology and their Application*, London, New York, Longmans, Green, 1920; L. Monden, *Sin, Liberty and Law*, New York, Sheed and Ward, 1965; Robert C. Mortimer, *The Elements of Moral Theology*, London, Adam and Charles Black, 1947.   ROBERT D. KNUDSEN

MORTIFICATION. See also *Asceticism*. Mortification finds its basis in the Biblical statements," mortify (*thanatoō*) the deed of the body. . ." (Rom. 8:13 AV), and "mortify (*nekroō*) therefore your members which are upon the earth" (Col. 3:5 AV). Both are translated in the more modern versions, "put to death" (cf. RSV, NEB). The apostolic imperative is based on the Lord's own demand for daily crucifixion (Luke 9:23).

The objects of mortification are the sinful actions of the flesh, or the old unregenerate self. These are called the "deeds of the body" (Rom. 8:13) or "your members. . . upon the earth" in the sense that sinful acts are concretely expressed through the bodily person. The manifestations whether in thought, emotion, or act, produced by the "law of sin" which still resides in the "members" of the believer (Rom. 7:23), are to be put to death. Ultimately it is self as self-centered rather than Christ-centered which is to be mortified. The Biblical expressions (present tense in Rom. 8:13; "daily" Luke 9:23) make mortification a matter of daily experience. The aorist (Col. 3:5) is probably the constantive use summarizing the process of many acts.

Mortification is not a meritorious work but rather an obligation to grace. It is based on the fact of a prior faith union with Christ in his death at Calvary. The imperative "mortify" (Col. 3:5) is preceded by the indicative "ye are dead" (v. 3; cf. Rom. 6:1-10). The reality of the believer's co-death with Christ is to be believed (Rom. 6:11) and lived out in life (v. 12-13), making effective in daily experience that death to self which has already taken place in Christ positionally in salvation.

Mortification is also performed by grace "through the Spirit" (Rom. 8:13). The same power of God which triumphed over sin in the death and resurrection of Christ is the only effective agency for making the death of the old self a reality in experience.

The believer's responsibility is simply to appropriate this power in faith and act upon it.

True mortification is not a morbid impoverishing asceticism by which the personal ego is gradually killed. It is a putting off of the old which results in the putting on of the new (Col. 3:5, 8, 12), a dying which results in life (Rom. 8:13; cf. 6:13).

ROBERT L. SAUCY

MOSES. See also *Decalogue; Jewish Ethics; Old Testament Ethics.* "As Moses the servant of the Lord had commanded" is the key to Joshua's career, and, although the phrase occurs rarely after this, it can be understood as the basis of all faithful Israelites. While modern liberal criticism would reduce the amount of authentically Mosaic writing preserved in the Pentateuch, only the most extreme critics would deny him a formative place in the infancy of Israel. Were little more than the rudiments of the Decalogue allowed to his agency he would stand as a giant among men. But the reasons advanced for divorcing him from a major part of the Pentateuchal Law appear groundless when examined in the light of well-attested ancient custom (cf. K. A. Kitchen, "Moses" in J. D. Douglas ed., *The New Bible Dictionary,* London, Inter-Varsity, 1962, Grand Rapids, Eerdmans).

Moses should be assessed, therefore, as he is presented in the whole of Scripture. This places him higher than any other man, unique in the Old Testament (Deut. 34:10), and in the New juxtaposed with God's perfect Prophet ("the law was given through Moses; grace and truth came through Jesus Christ," John 1:17). Emphasis on Moses as lawgiver is appropriate so long as it is remembered that the laws he drew up cover every aspect of life, forming the foundation of Israelite society, a society which only became an entity under his guidance. No other ancient Near East legislator has left so comprehensive a code. While this may be the chance of survival, no other leader known to us has made a nation of a horde of depressed slaves. Moses' success, however marred by the selfishness or dissatisfaction of the people, was due in a large degree to the fairness of his laws.

At this point his inspiration should be acknowledged; the laws which he gave to Israel were given to him by God. Scripture claims Moses had the whole law from God, although only the Ten Commandments were written by the divine finger (Deut. 5:22; cf. 31). Before the Sinai revelation, Moses dispensed justice to Israel, showing that some laws or standards were accepted already (Exod. 18:13ff.) and undoubtedly the experience and insight thus gained helped in formulating the body of Israel's laws. God did not speak to an empty mind, but prepared his servant from infancy. Accordingly, it is no surprise to find close parallels to some of the laws among Israel's neighbors. Their societies were similar, or were going to be, from the Wilderness viewpoint; so naturally their problems and solutions would often coincide, and the approach tried and proved by one community could be borrowed easily by another. By incorporating older laws, by adapting them, or by implicitly opposing them (as the Canaanite practice of seething a kid in its mother's milk, Exod. 23:19), Moses taught Israel what was right, that is, what conformed to God's demands; and it may be that a great deal more of his law was practiced in other societies than can be traced now.

Moses' whole career hung upon a successful conclusion, and this came only after his death. Had the nation Israel failed to occupy the Promised Land, his laws could hardly have survived, for the people would have lost their communal identity. Moses' imposition of a detailed, comprehensive law fostered Israel's unity by stressing the difference between right and wrong in every part of life, a difference required by Israel's position as God's selected people, his subjects by covenant. The absolutes of the Decalogue are the demands of a supreme authority, whereas all that is known of polytheistic societies suggests the impossibility of any definite law of this type; for even the best gods are merely enlarged reflections of their worshippers. Here, in contrast, is the assertion of uncompromising monotheism with the accompanying commands which penetrate "beneath action to its spring in motive" (H. H. Rowley, *Men of God,* London, Nelson, 1963, p. 13), the means by which Israel could "be holy" as her Lord was holy.

Moses, therefore, acted as God's spokesman, his prophet (Deut. 18:15f.), but he went beyond the simple giving of God's Word to interpret it for his people. In one way, the Torah (Law) itself is all interpretation of the primary demand to be holy, to love God, and to love neighbor as self; yet all was futile unless it could be put into action. Here Moses' personal example demonstrated the working of the covenant, God's love drawing out responsive, selfless devotion (cf. Exod. 32:32). Despite this impressive, life-long exhibition, despite continual appeals (e.g., Deut. 30:11-14), the majority in Israel never penetrated beyond the external symbols of the Mosiac faith, so that it had to be brought to fulfillment in a new covenant whose Maker himself gave a new ordinance: "If you love me, keep my commandments" (John 14:21ff.). Yet the kernel of Moses' law is embodied in the New Covenant; all the Ten Commandments are given again, except the sabbath law. The "old" that "has passed away" was concerned with the temporal needs of God's people as a nation, the birth of the church made those old rules obsolete; but without Moses' work the same church could not have come into existence (Gal. 3:24). And even if the ritual laws and the rules of hygiene given to ancient Israel are in force no longer, they are "profitable" for God's new people, to teach them of God's care for every aspect of life, the need for order and discipline, the high aims of a purity and holiness which reflect the very character of God himself as Moses reflected his glory (Exod. 34:29ff.; cf. II Cor. 3).   ALAN R. MILLARD

MOTIVES AND MOTIVATION. See also *Mixed Motives.* Motives and their dynamic effect, a condition or state called motivation, have concerned philosophers, psychologists, educators, and industrial managers for a long time. Motives are commonly defined as the thoughts and feelings that make a person act; motivation, as the urge to direct oneself toward goals which seem to the person to be worthy. Motives and motivation are, then, internal to the human being. Though personnel in education sometimes speak of motivating learners, psychologists usually say that all an individual or an institution can do to assist motivation is to establish conditions under which a learner or client will possibly be moved to act in prescribed ways.

In this sense, a Sunday School teacher is wrong when she refers to "motivating" her class. Because of certain conditions in their environment, of which her presence is one, her pupils presumably motivate themselves. Their hunger during the noontime class period, their boredom at the continuous droning of the teacher's voice, and the fatigue caused by sitting too long in one place create negative response resulting in restlessness and culminating in rebellion. The teacher tries to placate the pupils by offering them a reward: an outing which will occur next spring. Then she threatens them with the only punishment she can conscientiously administer: reporting their behavior to the department superintendent. Her efforts avail little. Suddenly she notices that two members of her class are cooperating by controlling themselves and seeking to regulate constructively the behavior of

their peers. The two cooperative pupils may feel as hungry, bored, and tired as the others. What makes them behave differently? Two possible hypotheses are as follows: (1) they are grateful, and therefore reverent, to God for what he has done for them; (2) they respect the teacher for her Christian witness and her unselfish devotion to the class.

This seemingly pat example illustrates certain recent developments in motivation theory as well as relevance of motivation to Christian ethics. The major theories of motivation now number four: (1) the associative theory, which holds that a given stimulus effects an expected response, with the bond between the two perhaps being strengthened by the hedonistic consequences of the response; (2) the drive theory, which says that the human organism is compelled by feelings of disequilibrium to behave in ways which establish equilibrium, or homeostasis; (3) the cognitive theory, a non-mechanistic interpretation which maintains that people take action as a consequence of having considered the ends or results of their behaviors; and (4) the psychoanalytic theory, which emphasizes the power of analytic thought and the function of unsatisfied wishes in driving people to behave in given ways. Though the four theories differ markedly, recent scholarship has identified some basic agreements among them. Theorists agree, for example, that behavior is complex, determined as it is by many influences. No single concept—of need, instinct, association, or whatever—is adequate to explain diverse ways of behaving. The notion of homeostasis as a basic principle of motivation is declining in importance. Human beings are now more often thought to be dynamically self-initiating, and therefore less dependent on outside stimuli as goads. Motives are being classified in hierarchies, with lowest-level motives often originating in biologically-based needs or drives like those associated with the hunger, boredom, and fatigue in the example above. Desire for rewards offered by superiors or associates and fear of punishment for failing to measure up to expected standards provide, at best, medium-level motivation. Motives which are permanently most effective are intimately life-related by being oriented toward one's values, principles, goals, and ideals. The two cooperative pupils mentioned in the example above were apparently behaving as a consequence of high-level motivation.

Recent theory-building and experimentation concerning high-level motivation have relevance for the study and practice of Christian ethics, even though they are centered in secularist thinking. Ausubel and others have discussed intrinsic, positive motives, including those for exercising curiosity, exploration, and mastery (D. P. Ausubel, *Educational Psychology: A Cognitive View*, New York, Holt, Rinehart and Winston, 1968, chap. 10). B. F. Skinner has favored arranging environmental conditions to reinforce worthy motivation *The Technology of Teaching*, New York, Appleton-Century-Crofts, 1968, chap. 7). McClelland has investigated "achievement motivation," which he believes can occur, for example, through knowing one's goals, perceiving one's progress, and taking responsibility for one's performance (D. C. McClelland, J. W. Atkinson, R. A. Clark, and E. L. Lowell, *The Achievement Motive*, New York, Appleton-Century-Crofts, 1953). White has described "competence motivation" as being a self-perpetuating process of dealing with one's environment because of a "feeling of efficacy" which has a motivating effect (C. N. Cofer and M. H. Appley, *Motivation: Theory and Research*, New York, John Wiley and Sons, 1964, *passim*). While many behavioral scientists are now preoccupied with the effects of society and culture on the individual, some of their number are exploring the significant role of the individual in determining his own behavior by what he himself thinks, feels, and values.

In the hierarchy of motives which affect Christian ethics, the highest-placed motive is showing gratitude for the grace of God in the atoning work of Christ. Unlike most of the high-level motives being upheld by secularists, this motive is directed away from self. A second, consequent high-level motive is manifesting love which is a response to God's love. Of course, the regenerated person may possibly be motivated to Christian behavior by his wish to emulate Christ. He may be thinking of his own future reward, or he may seek to avoid loss of joy. But, as in the example above, the worthiest of motives are directed vertically in an effort to give gratitude, obedience, and honor to God, and then horizontally in quest of the spiritual welfare and also the physical and material welfare of one's fellows.   RONALD C. DOLL

MOVIES. See also *Mass Media; Television; Theater.* Christian dramatic movies have generally been thinly disguised attempts at propaganda in the service of evangelism. Committed Christians should, however, be able to write from a heart full of Christ's glory and still deal honestly with characterization and plot so that nothing is forced. Movies used for evangelism that get to the conversion of the chief character and go no further display an unnatural preoccupation with the pre-Christian life, and a sad lack of creativity concerning the post-conversion life of obedience to the Lord Christ in this world of injustice, sex movies, machines, and societal break down.

Movies produced by Christians as advertisements for mission work are unethical if they fail to present the failures as well as the successes. To present only the positive side is to mislead the viewer. Should the church hang out its dirty linen? If it is claiming to "tell it like it is," it can scarcely overlook the facts of prejudice, organizational animosities, backsliding and other spiritual failures.

Should a Christian go to movies? We might as well ask, "Should a Christian read books?" Yes and no. If a movie leads him to sin, he'd best walk out. If his example of attending seems to overcome a new Christian friend with temptation, he might better stay away (cf. I Cor. 8-10, Rom. 14: Gal. 5). Some say simply, "Of course a Christian should go to movies." This is naive. Hollywood and Stockholm are ultimately not our friends. Some are drawn into the sins of Col. 3 or Eph. 5 by the vividness of dramatic productions. But to suggest that a Christian should never go is equal to saying that sin inevitably occurs, which is inaccurate. At present more perceptive films are being produced by the secular world than the Christian. A movie may not be Christian, but it often reveals the terrible stresses of people in today's society. It identifies problems, if not solutions. We need to profit from truth wherever found, since the Holy Spirit is the fountainhead of all truth.

Should a Christian act in secular movies (or plays)? Some say that due to evil parts or basic changes in the personality of the actor, Christians should not act. Certainly some parts displease Christ. And some become actors because they seek escape from themselves, so a Christian who doesn't know who he is probably should not act. But all parts aren't evil, and many people do not lose sight of who they are by acting. Subduing the earth and the cultural mandate require involvement. For the church to abandon its creative voice for righteousness and love in any area is unfortunate.

PAUL FROMER

MURDER. See also *Crime; Homicide.* It is God who providentially bestows life on human beings. Human life is the medium by which he is to be obeyed, served, and glorified. Hence while not an absolute value in itself, life is to be treated with profoundest reverence (cf. *Life, Sacredness of*) as a property held in stewardship for its rightful owner and donor, a trust to be retained or returned at his discretion. Life is therefore invested with a sanctity no mundane authority, not even a *de jure* government, ought to violate. He who intentionally damages or terminates it, aside from exceptional circumstances which God himself specifies, usurps presumptuously a prerogative which belongs exclusively to the Creator, and by so doing becomes a murderer. The command, "Thou shalt not kill" (Exod. 20:13), is simply the underside of the Biblical demand that man, down to the last breath he draws, acknowledges himself the steward of his sovereign Creator.

That death must remain under God's providential control is a pivotal assumption in the traditonal Christian ethic of self-defense. When Thomas Aquinas sanctions the use of force against an aggressor, he insists that the resisting force be no greater than what is required to frustrate the aggressor's evil purpose. To intend killing, even in self-defense, when lesser counter-violence would suffice, is to be guilty of murder and so, really, of sacrilege. Thomas could not be more laconic: "It is, therefore, wrong for a man to intend to kill another as a means to defend himself" (quoted by Paul Ramsey, *War and the Christian Conscience,* Durham, N.C., Duke University, 1961, p. 51).

The implications of this Biblically deduced position are enormously far-reaching. What about war (cf. *Peace and War*)? Does participation in a *jus bellum* exonerate soldiers from guilt? Traditionai theology has always so maintained despite the excruciating difficulty of certifying any specific *bellum* as *jus*. Again, what about suicide (q.v.)? Does God permit an individual to elect when and how he may close the door permanently on his continued existence here and now? What about euthanasia (q.v.)? Understandable, certainly, is the sufferer's desire for release from pain no drug can any longer mitigate or from the status of a humanoid vegetable. What, finally, about tolerating or abetting economic and/or political conditions which will insure, to a high degree of probability, unnecessary deaths by accident, sickness, or disease? In such situations of collective responsibility is the accusation of murder ever justified?

In a violent era when man's sacredness as *imago Dei* is being more and more scoffed at, Scripture's prohibition against murder stands as a bulwark of human dignity.

VERNON C. GROUNDS

MUSLIM LAW. See *Isamic Law.*

MYSTICISM. See also *Quietism.* "Mysticism" is a generic term covering a wide range of theories and activities centering in the effort to grasp and enjoy the divine essence. It has both philosophic and religious manifestations, and these may be Christian or non-Christian. A single person or movement may combine philosophic and religious emphases, concentrating in the first instance on grasping the divine essence and in the second on enjoying fellowship with the Highest. But there is an important distinction between rationalistic mysticism, which attributes to the mind a natural ability to rise to immediate intuition of the Absolute, and Christian mysticism, which ascribes the initiative to God in reaching out to man.

Mysticism is widespread. The earliest known forms came from the East, particularly from India and China. Hinduism and Buddhism have a strong affinity for mysticism. Eastern mysticism was translated to the West by Neoplatonism. It has exerted a strong influence on Christianity. Early reflections were found in the Alexandrian School and in Dionysius the Areopagite. Nearly all later Christian mystics reflect Dionysius' three stages of purification, illumination, and union.

The high point of Christian mysticism came in the Middle Ages, with Bernard of Clairvaux and the Victorines playing a prominent role. Meister Eckhart stood at the head of a large number of late-medieval mystics who reacted against the worldliness and rationalism in the church. Eckhart came under ecclesiastical condemnation, particularly because of accusations of pantheism. Mysticism became prominent in Germany, Spain, France, England, and the Low Countries. A sane and balanced form of this emphasis was found in the Brethren of the Common Life.

Mysticism prepared men for the Reformation by its criticism of prevailing systems, although the mystics did not protest against dogmas as the Reformers felt compelled to do. Mystic claims to spiritual freedom were soon seen to be in conflict with the Reformation. In the Reformation age, Protestant mystics included Tersteegen, Boehme, Arndt, and Sebastian Franck, and Catholic mystics included John of the Cross, Teresa of Jesus, and Ignatius Loyola.

Some general characteristics of mysticism can be discerned. Mystical theology emphasizes the love of God in contrast with speculative theology's emphasis on the knowledge of God. Mysticism therefore is frequently in tension with dogmatic theology and its periods of florescence occur particularly in reaction to dead orthodoxy. But many figures in Christian theology have sought to combine the two emphases. In the best of Christian mysticism it is held that the Divine Spirit vivifies the human soul, while, more incidentally, the soul cooperates in this process. As the soul becomes more responsive, the assimilation increases. The process culminates in contemplation, which, unlike meditation, does not require conscious effort.

Mysticism is inescapably individualistic.

There is a progressive inwardness in the mystic's development. Almost all Catholic writers stress three stages; purgation, contemplation, and union. Little value is set on external ceremonies. The progress is from the outward life to the inward life to the life of the spirit. Some mystics concentrate on the reconciliation of the soul with God, some aspire to ecstasy, and others emphasize the fruits of the Spirit.

Quietism is a form of mysticism which taught the necessity of utter passivity and "disinterestedness" in the relation of the soul to God, suppression of human effort so that the divine action can have full sway. Mystic death occurs, and God is the only reality that exists in the person who has undergone it. Found especially in Spain and France, Quietism disturbed the Catholic Church and came under its condemnation in the seventeenth century.

Mysticism has been viewed with suspicion by many in the church. An emphasis critical of doctrinal theology will understandably come off second best when judged by doctrinal theology's standards. An additional inherent difficulty resides in any attempt to describe mystical experience in rational terms. Furthermore, some mystics are known largely through the hostile representations of their critics.

Dangers inherent in mysticism have not been avoided with equal success by all. The mystic with alerted senses may find God everywhere and be subject to pantheism. Even some of the better mystics are sometimes at fault in claiming uncritically a likeness to God which amounts to deification. The *via negativa,* practiced by some mystics, appears to be an inappropriate way to arrive at the Divine essence. There is a constant danger of applying intensely personal experiences as a criterion for the spirituality of others. Mystic affirmations threaten also to denigrate the authority of the Scriptural revelation. Apocalypticism and antinomianism have appeared under the banner of mysticism. The outstanding mystics have sought consciously to avoid such dangers.

Mysticism broadly conceived hangs together with the possibility of a personal relation with God. The difficulty is in describing or seeking to regulate the Holy Spirit's work applying revelational truth to the individual believer. At its best, mysticism can serve as a corrective and balance to excessive rationalism and spiritual lethargy in the church.   JOHN H. KROMMINGA

MYTH. The Greek word *mythos* means an imaginative and fictitious tale, as distinct from a narrative of observed or reconstructed events. As such, myth is neither scientific nor historical, nor factually informative in any ordinary sense. The epistles warn against Jewish and Gnostic *mythoi* (fables) as being anti-Christian (I Tim. 1:4, 4:7; II Tim. 4:4; Titus 1:14; II Peter 1:16).

Often in the past century it has been affirmed that myth—aetiological, explaining cosmic processes; ritual-magical, seeking to control them; and existential, inviting identification with cosmic rôle—was the common coin of ancient religions and cultures, doing duty for both science and technology. The early chapters of Genesis have been cited as cases in point, though this begs questions about the nature of OT faith.

More recently, Rudolf Bultmann has classified virtually all the Christological narratives and doctrines of the NT as myth, i.e., according to Bultmann's distinctive existentialist definition, as extrapolated objectifications of the Christian "self-understanding" given through the *kerygma,* which (Bultmann holds) is the true and total content of apostolic witness. In other words, this material, instead of being what it seems, a window through which we may observe the historic Jesus who is also the cosmic Christ, is really just a mirror in which is reflected the self-understanding of the witnesses—their view of themselves as now freed from guilt and fear and made open to the possibilities of the future. Demythologizing, to Bultmann, means interpreting the New Testament in the light of this view of its nature. Whether this is a momentous clarification or a monstrous misunderstanding of the New Testament, and whether, theologically speaking, demythologizing would lead to renewal or to ruin, are sharply debated questions.

Some would salvage myth by equating it with anthropomorphic narration about God. That all Biblical narrative about God is anthropomorphic, and that the *imago dei* and the Incarnation show such anthropomorphism to be right and necessary, is undeniable, but to call the records of God's work in history myth just because anthropomorphisms are used is gratuitous confusion. Since pagan god-stories concern not history but nature, and since Scripture recounts nothing of Yahweh like the celestial goings-on of these god-stories, it seems clearer and sounder to follow Scripture's

own usage and reject myth as a non-Biblical category. All that Scripture tells us about God is historical, relating in one way or another to the outworking of his purposes in and for this world, and this is a fact which myth-talk can only obscure.

Biblical ethics gain their distinctive content from knowledge of the historically-revealed character and command of God, whom we must imitate and obey. Since myth is at best a category not of divine disclosure but of human interpretation, the more Biblical narrative one classifies as myth the less certainty can there be as to whether what purports to be God's deed and command really is so; and so the more existential, situationalist, and imprecise our theological ethics have to be. This correlation can be observed in many modern writers.

📖 P. E. Hughes, *Baker's Dictionary of Theology*, Everett F. Harrison, ed., Grand Rapids, Baker 1960; *The Theology of Rudolf Bultmann*, Charles W. Kegley, ed., New York, Harper & Row, 1966, p. 183ff.   JAMES I. PACKER

N

NARCOTICS. See *Drugs.*

NATIONAL ASSOCIATION OF EVANGELICALS. See also *Ecumenism and Ethics.* Harold J. Ockenga voiced the hopes of many evangelicals when he asserted to the 1942 founding conference of NAE, "If we are to guard our testimony and our purity, our great need is not for something which is negative but something which is positive, something which will launch a program, something which will marshal the enthusiasm and the resources and the strength of the people of Christian conviction throughout America."

Through the decades since NAE made its entry on the American ecclesiastical scene,

evangelicals have moved decisively from the protective withdrawal produced by the great fundamentalist/liberal debates to a renewed frontal assault on the strongholds of Satan through positive gospel witness in relevant areas of human concern.

Often evangelical reaction during the first half of the twentieth century to liberalism's "social gospel" understandably tended to equate humanitarian concern with weakness in gospel proclamation. It took a while to accomplish a swing back to Jesus' pattern of being "moved with compassion" by human suffering. It is noteworthy that the eight times in the Gospels that Jesus is characterized as "moved with compassion" all have human suffering in view, though these responses were always accompanied by spiritual concern.

The NAE has played a key role in the steering of Bible-believing Christians to honest involvement with social needs based on the gospel dynamic. Evangelicals have held consistently that an adequate social ethic is possible only when derived from the light of Biblical revelation and empowered by the imputed spiritual dynamics of regeneration. On the other hand, true spiritual regeneration should be evidenced before man through genuine acts of concern for people in need and against injustice of all kinds.

NAE concern for social needs led to the establishment in 1944 of a Committee for Postwar Relief to aid the victims of war in Europe. This initial relief ministry led the way to an expanded evangelical humanitarian ministry in Korea in 1950. The name of the original committee was changed to World Relief Commission to encompass the growing involvement in an integral part of NAE in social action worldwide. WRC today maintains a world-wide outreach with projects in the disaster and poverty-stricken areas of the world, including Korea, Vietnam, Pakistan, India, Chile, Peru, Nigeria and others. Its social/spiritual programs are administered primarily by evangelicals in each country through assistance to orphanages, schools, vocational centers, leper colonies, refugee programs, hospitals and agricultural development projects. In addition to WRC, Christians of evangelical commitment find expression for social concern in numerous other specialized humanitarian ministries that have come into existence since World War II. These ministries taken together reflect a renewed awareness of the social implications of the gospel and the commitment of an increasing number of evangelicals to give arms and legs to their faith through meaningful social action.

W. STANLEY MOONEYHAM

NATIONAL COUNCIL OF CHURCHES.

See also *Councils of Churches; Ecumenism and Ethics.* The National Council of the Churches of Christ in the USA is the country's chief organizational expression of the ecumenical movement. It aims to give tangible evidence of the unity Christians claim to possess. It promotes cooperative activity among denominations whose leaders seek a united approach to certain tasks.

Ethical Assumptions. The council's most noteworthy efforts have revolved around the quest for Christian answers to social problems. Considerable time and large sums of money have been spent on special studies. Many meetings have been called to propagandize proposed solutions. In a very limited way, the council has acted directly to alleviate human distress arising out of social ills. Mostly, however, it has been satisfied with trying to assign to the state the primary responsibility for their correction and treatment.

The council has been dominated by theologically-liberal churchmen and has therefore reflected liberalism's ethical ambiguities. Appeal to Scripture for ethical imperatives has been minimal. Love, liberty, compassion, and justice have been described as principles which form the council's objectives, but even these are not uniformily applied. At times it is difficult to understand exactly what the council uses for its ethical foundations. A 121-page handbook published by the council in 1966 sheds little light on what it uses to distinguish right from wrong. Although never expressed in so many words, the idea of a comfortable life for the greatest number surfaces repeatedly as a key objective. Little or no recognition is given evangelical Christianity's insistence that personal regeneration is pre-requisite to a spiritually vigorous social order.

Lack of an agreed-upon foundation seems not to deter the council from giving the impression that its conclusions bear an ecumenical imprimatur and are incumbent upon the entire Christian community.

History. The National Council of Churches was formed in 1950 out of the merger of twelve national interdenominational organizations. These were the Federal Council of the Churches of Christ in America (founded in 1908), the Foreign Missions Conference of North America (1893 and 1911), the Home Missions Council of North America (1908), the International Council of Religious Education (1922), the Missionary Education Movement of the United States and Canada (1902), the National Protestant Council on Higher Education (1911), the United Council of Church Women (1940), the United Stewardship Council (1920), Church World Service (1946), the Interseminary Committee (1880), the Protestant Film Commission (1947), and the Protestant Radio Commission (1947).

The council was organized by specifically instructed representatives of twenty-nine Protestant, Anglican, and Orthodox denominations or communions which then became charter members of the council. These included most of the large denominations in the country, with the notable exception of the Roman Catholic Church, Southern Baptist Convention, the Lutheran Church—Missouri Synod, and the American Lutheran Church. Several other small denominations joined during the fifties and sixties.

The Student Volunteer Movement, which dated back to the 1880s, merged with the council in 1953, evolving eventually into the University Christian Movement which phased itself out of existence in 1969. Church Women United separated from the council amicably in the late sixties. The Christian Ministry in the National Parks and the newsletter *Religion in Communist Dominated Areas* severed ties with the council in 1971.

Organization and Program. The council's constitution requires a General Assembly made up of eight hundred persons nominated by the member communions to meet every three years to chart broad policy, review programs, and to speak up on current issues. About one-fourth of the members of the General Assembly also serve on the General Board which is to meet three times a year for similar reasons. Day-to-day operations are handled by a paid executive staff, of whom there have been as many as 185. Most of these have offices in the Interchurch Center in Manhattan. The council has also had an overseas staff of up to forty-one people.

In addition to sponsoring many meetings, the council conducts valuable research on a wide variety of matters of interest to churches. The biggest and probably most rewarding task is the overseas relief arranged by the council's Church World Service. The most controversial aspect of the council is its practice of issuing pronouncements; in the first twenty years of the council the compendium of these grew to a sheaf almost an inch thick and covered thirty broad areas of subject matter—from agricultural policy to Vatican relations. Other noteworthy projects have included publication of literature (the Revised Standard Version of the Bible was a project of the council), lobbying in Washington, ministries for migrants, and voter registration drives. The Delta Ministry in Mississippi was its most controversial program; it supplied much food, clothing, medical aid, and housing to needy blacks but aroused considerable hostility through other activities which were suspect to conservative Southern whites.

Problems. The council is composed of four divisions: Christian Education, Christian Life and Mission, Overseas Ministries, and Christian Unity. While the goal of the organization is to coordinate ecumenical work via the General Assembly and General Board, the divisons and their agencies have their own boards which control income and expenditures. The council gets few undesignated funds so that interdepartmental coordinators have only the power to recommend priorities. The priorities are in reality set by the amount of subsidies the various agencies are able to attract to themselves. The situation illustrates the fact that coordinated effort is not necessarily achieved by merging organizations. Architects of the council inadvertently illustrated the problem when they created the nominal paradox the "Division of Christian Unity."

The council recognizes there is no union without mission. But mission seems invariably to divide, unless there is agreement on the ultimate authority for mission. Higher and form criticism have minimized the Bible's authoritative role for ecumenical leaders. Instead, the ecumenical ethic often reflects the arbitrary biases of humanistic philosophy and liberal politics. Those who accede are credited with being "prophetic."

Samuel McCrea Cavert's *Church Cooperation and Unity in America—A Historical Review: 1900-1970*, New York, Association, which came out in 1970, is a sympathetic treatment enhanced by a comprehensive bibliography.

DAVID KUCHARSKY

NATIONALISM. Most authorities accept the definition of nationalism formulated by historian Carlton J. H. Hayes. He points out that it is easier to define "nationality" than "nationalism." The former term most commonly designates a group of people who share a common language and a common historical tradition, and who believe they constitute a distinct cultural society. Hayes defines nationalism as: "a condition of mind in which loyalty to the ideal or fact of one's national state is superior to all other loyalties and of which pride in one's nationality and belief in its intrinsic excellence and its 'mission' are integral parts" (*Essays on Nationalism*, New York, Macmillan, 1926, p.6.)

Thus nationalism is a compound of many factors, some of which have roots in human nature and many of which have a long history. Obviously it is closely related to patriotism (q.v.) a concept at least as old as recorded history and indicative of a special feeling or love for a certain area, region, or country. But nationalism is more than patriotism and, according to today's usage, is a relatively modern phenomenon. Its modernity consists in the fusion of patriotism with nationality and the subordination of all other allegiances to one loyalty, the nation.

Most scholars agree that nationalism developed from the growing sense of national identity which accompanied the rise of the modern nation-state. However, it was not until the eighteenth century that nationalism emerged in clear form. The great landmarks of nationalism in England, America, and France were the revolutions in those countries in 1688, 1776, and 1789 respectively. Most important for the development of the concept in modern times was the French Revolution which emphasized not only "liberty" and "equality" but also "fraternity" meaning a feeling of national brotherhood. Liberalism and nationalism developed concomitantly from the ideals of the French Revolution and for many years the principle of "national self-determination" was an integral part of liberal policy. In nineteenth-century Europe nationalism was most commonly associated with the liberal principles of humanitarianism, freedom, and constitutionalism until the defeat of the German liberals by Otto von Bismarck (d. 1898) and the coming of World War I in 1914 which revealed the ugly side of a nationalism divorced from other moderating considerations.

On the positive side, nationalism historically has been a progressive force in the struggle of oppressed nationalities to free themselves from foreign domination, and still is in Africa and Asia among peoples now emerging from colonial control. Also, the humanitarian nationalism of men like Johann Herder (d. 1803) stressed the reasonableness and naturalness of nationality, the creative spirit of a nation and the intrinsic worth of every culture. Moreover, the liberal nationalism of leaders like Woodrow Wilson (d. 1924) with its emphasis on the principle of national self-determination was a logical extension of the democratic doctrine of popular sovereignty.

Negatively, nationalism has been used to support imperialist expansion, itself a contradiction of the principle of self-determination, and has become a divisive factor in international relations. It also led to the tragic war in 1914 and is still a leading cause of international conflict.

In terms of Christian concern, nationalism has become the popular religion of the modern world. The outright rejection of Christianity by many individuals and its secularization by others has created a religious vacuum that many have tried to fill with nationalism. Furthermore, nationalism is in a sense but an extension to the group to which one belongs of the pride that is inherent in fallen man.

The major dilemma modern nationalism presents for Christian ethics lies in the realm of primary loyalties. The Bible teaches obedience to duly constituted governing authorities (Rom. 13) and strongly implies that no believer should neglect proper devotion to the legitimate interests of his nation. Nevertheless, the Bible also clearly indicates that a Christian's allegiance to a particular nation or nationality cannot be absolute or unconditional because his highest loyalty is to God alone (Exod. 20:3; Act 5:29). The nature of the political system under which a believer lives largely determines the amount of tension he experiences in his personal response to the demands of nationalism. The more free the society, the less likely it is that a Christian will be forced to choose between God and country. In any event, "my country, right or wrong" is not a Biblical concept, and a Christian should never allow his faith to be prostituted by nationalism or any other ideology of man.

📖 Herbert Butterfield, *International Conflict in the Twentieth Century*, New York, Harper, 1960; Carlton J. H. Hayes, *Essays on Nationalism*, New York, Macmillan, 1926; Hans Kohn, *The Idea of Nationalism*, New York, Macmillan, 1944; Winthrop Hudson, ed., *Nationalism and Religion in America*, New York, Harper, 1970.

ROBERT D. LINDER

NATURALISTIC ETHICS. See also *Evolutionary Ethics; Humanism*. Philosophical terms are notoriously complex and elastic. Naturalism is no exception to this semantic vagueness. James Ward in 1899 defined it as the view which "separates Nature from God, subordinates Spirit to Matter, and sets up unchangeable law as supreme" (quoted by William Quillian, Jr., *The Moral Theory of Evolutionary Naturalism*, New Haven, Yale University, 1945, p. 2). His contemporary, Thomas Huxley, explained naturalism as "the extension of the province of what we call matter and causation and the concomitant . . . banishment from all regions of human thought of what we call spirit and spontaneity . . . (till) the realm of matter and law is coextensive with knowledge, with feeling, and with action" (ibid., p. 3). More recently and less explicitly, Sidney Hook has asserted that the term means "the wholehearted acceptance of scientific method as the only reliable way of reaching truth about the world of nature, society and man." He has also asserted that "the least common denominator of all historic naturalism, therefore, is not so much a set of specific doctrines as the method of scientific or rational empiricism" (quoted by Eliseo Vivas, *The Moral Life and the Ethical Life*, Chicago, University of Chicago, 1950, pp. 16-17). Equally sweeping is Jude P. Dougherty's statement: naturalism is the "philosophical position that affirms that nature is the whole of reality; that man has his origin, growth, and decay in nature; and that nature is self-explanatory—nature being defined as that which is amenable to scientific investigation" (Jude

P. Dougherty, Introduction, Part III, "American Naturalistic Thought," *Approaches to Morality*, Jesse A. Mann and Gerald F. Kreyche, eds., New York, Harcourt, Brace & World, 1966, p. 288). Hence the genus naturalism embraces a profusion of species—the atomism of a Democritus, the hedonism of a Bentham, the materialism of a Marx, the determinism of a Freud, the humanism of a Comte, the instrumentalism of a Dewey, the neo-positivism of a Ryle, and the existentialism of a Sartre.

Underlying these divergent unidimensional reality-systems, however, is the characteristic singled out by Vivas: "All naturalism is committed to secularism, since its essential meaning as a cosmological doctrine is irrevocably atheistic" (ibid., p. 124). Assuming that Vivas is correct in his appraisal, what ethical guidance can naturalism furnish its adherents? Can it logically espouse values? Can it effectively motivate their pursuit?

The Achilles-heel in any attempt to build an ethics on this foundation is the "inconceivable" transition which baffled David Hume two hundred years ago.

In every system of morality which I have hitherto met with, I have always remarked that the author proceeds for some time in the ordinary way of speaking, and establishes the being of a God, or makes observations concerning human affairs; when of a sudden I am surprised to find, that instead of the usual copulations of propositions, *is*, and *is not*, I meet with no proposition that is not connected with an *ought*, or an *ought not*. This change is inperceptable; but is, however, of the last consequence. For as this *ought*, or *ought not*, expresses some new relation or affirmation, it is necessary that it should be observed and explained; and at the same time a reason should be given for what seems altogether inconceivable, how this new relation can be a deduction from others, which are entirely different from it (quoted by

John Hospers, *Human Conduct*, New York, Harcourt, Brace & World, 1961, p. 532).

In 1903 G. E. Moore repeated this criticism in his celebrated *Principia Ethica*, labelling as "the naturalistic fallacy" the smuggling of moral evaluations into factual descriptions. By no legitimate process of ratiocination he contended, as Hume had previously, can imperatives be deduced from indicatives. The gold of right and good, norms and values—unless it proves fool's gold—cannot be refined out of the empirical ore of mathematics, physics, chemistry, biology, zoology, or any of the sciences, including psychology. Between the *is* and the *ought* a great gulf remains fixed and unbridgeable. Naturalism may profess its preferences, adjudging one mode of behavior good, one item in the spacetime continuum more significant than another. But it always fails to divulge where and how criteria for such an ethical assay are discovered.

A similar problem faced by this anti-supernaturalistic philosophy is a fact inexplicable on its premises, the fact that a creature has emerged who does indeed engage in evaluation, a creature whose whole history ineluctably demonstrates his inability to escape from the demandingness of Kant's categorical imperative. This creature believes not that he creates values, but that he finds them outside himself and that these values possess what Wolfgang Köhler has called "requiredness."

Allied to this problem is that of ordering values in some sort of hierarchy, deciding which values are of overriding weight and worth, which are subordinate. By what immaterial principle does a consistent naturalism assign rank to values, whether they are the desires John Dewey talks about or the interests Ralph Barton Perry discusses? When, if ever, does a value become valuable enough to fight and die for, or at least to warrant the sacrifice of lesser (comparison is inescapable though nature supplies no standard of comparison) values? That is a basic question.

In the end, then, naturalism founders ethically on its misunderstanding and misinterpretation of man—and thus, ultimately, its misreading of ontology. Instead of being empiricists, forming their theories only in the full light of all available data, naturalists turn out to be doctrinaire theorists who ignore the experiential facts which bear most decisively on ethics.

It is no wonder, therefore, as Robert Shafer remarks, that this philosophy has failed to build a viable ethics. Effort after effort has been made since the Renaissance, yet these efforts "have uniformly ended in self-contradiction, in paradox, in the justification or praise of immorality, or in more or less baleful absurdities" (*Christianity and Naturalism,* New Haven, Yale University, 1962, p. 290).

To avoid ethical bankruptcy, naturalism will be driven to imitate August Comte and deliberately develop a secular mythology and cultus. So Maritain pointedly inquires: "If naturalism really wants to be in a position to guide human life effectively, will it not have to resolve to be wholly normative, and thus (since this is impossible for it inasmuch as plain philosophy) make itself into a 'religion' in the whole sense of the word?" (*op. cit.,* p. 415). In short, naturalism can become ethically coherent and dynamic only by abandoning its atheism for supernaturalism.   VERNON C. GROUNDS

NATURALISTIC FALLACY. The most popular general argument against the naturalist's ethical theories is G. E. Moore's "open question" argument, which provides a test, or criterion, for sameness of meaning. The test requires that one compose a question of the form: "Is whatever is N (natural property, like pleasure) also E (ethical property, like good)?" and then proceed to ask if it makes sense to give an affirmative or negative answer. If it does, the terms in question

do *not* have the same meaning. Moore then argues, no matter what natural property N stands for, it always makes sense to ask, "Is pleasure, (N), also good, (E)?" But, on the other hand, if N were identical in meaning to E, the test question would lose its intelligibility, being reduced to the question, "Is whatever is N also N?" Moore's point is that "good" cannot be identified with any natural property, and that any attempt to define ethical terms in non-ethical ones like "pleasure" or "desired" is to commit the naturalistic fallacy.

⌦G. E. Moore, *Principia Ethica,* Cambridge, Cambridge University, 1903.   PETER GENCO

NATURAL LAW. Throughout the entire history of Western philosophy, appeals to laws of nature have been used to establish an authoritative basis for ethical judgments.

Broadly speaking, two major traditions of natural law speculation have emerged. One conceives of natural law in a *physical* and *descriptive* sense. It represents an essentially materialistic and naturalistic tradition which seeks scientific explanation and attempts to develop concepts of obligation by appealing to the physical laws of nature. Utilitarianism, Marxism, Social Darwinism, and behaviorism are examples of modern attempts to construct ethical theory in this manner. The second major tradition of natural law speculation—which usually uses the term in distinction from "laws of nature" or "physical laws"—represents an essentially idealistic and rationalistic tradition which seeks normative explanation and attempts to develop concepts of obligation by appealing to teleological meaning and ordering within nature. In this sense, natural law is conceived of in a *metaphysical* and *prescriptive* sense. It seeks, through the use of reason, to discover in human conduct absolute and universal principles of obligation which are believed to be lodged in the very nature of the human psyche and the universe. This essay expounds this latter concept of natural law; for the other usage of the term, the reader is referred to expositions of naturalism and physical laws.

Virtually all societies have established ethical prescriptions against murder and incest on the basis of what might be called a natural law instinct. The ancient Greek tragedians Aeschylus and Sophocles, however, first explicitly delineated the concept of natural law of ethical obligation by which conventional morality and the positive law of the government are both to be judged. The Socratic philosophers carried this still further. Socrates' *Apology* considers the problem of political · obligation and civil disobedience when laws of the state violate the higher natural law known by conscience. Plato suggested that human life should conform to rational forms. Aristotle transformed this into an avowedly teleological framework arguing that since man was uniquely capable of rational self-direction, personal fulfillment rested in living in accord with the dictates of reason. Roman Stoic philosophers utilized these concepts in the attempt to rationalize the divergent laws and customs of peoples throughout the Roman Empire. Insofar as possible, the precepts of human law, argued Cicero, are to be respected and evaluated in terms of the higher law of reason which is embedded in nature. "There is in fact a true law—namely, right reason—which is in accordance with nature, applies to all men, and is unchangeable and eternal. By its commands this law summons men to the performance of their duties; by its prohibitions it restrains them from doing wrong. . . . It will not lay down one rule at Rome and another at Athens, nor will it be one rule today and another tomorrow. But there will be one law, eternal and unchangeable, binding at all times upon all peoples; and there will be, as it were, one common master and ruler of men, namely God, who is the author of this law, its interpreter, and its sponsor" (*On the Commonwealth*,

III:22). Stoic concepts of natural law were reflected in the Emperor Justinian's codification of Roman law, and have ever since been fundamental to an understanding of Western jurisprudence.

Due to the prevalence of Stoic influences at the time, the early church was faced with the task of reconciling Christian concepts of grace and revelation with the Stoic concepts of nature and reason. The Prologue of St. John suggests that the concept of God as eternal reason is not antithetical to Christian teaching. Paul's allusions in the Epistle to the Romans to the natural theologies of pagan peoples also suggests that man's natural rational capacities are not antithetical to the revelation in Christ (1:20; 2:13-15). While there were exceptions such as Tertullian, many early church fathers utilized Stoic concepts of nature and reason in developing their social ethics.

Natural law concepts were an integral part of the social teachings of the church throughout the Middle Ages. There was little debate over the ontological existence of the natural law, but there was significant debate as to the epistemological basis for perceiving the natural law. Augustine maintained that man's fall into sin so thoroughly corrupted the *imago dei* within him that revelation and grace were necessary foundations for the right use of reason. Thomas Aquinas, on the other hand, emphasized the structures of the *imago dei* which remained intact despite the fall into sin, suggesting that grace and revelation serve as corrective supplements to the right use of reason. While Augustine did not deny that even pagans have some concept of natural justice, he obviously placed more emphasis on the supernatural and in social ethics than Aquinas. Generally speaking, Protestant thinkers have been "Augustinian" and Catholic thinkers have been "Thomistic" in dealing with the natural law question.

The seventeenth and eighteenth centuries saw the resurgence of secular concepts of natural law. Emphasis was placed on the ability to develop ethical norms on a purely rationalistic basis, independent of the teachings of church or Scripture. The individualistic temper of these centuries also affected the uses to which natural law concepts were put—for instead of emphasizing natural *law* (prescription), the emphasis was on natural *rights* (freedom) (q.v.). The nineteenth and twentieth century saw the demise of natural law concepts under the influence of positivism which questioned whether metaphysical inferences could be made with any validity whatever. Legal positivism refused to recognize any concept of law or obligation other than that formally promulgated by the state, a concept quite compatible with the totalitarian state. In reaction to the atrocities of Hitler's Germany, which were all perfectly legal in the technical sense of the term, theorists have again taken up natural law concepts as an attempt to delineate moral criteria by which the positive laws of states must themselves be judged.

B. F. Brown, ed., *The Natural Law Reader*, New York, Oceana, 1960; John Cogley, ed., *Natural Law and Modern Society*, New York, World, 1963; A. P. D'Entrèves, *Natural Law: An Introduction to Legal Philosophy*. London, Hutchinson, 1960. Illtud Evans, ed., *Light on the Natural Law*, Baltimore, Helicon, 1965; Otto Gierke. *Natural Law and the Theory of Society*, Ernest Barker, Boston, Beacon Hill, 1960.   PAUL B. HENRY

NATURAL RIGHTS. See also *Rights*. The notion of natural rights belongs especially to the eighteenth century when it was used as the grounds for the American revolution, in the Declaration of Independence (1776) and the French revolution, in the Declaration of the Rights of Man and Citizen (1789). It assumed, as an article of faith, that reality was mechanistic, machine-like, operating according to the laws of Newtonian physics. Such reality was termed "Nature," which as Carl Becker has shown, was deified and made to replace the Bible or the church as the revealer of the truth. All of human life (Human Nature)

and God (Nature's God) were recast to conform to the mechanistic worldview. The whole of Nature was believed to be rational, accessible to man by "Reason." Philosophically this view may be termed scientialistic rationalism.

Natural rights, then, were entitlements belonging to men by virtue of Nature, a condition existing, whether in Locke's or Rousseau's view of it, *prior* to the Social Contract which was said to have constituted human society. Each individual in the State of Nature held, as it were, a portfolio of rights by himself which, according to Rousseau, he transmitted to and then received back from the social system in a higher form; or according to Locke, some of which he deposited with government, to be withdrawn when necessary for their preservation. Since Nature was rational, and man as partaker in Nature was rational, then the appeal to Nature could be assumed to reveal natural rights as self-evident to all men, and so *universal* in character. This appeal made possible, in the American case, a radical break with English Common Law, the king, the parliament and political dependence on England, and in the French case, a destruction of the triple Estate hierarchical social system of the Ancien Régime in France and an extension of the individualistic democratic ideal throughout Europe.

The significance of the notion of natural rights lay in its claim that the rights of men originated independently of the king, the state, the church, social class, or any other institution. It was intended to limit the total claims upon the life of men by the eighteenth century social system, whether in its more secular absolute statist form or the Catholic clerical form. In the twentieth century, natural rights have been replaced by the notion of "human rights" as in the United Nations' Declaration of Human Rights (1945), reflecting a more personality-oriented idea of rights originating in man himself.

In Biblical perspective, an alternative idea of God-created rights appeals to constant norms inherent within the very constitution of God-created reality and which, rightly seen through the eyes of Biblical revelation, men may acknowledge and historically implement within the various social institutions and relationships God has ordained. Such creationally given rights serve as basis for acting and as standards which men and institutions may be called to observe if they are to enjoy the blessings of a full life of peace and health. The terms civil rights, social rights, economic rights, medical rights, and so on, reflect the many diverse ways man's God-given rights may be apprehended with reference to norms within the structure of creation.   C. T. McINTIRE

NECESSITY. See *Determinism; Fate; Free Will.*

NEGLIGENCE. The term refers to acts of careless neglect—in legal usage, to culpable acts resulting from either careless failure to become informed as to duties required by one's special occupation, or one's general legal obligations as a citizen, or from careless failure to act according to such knowledge. Failure to be aware that a lawyer has certain specified duties towards a client, careless neglect in failing to obey a red traffic light, neglect in learning that interest received on loans must be reported on income tax, careless failure to fence in a swimming pool, or to remove surgical instruments from a surgical operation, all would involve negligence.

Moral and religious usage is similar, though dealing with a more general concept. Moral negligence might involve carelessly forgetting to arrange for feeding a pet before going on vacation; or, acting on the assumption that morality has nothing to say about actions in the world of business. Religious negligence might involve carelessly neglecting to discover what God demands

we must do in order to be saved, when such information is easily available (cf. Heb. 2:3, "How escape if we neglect so great a salvation"), or careless failure to investigate the obligations a Christian has (cf. I Tim. 4:14, or II Peter 1:12). Negligence in this context, then, involves either careless failure to inform oneself as to the religious and moral duties required of the Christian; or, if having such knowledge, careless failure to act according to it. Negligence involves neglect, and is to be distinguished from trying seriously to do something and then failing.

Nor is negligence the same as ignorance; a man who does not know what his duties are, and has no easily available way of knowing, is ignorant rather than negligent (e.g., the pagan). Though related to the concept of sins of omission, the idea of negligence is not the same thing; for one can commit a sin of omission (q.v.) even after an ardent though unsuccessful effort to do something. The ordinary Christian can be negligent; so too a clergyman, who may neglect to inform himself as to the duties involved in his office, or who may carelessly fail to carry them out. So likewise can a church be negligent. In a given situation, a church may fail to consult the Word to see what action to take, even though aware that this is the obvious thing to do; or it may be aware that the Biblical demand would be to act in a given way, but carelessly neglect to act.

Negligence, in summary, roughly, is careless failure to try and do what is obviously required of us.   DIRK W. JELLEMA

NEIGHBOR. See also *Good Neighbor; Interpersonal Relations.* In several places in the OT the term simply indicates someone in close proximity (e.g., Exod. 32:27; Josh. 9:16; Ezek. 23:5, 12). Generally it refers to a fellow-member of the covenant community, one with whom there is a common religious bond and to whom there are stated moral obligations (cf. esp. Exod. 20:17; Lev. 19:18 and Deut. passim). Religious and ethical considerations therefore predominate over purely national ones.

In the NT the word occasionally signifies a person in geographical proximity and the more specialized Biblical usage also reappears in contexts where the OT itself is being paraphrased (Acts 7:27) or quoted (Heb. 8:11). It is noteworthy, however, that in every other instance it is either explicitly linked with the love-commandment (on the lips of Jesus: Matt. 5:43; 19:19; 22:39; Mark 12:31; Luke 10:27; from the writers of the epistles: Rom. 13:19-20; Gal. 5:14; James 2:8) or implicity related to it ("speak honestly to one's neighbor": Eph. 4:25; "please one's neighbor": Rom. 15:2). On all occasions in the epistles it refers to a member of the Christian community.

The command to "love one's neighbor" already occurs in the OT, a requirement that also embraces the resident-alien (Lev. 19:18, 34). It reappears in the pseudepigraphal (Jub. 36:7-8; cf. the possibly post-Christian references in Test. Iss. 5:2; Test. Dan. 5:3), Qumran (CDC 6:21; 1 QS 1:9) and rabbinic (Sif. Lev. 19:18) literature. However, all these writings uphold the equivalence of commandments from the point of view of obedience so that even where this injunction is accorded a fundamental position it is not given the status Jesus insists upon here.

Moreover, a new understanding of neighbor comes to expression in Christ's teaching, most dramatically in the parable of the Good Samaritan (Luke 10:29-37). Instead of providing a definition enabling one to discern who is the neighbor for whom there is responsibility, Jesus demands that one concentrate on *being* a neighbor to others—whomsoever they may be. In so doing he has set this ethical question in a wholly new perspective   ROBERT BANKS

NEO-NEPHALITISM. This refers to the teaching of Jakob Dobermann the Younger (1753-1815), son of a Bavarian archery instructor, in whose *Weltanschauung* pseudo-Hegelian elements improbably merged with a somewhat arrogant solipsism. The Neo-Nephalites had delusions of grandeur, and regularly walked on stilts, chanting "This is the way." The novelty of it attracted many (hence the derogatory alternative term Pied Piperism), but only the most recondite today recall the bizarre interlude.   JAMES D. DOUGLAS

NEO-ORTHODOXY AND ETHICS. See also *Barth; Brunner; Kierkegaard and Ethics; Niebuhr, Reinhold.* Ethics, narrowly defined, designates the science which seeks to determine right action between man and his neighbor. Christian ethics understands the horizontal dimension of man's relationship to his neighbor in terms of the vertical dimension of his relationship to God. Man, endowed with the *imago dei,* is made in and for fellowship with God, and this special relationship to God makes him uniquely responsible to his fellow man. Like all creatures, he receives his being from God, but he and he only is responsible before God for what he is and does. Hence the answer to the question: What ought man to do? ultimately cannot be discovered by man himself; it must, rather, be given by God and received by man in obedient submission to the revealed will of God. (Man as sinner, according to Christian teaching, never renders such obedience apart from grace.) According to the Christian view, this revealed will of God is contained in the Bible in the commandments (notably the Decalogue) (q.v.), in the exemplary lives of the saints, and especially in the life of Jesus who always did the will of his Father.

This theological approach to ethics is in contrast to the view that ethics is a descriptive science—that man discovers what is right and wrong by trial and error, guided by a pragmatic quest for happiness. If one takes such a pragmatic view, obviously what is right in one culture or era of human history may be wrong in another. Ethics then becomes relative; there are no absolute moral imperatives which transcend the historical realm.

Neo-Orthodoxy may be defined as that theological approach which seeks to preserve and affirm the insights of the Reformation, including both man's accountability to God and his sinful alienation from God. It follows, then, for the Neo-Orthodox, as for the older Orthodox, that the question of ethics cannot be separated from theology. The duty which God requires of man embraces and includes the duty which man owes to his neighbor. The right act is one which conforms to the revealed will of God. However, *Neo*-Orthodoxy holds that it is no longer possible uncritically to identify this revealed will of God with the commandments and precepts of Scripture.

Neo-Orthodoxy holds that we must stress that the words of Scripture are the words of man; the Bible is a human book, howbeit, one which uniquely bears and mediates the word of God in the moment of faith. In this "crisis of faith," the human words of the Bible became the divine, redemptive word of God.

This theological judgment is reflected in the Neo-Orthodox approach to ethics. The answer to the question, What ought one to do? is given in the moment, in the crisis of decision. The right act, the act which conforms to the will of God, cannot be determined in advance of the concrete moment of moral decision. To seek to determine what is right a priori, by appealing to the commandments of Scripture as abstract moral absolutes, is to exchange the freedom of the gospel for a legalistic casuistry. Love, which is the only moral absolute, finds in the precepts of Scripture and the example of the saints helpful pointers in the direction of the counsel of perfection, but the divine imperative for the

moment, can be had only in the moment as that moment is illumined by faith.

The one who lives thus by faith, i.e., the believer, finds himself in a world of men, the majority of whom do not confess Christ and therefore are not citizens of the Kingdom of God. In fact the believer himself, until the final eschaton, is a citizen, not only of the kingdom of God but also of the Kingdoms of this world. Therefore it is necessary, especially in questions of social ethics, to appeal to creation ordinances binding on all men, which, because of man's sin, have necessarily a legal, codified fixity about them. The state is not based upon the imperative of love, perceived in the moment, but upon laws of distributive and retributive justice. Even here, however, perhaps one should say, in this area, especially, one cannot appeal to the teaching of the Scriptures, uncritically, to establish the right. To do so would lead to a theocratic model of the state after the analogy of the Constantinian Establishment. It is in the area of social ethics that the ethical vision of the Neo-Orthodox is most fractured. Some have ought to ground the state in the redemptive revelation of God in Christ; others in some form of broken natural revelation or theory of natural law. It is also in the area of social ethics that the problem of a conflict of duty (tragic moral choice) has been most acute for Neo-Orthodox ethicists.

Emil Brunner, *The Divine Imperative*, Philadelphia, Westminster, 1947. Reinhold Niebuhr, *An Interpretation of Christian Ethics*, New York, Harper, 1935.   PAUL K. JEWETT

NEUROSIS. Neurosis (or psychoneurosis) is a major division in the classification of mental discorders. Neurosis is regarded as the result of intrapsychic conflict or stress, the principal symptom of which is anxiety or some alteration of attitude arising from anxiety. The defective reality-testing and disorganization of personality that are characteristic of psychosis are not seen in neurosis, although some degree of self-deception is usually present in the neurotic person.

Freud believed that the ego, under pressure from the superego, represses unacceptable instinctual impulses, and that the conflict signified by anxiety in neurosis is produced by the continuing clamor of these repressed desires for gratification. A different interpretation offered by some of Freud's contemporaries held that it is the voice of conscience, rather than instinctual desire, that has been repressed. From this viewpoint, the conflict in neurosis is essentially ethical, and the danger signalled by anxiety is moral in nature.

Psychoanalysis conceives of the therapist coming to the aid of the weakened ego as an ally against the instinctual demands of the id and the moral demands of the superego. For the resolution of neurosis, Freud advocated self-knowledge for the neurotic person and "the gradual demolition of the hostile superego."

When neurosis is viewed as an ethical or moral conflict, recovery of rejected and repressed moral standards is required for its resolution. Those who have looked upon neurosis as "the disease of a bad conscience" prescribe the restoration of the ideals that have been destroyed. According to this position, neurosis arises, not because moral force has been too strong, but because it has been too weak.

This understanding of neurosis, although consonant with Christian faith, does not obviate the need for the trained therapist, since devious forms of self-deception, some with unconscious roots, may block insight and self-understanding. If the resolution of neurosis is basically a moral enterprise, neither religious exercises nor technical skill alone will suffice. Therapy should seek both to bring insight that will cut through neurotic self-deception, and to reinstate the ideals that have been rejected.

Sigmund Freud, *Outline of Psychoanalysis,* New York, Norton, 1949, Chap. 6; Oskar Pfister, "What Transformations Does Psychoanalysis Require in Ethics and Moral Education?," *Psychi. Quar.* 5:407, 1931; Arvid Runestam, *Psychoanalysis and Christianity*, Rock Island, Ill., Augustana, 1958, Chap. III. ORVILLE S. WALTERS

NEUTRALITY. See also *Indifference; Judgment.* In the technical vocabulary of ethics and philosophy neutrality (or neutralism) is the equivalent of moral indifference. It refuses to attach importance to judgment. Neutrality is the attitude which assumes that the values of goodness and the corresponding anti-values of evil are either non-existent or of little consequence. If such a premise be conceded, ethics is no longer concerned with the ideal and is reduced to a report on how humans do in fact behave rather than an enquiry into how they ought to behave.

On Biblical grounds Christian ethics insists that moral neutrality is indefensible. The nature of God as himself both the source and expression of goodness, righteousness, and love, compels the Christian to recognize the importance of moral choice. The permissive society is the product of an age which has largely rejected God. "If God is not," observed Jean-Paul Sartre, "everything is changed and everything is allowed."

It is insufficient to assert that nothing is willed which is not first known. We must add that nothing can be willed unless it is presented as important. If an object stands before us as completely neutral, it lacks the capacity to motivate the will or elicit an affective response. In classical ethics what possesses positive importance is "good" and what possesses negative importance is "bad." A Christian interpretation supports the distinction and supplies it with a supernatural sanction.

Such a recognition of ultimate moral values does not, however, exclude the possibility that within the general framework of right and wrong there are some actions which in themselves may be regarded as neutral. Eating and sleeping, for instance, when not indulged in to excess, can hardly be considered as morally wrong, yet neither do they constitute positive goods.

A. SKEVINGTON WOOD

NEW BIRTH. See *Conversion.*

NEW MORALITY. See also *Contextual Ethics; Evolutionary Ethics; Situational Ethics.* It is not possible to pin-point the precise beginning of the New Morality since both its advocates and its opponents insist that it is nothing new. Its advocates do so because they wish to annex its ideas to Jesus Christ to leave the impression that it is basically a Christian ethic. Its opponents see its pedigree in the uninhibited paganism spawned by Neo-Hellenic mythology and running through the teaching of the French Encyclopaedists who proposed to enthrone a prostitute on the high altar of Notre Dame de Paris.

The New Morality received modern impetus in the Evolutionary ethic (q.v.) of Herbert Spencer (*Data of Ethics*, 1879), and Thomas Huxley (*Evolution and Ethics*, 1893), who taught that human beings seeking to maintain their existence in a natural environment must necessarily pursue those ends which make for their fuller life. The designation *moral* was then given to whatever process seemed best fitted to assure this result.

The immediate origin of the New Morality is to be found in a blend of ideas deriving from Freudian psychology (cf. *Freud*), and Existentialist philosophy (cf. *Existentialism and Ethics*). Freud regarded the sexual instinct, the "libido," as the dominant urge in the human unconscious which must be allowed uninhibited expression in conscious life and not be frustrated by the artificial curbs of conventional taboos. Existential ethicists deny outright

moral absolutes and glory in not knowing what to do. The acceptance of any law of conduct is an act of "bad faith" (Sartre), and a contradiction of man's fundamental freedom. These two ideas of sex and freedom are dominant themes among the New Moralitists.

The new moralists purport to restate these ideas in the context of an ethic of love. Traditional Christian ethics are condemned as legalistic, and as being naively suspicious of the world and the flesh. In the new morality nothing is prescribed but love. Rejected are the concepts of law and authority. Those who have less regard for historic Christianity virtually make the bed the altar of their new religion. Chastity is considered no more a virtue than malnutrition, and sexual intercourse is presented as the healthiest of "human sport" to which children should be early introduced. Those of more Christian commitment introduce "love" as the deciding factor, yet insist that this principle must find its application in each particular "situation." Fornication is then allowed as an act of Christian charity, and adultery a sacrament of divine healing (H. A. Williams). Of the new morality Situational ethics (q.v.) is the appropriate method.

The critique of the New Morality focuses upon its false view of love and freedom, and its failure to find for ethics an absolute norm and authority. Ethics must have a solid theological basis in God as Creator and Redeemer: in creation God is revealed in the love of law, in redemption is the law of love.

📖 H. L. A. Hart, *The Concept of Law*, Oxford, Oxford University, 1961; A. Lunn, and G. Lean, *The New Morality*, London, Blandford, 1964; H. D. McDonald, "The Concept of Authority" in *Faith and Thought*, Vol. 95, No. 2, Summer, 1966; D. Mumby, *The Idea of a Secular Society*, Oxford, Oxford University, 1963; Helen Oppenheimer, *Law and Love*, London, Faith, 1962; P. Sorokin, *The American Sex Revolution*, Boston, Porter Sargent, 1956; J. A. T. Robinson, "The New Morality," in *Honest to God*, London, S.C.M.; D. Rhymes, *No*

New Morality, London, Constable, 1964; J. D. Unwin, *Sex and Culture*, Oxford, Oxford University, 1934; H. A. Williams, "The Theology of Self-Awareness" in *Soundings*, A. R. Vidler, ed., Oxford, Oxford University, 1964.

H. D. McDONALD

NEW TESTAMENT ETHICS. See also *Jesus, Ethical Teachings; Johannine Ethics; Pauline Ethics; Petrine Ethics; Sermon on the Mount; Personal Ethics; Social Ethics.* Biblical ethics rests in its entirety on the assumption that the one sovereign and righteous God as man's creator approves and requires a specific moral stand and behavior. OT and NT morality share this recognition of a divinely-commanded ethic. To be sure, Jesus more intimately connected the Divine requirements of love for God and neighbor (Deut. 6:4f.; Lev. 19:18) by summarizing in the two-fold commandment the whole duty of man (Matt. 22:37), and he expounded and exemplified the meaning of love in depths exposing the shallowness of scribal and pharisaical views. But, contrary to situational ethics (q.v.), he made obedience to God's commands the evidence of love; he did not expound love as contravening a mandated ethic.

The main difference between OT and NT ethics is that the NT sets out with Jesus of Nazareth as the messianic Son in whom God's righteousness is perfectly fulfilled, and on the ground of whose active and passive obedience men as sinners may receive forgiveness of their sins and new life by the Holy Spirit. OT and NT alike disclose a morality of grace grounded in God's redemptive mercy, but the former does so in terms of promise and the latter of messianic fulfillment. The consciousness of being God's messianic Son not only pervades the Sermon on the Mount ("I am come," Matt. 5:17; "But I say. . . ." Matt. 5:22, 28, 32, etc.; "for my sake," Matt. 5:11) but it runs throughout Jesus' public ministry. Jesus is the example of uncompromised moral obedience; he stands head and

shoulders above moral philosophers both in virtue of his teaching and of his sinless life. The NT writings are replete with exhortations to live by the words and to walk in the way of Jesus (I Cor. 11:1, I Thess. 1:6; I Peter 2:21ff.). To be sure, his redemptive vocation imparted a special direction to his life, excluding for example marriage and fatherhood, so that Christians received ethical guidance not only from Jesus' example, but as well from his teaching, and from apostolic exposition authoritatively given in his name.

The NT writings everywhere expound God's love for man in the context of his gift of the divine son and his redemptive death. NT morality, in brief, is motivated by gratitude for God's grace in Christ (Rom. 5:8). It does not seek divine acceptance on the basis of one's own works, but pursues good works as evidence that one's life as a believer is directed by the Risen Lord and no longer dominated by the deforming grip of sin.

This introduces a further distinctive: NT ethics not only presupposes an already accomplished atonement, but it is resurrection-oriented (I Cor. 15:19, 32). Assuredly, the NT anticipated the general resurrection of mankind as a still future eschatological event. Yet Christian hope is consciously anchored to the historical resurrection of the crucified Jesus, and Christian virtue finds its center in the Spirit outpoured at Pentecost by the Risen Head of the church. Christians belong to a body whose Head lives already beyond death and resurrection, and who from the invisible eternal order bestows blessings anticipatively distinctive of the coming age of glory: "we have a sample of our inheritance" (Eph. 1:14). The Holy Spirit is not a divine source of blessing independent of the Son, nor does he qualify Christians only as isolated individuals; imparted at Pentecost to the church as Christ's body, the Spirit shapes a *koinonia*-ethic (cf. *Koinonia*) in view of the Risen Lord's ongoing presence in the community of faith.

The proclamation of the nearness of God's Kingdom was a central theme of Jesus' ethical teaching (Mark 1:15), and he correlated it with a summons to repent and to obey God's will. God's coming Kingdom has present, and not alone future, implications; men are to live by love, reflecting in neighbor-relations a whole-souled trust in God, unlimited forgiveness and unselfish concern.

Christian virtue is a fruit of the Holy Spirit (Gal. 5:22f.); it is not, contrary to Greek ethics, a "golden mean" (q.v.) achieved by a delicate balancing of unregenerate human capacities, nor, contrary to representations of modern psychology, the religious apex of a pyramidal rearrangement of values inherent in the natural man. It is to the image of Jesus Christ that the righteous are ultimately to be conformed (I John 3:2). The moral qualities that Paul details in his classic chapter on love (I Cor. 13) come alive if one substitutes the name of Jesus for the word *agape*. Christian love gains its profoundest exposition from Jesus Christ, not solely in view of his teaching, or even his example, but above all through his substitutionary and propitiatory sacrifice.

Although Jesus repudiated legalism (q.v.), that is, reliance on works for salvation, and lifted love (q.v.) to new priority, he did not—nor do the NT writers—displace God's commands by intimating, as does situational ethics (q.v.), that human love as a motivation itself determines the content of the divine will. He came to fulfill, not to destroy, the law and the prophets—indeed, to fulfill them in the spirit of love for God and neighbor. The Apostle Paul had to contend not only against those who sought to transmute Christian morality into a new legalism (cf. Gal.), but also those who made it an occasion for license (cf. I Cor.).

To say that there is no explicit interest in the Christian role in the world in the ethic of Jesus or the apostles is overstatement. To be sure, neither in the teaching of Jesus nor of the apostles will one find an anticipation of the modern humanistic confidence that the world can be transformed into an arena of peace and justice through human striving, sociological manipulation, or scientific alteration. For them the world has upon it the stamp of death; the church has a destiny in eternity. God's final judgmental intervention, to overthrow evil and vindicate righteousness in the decisive establishment of his coming Kingdom, are integral to NT expectation. Hence the writers ignore secular schemes for the restructuring of society in order to concentrate instead on the renewal of man. Yet the NT inherits and expands the divine demand of the OT for public justice, and its implications for social ethics are profound.

The NT sees justice as the only preserving dynamism in a fallen society, even as it sees regeneration as the only transforming dynamism of a sinful humanity. It roots the legitimacy of civil government in divine authorization (John 19:11) for the sake of justice and order (Rom. 13:1ff.).

Critics who reject the social adequacy of Christianity often ask whether uncalculating compassion is adequate to face the problems of political and economic order, in view of the Anabaptist-Mennonite regard for the Sermon on the Mount as a NT code for all the relations of life. Important as it is, one cannot find in the Sermon alone the exhaustive rule of Christian ethics expressing all that is important to NT morality. Reformed theology regards the Sermon as the divine rule for interpersonal relationships (cf. *Interpersonal Relations*), to be supplemented in official societal relationships by NT ethics in the larger sense (cf. Henry, *Christian Personal Ethics*, pp. 322ff.). Anticipations of ongoing social responsibility can be found in Jesus' own teaching ("render unto Caesar" Matt. 22:21). Just as the Sermon does not expound the atonement but presupposes it, and exposition of that doctrine awaits apostolic interpretation of its actual accomplishment, so exposition of the NT relationship of church and state awaits the emergence of the Christian community and apostolic instruction concerning Christian duty to government. The Pauline and Petrine letters indicate how government and society impose upon the believer duties beyond those of immediate neighbor-relationships, in the context of the validity of civil government (q.v.), the spiritual significance of work (q.v.), the stewardship of wealth (q.v.), and much else. It would be passing strange indeed were a theology as empty of significance for social ethics as some modern humanists imply to be the case with early Christianity to merit the tribute paid by the church historian F. J. Foakes-Jackson: "History shows that the thought of Christ on the Cross has been more potent than anything else in arousing a compassion for suffering and indignation at injustice. . . . The later Evangelicalism, which saw in the death of Christ the means of free salvation for fallen humanity, caused its adherents to take the front rank as champions of the weak. . . . Prison reform, the prohibition of the slave trade, the abolition of slavery, the Factory Acts, the protection of children, the crusade against cruelty to animals, are all the outcome of the great evangelical revival of the eighteenth century. The humanitarian tendencies of the nineteenth century, which, it is but just to admit all Christian communities have fostered, and which non-Christian philanthropists have vied with them in encouraging, are among the greatest triumphs of the power and influence of Christ" ("Christ in the Church," *Cambridge Theological Essays*, H. B. Swete, ed., 1905, pp. 512ff.).

📖 C. F. H. Henry, *Christian Personal Ethics*, Grand Rapids, Eerdmans, 1957; Paul Ramsey, *Basic Christian Ethics*, New York, Scribner, 1950; Hans Windisch, *The Meaning of the Sermon on the Mount*, Philadelphia, Westminster, 1951.

CARL F. H. HENRY

NIEBUHR, H. RICHARD. Helmut Richard Niebuhr (1894-1962) was a minister of the Evangelical and Reformed Church who served at Yale University from 1931-1962 as Sterling Professor of Theology and Christian Ethics. Although less well known than his brother Reinhold, H. Richard Niebuhr profoundly influenced the theological scene in America through his writings and students, some of whom contributed to a *Festschrift* titled *Faith and Ethics* (Paul Ramsey, ed., New York, Harper, 1957).

Niebuhr's contribution to moral theory has two theological roots. One is the post-Reformation emphasis on a sovereign God and the other is the nineteenth century theological emphasis on man's epistemological limitations. Niebuhr interprets these two traditions to mean that because God alone is sovereign and eternal, everything else, including moral judgment, must be relative and confessional.

Niebuhr characterizes moral theories in three ways: man-the maker, man-the-citizen and man-the-answerer. The maker-image suggests that man's moral life is judged teleologically; the citizen-image suggests that it is judged deontologically; and the answerer-image, which is Niebuhr's own, suggests it is judged by the situation.

Man's moral life, Niebuhr claims, is like the life of a motorist whose actions on the road are not judged simply by his destination, nor the rules of the road, but by a thousand other factors also, e.g, the condition of the road, the reliability of his vehicle, and the number of other motorists. The moral judgment must "fit" the situation.

Hence, the moral theory offered by Niebuhr has been variously defined as relational theory of value, *cathekontic* (or fitting) ethics, relativism, existential idealism, a type of absolutism, and an existential teleological theory of ethics. The relativity is an insistence on man's historical situation while the absolutism is an acknowledgment that from God's non-historical and non-relative situation there is but one fitting act.

📖 H. Richard Niebuhr, *The Kingdom of God in America,* Hamden, Conn. Shoe String, 1956; *The Meaning of Revelation,* New York, Macmillan, 1941; *Christ and Culture,* New York, Harper, 1951; *Radical Monotheism and Western Culture,* New York, Harper, 1960; *The Responsible Self,* New York, Harper, 1963.   HERBERT K. JACOBSEN

NIEBUHR, REINHOLD. Reinhold Niebuhr (1892-1971) was born in Wright City, Mo., trained at Elmhurst College, Eden Theological Seminary, and Yale Divinity School, and ordained in the Evangelical Synod of North America in 1915. After a notable ministry (1915-1928) at Bethel Evangelical Church, Detroit, he joined the faculty of Union Theological Seminary, New York, There, as professor of applied Christianity and later as Vice-President, he remained until retirement in 1960, earning an international reputation both for original thinking in Christian ethics and apologetics and for active engagement in public affairs.

Niebuhr always refused to call himself a theologian. His thought was worked out in the context of national and international events, in the light of which he tested all received doctrines, whether religious, social, or political. The experience of life in industrial Detroit and the stresses of the Depression led him to move, as he put it, "politically to the left, theologically to the right." Religious liberalism he found to be naive in its optimistic estimate of human possibilities, and he countered it with what came to be known as Christian realism. *Leaves from the Notebook of a Tamed Cynic* (Cleveland, World, 1929), written during his Detroit years, shows his dislike of religious sentimentality. In his Gifford Lectures, *The Nature and Destiny of Man* (I, 1941, and II, New York, Scribner, 1943), he drew on an Augustinian estimate of human sin. For this reason he is sometimes grouped with the neo-Reformation movement inspired by Karl Barth. Yet he gave only a limited approval to the Reformers, and he strongly opposed the doctrine of total depravity. He placed himself in the line of the American Social Gospel theologians, especially Walter Rauschenbusch (q.v.).

Niebuhr's Christian realism was first spelled out in *Moral Man and Immoral Society* (New York, Scribner, 1932). Niebuhr argued that the social expression of love was justice. Society cannot live by pure ideals. It must accept the limited possibilities given by political actualities. In *An Interpretation of Christian Ethics* (1935) he urged, on the other hand, "the relevance of an impossible ethical ideal," namely, Christian love as the inspiration causing individuals to strive for maximum social justice. The practical application of Christian realism was to be seen in Niebuhr's own changing opinions. Initially sympathetic to both Marxism and pacifism, he came to oppose their doctrinaire claims as destructive of positive human betterment in the name of abstract perfection. Neither was willing to look at man as he was, a sinful creature yet made in the image of God.

In his later writings, Niebuhr concentrated on the lessons to be learned from history, where all theories are put to the test. *Faith and History* (New York, Scribner, 1949), *The Irony of American History* (New York, Scribner, 1952), *The Self and the Dramas* of History (New York, Scribner, 1955), and *The Structure of Nations and Empires* (1959) show this concern. In opposition to his friend and colleague Paul Tillich, he contended that the basis for Christianity is not a metaphysic but the "dramatic" presentation of truth which Neibuhr assayed to find in Scripture.

Niebuhr is often criticized for having largely ignored the doctrines of the church and the Holy Spirit. But perhaps more fundamental is the inadequacy of his Christology, for he views Jesus simply as "a key of meaning" to the mystery of human existence and as a "symbol" of the enduring power of sacrificial love.

June Bingham, *Courage to Change: An Introduction to the Life and Thought of Reinhold Niebuhr*, New York, Scribner, 1961; John Edward Carnell, *The Theology of Reinhold Niebuhr*, rev. ed. Grand Rapids, Eerdmans, 1960; Gordon Harland, *The Thought of Reinhold Niebuhr*, New York, Oxford, 1960; Charles W. Kegley and Robert W. Bretall, eds, *Reinhold Niebuhr His Religious, Social, and Political Thought*, New York, Macmillan, 1956.   KENNETH HAMILTON

NIETZSCHE, FRIEDRICH. Friedrich Nietzsche (1844-1900) sought to revolutionize moral philosophy by rejecting both the goal and the substance of the tradition in ethics which extends from Socrates and Plato through Kant and Schopenhauer. The starting point for each member of this tradition, as Nietzsche sees it, is the self-evident validity of the values prevailing in his society or social class. Since these values were not to be questioned, the goal of reflection became their rational justification. Nietzsche mistrusts the appeal to self-evidence and takes as his starting point the empirical plurality of value systems. The goal of his philosophy, then, becomes not the rationalizing of "our" values, but the criticism of them, the evaluation of their value for human existence. Like the Hebrew prophet, the philosopher is to be an untimely presence, seeking a standpoint beyond the spirit of his times from which to judge that spirit.

The means to this end is genetic analysis. Nietzsche speaks of "the morality of mores," indicating that in every prevailing value system it is the customs and traditions of a concrete social unity which define the right and the good. What the philosophers have tried to present as rational because universal is in fact, for Nietzsche, only the interests of a very particular historical or sociological sub-division of humanity. Genetic analysis involves the employment of every available skeptical and suspicious perspective for uncovering these origins.

This uncovering is what Nietzsche calls psychology, and he claims that psychological insight is the key to evaluating values. While not claiming an absolute perspective for his own evaluations, he insists that honest evaluations are possible only when the unconscious motivations of various moralities are first understood. It is by overcoming the systematic blindness of a people to the unconscious meaning of their morality that the philosopher is able to free himself from the spirit of his times.

At the heart of Nietzsche's own psychology is the will to power. He agrees with psychological egoism that human acts are never altruistic, but he insists against the usual form of that theory that the self-interest which motivates all human behavior is the desire for power, not happiness. Power can be experienced in cruelty and domination over others. In other words, aggression is instinctive to man in Nietzsche's psychology. But the self-overcoming involved in coordinating the divergent instincts into the unified pursuit of a single goal is another and higher expression of the will to power.

From this psychology grows Nietzsche's critique of what he calls "slave morality" with its categorical imperative to altruism. Underlying Christian morality in both its theological and philosophical forms he sees the will to power of the weak. This makes it a fundamentally dishonest morality, for the profession of love as the highest value is seen as coming from the self-interest of the physically and socially oppressed. It is their resentment and thirst for revenge which Nietzsche hears in most talk about justice, their envy which makes equality an ideal, and their desire to be loved which places compassion at the heart of goodness. Nietzsche fails to realize the degree to which this critique is directed less toward the actual practice of genuine altruism than toward certain ways of preaching altruism to others.

Apart from the mendacity involved, the prevalence of slave morality allows the interests of the weak to prevail over those of the strong. Nietzsche repudiates this levelling effect because he holds the goal of human existence to be the production of those unusual individuals who tower above the herd. Since slave morality labels such persons evil while calling the weak and their interests good, Nietzsche describes his own stance with the slogan "beyond good and evil."

What lies beyond good and evil are the values of those who are not ashamed to think themselves above other men and to subordinate everything to their own self-mastery. The aristocratic-warrior values of Homeric Greece and Renaissance Italy become models, as do such individuals as Goethe and Napoleon. Here the will to power is honest about itself. Whereas slave morality is seen as turning against nature and the instincts, thereby slandering life and engendering illusions about other worlds, Nietzsche seeks to develop a tragic ethic, one which looks into the abyss of life as it is here and now, and says, Yes. Not with resignation, but with joy.

Christian thinkers find it easy simply to dismiss Nietzsche because of his claim that since God is dead the morality associated with his name should also be interred. But his value for Christian ethics lies in both his method and its results. His method is a reminder that the people of God are always in need of prophetic self-criticism; and his employment of that method is perhaps the most single-minded exposé of the pharisee-ism of practical reason since Jesus.

MEROLD WESTPHAL

The contemporary mood of human autonomy, which thrusts aside all relevance for supernatural authority and transcendent revelation and morality, was anticipated by Nietzsche, who saw that the admission of God is destructive of man's self-creativity of meaning and value (*Thus Spake Zarathustra*, Section 24). Nietzsche caps the Romantic emphasis on personal uniqueness and self-realization, but does so in anticipation of wholly secular experience for which history is relative, nature chaotic, and reason distortive of reality. Nietzsche is thus the prophet of a culture for which God is dead, and all recent death-of-God scribes echo his proclamation of the demise of deity. The outcome, as Nietzsche saw better than most of his contemporaries, is radical secularity. While his own perspective excluded a covering-theory of reality and religion, he anticipatively and significantly avoids the optimistic liberalism which turned God into bourgeois optimism about earthly progress (and the noncognitive transcendental myths of neo-orthodoxy of which Kierkegaard was a harbinger) and opts instead for the raw power of Superman, about as far as one can get from the self-giving God-man. The Twentieth Century has already beheld colossal manifestations of this totalitarian will to power, and its end is not yet.—Ed.

NIHILISM. See also *Cynicism; Pessimism.* Nihilism is the notion that ethical norms are rationally unjustifiable and a consequent mood of despair over life's emptiness or triviality.

Historically, several concepts have been mistakenly identified as forms of nihilism. *Cynicism* is often caricatured as nihilistic but this ignores that self-sufficiency and goodness are in fact its ultimate concerns. *Melancholy* is often erroneously identified as nihilism in disguise. *Pessimism* (Latin *pessimus*, the worst) finds expression in various outlooks that nonetheless escape nihilism by positing some value (Buddhism, nirvana; Schopenhauer, idea; Spengler, culture; Camus, freedom).

Nietzsche (q.v.) defined the concept as the situation which exists when "everything is permitted." Then every act has equal justification in the moral realm and every word is synonymous in the universe of discourse, and any effort to defend any particular word or act is indistinguishable from silence. The result of Nietzsche's nihilistic enthusiasm is the perennial pestilence of despair and loss of meaning which always follow the "absolutization of nothingness."

The charge of nihilism is raised over the central thesis of Heidegger's *Was ist metaphysik?* which posits non-being *(das Nichts)* as the foundation of being *(das Sein)*. This thesis is also pursued in *Sein und Zeit,* to being-there *(Dasein)* and Being-unto-end *(Sein zum Ende)* which emerges as Being-unto-death *(Sein zum Tode).* Heidegger responds to the charge of atheistic nihilism in his *Brief über Humanismus.* He also concurs with Holderlin's characterization of our age as a time of want, "want of God" *(Fehl Gottes).* Yet, Heidegger's analysis of the process of authenticity has no content and thus his nihilism shines through all being. Radical temporality of existence is the existential "moment of crisis between past and future." If all interpretative categories are radically temporalized, then nihilism is the inevitable termination of being through time.

Christian optimism is a superior option because the despairing man's last "ism" is not the last god. The last god is God, who is explained in Jesus Christ (John 1:18).

JAMES D. STRAUSS

NONCONFORMITY. Failure to observe a pattern of behavior or procedure established by authority or by general consent is termed nonconformity. Used by Paul in enjoining the Romans (12:2) against worldliness, nonconformity on principle has in our own age been espoused in the rebellion against society by youth—though its search for identity prefers Emerson's more secular text, "Whoso would be a man must be a nonconformist."

In its more restricted historical sense the term could be applied to the English Lollards. In the immediate post-Reformation era it described refugees from mainland Europe whose Protestantism clashed with Church of England practice that still evinced many Roman Catholic features.

In its most common usage, nonconformity relates to those Protestant dissenters who, following a simpler mode of worship such as that found in Calvin's reign (1558-1603) were designed to enforce adherence to the Book of Common Prayer. Many suffered deprivation and real persecution.

Other influences also were at work, and subsequently the body of nonconformists was to include Catholics, Independents, Presbyterians, Baptists, and Quakers. Under the Stuart kings, whose confidence of so-called Divine Right (cf. *Divine Right of Kings*) added new repressive measures, nonconformists endured even greater hardships and some sought sanctuary in the New World—until even that was forbidden.

The situation improved from 1690 with William and Mary, and full religious liberty came with the Hanoverian dynasty in the early eighteenth century. Equality, on the other hand, has been more difficult to achieve; some vestiges of discrimination against nonconformists, chiefly in the academic field, still linger on in England. But the battle was won. Like the Scottish covenanters, what English nonconformity had fought for and finally established was the principle that Church and State were distinct, not co-extensive, and that supreme authority belonged to God alone.

The "nonconformist conscience" in England led to the founding of the Salvation Army and of the Labour Party late in the nineteenth century. Early in the present century it motivated champions of Sunday observance and total abstinence, and opponents of gambling.   JAMES D. DOUGLAS

NONRESISTANCE. See *Neutrality; Passifism; Resistance.*

NORMS. See also *Absolutes, Moral; Principles.* Ethical norms are generally conceived of as the standards which govern, direct, or prescribe moral conduct. The term is sometimes used in a merely descriptive sense, for the average or most commonly occurring action. In ethics, however, its sense is usually evaluative, indicating the standard against which moral actions are measured.

Different ethical systems propound norms of different types. Some consider norms as rules, dilineating definite actions. In others, the norm is the type of act. An intermediate position makes principles the determinative factor.

Norms may apply to different elements of the moral act. An act may be judged according to the end that is intended and willed. Here the norm is definitive of good versus bad ends. Norms of means evaluate the means employed in accomplishing the desired end. When the motive of the person is considered, norms of motivation are relied upon. Finally, ethics may purport to scrutinize the consequences of an act, and would then have to refer to norms which distinguish good ends from bad. Some ethical systems evaluate an act in terms of only one or two of these norms. Biblically-based ethics, however, regard an act as truly good only when all four factors are good. Thus a good end does not justify an evil means (Rom. 3:8), nor is the motive behind the act insignificant (Matt. 5:23, 28).

Ethical theories differ also in terms of the locus of norms, i.e., whether they are objective or subjective. An objective ethical philosophy maintains that norms are somehow objectively present in reality. The task of ethics then is to discover these norms, so that one may relate himself to them. A subjectivist, on the other hand, locates norms within the person himself. The person creates these by his own decision or by the way he apprehends reality. Even objectivist ethical theories propose different sources for norms. Humanists teach that society formulates them. Vitalists or emergent evolutionists believe that forces at work within the natural process produce value, from which norms derive. Communists maintain that the dialectic is producing value through the historical process and that the state then formulates the norms. Theists hold that norms are created and propounded by God. Biblical ethics correlates this assertion with the self-revelation of the Creator, Redeemer, and Judge of mankind.

A distinction is also sometimes made between absolute and contingent norms. An absolute norm is one which applies and which consequently governs behavior independently of any other factors. Contingent norms, on the other hand, are dependent upon the presence of some additional factor. They apply only if that other factor is present. Similarly, norms vary in the extent of application. While some norms are incumbent upon all persons, others apply only to certain groups or classes. Thus, certain norms of conduct which apply to medical doctors or policemen on duty, do not pertain to all individuals.

📖 Paul Ramsey and Gene Outka, eds., *Norm and Context in Christian Ethics,* New York, Scribner, 1968; Carl F. H. Henry, *Christian Personal Ethics,* Grand Rapids, Eerdmans, 1957.

MILLARD J. ERICKSON

NUDISM. See also *Art.* Nudism is the dated phenomenon of families organizing themselves for the purpose of being nakedly at ease within an enclosed campground. In Germany, before World War I, men like Heinrich Pudor and Paul Zimmerman recruited enthusiasts for *Nacktkultur* and *Freikörperkultur* (cultivation of the unfettered, naked body) into groups with puritanic determination to achieve strong health: gymnastics were the rule, no drinking or smoking allowed, frequently vegetarian. Somewhat later Kurt Barthel brought this movement to the USA, and organized a nudist outing near Peekskill, New York, on Labor Day, 1929, which led to formation of the American League for Physical Culture. But in America Nudism relaxed its Germanic, physique-cult rigors (e.g., group athletics gave way to mostly just swimming and sun bathing), and its more noted camps in Southern California, Indiana, and New Jersey developed the easy atmosphere of a middle-class lodge for families week-end vacationing in the sun. Various nudist organizations like the American Sunbathing Association (ASA) and National Nudist Council (NNC) each have their journals and political infighting.

Contrary to general opinion and the legal harassment of the thirties, Nudism has not historically promoted enclaves of sexual promiscuity. Nudist sanctuaries have had a distinctly familial character, a club of married couples with their children socializing in a pot-luck picnic atmosphere. Single men and single women are relatively scarce; teen-agers are absent unless their parents are members. Tactile behavior like nude dancing is tabu; sexual arousal (e.g., male erection) is considered misconduct and grounds for expulsion. The program of Nudism aims at living out their basic tenet, that to be unclothed is wholesome and decent, and group nakedness in the sun a healthy, uncomplicated, relaxing pastime, that puts sexual matters into a normal, unexaggerated perspective—the very opposite of the titillation which semi-nude bodies may occasion.

A smack of fetishism will always cling to Nudism, however, because the practice cannot fulfil the demands of its devotees. The leveling anonymity of being naked among strangers and the nudist practice of using only first names (to prohibit close involvement and an intimacy with identity) all work to stop the socializing desired from being an opening-up, enriching experience, and truncates the interpersonal relations at the bland, coffee-cup talk and volley ball level. The unspoken attempt to become one big naked, happy family also runs amuck as a well-meant half-measure, because the primitivistic belief (cf. *Innocence*) that men can lose their problems by shedding their clothes is mistaken; and nakedness can never be an end for humankind, but always has an invitational note that must lead somewhere, to personal deepening or exploitation. Therefore traditional Nudism has an especially pathetic, dated, humespun inadequacy about it in our specialized and blatantly secularized environment grasping for satisfying (bodily) freedom. Today it is *amateur* "sensitivity groups" looking for wholeness, with a medicinal, albeit faddish, psychotherapeutic seriousness, and the routine of group intercourse among current "swinging" couples that make exposure of self and "nakedness" a casual yet pivotal matter—such movements are the living, humanistic residue of Nudism in decline.

The truth Nudism has lacked in its corrective openness about physical bodiliness is that clothes are a gift of God (cf. *Modesty*).   CALVIN G. SEERVELD

NULLITY. See also *Common Law Marriage*. Nullity is the declaration that there has not been a true marriage, regardless of how much or how long the reverse has seemed to be the case. The conditions on which such a declaration is made vary, but impuberty and coercion are prime examples. Nullity should be distinguished from annulment, the former revealing that marriage has not existed, and the latter dissolving the existing marriage bond.

MORRIS A. INCH

O

OATHS. Oaths as a moral problem and the conscientious refusal to swear (Quakers and some others) result from an unqualified application of Christ's command, "Swear not at all." However, this passage in the Sermon on the Mount (q.v.) is connected with commands concerning legitimate vows. Since in the same passage the sixth and seventh commandments are not abrogated, but extended to cover Jewish evasions, so too here Christ's command must not be interpreted as repealing OT oaths and vows. He was extending, or, better, applying the OT to the practice of repeatedly swearing on trivial occasions. Christ's accepting the oath at his trial confirms this interpretation.

The OT, in the places referred to, approves of oaths or vows seriously made. See also Gen. 24:2ff.; Exod. 13:19; Josh. 9:18-20. Not only so, God himself swears (Isa. 45:23; Heb. 6:13, 16, etc.)

There are also examples of sinful oaths: Saul's in I Sam. 14:24; Herod's in Matt. 14:7, Peter's denial, and the oath of Paul's enemies in Acts 23:12.

Best known among Protestants for making and keeping solemn oaths and vows are the Reformed Presbyterians, whose constancy under Claverhouse's massacres earned the Cameronians the name of Covenanters.   GORDON H. CLARK

OBEDIENCE. See also *Counsels; Monasticism.* The uniquely personal nature of Biblical religion is underscored by the pervasive emphasis that one learns of God's will and his calls to action by means of "hearing." "To see" and "to hear" are often the subjective responses to a word of Torah, covenant, or specific admonition which lead to willing compliance; but the words most often used for "obedience," "obey," are derivatives of the words "to hear" in Hebrew, Greek, and Latin. Normally, only authorized spokesmen for God were privileged to "see" visions, dreams, and theophanies, but every man could "hear" the word thus generated and could make appropriate decisions. Jesus' coming as the "Word" of God extended this idea to its limits.

Ultimate definition of moral or religious obligation was not subject to private human decision or divine-human negotiation, but resided in God's hands alone (Gen. 2–3). Personal fulfillment lay in choosing either to serve selfish ends or to find freedom in bondage to God. Love was to be the primary motivation for obedience to God (Deut. 6:4-5; Mark 12:28-34), but men's early adherence to personal or corporate covenantal relationships with God (Gen. 12; 15; Exod. 20–24; Deut. 5) was more often seen in terms of servanthood (cf. Rom. 6), a striving to adhere to absolute standards found in the Decalogue by means of an ever-developing case law responsive to cultural and temporal needs. In the NT the radical departure precipitated by Jesus' own obedience (John 5:30; Luke 22:42; Mark 14:36; Phil 2:8) led to a redefinition of the "servant" relationship to one of "sonship" (John 15:15). Obedience was thus based on the radical demands imposed by love for Christ, and called forth by opportunities for loving service to men everywhere for whom Christ cared. Obedience in redemptive living was fundamentally more cooperative (Phil. 2:12-13), and far more radical in its ethical demands (Matt. 7; 25; James).

Man has an obligation to be involved deliberately in God's reconciliatory mission in the world (II Cor. 5:11-21), and to decide always to "obey God rather than men" (Acts 5:29).

The Biblical means for learning God's will was by a "hearing" of the words of revelation offered by authorized spokesmen, conscious acceptance of Jesus Christ as the moral model (John 14), and deliberate attendance on the voice of the Holy Spirit as he spoke the truth given by Jesus Christ

(John 16:12-15). The church's historic task has been to address itself to those tensions generated by interactions of believers in a non-believing world order (Rom. 13), as well as by common tendencies toward legalism in rule-observance as contrasted with freedom in Christ-serving (Galatians).

FRANK H. THOMPSON

OBJECTIVISM. Broadly speaking, a particular ethical theory may be classified as objective if it gives credence to the claim that the truth-value of a given statement expressed by an ethical sentence is determinable without regard for the time and place of the utterance or the person uttering the sentence. Accordingly, an ethical objectivist would contend that the truth or falsity of a moral decision can be disclosed by objective conditions that provide objective control for deciding in favor of one alternative over another. Subsequently, the rightness or wrongness of an act is not contingent upon the approval or disapproval of the performer of the act (subjective theory) but, rather, is decided by such criteria as an insight of intuitive necessity, a rational disclosure, an observational investigation, a theological command, or the like.

Each criterion has coupled with it supporting reasons for adopting it, and each is open to serious criticism. The theological theory, for one, seems to fall short on three important counts. First, if God's commands are arbitrary fiats to be obeyed simply because they are backed by power, then one may still question the moral goodness of those commands. Second, if on the other hand God has good reasons for what he commands, then what one is obliged to do depends on those reasons, and not on God's commanding certain performances. Third, to say one acts from love of God and not fear of punishment presupposes he is morally worthy of love and worship on the grounds that he himself is good and commands only what he sees to be good. But

clearly this makes the goodness of an act logically independent of God's commanding it; the act would be good even if there were no God, or if he had not commanded it.

However, the seriousness of the particular difficulties bound up with theological and non-theological objective criteria alike is a secondary issue. The validity of all forms of objective theories depends primarily upon whether or not moral judgments are capable of being objectively true and if in fact there is objective moral knowledge.

Richard B. Brandt, *Ethical Theory*, Englewood Cliffs, N. J., Prentice-Hall, 1959; Immanuel Kant, *The Moral Law*, H. J. Paton, tr., London, Hutchinson University Library, 1948; G. E. Moore, *Principia Ethica*, Cambridge, Cambridge University, 1903; W. D. Ross, *The Right and the Good*, Oxford, Clarendon, 1930.   PETER GENCO

OBLIGATION. See *Duty*.

OBSCENITY. See also *Censorship; Pornography*. This word comes from the Latin *obscenus*. In ancient Rome it had virtually the same meaning as in modern English, being derived from the root words *ob* (for, or against) and *caenum* (filth). It literally designates something too filthy to be tolerated by decent society.

In current American usage, the word is used largely to describe material relating to sexual acts that are considered filthy and degrading. Obscenity when applied to language means the employment of crude words relating to sexual activity or human excrement that are instantly offensive to the ears of most normal persons. Photographs or drawings that depict sexual acts or the acts of urination or defecation are generally held to be obscene.

Obscene material is illegal and its dissemination is a crime punishable by fine or imprisonment. But the American courts in recent years have experienced great difficulty in establishing a precise legal definition of obscenity. The US Supreme Court has held that "obscenity is not within the area of constitutionally protected freedom of speech and press" (*Roth* v. U.S. 1957). The court reached this conclusion after reviewing the entire history of English common law and American judicial practice for 170 years, finding that legislative bodies and courts had never intended or assumed that obscenity could at any time be tolerated by an organized society.

However, the court warned that "sex and obscenity are not synonymous" (*Roth,* ibid.) They gave this definition: "Obscene material is material which deals with sex in a manner appealing to prurient interest." *Prurient,* in turn, was defined as "inciting lascivious desires or thought." In short, obscene material, in the legal sense, is that which is deliberately designed to arouse a desire for illicit sex activity, and, by this definition, sufficiently harmful or threatening harm to society to warrant its suppression.

The Supreme Court has several times applied this standard of definitions: "Whether, to the average person, applying contemporary community standards, the dominant theme of the material, taken as a whole, appeals to prurient interest" (*Roth,* ibid.). The key phrase in the legal definitions has turned out to be "contemporary community standards." These standards change and, in light of them, so does the definition of what is obscene. There can be little doubt, for example, that had a young woman appeared in public fifty years ago wearing as little adornment as the bikini suits now commonplace on most beaches, she would have been arrested. Annette Kellerman was successfully prosecuted in 1916 for wearing a much more conservative one-piece bathing suit. In 1913 a New York art dealer who exhibited the celebrated nude painting "September Morn" was convicted of displaying an obscene object. Today most art galleries contain paintings and sculptures far more explicit. The Supreme Court has held, in fact, that "nudity is

not obscene, *per se*" (Summerfield v. Sunshine Book Co., 1957), and that nudist magazines and other periodicals are now free to depict the nude human form. Thus, the definition of obscenity is any material which, in any given community at a given time, is regarded as deeply offensive to moral sensibilities.

While American standards have greatly changed, those of other cultures are markedly different. Thus, in Scandinavia where nudity in swimming, sunbathing, and sauna baths is quite acceptable, American motion pictures have been censored as obscene when they contain detailed scenes of brutal fist fights, stabbings, or wanton murder which to Scandinavian sensibilities are considered offensive to morals and peril to children. In India, where public acts of prostitution in temples and erotic art addressed to gods of fertility have been acceptable, American movies are censored if they show long kisses, which devout Hindus regard as too lascivious for public exhibition. Asian nations also censor Western movies that show slaughter of American Indians by cowboys, or gangster movies that show massacres by machine-gun wielding hoodlums. To many Asians such acts are utterly obscene.

As American standards of public morality have become more permissive, the courts hold less and less to be obscene in the legal sense. Presumably, we could arrive at a point where nothing would be held obscene and the word itself would become archaic. However, that point has not yet been reached. The US Postal Inspection Service reveals that thirty-five persons were successfully prosecuted for sending obscene material through the mail in 1971. A recent rash of convictions in lower courts of exhibitors of X-rated motion pictures will also afford another opportunity for a definitive test of what is obscene in contemporary society.

Those concerned with Christian social

ethics must understand that community standards now determine what is legally obscene.　　　　GLEN D. EVERETT

OEDIPUS COMPLEX. See also *Freud.* According to Sigmund Freud, the male child's development includes sexual desire for his mother coupled with a fear-conflict reaction toward his father. This phenomenon assertedly takes place during the Phallic-Oedipal period, which occurs typically between the ages of three and five. When this conflict has been resolved, the Phallic-Oedipal period ends. This period is preceded by the oral and anal stages, and is followed by the latent and genital periods.

Freud contended that this "sexual desire, fear-conflict" admixture toward his mother and father, respectively, constitutes a universal response, citing as his primary source for corroboration, Sophocles' *Oedipus Rex.* According to this famous legend, Laius, king of Thebes, learns from the oracle that his son, not yet born, will be his murderer. The son (Oedipus) is rescued, grows up as a king's son in another country. He consults the same oracle to ascertain his origin, is warned that he is destined to murder his father and marry his mother. Although in command of this revelation, Oedipus in his travels meets Laius, quarrels with him and kills him. Entering Thebes, he solves the riddle of the Sphinx, is elected king by the Thebes, and thus is rewarded with the hand of Jocasta. Many years of peace follow, during which time Oedipus and Jocasta become the parents of four children. When a plague strikes, the people consult the oracle, and the tragedy unwinds. Oedipus is discovered as the murderer of Laius, and, ultimately, as the son of Laius and Jocasta. His shock upon learning that he has murdered his father and married his mother causes him to gouge out his eyes and leave the country.

The two crimes of Oedipus, as Freud has interpreted them, represent the universal wishes of all male children, and when these are not handled effectively they form the basis for later neurosis.

　　　　　　　　　HAROLD W. DARLING

OLD AGE. See also *Senility.* Old age is the period in life covering the last decade or two before death, during which there is loss of both physical and mental capacity. In early cultures the aged were generally respected in both family and community for their experience and understanding. With the industrial revolution, and the weakening of family structure, economic security was provided by various forms of financial support which guaranteed a minimum income and more recently medical care to the aged.

However, economic security alone is not an adequate provision for the elderly. Still felt is the need for meaning in life—a concept often expressed in terms of useful work, purposeful goals, and significant interpersonal relationships. Many changes in the last few decades have acted to limit the fulfillment of these needs as well. Technological advances have had a profound effect, for both good and bad. Better medical care and low-cost housing have provided comfort.

At the current pace of advances in research into the causes of aging, it has been suggested that old age may be postponed as much as ten years within the next decade. On the other hand, the burden of a greatly enlarged population has been heaviest on those least able to compete. Then too, medical science has provided the tools to prolong life, but that life, in a lingering terminal illness, may be essentially meaningless and its prolongation extremely costly both financially and emotionally for those left behind.

The necessity for preserving life, basic to the Judeo-Christian tradition, is now being called into question (R. S. Morison, *Science,*

173, pp. 694-698, 1971). Its defenders point to a confusion over the definition of death. Death involves the whole organism, and so is more appropriately defined in terms of a "last gasp" than in terms of the patient's encephalogram as suggested by modern medical science. In the words of Leon Kass, "technological intervention (with all its blessings) can destroy the visible manifestations ... of natural phenomena, the recognition of which is indispensible to human community.... We need to keep company with the dying and to help them cope with terminal illness. We must learn to desist from useless technological interventions and institutional practices that deny to the dying what we most owe them—a good end" (*Science, 173*, pp. 698-703, 1971). Thus it is suggested that the tradition to preserve life does not imply that life itself is of absolute value. The quality of that life, and the dignity with which it is lived and finally relinquished is the central issue.

Just at this point does the Christian faith speak forcefully. For life is presented as a brief preparation for a future existence with God, "a vapor that ... vanisheth away," and old age the prelude to this other life (James 4:14; John 12:25). Studies by David O. Moberg and others have shown that religious beliefs have a significant positive influence on personal adjustment in old age. In addition to the profound conceptual difference in the meaning of life, there is also the operational difference of the church as a fellowship of believers. Here, every member is a part of the body of Christ and members one of another" (Rom. 12:5). The aged are to be ministered to equally with every other member, and their contribution through prayer and counsel to be viewed with respect and appreciation. Indeed, old age provides a perspective on life which is invaluable to the church fellowship. The preceding period of life is often filled with getting and begetting, high ambitions and lofty aspirations. By comparison, old age is a sobering stock-taking, a reappraisal of the meaningful in life, a reassertion of spiritual as opposed to material values. Where society has often failed its older members, the church has the responsibility to minister to them. And the rewards will be great, for in our essentially pagan culture we desperately need those who see more clearly those things which are eternal.

James W. Daley, et al., *Journal of Gerontology*, 23 134-139, 1968; J. G. Gilbert, and R. F. Levee, *Journal of Gerontology*, 26 70, 1971; D. O. Moberg and M. J. Taves, in *Older People and Their Social World*, A. M. Rose and W. A. Peterson, eds., Philadelphia, Davis, 1965, pp. 113-124; *Older People and Their Social World*, A. M. Rose, and W. A. Peterson, eds., Philadelphia, Davis, 1965; *New York Times Magazine*, Aug. 13, 1967, pp. 14-15; G. R. Taylor, *The Biological Time Bomb*, New York, World, 1968.   ROBERT L. HERRMAN

OLD TESTAMENT ETHICS. See also *Jewish Ethics*. Two factors fix the character and content of OT ethics: (1) the legal tradition of the ancient Near East and (2) the character and acts of Yahweh, the God of Israel. The ethical teaching of the OT is both continuous and discontinuous with the ethical teaching of its ancient world. A serious reading of Hammurabi's Code will reveal many sections comparable to some in the Pentateuch, and also many differences. These differences are due to Yahweh's character and acts. Three factors are determinative here: (1) Yahweh's role as Creator, (2) his holiness, and (3) his election of Israel.

Yahweh as Creator. It is not necessary to attempt to determine when Israel recognized the philosophical and theological implications of Gen. 1 and 2. The practical religious and ethical consequences appear from the beginning. There is an absoluteness in the ethic that results from the fact that Yahweh is One and is alone sovereign, without equal or rival. Polytheism presented a base for man's value system that was multiple and varied. There could be no unity. The OT doctrine of *ex nihilo* creation meant that one sovereign will dominated and gave unity to all. A rationale was not needed for his Word. He speaks and there is none to challenge. Yahweh is not a part of the process of things. He is not caught in the flux. Nor is he merely superior to other gods. He alone is God, and other objects of worship (the sun, moon, earth, heaven as in Gen. 1 and 2 and Ps. 121) are the works of his hands. He is transcendent, and so is his Word. The absolute character of the demand in that Word is lacking elsewhere in Israel's world just as it is lacking in our contemporary world where the authority of Scripture is not established. Sometimes a rationale is given for his commands (Exod. 20:11) but as often it is not (Exod. 20:13-17). The utilitarian worth of acting wisely is pointed out in the Wisdom Literature (Prov. 5). The common approach in the Pentateuch though finds this unnecessary (Exod. 20). Yahweh is the ultimate one and the fact that he has spoken is enough.

Given Israel's monotheism the inseparability of religion and ethics was inevitable. There was one base for both, Yahweh. The possibilities of religion without ethics or ethics without religion were precluded, and the beneficent interaction of the two guaranteed. Jesus could summarize all the law in love of God and neighbor (Matt. 22:36ff.), because these were already related in that both were commanded by Yahweh (Deut. 6:5 and Lev. 19:18). Religion and ethics support and pervade one another.

The transcendence of Yahweh permitted a universal application of the moral law in Israel that made it unique in the ancient world. Before the Creator all men stood alike. The moral law was as binding on king as upon commoner. The noblest and most powerful were bound like the humblest (see the stories of David and Nathan, II Sam. 12, and Naboth and Ahab, I Kings 21). There is one God and one law for all.

This unitary impact of monotheism meant also the mixing of cultic and moral. These often appear together in the OT. Leviticus 19 combines respect for parents, prohibition of idolatry, injustice, stealing, and immorality, with instructions on preparation of the sacrificial meal, gleaning the vineyards, the prohibition of meat with blood in it, and how to cut one's hair. The rationale is simply "I am Yahweh, your God" (v. 3). All of life is one. This does not mean that all is of equal value. The centrality of the Decalogue in the Sinai Covenant makes clear that the religious and ethical demands are crucial. The basis for the subsequent prophetic differentiation in value between the cultic and moral demands is already implicit (cf. Isa. 1; Jer. 7; Hos. 6; Amos 5).

Another significant consequence or Yahweh's transcendence is manifest in the OT sexual ethic. The pantheons of Israel's world were comprised of gods and goddesses who shared the same sexual drives and differentiation as men and women. The principles of sympathetic magic common throughout the ancient world inevitably led Israel's neighbors to imitation of "holy weddings" between gods and goddesses with the attendant sexual prostitution. Yahweh was not a part of nature and transcended this natural process. No sexual practices could be vindicated as an imitation of his divine activity. Man's sexuality was part of his createdness and thus must come under Yahweh's divine intention. This made sexual practices natural and good when performed according to his will, but ethically and religiously wrong when not. Thus the sacred prostitute, the pervert, bestiality, and immorality were precluded (Lev. 20:13; Exod. 22:19; 20:14) while the divine origin and sacred character of the sex act within marriage was maintained (Gen. 1:26-28; Song of Songs). Here Yahweh made the difference.

The Holiness of Yahweh. The Biblical

doctrine of creation indicates the single base for OT ethics, Yahweh. His moral nature, which determines the character of the ethical demands, is another matter. It is summed up by the Biblical writers in the word "holy." Israel is to be holy because Yahweh is holy (Exod. 19:6; Lev. 11:44-45; 19:1-2). This is an ethical matter as much as a religious one.

The root *qdsh* ("to be holy") is common in the ancient Semitic languages but it takes on a special meaning in Israel. This is because it is especially used of Yahweh. The word *qadosh* ("holiness") perhaps most clearly expresses the character of the transcendent Yahweh. It involves his *unapproachableness* (Exod. 19:11-16). It is closely linked with his *glory* (Ezek. 1:28). It is intimately related to his *jealousy* and his *wrath* (Exod. 20:5; 34:14; Deut. 4:24). The essential character of his holiness is seen in what evokes this jealous God to wrath. It is always a religious (as with idolatry) or a moral lapse that brings forth his anger. What this holiness demands in terms of conduct is found in the various codes of the OT like Exod. 20, Deut. 5, Exod. 21–23; Lev. 18–20, and in numerous summaries as found in Isa. 1, Jer. 7, Ezek. 18, Amos 5, and Micah 6. Often cultic demands are mixed with ethical, but this seems to reflect the unwillingness of the OT writers to divorce ethics from religious worship and practice. The priority of the moral-ethical demands over the cultic seem clear from Exod. 20 and Ps. 15 and 24. When the prophets are confronted with the choice between the cultic and the ethical, they place the premium on the latter. The revelation in the OT is progressive, yet the character and extent of the moral demand is remarkably consistent. It comes from the unchanging Yahweh.

The Election of Israel. The doctrine of creation provides a universalistic base and potential for the ethic of the OT. The calling of Israel gives a particularistic character. A different ethical standard prevails for Israel in the OT than for the other nations. Amos illustrates this (1–2). Damascus, Gaza, Tyre and others are judged by what appears to be a code based upon natural law while Judah is judged by "the Law of Yahweh" which has been given to her. Needless to say the standard based on Yahweh's revelation of himself is far more stringent. Yahweh's call is to higher responsibility as well as to higher privilege.

The election of Israel gives a historical character to the OT ethic. Israel is called to serve Yahweh within the historical continuum of the ancient Near East. She is called out, but her roots are not severed. Thus there is a continuity between the ethics of the OT and that of the Near East. Israel brought with her into the covenant much of the accumulated legal wisdom of its world. There is no conflict between that truth and the truth revealed in the covenant. Both are from Yahweh. It should not be surprising to find similarities between the legal lore of Babylon and the Pentateuch, nor between the wisdom of Egypt and the wisdom of Israel. There is a normative element within Israel that comes through its covenant knowledge of Yahweh that is lacking elsewhere. Thus there are the transient elements that were to be superceded in Christ mixed with the transcendent elements which found further illumination and confirmation in the NT.

Election results in a nationalistic character for the OT ethic that is not final. The particularism of Israel's ethic must be reconciled with the doctrines of Yahweh's creatorhood and his love. Isaiah sees a day when the nations of the earth will come to Zion to be taught "his ways" that they may walk "in his paths" (Isa. 2:1-5). The nationalism is not final but preparatory. It is thus possible to compare the OT ethic with that of Israel's neighbors. Yahweh chose a people within history to be his own. The OT ethic thus is inclusive of elements that are part of the legal tradition of the Near East, a legal tradition which was a human elaboration of natural law.

J. Hempel, "Ethics in the Old Testament," *The Interpreter's Dictionary of the Bible*, G. A. Buttrick, ed., Nashville, Abingdon, Vol. 2, 1962, pp. 153-161; John Murray, "Biblical Ethics," *The New Bible Dictionary*, J. D. Douglas, ed., Grand Rapids, Eerdmans, 1962, pp. 394-397; Th. C. Vriezen, *An Outline of Old Testament Theology*, Newton Centre, Mass., Branford, 1966; George E. Wright, *The Old Testament against Its Environment*, Chicago, Regnery, 1950.   DENNIS F. KINLAW

OMISSION, SINS OF. See also *Ignorance; Sin.* Most of the ten commandments are couched in negative terms and transgression of these commands is obviously overt sin. Other commands of God are positive in form, and not to measure up to these standards or keep these positive commands is also wicked. Such sins are called sins of omission. The Westminster Shorter Catechism succintly defines both sins of omission and commission: "Sin is any want of conformity unto or transgression of the law of God" (Q. 13).

It may be that sins of commission are more widely recognized, but that sins of omission are more common. The summary of the commandments enjoins us to love the Lord with all our hearts and our neighbors as ourselves. The Sermon on the Mount (q.v.) commands us to be perfect as our heavenly Father is perfect (Matt. 5:48). These absolute standards disclose how great are our human failings.

Sins of omission are not identical with sins of ignorance. We fail to perform many duties of which we are aware. The NT affirms "To him that knoweth to do good and doeth it not, to him it is sin" (James 4:17). But in respect to positive commands some sins of ignorance are also sins of omission. Fortunately all sin of all kinds when confessed and repented of is covered by the atonement. Christ both suffered the penalty of broken law and himself actively obeyed all God's holy law. R. LAIRD HARRIS

OPEN MARKET. See *Black Market.*

OPEN HOUSING. Open housing seeks to prevent racial discrimination in housing patterns. The term connotes the right of every American to buy or rent housing of his choice. Fair housing laws aimed at the private market (realtors, builders, home owners) began in 1944 with a New York City statute. The 1964 Civil Rights Act and the 1968 Housing Act make it illegal to refuse to sell, lease or rent to a person on the basis of race. Federal financing for housing projects now aim at a racially balanced environment to avoid urban blight and to enhance the overall quality of life. De facto segregation patterns still exist, however, often supported by "unwritten" rules of discrimination, thus underscoring the need for open housing ordinances at local levels.   PAUL D. SIMMONS

OPPRESSION. In ethical context, the term "oppression" usually means subjection to injustice or tyranny. Thus it is associated with socio-economic exploitation, the unjust exaction of services or homage, and the abuse of political authority. Opposition to oppression implies support of freedom and social justice.

The meaning of oppression in terms of public purpose can be determined by several different criteria. The primacy of the spiritual, natural law, the German common law tradition, and constitutionalism all have been used as standards to decide when a man or a group of men have been oppressed religiously, socially, economically or politically. Christian scholars at various points in history have acknowledged the validity of all four of these means of identifying oppression, both singly and in various combinations.

Most Biblical passages dealing with this subject speak of the need to end oppression and to establish social justice (e.g., Exod.

3:9; Deut. 23:15-16; 24:14; Ps. 10:17-18; Jer. 7:5-7; Ezek. 45:8; Amos 4:1; James 2:5-7). The Bible exhorts rulers to exercise righteousness and justice in dealing with their people, notes that the poor need a champion, and links oppression to the powerful elements of society (Ps. 72:4; Eccles. 4:1). Isaiah, speaking for the Lord, called upon God's people to repent and "cease to do evil, learn to do good; seek justice, correct oppression..." (Isa. 1:16-18 RSV).

Biblical authority indicated that Christians should attack the problem of oppression at two levels: individual and social. Individually, the answer is Christian love, both for other Christians and for all mankind (Rom. 13:8-10; I Cor. 13:1—14:1). Socially, the Christian response is to seek justice. Man's inhumanity to man can be curbed by incorporating justice into legislative, administrative and judicial institutions. Justice demands that no individual or group hold the power to exploit another. Righteousness and justice in personal and group life are commanded repeatedly in the Bible (e.g., Deut. 16:18-20; Ps. 82:1-4; Prov. 1:3; 21:15; Isa. 26:7; Amos 5:7-15; Rom. 12).

Unfortunately, although nearly all Christians agree that oppression is wrong, there is no apparent consensus on how to end it. Most believers accept the validity of legal-constitutional change, but this currently is not a live option in much of the world. Some Christians feel that in this case simple civil disobedience is the way to eliminate oppression while others agree with the phrase used by Franklin, Jefferson, and John Adams on the original Great Seal of the United States: "Rebellion to Tyrants Is Obedience to God."   ROBERT D. LINDER

OPTIMISM. See also *Eschatology and Ethics; Hope; Perfectionism; Social Darwinism; Utopianism.* Optimism is the confidence that everything is or will turn out well eventually. It can be viewed from philosophical, theological, Biblical and psychological grounds. Philosophical optimism includes those asserting "this is the best possible world" and those believing that man can improve himself and his environment, usually because the ground of all things is viewed as good and supportive of his efforts. Theological optimism varies from belief that only God and the good exist, and that evil is an illusion, to the triumphant expectation that, although evil abounds, God and the right will ultimately prevail. Biblical optimism includes those who believe the Bible teaches everything is good as part of an overall divine plan, as well as those who hold that Scripture affirms the existence of evil which God overcomes through present and eschatological intervention to serve his purposes, though it will survive eternally in some subjugated form. Psychological optimism is the practice of looking on the bright side of things, hoping and expecting the best regardless of any contrary consideration.

It is difficult to see how the evangelical Christian can be anything except optimistic concerning his personal destiny. The Bible provides many promises for his present welfare and as he holds true to his convictions and Biblical principles, insures his ultimate triumph and reward hereafter. The trials, temptations and persecutions of life develop his character and are occasions for rejoicing, being part of the majestic struggle against evil under divine leadership.

Evangelical optimism thrives on the glorious possibilities for the deliverance and improvement of even the worst of sinners. As they respond to God's love and mercy, the lowest of mankind can be transformed into the greatest of saints through the atonement of Christ, the power of his resurrection and the outpouring of the Holy Spirit.

It is more problematic to maintain optimism in the face of the natural and moral evils present in the universe. Natural disasters of earthquakes, hurricanes, volcanic eruptions, drouth and the carnivorous cycle of nature more easily sanction pessimism. The moral failures of war, crime, pollution, poverty and man's oppression of man add further pessimistic possibilities. The evangelical believes these faults are the result of man's fall and will eventually be overcome through divine eschatological intervention including the second coming of Christ. Meantime, these necessary evils can be accepted as part of this temporal order through which God is working out his designs and confronted with God's intended purpose for his creation and for man and society.

The greatest difficulty facing the evangelical optimist is the Biblically-based view that a vital segment of men and angels will never be redeemed in the final restoration. To meet this objection he must rely on faith that when the divine economy is fully consummated, the Judge of all the earth will do right in his omniscience, wisdom, justice and mercy. Christian optimism is therefore supported by a proper understanding of Scripture, the deliverance of sinful man through divine enablement, the integration of present inadequacies with corrective eschatological developments, and faith in the absolute goodness of the omnipotent God.   FLOYD F. McCALLUM

ORDER. See *Government; International Order.*

ORDERS OF CREATION AND PRESERVATION. Orthodox Christians have always identified the God and Father of Jesus Christ with the world's Creator. Both Jesus (Matt. 19, 22) and Paul (Rom. 13) taught that God the Creator employs his holy law to reign over all men throughout the nonredemptive dimensions of life. But what connection prevails, if any, between the sovereign will of the Creator and the societal structures and secular institutions of his sin-corrupted creation?

Roman Catholics synthesized some of Paul's testimony on the law of God (Rom. 1–2) with earlier Stoic teachings on the universality of a Natural Law (q.v.) perceived unaided by human reason and conscience. The syncretistic metaphysics and unevangelical anthropology inherent in this hybrid-system were incompatible with the Reformers' central doctrines of man's radical sin and his need for God's saving grace in Jesus Christ.

Hence Luther and the Augsburg Confession (Art. 16) opposed both the Roman domination of society and the sectarian separation from society. They defended the Scriptural witness to "ordinances of God," communal patterns of life based on the Creator's law that remained binding on all human creatures, whether redeemed or not, and ordained or not.

Luther radically distinguished God's twofold reign through the gospel as man's Redeemer-Sanctifier and through the law as his Creator-Judge. Moreover, he taught that God created continually, exercising his "left-hand reign" as Creator-Judge in three "orders" or "estates" of society. He wrote:

> The holy ordinances and foundations instituted by God are these three: the ministry, marriage and civil authority. . . . Service in them constitutes true holiness and pious living before God. This is because these three ordinances are grounded in God's Word and command (Gen. 1:28), and are thereby sanctified as holy things by God's own holy Word.
>
> —*Weimar Ausgabe* 26, 504

In the twentieth century, however, Luther's theonomous "ordinances of God" were blasphemously severed from the reign of the Creator's sovereign law, and secularized into autonomous "orders of creation" *(Schoepfungsordnungen)*. This perversion of

Reformation theology was promoted by some influential German Lutherans in the 1930 s. It moved in the direction of Idealistic philosophy, natural theology, and an independent primal revelation of God in creation. At its worst, it was twisted by the Nazified *Deutsche Christen* party to sanctify their Nordic heresies of "Blood and Soil" (Ansbach *Ratschlag*). They offered an uncritical glorification of counterfeit "orders of creation" (for example, the Nazi state and the German *Volk*), which made them sacrosanct sources of divine revelation parallel to and autonomous of God's normative self-revelation in Jesus Christ.

The prophetic task today is to reaffirm God's reign over all creation without either blindly identifying or rashly separating his divine authority and any particular societal pattern or relatively unjust social structure. In order to stress both sides of these theonomous but historical "orders"—that they are divinely ordained but also subject to God's law in a fallen world—post-war Protestant theologians often prefer to speak of the Creator's "orders of preservation" (Brunner), or "emergency orders" (Thielicke), or even "mandates of God" (Bonhoeffer).   WILLIAM H. LAZARETH

ORGANISM—FIELD THEORY. See *Psychology*.

ORGAN TRANSPLANTATION. See also *Heart Transplantation; Medical Ethics*.
Organ transplantation is fraught with philosophical and ethical problems. The morality of prolongation of life by transplantation, however, differs little from that of prolongation of life by other means. That this is in accord with the Christian ethic is evidenced by the major role of healing in the ministry of Jesus Christ.

It might be argued that the intermixing of tissues with the resultant almost inevitable rejection-reaction is evidence of interference with God ordained natural laws. In actuality, it represents nothing more than the body's defensive reaction against the invasion of anything foreign—the same mechanism activated against infection. Furthermore, blood transfusions, which represent a definite form of tissue transplantation, have long been accepted as ethical by the Christian community.

Other problems concern the organ recipient and donor and participating physicians. Kidney transplantation is at the present a widely accepted therapeutic measure for the treatment of end stage renal disease. There was a time, however, when it was but an experimental procedure, as has been true of nearly all other currently practiced organ transplants.

Can the Christian physician ethically participate in experimental clinic surgery? Under certain specific circumstances, the answer may be in the affirmative. An experimental procedure is considered morally acceptable when: all other modes of accepted therapy have been explored and exhausted; death or total incapacitation is inevitable within a short and predictable period of time; the surgeon has optimally prepared himself through laboratory experience; there is a definite, if small, chance of the procedure succeeding; and the patient is fully aware of the experimental nature and the risks of the procedure. If these criteria are fulfilled and if the procedure does not entail undue suffering or loss of human dignity, the physician may in good conscience proceed. The aim in organ transplantation is not simply prolongation of life with possible attendant suffering, but total rehabilitation of the patient.

Two types of organ donors must be considered from the philosophical viewpoint, the living related donor and the cadaver donor. The former is involved only in the transplantation of a paired organ, such as a kidney. The living related donor may be considered as acceptable only if thorough examination has revealed no impairment of his health, excellent function of *both* paired organs, a strong desire to donate the organ without any sense of direct family or physician pressure, and a minimal risk to his life during or after surgery. The current mortality among healthy kidney donors is < 1 in 2500. Life expectancy is a fraction of 1 percent less for a patient with one good kidney, than for one with both organs. Thus the principle of donation of one of paired organs by a living related donor is widely accepted.

The use of cadaver donors poses two distinct problems: the consent of the deceased and/or his relatives and an acceptable definition of brain death. It is the practice in all recognized transplant centers in the USA to obtain relative consent before using organs if the relatives are available. If they are not, and a reasonable effort has been made to communicate with them to no avail, the Uniform Anatomical Gift Act (enacted in 49 of 50 states) makes it permissible and legal to use the organs for transplantation without the consent of the next of kin.

Because of the many means currently available for maintaining vegetative (cardiorespiratory) function in patients, long after irreversible brain damage has occurred, new definitions of death have come into existence. The most widely accepted criteria of brain death are: (1) no spontaneous breathing whatsoever; (2) no reflexes; (3) no response to painful stimuli and where possible a confirmatory electroencephalogram run at highest sensitivity for thirty minutes with no evidence of electrical activity. If these criteria are met in a patient who is not under the influence of depressant drugs, anesthetics, or hypothermia, the diagnosis of irreversible coma or brain death may be unequivocally made. Under no circumstances should the declaration of death be made by a member of the transplant team. It should come from physicians or consul-

tants responsible for the primary care of the patient.

A final consideration is the question facing the potential living related donor of a paired organ. Is he morally bound to give an organ, if his physical condition, age, and circumstances permit? There is no Scriptural injunction that demands this. Many passages, however, indicate that the law of love operating in an individual may compel him to give of himself, not grudgingly or as under obligation, but joyously as privileged to give. "Greater love has not man than this...."   JOHN E. WOODS

ORIGINAL NATURE. See *Human Nature; Image of God.*

ORIGINAL SIN. See also *Fall of Man.* The meaning of original sin is dependent on a specific theological framework. This framework traditionally has been coordinated with the historical fall of Adam disclosed in Gen. 3. The sin of Adam has within it both a singularity and universality. The fall of Adam is interpreted not only as the first sin, but as the sin that has universal consequences, for the fall of Adam resulted in human solidarity in sin.

This double character of Adam's sin finds primary support in Rom 5:12-18. This passage contains the repeated emphasis that the "one" sin of the man Adam establishes the death and condemnation of "all" men. How further to interpret this relation between the "one" and the "all" has been debated throughout the history of the church. The two most prominent theories are realism and representationalism or federalism. Both theories assume the genetic unity of the human race through Adam but consider this unity inadequate to explain the universal responsibility for sin. According to realism the responsibility for Adam's sin is imputed to all men because all men in some form actually participated in Adam's sin. According to representationalism or federalism, imputation rests upon God's ordaining Adam as the representative or federal head of all men.

Some theologians replace the historical framework of original sin by an existential one. Original sin is interpreted as a factor in human consciousness to the exclusion of its historical origin as the first sin of Adam. It is interpreted as a "dialectical truth" rather than a historical truth. Individual man can discern in his consciousness solidarity with and participation in the universality of sin. This solidarity and participation means that sin is inevitable, yet human consciousness of responsibility for sin remains despite its inevitability.

The dialectical relation between inevitability and responsibility is maintained through the freedom of the self to ascend different levels of consciousness. On the level of concrete action the self inevitably wills something morally inferior to what the self discerns on the higher level of contemplation. In the moment of contemplation the self witnesses to a freedom over inevitability by acknowledging guilt for its morally inferior action. This paradox in which "man is most free in the discovery that he is not free" (Niebuhr) constitutes original sin.

The dialectical interpretation of original sin does have affinities with the moral failures found in human consciousness. But this approach tends to make human consciousness rather than Scripture the most determinative factor in its interpretation of sin.

G. D. Berkouwer, *Sin*, Grand Rapids, Eerdmans, 1971; Emil Brunner, *Man in Revolt*, New York, Scribner, 1939; John Murray, *The Imputation of Adam's Sin*, Grand Rapids, Eerdmans, 1959; Reinhold Niebuhr, *The Nature and Destiny of Man*, New York, Scribner, 1946.

THEODORE MINNEMA

ORPHANS. See also *Adoption; Children.* When the Athenian philosopher Aristides was called upon to defend his fellow Chris-

tians before Emperor Hadrian in A.D. 125, he said, "They love one another. The widow's needs are not ignored, and they rescue the orphan from the person who does him violence. He who has gives to him who has not, ungrudgingly and without boasting" (Helen Harris, *The Newly Recovered Apology of Aristides,* 1893).

Followers of Jesus Christ historically have demonstrated tender concern for children, especially the deprived or orphan child. Jesus reprimanded the disciples for attempting to keep children from "bothering" him and ordered, "You must let little children come to me—never stop them! For the kingdom of God belongs to such as these" (Mark 10:14, Phillips).

Christian influence during the fifth and sixth centuries brought legal protection for children in the Roman Empire. After Zwingli's break with Rome in the early eighteenth century, he instigated reforms in the Council of Zurich, Switzerland, that produced, among other things, the transformation of several monasteries into orphanages. A Christian statesman, Anthony Ashley Cooper, led the fight against child labor practices in Great Britain in the nineteenth century. And throughout history, Christian missionaries have led the way in establishing orphanages and child-care centers on every continent.

Christian concern for children is seeded in the OT view that children are gifts from God, rather than mere biological derivatives. "Lo, children are an heritage of the Lord," the Psalmist wrote, "and the fruit of the womb is his reward."

Care of the fatherless is commanded again and again throughout the Pentateuch. Providing for orphaned children was a sanctioned use of the tithe (Deut. 26:12). Blessings upon God's people were often conditional to meeting the needs of children who were deprived of normal parents, and harsh judgment awaited those who "oppress the fatherless" (Mal. 3:5).

The Bible lays great stress on the worth of an individual life, and this value is just as great for the newborn as for the elderly. In fact, the formative years of one's life drew special attention from Jesus. He cited child-like faith as the model for the kind of trusting confidence in Jesus Christ that gains entry into God's kingdom.

Pure religion, according to James, makes care for the "fatherless" of equal emphasis as living "unspotted from the world."

With childcare centers existing in most countries today, concerned Christians are provided not only the opportunity of caring for the physical needs of deprived children, but also the privilege of sharing in a positive way the good news of Jesus at the time and in the manner that makes the Christian message highly effectual.

In summary, caring for the needs of deprived children is both a moral responsibility and an ethical imperative consistent with the Biblical evaluation of the worth of a single life formed in the image of God. It is commanded by God in the Scriptures, and constrained by Christian love that demands expression in acts of love toward all who need it.   W. STANLEY MOONEYHAM

ORTHODOX (EASTERN) ETHICS. An essential element in the early Greek theology is the divinization of man *(theosis)*. Irenaeus, Clement of Alexandria, and Athanasius are cited, the last in the words: "He became man so that we might become divine." Bratsiotis states the Christian ethos in the words of Ignatius: "Since we have become his apprentices, let us live as becomes Christians." This ethos includes the piety which strives toward the ideal of divinization, perseverance under persecution, and an ascetic and mystical vigilance to aid in overcoming the world.

Catechetical Ethics. The *Didache* reflects the ethical encounter of early Christians with Jewish and pagan cultures and begins with "the way of life and the way of death." With Origen begins a growing literary tradition to strengthen the martyrs and guide the believers. The Greek Patrology (Migne) lists many writings treating general ethics in addition to special categories, such as virginity and continence, fasting, temperance, riches and benevolence. To the Eastern churches these treatises still form a backdrop for their ethical idealism, since Orthodoxy is conservative and the ancient language is not strange. Modern catechisms have as their purpose to remain in the continuity of a timeless Orthodoxy, even in other matters. Thus Platon (Petersburg Archbishop, d. 1812) curiously begins his catechism with a Socratic thesis: "Self-knowledge is the beginning of all human science," but the basis of his ethical thought is in the sentence: "Jesus Christ passed His life on earth in the most perfect fulfilment of the law." He continues: "The divine law is written in the heart of every man, and is contained in the following Ten Commandments, which God gave to Moses." The moral law is declared to be natural, impressed upon the hearts of all men. To Moses God gave a threefold law: ritual, civil, and moral. The written moral law is a facsimile of the natural, "as it contains no precept of which the conscience of every one is not convinced." The similarity to the natural knowledge of God and of law, as taught by Thomas Aquinas (q.v.), is apparent, but it would be rash to declare the Greeks dependent upon the Latins.

The *Greek Orthodox Catechism* of Constantine Callinicos is divided into three equal parts: dogmatical, ethical, and ceremonial. This emphatic treatment is unusual because systematic treatises on ethics have been rare in the East (Benz). According to Callinicos "the natural law is rigid and immutable . . . God's law is called *natural* as it applies to the constant phenomena of non-reasoning and non-free nature, and *moral* as it affects man. "The moral law is adaptable to human development through the ages." Callinicos emphasizes the free will of man, "that God-given capacity of man, thanks to which he can choose" his actions. "Upon free will is established man's responsibility." "The divine law is innate in our souls." "We call conscience that innate faculty," by which we behold our moral beauty or moral ugliness. Only that is good, which possesses the beauty and fitness of divine standards. Filial respect is equated with duty toward God. The duties toward man are described as presented in the decalog "in descending order of importance." "To sin by word is less than to sin in deed; and an evil desire is less than an evil thought uttered aloud." Labor becomes a sacred duty, and idleness is a profanation of the six days, even as the failure to santify the Sabbath is a profanation of the holy day. The honor due to father and mother includes patriotism (Gr. *he patris*, fatherland), "but patriotism must not be stained with a narrow-minded fanaticism and degenerate into *Imperialism* or *Chauvinism*." The Mosaic law was not yet perfect; it is negative, preparatory, superseded by the Evangelical law. Thus the moral law is capable of development. The Sermon on the Mount (q.v.) demonstrates the Evangelical law.

Historical Settings. Eastern Christianity has suffered dramatic changes which brought severe trials in their time. The Sassanian empire, the advent of Islam, the fall of Constantinople and the long captivity under the Ottoman empire were periods of testing for Orthodoxy. Only the twentieth century has seen its liberation. It is no wonder that Orthodoxy has remained more conscious of persecution and Christian resignation, more geared to compulsory compliance. The resurgence of Orthodoxy has been one of the miracles of this century. Whereas after 1918 its adherents were counted in the thousands, their numbers are now reported above fifty million. Their presence in the ecumenical movement (cf. *World Council of Churches)* has been greatly welcomed, but their Orthodox ethos has asserted itself more and more. The unity of the "visible church" is not the ecumenical objective of the Eastern church. Had the concept of the "Church invisible" been taken seriously by the ecumenists, most of their difficulties would have been greatly minimized or have vanished altogether (Spinka). The Russian Orthodox prize the term *sobornost,* declared an untranslatable term, whose meaning could be stated as "all for one and one for all." It is interpreted as "Where the Spirit of Christ is, there is the ecumenical Church" (Spinka).

Russian Orthodoxy has not shared the liberation since the advent of atheist communism; it has rather been subjected to persecution as massive as earlier catastrophies. Nicolas Berdyaev, who came from Marxism to Christianity, describes communism (q.v.) as "a rigidly orthodox, literalist, fundamentalist sort of religion." It destroys the individual personality and makes man a mere instrument of ideological policy; it has failed to realize a just society. Hromadka describes the projected classless society as an idealistic element in Marxism, a kind of secularized eschatology. What Russian communism means for the social ethics of the church is indicated in a paragraph from *Izvestiya,* April 26, 1929:

Religious organizations are prohibited: (a) from forming mutual aid associations, co-operatives, productive associations, and generally from making use of their property in their care for any other purpose except the satisfaction of their religious needs; (b) from rendering material aid to their members; (c) from organizing special prayer and other meetings for children, youth, and women, as well as general Bible studies; also literary, handwork, industrial, religious and other meetings, groups, circles, departments, as well as from organizing excursions and children's playgrounds, from opening libraries and reading-rooms, from organizing sanatoria and medical aid.

Ernst Benz, *Die Ostkirche*, Freiburg, 1952; Panagiotis Bratsiotis, *The Greek Orthodox Church*, London, 1968; Nicolas Bulgaris, *A Holy Catechism*, Constantinople, 1861-1961; Constantine N. Callinicos, *The Greek Orthodox Catechism*, New York, 1960; Josef L. Hromadka, *Impact of History on Theology*, Notre Dame, Ind., Fides, 1970; G. Potessaro (ed.), *The Orthodox Doctrine of the Apostolic Eastern Church* (Platon), New York, AMS Press, 1857-1969; Matthew Spinka, *Nicolas Berdyaev: Captive of Freedom*, Philadelphia, Westminster, 1950; Matthew Spinka, *The Quest for Church Unity*, New York, Macmillan, 1960; Nicolas Zernov, *Eastern Christendom*, London, 1961.

OTTO F. STAHLKE

OTHERWORLDLINESS. See also *Eschatology and Ethics; Secularism; Worldliness.* The idea but not the term "otherworldly" is Biblical, and stems from the Scriptural view of the world (the universe and its history) as: (a) created by God through and for Jesus Christ (John 1:3; Col. 1:16), and therefore good (Gen. 1:31); (b) in rebellion against God on account of man's sinfulness, and temporarily in the power of the evil one (Rom 5:12; I John 5:19); (c) the sphere of God's redemptive action in Christ, past, present and future (John 3:16; 4:42; Eph. 1:10). God as sovereign Creator and Savior is ultimately Lord of the universe and of history; there is no brief in Christian doctrine for a thoroughgoing dualism. But until the day when the kingdom of the world becomes finally "the kingdom of our Lord and of his Christ" (Rev. 11:15), there exists an ethical dualism; a tension between the control of God and of Satan in the world (cf. John 8:42-4). The Christian is not allowed to escape this tension. As a member of the body of Christ, he is to live responsibly in the world (John 17:18), even if spiritually he does not belong to it (John 17:14).

Here is the paradox. God is the Creator of the world; and in this sense the world is good. But the world is also corrupt when it is organized in opposition to God; and in this sense the believer is not to love the world or the things in it (I John 2:15-17). Because of this, the disciple must go into all the world, to evangelize it in the Lord's name (Matt. 18:19; cf. Mark 16:15, longer ending). Christians are thus to be world-affirming and world-denying *(otherworldly)* at the same time (cf. E. Brunner, *The Divine Imperative*, London, Lutterworth, 1937, pp. 170-8).

Since worldliness is an attitude before it is an act, the believer who walks in the Spirit may cultivate a disposition of what is sometimes called "holy worldliness." This is likely to be more positive and creative than "otherworldliness" in the sense of retreat or escape from the world, in order to be concerned with the world to come (but see also Heb. 13:14). It cannot be said, however, that the motives of anchorites such as Simeon Stylites (c. 390-459) and those who belonged to the monastic movement, from Anthony of Egypt to its flowering under Benedict, were entirely negative. They withdrew (and others still withdraw) in order to be quiet and pray for others and learn self-discipline; and their lives are often exemplary. Nevertheless, the dangers of introspection in this kind of existence are obvious; and it is still possible to live the Christian life unascetically and to love beauty, without being worldly in the non-Christian sense.

STEPHEN S. SMALLEY

P

PACIFISM. See also *Just War Criteria; Peace and War; Violence.* Absolute pacifism holds war to be morally indefensible; relative pacifism condemns only particular wars or types of war. A less carefully articulated view stems merely from a decent human hatred of violence in any form. Even more widely than in Christianity, pacifism is found in certain other religions (Buddhism, Confucianism, Hinduism) and in anti-religious groups.

Although the OT is not explicit on the subject (some would disagree citing the Sixth Commandment), the Gospels give Jesus' assurance that the peacemakers shall be called God's sons, that not the violent but the meek shall inherit the earth. But Jesus also could be both temple-scourger and sword-bringer. The NT generally stresses the divine love, leaving practical implications to the individual believer. There is sympathetic reference to the centurion Cornelius (Acts 10:47) who evidently was not compelled to change his profession; and the military allusions elsewhere (e.g., Eph. 6; Heb. 11) further suggest warfare to have been a normal feature of life.

Some of the early fathers (Hippolytus, Tertullian, Lactantius) were clearly pacifist, perhaps because a soldier in the Roman armies was exposed to pagan rites and swore allegiance to the emperor, thus clashing with his overriding loyalty to Christ. But weighty authorities on the other side—notably Clement of Alexandria—were convinced that the soldier who was converted should remain where he was.

After the Empire followed Constantine into technical Christianity compromise was increasingly found, and Augustine later was to lay down guidelines for modern Catholicism in declaring that while war was of itself evil, it was justifiable as a last resort. So far did this view develop that the *New Catholic Encyclopedia* (Vol. X, p. 856) declares that "absolute pacifism is irreconcilable with traditional Catholic doctrine."

Luther and Calvin just as readily acknowledged war's necessity on occasion, while the banner-carrying chaplain Zwingli

met death in battle. Anabaptists, Waldenses, and Quakers were among those who have condemned war on principle, and in this they have been followed by some later Protestant groups and by cultists such as Jehovah's Witnesses and Christadelphians.

In modern times Britain and the USA especially have come to extend freedom of conscience to this topic, though in some countries pacifism brings an automatic prison sentence when the draft call is disregarded. Even in English-speaking countries it is common for conscientious objection to be regarded as a mark of deficient patriotism, particularly by those given to invoking religion in support of a war effort.

For many the concept of relative pacifism became real only when the horror of nuclear and biological warfare came to be contemplated. A further moment of truth was the USA's involvement in Indochina, when increasingly questions were asked about what constitutes a "just" war. Young people began to associate Eastern mysticism with an anti-war ethic.

Apart from his hatred of violence itself, the percipient pacifist objects also to the tyrannical claims of war. He sees how truth is an early casualty when it becomes vitally important to deceive the enemy; to conceal some things, misrepresent others, stir up hatred, break off relationships, check Christian freedom, and stimulate a looking not at all on the things of others except with malevolent aim. The spirit of enmity seeps into the church itself: the chaplain who blesses military occasions is committed to a God-is-on-our-side posture which must necessarily infect his preaching, his pastoral ministry, and his personal integrity.

Nevertheless the case is anything but watertight. A major objection to pacifism is that its exponents demand for this single issue an absolute obedience which they are unprepared to concede over the whole range of life. How, too, can a Christian acquiesce in all the political necessities and advantages of peacetime, then abruptly dissociate himself from his country in time of war? While the non-pacifist is unlikely to deny that some men are called personally by God to stand in prophetic protest against this brutal way of settling differences, it is improbable that God's call will come to men who have not devoted their whole life to the service of God's love and the spreading of God's peace.

Even the philosophy of non-violence used so effectively by Gandhi cannot without challenge be identified with Christian love if it is merely a means of enforcing one's will on others—and is in a double sense the "line of least resistance" that might in turn provoke new antagonism. The pacifist demonstration that evinces aggressive attitudes and sends barbed words to war is suspect; if its motives are unimpeachable its position lacks comprehensiveness or logic.

Ultimately pacifist and non-pacifist are asking different questions. One asks what Jesus would do, and takes the path of non-resistance heedless of consequences; the other sees himself as holding dual citizenship, responsible for the maintenance of law and order and civilization as he knows it. The pacifist regards God's kingdom of pure love as a simple alternative to political action in this world, forgetting that the kingdom cannot have its perfect work in a fallen world wherein man with distorted vision is at odds with himself. The non-pacifist holds that whatever else God has in store for him, he means him to act as a citizen of the world in which he has placed him.

A double obligation is thus presented: to the absolute law of love, and to the relative law of justice, with a final synthesis between them all but impossible. It is a mistake to consider pacifism in itself, and to isolate war from other forms of enmity and sin. The outbreak of military hostilities is only an external symbol—albeit writ large—of man's attempt to live his life without Christ. The Christian also, in his capacity as citizen, must realize that he has in some measure contributed to situations that make war inevitable, and that he is called to repent for his share in the great common guilt.

📖 C. J. Cadoux, *Christian Pacifism Re-Examined*, Oxford, Blackwell, 1940; G. C. Field, *Pacifism and Conscientious Objection*, New York, Macmillan, 1945; L. P. Richards, *Christian Pacifism after Two World Wars*, London, Independent, 1948; F. M. Stratmann, John Doebele, tr., *War and Christianity Today*, London, Blackfriars, 1956; Paul Ramsey, *War and the Christian Conscience*, Durham, Duke University, 1961.   JAMES D. DOUGLAS

PAEDERASTY. See also *Homosexualism and Homosexuality.* Paederasty is homosexual behavior directed towards a young boy. The Biblical teaching against homosexuality is clear.

Paederasty is almost universally illegal. If it occurs many ethical issures arise. Whether or not the child was provocative, the least possible stir and publicity probably best serves the child's general development. Occasionally the adult has a major mental illness, but usually there is no abnormality beyond giving in to a sinful desire.

If the offense occurs among Christians, leaders should approach the offender firmly, encouraging him to resign quietly from his post. Enthusiasm to prosecute is tempered by the principle of Christians settling their own differences (I Cor. 6:18), and by consideration for the child. If serious doubt exists about the offender's mental state, prosecution may be the only way to persuade him to accept psychiatric evaluation.

NEIL YORKSTON

PAIN. See *Suffering.*

PANTHEISM AND ETHICS. See also *Idealistic Ethics.* Pantheism is the view that All is God or God is All. Unfortunately, the formula is not wholly illuminating. Is God the mere aggregate of existing things or their immanent unity? Is God the only reality, the world being only semi-real? Does the finite obscure or reveal God? These and similar questions render pantheism incapable of final definition. When Schleiermacher and Hegel deny they are pantheists, they are right given one understanding of the term and wrong given another.

Stoicism is the best known pantheistic system of the ancient world, though one with theistic strains. For it, the universe is an organic, rational, purposeful Whole that works for good under the determinism of Fate or Providence. The ethical task is to live according to nature—one's own or the universe's—since there are one under the all-embracing law of reason. Here begins Natural Law (q.v.) theory which holds that rational organization of one's life in conformity to Nature is virtue. Man has free will in that he can either acquiensce in Fate-Providence or be enslaved by his desires and emotions. Acceptance of what happens brings tranquility of spirit and forbearance and concern for all men who, because rational, are brothers.

For Spinoza, too, the universe is a rational organic Whole whose single, infinite, eternal substantial Reality expresses itself in the changing modes of the finite. Strict causality reigns. There is no free will, hence praise and blame are equally misplaced. Man's peace comes from rationally penetrating to the heart of things, understanding the immutable laws that bind all together, and affirming them. Freedom is action springing from self-knowledge aimed at fulfillment and preservation in being. Virtue is the full exercise of one's nature as guided by reason; whatever contributes to this is good and pleasurable. Since rational men need each other, self-interest demands altruism.

Two professing Christians of modern times, Schleiermacher and Hegel, reflect strong pantheistic tendencies. The influence of Spinoza on Schleiermacher is weighty; in the latter, familiar strains—modified at points—recur: the divine unity of the (non-personal) Whole, determinism, freedom as the rational expression of one's own nature, individuality as requiring friendship and society, virtue as the triumph of reason over the lower nature. For Hegel, virtue is acceptance of the part-relation to the rational Whole. In the human realm, this whole is the state to which the moral individual will be subordinate.

Pantheism stresses the part-whole relation rather than the person-Person relation of Christianity. The interpersonal at the human level is no longer grounded in the interpersonal of the Divine-human. The classical Christian motifs of divine sovereignty, the revealed will of God, sin, redemption, the moral dynamic of the Holy Spirit, the motive of a responding love, judgment and hereafter are either totally lacking or interpreted differently. Words like "ought," "obligation," "good," "love" acquire different content and connotation. The full value of the individual is missed.

CULBERT G. RUTENBER

PAPAL ENCYCLICALS. From the Greek *en-kyklos* (in a circle), an encyclical was originally a circular letter from a bishop to his flock. Later the word came to be used only of letters sent over the signature of the bishop of Rome. These *Litterae Encyclicae*, as they are known technically, are distinguished from other papal communications in that they are addressed to all the bishops of the world and the faithful everywhere. A common superscription used on all encyclicals reads: "To our venerable brethren, Patriarchs, Primates, Archbishops, Bishops, and other local Ordinaries in peace and communion with the Holy See," to which additional categories of persons within the church may be appended. When encyclicals are addressed to the hierarchy of one country or geographical area, they are called *Epistolae Encyclicae* and have often appeared in the vernacular. The salutation of some recent encyclicals has included persons outside the Roman communion, John XXIII's *Pacem in terris* and Paul VI's *Ecclesiam suam* and *Humanae Vitae* being addressed to "all men of good will." The apostolic benediction usually, if not always, appears in both the superscription and subscription of each encyclical and its date, the year of the pontificate, and the pope's signature are given in the end. The name, or title, of the encyclical is taken from the first words of the official Latin text.

Other Papal Documents. Whereas the term "encyclical" was common in the ancient church, its present designation of one class of papal communications dates from the eighteenth century. Other pontifical statements are called Apostolic Letters *(Litterare Apostolicae),* Apostolic Constitutions *(Constitutions Apostolicae),* Decretal Letters *(Litterae Decretales),* Motu Proprios *(Motus Proprii),* Letters *(Epistolae and Chirographi),* Rescripts *(Rescriptiones),* and Addresses *(Allocutiones).* Of all these, the Encyclical Letters *(Litterae Encyclicae)* are given the greatest publicity by far and are widely translated. The frequency of appearance varies, one encyclical, e.g., having appeared in 1965, two in 1967, one in 1968, and none in the two years following. On the other hand, Leo XIII issued eighty-six encyclicals during his twenty-five year reign, eight in the year 1888 alone.

Purpose. A wide range of subjects relating to the Christian faith and life and of concern to the church at large, or to the faithful in the geographical area addressed, is covered in the encyclicals. In their preparation the pope ordinarily uses the services of scholars or commissions of scholars who have expertise in the subject treated. Some popes have preferred to write their own encyclicals, Leo XIII, one of the greatest of all popes, being a notable exception. The purpose of papal encyclicals is pastoral. Through advice and exhortation, counsel, warning, and admonition the pope exercises his office as shepherd of the flock entrusted to him. Claiming the special guidance of the Holy Spirit, he instructs the church under his jurisdiction and all others willing to listen concerning difficult issues in the life of the people of God.

Authority. In thus carrying out his office as pastor and teacher of all the faithful, the pope claims to be exercising his ordinary magisterium, or teaching office. This is distinguished from his extraordinary magisterium which is invoked on very special occasions, when new dogma is defined or the pope promulgates some other utterance said to be infallible. In these latter instances special language is used including the terms "declare, pronounce, and define" (as in the new dogma concerning Mary promulgated in 1854 and 1950), or "teach and define," or "teach and declare," as in the new dogma concerning the new universal episcopacy of the pope and his infallibility, promulgated in 1870, or a similar formula. Moreover, the sanctions invoked in the event of non-acceptance are mentioned, such as, e.g., "let him be accursed."

This is not to suggest, however, that an encyclical does not carry great weight in Roman Catholic thought and life. It does, and Roman Catholics are under obligation to accept its teachings as coming from the vicar of Christ who, in matters of faith and morals, is said to be endowed with gifts of infallibility. Among his most solemn pronouncements are the encyclicals to some of which the attribute of infallibility is ascribed and to all of which the devout believer is expected to give an attentive reverence.

Yet it is also standard Roman Catholic teaching that one pope is not bound by the encyclical utterances of a predecessor. That is one reason that a study of this literature is confusing to the reader. Differing external circumstances or a change in inner disposition may call for variation in strategy, attitude, or conviction. New counsel, binding on pious members of the Roman Catholic Church, may seem the reverse of advice or admonition given a short time previous. Yet, throughout, it is believed, Christ is guiding his church and it is the Christian's privilege and duty to hear and to obey. This was stated clearly by Pius XII, in 1950, in *Humani Generis* where one reads:

> Nor must it be thought that what is contained in encyclical letters does not of itself demand assent, on the pretext that the popes do not exercise in them the supreme power of their teaching authority. Rather, such teachings belong to the ordinary magisterium, of which it is true to say: "He who hears you, hears me" (Lk. 10.16); for the most part, too, what is expounded and inculcated in encyclical letters already appertains to Catholic doctrine for other reasons. But if the supreme pontiffs in their official documents purposely [*data opera*] pass judgment on a matter debated until then, it is obvious to all that the matter, according to the mind and will of the same pontiffs, cannot be considered any longer a question open for discussion among theologians.—Denz 3885.

Later, Paul VI, in assessing certain teachings of Pius XII, implied the possibility of reversal when he declared in an allocution to a group of cardinals on June 23, 1964, that he did not consider these teachings "out of date and therefore not binding," and that therefore they were still the official position of the church until altered by papal declaration.

A Selected Listing. From the many hundreds of important papal documents it is arbitrary and presumptuous to select a few to illustrate the momentous character of many of these pronouncements. Whereas some Roman Catholic treatments begin with the First Epistle of Peter, we note first the famous bull of Boniface VIII *Unam Sanctam,* of 1302, claiming papal control over the temporal affairs of states and closing with the words: "We, moreover, proclaim, declare, and pronounce that it is altogether necessary to salvation for every human being to be subject to the Roman pontiff." In 1520 Leo X condemned Luther in *Exurge, Domine* and in 1570 Pius V excommunicated and deposed Queen Elizabeth I of England in *Regnans in excelsis.* Another unusual papal statement was issued in 1713 by Clement XI in *Unigenitus* directed against Jansenism and condemning the Pauline and Augustinian doctrines of sin and grace. Other interesting history centers around the bull *Dominus ac Redemptor noster* which suppressed the Society of Jesus in 1773. Clement XIV felt it necessary to disband the Jesuit order in order to save the church from schism. In the long, important pontificate of Pius IX the following are most significant: *Ineffabilis Deus* in which the Immaculate Conception of the Virgin Mary was defined; *Quanta Cura* with its accompanying *Syllabus of Errors* in 1864; and *Pastor Aeternus,* in which the universal episcopacy of the bishop of Rome and his infallibility when he speaks *ex cathedra* in matters of faith and morals is declared. *Casti connubii,* on Christian marriage, in 1930, by Pius XI, and the two encyclicals of Pius XII issued in 1943, *Mystici Corporis* and *Divino afflante Spiritu* were declared. These latter defined the church as the mystical body of Christ and encouraged the use of modern scientific tools in Biblical studies. In 1950 the same pope condemned opinions arising in the "new theology" in the encyclical *Humani Generis.* Encyclicals of Paul VI which have attracted wide attention are *Mysterium Fidei,* reaffirming traditional church doctrine on transubstantiation in the face of new interpretations of the eucharist, in 1965, and *Humanae Vitae,* which branded as illicit every effort to curb procreation in the conjugal act, in 1968.

Recent Challenges. This last encyclical brought to a head dissension which had been building up in the church for decades. The Second Vatican Council had given many the impression that the pattern of authority within the Roman Catholic Church might change. After growing disillusionment in the ensuing years, *Humanae Vitae* convinced many that the church was incapable of the radical reforms needed, that the pope was still controlled by the Curia, the vast bureaucracy without which he could not function, and that there had developed the most serious crisis in authority in the Roman Catholic Church since the age of the Reformation.

Reputable Roman Catholic scholars have openly challenged the official magisterium and the concepts of ecclesiastical and papal infallibility at a time that the church finds it most difficult to meet the criticism. The future of the Roman Catholic Church as it has been known may well depend on the outcome of the present struggle.

📖 Anne Fremantle, *The Papal Encyclicals in their Historical Context,* New York, New American Library, 1956; M. Claudia Carlen, *A Guide to the Encyclicals of the Roman Pontiffs from Leo XIII to the Present Day (1878 - 1937),* New York, 1939;_____, *Dictionary of Papal Pronouncements:* Leo XIII to Pius XII, 1878 - 1957 New York, 1958; P. Nau, *Une Source Doctrinale: Les encycliques* (Paris, 1952); G. K. Malone, *Mater si, Magistra, si! si!* (Chicago Studies 3, 1964); Hans Küng, *Infallible? An Inquiry,* New York, 1971; Leonard J. Swidler, *Freedom in the Church,* Dayton, 1969; G. K. Malone, "Encyclical," *New Catholic Encyclopedia,* New York, 1967, Vol. 5, pp. 332f.; Herbert Thurston, "Encyclical." *The Catholic Encyclopedia,* Vol. 5, pp. 413f.; *Acta Apostolicae Sedis,* appearing monthly from Rome.
M. EUGENE OSTERHAVEN

PARENTHOOD. Parenthood is based upon marriage, the oldest of God's institutions (Gen 1, 2), and upon one of its choicest blessings, children, who are described by Holy Scripture as God's gift (Ps. 127:3-5; 128:3), the delightful pledge of a loving marriage (q.v.) or, in Luther's inimitable terms, "the best wool on the sheep." Children exist not only for their parents; but parents also for them—for physical support and, above all, for careful nurturing, since children will bear not only their physical resemblance but moral, mental, and spiritual imprint as well. Scripture stresses the latter especially, holding parents responsible for bringing them up in God's fear and nurture (Gen. 18:19; Deut. 6:6, 7; 11:19, 20). Children are by nature the children of wrath, marked with original sin, like their parents (Eph. 2:3; John 3:3, 6), and need to be born again, to know God's salvation in Christ (Eph. 2:1, 5; 5:26; II Tim. 3:14-17). To bring them to Christ (Mark 10:14) is an obligation laid on parents by God (Eph. 6:4; Col. 3:21; Ps. 103:13).

History records how in the early years of pioneer civilizations children are usually prized and loved; sophisticated society, however, often despises, limits the number of, or, worse still, eliminates them. Abortion (q.v.) is probably the most "refined" of these control measures in a secularistic age. Christian parents, like the Hebrews of the OT, remember that children are not "protoplasmic accidents," but persons known to their Creator even before their forming in the womb (Jer. 1:5). Childlessness, thus, has rightly been viewed as a cross imposed by God in his inscrutable wisdom (cf. Luke 1, 25). Love-filled Christians, however, often compensate for this in a God-pleasing way by adopting neglected, forgotten, and unwanted children.

Parenthood imposes weighty responsibility. It is no understatement to claim that as parenthood goes, so goes a nation. The country which has to enforce its security and press obedience from its citizens with machine guns has a doubtful future. Where sons and daughters, on the other hand, willingly fulfill the precepts of the Fourth

Commandment, learn to honor and love parents, to regard the hoary head (Lev. 19:32), they are learning, too, and first of all, to fear and love God; proper obedience and respect for all constituted authority will follow.

Parental love which coddles, spoils a child; barbaric discipline crushes. Christian training keeps the apple near the rod, to use Luther's aphorism for proper balance in the control, guidance, and discipline of children. God's own handling of his people through law and gospel—through affliction and chastisement; through consolation, comfort, strengthening—provides parents a beautiful pattern of procedure, rightly dividing the Word of truth (II Tim. 2:15).

Whatever the burdens, duties, trials, Christian parents are convinced that, in spite of all, it is a great joy which God affords through the gift of posterity, and, contrary to contemporary secularistic thinking which seems obsessed only with birth control (q.v.), the Christian is ready to voice his joy and praise with the psalmist: "Happy is the man that hath his quiver full of them" (Ps. 127:5).

📖 Alfred Schmieding, *Parent-Child Relationship in the Christian Home*, St. Louis, Concordia, 1949; N. Taliaferro Thompson, *Adventures in Parenthood*, Richmond, Knox, 1959; John E. Crawford, *Being the Real Father Now that Your Teenager Will Need*, Philadelphia, Fortress, 1968; O. Ottersen, *Those Most Important Years*, Minneapolis, Augsburg, 1966; *Parent Guidance Series*, St. Louis, Concordia.   EUGENE F. KLUG

PASSION. The word "passion" (from the Latin *passio,* meaning "suffering") translates *to pathein* in Acts 1:3, where it refers to Christ's sufferings and death. It also relates in a general sense to inner emotions (cf. *homoiopathēs,* Acts 14:15, James 5:17). Linked to the latter word is *pathos,* meaning in the NT evil desire or lust (cf. Rom. 1:26; Col. 3:5; I Thess. 4:5), as does *pathēmata* also (Rom. 7:5; Gal. 5:24).

In relation to Christ's suffering, the term "passion" applies to the closing days of his life—to his agony in Gethsemane, the events relating to his trial, and very specifically to his crucifixion.

That various aspects of Christ's passion provide a moral or ethical pattern for believers is evident from such passages as Phil. 2:5-8; I Peter 2:21-25; Col. 1:24. In the Philippians passage the emphasis rests upon Christ's self-emptying humility as culminating on the cross; in I Peter 2 it is upon the manner in which he endured various aspects of his passion. Neither passage, however, should be interpreted so as to obscure the uniqueness and completeness of Christ's atoning work on Calvary. While his humble and patient endurance during his passion gives believers a perfect example of how they should meet suffering, only the atoning work of Christ, the God-man, has saving efficacy.

Likewise, Paul's reference in Col. 1:24 to completing "in my flesh . . . what is lacking in Christ's afflictions *(thlipsis)* for the sake of his body, that is, the church" cannot refer to any incompleteness or inadequacy in the atonement, which is indeed "a full, perfect and sufficient sacrifice, oblation, and satisfaction, for the sins of the whole world" *(Book of Common Prayer).* Rather is the apostle speaking of the suffering of the church, the body of Christ through the union of believers with their Lord (Acts 9:4, 5).

The Passion of Christ, though never in the ultimate sense reproducible in the believer's experience, because of Christ's unique Saviorhood, nevertheless provides the most powerful of all incentives for the practice of Christian ethics. In the words of Cecil Alexander, "Oh, dearly, dearly has He loved, and we must love Him too, and trust in His redeeming blood, and try His works to do."   FRANK E. GAEBELEIN

PATIENCE. See also *Longsuffering.* Patience is that virtue which enables a person to wait for something promised or hoped for and to bear with another who is at fault without anger or recrimination. In the LXX of Exod. 34:6 God announces himself as patient, where the meaning of the Hebrew is "slow to anger." This strain of thought appears again in Rom. 2:4-5, where the sinner is warned against presuming on the patience of God by failing to repent while judgment is deferred (cf. II Peter 3:7; Rom. 9:22-23). The implication of Jesus' parable of the unforgiving debtor (Matt. 18:23-35) is clearly this, that when God is patient to the point of exercising forgiveness, his people are to take the example to heart and deal similarly with one another.

Patience readily associates itself with kindred virtues such as goodness and kindness (Rom. 2:4). A connection with faith and hope is suggested by Heb. 6:11-12, and with love in I Cor. 13:4. The bearing of patience on the Christian's attitude toward the Lord's return is apparent. James provides a pertinent illustration by citing the attitude of the farmer who sows his crop and then must wait expectantly, without being disheartened, for the harvest (5:7-8).

Scripture does not point to patience as a native capacity which needs only to be cultivated to come to full flower. Rather, it is something which belongs to the Christian calling (Eph. 4:12 RSV) and is wrought in the believer by the Holy Spirit (Gal. 5:22 RSV).

The AV used "patience" at many points to render *hypomonē,* which is properly endurance or steadfastness under trial, whereas patience is accurately used to translate *makrothumia,* meaning long-suffering (literally, long spiritedness).

EVERETT F. HARRISON

PATRIOTISM. See also *Nationalism.* Is patriotism a Christian virtue or nationalistic vice? Samuel Johnson is quoted by Boswell as saying: "Patriotism is the last refuge of a scoundrel" (*Life,* April 7, 1775). True, the name patriot itself, assumed by disreputable people, fell into discredit in the eighteenth century. It was too often used to disguise hatred of other countries by love of one's own. However the *Oxford English Dictionary* defines patriotism as "love of, or zealous devotion to one's own country." Further definition includes the "dis-interested or self-sacrificing exertion to promote the well-being of one's country," or that which characterizes one who is concerned to "maintain and defend his country's freedom or rights."

The question partially resolves in to that of the attitude of the Christian to the State, and the tensions introduced by his simultaneous citizenship in the community of God's people. Jesus said, "My kingdom is not of this world" (John 18:36). When confronted by the question of the legality of Jews paying taxes to Rome, he also said, "Render therefore unto Caesar the things that are Caesar's, and unto God the things that are God's" (Matt. 22:21). The tale of the Christian life is thus the tale of two kingdoms, both having legitimate claims on the individual, each making demands of him as well as providing benefits in their particular spheres.

The Apostle Paul when persuaded he would be unfairly judged in Jerusalem, appealed to the highest court, Caesar himself (Acts 25:11). He thus expressed his confidence in the state as a neutral and just instrument. Furthermore, Paul required of the Christian that he be in subjection to the government, willingly pay taxes, respect the sword as an instrument of justice, give honor to whom it is due (Rom 13:1-7). He also exhorted believers to pray appreciatively for rulers, as for all men, so that Christian subjects might lead peaceful as well as godly lives—to the ultimate end that more men might be saved (I Tim. 2:1-7).

There is an additional consideration. The chief characteristics of the Christian are love (John 13:35) for God and fellow men, and devotion to justice and the means to accomplish it. If, in fact, government is that means, then it follows that the Christian should be supportive in every way possible. Love for fellow men thus manifests itself in a love for country, language, literature, culture—an intelligent and thankful appreciation of the blessings of God that come to him as a citizen of that nation. In so doing, the Christian is not chauvinist, but rather may be characterized by an enlightened internationalism which sees the hand of God in the affairs of all men. Simultaneously he must be alert to the likelihood of conflict between his dual nationalities. When such in fact arises, his primary patriotism is to a kingdom whose age is yet to come, but whose claims are immediate and unbending—such patriotism as ultimately led Jesus to his own death.

↪ Karl Barth, *Church and State*, 1939; H. F. R. Catherwood, *The Christian Citizen*, 1969; Oscar Cullmann, *The State in the New Testament*, 1957; P. T. Forsythe, *The Christian Ethic in War*, 1916.

PAUL E. LEONARD

PATRICIDE. Some Melanesian societies practiced patricide when the group's security and perpetuity were threatened by the aged chief losing his skill, wisdom, or agility. His eldest son was duty bound to the group to take over. He would not club or spear his father, as an enemy, but bury him alive with a public ceremony, saying respectfully, "Sir, your star has set." The father knew this was for the good of the group and considered it no injury, as he would be deified after death. Christianity places a high human value on the individual, but sometimes loses the group solidarity.

ALAN R. TIPPETT

PATRISTIC ETHICS. An ethical emphasis comprises a weighty part of the heritage from the Church Fathers, whose writings during the five centuries after the death of the apostles came to be considered orthodox.

The differences between the Fathers and the Apostle Paul are striking. They, unlike the apostles, were inclined, speaking broadly, to create the impression that a Christian became such not by the grace of God but by his own efforts by bringing his conduct into line with Christian standards. Such standards, while sought in the OT and NT, were strongly influenced by contemporary Greek and Jewish theory and practice. The Stoics saw natural law as the overriding principle. Human reason was to interpret it and declare how conduct should be brought into conformity to it. The Jews, both Pharisaic and Sectarian, had elaborated complex systems, based, in intention at least, upon the OT. Many Christian leaders paid more attention to these examples among their contemporaries or close predecessors than to the example of Jesus. The growth of gnostic systems increased the contemporary influence also.

Doctrine and life cannot be separated and the Fathers generally recognize this. In many instances it was the character of the lives of Christians which brought Christian teaching to the favorable attention of their neighbors and friends.

One of the earliest Christian post-canonical writings is the *Didache*. It is probably to be dated in the closing years of the first century despite the recent contention of Jean-Paul Audet that it should be placed in the period A.D. 50-70. It opens with the legalistic story of The Two Ways, which appears to have originally had an independent existence. Love to God and one's neighbor is explained as constituted of a long series of actions. The way of death likewise consists of actions, and these actions appear to determine our destiny. "A lifetime of faith will be of no advantage' unless you prove perfect at the last moment" (16.2).

This lack of comprehension of the grace of God is a marked characteristic of another first century document, the letter from the church at Rome to the church at Corinth, called, misleadingly, *I Clement*. There is much stress on repentance (e.g., chap 8) and good deeds (e.g., chaps. 33, 35) and little upon the work of Christ.

In the mid-second century Justin Martyr supports this trend in his *First Apology*. God "accepts those only who imitate the excellences which reside in him" (chap. 10). Another work, completed about that time, *The Shepherd,* moves toward the same objective. ". . . if they [your children] repent with all their heart, they will be written in the books of life with the saints" (Vis. I. iii. 2).

The major emphases in these works are concerned, first, with the superiority of temperance over luxury, of love over hate, of harmony over division and anger; second, with the importance of truth as against falsehood and pretence; third, with the maintenance of sexual temperance and the rejection of fornication, paederasty, and the exposure of infants.

One of Justin's pupils, Tatian, returned after Justin's death to east Syria, his home. His ascetic emphasis became stronger than that he had learned from Justin or from the Roman church. He discouraged marriage in principle.

In contrast to these basic demands, Clement of Alexandria offered a more superficial ethic. His *Paedagogos* is a manual of behavior. It contains directions for eating, drinking, sleeping, the wearing of clothing, the adornment of the person and sexual relationships. Removal of the facial beard is rejected as disrespectful of God's creation.

Alexandria became, with Clement, the capital of Christian asceticism. Origen reflected those tendencies in his early castration. The material, sensible world he placed on a lower plane than the spiritual realm and consequently favored ascetic practices. This emphasis on the essentially evil character of the material world contributed to the rise of monastic asceticism in the Egyptian deserts. Men escaped from the temptations of the world by dedicating themselves to solitary meditation. Athanasius encouraged such monastic practices by his idealized biography of the pioneer Christian ascetic, Antony.

In the Latin world ethical principles were prominent in the pioneer Latin theologian, the north African, Tertullian. Ascetic and benevolent practices supplemented the work of Christ in making satisfaction for our sins. The possibility of repentance and satisfaction for post-baptismal sins is limited. Many occupations, such as shopkeeping, or teaching in a pagan school, were incompatible with Christian ethical behavior. A Christian might, and usually should, refuse military service. If God wanted women to wear colored dresses he would have made sheep with purple and scarlet fleeces. Marriage was depreciated. In his mature years Tertullian found himself more in accord with the ascetic emphases of the Montanists than with the ethics of the regular catholic church.

Probably the most noisy ethicist among the fathers was Jerome. Jerome was convinced that sexual relationships were on a definitely lower level than virginity. He defended this proposition at great length and with amazing vivacity. He taught it to his pupils in Bible study classes in Rome. After his removal to Bethlehem he kept up a vigorous correspondence with various people in the West, dinning sexual asceticism into their ears for many years. It was his opinion that a cleric named Vigilantius, who thought some monastic practices immoral and against the best interests of the church, was misnamed. He should have been called Dormitantius! Jerome's views were more and more widely accepted.

As in many other areas Augustine of Hippo proved over the years to be an important influence in the field of ethical theory and practice. He argued for the Biblical principle that unregenerate man is incapable of doing good. All man's acts are tainted by the two chief ethical faults, pride and desire. Even apparently good works are tinged by them. Man's original nature has been vitiated. All sexual relationship in this dispensation is accompanied by desire, and desire is evil. But ascetic principles are only means to an end. They do not become good because they are unpleasant or because they "crucify the flesh." They are ways by which the more perfectly to serve God. Their value derives from this fact. Judgments as to the value of actions should be founded upon this test. Moderation is often better than abstinence in regard to a course of conduct. The eating of a particular food could be an example of this.

Both Jerome and Augustine were objects of the hostility of Pelagius, an exponent of Stoic morality in a pseudo-Christian guise. Man's nature is as free as was Adam's at his creation. The grace of God is seen in a free conscience, in the teaching and example of Christ. God made us human but we make ourselves righteous, said Pelagius. He found considerable sympathy in the eastern section of the church, but his western supporters were removed from their offices.

The first five centuries after the apostles are often a subjective disappointment to the modern evangelical Christian ethicist. The teaching of the Lord is misunderstood. Personal salvation appears to be suspended upon Christian conduct. The influence of judaistic work-righteousness remains strong. So does the impact of Greek and Latin stoicism. However, the influence of the Gospel accounts of Christ's acts and teachings get through to the members of the Christian congregations. They show life-patterns that are less selfish than those of their neighbors. Their concern for the welfare of that neighbor becomes apparent. Their worship is monotheistic and free from the influence of the licentious life-patterns of pagan deities. In particular, the attitude of reverence for human life apparent in abstinence from the exposure of infants and

in the respect shown to the physically weak and handicapped is impressive. Slaves are received as equals. The position of women is higher than in surrounding pagan society. The cruelty of the games is rejected.

The development of distinctive Christian ethical principles is slow, but the application of the teaching of Christ is influential ethically and, in consequence, evangelistically.   PAUL WOOLLEY

PAULINE ETHICS. See also *New Testament Ethics.* Paul, as a Pharisee, was intensely concerned with ethics. Judaism has always viewed right conduct as of supreme importance for the truly religious man, and this was no less true in Paul's day. When he became a Christian, he did not lose this interest in practical religion. On the contrary, his letters indicate that his moral sensitivity and understanding were heightened and brought into sharper focus by his conversion to Christ.

Basic Presuppositions. As a "Hebrew born of Hebrew parents" (Phil. 3:5; II Cor. 11:22), Paul shared many of the basic presuppositions of his Jewish contemporaries. He thought more theologically than philosophically, and he worked from the events of redemptive history and the deposit of revelation in the Scriptures rather than from the categories of human wisdom or the distillation of human experience. Right and wrong for the Jew, as G. F. Moore pointed out, were "not defined by the reason and conscience of men, naive or reflective, nor by national custom or the *consensus gentium,* but by the revealed will of God" (*Judaism,* Cambridge, Harvard University, 1927, II, p. 79), and with this Paul was in thorough agreement. Likewise, Paul thought of the ethical life primarily in terms of righteousness and its expression, not just in terms of civic rightness or social propriety. Ancient codes of jurisprudence, while represented as having been given by a god or gods, stressed almost exclusively the ideal of civic and social rightness; and modern man usually thinks along the lines of what is proper on the horizontal plane alone. But Paul, in accord with the Hebraic tradition upon which he built, thought first of righteousness and then of rightness, believing that only in the first is there an adequate basis for the second.

His Hebraic heritage also instilled within him a strong conviction regarding the interrelatedness and underlying unity of life: of thought and conduct, of the sacred and the secular, of the material and the immaterial, and of the visible and the invisible. In contradistinction to the Greek ideal of study and knowledge for their own sakes, Paul viewed the enlightenment of the mind as basically character education. Likewise, he was unable to isolate religion from the mundane affairs of men, but viewed the revelation of God as legitimately permeating and informing all of life. The apostle's thought was also "wholistic" in regard to the relations between the material or visible and the immaterial or invisible. Contrary to hellenistic religious speculation generally, he did not set the material *per se* against the immaterial or disparage the visible as a defiled reflection of the invisible. He recognized distinctions between the two (one cannot speak of a "unity" without noting varying elements comprising that unity), and he acknowledged that sin has invaded the material and visible realm. But he rested too heavily upon the OT to postulate that the world of matter and sense perception stands intrinsically opposed to all that is immaterial, invisible, and/or supernatural. God is the Creator of all that is, which means that nothing exists apart from him essentially or was created in opposition to him. The visible and material world, to be sure, has been taken captive by sin, but it is not the culprit itself; matter is indeed employed as the vehicle for sin, but it is not the source of evil. God's redemption is for the whole of created life, both the immaterial and the material (Rom. 8:19-24). And while Paul began his teaching on divine redemption by stressing God's provision for the "inner man" (spiritual life for spiritual death), he went on to speak of the expression of this spiritual life in the mundane world of men and things (e.g., Col. 3:18–4:6; Philem. 1-25; Eph. 5:22–6:9).

More particularly, however, the ethical teaching of Paul presupposes a regeneration and transformation of life effected by Christ through his Spirit. As the apostle never proclaimed salvation simply by a renewal of character, so he never taught the possibility of living the Christian ethic apart from being "in Christ." It is because the believer is "in Christ," and therefore a "new creation," that life has become transformed (II Cor. 5:17); and it is because Christ is in the believer through the Spirit that Christians can be exhorted to live in obedience to the Spirit (Rom. 8:10-14). Apart from this foundation, the superstructure of the Pauline ethic has no rationale or support.

The Determination of a Christian Ethic. Building upon being "in Christ" as the only basis for an authentic Christian ethic, Paul goes on to speak of the guidance of the Christian as a matter involving both the "law of Christ" (I Cor. 9:21; Gal. 6:2) and the "mind of Christ" (I Cor. 2:16). By the "law of Christ" he seems to mean not only the teaching of Jesus as the embodiment and true interpretation of the will of God (Rom. 12–14; I Cor. 7:10-11; cf. Acts 21:35; I Tim. 5:18), but also the person of the historical Jesus as the tangible portrayal and paradigm of the divine standard, as is suggested by his expression "according to Christ" (Rom. 15:5; Col. 2:8) and his frequent appeals to the character of Jesus (Rom. 15:3, 7-8; I Cor. 11:1; Eph. 5:2, 25ff.; Phil. 2:5-11; I Thess. 1:6). This new law of the Messiah abrogates the supervisory prescriptions of the Mosaic covenant for the believer in Christ (Rom. 7:1-6; Gal 3:23-26; Eph. 2:15). Yet, at the same time, it explicates more fully the divine standard in continuity with that code; and so it is for Paul the external expression of God's eternal principles, setting the bounds for the believer's life and indicating the quality and direction which his action should take within those bounds. By the "mind of Christ," Paul seems to have reference to the activity of the Spirit enabling the believer to discern the divine will and to form a proper ethical judgment at each given moment (Rom. 12:2; Phil. 1:10; I Thess. 5:19-22). Without the "mind of Christ," the "law of Christ" remains remote and unattainable. Where the two are in harmony, however, direction is supplied for Christian living.

The "love of Christ" and the "law of Christ" are not so much equated by Paul (as commonly supposed, based on an interpretation of Rom. 13:10 and James 2:8) as they are balanced, the latter being one aspect in the directing of a Christian ethic and the former a motivating and conditioning factor in a life so guided by Christ. That love which motivated and conditioned God's action on behalf of men "has been poured into our hearts through the Holy Spirit" (Rom. 5:5), with the result that now love has come to characterize the believer's ethic in the same manner. And as love provides the matrix and context for the Christian life, so the Spirit provides the dynamic and strength; for the same God who raised Christ Jesus from the dead also gives life to our "mortal bodies through his Spirit" (Rom. 8:11).

Of importance as well in Paul's teaching on determining God's will are issues having to do with the "Gospel of Christ," the "Body of Christ," and the "coming of Christ." In his more intimate pastoral letters, the apostle reveals that his own ethical decisions and personal life-style were influenced by his desire to advance the gospel and bring men to Christ. In writing to the Corinthians, for example, he speaks of being "all things to all men" that "by every means

I might save some" (I Cor. 9:22), "for the sake of the gospel" (I Cor. 9:23), and "that they might be saved" (I Cor. 10:33). And he urged his converts in this regard to "be followers of me, even as I am also of Christ" (I Cor. 11:1). All that he taught, wrote, or did was conditioned as well by his desire for the welfare of the church, the Body of Christ. There is in the Pauline writings and actions a delicate blending of the dual Christian doctrines of personal freedom and corporate responsibility. He expected his converts to emulate him in this, and his teaching and example in bringing together both truths serve as a paradigm for our lives and ministries today. Likewise, Paul taught that the coming of Christ has a direct bearing on the conduct of the Christian life. Such an expectation, he believed, comforted, encouraged, motivated, and gave direction in particular instances (I Thess. 4:13ff.; II Thess. 2:1ff.; I Cor. 7:29ff.; 15:51ff.; Phil. 4:5), and he urged believers to live with the consciousness that "the Lord is near" (I Cor. 15:58; Phil. 4:5).

The Expression of the Christian Ethic. The Christian, in Pauline teaching, lives his life between the polarities of what has been accomplished historically by Jesus Christ and what has yet to be fully realized in the future through God's consummation of the redemptive program. There exists, therefore, a temporal tension in the ethical experience of the believer. On the personal level, he is conscious (a) of what he is "in Adam" and "of himself," sobering him to the potentialities of his depraved nature, and (b) of what he is "in Christ," awakening him to the prospects of present victory and ultimate conquest. On the social and civic level, he is aware (a) of being a citizen of "the Age to Come," providing him a foretaste of heavenly perfection and heightening his conception of the ideal, but also (b) of being still inherently involved in "this Age" and its non-Christian orientation, challenging him to be a witness for God and to the ethical ideal, yet forcing upon him some type of accommodation without comprising this ideal or denying his Lord. It is this temporal tension in redemptive history which makes the expression of the Christian ethic so difficult, and which Martin Luther has rightly pointed out "no sophists will admit, for they know not the true manner of justification" (*Commentary on Galatians,* on Gal. 3:6). But it is the recognition of this temporal tension which, as O. Cullmann argues, "contains the key to the understanding of the entire New Testament" (*Christ and Time,* trans. F. V. Filson, Philadelphia, Westminster, 1949, p. 199).

Paul's primary emphasis in the expression of the Christian life was not upon adding virtue to virtue in the formation of a character, nor upon a compilation of certain "cardinal virtues," as was the endeavor of most ancient moralists. Rather, he laid stress upon the Spirit's permeation of the believer's personality and upon the "fruit of the Spirit" being produced in the life by the Spirit, with the result that the Christian's life will then manifest such qualities as "love, joy, peace, patience, kindness, goodness, faithfulness, gentleness, and self-control" (Gal. 5:22-23; cf. Eph. 5:9). One of Paul's constant designations for the ethical ideal is the expression *to kalon* (Rom. 7:18, 21; II Cor. 13:7; Gal 6:9; I Thess. 5:21), which is usually translated as "the beautiful, good, fine, or honorable." The concept incorporates nuances that are religious, rational, moral, and aesthetic, and signifies activity that is pleasing to God, thoughtfully enacted, morally honorable, and handsomely done. It is this type of ethic that the man "in Christ" is to express, with a "magnaminity of spirit" *(to epieikes),* to all men (Gal. 6:9-10; Phil. 4:5), "especially to those who are of the household of faith" (Gal. 6:10).

📖 C. H. Dodd, "The Ethics of the Pauline Epistles," *The Evolution of Ethics as Revealed in the Great Religions,* New Haven, Yale University, 1927, pp. 295-326; _____, *Gospel and Law,*

New York, Cambridge University, 1951; M. S. Enslin, *The Ethics of Paul,* New York, Harper, 1930; V. P. Furnish, *Theology and Ethics in Paul,* Nashville, Abingdon, 1968; R. N. Longenecker, *Paul, Apostle of Liberty,* New York, Harper & Row, 1964; M. Luther, "On the Freedom of the Christian," *Works of Martin Luther,* vol. II, W. A. Lambert, tr., Philadelphia, Holman, 1916; C. F. D. Moule, "Obligation in the Ethic of Paul," *Christian History and Interpretation,* W. R. Farmer, C. F. D. Moule and R. R. Niebuhr, eds., New York, Cambridge University, 1967, pp. 389-406; J. Weiss, *Die christliche Freiheit nach der Verkündigung des Apostels Paulus,* Göttingen, Vandenhoeck & Ruprecht, 1902.

RICHARD N. LONGENECKER

PEACE. See also *Virtues.* In common speech the word "peace" frequently has a negative connotation, particularly when the quality of personal relationships or the state of the individual are in view. In such contexts, the term chiefly refers to the absence or cessation of inter-personal conflict and mental tension.

However the Biblical conception has a consistently positive thrust. The OT term *shalom* does occasionally refer to the absence of strife (I Chron. 22:9; Prov. 17:1) but generally with wider associations. This is more emphatic in passages which designate the positive "well-being" of the individual (e.g., Ps. 4:8; Lam. 3:17), social and religious groups (I. Sam. 20:42; Mal. 2:5) or the nation (Exod. 18:23 et al). This involves physical (Gen. 15:15; Ps. 4:8; 38:3 ERV mg.) and material (Lev. 26:6ff.; Zech. 8:12) prosperity. In the prophetic writings the term possesses a more discernibly ethical (Isa. 26:3; Zech. 8:19; Mal. 2:6) and more profoundly salvific (Isa. 45:7; Jer. 33:9; cf. Ps. 119-165) significance, as well as an eschatological dimension (cf. Isa. 11:1ff.; Ezek. 34:25).

The coming of Jesus begins the establishment of this "peace" (Luke 2:14, 29; 19:42). He teaches its necessity (Matt. 5:9; John 14:27), demonstrates its presence through his miracles (Mark 5:34; Luke 7:50), and through his death (Rom. 5:1;

Col.1:20) and resurrection (John 20:19ff.) makes it available to men. Its ultimate author is God (Rom. 15:33 et al), it is potentially universal and cosmic in scope (Eph. 2:14-17; Col. 1:19-22), and its full realization will take place at the Last Day (I Thess. 5:23). In these passages peace is virtually equivalent with salvation and denotes the relationship in which the believer, church, and world is placed by God through Christ (Rom. 5:1; Eph. 2:14ff.).

However, the term also has implications for practical Christian living. It results in inward peace (Rom. 15:13; Gal. 5:22; II Tim. 2:22) though this does not necessarily involve the absence of stress or adversity (John 16:33; Heb. 12:11; cf. II Cor. 4:7ff.). It characterizes the relationship that should exist between members of the church (II Cor. 13:11; Eph. 4:3; Col. 3:15) though not at the expense of tolerating things which would seriously harm the community (see I Cor. 11:18ff.). Indeed it is to be the criterion for deciding disputes concerning such things as the inviolability of the bond between believer and unbeliever in marriage (I Cor. 7:15), differences on some ethical questions (Rom. 14:17), the conduct of gatherings for worship (I Cor. 14:33). In some situations it has material implications as well (James 2:16). It should also mark the attitude of Christians to outsiders (Rom. 12:18; I Peter 3:11) but this involves bringing salvation to them (Heb. 12:14; cf. W. W. Förster, *TDNT*, 11, 413-414) and may result in causing division among them (Matt. 10:34; Luke 12:51). It is only through spiritual discernment that one sees how peace is to be sought in these various circumstances (James 3:17-18).

                                                                    ROBERT BANKS

PEACE AND WAR. See also *International Order; Just War Criteria; Militarism; Pacifism.* One can correctly understand the Biblical perspective on peace and war only in view of the nature of Biblical theology and revelation. God has revealed himself through a series of historical events, as recorded in Scripture. God reveals more and more of his truth, and man's knowledge and responsibility increase as this salvation history proceeds to its final goal. The OT and the NT are not parallel presentations of the same truths, but the OT prepares for the NT and is necessary for its understanding. Thus in the Bible the chronological unfolding of God's will concerning peace and war is not fully developed until the NT revelation is completed. This does not mean that what the OT says about war is an inferior order of divine revelation. What is said about war in the OT revelation is incomplete, although it teaches much regarding God's holiness and his attitude towards man's sin and judgment.

Old Testament View. In the ancient world-view, war, not peace, seems to have been the normal relation between peoples, although peace was certainly desired. In the OT world each nation had its god or gods who fought with and for them, and this idea of "holy war" is also found in the OT where God calls his people to war and often fights for them himself (Exod. 14:14; Josh. 10;14, 42; 23:10). His role as a "man of war" served to impress upon Israel God's sovereign activity as the deliverer and preserver of his people (I Sam. 17:47). After the establishment of the kingdom the ideal of the holy war continued, although then it became primarily a function of the king and state.

A crucial point in the OT is the role which human sin and transgression play as the determining provocation for wars. It is because of the idolatry of the Canaanites, with its accompanying abominable practices, that they must be destroyed (Deut. 7:4, 16, 25, 26; 20:18). The holy war is always a response to the threat of war by Israel's foes, the Book of Judges being a prime example. All war is viewed as an evil brought on by human sin which is then incorporated into the plan of God and used as a weapon in his hand, serving to bring his people into a state of rest with the accompanying well-being and prosperity which go with peace.

While one finds in the OT an attitude of national exclusiveness and brutality, there is also a developing ethic regarding war and bloodshed. David was forbidden by God to build the Temple because he had "shed blood abundantly and made great wars" (I Chron. 22:8; 28:3). God is revealed as a redemptive God who is the God of the whole earth and peace is his ideal (Isa. 19:18-25; Jer. 16:19-21). He will redeem his people and all nations will share in this redemption (Isa. 42:6, 7; Jonah). It is God, not man, who will usher in a state of universal peace (Isa. 2:2-4; 11:1-9; Hos. 2:18; Zech. 9:9, 10). Sometimes the prophets were advocates of war, but more often they opposed it because the trust of the nation was not in God and therefore a war with his blessing was inconceivable (Isa. 37:5).

New Testament View. In the NT there is no notion of a holy war in behalf of the Messianic King. In fact, Jesus disassociated himself completely from the zealotic activity of his time. The only true pictures of war in the NT are the apocalyptic texts (Mark 13; Matt. 24; Luke 21; Rev. 6:4; 13:7; 16:14; 17:14; 20:7-9) and these do not teach that Christians are to take an active part in these wars. When Satan comes forth to deceive the nations (Rev. 20:8) he is unable to execute his plans and both he and war generally are struck down for good from above. The only reference in the NT to the God-ordained wars of the OT is an incidental statement in Heb. 11:34 which in no way gives justification for the waging of war in the name of God.

The existence of war is taken for granted by the NT and nowhere is it suggested that a soldier should seek to leave the service upon becoming a Christian. Military terms and analogies are frequently used to illustrate spiritual truths, but this does not mean that the institution of war as such was being legitimatized or glorified. James (4:2) indicates that war is the result of human passion and not compatible with the Christian life.

Basically *eirēnē* in the NT has the same meaning as *shalōm* in the OT: health, well-being, peace, salvation. Thus it is used in greetings (Mark 5:34; Luke 7:50; etc.), as a description of man's eschatological salvation (Luke 1:79; 2:14; 19:42), in terms of peace with God (Eph. 2:14-17), and of men with one another (Rom. 14:17; James 3:18). In the Kingdom of God there will be no discord. On one occasion the noun *eirenopoios* ("He who makes peace" in the sense of the opposite of war) is used and a blessing pronounced upon those who work for the establishment of peace among men (Matt. 5:9). Enemies are to be treated according to the law of love rather than with hate and retaliation (Matt. 5:43-44).

The rejection of military service on the part of the early church and subsequent Christian pacifism do not rest upon explicit NT teaching but upon an effort to apply the attitudes of Jesus to the problem of war. Throughout his ministry he sought to avoid association with the contemporary revolutionary movement of the Zealots and condemned as "men of violence" those who sought to bring in the Kingdom by force (Matt. 11:12). He clearly understood his ministry in terms of Isaiah's Suffering Servant. His final entry into Jerusalem on a donkey in fulfillment of Zech. 9:9 was a last attempt to show the people that the Messiah was not to be a mighty general upon a horse leading an army, but a humble man of peace intent upon establishing a spiritual kingdom.

Jesus and the early Christians had no voice in Roman policy and thus it is not surprising that the NT is silent concerning specific political problems relating to peace and war. Some principles are given, but it is often difficult to determine what belongs to Caesar and what belongs to God. The question concerning the obligation, if any, to protect others is never raised explicitly in Scripture. What should the Good Samaritan have done if he had arrived while the robbers were engaged in the act? Peter's use of the sword in Jesus' defense drew a rebuke from our Lord (Matt. 26:51-54). There are no specific precepts which clearly tell the Christian how to relate to the ambiguities of a world of sin where believer opposes unbeliever. Courses of action can only be extrapolated from NT principles.

📖 G. von Rad, *Der Heilige Krieg*, 1951; G. H. C. Macgregor, *The New Testament Basis of Pacifism*, 1953.   WILLIAM W. BUEHLER

PELAGIAN ETHICS. The adjective "Pelagian" is derived from the name of the British monk Pelaguis, whose precise views, like those of other men condemned for heresy in the ancient church, are quite difficult to ascertain. "Pelagianism," on the other hand, as developed by Pelagius' disciples Celestius and Julian of Eclanum, is comparatively well-known.

In the realm of ethics the hallmark of Pelagianism is the principle that ability is the measure of responsibility, and the view that man, even after Adam's fall, has an unimpaired ability to perform whatever God requires. In this scheme the freedom of the will to choose good or evil at any moment is deemed so essential that nothing can be allowed to infringe on it. Notably the new-born child must be in the same condition of integrity as Adam. Even our own actions cannot produce a settled disposition in us, and the significance of habit and character is denied in order to safeguard the freedom of each individual decision. The only way in which moral influence can be exerted on a free agent is by example and precept, and this is the most significant

aspect of the work of Jesus Christ. Pelagianism says man can in the exercise of his will attain unto perfection, and that men both in Scripture and outside the scope of Christianity have actually been perfect.

Pelagius' stand was meant to discourage defeatism and to commend ethics among Christians. Its real effects are to lure man into a tragic complacency and to prevent him from coming to grips with his own plight and from seeking refuge in the grace of God as the one way of escape from judgment and ruin. In severing the tie between Adam and his descendants, Pelagianism reduces the race to "a heap of unconnected units" (Warfield). In canceling the force of habit and character, it reduces human life to a succession of unrelated acts of volition without meaning or direction. In lowering the level of God's demands to what man can perform, it reduces the lofty Christian standards to the uninspiring level of naturalistic, heathen ethics.

Unfortunately the principles developed with almost ruthless consistency in the Pelagian controversies (411-429) and condemned at the council of Ephesus (431) did not disappear on account of this setback. They seem to surface again and to influence theology and ethics whenever men lose sight of the catastrophic nature of sin and of their tragic enslavement to it.

📖 Robert F. Evans, *Pelagius, Inquiries and Reappraisals*, New York, Seabury, 1968; R. Hedde and E. Amann, "Pélagianisme, "*Dictionnaire de Théologie Catholique*, XII, 675-715; G. Plitt, in *The New Shaff-Herzog Encyclopedia of Religious Knowledge*, Grand Rapids, Baker, VIII, 438-444; R. G. Parsons, in *Encyclopedia of Religion and Ethics*, IX, 703-711; B. B. Warfield, "Augustine and the Pelagian Controversy," *Studies in Tertullian and Augustine*, New York, Oxford University, 1930, pp. 289-412.   ROGER R. NICOLE

PENANCE. See also *Absolution; Confession; Restitution.* From the Latin *poena* (satisfaction, punishment, penalty), "penance" signifies (1) the sacrament of the Roman Catholic Church in which it is claimed that sins committed after baptism are forgiven through the absolution of the priest acting in Christ's name on condition of contrition, confession, and satisfaction; and (2) punishment imposed by the church for the infraction of divine law. In the latter sense public, then private, penances were observed on the ground that atonement for sin must be acquired in part through the work of the offender. This "satisfaction" usually took the form of fasting, prayer, or almsgiving, sometimes of pilgrimages, continence, flaggelations, or other penalties. It came to be called "heavenly medicine" to heal the wounds caused by sin. By the thirteenth century penance had become a part of the "sacramental system" and three centuries later the Council of Trent defined it as a sacrament. M. EUGENE OSTERHAVEN

PENITENCE. See *Repentance*.

PENOLOGY. See *Capital Punishment; Corporal Punishment; Prison Reform; Punishment; Retribution.*

PERFECTIONISM. See also *Holiness*. Perfectionism, as generally defined, is the doctrine that the Christian man, in this life, may be free from "defects" as well as filled with all positive "virtues." The nature of these "defects" and "virtues" is the subject of much disagreement.

The idea has its roots in the Scriptural terms *tamin* (Heb.) and *teleios* (Gk.). The Old Testament describes Noah (Gen. 6:9), Abraham (Gen. 17:1), Job (Job 1:1), and David (Ps. 18:32) as "perfect" men. In the Sermon on the Mount (q.v.), Jesus exhorts his disciples, "Be ye therefore perfect even as your heavenly Father is perfect" (Matt. 5:48). Paul exhorts, "let us therefore, as many as be perfect, be thus minded" (Phil. 3:15), and the author of Hebrews urges his readers, "Let us go on to perfection. . ." (6:1). James speaks of the one who controls his tongue as a perfect man (3:2), and John

writes of a "perfect love which casts out fear" (I John 4:18).

Building upon these Biblical concepts some early Christians developed perfectionism along two lines: (1) Christians are able to be kept from sin's dominion by God's grace; and (2) Christians who receive the Holy Spirit are made perfect in love. Justin Martyr stated that after Christians have received forgiveness, they must live sinless lives. Irenaeus termed Christians *pneumatici,* because they have put aside the lusts of the flesh and received the Holy Spirit.

Origen, the percursor of Monasticism (q.v.), distinguished two kinds of perfection—the final perfection of all Christian virtues which is not attained in this life, and the relative perfection of those who forget the past and mystically attain the knowledge of God's person. The monastics took seriously Jesus' words to the rich young ruler, "If thou wouldst be perfect. . ." and sought to attain perfection of virtues, of communion with God, and of personal discipline.

Medieval theologians like Augustine (q.v.) and Aquinas (q.v.) identified perfection with the beatific vision of God, but this was not normal Christian experience but was reserved for the few. However, in the *Summa Theologica,* after defining the absolute perfection of God and the perfection of the possibilities of the Christian soul in heaven, Aquinas spoke of Christian perfection in this life as being the "removal from man's affections of all that is contrary to love . . . and also whatever hinders the mind's affection from tending wholly to God."

After the Reformation (q.v.) the movements of Quietism (q.v.) and Pietism (q.v.) brought the idea of perfection to the ordinary Christian. Fenelon stated, "The very perfection of Christianity is Pure Love." Franke's essay on *The Perfection of a Christian* taught three stages of Christian progress necessary to reach the goal. Count

Zinzendorf taught a doctrine of sanctification which equated perfection with fulness of faith.

It was John Wesley who identified perfection with entire sanctification as a normal experience for every Christian subsequent to his initial Christian conversion. His *A Plain Account of Christian Perfection* attempted to define the doctrine by distinguishing it from Adamic perfection, angelic perfection, and sinless perfection. It does not imply freedom from ignorance, mistakes, infirmities, or temptation. Neither does entire sanctification free one from dependence on the constant mediatorial work of Christ, for "the best of men need Christ as their Priest, their atonement, their advocate with the Father." Wesley defined Christian perfection as "the loving God with all your heart, mind, soul and strength. This implies that no wrong temper, none contrary to love, remains in the soul; and that all the thoughts, words and actions are governed by pure love." Many of Charles Wesley's hymns express the theology and experience of perfect love, e.g., "Love Divine, All Loves Excelling," "O For a Heart to Praise My God," "O Glorious Hope of Perfect Love."

After Wesley, Methodism and its various branches continued to emphasize the experience of entire sanctification and the necessity of a holy life. In America Charles G. Finney espoused "an instantaneous change from entire sinfulness to entire holiness." Since 1867, the National Holiness Association has actively promoted the Wesleyan-Arminian heritage and the doctrine of perfect love.

The term is now avoided even by groups devoted to Christian perfection because of ready misunderstanding. A. H. Strong and B. B. Warfield expound the term as "sinless perfection," but no modern movement adheres to this.

📖 J. Wesley, *A Plain Account of Christian Perfec-*tion, New York, Jennings and Graham, n.d.; B. B. Warfield, *Perfectionism*, New York, Oxford University, 1931; R. N. Flew, *The Idea of Perfection in Christian Theology*, London, Oxford University, 1934.   BERT H. HALL

PERJURY. See *Lying.*

PERSECUTION. See also *Persecution; Religious Freedom.* Persecution is deliberate, persistent attack or harassment ostensibly because of the victim's religious identification or beliefs, ideological commitments or group membership. The psychological background of persecution may lie in conscious or unconscious motives or the sense of persecution may rest upon delusions.

Among the several conscious motives for persecution, the most obvious is strong personal dislike for another individual. The potential persecutor may have been predisposed to animosity by some previous encounter resulting in belief that his victim has given him cause to seek redress. Persecutory behavior is subsequently precipitated when the persecutor finds himself in a superior position from which he can take revenge with relative impunity. Thus, Absalom's resentment toward David (arising from the young prince's censure and exile by his father) finally erupted into a vengeful persecution of the king once he had usurped the throne (II Sam. 17).

Personal animosity may generalize to include all those identified with the one hated so that an entire group become victims of persecution. Scripture records that Simeon and Levi were so incensed over Shechem's rape of their sister Dinah that they put the whole clan to the sword in revenge (Gen. 34). Jacob recognized the danger that this aggravated violence could touch off a blood feud. The typical pattern of the blood feud is its generalization from vengeance toward one individual to persecution of an entire family, community or race. What is so alarming about generalized persecution is that the persecutor imagines himself justified in harming even those who have never hurt him personally, simply because the victims are somehow identified with a person against whom the persecutor holds a grudge. Generalized persecution, thus, exhibits a tendency to expand in ever-widening circles involving more and more innocent victims and constantly generates new personal and potentially generalizable grudges.

Persecutory animosity may also arise against individuals or groups strictly from miming the behavior of others. In this way, children imitate their elders' and idols' attitudes and behavior toward people with different skin color, or long hair or physical defects. Here we have an example of attitudes directed toward all members of a group no member of which has ever previously injured the persecutor. Again, the potential of this process for generating and amplifying persecutory behavior is appalling.

Finally, resentment against a particular individual may arise simply because he is a member of or associated with a hated target group. No knowledge of the individual's actual characteristics of behavior beyond his membership in the group is present to support this persecutory animosity. It is assumed that the victim shares the resented qualities presumed or known to exist in the group of which he is a member. As is generally characteristic of prejudice and persecutory attitudes, no individual experiential verification of such qualities is believed necessary. Furthermore, the fact that hostility by the individual may have been exhibited in response to hostility by the persecutor is overlooked.

Acting out of an overt persecution may stem not only from the persecutor's antipathy, resentment and/or thirst for revenge, but also from his enjoyment of a superior vantage point from which to attack. The element of "pursuit" and harassment typically found in persecutory behavior implies that it is the persecutor who is, at least for the time, in a position to chase, hound and badger the victim. That the element of superior power is essential to the exhibition of persecutory behavior is evident from the "conciliatory attitude" of many Nazi death-camp guards after the liberation of their prisoners (Victor Frankl, *Man's Search for Meaning*, New York, Simon and Schuster, 1962), and of Agag the Amelekite king after his capture (I Sam. 15:32). It follows that removal of the *power* to persecute by no means simultaneously eliminates an underlying causal resentment. Such hostility may continue to smolder unnoticed for years until it finds opportunity to break forth again. That is why demonstrations by an oppressed minority and civil rights legislation alone cannot assure attitudinal changes which will permanenlty dam up the wellsprings of persecution. Unless the unconscious motives feeding this animosity are eliminated, external pressure may only force displacement of persecutory behavior to a new set of victims or, at best, suppress its overt expression until a more opportune moment.

What are some of these "unconscious" motives? The chief one is fear—the feeling that one must fight to stay on top or be ground under, the instinctual defensive urge to "do others before they do you." Thus, persecution often arises from among those who are basically insecure, and who fear losing privileges they presently possess to a more vigorous, more competent, or more righteous person or group. When Jewish religious leaders could not resist the wisdom and power with which Stephen spoke, these staid defenders of the law stopped up their ears and took the law into their own hands (Acts 6:10; 7:51-58). In nearly every city, persecution arose against Paul primarily for this reason (Acts 13:45). Years before, the same basic motive had been paramount in the religious leaders' persecution of Jesus. Pilate himself recognized that it was jealousy, i.e., fear of losing the power and status, that had impelled the Sanhedrin to condemn Jesus (Matt. 27:18).

Closely related to fear of loss is the motive of resentment toward a source of frustration. Thus, Haman in his elevated rank could not completely enjoy the adulation accorded him because one lone Jew, Mordecai, would not bow to him. This frustration engendered in Haman a bitter persecutory animosity which generalized into a plot for genocide (Esth. 3:1-6).

Neither fear nor resentment, however, will necessarily cause one person overtly to persecute another. It may sometimes do the opposite, i.e., lead one to project his own persecutory animosity upon another so that he harbors the delusion that he himself has been singled out for persecution by some individual or group or nameless "them" (Anna Freud, *The Ego and the Mechanisms of Defense,* New York, International Universities, 1946). Such "delusions of persecution" provide an outlet for the animosity of those who would like to persecute if they dared but lack the boldness or the power to do so. The "delusions of grandeur" aid in compensating for the individual's felt weakness and incapacity to compete. Furthermore, for one whose conscience would condemn him for unjustified resentment against another, perceiving himself as a "victim" provides a pseudo-justification for any "defensive" or offensive measures he may wish to take against the alleged "persecutor." This sort of thinking turns attack into "self-defense" and, on a national scale, aggression into "liberation." Whether it be in the psychotic plotting of the paranoid or in the political purges and other machinations of the totalitarian state, the mechanism of pseudo-justified counter-persecution may be found at work.   JOHN K. TUEL

PERSON AND PERSONALITY. See also *Character; Mental Health; Psychology.* The nature of human personality is directly and intimately related to the consideration of ethics. Our understanding of man, his capacities and limitations, undergirds efforts to define appropriate ethical behavior.

Personality theory is but one segment of the more general discipline of psychology. Personality theory is characterized by its attempt to integrate and synthesize the disparate experimentally based psychological data on man into a coherent holistic view of human nature.

Psychology grew out of philosophy. Psychology is a word composed of Greek elements, yet the concept in its present form was not present in Greek thought. The word psychology is a neologism related to the human soul, that first was built up in the sixteenth century. Pneumatology and psychosophy were synonyms. Psychology and philosophy were indistinguishable for they addressed two major questions: (1) What is the nature of man? (2) What is good, healthy, moral behavior?

The demise of traditional philosophy in the nineteenth century followed upon the conclusion that on such questions philosophy could only speculate. Following the lead of Wittgenstein, philosophy became the scientific study of logic and syntax of language, ruling itself out of the discussion of man and his ethical behavior.

The philosophical mantle fell upon psychology. It dealt with these basic questions via the experimental method, typically without regard to philosophy. Recent trends in psychology have clearly been away from formal theory, toward a non-theoretical, or even anti-theoretical orientation.

Can the nature of man be encompassed by a rigorous experimentalism? The experimentalist would answer that he cannot deal with the totality of man and that he will be content to study man only insofar as it is experimentally feasible. The quest for what constitutes man as man is largely ignored. The concepts of reality, causality, mind, consciousness, and soul are rejected as experimental topics.

Personality theory represents a minor dissident voice in psychology. It is more closely linked to the medical tradition of psychiatry (q.v.) with its emphasis on human evaluation and methods for changing human behavior. The first half of the twentieth century was the age of the great personality theorists—grand global concepts of man. This style is now passe, because it was too global, too reductionistic, too far removed from experimental data and hypothesis construction. Currently, personality theory is more modest and circumscribed, tentative, oriented toward specific aspects of personality.

Personality theory is grounded in philosophy. Each personality theory is built upon certain assumptions about the nature of man, although a theorist may be unaware of his philosophic presuppositions. But various classical personality theories have been evaluated by theology more in terms of superficial attributes than basic assumptions. Thus Freudian psychoanalytic theory was rejected on the basis of its biological reductionism, whereas other psychoanalytic theorists appeared more sympathetic to religion. Carl Jung, (q.v.) spoke favorably about religious needs, but was just as caustic about organized religion as Freud (q.v.). Other psychoanalytic pioneers, Rank, Adler, Horney, and Fromm in turn won religious favor because they emphasized the social utility of religion; Carl Rogers because he championed positive ideals; Gordon Allport and Abraham Maslow because they stressed the altruistic potential of man; and O. H. Mowrer because he talked of the reality of sin. These are but some who have gained religious popularity because in one way or another their personality theories superficially seemed compatible with Christian doctrine.

But there is a serious danger in seeking some "one" personality theory to espouse. All personality theories have scientific assets and liabilities with no necessary Christian or anti-Christian bias. It is fatuous to assume that we will emerge with some definitive "spiritual psychology," for personality theory must remain at the level of scientific hypothesis. As such, every personality theory is temporary, expedient, and subject to new experimental and clinical data. We should be alert to any theology that attempts to take over and "Christianize" a particular personality theory.

The personality theorist and the theological ethicist converge in their interest in the nature of man, and the definition of ethical behavior. That is, they share a normative concern for human existence. But theology cannot produce a morality without a knowledge of human process and affairs. Nor can psychology produce a morality solely as a matter of science. The different contributions to the task can be highlighted. A theory of personality can define human unity but not human goodness. A theory of personality can describe how we create our values and show us how to act with integrity, but it cannot tell us how to choose our values or establish the criteria that we shall use.

As we move to a concern for ethical human behavior, a purely psychological theory of personality will not suffice. Rather we must frame personality in terms of the transection of intrapsychic, social, and cultural determinants of personality and resultant human action. This may be termed a behavioral science view of man, rather than a solely psychological view of man.

Morality has often been framed in individualistic terms, whereas morality is not limited to personal action but involves social and cultural dimensions. Thus morality cannot be considered solely as a psychological attribute of certain personality traits. The moral personality does not exist except within a socio-cultural matrix.

The development of moral capacity has been shown to be unrelated to the specific learning of set patterns of behavior. Rather, moral capacity is reflected in certain learned abilities of judgment and behavior: (1) the ability to withstand temptation and to behave honestly; (2) to act in conformance with social norms that require impulse control; (3) capacity to defer immediate gratification in favor of more distant rewards; (4) maintain focused attention on one task; (5) ability to control unsocialized phantasies.

The above attributes of personality reflect the fact that the individual is not alone in determining his value commitments and the determination of moral choice. His mature moral commitments are influenced by his social matrix, and his mature moral decisions are not his alone to make, but are dependent on the judgments and evaluations of his peers. Thus the nature of personality as a moral quality can been seen to coincide with much of the recent theological discussion on contextual and consensus ethics.

Traditional religious models of the moral aspects of personality have often failed to comprehend the notion of moral capacity versus the learning of specific morals.

A major mechanism of moral teaching has been to inculcate specific moral demands that are internalized as the "conscience," and experienced as feelings of guilt. But guilt feelings are learned phenomena, capricious, and no reliable guide to ethical decision making. Similarly, ethical precepts are often inculcated as idealistic goals, internalized as moral ideals; the failure to achieve them resulting in moral shame. The result is again capricious feelings, that afford no guide to ethical decision making.

Another major personality attribute of moral capacity is the ability to accept, respect, and love oneself. The capacity to act ethically in relation to others then is dependent upon the capacity to first deal charitably with oneself.

Moral capacity is intimately linked to personal maturity and personal integrity. Despite intellectual avowals and earnest intent, the neurotically distorted or immature personality will unwittingly fail to achieve consistent ethical behavior because of the contamination of dysfunctional personality structure.

Finally, morality in the religious context has often been construed as threat and constraint, rather than as freedom and fulfillment. To be a moral personality implies both the capacity to restrain within appropriate limits and the ability to choose and act with commitment.

The definition and commitment to moral values is central to human existence. The ethical nature of man is not a separable trait, but a reflection of the total personality. Therefore all aspects of personality play a role in the ethical process. No aspect of personality, from biological to cultural can be ignored in the construction of a systematic ethics of action.

📖 Calvin S. Hall and Gardner Lindzey, *Theories of Personality*, 2nd edition, New York, Wiley, 1971; Wayne E. Oates, *Religious Dimensions of Personality*, New York, Association, 1957; E. Mansell Pattison, ed., *Clinical Psychiatry and Religion*, Boston, Little, Brown, 1969.

E. MANSELL PATTISON

PERSONAL ETHICS. See also *Interpersonal Relations; New Testament Ethics.* As understood by secular writers, the term "ethics" (or its synonym "morals") refers to the problem of what is right and wrong, good and evil in human conduct. It thus covers the whole sphere of conduct in which men are involved in relationships with their fellow men. The Bible, however, is concerned with relationships not merely between men, but also between men and God. Consequently, it does not draw a very clear distinction between a person's duties to God and his fellow men, as if they were two separate spheres of conduct; on the contrary they are integrally related to each other. This means that in Biblical thinking there is no separate sphere of ethics distinct from the sphere of human-divine relationships; "ethics" in the Biblical sense embraces the whole of a person's relationships with God and with his fellow men.

If the term "ethics" is thus an exceedingly wide one, the addition of the qualification "personal" does nothing to limit it. For it is of the essence of Biblical religion that there is a personal God and that men are persons. Against any suggestion that man is merely a rather intelligent animal, the Bible insists that he was made in the image of God (and uses this fact, for example, as an argument against murder, Gen. 9:6), and hence that he stands over against God in a personal relationship. The effect of adding "personal" to the term "ethics" is thus not to limit the scope of the term but rather to define its character. It reminds us that our relationships with God and our fellow men must be conducted on the personal level. In other words, one may not regard another man as a "thing" to be manipulated and used for one's own ends and pleasure. He is to be treated as a person like oneself, and accorded his proper due.

However, the contrast drawn by the use of the term "personal" may be not so much with an implied "impersonal" as with an implied "social"; that is to say, "personal" may be taken to refer to the individual in his relationships with other individuals, by contrast with "social" ethics in which relationships involving groups of people are discussed. The differences between these two spheres of behavior, however, lie in details rather than in basic principles. The principles that animate the individual must also animate society, although the application may be different, especially when one considers the position of a ruler or a ruling group over against the rest of society.

Our task, then, must be to sketch the basic principles of the personal ethics found in the Bible. In the OT the conduct expected of men is regarded as a response to God. Israel was regarded as being bound by a covenant to God in which her divine suzerain laid down unilaterally the requirements which he imposed upon the people whom he chose as his special people. These requirements were not intended to be a means of pleasing God in the sense of a salvation by works; on the contrary, they represented the terms imposed by God upon the people whom he had redeemed out of Egypt.

A delicate question arises with regard to the universal validity of these requirements. In the OT it is axiomatic that God is holy and righteous, and that his demands are righteous; although men may sometimes grumble that the ways of God are "not fair" (Ezek. 18:25), it is generally assumed that what God does is right and good, and beyond argument (cf. Rom. 9:19-21). It follows that his commands are right and good. This means that they are of universal application, and it is a fact that God requires the same standards of ethical behavior from Israel's pagan neighbors as from Israel herself; the only difference is that Israel is the more culpable if she fails to keep them, since she should know God's will better (see especially Amos). Thus the covenant requirements of God are at the same time principles of universal morality, binding upon all men; the effect of the covenant is that men now accept these principles as God's law and begin to keep them out of love for the lawgiver. At the same time, it may be claimed that some of the covenant requirements were limited to the covenant people and were not necessarily universally or eternally binding. Some have, therefore, used the concept of "creation ordinances" to distinguish between universal laws and covenant requirements or the Jewish concept of "Noachian commandments," given before Sinai and binding upon all the descendants of Noah.

The teaching of the NT is not essentially different. Here the ethic is the outworking of the individual's response to the grace of God revealed in Jesus Christ through which he becomes a member of the people of the new covenant. As in the OT, the first requirement of Christian ethics is not that a person should *do* anything but rather that he should accept the saving grace of God by an act of faith. Man is a sinner who has failed to keep the law of God and to live ethically, and therefore his fundamental duty is to seek forgiveness for his sin. Put otherwise, man who has hitherto been a rebel against God must enter into a personal relationship with God through Christ the Mediator.

But, as in the OT, so in the NT the effect of this personal relationship with God is that the believer now comes under the obligation to serve God and to perform righteousness (Rom. 6:13). The believer is set free from the OT law as a means of gaining salvation (which was what the Jews had made out of it), but he is now "under law to Christ" (I Cor. 9:21); the law is not done away with but established (Rom. 3:31).

The basis of ethics thus becomes the two-fold command upheld and restated by Christ, to love God and to love one's neighbor (Mark 12:30f.; John 13:34). These two commandments, however, represent the summing up of the OT law (Rom. 13:8-10) at a deeper level (Matt. 5:21-48), and hence they can and must be broken down into individual commandments: "this is love, that we follow his commandments" (II John 6).

It is in this sense only that Biblical ethics may be regarded as "situational" (q.v.). This phrase can be properly used to indicate that the basic principle of love for God and one's fellow man needs to be applied in different ways according to the character of each individual situation. It must be emphasized, however, that it does *not* mean that every individual situation is so different from every other that it is impossible to establish sub-laws applicable to a whole series of situations. For example, the principle that adultery is sinful may be derived from an unfolding of the meaning of true love in situations involving relationships between married and unmarried persons; if so, it is false to claim that the application of the principle of love may sometimes condone adultery. Christian ethics accordingly finds expression in detailed principles which go beyond the formal command to love and bring out its specific applications.

It is not possible to separate off any "private" or "personal" aspect of an individual's life which does not involve relationships with other people and hence falls outside the basic principles enunciated above. Even if one can think of some acts which are so private that no other person is involved, even indirectly in them, it still remains true that every aspect of human life stands open before God (Heb. 4:12f.; cf. Rom. 14:9). Thus the whole of human behavior stands under the judgment of God, and becomes the area of response to his saving grace, by means of which we receive the strength to live a life worthy of him.

I. HOWARD MARSHALL

PESSIMISM. See also *Cynicism; Nihilism.* The word "pessimism" is derived from the Latin *pessimus,* meaning "the worst." Pessimism is an attitude toward the world, its events and one's life in it which magnifies evil and sorrow and often results in a gloomy and despondent view.

Several different kinds of pessimism should be distinguished: (1) psychological pessimism, built on subjective judgments about an individual's own experiences in life; (2) physical pessimism, which concludes that the world is largely evil; (3) historical pessimism, usually based on judgments about the corruptness of some societies or of society in general; (4) universal pessimism, resulting from the conclusion that the universe as a whole is evil, or at least that evil far outweighs the good.

Philosophies incorporating pessimistic emphases include Atomism, Stoicism, Skepticism, and Epicureanism. The most noteable example of pessimism in modern Western philosophy is Arthur Schopenauer, who influenced most subsequent pessimistic views.

In Arthur Schopenhauer's *World as Will and Representation*, (E. F. Payne, tr., Magnolia, Mass., Smith), he argues, with the help of Kant's rebuttal of theism, against Leibniz' "best of all possible worlds" thesis, concluding that this world is in many respects the worst of all possible worlds. Pain is the positive essence of life. The world has no sufficient reason at its base but only a blind and and irrational cosmic force. Human reason is only a byproduct of this blind force and man is actually worse off with reason, for unlike the animals without it, man cannot only experience present pain but he can anticipate pain and even meditate on the inescapability of death. Thus reason only enables man to outdo the other animals in evil and suffering.

In view of his essential pessimism about the universe Schopenhauer considers suicide as the best recourse Surprisingly, he decided against taking his life and sought release from life's tremendous tensions through artistic contemplation and moral action. Unsprinkled with any optimism or idealism, pessimism as a pervasive theory of life and of the universe, tends naturally to Nihilism (q.v.). Few pessimists carry out their view with brutal consistency. If release is not found in meditation or action, it is pursued in pleasure (as in Epicureanism) or by a passive resignation to the inevitable (as in Stoicism).

In the Orient, Hinduism and Buddhism place emphasis on the suffering and evil in human existence; both, however, seek release by better reincarnations and ultimately by nirvana. In the West, E. Hartman and Oswald Spengler are more recent exponents of pessimistic philosophies.

The Christian world and life view is opposed to pessimism. Life is worth living because God created it and preserves it for man's good and for his own glory. The evils of this life have a purpose and will ultimately yield a greater good. This is not the best of all possible worlds, but it is the best of all possible ways to obtain the best of all possible worlds which is to come. The Christian doctrines of Creation, Providence and the Last Things make pessimism untenable. God is in sovereign control of life and is working in everything for good (Rom. 8:28).   NORMAN L. GEISLER

PETRINE ETHICS. See also *New Testament Ethics.* The sources for a discussion about Petrine Ethics are the writings ascribed to Peter in the NT and a few Petrine speeches preserved in Acts. A number of critical problems relate to the Petrine writings, I and II Peter. Although challenged by some, Petrine authorship of I Peter is evident in the letter's apostolic authority and testimony. The use of Silvanus as amanuensis, suggested by I Peter 4:12, seems adequately to account for some non-Petrine features of style and language. II Peter contributes little beyond I Peter to the subject of ethics; hence, critical problems relating to its date and authorship need not be considered here.

The theme of I Peter is "The Living Hope in the Midst of Suffering." This must be seen against the background of impending persecution facing the Christians in north-central Asia Minor in the early 60s (shortly before Peter's death in A.D. 64). Prospects are that past afflictions will soon be multiplied and intensified (and perhaps become more official). This paradox of hope and joy in suffering (cf. Paul's discussion in Rom. 5:1-11) is spelled out and concretized in some thirty-five exhortations dispersed throughout I Peter. This unique feature of the epistle (in contrast to Paul's epistles where the hortatory section frequently is distinct from the doctrinal section) strongly suggests that the basic structure is that of a sermon (at least to 4:12). Certain allusions to baptism and its significance possible indicate that this was an exhortation to recent converts to live this new life style in a meaningful and God-glorifying way in their hostile pagan environment (2:11f.).

Following the characteristic introductory formulae designating the sender and recipients and the salutation, the author briefly reviews the redemptive work of God in Christ as the basis of the various injunctions (1:3-10). This redemption with its guaranteed consummation is now the occasion for joy (reading "in this you rejoice" rather than "rejoice in this" in 1:6). The Christian experiences suffering in order that the genuineness of his faith may be demonstrated (1:7)—a totally new perspective for these recent converts. Another significant dimension to the Christian's present life is the eschatological aspect of salvation which becomes the sure basis for his present hope (1:13). This futuristic element with its confident assurance permeates and motivates all of the ethical injunctions, rather than the emphasis on "realized eschatology" often found in Paul (e.g., Col. 3:1).

A holy, separated, consecrated, and dedicated life is urged upon the believer because God the Father is "holy." Peter spells out the implications of this with positive ("love one another," 1:22) and negative commands ("put away all malice and insincerity and envy and all slander," 2:1; "abstain from the passions of the flesh," 2:11).

Inasmuch as conflicts with government authorities were inevitable in these young churches, Peter advises his readers to recognize and honor these civil rulers (2:13-17). However, such instructions can be overruled by a higher principle in a crisis, e.g., when Peter before the Sanhedrin boldly declared "we must obey God rather than men" (Acts 5:29). This is the meaning of the injunction: "live as servants of God" (2:16).

Specific instructions regarding this new life in Christ are given for various classes of people. The appeal to servants to be submissive to their masters is based upon Christ's example (2:21). Suffering is part of a Christian's calling and he should bear it in the same spirit in which Christ did—obedient submission. Within the family, the relationship of husband and wife is conditioned by the new life in Christ. The submission and obedience of the wife to her husband, demonstrated in the holy women of the OT, can have a redemptive purpose and the consideration of the husband for his wife will promote their spiritual growth.

For the whole body of believers there must be "unity of spirit, sympathy, love of the brethren, a tender heart and a humble mind" (3:8). However, of paramount importance here is that the believer's suffering is for doing right (agathopoieō). This thought receives multiple emphasis in I Peter—2:15, 20; 3:6, 17. In a sense, this is the chief ethical injunction: "do right" (agathopoiei). This verb, a very significant term in Peter's ethical vocabulary, literally means "to do good, treat well" (as in Luke 6:9, 33, 35). The term is contrasted with hamartanein ("to sin, do wrong") in 2:20 and with kakopoiein ("to do evil") in 3:17. This clearly puts the term in the context of fulfilling the Christian moral law. This type of activity is the setting for God's approval (2:20), the method to refute foolish and ignorant men (2:15; cf. 3:16), the fulfillment of God's will (2:15; 3:17), and the antidote of harm, terror and fear (3:6, 13). Fulfilling this activity provides content for the hope of the Christian and gives unashamed confidence in the face of opposition (4:16). This moral good, synonymous with righteousness (3:13), must be the chief concern of the Christian—in fact, he must be enthusiastic and fervent for it (3:13).

The example of Christ's suffering functions very significantly in Peter's ethical injunctions as a paradigm for the believer. This is an *imitatio Christi* (2:21) as a consequence of Christ's redemptive work rather than the means. On the other hand, the experience of suffering has a sanctifying aspect to it. The striking formula "to suffer" is "to cease from sin" (4:1) has a partial parallel in I John 3:9 ("no one born of God commits sin"). The willingness of the Christian to suffer (following the example of Christ) means to live by the will of God and to resist the evil passions of the Gentile environment (4:2). This prospect of suffering, although somber and dire, nevertheless becomes an occasion for joy because of the future glory awaiting the believer (4:13, 14). The imminence of the end occasions some miscellaneous exhortations to the Christian community—love, hospitality, stewardship, mutual concern (4:7-11). The ultimate purpose of all Christian living is "that in everything God may be glorified through Jesus Christ" (4:11b). Another set of miscellaneous exhortations (5:6-11) concludes with the confident assurance that this present suffering will lead to victory and glory.

The unique features of Petrine ethics are (1) the present submission to suffering (including persecution) as a prelude to future glory; (2) the paradigmic character of Christ's suffering for the believer; and (3) the function of the living hope in the midst of suffering—stressing the expectation of future salvation and glory.

These dimensions of Christian living, with their strong eschatological emphasis, not only spoke meaningfully to the first century recipients in Asia Minor, but also can and should speak to the present-day church and her members in their tension-filled environment with its this-worldly emphasis which undercuts the futuristic perspective. The bridging of the gap between "this-worldly" and "other-worldly" by Peter for first century Christians in this "suffering-hope"

combination has significant present-day relevance.   BASTIAAN VAN ELDEREN

PHARISAISM. Historical Pharisaism is rooted in the period of the Babylonian Exile when Israel, deprived of Temple worship, became primarily a people of the Law. At this time one finds the beginnings of a conflict which ultimately surfaced in the Greek period. It eventually led under the Hasmoneans in the second century B.C. to a split between an aristocratic priestly element and a lay-oriented element of teachers and interpreters of the Law, a split from which gradually emerged the Sadducee and Pharisee parties of the NT. The name "Pharisee," of which the precise date or origin is moot, quite probably stems from the Hebrew *parush* meaning "separated" and reflects the sect's stubborn opposition to any inroads of paganism and religious defilement.

Although Pharisaism held distinctive doctrines such as a developed angelology, the resurrection of the dead, and divine control of history, doubtless its most distinguishing characteristic was concern for the Law. The Pharisees gave themselves to knowing and interpreting the Law. This interpretation of the Law, transmitted orally as the "tradition of the elders" (Mark 7:3) until codified as the Mishnah in about A.D. 200, was considered to be as binding as, if not more so than (Mark 9:9), the written Law. Indeed, the "traditions of the elders" was also viewed as part of the Law given by God to Moses and passed down orally through the ages.

Such concern for the Law arose from a practical, sincere desire to keep the Law, since the Pharisees believed that one's present and future standing before God was determined by conduct with reference to the Law. This religion of merit based on works led to a sense of self-righteousness and necessitated "separation" from all who failed to live accordingly to avoid temptation and defilement. Consequently, this life style came to be one of rigorous, legalistic separatism.

The view of Pharisaism prevalent in Christian circles has emerged from the Pharisees' opposition to Jesus and from Paul's rejection of it. Jesus charged the Pharisees with hypocrisy because their meticulous concern for the Law (Matt. 23:23f.) and inadequate righteousness (Matt. 5:20) had prevented them from responding to the true will of God expressed in his person and work (Matt. 23). Paul rejected Pharisaism as a religion of works of the Law leading to a deluded self-righteousness (Phil 3:5f.).

After the fall of Jerusalem in A.D. 70, the Pharisees emerged as leaders of the Jews and laid the foundations for rabbinical Judaism. Whereas historical Pharisaism has merged into orthodox Judaism, "Pharisaism" is reflected today wherever one seeks favor from, or sees himself favored by, God because of legal rectitude.

ROBERT A. GUELICH

PHENOMENOLOGY. See also *Existential Ethics*. Phenomenology, a modern philosophy, believes in interpreting appearances by means of essences intuited from those appearances.

Edmund Husserl, the most notable phenomenologist, flourished between 1900 and 1930. He rejected psychologism, phenomenalism, and scientism. He held that no abstraction is superior to an observed example. Thus, he parted with traditional empiricism.

Phenomenology deals with intentional acts. Statements about reality result from "bracketing experience." That is, they suspend belief in the existence of given objects. Examples are freely varied in imagination. Phenomenology is self-corrective, proceeding as it does from example to statement and vice versa. This process illustrates the "methodological circle" and the "epistemological circle."

Phenomenologists consider Kant and Hegel their forerunners. Husserl's successors include Heidegger, Sartre, and Merleau-Ponty, although these men interpret phenomenology in various existential ways. G. Van de Leeuw applies phenomenology to anthropology of religion; Donald Snygg and Arthur Combs to psychiatry; and Alfred Schutz to sociology. GEORGE S. CLAGHORN

PHILANTHROPY. Philanthropy (*philia*, love; *anthropos*, man) signifies love towards mankind. In ordinary usage it refers more particularly to acts of practical benevolence.

The Jews recognized the obligation of mutual love, but limited it to their own kind (Lev. 19:18). Jesus, however, insisted that the obligation to love one's neighbor includes anyone in need (Luke 10:25ff.). There are no limits to love: it includes and embraces friend and foe alike (Luke 6:27). The sons of the Kingdom must lend where there is no hope of repayment, and must practice love without expecting any reward (Luke 6:29-30).

The love Christians are to manifest is not emotional sentiment or idealistic "gas"; on the contrary, it is intensely practical, expressing itself not only in compassionate words but also in constructive deeds (Luke 10:33ff.).

It is instructive to see how this command was interpreted by the Early Church. Ernst Troeltsch, in *The Social Teaching of the Christian Churches* (New York, Macmillan, 1931, vol. 1, p. 134), quotes this testimony: "It is the aim of the Church to give parental care to the orphan, to be a husband to the widow, to help those who are ready for marriage to make a home, to give work to the unemployed, to show practical compassion to those who cannot work, to give shelter to the stranger, food to the hungry, drink to the thirsty, to see that the sick are visited and that help is forthcoming to the prisoners." In addition to all this, Troeltsch notes, help was given in time of public calamity.

During the Middle Ages the spirit of philanthropy became institutionalized as the humane impulse found expression more and more through the monastic system. The Reformation saw a determined effort to revive the tradition of private benevolence. The Reformed Church restored the order of deacons (cf. Acts 6:1ff.) and the Lutherans revived the duty of communal poor relief. In England, the poor became the responsibility of the parish under the State.

The Evangelical Revival was accompanied by an outburst of intense humanitarianism (q.v.). Wesley supported and encouraged Wilberforce in his herculean labors for the abolition of the slave trade. Although numerically a minority, evangelicals were directly responsible not only for the abolition of the slave trade (1807) but of slavery itself (1833); and, moreover, under the leadership of Shaftesbury, were instigators of a vast range of factory legislation. In every area of life they tirelessly promoted humanitarian reform and social righteousness. Lecky, the rationalist historian, acknowledges that the philanthropic spirit of the nineteenth century was the direct consequence of the stimulus of the evangelical revival.

The latter part of the nineteenth century saw the establishment, by extremely wealthy businessmen, of giant philanthropic trusts dedicated to furtherance of education and other good causes.

Today the public is often confused by the multiplicity of causes seeking support. The creation of the United Fund and the Community Chest is an attempt to deal with this problem by reducing the number of different appeals. Committed Christians also face a host of distinctively Christian enterprises, at home and abroad, demanding support and encouragement.

The practice of a wise and responsible philanthropy is an inescapable Christian obligation. It finds its ground in the initiative of God on our behalf. "We love, because he first loved us" (I John 4:19 RSV). At the judgment day the simple question will be whether we have ministered unto those in need, and thereby unto Christ (Matt. 25:31ff.).   STUART B. BABBAGE

PHILIA. See *Love.*

PHILOSOPHICAL ETHICS. See *Moral Philosophy.*

PIETISM. This was a religious movement within the Lutheran Church in Germany during the seventeenth century, reacting against rigid doctrinal orthodoxy and emphasizing the personal devotional life of the Christian and Bible study groups. Although there are evidences the Puritan piety of England and the Reformed Church of Holland influenced German Pietism, historically Pietism was initiated by Philipp Jakob Spener (1634-1705).

Spener had come to Frankfort as Lutheran pastor in 1666. In 1670 he organized his *Collegia Pietatis,* an informal system of Bible study which became very popular and spread among other churches and pastors. In 1675 Spener published his *Pia Desideria,* containing six proposals for the restoration of true religion. They included: greater emphasis on the Bible through preaching and private meetings for Bible study; more practical and less rhetorical preaching; more participation by the laity in the life of the church; deeper cultivation of the spiritual life by Christians, by ministerial students especially; a better attitude (of love rather than disputation) toward unbelievers. These proposals and his bold criticism of the clergy aroused open hostility. Spener accepted a call to Dresden in 1686 and to Berlin in 1691. Here he remained until his death.

Spener's strongest disciple was August Hermann Francke (1663-1727), who had remarkable success not only as a professor but in opening a poor-school, orphanage, publishing house, and a dispensary. Unfortunately, the jealousy of conservative pastors, combined with untimely criticism of the Leipzig theologians, aroused severe criticism and opposition.

Pietism was a reform movement in the direction of evangelical devotion based on the ethical teachings of Jesus. Spener never effected a formal organization; he did not want a movement outside the Lutheran Church, but only *ecclesiolae in ecclesia,* a leaven within the church. The Pietists emphasized not only a personal relationship with God, but regeneration and sanctification above justification and faith, and support of faith by living works. Criticisms were mostly doctrinal, as the Pietists denigrated correct doctrine in their extreme emphases upon the necessity of the new birth, and practical sanctification, and were preoccupied with individual salvation while ignoring the church and the world. They were also accused of undue emotion, subjectivism, mysticism, fanaticism, and social isolationism.

The overall contributions of Pietism, however, were wholesome, and indirectly spread far beyond Europe and the seventeenth century. The movement certainly instilled a new spirit and devotion into the churches, influenced preaching and stimulated pastoral care, initiated significant outreach in education through the establishment of the University of Halle in 1694, promoted a worldwide mission enterprise which reaped substantial results later in the labors of Count Zinzendorf and the Moravian Church, influenced John Wesley and the Methodists, and instituted orphanages and hospitals. The spirit of tolerance nurtured by Pietism and its low-key theology tended to develop an ecumenical atmosphere, while the beautiful hymnody of Pietism has been a great healer and unifier. It might well be said that Pietism is basically an attitude, more than a movement.

JAMES D. MOSTELLER

PIRACY. Piracy is (1) robbery or illegal seizure of goods at sea or on the shores of the sea, or (2) the unauthorized use of or appropriation of copyrighted or patented works.

Piracy is as old as travel by sea, dating to the Phoenician maritime fleet and flourishing to the middle of the nineteenth century. Such adventures have provided the material for countless romantic novels and movies. Some pirates, such as Lolonois and Bonnet, had little regard for human life; others, such as Captain Tew and Sir Henry Morgan, were known for kind treatment of prisoners. Pirates have been slaves and noblemen. One was an Italian priest, who, along with Captain Misson, set up a socialistic haven called Libertatia for aged and disabled pirates. For most, piracy was a convenient and highly profitable form of stealing. Robbery was often compounded by murder and kidnapping.

In modern usage, piracy refers to more sophisticated thievery: business and industry often use patented devices without authorization; musical pieces have been written by some only to be claimed by others; and writers (including theologians) have plagiarized written material. Famous (and embarrasing) instances involve using untranslated materials. Others unethically publish ideas gleaned from unpublished sources with no credit to the original author.

PAUL D. SIMMONS

PITY. Pity is a feeling of sympathy and compassion in the suffering of others (Ps. 69:20). It may also imply contemptuous sorrow, but the latter concept does not appear in Scripture.

God is compassionate and merciful (James 5:11); his compassions never fail (Lam. 3:22). He pities those who fear him as a father expresses concern and compassion for his children (Ps. 103:13). God's pity and love cause him to redeem those who are separated from him because of their sins (Isa. 63:9; Titus 3:15). This is aptly demonstrated in his mercy upon Nineveh and his lesson to Jonah (Jon. 4:10). Because of God's pity for Israel he will ultimately restore her to Palestine with his promised blessings (Joel 2:18), her captors having pity upon her (Ps. 106:46). However, when God judges, he judges without pity (Lam. 2:17; 3:43).

Man has the ability to express pity toward other men. He should have pity upon the ill-treated as David's pity for the poor man in Nathan's parable (II Sam. 12:6) and the good Samaritan's pity on the robber's victim (Luke 10:33-37). When men lack pity, God will judge them (Amos 1:11). When God judges men, others should not pity them in their judgment, because God is just (Deut. 13:8; 19:13,21).   RALPH H. ALEXANDER

PLAGIARISM. Plagiarism is the use or imitation of the language or thoughts of another writer and presenting them as one's own work. This contravenes the Decalogue at three points: stealing, bearing of false witness, and coveting. Clearly, thoughts and words are as much a person's property as more tangible goods. Appropriately enough, the Latin *plagiarius* (kidnapper) came to be applied humorously to the literary thief, for the stealing of one's original ideas is akin to the stealing of the person himself. In the academic world plagiarism ranges from a student's use of a term paper written by a friend to a professor's use of work by graduate assistants without credit.

There are many grey areas. Obviously, artistic borrowing and droll references to other works are acceptable, as is parody. Although plagiarism may be inadvertent among well-read persons, care in ethics and scholarship dictates careful attribution of sources. Copyright laws are modern society's major defense against plagiarism.

Though plagiarism refers to verbal concepts, the same ethical principle applies in other creative fields, such as the visual arts. The problem of idea-theft has been compounded by modern technological advances, such as the widespread "pirating" of tape and disc recordings, and reproduction of writing and music by photocopying machines without payment of royalties.   RICHARD N. OSTLING

PLANETIZATION. At this time only the moon appears subject to possible colonization, and then only as a totally dependent outpost of the earth. Whether it will be colonized depends on its scientific, economic, and military value in relation to the cost. Opposing claims to space on the moon will necessarily be settled by treaty or force.

The space program is a natural and worthy consequence of man's God-given intelligence and thirst for knowledge seen in the light of the command to subdue the earth (Gen. 3:28). It should give men increased knowledge of the sovereignty and glory of the Eternal God revealed in his work of creation (Ps. 19:1-6; Rom. 1:18-20).   WILLIAM K. HARRISON, JR.

PLATO. See *Greek Ethics.*

PLEASURE. Aristotle noted in his *Ethics* that there were two kinds of pleasures: one, a pleasure-state, which endures for a given period, varies in intensity and about which we can say that one "feels" it; the other, more difficult to describe, is the kind we allude to when we say, "I take pleasure in his company." In the latter instance, pleasure is not a state nor an episode; neither is it an event nor is it clear that it stops and starts like a pain, an itch or a tickle. Rather, it involves a way, acquired to be sure and not naive, of taking the world and summing up things. Here a judgment has entered in and also all sorts of qualities of the person involved are germane. It might be that good men would take pleasure in another's moral victory whereas an evil man would enjoy another's failure.

But what the NT authors refer to as a life "lived according to the course of this world" is a kind of pleasure-seeking of the former kind. The kind of pleasure that the Epicureans suggest as the secret of happiness—and which both Jesus and Paul refer to—is the kind that turns men into pleasure-seekers, who seek that which satisfies for the moment and the day. All of this the Bible repudiates. But it is a mistaken Christian austerity which sees a Christian as opposed to a life which pleases him.

On the contrary, a forgiven and transfigured life, lived in Christ Jesus, is one that never needs to be regretted. And because of Christ's atoning death it is as if God does not condemn us for all that we have done with ourselves. The work of Christ is also in our behalf so that we can take pleasure in our job, in our family, in our very life and its onerous tasks. Like the piano-player who may not relish each moment of practice but nonetheless takes pleasure in playing well and with beautiful effortlessness, so the Christian lives by grace and takes a deep and eventually an effortless delight in being one of God's children and living in such a world as this.

Surely there are disciplined ways to achieve this latter kind of pleasure, that free one altogether from the fretful pursuit that a sensible man improved by Christian teachings would also eschew. Also, it is easy enough to see that chasing pleasures and extracting them from sex, food and the uses of the body is vulgar, tiresome and plainly meritorious. One must become a technician; and the worst sort of connoisseurship is then necessary. From all of this, Christian teaching is a liberation, but not by making one indifferent or apathetic. That is the way of stoicism, which the New Testament also condemns.

Instead, it is as if we can learn to be pleased at the business of being a man. One can be glad to be alive, even if pain, injustice and death mark the path. For these, even if painful, become like the pains of surgery to a man who has a confident view of life. He might say: "It hurts terribly, but it makes no difference." So, too, with a Christian who takes pleasure in being in the company of God and his creatures—despite the pains involved.

PAUL L. HOLMER

POLITICAL THEOLOGY. In his pioneering volume Jürgen Moltmann noted that the primary implication of his theology of hope is a new perspective on social ethics (*Theology of Hope*, New York, Harper & Row, 1967, p. 304). The most ardent Roman Catholic disciple of theology of hope, Johannes Metz, coined the term Political Theology to express the essential character of this social ethic and to preserve its uniqueness. The antithesis of Political Theology is a purely personal religion and Christian ethic. In his essay "Religion and Society in the Light of Political Theology," Metz writes: *The deprivatizing of theology is the primary task of political theology* (p. 140, italics his). This odd verb, "deprivatize," intends to negate the idea that Christian faith can be restricted to personal religion and personal ethics (q.v.).

The theologians of hope contend that the real sins of man are social evils and social alienations. Therefore the church's primary concern must be with man's social, political and economic problems. Moltmann's definition follows: "Together with Joh. B. Metz, I call it *political theology* in order to make clear that ethics is not an appendix to dogmatics and also is not only a consequence of faith, but that faith itself has a messianic context in which it becomes meaningful and that theology itself stands in a political dimension in which it becomes relevant" (*Religion, Revolution and the Future*, p. 218).

The term as Metz uses it must not be

considered synonymous with state ideology; its context is modern political freedom, which is held to shape a need for theological critique of all governmental forms in view of the future reign of God. Moltmann sees it as a stimulus to the political consciousness of every theology.

The American reflections of Political Theology are linked more with an emphasis against political oppression than on deprivatizing theology. They pursue an enlarged role for the institutional church in national political life, tend to neglect theoretical concerns to concentrate on so-called immediate human needs, and seek a new society, man-made, linked to new political concepts. Harvey Cox calls for political incarnation of truth and is more programmatic than some. Roger Schaull stresses the need for structural transformation of social institutions.

It is unclear how much of this political emphasis is properly designated theology, in view of the primary concern of theology with knowledge of God. And, besides its man-centeredness, a further question arises whether the content of this social ethic is derived from Holy Scripture or is essentially a Marxian or Blochian concept in Christian garb.

📖 Johannes B. Metz, "Religion and Society in the Light of a Political Theology," *The Future of Hope*, Walter H. Capps, ed., Philadelphia, Fortress, 1970, pp. 136-154; Jürgen Moltmann, *Religion Revolution, and the Future*, New York, Scribner, 1969.   CARL F. H. HENRY

POLITICS. See *Ethics, History of; Government; International Order; State.*

POLLUTION. See *Environmental Pollution.*

POLYGAMY. See also *Bigamy; Marriage; Monogamy.* The state of marriage involving a simultaneous plurality of spouses includes polygyny (multiple wives), polyandry (multiple husbands), and communal marriage (multiple husbands in relationship with multiple wives). The usual form is polygynv which is practiced in parts of Africa, Australia, Melanesia, and elsewhere. Plural wives are usually the privilege of a small minority who thereby increase progeny, prestige, and wealth.

That monogamy was intended at creation is clear from Gen. 2:18ff. Subsequently, polygamy was allowed and its practice became rather common in ancient Israel (cf. Deut. 21:15ff.). Post-exilic Jewish teaching was basically monogamous. By the Christian era both Jewish and Graeco-Roman practice were almost universally so. In the NT, monogamy is largely presupposed. The creation order is clearly affirmed (cf. Matt. 19:3-9; Mark 10:1-12; I Cor. 6:16, 7:1, 2; Eph. 5:22-33; I Tim. 3:2).

The Biblical data are variously interpreted. In one view, the fact that the OT reports the polygamous relationships of upright men, and the relative silence of the NT on the subject, implies that the monogamous relationship of the creation order should not be taken too seriously (cf. Michael Keeling, *What is Right?,* London, SCM, 1969, pp. 51ff.). Another view grounds monogamy in the divine order of creation simply as reflected in the "givenness" of subjectively experienced monogamous relationships—i.e., the exclusivity of the relationship between one man and one woman in sexual love and procreation (cf. Emil Brunner, *The Divine Imperative,* Philadelphia, Westminster, 1947, pp. 340ff.). An approach consonant with a high view of Scripture grounds monogamy in the creation order as reinforced throughout the Bible, especially the NT. Polygamous marriages in the OT are understood as concessions, never as reflections of the Divine ideal. Lack of conformity to monogamy was to be punished. The progressive unfolding of God's will in the Bible clearly reveals that will to be the restoration of the original monogamous relationship (cf. Carl F. H.

Henry, *Christian Personal Ethics,* Grand Rapids, Eerdmans, 1957, pp. 328f.).

Historically the missionary problem has often primarily related to ways and means of dealing with polygamous converts and attaining the monogamous ideal. The confusing (and often debilitating) results of demanding that before baptism polygamous converts divest themselves of all but one wife has occasioned a reappraisal, and this approach has been abandoned in many areas. However, concessions made to those who have already taken plural wives should not be allowed for frustrate the Divine will. As reflected in the Bible itself, procedures for dealing with polygamists should ensure progression toward the creation prototype and the NT church pattern. Monogamy is clearly the ideal for the church's membership and an explicit qualification for her leadership (I Tim. 3:2).

DAVID J. HESSELGRAVE

POOR. See also *Poverty.* As an economic category this term designates in general those persons who do not have and are unable to obtain the means for sustaining life. If they are to survive they are thus dependent upon the resources of other people. Modern sociologists distinguish more specifically between ordinary poverty, where a person earns just sufficient to maintain himself and possibly a family at a bare subsistence level; real poverty, where a person does not possess or cannot earn enough to sustain life; and destitution, in which an individual requires the assistance of others if he is to continue to exist. Both sociologists and economists agree that individuals in the second and third categories must first have their poverty alleviated before preventive remedies can be undertaken.

The poor, as represented by one or more of the above classes, have been in existence for countless centuries (cf. Deut. 15:11), as reflected in a statement by Christ (Matt. 26:11). In the ancient Near East, and especially in Mesopotamia, poverty was often a relative concept depending partly upon the extent of personal freedom. While slaves as a class were the most deprived economically, some individuals of executive ability often rose to positions of major importance within large households, and even had their own slaves. Furthermore, since the insecure nature of ancient Near Eastern society turned princes into paupers with considerable frequency, there was no social stigma attached to either poverty or slavery.

The notable ethical and humanitarian concerns of the Mosaic Law made considerable provision for the economically deprived (Exod. 23:11; Lev. 14:21; 19:10; etc.), but forbade favoritism just because a person was poor (Lev. 19:15). The Song of Hannah described both poverty and riches as a work of God (I Sam. 2:7), reflecting normal Hebrew philosophical monism. Because the poor seemed natural targets for exploitation by the wicked (cf. Ps. 10:2ff.), they could cry to God for help (Ps. 34:6), since he had prepared for their needs (Ps. 68:10). Oppression of the poor was uniformly condemned in the OT (cf. Ps. 72:14; Isa. 3:15; Amos 2:6; etc.), and blessings were invoked on those who were charitable to them (Ps. 41:1; Prov. 14:21; etc.). Since the Hebrews believed that the increase of riches was generally correlative with individual spiritual stature, it followed that poverty was never regarded intrinsically as a virtue. The poor were to be objects of compassion, not of admiration.

Apparently from the beginning of the Greek period the Hebrew term "poor" took on an additional, non-economic meaning. The faithful minority at that time regarded themselves rather introspectively as the poor, harrassed remnant of spiritual fidelity in a vast morass of Hellenistic paganism. Thus "the poor" also meant "the faithful," a usage reflected consistently in the literature of the Dead Sea sect. This group, as their treasure scroll shows, was far from economically underprivileged, indicating that their use of "poor" actually described their fidelity to the spiritual traditions of the Law.

Christ used the term "poor" in Matt. 5:3, Luke 6:20 in this same sense, promising the Kingdom to the "spiritually loyal," not to the economically or spiritually deprived. Indeed, where "poor" occurs in the Gospels in the absence of an obvious or implicit economic connotation, it should be interpreted in terms of spiritual fidelity. Christ only condemned trust in riches (cf. Matt. 13:22; etc.), not their possession, and promised that when spiritual priorities had been established, other material things would follow (Matt. 6:33). The New Testament, like the Old, acknowledged poverty as an economic fact of life, but never extolled it as a virtue. When Christ asked a would-be inheritor of the Kingdom to become voluntarily impoverished (Matt. 19:21), he was challenging a specific individual and not issuing a general command to all his followers. Charitable gifts to impoverished widows was the first form of social work practiced by the Christian church, and this spirit of communal responsibility was developed by Paul and directed at indigent churches (cf. II Cor. 8:2f.). In the medieval period charity towards the poor endeavored to remedy the demoralizing effects of poverty, sustain individual independence, and promote the greatest good of the whole society. The ancient Roman view that the state alone should relieve poverty was revived by Adam Smith and Malthus, forming the basis for subsequent socialist theories, which however, were unable to eradicate poverty, and in terms of economic planning sometimes contributed to disparities within the system.

While the state should support the legitimate human rights of the poor, it should resist becoming a victim to parasitism.

Welfare must be administered justly and equitably, and the dignity of human labor must be promoted by the provision of appropriate opportunities and incentives. Though poverty is sometimes beyond individual control, it should be corrected as far as possible by means of self-help. In particular, professional indigents should be assisted to find remunerative employment. The mere fact of existence in the absence of productivity does not warrant mandatory state support for healthy adults (cf. II Thess. 3:10), since such citizens should be contributing to communal wellbeing.

R. K. HARRISON

POPULATION CONTROL. See also *Birth Control; Contraception.* The rapidly expanding population of the world has given increasing cause for concern. In 1830 it was one billion; by 1930 it had doubled; in 1960 it was three billion; by 1975 there will be four billion. It is estimated that seven and one-half billion people will inhabit the earth by the year 2000.

With overpopulation comes an increase in social ills. Techniques necessary to meet man's needs have not kept pace with the population expansion. Lack of food, housing, education, and medical help become overbearing problems. Overcrowding, inadequate housing, lack of sanitary facilities, lead to the spread of disease. Forecasts on the possibility of overcoming these problems within the foreseeable future are not optimistic.

Food quantity must be considered in relation to food quality. Malnutrition is a widespread problem. In some countries, even people who are receiving enough daily calories are ill or dying from a lack of proteins, vitamins, and minerals. Malnourished children are suffering permanent physical and mental retardation.

In many countries, illiteracy is gaining ground. Although progress has been made, in some underprivileged countries half the children of school age are not enrolled in school.

Basic to man's responsibility in God's creation is the Biblical statement, "Be fruitful and multiply and fill the earth and subdue it" (Gen. 1:28b RSV). History reveals that man has been more successful in multiplying, than in subduing the earth. Both must be accepted, however, as significant parts of the creation mandate.

To subdue the earth means at least that man is responsible to keep it under control. Coupling this with the Biblical admonition to help people fully realize themselves seems to necessitate some form of population control. Furthermore, the magnitude of the problem suggests that the Christian's responsibility goes beyond attention to the individual to support of organizational groups, including state and national government programs. Yet the heavy demand on essential goods already in insufficient supply may impoverish life by leading to the regimentation of society. Thus, other "inalienable rights" deemed necessary for sharing the gospel and for a full life may be lost.   LLOYD A. KALLAND

PORNOGRAPHY. See also *Obscenity.* This word comes into English directly from the ancient Greek word *pornographous* which meant writings about prostitutes (from the root words *porne,* "harlot," and *graphos,* "writing"). In English the word has come to have a broader definition, meaning all writings, photographs, or works of art that depict sexual activity, particularly illicit sexual acts or perversions.

In the legal sense, the U.S. Supreme Court has held that, to be banned as pornographic, a book must be "devoid of redeeming social values" (Kingsley Books vs. Brown, 1957). On the basis of possessing some literary and social values, such books as *Ulysses, Lady Chatterly's Lover,* and *Fanny Hill,* long banned from importation into the USA, have now been widely pub-

lished. However, when a prospective author sought to import pornographic pictures from abroad for purpose of publishing them in a book, the Supreme Court in 1971 held that they were intended to incite prurient interest and could be confiscated by the Customs Bureau (U.S. v. Twenty-six Photographs, 1971).

As with obscenity, the definition of legally excludable pornography has come to depend largely on contemporary community standards.

Pornography is generally divided into two classifications, "soft core" and "hard core." The former are books and photographs dealing with sexual acts that are not so offensive as to be illegal. "Hard core" material deals with sex in its rawest and crudest forms, using the language of the gutter, and making no pretense of any redeeming social value. It circulates only where enforcement of the law is lax.

Unfortunately, there has been great laxity in enforcing the law against pornography, so that many large cities have been literally flooded with "hard core" pornography, openly displayed for sale. In part, this laxity has come as a result of the rapidly rising crime rate, which has more than doubled in the years 1960-70, overburdened the courts with criminal cases, and has given police many more cases of easily defined crime, such as murder, bank robbery, and auto theft, than they have manpower with which to cope. In part, the laxity arises from the difficulty of obtaining convictions, since the courts have held that the prosecutor must present expert testimony as to contemporary community standards in order to convict. Such convictions are almost always appealed to the appellate courts, imposing a severe drain on the available manpower of the prosecutor's offices. A tendency has existed, therefore, to overlook the sale of pornography which could, if taken to court, lead to conviction. This, in turn, has posed a serious threat to the very community standards upon which successful prosecution depends.

Pornography has been described as a billion dollar business in the USA by Congressional investigating committees, which have asked for stronger laws to suppress it because of its effect on the morals of youth. A special Presidential commission appointed by President Johnson in 1968, after a two-year study of the problem, however, claimed that there was no proof that pornography was harmful to morals and recommended repeal of all laws prohibiting it. President Nixon repudiated the report and Congress has emphatically declined to act on its recommendation.

Pornography generally depicts women as mere sexual objects for male gratification and devoid of human personality or feelings. For this reason it has become a particular target of women's liberation groups. However, American churches, while still giving lip service to traditional Christian sexual ethics and marriage vows, have done little that is effective to stem the tide of pornography, preferring to address themselves to other social concerns.

GLEN D. EVERETT

POVERTY. See also *Poor*. The definition of "poverty" varies considerably. Perhaps the most common approach is "income-deficiency." Within this, three categories are used. One defines poverty in terms of a cost-of-living budget estimate. Thus the U.S. Labor Department establishes a "poverty line" based on an "absolute" minimum income needed by an urban family of four to "get by." Owing to inflation, the "poverty line" tends to edge upward. In 1966, it was $3,300; by 1969, it was $3,743. Using this standard, in 1969 there were 24.3 million persons with incomes below the poverty level, a decrease of 1.1 million since 1968 and 15.2 million since 1960. Those from nonwhite minorities constituted 31 percent of those below the poverty line in 1969, though they comprise only 12 percent of the population. By this criterion, about one out of ten families were poor in 1969, compared with about one out of five in 1959. While in 1959, 44 percent of all poor persons lived in metropolitan areas, in 1969 the figure was 51 percent.

Sixty-one percent of poor male family heads and 43 percent of poor female family heads worked in 1969. Not only, therefore, are most of the poor *not* idle (as the popular folklore has it), but 90 percent of poor male heads who did not work were either ill or disabled, or can be presumed to be retired. About 72 percent of poor female heads who did not work in 1969 gave family and home responsibilities as their main reason. Likewise, in 1966, among all poor persons in America were 18 percent of the nation's children and 30 percent of the nation's aged. In 1969, it would have taken $10.1 billion to raise the aggregate incomes of all poor families to the poverty level.

There are obvious difficulties in using the budget-estimate definition of poverty. The most obvious is that certain families, under certain conditions, can stretch X number of dollars further than other families.

A second category within the income-deficiency approach defines poverty as any income below 50 percent of the national median income of all workers. This definition, rather than emphasizing the minimum dollars it takes to "get by," is based on J. K. Galbraith's notion that "the poor are those who have fallen behind the grades and standards of the society as a whole." In 1970, for example, the median income of all American families was $9,870. Therefore, by this second definition, families with annual incomes of less than $4,935 are living in poverty. Using this definition, poverty has *not* declined in the USA since 1947.

A third category views poverty as "share of national income." In 1967, 20 percent of American families received only 5 percent of total national income. The next 20 percent got 12 percent of national income, so that 40 percent of families receive only 17 percent of available money. At the top end, some 5 percent of families received 15 percent of total national income, while the top 20 percent of all families received 41 percent of all income. As with the second category, this type of pattern has changed little since 1947.

Irrespective of which of the three definitions of poverty one accepts, there is general agreement that the element that is most difficult for the poor to bear is that they represent an island of deprivation in a sea of affluence. While the *relative* condition of American poor is vastly better than the impoverished of other lands, they are *relatively* behind a great many Americans. What is more, as a result of mass media (q.v.), those in poverty are keenly conscious of the life-style of the affluent. These very same media constantly seek to raise the consumption aspirations of poor and non-poor alike, so that there never seems to be any ceiling whatsoever on consumption aspirations.

The issue of ever-rising aspirations is especially pertinent if we look at the other broad approach to poverty besides income deficiency per se. It is complementary to the first and suggests that the poor are those who do not have access to resources such as fringe benefits (pensions, health plans, etc.), non-income compensation (stock options), liquid assets (savings and investments) that earn capital, adequate insurance, quality health care, quality legal counsel, the ear of elected representatives who might intercede on their behalf, and so forth.

The response of many non-poor is that the poor could escape poverty if only they *wanted* to. In the case of the blind, the aged, the lame, such an argument is obviously false. As for healthy adults who are in poverty, most received little or poor education as children; and although many work at low-paying, insecure jobs, most remain in poverty. To be black and poorly educated means, in addition, severe job discrimination. Compared to whites, there is clear evidence that blacks are indeed the last hired, are in fact paid less while on the job, and are first to be laid off. As for the great numbers of poor who are children (the poorest of all poor persons in our society are black children in households headed by females), through no fault of their own, their home environment is in many instances an inadequate preparation for public school. Equally discouraging is the fact that the schools attended by the poor are often inferior to other schools. In that case poor children on two counts (home and school) have little opportunity for social mobility, i.e., to go beyond the socioeconomic level of their parents.

Jesus' words about "the poor always being with us" can in no way be construed to be an excuse for ignoring the extreme poverty condition in America in the last third of the twentieth century. The OT prophets (especially Amos), Jesus' own behavior, Paul's example, the teaching of James, all compel the Christian to seek to relieve human poverty. There are at least two general strategies Christians should take. One is immediate: support programs designed to relieve the needs of the aged, the ill, the blind; provide nourishing food for all children (and adults) who need it; supply job-training for adults; replace welfare with a universal family assistance plan. The other strategy is long-range and is the fundamental solution to extreme poverty: revamp the educational system to provide genuinely equal educational opportunities for all children, irrespective of background, so that the promise of the "American Dream" can be more equitably fulfilled.

Christians, of course, must ever be alert to the dangers of materialism—and specifically to the lack of restraint on consumption aspirations, which is actually covetousness. Some of the youth of our day are, on humanistic grounds, warning of the emptiness of ever-expanding affluence; and Christians should certainly echo Jesus' words that a man's life does not consist in the abundance of the things he possesses. Nevertheless, Christians have a clear responsibility to the many persons in our society who are genuinely poor or near-poor. The Scriptural balance between poverty and covetousness is summed up in Prov. 30:8-9: "Give me neither poverty nor riches; feed me with the food that is needful for me, lest I be full and deny thee, and say, 'Who is the Lord?' or lest I be poor, and steal, and profane the name of my God" Toward the attainment of this balance for as many persons as possible Christians should strive.

S. M. Miller, and Pamela Roby, *The Future of Inequality*, New York, Basic Books, 1970; United States Bureau of the Census: *Current Populations Reports*, Series P-60, No. 78; Series P-23, No. 37; Series P-60, No. 37.   JOHN H. SCANZONI

POSITIVISM. See also *Language, Ethical.* Although the roots of positivism extend as far back as ancient Greek philosophy, the term "logical positivism" came to designate a powerful philosophical movement of the latter years of the nineteenth century and first half of the twentieth century. During the span of those years, philosophers, scientists, and mathematicians focused attention on a number of related issues that became hallmarks of their position. Of primary interest were questions about verifiability, metaphysics and theology, ethical judgments, logic, language, mathematics, the unity of science, and the legitimate function of philosophy.

Among discussants of these issues, later known as the "Vienna Circle" (1922), were Moritz Schlick, Otto Neurath, Friedrich Waismann, Herbert Feigl, Phillip Frank, Kurt Gödel, Hans Hahn, and Rudolf Carnap. Strongly influenced by Ludwig Wittgenstein's anti-metaphysical strain in the *Tractatus,* these men were already disposed to reject metaphysics as a logically untenable enterprise. Consequently, the scientific outlook was destined to be tailored to project a modern empiricism that would consist in a fund of knowledge restricted to descriptive analysis of experimental data. To this end philosophers, mathematicians, and scientists were joined in common pursuit, and out of the amalgamation there emerged a methodology designed to unify science and purify it of all metaphysical aspects. The philosopher's contribution to the union was providing a guiding principle that was equally applicable to all the sciences.

In its initial formulation, the verifiability principle ruled that the meaning of a statement is identical with another statement that expresses the method of its verification. Using this criterion as his pruning hook, the positivist peremptorily pruned the tree of knowledge of all its branches except those that were empirical or observational in form. Transcendental metaphysics, transcendental ethics, and epistemological theories about the reality of the external world were alike all severed from the tree and cast upon the pile for burning. Their fate was sealed because it was thought logically impossible to spell out the method of their experimental verification. Expressions such as "God exists," "Murder is wrong," and "The Real is Spirit," the positivist argued, are neither true nor false and thus are wholly devoid of significance.

In his zeal to cut away meaningless verbiage, however, the positivist had wielded his pruning hook all too indiscriminately. Unwittingly, the criterion permitted a given sentence to be empirically meaningful if it were analytic or if it followed from some finite set of logically incompatible observation sentences. The positivist could not accept this conclusion. To rectify the mistake, he divised a modified formulation of the criterion, which allowed for a sentence to be empirically meaningful if it could satisfy two conditions: (1) if and only if it is not analytic and (2) if it follows logically from some finite and logically consistent class of observation sentences. But it soon became apparent that even this reformulation was not enough, for there were other sentences condemned by the criterion that of necessity had to be redeemed as meaningful. "All iron rusts in the presence of damp air," for example, is not analytic, nor can it be conclusively verified by any finite set of observation statements. Accordingly, once more the logical positivist had to make a decision: either he had to concede that this reformulation was inadequate, or he had to conclude that all universal sentences—and consequently the laws of science—are meaningless. He chose to reformulate again, and in Alfred Ayer's mitigated or "weak" rendition, the principle of verification putatively provided the ground for snatching universal sentences from the burning and regrafting them to the tree of knowledge. Now a sentence was to be granted the label "cognitively significant" if and only if it were possible to indicate what observations would lead one to accept the putative statement as true or reject it as false.

As a result of the mitigated criterion, the contemporary empiricist no longer considered it necessary to reckon with metaphysician and theologian, nor with the epistemological or the normative ethical theorist. Their utterances were simply to be ignored as non-sense.

Consequently, in that normative ethics consists of pseudo-concepts, the positivist maintained there is not and can be no way of determining the validity or truth of any normative theory. Problems that had been considered the concern of the ethical theorist now became the burden of the social scientist. Hence, the best that could be hoped for in the field of ethics was articulation of functional codes of ethics relevant to various communities and possibly formulation of some socio-psycho-

logical hypotheses as to why human beings behave as they do. Given the criterion of verifiability, therefore, normative ethics as a discipline was ruled out, leaving only descriptive ethics as a viable course of study.

This parochial criterion was rejected by theological and many non-theological normative ethical theorists, who demonstrated that the positivist's position contained serious flaws. Perhaps the most significant flaw was the failure to distinguish between the logical possibility of sentence-significance and the logical possibility of verification. That is, the logical positivist did not take cognizance of the fact that knowing what a given sentence means is a prior consideration to knowing what observations would verify the statement made by the sentence. He inadvertently had assumed sentence-significance of the sentence in question in advance of the application of his test for meaningfulness. It was a mistake that had its source in the untenable conflation of the *evidence for* and the *meaning of* a given sentence. Thus, in the very act of application, the positivist disregarded his own criterion of meaning by *assuming* rather than *testing* for sentence-significance. Normative ethics, therefore, if it *could* be laid to rest as cognitively meaningless, certainly *was not* laid to rest by logical positivism.

Alfred Jules Ayer, *Language, Truth and Logic*, New York, Dover, 1946; _____, ed., *Logical Positivism*. Glencoe, Ill. Free Press, 1959; Brand Blanshard, *Reason and Analysis*, La Salle, Ill., Open Court, 1962; Rudolf Carnap, *Meaning and Necessity*, Chicago, University of Chicago, 1947; _____, "Testability and Meaning," *Philosophy and Science*, III, 4 (1936), 419-71; F. C. Copleston, *Contemporary Philosophy*, Westminster, Md. Newman, 1956; Herbert Feigl, and May Brodbeck, eds., *Readings in the Philosophy of Science*, New York, Appleton-Century-Crofts, 1953; Herbert Feigl and Wilfrid Sellars, eds., *Readings in Philosophical Analysis*, New York, Appleton-Century-Crofts, 1949; C. E. M. Joad, *A Critique of Logical Positivism*, Chicago, University of Chicago, 1950; Joergen Joergensen, "The Development of Logical Empiricism," *International Encyclopedia of Uni-*

fied Science, II, 9, Chicago, University of Chicago, 1954; Leonard Linsky, ed., Semantics and the Philosophy of Language, Urbana, University of Illinois, 1953; John A. Passmore, "Logical Positivism," Australasian Journal of Psychology and Philosophy, XXI (1943), 65-92; J. O. Urmson, Philosophical Analysis: Its Development Between the Two World Wars, Oxford, Clarendon, 1956.

PETER GENCO

POWER. See also *Force; Sovereignty, Divine.* Power is the strength, might, or ability to bring about intended results. Power takes many forms. We speak, for example, of military power, economic power and political power (i.e., the ability to control or command others). Power and authority (q.v.) are not the same. The New Testament recognizes this in its distinction between *dunamis* (physical or spiritual strength, the general ability to do something—II Cor. 8:3; Eph. 3:16) and *exousia* (lawful power, derived or conferred authority, the right or authorization to do something—Matt. 21:23-27). Authority is lawful or authorized power.

All power must been seen in its relationship to God. All power comes from God and belongs to God (Matt. 6:13; 26:64; John 19:11). God's sovereign power is evident in the creation and sustaining of the world. God delegates measures of his power to man (Gen. 1:26-28; Ps. 8:5-8) and permits man a measure of freedom in the exercise of this God-given power. When man misuses his power, he becomes a slave to the very forces God intended him to control. Governments derive their power not from the use of force or from the will of the people but from the sovereign power of God. "Every organ of power in the nation, whether cultural, political, or economic, is a stewardship under Christ, and can properly function only by obedience to his revealed word. Every abuse of power constitutes a breach of trust, destructive to the abuser and injurious to the glory of God among His creatures" (*Declaration of Faith Concerning Church and Nation*, Presbyterian Church of Canada). Proper governmental powers deal with the protection of human life, liberty and property. When political rulers claim a power other than that assigned by God, they become dictators.

The view that power itself is evil (cf. Jacob Burckhardt, *Force and Freedom*, New York, Meridian, 1955, p. 102) is mistaken. Power is not intrinsically evil (Rom. 13:4). Jesus recognized the legitimacy of political power (John 19:11). Power can be a good or evil depending on whether or not man uses it in conformity to the laws of God. Were the Christian to assert, on the specious grounds that power is intrinsically evil, the total abandonment of political power, he would be helping to create a power vacuum in which evil men would seize power. While it is true that power tends to corrupt (Lord Acton), it is just as true that the refusal to exercise power may, in certain situations, produce corruption.

According to Rom. 13:1-6, political power is made necessary by human sinfulness. The purpose of civil government (q.v.) is to restrain evil so that society can achieve some measure of civil order. If a state is to perform its legitimate tasks (e.g., protection of its citizens, maintenance of order, etc.), the state must have sufficient power to perform these tasks. In a condition of anarchy, there is little likelihood that human impulses to evil could be checked. But if the state is necessary because of human evil, the state is also a necessary evil because those who govern are sinful men. There is always a possibility that power will be abused. This can and has happened not only in the state but in the church, in the home, in every human organization. Montesquieu observed that "Constant experience shows us that every man invested with power is apt to abuse it, and to carry his authority as far as it will go" (*Spirit of the Laws* I, T. Negent, tr., New York, Hafner, 150).

It is necessary therefore that there be restraints and checks on the use of power. Augustine implied this when he taught that peace is always a kind of armistice between contending powers. The American Founding Fathers recognized the dangers implicit in political power and developed a system of government in which power would be dispersed among several agencies of government, each of which would tend to check the others. The most important check on power is law, not a law based on the caprice of the men who happen to be in power, but a law based on the moral law of God. Karl Barth distinguished between the good state that is characterized by *potestas* (power under law, power that follows and serves the law) and the evil state characterized by *potentia* (power that precedes and breaks the law). Power needs the effects of divine grace to temper its destructive impulses.

In Rom. 13, Paul clearly warned against the evils of anarchy. But this passage must not be made to support tyranny. Paul taught that God institutes civil government for the good of man. The man who defies this government, therefore, is also defying God and will suffer God's judgment (Rom. 13:1-2). When a state performs its tasks of defending right and punishing wrong, the good citizen has nothing to fear from the state (Rom. 13:3-4). But Rom. 13 does not oblige the Christian to all the decisions of the state. Man's first duty is to God (Acts 5:29). Where the state creates problems of conscience and obligation to God, resistance (q.v.) is justified. At all other times, the Christian must recognize and accept the responsibilities of his citizenship.

📖 Karl Barth, *Community, State and Church: Three Essays*, Garden City, Doubleday, 1960; Oscar Cullmann, *The State in the New Testament*, London, SCM, 1957; Friedrich Hayek, *The Consititution of Liberty*, Chicago, University of Chicago, 1960; Reinhold Niebuhr, *Moral Man and Immoral Society*, New York, Scribner, 1932; Helmut Thielicke, *Theological Ethics*, Philadelphia, Fortress, 1966; Paul Tillich, *Love, Power and Justice*, New York, Oxford, 1954.   RONALD H. NASH

PRACTICE. See also *Good Works; Pragmatism; Sanctification.* In the Bible God has given a revelation of himself and his will for man. It is the message of what God had done—he has given promises, established covenants, brought salvation to his people, redeemed men in Christ, promised a new heaven and a new earth; and it contains principles which should govern the life of man—the Law of Moses, the message of the ethical teaching of our Lord, the paraenesis of Paul's epistles, etc.

The foundation of Christian ethics is what God has done, i.e., the gospel. Ethical behavior becomes, for the Christian, the expression of the prior fact of his experience of the grace of God in Christ. In the Old Testament, God's choice of Israel is an act of grace and is independent of what Israel does; still, the covenant he establishes brings with it certain obligations. The same is true in the New Testament: God's grace is free and salvation cannot be earned, but salvation brings with it the responsibility to live out in life the faith one professes.

Nowhere in the Bible is this more clearly stated than in the writings of Paul and John. The basic structure of Paul's letters involves a spelling out of the doctrines of the gospel followed by an explication of what this means for believers (e.g., Rom. 1-11 is followed by 12:1ff.; Gal. 1-4, by 5:1ff.; etc.). A corollary of justification by faith is the changed life of the man who is "in Christ." John speaks not only of "believing" the truth but also of "doing" the truth (John 3:21; I John 1:6), and again of a radical restructuring of one's life as a result of faith (I John 1:6-10; 2:3-11; etc.)—thus emphasizing the close connection between faith and practice for the Christian. A faith which does not lead to exemplary behavior is no faith in the Biblical sense of the term.

W. WARD GASQUE

PRAGMATISM. See also *James, William.* Pragmatism is an epistemological theory initiated by William James, through a misunderstanding of Peirce, advanced by F. C. S. Schiller, and most consistently developed under the name of Instrumentalism by John Dewey (q.v.).

James held that the meaning of a concept is determined by the practical consequences of accepting it; and a theory is true if it works successfully to our liking. Because James varies his expressions and may not be entirely consistent, two difficulties emerge.

First, James seems always to consider the problem to be solved as one's personal, individual problem. This tends to make truth subjective. I choose my problem, you choose yours; our theories then may be formally contradictory, but since we each succeed, both theories are true.

James indeed tried to limit choices to what a healthy-minded activist would prefer; he deprecated "morbid minds... Buddhists... who are afraid of life." But this exception is an inconsistency. If belief in nirvana gets the Buddhist what he wants—not what James wants—this belief on pragmatic principles must be as true as any other.

F. C. S. Schiller, followed by John Dewey, avoided the individualism by making truth a social product. Buddhists who disagree with society are insane or sick. No matter how grotesque the formal fallacy of a theory may be, it is true if it advances the interest of an optimistic society. Pessimists are evil. Pessimism cannot be refuted logically, but it is false because it conflicts with social opinion.

Dewey also made society rather than the individual the test of truth; but his more important advance lays bare the second difficulty in James's several statements. "Is it meant," asks Dewey, "that when we take the intellectualistic notion and employ it, it gets value in the way of results, and hence has some value of its own; or is it meant that the intellectual concept itself must be determined in terms of changes effected in the ordering of life's thicket?" (*Essays in Experimental Logic*, Magnolia, Mass., Smith, pp. 312-316).

That the content of a concept consists of certain future actions makes ideas anticipatory plans. A law of science is not a statement of some antecedent condition: it is a plan for getting a desired result. An historical proposition does not signify any event in the past: its meaning is the future consequences in our actions.

That the content of a concept is actions at all is a behavioristic theory of truth. To remove all doubt Dewey says, "Habits formed in the process of exercising biological aptitudes are the sole agents of observation, recollection, foresight and judgment: a mind or consciousness or soul in general which performs these operations is a myth... knowledge... lives in the muscles, not in consciousness" (*Human Nature and Conduct*, New York, Modern Library, 1930, III i; cf. I vi; *Quest for Certainty*, New York, Putnam, pp. 86, 166).

This statement that knowledge lives in the muscles is not complete. Elsewhere Dewey says, "Although the psychological theory involved is a form of behaviorism ... behavior is not viewed as something taking place in the nervous system or under the skin of an organism, but always, directly or indirectly, in obvious overtness or at a distance through a number of intervening links, and interaction with environing conditions" (*The Philosophy of John Dewey*, Schilpp, ed., p. 555). Thus thinking is, literally, the interacting motions of a distant object and one's biceps or Achilles tendon.

Since physical bodies are constantly changing, since also men's problems and plans do so too, it follows that behaviorism disallows all fixed truth. This includes the logical principles of identity, contradiction, and excluded middle. Such principles are generated in action and change with action (*Logic*, New York, Holt, Rinehart & Winston, 1938, pp. 11-12; cf. *Philosophy and Civilization*, Magnolia, Mass., Smith, p. 129). The laws of logic are like civil laws on contract: they change. Accordingly one must be prepared eventually to abandon the law of contradiction (*Logic*, pp. 16-17, 102, 120, 372ff., 391).

In this Pragmatism meets its doom. The law of contradiction (and identity) requires a term to bear a single meaning throughout an argument. But if the term *muscle* in Dewey's argument can also mean soul, mind, and spirit, the conclusion will not be to his liking. He has built up his theory by arguments based on Aristotelian logic. He insists on his conclusions not only because he thinks that his premises are true, but also because his inferences are valid. Soon, however, society will have evolved to a non-aristotelian logic, and the logic Dewey used will be false. But if his logic is false, Pragmatism has no defense.

📖 Brand Blanshard, *The Nature of Thought*, Vol. I, pp. 313-393, London, 1939; Gordon H. Clark, *Dewey*, Nutley, N.J., Presbyterian and Reformed, 1960.   GORDON H. CLARK

PRAYER. See also *Lord's Prayer.* Prayer is the offering up of our desires to God for things agreeable to his will, in the name of Christ, by the help of the Spirit, with confession of our sins, and thankful acknowledgement of his mercies.

The Biblical concept of prayer is based on the nature of God and man. Presupposed is the idea that God is personal, and hence thinks and wills, and that man in the image of God reflects these same abilities. Also presupposed is the sovereign creatorship of God and the dependent creatureliness of man. In the image of God man was made for communion with God. Prayer is, therefore, a natural need, and this accounts for the universality of prayer.

Biblical prayers include praise, adoration, thanksgiving, confession of sins, and petitions. They are both an individual and a corporate expression of the covenant community.

Jesus taught that Christian believers are to approach God as their heavenly Father. He warned against mere formalism in prayer (Matt. 6:5-8), and stressed the spirituality of true prayer, as an expression of one's faith (Mark 11:20-24). We are to pray in his name. We are to persevere in prayer (Luke 18:1-8), and have a forgiving Spirit as we pray (Matt. 18:21-35). We are to be practical and direct in our prayers.

The NT church was a praying body (Acts 1:14; 2:42; 4:31; etc.). Paul teaches that the Holy Spirit helps us in prayer, both by moving us to prayer, and in assisting us in our praying with groanings which we cannot utter (Rom. 8:26f.). He also teaches that Christ continues to intercede for us (Rom. 8:34; cf. Heb. 7:25; John 2:1). Thus Christian prayer is prompted and aided by the Holy Spirit, and presented to the Father by the Son who is our advocate and intercessor before him.   MORTON H. SMITH

PREACHING. See also *Clergy, Ethical Problems of.* The preacher lives in a world torn by forces of immorality and vice which menace the people of God to whom he ministers, and himself the minister. If he is a preacher worth the name, one whom the Scriptures make wise to salvation through faith in Christ Jesus (II Tim. 3:14-17), then he knows how, and has the will to, train up his people in godly living (cf. Titus 2:1—3:8). This means that he warns his people against sins against God and injustices and lovelessness toward fellow men.

But he also conveys the power for good living. That power does not reside merely in advice and prescriptions, but in the good news of the liberating power which God has already brought into the world through the incarnation, life, suffering, death, and resurrection of his Son Jesus Christ.

The preacher will be tempted to make threats of penalty or misfortune the motivation for the good conduct of his people, but he will be careful to return to the power of the gospel. As he attacks wrong, he will not make his denunciations palatable by keeping them from striking his hearers. He will go to God for help to keep from being silent on wrongs which he is afraid to touch because they involve his own support. He will remember his kinship with all Christians and will refrain from attacks on other Christian preachers and groups, or to engage in ill temper which makes the Christian faith a "byword among the heathen."

The preacher will remember that his own person is the first corroboration of his gospel; that he is a witness and not merely a preacher; that he has to practice what he preaches. He will reflect on II Cor. 2-5 not merely for stimulus to his own sincerity and purity, but also for power in Christ to pursue it for the sake of the gospel.

Remembering Amos or Savonarola or Jonathan Edwards, the preacher will wonder if he should not lash out at the evils of his own time all around him. But he will need to remember that his clients are those who hear him—as a pastor, the members of his own congregation and community. A test of this criterion is whether the people to whom he has preached are available to stand by him in the ethical decisions and dilemmas of his ministry. His own congregation, praying for his guidance and ministry, is his first line of defense against the erosion of his character. He has a special endowment, as preacher, of the Holy Spirit; the Spirit functions as he reminds the preacher, and others through him, of what Jesus said and did (John 15:26; 16:13, 14). The Scriptures, and particularly the gospel, bring him not merely content for his messages and counsel, but courage and good character, faith under trial and the will to lead.

Especially gifted fellow Christians, and an occasional pastoral counselor, bring him continuing wisdom for the ethical decisions that he has to make for himself and others.

📖 P. T. Forsyth, *Positive Preaching and the Modern Mind,* London, Independent, 1907; H. H. Farmer, *The Servant of the Word,* New York, Scribner, 1942; John R. W. Stott, *The Preacher's Portrait,* Grand Rapids, Eerdmans 1961; Seward Hiltner, *Ferment in the Ministry,* Nashville, Abingdon, 1969.   OSWALD C. J. HOFFMANN

PREJUDICE. See also *Anti-Semitism; Race Relations; Racism.* Although prejudice as a concept is now usually related to intergroup conflict and animosity—whether racial, national, cultural, or socio-economic—it has profound ramifications. The modern empirico-scientific mood spawned the notion that man is ideally free of all presuppositions. In discussing Christianity as theological science, Barth reflects this demand for freedom from prejudice of any sort. To this, Gordon H. Clark (q.v.) replies that, if prejudice be understood merely as presupposition, neither science nor theology can accept such a restriction (*Karl Barth's Theological Method,* Philadelphia, Presbyterian and Reformed, p. 66), which in the nineteenth century was cherished as widely as another misconception, namely, that scientific laws are absolutely true.

As derived from the Latin *prejudicare,* however, prejudice means prejudgment without sufficient evidence either for or against persons, places, or things. The notion that Jews are sharp-dealing merchants ignores the Gentile propensity for being no less crooked in business. To say that Orientals are deceitful too much exempts Occidentals from similar vulnerabilities. To charge Negroes with inferior intelligence ignores the fact of human solidarity.

Race prejudice is the most common form, due partly to obviously visible differences between persons and groups, and also to philosophical or sociological theories that some races are intrinsically inferior.

But prejudice often extends to those of opposite sex (cf. *Women, Status of*) or to minority or ethnic groups. Prejudice differs from erroneous judgment in its resistance to correction.

Serious as are its consequences for those discriminated against, its consequences for the prejudiced person are even worse in terms of personality damage, intellectual, moral, and spiritual. Prejudice, moreover, provokes counter-prejudice, and prejudiced attitudes generate discriminatory actions based on prejudice. Social stability is then threatened or unlikely in a society that questions the dignity of fellow humans. To promote or protect discrimination by law inevitably weakens the faith of minorities in governmental processes and integrity.

Religion is a ready realm of prejudice, since it reflects the values men consider ultimate. Contemporary Ireland mirrors ongoing Catholic-Protestant rivalries compounded by political factors. In the USA champions of religious pluralism readily discriminate against evangelical Christians whose commitment to a final revelation resists syncretistic reduction, and neo-Protestant use of ecumenical power often disadvantages evangelical interests. Institutionalized Christianity, most conspicuously in the Middle Ages, made loyalty to commitments of the Catholic Church a basis for religious intolerance and discrimination. The modern trend is to nurture religious tolerance on the Syncretistic bias that one faith is as good or bad as another. The NT basis of religious freedom (q.v.) transcends both alternatives.   CARL F. H. HENRY

PRESCRIPTIVISM. See also *Descriptivism.* Underlying prescriptivism is the conviction that morality depends, at least in part, upon conforming to pre-established laws and ideals. To perform one's duty is to obey the moral law or to aspire to an approved ideal. Both are embodiments of the moral wisdom of the past, and each constitutes a kind of formula for moral rightness.

Prescriptivists resist the charge that theirs is a closed or static morality which stifles freedom and renders genuine morality impossible. Instead, they insist that laws and ideals make greater freedom possible by enabling the responsible person to avoid foolish mistakes in ethical judgment.

DELBERT R. GISH

PRIDE. See also *Fall of Man; Satan.* The word "pride" carries negative connotations throughout the Christian tradition and there is widespread, though not unanimous, agreement that pride is the basic sin of man. The serpent appeals to Eve with the words, "You will be like God" (Gen. 3:5); thus sin enters the human situation along with pride. The OT Wisdom Literature frequently focuses on pride as evil. "Pride goes before destruction, and a haughty spirit before a fall" (Prov. 16:18). In the Gospel narratives, the struggle of Jesus with the Pharisees is not the result of their immorality, but rather of the unbelief which accompanies their spiritual pride. Paul sees man's basic problem as his refusal to honor God and give him thanks, which results in worshipping and serving the creature rather than the Creator (Rom. 1:21, 25). Augustine pronounced pride to be the origin of all sin because it is precisely pride which makes repentance and faith impossible. Wherever man's situation in sin and his need for salvation have been viewed radically, pride has been taken to be man's basic problem.

Although the word "pride" carries this essentially theological content in the Christian tradition, there are many positive uses of "pride" by those more concerned about man's manners and morals than about his salvation. Aristotle, for instance, spoke of pride as the crown of the virtues, although it had to be seen as a mean between two extremes: in this case between undue humility and vanity (*Nicomachean Ethics* Bk. IV,

Ch. 3). Or in common usage, "pride" often carries positive connotations: a father says, "I'm proud of you, Son"; a craftsman takes pride in doing a good job. Pride can mean self-respect, dignity, justifiable satisfaction with one's situation in life.

Doubtless the church has at times failed to distinguish between pride as the worship of the creature rather than the Creator, and pride as that self-respect without which no man can serve either God or neighbor. In the confusion, the church has been, sometimes justly, accused of failing to give man his true dignity and humanity. The solution to that problem is not to water down man's radical need for God's grace, but rather to point up the ethical implications of salvation in Christ. When Paul exhorts the congregation at Philippi to act in humility, he bases his plea not on general morality but on Christ who "humbled himself and became obedient unto death" (2:1-11). Because the Christian glories in this Christ, he puts "no confidence in the flesh" (3:1). Knowing him and the power of his resurrection (4:10), the Christian is free to consider whatever in this world is true, honorable, just, pure, lovely, gracious (4:8). The life in Christ is incompatible with pride as self-glorification; but pride as genuine self-respect, or the dignity of true humanity, is impossible apart from life in Christ.

JAMES H. BURTNESS

PRIMITIVE ETHICS. See also *Cultural Relativism.* The word "primitive" in the expression "primitive ethics" is not used in an adjectival sense to describe the nature of an ethical system or to distinguish it from "advanced ethics." Rather, it refers to the nature of the group holding to these ethics. Primitive ethics are the ethics of primitive peoples, and although their values and ethical systems may seem strange and enigmatic to us, they cannot be considered "immoral" or "degraded." The ethics of primitive peoples and the ethics of indus-

trialized peoples are not distinguishable by the degree to which they are "ethical" or "moral." Many of the customs which would appear shocking to us at first glance or objectionable to us in light of Euro-American values, such as infanticide (q.v.), scarring the body, self-torture, cannibalism, and abandoning aged parents at time of survival crises, are "reasonable" and "justifiable" when seen in the context of their value systems and cultural frame of reference. In fact, our own culture has equally "objectionable" practices, such as discrimination, alienation, injustices, etc. Therefore, we are not to judge ethics of primitive peoples as being inferior to the ethics of complex societies.

Primitive ethical systems, like any ethical system, must satisfy certain basic requirements. These requirements relate to (1) the need of the individual, (2) the necessary conditions of group existence, (3) the nature of the environment, and (4) the history or heritage. In relation to (1), the individual requirements of primitive peoples are not significantly different from any other group of people in that certain biological and psychological functions must be satisfied. In relation to (2), there are certain functional prerequisites of group existence—systems for the production and distribution of goods, the replacement of members and the training of new members, systems of common goals and approved means of reaching them. In relation to (3), the techniques which a group utilizes to exploit the environment influence certain central values of the group. For example, the degree to which group effort is necessitated in exploiting the environment (as in walrus hunting, grasshopper drives, or irrigation farming), as opposed to individual effort (as in acorn gathering or crab fishing), influences the degree of group solidarity and communality. In relation to (4), the way the group perceives its history, whether in the historiographic or the mythological past, significantly influences its particular cultural perspective.

Although these principles are true for both primitive and nonprimitive peoples, certain fairly consistent differences arise in the resulting ethical systems. These differences arise not from the primitiveness or nonprimitiveness of the peoples but from such factors as the size of the group, the nature of the organization, their exploitative techniques, their relation to the environment, and their basic cultural orientation. For example, primitive groups, being smaller in size and more personal in their social relationships, built up a cultural solidarity based on a high level of group consensus, the type of solidarity that Emile Durkheim called "mechanical solidarity." Larger social groupings derive their solidarity more from their economic interdependence, "organic solidarity," according to Durkheim. In the smaller group there is greater homogeneity and greater social pressure to conformity. Also, in general, primitive value systems emphasize who people are rather than what they can do, are oriented to group goals more than to individual goals, are less atomized in their social relations, and tend to make fewer distinctions among peoples. Such values as these result largely from the size and nature of the group.

Another frequent characteristic of primitive ethical systems is a pervasive supernaturalism. This appears to be a function of their lack of control of their environment and of the uncertainty and unpredictability of success in their exploitative endeavors. The greater the danger involved in exploiting and the more unpredictable the success, the less will be their feeling of personal control over the contingencies of life. In order to compensate for these human inadequacies, one is forced into a supernatural dependency, or at least a frame of reference in which one can give supernatural explanations for that which is beyond human control (rain, natural catastrophies, death, etc.). Because modern, urban, industrialized man is further removed from a direct dependence on the environment and its uncertainties and because he has greater control over the contingencies of life, he no longer feels the necessity of a supernaturalistic orientation. This shift from a more supernaturalistic perspective to a more naturalistic perspective has occurred in similar fashion both in countries traditionally Judeo-Christian (Western Europe and America) as well as in non-Judeo-Christian nations (Japan).

Many of the characteristics of primitive ethical systems, such as supernaturalism, group-orientation, emphasis on ascription, mechanical solidarity, and emotional involvement, correspond more closely to Biblical ethics than do the ethical systems of modern industrialized nations, despite the fact that America lies in the Judeo-Christian tradition.

Primitive ethical systems are enforced by a wide variety of sanctions. Psychological sanctions have traditionally been classified to be either guilt or shame. Guilt is the personal feeling resulting from disobedience to what one believes are supernatural commandments which are highly internalized. Shame is the feeling resulting from being discovered by the group in behavior which is not in conformity with group expectations. Punishment more often takes the form of ridicule, teasing, being ignored, or even ostracism, than of corporal punishment. Shame cultures are far more numerous than guilt cultures in primitive societies.

In summary, primitive ethical systems are not significantly different from the ethical systems of complex societies with regard to the degree of "morality." Primitive systems share a common function and, to a large extent, a common structure, and they differ primarily with respect to content.

DONALD R. WILSON

PRINCIPLES. See also *Absolutes, Moral; Norms; Rule Ethics.* Principles are those more general precepts, expressions of value, or guides to thinking and action that enter into moral discourse and activity. While rules are concrete and thus direct action in definite ways, principles are more abstract and offer guidelines rather than directives. Several types of principles hold special relevance for ethics.

Logical principles are operative regardless of the content. They assist in unraveling the intellectual considerations involved, and guide us in correct thinking about ethical matters. Logical consistency tells us that if a given course of action is right or obligatory in a certain situation, then it also is the right thing to do when the same situation arises again.

Categorical principles tell us in what kind of actions we should be engaged. These tend to be rather formal. Examples are, "Always act lovingly," or "Always act in such a way that your actions could become a standard of action for all persons."

Definitional principles help us to relate such categorical principles to concrete problems and actions. They help to define the categorical principles, or to identify what type of case is involved in the categorical principles. Sometimes they are referred to as "middle axioms." An example is "Love does not unnecessarily prolong life of a person who is suffering terribly with a terminal illness." If the categorical principle being employed is "What is contrary to nature is wrong," then a definitional principle might say, "Artificially preventing the union of sperm and ovum is contrary to nature and hence wrong."

These principles do not in themselves constitute rules for action. Some ethicists, e.g., Joseph Fletcher, see principles as merely illuminating ethical problems, not guiding action. Others, however, make them the elements or building-blocks of rules, from which rules or concrete directives are constructed.

An entire ethical approach, sometimes referred to as principialism, bases itself upon principles. Many evangelical Christians subscribe to this position. God's revelation to man, as they see it, consists of certain principles having different applications in different situations, not of revealed rules, to be accepted and legalistically applied. In a particular cultural situation the principle might have been expressed in a definite rule or law. But the duty of the Christian is not to follow the rule precisely as therein expressed, but to determine what the underlying principle would dictate in the situation presently under consideration. This makes the principle the objective or absolute factor in Christian morality.

The principial method recognizes the presence of a number of revealed principles. All these must be taken into account, properly appraised, and combined to form rules of action or specific directives. Thus the Biblical command, "You shall not kill," is not to be absolutized as a law in abstraction from other revealed principles. When these are considered it is possible to determine what killing (cf. *Capital Punishment*) is prohibited in the Biblical injunction. The principle underlying this is evidently the value of human life and the importance of preserving it. Other principles are also set forth in Scripture, however, such as justice and the defense of innocent and defenseless persons. When the incidents of the OT are examined, it is seen that the prohibition of killing does not apply to engagement in a just war, or killing in self-defense. These principles carry the authority which they possess, because they accord with the very nature of God.

📖 John C. Bennett, "Principles and the Context," *Storm Over Ethics*, Philadelphia, United Church, 1967; Paul Ramsey, *Deeds and Rules in Christian Ethics*, New York, Scribner, 1967.

MILLARD J. ERICKSON

PRISONERS OF WAR. Twentieth century international agreements on prisoners of war constitute progress in humanitarian concerns deeply rooted in Christian ethics. The Bible resonates with the theme of God's compassion for captives (Ps. 68:6; 69:3; 102:20; 146:7; Isa. 42:7; 49:9; 61:1; Zech. 9:11; Matt. 25:36-40; Luke 4:18; I Peter 3:19). Thus the Christian has concern for prisoners and particularly for prisoners of war, whose capture occurs in their pursuit of duty to their country.

The Hague Convention of 1907 and the Geneva Conventions of 1929 and 1949, informed by Christian ethics, sought to formalize the neutral status of prisoners of war and assure their proper treatment, detention, and repatriation. The Hague Convention provided that to kill or wound an enemy who has surrendered is "especially forbidden" and stated that "after the conclusion of peace the repatriation of prisoners of war shall be carried out as quickly as possible." The current Geneva Convention, building upon the 1907 and 1929 conventions, was drawn up after the International Committee of the Red Cross formulated prisoner of war standards during World War II and the Swiss Federal Council convened a fifty-nine nation diplomatic conference in 1949. By 1970, 123 countries had ratified or acceded to the 1949 Geneva Convention. The six-part, 143 article document applied to "all cases of declared war or any other armed conflict between two or more of the High Contracting Parties even if the state of war is not recognized." It declares prisoners of war to be the responsibility of the detaining power, not the military units that captured them. It authorizes neutral states or other third party organizations such as the Red Cross to oversee the application of the convention to safeguard prisoners' rights.

Part II, Article 13, sets forth its fundamental provision for protection of prisoners of war:

Prisoners of war must at all times be humanely treated. Any unlawful act or omission by the Detaining Power causing death or seriously endangering the health of a prisoner of war in its custody is prohibited, and will be regarded as a serious breach of the present Convention. In particular, no prisoner of war may be subjected to physical mutilation or to medical or scientific experiment of any kind which are not justified by the medical, dental, or hospital treatment of the prisoner concerned and carried out in his interest.

Likewise, prisoners of war must at all times be protected, particularly against acts of violence or intimidation and against insults and public curiosity.

Measures of reprisal against prisoners of war are prohibited.

Among specific provisions pertaining to captivity are the requirements of good food, water, clothing, sanitary conditions, and opportunity for exercise, intellectual and educational pursuits, and religious practices. Prisoners may notify external sources of their capture within one week, may mail out no less than two letters and four cards each month, and may make complaints to authorities without fear of reprisal. Prior to the end of hostilities, seriously wounded or sick prisoners are to be returned to their countries when fit to travel. After cessation of active hostilities, prisoners are to be released and repatriated without delay whether or not an agreement exists between combatant parties. Deaths in captivity are to be reported.

Part VI, Article 130, defines "grave breaches" as:

Willful killing, torture or inhuman treatment, including biological experiments, willfully causing great suffering or personal injury to body or health, compelling a prisoner to serve in the forces of the hostile Power, or willfully depriving a prisoner of war of the rights of fair and regular trial prescribed in this Convention.

Combatant nations have frequently breached the prisoner of war conventions. In World War II non-ratifiers Japan and Russia ignored the 1929 Convention. Germany, a ratifier, did not apply it toward Russian prisoners. Germany and the USA generally observed it toward each other. In the Korean War, non-ratifiers North Korea and their Chinese Communist allies clearly breached both 1929 and 1949 conventions by inhumane and tortuous prisoner "death marches." Over 7,000 Americans were captured but only 4,428 survived.

The Vietnam conflict saw repeated violations by North Vietnam. North Vietnamese argued that the convention was not applicable because war was not declared. They classified Americans shot down under their laws. They refused to provide the Red Cross or other parties official lists of prisoners and drastically restricted prisoners' mail privileges. The USA and South Vietnam with some exceptions faithfully observed the Geneva Convention and allowed the Red Cross and the press to inspect prison camps.

Despite nations' limited compliance, the Geneva Convention remains a strong moral force to lessen the inhumane treatment accorded captured prisoners.

📖 American Enterprise Institute for Public Policy Research, *The Prisoner of War Problem*, Washington, D. C., 1970; Department of Defense, *Commanders Digest*, Washington, D. C., July, 1969; U.S. Congress, House, Subcommittee on National Security Policy and Scientific Developments of the Committee on Foreign Affairs, *Hearings on American Prisoners of War in Vietnam*, 91st Cong., 1st session, 1969.   ROBERT L. CLEATH

PRISON REFORM. See also *Punishment*. Jesus placed concern for the imprisoned on the agenda of Christian duty (Matt. 25:36). John Howard (1726-1790), to whom a monument was later placed in St. Paul's Cathedral, stirred debate in Commons over shocking abuses in English jails, and Elizabeth Fry (1780-1845) rallied public protest against wretched prison conditions. American prisons were conformed to compassionate concern as early as the 1780s when Quakers, carrying soup to Philadelphia prisoners, were so appalled by conditions that they sought facilities more conducive to solitude and meditation.

Evangelicals thus were in the forefront of prison reform. They helped shape the modern protest against widespread reliance on torture and death as punishment for a wide range of offenses, promoted humanity rather than barbarity such as flogging and mutilation in the treatment of offenders, and stirred widespread indignation over filthy, unventilated and crowded places of confinement.

Today the modern "correctional" system is widely conceded to have failed insofar as a reformation of criminals has been its goal. Before the nineteenth century the purpose of imprisonment was considered simply that of meting out punishment, particularly in vindication of God's righteousness and the moral law. Excessive resort to the death penalty in earlier generations encouraged some emphasis on improvement of the prisoner as a purpose of punishment. With the rise of modernist theology, subordinating all divine attributes to love as the core of God's being, the now prevalent notion emerged that punishment has as its decisive purpose the reform of the offender. The result has been not only declining respect for authority and law, but growing sympathy for the criminal element alongside mounting criticism of prison administrators and law enforcement agencies.

USA penitentiaries that opened in the forepart of the nineteenth century considered work performed by inmates a moral exercise, and emphasized punishment for the purpose of making amends and restitution. Unfortunately the exploitation of prison labor was a correlative. The National Prison Association organized in 1870 with a declaration of principles was hailed by penologists as promising a golden era, since work done by prisoners was henceforth to prepare them for a useful future role in society. But the new "reformatories" established in Elmira and elsewhere failed to achieve this goal. In recent years even the "exemplary" California correctional system has been shaken by the 1971 San Quentin riots, while those at Attica, New York, and elsewhere, have attracted public scrutiny to the prisons and jails of America.

Many prisons are today in numerous ways less than humane and in urgent need of change; some social critics even deplore their survival. There are too many differences in facilities to permit universal generalizations, but there can be no doubt that, taken as a whole, the prisons are not only solving problems but also creating them. Failure in their goal of correction is attested by the Attorney General's acknowledgment of a national recidivism rate of 80 percent: four out of five crimes are committed by ex-convicts.

The USA prison population today numbers almost 200,000. About 10 percent of these occupy federal prisons. An average of 8000 Americans daily enter locked cages which afford them less mobility than most animals have in the zoos. As they await trial in jails and serve out judicial sentences in prisons, they are subject to vast psychological pressures that leave many worse than when first isolated. In a single year, Manhattan's overcrowded Tombs reported eleven suicides and more than one hundred additional attempts among fourteen hundred inmates. Poor toilet facilities, roaches, and rats, exposure to sickness and disease are common complaints. Forced homosexualism (reportedly indulged in by an estimated 80 percent of female and 20-50 percent of male prisoners) prompts the question whether the natural connection between humanity and sexuality indicates that married inmates should have some periodic access to their mates. No less distressing is the fact that for many inmates prisons become an educational institution for later more serious crimes. About half of the 97 percent of all prisoners eventually returned to society subsequently commit new crimes.

The merely sociological view of crime has led to its ready rationalization by prisoners as politically and socially inevitable, and justifiable as a social protest "against the system." Criminals increasingly argue that their deeds merely reflect the failure of modern society to provide adequately for all human needs, and thus are vulnerable to revolutionary exploitation. The poor, the black and the young—who predominate— often not only blame the environment for their acts, but also the system of criminal justice for their confinement, since the affluent pursue bail bonds and legal appeals as ready alternatives. What needs correction, we are increasingly told, is not the criminal, but society, and the prison-system is deplored as one manifestation of society's sickness.

A prison system in which this mood flourishes cannot long serve any correctional principle aimed at the stability of society through a reform of criminals. But if the penal institution does not survive in some improved form, society will not long survive its collapse. Clearly the correctional system requires more than minor change. The whole notion of correction must be correlated not simply with the serving of time, but the serving of truth and right, and a new understanding of the purpose of punishment. No need is more conspicuous than that for moral guidane and spiritual care.

While rehabilitation does not lie within the power of the institution, and the offender himself has an indispensable decision to make in any change of purpose, Christian conscience must indict whatever conditions discourage reform and promote wrong, and whatever tends to worsen rather than to better the prisoner. The prisoner has a right to be spared degrading conditions, and no society can hope to profit where they prevail. In the face of today's large, isolated and overcrowded penitentiaries, socially-concerned evangelicals can show themselves a storehouse of understanding and compassion. Future planning can bring many prisoners within range of larger community services, including health, educational and social benefits of some minimal kind, with larger availability to their own families. Half-way houses may well show a better record of useful restoration to society than the present prison programs.

CARL F. H. HENRY

PROBABILIORISM. See also *Rigorism.* A doctrine of Roman Catholic moral philosophy popular among Dominicans and Jesuits during the seventeenth to the nineteenth centuries, its essence is that when one is in doubt about the understanding or application of a law, he must choose the way of strict adherence to the law rather than the way of liberty or inclination, unless opinions held by those who know the facts clearly make the way of liberty more probably right. This view seeks to remedy the laxity of Probabiliorism, which favors liberty in every case on the ground that doubtful laws cannot positively require obedience.   DELBERT R. GISH

PROBABILISM. Roman Catholic ethicists, notably those of the Jesuit order, have espoused the principle *lex dubia non obligat* in cases where allegedly thorough investigation and searching inquiry fail to dispel vestigial uncertainty that a particular command ought to be obeyed or a specific act performed. As explained by Joseph Mausbach, *"Probabilism* taught that as soon as any serious doubt arises regarding the existence of a duty, *a doubt after conscientious reflection, corresponding to the education and circumstances of the person concerned,* there is no obligation" (*Catholic Moral Teaching and Its Antagonists*).

Fathered by a fifteen-century Dominican, Bartholamus de Medina, this principle was later worked out in detail, especially by F. Suarez, and enjoyed widespread acceptance until the middle 1700s. It was then opposed in France by Jean Duvergier de Huranne, Abbe of Saint-Cyprian, Cornelius Jansenius, Bishop of Ypres, and Blaise Pascal whose devastating *Provincial Letters,* (trans. A. J. Krailsheimer, Baltimore, Penguin, 1968) directed in particular against the teaching of Antonio Escobar, exposed the hair-splitting logomachy which sanctions license under the guise of casuistry. For example, an individual may conscientiously follow the less probable of options if he is able to find even one reputable moralist who questions the bindingness of a law: a single somewhat authoritative expression of possible doubt is enough to justify the individual's refusal to obey. The anti-Jesuit sentiment aroused by the charge of chicanery in the name of ethics led eventually to suppression of the Society by Clement XIV in 1773.

No matter how subtly this principle is qualified, adherence to it has a tendency, its critics contend, to undermine morality *in toto.* In any specific situation calling for human decision and action the idiosyncratic circumstances are so complex that a measure of doubt almost invariably lingers, hence on probabilist premises the plainest of duties may be evaded with an unclouded conscience.   VERNON C. GROUNDS

PROCREATION. See also *Children; Contraception; Family; Marriage.* The Genesis account (1:28a) establishes procreation as the first creation mandate. In the context of Scripture, human procreation is always related to the institution of marriage. Although deviations are recorded throughout the OT and NT, monogamy (q.v.) is either stated or implied as the bounds of marriage. Therefore, procreation is moral only within the marital bond.

Furthermore, the highest form of marital relationship is enjoyed when both husband and wife are believers in the living God. Whereas the impulse for sexual intercourse is natural to man, total satisfaction of sexual experience comes only to those who practice godliness (I Cor. 6:19; 7:7).

In the Sermon on the Mount (q.v.) Jesus deals with the marital relationship and emphasizes the sanctity of sex relations: "But I say to you that every one who looks at a woman lustfully has already committed adultery with her in his heart" (Matt. 5:28 RSV). Jesus does not codemn sex desire as such, but he does condemn adulterous desire as well as the act when it follows. The sanctity of marriage is reinforced when Jesus adduces adultery as the only reason for divorce (Matt. 19:9).

In Eph. 5:22-33 Paul deals at length with the nature and obligations of marriage, and emphasizes the sanctity and dignity of the marital relationship. The apostle also stresses the relationship between the married couple and Christ. The awesome analogy between the marital relationship and the "body of Christ," the church, graphically underscores the sanctity of the institution of marriage.

Both the OT and NT emphasize love as playing a major role in the marital relationship. Contrariwise, particularly in the NT there is an emphasis on virginity (q.v.). The Gospel of Matthew relates this to the Kingdom, and in the Gospel of Luke Christians are told to "hate" parents, wives, etc., and there is a reward for "leaving" a wife (Luke 18:29; 20:34-36). In Rev. 14:1-5 it speaks of the 144,000 not being defiled by women and of virginity being possible (I Cor. 7:7). The context of these statements, however, appears to be related to the shortness of time that the Christian has for his earthly pilgrimage (cf. I Cor. 7:32-34), so that virginity ought not be viewed as normative for all believers.

Marriage as an institution is always viewed as good. In Eph. 5:25-33 husbands are required to love their wives, and intercourse is regarded as holy, even though not recorded as linked necessarily with procreation. Although Mark 10 and Matt. 19 declare monogamy as the correct marital relationship, it is noteworthy that the Gen. 1:28 injunction to multiply is not repeated here. Intercourse is a responsibility which husband and wife owe each other, a debt that should be paid (I Cor. 7:3-5).

Although love, happiness, and total fulfillment (which includes sexual intercourse) are aspects of marriage (as recorded in Ephesians) the Roman Catholic Church, due undoubtedly to Gnostic, ascetic, and Stoic influences, reacted by declaring that sexual intercourse in marriage is exclusively for the procreation of children. The rationale often cited for this interpretation is found in the "law of natural order." That is, God the Creator formed within creation a natural process uncontaminated by sin. If man (whose physical organs follow the natural process) is to understand the purpose for intercourse, he should observe the actions of the animal kingdom, wherein creatures engage in intercourse exclusively for the procreation of offspring. Clement of Alexandria wrote that Christian husbands were to use their wives moderately and only for the raising of children (*Stromata*, 3.11.71.4, *Die Grieschischen Christlichen Schriftsteller Der Ersten Jahrhunderte*, 15:228). Origen approved "intercourse with his wife only for the sake of a posterity" (*Third Homily on Genesis Six*, GCS, 29:47; cf. *First Apology of Justin*, XXIX, *The Anti-Nicean Fathers*, Vol. 1, p. 172, for a similar statement). Although there were groups such as the Cathars and many medical people (Arnold Zenanova, 1238-1311, John of Gaddesden, 1280-1336, and Magnino of Milan, ca. 1300) who voiced strong criticism of the theory that intercourse is exclusively for procreation, the tenet has remained a firm moral dogma of the Roman Catholic

Church through the encyclical letter (Humanae Vitae) of Pope Paul VI, delivered July 25, 1968.

The stress on love and total fulfillment, as well as procreation, as voiced by Luther and Calvin gave Protestant thought a more inclusive definition of the character and purpose of sexual intercourse. Protestant churchmen generally have been more open to contraceptives to prevent procreation, while the papal position has consistently disallowed the use of devices or methods of contraception other than what is natural to the body.

📖 John Murray, *Principles of Conduct*, Grand Rapids, Eerdmans, 1957; Salter O. Spitzer and Carlyle L. Saylor, eds., "Views and Position of the Christian Church—An Historical Review," *Birth Control and the Christian*, Wheaton, Tyndale, 1969, pp. 415-464.   LLOYD A. KALLAND

PROFESSIONAL ETHICS. See also *Industrial Espionage; Medical Ethics.* This essay is from the perspective of medical ethics (many parallels exist in other professions). A profession is committed to rationality, learning, and mastery of specific knowledge. To maintain a trustworthy status, professions have codes of ethics and self-discipline. A profession implies a service ideology. A professional relationship must be based on mutual trust.

In an ethically pluralistic profession, a detailed code of ethics presents a problem. When agreement is lacking over the nature, meaning, and purpose of man, discussions abound with phrases such as "honest human judgments" and "educated common sense."

The physician is primarily committed to welfare patients above personal and financial concern; ideally, the profit motive plays little role. Lewis Bird, following C. S. Lewis, notes Tao Principles of Medical Ethics compatible both with the world's major religions and the humanist position: (1) *Primum, Non Nocere*—"First of all, do no harm"; (2) The sanctity of life; (3) The alleviation of suffering; (4) The sanctity of the physician-patient relationship (n.b., confidentiality); (5) The patient's right to truth; (6) The patient's right to die with dignity; (7) The patient's right to informed consent (or dissent).

The Christian physician bases the sanctity of life (q.v.) on man's creation in the image of God. This view generally leads to a conservative position regarding abortion (q.v.) as a method of birth control (q.v.) and population control (q.v.) or euthanasia (q.v.). However, the Christian physician has the same difficulty as other physicians in determining both when life begins and when it ends. When a patient is in irreversible coma ("brain death") but his vital functions continue dependent entirely upon electronic technology, what is the balance between sanctity of life, alleviation of suffering for both patient and family, and the right to die with dignity?

Currently the medical profession in North America is much criticized as a profession not so much with service as the prime goal, as a guild protecting their vested interests. If their professional motives actually predominate, the health needs of our society shall be reassessed. If their guild motives predominate, they become defensive and justify themselves without analyzing the complaints.

The vast majority of physicians try to practice ethically, and work long hours with heavy responsibility. In respect to patient care and medical ethics, physicians tend to think only of relationships with *individual* patients. At this level many important ethical decisions must be made, and the family physician is ethically responsible and does the best he can by his patients.

Most patients speak well of their personal physician, while many citizens criticize the profession as a whole. Why is this? The ethical blind spot, I believe, has been the physicians' professional failure to look beyond their individual practice to the total health system. Society has changed drastically while the health system has lagged. Specialization has resulted in the treatment of diseases instead of persons, and this has added to fragmented care and alienated patients. Scarcity of physicians is compounded by maldistribution. There are more doctors available in wealthy suburbs than in poor, rural areas. The doctor-patient ratio has declined steadily in the inner-city areas of large cities which house many poor, minority, and elderly groups. For these, medical care often is not available, or inaccessible, as entry to the care-system requires cash. Urbanization contributed to the problem. In rural America, each physician looked after his share of the poor. Now geography tends to segregate physicians from the poor.

Public anger is not directed primarily at what physicians do, or their income levels, but concerns those who cannot get adequate medical care. Thus ethical concerns can no longer be narrowly confined to individual patients. Physicians' slowness to respond to consumer needs has resulted in increasing governmental involvement. Unmet needs are political issues, at best as a challenge to be met, at worst as political opportunities.

The distribution of physicians is not only a North American problem but a world problem, as shown by the ratio of doctors per population:

Israel, 1 doctor to 430 population; Canada, 1 doctor to 740; USA, 1 doctor to 750; Ghana, 1 doctor to 16,000; Indonesia, 1 doctor to 40,000; Nepal, 1 doctor to 72,000; Cambodia, 1 doctor to 95,000. One of the most immoral trends in medicine in recent decades has been the steady immigration of physicians from "have not" to "have" countries.

Physicians are confronted with needs and demands for change in health care delivery. The present system is over-run and the citizenry dissatisfied. Health is big business. In 1970, in the USA 70 billion dollars went into the health care industry; 16 billion from the federal government. Thus, the doctor-consumer relationship has already broadened. More money alone is not the answer; medicare and medicaid increased demand without increasing resources. Cost of health care, especially hospital costs, rise faster than the cost of living. If we are concerned with needs, we must cope with the duplications, competition, lack of planning and greed between hospitals that add unnecessarily to cost.

A major ethical goal at present is broadened concern for patients physicians do not see. In turn, this means planning and flexibility. Physicians have the responsibility of providing for the health of all people. The Christian physician should be especially aware of the ever-present danger of personal and corporate selfishness. North American medical achievements are great in biomedical technology, research, and education. Now physicians must concern themselves with sharing the results with equity, efficiency, and respect for human dignity. They may see the need, but resist change in a self-protective fashion, demanding proof that a new approach will work before cooperating, while ignoring vast areas where the present system is not working. Hopefully, they will become involved in creating a medical community that will respond creatively to the needs, even if costly to the profession in personal autonomy, prestige, finances, and "sacred cows." Their model of service is not the present economic or medical system, but is Jesus Christ. He found service costly. What does it say of the physician's professional motivation when it is said that medical care would deteriorate if the method of payment were changed? Many pastors work diligently without a "fee-for-service."

This is not an argument for any particular system. But the present system is dysfunctional and unable to meet all needs.

MERVILLE O. VINCENT

PROFIT. As contrasted with basic remuneration, i.e., wages for the performance of a given operation, profit consists of the excess of income over expenditure, an extra reward for skills employed and property committed to use or risk. Scripture thus speaks of *bêsa'*, literally, *threads cut off* in weaving (Jer. 51:13 RSV; KB, pp. 141-142), to identify *gain* (Ps. 30:9; Mal. 3:14), and also of *yôṭḗr, yiṭrôn, môṭār, what lies over and above* (Eccles. 7:11b; 1:3; Prov. 14:23). But when the AV refers to those "that could not be an help nor profit" (Isa. 30:5), the root *yā'al* means simply *to avail* or *benefit;* they are "of no use" (*Jerusalem Bible*). So too *chrḗsimos*, in II Tim. 2:14 (cf. 4:11) connotes *usefulness; prokóptō*, in Gal. 1:14 *make progress; sumphḗrō*, in Heb. 12:10, *be helpful, expedient; ōpheléō*, in John 6:63, *advantageous; sākan*, in Job 22:2; 34:9, *of service;* and *šāwâ*, in Esth. 3:8, *be appropriate for;* but all are rendered in the AV as "profit."

Scripture assumes the legitimacy both of the idea of "excess"—"The profit, *yiṭrôn*, of the earth is for all" (Eccles. 5:9)—and of its application as a motive for human effort. So while the patriarch Abraham may have refused reward from the king of Sodom (to obviate future dependence upon this corrupt monarch, Gen. 14:23), and while he remained content with remuneration for what his own "young men have eaten" (v. 23a), he insisted that his confederates receive their recognized share of the spoils that had been gained (v. 23b). The Book of Proverbs lays down the principle, "In all labor there is profit, *môṭār*" (14:23), and teaches, "The soul of the diligent shall be made fat" (13:4). When 31:31 praises the virtuous woman and enjoins, "Give her the fruit of her hands," its teaching goes beyond that of basic remuneration: for when she "maketh linen garments and selleth them" (v. 24; cf. v. 16), she perceiveth that her merchandise is not simply "good" (v. 18 AV) but also "profitable" (ASV, RSV); and

her husband "shall have no lack of gain," literally, *spoil* (v. 11). Solomon therefore urged endeavor as a way to prosperity (Eccles. 11:6); and he recognized God as the source of profit, who will reward his own in kind (Prov. 3:9-10).

Yet Proverbs lays a divine restraint upon an irresponsible devotion to the profit motive. It condemns illegal acquisition, whether by deceit (21:6; 20:17), false weights (20:10), shifted landmarks (22:28), oppression (23:10-11), or usury (28:8). Such unjustly gained wealth will not last (13:11; 28:22), and those who seek it will suffer punishment (28:20). The eighth century prophets inveighed against a lust for landed property to the detriment of the common good (Isa. 5:8; Mic. 2:2); in post-exilic days Nehemiah sacrificed to his community the allowance to which he was personally entitled (Neh. 5:14-16); and from patriarchal times onward Abraham's willingness to subordinate private gain in the matter of "Lot's choice" stands as testimony to the rule of generosity over greed (Gen. 13:8-9).   J. BARTON PAYNE

PROGRESS. See also *Eschatology and Ethics; Evolutionary Ethics; Perfectionism; Revolution; Santification; Social Darwinism; Utopianism.* The idea of progress is the belief that human history is moving inevitably in a desirable, upward direction.

Advocates of this view often disagree, however, on the means by which this direction is known and the goal to which it leads. They also differ on whether progress should be measured materially, economically, scientifically, ethically, or otherwise.

Progressivists agree on the continuity of history, the prevalence of change, and the certainty of improvement. They oppose doctrines of primitivism, senescence, entropy, and degeneration. They emphasize growth, optimism, purpose, and the overall increase of happiness.

Every major school of ancient Greek philosophy had doctrines of progress. Modern philosophers of progress were British and German, but chiefly French. Fontanelle, Abbé de Saint Pierre, and Turgot promoted the cause. The giants, however, were Condorcet, Comte, and Spencer. Condorcet wrote the classic *Sketch of a Historical Picture of the Progress of the Mind* in 1793. Comte presented his "positive philosophy" (1830-1854), a vision of science transforming the future. Spencer applied the principle of evolution to society and ethics in his "synthetic philosophy" (1850-1896). In the twentieth century, Teilhard de Chardin continues to link evolution and progress, adding mystical, monistic touches.

A broad spectrum of people have believed in progress. Some viewed progress as a scientific law for interpreting the past and predicting the future. Others saw it as a "trend" or "tendency." It was regarded on the one hand as an act of faith, for romanticists and rationalists, or on the other as scientifically provable fact. Among progressivists, some were secularists who rejected traditional religion entirely (such as Voltaire, Chastellux, Comte), while others retained religion as indispensable for progress (Hegel, Dilthey).

Knowledge, education, effective work, ideals, service are universally considered worth-while and uplifting. To progressivists, this proves that man has higher possibilities which he will realize.

Man has made indisputable advances in such fields as chemistry, electronics, medicine, and space exploration. But in some other crucial areas, he has failed. Wars, wasting of resources, pollution, rising crime rates, declining moral standards—all tend to make claims of general "progress" a mockery.

Christians believe that progress is not automatic. It will never be achieved by humanistic, naturalistic means alone. For individuals or the world, true progress consists of fulfilling God's will, according to his Word and way, by the power of the Holy Spirit.

J. B. Bury, *The Idea of Progress*, New York, Macmillan, 1932; Ludwig Edelstein, *The Idea of Progress in Classical Antiquity*, Baltimore, Johns Hopkins, 1967; Frederick Teggart, *The Idea of Progress*, Berkeley, University of California, 1949; Pierre Teilhard de Chardin (tr., Denny), *The Future of Man*, New York, Harper, 1959.

GEORGE S. CLAGHORN

PROHIBITION. See also *Temperance Movements.* Prohibition refers in general to the act of making something forbidden, usually in a moralistic or legislative way. In Christian morality the most effective prohibition is self-enforced, in line with "self-control" and "self-mastery." Paul illustrates it by the training of an athlete (I Cor. 9:25). The principle involved is that of concentration of all man's capabilities upon the one end of doing God's will, and the renunciation of everything, innocent or harmful, that interferes.

In a sociological sense, prohibition is legislation which prohibits the manufacture, sale, or use of alcoholic beverages. From 1920 until 1933 the USA enforced national prohibition. FRANK B. STANGER

PROHIBITIONS. See also *Commandments; Legalism; Pharisaism; Youth.* Prohibitions are edicts or decrees from a person or an organized society possessing authority forbidding specific acts or relationships. The prohibitions in the Commandments of Scripture are based on Divine authority over all things and should be viewed as the action of a gracious God determining man's life in accord with the Creator's moral purpose.

This raises the issue of the relation of legalism to religion and morality. Whatever misses the inner spirit of law and degenerates into a barren observance of externalities is contrary to New Testament Christianity. But a legal insistence which stresses the ethical manifestations of the moral life can provide valued insights.

FRANK B. STANGER

PROMISCUITY. See also *Sex*. The term literally means to "mix before." In the history of Christian ethics it has been employed to refer to indiscriminate sexual union, usually without any sense of responsibility on the part of the participants. Some interpreters, e.g., Emil Brunner (q.v.) and Helmut Thielicke, have pointed out the damaging effects of promiscuous sexual behavior upon the personalities of those involved.

The basic Christian attitude towards sexuality is one of reverent responsibility. The Christian sees sex as God given and views it as a trust. Thus, choosing that person to whom one is able to offer himself is a matter of extreme importance. The Christian, therefore, realistically recognizes not only the inherent dangers in promiscuous behavior, but also that it is sin against God. The OT account of David's sin involving Uriah's wife, Bathsheba, indicates it was God against whom David had sinned. This vertical dimension in ethics is conspicuously missing from popular expositions of sexual liberation.   WATSON W. MILLS

PROMISE. A promise is a declaration that one will perform a certain act in the future. Though no Hebrew word is expressly so translated, the idea is at the core of Biblical religion. The covenant of God with Israel may be viewed as a type of promise. The patriarchs, especially Abraham, lived by faith in the promises of God (Gen. 12:1-4; 13:15-17; Ps. 105:8-11; *etc.*). Also noteworthy are the promises of God to David (II Sam. 7) and those conveyed to the Israelites by the prophets. The word promise occurs much more frequently in the NT, especially in Hebrews, Galatians, Romans, and Acts. Jesus Christ is viewed as the fulfillment of all God's promises (II Cor. 1:20). Those who receive Christ in faith become heirs to these promises (Eph. 3:6) and receive the Holy Spirit as an earnest (Eph. 1:13-14; I Cor. 1:22). The fulfillment of God's promises are insured by God's faithfulness (Heb. 10:23), especially in Christ (Rom. 15:8) and God's ability to bring to completion what he promises (Isa. 43:12-13; Rom. 4:20-21).

God's promises and faithfulness are the model for the Christian's fidelity to his own promises. Failure to keep a promise reveals either deception in its making or inconstancy, both contrary to the character of God and the spirit of Christ. It may be argued that fidelity to one's word is an essential presupposition of community life. Many, especially Kant, have argued that the keeping of a promise is a duty that must be fulfilled regardless of the consequences. Others, especially some Utilitarians, have argued that promises may be broken when the consequences of performance would be more disastrous. Other exceptions may be made when the conditions were misunderstood, when performance is impossible, or when fulfillment would involve sin or an unlawful act. The more flexible approach must however take account of the consequences of undermining general confidence in the act of making promises.

DONALD W. DAYTON

PROPAGANDA. See also *Censorship; Lying*. Advances in communication theory and mass-media (q.v.) technology have made propaganda an increasingly powerful force in shaping men and nations. The term *propaganda* originally referred to the propagation of information or doctrines. It has come to denote persuasive methods that short-circuit critical processes and deviously manipulate the minds of men to gain a desired response. People are bombarded with propaganda to buy products, support causes, vote for political candidates, and embrace religious dogma. It has become a global weapon of war and is a primary means by which men gain and retain power.

Propaganda constitutes a major ethical problem because it limits a person's freedom of choice by its calculated avoidance of a fair presentation of factors necessary for sound decision-making. Propagandists frequently deal in outright falsehoods, but more often dispense half-truths and utilize special motivating devices that trigger immediate irrational responses. Commonly used propagandistic methods include oversimplification, band-wagon appeals, glittering generalities, identification with cherished symbols, slogans, "straw-men," name-calling, the "plain folks" approach, and "red-herring" issues. Emotional appeals are maximized and logical appeals minimized.

Propaganda must be assessed on the basis of end and means. Propaganda that serves the end of the persuader while detrimental to those persuaded must obviously be condemned. That which rests on a distortion of truth, however good is the end sought, or fails to offer the audience a rational basis for judgment, is also to be deplored.

The propagation of the gospel by Jesus Christ and the Apostles as recorded in the NT contrasts sharply with the sophistries of modern propagandists and exemplifies proper practices of persuasion. Jesus and his followers asserted truth based on the authority of the revealed Word, cited evidence of God's saving acts in history, and called for soul-searching decisions based on careful analysis of vital human needs. Jesus' persuasion was based on messianic prophecies, the demonstrated character of his life, words, and miraculous deeds, and the power of the Spirit to convince men that he was the promised Messiah. Likewise the addresses and letters of Peter, Paul and other apostles called for thorough analysis of truth. They persuaded men on the basis of solid evidence: God's interventions in the history of Israel, the supreme historical revelation of God's love and power in the life, death, and resurrection of Jesus Christ, and the amazing acts of the Holy Spirit in the lives of those called by God into the church.

Some Christian preachers have unfortunately used propagandistic methods that have maximized emotional appeals and minimized rational appeal. Such practices, in the long run, detract from the mission of the church. The church should avoid and oppose the use of propaganda devices, and encourage the people to "prove all things; hold fast that which is true" (I Thess. 5:21).   ROBERT L. CLEATH

PROPERTY. See also *Environmental Pollution; Rights.* A major element in the "abundant life" intended by Christ (John 10:10) lies in mankind's possession and use of property. At creation, God committed the world and its resources to human control (Gen. 1:28-29); and at Sinai, his eighth commandment, "Thou shalt not steal" (Exod. 20:15), provides the basis for property rights. The Decalogue thus establishes the principle of individual ownership, for it condemns as criminal the attempt to take from a man that which is his own. Ultimately, however, all property belongs to God (Lev. 25:23); and beyond the span of each man's life "there is nothing which he may carry away in his hand" (Eccles. 5:15; cf. I Tim. 6:7). Men are temporary stewards, as the Lord in each case designates (I Chron. 29:11, 14). Yet once God has delegated such possession, men are not to alter what he has granted.

Acquisition. Scripture teaches that property may be acquired (1) on the basis of reward. It legislates, "Thou shalt not muzzle the ox when he treadeth out the grain" (Deut. 25:4), indicating reward, even for animals, and more fundamentally for mankind (I Cor. 9:9-11). All forms of fraud are condemned, including the withholding of wages that are due (Lev. 19:13) or unwarranted exactions (cf. *Usury*) (25:36); compare Proverbs 29:24, on theft. The seeming approval of thievery in 6:30 describes it only as a lesser evil than adultery (v. 29; and cf. v. 31). Honor is demanded in the administration of trust funds (Lev. 6:2). The NT insists that gains through dishonesty have no place in the Christian's life (Eph. 4:28; cf. Prov. 11:1, 21:6, or Hos. 12:7; Mic. 6:10-11).

Property may be acquired (2) on a basis of assignment by those already possessing it, for example, through inheritance (Deut. 21:16; Prov. 19:14), though Scripture checks discrimination in bequests (Deut. 21:16). Moses' bestowal of double portions upon the first born (v. 17) appears to be limited to the OT situation, in which an eldest son had responsibility for the care of dependents. Israel's judges were warned not to permit economic need to influence their decisions (Lev. 19:15); for in the distribution of property the standard, "Thou shalt not steal," includes stealing, even by society as a whole.

The Book of Proverbs constitutes a prime Biblical source in support of the private acquisition of property. Wealth is recognized as stemming from God (3:9-10; 10:22; 22:4; cf. Job 1:21). Humanly speaking, substance is to be gained by wisdom (3:16; 24:3), by attention to corrections received (13:18), by the development of insight (14:15), but preeminently by industriousness (10:4; 13:4; 14:23). Proverbs emphasizes pride in labor and satisfaction in a job well done, plus power that results from it (12:24).

Possession. As early as Exod. 22:7-8 the right of a man to the possession of his property, even when someone else was using the goods involved, had been guaranteed; and Proverbs speaks of "precious substance, precious treasure" (12:27; 21:20). Property is valuable: it gains friends (14:20; 19:4) and authority (22:7); it pacifies (21:14), provides protection (10:15; 13:8), and outweighs social position (12:9). Yet at the same time the Book of Proverbs presents restraints: wealth at the price of unrighteousness is worthless (15:16; 16:8), and the possession of moderate amounts of property is viewed as the ideal (30:8-9). "A man's life consisteth not in the abundance of the things which he possesseth" (Luke 12:15).

To OT Israel God assigned the various portions of Canaan, according to families, on a basis of permanent tenure (Lev. 25:23). If a man in his need gave up the property, his relatives were empowered to redeem it back (v. 25); and in any event it reverted to him at the fiftieth-year jubilee (v. 10). This God-given right to the possession of property explains Naboth's refusal to surrender his ancestral inheritance, even at the demand of the king (I Kings 21:3); and his title was recognized by Ahab (v. 4). Such moral awareness contrasts sharply with the more natural (lack of) ethics demonstrated by the attitude of Ahab's Phoenician queen Jezebel toward Naboth's property (v. 7). The reason for the inalienability of Israel's land appears to have been symbolical, a testimony to the ultimate divine ownership (Lev. 23:25). It was also typical, in that its possession by the individual and family owners served as an acted prophecy of the Messianic age (Isa. 61:1-3). While charitable considerations were necessarily involved (for the Israelitish families concerned), the total concept was apparently not the socialistic one of possession upon the basis of need. The experiment of the early Jerusalem church in collective ownership (Acts 2:44-45; 4:34-35) was exceptional, voluntary even then (5:4; cf. 4:36-37), and proved impractical (Acts 24:17; Rom. 15:16). Such phenomena have reappeared sporadically in the history of the church, e.g., in monasticism or in certain utopian communities.

Ephesians 4:28 states that one of the purposes of man's possessions is "that he may have whereof to give to him that hath need." If it were not, in fact, for the possession of wealth and for the right of the

God-fearing individual to dispose of it privately, most evangelical institutions might long since have ceased to function. In present-day unregenerate society, the minority movement of Christianity may expect only to suffer loss from systems of economic collectivism.

Use. Scripture, however, is very clear in not elevating property rights above human rights; the possession, that is, of property finds its rationale under its proper use. Isaiah preached the dealing of one's bread to the hungry (58:7); and Jeremiah sacrificed his own substance for the sale of God's ministry (32:9, 15). The ideal for Israel was that of no poverty whatsoever (Deut. 15:4), and the law depicts a consistent social concern in the use of property (Lev. 19:9-10; Deut. 15:1, 9). The basis for Biblical charity lay in Israel's own deliverance from Egypt (Deut. 15:15); loving distributions to the neighbor (Lev. 19:18) and to all men (Luke 10:29-37; Gal. 6:10) thus reflect one's love for God (Lev. 25:55).

The highest possible use of property is to "honor Yahweh with thine increase" (Prov. 3:9). This includes one's support of public worship through recognized offerings (Mal. 3:10) and contribution to the propogation of the faith (II John 5-8). True faith embraces care for the needy (Prov. 3:27-28; James 2:16), but also the God-directed provision for one's own posterity (Prov. 19:14) and for oneself (Prov. 30:24-25; cf. I Tim. 5:8). Yet society possesses the right to intervene if men's employment of property leads to abuse, especially if the livelihood of others is involved. Nehemiah thus rectified economic oppression in post-exilic Judah (Neh. 5:7-13) and the early church enacted such measures as it could to insure care for its own (I Tim. 5:3-16). So even today's more complex concepts of property, e.g., of corporate or institutional ownership, though going beyond the situations of Bible times, are still guided by Scripture's teachings, both of God-insured possession and regulation to prevent abuse.

J. BARTON PAYNE

PROPHETS. See also *Old Testament Ethics; Moses.* The Biblical prophets were spokesmen for God. As the priest represented the sinful, needy people before God, bringing his sacrifice and offering his prayer, so the prophet represented God before the people. He reminded them of God's goodness in the past, and of their affirmation of loyalty to him, and pointed out the sins of the present, and the demands that a righteous God makes on his people. He asserted that God would meet his people in judgment in the future (cf. Amos 5:18-20), but that beyond the punishment there would be a consummation of history, a Messianic age of peace and righteousness when God's law would reach from Jerusalem to the ends of the earth (cf. Isa. 2).

The prophets affirmed that every Israelite was responsible to God, and that there was a basic law to which all people are responsible. When King David took Bathsheba and ordered the death of her husband Uriah (II Sam. 11) the prophet Nathan appeared to pronounce God's judgment on the king for his crime (II Sam. 12). Among Israel's neighbors the king could do as he pleased, but Israel's monarch was severely limited. The king was subject to the law of the Lord.

The lives of the prophets are sometimes used to convey a message. Hosea remained loyal to his wife, even though she forsook him and followed her lovers (Hos. 3). This act symbolized the continuing love of God for Israel, even after she had forsaken him to follow Baal and the other gods of Canaan. Jonah thought he could void his prophetic commitment by fleeing to Tarshish, but God brought him to the point where he was willing to go to Nineveh and present the claims of Israel's God to an Assyrian city. Jonah served as a lesson to Israel as well as to Nineveh, that God is concerned with the welfare of all peoples, even those normally considered enemies. When the people of Nineveh repented of their sins, their city was spared.

Prophets insisted that loyalty to the Lord must be accompanied by a concern for others. Isaiah said that God was tired of "vain oblations" (1:13). People assumed that bringing sacrifices to the temple was enough to win God's favor, but Isaiah insisted, "Cease to do evil, learn to do good, seek justice, correct oppression, defend the fatherless; plead for the widow" (1:16b, 17).   CHARLES F. PFEIFFER

PROPITIATION. See also *Expiation.* "Propitiation" *(hilasmos)* is used in the NT (I John 2:2; 4:10) to show the results of Christ's sacrificial work of redemption. It signifies that God's justice has been satisfied and his anger assuaged by Christ's atoning work. The idea is anticipated in the OT by the term *kipper* meaning "to cover," but also "to pacify by covering over," or "to propitiate." The AV renders the verb "make atonement," as when the priests are said to "make atonement for your souls" when they made an offering unto the Lord (Exod. 30:10, 15). That the term means "to pacify, to turn anger into friendship" is clearly indicated by its non-theological usage in the OT (Gen. 32:20; Exod. 21:30; Prov. 16:14; cf. Lev. 16:13).

The LXX usually translates *kipper* by *hilaskomai,* and the NT usage of the word points back to this idea of appeasement (I John 2:2; Heb. 2:17). In Rom. 3:25 Paul calls Christ metaphorically the *hilasterion* (Hebrew *kapporeth;* Luther: *Gnadenstuhl*), the mercy seat on which the blood of the sin offering was sprinkled, thus showing that Christ is indeed our propitiation before God.

Theologians, philosophers, and exegetes have objected to the idea of an angry God being propitiated. But the thought that God turns his wrath away from us is eminently Biblical (Ps. 78:38). And the justified pub-

lican knew this as his only hope when he said, "God, be propitiated *(hilastheti)* to me, a sinner" (Luke 18:13). The notion of propitiation (like reconciliation) is repudiated by neo-Protestant theologians who reject the doctrine of God's wrath.

ROBERT PREUS

PROSTITUTION. Most societies, past and present, have accepted prostitution. Acceptance has been based on the tenuous assumption that male sexual needs are very different from those of women, that males need a variety of sexual outlets before marriage, and that after marriage males have greater sexual needs than their wives could reasonably be expected to supply. The ancient Greek and some Eastern religions incorporated prostitution into their religious services. There is also evidence that Augustine and Thomas Aquinas felt that prostitution was a "necessary evil" in society to prevent seductions and rapes. During American colonial times, prostitution flourished much more in the South than in the Puritan North. The last half of the nineteenth and early part of the twentieth century has been called "the golden age of the brothel in the United States." During that Victorian era, women were divided into "good" (wives, mothers, and sisters—those who did *not* enjoy sex) and "bad" (prostitutes—women with whom men could enjoy sex) categories. Many accepted the prevalent "double standard" (men, but not women, need to sow some wild oats). Organized opposition to prostitution did not develop in the USA until World Wars I and II, and then not on moral grounds, but because it was believed to spread venereal diseases which, by infecting young soldiers, impaired the war efforts. Thus, brothels were deemed unpatriotic.

Today prostitution is illegal in all states except in thirteen of Nevada's seventeen counties. These counties contain some forty licensed brothels with an estimated annual gross of $3 to $5 million. After deducting living expenses, the girls average some $300 per week. Throughout the nation, laws regarding prostitution tend to be extremely vague; and penalties, where applied, are quite light. There is evidence that since World War II the number of prostitutes, and their use by men, has not increased and may even have declined slightly. The speculation is that this condition is because men today have greater sexual "access to" and "freedom with" women who are not prostitutes. Kinsey (1953) found that more than two-thirds of his white male sample had experience with prostitutes. the men had coitus with prostitutes no more than once or twice a year, and men with lesser education tended to visit prostitutes more frequently.

Prostitutes today may be divided into two categories: the street or "bar girl," and the "call girl." The latter tends to be more attractive, better educated, and makes more money. The call girl's clientele is usually from the upper-middle or upper class, and her emergence corresponds to the decline of the "old madam type of prostitution" and the sleazy brothel. The call girl is an "individual operator" uncontrolled by any "organization." Some work the middle-class cocktail lounges for "customers," but the most "successful" make all arrangements by phone, as a result of "contacts"—usually previous customers or referrals.

What little evidence exists as to why girls enter prostitution shows that physical force is not a reason. When questioned, these girls (who come mostly from the lower and working classes) admit candidly that the "big money" was the main motivating factor. There is indication that an increasing number of women are turning to prostitution to support an expensive drug habit. The "pimp," or the male who makes contacts for prostitutes, has traditionally lived off her earnings. But he, like the madam, may be in somewhat less demand than

before, owing to the call girl's greater independence.

Prostitution is one of the most severe ways possible to demean woman. Since she is made in the image of God, prostitution is a gross example of dehumanizing exploitation and a far cry from the glad use of sex that God intends. Made in God's image, women are not mere sex objects, but human beings, equal to men in all respects (Gal. 3:28) and not to be toyed with or exploited by them. Christians should be in the forefront of those extending equality of educational, occupational, and economic opportunity to all women, so that none need ever be economically coerced into prostitution. Above all, the Christian should be active in sharing Christ as a Person who demonstrated that he understands the needs of both prostitute and client, and that he can meet and refresh any person who is dissatisfied and disillusioned with exploitative sex.

📖 Robert R. Bell, *Social Deviance*, Homewood, Ill., Dorsey, 1971, pp. 226-247; J. H. Gagnon and W. Simon, eds., *Sexual Deviance*, New York, Harper & Row, 1967, pp. 105-166; A. C. Kinsey, et al, *Sexual Behavior in the Human Male*, Philadelphia, Saunders, 1948; Letha Scanzoni, *Sex and the Single Eye*, Grand Rapids, Zondervan, 1968.

JOHN H. SCANZONI

PROTAGORAS. See *Greek Ethics*.

PROTEST. See also *Demonstration*. Protest is an act or expression of opposition to the policies of some recognized authority. It may be a child's attempt to defy his father, a letter from an irate citizen complaining about dirty streets, the resignation of a bureaucrat who opposes his superior's judgment on a matter of policy, a sermon aimed at evil in high or low places, a petition, a march or public demonstration, or organized resistance. A protest requires a sense of moral order, an acknowledgement of legitimate authority which has somehow been abused—and the will if not the means to correct the abuse. It thus refers ultimately to some normative standard of morality which has been violated. It implies at least a partial acceptance of the legitimacy of this authority, but disagreement with one or more policies or decisions; should the disagreement broaden until the very legitimacy of the authority itself is challenged, then the protest becomes resistance, or—if organized, armed and open—rebellion (q.v.) or revolution (q.v.).

Protests have played a large role in the history of churches and states. One of the best known religious protests was Martin Luther's act of nailing his ninety-five theses to the door of the Castle Church at Wittenberg; eventually his protest developed into full-scale double rebellion, the North German churches declaring their independence of Rome, and the peasants, without Luther's blessing, making open war not just on the Catholic princes but on virtually all agents of established authority. At the turn of the last century Protestant church leaders who protested the humanist drift of the "social gospel" broke with more liberal church bodies to reassert the primacy of "fundamentals" such as the literal interpretation of Scripture. Many Catholic clergy today protest the doctrine of celibacy and are taking marriage vows without the sanction of Rome.

Political history is also full of protest, from the English barons' uprising against King John which resulted in the signing of the Magna Carta to such modern movements as women's suffrage. Protests have been especially characteristic of American history, perhaps because Americans have taken seriously from the start the words of the Declaration of Independence, that all men are created equal and endowed by their Creator with inalienable rights to life, liberty, and the pursuit of happiness. At different times in American history certain groups have felt this promise unfulfilled; accordingly they have risen up in rebellion or revolution, civil disobedience, abolitionist crusades, secession and civil war, and in our own day the civil rights, anti-poverty, peace and ecology movements. Economic, cultural and social history have also been punctuated by protests in the form of strikes and boycotts, book-burnings and avant-garde art, and women's liberation.

The stance of the Christian vis-a-vis protest movements is not an easy subject for generalization. On the one hand the Christian is expected to honor the Scriptural dicta that the powers that be are ordained of God, and that men should render unto Caesar those things which are Caesar's and unto God those that are God's; in this spirit many pastors and lay leaders have sought to dissociate themselves and the church from political dissent or any protest activity that might qualify their Christian witness. On the other hand, Christ taught that the chosen of God were called to be the salt upon the earth, or as leaven in a loaf of bread. This recalls Thoreau's response to Emerson when, upon seeing him in jail for refusing to pay taxes in protest against the Mexican-American War, Emerson asked, "Henry, what are you doing in there?" Thoreau is said to have replied, "Ralph, what are you doing *out* there?"

Some Christians have doubtless been guilty of confusing their own moral standards or political preferences with the divinely-ordained moral order. Yet protest has often been a necessary and effective agent of change, and it can be argued that the Christian bears responsibility for doing what he can to approximate the Kingdom of God.   JOHN B. ANDERSON

PROTESTANT ETHIC. See also *Weber, Max.* This term was popularized by the noted German sociologist Max Weber (d. 1920). Weber's seminal work on the subject was first published in 1904-1905 as two articles in the *Archiv für Sozialwissenschaft und Sozialpolitik* and later translated into English as *The Protestant Ethic and the Spirit of Capitalism* (New York, Scribner,

1930). However even before this translation, Weber's basic thesis had been disseminated to the English-speaking world by
historian R. H. Tawney in his book *Religion
and the Rise of Capitalism,* (Magnolia,
Mass. Peter Smith, 1926). The works of
Weber and Tawney touched off a debate
among scholars over the validity of Weber's
theory which has continued with un-
dimished vigor for nearly half a century.

Weber asserted the significance of religious and ethical ideas in the development of
capitalism. He set forth the thesis that
Calvinism in general and Puritanism in
particular associated moral obligation and a
highly developed sense of Christian calling
with business success, thus providing a
climate which contributed decisively to the
rise of modern capitalism. Tawney, an
English Socialist, accepted Weber's fundamental proposition in somewhat
diminished form. He recognized the existence of a "Protestant ethic" and admitted
its compatibility with the kind of economic
initiative necessary for the growth of
capitalism, while maintaining that no provable direct connection exists between this
ethic and the rise of a modern economy.

The spirited discussion of the Weber
thesis often has been marred by misunder-
standings of Weber's original premises, differing definitions of key terms like capitalism, personal animosities and biases, and a
seeming inability to agree to test the thesis
on a commonly acceptable geographic area
or religious group. In the meantime, many
scholars, journalists and popular writers
have used the term *Protestant ethic* as if its
existence were beyond question and its
meaning beyond misunderstanding. In reality, the term frequently is employed polemically by friends and foes of Protestantism
and capitalism alike to prove what they
want.

Although the exact nature of the impact
of Protestantism on the rise of modern
capitalism remains in dispute, most histori-

ans now accept some kind of connection
between the two movements. Weber's thesis
that Calvinism, especially Puritanism, provided an ethical rationale for the development of modern capitalism seems to have
some basis in historical fact. However, his
argumentation is fraught with many difficulties, not the least of which is his failure
to demonstrate a real link between earlier
Calvinist theology and social theory and the
modern capitalist ethos. On the other hand,
in support of Weber's views are the fact that
the Calvinist doctrine of election could be
interpreted to mean that a successful
businessman was one of the elect, and often
was in the eighteenth century and after; and
the traditional Protestant emphasis on the
virtues of hard work, thrift, honesty, sobriety, self-discipline and doing "all for the
glory of God" (I Cor. 10:31) which tended
to create productive workmen and aggressive businessmen.

Two conclusions seem warranted from
the mass of evidence produced by the Weber
debate: (1) early Protestantism stressed
that a man's Christian commitment should
have a practical effect on his social and
economic behavior, and (2) historically,
Protestants emphasized the dignity of a
man's vocation as a calling of God. In
combination, this produced the so-called
Protestant work-ethic which, from the
eighteenth century onward, was appropriated and secularized by capitalist entrepre-
neurs who found such a doctrine especially
helpful in furthering their own material
welfare, corporate prestige and business
power. Often this misapplication of the
Protestant ethic was simply an attempt to
legitimize the exploitation of workers, the
plundering of natural resources and the
depersonalization of economic life.

Thus it is important not to confuse
capitalism (q.v.) with Christianity or
Protestantism. The Christian faith does not
endorse any economic system and *bourgeois*
ethics are not necessarily Christian ethics.

The Christian is committed to seek economic well-being and social justice for all men. It is more sound, both historically and contemporaneously, to refer to a "Christian ethic" or a "Bible ethic" rather than a "Protestant ethic" since historic Protestantism embraces a Bible ethic while many nominal Protestants today do not. Therefore, the significant difference in ethical outlook is not so much between Protestants and other Christians but between Christians and non-Christians.

To try to make more of the Protestant ethic than this is to be on uncertain historical and ethical grounds, and to attempt to identify the negative aspects of modern capitalism with the widely-circulated WASP myth is not only slanderous but unwarranted by historical investigation.

⌘H. F. R. Catherwood, *The Christian in Industrial Society*, London, Tyndale, 1964; Robert W. Green, ed., *Protestantism and Capitalism*, Boston, Heath, 1959; Carl F. H. Henry, *Aspects of Christian Social Ethics*, Grand Rapids, Eerdmans, 1964; R. H. Tawney, *Religion and the Rise of Capitalism*, New York, Harcourt and Brace, 1926; Max Weber, *The Protestant Ethic and the Spirit of Capitalism*, New York, Scribner, 1958.

ROBERT D. LINDER

PROVIDENCE. Providence is God's supervision of creation. This can be contemplated in terms of Divine preservation, cooperation or concurrence, and government.

1. Preservation is God's uninterrupted regulation of creation by natural laws. From God's perspective, creation and preservation constitute one activity; from man's they are distinguished, although not separated. The constancy of God's will makes possible nature's laws and the natural sciences, whose theories are approximations of divine principles established in the creation. Without God's presence and activity each form would return to chaos and matter to nothingness. Each creature performs a God-given function in dependence on him. God is everywhere present, but differently in a stone than in a man. Jesus points to God's care of creation to convince men of his special love for them (Matt. 6:25-30). Even through nature's regulatory pattern, God calls men to repentance (Acts 14:17). Because it arbitrarily held to a closed universe, deistic philosophy denied the possibility of miracle. God's preservation permits a combining of extant forms. Creation, once perfect, is however now subject to corruption (Rom. 8:20).

2. Cooperation or concurrence asserts God as cause of every action without denying that the creature is also the cause of its own actions. For every action, God is the first cause and the creature is the second. Thus God causes the sun to rise and the sun rises. God also participates in all human decisions without circumventing man's will. He instigates all good (James 1:17). In unbelievers God works external or civil righteousness through the law written in the heart (Rom. 2:14). Rulers are God's instruments for good in the community and state (Rom. 13:4). In believers God originates the good thoughts, the ability to perform them, and the actions (Phil. 2:13). This is accomplished by the Spirit at work in the Word. Divine participation in evil is more problematical. God neither is nor can he be the cause of evil; evil is by definition that which is opposed to God and thus not approved by him. God's atoning work in his Son is directed to victoriously overcoming it. Evil is not absolute, but subject to God. While not forcibly eradicating it, he directs, suppresses and uses it for his ultimate good (Gen. 50:20).

3. Government is God's direction of everything to his goals so that they are always attained. For God all things happen out of necessity, being determined by him. Christians realize that God directs the world for their good (Rom. 8:28). God's predetermined direction of everything is rationally irreconcilable with man's ability to change things. Man is a moral creature and is

responsible for making decisions and suffering their consequences. Still his will is God's instrument for his own purposes. Jesus dies by God's predetermined plan, still his executors are responsible (Acts 4:27f.). Judas is morally responsible for betraying Jesus, still God has ordained his actions (Matt. 26:24). Prayer is based upon the real possibility that the future can be changed (James 5:16). Hezekiah prayed God to lengthen his life (II Kings 20); nevertheless God decides the length of man's life (Job 14:5).

4. Providence is denied by fatalism and casualism. Fatalism, the major tenet of Stoicism, holds that everything is inevitable, including moral decision. This relieves man of ethical responsibility and makes resignation the proper attitude in the face of the inevitable. Manicheanism, Taoism (q.v.), and Mohammedanism are also fatalistic. Contemporary interest in the horoscope reflects a form of fatalism in which the zodiac signs are thought to determine personality and fate. Casualism holds that everything happens by chance. Epicureanism is its classical expression; the world came together by chance, and it continues without direction. This results logically in atheism or agnosticism.

5. Christians believe both that God directs all events for his glory and purposes, and that he holds man personally responsible for his deeds. Christians in their decision consciously align themselves with God's goals revealed in Christ.

📖 P. R. Baelz, *Prayer and Providence*, London, SCM, 1968; Harry Blamires, *The Will and the Way*, London, SPCK, 1962; L. Berkhof, *Systematic Theology*, Grand Rapids, Eerdmans, 1965, pp. 165-178; M. C. D'Arcy, *The Pain of This World and the Providence of God*, London, Longmans, Green, 1952; Reginald Garrigou-Lagrange, *Providence*, London, B. Herder, 1957; William G. Pollard, *Chance and Providence*, New York, Scribner, 1958.

DAVID P. SCAER

PROVOCATION. "To provoke" may in the Biblical usage refer to the calling forth of any action, good or evil, as in II Cor. 9:2 (KJV; RSV renders "stirred up"). "Provocation," however, was usually used in a negative sense (II Kings 23:26; Job 17:2; Ezek. 20:28).

Provocation has both a vertical (man to God) and a horizontal (man to man) dimension. Psalm 95:8 is an example of the former. Here the term refers to the conduct of the Israelites towards God in the wilderness. The Psalmist here recalls the murmurings of the chosen people. Again, in Jer. 44:8 the reader is warned against provocation of God's anger ("wrath" in KJV) through idolatry.

Provocation considered in terms of relationships to one's fellow man (Eph. 6:4) has been a debated aspect of the non-violent approach among civil rights advocates. Is a person responsible when his action, however peaceful and non-violent, "provokes" someone else to act in a manner which is itself violent? Some critics claim that this dimension puts civil disobedience in an entirely different light. Those who reject such reasoning point to the fact that Jesus "provoked" certain violent responses among some of those with whom he disagreed, apparently without violating his conscience.

WATSON E. MILLS

PRUDENCE. Prudence, like providence (q.v.), is etymologically connected with the Latin *providens*, foreseeing. In popular usage, elements of selfish caution and cleverness have influenced the significance of prudence, obscuring the confidence, enterprise, and generosity which rightly belong to it. It is not, as William Blake wrote, a "rich, ugly old maid, courted by incapacity." Rather, it is the first of the "cardinal virtues" of classical tradition and should be desired by all. It is practical wisdom and sagacity in adapting means to ends. Among its components are reasoning, teachableness, memory, ingenuity, foresight, preparation, circumspection, and caution.

If a man's basic principles are wrong, he

cannot be prudent; and what he considers prudence may be cowardice, miserliness, or self-indulgence. If, on the other hand, he lives in service to God, he is still responsible for the practicality of his use of the means to attain his purposes. Both the OT and NT teach that we should use our wits. This is no slight task. Innumerable contingencies can arise that will make it difficult for even the instructed Christian to determine what is prudent. Having prepared for an intended action, taking into account its probable and possible results, and having prayed for wisdom, he is empowered to act in confidence, trusting the prudence of his action to God's providence.

Those who deny the necessity of human prudence on the grounds of God's predestination of events are wrong. John Calvin expresses a generally accepted Christian principle (*Institutes* i. xvii, translated by John Allen, Philadelphia: Presbyterian Board of Christian Education, 1936, Vol. 1, p. 237):

... Solomon easily reconciles the deliberations of men with the providence of God. For as he ridicules the folly of those who presumptuously undertake any [sic.] thing without the Lord, as though they were not subject to his government, so in another place he says, 'A man's heart deviseth his way; but the Lord directeth his steps [Prov. 16:9]; signifying that the eternal decrees of God form no impediment to our providing for ourselves, and disposing all our concerns in subservience to his will.... He who has fixed the limits of our life, has also intrusted us with the care of it; has furnished us with means and supplies for its preservation; has also made us provident of dangers; and, that they may not oppress us unawares, has furnished us with cautions and remedies.

STEPHEN M. REYNOLDS

PSYCHIATRY. See also *Behaviorism;*

Psychology; Phenomenology; Psychoanalysis. The first significant steps toward a scientifically-based psychiatry were taken during the eighteenth century as the Enlightenment swept in experimentation and observation to take the place of deductive speculation and superstition. As other medical sciences became modernized by incorporating the scientific-causal methodology of chemistry and physics, similar efforts were made to explain mental illness by diseased brain cells. Even though evidence was lacking for an organic explanation of some important types of mental disorder, early workers assumed that brain lesions would ultimately be found in all. The science at this stage was "a psychiatry without psychology."

Three names stand out in twentieth century psychiatry, combining the diagnostic categories of Emil Kraepelin, the dynamic concepts of Sigmund Freud, and the longitudinal study of the whole person emphasized by Adolph Meyer. The careers of these three men overlapped closely in time, but they traveled separate ways. Each has left a deep influence upon today's psychiatry.

Kraepelin, a German, after spending years studying the behavioral disorders of hospitalized patients, developed a descriptive psychiatry and a system of classification, much of which is still in use. His emphasis upon careful observation, exact description, and orderly diagnosis was very beneficial.

Freud's contribution was to challenge the organic-descriptive psychiatry of his time and turn it in a psychological direction. After some years in the study of neurology, he turned to personality theory, creating a conceptual system based upon unconscious mental activity. When his topographic system, with its hypothetical personality strata, proved to be too rigid, he replaced it with the structural theory, postulating a psychic apparatus consisting of id, ego, and superego. Freud's elaboration of these concepts has strongly influenced contemporary psychiatry. Even those who disagree with his deterministic premises and his scientism make use of some insights resulting from Freud's observations.

Adolph Meyer, a Swiss physician who emigrated to America, originated psychobiology, an orientation that emphasized man as a whole person, who could be fully understood only in terms of all his life experiences. Meyer accented the importance of examining the entire life-history of the patient. These features of his "common sense psychiatry" became firmly established in American psychiatry.

During the early part of the twentieth century, the descriptive psychiatry of Kraepelin was dominant, often with a blend of Meyerian psychobiology. Freudian psychoanalysis gained its greatest impetus following World War II when increasing numbers of physicians sought psychiatric training in psychoanalytic centers. Psychoanalysis was torn by conflicting ideologies from the beginning, and diversity continued to be the rule in America. Neo-Freudians, especially Horney, Sullivan, and Fromm, emphasized social causes of psychopathology, which had been largely neglected by Freud. Ego psychology soon eclipsed the id-psychology of Freud by recognizing and giving preeminence to the conscious autonomy of the person.

Existential analysis and phenomenology, which were active in Europe for decades, became increasingly influential in American psychiatry in the 1950s and 60s. Existential psychology reacted against applying the cause-effect relationships of physics and chemistry to human personality, rejecting alike the positivism and determinism of psychoanalysis and behavioral psychology.

Phenomenology seeks to understand, rather than explain, and tries to enter into the patient's feeling, perceiving, thinking world, and to examine his experience from within. Existential psychology considers man-in-the-world as a unity. Personality is not static, but is always in the process of becoming. The patient is a person, rather than an object. These concepts, originating within European psychiatry, have found considerable acceptance in America.

The efforts of psychology and psychiatry to divest themselves of philosophy have been recognized as futile, since every system requires the assumption of premises that cannot be proved. Moreover, these disciplines have inevitably found themselves, when they set out to help troubled people, working in the ethical realm, where values cannot be evaded. The psychiatrist has come to recognize that, in seeking to relieve his patient of intrapsychic conflict, he cannot avoid value judgments, for he sets the boundaries of illness and health, determines therapeutic goals and methods, and tacitly ratifies or amends the patient's code of conduct. In a more direct way than in any other medical specialty, the psychiatrist's philosophy of life becomes involved in the therapeutic relationship. Psychiatry remains "a practical art with scientific aspirations."

In recent decades, psychiatry has been accepted into the main stream of American medicine, and, with variable success, has been seeking integration with psychology, sociology, philosophy, and religion. Psychiatry has also become involved in education, law, and social work, as well as in military and governmental affairs. Preventive and community variants of psychiatry represent efforts to identify and neutralize the precursors of mental illness, to treat such disorders in their incipiency, and to improve rehabilitation.

Psychiatry has passed through various stages, from the scrutiny of present and outward behavior, to an emphasis upon past and inward mental process, and, more recently, to an increasing focus upon the whole man and his purpose as a consciously choosing person. While reductive naturalism and humanism continue to inform much of today's psychiatry, these ideologies must compete with the Christian understanding of man and the universe on the basis of explanatory breadth and cogency. To such a competition, the Christian world-view brings coherence and comprehensiveness, both rooted in human history. Christian faith has been found to offer a congenial context for psychiatry, where illness and health are so closely intertwined with the ultimate questions of man's origin and destiny.

🗎 Franz Alexander & S. T. Selesnick, *The History of Psychiatry*, New York, Harper & Row, 1966; Gordon W. Allport, *Pattern and Growth in Personality*, New York, Holt, Rinehart & Winston, 1961, Chaps. 7, 22; Alfred Lief, *The Commonsense Psychiatry of Dr. Adolph Meyer*, New York, McGraw-Hill, 1948, Chaps. 10, 12; Rollo May, et al, (eds.) *Existence*, New York, Basic Books, 1958, Part I.   ORVILLE S. WALTERS

PSYCHOANALYSIS. See also *Freud, Sigmund.* Psychoanalysis is best known as a form of treatment for emotional disorders, but is also a method of psychological investigation, and a theoretical system resulting from the application of that method. As conceived and elaborated by Sigmund Freud, psychoanalysis is a philosophical system as well.

The therapeutic aspect of psychoanalysis was developed after Freud learned that some hysterical symptoms could be resolved by encouraging patients to recall and describe earlier happenings having strong emotional content. When hypnosis proved to be unreliable for evoking such recall, Freud devised the system of free association, in which the patient reports without conscious selection all the thoughts that come into his mind during the treatment hour, no matter how trivial, embarrassing, or painful. The analyst selects from this flow of recollections the material he considers significant, and, over a period of months, constructs a hypothetical pattern of motivation to account for the patient's symptoms. At ap-

propriate points in the therapy, he conveys to the patient his interpretation of the meaning of prior events and their relationship to the emotional disorder. In the course of analysis, the patient is expected to develop a relationship to the therapist known as transference (q.v.), in which the patient treats the analyst as some important person in his earlier life. The analysis includes the resolution of this relationship by the analyst's interpretation.

Free association became a method of disclosing attitudes and motives outside of awareness, which were designated by Freud as unconscious. By the use of the method in the treatment of patients, Freud gradually created a psychological system based upon the assumption that the little-known unconscious stratum of mental life is more important than the conscious. He assumed that disagreeable or unacceptable ideas and memories are removed from awareness by a process of selective forgetting called repression. The difficulty of recalling such repressed material was called resistance. The entire system of psychology rests upon the basic postulates of unconscious, repression and resistance.

Freud's first system was designated as the topographic theory. Mental life was thought of as stratified into conscious and unconscious, with an intermediate preconscious. This model was later superseded by the structural theory, in which the psychic apparatus was assumed to consist of three hypothetical elements: id (q.v.), ego (q.v.), and superego (q.v.).

Freud taught that the id represented the inner world of subjective experience, apart from direct knowledge of external reality. He believed that the id is a reservoir of instinctual psychic energy that drives personality. Unconscious processes are amoral and are regulated by seeking of pleasure or the avoidance of pain. The ego comes into existence under the influence of the objective world and serves as intermediary between the id and external reality. Its power, according to Freud, is derived from the id, but its function is to integrate the conflicting demands of id, superego, and reality. The superego is the moral component of personality, and guides conduct along the lines of right and wrong that have been incorporated from the parents. Other theoretical concepts essential to classical analysis are infantile sexuality and the universal oedipus complex.

Many deviants from orthodox psychoanalysis continued to use the name. Among those leaving Freud's intimate circle to establish systems of their own were Adler, Rank, and Jung (q.v.). Adler assumed that man is motivated primarily by social urges, and minimized the sexual instinct. Rank assigned a primary role to the birth trauma, and emphasized the will as an integrating element. Jung's primary emphasis was upon the collective unconscious and its structural elements, the archetypes, believed to be inherited from man's past.

In America, a neo-Freudian psychoanalytic movement developed, based upon a belief in the influence of culture as a dominant factor in the formation of personality. Horney, Sullivan, and Fromm are included in this group, all three emphasizing the role of social factors in producing distortions of personality. Most neo-Freudian theories have humanist or naturalist presuppositions.

After Freud's death, a movement developed within psychoanalysis known as ego-psychology, that dropped the earlier emphases upon instinctual drives and emphasized, instead, the autonomous character of the ego. In departing from the determinism that characterized classical psychoanalysis, ego psychology converges upon a view of human autonomy and responsibility that has always been central in the Christian doctrine of man. This has resulted in a wholesome turn toward conscious functions and healthy personalities, in contrast with the early focus of psychoanalysis upon psychopathology, which led Freud to formulate universals from the distorted personalities that he treated in his consulting room. Freud's view of religion as a collective neurosis became associated with psychoanalysis and is still held by many analysts.

Freud assumed that the laws governing physical processes are applicable to human personality. The resulting system of psychology is basically materialistic and deterministic, with no place for human freedom. If the motive power of personality derives from a pleasure-seeking id, a subjectivist, hedonistic ethic follows.

Freud claimed from the beginning that his system was a legitimate segment of science and that he had no concern with philosophy. The *Weltanschauung* of psychoanalysis, he declared, is identical with that of science itself. While it is true that Freud has deeply influenced contemporary psychology, the Freudian scientism is implied in every psychoanalytic observation. Psychoanalysis has never succeeded in winning acceptance as a scientific discipline.

Sigmund Freud, "Two Encyclopedia Articles," *Collected Papers*, London, Hogarth, 1957, Vol. V, pp. 107-130; *An Outline of Psychoanalysis*, New York, Norton, 1949; *New Introductory Lectures on Psychoanalysis*, London, Hogarth, 1933, Lecture XXXV.   ORVILLE S. WALTERS

PSYCHOLOGY. See also *Behaviorism; Humanism; Psychoanalysis.* Psychology is the study of the mind, or, more correctly, the behavior of the individual. Its domain includes how man thinks and learns, how he reacts or behaves, how he feels and expresses those feelings; in short, what he does and how he does it.

While man always has been concerned with his behavior and the behavior of his fellow human beings, psychology is generally considered as having become a separate field with the establishment of the first psychological laboratory by Wilhelm Wundt in Leipzig, Germany in 1879. The concern of these early psychologists, who were called Structuralists, was conscious experience, which they studied by introspection. By the turn of the century, two more schools had emerged. First was the peculiarly American school, pioneered by William James (q.v.) and John Dewey (q.v.), called Functionalism, which focused upon man as a reacting person, and how he adjusts and functions in society. The other was Psychoanalysis, developed by the Viennese physician Sigmund Freud (q.v.), which viewed man's behavior as largely the result of unconscious factors. Freud saw man's personality as composed of three parts; a superego (q.v.), roughly equivalent to the conscience; an id (q.v.), repository for sexual and agressive instincts and drives; and an ego (q.v.) the referee between the superego and id.

By 1915 two other major schools appeared on the horizon; the school of Behaviorism, a distinctly American school, and Gestaltism, which began with German-born psychologists, notably Max Wertheimer, Kurt Koffka and Wolfgang Köhler, who came to America as a result of the perilous times immediately preceding World War I. Behaviorism, led by J. B. Watson and E. L. Thorndike, and aided by the discoveries of Russian Physiologist Ivan Pavlov, provided a "scientific," deterministic and atomistic viewpoint of man. They viewed man as composed of an infinite number of Stimulus-Response bonds. His behavior was therefore predictable in the sense that if the Behaviorist (observer) knows the stimulus situation he can anticipate the person's response. The totality of man, then, is reduced to the sum of the parts (Stimulus-Response bonds).

Gestalt psychology came into being for the express purpose of refuting the claims of the Behaviorists. Gestaltists maintained that we must know the total situation or set of circumstances and see life in its totality if we are to have a true conception of human behavior. They viewed man as a Gestalt—as a whole integrated being, functioning as a totality, acting as he does because of all of the varied experiences of life impinging on him. The five major schools named have wielded a notable influence in the new emerging science of psychology. Largely because of Functionalism, the fields of Clinical Psychology, Counseling Psychology, Abnormal Psychology, Tests and Measurements and Educational Psychology have developed into significant subfields in Psychology.

The field of Learning Theory constitutes an important branch of psychology. To explain fully what happens during learning two distinct theories of learning have been proposed: associationist and field theories. Thorndike was the prime theoretician behind associationism. Experimentally based, rooted in animal learning, associationism built upon familiar behavioristic tenets, most notably trial-and-error learning and the law of effect. This law states that we tend to remember pleasant experiences and forget the unpleasant. This law led to the principles of reinforcement, that is, that we repeat responses that are positively reinforced when we are placed in the same (or similar) stimulus situation.

Modern field theory challenged the foundations of associationist theory. Stimulus-Organization-Response is a much more viable option, they said, than simply Stimulus-Response. Specifically, learning, functioning and behaving are comprehended much more fully when adequate place is given to the internal conditions and organizing processes which are assumed, even though at times it is difficult and even impossible to observe them. Hence, human experiences are much more than simply the sum of the separate elements of these experiences.

The term "field" is derived from physics, where it has been substantiated that gravitational and electrostatic forces surrounding an object help determine its physical properties. Therefore, field theorists contended, we must go beyond the behaviorists' objective, physical world into the perceived, phenomenal world, which is truly the world to which the individual reacts. Field theorists interpret learning as the organization (or reorganization) of one's perceptual and conceptual patterns, and place stress upon the role of cognitive processes in learning.

The two major forces in American psychology today, however, are Behaviorism, with its view of man as amoral, neither good nor evil, but simply the product of his environment and past experiences, and Psychoanalysis, which views man pessimistically, as caught between the forces of past moral teachings (superego) and inner drives and tensions pressing for expression (id). In such a predicament he is likely, on the one hand, to inhibit his desires and drives which may well lead to unhappiness and/or neuroticism. On the other hand, he may violate his conscience and engage in irresponsible self-expressive acts which can result in social disapproval, legal entanglements, loss of self-respect, neuroticism, and even psychoticism.

Some psychologists who followed Freud, called neo-Freudians, such as Otto Rank, Erich Fromm and Karen Horney have been more optimistic than Freud in their viewing of the ego, maintaining that individuals can overcome inhibiting and potentially destructive elements connected with the id and superego through strengthening the ego or basic personality, and thus become fulfilled persons.

A third force in contemporary American psychology, Humanism, represented by such thinkers as Carl Rogers, A. H. Maslow and Sidney Jourard, has built upon some of the ideas of the neo-Freudians. They have maintained that man may develop toward his fullest potential, moving away from his hangups and facades through openness, peak experiences and the ability to relate lovingly, more fully and more appropriately to oneself, others and nature (or God).

A Christian perspective is not readily apparent as we view the three above-mentioned positions. The rigid determinism and utter hopelessness of Freudian psychoanalysis stands in stark contrast to the message of deliverance from our inherently sinful condition through Christ, so that we become new creatures, old things passing away and all things becoming new (II Cor. 5:17). Neither is the Christian position reconcilable with Behaviorism, which accords man neither a spirit nor a mind. Humanism is at least a step closer than the others to Christianity with its emphasis upon love, proper relationships and movement toward personal fulfillment. The Christian will insist, however, that a proper relationship to ourselves and with our fellow men is possible only as we are in proper relationship to God through Christ, and that agapé love and personal fulfillment become the by-products of that relationship.

HAROLD W. DARLING

PUBLIC OPINION. Public opinion refers to the expressed or unexpressed views of the citizenry that influence their behavior in a socially significant way. The advent of modern political democracy (q.v.) has given public opinion an importance not accorded it under autocratic governments. The efficient functioning of a democracy requires leaders to take cognizance of it and responsibly try to mold it—so that their policies will be supported by the people.

Public opinion is difficult to assess, and at best a generalization with inherent limitations. A pluralistic society contains many publics; attitudes and convictions are not always openly expressed on a broad scale; and opinion is subject to rapid change.

Findings of public opinion surveys such as the polls of George Gallup, Elmo Roper, and Lon Harris have become accepted barometers of public sentiment on candidates and issues. The accuracy of their findings is dependent on the nature of their population sample and methods of collecting data. The many uncontrolled elements in such polling—the interviewer-interviewee relationship, the possible bias in questionnaires, the frequent disparity between expressed opinion and behavior, the changes that occur in one's psychological set and attitude, and statistical errors—make them less than scientific and require a degree of skepticism about their conclusions. But regardless of their inherent limitations, people treat them as factual so that they in turn become instruments that influence public opinion. Political candidates eagerly cite polls favorable to them because many uninformed or uncommitted people gravitate toward what they believe to be majority opinion. Since polling results tend to influence public opinion, it is ethically questionable whether they should be published shortly before an election. Voters would do well to judge candidates and issues on their merits and not by opinion surveys, which at best are probable generalizations and at worst contrived propaganda.

Public opinion is also often judged by the visibility given certain viewpoints through the mass media. But the widely disseminated views of television reporters, commentators, and documentaries, newspaper and magazine editors and columnists, and organized, vocal pressure groups do not necessarily reflect majority opinion. They do, however, shape public opinion. If biased minority opinion is effectively presented often enough through the mass media, it will not take long for it to become majority opinion. The power of mass media to propagandize must not be underestimated. Every effort must be made to insure fair opportunity for all viewpoints to be communicated through the mass media, particularly on television, which is probably the most influential medium and affords limited opportunity for exposure of views, compared with the press.

Leaders in a democracy must consider public opinion carefully but in the final analysis make their judgments on the basis of informed, reflective thought anchored in moral considerations. Effective leaders cannot run too far ahead of public opinion, but they ought not forsake principle and defer to it for the sake of expediency. To do so is inevitably to do harm to the public they serve. The Apostle Paul was well aware that public opinion is fickle and can be desperately wrong when it is favorable (Acts 28:6) no less than when it is unfavorable (28:4).   ROBERT L. CLEATH

PUBLIC OWNERSHIP. See *Socialism.*

PUNISHMENT. See also *Capital Punishment; Corporal Punishment; Prison Reform; Retribution.* According to the Scriptures no human action ever stands isolated from consequences. Sinful conduct always results in some form of punishment. This principle is established in the *lex talionis* of the OT (Exod. 21:23-25) where harmful actions are to be punished "life for life, eye for eye, tooth for tooth, hand for hand...." Paul confirms this foundational truth, "Do not be deceived; God is not mocked, for whatever a man sows that he will also reap. For he who sows to his own flesh will from the flesh reap corruption; but he who sows to the Spirit will from the Spirit reap eternal life" (Gal. 6:7-8).

The principle is not intended to be vindictive or a basis for cruel or unusual punishment, but to supply a foundation of ethical responsibility that gives moral significance to the actions of man. The verb *paqad,* primarily translated "to punish" has the root meaning, "to visit." Thus punishment is not vindictive but reflects God's visiting his people in regard to their conduct. The intent is to remove the resort to vengeance and to assure that justice will be available and applicable to all. It is also intended to curb man's destructive and depraved nature so that men may live in safety and security.

This process of rewards and punishment is seen by some to reflect a development in the process of revelation. The early statements of punishment (e.g., Cain, Gen. 4:13 and the Law) primarily inflict an eventual punishment in kind as the consequence of wicked action. This is illustrated further in God's judgments upon Israel for her unfaithfulness (Jer. 19–23), consisting of physical destruction and captivity. Later the prophets attach eschatological significance to Israel's conduct. "And many of those who sleep in the dust of the earth shall awake, some to everlasting life and some to shame and everlasting contempt" (Dan. 12:2).

Jesus more fully elaborated the eschatological as well as temporal significance of conduct and punishment. He recognized that temporal punishment was accorded to Sodom because of its sin, but added that because of unbelief Capernaum would be liable for far greater punishment in the judgment than was meted out to that earlier wicked city (Matt. 11:23ff.).

The concept of punishment was brought into sharp focus through Jesus' moral indignation against the Pharisees (Matt. 23:13 ff.). Jesus' teaching included much about eternal punishment and hell (Matt. 5:22; 8:12; 13:41ff.; 25:31ff.; Mark 9:43-48; Luke 16:22-24).

The principle of reward and punishment is reiterated in the NT Epistles by James (2:14), Paul (Rom. 2:5; I Cor. 3:8, 13-15; II Cor. 5:10; Col. 3:23-25) and John (Rev. 5–6; 8–9; 10:7-15).

Throughout church history the large part of orthodox Christianity accepted the Scriptural teaching on punishment. Exceptions were few before the rise of rationalism in the later centuries. One exception was Origen, who held that punishment was temporal and purifying, and largely a matter of conscience.

Contemporary rejection of the concept of punishment takes three forms. The first is the normal argument that punishment, and particularly eternal punishment, contradicts the nature of a loving and forgiving God. This view regards punishment as vindictive, an outburst of anger unbecoming to God. A second objection is voiced by educators who hold that positive reinforcement is more effective than punishment in teaching and controlling behavior. This philosophy, is set forth in B. F. Skinner's *Walden Two* (New York, Macmillan, 1969); in that idyllic community there are no punishments. A third objection to punishment comes from psychology, and finds its primary proponent in Freud, who taught that the trauma that results from punishment has long-lasting effects throughout the life of the individual thus negating any temporary benefits.

The Biblical understanding of punishment is predicated on a higher view of both man and God than these criticisms accept. Scripture teaches that man, created in the image of God, has a responsibility that exceeds all else in creation. His actions then take on significance for both time and eternity. The Biblical view expounds punishment neither as vindictiveness nor that out of which God gets pleasure. In God's design all human actions are significant. God respects the principle of punishment in the provision of redemption by taking upon himself man's punishment so that he might forgive.

The concept of punishment permeates the Scriptures. Few concepts are more consistently taught than that of the law of harvest: "Whatever a man sows that also shall he reap" (Gal. 6:7).   H. PHILLIP HOOK

PURITAN ETHICS. "Puritan" was a nickname applied after 1564 to non-separating Calvinists who desired more reformation of worship, discipline, and government, and more support for preachers, than the Elizabethan settlement of English religion provided. Spurred by memories and reports of church life in Geneva and Zurich, plus a radical Biblicism going back through Tyndale to the Lollards, the Elizabethan Puritans pursued a threefold quest: first to purge Anglican worship of residual Popery, second to replace episcopacy by presbyterianism, and third to lead Englishmen into vital godliness so that England's calling to serve God might be fulfilled. Following their crescendo of opposition to Laud's Arminianism and Charles I's absolutism, Puritans gained brief political power under the Long Parliament and Commonwealth, but lost it again, and with it through ejection and persecution much religious influence too, after the Restoration in 1660. Under Cromwell congregationalism (a polity already established in Puritan New England, and embraced by most Baptists as well as some paedobaptists in old England) gained respectability alongside presbyterianism in Puritan circles.

Puritan theological leaders (Perkins, Sibbes, Ames, Owen, Goodwin, Baxter, Howe, etc.) were mostly learned Calvinists, supralapsarian, infralapsarian, or Amyraldean. Being also gifted preachers and pastors, in demand for their counselling skill as "spiritual physicians," "comforting afflicted consciences," they were in addition deeply versed in what they called "practical theology," the study of the theory and practice of devotion and the problems of Christian behavior. This interest was shared by non-Puritan Anglicans and Roman Catholics, though Puritan practical teaching, being based on the axioms of justification by faith only and salvation by grace only, through a converting regeneration, has often a different cast and flavor from the moralism of the former and the legalism of the latter. The comprehensive works of William Perkins

(*The Whole Treatise of the Cases of Conscience,* 1606), his pupil William Ames (*Of Conscience with the Power and Cases thereof,* Latin 1630, E.T. 1643), and Richard Baxter (*A Christian Directory,* 1673), together with the exposition of the moral law from the ten commandments in the Westminster Larger Catechism (questions 91-152), summarize most of the Puritan lore in this field.

Puritan ethics assumed the Reformed confession of the sovereignty and majesty of God as the source, lord, and end of all things, and of the natural man's radical perversity as a rebel who will not glorify his maker. To the doctrines and perspectives of classical Calvinism the Puritans added an interest in inward experiential communion with God which, like some aspects of Puritan biblicism, seems to have mediaeval roots. The divines focused this interest in detailed studies of the work of the Holy Spirit in the believer (see especially John Owen, *Works* III, IV, London, Banner of Truth, 1966-7). Puritan teaching has been described as a theology of regeneration, whose central theme is walking with God. That in all "duties" Christians must by meditation, prayer and self-scrutiny "keep up communion with God" is a recurring Puritan refrain.

Keynotes of Puritan ethics include:
Pilgrimage and conflict. Bunyan's allegories, *Pilgrim's Progress* and *The Holy War,* focus vividly the view of life which possessed Puritans' minds and fired their imaginations. Christians must travel through this treacherous and distracting life with hearts in, and eyes on, heaven, not permitting desire to center on things below. By watchfulness and prayer they must contend daily against the world, the flesh and the devil, enemies which once enslaved them, but from which Christ has now freed them. Ordered self-discipline, based on knowledge of God's law and promise, are essential for the warrior-pilgrim's well-being.

Work in one's calling. God is glorified and sin kept at bay by hard work, and everyone needs a lawful calling. Money, time and talents must be used for God; idleness shows a bad heart. Thrift, capitalism, and philanthropy were encouraged.

Education and culture. Puritans fostered education everywhere. They were not, as some suppose, Manicheans, but cultured men who embraced science and the arts as field of enjoyment and responsibility (though moral and mystical concerns evidently inhibited their artistic energy). They only opposed art which was debased and debasing (e.g., commercial theater and "pulp" literature). In art and life they held that sincerity requires simplicity.

Sabbath and family. Treating God's law in both Testaments as one, they viewed the Lord's Day as the Christian sabbath and the family as a patriarchal clan, a miniature church and commonwealth under Father. Yet they expounded these OT-inspired emphases in a humane NT spirit. Puritan Sunday observance and domesticity have been long-lived elements in their legacy to the English-speaking world.

📖 M. M. Knappen, *Tudor Puritanism*, Magnolia, Mass., Smith, 1963; W. Haller, *The Rise of Puritanism*, Magnolia, Mass., Smith; G. S. Wakefield, *Puritan Devotion;* C. H. and K. George, *The Protestant Mind of the English Reformation*, Princeton, Princeton University, 1961; P. A. Scholes, *The Puritans and Music*, New York, Russell, 1962; H. G. Wood in *HERE*; T. Wood, *English Casuistical Divinity in the Seventeen Century,*   JAMES I. PACKER

PURITY. See also *Holiness.* As a term in personal ethics the mandate of purity has a long history. Undoubtedly in both non-Biblical religions and Biblical faith its original connotation was ceremonial and cultic. Purifications by ritual acts of washing and abstinence from food and sexual activity became part of the worshipper's preparation for taking part in the cult. See Exod. 19:10-15; 30:17-21 for obvious examples.

The work of the writing prophets in the eighth and seventh centuries B.C. was to direct the nation's religious attention, under God, to the inner aspects of purity. They did this by denouncing the emptiness of ritual forms by themselves, and (more importantly) by insisting that God requires a holy life of moral righteousness expressed in sincere worship and whole-hearted obedience to his law, both personally and socially (Amos. 5:21-24; Mic. 6:6-8; Isa. 1:11-20).

The same concentration on the inwardness of moral purity is carried over into the NT. The church was born in a Jewish culture of ritual observance, seen in dietary laws, ceremonial washings and the practice of strict "separation" from contact with the defiling Gentiles. Jesus opposed this preoccupation with the outward at the expense of the inner disposition of personal sanctity (Mark 7:1-13) and taught his followers that a "good heart" (i.e., an inner life, rightly related to God) is all-important, just as a sound tree will yield only healthy fruit (Matt. 7:16-20).

Paul, in his struggle for Gentile freedom from Jewish legalism, sets this teaching in perspective for the universalistic Christianity which followed the Gentile mission. Jewish ritual "purity" gave way to an insistence on personal ethical seriousness which was shown in the way he taught his Gentile converts to avoid sexual misbehavior (I Cor. 6:9-20; I Thess. 4:1-8), to practice fair dealing and honesty in business ethics (II Cor. 8:21; I Thess. 4:6 RSV marg.) and especially to cultivate the fruit of the Spirit (Gal. 5:22, 23) by refraining from vices (Gal. 5:19-21). "Keep yourself pure" (I Tim. 5:22) is his counsel to all his converts. This was revolutionary teaching in a world of accepted immorality and social vice. "He set up, for the first time ... a standard of personal purity, and proclaimed that it was to this that God had called men" (C. A. A. Scott, *New Testament Ethics,* Cambridge, 1948, p. 118). RALPH P. MARTIN

Q

QUAKER. Though Quakerism has been primarily a religious system, it has always had strong ethical influence. What has been especially effective in its effect upon general culture has been the rare combinations of inner piety and outer social action. The most significant exemplar of this combination is John Woolman (1720-1772). Woolman was a simple-hearted New Jersey tailor who, as a part of his profound religious experience, became convinced of the evil of slavery. Woolman's recognition of the wrongness of human slavery arose from his realization of the truth of the Biblical idea that God has made all men in his image. Therefore, reasoned Woolman, we dare not treat humans as chattels. Though he was almost alone, he finally was able to convince enough of his fellow Quakers of the truth of his moral insight that he was allowed to publish his book on the sin of slavery. Part I was published in 1754 and Part II in 1762. This is rightly considered the first serious book combining Christian experience with the sin of slavery.

Quakers have, through more than three centuries, been moral pioneers in many fields. One of these is the treatment of the mentally ill. In 1796, long before most people had any understanding of the modern approach to mental illness, William Tuke and other Quakers established the Retreat at York. A great moral advance was made by the decision to give up punishment and to treat the insane with imaginative compassion. The fruits of this action have been numerous.

Another moral advance inaugurated by Quakers has been that of a new attitude toward offenders. The pioneer of this work was Elizabeth Fry, who did her first redemptive work with the female inmates of Newgate Prison, London, beginning in 1813. Comparable to this is the pioneering work of Quakers in seeking to produce peace in the world. When most Christians accepted war uncritically as something inevitable and justifiable, the Quakers of the seventeenth century already regarded it as an evil to be eliminated.

D. ELTON TRUEBLOOD

QUARRELING. A quarrel may result from a complaint or objection. In this sense, it may be based on an a-moral factor and not be in itself evil. Merely as a "cause" to be disputed or a "case" to be defended (as in Lev. 26:25) it may be a potential good.

A quarrel, however, usually implies strife —heated verbal exchange often leading to angry outburst. In this sense it may express deep resentment; thus it often initiates a continuing hostility that affects an increasing number of people and areas. As such, it is evil.

Jesus was angry when cleansing the Temple (Mark 11; John 2) but this was righteous anger. The money-changers involved in that scene gave ample grounds for Christ's action. It was their misappropriation of the place and function of worship in the House of God, to which Jesus addressed his rebuke. He expressed his quarrel with them in a righteous manner, not in hostile resentment.

Most quarrels, however, are not righteous. When a quarrel emerges into angry inter-personal relationships, involving jealousy and/or reflecting self-centeredness, then that quarrel is evil and leads to evil. It is sin. God purposed in redemption to overcome the failures and quarrels of mankind. In his redemptive act, he proffers victory over our quarrelsome selves and a way of peace with one another and with God himself.   FRANK J. KLINE

QUIETISM. Quietism is a form of mysticism which was fostered primarily in Spain and France during the seventeenth century. It held that spiritual ecstasy is attained via self-abnegation and withdrawal from all outward activity. Union with God and purity of soul were to be achieved in passive contemplation and interior annihilation. In the Eastern church a form of quietism known as Hesychasm advocated a meditative faith which dealt only with the interior life of the believer. Among the Quakers quietism was predicated upon the absolute inability of man to establish contact with God. Man had to remain absolutely silent if he was to hear the divine voice and thereby achieve mystical union with God. Quietism confuses the Biblical concept of the *unio mystica* and impairs the ethical thrust of the Christian faith which holds that the believer in Christ is God's handiwork, created by the Spirit of God to perform works of love toward the neighbor in the name and for the sake of the Savior.   JOHN F. JOHNSON

R

RACE RELATIONS. See also *Intermarriage; Racism; Segregation.* Race relations descriptively refers to an area of social inquiry concerning the relationships of groups of people who share distinct physical and genetic characteristics and are designated by society as racial groups. Race relations is also an activists' term indicating both religious and secular efforts to ameliorate conflicts between the dominant group or groups and subordinate racial groups.

The subjugation of one group of people by another is by no means a recent development; the origins of slavery (q.v.) date so far back in antiquity that present explanations can only be speculative. What is of concern to our day is the emergence of slavery in the Western world within the last four hundred years, and the painful aftermath which now threatens the very existence of a number of countries that confess some degree of Christian commitment. Germany, the Republic of South Africa, and the United States are examples of great Western nations in conflict over the exploitation of racial and ethnic minorities in the context of a tacit Christian ethic. This conflict between the Biblical view of the unity of man as a creature in God's likeness and the presence of social, political, and economic institutions that exploit and degrade a group or groups of people for the profit and pleasure of the dominant group is what Gunnar Myrdal called the American dilemma (*An American Dilemma,* Vol. I, New York and London, Harper, 1944, Intro. and Chap. 1). This disjuncture between the American creed and the institutional realities of a racist society has undoubtedly produced the major causes of guilt, fear, and violence in race relations since 1950.

In early American history, before slavery came to be regarded as an economic necessity, little effort was made to prove the fundamental inferiority of the Negro. But the invention of cotton processing machines and the rapid growth of agriculture in the South produced an increased demand for slave labor, and a widespread effort followed to provide a moral basis for the institution. As a result, a Southern ideology emerged in contradiction to the democratic creed of the earlier Virginia statesmen.

As long as the slave trade was taken for granted with no opposition, slaves were conceded to be human. Some captors wrote that the slaves they brought back from Africa were clearly their mental equals, and even superior to many Caucasians back home.

When voices were raised against this inhuman traffic, particularly by influential men and representatives of powerful organizations, the slave holding interests were driven to find moral justification for enslaving human beings (Ashley Montagu, *Man's Most Dangerous Myth,* Cleveland and New York, World, 1964, p. 39). As a result a vast literature developed on the Scriptural justification for slavery, to which large segments of the church in the South gave support. The churches' defense of slavery became so wide spread that: "the American Anti-Slavery Society observed in their 'Resolutions' of May 7, 1844 that no institution is more hostile to the anti-slavery movement than the professedly Christian church in this country" (J. Oliver Buswell III, *Slavery, Segregation and Scripture,* Grand Rapids, Eerdmans, 1964, p. 13).

Following the American Civil War constitutional amendments outlawed slavery but, as Alexis De Tocqueville predicted, the end of servitude did not solve the problem of Negro-white relationships. The former owners had lost their slaves, but they were, for the most part, as determined as ever to define the Negro's role in America as that of the white man's servant, and to find legal means of keeping him in an inferior status as a resource for cheap labor.

Racial segregation laws were passed in the Southern states; they not merely separated the races but provided a means for white domination of the Negroes. As in the case of slavery, the Bible was cited as authority for segregation on the basis of racial in-

feriority. It was also fortuitous for racists' intentions that during the nineteenth century three lines of research appeared to give support to the arguments for racial inferiority.

Charles Darwin's *The Origin of Species by Means of Natural Selection, or the Preservation of Favoured Races in the Struggle for Life,* seemed to lend strong support for the inequality of races. Although Darwin in his book, *The Descent of Man,* published in 1871, clearly states his conclusions that all races were of the same species and came from the same parentage, those who were seeking proof of Negro inferiority found in Darwin's formulations of "natural selection" and "survival of the fittest" the unverified facts for a genetic theory of superior and inferior races (Eugene Nida, *Customs and Cultures,* New York, Harper, 1954, pp. 56-57).

Anthropology was the second area of study to which the defenders of slavery appealed in support of their views. Early anthropology was concerned primarily with "the task of establishing criteria by means of which 'races' of mankind might be defined" (Montagu, *Man's Most Dangerous Myth,* p. 66). The word "race in its zoological sense was first introduced in scientific literature by George L. L. Buffon in 1749, but was not intended to describe any rigid separation of natural distinctions between men. Buffon was widely read in several European languages and the term "race" was appropriated by those who supported a doctrine of human inequality Montagu, *Man's Most Dangerous Myth,* pp. 46-47).

Just prior to 1900 the third of these scientific areas, the new field of psychological testing, became the battleground for the question of racial inequality. Early studies seemed to support the hypothesis that Negroes in America were less intelligent than whites. In 1961 R. S. Woodward examined these studies and raised serious questions about the methodology employed in comparing white and Negro children from dissimilar cultural backgrounds (Otto Klineberg, *Characteristics of the American Negro,* New York and London, Harper, 1944, Chaps. I, II).

During World War I a massive testing of troops brought into question the alleged disparity between the average intelligence of Negro and white soldiers, and within the next thirty years the accumulated psychological data on the relative intelligence of races indicated no essential difference when motivation and cultural opportunities were controlled.

After World War II churchmen, social workers, sociologists and other citizens concerned about the segregation and exploitation of American Negroes turned to the human sciences for their proof of racial equality. The social sciences were all in virtual agreement on the fundamental unity of the human race and the equality of average capabilities of the major racial groups. Race relations experts turned to the massive accumulation of these data for support of their efforts to desegregate and racially integrate the nation. They turned to the same sources of authority as did the racists in earlier days when these fields were still in their infancy. The difference was that by 1950 these disciplines had been refined and the consensus in these areas was overwhelmingly on the equalitarians's side.

From the point of view of Christian ethics, the results of the scientific study of race are informative and supportive but they cannot be the final basis of moral judgment. Science can be helpful in determining what empirical relationships exist and the conditions or actions that are causal antecedents of observed facts about which men are endeavoring to make decisions. Science can state probable results of contemplated action but it cannot determine what ought to be done in the ethical sense.

The fallacy of many race relation experts in recent years was their effort to "prove" the equality of the races as justification for equal treatment and equal justice. Therefore the fate of disadvantaged classes, races, and cultures rested upon the scientists' ability to prove human equality. Scientific research has overwhelmingly supported the essential equality of races in many basic characteristics, but this equation falls far short of the Christian ethic.

For the evangelical believer the source of ethical truth is the Word of God whether in limited prescriptive form or in broad basic principles. As in other areas of theological inquiry it is appropriate to begin with God's creative purpose "in the beginning" to develop a human relations ethic. God created man in his own image and all men are direct descendants of that first set of parents; despite sin, every man carries the divine image of God. There is a fundamental unity in the human race that transcends all pretenses of claims of race; every human being is the object of God's love and is offered redemption through Jesus Christ.

Despite man's common humanity and the love of God for every human being, men have been alienated, degraded, rejected, exploited and enslaved by other men. Racial mythology, economic privilege, and even perversions of the Biblical doctrines of election and predestination have been employed to set men apart and to justify man's inhumanity to man.

The church, the body of Christ, is the prototype of society, and it is ordained and empowered to live its life as a witness to God's will in human relationships (cf. Eph. 2:13-19). As members of God's household they are overcoming the worldliness of separation, hostility, and prejudice in their own common life. The body is not bound together by proven equality, or cultural sameness, nor by intrinsic worth (cf. I Cor. 12:22-26).

The Christian's responsibility in human relations in general, and race relations in particular, is both personal and corporate. As an obedient servant of Christ in the world he will bear witness in his personal relationships to God's love for all men and his judgment on those who would oppress others. As the body of Christ the church will discipline its life that it may witness to the world the message of reconciliation which God has committed to the church.

GILBERT M. JAMES

RACISM. See also *Apartheid; Segregation.* Race and racial matters are facts of life. There are different races and different racial cultures. Skin color or different national origins are racial differentia. These differntia are incidental and relative to what constitutes authentic humanity. When these relative differences are turned into absolutes, race turns into racism. When the relative factor of white skin color is absolutized, white racism emerges. When Hitler absolutized Nordic origin, Nazism was born. When a feature of race incidental to our humanity is absolutized, the race processing this feature exalts itself as a superior race, develops the consciousness that it is the historic bearer of a transcendent destiny to lead the world, by whatever required means, into its future. Its manifest destiny, however, is only manifest in its peculiar racial difference. In white racism, superiority is manifest in white skin; in Hitler's Germany it was Nordic soil and blood.

Racism of whatever kind, and there are many kinds, is at best dangerous. At worst it is demonically destructive, for the demonic by definition is that which exalts itself against God and projects itself as though it were God. Theologically understood, racism is a vaulting, arrogant human attempt to seize for itself that special status which in Biblical thought is called election. As such racism is a profound perversion of election, for in Biblical definition election belongs to God alone, the God who exalts the humble and casts down the proud.

So far from supporting racism, the Scriptures condemn it and God in history judges it. This much the twentieth century should learn from the rise and fall of the Third Reich.

While the Scriptures abhor racism, they do project the Jewish nation as a chosen people to whom God gave a messianic consciousness, special advantage, and a manifest destiny for the sake of the world. All this stems from Israel's election, for election constitutes one's existence before God. Moreover, all this became manifest in Jesus Christ, the Elect of God *par excellence,* in whom the true character of the special status of the Jewish people was revealed. In him we have the true counterpart to all racism, and the promise of its final elimination; for this Bearer, chosen by God to carry the destiny of mankind, goes the divinely appointed way of humble sacrificial love with no recourse to the coercion of brute force and power and the horrors of war and tyranny.

Election is God's answer to and triumph over racism. Racism—whether white racism, antisemitism (q.v.), or any other brand—is essentially anti-Christ. It takes to itself what God chose to give to Christ.   JAMES DAANE

RAMSEY, PAUL. Paul Ramsey (1913-) is Harrington Spear Paine Professor of Religion at Princeton University. He has promoted a distinctive Christian ethics and its application to contemporary social issues. In *Basic Christian Ethics,* Ramsey worked out a systematic understanding of the distinctive contribution of the Bible to ethical theory and suggested guidelines for Christian social action. The basic Christian moral norm is obedient love revealed in the incarnation and death of Christ. This fundamental concept is considered the key to an understanding of all other related concepts—justice, right, obligation.

In reaction to the social inadequacy of

situation ethics, Ramsey veered from an earlier view to unite obedient love with a modified theory of natural law. The unifying theme of *Nine Modern Moralists* is Christ transforming natural law, or love interpenetrating and refashioning justice. The prudence of human reason which expresses itself in justice is refashioned by a prudence which embodies divine love, so that the tension of personal and principial ethics is transcended. The structures of the world are not replaced by agape but are recognized to be inadequate in themselves and in need of the transcendent, transforming power of divine love. In *Deeds and Rules,* Ramsey criticizes the defective assumptions of situation ethics emphasizing that love makes no rules, and there is no continuity of principles between situations. He shows that Christian moral deliberation not only issues in what love requires, but also is the source of general moral rules which bridge the gap between individual and society.

Ramsey's social ethics is predicated on the Biblical idea of Creator-covenant by which God's justice is promulgated on earth. Unlike Greek justice, "giving every man his due," Christian justice, "man's due according to the righteousness of God," shows the influence of Augustine's theory of two cities. From the vantage point of the city of God, the church must develop political theory, but has no right as church (the city of God) to engage in politics.

Most significant is Ramsey's extensive work in medical ethics and his distinctive defense of the legitimacy of war under the necessities of justice in an age when the tide is pacifist.

📖 Paul Ramsey, *Basic Christian Ethics,* New York, Scribner, 1950; *War and the Christian Conscience,* Durham, Duke, 1961; *Nine Modern Moralists,* Englewood Cliffs, Prentice-Hall, 1962; *Christian Ethics and the Sit-in,* New York, Association, 1962; *Deeds and Rules in Christian Ethics* (co-ed, Gene Outke), London, SCM, 1968; *The Just War,* New York, Scribner, 1969; *Fabricated Man,* New Haven, Yale University, 1970; *Patient and Person,* Exploration in Medical Ethics, New Haven, Yale University, 1970.   ROY W. BUTLER

RAPE. See also *Abortion; Life, Sacredness of.* Rape is a man's unlawful carnal knowledge of a woman, without her consent, by resort to force or fraud. Mosaic Law made it liable to the death penalty if the woman was betrothed (Deut. 22:23-30). In the USA a few southern states made death a penalty for rape. In circumstances of rape, abortion of a fetus is considered moral and legal. In modern times whether the woman is married or single, chaste or unchaste, is usually considered immaterial. But corroboration by evidence other than the woman's testimony, and initiation of prosecution within a given time after the alleged offense, are required.

CARL F. H. HENRY

RATIONING. See *Black Market.*

RAUSCHENBUSCH, WALTER. Walter Rauschenbusch (1861-1918) was a Baptist church historian and "prophet" of the Social Gospel. He hailed from seven generations of Lutheran ministers in Germany. His father, August Rauschenbusch, left a large United Evangelical-Lutheran Church in Altena, Westfalia, in 1845 in order to emigrate to the USA. In 1850 his father became a Baptist, and in 1858 he became professor and head of the German Department of Rochester Theological Seminary.

Walter, born in Rochester, N. Y. was a graduate of the German Gymnasium in Guetersleh, Westfalia, University of Rochester, and Rochester Theological Seminary. From 1886 to 1897 he was the pastor of Second German Baptist Church, New York City. Here, at the height of the "Gilded Age," he was awakened to the perils and needs of a social order that violated practically every law, human and divine. In his parish and community work he sensed the sharp incongruities of a social order that tended to depersonalize humans destined for a life of beauty and holiness. In 1912 he wrote of the Kingdom of God as an all-embracing, all-compelling, redemptive message and redeeming fact for people and nations lost in the web of personal and collective sin:

> So Christ's conception of the Kingdom of God came to me as a new revelation. Here was the idea and purpose that had dominated the mind of the Master himself. All his teachings center about it. His life was given to it. His death was suffered for it. When a man has once seen that in the Gospels, he can never unsee it again. . . . I found that this new conception of the purpose of Christianity was strangely satisfying. It responded to all the old and all the new elements in my religious life. The saving of the lost, the teaching of the young, the pastoral care of the poor and frail, the quickening of starved intellects, the study of the Bible, church union, political reform, the reorganization of the industrial system, international peace—it was all covered by the one aim of the Reign of God on earth. That idea is necessarily as big as humanity, for it means the divine transformation of all human life (*Christianizing the Social Order*, pp. 93f.).

Rauschenbusch left his pastorate in New York City in 1897 to become professor of New Testament in the German Department of Rochester Theological Seminary. In 1902 he transferred to its English Department as professor of church history until 1918. In 1907, while on a sabbatical leave at Marburg University, he published his first major work *Christianity and the Social Crisis*. Two years later his contribution to the *Handbuch der Kirchengeschichte*, edited by Gustav Krüger, appeared in volume IV—*Die Neuseit*, in Tuebingen. *For God and the People: Prayers of Social Awakening* appeared in 1910; then *Christianizing the Social Order*, 1912; *Dare We Be Christians*,

1914; *The Social Principles of Jesus*, 1916; and finally *A Theology of the Social Gospel*, 1917. As editor of *Der Jugend Herold* he influenced German Baptists of the USA and Canada. It is hardly known that Rauschenbusch translated many of the Ira D. Sankey-Moody Gospel hymns in *Evangeliums Sänger* Nr. 1-3, Kassel 1897, 1907, 1910, 1929 (121,000 copies) into beautiful German.

Critical works on Rauschenbusch have appeared through the years. I. M. Haldemann wrote a withering attack, *Professor Rauschenbusch's Christianity and the Social Crisis* (c. 1908). This forty-two page pamphlet, according to Henry Conrad Moehlmann, successor to Rauschenbusch in 1918, was "a keen analysis of a college professor's new book in the light of THE OLD BOOK," and deserved a better answer from defenders of the Social Gospel than it received. W. A. Visser't Hooft in 1928 brought out his *The Background of the Social Gospel* critically tracing its origin and basic outlook.

📖 A. M. Singer, *Walter Rauschenbusch and His Contribution to Social Christianity*, 1926; V. P. Bodein, *The Social Gospel of Walter Rauschenbusch and Its Relation to Religious Education*, 1944; Reinhart Muller, *Walter Rauschenbusch*, 1957, a Marburg dissertation under Prof. Ernst Benz, with excellent bibliography and appreciative though critical content; Charles H. Hopkins, *The Rise of the Social Gospel in American Protestantism, 1865-1915*, New Haven, Yale University, 1940.   WILLIAM A. MUELLER

REASON. See *Knowledge and Ethics*.

REBELLION. See also *Government; Resistance; State*. Rebellion is an act or course of open defiance, effectively a declaration of war, against an authority or ruler no longer recognized as legitimate. The term may be used in several senses—theological, political, social—but in each case the aim of rebellion is independence, the power to decide one's own fate.

Proverbs 17:11 affirms, "An evil man seeketh only rebellion; therefore a cruel messenger shall be sent against him." There is an expression of rebellion which is evil—rebellion against the will of God. The fall of Adam and Eve in the Garden was clearly a rebellion against God, as was the primordial struggle of Lucifer, once highest of the angels, whose revolt John Milton dramatized in *Paradise Lost*.

However, rebellion against the will of man, as represented by a civil government, or rebellion against societal conventions, cannot be as easily categorized. Politically the term connotes organized and armed resistance, an open attempt to throw off the shackles of an allegedly oppressive ruler or government. It is the most serious form of political protest, and there are certainly times when it can and must be justified. The rebellion of the thirteen colonies against the arbitrary rule of the British crown was justified because it flowered in the creation of the American Republic, where men have enjoyed a far greater measure of both temporal and religious freedom than would have been possible under some vestigial form of governance based on the old divine right of kings. The rebellion of seventy-five million Bengalis against the repressive policies of the government of Pakistan is a modern example of a political situation where rebellion against established authority appears justified from the standpoint of man's right to live in freedom and dignity.

This is not to deny that rebellions have often been attended by acts of cruelty and barbarism which run completely counter to the goals of freedom and dignity. The tumbrils which rolled through the streets of Paris during Robespierre's "Reign of Terror" were filled with innocent victims, and this same unhappy feature has marred many of the rebellions recorded by history. Therefore, the Christian who is confronted by a choice of rebellion or some lesser form of opposition to the established order often faces a very difficult moral decision in view of the cruel consequences which may well flow from acts which kindle a rebellion.

Anarchy and a complete breakdown of all existing values are often a temporary result. Accordingly for the Christian rebellion is a course of action which must be a final resort after he has exhausted all other efforts to bring about a more peaceful solution. But when he acts *in extremis* to right the wrongs perpetrated by evil men, he may be acting in consonance with the higher morality confided to him by an all-powerful, all-wise, all-knowing God.

JOHN B. ANDERSON

RECONCILIATION. Reconciliation is the process of restoring unity after an enmity or a quarrel. The Bible pictures an original harmony in the Garden of Eden. But this harmony was broken by the entrance of sin which separated man from God (Isa. 59:2) and made the two into enemies (Rom. 5:10; Col. 1:21; James 4:4). When enmity exists harmony can be restored only by dealing with the root cause of the hostility and taking it out of the way. It is the consistent witness of the NT that that is what Christ did when he died on the cross. He dealt there with man's sin and took it out of the way, thus making it possible for man to return to God.

The NT speaks of man as having been reconciled to God (Col. 1:21) or it exhorts him to be reconciled (II Cor. 5:20). But it never speaks of God as being reconciled to man. From this some have drawn the conclusion that all the hostility is on man's side and that nothing is necessary but that man should repent of his wickedness and return to God. Such writers often maintain that reconciliation is the most significant way the NT has of viewing the atonement, which makes their contention all the more important. On this latter point it should be borne in mind that the NT passages dealing with reconciliation are few and entirely Pauline (Rom. 5:10f. 11:15; II Cor. 5:18-20; Eph. 2:16; Col. 1:20f.). That the concept is important is undoubted, but it is a long way from being the characteristic way of viewing Christ's atoning work.

As to the view that reconciliation applies only to man and that God does not need to be reconciled, we should not overlook the fact that it is God's demand on man that creates the rift, not any attitude of man. Man is not worried by his sin and is content to let bygones be bygones, if only God will do the same. But a holy God will not and cannot do this. Because he is who and what he is, he insists that sin be treated with full seriousness and an adequate atonement effected. Under these circumstances it is nonsense to say that there is no sense in which God is reconciled. Granted that the NT writers do not say this in so many words, yet what they say about the nature of God, about his demands on men and about the atonement in general makes the conclusion inescapable.

We should also bear in mind the meaning of reconciliation. When we speak of two people as being reconciled we do not mean that the offender has allowed himself to be persuaded. We mean that the one against whom the offense has been committed has agreed to forego enmity. It would be a curious way of speaking to say that when man had insulted and rejected God by his sin reconciliation meant no more than that man had changed his mind.

This does not mean that God is vindictive, insisting on a full recompense from man before he is ready to forgive. On the contrary, it is God who takes the initiative. It is he who, in the person of the Son, effects reconciliation and takes away the deep-seated cause of offense. God did not have to be persuaded to be gracious. The whole Bible witnesses against so monstrous a conception. But it is God's hostility to every evil thing that is the significant thing and it is reckoned with in the manner in which Christ wrought the atonement.

In recent times some have thought that reconciliation ought to be seen in what we may term a horizontal rather than a vertical direction. Sin is thought of as something that erects barriers between a man and his neighbor, rather than between a man and his God. Reconciliation then becomes a way of enabling men to live together in meaningful community. There is, of course, something in this, for the man who has felt the healing touch of Christ upon his life is concerned with breaking down barriers which divide men. But there must be a right order here. First comes reconciliation of the sinner with God, then reconciliation with man follows. Ephesians 2 is instructive in this connection. There, in connection with the great division of men into Jews and Gentiles, it is pointed out that Gentiles were separated from Christ as well as from one another. But the blood of Christ that brought them near to God brought them also near to one another. Peace was made between man and man, but it was the consequence of peace between man and God.

J. Denney, *The Christian Doctrine of Reconciliation*, New York, Doran, 1918; V. Taylor, *Forgiveness and Reconciliation*, London, MacMillan, 1946 (2nd ed.); L. Morris, *The Apostolic Preaching of the Cross*, Grand Rapids, Eerdmans, 1955.   LEON MORRIS

RECREATION. See *Amusements; Leisure.*

RED CROSS. See *Christian Social Movements.*

REDEMPTION. See also *Salvation.* Redemption is a term used in Scripture and throughout the history of theology to describe the renewal of a right relationship with God. The metaphor was originally taken from the slave market where freedom was bought back for people who had been held as slaves. To redeem means to buy back freedom, and in Christian usage it means that freedom from sin, death, and the power of the devil has been paid for with a price. The kind of price paid, who pays it and to whom it is paid have been the subjects of theological debate. If we look at this Biblical metaphor alongside other metaphors used in Scripture we can get a rounded and fully adequate picture of what is meant by a restored relationship of freedom between God and man. Some of the other metaphors are justification (q.v.) taken from the law courts; or sanctification (q.v.), which is ritual cleansing taken from the temple sacrifices; or adoption (q.v.), taken from family relationships.

Various theories of redemption have arisen in the historical career of this metaphor.

Irenaeus taught that we are redeemed by a recapitulation that is wrought by God's love as he puts down the enemy powers of sin, death, law, and wrath by means of self-sacrifice.

Origen developed the theory that redemption is accomplished by paying a ransom for sinners. The breach in God's justice is overcome by the holy sacrifice that is offered by Christ, and the payment is made to the devil who is tricked into accepting it.

Athanasius developed a doctrine of redemption in which Christ is our vicar or substitute. Redemption is accomplished because Christ accepts all men into his divine fullness.

The Latin theory of atonement stressed the satisfaction idea in the theology of redemption. Redemption is accomplished because Christ provides satisfaction and merit which removes God's wrath. Anselm answers the question "Cur Deus homo?" by saying that God frees us from sin by means of the satisfaction the God-man offers. "God alone can make satisfaction and man alone owes it; therefore it is necessary that the God-man does it (2, 6)."

Luther, in accord with the early church views of Irenaeus and Paul, emphasizes the victory over wrath and the redeeming work of Christ as God. God in Christ died for us,

freeing us from sin, death, and devil.

After the Reformation Albrecht Ritschl revived Abelard's moral influence theory of redemption which stresses the forgiveness of sin as a reception into the fellowship of believers.

Today there is renewed emphasis on the Biblical and Reformation interpretations with a recognition that the mystery of redemption has many facets.

ROBERT P. ROTH

REFORMATION. See also *Reformed Ethics*. The main causes of the Reformation have been variously described as economic, political and ecclesiastical. While it is true that the disintegration of manorialism was related to the emergence of Reformation culture and life, that nationalistic sentiment often supported the Reformers' cause, and that ecclesiastical abuse precipitated the reforming movement (e.g. Luther's *The Ninety-Five Theses*), the Reformation nevertheless cannot be wholly explained by any of these causes. Building on the critical work of Julius Hare and Karl Holl, scholars in recent years have become increasingly more certain that the Reformation was at heart a *religious* movement. At its center was a saving encounter with Christ mediated through the written Word and facilitated by the work of the Spirit. It is misleading to see Luther merely a man who defied tradition on the grounds of esoteric insight (Hannock, Carlyle) and it is unhistorical to claim, as earlier Catholic critics did, that he was either a profligate (Denifle, Grisar) or a proud egocentric (Maritain) whose theological competence could, in consequence, be impugned. Similarly, Doumergue's brilliant pioneering work has stimulated fresh studies on John Calvin which have now largely invalidated those studies which have either questioned the genuiness of his faith (Audin) or assailed the integrity of his character (Galiffe, Fromme, Pfister).

Continental Reformation. The progress

of Luther's theology is inseparable from the struggles of his inner life. *Anfechtung* (violent temptation) is one of Luther's favorite words. He refused to concede to medieval moralists like Biel and Casian, however, that his deep *Angst* was merely a subjective state ("Scruples") which could be overcome by the right "technique." His deep despair was rooted in guilt and guilt, in the sense of subjective shame, was caused by a more profound sense of guilt, that of objective blame before God. Romans 1:17 then led him to see that the Schoolmen's "passive justice" of God was actually the divine justifying action in Christ whereby condemnation is replaced by forgiveness, alienation by union with Christ, and guilt by the imputation of man's sin to Christ and Christ's righteousness to man. By the instantaneous action of God, the sinner is *declared* rather than made righteous. In consequence, Luther repudiated the penitential system because it softened the sense of guilt without changing the sinner's relationship to God. Requiem Masses, self-mortifications, pardons and prayers to the saints obscured rather than illuminated the ethical and religious issues at stake.

Calvin was able to build on and to some extent refine Luther's gains. Calvin's theme in the *Institutes* is the knowledge of God. At the center of the work is the doctrine of justification (*Institutes* III, xi-xviii). This is preceded by what the sinner needs to know to be justified and followed by what he needs to do to live consistently with his justification. Thus the early chapters of the work lay a careful theological foundation for the later discussion on ethics which set the course for discussion in this field for the next century (cf. especially *Institutes* III, vi-x). The Reformers' doctrine of justification *sola gratia, sola fide*, was reiterated in most of the Protestant credal documents from this period: Augsburg Confession, arts. iv, vi, xv; Formula of Concord, art. iii; Zwingli's Sixty-Seven Articles, arts. xviii,

xxii; Second Helvetic Confession, cap. xv; French Confession of Faith, art. xvii; Belgic Confession, art. xxiii.

English Reformation. At least eleven of the Thirty-Nine Articles appear to have been drawn out of the Augsburg Confession and the remainder all closely parallel statements in other Continental formulations. Article xi states: "We are accounted righteous before God, only for the merit of our Lord and Saviour Jesus Christ by faith, and not for our own works or deservings; wherefore, that we are justified by faith only is a most wholesome doctrine." This belief is magnificently translated into worship by the *Book of Common Prayer* as, for example, in the following prayer:

Almighty God, father of our Lord Jesus Christ, Maker of all things, Judge of all men, we acknowledge and bewail our manifold sins and wickedness, which we, from time to time, most grievously have committed, by thought, word, and deed, against thy Divine majesty, provoking most justly thy wrath and indignation against us. We do earnestly repent, and are heartily sorry for these our misdoings; the remembrance of them is grievous into us; the burden of them is intolerable ... for thy Son our Lord Jesus Christ's sake, forgive us all that is past; and grant that we may ever hereafter serve and please thee in newness of life. . . .

The broad consensus which developed among Protestants over the meaning of man's moral dilemma grew out of a new understanding of the Biblical Word. It is not to be attributed to esoteric insight. It was in Erasmus, not in Luther, that religious consciousness came to the fore. Luther, perceived the noetic consequences of sin far more acutely than did Erasmus. And it was Luther, rather than Erasmus, who expounded the mediating role of Scripture in bearing Christ's message of grace to the sinner and its consequent role in structuring his new found faith. Erasmus recovered the Biblical text for his century; Luther recovered the Biblical message.

Gordon Rupp, *Luther's Progress to the Diet of Worms*, New York, Harper, 1964; *The Righteousness of God*, New York, Philosophical Library, 1954; Francois Wendel, *Calvin*, New York, Harper, 1963; G. E. Duffield, ed., *John Calvin*, Grand Rapids, Eerdmans, 1966; P. E. Hughes, *Theology of the English Reformers*, Grand Rapids, Eerdmans, 1965.

DAVID F. WELLS

REFORMED ETHICS. See also *Calvin and Calvinistic Ethics; Luther and Lutheran Ethics; Reformation.* The Reformed branch of Protestantism (as contrasted with the Lutheran and Radical branches) began with the work of Ulrich Zwingli (1484-1531) in Zurich, Switzerland. (Cf. *Calvin and Calvinistic Ethics* for the contribution of John Calvin.)

Zwingli was not an ethical theorist in the formal sense, but he was a practical man who treasured actions above talk, and whose writings display a profound ethical concern. This practical bent, more than his "humanistic" background, led him to a greater emphasis than Luther on the positive functions of the law of God in the Christian life. To Zwingli, the law is not only a threat, but a gift of God's grace. It reveals the believer's sinfulness, not to slay him, but to kindle in him love for the gracious lawgiver and therefore true repentance. The Ten Commandments stand as an eternally valid standard of Christian conduct, not annulled, but vindicated by the grace of God in Christ. They represent God's fundamental demand upon all men, a demand known "by nature" even to those men unacquainted with the written law. Zwingli did not feel, however, that the law made life easy for the Christian. He was deeply aware of the inner conflicts pictured in Rom. 7, and of the tensions between joy and sorrow, struggle and satisfaction, conflict and peace in the Christian life. In his catalogue of Christian virtues, he laid particular stress upon discipline, temperence, sobriety—traits which fit the believer for the fierceness of the spiritual battle. He regarded the law, moreover, as bearing not only upon individuals, but upon society as a whole. The civil magistrate is a minister of God who is called upon to bring both believers and unbelievers into external conformity with God's law as much as possible, though of course true inward conformity to the law is possible only through the working of faith in the heart by the power of the Holy Spirit.

Since Zwingli, Reformed ethics has maintained his basic emphases. It has generally rejected his view that salvation is open to the heathen on the basis of natural law alone, and thereby has set itself off more sharply in distinction from Roman Catholic ethics while underscoring more emphatically Zwingli's own emphasis on the necessity of written Scripture. Reformed ethics maintains the distinctive Reformation teaching that man is unable to please God in any way apart from the grace of God in Christ and the regenerating power of the Holy Spirit. Yet, in contrast with other forms of Protestantism (and in sharp antithesis with modern liberal thinking), Reformed ethics maintains a distinctive emphasis upon the eternal authority and relevance of God's moral law. Reformed thinkers are, of course, not blind to the fact that God often requires different things of different people in different situations; but they will not concede that this fact in the least diminishes our responsibility to obey these requirements. Nor do they concede the objection that such a position is "legalistic." Recent studies have confirmed that law is an indispensible element in the very concept of a covenant between God and man. Obedience to divine commands is an essential requirement of both Old and New Covenants (Deut. 6:1-9; Matt. 5:17-10; John 13:34f.; 14:15, 21, 23; 15:10; I John 5:3; II John 6). Keeping the law cannot save a man, but those who are saved will want to keep the commandments of the Lord who redeem them.

It is an oversimplification, however, to describe Reformed ethics as purely and simply an ethics of law. The Reformed confessions and theologies emphasize other aspects of ethics in addition to the legal aspect: (1) Reformed ethics is "situational" in the sense that it sees the ethical task as one of directing present circumstances toward a future goal (that of the Kingdom of God), and therefore as one which requires an analysis of the present "situation." It recognizes that present situation as already structured by God's great redemptive acts in the past, and as being directed by God's providence toward the final consummation. The Christian life, therefore, is characterized by a tension between the "already" and the "not yet." Unlike modern "situationism," however, Reformed ethics recognizes that the most important factor in the present situation is the ever-living God who continues to speak his will to us through the Scriptures of the OT and NT. (2) Reformed ethics is also "existential," in that it sees faith and love as necessary and sufficient conditions for genuine good works, and therefore sees the ethical task as that of purifying the inner man that his righteousness may be more than merely external. Unlike modern "existential" ethics, however, the Reformed position recognizes the power of God's commands to purify the soul (Ps. 19) when addressed to a believing heart.

G. W. Bromiley, ed., *Zwingli and Bullinger*, Library of Christian Classics XXIV, Philadelphia, Westminster, 1953; J. Murray, *Principles of Conduct*, Grand Rapids, Eerdmans, 1955; C. Van Til, *Christian Theistic Ethics*, unpublished class syllabus privately reproduced, 1970.   JOHN M. FRAME

RELATIVISM. Relativism is a theory that the basis for judgments in knowledge, culture, or ethics differs according to persons, events, or situations. It connotes a state of mind or a way of thinking inhospitable to absolute claims.

The philosophy which underlies contemporary culture has been influenced profoundly by the general acceptance of theories of relativity in modern physics. In general, these theories have for a common denominator the hypothesis that one cannot detect the absolute movement of any body in space, and that motion can correctly be defined only in terms of relation. The more sophisticated type of relativity theory is that formulated by Albert Einstein. Central to his system is the hypothesis that the mass of any body is relative to motion and varies with its energy content. The only constant permitted by the system is the speed of light, beyond which it is hypothesized that no body-velocity is possible.

Epistemological Relativism. As a form of knowledge-theory, relativism stresses the mood of scientific detachment. This is implied in the description of all scientific data and of all epistemological phenomena. It is held that the observer must transcend his own conditioning and his private valuing, and must relate himself empathetically to data in their context.

A corollary of this is that things can be known only through their impact upon minds, so that Reality as such is inaccessible to the knower. In Classical times, this epistemological trend led to the Skeptical movement (cf. *Skepticism*), associated with the name of Pyrrho, who taught that all knowledge must be held in question. Inquiry thus resolved itself into terms of habitual doubt and a perennial suspension of judgment.

In modern times, René Descartes sought to reach a posture of belief through a methodological doubt akin to that of the ancient Skeptics. Immanuel Kant (q.v.) sought to place limits upon skepticism; his view that the content of knowledge derives from a priori categories of the mind is, however, the modern forerunner of epistemological relativism. In more recent times, the procedures of the scientific method have served to save epistemology from pure privatism and skeptical solipsism.

Cultural Relativism. Cultural relativism represents a specialized application of the relativistic mood. In a broad sense, it centers in a rejection of stable and universal cultural norms, and in the assertion that cultural forms are in every case the social products of those with whom they originate. In a more technical sense, cultural relativism is a metaphysics of society. Articulated most clearly by Ernst Cassirer, this form of cultural analysis holds that man exists in a symbolic universe which he himself has constructed. Social reality is thus to be found by investigation of the symbolic forms which a society expresses.

It is here assumed that the conventions of a given group mediate its values, since all experience is to some extent culturally mediated. Values are dogmatically held to be cultural products, reflective of a society's interests. Each social system is held to be unique, and the social milieu forms a context or arena within which value systems are developed.

Cultural relativism reprobates any uncritical preference for one's own culture and insists that other cultural forms be acknowledged as its equivalent. Discriminatory judgments with respect to any given culture are said to be ethnocentric in origin and existentially invalid.

Moral Relativism. Moral or ethical relativism is a specialized form of cultural relativism in which any universally acceptable criterion for measuring values is rejected. All value systems are viewed as being of equal validity, since they are all culturally conditioned and determined. Hence, no value system may correctly be held to be either true or false; the most that can be said is that such a system is valid within a given context.

Friedrich Nietzsche (q.v.) in his *Gene-*

alogy of Morals held that all traditional value systems reflect group interests, and serve to reinforce the privileges of "stronger" persons. Some have called the "interest theory" into question, and hold rather that moral evaluation rests upon psychological factors. E. Westermarck, for example, held that value systems reflect emotional preferences rather than external interests.

A distinction is frequently drawn between moral universals and moral absolutes. It may be shown empirically that a limited range of behavioral forms (e.g., the prohibition of incest) are almost universally rejected. The ethical relativist will not entertain the conclusion that such a prohibition represents anything metaphysically absolute, holding rather that common categories or patterns of behavior emerge from commonly-experienced needs.

The ethical relativist insists that there exists no single scale of values applicable to all societies. Insistence upon such a value-scale is held to be an expression of the fallacy of ethnocentrism—the prideful error of judging other value systems by one's own, usually in a self-congratulatory manner. A specialized form of ethical relativism is elaborated in the ethical form known as Situational Ethics (q.v.).

Impact of Relativism upon Christian Theology. The rapid development of means of communication has brought all religious systems, including the Christian system, into close juxtaposition. Those systems which make claims to universality, and Christianity in particular, have been influenced profoundly by the mood and methods of relativism. In particular, the claim that Jesus Christ is uniquely related to the human race through the Incarnation has been called into question. The issue between the Christian and the relativist finds its crux at the point of such claims as that of our Lord, "I am *the* way, and *the* truth, and *the* life," and the apostolic proclamation that "there is none other name under heaven given among men whereby we must be saved."

HAROLD B. KUHN

RELIGION AND ETHICS. See *Confucian Ethics; Metaphysics and Ethics.*

RELIGIOUS FREEDOM. See also *Persecution.* The problem of religious freedom is a perennial one, and the battle for religious liberty is never completely won.

The course of Christian history discloses three basic approaches to the issue. From the days of Emperor Constantine (fourth century) and Emperor Theodosius I (c. 381) there have existed established or state churches to this very day. The three major branches of Christendom—Orthodoxy, Roman Catholicism, Protestantism—have existed, in the main, both in the old world and the new, that is, Europe and the Americas, as established church systems. Since the days of Emperor Theodosius the denial of the Trinity was considered both a theologico-religious error as well as lése majesté, offense against the state, hence punishable with death by the "secular" powers. The Protestant Reformation (q.v.) in its magisterial expression—Lutheran, Calvinist or Reformed, and Anglican—did not break with the Constantinian establishment of the church. Today we sadly recall that in the sixteenth century Catholics persecuted Protestants, and Protestants persecuted both Catholics and Dissenters such as the Anabaptists. Michael Servetus was burned at the stake in Geneva for the denial of the doctrine of the Trinity. In Lutheran Thuringia, heartland of the German Reformation, a minister of state, Kerrl, was put to death for being a crypto-Calvinist. The churches of the Standing Order of New England in the seventeenth century witnessed the expulsion of Roger Williams in 1636 from Massachusetts Bay Colony; Baptists, Quakers and other sectaries were publicly whipped in the pillory, driven from their homes, and some were even killed for the sake of defense of the religious, orthodox establishment. France and Spain rid themselves of the hated Protestant Huguenot heretics through edict, civil wars, massacres, and other measures. In the countries where Orthodoxy was established by law, in Moscovite Russia and the Balkans, harrassing of Evangelicals and other Dissenters has been the order of the day until World War I and beyond. The Communist regimes in these lands have espoused an open, intolerant, and persecutory attitude toward all religions, even though, for reasons of expediency, this attitude abates at certain times. In Lutheran Germany Baptists emerged after 1834 under the leadership of Johann Gerhard Oncken. The orthodox Lutheran clergy assumed a persecutory stance toward Baptists and other free churches all through the nineteenth century. Minor persecutions continued into most recent times.

What lay behind this nefarious tendency of Christians persecuting Christians? Or harrassing dissenters and putting flagrant heretics to death? Or forcing large contingents of believers such as the Mennonites to migrate to the Americas?

The simplest answer to this question is this: Christian churches, established by law in a given nation, considered soul-murder brought on through heretical teachings, worse than bodily murder. Moreover, the principle "One King, One Faith, One Nation" made for clear cut intolerance in religious matters. Most of the Anabaptists of the sixteenth century were put to death by both Catholics and Protestants on the basis of the ancient laws of Emperor Justinian. These Baptizers were considered both heretics and seditionists. And Calvin could in good cónscience assent to the burning of Servetus because he identified the Old Testament law against idolatry with the New Testament doctrine of heresy.

The second approach to the matter of religious freedom is the tolerance granted to religious practitioners and ecclesial societies by the state or government. The rise of modern secularism since the Enlightenment (1675 onward) has been partially responsible for the principle of tolerance adopted by rulers, kings or republics. It is to the discredit of established church systems, all trying to enforce their brand of Christian orthodoxy by means of police, courts and other state agencies, that often "enlightened despots" like Frederick the Great of Prussia (1740-1785) were advocating religious tolerance while these religious establishments strongly resisted such tolerance. Voltaire in eighteenth century France valiantly fought in the defense of Huguenot families who had been unjustly robbed of their possessions or had been innocently put to death. Men of latitude and breadth of mind, often sub-Christian in their theologies, frequently have been more tolerant toward religious dissent than orthodox Christians.

The third approach to religious freedom is that espoused by both Anabaptists like Balthasar Hubmaier in the sixteenth century and English and American Baptists who emerged in the early part of the seventeenth century.

While Beza, Calvin's successor in Geneva, brazenly declared the concept of religious liberty "a most diabolical dogma, because it means that everyone should be left to go to hell in his own way," Hubmaier in his *Von Ketzern* (Regarding Heretics) clearly broke with the pernicious and ancient doctrine of persecuting heretics or destroying them with the sword or fire. Hubmaier appealed to all Christian men to disavow force in religious concerns once and for all. "If I have taught truth, why abuse me and others of my convictions? If falsehood and error, I plead with Christians to show me my error and correct me with a spiritual word . . . ."

In the new world, i.e., colonial New England, it was Roger Williams (c. 1604-83) who sounded the tocsia in favor of complete religious freedom within a given com-

monwealth of people. To Williams, religious liberty within the context of a nation is a God-given and inalienable right bestowed upon man by the Creator. Interestingly enough, Williams, a Puritan of Puritans and radical Calvinist, based his theory of religious liberty not on any rights of man doctrine but on the awesome doctrine of predestination. God, from eternity, has determined some men to be saved, others to be damned. Therefore let moral man, be he king or potentate, pope or Puritan oligarch, keep out of God's sovereign domain. Let men travel to their ultimate destiny in freedom and at their own peril if they defy the wooing call of God and salvation. To force a man to espouse this or that religion is soul rape, thus Roger Williams. But it must also be remembered that Williams was thinking strictly in terms of religious freedom within a state or nation. He did not endorse doctrinal license within the church. There where Christ is Lord and head heretics, if unrepentant, are to be dealt with in terms of "spiritual artillery," that is, through excommunication from the Christian fellowship.

Coercion in religious matters is clearly against New Testament teaching. Spiritual sickness and blindness are subject to God's final judgment. Tolerance of religion, granted by government, may be taken away by such government. Soul freedom is a divinely given right. Those who knew Jesus Christ as Lord and Savior pray for their enemies as he did. For as Augustine put it, the enemies of today may be God's friends of tomorrow. And, as Leonard Busher said, only God is the Lord of the conscience.

Roland Bainton, *The Travail of Religious Liberty*, New York, 1951; W. R. Estep, *The Anabaptist Story*, Nashville, 1963; W. L. Lumpkin, *Baptist Confessions of Faith*, Philadelphia, 1959; Thorsten Bergsten, *Bathasar Hubmaier*, Kassel, 1961; William A. Mueller, *Luther and Calvin on Church and State*, Nashville, 1954; Roger Williams, *The Bloody Tenent of Persecution*, 1644;_____, *The Bloody Tenent Yet More Bloody*, 1651.

WILLIAM A. MUELLER

REMARRIAGE. See also *Marriage*. The NT adduces only three situations in which a person is allowed to remarry: (1) when the spouse has been put away on the grounds of adultery (Matt. 5:31, 32; 19:3-9; Mark 10:2-12; Luke 16:18); (2) when an unbelieving spouse leaves or divorces a believer (I Cor. 7:10-15); and (3) when a spouse dies.

Matthew 5:32; 19:9 clearly states that adultery is the only reason for divorce. When remarriage takes place following a marriage broken on grounds other than adultery the parties involved in remarriage become guilty of adultery. Jesus abrogates the OT penalty for adultery, which was death (Lev. 20:10; Deut. 22:22-27), and he also repeals the allowance found in Deuteronomy 24:1-4 to put away a spouse for a reason other than adultery. Although Mark 10:11, 12 and Luke 16:18 make no mention of the fact that the innocent party is free to remarry, it is clear from the Matthew 19:9 text that this privilege is granted.

According to the Apostle Paul, when there is a mixed marriage—one spouse a believer and the other an unbeliever—the believer is to remain with his unbelieving spouse (I Cor. 7:12. 13) in that the children from this marriage are sanctified in the believer (v. 14). However, if the unbeliever separates himself from the believer, the marital relationship is broken and the believer is free from obligations of marriage. Nothing is said in the text forbidding the believer to remarry.

Romans 7:1-3 and I Corinthians 7:39 plainly state that the death of one spouse dissolves the marriage and, this being the case, the surviving spouse would be at liberty to remarry. Although this is not expressly stated, neither is remarriage explicitly forbidden.   LLOYD A. KALLAND

REMORSE. See also *Repentence*. It is important to distinguish between repentence and remorse. Richard Hooker defined remorse as the fruit of our own ill doing. Repentence involves turning from sin to God and combines sorrow for the past with the promise of amendment for the future; remorse, by contrast, combines the barrenness of regret with the hopelessness of despair. The Bible puts it this way: "Godly grief produces a repentence that leads to salvation and brings no regret; but worldly grief produces death" (II Cor. 7:10 RSV). Remorse, in the last analysis, is self-destructive. The classic illustration is Judas, who "seized with remorse" (Matt. 27:3 NEB), went and hanged himself.

STUART B. BABBAGE

RENAISSANCE. See also *Enlightenment*. "The Renaissance" is the name applied to a major development in learning and the arts which took place in Europe between the middle of the fourteenth century and the early years of the sixteenth. It had its earliest appearance in Italy, with the city of Florence as its center. The movement spread to other areas of Europe, developing later and with somewhat different emphases north of the Alps. The term "Renaissance," first applied to the movement in the nineteenth century, reflects the recognition that European civilization during these centuries enjoyed a particularly brilliant cultural outburst.

The Renaissance was a complex movement which affected many areas of life. The one unifying feature is the secularization of life, thought, and culture. The revival of the classical literature of Greece and Rome and the study of man as a terrestrial being were two dominant motifs. Painting, sculpture, architecture, music, literature, philosophy, science, and technology were all deeply involved in the movement. Politics, statecraft, explorations, and many other human endeavors were also deeply influenced by it.

A great deal of controversy has centered in the question of the interpretation of the Renaissance. Nineteenth century scholarship, following Jakob Burckhardt, viewed the movement as a burst of new light against the background of medieval ignorance. Later scholarship, reflecting better knowledge of the state of medieval learning, has sometimes questioned whether the Renaissance reflected any basic change at all. It is generally recognized today that neither extreme of interpretation is correct. The Renaissance was the fulfillment of the medieval promise. It gave a new direction to intellectual endeavor, turning the thoughts and minds of men toward what is now called modern civilization.

One of the major Renaissance emphases was the revival of antiquity. The Latin classics were not unknown in the Middle Ages, but the Greek classics were little known. Close attention was directed to these classics in the Renaissance. Enthusiasts sought not only to study, but to imitate classical life. Many lost manuscripts were discovered and published, and grammars and dictionaries were produced to help scholars in their work. Such attention to classical antiquity was generally called "humanism." Earlier revivals of antiquity had shaped the classics to church and dogma; the Renaissance studied them for their own sake.

A similar concentration on man and his achievements characterized the brilliant productions of the Renaissance in art and architecture. Art turned from other-worldly symbolism to the beauty of the external world. Religious subjects continued to be used in art, but with much more naturalism than before. Renaissance architects, likewise, departed from the mysticism and symbolism of the Gothic style and revived such classical elements as the rounded arch and the Corinthian column. The literature of the age emphasized mundane pleasures. Drama and music exhibited similar trends.

The men of the Renaissance bore a varied relation to the church and religion. Some of them were clergymen, many were pious,

nearly all were in outward conformity with the church. But the worldliness and paganism of classical Latin literature encouraged a critical and skeptical attitude. Poggio Bracciolini was an example of a humanist who openly flouted the morality of his day. In general, the humanists were so preoccupied with other things that they gave little attention to the church. The past was regarded as the record of human achievement, not as the divine plan of salvation. There was some reaction to this secularism, but ultimately it prevailed.

The Renaissance north of the Alps was an adaptation and modification of the Italian version. Beginning later than the Italian Renaissance, the northern Renaissance also continued longer. Although impatient with superstition, the northern Renaissance was much less anti-clerical and anti-religious than in the south. Some, indeed, wish to call it "the Christian Rennaissance." Reuchlin and Erasmus, prominent figures in the northern Renaissance, made important contributions to the revival of Biblical studies. German humanists gave the Bible and the writings of the Church Fathers a place alongside of classical literature. They were not much interested, however, in the hereafter. Their concern was for the improvement of morals and learning and other conditions here on earth. The greatest influence of German humanists was in the sphere of education.

There is no agreement as to who the originator of the Renaissance was. The poet Dante is thought by some to have earned that honor, but by others he is judged to be essentially medieval. Petrarch's revival of classical letters is widely recognized to be an outstanding early Rennaissance impetus. Other prominent figures, selected from a great host, include Michelangelo in art, Brunelleschi in architecture, Lorenzo Valla in historical criticism, and Machiavelli in politics. Leonardo da Vinci may be taken as representative of Renaissance man, participating brilliantly in art, science, and technology.

The Renaissance contributed much to the Protestant Reformation, even in its secularism. But the two movements are radically different, particularly in their basic loyalties. The Reformation temporarily blunted the secularist influence of the Renaissance. But the secularism of the modern age may be said to be the flowering of the seed of the Renaissance. In that respect this movement marks a decisive turn in history, the end of the Middle Ages, and the beginning of modern times.   JOHN H. KROMMINGA

RENUNCIATION. The sacrifice of all in absolute loyalty to God, depicted in Abraham's leaving his country and kindred, is even more prominent in the NT. As conditions for discipleship Jesus demanded the renunciation of one's own property, family, and life itself (Matt. 19:16-30; Luke 14:25-27, 33), demonstrating this in his own experience. Similarly the apostle reckoned everything as loss for the gaining of Christ (Phil. 3:7-11).

The call for renunciation is not based upon contempt for self and the world but upon priority of values. In contrast to man's tendency to exalt himself and the wealth and comfort of this world as the highest good, Christianity places the highest good in God and a devotion to him. Anything and everything which clashes with this loyalty, standing as an idol in the place which is rightfully God's, must be sacrificed.

Christian renunciation results in the paradox of gain through surrender. True self-realization comes through losing one's life for Christ's sake (Matt. 10:39). Even the sacrifice of family and possessions for the sake of God's Kingdom results in irradiating and enriching of these provisions in this life and above all in the eschatological life to come (Luke 18:28-30; Matt. 6:33). The final motive, however, is not selfish gain, but the glory of God and his Kingdom

which is the highest good not only of the sacrificing individual but for all creation.

True renunciation can only be accomplished in Christ, for in the last analysis it is the giving up of one's own life with its old values that it might be established in him.
                                    ROBERT L. SAUCY

REPENTANCE. Jesus' message and that of his immediate disciples was characterized by the demand that men should repent (Mark 1:15; 6:12; see also Luke 10:13; 11:32; 13:3, 5; 15:7, 10). The call for repentance (and promise of forgiveness) was also a fairly regular feature in the gospel of the early church (Acts 2:38; 3:19; 17:30; 20:21; 26:18, 20; see also Heb. 6:1). On the other hand, "repentance" is seldom mentioned by Paul and never appears in John's writings.

In Greek the two predominant meanings of *metanoeō* are "to change one's mind," and thus secondarily, "to regret, feel remorse" (over the previous view held). The note of remorse (q.v.) is present in the parable of the tax collector (Luke 18:13; see also Luke 17:4; II Cor. 7:10).

The distinctively OT concept of repentance however is far more radical. The nearest Hebrew equivalent would be *sūb*— "to turn around"; e.g., Ezek. 33:11, "Turn back, turn back from your evil ways"; Hos. 6:1, "Come, let us return to the Lord" (RSV). Thus repentance means not just feeling sorry, or changing one's mind, but turning right around, radically altering the course and direction of one's life, its basic motives, attitudes and world view (cf. Luke 15:17-21; Matt. 18:3). This is why the best translation for *metanoeō* is often "to *convert*" understood literally, "to turn around." A full fledged theology of conversion would have to resolve the relation between repentance as gift of God (Acts 5:31; 11:18) and repentance as responsibility of man (e.g., Mark 1:15; Acts 2:38).

Repentance and faith go together as two

sides of the one coin (Acts 20:21; I Thess. 1:9, Heb. 6:1), repentance being more typically understood as a turning away *from* sin, faith as a turning *to* God. Although the one implies the other, the NT gospel puts the emphasis on the more positive call for faith; Christians are often called "the believers," never "the repentant ones" (note also the almost total absence of the concept of repentance in Paul and John). The Christian ethical life is at basis positively motivated, not negatively renunciatory.

In NT repentance is seen as a *decisive* step; this is why from the Baptist onwards baptism is demanded as the expression of repentance—a decisive act of renunciation of the old way of life, a throwing oneself wholly on God's mercy (Mark 1:4-5; Acts 2:38; 22:16). Too strong an emphasis on the once-for-allness of repentance caused much debate in the early centuries on the possibility of a second repentance (cf. Heb. 6:4; but I John 1:5–2:2).

The *unconditional* nature of repentance is underlined by the parable of the tax collector and the Pharisee: the Pharisee states his claim on God and is not justified; the taxcollector is justified because he makes no claim or condition: "God, be merciful to me a sinner!" (Luke 18:13).

The *comprehensiveness* of repentance is indicated by Matt. 12:33; 23:26: repentance is a root *and* branch, inside *and* outside matter, affecting man from the depths of his personality and right through the whole of his life (see also Luke 3:8-14; Mark 10:21; Luke 19:8; Acts 26:20). It can never be reduced to either one or other, a hidden affair of the heart without visible consequences, or a mere doing of penance (Vulgate, Douay).   JAMES D. G. DUNN

REPRESSION. Freud defined repression as the function of rejecting and keeping something out of consciousness. Usually, he believed, repressed material consists of instinctual urges which continually strain to re-enter consciousness, but are prevented from doing so by a constant expenditure of energy. According to Freud, repressed material may be revealed through hypnosis, dreams or the psychoanalytic process of free association. The effort to release repressed material meets resistance to the process by the patient. The more sensitive the material outside of awareness, the greater the resistance to its disclosure. Hence, the task of the analyst is to recognize and overcome resistance, to facilitate recovery of the repressed.

Repression at first signified only the process of selective forgetting. The term was later broadened by Freud to include all "mechanisms of defense," of which rationalization, denial and displacement are examples. However, these devices may not be unconscious in the psychoanalytic sense, even though they are self-deceiving strategies.

At first, the goal of psychotherapy for Freud was to undo the process of repression and make the unconscious conscious. Later, he recognized the inadequacy of that operation and offered a new objective, to place personality under the control of a conscious ego rather than the unconscious instinctual id (q.v.)—"Where id was, there let ego be."

Freud at first believed that when repression occurred, the instinctual energy thus freed appeared in the form of anxiety. He later concluded that anxiety appears first as a danger signal, warning of instinctual urges that must be repressed. This means that instead of resulting from repression, anxiety comes first and leads to repression of the dangerous id-impulse.

Repression is often prominent in neurotic or psychotic illness, but should be considered unhealthy only when it leads to the evasion of some issue that should be faced instead of forgotten. Several of Freud's contemporaries defended the view that anxiety arises from repressed conscience rather than from repressed instinctual urges, a position that is compatible with Christian faith. From this standpoint, neurosis is regarded as the disease of a bad conscience which may be healed by restoring the moral standards that have been rejected.

↪ Sigmund Freud, "Repression," *Collected Papers*, London, Hogarth, 1957, Vol. IV, p. 84; *The Problem of Anxiety*, New York, Norton, 1936, Chap. VIII; Oskar Pfister. "What transformations does psychoanalysis require in ethics and moral education?," *Psychiatric Quar.*, 5:407, 1931.

ORVILLE S. WALTERS

RESIGNATION. See also *Providence*. Christian acquiescence before evil, frustration, and ill-usage is not the rigorous, emotionless self-composure of the Stoic (cf. *Stoicism*), but rather an attitude rooted in agreement with the will of a loving and sovereign God who accomplishes his purposes through all experiences, who grants peace of heart in the face of threat, and who holds before his children the joy of winning goals through endurance.

In the OT murmuring was forbidden. Temptations to cynicism could be met by seeing that all of life was under the personal jurisdiction of God (e.g., Isa. 45, esp. v. 7), and by worshipful reflection and praise (e.g., Ps. 73:15-26; Jer. 20:7-13). Jesus' dictum, "But I say to you, Do not resist one who is evil . . . " (Matt. 5:39 RSV) is best understood in its setting in the "blessedness" or health of the Christian's life. There resignation is redemptive rather than a defensive response, and is a testimony to the power of the Christian spirit. Paul's secret of contentment in the face of all circumstances (Phil. 4:11-13) was won through the help of the Spirit of Christ, and was sustained by constant thanksgiving.

The church has seen that resignation is not incompatible with the Christian's capacity for righteous anger (q.v.) or decisive action against evil, where this will more likely move persons to salvation than would quiescence. As in the OT, aggressive action must be counselled only by God, through an authorized spokesman.

All other forms of resignation, including mysticism, quietism, and non-violent resistance, are one-sided aspects of Christian realism which submits all human emotion to God's purposive control. FRANK THOMPSON

RESISTANCE. See also *Rebellion*. Resistance is an organized, sustained protest movement characterized by non-cooperation with the authorities rather than by open rebellion against them. Often members of a resistance movement do not accept the legitimacy of the authority which governs their society, but find themselves too weak to challenge it openly; hence resistance is often associated with underground movements. The term has largely political overtones. Often it is used to describe a native population attempting to thwart an occupying army, as in the case of the resistance organized by the French *maquis* against the Germans in World War II. It may also refer to a more particular protest, such as the resistance organized by American opponents of the Vietnam War in an effort to provide support and counsel to draft evaders.

However, resistance movements need not be purely political. The Scottish Covenanters of the 1600s, protesting the high-church heresies of the Stuart kings, organized a resistance based on principles of church government and doctrine, though it had serious political implications. And Korean Christians participated in resistance movements against the Japanese in the 1930s, not so much because they challenged Japan's temporal power as the conqueror of Korea, as because the Japanese insisted that they abjure their faith and worship the Emperor. The Christian's attitude toward resistance as a form of protest must be tempered by an acknowledgment that his primary purpose is not to subvert the kingdoms of men but to prepare men for the Kingdom of God. However there are times, as during the extermination of the

Jews in Europe in the last great war, when love and conscience demand a more active role in resisting a force which is too strong to defy yet too malignant to ignore. The young German pastor, Dietrich Bonhoeffer, set such an example of courage and faith when he took up the burden of protest on behalf of the Jews by creating a resistance of moral force within the concentration camp itself. JOHN B. ANDERSON

RESPONSIBILITY. See also *Duty; Rights.* Responsibility and morality are inseparable. The one cannot exist without the other. A mechanistic or behavioristic philosophy has no place for either. Other philosophers differ among themselves concerning the basis or nature of obligation.

Plato found responsibility in a suprasensory, supratemporal World of Ideas; Aristotle, in the nature of man; Kant (q.v.), in the force of logic. Fichte made obligation an original datum. Christianity, of course, bases responsibility on the imposition of the Creator's commands.

Ethical writers usually spend more time on the extent of responsibility. Probably there is universal agreement that a man is not responsible for involuntary actions: if a man is knocked down by an auto, he is not responsible for falling. Trivial? Not so trivial when a man is knocked down by insanity, sets fire to his house and kills his children.

The Stoics put great stress on volition; but it was Aristotle who best enumerated the details. He examines actions done through fear. What, then, about actions done under the "compulsion" of pleasure? How about drunkenness? Some other actions are done in ignorance. There are various kinds of ignorance. A man may be ignorant of who he himself is (he thinks he is Napoleon or Christ); he may not know what he is doing ("Father, forgive them, for they know not what they do"); he may not know the person on whom his act terminates (mistaking a friend for an enemy); he may not know the instrument (the gun that "wasn't loaded"); he may not know the manner of his doing the act (he intends to shake your hand cordially and nearly breaks your joints). Ignorance in any one of these particulars relieves one of responsibility. Aristotle continues with other details.

The Bible does not give any systematic account of these matters, but both in the Mosaic Law (e.g., the cities of refuge) and in the NT examples occur. I Timothy 1:13 says, "I was before a blasphemer, and a persecutor, and injurious, but I obtained mercy because I did it ignorantly in unbelief." In addition to particular cases, general statements occur in Luke 12:45-48 and John 15:22; but particularly in Romans 1:32, "Knowing the ordinance of God, that they who do such things are worthy of death, not only do the same, but approve of those that do them."

This last reference meets the objection that the heathen are not responsible because they have never heard the gospel. They are responsible because they know the law. "When the Gentiles, who do not have the [Mosaic] law, act lawfully by nature, they are, without the [Mosaic] law, a law to [or, for] themselves: they show the work of the law written in their hearts" (Rom. 2:14-15). Thus responsibility is both established and limited by knowledge.

Theologians and popular preachers who do not care to emphasize knowledge sometimes try to base responsibility on free will. But, aside from the fact that the Scripture does not so teach, a will free from and independent of knowledge, of one's own character, and of God furnishes a poor foundation for morality.

Archibald Alexander, *Theories of the Will*, New York, Scribner, 1898. GORDON H. CLARK

RESTITUTION. Restitution is the return to the rightful possessor of what has been misappropriated, or reparation for an injury done. It is based on the principle that a right has been violated.

An elaborate system of compensation was laid down in the Mosaic Law in the OT, on the general principle that restoration should as far as possible be equivalent to the loss. In some cases the penalty to the injured was four, five, or even seven times the loss inflicted (Exod. 21:18-36; Lev. 24:18-21; Deut. 19:21; Prov. 6:31).

In the NT Zacchaeus said he would restore fourfold for any wrongs he had done to another (Luke 19:8).

In Roman Catholic moral teaching the duty of restitution is based, first of all, upon natural law, to restore the balance of rights, reconstruct the natural order of justice, and maintain social security and peace.

The duty is implicit in the seventh and tenth commandments which forbid stealing and covetousness. Restitution is a Christian obligation, prerequisite of an acceptable relationship to God (Matt. 5:23f.). Genuine sorrow for sin implies not only the desire for future amendment of life but the desire to repair or minimize the injuries inflicted by sins already committed and now repented of. If the right violated is one of great moment, then salvation requires that actual restitution be made, if at all possible. When impossible, there must be an inward intention to make restitution when and if the opportunity arises.

Sometimes the word restitution is used in the special theological sense of restoration. Scripture affirms the restoration of all things, including man's life and the entire creation, to its original design, through God's triumph over all that has marred his work.   FRANK B. STANGER

RESURRECTION. See also *Body; Eschatology and Ethics; Immortality.* Christian belief in the resurrection of the dead has its roots in both the OT and Jewish intertestamental literature. In these sources

resurrection assumes an ethical dimension in that it is seen as a vindication of the righteous who have suffered unjustly (e.g., Isa. 25-26; Dan. 12:1-3; II Maccabees 7). This is reflected in the NT in, for example, Romans 8 and Revelation.

As it is associated with the final judgment, the resurrection of the body becomes an ethical sanction in the NT (e.g., Matt. 25:31-46; II Cor. 5:6-10; Acts 17:31-32; Rev. 20-21).

Perhaps the most important ethical considerations based on the future resurrection refer to the character of present behavior. In I Corinthians Paul argues for a *future* resurrection against those who denied it because they held that the Christian already possessed the "resurrection life" (I Cor. 15:12; I Cor. 4:8; cf. II Tim. 2:18). Undoubtedly the arrogant and deviant behavior of Paul's detractors in Corinth was an outgrowth of their "over-realized" eschatology.

Paul argued that although the Christian is completely identified with Christ's death, his union with Christ in resurrection is yet future. The present implication of this future reality is the moral exhortation to walk in newness of life (Rom. 6: cf. also I John 3:2). In another context, presumably when the historical situation differed, the expressions of Paul indicate present possession of resurrection and union with Christ as a moral force (Eph. 2:1-10; Col. 3:1-4).

📖 Calvin K. Staudt, *The Idea of the Resurrection in the Ante-Nicene Period*, Chicago, University of Chicago, 1909; John T. Darragh, *The Resurrection of the Flesh*, London, SPCK, 1921; C. F. Evans, *Resurrection and the New Testament*, London, SCM, 1970, pp. 1-40.   DAVID M. SCHOLER

RETRIBUTION. See also *Punishment; Rewards.* The Bible insists that retribution must inevitably follow sin. Although the word is not used in Scripture the idea of retribution appears frequently and is clearly expressed by Paul in Rom 2:5, 6, where the sinner is described as storing up for himself the wrath of God on that day "when God's righteous judgment will be revealed. For he will render to every man according to his works." Such statements as, "For he that sows to his own flesh will from the flesh reap corruption" (Gal. 6:8), indicate that retribution is the natural result of sin. It is significant that the Hebrew word 'awŏn means both sin and its penalty and most frequently denotes the first of these. Consequently, Cain's statement, usually translated, "My punishment is greater than I can bear" (Gen. 4:13), may just as accurately be translated, "My sin is greater than I can bear." This means that retribution is inescapable.

Biblical teaching leads one to conclude that retribution, except for those who repent, is eternal (Dan. 12:2). Matthew 25:46 uses the same terminology for "eternal punishment" and "eternal life." The more exhaustively this subject is explored the more apparent it becomes that divine retribution for iniquity is reasonable and inevitable.   ARNOLD C. SCHULTZ

REVELATION. See also *Christain Ethics; Old Testament Ethics; New Testament Ethics; Pauline Ethics.* Revelation, which means the work of God making known what was previously unknown, has been much discussed in this century, and some Biblical emphases are now more widely accepted as a result.

Revelation in the Bible means God *communicating,* making himself and facts concerning himself known to his rational creatures. All knowledge of God springs from and is correlative to revelation, as Augustinians have constantly insisted. God gives knowledge of himself by *enlightenment,* a process transcending ratiocination which imparts the intellectual equivalent not merely of perceptions of what is "there," but also of sight itself. Man knows God only through this self-disclosing action on God's

part. This was true of man as such (Adam in Gen. 1, 2) before it was true of man as sinner (Adam in Gen. 3). The Christian gospel, itself a message which claims revelatory status (cf. I Cor. 2; Gal. 1; I Thess. 2:13), calls for the receptivity of faith in relation both to the knowledge and the salvation of God; for it requires us to receive Jesus Christ not only as our sacrifice and mediator Godwards but also God's image and wisdom manwards.

God's revealing activity has two modes. As Maker, Benefactor, Lawgiver, and Judge, God reveals himself in and through the created order—nature, history, conscience—to all men. The revelation reaches us by virtue of our being alive in God's world, and is inescapable (Rom. 1:18ff., 32, 2:14ff.; Acts 14:17; Ps. 19:1-6). The way of sinners, however, is to suppress and distort, more or less, this "general," "natural" revelation, and none are brought by it to acknowledge their holy Creator as they should (cf. Rom. 1:18—3:20; Acts 17:24-31). In any case, no knowledge of saving grace for sinners is communicated by this means, even though it is through the second Person of Godhead that general revelation comes (John 1:4, 9). Knowledge of God as Saviour comes only through knowledge of the acts of God in redemption—knowledge, that is, of Jesus Christ the incarnate Son, and his cross and resurrection, and of the saving history in which Christ is central. Through this "special," "supernatural" revelation, given and proclaimed on the stage of world-history and brought home to individuals through the sovereign enlightenment which is an aspect of spiritual regeneration and creates in us eyes to see (I John 5:20; I Cor. 2:14ff.; II Cor. 3:12—4:6), we learn to read the "book" of general revelation, too. Calvin's illustration is that the Biblical knowledge of God acts as spectacles, focusing for us and making distinct our hazy sense of God gained from created things (*Institutes* I.vi.1).

The Bible presents the communicating work of God as a complex of activities involving three distinct "moments," or classes of moments. First, revelation came in history, as God sent messages to, and dealt with, chosen people and worked out through them his redemptive plan. Second, and largely in parallel with ongoing revelatory events, God caused his words and acts, set against their background and supplemented by details of his people's response or lack of it, to be recorded and interpreted in the "public records" (Calvin) of the Scriptures. Third, God gives men understanding of the meaning and bearing of his redemptive work, and through this understanding and the response to which it leads he involves them in the power and benefit of that work. Central to this understanding and response is recognition of personal deity in Jesus and divine authority in the Scriptures, according to the explicit witness of Scripture in each case. "Reveal" (apokalupto) relates to this third "moment" in Matt. 11:25, 16:17; Gal 1:16; I Cor. 2:10; etc.

The polemics of the revelation-debate are complex. Since Lessing it has often been held that to seek absolute truth amid the relativities and contingencies of history is vain. Since Kant and Schleiermacher, the idea of God sending verbal messages and inspiring a record of his ways which, though thoroughly human, is also thoroughly trustworthy, has seemed to many incredible, while the idea that our critical and selective evaluation of the Biblical witness is more authoritative than the witness itself has been taken as a self-evident truth. Neoorthodoxy has re-established our dependence on the Word of God for knowledge of God, but has tended to set Christ, the living Word, against the written Word, rather as the Anabaptists of Reformation days set the Spirit against the Word. Brunner, and even more Bultmann, have maintained that what is given in relevation (third "moment") is a divine claim with little or no conceptual content (both writers being radical skeptics about Bible history).

Biblical ethics rarely enter into the revelation-debate, but it is noteworthy that all Old Testament moral teaching in the law and the prophets claims to come verbatim from God, and if this claim is not accepted one can scarcely rise, whatever one intends, above a situationism controlled by a more or less subjective conception of what it means to love one's neighbor. In the ethical contributions of Brunner and Bultmann this becomes obvious.

▱ Calvin, *Institutes* I. vi-ix; B. B. Warfield, *The Inspiration and Authority of the Bible*, Nutley, N. J., Presbyterian and Reformed, 1948; C. F. H. Henry, ed., *Revelation and the Bible*, Grand Rapids, Baker, 1959; J. Baillie, *The Idea of Revelation in Recent Thought*, Irvington-on-Hudson, Columbia University, 1956.   JAMES I. PACKER

REVENGE. See also *Enemy; Retribution.* The same Hebrew (nakam) and Greek (ekdikeo) roots underlie the terms "to avenge" and "to revenge"; the latter commonly reflects a malignant or resentful spirit in inflicting punishment upon a wrongdoer. The word occurs six times in the NT, in some passages (Luke 18:2; cf. v. 5) in the forensic sense, while others convey the meaning of revenge.

In Christianity the Golden Rule decides the matter of private and personal revenge. Christ's teachings resolutely condemn personal malevolence and retaliation. Love is to motivate the Christian in interpersonal relations (q.v.); in public affairs his interests are to be preserved by legal tribunals that reflect the divine ordination of civil government for a fallen society (Rom. 13).

Instead of seeking revenge, Christians are to rely on God's judgment (Rom. 12:19). Punishment has moral significance only if it vindicates righteousness and law. The NT term vengeance (ekdikesis) does not carry the sense of arbitrary or vindictive reprisal, but of just retribution inflicted by God or his agents. Its association with wrath (q.v.), as in Rom. 3:5; 13:4, has divine righteousness in view.   CARL F. H. HENRY

REVOLUTION. Revolution is a sudden and violent socio-political process aimed at the overthrow and/or seizure of governmental power. It is to be distinguished from lesser forms of political violence such as riots, violent political strikes, assassinations, small-scale terrorism, mutinies, ethnic clashes, and sabotage. These socio-political dimensions of violence, however, may be embodied in a revolution. Revolutions are often distinguished from rebellions. In his celebrated work *The Rebel,* Albert Camus maintained that while revolution aims at the complete variegation of the government, rebellion has a more limited objective—the endeavor to achieve certain moral ideals such as justice and freedom. Others claim, however, that the difference is simply quantitative. Revolutions are rebellious, but on a more comprehensive scale. Revolution is a socio-political process, rather than a simple act. Its historical development usually begins with social and political alienation, followed by creation of a revolutionary organization, a dramatic revolutionary appeal, and a period of movement-building. Usually an unproductive period of non-violent bargaining precedes the outbreak of revolutionary violence. The post-violent stages vary according to the success or failure of the revolution.

Typologies of revolution differ according to objectives, magnitude and degree of organization. Usually three general types of revolution are distinguished: (1) social revolutions aiming at radical social change, (2) political revolutions directed against the whole governmental structure, and (3) palace revolutions seeking to oust a particular regime or its leaders. Chalmers Johnson presents the following classification: (1) the *Jacquerie* or mass rebellion of peasants with the limited aim of airing specific grievances, (2) the *Millenarian* rebellion which incorporates supernatural forces into radical change, (3) the *Anarchistic* rebellion, perpetrated by those who nostalgically react to change, (4) the *Great Revolutions* which aim at fundamental change throughout the total socio-political structure, (5) the *Coup d'etat* or planned overthrow of the government by ideologically inspired élites, and finally (6) *Mass Insurrection* or massive guerrilla warfare guided by a conspiratorial élite (*Revolution and the Social System*, Stanford, 1964, pp. 45-68).

Only within recent years have the churches begun to reflect theologically on engagement in violent revolution. One stimulus has been the many "revolutionary situations" throughout the Christianized world. Out of the 1966 Prague Christian Peace Conference and the World Conference on Church and Society in Geneva emanated the literature which has been a springboard for the so-called "theology of revolution." Here the task of theology is conceived as one of relating the Christian faith to revolutionary struggles around the world. The rationale for this emphasis has included appeals both to precedents within church history (Thomas Munzer, the Puritans, etc.) and to Biblical categories as entailing revolutionary change. Certainly the liberation of the oppressed is a commendable task if properly formulated. If the argument affirms that only in certain very limited circumstance some kind of compatability (not identity) may exist between the Biblical categories and revolutionary activity, there is little room for disagreement. But, if the approach assumes that church history and Biblical categories necessarily entail participation in revolution, serious objections must be raised.

As it stands, the phrase "theology of revolution" seems no less monstrous than the comparable phrase "theology of war." This led Joseph Hromadka and others to speak, instead, of a "theology *for* revolution." The basic issue is the theological foundation for Christian participation in a revolution and next to that the justifiable limits of such participation. It will not do simply to invoke a modified understanding of Just War (q.v.) theory, for revolution raises unique issues not discussed in questions of war. One of these concerns political obligation; i.e., whether or not Christian moral obligation to the state is absolute or only *prima facie*. The theological task, then, is not just one of relating the Biblical categories or church history to the revolutionary struggles that are occurring throughout the world, rather it becomes one of reflecting ethically upon the possibility and limits of revolutionary participation in light of certain Biblical criteria.

The theologians of revolution appeal to four Biblical concepts to provide the theological framework and perspective to justify the Christian's participation in a revolution. First, God is the Creator and Ruler of all the spheres of nature and society. Because the orders of creation purpose to serve man, they must of necessity continually change in line with human needs. A corollary of this affirms the necessary de-sacralization of the ontocratic structures of reality. Consequently the Christian must make common cause with all those movements that are promoting liberation from all mythical forces and are moving toward the renewal of the social and political structures in the direction of a secular and man-made order of life. Secondly, God's activity is dynamically historical. Historical existence is characterized as a pilgrim people's perpetual struggle for new forms of freedom. Thirdly, revolutionary activity grows out of the Biblical notion of radical renewal that accompanies repentance. Repentance is a call to renewal, to new life, to revolution. Fourthly, the agonizing struggle for historical liberation embodies the constant realization that it is moving forward to God's open future, i.e., it is an eschatological struggle.

For the theologians of revolution the most important theological perspective upon revolution is given by the revolutionary character of Biblical Messianism. They conceive of the Messiah as a political revolutionary who has come in the past, yet who still continues his liberating work as a possibility toward which men are constantly moving.

These Biblical concepts of de-sacredization, historicalization, transformation and futuralization which, according to the theologians of revolution, necessarily entails revolution, are capable of being mated with any set of values. Barrington Moore has noted that a revolution might proceed in any one of three distinct directions—communist, facist, and democratic (*Social Origins of Dictatorship and Democracy*, Beacon, 1967, p. 413). Certainly most people would claim that there are significant moral differences between these various ideologies. Revolution as social process is morally vacuous. Merely to argue that the Biblical categories imply revolution, even were that the case, is hardly rigorous reasoning about the nature and direction of that revolution. Furthermore, while few would disagree that at any moment, somewhere, something should be changing, this cannot pass for stringent moral and theological reflection upon the significance or the justification of the particular direction of that change. Moreover, while it is difficult to dispute the fact that the Biblical categories imply change, it is pressing the data to argue that this change necessarily entails revolution.

Some of the renewed interest in the historical Jesus has been stimulated by the suggestion that Jesus lived and died as one who was a part of or sympathetic to certain militant nationalistic movements in first century Palestine (S. D. Branden, *Jesus and the Zealots*, Scribners, 1967, p. 358). Certain allusions in the Gospels might be fashioned to support the position that Jesus was a Zealot (q.v.), such as his reference to

Herod as a "fox" (Luke 13:32); his declaration that he came not to bring peace, but a sword (Matt. 10:34); his choice of a Zealot as one of his disciples (Luke 6:15); his cleansing of the temple (John 2:13-17); the possessing of weapons by his disciples in the garden of Gethsemane (John 18:10-11); and the inscription over the cross. Oscar Cullman has pointed out that to assert Jesus was sympathic to the Zealot cause based on this evidence is quite dubious. According to Cullmann Jesus' concept of eschatology was not cast in a national earthly framework like that of the Zealot's, but rather focussed attention of God's Kingdom as outside the framework of worldly institutions (*Jesus and the Revolutionaries*, Harpers, 1970, p. 20). Furthermore, contrary evidence would suggest that Jesus was not at all in sympathy with the Zealot cause. This is seen in his command not to draw the sword (Matt. 26:52); the fact that he preached peace (John 14:27); and that a Roman sympathizer was one of his disciples (Matt. 9:19).

Yet the Biblical evidence suggests that Jesus vigorously challenged the religio-political status quo. His rejection of the system, however, was more than simply the result of a disdain for the status quo. Rather he refused to condone a situation that did not measure up to the ideals of the past. Jesus, like the prophets, attempted to restore, for the present generation, the divine intent of the past traditions in light of the possibilities of God's future Kingdom.

📖 Tariq Ali, *The New Revolutionaries*, New York, William Morrow, 1969; Hannah Arendt, *On Revolution*, New York, Viking, 1965; William Beardslee, "New Testament Perspectives on Revolution as a Theological Problem," *The Journal of Religion*, Vol. LI, Jan., 1971, pp. 15-33; V. Borovoy, "The Challenge and Relevance of Theology to the Social Revolutions of Our Time," *Ecumenical Review*, Vol. XIX, Oct. 1966; Crane Brinton, *The Anatomy of Revolution*, New York, Random, 1965; Albert Camus, *The Rebel: An Essay on Man in Revolt*, Anthony Bower, tr., New York, Random, 1956; Harvey Cox, ed., *The Church Amid Revolution*, New York, Association, 1967; James C. Davis, ed., *When Men Revolt and Why*, New York, Free, 1971;

Leslie Dewart, *Christianity and Revolution*, New York, Herder and Herder, 1963; Hans-Werner Gensichen, "Revolution and Mission in the Third World," *Lutheran World*, Vol. XVI, Jan. 1969, pp. 29-46; J. M. Lockman, "Ecumenical Theology of Revolution," *Scottish Journal of Theology*, Vol. XXI, June, 1968, pp. 170-186; Jürgen Moltmann, *Religion, Revolution, and the Future*, New York, Scribner, 1970; Eugen Rosenstock-Huessy, *Out of Revolution*, New York, Four Wells, 1964; Richard Shaull and Carl Oglesby, *Containment and Change*, New York, Macmillan, 1967; H. Wendland, "The Church and Revolution," *Ecumenical Review*, Vol. XIX, Oct. 1966, pp. 440-453).

DOUGLAS J. MILLER

REWARDS. See also *Punishment*. The Christian idea of rewards is an extension of the Biblical law of retribution (q.v.). The Scriptural vocabulary of reward is primarily of just and fair payment for goods purchased or services rendered (Gen. 30:32; Luke 10:7). Its extension into ethical and spiritual realms was inevitable (Gen. 15:1; Deut. 28; Matt. 5:12). Hard work, diligence, and astute self-advocacy bear suitable fruit in this life, but ultimate rewards and punishments are conferred by God on the faithful and on sinners. These are not payments for merit or demerit, but express the justice and lovingkindness of God, and underscore each man's faith decisions toward God and love-decisions toward neighbors (e.g., Matt. 25).

FRANK THOMPSON

RICHES. See *Stewardship; Wealth*.

RIGHT AND WRONG. Right and wrong stand for objective characteristics which attach directly and inalienably to acts and their consequences. Christians agree with moral realists that we are each subject to an unconditional standard of value. But Christians hold that right and good are judged morally by more than the standard of being conducive to the maximum possible good (conversely wrong and bad by what is inimical to it). Christians are also sympathetic to the idealist premise (as in Plato) that right and wrong relate to the standard of the ultimate good and that it is always better to do right than wrong. But they relate the rightness or wrongness of acts not simply to intrinsic good but to the Biblical revelation that the good and right are what God wills. To ask whether the will of God is good is redundant.

In their efforts to clarify moral language Analytical Philosophers generally accept the language of ethics as meaningful but not as relating to objective moral standards (cf. *Language, Ethical*). Clarification entails for some the prior assumption that the answer be cast in terms specified beforehand, i.e., the measure of our understanding. This does not deny the possibility of mystery and revelation, but gratuitously assumes the impossibility of saying anything about them, as language is the vehicle of revealed truth.

Christians insist that the Bible reveals the will of God in specific terms. Christian morality is not based upon situational ethics (q.v.) in which every man does what is right in his own eyes (Judg. 20:25). Moral judgments are more than culturally fashioned and biologically induced responses. Nor are they simply expressions of feeling so that "That is wrong" really means "I don't like that." Nor do Christians teach that good and right are dictated arbitrarily by God.

In Christian teaching no tension exists between the morality of right and wrong and the concept of growth toward the moral ideal. Redemption from the consequences of our wrongdoing in relation to God's laws is available through Christ's perfect sacrifice. The will of God is revealed personally and historically in Jesus Christ, whose beneficiaries delight to conform to the divine commandments. The Holy Spirit assists the believer's growth into the ideal of our Lord's perfect humanity. Christian morality is not only a matter of right and wrong but also of divine enablement toward the Christ-centered ideal (Rom. 8:11; Phil. 2:13).

A. R. C. Duncan, *Moral Philosophy*, CBC, 1965; C. F. H. Henry, *Christian Personal Ethics*, Grand Rapids, Eerdmans, 1957; T. E. Hill, *Contemporary Ethical Theories*, New York, Macmillan, 1950; A. N. Prior, *Logic and the Basis of Ethics*, New York, Oxford, 1961; I. T. Ramsey, ed., *Christian Ethics and Contemporary Philosophy*, London, SCM, 1966.   SAMUEL J. MIKOLASKI

RIGHTEOUSNESS. Mankind understands righteousness by standards distinguishing right from wrong. Though human standards differ, the ability to make moral judgments in one sense or another is universal; no people are amoral in the sense of unconcern about good and evil (Rom. 2:14). Christianity understands righteousness as an attribute in God and as a positive relationship to him in which man acts according to God's righteous standards (Ps. 1).

God is eternally righteous and the source of all righteousness. God as a source of all righteousness cannot be judged by external standards, hence a discussion of God's righteousness in the abstract is problematical. God's righteousness can only be understood in his revelation. Though not by nature bound to external standards, he binds himself to what he reveals; all his revelations reflect his righteousness, and these righteous revelations he can deny as little as he can deny himself (Ps. 145:17; Heb. 6:18). In a special way, man, as created in the image of God, possessed God's righteousness; patterned after God, he stood by creation in a positive relationship with his Creator and naturally did God's desires.

God's righteousness becomes retributive when man sins and steps outside the moral relationship God intended by creation (Rom. 1:18). Divine wrath overtakes man in the world in several forms. First, it results in man's alienation from God. Divested of God's righteousness, man may not and cannot stand in harmonious relationship with God. If this breach is not corrected, it becomes permanent and damns man eternally. Hell is the final righteous manifestation of God's wrath. In spite of man's alienation from God, God continues to act righteously toward man in his condition of unrighteousness (Rom. 3:19). Second, it appears in the law which survives in the hearts of all men and which God has most clearly articulated in the Ten Commandments. These are the negative expressions of God's righteousness to inform man that he is no longer in proper relationship, and as such are incapable of returning man to his original state (Rom. 3:20). Third, in the community the state is God's instrument of wrath in effecting civil righteousness, or outward conformity to the civil law. The state manifests God's righteousness by containing overt unrighteousness which threatens the security of others (Rom. 13:1-7). Working through a system of rewards and punishments, the state promotes outward harmony among men and preserves them from gross offense against God (I Peter 2:14). Through war God punishes national unrighteousness (Lev. 26:14-20). Fourth, God's demanding and punitive righteousness becomes most evident in the life and death of Jesus. He lived in perfect harmony with God and fulfilled all God's righteous demands (Matt. 3:15). In his death he assumes all penalties of God's punitive righteousness on mankind's unrighteousness (Matt. 20:28; Rom. 5:18-21).

God's vindicating righteousness is seen in declaring the sinner righteous for Jesus' sake. In love God offers Jesus in the sinner's place to fulfill his righteous requirements (I Peter 3:18). Forgiveness does not annul righteousness, but is required by it. By faith sinners receive Jesus' righteous life and payment of all penalty for their own unrighteousness. Therefore God remains righteous in his verdict of forgiveness (Rom. 3:21-26). Eternal damnation is due to the individual's self-exclusion from God's righteousness.

Since man is placed in a righteous relationship with God through faith, he is capable of fulfilling God's righteous demands in the law. In faith man sees God's law positively and leads a life pleasing to God. He also refrains from displeasing God (Rom. 6:15-19). Thus believers are righteous in two ways. First, they stand in the proper relationship with God. Second, they conform their lives to God's revealed will. Total righteousness in this life is never possible to redeemed man (I John 1:8), but death ushers the sinner into a totally righteous life (Rom. 6:7).

The ancient Greeks understood righteousness as an ethical life lived in conformity with certain virtues. Righteousness existed independent of religious commitment. Many modern philosophies and movements also separate ethics from a consideration of God's righteousness. The Judaism confronted by Jesus regard righteousness as what men do rather than what God is, and the relationship he establishes with men (Matt. 5:20; Luke 18:9-14). In the post-apostolic church righteousness deteriorated to an organically infused quality by which the faithful could live righteous lives. When righteousness is considered a quality in man distinct from a relationship to God, it becomes a quantity measured by the amount of good works outbalancing the bad. In the sixteenth century the Reformation's prime contribution was Luther's renewal of the Pauline concept that righteousness is that attitude in God by which he declares righteous in his sight sinners who by faith appropriate the merit of Christ alone.

📖 Wilhelm Dantine, *Justification of the Ungodly*, Concordia, St. Louis, 1968; *Formula of Concord*, IV; Malanchthon, *Augsburg Confession* and *Apology* IV.   DAVID P. SCAER

RIGHTS. See also *Bills of Rights; Civil Rights; Natural Rights; Property; Responsibility.* The American Declaration of Independence of 1776 declared that "all men are created equal, that they are endowed by their Creator with certain inalienable Rights, that among these are Life, Liberty, and the pursuit of Happiness." This is only one of several statements about human rights to be written in the past three hundred years. Similar notions of inherent human rights have been central in much modern thinking about man's relationship to others and to his government. But the American affirmation differs from two other major statements in a significant way. Unlike the French Declaration of the Rights of Man (1789) and the Universal Declaration of Human Rights adopted by the United Nations general assembly in 1948, the Declaration of Independence clearly related human rights to man's creaturely relationship to God. Whereas the United Nations statement simply avoids reference to any transcendent and divine ground of human rights, the French Declaration is openly hostile to theistic presuppositions. The French philosophes of the eighteenth century, rejecting the view that man is essentially evil and unable to save himself, developed a doctrine of the rights of man in conscious opposition to the Christian view of man. Then as today, humanism (q.v.) erred in regarding human rights as ends in themselves divorced from any reference to God.

The Christian recognizes that God is the source and sanction of human rights, that human rights are a means to the end of aiding men in meeting their duties to God, and that government exists for the primary purpose of protecting basic human rights. As men exercise their rights properly, they fulfill their obligations to God and to other men. Man's rights are subordinate to the duties he owes God.

To have a right is to have a legally or morally justifiable claim to possess or obtain something or to act in a certain way. Having a right is a triadic relationship involving the person possessing the right, other persons having a duty to observe that right, and the object or thing which the right concerns.

An important distinction exists between positive rights and natural rights (q.v.). Natural rights are rights that men possess regardless of the decrees and policies of a state. Natural rights are grounded on natural law (q.v.) (which the Christian interprets as the law of God) and on human dignity, a dignity that man (q.v.) possesses by virtue of his creation in the image of God. Positive rights are given by the state, grounded on positive law and backed by some sanction. While natural rights must be expressed in positive rights, the Christian must avoid the positivist view that rejects the notion of natural right. Leo Strauss has observed, "To reject natural right is tantamount to saying that all right is positive right, and this means that which is right is determined exclusively by the legislators and the courts of the various countries" (*Natural Right and History*, Chicago, University of Chicago, 1953, p. 2). However, many theories of natural rights are as unbiblical and unchristian as the positivist position. Theories of human rights that based those rights on naturalistic and humanistic grounds (e.g., the French Declaration) are incompatible with revealed truth. If there is no God and man is not a creature of God, why should man possess rights that a tree, dog or camel does not possess? Surely the Christian hypothesis that man carries the image of God (q.v.) supplies a ground for human rights that secular theories fail to provide.

Some might argue that no doctrine of human rights can be found in Scripture. This is certainly true if one searches the Scriptures for any statement similar to those produced by the Enlightenment. Some might also appeal to the fact that the concept of human rights is a post-medieval development and cannot therefore have any necessary relationship to Christian thought. There is, however, a simple answer. In many cases (those that philosophers call Demand Rights) rights and duties are correlative. That is, if A has a right with respect to B, the B has a corresponding duty with respect to A. In this sense, every demand right is simply a duty looked at from a different perspective. In other words, certain notions that at one time are stated in terms of rights can at other times be expressed in terms of duties. When the Scriptures assert that A has a *duty* to B, it is also implying that B has a right with respect to A. Thus the second table of the Decalogue can be seen not only as a list of man's duties to other men but also as a list of man's rights. In this way, Scripture implies that men possess rights to life, property, truth, etc.

It seems best not to regard any human rights as absolute or inalienable, however. Human rights sometimes come into conflict and require adjudication. Scripture, for example, recognizes that while man possesses the right to life, that right can be sacrificed for a capital offense. The proponent of natural rights should, moreover, avoid the erroneous view, inspired by Thomas Paine's *Rights of Man* and the French Declaration, that confuses human rights with human wants. This confusion is found, for example, in the United Nations Universal Declaration. Such alleged rights as the right to equal pay, right to marry, right to enjoy the arts and even the right to be idle are more aspirations than rights.

William K. Frankena, "The Concept of Universal Human Rights," in *Science, Language and Human Rights,* Philadelphia, University of Pennsylvania, 1952; "Natural and Inalienable Rights," *Philosophical Review,* vol. 64, 1955; A. I. Melden, ed., *Human Rights,* Belmont, California, Wadsworth, 1970; Leo Strauss, *Natural Right and History,* Chicago, University of Chicago, 1953.

RONALD H. NASH

RIGHT TO WORK. See also *Labor Relations.* The term "right to work law" is ordinarily used to describe legislation which protects the right of an individual to work whether or not he chooses to join or pay dues to a labor union. In the absence of such legislation, collective bargaining agreements between an employer and a union have included a provision which obligates the employer to discharge an employee who fails to pay money to a union even when support of that union's policies and practices may violate the employee's conscience. Opponents of such legislation charge that it encourages "free riders" who nonetheless derive benefits from union representation. Advocates of "right to work" legislation respond that unions, like all human institutions, may be good or bad, and that a "right to work" law gives the individual the opportunity to exercise his own discretion by supporting the organization only if he believes it operates in his interest and that of society. The Biblical ethic considers work a human duty to be fulfilled as a divine calling, and man's right to work ought in these circumstances to be protected from all discriminatory practices. The right to work law copes with one such restrictive policy.

REED LARSON

RIGORISM. See also *Probabiliorism.* The term "rigorism" is applied to a variety of views. Included are the following: (1) Those systems of ethics which insist upon the rigid universal application of moral law without regard for pleasant or unpleasant consequences. Examples are the ethical systems of the ancient Stoics and Immanuel Kant, whose views are also called Formalism. (2) Extreme ascetic practices such as those found among the Flagellants and the German mystics (Tauler, Suso), as well as among the Puritans of England and colonial America. (3) The Roman Catholic doctrine of Tutiorism (from Lat. for "safer"). The kinship appears in the fact that while Rigorism requires radical renunciation of hedonism and avoidance of laxity, Tutiorism counsels that when one is in doubt over two opinions, right action takes the course more conducive to moral safety. (4) Any insistence on obeying the letter of the law, or combining legalism with literalism.

DELBERT R. GISH

RITSCHL AND PROTESTANT ETHICS.

Albrecht Ritschl was born in Berlin, March 25, 1822. Subsequently trained at Bonn and Halle, he studied for short periods also at Heidelberg and Tübingen. He held full professorships at Bonn (1846-64) and Göttingen (1864-89). His principal works include *Die christliche Lehre von der Rechtfertigung und Versohnung, Die Geschichte des Pietismus, Unterricht in der christlichen Religion,* and *Theologie und Metaphysik.* He died March 20, 1889.

The early influences on Ritschl were the Tübingen school and Hegelian metaphysics. He left these positions behind, however, and came greatly under the influence of Kant and Lotze. Ritschl accepted the Kantian rejection of metaphysics, and sought to examine Christianity in light of this commitment. Thus, he accepted the fact that there was a God who revealed himself in Christ, but rejected the belief that he could be reached through theoretical reason. Thus, Ritschl was led to radical disjuncture between scientific and theological discourse. The former makes theoretical judgments, while the latter is characterized by value-judgments. To say that Christ is God does not make a metaphysical claim (although such a claim may be implicit in such a statement) but acknowledges his supreme worth (the making of a value judgment). Thus special stress was laid upon the ethical and practical aspects of Christianity rather than on the intellectual and speculative.

Unlike Kant, however, Ritschl accorded primacy to religion over philosophy, since the spiritual (noumenal) is greater than the material (phenomenal). For Ritschl Christianity is the highest form of religion since it is absolutely ethical as founded upon Christ the founder of the Kingdom of God. Original sin is rejected as unhistorical and therefore unverifiable. Sin is to be understood as the result of finitude, particularly ignorance. It may be forgiven so long as it has not hardened into a final rejection of God, of which there are no known cases. Thus, Ritschl holds out the possibility of universalism (q.v.) without affirming it. Evil, on the other hand, has a specialized meaning. It refers to possible restrictions on purposeful activity. It may be allowed as disciplinary or for some ultimate benevolent end. For this reason, man is commanded to have faith in providence.

Ritschl rejects the idea that the death of Christ was substitutionary appeasement. The death was not some payment which the justice of God demanded, but rather was a bridge for reconciliation with God. The emphasis is on the removal of the alienation and the restoration of communion, not on a payment of any kind to God. Thus, Christ restores sinners to fellowship, as well as enlists their discipleship in the Kingdom.

The Kingdom of God comes into being wherever Christlikeness prevails among men. While the goal of the Kingdom is the transformation of society, Ritschl's ethics does not lead to a simple utopia. The Kingdom is more within and above history than at its end. Futhermore, it is impossible to rigidly codify imperatives for the Kingdom, since love, the highest form of righteousness, cannot be translated into legal prescriptions.

While the Kingdom of God is central to Ritschl's ethical position, he talks at greater length about the church. The church, however, is not the Kingdom of God in fact or principle. On the contrary, the Kingdom is manifest from within the church, but does not define the essential nature of the church. In the church the concrete life of the forgiven is seen, worshipping and seeking fellowship. The church is given a peculiarly Ritschlian interpretation. One does not first acknowledge the gravity of his sins, then come to Christ for forgiveness, and thereupon enter the church. The church is not for the redeemed. It is the means of reconciliation; through and within the church one gradually comes to understand his sin, and also to grow in the grace and knowledge of Jesus Christ. As might be expected, Ritschl placed a great emphasis on Christian education.

Ritschl's views influenced an entire generation of Protestant theologians. His followers included such diverse personalities as Julius Kaftan, Wilhelm Herrmann, Ferdinand Kattenbusch, Friedrich Loofs, and Adolph von Harnack.   PAUL D. FEINBERG

ROBINSON, JOHN A. T. J. A. T. Robinson (1919) was lecturer in Divinity at Cambridge University from 1954-59; then became bishop of Woolwich (1959-69). Since 1969 he has been Dean of Chapel of Trinity College, Cambridge, and lecturer in Theology.

Early writings, *In the End God* (New York, Harper & Row, 1950), *Jesus and His Coming* (Nashville, Abingdon, 1957), *Christ Comes In* (1960), *Twelve New Testament Studies* (Naperville, Allenson, 1962) reflect his interest in New Testament studies. They are generally characterized by an extreme statement of the so-called "realized eschatology." His *Honest to God* (Philadelphia, Westminster, 1963) followed by *Christian Morals Today* (Philadelphia, Westminster, 1964), *The New Reformation* (Philadelphia, Westminster, 1965), *Exploration into God* (Stanford, Calif., Stanford University, 1967), and *Christian Freedom in a Permissive Society* (Philadelphia, Westminster, 1970) are marked by an ethical concern under the influence of Dietrich Bonhoeffer (q.v.), Rudolf Bultmann (q.v.), and Paul Tillich (q.v.).

Considering the framework of the Biblical message as prescientific and therefore antequated, Robinson drops the supernatural element from Christian faith and opts for a secular understanding of the gospel and a non-religious understanding of God. "God" is not met by a "religious" turning away from the world but in an unconditional regard for other persons seen through their ultimate concern. Robinson's "God" is no longer the personal God of the Biblical revelation, but is identified with the all-in-all of Tillich's "ecstatic naturalism"; and language about such a Being is resolved ultimately into language about man. In the specific area of ethics, Robinson gives bold advocacy of the New Morality (q.v.) in which Christian behavior is reduced to a form of baptized hedonism (q.v.). The law of God is replaced by a concept of love which allows no restraints outside its own judgment of love. The result of such views is to give episcopal blessing to practical epicureanism, and to ease the conscience of those who wish to fall in with the unrestrained license of the permissive society.

📖 *The Honest to God Debate*, J. A. T. Robinson & D. L. Edwards, eds., London, SCM, 1963.

H. DERMOT McDONALD

ROMAN CATHOLIC ETHICS. See also *Aquinas and Roman Catholic Ethics; Canon Law; Papal Encyclicals.* Roman Catholic ethics and moral theology today are dependent, in their main lines, upon the massive structure of moral theory constructed by Thomas Aquinas (q.v.) in the thirteenth century. While contemporary Catholicism displays an interesting variety of opinion in moral theory, all of it can be measured in distance from Thomas. The main body of theory appears to be close to the Angelic Doctor in form and substance. That has not prevented a number of Catholic ethicists from developing selected accents in the Thomistic structure to the apparent disparagement or neglect of others. Perhaps in no other areas of Catholic thought have the changes been more pronounced.

The main traditional Thomistic accents conserved are those summed up in the insistence upon the rational, legal, and therefore objective, character of the moral order approved by God. These have been the characteristic marks of Catholic moral theory for centuries. At times this has resulted in reliance upon a lifeless legalism in practice, a mere reckoning with objective rules. In the application of canon law, especially, specific forms of conduct are required in an amazing range of behavior attitudes and practices. The continuance of this legalistic strain varies today from place to place in the Catholic world. It is much less significant in the USA, for example, than in Spain or Portugal.

Many Catholic ethicists today approve an explicit distinction between moral philosophy (q.v.) or ethics and moral theology (q.v.), a distinction implicit in Thomas. Ethics is the behavioral province of every rational man. The supposition is that the natural man has the basic rationality by which he can discern the difference between right and wrong, as well as the rational will by which decision and action are taken. Men everywhere share the moral norms provided them by the natural moral law. Moral theology, on the other hand, has its source in divine revelation. It provides the ethic of the supernatural life, that of the Christian in his advance to his ultimate goal, the vision of God in the next life. Faith, hope, and charity are graces provided him by God, and he is sustained and energized throughout by supernatural resources. He is enabled to make a much better use of the principles of natural morality than the non-Christian. Much of the resources are supplied, not directly by divine gift, but through the ecclesiastical structure, teaching, and sacramental system of the church. It is at this point that the dicta of canon law (q.v.) play so significant a role, taking up the definitions furnished by moral theory and detailing them in specific requirements of conduct. A refined casuistry (q.v.) also has its exercise here.

As indicated above, Catholic moral theory today is not a monolith of ideas and practice with which all Catholics concur. Leading spokesmen (e.g., Bernard Häring, Karl Rahner, Dietrich von Hildebrand) are greatly concerned, on the one hand, to develop the "new law" accent in Thomistic theory, with its emphasis upon the dynamics of the inner life in active relationship with God's self-giving love through Christ (personal commitment and decision, an active moral conscience, etc.), and on the other, with the application of moral theory to the whole range of social questions troubling today's world. Remarkable work is being done in both areas. In the first, genuine evangelical ethical accents come forth. The Christian stands in direct and personal relation to his God, exercises moral freedom over against his dilemmas in that context, and simply lives as a Christian person without undue specification of behavior by the church. If given to egoism and concupiscence, the Christian becomes subject to the law's condemnation. The above interpretations, however, are as yet isolated, and often lonely, accents in the vast Catholic world.

Social theory, encouraged in modern times by papal documents of enormous significance (e.g., *Rerum Novarum* of Leo XIII; *Quadragesimo Anno* of Pius XI; *Divinis Redemptoris* of Pius XII; *Mater et Magistra* and *Pacem in Terris* of John XXIII), aim to spell out the demands of natural law in the realms of politics, international law, economics, family life, racial concerns, and wherever else Christian principle requires application. When the teaching church, particularly the pope, speaks authoritatively on such matters, they assertedly do so with the authority of God. Official decrees and encyclicals, however, require interpretation, and at this point Catholic scholars, conservative and liberal of varying degrees, are often in substantial conflict. Whatever the viewpoint, however, an objective moral order remains in focus.

📖 Henry Davis S.J., *Moral and Pastoral Theology*, 4 vols. New York, Sheed and Ward, 1959; Bernard Häring, *The Law of Christ*, 3 vols., Westminster, Md., Newman, 1963-66; Joseph Maasbach, *Katholische Moraltheologie*, Eleventh Improved Edition, by Gustav Ermecke, 3 vols., Muenster, Aschendorff, 1955-61; Dietrich von Hildebrand, *True Morality and Its Counterfeits*, New York, McKay, 1955.   ELTON M. EENIGENBURG

ROMANTICISM AND ETHICS. Romanticism was the first phase of German Idealism in the transition from Kant to Hegel. It had a strong influence on Western literature and the arts between 1775 and 1815. The ideas of Rousseau, Vico, Lessing, and Diderot are basic to the later Romanticists. Of other major Romanticists, such as Schlegel, Fried, Novalis, and Schleiermacher, perhaps Schelling is the most typical and expressive philosophical figure.

Romanticism stressed idealism in thought and individualism in ethics and politics. Taking Kant as a point of departure, the Romanticists sought to reject both revelation and reason as means of approaching reality, and turned to man's inner subjective or intuitive experiences. They believed that Nature was Spirit made visible and that behind Nature lay Absolute Spirit which is the creative force behind all phenomenal manifestations in human consciousness. Hegel later modeled this Absolute on a dialectic of thesis, anti-thesis, and synthesis which unfolded itself in human history. For the Romanticists, however, the Absolute was more an artist than a logician.

In contrast to Kant's strict ethic of duty for duty's sake and the radical evil within man, romanticists like Jacques Rousseau stressed human feeling and freedom as well as the natural goodness of man. Rousseau encouraged self-expression instead of harsh discipline. He strongly opposed tyranny, declaring that "we have a duty to obey only legitimate powers." The only rightful leaders are those whom the people freely choose, for the rulers right to rule is derived from the citizenry, not from the Deity.

Rousseau's ethic was a strong force behind the French revolution and modern democracy. The only proper government, he held, is a completely democratic one.

NORMAN GEISLER

ROYCE, JOSIAH. Josiah Royce (1855-1916) was the most influential idealistic thinker in the USA. He stands in the Hegelian tradition and through a lifetime of influence as a professor at Harvard University won many followers in America. His *The Problem of Christianity* (2 vols., 1913) contributed greatly to the development of liberal Christianity. Royce's ethical theory is presented in *The Philosophy of Loyalty* (1908). He defines loyalty as "the willing and practical and thoroughgoing devotion of a person to a cause." A problem is bound to arise when one faces conflicting loyalties. What is one to do? This solution lies in his proposed principle of loyalty to loyalty, that is, loyalty to a cause which will produce the highest possible loyalty. This is achieved by finding a cause large enough to include the ideals of opposing interests or sides. Loyalty, then, implies, belief in a universal cause, a highest good, a supreme value. One must be loyal to what works best for both sides, and ultimately what works best for all. The similarity to Kant's imperative is evident. For the Christian, Royce's commendable aim falls short of the ideal. For the Christian, conflicts and opposing interests are resolved, not by appeal to an abstract principle but to the life and teachings of Jesus Christ, and the inner dynamic of the Holy Spirit turns principle into a vital reality in human experience.

WARREN C. YOUNG

RULE ETHICS. See also *Act Ethics*. Rule ethics relates moral decision and activity to specific rules. In arriving at a course of moral action, one would typically inquire as to rules governing the type of action under consideration, and follow the relevant or applicable rule. This approach to ethics presupposes enough similarity among moral cases, so that some type of inclusive statement can be made. If one can determine to which class an action belongs, he will then know what rule should be followed.

Two basic views of the derivation of such rules are generally found within Christian ethics: the view that these are divinely revealed and the conception that they are rules of nature. These two theories are sometimes called "revealed rules" and "natural rules," respectively. The former says that God has communicated his will to man in such a way that man may determine it by examination of the revelation. The latter employs the methodologies of natural sciences and social sciences to discern characteristics of reality. For example, with respect to a rule prohibiting incest, a revealed rule ethic would appeal to a sacred Scripture (in Christianity, the Bible), while a natural rule ethic would note such data from behavioral and biological sciences as the nearly universal taboos, the adverse genetic effects should pregnancy result, and the consequent guilt feelings. While any generalization here is somewhat misleading, Protestant rule ethics have generally been based upon revealed or Biblical rules, while Roman Catholic ethics has given considerable place to natural rules.

One problem that must be faced by all rule ethics is the question of how to deal with cases which appear to be exceptions to any applicable rules. Some would say that there are genuine exempting conditions which dictate that in this case the rule ought to be broken. These exempting conditions would then constitute "rules for breaking rules." Another conception, however, says that the seeming exception simply serves to define the rule more fully. It indicates that the rule is more complex than originally believed. Thus, when the rule, "Always do A," is seen in case X not to apply, one ought to conclude that the more comprehensive rule is, "Always do A, except in cases of X, where one ought to do B." The Biblical commands of capital punishment and participation in just war are not exceptions to the rule, "You shall not kill." They serve rather to define it more accurately.

Rule ethics vary in the degree of specificity and detail of the rules. On the most specific end of the spectrum, a rule would dictate a rather concrete action and would apply to relatively few cases. On the other end of the spectrum, that of maximum generality, the rule approximates a principle.

Rule ethics is sometimes caricatured as legalism. It should be noted, however, that the essential tenet of rule ethics is that values are objective, so that normative generalizations can be formulated regarding these values. It is only when the rule becomes detached from the value and morality becomes attached to the rule as an end in itself that this ethic can be described as truly legalistic.

Christian rule ethics must always make certain that its rules are God's rules, not man's. While relatively few action rules as such are given in the Scriptures, all rules formulated should be based upon principles derived from the Bible by correct exegesis.

William Frankena, "Love and Principle in Christian Ethics," *Faith and Philosophy,* Alvin Plantinga, ed., Grand Rapids, Eerdmans, 1964; Paul Ramsey, *Deeds and Rules in Christian Ethics,* New York, Scribner, 1967.   MILLARD J. ERICKSON

S

SABBATH OBSERVANCE. See *Sunday*.

SACRIFICE. See also *Atonement; Expiation; Propitiation*. Many religions have had sacrifices as part of the accepted ritual by which man rightly approaches the deity. The Christian understanding of sacrifice rests on the complex and changing OT sacrificial system, where at least three different aspects may be identified. (1) Sacrifices were a gift to God as the sovereign lord. The costliness of the gift gave it ethical value, and by accepting it God committed himself in some way to the worshipper. (2) Sacrifices were a means of establishing communion with God. (3) Sacrifices expiated or atoned for sin. Each of these aspects has ethical significance: Did the sacrifice compel God to bestow mercies and favors? or to accept the worshipper? Did the sacrifice relieve the worshipper of the necessity for moral attitudes and actions? The latter is a particularly important point, and the opposition to sacrifice which was expressed by some of the OT prophets (Amos 5:21-25, Jer. 7:21-22) must be understood as a protest against perfunctory sacrifices offered without the appropriate moral attitude. Thus sacrifices were not a substitute for love and loyalty to God, but a means of covering man's failure to respond to God perfectly.

The tendency in current Biblical scholarship is to distinguish expiation from propitiation. Propitiation has as its object an angry God who must be appeased; expiation has as its object the offense of sin which must be covered. While both ideas are present in the Bible, the latter may be the better expression for the meaning of Christ's death. God himself the mover in reconciliation (II Cor. 5:17), as Christ is himself not only the sacrifice for sin (Mark 10:45; Eph. 5:2; Rom. 3:25, I Cor. 5:7) but also the priest who offers sacrifice (Heb. 2:17; 10:12). God gives himself the gift which men are unable to give, and thus he himself covers the sin which offends his holiness. This costly mercy remains partly mysterious and inexplicable, but flows from the dual essence of the divine character: holy love (cf. *Salvation*).

The benefits of Christ's death are not automatic, but follow from penitence and personal commitment to God through Christ. Thus Christian forgiveness, as OT atonement, is not a substitution for moral commitment and renewal or for rectitude of life.

📖 Roland de Vaux, *Ancient Israel*, New York, McGraw-Hill, 1961, pp. 447-56; Y. Kaufmann, *The Religion of Israel*, Chicago, University of Chicago, 1963, pp. 110-15.   STANLEY D. WALTERS

SAINTLINESS. Saintliness is that quality which is proper to or befits a saint. A saint (*hasidim*: saints, holy ones, I Sam. 2:9; II Chron. 6:41) is one who has been sanctified (*sanctus*: made holy). He is recognized as possessing a certain degree of kindliness, godliness, moral virtue, and piety. Holiness is generally conceived in a theological context, as relating to deity. The OT word *qadosh* (holy), while sometimes used to designate heavenly beings, as in Dan. 8:13, usually refers to persons of high spiritual and moral status. Its root suggests separateness, implying that a person has been set aside, consecrated, devoted to God and separated from all profane usage and conduct. The Greek word *hagios* (holy) derives originally from a cultic concept indicating that sacred quality possessed by persons (or things) which could establish or preserve contact with deity. Its *usus loquendi* is aptly demonstrated by its frequent appearances in the NT. Jerusalem—the Holy City—was reserved for God and his service (Matt. 4:5). The holy prophets of old were consecrated to the service of God

(Luke 1:70). In particular Christians were to manifest the quality of holiness or saintliness in their lives (I Peter 1:15-16). There is little question that Christians were held to be saints in the Lord (I Cor. 1:1-2; Eph. 2:19). Adherents of the Christian community were named the saints at Jerusalem, Rome, etc. Saintliness is therefore that virtue of holiness, godliness, or piety manifested by one who is motivated by divine relationship and prompting.

A Christian confesses that he has been called, enlightened, and sanctified by the Holy Spirit. Paul reminds the Corinthian Christians that they were washed, sanctified, and justified in the name of the Lord Jesus Christ and by the Spirit of God (I Cor. 6:11). Christ loved the church and gave himself for it to sanctify and cleanse it (Eph. 5:25-26). In the redemptive work of Jesus Christ God has reconciled the world to himself. In the resurrection of Christ he has pronounced his verdict of justification and restoration. By faith in Jesus Christ and his atoning work the sinner becomes saint, i.e., is declared righteous and holy in the eyes of God (*propter Christum,* for Christ's sake). By the same faith with which the sinner clings to Christ for pardon and cleansing he is at the same time internally renewed.

This renewal by the Holy Spirit is the basis for personal saintliness. Christians are bidden to present their bodies as living sacrifices to God, an admonition which Paul characterizes as resulting in reasonable service acceptable to God (Rom. 12:1). This is a spiritual offering of ethical and moral life, conformable to the will of God and to one's new status as a saint of God.

JOHN F. JOHNSON

SALVATION. The Biblical doctrine of salvation may be briefly summed up as God's answer to man's need. It is, therefore, related to many other Biblical doctrines, such as the doctrine of God, the doctrine of the person of Christ and the doctrine of the Spirit. Moreover, it may be summarized under two main divisions: (a) its main characteristics; (b) its implications. The latter section is most relevant to the sphere of ethics, but apart from a comprehension of the former it cannot be appreciated.

Since salvation is essentially an answer to a specific need, it is necessary to begin with the Biblical concept of sin as rebellion against a holy God, as transgression against God's laws, as a basic bias against righteousness. This at once puts man in a position of condemnation from which he needs to be delivered. It is for this reason that the need for repentance is everywhere enjoined as an essential prerequisite to the application of the saving acts of God. It is basic to the Biblical doctrine of salvation that man can do nothing to save himself.

Salvation, therefore, begins with God. It is he who takes the initiative as is seen in both OT and NT. In the provision of a covenant relationship between himself and his chosen people, God kept to his part, but man failed in his. The sacrifical system which formed the basic part of the cultus for Israel was intended to teach man his inability to meet his own need. The system itself, although instituted by God, could never solve man's condition, for the offerings to be effective had to be constantly repeated. In the NT the death of Christ is viewed as a final and effective sacrifice for sin.

Closely allied to the sacrifical aspect of the work of Christ in salvation is the idea of substitution in which he is seen to have done for man what man could not do for himself. He is seen as a shepherd who has laid down his life for his sheep and as a lamb who takes away the sin of the world. In this sense therefore Christ is seen as the remover of guilt. Through his death man obtains the possibility of a clear conscience before God.

Another aspect of salvation which has

often been misunderstood is that of propitiation (q.v.). Although the term has its origin in the pagan sense of placating an angry deity, in its Christian meaning this sense is missing. It is God himself who provided the propitiation in Christ, which transforms any notion of placating his anger. What is essential to this concept, however, is that salvation must be considered against the background of God's righteousness and the fact that wrath is an essential element in his holiness.

The Biblical concepts of redemption and reconciliation are along the same line. Redemption is based on deliverance at a cost. But the Christian is not redeemed by corruptible things but by the blood of Christ. Redemption means the breaking of the stranglehold of sin and the possibility of a new life. Reconciliation, much stressed by the apostle Paul, involves the restitution of the believer to fellowship with God, in the knowledge that all past hindrances are done away in Christ. The further concept of adoption shows that the believer is not only reconciled but is adopted into the family of God in a new relationship. He receives authority to become a son of God with all the privileges and responsibilities of sonship.

It is in the light of the saving work of Christ that the implications for human behavior must be considered. The NT never supposes that an act of faith in Christ is sufficient of itself. Believers must work out their own salvation with fear and trembling. This at once points to the ethical implications of the Christian position. The basic idea is that God who has taken the initiative in providing salvation sets himself as the new pattern for human behavior. "Be holy as I am holy" becomes the norm. Jesus insisted on perfection after the manner of God the Father's perfection. The Christian life is therefore seen as a constant striving towards a goal which must be considered as beyond man's natural reach.

Involved in the NT doctrine of salvation is the obligation to perform good works. Although Paul particularly opposed any suggestion of salvation by works, he nevertheless admitted the resonsibility of believers to demonstrate the effectiveness of their faith. James is specific on this point: "I by my works will show you my faith." It is essentially because of the new relationship with God which comes as a result of the saving work of Christ that new obligations are imposed. Salvation is more than an objective work of God. It involves the subjective response of faith and obedience.

DONALD GUTHRIE

SALVATION ARMY. See *Christian Social Movements.*

SANCTIFICATION. See also *Holiness; Perfectionism.* Sanctification may be defined as the gracious work of the Holy Spirit, by which he frees the justified sinner from the pollution of sin, renews his entire nature, and enables him to live a vital Christian life.

Biblical References to Sanctification. In the OT, the root of *quadash* is used to express the concept "sanctification." Although the etymological origins are somewhat obscure, most Biblical scholars believe that the root is *qad,* to cut. The fundamental meaning would be to set apart an object from common ordinary usage for special and sacred purposes.

Hagios is the characteristic term in the NT, and from it, various meanings of sanctification are derived. Basically, it means separation for service of God. The primacy of separation for service of God inherently required separation from the natural characteristic of man and the world which would obviate such service. Thus, it is easy to understand why *hagios* acquired an ethical connotation in the Christian faith. The *hagios* of sanctification implies not only an inner subjective reality but also external relationships. "But as he which hath called you is holy, so be ye holy in all manner of conduct. Because it is written, Ye shall be holy because I am holy" (I Peter 1:15f.).

Derivative of *hagios* is the verb *hagiazo* which is used in I Peter 3:15 and Matt. 6:9 as the process of rendering an object holy. In John 10:39 *hagiazo* is used in the ritual sense of separating from the common for sacred purposes. In John 17:17 the term is used to declare the action of God through the truth for the subjective quality of sanctification. The context shows that the setting apart is for the believer's consecrated service in Christ's mission in the world. This passage illustrated that even though the primary meaning is formal and personal, the practical connotation is ethical because of its direction "in the world."

A form of *hagios* particularly related to ethics is *hagnos* which occurs in II Cor. 7:11; 11:2; Phil. 4:8; I Tim. 5:22; James 3:17; I Peter 3:2; and I John 3:3: "And everyone having this hope in him purifies himself as that one is pure." Purity in the ethical sense is fundamental to these passages.

The term sanctification in the NT is the translation of *hagiasmos*. This word occurs ten times: Rom. 6:19, 22; I Cor. 1:30; I Thess. 4:3, 7; II Thess. 2:13; I Tim. 2:15; Heb. 12:14; I Peter 1:2. The teaching of these passages is primarily separation and ethical purification. The work of sanctification is the separation from all that is contrary to purity of the Spirit.

Theological Development of the Doctrine of Sanctification. The doctrine of sanctification was more implicit than explicit in the writings of the Church Fathers. Not until Augustine was the teaching formulated. Augustine regarded sanctification as a gift of the Holy Spirit freely and spontaneously bestowed on man, and included sanctification in justification. With Aquinas, the doctrine took its scholastic Catholic form according to which sanctification is worked out practically through the sacraments.

Luther rejected the idea that the Spirit was infallibly infused by the sacraments *ex opera operate*. Luther wrote: "The soul, through faith alone, without works, is, from the Word of God, justified, sanctified, endued with truth, peace, and liberty, and filled full with every good thing, and is truly made the child of God."

The Westminster Confession reflects Calvin's position: "They who were effectually called and regenerated, having a new heart and a new spirit created in them, are further sanctified really and personally, through the virtue of Christ's death and resurrection, by his Word and Spirit dwelling in them, the dominion of the whole body of sin is destroyed, and the several lusts are more and more weakened and mortified, and are more and more quickened and strengthened in all saving graces, to the practice of true holiness, without which no man shall see the Lord." (Chapter XXIII).

The Wesleyan Doctrine, from the teachings and writings of John Wesley, is distinct in that by such terms as "Christian perfection," "perfect love," and "holiness" (q.v.) it teaches the possibility of entire sanctification completed in this life. Generally, Wesleyanism teaches that the believer grows in grace and in knowledge until, by a final all-surrendering act of faith in Christ subsequent to regeneration, he reaches an instantaneous completion. This Wesleyan doctrine of sanctification stresses II Cor. 7:1; Eph. 4:13; Rom. 6:6; Gal. 2:20; I Thess. 5:23 and John 17:19. Much emphasis is placed on the Greek aorist tense which signifies an act, not a process.

Ethical Implications of Sanctification. Sanctification can be called the crowning attainment of human character. The core of Biblical teaching builds a bridge between death and life, sin and holiness, guilt and glorification. The entire Levitical system focuses on separating common objects for sacred offerings, all with a view to a pure life. Sanctification in the ethical sense is the essential element and summit of Christian life and experience.

The richer meaning of sanctification lies not merely in separation from, but in one's relation to the living Christ. Life in the Son is the aegis of an abundant life in the world. The texture of life is determined by the believer's sanctification in the Holy Spirit. Sanctification is the Christianizing of the Christian. Whether we can express love for hate, faith for fear, peace for persecution, truth for slander, strength for weakness, trust for mistrust turns upon our new being in Christ. A believer weaves into the detail of living the purity of the Spirit of Christ until the whole life style reflects sanctity in Christ.   JOSEPH R. SHULTZ

SANCTION. In ethics the term "sanction" is used in at least two ways.

First, it may mean any consideration, influence, or principle that requires or demands some ethical response; hence it is the very source, ground or authority for ethical decision and action. For Kant (q.v.) it was the essential motivation for conformity to the moral law in terms of the categorical imperative. One's moral obligation is found in obedience to this external, universally valid moral principle. Hence the virtuous individual is the one who always fulfills his duty of absolute obedience to the imperative. For the Christian the determining factor in ethics is the revealed will of God. While the ultimate authority or sanction is found in the Hebrew-Christian Scriptural revelation, the immediate and guiding factor is to be found in the fulfillment of divine revelation in the life and teachings of Jesus Christ. Stated in the simplest terms, the moral and ethical sanction of the Christian is the ethical teaching of Jesus. The love of God should be the central factor about which the life of the Christian is built. This divine love is most fully and clearly revealed in Jesus Christ, the norm for all Christian teaching and conduct.

Secondly, the term may be used to describe any measure invoked by an individual or group to secure compliance to a rule or law. As such it has been used by a group of powers to bring about conformity to some established principle or law. Thus, coercive power is used to assure moral or ethical conduct. Penalties or sanctions are usually imposed for non-conformity.
                                        WARREN C. YOUNG

SATAN. See also *Evil*. The non-existence of Satan is taken for granted today by any theology which prides itself on compatibility with the scientific world-view. Disembodied suprahuman intelligence, whether benign or malignant, are dismissed as intellectual archaisms, mere personifications of impersonal forces, or vestigial remnants of mythological (i.e., prescientific) philosophizing. Any attempt to rehabilitate belief in the demonic—whether, e.g., Edwin Lewis' speculative *The Creator and the Adversary*, Denis De Rougemont's urbane *The Devil's Share*, or C. S. Lewis' sophisticated *Screwtape Letters*—is tolerated only as the futile rear guard action of a routed supernaturalism.

Yet loyalty to revelational data requires the dogmatic postulation of a world-view in sharpest conflict with *avant garde* theology. Scripture discloses nonmaterial dimensions of reality which interpenetrate space-time and in which diabolical spirits operate. These are personal beings, possessing intelligence and will, set in unyielding rebellion against God. They are agents of a supreme spirit, himself the very essence of evil, as inconceivably mighty as he is inconceivably malignant, no second deity, though, by the dimension of infinity. Scripture variously designates him as a liar and murderer (John 8:44), the wicked one (Matt. 6:13; 13:9; I John 2:13-14), the strong one (Matt. 12:19), the prince of the air and this age and devils (Eph. 2:2; John 16:11; II Cor. 4:4; Matt. 10:25, 24-27), the tempter (Matt. 4:3; I

Thess. 3:5), the destroyer (I Cor. 5:5; 10:10), the enemy (Matt. 13:28-39), and the accuser (Rev. 12:10; Job 1:6-12); it symbolizes him as a lion, a serpent, and a dragon (I Peter 5:8; Rev. 12:3-17; 20:2).

While, to be sure, Scripture repudiates Manichean dualism, it portrays this perverted power as God's creature who somehow has become his antagonist. That Satan was brought into existence by God and that, as divinely formed, he was good, are legitimate deductions from the OT creation narrative. The dark hiatus between Satan's pristine condition and his present perversion is illuminated dimly by the statements in II Peter 2:4 and Jude 6 concerning those angels who left their first estate. Even less certain in their application to Satan's metamorphosis are Isa. 14:12-17 and Exek. 28:12-19, passages which depict enigmatically the fall of an exalted cherub. But, assuming their applicability to this transformation from submissive creature to wilful rebel, some light is shed on the origin of God's formidable rival. Prompted evidently by a lust for autonomy and selfglory, Satan refused to acknowledge his ultimate dependence on his sovereign Maker whom he hates and whom he aspires to dethrone.

With a vast host of subordinate spirits as his allies, Satan is able to exert an indeterminable influence on human bodies and psyches (Mark 1:23; 5:1-18; 9:17-26; John 13:2, 27; Acts 5:3; etc.). He is able to manipulate circumstances and events (I Thess. 2:18; Rev. 2:10). He also works in political affairs and through governmental machinery (Rev. 12-13). He is active, moreover, in the shaping of philosophies. As the prince of the power of the air—to follow Heinrich Schlier's explanation of Eph. 2:2 (*Principalities and Powers in the New Testament*, Freiburg, Herder, 1961, pp. 30-33)—he produces a certain climate of opinion in a culture, a *Zeitgeist*, a prevalent interpretation of life grossly misinterpretative of reality, a widely-accepted life that

passes as profound insight (II Thess. 2:3-11). He works, furthermore, in religion, imbuing idolatrous systems of belief and worship with a numinous aura (I Cor. 8:5; 10:19; 12:2; Rev. 2:13; 9:20). He even works to pervert God's own revelation, whether in a distorting legalization of the OT (Gal. 4:8) or heretical twisting of the gospel itself (II Cor. 11:13-15; I Tim. 4:1; I John 4:1-4). He endeavors to induce professed Christians to adopt the God-denying standards of his aeon (Rom. 12:1-2; Col. 2:20-23). Destructively bent on the undoing of divine creativity with its light, order, wholeness, peace, and love, he purposes to maximize discreativity with its darkness, doubt ("Yea, hath God said?"), disobedience, denial, disease, deception, disorder and divisiveness.

It is impossible to do full justice to the Gospels unless one sees them from the standpoint of a cosmic struggle between God's satanic antagonist and God's obedient Son. After the wilderness encounter with his adversary, the Saviour announced in a sort of manifesto at the outset of his public career that he had come to set the captives free (Luke 4:18). From then on, as his miracles demonstrate, he was locked in battle with the sinister fomenter. Peter puts it tersely in Acts 10:38, "God anointed Jesus of Nazareth with power, who went about doing good, and healing all those who were oppressed of the devil." The struggle mounted in intensity until it culminated on Calvary. There the enemy and his allies rashly overreached themselves, using their ultimate weapon, death (I Cor. 2:8; Heb. 2:14). But precisely by dying and rising again Jesus became *Christus Victor,* who broke the power of death, defeating his and God's and man's enemy (Col. 2:14-15).

Yet Jesus' victory did not completely nullify Satan. That victory, in Cullmann's apposite figure, was D-Day, a turning-point in the war when the enemy's power was decisively shattered. Now, though he is still struggling, the prolonged struggle is really a painful mopping-up operation. The enemy continues to oppose the will of God, motivated to frenzy by the knowledge that his prophecied doom is inexorably closing in upon him (Rev. 12:12; James 2:19).

Aware of this invisible struggle the believer is not surprised at the course of contemporary events by the development of heresies which almost deceive the very elect, the irrationality and violence of his era, the intellectual and cultural aberrations of civilization, the corruption and pride of so-called statesmanship, the hate and greed and lust which disrupt interpersonal relationships, the pride and pretense and power-seeking guised as religion. Aware that he is contending against powers too awesome and sinister for his own unaided strength (Eph. 6:10-18), the believer follows the directive of I Peter 5:8, relying on the Spirit and the Word, as Jesus did. He also watches prayerfully, asks for the gift of discerning the spirits (I John 4:1; I Cor. 14:1), and true nature of the tendencies and issues of our day.   VERNON C. GROUNDS

SCANDAL. Scandal is generally a false report intended to be injurious to others by casting undeserved doubt and aspersion upon an individual's or group's reputation. It may also be deserved by the performance of a disgraceful or immoral act.

In the first sense it refers to instances in which persons are caused to distrust and disobey others without legitimate reason. In Greek usage the *skandalon* was the movable stick or trigger for a trap, and refers to that which blocks a person from his proper course in living or that which causes him to stumble. In this sense offense and stumbling-block are often used synonomously with scandal. The NT contains stern warnings against persons whose scandal causes others to stumble, sin, or believe a false doctrine (Matt. 18:6-9; Rom. 16:17).

In the second sense scandal refers to true reports which are, nevertheless, offensive, disreputable, or slanderous. Scandal in the second sense is of two kinds. A true report may be offensive because the point of view does not easily permit a favorable interpretation. Jesus, for example, was a scandal to the Jewish community because his life was so contrary to the Jewish messianic expectations (I Cor. 1:23-24). The other presupposes the performance of a disgraceful or immoral act.   HERBERT K. JACOBSEN

SCHLEIERMACHER AND PROTESTANT ETHICS. Friedrich D. E. Schleiermacher (1768-1834) is sometimes known as the "father of modern theology." Perhaps the most important of his influential innovations is that his view on the final authority in religious matters is not Scripture (as in orthodox Protestantism), nor natural reason (as in pre-Kantian rationalism), nor a combination of these plus tradition (as in Roman Catholicism), but intuitive religious feeling. For Schleiermacher, "Christian doctrines are accounts of the Christian religious affections set forth in speech" (*The Christian Faith*, Edinburgh, T. and T. Clark, 1928, p. 76). The influence of this principle upon modern liberal Protestantism, and not least upon modern liberal Protestant ethics, is incalculable. Schleiermacher's specifically ethical writings, however (*Grundlinien einer Kuitik der Bisherigen Sittenlehre, Grundriss der Philosophischen Ethik*), have had comparatively little impact on recent thought. This fact would have disappointed Schleiermacher, for he regarded his ethical works as in one sense the capstone of his theological labors and even regarded dogmatics itself as a kind of subdivision of ethics (*The Christian Faith*, pp. 3ff.).

Schleiermacher virtually identifies ethics with what we would ordinarily call "history"—i.e., a descriptive account of the ways in which man's reason acts upon nature to accomplish its purposes. Specifically Christian ethics then, describes the ways in which the Christian's communion with God through Christ influences his actions. In line with this conception, Schleiermacher presents detailed "descriptions" of various goods, virtues and duties and the relations between them. Essentially he sees the ethical life as a struggle to attain "unity" or "peace" between apparently (but in his view not actually) conflicting realities—spirit and flesh, ideal and real, reason and nature, individual and universal, production and appropriation. etc. In this spirit he supports the development of "unity" in the political and social realms— the developing Prussian state and the Lutheran-Reformed ecclesiastical union—at least insofar as he feels that these unions had a firm basis in the popular cultural consciousness. He advocates broad social reforms, particularly improvements in the condition of the poor.

Schleiermacher contrasts this "descriptive" approach most often with what we might call a "normative" approach—i.e. the exposition of an eternal, authoritative standard which demands man's obedience (*The Christian Faith*, pp. 517ff.). Like the modern "situationist," Schleiermacher belittles the value of "law" to exalt that of "love." In his view, law "does not pierce behind the outward act" and thus cannot deal with inward motives. This view leads him to the paradoxical position that the two great commandments of the law (Matt. 22:36-40) are not commandments at all! Such a view has a substantial weakness: if consistent it has no basis for declaring *anything* to be right or wrong! Mere description cannot yield such evaluations, which require a Biblical appreciation of the law of God (Deut. 6:1-9; Matt. 5:17-19; John 14:15).   JOHN M. FRAME

SCHWEITZER, ALBERT. See also *Interim Ethics.* Albert Schweitzer (1875-1965), world-famous theologian and missionary doctor was born in Alsace in 1875, the son of a Protestant pastor. He was distinguished not only in theology and medical service, but also as a musician, becoming an authority on Johann Sebastian Bach. During theological and philosophical education at the University of Strasbourg he came under the influence of the New Testament professor, Heinrich Holtzmann, whose commentaries on the Synoptic Gospels challenged Schweitzer to think out his own independent line. His theory strongly challenging Holtzmann's position, was incorporated in a book published in 1906 dealing with criticism from Reimarus to Wrede. Translated into English four years later as *The Quest of the Historical Jesus,* it exerted wide influence in the ongoing debates in New Testament criticism. The gist of Schweitzer's theory is that the Gospels were the product of early Christian theology and could not be considered to be reliable guides to the historical Jesus. His own view was that Jesus was a disillusioned eschatological prophet, who had mistakenly but fervently believed in the imminence of the eschatological kingdom. The radical nature of the hypothesis exposed him to severe criticism. It was in the context of this near expectation of the kingdom that Schweitzer's theory of *Interim Ethik* has relevance. The teaching of Jesus was regarded as strictly temporary until the kingdom was established.

Schweitzer wrote other books, among them *The Mysticism of Paul the Apostle* (1931) and *Paul and His Interpreters* (1912), both works of great erudition. His practical missionary work at Lamborene in French Equatorical Africa made him one of the most notable humanitarians of the first half of the twentieth century. It illustrated much of the ethical theory which he set out in his book on *Civilization and Ethics* (1923) stressing "reverence for life" in a pantheistic manner.   DONALD GUTHRIE

SCIENCE AND ETHICS. See also *Atom-*

ic Energy; Environmental Pollution; Technocracy and Technology. The inter-relationship of ethics and science has rapidly become a crucial issue of our time. Precipitated by the development of atomic warfare, awareness of this issue has been augmented by the ecological crisis, the technological rape of our environment, the mounting understanding and manipulation of human genetic material at the biological level, and the advances in medical science. When the author of *Ad Diognetum*, in the second century of the Christian era, likened the function of the Christian in the world to that of the soul in the body, he reminds us of our own position in today's world. The church has no right to oppose scientific advance, but, as the prophetic voice and the Christian conscience of the human community, it must make itself heard in proper direction and use of such advances.

We need to clarify in our thinking the method and function of natural science and the limits which are set by its very approach to nature. Modern science with its emphasis on the experimental approach to nature first came to birth within our Western culture in the breakup of the great age of faith in the later medieval period. It has one root in Greek rationalism, with its emphasis on the rational and mathematical structures implicit in reality. The other root lies in the world-affirming nature of the Christian faith. The Biblical faith is not world-denying like so many Eastern religions (e.g., Hinduism and Buddhism). Its doctrine of creation sees God as declaring the world to be good (Gen. 1). Its understanding of man as made in the divine image sees him as given dominion over the lower orders of creation (Gen. 1:26, 18ff.; Ps. 8:5ff.). Its prophetic voices declare history to be the scene for the fulfillment of the divine purpose. Its central disclosure is found in Jesus of Nazareth as the incarnate presence of the living God in one genuine human life, in which our humanity and our historicity are affirmed as significant in the purpose and life of God himself. The healing miracles of our Lord link up our world and our natural environment with the divine concern. And the Christian hope finds a place for the redemption of the whole universe so that the whole creation is groaning and travailing waiting for the final unveiling of the sons of God (Rom. 8:22). In that day, Christ will sum up all things in himself, things on earth and things in heaven, and there will be a new heaven and a new earth in which righteousness is regnant (Col. 1:19f.; Eph. 1:10; II Peter 3:13; Rev. 21:1ff.; Isa. 65:17; 66:22). Furthermore, the disclosure of God comes to us through what is observable by the senses, through nature, through the movements of history, through the behavior of human beings like the prophets, and supremely through Jesus of Nazareth. From the Christian faith, science derived its concern for nature and its empirical approach to nature.

With such a background, the methodology of science developed as a combination of rationalism (especially in its mathematical form) and empiricism. Believing nature to be intelligible, the scientist seeks for rational models (initially mechanistic and increasingly mathematically symbolic and statistical) by which such intelligibility may be represented. Believing that the approach must be through sensible observation, the scientist seeks to devise experiments by which the validity of such models may be tested. The scientist is looking for general relationships in nature and seeking to describe its regularities. Hence his models must be universally applicable, while the more mathematical they are, the more they are susceptible to accurate validation by experimental measurement. Furthermore, he is concerned to predict the future behavior of nature and to control it to some degree. Hence he is concerned with past behavior, believing that like conditions will issue in the like results.

All this means that the scientist is not concerned qua scientist with what cannot be experimentally observed, with what is not susceptible to measurement, tabulation and his causal machinery. The first philosopher of modern science, Sir Francis Bacon, made this quite clear when he argued that science has no place in its methodology for dealing with what cannot be, theoretically or practically, subject to empirical observation. First and final causes, forms, human souls, categories like "God," "teleology," "purpose," "soul," "creation" find no place in the scientific vocabulary. This means that purely at the scientific level, the scientist cannot deal with ethics and conscience.

There are, of course, scientists like Julian Huxley and C. H. Waddington who believe that a system of ethics can be derived from the scientific approach to nature. But such derivation is not really a part of the scientific discipline. It arises from a certain philosophical approach, a faith-stance. When scientists affirm that the scientific approach to the world is the only viable way of knowing, and ban all spiritual and revelatory insights which are not scientifically verifiable, such naturalism or "scientism" is itself not science but imposed on science. Science is itself ethically neutral.

Only one dimension of a scientist's human personality, however, is concerned with the pursuit of scientific truth. Man is a multidimensional being. He is, as W. H. Thorpe has emphasized, distinguished from the animal order by his concern for absolute values. These values embrace goodness and beauty as well as truth. Too often, in the past centuries, the pursuit of truth has been divorced from the vision of the good at the moral level. The scientist does have a conscience, however much his scientific interests may tend to submerge it. He is a responsible being, both to pursue the truth and to pursue the good. In the Western culture both the scientific pursuit and the

moral obligation alike have their source in the Christian disclosure. We have divorced them at our own peril, and, in so doing, we have dehumanized man. A scientist with no moral concern is a mere shadow of man at his noblest, however much his scientific work may betray genius and insight. Certainly, at the Christian level, scientific and moral judgment should go hand in hand.

In the early years of scientific development, most scientists were men with Christian commitment—e.g., Copernicus, Galileo, Descartes, Bacon, Boyle, Newton, Ray, Priestley. Their ethical judgment on the consequences of scientific discovery is very evident, for they believed that in their scientific work they were studying the mind and wisdom of the Creator. Man in God's image was man the scientist, for science was the means by which dominion could be exercised over nature. It gave man an understanding of *The Wisdom of God in Creation* (the title of John Ray's book). We find Michael Faraday refusing to condone the use of poison gas (eighteenth century!) and Sir Isaac Newton caustically condemning an invention for making artillery more destructive. In our own day a large group of international scientists protests the prostitution of atomic science to nuclear warfare. Some of them humanist and even Marxist, many with no Christian commitment, they testify to the scientist's ethical concern. Hence we have Thorpe's affirmation that what differentiates man from the animal order is his concern for values.

At the level of Christian disclosure certain moral principles stand clear. As the conscience of the community, Christians need to emphasize these prophetically, in preaching, teaching and all forms of Christian witness. Central is the emphasis on concern for the human person as potentially a child of God, for whom the Christ was pleased to die. This principle needs to be applied to the enormities of modern warfare, chemical and nuclear, and to the technological exploitation of human beings by modern industry. The supreme worth of the human person also carries with it the issue of the morally responsible relationship of human beings, particularly with regard to the relationship of the sexes and the nature of the marriage covenant. Christian thought needs to be brought to bear upon issues now coming to the fore—the indiscriminate use of abortion, the artificial insemination of female eggs by selected male sperm, the possibilities opened up by the new understanding of the coding of human genetic material and its possible manipulation. Again, the new psychological methods and also the chemical devices employed for "brain washing" and robbing people of their God-given freedom and capacity for free decision call for a prophetic judgment by Christian thinkers. Finally, the church has never developed an ethical approach to nature, and now the environmental problem confronts us all. Yet the material for this ethical approach lies in the Biblical disclosure with its emphasis on a covenantal structure which applies to man's relation to nature as well as to his relation to God and to his fellow man. Only when we have accepted this level of moral responsibility, can we speak responsibly to the ecological issues of our time.

📖 L. Augenstein, *Come Let Us Play God*, New York, Harper and Row, 1969; C. A. Coulson, *Science, Technology and the Christian*, Nashville, Abingdon, 1960; F. T. Ebling, ed., *Biology and Ethics*, New York, Academic, 1969; J. S. Huxley, *Evolution and Ethics*, New York AMS, 1896; A. Rosenfeld, *The Second Genesis: The Coming Control of Life*, Englewood Cliffs, Prentice-Hall, 1969; E. C. Rust, *Science and Faith: Towards a Theological Understanding of Nature*, New York, Oxford University, 1967; _____, *Nature and Man in Biblical Thought*, London, Lutterworth, 1953; _____, *Nature: Garden or Desert?*, Waco, Word, 1971; W. H. Thorpe, *Science, Man and Morals*, Ithaca, Cornell University, 1966.

ERIC C. RUST

SCRIPTURES. See *Bible; Revelation*.

SCRUPULOSITY. This term refers to the extremely conscientious attitude—hesitant, laborious, uncertain—which some persons manifest in the presence of moral alternatives. The victim of scrupulosity seeks a degree of certitude which the more self-confident person regards as impossible to achieve. He demands of himself a standard of righteousness quite inconsistent with the realities of life in the normal social order.

The difficulty appears most noticeably in early adolescent years. Typically it arises with reference to sexual behavior, but may focus upon any moral issue. A person who condemns himself for a selected fault not infrequently fails to recognize how insensitive his conscience is at another point. On the one hand he agonizes over a trifle; on the other he excuses or ignores fundamental sins. Moreover his punctiliousness in some details of conduct and his anxiety over failure lead him in the direction of exaggerated preoccupation with himself. Thus a greater evil occurs: self-giving, outgoing love for one's neighbors cannot come to fruition.

Thus scrupulosity precludes the most wholesome ethical relationships. The conduct of life cannot safely be decided on the basis of private thoughts and feelings, but must be supported by more stable and enduring authority. Yet it may bring benefit; extreme conscientiousness stimulates some persons to rectify bad conduct. If they will honestly face their problem and seek out wise teachers, there is hope for them. One difficulty is that the scrupulous tend to suspect counselors and refuse to co-operate with them.

Christian ethical teachers can aid the overly-scrupulous person by sharing relevant Biblical truth with him. The troubled one must grasp firmly the truths of God's love and primary concern for men's motives, the frustration of legalism and literalism, and the truth that no man lives to himself.

DELBERT R. GISH

SECRECY. In personal matters, Christian ethics has long respected the right to privacy as part of its regard for the individual. In Catholicism secrecy undergirds the sacrament of penance by ensuring the total confidentiality of confessions. The law upholds the confessional "seal" but is more ambiguous on counselling involving the laity or Protestant clergy. The professions (law, medicine, psychiatry) have similar traditions.

Invasions of privacy by the government, such as wiretapping and other forms of surveillance, have been justified because they enhance the social "common good" by limiting crime or subversion, but Christians are divided on this issue. Mass media spokesmen argue that persons in public life necessarily sacrifice their absolute right to privacy.

Christian ethicists have largely ignored the related topic, freedom of information in social affairs. In secular democracies, full information on public policy is a necessary component of citizen participation, and is generally accepted (though often ignored) as a means of extending individual freedom. Typical arguments against official secrecy are that it implies a low opinion of the public, gives advantages to the elite, enhances suspicion and rancor, limits the flow of useful ideas, protects the guilty and harms the innocent, and is—in any event—impossible to maintain in modern society. A degree of legitimate secrecy by government is usually recognized, particularly in matters of diplomacy and military security, but government has an innate tendency to over-extend its use. A classic conflict between government's right to secrecy and the public's right to information occurred in 1971 with the *New York Times'* publication of classified documents on formation of Vietnam War policy.

Within the church, democratic information procedures are largely accepted by Protestants, but Catholics are only gradually accepting the right of the clergy and laity to full disclosure on the part of the hierarchy.

RICHARD N. OSTLING

SECRET SOCIETIES. The term secret society has been used loosely for a medley of associations having little in common beyond an element of secrecy, and this may vary from a mere password to an elaborate ritual of initiation with a private language, peculiar ceremonials and symbols, and practices calculated to lend an air of mystery. It may be applied to Freemasonry or the Klu Klux Klan as well as to phenomena in primitive cultures. From this angle Maciver's definition of an association as "an organization of social beings . . . for the pursuit of some common interest or interests" applies equally to secret societies with the added proviso of re-enforcement by secrecy, either for the maintenance of the internal solidarity of the society or for more effectual domination over non-members.

The history of secret societies reveals certain identifying characteristics: initiation, secrecy, taboos, dress, rites and ceremonials, secret language, masks, and badges. Secret societies are found in primitive cultures and in more modern times have been prominent in times of marked religious decline. Among the early tribes in America, as among primitive peoples elsewhere, secret societies were intended not only to link together certain clans or tribes protectively, but also achieve a closer link with the gods or spirits.

In contemporary Western culture Freemasonry has been the best known and most extensive secret organization, tracing its origin to the sixteenth century and its formal organization two centuries later in Great Britain. In internal organization Freemasonry involves symbolic ritual, initiation, and the practice of secrecy.

The Communist Party has sometimes been depicted as a secret society, but this is not technically correct. The Communist

Party does operate in secret in many instances, but in an attempt to represent itself as a legitimate political organization it also carries on above-ground activities.

The Bible does not mention secret societies as such. Certain Biblical teachings, however, have led many Bible-believing persons to the position that spiritually minded Christians should not participate in secret societies. Such societies have often become a substitute for the church. Activity in secret societies has taken the place of religious devotion. Usually there is an emphasis upon "justification by works." Secret societies have generally tended to be exclusive rather than inclusive, and ofttimes they have appeared to be racist. Some believe that the New Testament teachings against the multiplication of occasions for taking oaths also exclude the numerous demands of secret societies.

In any event, both the history of governments and of the church confirm that a good society requires no cadre of secret leadership.   FRANK B. STANGER

SECULARISM AND SECULARIZATION. The word *secular* and its derivatives *secularism, secularity,* and *secularization* take their modern meaning from the medieval distinction between that which came under ecclesiastical (or, more particularly, monastic) jurisdiction and that which did not. Parish priests, for example, were called secular clergy because they were not under monastic rule. Until the last century *secularism* ordinarily referred to the theory of the separation of civil from ecclesiastical authority. Then G. H. Holyoake (1817-1906) applied the term to his own anti-religious views, and secularism became synonymous with a denial of all supernatural causality and an affirmation of a non-religious approach to existence. Today "the secular" is usually contrasted with "the sacred," taking the place of the earlier contrast made between the sacred and the

profane. Likewise, *secularization* is the name given to the process whereby a supernaturalistic understanding of the world is replaced by a naturalistic one, and religion ceases to be an effective social or cultural influence.

In the 1960s the relation between secularity and Christianity became a topic of widespread debate, to the extent of almost dominating the theological scene. The fuse igniting this explosion was fashioned from a few scattered phrases found in Dietrich Bonhoeffer's prison letters. These letters had been published by his friend Eberhard Bethge in 1951, and translated in 1953 under the title *Letters and Papers from Prison* (New York, Macmillan, 1967). Although Bonhoeffer there hardly used the word *secular,* he included an Outline for a Book containing a section on "God and the secular." He also wrote of a "non-religious interpretation of biblical concepts" which he felt that the age required, and said of the contemporary Christian that he should "live a 'secular' life." Taken by themselves, Bonhoeffer's references to the secular scarcely seem sufficient to have sparked the debate about secularity and Christianity that so engaged theologians during the sixties. Bonhoeffer's account of "non-religious" or "worldly" Christianity shows that it was not what ordinarily goes under the title of secularity that he had in mind, any more than a "secular" life can be taken to mean a secular life and nothing more. And, in fact, the use made of Bonhoeffer in this connection gives clear indication that those who referred to his advocacy of a Secular Christianity had taken their idea of the secular from other sources.

Paul van Buren's *The Secular Meaning of the Gospel* (New York, Macmillan, 1963) was one of the first books of the 1960s to lend prestige to the secular. Though appealing to Bonhoeffer as a forerunner, van Buren did exactly what Bonhoeffer had consistently abhorred, namely, allowed "the world" (in this case, linguistic philosophy) to dictate the essential content of the Christian message. Whereas Bonhoeffer had stated that the modern Christian should live a "secular" life in the world, van Buren insisted that the modern Christian must *be* a secular man tied to a secular understanding of existence—a very different thing. Other books following van Buren's showed a similar tendency to regard secularity as a norm to which any contemporary statement of the Christian gospel must be prepared to submit without question. Arend Th. van Leeuwen's *Christianity in World History* (1963), Harvey Cox's *The Secular City* (1965), and Ronald Gregor Smith's *Secular Christianity* (1966) all made reference to Bonhoeffer; yet, in their estimate of the secular, they followed the theory advanced by Friedrich Gogarten, who interprets the process of secularization as the direct and proper outcome of Biblical faith. (In 1966 Larry Shiner presented Gogarten's views for the English-speaking public in *The Seculari-zation of History: An Introduction to the Theology of Friedrich Gogarten,* Nashville, Abingdon.) Many other writers took up the same theme, advocating a secular Christianity with a secular Christ, a secular salvation, a secular conversion, a secular mission, and a secular future. Thus secular theology was ready to blend with the death-of-God theology of the later 1960s and with the theologies of hope and the future which were next in line and which fused NT eschatology with Marxist doctrines of world-historical progress.

While theologians have so widely assumed secularization to be an unquestion-able fact to which Christian faith must adapt itself, many sociologists are skeptical about the so-called "radical secularism" of modern man. They point out that present-day societies are "secular" only if Medieval Europe is taken to be the norm of a "religious" culture, and that even the most "secularized" societies provide no evidence of a withering-away of religion. In *The Religious and the Secular* (1969) sociologist David Martin argues that "the process of secularization" is an invention of ideological thinking, born of the wish to see religion disappear, and that it is supported by no rationally consistent body of facts. He states flatly, *"Secularization should be erased from the sociological dictionary."* Perhaps it should be erased from the theo-logical dictionary also. The secular and the sacred (or the religious) are correlative terms, and the one exists only in co-exis-tence with the other. If nothing is sacred, nothing is secular either. The secularist can deny only what the religious man affirms, and the debate between them seems likely to continue in spite of the predictions of the secular theologians.

Daniel Callahan, *The Secular City Debate,* New York, Macmillan, 1966; Harvey Cox, *The Secular City,* New York, Macmillan, 1965; Martin Jarrett-Kerr, *The Secular Promise,* London, 1964; Arnold E. Loen, *Secularization,* London, 1967; David Martin, *The Religious and the Secular,* New York, Schocken, 1969; Martin E. Marty, *The Modern Schism: Three Paths to the Secular,* New York, Harper & Row, 1969; Ronald G. Smith, *Secular Christianity,* London, Collins, 1966; Arend Th. Van Leeuwen, *Christianity in World History,* New York, Scribner, 1963.   KENNETH HAMILTON

SEDUCTION. Seduction is the act of beguiling an unsuspecting person to con-form to another's wishes and to act im-morally. Usually seduction involves the sex-ual exploitation of a woman's chastity. There are several Biblical examples (e.g., Dinah, Gen. 34:2, and Tamar, II Sam. 13:1-4; cf. Gen. 19:30-35; 35:22; Deut. 27:20; I Chron. 5:1). Biblical injunctions are found in Exod. 22:16-17 and Deut. 22:23-29. Prov. 6:23-35; 7:4-27 and 9:13-18 also counsel against seduction. The word need not, however, refer to sexual acts. To divert a person from performing his duty by enticing him into another path is also to seduce him or to lead him astray. The prodigal son was seduced by the glitter of riotous living. Men are seduced by any obsessive and/or inordinate desire that diverts them from their responsibilities.

HERBERT K. JACOBSEN

SEGREGATION. See *Apartheid; Race Relations; Racism.*

SELF. See *Ego; Person and Personality; Psychology.*

SELF-CONTROL. See also *Temperance.* Though the word does not appear in the AV, later versions, including ASV and RSV, have adopted "self-control" in preference to the AV rendering "temperance" in the three passages where *egkrateia* is found (Acts 24:25; Gal 5:23; II Peter 1:6). The verb, used in the sense of exercising self-control, occurs twice (I Cor. 7:9; 9:25). Only once is the adjective employed (Titus 1:8). Despite the absence of the word from the OT, the phenomenon is there. Joseph with difficulty restrained himself, that is, his emotions, when he conversed with his brothers who were unaware of his identity (Gen. 43:31). David, despite pressure from his men to kill Saul in the cave, refrained from taking revenge (I Sam. 24).

Lack of self-control in the regenerate produces a sense of failure and shame; in the unregenerate it produces ever bolder ventures into sin, accompanied often by wantonness, and utter lack of shame that parades moral failure as though it were a virtue.

A seeming contradiction presents itself in the listing of self-control as part of the fruit of the Spirit (Gal. 5:23). If the Spirit produces it in the life of the believer, how can it rightfully be called self-control? One may say that the meaning is control of the self rather than by the self. Further, the operation of the Spirit is not to be thought of as being so unilaterally compelling as to exclude the element of human cooperation in the achieving of the desired result (cf. Phil. 4:13).

The areas in which self-control operates are many: the appetites, ambition, temperament, speech, etc. What might in itself seem to be repression and therefore psychologically hazardous is relieved of this danger when self-control is harnessed to Christian service. Paul notes that the athlete in training thinks nothing of limiting himself, since only thus can he hope to win the race (I Cor. 9:24-27). If our goal is sufficiently worthy, sacrifice is not burdensome but welcome. Self-control is highly personal but its effects can be felt in many lives through the inspiration of example.

EVERETT F. HARRISON

SELF-DEFENSE. The teaching of Jesus as recorded in Matt. 5:38-42 (Luke 6:29, 30) is definitive. Proportional retaliation was permitted by the *lex talionis* (Exod. 21:23-25; Lev. 24:19-21; Deut. 19:21). It was exacted, however, by a judicial sentence and the individual had no license to take the law into his own hands. In any case, the intention was restrictive rather than permissive and vindictiveness was explicitly prohibited (Lev. 19:18; Prov. 20:22; 24:29).

Jesus repudiated any right to self-defense in unambiguous terms. Even under extreme pressure the Christian refuses to assert the claims of self-interest. Mention of the right cheek in Matt. 5:39 may indicate a blow delivered by an aggressor with the back of the hand which literally added insult to injury and, according to the Mishnah, incurred an exceptionally heavy fine (*Baba Kamma* 8:6). The Christian method is to meet violence with love (Rom. 12:17-21; I Cor. 13:4-7; I Thess. 5:15).

The personal example of Jesus confirms and interprets his teaching (John 18:10, 11, 22, 23; I Peter 2:23). Did he find the principle of non-resistance in the character of the Suffering Servant (cf. Isa. 50:6; 53:7)? To acknowledge Jesus as Lord involves conformity to his standards. The challenge of this higher ethic must not be evaded by reference to supposedly mistaken eschatological assumptions or by over-subtle attempts to distinguish between self-defensive self-protection, and neighbor-regarding self-protection. Certainly Jesus was suggesting an attitude rather than drawing up regulations, but it is an attitude which must be reflected in actual behavior in such circumstances as are described in Matt. 5:39-42.

This raises the ethical problem of reconciling our Lord's teaching with the claims of the state, particularly in time of war (cf. *Pacifism; Peace and War*). Some may ask whether non-resistance does not threaten the stability of social order and actually encourage wrong-doing. It is clear, however, that Jesus was not proposing universal legislation. He simply told his disciples how they themselves must act in a unilateral situation.					A. SKEVINGTON WOOD

SELF-DENIAL. In the symbolism of religious sacrifice the offering of a gift or animal victim represents the inner offering the worshipper makes to God. "Let a man deny himself," Jesus said, "and take up his cross and follow me" (Matt. 16:24). This invitation follows the announcement of his forthcoming sacrificial death (Matt. 16:21). The disciples were also to pursue a path of self-denial.

Paul cites the "mind of Christ" to the Philippian congregation: ". . . who, though he was in the form of God, did not count equality with God a thing to be grasped, but emptied himself, taking the form of a servant . . . " (Phil. 2:6-7). He himself had been "crucified with Christ" he writes, and thus "it is no longer I who live, but Christ who lives in me" (Gal. 2:20). He exhorts his Christian brethren to follow this example: "I appeal to you therefore by the mercies of God, to present your bodies as a living sacrifice, holy and acceptable to God, which is your spiritual worship. Do not be conformed to this world . . . " (Rom. 12:1-2).

In order to share more intimately in the cross of Christ, his followers throughout the centuries have frequently deprived themselves of certain pleasures and comforts. Among Roman Catholics the desire to offer oneself to God in a life of prayer and sacrifice has led to the establishment of religious communities. Desire for extraordinary sanctity led in some instances to denial or mortification amounting to bodily abuse. Prior approval of a wise confessor was designed to correct this circumstance.

Among Protestants the quest for holiness has also led to excesses. Yet the call of Christ to take up one's cross introduces one to the cost of discipleship. "When Christ calls a man," Bonhoeffer reminds us, "he bids him come and die" (*The Cost of Discipleship,* New York, Macmillan). But the joy of sharing the victory of the Lord remains. One is to "count it all joy" in the Christian life as he reaches toward completeness in Christ (James 1:2-4).

STEWART D. GOVIG

SELF-DISCIPLINE. See *Self-control.*

SELF-EXAMINATION. Many of the distinctive features of the human situation spring from man's capacity for self-awareness. From this unique fact emerge the perennial questions which are basic to the religious life: Who am I? Why am I alive? and Whence?

Jesus challenged his listeners to self-examination when he reminded them that where their "treasures" were their "hearts" would be also" (Matt. 6:21).

Knowledge of self is important for the believer's spiritual progress. Regarding participation in the Lord's Supper, Paul counseled the Corinthians, "Let a man examine himself and so eat of the bread and drink of the cup" (I Cor. 11:28). Moreover, all were to examine and test themselves to see whether they were "holding to the faith" (II Cor. 13:5).

For the Christian, self-concern explores the relationship of dependence upon God over against merely psychological supports and treatments.   STEWART D. GOVIG

SELFISHNESS. See also *Self-love*. Christian anthropology holds that man is God's highest earthly creature, lifted above all other earthly creatures in being made in the "image of God." Thus man becomes responsibly aware, meant to be God's child.

Sin involves man's self-centered denial of this distinctive endowment. The radical realism of the Bible insists that even the purest ideals and the most disinterested achievements of individuals and societies are stained by sinful self-interest and pride. Selfishness is a measure of the world's tragedy and man's proud unwillingness to accept the authority of God in whose image he has been made remains the mystery of evil.

Yet this very misdirection of human life is the presupposition of the gospel. To despair of man in his egocentricity toward God may be inevitable for some. But to despair of man in such a way that one really despairs of God is blasphemous. Although no individual can dissociate himself from a humanity so subject to possession by evil, God in Christ has reconciled the world to himself, "not counting their trespasses against them" (II Cor. 5: 19).
          STEWART D. GOVIG

SELF-LOVE. See also *Selfishness*. If "self" is defined as "soul" or "unity of consciousness," self-love is the instinctive as well as reflective self-concern or self-regard which is part of man's legacy and givenness as a creature of God. The Biblical view, however, requires an important distinction between self-love on the basis of creation and the implications for self-love of fallenness or sinfulness.

On the basis of creation, man was created with a natural and normal self-love; however, due to the fall of man, he is disposed and inclined toward unnatural and sinful self-love. Because of the adulterating influence of sin, self-love is now unacceptable as a sufficient norm for love. The description of men as "lovers of self" (II Tim. 3:2) is a warning against self-love under the dominion of sin. The self in sin appears to share a mysterious character, fluctuating between knowing that the true good and happiness are in God and in seeking for that good and happiness in alternatives that involve inordinate self love.

Since self-love provides no norm or standard adequate for the measurement of love, some other norm is needed. The Bible views God-love, or the love which comes from God, as the only approved standard for love. For example, for a person to love his neighbor as he loves himself (cf. Luke 10:27) he needs the love of God to regenerate self-love in order that there may be God-like love. Any effort to use fallen or sinful self-love to define true neighbor-love inverts the Biblical view, for not love to self but love to God is primary in Scripture. Furthermore, fallen self-love belongs to secular ethical norms rather than to Biblical norms. Screwtape wrote to Wormwood that God "wants to kill their animal self-love . . . to restore to them a new kind of self-love" (C. S. Lewis, *Screwtape Letters,* New York, Macmillan, p.74).
          CHARLES R. WILSON

SELF-REALIZATION. See also *Idealistic Ethics*. The Christian view is Biblically oriented, in contrast with the non-Christian view, which is anthropologically oriented. The non-Christian view holds that within man himself lie all the capabilities for bringing his essential self to full development. The Christian view is that man must realize the death of the old nature and be "born anew" with a new self (cf. John 3:3).

The non-Christian view is optimistic regarding the inherent goodness of the self; the Christian view is realistic regarding its inherent sinfulness. To seek self-realization on the non-Christian view is like seeking justification by sanctification. The Christian view seeks sanctification through justification.   CHARLES R. WILSON

SENILITY. See also *Aged, Care of; Medical Ethics.* This is a term applied to those physical and psychological deteriorations associated with old age. Some of the most obvious physical manifestations are the reduction of muscle strength, diminished coordination, wrinkled skin and stooped posture. Psychological and mental manifestations include decreased learning capacity, impairment of memory and emotional instability.

The process of senescence begins in the third decade of life but it proceeds at dramatically different rates in different individuals. Furthermore, there is no even rate of deterioration among the various manifestations of senility. Therefore, manifestations range from serious and wide-ranging impairments of some who are relatively young to only minor impairment of others relatively old.

When the effects of senility are limited in nature the moral and social problems are akin to those usually associated with the aging process. For the individual there is the need to accept and adjust to new limitations. For society there is the task of defining new and meaningful roles for those who are aging.

In the case of advanced stages of senility the moral issues become more intense. With advances in medical science the vital functions of life can be maintained long after senescence has destroyed the individual's capacity to function as a human being. Our folk language reflects awareness of the radical change in a person's life when we refer to a "vegetable existence." Such a reference assumes that the loss of capacities has proceeded to the point where distinctively human life is no longer present.

The basic moral questions emerging from this situation are: (1) What characteristics or capacities of human life must be absent before death is acknowledged? (2) How can this loss be determined clinically? (3) What behavior pattern can best retain our traditional reverance for human life in the context of our having the capacity to maintain indefinitely "vegetable" existence for many.

Christian concern for the elderly is rooted in an ancient tradition that affirms respect toward those who suffer the infirmities of old age. This respect is reflected in the story of Isaac and Esau (Gen. 27:1-4), which displays the responsibility of those who have wealth and strength to care for those weakened by old age (cf. Lev. 19:32; Zach. 8:8; Ps. 71:1-24 and Exod. 20:12).
                          DANIEL B. McGEE

SENSUALITY. Sensuality involves the gratification of the senses. It engages sense perceptions much more deeply than the normal stimulus-response reaction to environmental changes. As a person can exclude all direct conscious sensory input through methods such as transference of mental concentration to theoretical problem, so overstimulation can be induced by centering the mind on past or anticipated pleasurable experiences. Any of the senses may be involved, but the pleasure of reasoning is excluded. The results are reflected in voluptuousness, greed, licentiousness, debauchery, and addiction.

Aristippus, an early Hedonist, declared that man should do the pleasurable and refrain from the painful, and proclaimed pleasure the chief goal of life, even though unattainable for most men. Epicurus asserted that absence of pain and stilling of every natural craving would produce the highest form of pleasure.

Others have urged the fulfillment of all sensual desires, claiming not to do so would be sublimate and repressive, producing trauma and frustration injurious to bodily and mental health. Freud is often cited as affirming this view. Actually he stated that one must beware of overestimating the importance of abstinence in affecting neurosis.

New Testament teaching emphasizes joy as distinguished from pleasure. Jesus suggests that inward violent passion (Matt. 5:28) should be avoided. Paul frequently condemns the "lusts of the flesh" (Rom. 6:12-14; Gal 5:16, 17, 24; Eph. 2:3; cf. I Peter 2:11; 4:2; II Peter 2:10, 18; I John 2:16). Christians are warned to avoid "worldly lusts" and "pleasure" *(hedone)*.

Some Christians mistook these teachings as commending asceticism and mortified the flesh, hoping thereby to sanctify the body by pain. Paul affirmed that joy comes as a fruit of the Spirit.   W. IVAN HOY

SEPARATION, ECCLESIASTICAL. See also *Apostasy.* This term designates action of believers who separate themselves from their church because the latter has become unfaithful to the Word of God. In distinction from schism (a division without sufficient ground) and separatism (the attitude of those who motivated by some form of ecclesiological perfectionism leave their church), true separation occurs only when all means of reforming the church have been exhausted. There is neither a direct prescription nor a direct prohibition in the Bible. The OT portrays an entirely different situation (the theocracy!), while the NT does not know of a church that to a large extent has become heretical or preaches a severely reduced gospel. The matter must therefore be determined by the NT teaching concerning the true nature of the church and its unity. The Augsburg Confession summarizes it well: "The church is the assembly of all believers among whom the gospel is preached in its purity and the sacraments are administered according to the gospel" (Ch. VII). Believers have their unity in Christ, but it is also a unity-in-truth. Heresies may not be tolerated. The first task of believers is always to reform the church from within. If this appears impossible the believer has to decide before God's face whether he can stay in his church and share responsibility for what is going on. Some evangelicals believe that in certain situations separation is not only allowed but even mandatory as when: (a) the church itself in its official doctrinal statements opposes the gospel and refuses to repeal its errors; (b) the church compels members to believe or do things which are clearly contrary to the Word of God; (c) the church no longer gives freedom to believe or do what is clearly demanded by the Word of God; (d) the church in its official capacity refuses to deal with notorious heretics, in spite of protests or charges.

John Calvin, *Institutes,* Book IV, Chaps. 1, 2; W. Elert, *Eucharist and Church Fellowship in the First Four Centuries,* St. Louis, Concordia, 1966; S. L. Greenslade, *Schism in the Early Church,* Naperville, Allenson, 1964; F. H. Littell, *The Anabaptist View of the Church,* Boston, Beacon, 1952; M. Lloyd-Jones, *'Ecclesiola in Ecclesia'* in *Approaches to Reformation of the Church,* London, Evangelical Magazine, 1966; K. Runia, "When Is Separation a Christian Duty?", *Christianity Today,* Vol. XI, Nos. 19, 20.   KLAAS RUNIA

SEPARATION, MARITAL. See also *Divorce.* Marital separation refers to a wide range of situations in which marital discord or lack of troth (cf. *Marriage*) is so serious that, although it has not yet been legally acknowledged by a writ of divorce, there is in reality no longer any marriage. It can refer to persons temporaily or permanently estranged from each other due to marital breakdown even though for social, economic, family pressure, or religious convictions they have not sued for divorce. Often it refers to couples living apart in every way by mutual consent usually with intention of final divorce. At the same time it may refer to couples whose separation and the accompanying arrangements have been legally recognized and sanctioned.

Legal separation as separation from "bed and board" *(divortium a mensa et thoro)*

for a determinate or indeterminate time is to be distinguished from "absolute" divorce or dissolution of nuptial tie *(divortium a vinculo matrimonii)*. Legal or judicial separation is the usual arrangement for those who cannot tolerate their marriage even though for a variety of reasons they do not contemplate remarriage or seek complete release from the marriage bond. The strangeness of this arrangement (e.g., although physical intercourse with marriage partner is illegal, intercourse with another party is adultery) is explained by its rootage in canon rather than in statutory law.

Faced with the Council of Carthage's decision in A.D. 407 that marriage was indissoluble except by death, early ecclesiastical courts nevertheless recognized that in some cases the marital situation was intolerable and permitted the couple to live apart. Since the Roman Catholic Church, having further declared in 1563 at the Council of Trent that marriage is a sacrament, still does not recognize divorce; legal separation (in effect divorce without right to remarry) is still utilized extensively in countries heavily influenced by Roman Catholicism.

To justify legal separation without divorce Catholics traditionally appeal to I Cor. 7:10-11. However, since the thrust of the passage is the antinormative character of separation itself, the parenthetical clause—"if she does leave him, she must remain unmarried or else make it up with her husband"—cannot be read as legitimatizing it. Paul is simply stating that if a wife does leave—according to the norm she ought not—there are ways of regulating the wrong.

JAMES H. OLTHUIS

SERMON ON THE MOUNT. See also *Beatitudes; Interpersonal Relations; Lord's Prayer.* The Sermon on the Mount has achieved pinnacle status in the West as an expression of the highest moral idealism. It has been understood as the premier amplification of the "love thy neighbor" (cf., *Love*) ethic and of the Golden Rule (q.v.) which it contains.

Within Christendom, its status no less high, its thrust has been understood in quite different ways. Closest to its general cultural appropriation, and probably closest to the way it actually operates for most churchmen, the Sermon has been seen as enunciating a set of *generalized* moral principles (Ritschl), sometimes including a program for societal renovation (Rauschenbusch). When the *radicality* and particularity of the Sermon are stressed, it has been read as: (1) a call to particular perfectionist action (Windisch), perhaps (2) for a special group of believers (a monastic or sectarian ideal); (3) a now-dated interim ethic (Schweitzer, q.v.); (4) or internalized, as proposing an ethic of radical inner attitude (Bultmann, q.v.); (5) or, in its impossibility, as the law which drives men toward repentance (Luther, q.v.).

What is this document which is so variously viewed? With parallels in Mark and Luke, the Sermon comprises Matt. 5–7. Chapter 5, including the Beatitudes, discloses the righteousness of God's new Kingdom and applies its meaning to anger, adultery, oathtaking, resistance, and love. As well, it proclaims Jesus as the one who fulfills the law and the prophets and calls for perfection. Chapter 6, including the Lord's Prayer, treats the renewal of divine devotion—in prayer, almsgiving, and fasting—and enjoins that appropriate trust in God which will "seek first the kingdom," "serve one master," and thereby overcome anxiety. Chapter 7, including the Golden Rule, incorporates a number of injunctions—against judging, building on the sand, and false prophets—but also urges men to ask for the good gifts of the Father. Perhaps more important than a summary of its contents, though, is the tone of intense polemic and contrast which pervades the Sermon, captured well in Jesus' "It was said of old . . . but I say. . . . "

All too often, Christian ethical interpretations have been misled by secular appropriations of the Sermon—which could give credence *only* to the *teachings* as high moral wisdom, a kind of "Morals on the Mount." For the believer, the Sermon has no independent status as a compend of ethical wisdom. Its significance is determined solely by its relation to the Lord who gives it. Thus, one must ask about the Sermon as a whole in light of its speaker.

The Sermon would not *be* at all (nor would the NT itself) were it not for the Lord, crucified and risen; and interpretation must proceed from this foundation. Jesus Christ is "good news." Prior to the Sermon, in Matthew, he has been baptized obediently, granted authority, and has defeated Satan's temptation. Dominantly, for Matthew, Jesus is the *fulfillment* of law and prophets and "all righteousness." In this context, the Sermon is itself a fulfillment and an explication of what is meant that Jesus is fulfillment. As it represents an embodiment of the promises of the Kingdom in the mouth of its agent, the Sermon is both evidence that the Kingdom is "at hand" and an authoritative interpretation of the law of God, the norms of that Kingdom. The Sermon's particular imperatives are normative as the "prominent lines" (Barth) along which God's will confronts men. Less often seen, Matthew's insight into the Lord's fulfillment stresses the availability of divine *mercy*. The operation of mercy accompanies every deed of the Messiah, and he demands "mercy, not sacrifice" (9:13). The Sermon, then, spells out the implications of the nearness of the Kingdom: the transformation initiated by the presence of its agent, the mercy granted, and the righteousness demanded.

Whatever else it does, the Sermon points one toward the Lord, forcing thereby a decision as to whether one will be *obedient*. For the believer, to fulfil "righteousness which exceeds the scribes and Pharisees" is to be committed in a personal way to the one who fulfils. Thus, Matthew has linked obedience with the Christian understanding of discipleship: in following Jesus the perfection demanded by the law if fulfilled (cf. 19:27ff.). And the ideal of righteousness demanded is not abstract but belongs with redemptive events. Moreover, the righteousness *required* is both radicalized and resistant of codification. For example, "fruits" are one criterion of righteousness; but how difficult they are to assess if men are praying and giving alms "in secret"! Also, against its solemn, oft-hypocritical display, a king of "cheerful fasting" is enjoined. But if one is so joyful in fasting, how can other men help but know; and is this kind of joy really "fasting"? Such new righteousness is difficult to legislate! The new community is forced continually to bring its own internal-critical faculties to bear in scrutinizing its behavior and to persist in reliance upon its Lord.

Is the Sermon practical and relevant? Surely not as a general ethic or social program. It is as practical and relevant as new life in Christ—and, as such, at once a gift and a task.   RICHARD DAVIS

SERVICE. See *Social Service; Vocation.*

SEX. See also *Kiss, Kissing; Marriage; Procreation.* The Christian understanding of sex is based on the OT revelation of creation and the Biblical psychology of the wholeness of personality. Jesus described the relationship between a man and a woman as that of being made one flesh through the covenant-responsibility they accept for each other as persons. Sexuality cannot be separated from the totality of the rest of the life of a person. What he or she does sexually involves him or her as a total person and what they do together sexually is either potentially or actually effective for the rest of their lives. Yet marriage is a basically human, finite, and earthly institution, for in the resurrection there will be neither marriage nor giving in marriage. Consequently, the most important criteria for sexual behavior are considerate care for each other above all others, the refusal to let anything but death separate man and wife from each other, and the steadfast fidelity of one man to one woman to each other.

In Jesus' day, the double standard of sexual morality defined immoral sexual behavior as something a *woman* does. The good news of the gospel of Jesus Christ came especially to women in Jesus' teachings that men and women are equally responsible morally for their sexual behavior. The liberation of women from the position of being the victims of male chauvinism has its deepest and clearest expression in the teachings of Jesus.

In contemporary sexual ethics, however, the assumptions just stated concerning the sexual life of persons have undergone and are undergoing some severe challenges and tests.

The first challenge and test comes from within the ranks of Christendom itself. Several groups of Christians see the intimate relationship of sex between a man and a woman to be the domain of church legislation. The main thing that is here kept alive is the power structure of the church. This forensic or legalistic attitude resorts to the letter of the law while destroying the spirits of men and women. The Roman Catholic Church and to a considerable extent Protestant churches whose reformation did not revise inherited teachings about the family and the correlation of marital intercourse only with procreation must be severely criticized in New Testament perspective.

The second challenge to the spirit of Christ concerning the nature of men and women's relationship to each other is the psychoanalytic test of health. The moralisms of the Roman Catholic interpretation of sex were the kind of "victorianism" against which Sigmund Freud threw his weight. He established the truism that such a morality contributed to modern nervousness. But the reactionary teaching of Freud was itself distorted, and became, not an effort to recover the Biblical view of the unity of sex within the total personality of an individual, but an additional occasion to license, antinomianism, and sexual irresponsibility. These were results that not even Freud himself intended.

A third challenge and test of the Christian ethic of sex has come in the shift away from the cultural assumption that marriage is a permanent commitment of a man and a woman to each other. Margaret Mead, the noted anthropologist, observed in the 50s that a mood of tentativeness prevailed over the decisions of Americans to be married. Alfred Kinsey earlier said that one of the major contributing factors to divorce was the lack of determination to make the marriage last. Mead and others have recently gone on record proposing that the marriage commitment be a limited one in which persons would agree to be married for three years to see "if it worked." At the end of this novitiate period. they would then reassess their relationship and decide whether to make it permanent. This has even taken the form of a proposal on the floor of the Maryland State Legislature that the marriage contract be so written into law. Yet, as Douglas Heath has observed concerning the different communes in which "free love" seems to be the order of the day, the commune is itself short lived unless there is some clear understanding about "who belongs to whom" sexually, and unless the group has a purpose larger than itself and its biological gratification to give its existence meaning. The visceral meaning of the teachings of Jesus seems to be that in the biological tissue of one's being the *need to belong* in a lasting commitment "will out" in situations even where the teachings of

Jesus are never mentioned nor thought of consciously.

The fourth challenge and test of the Christian assumptions concerning sex has come in the form of situational ethics. This challenge, too, has come from within the Christian fellowship. It is based upon the insistence that the love of God and neighbor may make what would be right in one situation actually wrong in another situation because the context of an act assertedly gives the same act a different meaning. However, situation ethicists overlook the centrality of personal commitment in starting and keeping a situation going. Situation ethicists react against legalism. They fall into the same trap of the legalist, however. That trap is the tendency to make the act or the behavior itself the center of attention and to ignore the issues of the heart, that is, the kinds of promises, covenants, and commitments that set the behavior into motion at the outset.

The final challenge to Christian assumptions about sex is being posed by the contemporary practices of group or cummunal sex. Whereas even ten years ago these kinds of behavior were considered psychiatric aberrations, *Newsweek* describes them in detail as a new morality of normative rather than abnormal sex. Strange as this may seem, the real issue that group sex raises for Christians is the place of sex at the community level as well as the private and personally possessive level. Do we *own* our husbands and/or wives? Are they our possessions? We know that in the resurrection there will be neither marriage nor giving in marriage. Does this also refer to the quality of life in the here-and-now? Or, is this a reference that points only to the life after death? In more specific detail, does not the Christian understanding of human life first expose the raw nerve of jealousy and possessiveness in relation to our husbands and/or wives? Then does it not heal the infection with the capacity of sharing—at least at the level of

ministry to others, such as widows and orphans, etc.—attention, considerateness, care, and the other sublimated forms of the love of people of one sex for the other? Experiments throughout Christian history have sought to answer this question. The appointment of deacons in the NT to care for the Greek widows, the injunction of the book of James that pure religion involves visiting the widows and fatherless in their afflication and keeping oneself unspotted from the world are two specific examples. More recently the Oneida experiment, the Shaker experiment, and the Mormon experiment are cases in point. However, no all-inclusive, culturally convincing answer has been devised to the question of a person's positive relationship to persons of the opposite sex except his or her spouse. We have only a set of negative prohibitions, not positive affirmations.

In summary, it can be said that the deepest meaning of the sexual life is that in the Christian fellowship sex is the nonverbal expression of tender gratitude, personal adoration, and accepted responsibility before God. It cannot take the place of God, but it can infuse our service of God and neighbor with joy.   WAYNE E. OATES

SHOPLIFTING. See *Theft*.

SICK, CARE OF THE. See also *Christian Social Movements; Hospitals; Medical Ethics; Senility*. The ethic of prophetic Israel as well as rabbinic Judaism evidenced particular compassion for the poor, the oppressed, and the sick. In covenantal continuum the NT ethic takes up the concern for "the lame, the maimed, the blind and the dumb" in both the ministry of Jesus and the mission of the apostles. The cause of illness could not be so readily ascribed to either demonic presence or sinful practice; serious pathology provided the matrix for the "works of God to be manifest" (John 9:3). From the parable of the Good Samaritan (Luke 10) through the imagery of the Final Judgment ("I was sick and you visited me," Matt. 25:36) runs the theological thread of Christian charity. On this basis, in distinct contrast to the Graeco-Roman hospitals open only to the rich and the privileged, the early Christians founded the first public hospitals.

All disease and personality dysfunction usually exhibits physical, emotional, social and spiritual disorder. C. S. Lewis' observation is particularly trenchant: "God whispers to us in our pleasures, speaks in our conscience, but shouts in our pains: it is His megaphone to rouse a deaf world" (*The Problem of Pain*, London, Fontana, 1957, p. 81). Gradations of physical and psychic discomfort merit varying degrees of pastoral care and communal support. Patient care requires a skilled balance between spiritual and psychological counseling; the former provides moral and eternal insight, the latter support for morale and maturity. The one is redemptive, the other therapeutic. Most patients need both.

Ethical concern in patient care must exhibit itself where persons become totally dehumanized "cases." The strain on both patient and family in transplantation procedures, radical cancer surgery, borderline psychotherapy, terminally intensive care, etc., all engender overriding ethical considerations which may invalidate their initiation or continuation. Both the sanctity of life and the inviolability of personhood argue for comprehensive medico-moral treatment.

The followers of Christ are called upon to assume a role in the care of the sick. The injunction to "weep with those who weep" (Rom. 12:15) suggests openness to trauma, bitterness, anxiety and loneliness. The 1964 Tübingen Consultation ("The Healing Church") specifically and creatively relates Christian healing to the responsibilities of the local congregation. Here the spiritual and therapeutic gifts of the Christian community can be supportive of the disabled member. The oil of anointing (James 5:14) and the prayer of the faithful add their balm to the medical care being given. The Order of St. Luke has sought to provide in various denominations a systematic, weekly prayer service for sick or disabled parishioners.

Care of the sick has been a concomitant feature of the message of Christ throughout church history. The will to live, the faith to endure, the basis for hope and the support of love are all grounded in the gospel. The Christian's concern for humanity argues for the broadest distribution of total health care in the context of an agape ethic.

LEWIS P. BIRD

SIN. See also *Ignorance; Omission, Sins of.* Sin (derived from a Latin word meaning "guilty") is that which is contrary to divine law; or, more broadly, that which is contrary to what ought to be done. A sense that some things are right and ought to be done, other things wrong and ought not be done, appears in all cultures at all times. Despite many variations within ethical codes throughout history, there is a basic pattern of similarity among them. Such things as murder, lying, adultery, cowardice are, for example, almost always condemned. The universality of the ethical sense itself (the "oughtness" of conduct), and the similaries within the codes of diverse cultures indicate a common moral heritage for all mankind which materialism or naturalism cannot explain.

The term "to sin" usually denotes a deliberate transgression, for which a penalty or punishment may justly be imposed. In this usage, therefore, it is distinct from inadvertent acts contrary to what ought to be done, and from transgressions committed in ignorance. Related considerations are the concepts of "innocence" and of moral incompetence, associated respectively with young children and mental defectives.

A fundamental topic in man's ageless study of ethics is that of the origin, or origins, of the code which sin transgresses. Is the code "natural," inherent in the nature of things, as hardness is the nature of stone? Is it entirely subjective, the individual's highest view of himself? Is it the accumulation of the highest thoughts all men have had of themselves as human beings? Is it utilitarian, that conduct which generates the greatest good for the greatest number? Is it divine? Or is it a composite of all of these, and possibly of others as well?

In the great Mesopotamian cultures, and early Egypt, the ethical code was held to originate in the divine, revealed through kings, who were conceived to be the gods' earthly representatives.

Although the Greek and Roman writers who collectively compose "classical" thought were of several minds about sin, their major tendencies may be identified. Most significant, perhaps, was their rationalization of the subject—their attempt to eliminate the mysterious, the supernatural, and the imponderable. Not that the divine was eliminated entirely, for one cannot read Socrates (through Plato) or Aeschylus or Seneca without finding that the concept of one god permeates their thought; but the divine being in their works is more expressive of the best human ethics, carried to a level of perfection, than of a unique and super-human moral consciousness. There is nothing, in sum, of the Biblical teaching of the unthinkable holiness of God: "For my thoughts are not your thoughts, neither are your ways my ways, saith the Lord" (Isa. 55:8).

As to the culpability of sin—the pinch of personal responsibility, making the imposition of punishment just and inevitable—the classical writers were of at least two minds. For Socrates, sin results from ignorance, not wilful transgression. All men at all times, he asserts, desire the good. If a man knows what is right, he will do it. (This view is common in contemporary thought, as seen in the faith in education as the pathway to social and individual righteousness.) Greek dramatists, on the other hand, speak commonly of an inner flaw, pride (hubris); and in almost OT terms they depict the grim working out of the bitter fruits of sin through several generations. Stoicism, too, identified an inner flaw—the emotions—but did not assign moral culpability to acts contrary to virtue; only folly. The distinction is between the wise man and the fool, not the righteous man and the sinner. Platonism as elaborated on and expanded in the centuries after the death of Socrates and Plato, identified the inner flaw not as moral depravity but as imperfection inherent in matter owing to its temporality. In this imperfect environment, the body, the soul dwells as in a prison. Platonic dualism—"the soul is eternal and good; the body temporal and imperfect"—plays a persistent and permeating role in all later ethical theories of the Western world, being most notable in the early days of the church in Gnosticism (q.v.) (although that complex doctrine has other origins as well).

Since the beginning of the Christian era, the predominant view of sin in the Western world has been ostensibly Judeo-Christian. It has, however, been far from unified, owing not only to the rivalry of secular philosophies, but also to disunity and controversy within the Christian communion. Brevity requires that we limit our comments to the latter.

From the earliest days controversy raged. Typical were the contrary views held by two early (fifth century) contemporary Christian leaders, Pelagius and Augustine. At issue (over-simplified a bit) was the doctrine of original sin. Is man, as the natural descendant of sinful Adam, born a sinner, justly under the condemnation of God (as Augustine would have it)? Or is he born neutral, as it were, with the capability for both good deeds and bad deeds, one balancing the other, with the final accounting determining the individual's destiny (as Pelagius believed)? Though Pelagianism (q.v.) was officially condemned by the Roman church, it is essentially the Pelagian position, heavily larded with Platonic and Aristotelian dualism, that is most visible in medieval Christianity. To help in keeping accurate the balance of good deeds and bad deeds (sins), there developed elaborate schemes of sins of various degrees of heinousness, and of good deeds of various degrees of worthiness. Seven sins were "deadly" (unpardonable): pride, covetousness, lust, anger, gluttony, envy, and sloth. Thousands of other sins were catalogued in various ways as "venial," or pardonable. The heavy infusion of Platonic dualism in the Pelagian pattern produced emphasis on asceticism, or afflication of the flesh, which because it is temporal, was considered inherently imperfect (evil). Growing naturally out of these theories was emphasis, too, on penances, or deeds of self-inflicted mortification designed to "pay for" and cancel sinful deeds. And finally, most grossly, appeared the practice of selling "indulgences," either for sins committed or planned; the purchase of masses for the soul's welfare; and other human deeds calculated to counter-balance the sinner's sins and to cleanse him in the eyes of God.

From this moral environment (which would have appalled the most elevated classical pagans) there burst the Reformation (q.v.), returning to the Biblical view of sin. It is presumptuous to try, in a few words, to summarize this view; but the attempt must be made: sin is the wilful disobedience of God—the knowing transgression of his law, the conscious denial (in effect) of his absolute sovereignty in the universe. This sin Adam committed uniquely, for he alone of all created men knew God perfectly (not that he knew him totally, but his knowledge was without flaw and was perfectly suited to his condition

and need), and he alone, before the Fall, was without predisposition to sin. By Adam's sin was man (Adam and all his natural descendants) alienated from God, infected in all his original capabilities ("total depravity") through self-corruption, given a "natural" disposition to sin, and justly sentenced to physical and spiritual death, the latter being eternal separation from God. "By one man sin entered into the world, and death by sin; and so death passed upon all men, for that all have sinned" (Rom. 5:12).

To this imputation of Adam's sin to all humankind, rendering man incapable by his own efforts of conforming to God's perfect righteousness, are added those sins each individual knowingly and culpably commits. Degrees of knowledge vary, but " . . . to him that knoweth to do good, and doeth it not, to him it is sin" (James 4:17). Man's sinful nature before God is thereby doubly confirmed: by natural condition, within which he cannot please God by good works; and by individual acts of transgression. There is thus no human solution to the problem of sin. Only by God's direct intervention in human life through his Son, born in the flesh (incarnate), is man, through faith, able to have Christ's righteousness imputed to him, to be made alive spiritually, to be restored to fellowship with God, and to live a new life in the power of God.   CALVIN D. LINTON

SINGLEMINDEDNESS. See also *Mixed Motives; Zen.* The life and ethical behavior of a Christian are to be Christ-centered. The committed believer is constantly to love God with all his heart, soul and mind (Matt. 22:37), and to work out his salvation by showing this love to others (Phil. 2:12f.). This may not mean that, like the Zen Buddhist, it will be possible to spend unlimited time exclusively in meditation. But singleness of purpose in life will refer everything that is done in the course of daily duty ultimately to the Lord. The Christian is to serve Christ as slaves serve their masters, with singleness of heart (Eph. 6:5; Col. 3:22; cf. I Chron. 12:33, 38). This will not prevent the performance of "secular" work and menial tasks; but these can be carried out for God's sake and in his strength. (Contrast the "double-minded" man of James 1:7 and 4:8, who lacks faith and is torn between God and the world.) What is true of the individual Christian should also be true corporately of the church; Christians are to be "of the same mind" (Phil. 2:2). In both cases, the secret is to "have the mind of Christ" (I Cor. 2:16), and consistently to "set the mind on the Spirit" (Rom. 8:6).

STEPHEN S. SMALLEY

SITUATIONAL ETHICS. See also *Fletcher, Joseph; Utilitarianism.* Situational ethics, though popularly and correctly associated with the name of Joseph Fletcher, has a background in Nietzsche (q.v.) and Dewey (q.v.).

Nietzsche's evolutionary logic, repudiating Kantian a priori forms and making our learning processes nothing more than practical expedients for handling things, is the extreme of nominalism in the thesis that there are no identical cases in nature. Observed similarities are due to the coarseness and inadequacies of our perceptive organs. The use of moral rules therefore, treating different cases as if they were alike, falsifies the situation. Intelligence should evaluate each case uniquely.

Dewey invites the same inference. He constantly stresses the concrete (i.e., the individual) situation. For example, since the rationalistic theory affords no guidance and by its futile attempt to construct an hierarchical scheme of values or duties confesses it inability to judge the concrete, the implication seems to be that general rules should be replaced by an intuition of the individual situation (*Quest for Certainty,* New York, Putnam, 1960, pp. 265ff.).

If perchance Dewey would not word it just that way, there is no doubt whatever that Fletcher fulminates against moral rules and universal laws. He urges us to break every one of the Ten Commandments and insists that "Any ethical system is unchristian.... Jesus had no ethics, if ... ethics [is] a system of values and rules intelligible to all men."

The attack on system is sustained: "System is that which is most opposed to life, freedom, and variety." Later on he says, "Christian situation ethics ... denies that there are ... any unwritten laws of heaven, agreeing with Bultmann that all such notions are idolatrous and a demonic pretension." (Why did he say *unwritten* laws? It is the written Commandments he does not like).

Apparently in an effort to avoid complete anarchy Fletcher inserts a sub-head: *Principles, Yes, But Rules, No.* What follows is pretty much a play on words, but the pretense cannot be maintained, for two pages later he returns to his first love, "In situation ethics even the most revered principles [!] may be thrown aside if they conflict in any concrete case with love" (pp. 31-33).

Presumably he does not mean to throw aside his own revered principle, but clearly he has no sympathy with the universal laws of the Ten Commandments.

Love is what Fletcher wished to substitute for system, commandments, or rules intelligible to all men. On the page before the Table of Contents he quotes Tillich: "The law of love is the ultimate law because it is the negation of law; it is absolute because it concerns everything concrete." In his own words he says, "Christian ethics posits faith in God and reasons out what obedience to his commandment to love requires in any situation." Again, "the ruling norm of Christian decision is love: nothing else."

Ignoring his own prescription here, Fletcher never "reasons out" what love requires.

To be sure, he asserts that love dictates abortion on the ground that no unwanted and unintended baby should be allowed to live. He approves of bachelor mothers; and very clearly states, "Whether any form of sex—hetero, homo, or auto—is good depends on whether love is served." But there is no reasoning to support these assertions. Could not love for babies prohibit abortion? Could not love for God abominate homosexuality?

Fletcher indeed has some apprehension that love furnishes no guidance in the concrete situations of life. Accordingly he appends a method or system to remove the deficiency. Even so he never makes use of the method in solving any concrete problem. The method is simply the utilitarian calculus applied to love: "Love can calculate."

But if Bentham could not calculate pleasures, Fletcher has no easier problem. First, he does not make it clear whether an adulterer should try to maximize his own feelings of love, or those of his paramour, or those of his paramour and his wife, or perchance of the whole human race. Since in one place he uses the phrase "on the whole," the last possibility is probably the correct interpretation. But how does a man measure the feeling of both women? Second, the measuring is impossible because there are no identifiable units of pleasure or love to make counting possible. Third, if there were units, there is no way to total them for a single individual and a total for the whole human race is so impossible as to be ridiculous.

Finally, Fletcher rejects the Scriptures. He denounces Paul's "obscure and contradictory" views of the justice of God—"a confused wrangle in which Paul did not provide a cogent answer to the questions he raised." Fletcher seriously misinterprets Gal. 5:1 and Matt. 5:27-32; and, of course, discards the Ten Commandments. How then can he appeal to the Bible for the one phrase, "Thou shalt love"? A person who believes all the Bible can consistently appeal to any verse, as Jesus did in John 10:35; but a person who does not, must give reasons for accepting one verse rather than another. Fletcher gives no reason. To all intents he treats it as if it were a verbally inspired revelation to himself alone. Strange that Fletcher is inerrantly inspired and the Scripture is not.

📖 Joseph Fletcher, *Situation Ethics,* Philadelphia, Westminster, 1966.   GORDON H. CLARK

SKEPTICISM. See also *Doubt.* Skepticism as popularly conceived means only a doubt or questioning attitude toward one thing or another. Ethical skepticism would be a doubt, or rather, a denial of moral principles. This is often the result of a non-skeptical, a dogmatic, scientism. Physics seems so certain as to compel acceptance, whereas everybody has his own moral standards; therefore these latter are regarded as relative, subjective, and without universal application.

Philosophical skeptism is a denial that knowledge is possible. It is the normal result of empirical epistemology and has uniformly been opposed by realists such as Plato, Augustine, Descartes, Hegel, and, unsuccessfully, by the non-realist though non-empiricist Kant.

Skepticism began with the Sophists before 400 B.C. Plato showed that their identification of knowledge as perception implies that knowledge is impossible.

Pyrrho (365-275) originated a continuous skeptical school that lasted to A.D. 200. He denied knowledge, considered virtue to be conventional, and therefore recommended a life of impassiveness or apathy.

Arcesilaus (315-240) attacked the Stoic criterion of truth—the comprehensive representation—and urged suspension of judgment. Carneades (219-129) also opposed the Stoics: there is no criterion, for any sensory image may be deceptive. The insolubilia show that logic is untrustworthy. Practical action requires no opinions: as living beings men cannot avoid doing something. There is some evidence that Carneades admitted that some actions were preferable to others. This would be an inconsistency.

Aenesidemus (80 B.C.-A.D. 130) collects ten arguments, of which some are: sensory images depend on organs, these differ from animal to animal, therefore no image is truer to nature than any other; one sense contradicts another sense, as the pole half in water looks bent but feels straight; no object is ever experienced in isolation and the surroundings alter its appearances; customs and morality vary—no one view can be insisted upon.

Sextus Empiricus (c. A.D. 200) was the last of the ancient skeptics. Plotinus (205-270) and later Augustine (354-430) defeated the skeptical school by refuting the empiricism on which it was based.

In modern times, passing over Montaigne as a non-philosophical popularizer, the greatest skeptic of all was David Hume. For him knowledge consisted in sensory images that were images of nothing occurring in a mind that did not exist.

Kant tried to reinstate space, time, and causality. This presumably permitted a science of appearances, but the "real" world of things in themselves remained unknowable. After Hegel, for whom nothing was unknowable, there came an irrationalism exemplified in Kierkegaard, Nietzsche, James, and Dewey. Though the appelation is infrequently used, these two are skeptics. (See entries on names mentioned.)

✦ Gordon H. Clark, *Thales to Dewey*, Boston, Houghton, Mifflin, 1957, chapter on Hume; Plato, *Thaetetus*.   GORDON H. CLARK

SKYJACKING. *See* Hijacking.

SLANDER. See also *Scandal*. Slander, like libel, is false and defamatory imputation that exposes another to hatred, contempt, or ridicule. The legal criterion of both slander and libel is the effect on another's reputation, but libel involves the use of more permanent means. Whereas slander may involve significant signs, gestures or looks, or the spoken word including extemporaneous broadcast comment, libel assails another's reputation in writing or print or by broadcast of prepared remarks. Some courts attach responsibility for what is spoken or written to owners of broadcasting stations, but most decisions limit liability to those persons who actually participate in producing and broadcasting what is defamatory.

Successful legal defense of what is communicated may show an imputation or insinuation to be (1) justified by the facts; (2) fair comment—that is, legitimate opinion rather than allegation, and a matter of public interest; (3) absolute privilege (as part of legislative or judicial proceedings); (4) privileged reporting, such as the qualified privilege of newspapers. Often a public apology is accepted in mitigation of damages.

The NT includes a variety of terms to designate evil-speaking, which it everywhere deplores (cf. *kakalogein*, "to speak evil of," Acts 19:9; *katalaloi*, "backbiters," Rom. 1:30; etc.). *Blasphēmia* includes evil-speaking against God as well as man (cf. Rom. 3:8; I Cor. 10:30). The chief slanderer is the devil (*diabolos*, from *diaballō*, Luke 16:1). Women called to the diaconate must not be slanderers (I Tim. 3:11) nor must any who by their word and example would influence the young (Titus 2:3).

The Christian learns to accept *dusphēmia*, evil report, as part of his lot (II Cor. 6:8), but returns such defamation with blessing (I Cor. 4:13). The Greek term *skandalon*, snare, has given rise to our word scandal, or offense to another. The NT makes clear that people may be scandalized through their own misunderstanding and pride, rather than through misrepresentation: thus Jesus

Christ became a scandal to those Jews who expected an earthly Messiah (I Cor. 1:18). In a pluralistic society the Christian is called not to the avoidance of any and every offense but rather to positive witness.

CARL F. H. HENRY

SLAVERY. Slavery had its roots in problems common to man until the industrial revolution. A labor force greater in number than the needs of an agrarian society put men under great economic pressure. Throughout ancient times prosperity was tied to land. The landless poor had almost no access to a livelihood in earliest times. Conditions had improved only slightly by the Graeco-Roman period. The limited development of handicraft employment did little to relieve the situation because free labor, surplus itself, was always in competition with slave labor.

Slavery in OT times is known to us only by the law of the Pentateuch. Their apparent contradictions make it clear that they originated in different tribal groups. However, contrary to more usual opinion, the law which forbade antichresis (Lev. 25:35-38), and the laws of bride sale (Exos. 21:7-11), and of betrothed slave girls (Lev. 19:20) must originate from the second millennium B.C. because of their close relationship to Nuzi laws. These and many other parallels argue for an early date for the laws.

This early date of the slave laws makes them most remarkable in their intent. They indicate to us that Biblical revelation is neither revolutionary nor reactionary. The laws attempt to deal with men in their immediate situation and to offer a better way of treating their fellows. The solution to the dilemma of those without land or capital in an agrarian society is to be found within the family. The slave was to be considered as a member of the family He was protected from physical abuse He shared in the religious rites and wealth of the family, as if an immediate member of it. Within a specific period of time, either seven or fifty years, he was to be restored to his ancestral land and he was to be provided with goods sufficient to give him a new start.

These terms of enslavement are the more remarkable when one reflects that most slave contracts in the ancient world were legal fictions which offered little promise of manumission. The OT legislation is unique because it guaranteed the integrity of a man or woman based on the sovereignty of God over his people and the land.

By NT times some aspects of the slave system had changed radically, others little or not at all. Dependence on an agrarian economy remained much the same. Some progress was made in the development of handicraft industrialization, but there still remained a huge labor surplus because of the massive infusion of slave labor in the form of prisoners of war.

Ethnic differences between master and slave worked to the detriment of the latter. The prisoner of war was an "outsider" instead of the "insider" of previous eras who fell into slavery within his own society because of debt. It is always said that the Graeco-Roman system was less humane than that of the earlier New East because of the cultural remoteness of the slave to his new home. The slave system of the American South may have been most brutal of all for this reason.

Jesus never passed judgment on slavery. Examination of the vocations of Palestinians in the first century shows that the Jews were less dependent on slaves than were the inhabitants of peninsular Italy. But it is clear from Jesus' parables that he did come in contact with slaves and slave owners on occasion. For both Jesus and Paul the determining factor in their attitude towards slavery was the impending *eschaton*. Paul nowhere encourages slaves to seek their freedom. Instead, he tells them to obey as unto Christ and he exhorts slave owners to treat slaves fairly because they too have a master—in heaven (I Cor. 7:20-24; Eph. 6:57-7; Col. 4:22-25). The principal consideration seems to be the same as that of the OT. The slave should be granted all the privileges of other members of the family because he is a member of the household of God.

One of the great regrets of anyone who deals with the subject of slavery in any period of history except our own is the lack of historical documents or demographic figures. We know, for instance, from a great deal of circumstantial evidence that the Romans freed slaves in enormous numbers during the late Republic and early Empire. What we do not know is in how great numbers, whether manumission was as common in the East as it was in peninsular Italy, or whether this affected the thinking of the NT on the subject. All we do know is that this was happening during the NT era because of a population decline over a long period of time.

For those who would judge Christianity harshly for not freeing the slaves, it must be pointed out that they are quick to find fault from our vantage point in economic history. We have some rather exact figures on cost of living and wages for the NT era. They show that the slave was at least as well off as his free counterpart. There simply was no means of livelihood for a free man who had neither land nor capital. The parallel in the American South is again significant. The slaves were set free, but the Northern industrialists turned to Europe for labor immediately after the Civil War and left many ex-slaves in worse circumstances than they were before emancipation.

The Bible reaches beyond mere conomic systems. It demands that, no matter what the system, human beings be treated as if members of the family. In our affluent world this should be translated into decent employment and a living for every man. The free enterprise system carries with it the risk that men will disregard their neighbor in utter disregard of the Biblical view of the economic relationship of men to each other.

ARTHUR A. RUPPRECHT

SLOTH. Usually the most neglected of the "seven deadly sins" as listed by Pope Gregory the Great, sloth or *acedia,* as it was known to the Greeks, is normally defined as a disinclination to exertion, or as physical and mental inactivity; a compound of sluggishness, laziness, idleness and indolence. In recent years there has been a revival of interest in the subject. Billy Graham in *The Seven Deadly Sins* (Grand Rapids, Zondervan, 1955) considers sloth to be "apathy and inactivity in the practice of our Christianity." Failure to spend time in prayer, to read the Bible, to witness for Christ, indicates "spiritual drowsiness" and slothful behavior. Dorothy Sayers says that sloth "believes in nothing," cares for nothing, seeks to know nothing, interferes with nothing, enjoys nothing, loves nothing, hates nothing, finds purpose in nothing, lives for nothing." She equates it with "tolerance." In *On Not Leaving It to the Snake* (New York, Macmillan), Harvey Cox says that sloth is not laziness so much as man's "unwillingness to be everything he was intended to be." Thus the first human sin was not just pride; it was *acedia.* Cox's exegesis attempts to eliminate the issue of sin and morality and substitute a wholistic humanism. Sloth thus becomes not sinful neglect so much as weakness and failure to take responsibility. The Biblical position is that sloth is not inadequacy or irresponsibility (although these are included) but inertia, and the Biblical remedy for sloth is Eph. 5:14, "Awake, thou that sleepest, and arise from the dead, and Christ shall give thee light."

SHERWOOD E. WIRT

SMOG. See also *Environmental Pollution.* Smog is a combination of fog and chemical or solid particles in the air, and may appear in conditions ranging from haze to a dense fog. Photochemical smog, the most serious form, results from complex chemical interactions between heat from the sun and chemical air pollutants.

The basic cause of air pollution is the imperfect burning of fuels and other materials. Homes, factories, and power plants emit solid wastes such as fly ash, smoke, and soot, as well as damaging sulfur oxides from burning coal and heavy fuel oil. Automobiles, trucks and buses contribute the major portion of pollutants, however, in the form of dangerous hydrocarbons from evaporating gasoline, carbon monoxide from imperfect combustion, and nitrogen oxides from engine heat. Americans pour at least 183 million tons of toxic materials into the air each year.

Harmful effects of smog include deaths, respiratory illnesses such as emphysema, damage to homes, works of art, buildings, increased auto and other accidents due to decreased driver visibility, and damage to vegetation such as smog-induced X disease among the Ponderosa Pine in California. Air inversions caused extensive deaths in Donora, Pa., New York City, and London, England, when a killer smog was trapped over the city by a warm air layer above.

Ethically considered, smog is evidence of man's sinful attitude toward God's creation (cf. Gen. 3:1-7). His suffering from pollution may be an experience of the judgment of God (cf. Luke 15:11ff.). Genuine repentance will involve a changed attitude toward man's natural environment.

PAUL D. SIMMONS

SMOKING. When Columbus first introduced tobacco to the Indians in the Caribbean Islands it was bitterly criticized. King James I objected to the obnoxious odor. In colonial America many questioned the prudence of using fertile lands to grow tobacco instead of needed food crops. Some early New England laws prohibited smoking as a non-productive pastime.

More recently the causal relationship of smoking to lung cancer, laryngeal cancer, peptic ulcer, cardiovascular disease, bronchitis, and emphysema has been proved beyond all doubt (*The Health Consequences of Smoking, A Public Health Service Review,* U.S. Department of Health, Education, and Welfare 1967). Cessation of cigarette-smoking sharply reduces the risks of dying from these diseases. There is strong evidence that other diseases are related to smoking but there is no indisputable proof of a causal relationship. The higher incidence of cirrhosis of the liver in smokers is probably associated with a greater use of alcohol by these same individuals. Annually approximately 300,000 people die ten years prematurely in the United States because of smoking. The average life span of moderate smokers is shortened about eight years.

Smoking is probably not a true addiction. One does not develop biologic dependency upon tobacco as in the case of narcotic drugs. An infant born to a morphine addicted mother must be placed on token doses of the drug in decreasing amounts after birth to overcome dependency, whereas no similar phenomenon has been demonstrated for babies born to mothers who smoke cigarettes. Women who smoke tend to have smaller babies, but it is not known whether the maternal smoking has any influence on the biologic fitness of the newborn.

Within the family context, money is often used for tobacco when there are more urgent needs such as food and clothing. The beginning, habituation, and discontinuation of smoking are for the most part psychologically or socially determined; whether there are also predisposing constitutional or hereditary factors is uncertain. Cigarette smoking which has become a socially acceptable means for fulfilling psychological need of prolonged oral satisfaction is hedonistic. Noyes and Kolb in discussing "Oral Personality" state that: "if the individual, far beyond the age when the mouth should have ceased to be a focus of satisfaction, continues to be mouth-centered, he is said to be of an oral type of personality" (A. P. Noyes and L. C. Kolb, *Modern Clinical Psychiatry,* Philadelphia, Saunders, 1963, p. 23).

In addition to dangers to oneself one must consider the effect smoking has on others. Smoking in public places is offensive to many individuals. The extent of irritation probably reflects varying degrees of allergic response or susceptibility.

The US Government has found itself subsidizing tobacco farmers and at the same time spending much money in publicizing the dangers of tobacco. Only in 1971 was the commercial advertising of tobacco on radio and television banned. The total budget of such advertising was estimated at well over $200 million per year.

CHRISTOPHER T. REILLY

SMUT. See also *Pornography.* This Anglo-Saxon word means pornography. It is derived from the word *soot* and originally meant the dirt on the hands, faces, and clothing of chimneysweeps that would besmirch anything they touched or brushed against.

In modern American usage, it has come to mean those pornographic writings or photographs which are so evil and obscene that they will soil the mind and virtue of anyone who comes into contact with them, particularly children. The fact that "Smut Peddler" fits into a newspaper headline much more conveniently than does "Pornography Merchant" probably accounts for its emergence as a common noun (and, as "smutty," an adjective) in current American English.

"Smut" is often used by state legislatures as a synonym for pornography in describing what is prohibited by law, along with another Anglo-Saxon word of low social value, lewd. It adds to the onus of the charge against the accused. It is a derogatory word to describe material that offers a cheap, illicit sexual thrill and to characterize those who deal in it for profit.

GLENN D. EVERETT

SOCIAL CHANGE. It is now an accepted fact that society is in the midst of rapid social change. We are here concerned with means of adaptation by the church to this situation (see the reports of the Ecumenical Council on this subject).

1. The driving forces of this social change are on the one hand demographic growth and on the other, technology. It is impossible to say which of the two is the determining factor. The demographic explosion is to a large extent caused by applications of technology (medicine), and conversely, the development of techniques is brought about by the demands of the size of world population. The two are interdependent. Thus they cause an upheaval of the whole of life and of society. Population growth beyond a certain level brings with it a modification of structures and social forms, and of modes of thought. Thus it is that beyond a certain point of population density the quantitative becomes qualitative. Technology modifies not only courses of action and the *levels* of life, but also the *mode* of life and finally the entire *milieu* of life. All this takes place very rapidly: technology evolves, it seems, more and more quickly. There are a certain number of applied inventions which grow in geometric progression, and we know that the population growth rate has taken on the speed of an exponential curve. Thus one has the impression of rapid social change.

In order to evaluate the situation correctly, two very different levels must be distinguished. On the superficial level, we do indeed see all the traditional forms of life and society in upheaval. So we have the feeling that there is nothing stable in our world, that the future is completely unforseeable, and that situations are completely fluid. But on a deeper level, one is aware that there exists a coherence, a continuity of stable structures. It is a question of the technological structure: techniques evolve, applied technology multiplies, technical products replace each other rapidly; but this is appearance. The technological system (taking "system" in the sociological sense) remains coherent, develops according to its own law, and behind the facade of rapid change, is slowly "getting its house in order."

The evolution of other factors now depends upon this technological system. These factors are therefore neither free nor unforseeable, and one cannot hope to modify this social change in a voluntaristic way with regard to the economic, political or psychological levels, which are the superficial aspects. The only decisive intervention would take place on the level of the technological system. But that level is very difficult to attain, and even more difficult to transform. Here, we are, nevertheless, summoned only to consider social change, or the "surface effect" of the phenomenon.

How does social change present itself? It seems to me that one can hold to three principal aspects. The first is the destructuralization of the body social — which implies two reciprocal facts: the disappearance of intermediate groups, and the tendency to "massification." The traditional sociological structures (family, trade guilds, groups of friends, neighborhood networks, stable social strata, etc.) used to correspond to a demographically small society in which professional relations were constant, social upward mobility slow, and interchanges very infrequent and small in number. All this has changed. We are witnesses to the disappearance of "intermediate bodies," i.e., to the setting up of direct contact of the individual with global society. The tragic period in the

Western world was between the end of the nineteenth and beginning of the twentieth centuries. Since then, we have progressively recreated new groups (for example, the unions, numerous associations), but ones which do not have the vigor and the protective role of the old groups. And the crisis becomes more grave in countries of the Third World where the destructuralization of the traditional family, of clans, of tribes, of marriage relationships, is a veritable catastrophy. We know, moreover, the debate concerning massification. That this is taking place is indisputable, however, if one considers that modern man lives constantly in contact with the masses (urban). But one must not draw from it catastrophic consequences (anonymity, up-rooting, etc.).

The second aspect is that of equalization. By the diffusion of technology and by the demographic burden, a double social equalization is produced: legal and economic. Legal equalization is felt in the growth of democratization at all levels. Similarly from the point of view of economic life there is a tendency towards a redistribution of goods in such a way that the intervening gulf is diminishing more and more. But, of course, it is a question of tendencies (that is, the direction of the evolution which unquestionably cannot be rapidly achieved), and not of totally accomplished realizations. What is nevertheless very characteristic is that this double democratization is so very evident to our eyes that any exception, any contradiction, takes on the aspect of scandal: scandal of economic inequality, be it between rich and poor nations, be it the fact of the existence of pockets of poverty in Western countries; scandal of racial inequality; scandal of the limitation of democracy due to the non-participation of workers in the administration of enterprises. But these facts are scandals not by relation to moral values that we would have chosen, but by relation to the inevitable process of evolution of modern society.

Finally, the third aspect is the tendency towards the disappearance of ideologies. We are witnessing a more and more radical questioning of all beliefs; moral, religious, social, political. Traditional ideologies are at once intellectually criticized and abandoned as beliefs. Ethical values are rejected. There is no longer a common behavior, and we are also losing, as much from the psychological point of view as from the moral or spiritual, the necessary reference points for the conduct of life. This summary description may appear as a description of crisis. But it must not be forgotten that any social change is actually a crisis which takes for granted criticism of what used to be and the separation between what is in the process of dying and what asks to live.

Finally, one must point out that this social change happens either by voluntary intervention by men and groups of men, or by an involuntary process. It is evident that demographic growth brings with it completely involuntary consequences and that there is in it a process of change that we cannot direct or master except if we were to modify the demographic evolution itself. Voluntary interventions can be of two types: either violent (revolutionary and of a political nature) or non-violent (reformation of the Technostructure, whether by psychological action, by use of political power, or by what would seem to be more effectual, decisions by groups of technicians).

2. Of course, Christianity, Christians and the churches find themselves situated in the midst of these changes and undergo the counter-blows of the crisis. The true danger is not that Christianity be eliminated as an ideology, nor that the social power of the churches be contested. It is double: on the one hand, that Christianity in this society be readapted as religion (i.e., as means of not seeing the obligations implied by transformation, as refuge, as false consolation, as illusion); on the other hand, that the churches seek at any price to adapt Christianity to these changes (politicization of Christianity, total engagement on the social level, modification of the basis of the message by hermeneutics, attempts to synthesize modern cultural aspects with Christianity, etc.). The first error is conservativist, the second progressivist. But the two exist at the most superficial level of social change. Nor can it further be a question of approving or disapproving this social change and of bringing a moral judgment to it: it exists, and we must take it into account. It seems that the responsibility of churches and of Christians in these questions would be considerable, but of a completely different sort than either the mystical or the political. I will give only two examples.

One of the serious elements of the situation is the absence of reference points of evolution — points of stable values by relation to which we can measure the meaning and orientation of the change. This change cannot be borne by man except if man conserves a certain number of fixed points to know where he is going — like the navigator's use of the stars. One of the essential roles of Christianity presently is to furnish modern man with these fixed points. By this is not meant the repetition of traditional values, but rather it implies the radical refusal to justify and to adapt oneself to all that takes place (for example, Cox justifying the large city). With revelation as a starting point, new values are to be *created* which are sufficiently certain so that man can by relating to them judge social evolution and choose a certain orientation not for political or ideological motives, but based on a judgment conforming to the coming of the Kingdom of God. This is what the church has always done at the time of great mutations of civilization (first, fourth, ninth, sixteenth centuries), and we must do it again. This is the first great service that we can render to men. (The rest, the struggle for social justice, etc., is very secondary in relation to it.)

The second facet of the Church's responsibility is very different. The problem is occasioned by the fact that technology always has the effect (resulting from its constant striving after perfection) of producing in each group a certain uniformity of essential objectives and a closing up of the society which is crystalizing itself. (Contrary to what is often said, that technology incessantly produces the bursting forth and change of society, it is here that the difference between the two levels of evolution intervenes.) A group which tends to close up, to become uniform, is a condemned group. It ceases to evolve fundamentally (and *that* is what is threatening for us today, much more than rapid change), because it is fixed upon principles which no one questions any more (the technical principle, for example). The role of Christianity is then to introduce into such a society a group of new tensions, to challenge the structures, and to bring about the birth of a critical mind (much more profound than the hippy movement, but of the same order). These are the three conditions for a society continuing to evolve positively, instead of becoming sclerosed and abandoning itself to the apparent disorder. In sum, Christianity must above all instigate the possibility of a true social change in a society where there are only apparent changes.   J. ELLUL

SOCIAL CLASS. Our Lord Jesus Christ was heard gladly by the poor. He chose his disciples from the skilled laboring classes of people. Many of his followers were from the dispossessed of the land. However, he conferred with rich young persons, with educated men of the power structures of his day, and fell into conflict with those who were comfortably secure in positions of religious leadership and political power. He could, in other words, communicate the truth which he perfectly incarnated to people of all social classes. Yet, not long after the death, burial and resurrection of Jesus Christ it became evident that in the development of the church class distinctions were becoming a basis for preference in the fellowship of Christians. James 2:1-9 asks: "Are ye not partial in yourselves . . . ? . . . But ye have despised the poor." The whole context of this passage is a mood of challenge to the Christian fellowship for building on social class distinctions. This failure often has been repeated and we can profit from recent studies of Christian history.

Max Weber, in his book, *The Protestant Ethic and the Spirit of Capitalism* (New York, Scribner, 1958), first made the distinction between the kind of religious expression which he called a "sect" (which lays heavy emphasis upon personal spiritual conversion, spontaneous religious testimony, and moral standards that stand apart from and in critical contrast to the rest of the worldly culture around them), and a "church" (which lays heavy emphasis upon accommodation to the secular order, the development of ritual and organization or religion, and the use of the power of the church as an agent in society). The "sect" is exclusive in its membership along moral and religious lines. The "church" is exclusive in its membership along cultural and prestige lines. Whereas Weber is credited with this original formulation, Ernst Troeltsch in his lengthy *The Social Teachings of the Christian Churches* (New York, Harper & Row), attempted to document the ascendency of the church-forms over the sect-forms of the Christian faith as the churches sacrificed and compromised Christian ideals in an effort to "get ahead" in social class. Richard Niebuhr, in his book, *The Social Sources of Denominationalism,* (Magnolia, Mass., Smith), documents the American accommodations of this process.

The neat distinctions of Weber,

Troeltsch, and Niebuhr do not, however, give specific practical help in understanding the social class structure of America. Here W. Lloyd Warner's book, *Social Class in America* (Magnolia, Mass., Smith), is helpful. He challenges Aristotle's conclusion that the development of a middle class, a "golden mean" group, is the best solution to the excesses of a class system of rich and poor, of masters and slaves despising and envying each other. Aristotle assumed that middle class people would not envy and plot against each other, but would "pass through life safely" (*Politics,* tr. Benjamin Jowett, New York, Modern Library, 1943, pp. 190-193).

Warner points out that each of the three social classes can be divided into two classes within the class. He enumerates six "social status characteristics": (1) the amount and kind of education, (2) the amount and source of income, (3) the kinds of groups, clubs, organizations, and associations to which one belongs, (4) the kind of occupation one has, (5) the location of one's place of dwelling, (6) the kinds of furnishings, gadgets, and luxuries one has. The subtlest sources of conflict are *within* the social classes. For example, the lower class is divided into two groups, the lower-lower, who are unskilled laborers, and the upper-lower, who are skilled laborers. The conflict between these persons is intense at the point of their occupation. What often is mistaken as race conflict is conflict between labor classes, as in the case of blacks who for centuries have been in an unskilled labor caste. "Caste" differs from class in that a caste is a status into which one is born and must remain. Another example of conflict *within* classes is that of the difference in the *source* of income among wealthy persons. Two families may have hypothetically the same amount of wealth, but one of them has inherited it, or uses wealth as a way of making money make money, while the other family is newly rich and has earned all

its money by personal effort. The former would likely be thought of as upper-upper class and the latter would be lower-upper.

Several problems of religious and moral significance can be understood better by social class reference. For example, as early as 1952, Herbert Schneider demonstrated that denominations vary widely in their constituency along social class lines. "At the high status extreme, nearly one-fourth of the Christian Scientists, Episcopalians, and Congregationalists are from upper class; fewer than one-half are from the lower class. At the other end, fewer than one-tenth of the Roman Catholics, Baptists, and Mormons are from the upper class; roughly two-thirds are from the lower class" (N. J. Demerath, *Social Class in American Protestantism,* Chicago, Rand McNally, 1965, pp. 2f.).

Another factor that has specific social class overtones is that of sexual behavior. For example, the lower-lower class person whose daughter becomes pregnant out of wedlock is more likely to keep the child in the home than is the upper-middle class person who would tend to seek an abortion in a state where it is legal or to seek the child's adoption by another family. Value structures about the family and sexual behavior are shaped by the milieu of the social class. "Thus the pivotal meaning of social class . . . is that it defines and systematizes the different learning environments for children of different classes" (Robert M. Goldenson, *The Encyclopaedia of Human Behavior,* Vol. II, New York, Doubleday, 1970, p. 1221). Sexual behavior is only one of the kinds of learning involved; attitudes toward property, the necessity of going to school, and differences from other persons are also defined and systematized by these learning environments.

Within the life of the churches, one finds church atmosphere considerably conditioned by social class factors involved in the life of the people. For example, in the post-World War II suburban development of city life, suburbs were built so as to include only one social class. Churches establishing themselves in these areas found a very narrow spread of social class representation in their membership. As a result, they became captive to the particular social attitudes, beliefs, and customs of that group. Children grew from birth to maturity and never met and knew people out of their own social class until they went to college. Even then, they met only people from the very few other social classes who attended the same college.

When we return to the ministry of our Lord and see the infinite access he had—and as a Risen Lord now has—to people of all strata of society, one concludes two things: First, that Christians have their work cut out for them in breaking down the walls that separate them from other social classes, and second, that when we do so our own human development under God will find a new and larger environment more pleasing to God.   WAYNE E. OATES

SOCIAL DARWINISM. See also *Evolutionary Ethics*. Social Darwinism is a social philosophy of the nineteenth century whose proponents found in the prevailing theories of evolution a naturalistic justification for processes of social stratification and social change. Some theorists such as Herbert Spencer (1820-1903) in England and his American disciple, William Graham Sumner (1840-1910), saw in the biological principle of "survival of the fittest," the scientific and ethical sanction for laissez-faire (q.v.) capitalism and the limited state. Others, such as Ludwig Gumplowicz (1838-1909), the Austrian Polish sociologist, found a naturalistic explanation for the origin of human institutions, particularly the state, in the older theory of group conflict. Still others, such as Lester F. Ward (1841-1913), the American sociologist, conceived a scientific explanation for social change which combined a zig zag view of evolutionary movement in society, a theory of natural inequalities in men, and the idea of rational manipulation by men of evolutionary processes to justify a scientific answer to the problems of politics. Through "sociocracy," affirmed Ward, society could be ruled by scientifically determined laws.

Social Darwinism in America marks the transition from a society based upon natural rights grounded in the divinely sanctioned concept of natural law to a concept of society based upon individual rights revealed in the evolutionary process of social conflict. "All the rights, freedom and social power which we have inherited," wrote Sumner, "are products of history." Undergirding the generalization was the Darwinian doctrine of natural selection through "survival of the fittest" which was used to justify the results of industrial change in a laissez-faire economy. Sumner sought thereby to approve economic individualism and to provide a self-evident scientific sanction for the ethical hedonism of post-Civil War society in America. The new industrial entrepreneur must be accepted as a legitimate product of his society. By following the utilitarian principle of self-interest he had discharged his duty to man and won the right of social acceptance.

Social Darwinism waned as Mendelian theories of genetical transmission of individual traits displaced environmental explanations of social and individual change. Simultaneously, monopolistic tendencies in laissez-faire capitalism gave rise to idealist and common law theories of social control of the economy through statutory law. Even the courts sought to discover a new balance between the Darwinian concept of individual freedom, commonly expressed in "freedom of contract," and the concept of the public interest as they rendered opinions defining the relations between employers and employees. SAMUEL R. KAMM

SOCIAL ETHICS. Ethics is conveniently defined as the science of morality, morality being understood as the set of judgments people make regarding what is right or wrong, good or bad, in the relations within or between individual or collective centers of intelligence and will.

It is sometimes said that all ethics is social, since man, the agent of morality, is by nature, and therefore inalienably, social. There is no doubt that man is social in this way; he does not so much exist as co-exist, and he has no ultimate privacy. It is true, accordingly, that when he acts others are unavoidably affected by what he does; his choices and decisions have social consequences. It is equally true that a man's moral behavior is significantly influenced by the community in which he is imbedded and by the social history which is his heritage and, in a sense, his destiny. It is true also that more often than not man acts not as a single individual, but as a member of a group which includes and overarches him, and of which he is ineluctably representative. But these facts, important as they are, do not as such render all ethics social. At any rate, they do not make meaningless or unimportant the traditional distinctions between personal, inter-personal, and social ethics.

As already observed, men are not sheer unrelated atoms of being. But they nevertheless are individuals, unique centers of consciousness and power. And because they reside on a vertical as well as on a horizontal plane of existence they are able through the exercise of their God-oriented freedom to transcend the social matrix. This transcendence is indeed the reason why individuals are able to work creatively on social structures and processes. But this feature of man's existence also provides a charter for that department of ethics which has come to be called Personal. Christian Personal Ethics (q.v.) cannot be finally isolated from Christian Social Ethics, but, unlike the latter, it does not concentrate on collectivities and communities or on impersonal structures and arrangements. It concentrates instead upon the individual moral agent who lies behind and participates in these. Personal ethics contemplates man as a centered self, and it observes and evaluates the development within him of those habits, postures, attitudes, and traits which characterize him as a person. Since in Christian perspective true personhood is unthinkable outside a man's relation to God, Christian personal ethics is as much concerned with the "supernatural graces" of man as it is with man's "socially redemptive virtues," though it never regards these as antithetical or unrelated. Personal Ethics, then, may be said to be chiefly concerned with self-discipline, with character formation, and with the cultivation and development of those virtues and graces which fit him for the discharge of his religious and social responsibilities.

Since an individual or person is never merely centered upon himself, but always stands in relationships, ethics cannot restrict itself to a consideration of the moral agent as such. It must also contemplate the person in his attitudes and actions toward others, and in the first instance toward those others whom he meets in individual or one-to-one encounter. These sorts of encounters take place all the time; individuals meet other individuals in a vast variety of situations, and they are required to respond to each other in morally appropriate ways. Inter-Personal Ethics is concerned with human behavior on this level and in these restricted contexts. Enveloping social structures can not be ignored in this branch of ethics for they simply exist and must be reckoned with, but critical attention is not focused on them. What is chiefly considered here is the moral response an individual makes to the neighbor who is immediately present to him—a response not mediated through the structures and agencies of society, but a response made directly and with a certain degree of intimacy. The case of the Good Samaritan may be taken as typical of those contemplated in Inter-Personal Ethics.

Social Ethics derives its special character from the explicit attention it pays to the social dimensions of human existence. One consequence of its social orientation, and one mark of its distinctiveness, is its unique awareness of and preoccupation with super-individual entities—its concern with the moral significance of more or less integrated human groups, collectivities, and communities. In this respect it is significantly unlike Personal and Inter-Personal Ethics.

It is not true, however, that in Social Ethics the individual falls out of purview. Social Ethics is concerned with the moral behavior of individuals as well as with that of super-individual corporate realities. Its concern with the individual is, however, of a special sort; it is socially qualified. It contemplates the individual not merely as the centered self it is, nor specifically as one who responds without explicit intermediation to the neighbor who in his singleness or indeterminate plurality directly confronts him. It rather contemplates him as one who either makes an individual response to some super-individual community, or as one who, functioning communally, acts in concert with others through the agency of some group with which he is affiliated.

But since Social Ethics is concerned not only with the behavior of individuals in relation to or from within community, but also with the morally significant vitalities and interactions of communities as such, at least four sets of moral problems are customarily considered by those who work within it.

As the foregoing has already suggested, one important area of concern in Social Ethics is that in which the individual is confronted by and set over against some social magnitude, such as the State (q.v.), which while embracing and assisting him also limits and sometimes threatens him. The central problem here is how to harmonize the interests of the individual and the community. The problem arises from the fact that individual and collective centers of life and purpose, though interdependent, are always in tension; the freedom and spontaneity espoused by the one is balanced by the authority and order espoused by the other. The moral task here lies in establishing such social arrangements as will prevent a lapse from balance into conflict. What needs to be secured is that delicate adjustment of freedom and order which will exclude both anarchy and tyranny, that measure of harmony which will prevent either individualism or collectivism from taking root.

Another set of problems arises in Social Ethics from the fact that not infrequently the individual acts not singly but jointly, not on his own but in concert with others, not against but from within some organization or community by which he is embraced. The chief issues arising here concern the existence or non-existence of common ground for deliberation and action, and the reality and meaning of such things as corporate responsibility (q.v.), collective guilt, exemption from the effects of majority decision by reason of conscience, and the like.

A third set of problems in Social Ethics arises from the fact that there are many organizations and communities in society whose relations and interactions require definition and regulation. At issue here is the exact nature of these communities, the fixity of their boundaries, the status of their claims, and the nature and extent of their possible cooperation. Typical of the problems in this area of existence and inquiry is the age-old problem of the relation of Church and State. Calling for attention here too are the economico-political issues involved in Socialism (q.v.), Communism (q.v.), and the Welfare State (q.v.). Involved here also are such inquiries into the nature of family, state, church, and school as may provide warrant for public, private, or parochial education.

Closely related to the set of problems just referred to, but distinguishable from them, are the problems arising around the issues of plurality and unity. In Social Ethics one is concerned not only to determine and appraise the relative claims of the several communities existing within society, but also to discover under what conditions and by what sanctions all the particular groupings can be joined and harmonized. During the Middle Ages occidental society achieved a kind of unity under the hegemony of the church. Since then, through the impulses set loose by the Reformation (q.v.) and the Renaissance (q.v.), religious diversity, ethnic heterogeneity, cultural variety, and social pluralism has characterized the society of the West. The big question in Social Ethics is whether a society so characterized can endure, and if so, what view of man and God is calculated to make it viable. It is at this stage of its inquiry that Social Ethics impinges on the ultimate question of metaphysics and theology, the answers to which relate not only to the questions here raised but to all the questions considered in the other departments of ethics.

 Emil Brunner, *The Divine Imperative*, London, Lutterworth, 1937.   HENRY STOB

SOCIAL GOSPEL. See also *Rauschenbusch, Walter*. Until Timothy L. Smith wrote *Revivalism and Social Reform* (Nashville, Abingdon, 1957) it was generally assumed that the social gospel was an American theological aberration. Evangelicals branded it the product of preachers who had strayed from the gospel of the grace of God and reached for "good works" as a lame substitute. Doubtless the social gospel often deserved this characterization. Yet Smith has shown that the preoccupation with social problems that later dominated a large segment of American Protestantism actually stems from the zeal and compassion which revivalists of the mid-nineteenth century awakened for sinning and suffering men. The social theories of the evangelists became the working basis of the social gospel.

As an historical phenomenon, the rise of the social gospel in the American churches is a well-documented episode. It accompanied the emergence of the labor movement, the growth of urban ghettos, the increase in crime, poverty and disease. It took the form of active Christian concern for victims of the industrial revolution, together with persistent efforts to ameliorate the festering social conditions in factory towns and big cities.

As an expression of love for one's fellow men, however, the social gospel may be considered to have originated in the Hebraic environment of the OT and NT. Seen thus classically, it is the outward accompaniment of the proclamation of the gospel of salvation in Jesus Christ. Just as Jesus interpreted his messianic mission through acts of love, so his followers since the Acts of the Apostles have engaged in a multiplicity of works intended to benefit and bless their fellow men (cf. Titus 3:8).

The social gospel is best understood through its sociological background. Over the centuries the human race has been engaged in a long, uphill battle against entrenched economic forces that have refused to yield power or to acknowledge the right of a man to be himself. In many parts of the world oppression and wretchedness are still a way of life for the great majority of people. Sin is always at its ugliest when it involves the exploitation of man by man. That Jesus was deeply conscious of human social struggle is evident throughout the Gospel record. The later history of the church reflects (though often too dimly) his interest in human welfare. Despite the unholy alliance of church leaders with imperial interests, there is evidence that many Christian pastors, missionaries, laymen and laywomen were active in implementing the social imperatives of the gospel.

Even in nineteenth century America it appears that the evangelists and revivalists who roamed the frontier were not only preaching the gospel of inner salvation, but were also championing the friendless, the jobless, the drunkard, the illiterate, the widow and orphan, the hunted Indian and the enslaved Negro. Nevertheless at the end of the Civil War the torch of compassion passed from the evangelical Christians to the growing liberal movement within the American churches. Causes were many and complex: the increasing racial standoff, the new immigration, the evolution controversy, the growing strength of the working class. Evangelical churches established store-front rescue missions and sent missionaries to many lands. Yet many churches were asleep on the home front while liberal prophets such as Washington Gladden, Stephen Peabody, Graham Taylor and Walter Rauschenbush challenged the economic royalism of the time, fought the prevailing racist approach toward minority groups, struggled against poverty and misery, and defended the right of workers to organize and to strive for a better standard of living. In these matters they did what more orthodox men should have done.

During the century 1865-1965 many organizations that had strong evangelical beginnings, such as the Y.M.C.A. and Y.W.C.A., were reoriented toward social work. The Salvation Army's social program assumed increasing importance. In Britain F. D. Maurice, Charles Kingsley and the Chartists led a parallel movement within the Church of England. In many leading Protestant denominations (Methodist, Congregational, Unitarian, Presbyterian, Quaker) the social gospel made such headway that the gospel of redemption through the sacrificial death of Christ was muted or else eliminated entirely. By the late 1950s some younger churchmen were redefining the word "evangelism" as "social action." The emergence of the "secular Christianity" emphasis in 1963 made the issue even sharper. The social ethic of the gospel was not interpreted in some churches affiliated with the conciliar movement to sanction the espousal of political activity, even violent political activity depending on the circumstances.

The theological revival associated with Karl Barth had brought about during the 1940s and 1950s a sharp reevaluation of the social idealism that had led many American liberals to think that they were "building the Kingdom of God" (as the Kansas City Congregational creed of 1913 had suggested). The term "social gospel" now began to fall into disrepute, even among some liberals. The movement itself, however, was far from dead, as witness the identification of churchmen with a variety of "liberation" and anti-war movements in the 1970s. It is no exaggeration to say that the social gospel has become a prisoner of radical interests. Lacking the correction of Scripture and the direction of the Holy Spirit, it ceased to be a healthy expression of the church's social conscience and too often becomes a refuge for borderline freaks and anarchists. One victim of this diffusion of purpose has been the National Council of Churches, whose future is now in doubt.

Meanwhile the evangelical community in America and Britain at last has shown signs of awakening from its Rip van Winkle sleep. Since the sounding of the first alarm by Carl F. H. Henry in *The Uneasy Conscience of Modern Fundamentalism* (Grand Rapids, Eerdmans, 1947), the evangelical churches have come to an increasing recognition of the commands of Christ in the social sphere. In 1966 the Wheaton Declaration was issued in the USA and the Keele report in Britain, both expressing concern for an evangelical approach to the social questions of the day.

At the Minneapolis Congress on Evangelism (1969) this trend was pushed further. With the issues of race, poverty, ecology, war, drug addiction, and sexual permissiveness mounting into crises that threaten to engulf and destroy Western civilization, the evangelical social conscience has come to life none too soon.   SHERWOOD E. WIRT

SOCIALISM. The trend away from ecclesiastical authoritarianism in the post-Reformation period gave rise in the eighteenth century to popular sovereignty in the political realm, with such characteristic documents as *The Federalist Papers* and *The Wealth of Nations.* A different kind of dream gathered momentum during the nineteenth century, contemplating the perfected temporal life of man in a planned society, to be achieved by governmental direction of economics and technology. Socialism is the appropriate generic term for this movement.

The quintessence of modern Socialism is government ownership of productive property and the centralized management and direction of economic life. Socialists are divided into parties, sects and hostile factions, but beneath the clash of labels they all advocate the planning of economic affairs by political authority—control over production and exchange being the key to leverage over other sectors of life and the means of achieving national goals.

Such practices as voluntarily pooling goods, sharing the common tasks of a community, working with the hands, reviving interest in folk arts, do not constitute Socialism. And it goes without saying that concern for justice is not limited to socialists; the noblest work in behalf of slaves, prisoners, the sick, the handicapped, children, and animals has been done by non-Socialists. When it comes to improving man's lot on earth, the influence of Adam Smith probably did more to upgrade the poor than any other single factor, and the major thrust of Classical Liberalism maximized civil, intellectual, and religious liberty for all men by limiting government to the tasks of policing.

Socialism is in contention against the Free Society, and we know a thing better if we understand its adversary. To insist that centralized political planning of the economy is the essence of Socialism may plant the misleading suggestion that the Free Society—call it the free economy, the market economy, or capitalism (q.v.)—is characterized by lack of planning. Such is not the case. There is individual planning of all sorts in the Free Society, but no centralized economic planning. The Rule of Law is not a random development; it is intentional, the result of generations of planned effort by men seeking to establish institutions which maximize human freedom. The market economy operates within the framework of the Rule of Law, and is regulated by millions of consumers making billions of decisions as they carry out their private plans for the achievement of their personal goals—as well as by other millions who plan ahead for their businesses, their churches, their schools, their hospitals and other corporate ventures.

There are two radically opposed ways of life here; Socialism versus the Free Society, and they lock horns over the questions: Who shall plan? and For whom? Socialism has an overall plan which the handful of men who wield political power must impose on the mass of citizenry in order that the intended national goals and purposes may be realized. But, millions of people have billions of plans of their own, and because many of these private plans do not fit into the government's plan they must be annulled; and if persuasion does not suffice punishment must be invoked. The ideal blueprint for ordering the life of a beehive may be identical with the private plans of the last little bee; but it is not so in human society, where each person is a unique self. Socialism means a nation with two kinds of men; the few who have the power to run things and the many whose lives are run by other men.

What kind of men are best adapted to the task of fitting the lives of other men into the Plan? Men possessed by an ideology which convinces them they are carrying out History's mandates when they conform the lives of citizens to the social blueprint. As History's vice-regent, the Planner is forced to view men as mass; which is to deny their full stature as persons with rights (q.v.) endowed by the Creator, gifted with free will, possessing the capacity to order their own lives in terms of their convictions. The man who has the authority and the power to put the masses through their paces, and to punish nonconformists, must be ruthless enough to sacrifice a person to a principle. The operational imperatives of a socialist order demand this kind of action; a commissar who believes that each person is a child of God will eventually yield to a commissar whose ideology is consonant with the demands of his job.

The ideology which facilitates the Planned State was not invented by Marx; it was at hand in the form of nineteenth century materialism. Man, in terms of this ideology, is a mere end product of natural and social forces, inhabiting a universe which does not reflect the handiwork of the Creator, but is reducible instead to the mechanical arrangement of material particles. There is no transcendent end for men to serve, and no soul needing salvation; mankind will be regenerated by altering its environment so as to put men fully into the service of the State. In Socialist eschatology the Stage will finally wither away and men will enjoy an earthly paradise.

The skewing of the Christian vision here is obvious; Socialism needs a secular religion to sanction its authoritarian politics, and it replaces the traditional moral order by a code which subordinates the individual to the collective. This inversion of values is intended to enhance economic well-being, but in vain. Socialism promises to distribute abundance but is at a loss as to how to produce it. A classic study by the eminent economist, Ludwig von Mises, *Socialism* (1922), demonstrates the impossibility of economic calculation in a planned economy, and experience attests to the chronic shortages of goods which afflict Socialist nations.   EDMUND A. OPITZ

SOCIAL SERVICE. See also *Christian Social Movements.* Evangelical Christians have been social service minded since the time of Christ. To be sure, the primary mission of the apostolic church was leading people into a transforming experience in Jesus Christ. But as these regenerated and Spirit-filled people began to share their experiences with others, they also started sharing their material possessions with needy brethren.

Assistance to the poor continued to some extent after the first century. Not until the eighth century, however, did the Roman Catholic Church provide a system of general aid, funded by compulsory payments from members of the church. Somewhat in contrast to apostolic practice, this relief diluted the element of love between the giver and the recipient; giving became a religious duty and even a ticket to heaven. Some orders within the established church, however, reflected a genuine concern for the unfortunate. The Sisters of Charity of St. Vincent de Paul provided aid to the sick and poor beginning in 1633.

But the church of the Middle Ages lost most of the transforming message of the first century church. A return to an evangelical emphasis began in the sixteenth and seventeenth centuries with such Reformers as Luther, Knox, and George Fox.

At the beginning of the Wesley revivals, the poor were neglected and degraded. The enclosure system, emergence of cities, and the rise of the industrial system were undoubtedly contributing causes of the serious plight of large sectors of society. The economist, William Petty, estimated that over half of England's population was a liability at the end of the seventeenth century. With the resurgence of evangelical Christianity, apostolic concern for the poor reappeared in the great revivals that swept England in the eighteenth century.

Even though the social and industrial revolution (q.v.) contributed to miserable social conditions, the century of evangelical revival which followed and brought with it extensive social service suggests that the ecclesiastical failure to emphasize evangelical concerns in the Middle Ages was a contributory cause of degenerate social conditions.

John Wesley taught that a Christian was entitled to supply his "own reasonable wants together with those of (his) family." But beyond such expenditures money should be spent "in doing good to others" or, as he said, "you (would) spend it to the hurt of yourself." Social assistance was extended beyond their membership to strangers after 1770. They commonly worked extra hours to earn more to give to the needy. They gave not only money but also time and energy in personal involvement. Methodist societies provided employment, loans, housing and schools for the poor, as well as assistance to the sick and dissemination of literature.

Other evangelical churches including the Baptist, Presbyterian, and Congregationalist for the most part had adopted the Methodist approach to revivals and social assistance in England in 1800.

A new evangelical ferver arose in America in the 1820s with the revivals under Charles E. Finney. By 1840 the revival movement brought with it a corresponding resurgence of evangelical social service. Samuel Allibone estimated that in the 1850s 5,000 volunteers from 150 churches were working in charitable activities in Philadelphia alone.

A decade after Phoebe Palmer started an independent evangelical effort in New York City's slums in the early 1840s her work involved extensive relief projects, including boarding houses, a young women's home, a rescue home for young delinquents, an asylum for the deaf, and an orphan's home for 500 Negroes.

Evangelical groups sponsored seamen's bethels in eastern cities, and interdenominational societies for distributing food and clothing, finding employment, resettlement for children and medical aid for the poor, and other rescue work. In personal work in Chicago's slums the evangelist, Dwight L. Moody, would ask "Do you have food, clothing, and fuel?" and provided such as a part of his evangelistic effort.

Some types of social service started in the mid-nineteenth century are carried on by evangelical missions and churches today. The Salvation Army is an example of one continuing evangelical social service organization. The Pacific Garden Mission founded in 1827 is still engaged in rescuing alcoholics; in 1970 it provided 250,000 meals, 73,500 lodgings and 126,500 items of clothing. Their evangelical approach yielded 2,361 professed conversions to Jesus Christ.

David Wilkerson started a rescue work for drug addicts among the youth in New York City in the 1950s. His work has resulted in about 85 percent cure of drug addicts who come to his Teen Centers, which have spread to most major cities of the USA.

From the apostolic church to the present time the personal love and concern in social work intensified or waned as the evangelical emphasis on the conversion of individuals was stressed or ignored. Likewise, major social reform movements followed the rise of evangelical emphasis on conversion and Spirit-filled lives. These reform movements followed both the American and English revival periods. In contrast, the rise of the social gospel (q.v.), detached from an emphasis on personal transformation, led to a transfer of social service to the State and has yielded much inner-societal hatred and general disillusionment.

📖 Raymond G. Cowherd, *The Politics of English Dissent*, New York, New York University, 1956; Timothy L. Smith, *Revival and Social Reform*, Nashville, Abingdon, 1957; Wellman J. Warner, *The Wesleyan Movement and the Industrial Revolution*, New York, Longmans, Green, 1930.

MORRIS L. STEVENS

SOCIOLOGY AND ETHICS. Since the days of August Comte (1798-1857) in France, sociology has emerged as the social science concerned with the study of man as a social being. Comte viewed sociology as an all-inclusive study of society and even initially called it social physics in support of his belief that a proper study of mankind would require the use of the methods of the physical sciences in its analytical schemes. Comte was so convinced that the positivistic or scientific approach to human affairs was the only one to take that he sought to apply it even to the realm of religion. As a consequence he lost many of his scientific followers.

In England Herbert Spencer (1820-1903) followed Comte as a strong exponent of the evolutionary principle in human affairs. He laid the groundwork for a complete rejection of the supernatural in the affairs of men. Spencer carefully defined evolution in such a manner as to imply an automatic, non-reversible process of development operating in such a mechanical fashion as to sweep the human being relentlessly along a path of no return. Man was a pawn in the hands of fate.

It remained for Lester Ward (1841-1913) in America to react rather sharply to the type of thinking represented by Spencer. Ward argued vigorously that man is a self-determining creature, not a helpless victim of the evolutionary process. He held that it is within man's province to shape his future if he really wants to do so. His concept of social telesis embodied this thought.

William Graham Sumner (1840-1910) in America pushed further the idea that man is a victim of his own creations. By the concepts *folkways* and *mores*. Sumner represented the customs, the group habits, that man has created over the years of his existence as a result of trial and error. His famous statements, "The mores can make anything right or can make anything wrong," still stands to-day as the classical foundation of an ethic based on man alone. Man and man alone is held to determine what is right and what is wrong.

It is necessary, however, to read the works of Emile Durkheim (1858-1917) of France in order to see the development of sociology toward a complete separation of supernatural elements from the affairs of men and to witness the almost fanatical worship of the "social fact" as the datum of the discipline. The "social fact" was the empirically demonstrable finding of social life and was regarded as the basis for truth in sociology. Statistics became one of the principal techniques used for presenting the "social fact" in an unbiased and objective manner. As Lord Kelvin once put it, "When you cannot measure what you are speaking about; when you cannot express it in numbers, your knowledge is of a meager and unsatisfactory kind." This statement characterizes the kind of intellectual vacuum in which one becomes entombed if he uses only one approach to the discovery of truth.

Since Durkheim, sociology has experienced its most significant development in the USA. The emphasis in the USA is, of course, on the empirical approach and the validation and testing of hypotheses and theories is the first order of business. Trouble develops when this approach is used in areas where it is questionable that application should or could be made. The field of ethics is a case in point.

As we have seen, sociologists historically have avoided consideration of *ought* behavior and have emphasized *what is* behavior. Then some of them turn around and contend that the *what is* behavior should be the *ought* behavior. But not all sociologists reveal such inconsistency. Many of them adhere to the canons of scientific inquiry and their studies are highly professional in every way. The so-called sociologists· who deviate from the path of the established procedure provide a false impression of the discipline and its practitioners.

The pseudo-sociologist needs to be reminded that the task of delineating the actual areas of human behavior is quite distinct from that of a prophetic seer who can tell man what he ought to do. As George Lundberg has suggested, the job of the sociologist is to ascertain the possible alternatives for the courses of human behavior and to indicate the possible outcome of the alternative courses of action. He should not do less nor should he try to do more.

Alvin Boskoff, *Theory in American Sociology*, New York, Crowell, 1969; Lewis A. Coser, *Masters of Sociological Thought*, New York, Harcourt Brace Jovanovich, 1971; Emile Durkheim, *The Elementary Forms of Religious Life*, New York, Free Press, 1947; Charles A. Ellwood, *A History of Social Philosophy*, New York, Prentice-Hall, 1938; M. C. Elmer, *Contemporary Social Thought*, Pittsburgh, University of Pittsburgh, 1956; Paul B. Horton and Chester L. Hunt, *Sociology*, New York, McGraw-Hill, 1964; George A. Lundberg, *Can Science Save Us?* London, Longmans, Green, 1961; Pitirim A. Sorokin, *Sociological Theories of Today*, New York, Harper and Row, 1966; Margaret Wilson Vine, *An Introduction to Sociological Theory*, London, Longmans, Green, 1959.

EDMUND G. McCURTAIN

SOCRATES. See *Greek Ethics.*

SODOMY. See also *Sex.* Sodomy is an act of sexual perversion originally associated with male temple prostitutes for which the city of Sodom became infamous. It also refers to the intercourse of men with animals (cf. *Bestiality*). The Bible contains numerous references to this practice and its proscription (Gen. 19:1-14; I Kings 14:24;

II Kings 23:7; Rom. 1:26; etc.).

HERBERT K. JACOBSEN

SOPHISTS. See *Greek Ethics.*

SORCERY. See *Witchcraft.*

SOVEREIGNTY, DIVINE. See also *Divine Right of Kings.* The doctrine of divine sovereignty is foundational to Christian ethics.

This may be illustrated by reference to the Ten Commandments. The Commandments are not a series of simple ethical imperatives: they are rooted in the context of God's sovereign acts in the redemption of his people. Thus the Commandments are prefaced with the words: "I am the Lord your God, who brought you out of the land of Egypt, out of the house of bondage" (Exod. 20:1-2).

The doctrine of divine sovereignty affirms that God is the one "who accomplishes all things according to the counsel of His will" (Eph. 1:11 RSV). It affirms that God is not only the creator, but also the sustainer and the ordainer of all things. The Bible teaches that God's sovereignty extends to the minutest particularities of life. Even a sparrow does not fall to the ground, Jesus explained, apart from the Father's will (Matt. 10:29).

If God not only creates but also ordains all things, the question may be asked: What place is left for the exercise of human freedom? The answer is that the Bible affirms, at one and the same time, the truth of both divine sovereignty and human responsibility (q.v.). The events of the crucifixion illustrate this fact: "The Son of Man goes as it has been determined; but woe to that man·by whom he is betrayed" (Luke 22:22 RSV; cf. Acts 2:23; 4:27). Through Scripture the connection between the doctrine of divine sovereignty and the fact of human responsibility is inseparably maintained. In the parable of the talents the good and faithful servants were those who were enterprising in using to the best advantages the gifts they had (Matt. 25:14-30).

The doctrine of divine sovereignty is not an invitation to sloth, but an incentive to service. J. I. Packer writes: "The doctrine of divine sovereignty would be grossly misapplied if we should invoke it in such a way as to lesson the urgency, and immediacy, and priority, and binding restraint, of the evangelistic imperative. No revealed truth may be invoked to extenuate sin. God did not teach the reality of His rule in order to give us an excuse for neglecting His orders" (*Evangelism and the Sovereignty of God*, London, Inter Varsity Fellowship, 1961, p. 341).

On the contrary, the doctrine of divine sovereignty braces Christians to ethical endeavor. Thus the apostle enjoins the Philippians to work out their salvation with fear and trembling, and then he immediately reminds them that it is God who is at work in them, both to will and to do of his good pleasure (Phil. 2:12-13). On the one hand, the apostle exhorts them to diligence and perseverance; on the other hand, he reminds them that it is God who gives us both the desire and the ability to serve him.

Historically, the doctrine of divine sovereignty has moved Christians to the highest heights of spiritual endeavor and moral achievement. It was said of the Scottish convenanters that they abased themselves before God and put their feet on the necks of kings.

The fact that Christians are, by and large, weak and aenemic, is to be attributed to the fact that we have so largely neglected the doctrine of the divine Lordship in relation both to the world and to ourselves.

STUART B. BABBAGE

SOVEREIGNTY, NATIONAL. See also *Government; Independence; Nationalism; State; World Government.* No term in political science has been subject to more variation of meaning and, therefore, to controversy, than the idea of sovereignty. Indeed, sovereignty implying supreme authority and dominion is not so much a fact as a theory or assumption about authority. Its characteristics have altered with the changing circumstances of political communities.

In the OT the people of God accepted the rule of God. As king, there were no boundaries to his rule (Ps. 47:8). In contrast to other nations, Israel recognized no divine king but Yahweh. All nations were under his rule whether his sovereignty was recognized or not (Ps. 103:19). But God's rule was not tyrannical. The Incarnation confirms the fact that God in Christ established rule on behalf of man (Rev. 5:6). The primary meaning of sovereignty, then is the rule of God over the created world—a power and authority, independent and transcendent, that God exercises from above (cf. *Sovereignty, Divine*).

In its historical evolution, the term "sovereignty" has passed through numerous phases of development. In Greek political theory, the state was not sovereign in the sense of being above classical law; the authority of customary law, embodying the dictates of the gods, ranked higher. In Roman law, the rule of the emperor was likewise not vested with sovereignty; in theory it was vested in the popular will of the people. In the Middle Ages, the concept of sovereignty was also unknown since the sources of power were so divided. Papal rule was too weak to enforce unity of political rule, while the powerful ritual of Christendom inhibited separate territorial rulers from claiming sovereignty.

Only when Christendom was conceived as a single political society at the end of the Middle Ages, did the notion of sovereignty of individual states come into its own. In the transition between feudalism and nationalism, the idea of a supreme monarchy developed in France under Louis XI. In the late sixteenth century, Jean Bodin used this new concept of sovereignty as a boost to the power of the king over his rebellious lords. Under the stress of civil war, the Reformation with its rejection of papal rule, and other stresses, theorists such as Hobbes, Grotius, and Vattel, sought legal and moral bases for territorial sovereignty. Preoccupied with the preservation of the state's identity, this was the motive for the formulation of the classical concept of sovereignty. The doctrine of the divine right of kings (q.v.) came into full expression in the seventeenth century as a legitimacy for the disavowal of papacy.

The close connection between the concepts of sovereignty and absolutism was given another twist with the American Revolution. In the absence of a monarch, and with the experiment of federalism, where could sovereignty be said to reside? Sovereignty, it was agreed, must reside in the Constitution. Later, in the 1860s, John Austin, thinking of the British model, argued that sovereignty was vested in Parliament. Since the Hague conferences of 1899 and 1907 that established international rules for the conduct of war, the whole development of international law has sought to protect the sovereignty of states by the restriction of the classical theory of unlimited power. Further, the nineteenth century distinction of sovereign states and less sovereign territorial units has been diluted. Since the formation of the United Nations (q.v.), non-self-governing territories have been placed under United Nations trusteeship. Thus the theory of divided sovereignty first developed in federal states has been elaborated within the whole family of the United Nations.

The concept of sovereignty today has no single, precise meaning. Many types of sovereignty have emerged: political, legal, de jure, de facto, internal, external, popular, coercive, influential, positive, negative, absolute, and relative. Sovereignty does not refer to a fact that can be defined empirically. Rather it is a logical system of authority and power, an explanatory principle rather than a generalized description of government.

📖 J. N. Figgis, *The Divine Right of Kings*, Cambridge, Cambridge University, 2nd edit. 1914; Bertrand de Jouvenal, J. F. Huntingdon, tr., *Sovereignty, an Inquiry into the Political Good*, Cambridge, Cambridge University, 1957; C. E. Merriam, *History of the Theory of Sovereignty since Rousseau*, New York, Columbia University, 1900; W. J. Stankiewiez, *In Defense of Sovereignty*, New York, Oxford University, 1969.

J. M. HOUSTON

SPORTS. See also *Athletics*. The great interest and time our society devotes to sports is evidenced by the space daily newspapers give this subject.

Such activities are not just an idle pastime, for the values associated with sports include physical wellbeing, mental relaxation (for spectators as well), and the formation of friendships. Some of the finer qualities of human behavior are demonstrated by the competitors. Even politically diverse and alienated countries have been able to cooperate in this sphere. The Apostle Paul reminded Timothy that "bodily exercise is of some value" (I Tim. 4:8), contrary to the translation in AV, "bodily exercise profiteth little," but godliness by contract is profitable to both our physical and spiritual life. I Cor. 9:26 is probably a reference to both racing and boxing.

As with other gifts, however, misuse results in disorder, such as the spending of $1,000 for ringside seats at a world championship boxing bout (Frazier-Clay) to see two men attempt to inflict injury or reduce each other to unconsciousness. At least six professional boxers have died after contests in Britain since 1945. In the USA boxing takes an average of two professional and two amateur lives a year (Statistical Bulletin of Metropolitan Life Insurance Co., Vol. 48, Sept. 1965).

The proper amount of time devoted to individual non-competitive sports (e.g., swimming) is commendable. Competitive sports, whether an individual or team effort, should ideally involve no intention to injure the opponents. Nevertheless in vigorous games such as football injuries are inevitable (L. A. & D. K. Clawsen, *Clinical Orthopaedics,* Vol. 69, March-April 1970, Philadelphia, Lippincott, p. 219). It has, however been demonstrated that the risks in these sports are minimal. In the USA approximately twenty-six deaths per year (only an indirect measure of less serious injuries) are related to high school and college football. But almost as many would have died during the same period of time had they been involved in a substitute activity. For example, it would have been more dangerous to ride an automobile.

The overwhelming considerations as to the morality of a given sport would therefore be: (1) the intent to injure (cf. Exod. 20:13); (2) the emphasis placed on the activity as related to other responsibilities (cf. Exod. 20:3), and (3) the use of adequate safety precautions (cf. Matt. 19:19).
CHRISTOPHER T. REILLY

STATE. See also *Government; Justice; Nationalism.* The NT pictures the state as God's instrument for bringing justice and fair play in the affairs of men. If the state ceases to do this and gives itself to evil, it becomes a demonic tyrant and an evil harlot that God himself will personally judge. The evil role of the state is described in the book of Revelation. The proper role of government—bringing justice and fair play—is set forth in the rest of the NT.

Paul's letter to the Romans describes emphatically the role of the state. Why should every person be subject to the governing authorities? Paul says there is no human authority except by God; those that exist have been ordained by God (13:1). Paul does not enumerate the various ways in which governments come to power, but he says that government in human affairs is a reality that God maintains. In the context Paul describes government when it is functioning correctly. The one who resists this kind of governing authority finds himself resisting the ordinance of God. Those who resist will receive God's condemnation (13:2). This governing authority is God's servant, bringing his wrath to bear upon the evil doer (13:4). Without government functioning as Paul describes it in 13:1-7, there would be anarchy. If everyone does what is right in his own eyes, chaos will result. Man's selfishness may even blind him to enlightened self-interest that would encourage him to seek the welfare of many because it would benefit him. The spheres of the government's responsibility are large, and the task is enormously complicated.

Relationship of the State to Evil. When government is functioning correctly, it curbs evil. To the degree that it is not functioning correctly, government assists evil in its deadly attack upon the good.

Of the properly functioning government, Paul asserts: "Rulers are not a terror to the good work but to the evil work (Rom. 13:3). The man who does evil should certainly fear because the ruler does not carry the sword to no purpose" (Rom. 13:4). Here Paul insists that force is absolutely necessary to maintain justice. But since this force or power is wielded by imperfect men, it can be misused. Nonetheless, without the force of governmental authority, private or personal might would make right. Isolated individuals would not be able to stand up against pressure groups which are out to further their own ends.

Relation of the State to Good. Some people think of government only in negative terms. The purpose of the state is to punish evil doers. Yet there is also a positive side. The good is to be exalted and honored; government is to praise the one who does good (Rom. 13:3; I Peter 2:14). When the state gives official recognition to a citizen who rescues a person from a burning house, the state is exercising one of its true responsibilities.

Response of Christians to the State. When the state functions correctly, the Christian must subject himself to that government on two grounds: (1) the threat of wrath if he disobeys; (2) his conscience reminds him of God's sovereign control of government.

The Christian shows his subjection by paying various kinds of taxes and by cooperating in other ways to show respect and honor (Rom. 13:6-7). However, whenever respect and honor has included even mild worship of a human ruler, Christians have adamantly desisted (cf. *Protest; Rebellion; Resistance*).

Prayer for kings and all who are in authority (I Tim. 2:2) is essential for their carrying out their God-given tasks.

Jesus pointed out two spheres: the things that belong to the state and the things that belong to God (Matt. 22:15-22; Mark 12:13-17; Luke 20:20-26). Men must function in both spheres. However, if the state begins to arrogate to itself idolatrous powers, then the Christian must assert his loyalty to God. He will listen to and obey God rather than men (Acts 4:5-7; 5:21, 29).

The state in the NT has a clear-cut exalted role. To help keep it faithful to that role is the responsibility of every Christian.

A. BERKELEY MICKELSEN

STERILIZATION. See also *Eugenics; Sex.* The indications for voluntary sterilization may be eugenic, prophylactic (sometimes called therapeutic), socio-economic and personal convenience. Not to be confused with castration, sterilization involves a surgical procedure whereby the reproductive cells of either the male (sperm) or the female (ovum) are effectively blocked (1) from further travel through their respective tubes, and thus (2) from any ultimate union

(fertilization) in the uterus. Neither sexual performance nor gender identification is impaired thereby. For males the surgical procedure is known as a vasectomy whereby the *vas deferens* are tied off. While only about 1 or 2 percent of the cases return for reversal procedures, success here amounts to only about 25 percent; the procedure is considered essentially permanent. The basic operation for women is known as a salpingectomy or tubal ligation. Most desirably done just following delivery, the Fallopian tubes are cut, a section excised and the remaining tubal ends tied. Again, the results are permanent, with some small degree of tubal restoration surgically possible. A newer procedure of promise is the laparoscopic tubal sterilization whereby a small incision near the navel admits a telescopic surgical instrument to the Fallopian region.

According to the Association for Voluntary Sterilization about two million living Americans have been sterilized with over 100,000 men and women currently utilizing this method of fertility control annually. It is legal in all fifty states; only Utah limits sterilization to cases of medical necessity. Current medical criteria views the procedure to be a matter solely between the physician and the patient (and, if married, the patient's spouse). While Denmark has experimented with "voluntary compulsion" by the state of "problem" individuals (mental defectives, welfare recipients, and hardened criminals), significant moral problems attach themselves to involuntary sterilization. However, long-term benefits both to the individual and to society may warrant involuntary sterilization when the rights of the individual are counterbalanced by morally compelling circumstances.

Until modern times Christian theologians have not had to comment on this procedure. Both Deut. 23:1 and the Council of Nicea (A.D. 325) condemned castration, but sterilization is *sui generis.* In a historical continuum of consistent denunciation of the operation by Roman Catholic moral theologians, *Humanae Vitae* also pronounced against sterilization. Mutilation of the body's integrity has not been a compelling argument for Protestants, however. Seeking to balance overpopulation and unanticipated pregnancies with the values of family, society and individual rights, Protestant thought has walked an ethical middle road. Until an effective, long-term contraceptive is found, sterilization may continue its growing popularity as a physically certain, morally permissible means of birth control for married couples. The advent of sperm banks will permit future artificial insemination procedures for males who opt for vasectomies now. As a procedure which seeks to anticipate an unwanted pregnancy, sterilization has more to commend it than the *post facto* "remedy" of abortion.

The State has in any event no right to deprive innocent persons of parenthood, and where sterilization is voluntary, wrong motivation will constitute it an immoral means. LEWIS P. BIRD

STEWARDSHIP. Stewardship is a spiritual principle and Biblical teaching. It recognizes God as the owner of all things; man as responsible for his use of these things in keeping with God's purpose; and that man must give account for the quality and results of his management. The principle is of importance in Christian ethics beyond the familiar applications relating to giving of funds and church finance.

The NT words steward and stewardship signify "house management." A steward was a trusted and responsible servant with large authority in handling the household or business affairs of another. The NT applications include stewardship of the gospel and of the office of minister (I Cor. 4:1; Titus 1:7; I Peter 4:10). Stewardship involves responsibility for all that is entrusted to one. It encompasses all of life.

Stewardship is based on the fact that God created all things and retains sovereignty over all. Christian faith affirms that God's creation is "good" as asserted in God's own declaration on six occasions as reported in the creation story in Gen. 1 (vv. 4, 10, 12, 18, 21, 25, 31); that created things are good in themselves and in relation to the purpose of God; and that their qualities of good or evil may be determined by their use. This is in strong contrast to other concepts of the material world, e.g., Gnostic (evil in essence); Manichee ("dark" in eternal conflict with the "light"); Hindu (worthless illusion); Buddhist and present-day popularized derivations (valueless, harmful since it contributes to desire, and is to be rejected by ascetic practices); and Marxist Socialism (absolute and ultimate value).

God's revealed purpose, the redemption of mankind through Jesus Christ, involves witness of redeemed persons and the use of created things in this witness. God has committed his created things to man for administration and utilization in keeping with this purpose, his own sustenance, his spiritual development, the welfare of humanity, bringing the message of redemption to all mankind, and the glory of God. As responsible steward one will be judged and give account for his use of all (Luke 12:42; 16:2f.; I Cor. 4:2).

The historic and most familiar application of the principle relates to gifts. The OT contains detailed requirements concerning the tithes to be brought by the worshipper (e.g., Lev. 27:30-32; Mal. 3:8-10). The NT does not bind the Christian to the old Mosaic law but to the new and higher law of love which expects more, rather than less, of the redeemed believer (Matt. 5–7, esp. 5:17, 21, 27, 33, 38, 43, 48; 23:23; John 14:15; Rom. 6:15; 13:10; II Cor. 5:14). Stewardship as seen in giving is one facet of the whole doctrine, which includes much more. This does not, however, in this particular area, dilute its application, weaken its significance or justify neglect.

Properly understood the principle includes all of life; all men's actions and attitudes; personality and personal influence; in money matters, the acquisition, handling, spending, saving, investing, giving, and final disposition; use of the land, resources and tools; one's profession, job or place of service; education and the use of education; one's worship, the witness of his life, his personal testimony, his purpose and goals in life.

Stewardship continuously speaks to current problems in each age and area of life. Measured against God's purpose for his creation: What relation has one steward to another person in God's image, whatever his nation, place, or race? What of exploitation of persons? What is the Christian's responsibility for the land, its natural resources, its ecology? What is the Christian's part in social change? his relation to the centers of power? What of his use and placement of money? What of the stewardship of the church itself? what of its budget and the division of its funds for itself and others? What of churches that pay more in interest on church building debts than they contribute to all mission activity beyond their states?

Simply stated, stewardship prompts one to ask: What is God's purpose for me in my specific interpersonal relationships, my use of resources, my attitude toward and my use of this created universe?

MERRILL D. MOORE

STOICISM. See *Fate; Greek Ethics.*

STRIKES. See also *Industrial Relations; Labor Relations.* The employee strike, as well as the employer's lockout, should not be viewed in isolation; it forms part of the overall collective bargaining, free enterprise system currently functioning in our predominently sub-Christian society. Accordingly, any responsible ethical evaluation of the strike as an economic weapon cannot overlook the fact that most participants have not made a Christian commitment. If one further accepts the view that full discipleship can be required only of disciples, the ethical complexity of the situation becomes evident. Assuming that it is undesirable to have governments dictate all job conditions and that it is highly improbably that any contemporary society will adopt the Christian love ethic as its norm, we are left with two major options—compulsory arbitration or an improvement of the present situation by enlightened legislation. While arbitration appears to be gaining acceptance, there is no indication that it will totally replace the strike. Thus, unless we want to flee from society, we should press for laws which protect the public interest (which probably means prohibition of strikes in all essential services, particularly in the public sector), ensure justice for all employees, respect individual conscience scruples, while still permitting organized employees collectively to withdraw their services while retaining their status as employees.

A Christian employee, one can surely argue, should have the same right as anyone else in the matter of withdrawing his service, provided such action does not constitute breach of promise. He should, however, exercise it with great caution, keeping in mind that ultimately a union decision is not the basis for his ethical code. He should reject all violence and in general be reluctant to support "sympathy strikes" and "target company" strikes. Indeed, he does his utmost to prevent strikes. However, in situations where the employer fails to maintain safe premises, breaks his commitments, refuses to negotiate, or persistently exploits his employees, the Christian employee might well be justified in supporting the strike as a means of last resort. Before making such a decision or complying with a union ultimatum he should seek counsel from fellow believers. Concerning the whole matter of "striking," Christians should constantly evaluate each case on its particular merits. Such a stance is equally valid for trainmen and truckers, electricians and physicians.   JOHN H. REDEKOP

SUBJECTIVISM, ETHICAL. See also *Ethical Relativism; Situational Ethics.* In ethics the term "ethical subjectivism" is used to describe the view that moral judgments are not to be isolated from the psychological states or attitudes of the persons making them. All moral or ethical theory is determined by reference to the feeling of the subject involved. Stated the other way, it is a denial or rejection of all objective or universal standards as applied to moral or ethical conduct. The Sophists were ethical subjectivists who regarded man as the sole factor in determining all matters of personal conduct. Likewise, hedonism in all its forms is an expression of ethical subjectivism. The subjective reference is present in the sensuous hedonism of Aristippus, the aesthetic emphasis of Epicurus, and in Bentham's principle of the greatest happiness for the greatest number. In the last analysis it is the individual or subject who here determines pleasure, and this is the essence of hedonistic virtue.

WARREN C. YOUNG

SUFFERING. Suffering is a constant in the human condition, so universal in time and in place, so personal and subjective in its experience, that it need not be described; no man has reached his maturity who does not know what suffering is. It is not the "what" or the "whether" of suffering but the "why" which beggars analysis. And closely allied to the why of suffering is the perennial question of how it may be faced.

Apart from the Scriptural approach two answers have been offered. From the Stoics to Sarte suffering has simply been accepted as descriptive of the way things are, where one does not evade the reality but endures it. Man is either the end product of some evolutionary series of accidents or the helpless object of impersonal determinative forces and therefore no answer is to be sought outside the nature of things. From this kind of fatalistic acceptance there have been produced great examples of courage and patient endurance which are not entirely foreign to the requirements of Christian fortitude.

The other approach has classical expression in Buddhism where the "solution" to the problem is escape from human existence in a disciplined program by which the desires of life are eliminated and there is eventual escape into Nirvana by rigid self-denials which solve the problem by eliminating it. Christian Science and its friends need not be given serious consideration here since, in essence, the question itself is unreal.

In the Biblical approach and more exactly in the Christian approach the question is squarely faced, but the question is intensified because the extent to which one is able to accept a God who is Love, to that extent one finds it even more puzzling to grasp how a universe governed by personal omnipotent Love can be a place of blindness, torture, separation, helplessness, hopelessness, "strong crying and tears."

According to the Bible the mystery of suffering rests on the mystery of iniquity. Suffering then is caused by sin and sin is the condition of a creation which has rebelled against the Creator, so that the disharmony which necessarily follows throws all things out of joint; the new condition is cosmic, the whole creation groans, and over and above such apparently causal relationships is the wrath of a holy personal God whose face is set against all unrighteousness. That sin and suffering are thus interrelated is clear from the bliss of Eden at one end of the story and the bliss of heaven at the other; in between Eden and heaven both sin and suffering are rampant.

But further explanation is needed. It is true that sin produces suffering and we can assume that all suffering somewhere, somehow is caused by sin. The difficulty lies in the inequality of what ought to be an equation. Why, for example, do the righteous suffer? Why do the wicked apparently flourish? These questions and their variants appear over and over again in both the OT and NT. When the necessary equation between sin and suffering is individualized instead of generalized the equation seems to break down. Job gives classic expression to this kind of problem. The question in Job is how to read his suffering back to his sin, his suffering as against the apparent easy-going life of his critical friends. Significantly the book of Job does not give any final answer except to lay to rest the easy criticisms of his friends (the popular easy criticisms of every generation) and to open up a whole realm of other possibilities resting in the over-powering greatness of God and the endless mystery of God's ways with his creation. Greater things are at stake and greater things are underway than will appear to Job and his friends.

The NT offers two further ways to understanding. The first is that there is a mass and morass of suffering which must be paid for by sinful humanity. There will never be any neat score-keeping here (at least from man's limited viewpoint) but the price will be paid by humanity in human history and paid in full. The other answer is on the cross where one who knew no sin took on himself the sin of the world. Among many other things the cross reveals that suffering may be made into something redemptive, if the suffering is chosen for love's sake, if the cross is taken up in discipleship. As co-workers with Christ the disciple accepts God's judgment on sin, accepts in faith such suffering as is laid upon him in God's wisdom and love, but more than merely doggedly accepting he positively takes upon himself the cross of discipleship, knowing that final answers rest in the great finalities which remain with God in another world. "Shall not the judge of all the earth do right?"

ADDISON H. LEITCH

SUGGESTION. See also *Brainwashing; Hypnotism; Propaganda; Witchcraft.* Suggestion is a process of human communication in which an idea is implanted or behavior induced in an individual who responds uncritically. This process, because of its potential for exerting constructive or destructive influence, has moral implications.

Suggestion plays a role in many forms of human interaction. Advertisers use it to influence people to purchase their products; politicians, to persuade people to vote for them. Suggestion forms the basis of hypnosis and certain forms of brief psychotherapy.

The effectiveness of suggestion depends on the ability of the source to convey authority and on the degree of suggestibility of the subject. Adults possessing certain character traits and children are highly susceptible to suggestion and thus vulnerable to exploitation.

Suggestibility may be increased by drugs (q.v.), and by states of emotional and physiological stress. Drugs such as scopolamine and thiopental sodium produce a hypnotic trance which in turn heightens suggestibility. Increased suggestibility occurs in some neuroses—e.g., conversion reaction—and certain types of psychoses—e.g., where two closely associated individuals manifest the same symptoms, one apparently inducing symptoms in the other *(folie a deux)*. Malnutrition and excessive fatigue also increase suggestibility. Thus, suggestion has been used in brainwashing (q.v.) techniques and in the treatment of combat fatigue.

Negative suggestibility, a tendency to do the opposite of what is suggested, occurs normally in children and abnormally in certain forms of schizophrenia (catatonic).

Usually the idea or attitude suggested comes from a source outside of the subject (heterosuggestion). In autosuggestion, the source of the idea or attitudes stems from within the individual.

ARMAND M. NICHOLI II

SUICIDE. See also *Euthanasia; Genocide.* Is it wrong for an individual to terminate his life? If so, precisely why is self-destruction immoral?

The ancient Stoics—e.g., Seneca—vigorously defended the right of suicide as a corollary of man's radical freedom, his lordship over every aspect of his own being. Hence their famous shibboleth, "The door is open," expressed the conviction that one may at any time choose to liberate himself from pain and evil (Adolf Wuttke, *Christian Ethics,* Edinburgh, T. & T. Clark, 1873, vol. I pp. 139-140). In modern Japan suicide is considered as indication of "magokoro" or sincerity. According to that country's leading authority on the subject, psychiatrist Kenshiro Ohara, when a Japanese mother decides to kill herself, she usually first kills her children. Instead of calling forth indignation, such a deed elicits praise since children are not only regarded as parts of their parents but, in addition, to leave them motherless would be cruel (*The New York Times,* April 30, 1973, p. 10).

In Christian thought suicide has found few apologists. John Donne and Thomas Moore are notable exceptions. The almost unanimous opposition to what is stigmatized as self-murder does not appeal to explicit texts. (The Biblical instances of suicide are inferentially condemned—Haman, Saul, Ahithophel, and Judas. Even Samson's heroic death was evil, says Augustine, unless God specifically granted him inner guidance to destroy himself with the Philistines [cf. Paul Ramsey, *War and the Christian Conscience,* Durham, North Carolina, Duke University, 1961, p. 47]). Traditional opposition to suicide rests, rather, upon an extrapolation from the Sixth Commandment, "Thou shalt not kill" (Exod. 20:13; cf. Gen. 9:6). Human life is God's sovereign gift. Crassly stated, it is his property; and, as divinely bestowed, it is of measureless though not absolute value. Only God, consequently, is entitled to determine when and how life is to end. Thus its termination, whether by illness or old age or accident, is under his providential control. There is, to be sure, the possibility that life may be ended in battle or by execution, but, providing the ending is sanctioned by a legitimate authority which is functioning as God's surrogate, no sin is committed. There is, moreover, the possibility of a voluntary self-sacrifice which entails no condemnation—a husband dying to save his wife, or a sailor guiding a one-missile torpedo toward an enemy ship. But, aside from a few cases of these sorts, to end one's life intentionally is to be guilty of *lese majesty,* rebelliously usurping God's prerogative.

With the widespread undermining of Christian faith and the increasing stress on human autonomy, the traditional appeal to divine providence as determining when and how one's life ought to end comes under attack as an irrational submission to blind "theological positivism" or the impersonal caprices of nature and history. Even if one accepts Biblical revelation, he may feel constrained to agree with seventeenth century John De Lugo as he argues that suicide is wrong. "The whole difficulty lies in assigning a reason for this truth. For though the evil in question be immediately clear, it is still not easy to find its basis. Consequently, it happens here as in many other questions, that the conclusion is more certain than the reasons which, being of various kinds, are adduced from different sources to prove the point" (cf. John C. Milhaven, "Moral Absolutes and Thomas Aquinas," ed. Charles Curren, *Absolutes in*

Moral Theology, Washington, Corpus Books, 1968, p. 184).

Though a Biblicist, one may also agree with F. B. Barry that suicide should be removed from the category of felony (*Christian Ethics and Secular Society*, London, Hodder & Stoughten, 1966, p. 252).   VERNON C. GROUNDS

Despite gains over poverty, rising living standards, and progress in battling disease and pain, suicide rates in the USA continue to rise and do so even among younger and affluent persons. The latest reliable estimates available, from the demographic yearbook of the U.N. World Health Organization, ranks the USA fifteenth highest in respect to suicide rate (as of 1968); Hungary tops the list, followed by Czechoslovakia, Austria, Sweden, Finland, West Germany, Denmark, Switzerland, France, Belgium, Japan, Taiwan, Australia, and Singapore. Final USA vital statistics show a suicide rate of 10.6 per 100,000 population in 1960, 10.8 in 1964, 10.7 in 1968, and 11.1 (or 22,364 suicides) in 1969. A preliminary sampling indicates no decline in the 11.1 rate for 1970 and 1971. The statistical bulletin published by Metropolitan Life shows a decrease in suicides at ages 55 and over and, in fact, a small decrease in the 45-54 year bracket. But other age brackets reflect an increase between 1960 and 1967, as follows: 15-24 years, from 5.2 to 7.0 per 100,000; 25-34, from 10.0 to 12.4; 35-44, from 14.2 to 16.6—Ed.

SUNDAY. It would seem that from a very early period Christians adopted Sunday as their distinctive day of worship. The name itself is not mentioned in Scripture, since, of course, it is derived from pagan sources and denotes the day devoted to the sun. The diary portion of Acts refers to the custom at Troas of breaking bread on the first day of the week (Acts 20:7) and Paul instructed his converts in Corinth to set aside money for Christian aid on the same day (I Cor. 16:2).

Apparently it was felt unsatisfactory to designate such an important occasion merely by a number, whether "first" or "eighth" (*Ep. Barn.* 15.9), and by the time the Apocalypse was written the title "Lord's day" had gained currency (Rev. 1:10). Some have surmised that the practice originated in Syria and was the creation of Gentile Christendom. The Graeco-Roman world was familiar with the Babylonian arrangement of days to form weeks and Justin Martyr spoke of Sunday as if well-known to all (1 *Apol.* 67).

But were there older roots in Jewish Christianity and in Palestine itself? Evidence in Eusebius (HE III, 27.5) indicates the existence of an Ebionite group who kept Sunday to commemorate the Saviour's resurrection. H. Dumaine believes that such a Jewish-Christian observance went back to the primitive church (DACL IV, col. 893).

The obvious reason for recognizing Sunday as the Christian's holy day is thus no doubt the real one. The association with the first appearance of the risen Lord is paramount. This factor is determinative for the Christian conception of the Lord's day and consequent patterns of behavior. It immediately emancipates it from any traces of sabbatarian legalism or gloom. "Sunday we give to joy," announced Tertullian (*Apol.* 16). Later the Fathers were to explain the symbolism of the sun by reference to Mal. 4:2.

This was what Theodor von Haering had in mind when he insisted that it is not strictly evangelical to ground Sunday observance on the Decalogue (*The Ethics of the Christian Life*, ET, London, Williams and Norgate, 1909, p. 162). It is rather to be interpreted in terms of the teaching of Jesus (Mark 2:23-28; 3:16; Luke 13:10-17; John 7:23) and the Pauline stress on Christian liberty (Gal. 5:1). These are the salient Biblical criteria by which ethical attitudes to Sunday observance are to be assessed. The reintroduction of obligatory sanctions would be a retrogression. On the other hand it is necessary to realize that the Christian use of Sunday as the Lord's day embraces two major OT emphases relating to the Jewish Sabbath. It was not only a day of rest, but a memorial of the creation (Exod. 20:8-11) and the covenant (Exod. 31:13-17; Isa. 56:4, 6). It was devoted to God as a sign of sanctification (Ezek. 10:12). The Christian Sunday marks the recreation of man in Christ the Second Adam (I Cor. 15:22; II Cor. 5:17), and the inauguration of the new covenant in the Saviour's blood (Matt. 26:27, 28).

The Jewish idea of Sabbath rest in the sense of cessation from labor did not infiltrate Christian thought until the fourth century. Before the decree of Constantine in A.D. 321 constituting Sunday a public holiday, Christians went to work like everyone else. Although strongly under Christian influence, Constantine seems to have exempted the day primarily on humanitarian grounds—a factor which must still be taken into consideration. Even after 321, however, Christians continued to maintain the essential difference between the Lord's day and the Sabbath. They regarded it as a day of worship rather than as a day of rest.

As they followed Jesus in rejecting any arbitrary enforcement of sabbatarian regulations, the early Christians in fact fulfilled the essential implications of the divine rest on which the Jewish institution was based. God's own rest after creation is far from passive (John 5:17; Eph. 1:10). He pursues his redemptive purpose, and it is in active identification with it that the Christian best reflects the spirit both of the Sabbath and the Lord's day.

W. Hodgkins, *Sunday: Christian and Social Significance*, London, Independent, 1960; H. P. Porter, *The Day of Light: the Biblical and Liturgical Meaning of Sunday*, London, SCM, 1960; W. Rordorf, *Sunday: the History of the Day of Rest and Worship in the Earliest Centuries of the Church*, ET London, SCM, 1968; M. G. Glazebrook, "Sunday," *HERE* XXI, New York, Scribner, pp. 103-111.   A. SKEVINGTON WOOD

SUPEREGO. See also *Conscience; Freud; Id.* The superego is one of the three divisions of personality as conceived in Freud's structural theory. The ego acts as middleman between the pleasure-seeking, instinctual drives of the id and the reality demands of the external world, while the superego represents the moral demands that have been taken over from other people, such as parents, teachers, or similarly admired persons. Racial, national, and family traditions, as well as the demands of the immediate social milieu, were included in the standards considered to be upheld by the superego.

In the Freudian structural theory, the chief function of the superego was to limit satisfactions. The superego was considered the vehicle for the phenomenon called conscience, perpetuating the strictures formerly exercised by parents through observation, criticism and punishment. The functions of the superego, however, were regarded as largely or completely unconscious. Freud imagined the superego dealing with the ego as a strict father would deal with a child, often administering excessive punishment. Feelings of inferiority or guilt were attributed to the disapproval of the superego, leading to an unconscious need for expiation or self-punishment. Freud postulated that when the oedipus complex—based upon sexual attraction toward the parent of opposite sex—is resolved by age five, the energy associated with that drive becomes expressed in the superego. This is the Freudian doctrine that the superego is the precipitate of the oedipus complex. The superego thus is believed to have a purely naturalistic genesis, and conscience is regarded as an aggregation of parental and social precepts that derives its force from biological drives. Freud acknowledged his acquaintance with the universal belief in a divine spirit that has implanted in man both a knowledge of his perfection, and a striving toward it, but he rejected the idea as contrary to reason and science.

 Sigmund Freud, *Outline of Psychoanalysis,* New York, Norton, 1949, pp. 16ff., 121ff.; *Moses and Monotheism,* New York, Vintage, 1955, Part III, Section II.   ORVILLE S. WALTERS

SUPEREROGATION, WORKS OF. See also *Merit.* Linked to the Roman Catholic teaching of the merit of good works, is the claim that believers are able to merit more than is necessary for their own salvation. The term comes from the Latin *super-erogare* which means to do or to pay more than is required or necessary. The Vulgate translation of Luke 10:35 uses this term, but its technical sense was developed in the Middle Ages. Clement VI in 1343 proclaimed the doctrine (Denzinger 550ff.), and it was implicitly sanctioned by the Council of Trent in its affirmation of the doctrine of indulgences.

Works of supererogation are not obligatory but rank as something good over and above what is required, such as the "counsels of evangelical perfection" involving vows of poverty, celibacy, and obedience. These superabundant merits of the saints and of Mary are added to the infinite merits of Christ, which were beyond the needs of our salvation, and become the "spiritual treasury" of the church. These are at the disposal of the pope and by way of indulgences can be transferred to others in need, including the dead.

Biblical support for the doctrine was sought in the account of the rich young ruler (Matt. 19:16ff.) and in Paul's teaching on virginity (I Cor. 7). The Reformers repudiated the doctrine as unbiblical and as arrogant and impious.   FRED H. KLOOSTER

SUPERMAN. See also *Nietzsche.* Superman is the name given by Nietzsche to what he considered a higher type of humanity. Nietzsche did not coin the word *Über-mensch* (literally, "overman"); the term was used by Herder, Muller, Goethe, and Faust before Nietzsche. The hyperanthropos is found in the works of Lucian (Second century A.D.) to whom Nietzsche had made frequent reference as a classical philologist in his *Philogica.* Nietzsche first used the word "superman" as a youth in describing Byron's Manfred as a "superman who controls spirits," thus closely paralleling Goethe's usage in his poem *(Zueignung).* He later applied it to Shakespeare's heroes as well. The "superman" is a human being *(Mensch*—male or female) who has organized the chaos of the passions, given style to one's character, and become creative.

Except for an ironic, self-critical reference in the chapter on Poets in *Zarathustra,* Nietzsche uses the word "superman" in the singular. It is intended to indicate a this-worldly antithesis to God. Despite its singular form, the word is never applied to an individual, and Nietzsche plainly considered neither himself nor Zarathustra, whom he often ridiculed, to be "superman." Nietzsche rejects the idea of a kind of superior man or the deification of a specific individual. Even the most superior men fail us. Hence, the idea of superman is not to be identified with what is visible nor with what is concealed in man. Rather, the superman stands for the future, for what is beyond man but can be realized through man.

To bring forth the superman is our task, contends Nietzsche. For "It lies within our nature to create a being higher than ourselves. To *create beyond ourselves!* That is what drives us to procreate, and that is the urge behind our activities and our achievements." Man is a rope stretched between animal and superman—a rope over an abyss.

In order for superman to come there must be a radical break with all traditional values. Absolutes like myths of the past are completely defunct. God died and all value died with him; we must now transvaluate all values. The values of the past, especially the

Christian ones, must be transformed from other-worldly to this-worldly. The former "soft" virtues of the flock morality must be replaced by the new "hard" virtues of the individual. For example, one must not love out of weakness or sentimentality, but engage in generosity that gives as an overflow of one's individual strength.

The superman, then, is a personification of this higher man envisioned by Nietzsche. It is an ideal toward which men should strive in the transvaluation of all traditional values in view of the claim that God has perished.   NORMAN GEISLER

SUTTEE (SATI). Especially in Bengal, Hindus burned widows (often mere children) on the funeral pyres of their husbands, voluntarily or otherwise, regarding it as a religious duty. The custom so symbolized the "mystic unity of souls," that the victim could laugh at the flames. It also aimed at preventing second marriages. Christian missionaries, emphasising the ethical outworkings of the gospel, naturally opposed suttee; also many Hindu reformers under Christian influence did so. In 1829 Lord Bentinck outlawed suttee. Brahmins declared this dishonorable to womanhood, but once prohibited in British India several Native States followed voluntarily.

ALAN R. TIPPETT

SYMPATHY. See *Compassion.*

SYNCRETISM. Syncretism was originally a political term. Plutarch described the unity of the Cretans against the common enemy as a *synkretismos.* Later the term was used of harmony in the sphere of philosophy and religion. The fifteenth century Cardinal Bessarion, used the term in his endeavor to reconcile Plato and Aristotle. In the seventeenth century, the Lutheran Calixtus was called a syncretist for his attempted reconciliation of Protestant theologies. The derivation of syncretism from *synkerannumi* (to mix) now became normative.

Gunkel, Harnack, and Bultmann use the term widely to describe Christianity as a syncretistic religion assimilating Judaistic, Hellenistic and gnostic concepts, while Russell Chandran argues that all formulations of Christian theology are of necessity syncretistic. This is a misuse of the term. The NT writers boldly used terms common to Hellenistic and gnostic culture, such as *gnōsis, logos, plērōma, mystērion,* in their zeal to communicate the gospel to the pagan world, but there is little evidence that they accommodated their message to pagan thought-forms or ideas. Christianity as a prophetic religion based on belief in God's self-revelation in historic act, propositional word and finally in the incarnation, cross, and resurrection of Jesus Christ, was from its inception thoroughly anti-syncretistic. The use of pagan terminology by the NT writers in the interests of evangelism is no proof of syncretism. Without the adaptation of non-Christian terminology, there can be no effective communication of the gospel.

Syncretism is essentially of two types: overt and primitive. The systematic and intentional attempt to reconcile diverse or conflicting tenets or religious practices frequently occurs in religious history. Mithraism in the first four centuries A.D. and Manichaeism which persisted up until the tenth century attempted to give the ancient Hellenistic-oriental world universal religion. The Theosophical Society founded by Madame Blavatsky and the Ramakrishna Mission of Swami Vivekananda stem from Hinduism, Bahai world faith from Islam and numerous sects such as Oomoto and Ittoen from Shintoism and Buddhism. Modern advocates of the convergence of world religions in a universal religion include W. E. Hocking, Arnold Toynbee and S. Radhakrishnan. The history of Christian theology evidences many attempts to synthesize Biblical faith with non-Christian philosophy. Thomas Aquinas' synthesis of Biblical faith and Aristotelian philosophy and the current attempts of Raymond Panikkar (*The Unknown Christ of Hinduism*, New York, Humanities) to baptize Shakara's Advaidic Vedanta are well known. In Africa some of the Independent Churches are attempting to synthesise Christianity and African Spiritism.

Primitive Syncretism, as an unreflected spontaneous assumption that all religions and theologies are inadequate expressions of universal and eternal religion, is widespread. It is an attitude of mind rather than a set of convictions, reflected in the famous defense of the pagan Roman Symmachus against the removal of the statue and altar of Victory, "it is impossible that so great a mystery should be approached by one road only." Primitive syncretism reflects both man's search for integration with the totality of the cosmic and natural order and his rebellion against God's lordship (Rom. 1). It is normative religion for man seeking the realization of Self.

Several patterns of syncretistic thinking are discernable. On the principle of regression, syncretism abstracts universal ideas from historical facts and regresses from God as personal in his attributes and relations to the impersonal and unknowable being of God. On the principle of universalism, religious tenets and practices complement each other so that the sum total of particular truths is greater than the partial truth of any one.

The *Lebensmitte* or creative center of syncretistic thinking tends to be either deistic or pantheistic. The former emphasizes the transcendence of God and is rationalistic and moralistic. Religion is essentially ethics independent of creed and cultic practice. The latter emphasises the immanence of God and the mystical identity of man with the cosmos. Ethics which are subordinate to religion are grounded in abstract principles or social customs. While claiming to champion religious tolerance, syncretistic thinking is normally intolerant of all systems which do not accord with its own *Lebensmitte*. The Biblical rejection of syncretism in all forms is clearly evident in the prophetic protest against the Baalisation of Yahweh-worship and the Babylonian-Assyrian cults and in the attacks of the NT writers on Hellenistic and gnostic cults prominent in Antioch, Ephesus, Corinth, Colossae, Rome. Successive waves of syncretism are discernable in church and secular history (W. A. Visser't Hooft, *No Other Name*, London, SCM). Primitive syncretism underlies the synthesizing tendencies of modern liberal and radical theology, both Protestant and Catholic. The Christian church has failed to take the challenge of world-wide syncretism sufficiently serious. Only a reforming faith proclaiming a Biblical theology will offer a satisfactory apologetic. BRUCE J. NICHOLLS

T

TALMUD. See also *Jewish Ethics*. The literal meaning is "teaching" (*lamad*, to teach). As a technical term it refers to a body of literature which in the broadest sense describes the rabbinic way of life.

The Talmud is a composite work with a long history. It comprises the rabbinic discussions on points of *torah* (q.v.) and contains an accumulated treasure-store of ancestral wisdom and tradition over several centuries. In the English translation the *Babylonian Talmud* runs to thirty-four volumes plus an extra Index volume (edited under the direction of Rabbi I. Epstein,

New York, Soncino Press, 1935-48, Index, 1952).

Behind the written text is a long oral tradition transmitted through the rabbinic academies in Palestine ("Jerusalem" Talmud) and in Babylonia (Babylonian Talmud) on matters concerning the Mosaic text and its applicability to daily practice. The need arose from the fact that the *torah* provided no "clear cut" answer as to the interpretation of its ordinances.

The core of the Torah is the Mishnah (lit., "learn," "recite"). The Mishnah is the deposit of oral tradition as codified by Rabbi Judah the Prince (c. A.D. 200). Its purpose is to elucidate *halakha* (lit., guidance), i.e., definitive ruling as to the application of the laws arising from the *torah*. These rules are presented in the form of minority and majority views. The Sages who appear in the Mishnah are described as Tannaim (sing. *tanna:* one who repeats or teaches) as distinct from the Rabbis of the post-mishnaic period who are called Amoraim (sing. *amora:* speaker, interpreter).

Here is an example of mishnaic discussion: Tractate *Shabbat* deals with matters of Sabbath observance. Exodus 16:29 reads: "Let no man go out of his place on the seventh day." To the Rabbis "to go out" implied carrying a burden (cf. Jer. 17:22). The Mishnah lays down: "A tailor should not go out with his needle (on Friday) near nightfall lest he forget and 'go out'" i.e., find himself carrying a burden (1:3). Here is another passage dealing with "going out": If a man throws ought from a private to another private domain with the public domain in between, R. Akiba declares him culpable, but the Sages declare him not culpable (11:1) (E. T. by Canon H. Danby, Oxford, 1933). Rabbinic decision is always by majority, though the minority view is recorded, and is important.

The other component of the Talmud is called Gemara (lit., "completion"). Its purpose is to explicate, illustrate and elaborate the mishnaic text. The Gemara thus contains a wealth of folklore, anecdotes, edifying examples and wise maxims. Mishnah plus Gemara constitute the bulk of the Talmud. There is however one more component which must be mentioned.

Baraitot (sing. *baraita:* "outside" teaching) refers to tannaitic traditions of ancient provenance which have been left "outside" the Mishnah as edited by R. Judah the Prince. These Baraitot are frequently quoted in the Gemara to clinch a decision or to record an opposite opinion.

The Mishnah is divided into six "orders," and each "order" is subdivided into a number of treatises, chapters, and paragraphs. The six "orders" are:

1. Seeds—laws and regulations appertaining to agriculture.

2. Feasts—rules in respect to festivals.

3. Women—laws regarding marriage, divorce, etc.

4. Damages—criminal and civil law.

5. Hallowed things—laws dealing with matters regarding sacrifice, temple, etc.

6. Cleannesses—problems relating to ritual purity.

Embedded in the text of the Talmud is aggadic material (*aggadah:* tale, lesson). This represents the non-legal aspect of the talmudic teaching and consists of legends, stories, anecdotes, theological quibbles and some historical data.

The printed text in the original is so arranged as to convey the composite nature of this literature. The Mishnah is placed in the middle of the page and appears in bold lettering. Surrounding the mishnaic text on all sides is the additional material which makes up the whole.

Traditionally, on the same page appear in a separate column the Tosaphot (pl. additions) or *novellae,* views and explications by later scholars from the twelfth to the fourteenth centuries. The tosaphists are European sages mainly from the north of France and Germany. The Tosaphot have been described as a Talmud on the Talmud.

The redaction of the Talmud was completed in the sixth century A.D. Its language is non-classical, rabbinic Hebrew, with a strong admixture of Aramaic and the use of loanwords from Greek and Latin.

The Talmud carries supreme authority in orthodox Jewry. Rabbi Mendell Lewittes explains: "Each opinion, each individual interpretation by a master of tradition is considered part of the divine revelation. . . . " Even the minority views conflicting with the majority are understood as the words of the living God (cf. *Studies in Torah Judaism,* ed. by Leon D. Stitskin, Yeshiva University, 1969, p. 259).

Judaism, explains Rabbi Immanuel Jakobovitz, is a "Halakhah-centred system, employing laws to convey and inculcate concepts in much the same way as the artist uses his material for communication of his notions" (ibid. 331). Given this premise, the Talmud has proved its value in keeping Judaism alive.   JAKOB JOCZ

TAOISM AND ETHICS. China has been the historic matrix for the unique blending of the *San Chiao,* the "Three Religions," as they are commonly called: (1) Confucianism, with its emphasis on socio-political morals, ceremonies, and the active life; (2) Taoism, with its concern for idyllic idealism, superstitious geomancy, and the mystical life; (3) Buddhism, with its affirmation of reincarnation, ritual, and the philosophical life. For at least 2,000 years Taoism (pronounced Dowism) has been an integral part of the lifestyle of China, moving from its formative stage of ancient mysticism through its magical and then formally religious stages until the present time, when Chairman Mao's Marxism largely has replaced the *San Chiao* of the ancestors.

The amalgam of mysticism and magic, naturalism and religion dates from the time of Lao Tzu (b. 604 B.C., according to tradition). The sayings of this legendary curator of historical documents turned mystic seer form the core of the book bearing his name, the *Lao-tzu* (compiled by the fourth century B.C.). The *Lao-tzu* is a collection of crisp sentences and cryptic poems, also known as the *Tao Te Ching* ("Classic of the Way and Power"). The Saint Paul of Taoism is Chuang Tzeu, a fourth century B.C. mystic whose name and fragmentary contributions are attached to the thirty-three essays of the *Chuang-tzu.*

The *Tao* defies definition: "The *Tao* that can be comprised in words is not the eternal Tao; the name that can be named is not the abiding name" (*Tao Te Ching,* I). For practical purposes, *Tao* means a path, a road, the way of nature, the Way of Ultimate Reality. Oriental Christian apologists have linked the *Tao* of the Far East with the *Logos* of Johannine theology for kerygmatic purposes, for better or worse.

Of special interest to the Evangelical ethicist is the unique adaptation C. S. Lewis gives the *Tao* (cf. *The Abolition of Man,* New York, Macmillan, 1947). Defining it as the universal moral sense of mankind, Lewis utilizes the *Tao* to specify and affirm those elementary principles of general ethics shared by all representative viewpoints in a pluralistic society. The articulation of such *Tao* principles in the fields of social ethics, medical ethics, family life, sex education, etc., is mandatory if common ground for ethical debate is to be found within multiple value systems.

The traditional Taoist Philosophy of nonaction leads to mystical quietism, nonagression and a laissez-faire attitude toward life. Taoist ethics are relativistic; in typically paradoxical language the *Chuang-tzu* counsels: "When there is life, there is death, and when there is death, there is life. . . . Let us forget life. Let us forget the distinction between right and wrong. Let us take our joy in the realm of the infinite and remain there" (*Chuang-tzu,* II). Taoists are advocates of individual autonomy, spiritual freedom, personal simplicity and pacifism; they are opposed to materialistic acquisition and capital punishment. In contrast to Confucianism's laborious moral code, Taoism's emphasis is upon the rule of Nature over the institutions of men. In contrast to Christianity, Taoism is essentially amoralistic and pantheistic, with neither an historic ethical model nor a loving relationship with a personal God.

🕮 H. G. Creel, *Chinese Thought from Confucius to Mao Tse-tung*, Chicago, University of Chicago, 1953; Allie M. Frazier, ed., *Readings in Eastern Religious Thought*, Vol. III, Philadelphia, Westminster, 1969.   LEWIS P. BIRD

TECHNOCRACY AND TECHNOLOGY.
See also *Atomic Energy; Cybernetics; Science and Ethics; Urbanization.* Technocracy is a theory and movement originating in the USA about 1932 and urging that control of industrial resources and reorganization of the social order pass from the politicians to engineers and scientists. Technology is the branch of knowledge that deals with industrial arts. In any age technology has been "the systematic modification of the physical environment for human ends." Hence man as tool-user.

Today technology dictates so much of material change and determines so deeply the social fabric in the Western world that it is proper to speak of ours as a technological society. So deeply is science involved with our Western civilization that a recent Advisory Committee of the President of the USA reported that "science is a necessary element in national survival." We need, therefore, the widest possible diffusion of scientific and technological knowledge lest society fall captive to a scientific-technological elite which could become, if the history of man is any guide, "as pernicious as every other all-powerful priesthood."

Dynamic Balance. The dynamic balance of science, technology, and society should be more widely understood. Each new discovery in science can be used in two ways: fed back into the main stream of science and discovery, it encourages further science; used by industry it becomes catalyst for superior technology with inevitable effect upon social patterns. The mutual stimulation of science and technology has been fostered by professionalization of the scientific and engineering communities and by increasing emphasis upon the "systems" approach (attack of problems by teams considering all possible "angles" for solution, thus endowing it with "global" rather than "local" significance).

Technology and Human Values. With greater control by machines has come less ethical concern for the people affected by the change, subordination of the individual to the organization, and with increase in the level of production has come the rigidity implied by precision machinery moving at high speeds.

The changes induced by new technologies have the proportions of a "second industrial revolution," but with a difference. The essence of the current revolution is not invention of new items (such as plastics, TV, computers, or even nuclear energy) but lies rather in the idea of thoroughly integrated research and development, a technology for producing new technologies. It is captured in the machine which duplicates itself. Men who become enamored with this ideal do well to ponder that this is what the Creator was about during the sixth day of creation: making beings who could go on duplicating themselves. The difference was that God's work bore his image.

The central ethical question about technology is what happens to human beings in the process: both the creators of technology, its consumers, and all indirectly affected by it. Because technology involves *how* something is made or done, it is, *per se,* ethically neutral. What it does to man is to magnify his humanity, his character, the ethical nature of his decisions. It makes possible vast consequences from one decision, and thus holds up to man's heart a huge magnifying glass. In Abraham's day the king by his mere decision committed whole armies to the field of battle. Today machines create this magnification effect of the will of the few or even of one. Machines have thus moved from periphery to the center of human life, from optional to necessary. The illusion is current that the machine relieves man of ethical responsibility. Hence the rash of hatred for the machine as such is juvenile, if not irrational. The pathos is misdirected, for only *men* use machines. It is man who makes neutral technology a thing of good or evil. If and where it is allowed to usurp control in the form of a coterie of expert teams and professional groups, there is danger that technology "foster a false ethic of limited responsibility." It is fatally easy to persuade conscience of the necessity of "progress."

Another danger is psychological. It is well known that mental illness is related to rapid social change. "If psychiatric illnesses are truly increasing in the Western world, the reason is . . . in the accelerated rate at which old habits and conventions disappear and new ones appear" (DuBos). The nagging question, often thought, was put by an Asian to an American scientist: "There is one thing that you in the West can teach us in the East. It is something that matters tremendously. Show us that it is good to live in an industrial community."

Christian Response. Technology can sharpen our sense of responsibility by reminding us that material means can serve spiritual ends. A superior technology can become a wider means to serve God. Machines can underline something about the way God has made the universe and man's mind compatible with understanding it. And they illustrate the "habit of truth," for machines do not lie. They follow the laws of their being. The sad fact is that the scientist is often more ready to admit interpretative error in his field than the churchman is in his. Is the scientist's stance toward nature better than the churchman's toward the Bible?

There is great need for Christian consciences, sensitized to Biblical norms, to be heard at all levels of the technological order, especially in management. The Christian is uniquely situated to help create a climate of justice and equity in behalf of all affected by change; he knows the threat of technology to a new brand of materialism—that of reliance upon technology to pilot the ship of life; he knows that to succumb to it is to forsake the spiritual purpose God assigned to human life; he knows that the Creator of human life is Lord of its meaning; that the new technologies (or the old) are powerless to solve the peculiarly "human" problem; and he knows that the grace of God is ever available to transform men and fuse them with his purpose in the midst of a technologically dominant culture.

John G. Burk, ed., *The New Technology and Human Values*, Belmont, Calif., Wadsworth, 1966; Lynn White, Jr., *Machina Ex Deo*, Cambridge, Mass., Massachusetts Institute of Technology, 1968; Melvin Kranzberg and Carroll W. Pursell, Jr., eds., *Technology in Western Civilization*, New York, Oxford University, 2 vols., 1967; Jacques Ellul, *The Technological Society*, New York, Knopf, 1964; R. J. Forbes, *The Conquest of Nature*, New York, Praeger, 1968; W. H. G. Armytage, *The Rise of the Technocrats*, Toronto, University of Toronto, 1965; Charles Singer, et al., ed., *A History of Technology*, New York, Oxford University, 5 vols., 1957.   CHARLES HATFIELD

TELEOLOGICAL ETHICS. See *Ethics, History of; Utilitarianism.*

TELEVISION. See also *Mass Media.* The electronic transmission of pictures and sound via airwaves or cable has become pervasive in developed societies since World War II, while radio, its sound-only predecessor, remains predominant in the "Third World." It has extensive social value, providing rapid news, inexpensive entertainment (which in balanced use is an ethical good), as well as vast potential for education and cultural development. Often, however, this potential is neglected. Because of its effectiveness and accessibility, "TV" compounds many of the difficulties inherent in all mass media. An example is the problem of stewardship of time. Surveys show that many persons are tempted to spend long periods watching TV, thus stunting more creative activity, including religious, interpersonal, and benevolent engagement.

TV also has intrinsic problems of its own, and the moral impact of these is only gradually being realized. They stem from the power and peculiarities of visual communication. Unlike the more abstract medium of radio, TV encourages audience passivity, and can be particularly harmful in crimping children's use of imagination. TV has enhanced radio's tendency to divide news and entertainment into small segments. The use of short bits of entertaining, visually effective material can easily distort news coverage. The compact excitement and fast pace bombard the senses, perhaps numbing normal human responses, and downgrading the rational-intellectual-meditative aspects of culture. And TV can trivialize important matters and blur the distinction between the real and the unreal when, for example, war coverage or dramatized murders are piped into the living room and can be eliminated with the twist of a button. Most problems are "solved" dramatically within sixty minutes, or even sixty seconds (e.g., by deodorant and aspirin commercials), so that TV may subtly exaggerate demands for swift gratification, and unreasonable impatience with deep-seated social ills, leading to despair when personal or social affairs prove more troublesome.   RICHARD N. OSTLING

TEMPER. The root words for "temper" are variously translated in the OT: "moisten" (Ezek. 46:14); "dewdrops" (S. of Sol. 5:2); "seasoned with salt" (Exod.

30:35); "mixed," "mingled" (Exod. 29;2).

Paul uses the term when he says that "God has tempered the body together" (I Cor. 12:24). Paul is arguing in favor of the unity of the church and of full cooperation on the part of individual members. He uses as an illustration the human body, which consists of various parts with various functions. It is God who has "tempered," "compounded," "blended," "mingled in due proportion," the body. Each member has its place and function and is intended to contribute to the good of the whole frame.

In a psychological sense, temper refers to a person's disposition, especially to affections and passions. In Scripture temper is a neutral word colored by its manifestations. Temper is good when composed and manifested in equanimity, bad when fiery and given to destructive rage. Scripture presents as ideal a "temper of personality" manifest by Christian graces (Gal. 5:22f.). The Christian "temper of personality" is the opposite of the "old life" (cf. Eph. 4:31, 32) and is made possible by the regenerating and sanctifying power of the Holy Spirit. FRANK B. STANGER

TEMPERANCE. See also *Abstinence; Prohibition; Self-control; Temperance Movements.* By definition temperance means moderation. Less aptly it is used at times for total abstinence, especially with reference to intoxicants. Though the word is absent from the OT, the thought is common, notably in Proverbs. Some of the prophets have stern warnings against excess, particularly when it is practiced at the expense of the poor (e.g., Amos 4:1; 6:4-7). The NT employs two words for the idea of temperance: one of them *(egkrateia)* having the meaning of self-control (Gal. 5:23; II Peter 1:6), the other *(sōphrosunē)* emphasizing soundness of mind which provides insight into the right course of action for the well-disciplined life (Titus 2:2).

The Greeks and Romans recognized the worth of temperance by including it among the primary virtues. But what was a virtue with the pagan, suggesting an ideal which if measurably attained was attributed to self-effort and lauded as a distinguished achievement, became in the Christian context a necessity. To make clear that temperance is the result of a divine operation in the believer, Paul includes it as part of the fruit of the Spirit (Gal. 5:23). In line with this the apostle contrasts drunkenness with being filled with the Spirit (Eph. 5:18).

Whereas endurance is the response of the believer to pressures which come upon him from without, such as persecution, temperance is his refusal to yield to the desires of the flesh and the mind which come from within. The most prominent of these relate to eating, drinking and sex. All of them are acquisitive and therefore cater readily to selfishness. All of them relate to normal and proper activities of the creature, so that the element of evil is not in the area of use but of abuse. It has been well said that, "Temperance is the form which true self-love, duty to self, necessarily takes" (R. L. Ottley).

Paul did not hesitate to recommend to Timothy the use of wine for his habitual stomach ailment, but he was careful to specify "a little" (I Tim. 5:23). He did not wish his helper in the gospel to become a drunkard. Proverbs 31:6 recommends strong drink for one who is perishing. In line with this is the use of brandy to restore the victim of exhaustion.

To many people temperance is synonymous with total abstinence, even though this is not the meaning of the word. A case for this position can be made out on Scriptural principles. For example, Paul insisted on his right to eat meat, even that which had been offered to an idol, but nevertheless was prepared to forego the eating of meat entirely if the practice caused a brother to stumble (I Cor. 8:13). So voluntary abstinence under certain conditions is thoroughly Christian. In the area

of sex, the maintenance of the unmarried state is recommended if one has the gift of celibacy and pursues this course for the sake of service to the Kingdom of God (I Cor. 7). But if this choice is made on the assumption that it means embracing a superior type of piety, it is misguided.

Abstinence may also be defended on the ground that the body of the believer is the temple of the Holy Spirit and should therefore be kept as pure as possible. However, difficulties arise when one faces the fact of individual differences. What may be injurious to one person may not be physically harmful to another. Above all for the total abstainer is the threat of pride as he compares himself, albeit secretly, with his brethren who do not share his position. Renunciation of what is lawful is legitimate only if the motive is to please the Lord.

Hugh Black, *Culture and Restraint;* Grundmann in *TWNT,* Grand Rapids, Eerdmans.

EVERETT F. HARRISON

TEMPERANCE MOVEMENTS. Since the first discovery of fermentation by which sugar is converted into alcohol and carbonic acid and the first experience of intoxication there has been a temperance problem. The records of ancient oriental civilizations refer to it. Priests, lawgivers and sages in Palestine, China, Persia, Egypt and Greece tried to alleviate the problem of drunkenness as it affected both the individual and society.

Distilled intoxicating liquors were not produced until the thirteenth century A.D. Since distilled liquors contain much higher alcoholic content, their potency for intoxication is considerably greater. Along with the development of the technique of distilling, an ever-increasing market arose for distilled liquors. By the eighteenth century excessive intemperance had widespread effects such as ill-health, poverty and violence, among others.

Early in the nineteenth century the beginnings of a reaction to excessive drunkenness were noticeable. At first, efforts for abstinence from alcohol were promoted by individuals and some small groups. Father Theobald Mathew in Ireland as well as Great Britain and J. B. Gough in America began preaching that crime and poverty were the results of alcoholism. Father Mathew was the greatest of all temperance missionaries. In the course of his preaching and traveling, he secured no less than approximately a half million pledges of abstinence in Ireland and Great Britain. Pledges were the most popular means employed to combat intemperance, and many were ready to pledge themselves to abstain.

Organized group efforts arose early in the century. In 1808 a temperance group was formed in Saratoga, New York. In 1826 societies in Boston pledged their members to abstinence; by 1830 a thousand similar societies existed in America. Scores of additional societies appeared in Great Britain, Ireland, Norway and Sweden.

In 1846 the state legislature of Maine passed the first prohibition law in America. By 1856 at least thirteen states had passed laws aiming at the abolition of alcoholic liquors. Particularly in America, there was vigorous and dramatic renewal of temperance activity in the latter part of the 1860s and the early part of the 1870s especially because of the impressive involvement of liquor manufacturers in politics along with the truly phenomenal growth of the liquor business. In America, the liquor business had doubled its assets within a decade.

Concerned over these developments, temperance forces in America formed the Prohibition party in 1869 in Chicago. Here for the first time in any American political convention women had equal rights with men. In 1874 the Women's Christian Temperance Union was formed. Outstanding workers in this organization were the W.C.T.U. leader, Frances Willard, and Carry Nation. In 1893 the Anti-saloon League was formed. This organization became influential in American political life.

These temperance movements received strong support from church groups and some important industrialists. Efforts were formed to press for more and more governmental control of the liquor business. Temperance-minded individuals and organizations saw the law as the most effective means to deal with the rising tide of alcoholism. Many liquor-control laws were passed in the various states. Eventually in 1917, the temperance movement succeeded in achieving federal prohibition of alcoholic liquors by the adoption of the eighteenth amendment to the Constitution. This was newsworthy throughout the world, as was its repeal in 1933.

The temperance movements attained their greatest influence in the nineteenth century and the early part of the twentieth. Two important factors gave vital support. One was the popular moral concern regarding the evils brought on by drunkenness and alcoholism. Wherever distilled liquors became available, there was a startling increase in ill-health, crime and violence, poverty and broken homes. Both the individual and society reaped the harvest of these evils. The result was the increased public concern over the obvious cause, namely distilled liquors.

Another important concern was political. The temperance organizations observed the growing involvement of the liquor industry in political affairs to protect its own vested interest. There was strong opposition to the influence of liquor manufacturers in government. This was especially true in America and Great Britain. Out of this negative opposition emerged a positive attitude that the government must regulate and control the liquor business.

During the twentieth century the great influence the temperance movements formerly held has faded. However, the interests they initiated in the influential days of the nineteenth century remain highly important in the twentieth century. One of those interests was the scientific study of alcoholism. Today there is a remarkable store of knowledge regarding alcohol and its effects. A second interest is alcohol education in the public schools, providing opportunity to inform children about alcohol and its effects.

There is favorable evidence that the Christian churches have been influential in the temperance movements. They have often opposed alcoholic liquors and those who engage in their manufacture. On the other hand, there has been a permissiveness on the part of the churches when it comes to confronting the moral issues regarding alcohol. The spirit which rested upon the prophets and sages of ancient times is absent in many churches of modern times: "Wine is a mocker, strong drink is raging: and whosoever is deceived thereby is not wise" (Prov. 20:1).   CHARLES R. WILSON

TEMPLE, WILLIAM. Successively Archbishop of York and Canterbury, William Temple (1881-1944) has been acclaimed as the outstanding Anglican ecclesiastic of the present century. A man of many parts, he was consistently concerned with the ethical implications of the Christian faith, particularly as they affected society.

Trained in philosophy at Oxford under Edward Caird and influenced also by Bernard Bosanquet, he moved from a neo-Hegelian position towards what he described as Christo-centric metaphysics. In his ethical theory he recognized the distinction between right and wrong as ultimate and defined it in terms of love and selfishness. He never lost sight of the fact that the problems of ethics arise within the complex of personal relationships. He contended that all moral obligations are social in character and that duty is a term never applied strictly to the isolated individual. Hence he could assert that "the Atheistic Debauchee upon a Desert Island is not liable

to moral censure" (*Mens Creatrix*, London, Macmillan, 1917, p. 182). Later pronouncements, however, reflect his realization that ethical societism can be misleading if it excludes intrinsic values.

In recognizing the promotion of love as the ultimate goal of conduct Temple anticipated modern emphases. But love was conceived in Biblical terms and presupposed justice while surpassing it. "No formula except the Golden Rule expresses the whole of morality" (*op. cit.,* p. 206). The climax of morality is devotion to the common good, realized perfectly in Christ. Temple's ethical system tended to lack definition at certain points because of his reluctance to recognize the propositional aspect of revelation.

His greatest contribution lay in the attempt to reach a statement of Christian social doctrine. Since Christian principles represented the fulfillment of natural law, he was convinced that authoritative Christian pronouncements on political and economic issues are not only possible but necessary.
          A. SKEVINGTON WOOD

TEMPTATION. The word "temptation" is used in the Bible in a variety of ways. Of primary concern are (1) enticement to sin, (2) man testing God, (3) God testing man, and (4) overcoming temptation.

Enticement to Sin. The impulse for man to do evil is often attributed by the Bible to Satan. Peter warns, "be sober, be watchful. Your adversary the devil prowls around like a roaring lion, seeking someone to devour" (I Peter 5:8). Paul is concerned lest the believers in Corinth might be turned away from the gospel by the "tempter" (I Cor. 3:5). In Ephesians, he encourages his readers "to stand against the wiles of the devil" (Eph. 6:10). The NT teaches us that there is a personal archdemon whose work includes the tempting of the faithful.

Not all responsibility for man's temptation to sin, however, is to be placed outside himself, and least of all can it be attributed to God. Replying to those who wanted to blame God for temptation, James says, "Let no one say when he is tempted, I am tempted by God; for God cannot be tempted by evil and he himself tempts no one" (1:3).

Part of the blame for temptation rests squarely on the individual who is "lured and enticed by his own desire" (James 1:14). In Judaism, the rabbis spoke of the "evil impulse" (*Evil Yezer*) within man. Thomas Aquinas argued that since it is the will of man which says "Yes" or "No" to temptation, the ultimate blame for sin must rest upon each individual.

Man Testing God. Temptation may include the idea of man challenging God or putting him to the test. By demanding water at Rephidim as a sign of God's presence, Israel placed a stain upon their heritage for centuries (Exod. 17:1-7; cp. Ps. 95:8-11; Heb. 3). Peter warns the Jerusalem conference not to "make trial of God" who has shown through the example of Cornelius the freedom which Gentile Christians have from the Law (Acts 15:10). By refusing to jump from the pinnacle of the temple in order to prove God's providence, Jesus furnishes an example of trust to all his followers (Matt. 4:6-7). Man is "tempting God" when he refuses to acknowledge his will and ignores his power to save through Jesus Christ.

God Testing Man. As man tests God, so God tests men. What is immoral for man and moral for God is precisely so because God is God. Thus God tests Abraham's faith by demanding the sacrifice of Isaac (Gen. 22:1-8). Abraham's trusting obedience when "tempted" by God marks him as a shining example of faith (Heb. 11:7). James reminds his readers who may have been experiencing persecution to "Count it all joy, my brethren, when you meet various trials, for you know that the testing of your faith produces steadfastness" (1:2). Al-

though God's testing is never an enticement to evil, faithfulness in spite of adversity is an indication of the integrity of one's faith.

Overcoming Temptation. The Bible teaches us that temptation to sin can be successfully resisted. Since it is the will of man which must finally give consent to sin, then that will strengthened through the power of Jesus Christ can give victory to the tempted.

Overcoming temptation one time gives the individual more ability to overcome the next time. "Resist the devil," says James, "and he will flee from you" (4:7). On the other hand, each time one yields to temptation, its power grows stronger. Rabbi Akiba reportedly said, "At the beginning it (sin) is like a thread of a spider's web, but in the end it becomes like a ship's cable."

The Rabbis were famous for their "hedge" around the law. For example, since the law says, "You shall not commit adultery," it was best to provide a series of obstacles between the individual and the actual breaking of the commandment. Hence they said, "One who walks behind a woman crossing a stream has no share in the World to Come." Although it fell into disrepute because of endless legalism, the idea of "hedging" is not without merit. The best way to resist sin, however, is through "the expulsive power of a new affection."

PAUL BENJAMIN

TEMPTATIONS OF JESUS. The explicit accounts of Jesus' temptations are recorded prior to the beginning of his ministry, suggesting that they served a preparatory function (Matt. 4:1-10; Mark 1:12; Luke 4:1-13). The emphasis that the Spirit sent Jesus into the wilderness of temptation implies that the Father was testing him to develop his loyalty and faith. This interpretation is supported by the fact that *peirazo* is sometimes used with this meaning (Gen. 22:1; Deut. 8:2; John 6:6).

However, it was undoubtedly Satan's purpose to seduce Christ to do evil. The three temptations have a striking similarity to the account of Gen. 3, for they too appeal for the use of one's resources in violation of divine authority. The initial temptation enticed Jesus to employ his powers for selfish purposes by changing stones into bread to alleviate his hunger. This same egocentric appeal was related to his Messianic program by the temptation to use the spectacular means of jumping from the pinnacle of the temple and to submit to Satan's compromising plans to gain the world's kingdoms. By complying with these temptations Jesus could have avoided the tragic suffering of the cross and fulfilled the false Messianic expectations of his day.

These temptations assumed Jesus' suprahuman, Messianic power. The conditional element was introduced by Satan to challenge Jesus to demonstrate his power, and messiahship, thus making the temptations all the more forceful.

It is likely that Jesus' temptations were continual throughout his life and were fundamentally similar. The record indicates that men, including his disciples, sometimes acted as agents of the demonic in these temptations (Luke 4:13; 22:28; Mark 1:24; Matt. 16:23; John 6:15; 7:3-5). The temptations came to a climax in Gethsemane and on the cross, where Jesus struggled between doing his will and that of the Father and questioned the fidelity of the Father.

Jesus' temptations indicated his humanity as well as his divinity and were essential to a genuine incarnation. Like other men, Jesus constantly and freely faced real and opposing choices between God and anti-God. Like men he experienced the full, agonizing force of temptation and overcame by dependence on the strength of the Father mediated through God's word and through prayer. This fellow feeling with man in temptation makes possible Christ's high-priestly sympathy for the human predicament (Heb. 2:18).

Christ's unfailing victory in temptation ultimately differentiates him from men and enables him to become their Saviour and Lord. He was tempted in all points as men are yet he was without sin (Heb. 4:15) Because he overcame the world, his disciples may also overcome the world, for he conquered the demonic powers which are the source of all temptation and evil (John 14:33; Col. 2:15; Heb. 4:16).

📖 E. Best, *The Temptation and the Passion*, New York, Cambridge University, 1965; W. J. Foxwell, *The Temptation of Jesus*, New York, Macmillan, 1965; H. Seesemann, "Temptation," Kittel's *Theological Dictionary of the New Testament*, Vol. VI, Grand Rapids, Eerdmans, 1968; H. Thielicke, *Between God and Satan*, Grand Rapids, Eerdmans, 1958.   ROBERT A. TRAINA

TEN COMMANDMENTS. See *Decalogue.*

TERRORISM. See also *Revolution; Violence.* Many Biblical terms reflect the idea of terror, or something that affrights men by its power (cf. Deut. 26:8), awesomeness (cf. Dan. 2:31) or cruelty. Fear (q.v.) is a basic response of man as sinner to God's moral demand. Almighty God is depicted as terrible in view of his infinite power, strict justice and awesome holiness.

Where "fear of the Lord"—a dominant OT thought—is weakened, men employ terror-techniques more readily to achieve their goals. Conscious of the "terror of the Lord" (II Cor. 5:11), the Christian seeks to reach others by reason and persuasion. But the resort to violence (q.v.) is a hallmark of a revolutionary spirit.

Modern escalation of terrorism reflects an easy reliance on violence as a way to promote social and political change. For example, to challenge the role of Israel in the Near East, terrorists have resorted to bomb-threats, actual bombings, hijacking (q.v.) of international flights, the destruction of planes, ransoming of passengers, crews and planes. World opinion was outraged by the Palestinian terrorist killing of eleven Israeli Olympic athletes in Munich in 1972, and of two American diplomats in Sudan in 1973 despite official immunity. The multiplication of organizations, some ideological, that espouse hatred and contempt, promote the distruption of law and order, and appeal to force and violence by guerilla-like tactics, is a sign of the times. In March, 1971, J. Edgar Hoover, late director of the Federal Bureau of Investigation, reported a stepup of violent and terrorist tactics by the New Left and black extremists. He identified the Weatherman organization as a terrorist group that promotes revolution, and the White Panther Party and Youth International Party (Yippies) as supporters of Weatherman-type terrorism. Law enforcement agencies are the principal target of some terrorists. A number of "urban guerillas," for example, make police officers their special objective. In a manual for revolution, Charles Marighella, a former official of the Brazilian Communist Party, said that "every urban guerilla can only maintain his existence if he is disposed to kill the police." CARL F. H. HENRY

THANKFULNESS. See *Gratitude*.

THEATER. See also *Mass Media; Movies*. Here we refer to the legitimate stage, not movies. One question concerns the legitimacy of the dramatic. It appears that the creation mandate (Gen. 1:26-28) has significance only if we understand the world to have unrealized potential. Presumably Adam had to study out the universe and both tend and develop it.

The dramatic is a way of tapping the potential of creation, of created men. We have the capacity to dramatize human relations and aspirations. Children naturally dramatize their parent's normal activities, a simple form being a child with a doll. Children also dramatize by fantasy, in which their minds explore "impossible" worlds. This would appear to be a creative aspect of the image of God.

In the OT the temple rituals were dramatic productions, with heavily symbolic elements carrying theological and psychological content, but encompassed by artistry. Psalm 24 would appear to be an antiphonal dramatic recitation between the priest behind the closed temple gates and the people outside with the ark. Christ's parables are likewise terse dramatic productions. The prophets also taught in dramatic form. Surely Isaiah would not have named a son Mahershalalhashbaz for any other reason (8:1). The unbelievable visions of Zechariah, Ezekiel, and Daniel are likewise dramatic means of displaying truth.

Sunday itself is a dramatic display of conviction that God created the earth (Exod. 20:8), redeemed Israel from Egypt (Deut. 5:15) and raised Christ from the dead. Easter and Christmas celebrations are of the same sort.

Drama was lost in the West after the collapse of Rome, and rediscovered by the church in the eleventh century. Modern drama was born in church. The drama reenacted the Easter story in the church or churchyard. Various people read the parts, and gradually appropriate settings and clothing were added. Then the trade guilds developed and the actors became professional, using wagons and carrying the necessary materials with them. So the drama moved out of church and in time became secularized.

The tendency is for the legitimate theater to become illegitimate, as with *Hair*, when sensuality or violence are the subject, and the result is the stimulation of inordinate desire, reducing the drama to pander.

Subduing the earth means doing one's best in his calling, even if it means playing a part in a dramatic presentation. The disaster is that Biblical Christians have left the theater pretty much to the secularists and only semi-Biblical religious groups. Without adopting the ways of the world, or opting out, we must say our word, and act and write to the glory of Christ. Churches should be preparing their members for aggressive involvement, not fearful isolation.

PAUL FROMER

THEFT. See also *Decalogue; Property.* The exact nature of personal property rights as Christians understand these is complex. Certain restrictions guarantee this right of property. These include the prohibition of damage, theft, and robbery (Exod. 21:33-34; 22:5-6; 22:4, 7. 9; 20:15; Gen. 31:31; II Sam. 23:21).

A thief is one who acquires the property of another without his consent and knowledge. The ethical position of the Judaeo-Christian heritage is built upon Exod. 20:15. While all stealing is forbidden, some specific cases are difficult to isolate and discuss. Overt acts of hold-up or mugging represent obvious examples of theft. More sophisticated instances such as finding unfair loopholes in tax laws or bribing an official present specific ethical problems. Popular opinion is frequently lenient toward theft when it involves methods which are covert and not in flagrant opposition to the law. Dubious banking or stock-marketing practices constitute theft as well as the petty pilfering by ghetto juveniles. It is possible to denounce theft by force when perpetrated by the poor, and to condone underhanded fraud used by the rich. Roman law, for example, might decree crucifixion for a poor thief while assigning to a wealthy politician a province to be looted for his own personal gain. But the Biblical record interprets "thou shalt not steal" in light of divine justice, not of worldly expediency. While theft is sin anywhere and when committed by anyone, the OT prophets condemn the dishonest rich far more vigorously than the desperate poor.

WATSON E. MILLS

THEISM. The term connotes an approach to the universe which sees behind all things a personal deity, and designates a corrective to alternate God-forms. As Immanuel Kant wrote, "the theist believes in a living God." Theism does not specify any concrete form of empirical religion, but affirms the most vital element, a personal God. The chief theistic religions, in order of historical appearance, are: Judaism, Christianity, and Islam.

Theism stands in antithesis to atheism (q.v.), which has historically appeared chiefly as a defensive countermovement to theistic forms. In its typical form, atheism is a radical denial of the existence of any being properly considered as "deity"; it thus differs from agnosticism which claims only that no evidence has been adduced to support a theistic belief. While related etymologically to deism, theism diverges radically from it in asserting that God does not merely support or maintain the cosmos, but is an active participant in all of its events. Against henotheism, which allows or owns the existence of many deities, but specializes in worshiping and honoring but one, theism insists that the proper definition of "God" implies absoluteness, which rules out a plurality of beings properly denoted as deities.

Theism stands as a challenge of polytheism on the same ground of basic definition and of logical consistency. It opposes polytheism, further, in insisting that with every multiplication of supposed deities, distinctions between "God and world" are blurred, and divine activities within and upon the empirical world are lessened, and even imperiled. Theistic thinkers recognize, of course, tendencies toward theism in some non-Christian systems, especially in Advaita Hinduism and in parts of the Bhagavad Gita, and likewise in some popularized forms of Buddhism.

Theism rejects all ultimate dualism, and sees all things as finally traceable to a single Being. It holds that the empirical universe is distinct from God, having its source, not in some preexisting conditioning factor or element (as in Plato or Jakob Boehme), but in God's free creative act. It holds as an article of faith that, at some point in the Divine career, God projected into being that which previously was not, conferring upon it both existence and structure.

Contemporary theism holds no particular theory of the inner nature of world-reality, but is not essentially averse to the position that matter is a configuration of energy. Theists would, in general, be able to live comfortably with the view that in the primal origination of things, God released his creative abilities in terms of the "imprisonment" of energy in such a way that it became the material basis for the physical universe.

Against pantheism (q.v.), theism insists that the cosmos is essentially distinct from God, being in no sense an emanation or mere externalization of his Being or inner experience. Its critique of pantheism centers in the proposition that the latter seeks a substitute, in the cosmos and its regularities, for the deity lost in more recent scientific theory. In this quest, it has surrendered deity by identification of it with the world itself.

Christian theism rests upon a positive and actual self-revelation on the part of God, and implies a real, as well as a possible, sovereign invasion of the universe. It is not the product of natural revelation, but the result of God's self-disclosure. Nor does it depend in any major sense upon so-called "proofs" for God. Recognizing that the traditional arguments are just that (i.e., arguments), theists allow that these rely upon commitments to reality which are less persuasive today than earlier.

Theism thus finds its center in belief in a personal, self-conscious and self-sufficient being, "above" the world and "outside" the world. As utterly free, God combines sovereign ability and holy love. Having called the empirical universe into being, he sustains and rules that universe. Having created man in his own image, he has ordained basic moral requirements, which remain valid for man in spite of his Fall. Toward man in his fallen condition, God extends a hand in saving love through the sending of his Son as Redeemer.

In Christian theism, ethics derives from God's revealed standards and requirements. Thus ethics springs from the basic premises of theism, and not the contrary, as in the Kantian system. Christian theism is totally inhospitable to ethical relativism. It resists the view that moral values are mere human products, whether they be' of individual preference, or of social derivation. It must, moreover, go beyond good will (or proper intent) as the unqualified good. The criterion for moral goodness is located in the divine will, and is conditioned by his absolute perfection and complete holiness.

HAROLD B. KUHN

THEOCRACY. See also *Church and State*. This term is used of those governments or states which are, or are thought to be, under the immediate direction of God. The divine will is mediated through a leader or some authoritative body such as a priesthood.

While "theocracy" is not a Biblical term, it was coined by Josephus (*Contra Apion.* II. 16, 165) to describe God's rule over Israel. The OT indicates that this control was accomplished through the Patriarchs, then through Moses and the Pentateuchal legislation, the priesthood and the judges (cf. Exod. 19:6; Deut. 17:14ff.; Judg. 8:23; I Sam. 8:7; 12:12, etc.). Even the Hebrew monarchy was ideally theocratic, though individual rulers often ignored the concept. The prophets also cherished theocratic ideals, and prior to 520 B.C. looked for a time when the nation would return from exile to establish a theocratic community in Palestine (cf. Ezek. 37:14, 22ff., etc.), an event occurring under Ezra and Nehemiah.

By NT times, however, the religious leadership of the priests had been contaminated by political activities, one result of which was the separation of the Qumran group, which was also theocratic in nature. In the OT the theocratic concept was subsumed under the larger realization of divine rule over all creation. The NT theocratic ideal found its greatest expression in terms of the church and the kingdom of heaven. Because of the other-worldly values emphasized by the early Christians, a significant shift of emphasis concerning the theocracy resulted. In the pre-Christian period, the principal problem for the Jews was that of maintaining priority for a personal relationship with God in the midst of a concrete social order bearing a Hellenistic, and therefore a pagan stamp. For the members of the early church, who claimed the regeneration of the new birth, the predominant concern was to ensure a proper balance between membership in the Kingdom of God and the responsibilities incurred by being accredited citizens of a temporal social order. Christ gave general guidance for resolving the tension (cf. Luke 20:25), and this was made more explicit by Paul (cf. Rom. 13:1ff.; Titus 3:1, etc.) and Peter (cf. I Peter 2:13ff.) in their statements concerning Christian life in the world.

In subsequent periods the theocratic ideal was given special emphasis in the social and theological configurations of Islam, while in a different form it appeared with equal force in the medieval papacy, where the pope claimed the title of *Vicarivus filii dei,* and purported in *ex cathedra* pronouncements to be mediating the divine will. The developed doctrine of the divine right of kings (q.v.) had obvious affiliations with ancient Near Eastern theocratic ideals as reflected in sources depicting kings being nursed in infancy at the breasts of goddesses, thereby becoming effectual surrogates of deity.

During the period of the European Reformation, Calvin's political teachings in Geneva were based firmly upon theocratic ideals. Since God was sovereign of the world, kings and secular rulers were to be obeyed since they were his ministers. The secular power was responsible for protecting the church, and politics was recognized as a legitimate sphere for Christian activity. Civil law was to be based on the moral law, which in turn reflected the *naturalis legis testimonium* imprinted by God in the human heart. If princes endeavored to usurp divine authority, however, it was proper to resist them since their actions threatened the entire theocratic structure.

The Puritans also respected theocratic ideals, as seen, for example, in the Puritan government of Massachusetts. Modern sects with theocratic leanings include Mormons and Jehovah's Witnesses.   R. K. HARRISON

THEOLOGICAL VIRTUES. See *Virtues.*

THOMAS AQUINAS AND THOMIST ETHICS. See *Aquinas and Roman Catholic Ethics.*

TILLICH, PAUL. Paul Tillich (1886-1965), born and educated in Germany, spent most of his academic career at Union Theological Seminary in New York. After retirement he lectured at Harvard University and at the University of Chicago.

Tillich may be said to take his place along with Barth and Schleiermacher as a modern counterpart of ancient theologians. Tillich did not erect a rationally deductive system, but attempted in dialectical fashion to speak comprehensively to every theological issue. Two things characterize his systematic theology: his method of correlation and his symbolic use of theological language.

Tillich's method was an attempt to bring together human questions and divine answers. He says we must start with the human situation because this is where we stand and to begin with this is all we know; but nevertheless we seek for ultimate reality and our search leads us to correlate the answers given by divine disclosure to our human needs. Tillich faults Christian orthodoxy for proclaiming the message of Christian faith without correlating it to scientific, aesthetic, economic, political, and ethical forms of our day. He also charges neo-Reformation theology with undue emphasis on eternal truth, and not enough attention to the relativities of human existence. Kerygmatic theology must, therefore, be balanced with apologetic theology which starts with analysis of the human situation and then applies the gospel to it.

After he has made analysis of existential questions Tillich tries to demonstrate that the symbols used in the Christian message are answers to these questions. Symbols are words that point to basic reality. The words are always broken symbols because they merely point and they must never be taken literally. Christian symbols are not identical with the reality they designate, but they provide a correlation of disclosure. Thus, for example, the historical Jesus is proclaimed as Christ in the kerygma. This means that Jesus is the symbol for the reality of Christ. Strictly speaking we must say that Jesus is proclaimed *as* Christ, but we should not say that Jesus *is* Christ. This use of language as broken symbols leads Tillich to a Christology not too different from that of Bultmann. Words like heaven and hell must not be taken literally, but must be abstracted to mean various qualities of reality.

In addition to his correlation method and his symbolic use of language Tillich is marked by his translation of Biblical categories into philosophical concepts. What the Bible calls life and death Tillich treats in terms of the Platonic dialectic of Being and Nothing. What the Bible calls the fall into sinful separation Tillich describes as essential anxiety and individuation. Biblical *koinonia* becomes participation. Faith becomes the courage to be. Redemption becomes the New Being.

Tillich's theology may be presented in three parts: (a) Man, Existence, and God; (b) Estrangement, Salvation, and Christ; (c) Society, Ambiguity, and the Spirit. The first part deals with the question of being and non-being, or the question of life and death; and the answer is God as the Ground of Being. The second part deals with the question of estrangement, or in Biblical language, sin; and the answer is the New Being in Christ. The third part deals with the question of the ambiguity and meaninglessness of our social striving, or in Biblical terms, the judgment of God in history; and the answer is the life of the Spirit.

Biblical Religion and the Search for Ultimate Reality, Chicago, University of Chicago, 1955; Christianity and the Encounter of the World Religions, New York, Columbia University, 1963; The Courage to Be, New Haven, Yale University, 1952; The Protestant Era, Chicago, University of Chicago, 1948; The Shaking of the Foundations, New York, Scribner, 1948; Systematic Theology, 3 vols. Chicago, University of Chicago, 1951-57; Theology of Culture, New York, Oxford University Press, 1959.   ROBERT P. ROTH

TOLERANCE. See *Religious Freedom; Persecution.*

TORAH. See also *Jewish Ethics.* The noun is derived from the Hebrew verb *yarah* (to throw, to shoot). In Biblical usage it covers a variety of meaning: to inform, instruct, guide, lead, etc. Torah exists to provide direction, to aim at the purpose of doing God's will. It is only when *torah* is understood as *nomos* (=LXX), lex, law, that it acquires a purely legalistic connotation.

1. Torah in Jewish tradition is never just law in the legal sense. It is wisdom, grace, an expression of devotion to God, a style of life. Technically, the term covers two aspects: (a) the written text of the Pentateuch

(most scrupulously copied and greatly honored because of the sanctity of the text), and (b) the unwritten tradition ("*torah* by word of mouth"), handed down from generation to generation.

Though the written text remains unaltered, the verbal tradition is flexible to accommodate the changing exigencies of life. It aims at re-interpreting the text in such a manner that life is not hindered. A crisis arises when change is more rapid than rabbinic adjustment of the law, as is the case in Israel at present.

The rabbis do not regard the *torah* as a universal obligation but only as the distinctive mark of the Jew. The Gentile is under no obligation to the Torah, only to the basic rules of morality. Traditionally, the Seven Commandments to the Sons of Noah (cf. Gen. R., 34:8) is all that is required of him, namely refraining from idolatry, incest, shedding of blood, profanation of God's name, injustice, robbery, and eating the flesh of a live animal (cf. Acts 15:19f.). Whosoever of the nations observes these rules will have a share in the world to come (Mamonides, *H Mel.* 8:10).

For the Jew the Torah is a mark of God's special favor: "If somebody says to you: there is wisdom among the nations believe him ... but if he says there is *torah* among the nations believe him not," for even the true prophets of the nations are false (*Midrash R.,* Lam. 2:9). For the Rabbis' study of the *Torah* is a primary duty. They refer to Josh. 1:8: "this book of the *torah* shall not depart out of your mouth, but you shall meditate on it day and night." A later addendum to *Pirke 'Abot* contains the passage: "This is the path of *torah:* a morsel with salt shalt thou eat; water by measure thou shalt drink; thou shalt sleep upon the ground and live a life of painfulness while thou toilest in the *torah* (ib. 6:4; cf. also Ps. 119).

2. In the NT as also in the LXX *torah* is translated with *nomos,* but not necessarily in the legalistic sense. Jesus came not to destroy the law but to "fulfil" it. Here *plerosai* means not only to complete but to establish (cf. Jocz, "Jesus and the Law," *Judaica,* Heft 2, 1970, pp. 120ff.). The same applies to the Pauline text: Christ is the "end" *(telos)* of the law that everyone who has faith may be justified (Rom. 10:4). In the context *telos* means to accomplish what the *torah* left incomplete, namely man's justification. Paul knows the value of the law: it convicts of sin (Rom. 7:7-11); it serves as tutor *(paidagogos)* in preparing the way for Christ (Gal. 3:24). The ultimate intention of the Law is the motive of love (Gal. 5:14). This can only be achieved as the fruit of the Holy Spirit (Gal. 5:22) and not by the letter of the Law (II Cor. 3.6). This "radical inwardness" (cf. C. F. H. Henry, *Christian Personal Ethics,* Grand Rapids, Eerdmans, 1957, p. 353) is a mark of messianic fulfilment: "I will put my law within them, and I will write it upon their hearts" (Jer. 31:33).

3. Both Luther and Calvin opposed antinomianism. Luther rejected the views of Jacob Schrenk and John Agricola that there is no place for the law in the church (cf. *Table Talk,* Oct. 10, 1538). Calvin refers to the antinomianists as "unskilful persons," (*Institutes,* II, VII, 13). The Reformers acknowledge that the law performed a threefold function *(primus, secundus et tertius usus legis):* (1) like a mirror it reveals man's true condition; (2) it curbs and bridles sinners; (3) it encourages obedience to God's will (*Institutes,* ibid. 6ff.). In Calvin's words: "the law acts like a whip to the flesh urging it on as men do a lazy sluggish ass." He rejects the view that Paul regarded the law as abrogated (ibid. 15). Luther took a similar view (cf. H. H. Kramm, *The Theology of Martin Luther,* 1947, pp. 60ff.). The Christian is always under the law and under grace, for he is "at the same time sinner and justified, but always a penitent" (*Vorlesungen über den Römerbrief.* 1515/16, II, 108).

"Situation ethics" (q.v.) which takes the view that the Christian is under no law, except the law of love (cf. Joseph Fletcher, *Situation Ethics,* Philadelphia, Westminster, 1966, pp. 46, 69, 146), misinterprets the human condition. Because of man's fallen nature law and grace belong together: "The forgiven Christian is not a lawless Christian" (C. F. H. Henry, *op. cit.* 362). He is a man who knows more about the law because he knows more about grace.   JAKOB JOCZ

TOTAL DEPRAVITY. See *Depravity.*

TOTALITARIANISM. Totalitarianism is a highly centralized form of government, controlled by a despot or clique, admitting of no political opposition and seeks to regulate all aspects of life. The term is of twentieth century coinage, even though the idea and various forms of totalitarianism have appeared throughout history. What is new in our century is the degree to which propaganda and regimentation pervade every aspect of the government's activity. Also new is the philosophical rationale presented for the elevation of authority, and the means to check any deviation from the required norm.

One clear form of authoritarianism is the totalitarian state. In it we find a metaphysical enhancement of the state, demanding unconditional obedience and usurping the place of God. Since the Scriptures outline the role of the state as being God's servant for man's good, to preserve order and punish evildoers, a totalitarian state constitutes a perversion in which the state no longer renders divine service (Rom. 13). In short, totalitarianism is the deification of the state and the dehumanization of man.

What is the Christian to do? Is he to submit to such a demonic unjust state, or is he called upon to resist? Where does he find guidance and direction? The Scripture does not address itself specifically to this prob-lem. The early church was convinced of the temporal character of this world. Because of "this time bomb on board the world, ticking away," it did not seem necessary to bother about forms of government. Mark 12:16, which at first sight seems to order the Christian's relationship to the state by telling him to render unto Caesar the things that are Caesar's and to God the things that belong to God, can be interpreted in this same light. It may mean: Why do you get sidetracked by trivia connected with duties to the state? The state is taken for granted by Jesus, therefore he does not question certain obligations, but neither does he find it necessary to change things. In the coming kingdom the state will no longer exist. The Apostle Paul follows the same path. While he acknowledges the positive value of the state in maintaining order he also shows the incompatibility of the present system with the lordship of Christ (Phil. 3:20; I Cor. 6:1).

The theologians do not give much more help. Some, like Karl Barth (q.v.), have openly attacked social injustice in Nazism, but have never attacked other forms of totalitarianism. While some have voiced strong protest and resisted the claims of a godless state, others have regarded such systems as an historical necessity (Hromadka). German theologians Helmut Thielicke and Walter Künneth have come up with some guidelines. Based upon actual experience with totalitarianism in the form of Nazism, their positions see resistance as a necessity. The only question concerns how to resist most effectively. They have stated that generally only certain persons are called to acts of resistance because such acts affect the whole order of government and the entire people's existence. First, forethought and planning are necessary to anticipate some of the consequences, since even a totalitarian system may be preferable to total anarchy. Furthermore, only in extreme cases may force be justified, and only after all other means have been exhausted and proven of no avail. Third, absolute claims must be opposed with a strong confession, backed by willingness to lay down one's life as the early martyrs did. Fourth, Thielicke offers an alternative to forceful, direct resistance through *Unterwandrung*. By this he means a counteracting of injustice from within. This amounts to working for change from within the system. He illustrates this by referring to the Paul-Onesimus incident. Paul did not attack slavery—this might have proved utterly futile. It most certainly would have led away from Christ to a concentration upon the order of society. But by sending Onesimus back to Philemon as a Christian brother, Paul in effect breaks the old order of a slave-master relationship from within. This is the meaning of *Unterwandrung*. Thielicke advocates such inroads as an alternative to political action.

There is little question about the fact that totalitarianism leads to complete bondage regardless of the form it takes. Even Christianity is a totalitarian system, but the bondage it produces leads to genuine freedom. A need for authority lies imbedded in human nature. Not only children, but people in general cannot live without some authority. While Christians may submit gladly to divine guidance, others submit to different authorities or absolutes. At the same time, there is a strong desire for independence from authority, which expresses itself in the overthrow of existing authority. Men often become content with the overthrow of the old without offering constructive alternatives. Various new forms of totalitarianism emerge, all of which again lead to bondage. The totalitarianism of God alone brings freedom.

Helmut Thielicke, *Die Evangelische Kirche und die Politik*, Stuttgart, Evang. Verlagswerk, 1953; Walter Künneth, *Politik zwischen Daemon und Gott, Eine Christliche Ethik des Politischen*, Berlin, Lutherisches Verlagshaus, 1954.

HERBERT R. DYMALE

TRADITION. The term tradition comes from the Greek *paradosis* and means "a giving over" either by mouth or in writing. The concept implies (1) a deposit which is handed on and (2) depositaries or persons in possession of the deposit and commissioned to preserve and transmit it to successors. Tradition is the teaching that is handed down from one to another.

Paul seems to use tradition in two senses: (1) tradition as the primitive Christian teaching (I Cor. 15:1-4), including his "instruction" to the churches at Corinth (I Cor. 11:2) and Thessalonica (II Thess. 2:15; 3:16), and (2) the "tradition of men" in contrast to divinely revealed tradition (Col. 2:8).

Roman Catholic thought expands "tradition" in the sense of revealed truths beyond the canonical Scriptures. The Reformation was in essence a revolt not against the authority of the "deposit" or its Founder but against the existing depositary class in Western Europe, occasioned by the corruption and exactions of the pope and hierarchy. The Reformers restored the Bible as the authoritative Christian tradition.

In contemporary Christendom a clear line of distinction marks evangelicals from non-evangelicals at the point of the authority of "revealed tradition." Evangelicals are committed to "the faith once delivered to the saints" as authoritatively revealed in Holy Scripture.   FRANK B. STANGER

TRANQUILITY. Tranquility is one of the fruits of contentment (q.v.). If a person is satisfied, he is relieved of restlessness and is at peace with himself and the world about him. The word has very limited use in the Bible (in Dan. 4:27 it refers to royal prosperity and freedom from disturbance throughout the realm). It is closely related to quietness, which has additional applications. "Better is a dry morsel with quiet than a house full of feasting with strife"

(Prov. 17:1 RSV). Domestic and social relationships can be spoiled by quarreling. To live in peace with little is better than to live in abundance with bitterness and tumult. On a wider front, God through the prophet pictures the messianic age as a time of tranquility for his people: "And the effect of righteousness will be peace, and the result of righteousness, quietness and trust for ever" (Isa. 32:17 RSV). Human guarantees of peace are frail and easily broken. Only divine rule in the earth can furnish a sound security. Of special interest is the counsel of the apostle Paul to the young church at Thessalonica in which he twice exhorts to quietness (I Thess. 4:11; II Thess. 3:12). The thrill of belonging to a new movement plus the possibility that the Lord might be returning at any time proved so exciting that some of the saints were not applying themselves to their daily work. This restlessness needed to be rebuked. The successful Christian is one who has learned to excel in the ordinary. Such a life-style can be a stabilizing influence on a society in ferment.   EVERETT F. HARRISON

TRANSFERENCE. Transference is a psychoanalytic term referring to an emotional attitude that tends to develop on the part of the patient toward the therapist in the course of psychotherapy. In this relationship, the patient forms a more or less intense attachment to the analyst, transferring the attitudes which he held as a child toward some person close to him, usually a parent. His behavior may express either excessive love or hate, being designated as positive or negative. Such a relationship increases the suggestibility of the patient and heightens his desire to please the therapist. Transference may also develop outside the therapeutic relationship, wherever an authoritative relationship exists.

Since an attitude carried forward from childhood is likely to be inappropriate in the adult situation, transference in analysis is looked upon as neurotic, requiring resolution by working through and interpretation. The termination of an analysis is considered to depend upon the successful dissolution of the strong but illogical transference bonds that may exist between patient and analyst. Psychoanalysis has long been adversely criticized on the ground that it proceeds by creating a neurosis that must subsequently be resolved, giving rise to the quip that analysis creates in the patient a disease of which it claims to be the cure.

The authority vested in the therapist by the patient through the transference has been called the crux of psychotherapy, since moral direction, expressed or covert, is a consequence. By the communication that occurs in this authoritative relationship, the therapist reveals his own world-view, with its moral implications. In selection, omission, gesture or inflection, even as he may seek to practice ethical neutrality, the psychotherapist conveys cues that approve, criticize or reject the offerings of his patient. The patient thus tends to become what the therapist wants him to be. Since the ethical neutrality professed by Freud and many of his followers does not exist in fact, it is important to take into account the attitude of the therapist toward Christian faith in making a choice.

Sigmund Freud, *An Outline of Psychoanalysis*, New York, Norton, 1949, p. 66-70; Sebastian de Grazia, *Errors of Psychotherapy*, New York, Doubleday, 1952, Chaps. 3-5.

ORVILLE S. WALTERS

TRANSPLANTING OF ORGANS. See *Organ Transplantion*.

TREATIES. A treaty is an instrument used to bind two or more states under contract, covenant, compact, or agreement. It is especially a contract relating to peace, truce, alliance, commerce, or other international concerns, or the document embodying such a contract. As a general rule, only states and international organizations have the capacity to enter into agreements, but political subdivisions and the Holy See have exceptionally become parties to some treaties. International law does not require any particular form, although written agreements are normal; oral agreement however is not unknown. But many treaties have not been binding until ratified by the states concerned.

Treaties are as old as states themselves. The negotiation of treaties of peace, alliance, commerce and other motives was a regular feature of international relations in the ancient Near East. The earliest written treaty known is for the settlement of a boundary dispute between the kings of Umma and Lagash, concluded about 3000 B.C., in Mesopotamia. From an analysis of some thirty international treaties, dating from the second to first millennia B.C., K.A. Kitchen has shown that the covenant of Sinai closely reflects the structure of treaties extant in the thirteenth century B.C. This is strong evidence for rejecting a later date for the long cherished theories of Hebrew religion in the Pentateuch and of their literary criticism. Thus indirectly, it is this knowledge of ancient treaties, their literary form and structure, that has profound implications for the dating of the Mosaic covenant, which stands at the heart of ancient Israelite religion.

The Israelites were forbidden from making treaties with the Canaanites because of their covenant with Jehovah and avoidance of moral contamination (Exod. 23:32; 34:12; 7:2, Judg. 2:2). But, surrounded as they were by other nations, treaty relations were from time to time inevitable. Such were the commercial treaty David and Solomon made with Hiram, king of Tyre (I Kings 5:15ff.); the military alliance Asa made with Ben-hadad, king of Syria (II Chron. 16:1ff.); and the political pact the kings of Israel and Judah made with the kings of Syria and neighboring states to preserve their identity against the pressures of Assyria, Babylon, or Egypt. The prophets denounced these alliances in vain (Isa. 31:1; Jer. 27:3ff.).

Complexities in the growth of national sovereignty (q.v.) have multiplied the number of treaties during the past three centuries. By the mid-1960s, the sixty-odd sovereignties of the world had created some 10,000 treaties, covering every international interest. The USA alone had more than 850 treaties with other powers, over 500 of which had been created since 1900. It is reasonable to expect the United Nations (q.v.) membership to reach some 125-130 members in this decade, and a further proliferation of treaties. These developments are leading to a political reality of a world of great diversity with many centers of power, and no longer divided between two or three overwhelming power blocs.

Many treaties are multilateral rather than bilateral. The Treaty of Westphalia in 1648 saw the emergence of a genuine society of European states and the development of public law throughout the continent. Subsequently great international congresses represented major shifts of power in complex multilateral agreements, such as the treaties of Utrecht in 1713-14, of Vienna in 1815, and of Versailles in 1919. In contrast, a continent like Africa was carved up by arbitrary colonial agreements that often lacked ethinic or geographical realism. The Antarctic Treaty of 1959, signed by twelve nations dedicated this continent for peaceful purposes, so that it is under the supervision of S.C.A.R. (Special Committee for Antarctic Research) under the International Council of Scientific Unions, and all national claims have been postponed for thirty years. A further treaty on the Peaceful Uses of Outer Space, signed in 1967, now provides that celestial bodies should be used only for peaceful purposes. Thus treaties now formulated cope with new challenges of sovereignty, scientific and economic co-operation, and environmental issues never faced before.

📖 D. R. Hillers, *Treaty-curses and the Old Testament Prophets*, Rome, Pontifical Biblical Institute, 1964; K. A. Kitchen, *Ancient Orient and Old Testament*, London, Tyndale, 1966; Sir Arnold Duncan McNair, *The Law of Treaties*, New York, Columbia University, rev. ed. 1961; A. Oakes & R. B. Mowat, eds., *The Great European Treaties of the 19th Century*, Oxford, Oxford University, 1918; Quincy Wright, "The Legal Nature of Treaties," and "Conflicts between International Law and Treaties" in *American Journal of International Law*, vol. X, 1916, 706-36, and vol. XI, 1917, 566-79.   J. M. HOUSTON

TROELTSCH, ERNST. Ernst Troeltsch (1865-1923) was born near Augsburg in Bavaria, and educated at Erlangen, Berlin, and Göttingen. He taught at Göttingen (1891), Bonn (1892-94), Heidelberg (1894-1914) and Berlin (1915-23), and also served in government as a member of the Bavarian upper house. Numerous of his writings have been collected in the four volume *Gesammelte Schriften* (1912-25). His most important contribution is *The Social Teachings of the Christian Churches*, published in 1912 and translated into English in 1931 (New York, Harper & Row).

Troeltsch accepted and was desirous of preserving the Kantian primacy and the underivative nature of human moral imperatives. However, he involved himself in intractable problems when he sought to combine the aforementioned view of morality with historical relativity. He held that the two basic principles of historical method were "analogy" and "correlation." By analogy he meant that historical events must be analogous to events occurring in our present experience; by correlation he intended that all events belong within an immanent process. Therefore, while the moral awareness was basic to the human constitution, it was within the course of historical development that morality and religion became interdependent and related.

Troeltsch was vulnerable, therefore, to what has been called the "crisis of historicism." While he insists on the a priori nature of ethics and the necessity of some values or norms that transcend historical change and accident, he cannot avoid the conclusion that any phenomenon may be accounted for adequately merely by describing its origin and development. Troeltsch was aware of the difficulty, and able to reconcile the conflicting claims.

Troeltsch's importance rests in the fact that his *The Social Teachings of the Christian Churches* was a first on social ethics. H. Richard Niebuhr and Paul Tillich as well as the Roman Catholic theologian Friedrich von Hugel admit special indebtedness to him. On the other hand, both Karl Barth and Emil Brunner consider him a major interpreter of Reformation and Christian faith.   PAUL D. FEINBERG

TRUST. See *Faith*.

TRUSTS. See also *Business Ethics*. Trusts are legal arrangements or agreements among two or more parties to the trust, whereby the trustee receives from the trustor (grantor) some property or right which the trustee holds as temporary owner and custodian for the benefit of the trustor or a third-party beneficiary. Income from the trust is either added to the principal or distributed to designated beneficiaries. The trustor and trustee each owe certain obligations to the other party.

The trustor should clearly indicate to the trustee the terms of the trust, including the property or right to be placed in trust, any desired use or restrictions, the expiration date or event, the amount of any compensation for the trustee, and the method for periodic and final disposition of the principal and income, if any, to designated beneficiaries or to the trustor.

The trustee should faithfully adhere to the terms of the trust agreement; in addition, the trustee has an implied or expressed obligation to use reasonable care to protect the item in trust and to give to the trustor periodic and a final accounting of what was received and the disposition of the trust. Within the latitude of independence granted the trustee is the implied duty to use the trust in the best interest of the trustor. Unless restricted, the trustee should not permit the trust to lie idle (Matt. 25:14-28), nor be squandered on risky ventures.

Trusts may be illegal and immoral if they are a detriment to the public or an individual. A trust created to combine two or more businesses under a common owner (trustee) for the purpose of unreasonably restricting trade or commerce is prohibited by common law, state laws, and the Sherman Act of 1890 and the Clayton Act of 1914, as interpreted by the Supreme Court.

ROBERT P. BENJAMIN

TRUTH. When Pilate asked Jesus "What is truth?" (John 18:38), he had in mind the abstract, intellectualist meaning truth had for Greek minds. Truth for them was something to be thought or believed. This meaning has influenced the English terminology most profoundly. Truth refers to an actual state of affairs as contrasted with a rumor or a false report. A sentence is thought to be true if its assertions either agree with the laws of the intellect, or correspond to what is really factual.

Biblical usage does not stop here. The OT term for truth *('emeth)* suggests notions of firmness, stability, reliability, faithfulness. The Lord is called a God of truth because he is one on whom his people can safely rely. For this reason the versions frequently render *'emeth* as faithfulness (e.g. Deut. 32:4; Ps. 146:6).

Truth is not solely something one thinks, but also something to be done. God does truth forever (Ps. 146:6). Truth is a quality of God's nature. He is the only unchanging and constant reality in a world in constant flux. It follows that his word to man will likewise be reliable and sure (Ps. 43:3; 119:43). God's people are expected to be "men of truth" (Exod. 18:21; Ps. 45:4; Hos. 4:1). The dominate meaning of stability is carried over into the NT. Truth is something to be done (John 3:21). Faithfulness and truth are set over against human sin and falseness (Rom. 3:3-7). Truth is something that can set men free (John 8:32). By truth John means the redemptive divine self-disclosure in Jesus, and by freedom he means, not freedom of thought, but freedom from bondage to sin.

The sustained emphasis of Scripture condemns falsehood and commends the speaking of the truth. God is one who never lies (Titus 1:2). He cannot deny himself (II Tim. 2:13). We are commanded not to bear false witness (Exod. 20:16), not to lie to one another (Col. 3:9). "Therefore, putting away falsehood, let everyone speak the truth with his neighbor" (Eph. 4:25). Deception and untruth are hallmarks of godlessness. The tempter in the garden impugned the truthfulness of God and deceived our first parents. Lost men have exchanged the truth of God for a lie (Rom. 1:25).

Is it, however, necessary always to tell the whole truth? Does "speaking the truth in love" (Eph. 4:15) entail the occasional concealment of the truth? God certainly authorized Samuel to conceal from Saul the main purpose of his visit to Jesse (I Sam. 16:2). There was no untruth in our Lord's command. A partial truth need be no lie (cf *Lying*). Concealment of truth may well be the proper action which certain situations call for and require.   CLARK H. PINNOCK

TRUTHFULNESS, See also *Lying, Truth.* The Christian lives under a speech imperative, to tell the truth, or, to "not bear false witness" (Exod. 20:16; Matt. 19:18). This commandment is no merely arbitrary or trivial matter. The universe itself is formed by a God whose fundamental creative activity is speech (Gen. 1:3) and who desires truth (Ps. 51:6). The Lord, in speech and act, is "the Word" and "the truth" (John 1). And sin first entered the world embodied in a lie (Gen. 3). In the latter instance the significance of truth is clarified precisely in seeing what is wrong with lying: it is the placing of oneself above both the truth and the other—and God. That it is an act of inordinate self-love is why the lie poses a constant temptation and is listed among the most heinous of sins (Rev. 21:8). In contrast, the Christian is to speak the truth.

Truthfulness involves an assessment of both the words and the speaker. Since if one makes an "honest mistake" he is not considered morally a liar, it is clear that truthtelling is not just a matter of verbal infallibility. It is a question about the agent as well as about his actual words.

Truth itself, a congruence between words and reality, stands over against the extremes of incomplete speech and a "blurting it out" topheavy word. The half-truth is no truth at all. Moreover, since words "mean" differently in different contexts, a mechanical notion of truth and an abstract, total frankness are distortions as well. The latter, though less frequently recognized, may be aggressively injurious and a violation of the Christian's responsibility to be "speaking the truth in love" (Eph. 4:15). Thus, the truth must become a living word. Here one moves to an important Christian perspective: the *relationship* between speaker and hearer under God—the very thing violated by the false witness—must be included in a description of truthfulness. Responsible speech is extending the truth to those who have the right to know.

This "relational" perspective enables the Christian to contribute positively to the sorting out of the "truth question" at its current frontier. Complex societal issues— like truth in advertising and lending, privileged communication, governmental secrecy, and a medical patient's right to know—are questions of the relation of truth, speaker, and hearer. Considered as such, they are occasions for a serious extension of the range of applicability of truthfulness.   RICHARD DAVIS

TWOFOLD REIGN OF GOD. See also *Orders of Creation and Preservation.*

Biblical realists have tried to live ethically in both the world and the church by distinguishing God's twofold reign through the law as Creator-Judge and through the gospel as Redeemer-Sanctifier. In this spirit, the social ethics of Augustine, Martin Luther, and Reinhold Niebuhr were all variously grounded in Paul's inaugurated eschatology.

Paul encompasses all mankind in his dramatic contrast of Adam and Christ (Rom. 5:1-2, 17-18). In and through Adam, we are all fallen creatures in the "old age" of sin and death. In and through Christ, all who believe in him are incorporated into the "new age" of righteousness and life. The fall of Adam stands at the head of the "old age" and subjects all creation to the wrath of God. The cross of Christ stands at the head of the "new age" in which men are justified by grace through faith and come to know the peace of God.

Three consequences are of great importance for Christian ethics. First, the Christian belongs to both ages at the same time. In the providence of God, the new age does not supplant the old but interpenetrates it (Rom. 5:8). The Christian does not cease to be a sinful creature even though he receives forgiveness and new life in Jesus Christ. He is simultaneously righteous in Christ and sinful in Adam. Hence, believers are admonished, "Do not be conformed to this world [age] but be transformed by the renewal of your mind" (Rom. 12:2).

Second, the law and the gospel have very different functions to perform in the two ages of Adam and Christ. The gospel belongs to the new age of Christ and is "the power of God for salvation to every one who has faith" (Rom. 1:16). The law belongs to the old age of Adam "since through the law comes knowledge of sin" (Rom. 3:20).

The Christian is then related both to the gospel insofar as he is already righteous, and to the law insofar as he still remains sinful. The civil function of the law is to compel all sons of Adam to govern their public affairs with due regard for peace and justice. The ethical function of the gospel is to empower all followers of Christ to serve their fellow men in the world by working to make peace more wholesome and justice more loving.

Third, the church is primarily the agency of the gospel in the new age of Christ, while the state is primarily the agency of the law in the old age of Adam. Since the two ages interpenetrate, however, the church also has an obligation to support all just law, as the state is likewise obliged to sustain the kind of open society in which the gospel may be freely proclaimed.

This twofold reign of God through both law and gospel in both church and world permits of no absolute divorce between the realms of the "sacred" and the "secular." Consequently, Christians exercise their dual citizenship in the two ages of Adam and Christ by means of their responsible participation in both church and world (Rom. 12–13).   WILLIAM H. LAZARETH

TYRANNICIDE, TYRANNY. The English word tyranny is derived from the Greek *tyrannos.* (Since *tyrannos* is not Greek in origin, some think that it was borrowed from the Lydians.) Today, tyranny is used almost exclusively of cruel and oppressive rule.

In antiquity the term had a more ambiguous or neutral meaning than its present negative connotation. Grammarians have noted its first-known use in a poem of Archilochus of Paros, in the middle of the seventh century B.C. In subsequent poetry it often appears as a synonym for king *(basileus)* with no observable connotation,

bad or otherwise. The seventh century B.C. has often been called "the age of tyrants." However this expression might easily mislead. The tyrannies first came into existence at this period, and there was a large group of tyrants at the same time in different parts of Greece. Yet tyranny was not as a form of government confined to this span of Greek history. Tyranny was always with the Greeks, and no age in subsequent history was exempt from the rise of tyrants here and there.

A tyrant was usually a ruler who had acquired power unconstitutionally or inherited it from someone who had gained power in such a manner. Such seizures of power became quite common, because in most states the reigning aristocracies were widely resented. This resentment on the part of the populace presented opportunities for ambituous men to seize power in the name of the oppressed. However, these early tyrannies did not gain their power from the support of the poorest classes, whose cause was championed in the rise of democracies, but rather from the class just below the nobles, roughly the class that supplied the hoplites or infantry soldiers. The best known tyrants of this period were Cypselus at Corinth and Orthagoras of Sicyon.

The best tyrants were builders and patrons of the arts. Many, like Pisistratus, showed concern about the well-being of their subjects, and did much to ease the change from aristocratic to democratic rule. Nevertheless, tyrants quite early acquired a bad name, because many used their power unscrupulously. It was not uncommon that those who killed tyrants received highest honor, like Harmodius and Aristogiton in Athens.

Tyrants and tyrannies have found their way into literature. In Plato's *Republic* the wise king is placed at the top and the tyrant at the bottom of his classification of constitutions. The aforementioned form of govemment, on the other hand, has been most eloquently argued for in Machiavelli's *The Prince*.

Tyrannicide, the act of killing a tyrant, is a doctrine that has falsely been attributed to the Jesuits. In the treatise *De rege et regis institutione* (Toledo, 1599), the Spanish Jesuit Juan Mariana permitted such killings in extreme cases. However, this view was never adopted by the order as a whole; in fact, they explicitly reputiated it in 1614.

The Scripture neither advocates nor condemns forms of government *per se*. The crucial matter is the manner in which the ruler conducts himself with respect to God and those ruled. The ideal is to be seen in Israel's theocratic monarchy and paramountly in the millennial reign of her Messiah, the Lord Jesus Christ. The ruler is to recognize his authority is delegated by God. This is vividly portrayed in the anointing of the king by the prophet. Once in authority he is to rule justly and righteously. Hence, those tyrants who ruled in the fear of God and for the good of the people, did not misuse their position. On the other hand, those who administered affairs unjustly and for their selfish ends, violated God's standards for those who rule.

PAUL D. FEINBERG

U

UNBELIEF. See also *Doubt*. In the NT, unbelief *(apistia)* is not merely the withholding of intellectual assent or the complete ignoring of God, nor is it simply lack of belief in God. Rather it is the active rejection of God's self-revelation in Jesus Christ (see Luke 22:67; John 5:38; 8:24; 10:24-26; Acts 19:8f.; 28:23f.; II Cor. 4:4). The fate of Judas (Matt. 27:3-10; Acts 1:18f.), the son of perdition (John 17:12), who is said to have gone "to his own place" after falling from apostleship (Acts 1:25), is perhaps the saddest NT example of the outcome of that persistent repudiation of Christ which constitutes unbelief (John 6:64). Unbelief stems from an obstinancy of heart in reaction to learning the truth (Heb. 3:7f., 12), and manifests itself in the assertion of independence from God.

Throughout the Bible, unbelief is closely related to sin, rebellious disobedience, divine judgment, and spiritual impotency. Behind sin lies unbelief; for the Christian, any action which does not proceed from his faith in God is sinful (Rom. 14:23). Unbelief itself is the principal sin (John 16:8f.) because to doubt God's testimony concerning Christ is to make God a liar (I John 5:10). Also unbelief readily gives rise to disobedience (Deut. 9:23f.; II Kings 17:14; Heb. 3:12, 18f.; 4:6); the regular NT word for disobedience *(apeitheia)* sometimes signifies disbelief. Again, the unbeliever stands under God's judgment (Num. 14:11f.; Deut. 1:32-36; Ps. 78:21f.; John 3:18, 36; Rom 11:20; II Thess. 2:12; Jude 5) which will undoubtedly fall (John 8:24). The reality of unbelief makes intelligible the Christian concept of hell; given the possibility of a man's lifelong repudiation of God, there follows naturally the possibility of his permanent deprivation of fellowship with God. Lastly, unbelief may hinder or totally exclude God's miraculous working (Matt. 13:58; 17:19f.). It was because of unbelief that most of those who left Egypt under Moses incurred God's displeasure and were not permitted to enter the promised land (I Cor. 10:5; Heb. 3:19).

Although belief is the hallmark of the Christian (II Thess. 2:13f.) and unbelief characterizes the non-Christian (Rom. 15:31; I Cor. 14:22-25), unbelief may be shown, at least temporarily, by believers who refuse to obey God or to believe the truth (Luke 24:11, 41; John 20:24-28; Heb. 3:12; 4:11; see also Gen. 17:17, Abraham; Num. 11:21; 20:2-12, Moses; Luke 1:20, Zechariah).

The state of the natural man as a guilty, disobedient unbeliever who is spiritually dead (Eph. 2:1-3) is reversed when he acknowledges his need of God's forgiveness and thus becomes a new man in Christ (Eph. 2:4-10), who, through his belief in Christ, has passed from spiritual death to spiritual life and no longer stands under God's judgment (John 5:24).

MURRAY J. HARRIS

UNCLEANNESS. See also *Health Laws.* The terms clean and unclean occur frequently in the Bible, particularly in connection with the Levitical system. The terms convey the sense of holy and common, purity and impurity, and ultimately acceptance or non-acceptance by God. The Hebrew word *tame* and and NT Greek *akathartos,* unclean, and *katharos,* clean, connoting "uncleanness," fundamentally mean to be contaminated by impurity. The "uncleanness" represented by the Biblical writers is physical, ritual, and moral.

The Hebrew understanding of the nature of Yahweh as holy was the basis for the development of the Levitical laws. The Levitical laws concerning uncleanness pertain to (a) persons, (b) animals, (c) places, and (d) objects. Serious forms of uncleanness were leprosy (Lev. 13, 14; Matt. 8), uncleanness caused by sexual immorality (Lev. 18; John 8) and impurity resulting from contact with the dead (Lev. 11; Matt. 23:27). Exclusion from society was the result of being declared "unclean."

Christ's teaching in Matt. 15:3-20 epitomizes the New Testament teaching of clean and unclean as spiritual, not physical. The Essenes at Qumran sought cleansing through many ceremonial washings. Christ abrogated the idea of becoming clean through ritual.

Spiritual cleansing is effected only by faith in the atoning work of Christ (I John 1:7, 9; Acts 10:15; 11:9; Eph. 5:26, 27; Heb. 10:22; James 4:8). A symbolic affirmation of cleansing is found in John 13. The early church experienced intense struggles in abrogating the Levitical traditions of cleansing and proclaiming Christ the perfect sacrifice, as attested by the apostle Peter (Acts 10), the apostle James and the church (Acts 15).   JOSEPH R. SHULTZ

UNCONSCIOUS. Freud is popularly credited with the discovery of the unconscious, but the concept had been the subject of insightful comment and speculative conjecture for centuries. Especially during the nineteenth century, the general conception of the unconscious mind was commonplace among European philosophers. Janet, a contemporary of Freud's, preferred the term subconscious. He also recognized that ideas excluded from awareness could generate emotional disorders and produce conscious effects.

Freud maintained that the great bulk of mental activity is unconscious, and that conscious processes represent a small and subordinate part of psychic life. He described the unconscious as a mental process of which we are not aware, but whose existence could be proved by psychoanalysis. Since psychoanalysis rests wholly upon the reality of the unconscious, this process of reasoning begins by assuming the truth of what is to be proved, a well-known logical fallacy.

The term "unconscious" has become burdened with a multiplicity of imprecise meanings, including such variations as unremembered, incommunicable, ignored, involuntary, and unavailable to awareness. The psychoanalytic meaning of unconscious signifies that processes are (1) dynamically repressed; (2) available to consciousness only by special techniques such as hypnosis or psychoanalysis; and (3) not under voluntary control.

The relative character of the unconscious has long been recognized. There are widely varying degrees of awareness or unawareness. Many emotions and desires described as unconscious are, in fact, quite literally conscious, and can be recognized if one introspects honestly and carefully enough. Because they cause us to think badly of ourselves or cause others to think badly of us, we may *ignore* the existence of emotions, we may *dislocate* emotions, ascribing them to some other object, or we may *misdescribe* emotions as some more respectable attitude. Emotions that are thus habitually ignored, dislocated, or misdescribed, are often conscious rather than unconscious.

Following Freud's usage, the term "unconscious" was enlarged in psychoanalytic usage to include not only psychic content excluded from consciousness, but also content distorted in consciousness by various defensive devices. While amnesic forgetting *omits* something from consciousness, other defense mechanisms may *misrepresent* something to consciousness. The latter are not unconscious in the strict psychoanalytic sense.

Freud's theories led to a depreciation of the conscious and a widespread view that human nature is predominantly irrational. Preoccupation with irrational man has subsided, permitting a return to the more balanced view long inherent in Christian faith, which recognizes not only that man has an evil inclination, but that he bears the *imago Dei*, and may be redeemed by divine grace. Primacy of the unconscious, implying a philosophic determinism, has been largely abandoned in recent decades in the face of overwhelming evidence for the autonomous activity of the person. Many theories of personality have converged in an emphasis upon conscious, purposive, future-oriented motivation of the self that is increasingly superceding the classical Freudian view of the unconscious. The newer viewpoint allows that neurotic compulsions may be based upon unconscious motivation, but gives preeminence to the conscious in normal persons.

Gordon Allport, *Personality and Social Encounter,* Boston, Beacon, 1960, Chaps. 5 & 6; Henri F. Ellenberger, *The Discovery of the Unconscious,* New York, Basic, 1970; Orville S. Walters, "Theology and Changing Concepts of the Unconscious," *Religion if Life,* XXXVII, 112-128, Spring, 1968. ORVILLE S. WALTERS

UNDERDEVELOPED NATIONS. The phrase came into prominence in 1949 when President Truman in his inaugural address announced as Point Four, "a bold new program for making the benefits of our scientific advances and technical progress available for the improvement and growth of the underdeveloped areas." It can be understood only in relation to the foreign aid programs. As a political definition *underdeveloped areas* included practically the entire non-communist world except the English speaking countries, Europe, and Japan. Countries were considered underdeveloped if they were not furnished with the institutions and equipment of modern industry, regardless of their historical contributions to the art and literature of the world, their religious concepts and moral standards, the refinement of their customs, the security of their cities and countryside, the stability of their regimes, the excellence of their arts and crafts and husbandry.

The policy of giving aid by way of goods, money, and services to other countries was accepted by the USA electorate. In the course of the following twenty years some $150 billion was devoted to the purpose, while the idea was also taken up and promoted by the United Nations Organization. Many peoples with ancient lineage and long traditions gladly classified themselves as "underdeveloped" with the object of sharing in this largess. A few, Burma for instance, refused to be reckoned in the category, and the increasing sensitivity of certain peoples, particularly in Latin America, where a European colonial culture had long flourished, led to the use of euphemisms like "less developed" or "emerging" countries. Nevertheless, the scale of values implied by the definition remained: the standard of excellence was not the moral quality of the culture, nor the degree of political sophistication, even less the stability and suitability of the livelihood system, but the level of the GNP, or gross national product. This is a term in itself of equivocal meaning defined as the monetary value of goods and services produced by an economy and moving to market—a definition that ignores all the values, both economic and cultural, that are produced and utilized in the home. Thus, a country with GNP of say $200 per capita—one may wonder how this figure is determined in countries where statistics are either unknown, or the plaything of bureau planners—is regarded as "underdeveloped" by comparison with a country with GNP of say $1,000. By this standard, the desert sheikhdom of Kuwait, inhabited largely by nomad Arabs but enjoying a computed per capita GNP of $3,540 (in 1968) as a result of oil royalties, would rank as a highly developed country in comparison with Ireland with its GNP of $980, or even with the USA with GNP of $3,980.   ELGIN GROSECLOSE

UNDERSTANDING.
Understanding is the act of grasping mentally, of comprehending, discerning, interpreting.

The first step in understanding is procuring information about the indicated topic. The next is analyzing that information by relating it to information which might explain it and to consequences which might result from it.

Basic questions confronting the search for human understanding are what, where, when, who, how, why, and so what? What are the consequences of my being as I am?

The effort to understand society or any other topic involves the same questions.

Man's unaided reasoning can think its way through to only partial answers to those questions. He is incapable of arriving at adequate understanding. Apart from God, the source of all wisdom, our understanding at best, will be, only partial. Genuine understanding, particularly of spiritual truth, is the Lord's gift. "And I have filled him with the spirit of God in wisdom, and in understanding" (Exod. 31:3). "God gave Solomon wisdom and understanding" (I Kings 4:29). The psalmist asks for this gift, "Give me understanding that I may learn . . . " (119:73).

Through the Scriptural revelation man receives this gift. "Through thy precepts I get understanding" (Ps. 119:104); "The unfolding of thy words gives light; it imparts understanding" (Ps. 119:130). Our own understanding is neither omniscient, infallible, nor adequate. "Trust in the Lord with all thine heart and lean not unto thine own understanding" (Prov. 3:5). The Lord will bring to futility the reasoning of men who omit him from their thinking. They are unable fully to discern the truth about themselves as individuals, about society, about the environment, or any other topic. "I will destroy the wisdom of the wise and will bring to nothing the understanding of the prudent" (I Cor. 1:19).

The Lord acts upon the minds of men so that they can comprehend spiritual truth in Scripture. "Then opened he their understanding that they might understand the Scriptures" (Luke 24:45).

Through Jesus Christ, who said "I am the truth" (John 14:6), we receive genuine understanding, which is one of the dimensions of truth. Jesus attached specific qualifiers to knowing the truth and to the acquiring of understanding. "If you continue in my word you are truly my disciples and you will understand" (John 8:31f.).

Even with Christ's gift, our understanding

at present is not complete, but when he establishes his kingdom, we shall understand completely. "Now I know in part; then I shall understand fully, even as I have been fully understood" (I Cor. 13:12). But for the present, we live by faith in the Lord and his word and "by faith we understand" (Heb. 11:3).   JOHN W. ALEXANDER

UNEMPLOYMENT. See also *Employment; Guaranteed Income; Work.* Unemployment, in the broad sense, is the condition in which an individual does not have a paying job or occupation. Receiving income from passive investments (stocks, bonds, savings accounts, some real estate investments, etc.) by itself does not remove a person from the status of unemployed.

A more restrictive use of the word would limit a person to being unemployed if the individual desired a paying job or occupation. This meaning would eliminate most young people as unemployed up to the appropriate beginning working age for that geographical area, race, creed, religion, sex, or family life style. Also excluded as unemployed would be those workers who voluntarily left their employed status, say through retirement or because they have no desire to work. Technically, a person who was forced to retire and who still desired to work should be classified as unemployed; in practice, such a person would be considered retired, not unemployed. A disabled, handicapped, or mentally deficient person desiring work, but unable to find work because of his physical or mental condition, is unemployed; however, from a social viewpoint, such persons are generally accorded a higher status of respect than an unemployed, able-bodied person.

Since the 1930s, many free-world countries have enacted various types of unemployment compensation plans. In the USA, each state enacts its own unemployment laws for workers becoming unemployed within the state. The duration of weekly payments is generally twenty-six weeks. The amount of weekly benefits, with minimums and maximums, is based on earnings for some previous period, generally, four of the last five calendar quarters. State laws usually provide that, to draw the benefits, an unemployed worker "shall make such personal efforts to find work as are customarily made by persons in the same occupation who are genuinely interested in obtaining work" (*Handbook for Interstate Claims Taking,* June 11, 1953, ii.) As the length of unemployment increases, the unemployed may be required to accept work in another occupation or area, or be retrained for a new occupation. Benefits may be reduced in amount or number, or terminated entirely, for various listed causes, such as failure to accept an offered job. Many potential workers prefer to draw the benefits, rather than to work; as a result, they circumvent the spirit of the laws by various means.

A worker drawing unemployment benefits has a duty to himself, the state, and his employer when laid off or discharged to obtain a job as quickly as possible; such a new job should be taken even at reduced pay or desirability. The Apostle Paul wrote that "if any would not work, neither should he eat." (II Thess. 3:10b). The Christian who emphasizes this text must also be concerned with the employment opportunities for the jobless. With an agrarian economy, an unemployed individual could work on the farm to support his family. The industrial revolution created a work force more dependent upon non-farm jobs. The present situation of the new worker dependent upon industrial jobs and the Federal and State unemployment laws enacted to help the industrial worker may obscure the moral force of the "no work, no eat" Biblical doctrine.   ROBERT P. BENJAMIN

UNION WITH CHRIST. See *Atonement.*

UNITED NATIONS. Just as the League of Nations was the form of international organization which emerged from the First World War, so the United Nations is the form of international organization which arose from the upheaval of the Second World War. The idea began to take shape in the mind of President Roosevelt during the course of the war, and several drafts were prepared by the Department of State. In the fall of 1944 and early in 1945 a conference was held at Dumbarton Oaks in Washington, D.C., in which representatives of the United States, the Soviet Union, the United Kingdom and China worked out the final proposals. At the Yalta Conference in February, 1945, when agreement was reached between Roosevelt, Stalin, and Churchill on the representation of Byelorussia and the Ukraine, and on the method of voting in the Security Council, it was decided to convene an international conference on international organization in San Francisco in April of the same year. The San Francisco Conference met on April 25 and concluded its labors on June 26 by the signing by the nations taking part in the Conference of the Charter of the United Nations which was elaborated on the basis of the Dumbarton Oaks proposals.

According to its Charter, the United Nations is composed of six principal organs: the General Assembly, the Security Council, the Economic and Social Council, the Trusteeship Council, the Secretariat, and the International Court of Justice. Every member nation has a seat in the General Assembly. The composition and functions of all organs are determined by the Charter and by special rules of procedure. In the Security Council, which is charged with primary responsibility for the maintenance of international peace and security, there are five permanent members: China, France, the Soviet Union, the United Kingdom and the United States. The permanent members enjoy the right of veto, which means that no substantive motion can be considered a decision by the Council if one of these members votes against it, even if all other members voted for it. Since 1950 the General Assembly has been considering matters appertaining to international peace and security in those cases where the veto interferes in the effectiveness of the Security Council.

New York is the Headquarters of the United Nations, but the world body has offices also in Geneva and in other parts of the world. There have been meetings of the General Assembly in London and Paris, and other organs and commissions assembled in these and other capitals. Up to 1972 three Secretaries-General served the United Nations: Trygve Lie of Norway, Dag Hammarskjöld of Sweden, and U Thant of Burma. Kurt Waldheim of Denmark presently serves.

Belonging to what is called the United Nations system are a dozen or more intergovernmental organizations, such as the International Labor Organization (ILO), the Food and Agriculture Organization (FAO), the United Nations Educational, Scientific and Cultural Organization (UNESCO), the World Bank, the World Fund, etc. These specialized agencies, as they are called, are each wholly autonomous with respect to the United Nations, but they all have special relations to the United Nations through individual agreements with it.

The United Nations is limited by the terms of its Charter, by the right of veto exercised by the great powers, by the sovereignty of its members, by the rivalries and jealousies among the great powers, by the vast differences and inequalities between the developed and underdeveloped nations, and by the turbulence of the world which reflects itself in its halls. To the extent to which the United Nations has been ineffective in the discharge of its responsibilities, it was these essential limitations which handicapped it.

Despite these limitations and weaknesses,

the United Nations can boast of a good record of achievements. The public discussion of many a tense situation with the whole world looking on has often helped to defuse the tension. Its great debates, especially the opening general debates at the beginning of each session of the General Assembly, provide the best education that can be had about the concrete international situation. Its very location in New York has helped in educating the USA about the world and the world about the USA. Through the permanent opportunities which it offers the great powers to confront one another in its debating councils and to discuss their conflicts and differences in an orderly and peaceful manner, it has helped them to adjust their differences among themselves.

The small and exposed nations look upon the United Nations as their principal guarantee, such as it is, against encroachment and aggression, and they have often referred to it their complaints as a last resort. It has served as an ideal multilateral agency for the disbursement of billions of dollars in economic and technical aid for the underdeveloped nations. Many of the leaders of the emerging nations have received their apprenticeship in international responsibility in its councils and halls. The climate of equality and internationalism which the permanent delegations enjoy under the Charter in their daily contact with one another in New York is conducive to civility, harmony, peace and mutual understanding. No sooner did forty or more new nations in Asia, Africa and the Middle East attain independence than they became members of the United Nations; for many of them the United Nations served as a midwife for their birth; for others it sealed their new status with its fellowship and special blessing; for all it became the principal matrix for growth in the exercise of international responsibility.

The United Nations elaborated and proclaimed in 1948 the Universal Declaration of Human Rights, which is one of the principal documents of this age, and which has given a mighty impetus to the movement for human rights throughout the world. The United Nations publishes an immense body of literature embodying authoritative facts and figures on economic, social, political, demographic and other conditions in all countries. The Secretariat of the United Nations is a unique body of international civil servants of whose like no capital can boast, so far as competence, experience, knowledge of world affairs, impartiality and a detached world view are concerned.

The United Nations actually intervened, in some cases with a measure of success, in numerous situations of actual war or of threats of war, in Iran and Greece, in Cyprus and the Congo, in Korea and Berlin, in the dispute over Kashmir between India and Pakistan, in many international tensions in Africa and Latin America, and in the many wars or threats of war of which the Middle East has been the scene since 1945. Finally, the mere existence of the United Nations serves somewhat as a deterrent against adventurers and would-be aggressors who know that in a watchful world they would be exposed and judged at its bar.

It follows from all this that, despite its many limitations and failures, the United Nations has certainly served the cause of international peace and security, and that with it the world would be distinctly a safer place to live in than without it. And while it is true that its financial troubles are mounting, still, were the United Nations to die today, it would inevitably resurrect tomorrow from its own ashes. CHARLES H. MALIK

UNIVERSALISM. Belief in the ultimate salvation of all mankind was espoused early in the history of Christianity by Clement of Alexandria (d. c. 215) and his pupil, Origen (d. 254). Though subsequently embraced by

Gregory of Nazianus (d. *c.* 389), Gregory of Nyssa (d. *c.* 394), Didymus of Alexandria (d. *c.* 395), and later by John Scotus Erigena (d. 877), it found no acceptance in any of the major branches of the church. After the Reformation it occasioned serious controversy, was condemned in the Augsburg Confession (1530) and was at variance with the conclusions of the Heidelberg Catechism (1563), the Council of Trent (1563), and the Westminster Confession (1646). The doctrine has persisted, however. Influential proponents have included Jonathan Mayhew, John Murray (founder of the Universalist Church) and Nels F. S. Ferre in America; Friedrich Schleiermacher and implicitly Karl Barth (d. 1968) in Germany; and Frederic W. Farrar, Charles H. Dodd, Herbert H. Farmer, and John A. T. Robinson in England.

The neo-universalism pervasive in contemporary theology has added certain nuances to the doctrine. Ferre speaks of a radical love that will pursue every man until he is redeemed. Ethelbert Stauffer postulates an irresistible grace that overcomes the most obdurate opposition. Emil Brunner takes the Biblical mention of hell as a challenge to right action rather than as a description of an objective condition.

Perhaps the most influential voice recently has been that of Karl Barth who taught that all men are in Christ through the will of the electing God. In Christ all men are reprobate and also elect—their division into two classes rendered impossible because as the only reprobate he bore the judgment for all that all might be in him who is the only elect. Thus for Barth, the objective reconciliation of all men to Christ is a fact which means that the difference between Christians and heathen is "noetic," not "ontic." Barth, however, took the Biblical warnings of punishment seriously enough to state that "there is no divine election that cannot be followed by rejection and no rejection that cannot be followed by election" and thus is open to the charge of inconsistency (*Die Kirchliche Dogmatik,* II/2, p. 205).

Universalists have supported their position by pointing to Bible passages which declare the salvation of all men to be God's will (e.g., I Tim. 2:4); or that allegedly predict the salvation of all (e.g., I Cor. 15:22-28); or seemingly include all in a salvific relationship with God (e.g., II Cor. 5:19); or purportedly give grounds for hope after death to all (e.g., Matt. 18:18-22). But, careful exegesis of these and similar texts will not allow a universalistic interpretation. Moreover, numerous passages convey warnings of wrath and judgment without consolation of any kind (e.g., John 3:36; II Thess. 1:6-10).

The more important ground for universalism is discoverable in the universalists' view of the nature of God. If the ultimate attribute of God is love to the exclusion or diminution of his wrath and righteousness, a universalistic conclusion becomes compelling. The force of this thinking is weakened, however, by the realization that this love-dominated God has nonetheless allowed the present state of affairs with its attendant suffering; and it is demolished by a consistent Biblical portrayal of a God whose perfections of righteousness and love are equally ultimate (cf. Carl F. H. Henry, *Aspects of Christian Social Ethics,* Grand Rapids, Eerdmans, 1964, pp. 146ff.).

The implications of universalism are most painfully evident, especially as they concern the church's mission. It tends to nullify that motivation for evangelism which links the eternal destiny of the lost with the responsibility of the church to share the good news through which men can be saved. Moreover, it redefines evangelism and transmutes the message from "Be ye reconciled to God" to "You are reconciled to God" (cf. D. T. Niles, *Upon the Earth,* New York, McGraw-Hill, 1962, p. 104). It is understandable, therefore, that evangelical Christians have staunchly opposed universalism.

Delegates to The Congress on the Church's Worldwide Mission meeting at Wheaton, Illinois, in April, 1966, joined in the declaration that "the repudiation of universalism obliges all evangelicals to preach the gospel to all men before they die in their sins" (cf. Harold Lindsell, ed., *The Church's Worldwide Mission,* Waco, Tex., Word, 1966, p. 225).   DAVID J. HESSELGRAVE

URBANIZATION. See *Social Change.*

USURY. In Biblical Hebrew the verb *nāšâ, nāšâ,* may mean to grant a loan (Deut. 24:11; Isa. 24:2; Jer. 15:10 AV) but also to lend on interest or to exact usury (Exod. 22:25). Similarly, the noun *maššâ,* may connote only a debt or claim (Neh. 10:31, and perhaps 5:10), but also usury (5:7). The verb *nāšāk,* clearly means to claim interest (Deut. 23:19); hence the Bible's most frequent noun for usury, *nesek.* Though sometimes traced to a verbal root meaning to bite, *nesek* seems related to an Akkadian word for settling accounts. Parallel is *tarbît,* increment (Lev. 25:36), used only in conjunction with *nesek,* cf. the poetic lines in Ezek. 18:8. So while the man who practiced *maššâ* may often, indeed, have been an extortioner (Ps. 109:11), the OT terminology does not in itself imply excessive or illegal rates of interest, as does usury in later English usage. The NT term for interest, *tókos,* means literally birth, offspring, i.e., money that "breeds."

For the semi-nomadic Hebrews of the Pentateuch, loans existed, not to gain temporary capital, but to maintain a poor man's very life. The richer brother was thus obligated to "lend him sufficient for his need" (Deut. 15:7-11). Correspondingly God's wilderness legislation forbade the taking of interest (Exod. 22:25; Lev. 25:36-37; Deut. 23:19-20). In contrast therefore to the advanced Babylonian economy depicted in the Code of Hammurabi, David's Israelites would not seek interest (Ps. 15:5); and Solomon and the prophets condemned those who did (Prov. 28:8; Ezek. 18:13; 22:12). Christ spoke of lending "in order to receive back the same amount" (Luke 6:34 NAS); and while Nehemiah *lent* to his poor brethren in post-exilic Judah (Neh. 5:10), he condemned those who would exact interest of them (vv. 7, 10). The lenders thus agreed to "require nothing of them" (v. 12), as opposed to their former 1 percent per month (v. 11), which was still considerably under the normal annual rate of 20 percent.

Yet even the Mosaic law had authorized collecting interest from foreigners (Deut. 23:20), and charges for loans characterized the NT economy (Matt. 25:27; Luke 19:23; Josephus *Wars* ii. 17, 6). Usury was condemned by the Third Lateran Council, A.D. 1179; but medieval Christian theory also justified interest on capital loans in which the lender suffered the loss of other potential gain, which is now almost universally the case.   J. BARTON PAYNE

UTILITARIANISM. Utilitarianism, dimly forshadowed by Helvetius, Beccaria, and Hume, was perfected by Jeremy Bentham (1748-1842). The immediate stimulus was the imperfection of the British legal system. Utilitarianism was a theory to support reform.

The philosophical basis is psychological hedonism: "Nature has placed mankind under the governance of two sovereign masters, *pain* and *pleasure.* It is for them alone to point out what we ought to do, as well as to determine what we shall do."

If pleasure is the only human motive, it is plausible that we should aim for the greatest amount. To calculate the amount we must measure the intensity, the duration, the certainty, the propinquity, the fecundity, and the purity of the pleasure.

Then Bentham adds a seventh dimension: "the extent; that is, the number of persons to whom it extends."

Now, psychological hedonism surely means that a man is motivated by his own pleasure. The pleasure of others are not pleasures and therefore not motives to him. Thus Bentham seems to have made a fallacious inference from psychological hedonism to utilitarianism—the theory that the good life is the one that produces the greatest good for the greatest number. Yet if the greatest good of the greatest number prevents a man from getting the greatest good for himself, what reason can be given to convince him to sacrifice his own good? Surely not psychological hedonism.

Bentham tries to minimize this conflict by a theory of four sanctions. The physical sanction is merely the natural consequence of one's action. This has little to do with inducing us to seek the pleasure of others. The political sanction is the power of the state. Such a sanction by imposing penalties can make one's personal pleasures result in pain and so produce a certain amount of harmony in the state. The social sanction still further makes it painful to seek personal pleasure at the expense of the greatest number. The religious sanction, i.e., God's inflicting pain in order to harmonize private and universal pleasure, would guarantee the result, if only these punishments could continue into the world to come. But Bentham rejects this solution: God is supposed to operate only in this life and only through the powers of nature. Since these four sanctions do not produce a perfect harmony, utilitarianism is left without a justification of its principle of universalism.

The principle of the greatest good for the greatest number envisages at least some people, the smaller number, who must suffer. Thus utilitarianism justifies massacre. To be sure, Henry Sidgwick in the late nineteenth century tried to avoid justifying massacre by replacing the notion of the greatest good of the greatest number with the assumption that the greatest sum of pleasures for any one individual actually contributes to the greatest sum for every other individual. Thus a murder could never be beneficial to anyone. But there is no empirical evidence to support this assumption.

Bentham's original principle of the greatest good "on the whole" is quite consistent with Stalin's murder of millions of Ukrainians, his slaughter of the captured Polish officers, and his suppression of the Hungarians. These actions caused considerable pain to many people; but they will all be overbalanced by the pleasures of the greater number of happy communists in the centuries to come.

This is true, of course, provided that the calculation is correct—provided, of course, that the calculation is possible. The possibility of measurement depends on the identity of a unit. In order to measure heat, a degree of temperature had to be invented. No one has yet invented a unit of pleasure; therefore there can be no sum. There must also be a unit of pain, and this unit must be commensurable with the unit of pleasure. One cannot add an inch to a degree to an ounce and get a total. It is doubtful that pains and pleasures are commensurable, and at any rate there is no unit. Therefore the required calculation is impossible.

If it were possible, the question would still remain whether the calculation could be complete and correct. To count the pleasures, not only of all people living today, but also of all future generations all over the world, is a superhuman task. For example, how much pleasure or pain will my action today produce for a Chinese peasant a few hundred years from now? Must morality depend on my knowing this amount before I decide between two proposed decisions?

God and immortality, though in one way or another they may avoid the difficulty of conflicting goods, cannot help one to calculate. Practicability as well as consistency is needed. This requires a verbal revelation, such as the Ten Commandments. Only these can inform us which decisions are right and wrong.   GORDON H. CLARK

UTOPIANISM. See also *Optimism; Social Darwinism.* The word "utopia" was coined by Thomas More in 1516. It is a combination of two Greek words meaning literally, "no-place." Its close similarity to *eutopia,* meaning "good place," has been pointed out. Since the time of More the word has appeared in all major languages with application to both imaginary and real societies.

Although the term was not then used, primitive myths of Golden Age are forerunners of modern utopias. Many ancient civilizations contain stories of original paradises as do the Hebrew Scriptures. This is amply illustrated in Mircea Eliade's analysis of primitive mythology as a retrospective thrust to the perfect point of beginning for human society.

Plato's *Republic* can be viewed as the first great attempt of the Greeks to design a perfect state of their own, as opposed to mere nostalgia for the original one created by the gods. The OT anticipates some kind of utopian kingdom from at least the time of the Hebrew prophets, on distinctive messianic assumptions. In more recent years Communism, presupposing an economic dialectic within history, has held out hope of a political utopia. Still more recently, speculative utopias attempt to go beyond traditional Marxism, as that of Marcuse.

Five main types of utopias are widely recognized. First, *literary* utopias present highly imaginative descriptions of perfect or nearly perfect societies such as may be found in novels. Second, *political ideals* arising out of works on political theory, such as Plato's *Republic,* are utopias with more than a purely imaginary or literary intent; they are idealized and hoped-for political systems designed for adoption in the real world. Third, *philosophical anthropologies,* although not consciously utopias, nevertheless discuss the potentiality for human perfection. Fourth, *philosophies of history* such as those of Hegel or Marx culminate in a vision of achieved perfection. Fifth, *religious eschatologies* look to a day of divine intervention designed to regain Paradise lost. Different forms of millennarianism and chiliasm fit into this category.

There are many motives behind man's persistent aspiration for utopia. Discontent with the present state of affairs, the psychological tendency to illusion, incurable optimism, and religious expectation have all been offered as possible explanations of this phenomenon. From the Christian point of view, however, utopian hope has always been a part of God's redemptive plan for planet earth. A gracious God holds out to sinful and rebellious man the hope of a renovated and restored world in which "God shall wipe away all tears from their eyes: and there shall be no more death, neither sorrow, nor crying, neither shall there be any more pain: for the former things are passed away" (Rev. 21:4).

NORMAN GEISLER

V

VALUES. Value theory or axiology is a general theory based on the assumption that aesthetic value, moral value, political value, and (consistently) physical value or health, are all species of one genus.

A distinction must be made. The criteria

for judging a work of art, the criteria of good health, and the criteria of moral action are not plausibly species of one genus. How often have we heard the aesthetes decry moral norms in art! On the other hand, a combination of health, wealth, morality, and art may define the good life. In this sense Aristotle's ethics is axiology, for his good life has the proper proportion of each. However, this is not axiology in the modern sense of making every value a species of an inclusive genus.

As a distinct modern movement axiology first came to notice in the neo-realist school of Brentano and Meinong. Values as well as chairs and tables exist independently of consciousness. Green exists in a chair; good exists in a proposition. Whether or not minds exist or bodies exist, the *proposition* "a diseased appendix ought to be removed" is a good proposition. But one wonders whether a proposition can exist without a mind or an appendix without a body.

Meinong was followed by Scheler and Husserl. In America axiology was popularized by Ralph Barton Perry, John Dewey (though not a realist), S. C. Pepper, and others. C. I. Lewis uses the term *value* in a narrow sense and approximates Aristotle by subsuming axiology under ethics; but most make ethics a subdivision of axiology. In some cases a good amount (or is it a bad amount) of pedantic linguistics is mixed in.

Neo-realism seems to imply a theory of valuation that is both cognitive and empirical. Absolute idealism and Calvinsim are both cognitive, but not empirical. The emotive theories of A. J. Ayer, Charles L. Stevenson, et al, are empirical, but non-cognitive. These latter make valuation arbitrary and irrational, and remove it from the sphere of discussion. Ayer and Sartre are good examples.

The great difficulty with the cognitive, empirical view is its empiricism. Appendectomies, lies, and wars are as natural as plants and planets. None of them comes with a tag, saying, "I am valuable." An example is the war in Viet Nam from 1962. The American effort was widely denounced as immoral and bad. But the denouncers think that riot, arson, murder, and treason are moral and good. Anti-communists hold a different view. The difficulty is how to determine by empirical observation which view is right.

The same difficulty occurs in music. Some people value Bach, Beethoven, and Brahms; but others prefer ear-drum-splitting rock.

Empiricism is incapable of establishing norms. Perry may say that "any object, whatever it be, acquires value when any interest, whatever it be, is taken in it." But this may make heroin as valuable as, or even more valuable than chocolate ice cream. To avoid this embarrassment Perry tries to show how one value is better than another. The better value is the one that harmonizes many interests. But though this definition complicates the observation, it is of no help to empiricism. There could be several harmonies, each of ten different values. How then shall we choose one from among them? Or, again, one harmonious combination might integrate five values, while a second includes twenty. But could not a life of five values be better than a life of twenty? The example of drug addiction prevents the theory from advocating a highest value that includes all. Therefore observation cannot decide among combinations; empiricism justifies no *ought*.

Various empiricists have tried to defend their theory against this charge. But there can be no value in their arguments because it is always and everywhere fallacious to insert into the conclusion a concept that nowhere appears in the premises. The observational statement, X values rock, does not imply that X ought to value rock, that Y and Z should value rock, or that Bach and Brahms are disvalues. If the rock example is not convincing, try heroin.

⟳Brand Blanshard, *Reason and Goodness*, London, 1961; John Dewey, *Theory of Valuation*, Chicago, University of Chicago, 1939; R. B. Perry, *Realms of Value*, Cambridge, Mass., 1954, Westport, Conn., Greenwood, 1968.

GORDON H. CLARK

VENEREAL DISEASE. Venereal diseases are communicable diseases spread by sexual contact. Long with us, they are named after Venus, the goddess of Love.

Two major venereal diseases are gonorrhea and syphilis. Sharp increases of these were related to two world wars. The advent of penicillin then brought a sharp decline. Since about 1957 the incidence of V.D. has been increasing. The rate sky-rocketed from 1967 through 1970. Gonorrhea is the number one communicable disease in the USA. An estimated two million new cases occurred in 1970. The syphilis rate in the USA is higher now than in the mid-fifties; in 1970 it was the third most commonly reported infectious disease. Trends are similar worldwide, with many reports of gonorrhea reaching epidemic proportions.

Medical history indicates that when the cause, method of spread, and treatment of an infectious disease is known, it is soon controlled. Why has this not been true of V.D.? Some reasons are: increase in world population, especially of the young and sexually active; increased urbanization with anonymity, loneliness, and decreased social controls; increased travel and mobility; ignorance; more promiscuity because of better and available birth-control means; increased gonococcal resistance to antibiotics; changing sexual mores with increased heterosexual and homosexual promiscuity.

Thus, prevention involves educational, medical, and moral efforts. The greatest of these is moral. Promiscuity is clearly the great perpetuator of V.D. God's standard of Christian monogamy is clearly society's great untried remedy. Jesus said, "If you love me, you will keep my commandments" (John 15:15 RSV). "Love Jesus and eradicate V.D." has more relevance than many think.   MERVILLE O. VINCENT

VICE. See also *Crime; Gambling*. Strictly defined, vice is "an immoral or evil habit or practice; ... immoral conduct; depraved and degrading behavior ... sexual immorality, especially prostitution" *(Random House Dictionary)*. It is the opposite of virtue as darkness is of light, and wrong of right.

While the term "vice" is not used in the Authorized Version, more recent versions employ it (e.g., Rom 13:13; Eph. 4:19 NEB; I Cor. 5:8 Berkeley). Vice dominated the Graeco-Roman world in NT times. Pre-marital and extra-marital sex (q.v.), along with incest (q.v.), were indulged in without shame. From the emperor's palace down to the lowest hovels, society was riddled with homosexuality (q.v.) (William Barclay, *Flesh and Spirit*, Nashville, Abingdon, 1962, p. 26). Early Christians faced a culture in which prostitution (q.v.) was sanctioned by and connected with heathen temple rites. No wonder then that Paul began his list of "the works of the flesh" with the rampant sex-sins of his day (Gal. 5:19). "It has been said that chastity was the one completely new virtue which Christianity introduced into the pagan world" (ibid., p. 27). Paul set the Christian ethic clearly and solidly against all forms of sexual immorality (I Cor. 5:1; 6:13-20; I Thess. 4:3-8).

In theological and ethical literature the term "vice" usually denotes any principle, practice, or habit which produces unrighteous character and life. During the Middle Ages theologians set out seven vices—often called "capital" or "deadly" sins—as the categories under which all forms of sin could be classified. Every overt sin could be traced to one or more of these deadly vices: pride, covetousness, lust, envy, gluttony, anger, and sloth. Lust and gluttony are fleshly evils; pride, covetousness, envy, and anger are evils of the spirit; and sloth may be a sluggishness of either body or spirit, or both.

In most strata of current society vices abound in glamorized forms. Paganism's age-old immoralities are once more flourishing and fashionable, even endorsed by some trained in the psychological and social disciplines, the natural sciences, philosophy and religion. A new hedonism, frequently expressed in the playboy philosophy, has gained widespread acceptance. The avenues of expressing vicious practices multiply with the advances of technology. A growing list of personal and social vices threaten modern society: illicit sex, abortion (q.v.) and divorce (q.v.) on demand, alcoholism (q.v.), drug abuse (q.v.), pornography (q.v.), theft (q.v.), lying, cheating, gambling (q.v.), cigarette-addiction, wasted leisure-time, unnecessary environmental pollution (q.v.), needless dependence upon others, and demoralizing recreations.

Many thoughtful persons believe that if these moral vices are given continued prominence, tolerance and justification, especially by the social sciences, they will propel this civilization to its death.

In Eph. 2:8-10, evangelical Christianity finds the antithesis to mankind's vice-problem (Rom. 1:29-32). "Good works" become the norm in daily living for those redeemed by Divine grace.

DELBERT R. ROSE

VIOLENCE. See also *Pacifism, Revolution*. The terms *violent* and *violence* are rooted in the Latin word *vis* meaning "force," "vigor," "power," and "energy" (*The Oxford Dictionary of English Etymology*). The Latin term suggests performing an act with all one's might, hence with considerable mental or physical strength. Violence is accordingly defined as the exercise of force so as to harm, injure, or destroy persons and property, and such harm may include psychic and spiritual as well as physical harm. Furthermore, the threat of actual harm is also included.

The task of the theologian is not to formulate a theology of violence, but rather to deal with the question, "Is it ever permissible for the Christian *qua* Christian to act in a violent manner?" Answering this question requires wrestling with the philosophy of non-violence which has always found some degree of support in the Christian community. Those who maintain this position assert that it is always wrong to use violence to prevent violence.

Certainly all Christians ought to abhor violence. But is it true that if he ever engages in violent activity, he will be held morally culpable?

The Christian pacifist bases his position upon two general premises: (1) the means of any human action must always correspond to the ends, and (2) it is essential for Christian witness that the believer obey Jesus' teaching about love. The first contention assumes that violent means will never produce non-violent ends. In most cases this assertion is probably correct, but it does not always seem to be the case. For instance, delivering a solid blow to the bald head of a friend upon which a malaria-carrying mosquito has alighted, or belting a panicked man drowning in a lake, may contribute to the other's well-being as an end. It would be improper, however, to claim that these means correspond to this good end. Nor does it make sense to argue that these violent means necessarily entail violent ends.

There is little question that obedience to the teachings of Jesus Christ is essential to the Christian life. This includes his teachings about peace and love. Is it the case, however, that the Biblical concept of love necessarily excludes the exercise of violence in any and all circumstances? Part of the answer to this question depends upon the definition of love. If the definition is limited to some particular form or type of action such as that which is non-violent, then it is evident that love excludes the use of violence. But if love is primarily understood as intending the well-being of the other, then it is conceivable that violent action might be performed. This is especially true when third parties are involved; i.e., in cases where, for instance, one stumbles upon an aggressor who is maliciously harming some innocent or helpless person, such as a rapist, or is confronted by a political madman such as Hitler. It is conceivable that in cases like these the most loving thing would be to help the one in need even if it meant acting violently against the aggressor. It is even conceivable that violently restraining the aggressor may be the most loving thing that could be done to him. Knocking out a would-be rapist could save him from the gas chamber.

To claim that violence may be used by the Christian to defend another from attack or to fight for his country is not to claim that there are no limits upon the use of that violence. The limiting criteria, as traditionally formulated in so-called Just War (q.v.) Theory has relevance here (Paul Ramsey, *The Just War*, New York, Scribner, 1968). This means that the Christian must reject the theories which tend to glorify violence as is found in the Crusader ethic or, in a more philosophical vein, as is expressed in the writings of Sorel, Pareto, and Frantz Fanon. In this view revolutionary violence is conceived as a positive value; i.e., as being intrinsically good. For instance, Fanon argues that violence invests the characters of a colonized people with positive and creative qualities (Frantz Fanon, *The Wretched of the Earth*, New York, Grove, 1968, p. 93). Besides being scientifically dubious, since its validity rests upon the application of organic and biological models to the social and political realm, this theory permits the most cruel forms of violence, which all men of goodwill would morally reject.

Certainly violence has been a common phenomenon in the history of mankind. Even God's chosen people, the Israelites, were not exempt from participating in violent activity. The holy war permeates the writings of the OT. The Maccabees and the Zealots believed that there was no contradiction between prayer and the sword (II Macc. 15:16). The Qumran community expected God's coming to include a war between the sons of light and the sons of darkness. Even in the Christian Apocalypse the concept of a great battle (Armaggedon) is one of the attending events of the eschaton (Rev. 16:16). It should not be inferred from this data, however, that God considers violence to have a positive value. Rather its use is justifiable only in the most extreme situations. Violence is a result of man's sin and rebellion. Only in the Messianic Age when men shall beat their swords into plows will violence finally cease from this earth. It is to this end that all Christians pray.

Hannah Arendt, *On Violence*, New York, Harcourt, Brace and World, 1969; Henry Bienen, *Violence and Social Change*, Chicago, University of Chicago, 1968; Harry Eckstein, *Internal War*, Glencoe, Ill., Free, 1964; Jacques Ellul, *Violence*, New York, Seabury, 1969; J. Glenn Gray, *On Understanding Violence Philosophically*, New York, Harper and Row, 1970; Ted Robert Gurr, *Why Men Rebel*, Princeton, Princeton University, 1970; H. L. Nieburg, *Political Violence*, New York, St. Martin's, 1969; Thomas Rose, *Violence in America*, New York, Random, 1969; Jerome A. Shaffer, ed., *Violence*, New York, McKay, 1971; George Sorel, *Reflections on Violence*, New York, Collier, 1961. DOUGLAS J. MILLER

VIRGINITY. See also *Continence; Sex.* Virginity denotes absence of sex experience or abstinence from it. The reference may be to either men or women, although in popular usage a virgin is normally a woman.

Great importance has been attached to virginity in some religious and philosophical systems. Dualism in particular regards the physical as intrinsically base or evil, so that the sex relationship is viewed as either sinful of defiling. Virginity might be demanded of special groups, and the higher life is that of the virgin untouched by sexual impurity.

The Old Testament, however, finds no superior ethical merit in virginity except in so far as it might be avoidance of fornication. On the contrary, virginity, like infertility, is something to be bewailed as in the case of Jephthah's daughter. The proper fulfilment of life, with its strong psychosomatic unity, is found in marriage and the family. These are divinely instituted at creation, so that there is no cause for a sense of inferiority, shame, or guilt in marital sex.

Generally speaking the NT follows the same pattern. Thus the disciples may be married men and bishops are to be the husbands of one wife. Nevertheless, some new factors do come into play. Jesus was born of a virgin and seems to have remained unmarried for the sake of his saving mission. The gospel can also carry with it a challenge to virginity for some hearers. Paul, too, sees that celibacy may in some instances be a better choice for more effective Christian service. Virginity is also integral to the resurrection life, since there will be no marrying or giving in marriage in heaven.

These factors do not imply disparagement of marriage. Unfortunately, however, the church increasingly tended to construe them along these lines in reaction to sexual licentiousness of paganism and under the influence of dualistic movements like Gnosticism and Manicheanism. By the fourth century Mary's perpetual virginity was being made an article of orthodoxy, celibacy was being stressed as the proper life for the clergy, and there was even a tendency, as in Augustine, to regard marital sex as intrinsically degrading and sinful, even though permitted and sanctified.

This movement came to a head in the Middle Ages with its exaggerated estimation of virginity. It produced a whole set of problems of both thought and action from which even Protestantism did not entirely escape and to which sexual permissiveness is a reaction rather than an answer.

In Biblical ethics two important points must be made regarding virginity. The negative point is that it is of no higher rank than marital sexuality and merits no special adulation. The positive point is that the demands of Christian discipleship may entail virginity for some Christians, and in this case it is to be accepted with humility and glad dedication.   GEOFFREY W. BROMILEY

VIRTUE, VIRTUES. See also *Cardinal Virtues.* The word virtue is a translation of the Greek *aretē,* which is a term of many and varied meanings. The primary sense seems to be eminence or excellence, and this may refer to other things, e.g., animals or plants, apart from man. In Homer excellence in war is important and this gives the sense of martial valor. But excellence is also deserving, and hence the idea of worth or merit is present. This leads on ethically to the sense of virtue, i.e., what is good, excellent, or worthy. In Jewish Hellenism this can be more or less the same as righteousness, although in Greek thought this is one of the virtues rather than virtue itself. Virtue obviously sub-divides into (a) its essence, or what constitutes goodness, (b) the aptitude or power to achieve it, and (c) a specific expression of it, i.e., an individual virtue such as courage or wisdom. Two further senses may be noted. Since there is also an *aretē* of the gods, this takes the form of a self-manifestation in power. Finally, *aretē* can be an equivalent of *doxa* or glory.

Virtue is a very important word in pagan ethics. Fundamentally the reference is to virtue in its unity as goodness, whether in essence, power, or achievement. But there is an irresistible pressure towards differentiation, especially in relation to the different areas of human life or personality. This differentiation produces already by the time of Plato an attempt to single out the chief virtues in the various spheres. These have come down to us as the cardinal virtues of wisdom, courage, temperance, and justice, and the importance of these is reflected in the continuing role they have played in philosophical ethics.

In ethics, as in theology, the early church inherited the wealth of classical thought as well as the Biblical legacy, and we quickly find attempts to compare and then to combine the two. Indeed, Ambrose of Milan seems to have been the first to use the actual term "cardinal virtues," and Augustine of Hippo made an early attempt to integrate the classical virtues with the predominant Christian "virtue" of love. The medieval church completed the synthesis. It saw two main categories of virtues, the natural and the supernatural (or infused). The four cardinal virtues are an apt summary of natural virtues, while faith, love, and hope form a trio of supernatural or theological virtues in an by which grace perfects nature. Seven virtues are thus achieved in suitable antithesis to the seven deadly sins. This integration is also an appropriate parallel to the similar theological integration of reason and revelation in medieval theology. So much can be known or done by nature; so much can be known and done only by grace.

Although Reformation ethics rejected the medieval synthesis, the Lutheran concept of civil righteousness provided a sphere in which pagan thought might still make a contribution. Thus Melanchthon regarded such general virtues as justice, truth, and moderation as normative in this area. The Reformed idea of common grace provided a starting-point for similar ideas, since it postulated a sphere in which a measure of natural righteousness may be achieved even though this does not avail to salvation and cannot constitute the righteousness of the Christian. The secularized version of common grace, namely, natural law, became an influential postulate in the eighteenth century and opened up the door to new discussion of virtue and the virtues in both philosophy and philosophical theology, with Kant as an important figure in the one and Schleiermacher in the other. In orthodox prolegomena to ethics this has often led to a scheme very similar to that of the Middle Ages. A basic investigation of the meaning of virtue and of what may be known and achieved as virtue in terms of civic righteousness or common grace is followed by exposition of the ethics of revelation, i.e., of the virtue which may be known and achieved only through revelation and in Christian faith.

A point that should not be forgotten, however, is that Scripture itself gives little or no support for the discussion of "virtue" in Greek categories. In fact the word *aretē* is noteworthy only for its extreme infrequency in both the OT and the NT. As far as the Old Testament is concerned it is avoided altogether in the Greek rendering of Hebrew originals, even though one might have thought that so important a Greek concept could have been pressed into service in some capacity. The only instances, and these are few, are in apocryphal works with no Hebrew original. Unless this absence of *aretē* is an accident—which seems most unlikely—the probable reason for it is that the translators saw or sensed an incompatibility between the anthropocentricity of the Greek term, with its reference to human excellence, ability and achievement, and the theocentricity of the Bible, with its emphasis on the righteous acts of God on behalf of unworthy, inadequate, and impotent man.

Aretē does occur a few times in the NT but in view of the importance of the word in classical thought its insignificance in the NT is striking. For the NT has a great deal to say about the Christian life. It refers to its basis, speaks of its power, and portrays its nature even to the extent of giving lists of what might elsewhere be called virtues and vices. Nevertheless, in doing this it has a completely different working vocabulary which is governed for the most part by the OT. Virtue is righteousness or sanctification, while virtues are the fruits of the Spirit or good works prepared already by God. The so-called cardinal virtues might occur, but with no special emphasis and in a very different orientation, while faith, love, and hope, although important, are not singled out as specifically theological virtues. Even a little study makes it quickly apparent that the Biblical presentation can be fitted into the Greek understanding only by a process of adaptation, compression, and reconstruction.

Even in the few instances in which *aretē* is used, the relation to classical virtue is by no means self-evident. In the whole Pauline corpus, with its wealth of ethical teaching, the only example of the term is in Phil. 4:8: "If there be any virtue." Even here the meaning is not wholly clear. The reference may be to excellence or goodness, as other renderings have it, or it may be that the combination with praise, or with some of the items in the preceding list, is important. In any case the mention of *aretē* is incidental, and in the context of Paul's theology excellence or goodness is obviously the work and gift of God.

The other instances are all in the Petrine writings. Only one of these relates to man, i.e., that in II Peter 1:5, where virtue comes between faith and knowledge in an extended sequence. Since both faith and knowledge have a specific Biblical thrust, one must conclude that virtue has its own nuance too, in spite of a famous secular parallel in which faith and virtue are similarly combined. In I Peter 2:9 and II Peter 1:3 the reference is obviously to God or Christ. "Praises" in the former are the wonderful acts of God rather than his individual attributes. In the latter the thought is usually taken to be that we are called to (or by) the glory and virtue of God (or Christ), the sense being either "praise" or again God's self-manifestation in his mighty acts. Even if the glory and virtue were taken to be the goal of Christian calling, they would have to be understood as the virtue and glory that God himself imparts, not as an inherent or achieved renown, excellence, or worth on the part of man himself.

The Biblical teaching, then, would seem to confront us with an antithesis to the classical idea of virtue and virtues. This does not rule out ethical study of the classical and modern conceptions. A place might even be found for an ethics of civil righteousness or common grace. In the last resort, however, it is hard to see how such ethical discussion can be a solid basis for the completely different approach of Biblical ethics. The main purpose it can serve is that of contrast rather than of introduction with a view to synthesis.

GEOFFREY W. BROMILEY

VIVISECTION. See also *Animals.* Literally the term means surgery on a living, non-human animal. It has come to refer to a wide variety of experimental practices on animals for the purpose of advancing the sciences of medicine and biology. These include testing new drugs and medical procedures, training medical personne in surgical techniques, manufacture of medicines, use of animals in diagnosis of disease, and basic research into life processes.

While experimentation with live animals can be traced back to Alexandria in the fourth century B.C., its widespread practice has developed as a concomitant to modern science. This development stimulated vigorous anti-vivisection sentiment. Its organized expression in mid-nineteenth century England spread to the United States, Germany, and other European countries. Anti-vivisection sentiment rests upon three arguments, viz., that vivisection (1) is of little value to medical science, (2) brutalizes the humaneness of society, and (3) disregards the inherent and immutable value of animals.

Those who call for extensive use of experimentation with animals contend that: (1) it is essential for medicine, (2) it can be performed with a minimum of suffering; and (3) man is responsible to use animals for his own good.   DANIEL B. McGEE

VOCATION. See also *Work.* The idea of work as a vocation or divine calling dates from the Reformation, when it was advocated first by Luther and afterwards by Calvin. Medieval Catholicism knew the concept of vocation only as calling to the "religious life," a view which resulted from its distinction between the natural and the supernatural. The realm of the supernatural was regarded as of a higher order, into which one can enter only by a divine calling. Luther's starting point of justification by faith led of necessity to the doctrine of the priesthood of all believers, which meant the end of the old distinction between sacred and profane work. Every one may see his work as a divine vocation. Luther translated I Cor. 7:20 "Let every one stay in the vocation *(Beruf)* in which he is called." Although there are comparatively few explicit references in Calvin's works, there is no doubt that basically he agreed with Luther (cf. *Institutes* III, x, 6; *Commentary* on I Cor. 7:20). Calvin, however, related it to sanctification rather than to justification and also had a more positive appreciation of commerce and business. This view of vocation later became one of the most prominent ideas in Calvinism.

The concept of the priesthood of all believers as developed by the Reformers and their rejection of all dualism is in full agreement with Scripture. Nevertheless it should be noted that the term "vocation" *(klēsis)* in the NT is never used for a secular occupation. The NT always takes it in a spiritual sense: (a) God calls people to become his children (cf. Rom. 8:29f.); (b) God calls people to special service (cf. Matt. 4:21; Rom. 1:1; etc.). *Klēsis* implies service of Christ in his Kingdom. I Corinthians 7:20 also has this meaning. The text first of all means that the believer has to remain faithful to the calling of God by which he was brought out of darkness into light. Yet Paul also refers to the circumstances in which the Christian is called and the latter is urged to serve God in that place of life in which it pleased God to call him. According to the Bible therefore to be a Christian is the main thing. The secular occupation is always secondary, yet it is a definite service and in a derivative sense it may be called a vocation.

This also implies that not all occupations can be accepted by a Christian as vocation. The NT itself gives both positive (cf. Titus 2:10) and negative (cf. I Tim. 6:1) directives. There are at least three classes of occupation which a Christian may hesitate to enter: (a) occupations dealing with matters which are likely to hurt others (such as gambling enterprises, large areas of today's entertainment, etc.); (b) occupations not providing any useful service to society (such as conducting football pools, producing certain kinds of popular literature, etc.), and (c) occupations which, though permissible in themselves, are harmful for the particular Christian (e.g., youth work for a homosexual).

The view of daily work as a divine vocation does not exclude the idea of special vocations. The NT speaks of people called to a special service within the church (cf. Mark 3:13ff.; Eph. 4:11; I Cor. 12:28; Rom. 12:6-8). This includes all those called to specific ecclesiastical offices, whether fulltime or not. Their vocation is not a "higher" vocation, but they are called to a special task, which requires special qualifications (cf. I Tim. 3 and Titus 1) and entails special responsibilities.

E. Brunner, *The Divine Imperative*, Philadelphia, Westminster, 1937; W. R. Forrester, *Christian Vocation*, 1951; G. Harkness, *John Calvin, The Man and His Ethics*, Nashville, Abingdon, 1958; C. F. H. Henry, ed., *Aspects of Christian Social Ethics*, Grand Rapids, Eerdmans, 1964; W. Lillie, *Studies in New Testament Ethics*, 1961; A. Richardson, *The Biblical Doctrine of Work*, Naperville, Allenson, 1952; E. Troeltsch, *The Social Teachings of the Christian Churches*, New York, Harper & Row, 1960, Vol. I, II.   KLAAS RUNIA

VOLUNTARISM. This term is applied to any philosophical theory which views the will as prior or superior to the intellect or reason. Since in general the voluntarist regards self-preservation as the goal of the moral life, this doctrine may be regarded at least as old as the Sophists. Arthur Schopenhauer (1788-1860), through his *The World as Will and Idea*, contributed greatly to the modern development of the doctrine that the dominant factor in the individual or the universe is the will. In ethics, if the ends or goals are entirely the product of the will, they no longer can be considered as rational. In that case, it is meaningless to inquire whether the end is good or evil, right or wrong, as independent of being willed. Thomas Hobbes argued that the good is the object of one's desire or passion, and the bad is what one does not like or desire. Hence terms like good and evil are relative to desires or dislikes.

The modern pragmatic philosopher, William James (q.v.), was essentially an ethical voluntarist. He rejected the thought that ethical theory could be based on reason alone. In his *The Will to Believe* (1897) and elsewhere he appealed to the will as an inescapable element in determining one's world view. Existential ethics (q.v.) is likewise voluntaristic.   WARREN C. YOUNG

VOTE. Voting is a formal expression of will or choice in matters undergoing decision. It is a cherished privilege whereby the governed indicate their will in political matters. This corporate expression of will is the manner in which participatory as well as representative-type democracy is carried out. Effective guarantees and consistent exercise of this opportunity are the only safeguards to continued government by the people.

In view of the Christian's responsible relationship to government (Rom. 13:1ff.) he should be politically involved to the limits of his ability and competence. In totalitarian lands, the ability for free participation is restricted; elsewhere, the opportunity for competent engagement is too often neglected.

The 26th Amendment to the U.S. Constitution guarantees the right to vote to every citizen age eighteen or over. This represents a checkered history: Article XV (1870) extended the right to vote to all citizens regardless of race or previous condition of servitude; and women's suffrage, granted first by the Wyoming territory in 1869, was not nationally recognized until 1920 (Article XIX). The Voting Rights Act of 1965 abolished literacy tests and Article XXIV eliminated the poll tax as extensions of Article XV. Federal courts are still seeking ways to assure the one-man one-vote rule to prevent disproportionate power being exercised by population blocs.

The vote is a corollary to the notion that citizens are responsible for the government, just as elected officials are responsible to the electorate. This Constitutional Right is one of the main ideological differences between East and West. Even so, the democratic process is weakened by local politics, which may subvert the voting rights of minority groups; the apathy of eligible voters toward political processes; and the difficulty of translating voting results into concrete political action (cf. *Democracy*).
              PAUL D. SIMMONS

VOWS. A vow is a promise made to God whereby a man binds himself to do (Gen. 28:20ff.) or not to do (Ps. 132:2) a certain thing.

A vow ought never to be made lightly (Prov. 20:25). It is always solemn and ought to be ventured only after due deliberation. To be truly acceptable, a vow must be free. Voluntarily made, it is sacredly binding (Deut. 23:21-23).

The case of Jephthah is instructive. Living among heathen who offered human sacrifice, he rashly vowed, if successful over the Ammonites, to offer up to the Lord, as a burnt offering, whoever first emerged from the house to meet him (Judg. 11:30ff.). Doubtless he took it for granted that it would be a slave. When his only child, his daughter, came forth to meet him, he was greatly distressed. " 'Alas, my daughter! You have brought me very low, and you have become the cause of great trouble to me; for I have opened my mouth to the Lord, and I cannot take back my vow' " (Judg. 11:35 RSV). Jephthah rightly understood that a vow made to God is binding; what he did not understand is that only vows that conform to the known will of God are acceptable (Deut. 12:29-31).

The man who fulfills his vows is blessed (Job. 22:27), and the man who makes a vow and then cheats is cursed (Mal. 1:40). Ananias and Sapphira were guilty of this latter hypocrisy (Acts 5:1ff.). The Israelites looked forward to that time of future blessedness when, delivered from their enemies, they would be able to fulfill their vows (Nah. 1:15).

The motivation and spirit of the one making the vow is important (Ps. 51:16-17). Vows by some of the OT patriarchs were of the nature of a bargain, being conditional on deliverance from danger (Judg. 11:30) or the obtaining of some benefit (Gen. 28:20-22; I Sam. 1:11). Absalom's vow was a mask for treachery and deceit (II Sam. 15:7ff.). Jesus condemned the hypocrisy of those who evaded their duty to parents by pretending that what was due to them was Korban (Mark 7:11).

The Bible does not prescribe the taking of vows. If vows are made, they are to be fulfilled. But the man who refrains from making vows is guilty of no sin (Deut. 23:21-22). The Reformers recognized that the baptismal promise has the nature of a vow, a vow continually renewed throughout the life of the believer. They emphatically condemned the taking of life-long monastic vows as requiring that which we are not in a position to promise. Luther insisted that monastic vows are not merely invalid but sinful and idolatrous; Calvin, while placing the baptismal vow above all, recognized the utility of voluntary special vows, as a means by which a Christian might progress in the spiritual life or express his gratitude to God.

STUART B. BABBAGE

W

WAGES. See also *Business Ethics; Capitalism; Communism; Industrial Relations; Socialism.* Wages are payment for work performed.

In the Middle Ages, the just wage would enable the common worker to live decently within his social station (George O'Brien, *An Essay on Medieval Economic Teaching,* New York, Kelley, 1967, pp. 120-127).

Thomas Malthus later postulated that wages would tend toward subsistence since the population increased geometrically and the food supply arithmetically (Frank Neff, *Economic Doctrines,* New York, McGraw-Hill, 1950, p. 146).

In the Industrial Revolution (q.v.), many employers held factory workers in virtual economic slavery with long working hours and bare subsistence wages. Karl Marx, reflecting on such abuses, fathered communist ideology by contending that all value is created by labor, and returns in the form of interest, rent, and profits are unjustifiable exploitation. The communist doctrine "to each according to his needs" conflicts with the capitalist ideal of "to each according to his contribution." Complete equalization of incomes would destroy the competitive forces which place workers where they are needed in a free market and necessitate punitive incentives to maintain motivation. Modern Russia has found that wage differentials are necessary to stimulate workers.

In a constitutional republic, capital, rent, and profits are somewhat protected. When a nation moves toward a pure democracy by extending the franchise and liberalizing its constitution, however, a tendency is exerted toward equalization of incomes and socialism. The absence of a strong positive incentive may weaken pure socialism and there is danger that the negative incentives of a totalitarian government may be instituted. The ethic of a more equitable distribution of income conflicts at some point with the ethics of freedom and positive motivation. The progressive income tax, social security, welfare programs, and socialized medicine programs should be evaluated both for their aid to the poor and for their effect on worker motivation.

Political response to the labor vote has resulted in labor monopolies by exempting unions from anti-trust legislation. Without union power, labor could hardly bargain and was at the mercy of the large corporation. With power, union officials in important industries press for much higher wages and union workers gain larger proportions of national income. However, inflation results as wages increase near full employment beyond productivity, and those on fixed incomes lose purchasing power (Gilbert Burch, "The High Cost of Wage Inflation,"

Readers Digest, April, 1971, p. 139). A more significant threat of the wage-price spiral to the economy is the pricing of domestic goods out of both foreign and domestic markets. This can cause domestic unemployment, an unfavorable balance of trade, and currency devaluation. The minimum wage when extended to marginal workers also creates unemployment. Employers must gain a return from the workers' contribution at least equal to the wage paid or institute layoffs. The increasing welfare burden may conflict with the work/eat ethic. With major political influence, workers must consider the devastating long-run effects of wage demands beyond productivity.

The Bible speaks often about money (q.v.) matters. Wages should be just and equal (Col. 4:1) and promptly paid (Deut. 24:14f.).   WALTER P. GORMAN III

WAR AND PEACE. See *Peace and War.*

WATERGATE. A summary term for the tangle of political corruption that rocked the Nixon administration in 1973, growing largely out of illegal acts by those close to the president who electronically bugged and burglarized Democratic party headquarters in the Watergate complex in advance of the 1972 election, or who sought to cover them up. The events led to resignation of L. Patrick Gray as acting F.B.I. director, dismissal of John W. Dean III as counsel to the president, and resignations of top White House aides John Ehrlichman and H. R. Haldeman following grand jury indictments of G. Gordon Liddy and E. Howard Hunt and others for political espionage. Watergate also led to the resignation of Attorney General Richard Kleindienst, who had personal and professional acquaintances among those allegedly implicated, including former Attorney General John Mitchell.

It developed further that the White House had ordered its own investigation of

Daniel Ellsberg, who had leaked and duplicated Pentagon papers bearing on the Vietnam War, and that Watergate spymasters, whom Erlichman assigned to the Ellsberg probe, burglarized the office of Ellsberg's psychiatrist, and that Erlichman had later knowledge of this illegal activity.

Although President Nixon's was a "law and order" administration, pleading with discontents to "work within the system," administration credibility declined and confidence in the federal political process waned following its subversion by some White House aides and members of the Committee to Re-elect the President. Disclosures involved rigging of a newspaper opinion poll and advertising, and vast unreported gifts of money to assure the president's re-election. Calls for election reforms followed estimates that the Democratic and Republican parties may have raised $100 million in 1972 contributions without adequate accounting. President Nixon did not at once name an independent investigator, but authorized his new acting F.B.I. director to do so. Despite wide doubts whether the president could be wholly unaware of what his closest associates were doing across nine months in the worst national scandal since Teapot Dome, Nixon was professedly not involved, contrary to Dean's contentions. He stressed that the administration shakeup had not been frustrated but in fact had been made possible by the American political system, though he acknowledged also that it had been stimulated by a free press, which the administration had often castigated politically, as well as by the insistence of a federal judge and grand jury.

CARL F. H. HENRY

WEALTH. See also *Stewardship*. Some extraordinary statements of Christ's must be noted in any discussion of wealth. To the rich young ruler, he said: "Sell what you have and give to the poor; and come, take up your cross and follow me" (Matt.

19:21). Again, he says: "Sell that ye have and give alms; provide yourselves bags that wax not old, a treasure in the heavens that faileth not, where no thief approacheth neither moth corrupteth" (Luke 12:33). When he sent his disciples out on mission, he counselled them to "take nothing for your journey, neither staves, nor scrip, neither bread, neither money; neither have two coats apiece" (Luke 9:3). Money, in short, was to have little place in their lives if they would be his disciples. Seeking first the Kingdom of God, "all other things would be added unto them" (Matt. 6:33). Evidently he himself had nothing with which to pay the tribute money though he commanded "Render to Caesar the things that are Caesar's" (Luke 20:25).

Yet at no point does Christ dispute the right of private possession. Material gifts come from God. They are to be used for God's glory. The unjust steward was commended because he made to himself "friends of the mammon of unrighteousness" (Luke 16:9); yet at the same time he warned his disciples of the deceitfulness of riches and of the impossibility of "serving God and mammon" (Matt. 6:24). Material gifts come as the result of the use of God-given talents and always should be used for the glory of God alone. However, when the pursuit of riches becomes an end in itself, the danger is great that God will be blotted out even as the sun can be blotted out when a nickel is pressed close enough to the eye.

The right use of money is frequently noted by Paul. Writing to the Corinthian Church, he cites the example of the Macedonian brethren and says: "Out of their abject poverty their liberality shone forth" (II Cor. 8:2). They were down to their last penny, Phillips paraphrases, yet they persuaded the apostle to take something for the poorer brethren in Jerusalem, having "first given themselves unto God" (II Cor. 8:5). Writing to Timothy, he urges:

"Charge them that are rich in this world, that they trust not in uncertain riches but in the living God," and he goes on to indicate the right way in which they ought to use their money: "that they do good, become rich in good works, be ready to share, and thereby lay hold on eternal life" (I Tim. 6:18). In this way, he adds, they will "lay up in store for themselves a good foundation against the time to come" (I Tim. 6:19).

Stewardship of the gifts of God is implied at every level of gift. Whether the gift be one of possession or faculty, the basic rule is that "each man is given the gift of the Spirit that he may make the most of it for the good of all" (I Cor. 12:7). We are called to be "good stewards of the manifold gifts of God" (I Peter 4:10). This comes immediately after the apostle's urging his readers to "use hospitality one to another without grudging" (I Peter 4:9). Christian stewardship recognizes that all gifts come from God and that they are held in trusteeship for God. We have in ourselves no right of self-determination. We are trustees. Our first duty is faithfulness to the trusteeship we hold. This implies that as God has blessed us richly, we must share these gifts as God appoints. Nothing has to be selfishly preserved for one's own gain. All has to be used on the principle of "each for all and all for each."

Under communism (q.v.), the means of production and property in general are held in common, that is, by society in general, and not by individuals. Karl Marx and Friedrich Engels attempt to apply the idea of commonly owned property to industrialized societies. Socialism (q.v.) challenges the belief in the sanctity of private property and favors all use of material, property, real estate and goods, for the general benefit of the entire community. Admittedly, there was a period in the times of the Early Church, when a practice somewhat resembling this obtained. But it was short-lived, had a specific objective in mind, and was soon superseded. Throughout history in general, the right of private possession of goods has not been regarded as evil in itself. But from the time of the industrial revolution in England and on the Continent of Europe, there came a significant growth of the middle classes and in a relatively brief period to the fulfillment of the Chartists' demand that "every man in the land has a right to a good coat on his back, a good roof over his head, a good dinner upon his table, no more work than is necessary to keep him in good health, and as much wages for his work as would keep him in plenty, and afford him the enjoyment of all the blessings of life which a reasonable man could desire." This involved the principle of a just wage for work done. And with this, the NT and OT appear in perfect agreement.

Over against this, the doctrines of Marx and Engels as stated in *The Communist Manifesto* (1848), setting forth the principles of class conflict and inevitable revolution, are very extreme. John Stuart Mill used a dexterous pen to demonstrate that all men, irrespective of rank or class, were due a just and reasonable recompense for work done. This however was only accomplished as the Trade Union Movement developed and the hard bargaining to which we have grown accustomed at the resigning of contracts for work came into prominence.

In assessing the true place of wealth in the life of the Christian, one must go back to the words "What doth the Lord require of thee, but to do justly, to love mercy, and to walk humbly with thy God?" (Mic. 6:8). A just wage is the equivalent of the "just balances" that are extolled in Proverbs. No true Christian can possess great wealth and use it only for selfish gratification. It is given to him to share what he has with others remembering the word of his Lord: "Give and it shall be given unto you" and "With what measure you mete, it shall be measured to you again" (Matt. 7:2).

Our twentieth century world has not yet realized the potential of wealth as a sacred trust from God. Possessions hoarded are useless. The only gold that is good is the gold that goes. Which raises the question: How much of my money does Christ demand? There is only one possible answer: He demands it all. What we have is his by right. We are only trustees of his property and must use it for his glory and the good of many. There are some whom Christ asks to make money for himself. Others are called like Antony of the Desert or St. Francis of Assissi, to serve him in poverty. But the call of God is always clear. He never leaves us in doubt as to what he wants us to do.

Wealth should be used by the Christian to care for the saints, who by force of circumstance, sickness or accident, are unable to help themselves. There will always be need to give money for the preaching of the gospel and to spread abroad the good news of the Kingdom of God. Let God have first claim on what we call our own. Let him be the first benefactor from our earnings. When you do this, you discover soon that God will be no man's debtor. As John Bunyan says: "I shovel out, and God shovels in; but God's shovel is bigger than mine." In an affluent society, Christians must learn the art of using their affluence for the advantage of the disadvantaged. Privilege begets responsibility. "To whom much is given, of him shall much be required" (Luke 12:48). Spurgeon reminds us that the Scripture never tells us to pay our debts; it tells us not to have any. As God has given, so must we give—prodigally, lavishly, liberally. To do so is to have learned the secret of abundant life—to live is to give.   WILLIAM FITCH

WEBER, MAX. Max Weber (1864-1920), a truly seminal social thinker, made outstanding contributions in such diverse areas as sociology of religion, class stratification, sociology of law, political theory, economic behavior, and bureaucracy. Born into the home of a prominent political figure in Imperial Germany, he grew up in a stimulating intellectual environment. Besides studying law, he acquired professional competence in economics, philosophy, and history. He completed formal training in 1891, but poor health rendered him unable to hold a permanent academic position. He briefly held professorships at Freiburg, Heidelberg, and Munich, served as government consultant in several agencies, and was an editor of the *Archiv für Sozialwissenschaft und Sozialpolitik,* but was primarily a private scholar.

Although Weber's most significant sociological work *Wirtschaft und Gesellschaft* was posthumously published, he is particularly known for his provocative ideas on religion and society. In *The Protestant Ethic and the Spirit of Capitalism* he contended that important affinities exist between Calvinism and capitalism, especially the incentives for action in this world implicit in its theology, the manner in which Puritan divines interpreted Calvinist views to their congregations, and the transformation of these doctrines and pastoral exhortations into social controls. The anxiety over salvation was allayed through an "inner-worldly asceticism" and the believers demonstrated their spirituality by leading frugal but active lives. The accumulation of wealth was the natural if not conscious result of such a life style.

In his comparative sociology of other world religions, above all Confucianism and Hinduism, Weber argued that their beliefs and practices inhibited economic development, thus reinforcing his contention that Western religion was a major influence in the development of capitalism which, in turn, was the great distinctive of Western civilization. He also pointed out significant types of relationships between religious ideas and social organization, namely, social groups with particular economic interests were receptive to certain religious conceptions (peasants tend toward nature worship), religious ideas led to the formation of certain groups (monastic orders, guilds of magicians), and the distinction between the elite and the masses was as prevalent in the religious sphere as elsewhere.

Max Weber, *The Protestant Ethic and the Spirit of Capitalism*, New York, Scribner, 1958; *From Max Weber: Essays in Sociology*, New York, Oxford, 1946; *The Sociology of Religion*, Boston, Beacon, 1963; *Economy and Society: An Outline of Interpretive Sociology*, New York, Bedminster, 1968; Reinhard Bendix, *Max Weber: An Intellectual Portrait*, Garden City, Doubleday, 1962; Bendix and Guenther Roth, *Scholarship and Partisanship: Essays on Max Weber*, Berkeley, University of California, 1971.   RICHARD V. PIERARD

WELFARE STATE. During the past ninety years all developed nations have been moving towards the welfare state, although the term itself came into general use in English only after World War II and in the USA may still be used as a term of contempt.

The Roman and Germanic heritage of Europe and North America is characterized by *voluntary associations* of all sorts, from burial societies to sports clubs. Churches (whether "church" or "sect" in Ernst Troeltsch's sense) appear as the largest of such associations. The Roman state encouraged voluntary societies for benevolent purposes, including the church after 313. The Christian successor states of the Roman Empire followed this pattern. Although the Roman state itself provided bread and circuses (i.e., entertainment) for the unproductive urban masses, in the provinces people had to turn to national, religious, craft, or other associations or to private benefactors for help in distress. Wealthy individuals often were expected (or obliged) to build or maintain public works at personal expense in exchange for public honors.

Gradually the state began to take a more positive hand in structuring society, especially as industrialization progressed. During the 1880's German Chancellor Prince Otto von Bismarck pioneered a comprehensive scheme of social security to insure workers against accidents, sickness, and old age. This early German welfare legislation was less inspired by a concern for social justice than by the paternalism characteristic of Bismarck's conservative outlook and by the practical observation that the increasing specialization of labor and the concentration of economic power in a rapidly developing industrial state imperil not only the personal dignity and economic security of the individual, but also his civic spirit and his ability to function productively. Thus leading industrial concerns such as I. G. Farben in Germany and the Ford Motor Company in the USA were ahead of their respective governments in making broad provisions for the welfare of workers.

The world-wide Great Depression led more countries to introduce government social services and insurance. Social Security began in the USA in the Depression under Franklin D. Roosevelt. In Germany and Great Britain, World War II brought destruction and impoverishment and with it increased welfare services, introduced by the ruling conservative Christian Democratic Union in Germany and by the socialistic Labour Party in Britain. (The British Labour Party, unlike other European socialist parties, owes much to non-conformist piety and little to Karl Marx.) Although the USA suffered little in World War II and enjoyed unprecedented prosperity afterwards, Presidents Eisenhower and Johnson vastly expanded the federal role in all areas of social concern, especially in Health, Education, and Welfare, a new department created by Eisenhower in 1953. Federal welfare expenditures now exceed defense spending in the USA.

Vastly increasing expenditure at all

government levels and a generally rising standard of living in the USA have nonetheless failed to resolve many health, educational, social and economic problems. The record of Britain, Germany, and the Scandinavian countries is more successful, although in those countries too social services consume a growing proportion of national productivity. In the non-communist countries without a Reformation heritage, welfare legislation is less developed. In Japan, the workers' welfare is largely a concern of industry and business. Underdeveloped countries do not have the wherewithal to provide significant welfare services, with or without the expropriation of private property. In communist nations, where the state is virtually the sole employer, unemployment can be treated as a crime or as a punishment for a crime; educational and health services are generally freely available, although educational opportunities are often withheld from those whose political or religious associations seem undesirable.

Christian churches have tended to oppose the welfare state, although once in existence, it has been supported by many churchmen and theologians. Early opposition stemmed partly from a legitimate fear that government welfare would reduce personal concern for human suffering, a Christian duty, as well as from concern about the impact of mounting welfare taxation on church revenues. In the USA the growth of the welfare state has had a particularly severe effect on private educational institutions, which suffer both from increasing competition by public institutions as well as from mounting tax pressure on private donors. In most non-English-speaking welfare states, private and church-related education, whether by economic pressure or government decree, has been reduced to a minimum or abolished. The oft-repeated charge that evangelicals have been concerned only with saving souls and not with

helping people in distress is demonstrably false, unless one follows historian William G. McLoughlin in disqualifying as social action any evangelical work which ministers not solely to physical needs but also preaches the gospel.

The statesman-theologian Abraham Kuyper, Prime Minister of the Netherlands 1901-1905, held that welfare legislation is essential but must always be accompanied by the attempt to influence the moral and spiritual attitudes of the recipients of benefits. During the 1950s and 1960s American social reformers rejected this common-sense or paternalistic view as a violation of the recipients' human dignity and argued for benefits "with no strings attached." This view has been widely adopted in ecumenical religious circles, as the Fourth Assembly of the W.C.C. in 1968 made clear. Jacques Ellul's concept of Christian presence has been interpreted, despite his objections, to mean that the Christian must work in secular society but may not witness to it.

Christian thinkers such as Jacques Ellul stress that it is the technological society rather than capitalism which threatens the economic and personal freedom and the human dignity of individuals (cf. *Social Change*). Both capitalist and socialist economic systems are merging into a unified world-wide economic system embracing all national economies and creating what F. G. Jünger calls the "total work plan." Both capitalism (q.v.) and communism (q.v.) can provide a measure of economic welfare but both exploit the individual, programming him either to produce or to consume as the system requires. In such a technological society, the call to individual repentance and conversion cannot of itself solve the social and economic problems which necessitated the welfare state. Without personal conversion and commitment to Jesus Christ, however, such social justice and economic welfare as governments can provide remain relatively hollow accomplishments, for individuals who lack the perspective of an enduring city built by God (Heb. 11:10) must necessarily become totally dependent on and subservient to the total planning of an increasingly organized society.

📖 Ernst Troeltsch, *The Social Teachings of the Christian Church*, 2 vol, New York, Harper, 1960; Helmut Thielicke, *Theological Ethics*, Philadelphia, Fortress, 1966, 1969; Vol. II, *Politics;* Jacques Ellul, *The Technological Society*, New York, Knopf, 1964;_____, *Propaganda*, New York, Knopf, 1965; Friedrich George Jünger, *The Failure of Technology*, Chicago, Regnery, 1949.

HAROLD O. J. BROWN

WIDOWS. It is a noteworthy fact that the Bible has much to say about widows. Each book of the Pentateuch refers to them and always with compassion. It was a widow who was commanded by God to feed Elijah (I Kings 17:9). The Psalmist speaks of God as " a judge of the widows" (Ps. 68:5). The prophetic message of Isaiah is summed up in the words: "Learn to do well; seek judgment; relieve the oppressed; judge the fatherless; plead for the widow" (Isa. 1:17). Oppression of the widow under any circumstance was counted a sin of sins. Ezekiel's flaming words burn in his hearer's ears: "There is a conspiracy of her prophets in the midst thereof; they are like a lion roaring for the prey; they have devoured souls; they have taken the treasure and precious things; they have made her many widows in the midst thereof" (Ezek. 22::25). Against the Pharisees our Lord spoke vehemently for "they devoured widows' houses" (Mark 12:40). One of the loveliest of incidents ever noted concerns a widow whom our Lord saw casting into the treasury "two mites which make a farthing" and he said of her: "She has cast in more than all they that went before her" (Luke 21:2-3). In the early church one of the first major problems to which the apostles had to give attention was the need of "those widows who were being neglected in the daily offering" (Acts 6:1). Timothy re-

ceives extensive counsel from Paul concerning widows and James says that "pure religion and undefiled is to visit the fatherless and the widows in their affliction and to keep oneself unspotted from the world" (James 1:27).

From all this, it is clear that the care of women whose husbands had died was always regarded as a prime duty of the people of God. They were free to remarry; and in that case the situation was totally altered. But as long as they were "widows indeed" (I Tim. 5:3) they were to be treated with solicitude, care, and concern. Indeed, under the Deuteronomic law, if a man died leaving his wife without issue, it became the responsibility of the man's brother to act as husband to the widow. Widowhood carried with it some sense of reproach, as we see in Isa. 54:4: "Thou shalt not remember the reproach of thy widowhood any more." It is in perfect harmony with this that Abraham Lincoln in the *Second Inaugural Address* said. "With malice toward none, with charity for all, with firmness in the right as God gives us to see the right, let us strive on to finish the work we are in, to bind up the nation's wounds, to care for him who shall have borne the battle and for his widow and his orphan, to do all which may achieve and cherish a just and lasting peace among ourselves and with all nations." Compassion as taught in the Bible is unfailingly associated with the distressed, the needy, the outcast, the refugee, and with the widow. Kindness to widows is a sign of divine grace; oppression of the widow and the fatherless is on the other hand, a most definite cause for divine retribution.

Writing to Timothy, Paul urges that *young* widows should remarry (I Tim. 5:11). At the same time, he stresses that those who are definitely widows, i.e., those without relatives to support them, so long as they are regular in their attendance and observance of their religious duties, should be accorded a special status within the church and become a first charge on the financial resources of the church. A roll of such women should be kept, they being over sixty years of age, having borne children, well reported of for good works, given to hospitality, caring for the stranger. The particular status of widows within the church today should never be forgotten. Most churches have numbers of such godly women, and to their prayers and practical piety much is due. It should be the unfailing responsibility of the church to cherish and nourish such. To leave them to the ravages of want and fear is totally un-Christian. Even though it may be true that in our Western world the situation of widows may be free from anxiety and care, it is still true that in many parts of the world the Biblical injunction towards compassion for such as have lost their husband must never be forgotten. No kind of social insurance can compensate for forgetfulness by the Christian fellowship.   WILLIAM FITCH

WIDOW-STRANGLING. In some societies wives of chiefs have been strangled on the husbands' deaths and buried with them. The idea was theological, being based on their view of the afterlife, where prestige depended on wives and servants accompanying the deceased. This was essential for ancestor-worshippers.

Widows accepted this duty and resisted missionary and colonial reforms. Strangling was ceremonially performed. In Fiji the strangling-cord was operated by two persons of higher rank than the victim. Honorable or mercy killings of females were always by strangulation in Melanesian ethics. The custom disappeared with the new eschatology and ethic of Christianity. ALLAN R. TIPPETT

WILL. See also *Determinism; Free Will.* Will is the disposition of the mind to action. The will has two distinct characteristics: the Liberum Arbitrium and the Voluntas.

The Liberum Arbitrium is the irrational disposition of the mind expressing spontaneous intention, want, or desire. It is completely unreflective and is defined only by its intentionality. Thus on the unreflective level of consciousness the will is pure spontaneity. The Voluntas is the conscious disposition of the mind to action.

The Liberum Arbitrium is ontologically prior to Voluntas. One therefore must will to think. Only on the level of Voluntas does conscious deliberation and intention take place. On the level of pure spontaneity sin is existent only in potency. Only when this potency is actualized by deliberate assent into action can one judge an action as sinful or evil.

For example, on the level of Liberum Arbitrium if I want to take one thousand dollars from John Doe's safe I am only conscious of the thousand dollars to be taken. The act of knowing that this money is John Doe's and judging the action of taking the money as bad or evil has not arisen.   ROBERT G. CLOUSE

WISDOM. The confident assumption underlying Biblical wisdom is that God created man with sufficient perceptual and rational powers to live in this world efficiently and effectively, carrying out practical enterprises with skill and satisfaction. Prudential wisdom was pursued by men of all nations (I Kings 4:30-31). Generalizations were drawn from domestic, economic, and political experiences, and this knowledge transmitted to any with open minds and the wit and will to learn. Biblical wisdom never attained the status of a philosophical system, and such systems were viewed with suspicion in the NT. The Hebrew holistic view of life was hospitable to the dictum that obedient reverence for Yahweh was the first component of right knowledge (Prov. 1:7). An ethic of just and altruistic conduct was advocated, with emphasis on protection of the rights of the poor and alienated

(Prov. 14:21, 31; Job 31). In contrast with the wise man, the fool was the imprudent, selfish, rebellious man who flouted the fundamental insights into reality available to all men of good will. Proverbs 1:1-7 defines the characteristics of the wise; Ps. 1 and Prov. 9 show the joyous felicity or "blessedness" of a wise life.

Wisdom literature displayed an appreciation for careful observation, disciplined reasoning, and thoughtful, terse statement. Delight was shown for proverbs and riddles as distilled microcosms of life's aspects. These utterances, rooted in long experience, appeared to have the finality of Torah, changing the lives of learners and preserving the lives of the thoughtful. In fact their paradoxical rhetoric was an exposition of crucial alternatives in life situations, a concept invaluable in assessing Jesus' teachings in the NT. Purely practical wisdom as seen in Proverbs was challenged and enriched in the theological struggles of Job and Ecclesiastes.

Theologically, the wisdom outlook affirmed the view of Gen. 1 that this is a good world, and that this life is essentially worth living (Prov. 1-4). It accepted a mandate to examine the universe with encyclopedic thoroughness (I Kings 4:32-34; Eccles. 1:13-14). It seemed to affirm God's imprimatur on sanctified common sense as a useful means of learning truth about reality. Its highest OT expression appeared in the near-personification of Prov. 8, where wisdom is revealed to have accompanied God in the creation, sustenance, and aesthetic appreciation of the universe. This may have facilitated the later identification of Jesus as Word and Wisdom, the incarnation of divine, life-giving knowledge and insight into the true nature of things (John 1; I Cor. 1-3). Jesus' life was one of wisdom (Luke 2:52; Matt. 13:4), and he often spoke in the parables and aphorisms of the wisdom teacher (Mark 4:10-34; Matt. 5-7). New Testament wisdom was then much

more spiritual and theological (Acts 6:3, Eph. 1:8, 17), amplifying the former content of the idea.

Wisdom was and is to be attained by a single-minded search for understanding and insight from the hands of God (Prov. 2; James 1:5-8), by wide and accurate observation of the realities of life, and by commitment to godly living.

FRANK H. THOMPSON

WITCHCRAFT. Throughout history each tribe and nation of mankind has practiced witchcraft in some form or another. Professor C. G. Jung described it as a magical archetype.

In the OT Israel had to contend with the Canaanite sorcerers (Deut. 18:10-12; II Chron. 33:1-6), and the sin of sorcery was punishable by death.

In the NT we meet the magicians Simon Magus and Elymas (Acts 8:9; 13:8), and find that sorcerers themselves will have their end in the lake of fire (Rev. 21:8).

In church history the Papal Bull "Vox in Rama" (1233) and the famous "Witches Bull" of Innocent VIII (1484) were both concerned with the problem of witches, and the pernicious "Hammer of Witches" (Malleus Maleficarum) of 1489 resulted in the horrific witch hunts in which many innocent people died. Although the age of Enlightenment (q.v.) saw decline in the belief in witches, this belief never completely disappeared, and today we are witnessing a resurgence of interest in both black magic and Satan worship.

Forms of witchcraft which are still practiced today include: love and hate magic; magical persecution and defense; casting and breaking of spells; death magic. Transfigurations (changing into animals, etc.); translocations (travelling in a supernatural way), and worst of all, devil marriages (incubi and succubae) also exist.

Although some witchcraft can be attributed to delusion and autosuggestion, much can be traced back to actual satanic forces. It is the Christian worker's duty therefore, rather than that of the psychiatrist, to clarify, warn, and counsel those entangled in this field.

📖 K. E. Koch, *The Devil's Alphabet;* _____, *Between Christ and Satan,* Grand Rapids, Kregel, 1968.   KURT E. KOCH

WOMEN, STATUS OF. *Status of Women to NT Times.* In Greek Culture women were placed almost on the same level with slaves and were under the control of their husbands by custom and by law, although they were accorded somewhat higher respect than women of other ancient pagan societies. Plato, whose views were exceptional, affirmed the equality of the sexes and the community of wives *(The Republic,* v. v. 455-466). The honor of wives was jealously guarded, though most of their time was spent in confinement at home. Demosthenes' summary is brutally frank: *"Hetairai* we keep for the sake of pleasure, concubines for the ordinary requirements of the body, wives to bear us legitimate children and to be faithful guardians of our households" *(Theomneustus and Apollodorus Against Neaera* 122). Only in Macedonia at the time of Christ did a minority of Greek women enjoy a greater measure of freedom.

In Roman society a woman enjoyed greater practical, though not legal, freedom. She shared her husband's life and was at liberty to appear with him in public. With this partial emancipation came increased moral laxity including more frequent divorce (Seneca *De Beneficiis* iii xvi 2). Stoicism tended to elevate the position of women and sought to inculcate a high ethical standard; on the other hand, Roman religions often incorporated shameful vices which greatly degraded their position.

Status of Women in OT Sources. In Judaism the status of women can only be understood by recognizing the distinction made between her proper and improper spheres of service. In the home her position was one of dignity and responsibility (Prov. 31). Children were the special charge of the mother (Exod. 20:12; 21:15; Lev. 19:3). Though she took part in religious activities (Deut. 12:12, 18; 14:26; 16:11, 14), "the majority of women were entirely dependent on man, and became in religious matters a sort of appendix to their husbands" (S. Schechter, *Studies in Judaism,* London, Adam & Charles Black, I, 388). Men dominated the public scene. The general principle which applied to the status of women in Judaism was, "The King's daughter *within the palace* is all glorious (Ps. xiv. 14), but *not* outside of it" (Schechter, I, 391).

Status of Women in NT Christianity. Jesus taught women and received their ministrations and financial support (Luke 8:3; 10:38-42; 23:56; John 4). In his parables he frequently included references to their everyday life (Matt. 13:33; Luke 15:8ff.) He opened the privileges of religious faith equally to women and men. We must conclude that as regards spiritual privilege Jesus considered the two sexes equal. But as regards spiritual activity he recognized a difference. What Christ did not say about women is as important as what he did say. It is significant that no woman was chosen to be among the twelve disciples. The Lord's Supper was instituted in the presence of men only. The apostolic commissions of John 20:19-23 and Matt. 28:16-20 were given to men only (though the Spirit fell on women as well as men on the day of Pentecost). Concerning the status of women "Jesus is not the radical reformer who proclaims laws and seeks to enforce a transformation of relationships. He is the Saviour who gives himself especially to the lowly and oppressed and calls all without distinction to the freedom of the kingdom of God" (Kittle & Kittle, eds., *TDNT,* Grand Rapids, Eerdmans, I 784.

With the founding of the church, women

were among the first believers after Pentecost and the objects of persecution after the first scattering of Christians (Acts 5:14; 8:3). Mary the mother of John Mark apparently donated her house as a meeting place in Jerusalem (Acts 12:12), and some suggest that Euodia and Synthyche acted as hostesses for house churches in Philippi (A. Harnack, *The Mission and Expansion of Christianity in the First Three Centuries*, London, William & Norgate, II, 64). When the Christian message went first into Europe the first converts were women (Lydia at Philippi, honorable women at Thessalonica and Berea, and Damaris at Athens, Acts 16:14; 17:4, 12, 34). At Corinth, Priscilla and Phoebe were active in the work of the church, though the exact nature of their activities is unclear (Acts 18:26; Rom. 16:1-3). Though women played an important role it was not a leading one, missionary work, writing of the NT and leadership of the churches were entrusted to men.

The teaching of the Epistles is instructive. The difficult passage in I Cor. 11:2-16 seems to teach the concept of subordination (though not inferiority) of women especially as it relates to public ministry in the churches. Further, I Cor. 14:34 and I Tim. 2:12-15 apparently restrict women from teaching in the assembly. These regulations are given as an expression of true Christian doctrine—principally that of the subordination of women to men in the original order of creation. Though this public spiritual activity is restricted, the equality of spiritual privilege is clearly asserted (Gal. 3:28).

Widows were cared for by the church from the very first (Acts 6:1) and were the first to be honored in any way as a group (I Tim. 5:3, 9). Younger widows were advised to remarry, and no preference was given to celibacy. The activities of women were primarily connected with the home (I Tim. 5:14; Titus 2:4-5).

Two passages are used to support the existence of the office of deaconess (I Tim. 3:11; Rom. 16:1-2), but neither furnishes clear evidence. It seems more likely that the women referred to in the former are the wives of deacons who accompanied them in their ministrations especially in the homes of widows and others, and Phoebe's being designated a *diakonon* (servant) of the church scarcely implies an official order (in that case one would expect a feminine article or the word *diakonissa*). Deaconesses are not unequivocally attested as a recognized order until the third century, and the order probably arose out of the order of widows.

Status of Women in Contemporary Times. The ordination of women to full clerical activities is now practiced by major denominations. The arguments for this are based on the equality of spiritual privilege granted women in the NT and the examples of women who were active in the life of the NT church as cited above. The NT teachings on subordination and silence in the assembly argue against ordination. A distinction may be made between prophecy given to men and women in the NT in which the person acted simply as God's mouth without conveying any message of his or her own, and teaching and governing in which the individual does use subjective judgment and from which activities women are excluded.

The second half of the twentieth century has seen increased activity among women's liberation movements in and outside the church. In areas where activity relieves oppression (e.g., suffrage, equal pay) it is helpful. If the goals of such movements run counter to God's established order, this is wrong (e.g., removing children from parents to communal centers). When a woman tries to usurp the place and responsibilities given to a man (and vice versa), there will be a disruption. For the believer true liberation comes through obedience to the truth of God and renouncing one's rights in the service of others (John 17:17; Rom. 15:1-3; Gal. 5:13).

R. C. Prohl, *Woman in the Church*, Grand Rapids, Eerdmans, 1957; C. C. Ryrie, *The Role of Women in the Church*, Chicago, Moody, 1958; L. Zscharnack, *Der Eienst der Frau in den ersten Jahrhundertan der christlichen Kirche*, Göttingen, Vanderhoeck & Ruprecht, 1902.

CHARLES C. RYRIE

WORK. See also *Vocation*. Not many areas of human behavior have been more radically affected by the Christian gospel than that of daily toil. Wherever the gospel has been truly influential the concept of the dignity of work has emerged. The change from the conception of work as a curse to work as partnership with God owes more than we ordinarily realize to the witness of Christ. In the first place, far from being a parasite or one above the battle of toil, Christ was a carpenter and his followers were working men. The fact that he was identified with common life rather than with a career in professional religion is fundamental to our understanding of him and of his message. He seems to have turned deliberately from the priests to those who were hard working fishermen.

Samuel Johnson was so impressed with Christ's teaching about work that he posted across the dial of his watch the Greek words of John 9:4. In the English of the Authorized Version these words are: "I must work the works of him that sent me, while it is day; the night cometh when no man can work." Johnson felt the impact of these words keenly because he was constantly aware of his own failure to produce what was required of him. Being aware of extraordinary gifts, he believed that, so far as production was concerned, he was always in arrears. The time in which we may make our contribution is one which becomes shorter every day of our lives. The keen sense of indebtedness led Johnson to write a short prayer as he began the prodigious work of compiling the *Dictionary* of the English Language. The famous prayer is as follows:

> O God, who has hitherto supported me, enable me to proceed in this labour and in the whole task of my present state; that when I shall render up, at the last day, an account of the talent committed to me, I may receive pardon, for the sake of Jesus Christ.

The Christian understanding of the significance of work derives, in large measure, from the central conviction that each human being is actually made in the image of the living God (Gen. 1:36). Any reasonably thoughtful person knows that this does not refer to our bodies, because no literate Christians think of God as physical. Man exists not physically, but functionally, in God's image. We are like him, in spite of our sin and finitude, because he is the infinite Creator and we are finite creators. We are creators because we are born free and consequently able to make a difference. The chief way in which we make a difference is in our daily work. By means of toil we can leave the world different from the way we find it. A human is, therefore, both creature and creator, and in this paradox lies much of the meaning of personhood. Part of the power of the Christian view of life lies in the way in which simplistic views of man are rejected and the ultimate paradoxes are faced with boldness.

The ethical significance of man as finite creator is immense. The conception, being far removed from that of natural human goodness, is logically compatible with the doctrine of original sin. Some of the differences which men are free to make may actually be disastrous in human consequences. The dignity of man lies not in his goodness, which is often conspicuously lacking, but in his responsibility, which arises from his freedom to act. This bears mightily on the entire science of ethics.

The Christian ethic about work is greatly needed in the modern world. Part of the need arises from the fact that much work is really hated and only endured for the sake of the wage. Such an attitude is bound to be destructive to the entire social order. Much of the conception of an honest day's work for an honest day's wage derives from Christian sources. Pride in good workmanship must be restored, and this cannot be accomplished without the introduction of deep conviction.

The most profound conception of work is that which is connected with a divine calling. There was a time when the idea of calling was applied, almost exclusively, to the work of clergymen and missionaries, but this limitation is now widely seen as being obsolete. A great part of what it called Church Renewal in the latter half of the twentieth century has come from an extension of the idea of calling, so that it now includes all aspects of common life. Why, it is now asked, should not a man be called to be a brick mason or a banker? Why should not a fireman be conscious of a holy vocation? After all, he is certainly engaged in a work which saves lives and prevents much misery. Why should not a woman sense that she is called to be a mother, a wife, or a librarian?

It is wholly possible that some of the mose effective groupings of Christians in the future may be based on vocational considerations.

One important new development in the relation between Christianity and daily work is preparation for retirement. For the Christian, retirement is really liberation for service. The retired person may start a wholly new chapter rather than do nothing. The Christian philosophy of work is one which never ends.   D. ELTON TRUEBLOOD

WORLD COUNCIL OF CHURCHES.

See also *Ecumenism and Ethics.* The World Council of Churches has attempted to perform worldwide what the National Council of Churches does in America. Formed in August, 1948, at the Amsterdam assembly, it is now made up of 252 church bodies of Protestant, Anglican, Orthodox, and Old Catholic confessions. Subsequent W.C.C. assemblies were held in Evanston (1954), New Delhi (1961), Uppsala (1968). The movement seeks to overcome the proliferation of Christian churches (the Orthodox are now the largest single group in W.C.C. because of membership masses in their state-church contexts).

The membership basis defines W.C.C. as "a fellowship of churches which confess the Lord Jesus Christ as God and Saviour according to the Scriptures, and therefore seek to fulfill together their common calling to the glory of the one God, Father, Son, and Holy Spirit." Since no test of doctrine is intended, but emphasis falls rather on confession, this formula has accommodated the whole range of neo-Protestant divergence; even Unitarians found shelter in it, for what was "according to the Scriptures" varied greatly in expositions, for example, by Bultmann and Barth. At the theological level, evangelicals protest the ready exploitation of semantic ambiguity as serviceable to church merger and union.

W.C.C. properly concerned itself with Christian duty in respect to human communities of nation and race, with problems of war, peace, and international order, with the estrangement of larger classes in modern society from the church, with the general disintegration of the social order, with the challenge of Marxism as a critique of social injustice, with large areas of contemporary societal bias, including apartheid, with issues of life and labor and economics. But it devoted itself less to the exposition of Christian principles in the context of Scriptural revelation than to free-floating espousal of particular positions. Its neglect of personal ethics has been conspicuous.

From the outset W.C.C. disclaimed intentions of becoming a super-church. But extensive publications, public pronouncements, highly publicized forums, and political lobbying have promulgated the special slant of W.C.C. spokesmen as that of the world church. W.C.C. positions on socio-political issues were so routinely liberal and pro-socialist, so onesidedly critical of capitalism and American policy, while characteristically maintaining silence over Soviet and communist offensives, as to be highly predictable.

W.C.C. political policymaking reached a peak at the Geneva Conference on Church and Society in 1966, the year twelve hundred evangelical leaders gathered in Berlin for the World Congress on Evangelism independently of conciliar inspiration. The two world conferences expounded the respective priorities of conciliar ecumenism and of world evangelicals, i.e., preoccupation of the former with political specifics, and devotion of the latter to fulfillment of Christ's commission to evangelize the earth.

A Princeton professor, Paul Ramsey (q.v.) characterized Geneva 1966 as the worst incursion of churchmen into political affairs since the Middle Ages, not only shattering all reformation precedent but also an unwelcome contrast even to the modern Roman papacy. Ramsey's complaints against the W.C.C. - sponsored conclave were that its policy-making specifics outran both the competency of the church and factual data; that the church has a questionable right to a particular stand on controversial secular issues; that the ecumenical church possesses no "common" mind on the meaning of a "responsible society"; and that, instead of pretending competence as a maker of political policy, the church should ideally nourish, judge, and repair the moral and political ethos. He scorned leading ecumenists who closely identify Christian social ethics with the policy-making of the secular city and consider their specific pronouncements and solutions as "events in salvation history."

Behind the Geneva conference stood the influence of John C. Bennett (q.v.) and an American neo-Protestant "curia" that sought show-window prestige for partisan socio-political views. In telling statesmen what is required of them, Geneva enunciated specifics while excluding as discussants the very churchmen in high political echelons holding access to most of the relevant facts, e.g., with regard to Vietnamese military policy and strategy. The magazine *Christianity Today* declared in protest that the institutional church "has neither a divine mandate, nor competence, nor jurisdiction in such matters" (Oct. 8, 1965, p. 34). But its editor urged evangelicals not to react into mere polemics at the cost of neglecting urgent questions of social justice.

W.C.C. has been increasingly interested in Christian-communist dialog, and through this, in political theology (q.v.) correlated with a future-oriented ethic. Radical social change, including revolution (q.v.) is welcomed on the premise of God's redemptive activity in history. A recently emerging emphasis on transcendent spiritual factors implies no clear alteration of W.C.C. socio-political stance. What began in Amsterdam (1948) as an economic quest condemnatory of both communism and capitalism and seeking a socialist third way, has more and more tilted leftward as ecumenical spokesmen have espoused revolutionary theology and one-sidedly deplored the West in the power-struggle between so-called free and communist worlds. More recently W.C.C. has made supportive grants to political liberation movements, none of them operating against a Marxist regime; in Greece, in order to placate the Orthodox, it skirted criticism of a military dictatorship, and it has often wavered in promoting religious liberty.

The W.C.C.'s deliberative body is its 100-member central committee. Its general secretary is Phillip Potter, Methodist, of the West Indies, who succeeds Eugene Carson Blake, Presbyterian (U.S.A.), active with the late Bishop James Pike in sponsoring the *Consultation on Church Union* (C.O.C.U.) as the hopeful American successor-movement to the faltering National Council. W.C.C. more energetically pursues liason with the Vatican (Catholic observers regularly attend major ecumenical occasions and in some instances have ironically introduced a much-needed spiritual note) than with conservative evangelicals (as reflected by World Evangelical Fellowship, International Council of Christian Churches, Evangelical Foreign Missions Association) whose views are largely smothered in the ecumenical polyglot.

Although W.C.C. at New Delhi (1961) integrated the International Misssionary Council, the foreign mission movement world-wide is predominantly represented in Evangelical Foreign Missions Association and the Interdenominational Foreign Mission Association. This is due not only to the ecumenical priority for nationalization, but to declining missionary interest in theologically inclusive and non-evangelical churches, and to theories of universal salvation. In recent years W.C.C. has pursued the question of common values in all religions in dialog with representatives of other faiths.

While W.C.C. has a Department on Studies in Evangelism, it tends to minimize the indispensability of personal conversion to the point that official enthusiasm for ministries such as that of Evangelist Billy Graham is mitigated. The new evangelism is pointed more toward external sociological than toward internal spiritual needs.

Theology is no longer the integrating factor in ecumenical engagement. The 1963 Montreal conference on faith and order displayed such lack of cohesion that many despaired of another. The heartbeat of ecumenical advance is dialogue, and it elevates unity above truth; although it emphasizes unity in mission, its destination is patently unsure.

📖 John C. Bennett, ed., *Christian Social Ethics in a Changing World*, New York, Association, 1966;

E. Duff, *The Social Thought of the World Council of Churches,* New York, Fernhill, 1956; David P. Gaines, *The World Council of Churches,* Peterborough, N. H., Bauhan, 1966; Carl F. H. Henry, *Aspects of Christian Social Ethics,* Grand Rapids, Eerdmans, 1967; Paul Ramsey, *Who Speaks for the Church?* Nashville, Abingdon, 1967; C. C. West, "Ethics in Ecumenical Movement," in John C. Macquarrie, ed., *Dictionary of Christian Ethics,* Philadelphia, Westminster, 1967.

CARL F. H. HENRY

WORLD GOVERNMENT. See also *International Order; United Nations.* There is no world government. Nor is there any likelihood that there will be one in the foreseeable future. What there is, is only the United Nations and the United Nations is notoriously not a world government. There are, to be sure, schemes no end for some world government, in the brains of this or that thinker, or in the constitution of this or that idealistic organization or movement, but the probability that these schemes will ever pass from thought to reality is almost nil. A discussion of our topic therefore can only cover the reasons why world government does not exist and will not come into being soon, the reasons why the urge towards world government is nevertheless real and persistent, the sort of order and unity that obtain in a world without world government, and some idea of some of the schemes that have been proposed.

There are about 150 nation-states in the world today, of which 130 are members of the United Nations. The formal principle which constitutes a nation-state is the principle of sovereignty. This means that the government of the nation-state is the final determiner of its own laws and policies. It may consult or negotiate with others, and the consultations or negotiations may last days or months or years; it may take endless factors and situations into consideration, internal or external, including its resources, commitments and all sorts of political conditions; but in the end when the law or policy is decided and decreed, it, and it alone, must bear responsibility for the decision. The sovereignty of a nation is ultimately vested in a king or president or council or parliament, and the seal of the sovereign act is the signature of the sovereign; and at the moment of signing, the sovereign alone is signing and nobody else is signing for him. When the Charter of the United Nations speaks of "the principle of the sovereign equality of all its Members" as the first principle of the Organization (Article 2, paragraph 1), the Nation-states are guaranteed by this most solemn affirmation their absolute juridical equality so far as sovereignty and freedom of action are concerned.

A nation assured of this highest of national rights will be most jealous to protect and preserve it. There are limits beyond which it will not go without coercion in limiting this right. If it goes beyond these limits, or if it is coerced to go beyond them, it will cease to be an independent nation and it will become incorporated into another. These limits may vary from nation to nation (say, as between the Eastern European nations in relation to the USSR and the Latin American nations in relation to the USA), but essential limits there always are. Within these limits, any act of limiting the nation's sovereignty, by entering into international agreements of any kind, is sovereignly and freely taken by the nation itself, and therefore in the very act of taking it, it affirms its own freedom and sovereignty. Group life, and *a fortiori* national life, develops a soul of its own, which is made up of a whole complex of material interests and moral and spiritual values, interests and values which the nation most jealously protects, and seeks to promote and deepen and render as secure as possible. Freedom, independence, sovereignty, exclusive interests and laws, faith in certain distinctive values, and therefore the fear that these values will be contaminated or undermined or destroyed if the nation compromises its sovereignty beyond a certain point—it is these things, constituting the very essence of the concept of the nation-state, which stand in the way of real world government. Senators Connally and Vandenberg made it quite plain to their colleagues at the San Francisco Conference in 1945 that without the right of veto in the Security Council the United States Senate would not ratify the Charter of the United Nations, and this right of veto is the most important provision in the Charter for the preservation, quite intact, of the national sovereignty of the great powers in all important matters affecting international peace and security. One can be perfectly sure that the Supreme Soviet of the Soviet Union would not have ratified the Charter either without the right of veto. Indeed the securing of this right for the great powers was the principal agreement at Yalta between Roosevelt, Stalin, and Churchill. The proof of how deep-seated the sense of sovereignty is can be gauged from the simple reflection that an American running for the Senate or for the House of Representatives of the USA on the explicit platform of relinquishing the sovereignty of the USA will have no chance whatever of being elected.

And yet the old dream persists: it is more tidy and orderly to have world government; there must be world government to prevent disastrous world wars occurring; the physical unification of the world through satellites, rockets, and faster and faster transportation, and through instantaneous communication, makes such government an absolute necessity; all the more so with the proliferation of nuclear weapons and the unheard-of other means of mass destruction. Thus, so goes the argument, as world war has become absolutely unacceptable and unthinkable, world government, the only effective and sure means of preventing such war, has become an absolute necessity; and what is absolutely necessary is certainly possible and must be sought. Because all fear, including the awful fear of the atom, is essentially negative and unstable, the search for a positive principle of order must go on. And this is world government. This is a perfectly valid rational argument, but man is not pure reason, nor certainly are human groups; and the nation is perhaps least rational of all groups—what with national interests, national honor, the sense of great traditions worthy of being loved, defended and perpetuated, and certain national class ideologies with messianic content. World government will always hover as a regulative idea before the human mind, and men will ever seek to approximate it as much as possible in actual, historical embodiment. But it will always run up against the pride of nations and cultures and the agressiveness of ideologies.

If world government is necessary ideally but impossible practically and politically, what is it that replaces it in actual international existence? The order that serves as a fragile substitute for world government under present conditions is whatever is regarded as binding in international law, including the law and tradition of the United Nations; the balance of power among nations and groups of nations; and the powerfully deterrent effect of the atom and nucleus. The unimaginable horrors of the modern weapons of war, ushering in an absolutely new phase in human history so far as any calculations for war and peace are concerned, have rendered war rationally obsolete and are forcing mankind to a tacit order, if not yet of peace, at least of no war. If world government means world order, there is already an informal world government through the order that obtains from the balance of terror and the slow growth of international law and organization.

Many drafts have been drawn up for a world government. Grenville Clark and Louis Sohn worked out in their *World Peace through World Law* (Cambridge, Harvard University, 1966) "a comprehensive and detailed plan for the maintenance of world peace in the form of a proposed revision of the United Nations Charter." They suggest "an effective system of *enforceable* world law in the limited field of war prevention," "world judicial tribunals to interpret and apply the world law," "a permanent world police force," a system of "complete disarmament of all the nations," and "effective world machinery ... to mitigate the vast disparities in the economic condition of various regions of the world." A committee to Frame a World Constitution was established at the University of Chicago in 1945, and the constitution it proposed was republished in 1965 by the Center for the Study of Democratic Institutions at Santa Barbara, California. Movements for world government have also arisen, including the United World Federalists, the World Movement for World Federal Government, and the British Parliamentary Group for World Government. The stubborn fact of national sovereignty, including the arrogance of culture and ideology, has consistently vitiated all these good intentions.

The ultimate problem is how to reconcile freedom with security, the value of the individual and distinctive with the value of the general and inclusive, the warmth and joy of the personal with the deadness and inanity of the impersonal, the intimacy and intensity of the home and hearth with the vague universality of the world. Without a fundamental spiritual outlook under a transcendent lure this reconciliation is impossible. Thus man alone cannot through his unaided powers achieve either world government or world peace. The dark forces of rebellion and corruption will always break through. Working very hard and in all sincerity for world peace and order, man must be thankful for any measure of success. But the essential fragility and instability of every human attainment must also make him exceedingly humble before the awesome mystery beyond. In the presence of this mystery, while working harder than ever, he can only fall on his knees and pray. Freedom and security can only be reconciled in God.   CHARLES H. MALIK

WORLD-LIFE VIEW. See *Metaphysics and Ethics.*

WORLDLINESS. In the NT the world is the object of God's love (John 3:16) yet has no understanding of God's action in it and for it (John 1:10). So "this world" is the name given to the whole realm of unbelief which is under the control of the powers of evil (John 14:30; I Cor. 2:8). The "children of this world" are contrasted with the "children of light" (Luke 16:8; cf. John 3:19). And Christians are frequently admonished to oppose themselves to the ways of the world (Rom. 12:2; II Tim. 4:10; I John 2:15-17).

In *Pilgrim's Progress* (1678) John Bunyan describes how Mr. Worldly-Wise-Man persuades Christian to leave the path pointed out by Evangelist and to go to his own town of Morality. There is here an evident reference to the NT description of the world which "by wisdom knew not God" (I Cor. 1:21) and to the worldly rejection of the gospel of God's grace in favor of the effort to find salvation through good works. But, even in Bunyan's time, worldliness had largely lost its specifically NT reference. Instead of meaning the choice of works over faith, it had come to mean the absence of good works. Perhaps under the influence of Titus 2:12 ("Denying ungodliness and worldly lusts") its connotations were almost wholly moral. The change in meaning reflected the separation of "temporal" from "spiritual" orders and ideals. Worldliness was not opposed to *un*worldliness; and the contrast lay in the choice of the *mores* of secular society over against the *mores* taught by the church. Thus, while a layman might pride himself on being "a man of the world," he would strongly condemn any

sign of worldliness in a clergyman. Similarly, a dedicated Christian would seek to avoid conduct that might be judged worldly and therefore cast doubt upon the genuineness of his commitment to the life of faith.

It was in order to overcome the identification of the Christian life with unworldliness or other-worldliness that Dietrich Bonhoeffer (q.v.) advocated Christian this-worldliness. In *Letters and Papers from Prison* (London, SCM, 1967, 3rd ed.) he explained, "I don't mean the shallow and banal this-worldliness of the enlightened, the busy, the comfortable, or the lascivious, but the profound this-worldliness, characterized by discipline and the constant knowledge of death and resurrection. I think Luther lived a this-worldly life in this sense" (p. 201). Bonhoeffer's call was to a return to the Reformation understanding of all life being sanctified for the Christian, who is sent "into the world" (John 17:18).

KENNETH HAMILTON

WORSHIP. The Biblical idea of worship stems from the Creator-creature relation. "Worthy art thou our Lord and God, to receive the glory ... because thou didst create the universe" (Rev. 4:9). Additionally, God's acts of providence, and particularly his work of salvation, are proper motivations for worship. "Worthy is the Lamb that hath been slain to receive the power, and riches, and wisdom, and might, and honor, and glory, and blessing" (Rev. 5:12).

True worship is essentially spiritual, the heartfelt expression of the worshipper to his Maker and Redeemer. "God is Spirit; and they that worship him must worship him in spirit and truth" (John 4:24). Its proper expression by various external actions is carefully prescribed by Scripture. Much of the Mosaic Law is devoted to directions for worship. Mere formalism was totally unacceptable to God (Jer. 7:22; Hos. 6:6; cf. I Sam. 15:22f.).

With the coming of the Messiah much that was foreshadowed in the OT worship was fulfilled and set aside. The forms of Christian worship were derived from the synagogue instead of the temple. Elements of worship clearly attested to in the NT include the preaching of the Word, prayer, singing of praise to God, and observance of the sacraments of baptism and the Lord's Supper. Creedal forms and perhaps hymns are found in passages such as I Tim. 1:12).

Through the gradual addition of forms and traditions church worship in the Middle Ages became very elaborate and formal. The Protestant Reformation (q.v.) attempted a return tb Biblical forms of worship. Lutherans excluded what was not permitted by Scripture, but allowed much that is not prescribed by the Word. The Reformed principle was to include only that directly taught in Scripture. The strictest adherence to this principle disallowed the use of instruments and permitted singing only of the Psalms.

Since the Reformation a wide divergence has overtaken Protestant churches. The "liturgical movement," which had its beginnings in the middle of the nineteenth century, developed along two lines of interest. One was a return to a pre-Puritan period of the Reformation, with a study of the liturgies used in the early Reformation churches. The other was more ecumenical in character, embracing liturgical elements from the Roman church and Eastern Orthodox churches as well as the Protestant churches. This movement is exerting great influence in contemporary churches.

The decade of the 1960s and early 1970s saw a revolution in worship. Under the influence of existentialism, worship was to be a "happening" or an "event." There has been an attempt to recover the purportedly neglected area of celebration, joy, and personal communication. The result has been an abandonment of traditional patterns of worship and the introduction of novel forms, including jazz and "rock" music, dancing to the communion table and dialog instead of preaching. When used by those who have lost the content of the gospel such services fail to restore NT worship or to proclaim the gospel of Christ, the pressing need of our time. The so-called Jesus Movement purports to be much more interested in the message of the gospel alongside a strong emphasis on the emotional elements of worship.   MORTON H. SMITH

WRATH. See also *Judgment; Punishment; Retribution.* In both the OT and NT God's reaction to sin is expressed in terms borrowed from the human emotion of anger. But this does not mean that wrath is an irrational passion in God; rather it means his opposition to evil and his judgment on evil. Nor is it a permanent attribute of God. For whereas love and holiness are part of his essential nature, wrath is contingent upon human sin: if there were no sin there would be no wrath.

Old Testament. God's wrath is provoked by evil of all kinds, but particularly by Israel's rebellion against the God who has made a covenant with them (e.g., Exod. 32:10; Num. 11:1; Isa. 1:2-24; Jer. 4:4; 32:30-35; Hos. 13:4-11).

The wrath is inflicted by means of natural phenomena—disease (Num. 11:33), famine (Ezek. 5:12), etc.—or through God's providential ordering of history (Isa. 10:5; 13:5). The Exile is the supreme example of divine wrath (II Kings 17:18; 23:26-27; Jer. 7:29; Lam. 2:1ff.). But as well as these physical expressions of wrath there sometimes occurs the more spiritual idea of wrath as the experience of being deprived of fellowship with God (Ps. 27:9; Isa. 64:7; Lam. 5:20-22; Ezek. 39:23-24). After the Exile there was a tendency to look forward to a judgment of wrath on the nations rather than on Israel (Ps. 79:5-7; Joel 3:11-17; Zeph. 1:15, 18; 3:8).

Despite the frequency of references to

God's wrath, it is constantly affirmed that God is "slow to anger and abounding in steadfast love" (e.g., Ps. 103:8; 145:8).

New Testament. Paul takes up the prophetic expectation of a future day of wrath for unbelievers (Rom. 2:5; I Thess. 1:10), but thinks also of wrath as already realized in men's present experience (Rom. 1:18-32; I Thess. 2:16). Wrath is brought about by "all ungodliness and wickedness" (Rom. 1:18; Eph. 5:6), but these are only outward expressions of a basic estrangement from God (Rom. 1:21; 2:5; 5:9-10). Since all men are sinners, all are "by nature children of wrath" (Eph. 2:3), and in need of salvation.

According to C. H. Dodd, Paul thinks of wrath as an impersonal "inevitable process of cause and effect in a moral universe" (*The Epistle of Paul to the Romans,* London, Hodder, 1932, p. 23). But although Paul sometimes uses the word "wrath" absolutely, rather than the phrase "wrath of God," he clearly regards God as its source. Even in Rom. 1:18-32, Dodd's *locus classicus* for impersonal wrath, God's involvement in the wrath is clear (see vv. 18, 24, 26, 28). In a divinely governed universe, if men sin and evil consequences follow, that is because God has willed it so.

However, wrath in the NT is not an emotional reaction within God so much as an activity of God—his judgment upon sin. It is striking that although the noun (Greek *orge*) occurs twenty-nine times in the NT with reference to God's wrath, God is never said to "be angry"

Although in Rom. 13:4-5 God is said to use the State as the agent of his wrath, the judgment of wrath normally affects men as a spiritual condition of alienation from God. It is said of those who refused to enter into relationship with God, that "God gave them up . . . " (Rom. 1:24, 26, 28)—God allows men to experience the consequences of their refusal to live in relation to him. "The enterprise of setting up the 'No-God' is avenged by its success" (K. Barth, *The Epistle to the Romans,* London, Oxford University, 1933, p. 51). The judgment of the Last Day will be a consummation of this alienation. It will be the negation of salvation (I Thess. 5:9), justification (Rom. 1:17-18; 5:9), eternal life (Rom. 2:7-8), membership in the Kingdom of God (Eph. 5:5-6). This destiny, terrible though it is, is the outworking of God's respect for human freedom. The author of Revelation, with marvellous insight, describes this judgment as "the wrath of the Lamb" (Rev. 6:16): it is the wrath of one who himself experienced this alienation (Mark 15:34; II Cor. 5:21) so that those who have faith in him might be delivered from it.

Numerous commentaries on Romans; *TDNT,* Grand Rapids, Eerdmans, Vol. V, pp. 382-447; K. Barth, *Church Dogmatics,* Edinburgh, Clark, Vol. IV, 1956; W. Eichrodt, *Theology of the Old Testament,* London, SCM, 1961, pp. 258-269; A. T. Hanson, *The Wrath of the Lamb,* London, SPCK, 1957; R. V. G. Tasker, *The Biblical Doctrine of the Wrath of God,* London, Tyndale, 1951.

STEVEN TRAVIS

WRONG. See *Right and Wrong.*

Y

YOUTH. See also *Family; Juvenile Delinquency.* Youth is the period between childhood and maturity, characterized by vigorous appearance of body. The term may be employed favorably (e.g., vigorous) or unfavorably (e.g., naive).

Youth is the stage in which many individuals adopt for life the value system by which they determine their answers to two of life's basic questions: "What is right?" and "What has value?" In reaching their answer they have two major voices to listen to: the voice of the Lord and the voice of the world. The voice of the Lord confronts them primarily through the external Holy Scriptures and the internal Holy Spirit.

The Lord thereby convinces the young person that there are absolutes (q.v.), some things absolutely right, some absolutely wrong, others absolutely valuable, some absolutely worthless. During youth many awaken to the truth of Scripture and to the witness of the Holy Spirit in a godly life.

Simultaneously youth is barraged by the voice of the world saying that there are no absolute values, and that all is relative. Christ's warning is still timely: "Do not lay up for yourselves treasures on earth where moth and rust destroy and where thieves break through and steal. But lay up for yourselves treasures in heaven where no moth or rust destroys and where thieves do not break through or steal. For where your treasure is there will your heart be also."

Youth is the time when most people decide where their hearts will be. Youth is the "peak period" for favorable responses to Christ. Random samples of Christians in terms of age at which they came to him indicate that over 80 percent responded before they were twenty. Beyond the teen years there is an inverse correlation between age and percentage of response to Christ, so that by the time a person reaches seventy the probability that he will become a Christian is exceedingly low.

As youth go today, so will go the leaders of tomorrow. Tomorrow's presidents, managers, editors, teachers, parents, and other leaders are currently in the ranks of youth and in process of forming thought patterns and values systems which will determine the direction society will take. This is true in the religious sphere as in all others. To whom do youth respond in terms of religious persuasion? Mostly to peers. To be sure, there have been unusual periods in which youth were strongly influenced by adult Christians (e.g., Moody at Cambridge in the 1870s, Graham at some universities in the 1960s) but these are exceptions.

A trap ensnares many Christian youth, partly because of poor teaching by their Christian elders. They are misguided to believe that everything is absolute and that nothing is relative. The world contends that there are no absolutes and that everything is relative; the church often seems to contend that everything is absolute and that nothing is relative. The solution can be found in a three-category system in which one extreme consists of God's *absolute positives,* the other extreme consists of God's *absolute negatives,* and in between is the zone of the *relatives* (or "the zone of the ambiguous"). Scripture identifies what belongs in the two absolute categories. Youth is the time when a person's mind is unusually receptive to information as to what these absolutes are and his will is unusually ready to decide whether or not he will obey God's absolute commands of *do* and absolute commands of *do not.* But youth also is alert enough to know that many questions of value and of ethics are in that middle zone covered by God's admonition: "Let every one be fully persuaded in his own mind" (Rom. 14:5).

In developing a value system, youth is the impressionable period in which a person works out his answers to the basic values questions of life: What is worth learning? What is worth remembering? What is worth doing? Who is worth knowing? What is worth experiencing? Particularly relevant at this point is the Lord's promise, "I will instruct you and train you in the way you shall go. I will guide you with my eye upon you" (Ps. 32:8). The Lord's basic guideline for such decision-making is "Seek ye first the Kingdom of God and his righteousness" (Matt 6:33).   JOHN W. ALEXANDER

Z

ZEAL, ZEALOT. Derived from the Greek *zēlos*, whose root means to boil, the word "zeal" connotes intensely passionate, singleminded devotion to a cause. The Bible records numerous examples of both godly (Ps. 69:9; II Cor. 9:2; 11:2) and misguided (Acts 10:2; Phil. 3:6) zeal. Intense zeal for the law exemplified in Num. 25:1-13 became the standard of piety during the Maccabean resistance to Hellenism (see I Macc. 2:24-27, 54). During the Roman period, those whose zeal for Jahweh was most fanatical, nationalistic and violent formed a party of revolt called the Zealots.

The Zealots' goal was the violent overthrow of Roman rule. Asserting that God was their only ruler and Lord, they viewed payment of taxes to the pagan Roman emperor as treason. Judas the Galilean led an armed revolt against Rome because of the census in A.D. 6. More visible Roman domination after the death of Agrippa in 44 led to increased hostility toward Rome which the Zealots fanned until it burst into a full scale war against Rome (66-74).

Recently, some scholars have argued that Jesus was closely connected with the Zealots. One disciple (Simon) had probably been a Zealot (Luke 6:15; Acts 1:13). Misunderstanding Jesus' teaching about his kingdom, the Roman governor executed him as a political rebel. But Jesus, unlike the Zealots, did not oppose payment of Roman taxes (Matt. 22:15-22). His command to love enemies and not to resist evil persons (Matt. 5:38-48) was anathema to the Zealots. Although intensely concerned with the needs of the world (Luke 4:18; Matt. 9:35; 25:31ff.), Jesus declared unequivocally that since it was not of this world, his kingdom—unlike that of the Zealots—could not be ushered in by politics and violence (John 18:36-37).

📖 Josephus *Antiquities* XVIII. i.6 and *BJ* IV. iii.9; Vii. viii.1; William R. Farmer, *Maccabees, Zealots and Josephus*, New York, Columbia, 1956; Martin Hengel, *Die Zeloten*, Leiden, Brill, 1961; S. G. F. Brandon, *Jesus and the Zealots*, Manchester, Manchester, 1967; W. Wink evaluates Brandon's radical thesis in *Union SQR*, 25 (1969), 37-59, as does Oscar Cullmann, *Jesus and the Revolutionaries*, New York, Harper, 1970.   RONALD J. SIDER

ZEN. Zen is the Japanese pronunciation of the Chinese word, *Ch'an,* an abbreviated form of *Ch'an-na,* which in turn is the Chinese transliteration of the Sanskrit *Dhyana* and the Pali *Jhana,* meaning "meditation." The purpose of Zen is to discipline the mind through meditation and to make the mind its own master through insight into its proper nature.

According to the Prajnaparamita and other Mahayana Sutras the ultimate nature of all things is emptiness. In the *Tan-chin* ("Platform Sutra"), Hui-neng (d. A.D. 713) points out that "since all is void, originally there was nothing." This teaching is the inmost essence of Zen, and to understand it is the way to attain satori ("enlightenment").

Zen is not a system of philosophy or religion. While some authorities regard Zen as the "pinnacle of Buddhism," it is really the "Chinese revolt against Buddhism." In fact, Zen is a revolt against all authority. According to Lin-chi (d. 867), "There is no Dharma (truth) as long as you seek it outwardly ... smash whatever you come across ... smash the Buddha ... smash your parents and relations if you come across them. Then you will be in real emancipation." According to the *Tan-chin* and the *Chih-yueh-lu,* scriptures are only "fingers pointing at the moon" or a "ferryboat in which to cross a stream."

However, Zen is futile as an attempt to gain insight into man's nature because man cannot in fact have true knowledge of himself until he has true knowledge of God. The total depravity of man moreover, not only precludes every attempt to deify human nature but requires that human nature instead be regenerated in the image of God by the Holy Spirit.

Zen is not only futile, it is also dangerous. In the first place, it is a subtle form of atheism. It denies the personality and transcendence of God by identifying him with Nature, the Absolute, Oneness, and Tathata ("suchness"). Secondly, it disregards the righteousness of God. According to the *Prajnaparamita Hrdaya Sutra,* if one understands that reality is neither pure nor impure, he finds the Buddha in the dung as well as in heaven. Hence we are told, one should love the devils as well as God. This is radical moral relativism. Thirdly, the so-called satori ("enlightenment") is really a state of mystical intoxication and it may cause a mental breakdown by means of "Koan"—a mental exercise that rejects all logical norms. Finally, Zen's attempt to liberate man from all external authority, even divine law, exalts man as his own master. Untimately this teaching of radical freedom and subjectivity would lead to the darkness of nihilism and anarchy.

John Blofeld, tr., *The Zen Teaching of Haung Po,* New York, Grove, 1959; Chen-Chi Chang, *The Practice of Zen,* New York, Harper, 1959; Lit-sen Chang, *Zen-Existentialism,* Philadelphia, Presbyterian & Reformed, 1969; Paul F. & George D. Fung, trs., *The Sutra of the Sixth Patriarch on the Pristine Orthodox Dharma,* San Francisco, Buddha's Universal Church, 1965; D. T. Suzuki, *An Introduction to Zen Buddhism,* New York, Philadelphia Library, 1949;_____, *Essays in Zen Buddhism,* 3 Vols., London, Rider, 1949-1951.

                                    LIT-SEN CHANG

ZOROASTRIAN ETHICS. Christian life begins with and is rooted in justification by faith alone; which blossoms into character rich in the ethical excellences. The religion of the Prophet Zoroaster ("Zarathustra" in the original Iranian) occupies the opposite end of the spectrum projecting a salvation permanently rooted in good works. Zarathustra's answer to the question in John 6:28f. ("What shall we do, that we might work the works of God? And Jesus answered and said unto them—This is the work of God, that ye believe on him whom he hath sent.") would no doubt have been along the lines of that already given, "Make thine own self pure, oh righteous man; every man in the world below can win purity for himself, by cleansing his heart with good thoughts, good words and good deeds" (Vendidad F. X. 19).

The Zoroastrian creed, described in one of its hymns as "the Holy Faith which is of all things best," was announced by the Prophet Zoroaster in the ancient land of Persia during an epoch whose exact place in the time scale is subject to widely divergent interpretations, ranging from 6000 B.C. (according to certain Persian writers) to 600 B.C. Whatever the date, the cultural milieu in which he lived partook to an appreciable extent of ideas and religious beliefs traceable to early Vedic sources, as recorded in ancient Indian sacred writings. Even in the new creed, many terms betray their Indo-Aryan origins, though Zoroaster parted company with Vedic ideas in abandoning altogether the world-negating asceticism and renunciation that are so persistent a theme in classical Vedic lore. Although much more world affirming, it nevertheless retained some traces of the Indo-Aryan system. For one thing, the idea of human perfectibility, part of the larger idea that the whole universe is structured by God for orderly progression to nobler and more elegant levels of excellence, is strongly present in Zoroastrianism.

A religion built upon this anthropology—i.e., that man is perfectible and that man is the architect of his own perfectibility—must necessarily be a religion of works. Somewhat analogous to Vedic Monism, the world and life outlook was symbolic of the integral unity of the Universe. The whole of the created order is so organized by the Creator, *Ahura Mazda,* that it forgets its path towards the ideal of perfection, and man, as the self-conscious agent with independent free will, has the supreme destiny of hasten ing the advance to this goal by his consciously willed efforts. The only way man can fulfil his high calling is to travel on the royal highway of Asha, or Righteousness.

We begin now to discern why this religion is pre-eminently the religion of Pure Ethics, the religion of the Good Life. How do I live the good life? By attuning the mind to the Greater Mind, the Mighty *Ahura Mazda,* the source and repository of the Highest Good that the mind is capable of. And why is this the method leading to the good life? Because the Good Mind is the only soil in which the twin blossoms of Right Speech and Right Conduct will flourish. The ethical system, indeed the whole system of this faith, rests upon the triple pillars of Pure Thought, Pure Speech and Pure Action. The only acceptable sacrifice to God is the sacrifice of a life dedicated to the diffusion of noble thoughts, noble speech, and meritorious acts of loving kindness and service.

The Gathas or Hymns of Scripture leave no doubt that the doctrine of Zoroaster is a sublime monotheism. The persistent myth that Zoroastrianism is an ontological dualism is one more example of a much repeated fallacy that dies hard. Where do the crucial issues of evil and sin fit in? Over and against the One Supreme God and the lesser spirits ranged on his side, there looms the dark figure of the great spirit of Evil, Angra Manyu, later called Ahriman. The two are almost equally matched and are locked in a relentless warfare with each other. But there is no real dualism, for the ultimate triumph of God and his Angels of Light is a certitude. The physical world, the habitation of man, is the arena "par excellence" where the powers of darkness *unleash* their venom. There is, within the heart of man and without, a continuous conflict between the good and the evil, between the divine and the demonic. The destiny of man is not renunciation or ascetic withdrawal or self-isolation, but rather to accept the great challenge and to throw all his resources into

the conflict by allying himself with the Author of Goodness. Man then becomes a co-worker with God, a partner in the work of works, which is the destruction of the malevolence of Ahriman. This is the royal road along which the human instrument achieves the double purpose of saving himself (i.e., attaining salvation) and paving the way for the triumph of Righteousness.

Sin in this context, is the short-sighted choice of any of the allurements of error, like deceit, falsity, murder, adultery, and such like, for the attainment of some fleeting satisfaction. It is born of ignorance, not human depravity, as it is written in the Aögesnaïde Nask (56)—"Ignorance it is which ruineth most, ruineth them that know not aright. . . . " Right knowledge and the dawn of true awareness is thus the remedy for sin and error. Sin in this sense, as a violating of moral law, of the law of conscience, can be expiated by a corresponding balance of righteous acts; the social virtues, such as philanthropy, the diffusion of sound knowledge, mutual aid and social welfare works are considered powerful solvents for accrued sin. Followers of this faith are generally reputed to be desirable citizens for their social concern. Zoroastrianism presents the clear prospect of a life after death, either of blessedness or of deprivation and suffering. The highway to Heaven calls for discipline of concentrating on works of moral purity and righteousness and the avoidance of every action that vitiates the principle of goodness and well-being.

Two nagging questions keep intruding upon the mind: (a) Can man be trusted to keep up a lifelong tension of endeavor that will always ensure his choosing the right? (b) Even if he could, would a heaven attained by one's own external conduct, in the long run, prove a satisfactory resting place for the human spirit?

PEROSHOTMAN MUTHU KRISHNA

ZWINGLI. See *Reformed Ethics.*